ENCYCLOPEDIA OF SOCIAL HISTORY

Garland Reference Library of Social Science
(Vol. 780)

ENCYCLOPEDIA OF SOCIAL HISTORY

Edited by Peter N. Stearns—Carnegie Mellon University

Associate Editors

Stephen P. Frank—University of California, Riverside

Michael P. Hanagan—Vassar College

Julie Roy Jeffrey—Goucher College

Erick D. Langer—Carnegie Mellon University

Paul E. Lovejoy—York University

Abraham Marcus—University of Texas at Austin

Sarah Pomeroy—Hunter College, City University of New York

Evelyn S. Rawski—University of Pittsburgh

Joe William Trotter—Carnegie Mellon University

Anand A. Yang—University of Utah

Editorial Assistant

Ria David

Production Manager

Donna Scheuble

Encyclopedia
of
SOCIAL
HISTORY

Edited by
PETER N. STEARNS

GARLAND PUBLISHING, INC.
New York & London
1994

Library of Congress Cataloging–in–Publication Data

Encyclopedia of social history / edited by Peter N. Stearns.
       p.   cm. — (Garland reference library of social science ; v. 780)
    Includes bibliographical references and index.
    ISBN 0–8153–0342–4
    1. Social history—Encyclopedias.   I. Stearns, Peter N. II. Series.
HN28.E53   1994
306'.09—dc20   93–29230
                                                 CIP

Printed on acid-free, 250-year-life paper
Manufactured in the United States of America

Table of Contents

Introduction

The Domains of Social History

Since the 1960s social history has become a dominant form of research in the United States and around the world. It has expanded the subjects open to historical analysis. It has revised the ways historical change is presented and explained. Its impact has spilled over into other social science areas, and even into the study of literature. Many sociologists embrace the findings and analytical framework of social history in dealing with such topics as professionalization, mobility, or even the social functions of emotion, thus incorporating an understanding of change into their own generalizations. The new historicist school of literary criticism sees intimate and mutual interactions among authors, readership, and the larger social context of a period. Social history, in sum, has become one of the key sources of expanding knowledge about human social behavior.

The novelty of the study and the impact of social history makes a basic encyclopedic work on the subject particularly welcome. Users seeking a fuller introduction to this vital subject area, but unfamiliar with key findings, can gain a starting point here, with a host of references and suggestions for additional reading.

The basic features of social history also complicate the organization of a manageable encyclopedic work. This introduction, after briefly embellishing the picture of what social history is all about, explains the way this *Encyclopedia* is organized, how its topics were selected, and how the volume can best be used to explore one of the key growth areas of modern research.

The Nature of Social History

One of the entries in this volume, unsurprisingly entitled "Social History," offers a more elaborate definition of this field and its emergence. For starters, it is essential to emphasize two points: first, the range of subjects social history covers, and second, the characteristic analytical style of the field.

Social historians pay great attention to groups of people, particularly those remote from the summits of power (though elites are examined also). Their passions frequently center on the activities and beliefs of the working class, or peasants, or racial or ethnic minorities, or women, or youth. In dealing with social, gender, and age groupings, social historians at once seek to show the rich histories of these groups, arguing that they are not merely passive recipients of orders and guidelines from above, and to demonstrate how the values and behaviors of these groups affect the larger historical record. The second topical emphasis of social history involves a wide range of social behaviors and ideas, not simply the formal political and intellectual strands that organize most conventional history. Social historians thus deal with, among other things, sexuality, crime, family life, leisure activities—they deal with every aspect of human behavior, in other words, that is not simply biologically determined. Here too, the goal is to explore patterns of change in these areas, subjecting them to serious analysis and not merely human-interest storytelling. Social historians are also eager to show how the new topics, sometimes remote from mainstream historical interest, actually interact with other trends, reflecting changes in economic or political structure but also causing changes in turn.

Social history, in sum, greatly expands the subjects of historical inquiry, in terms of the groups of people and the range of activities open to investigation. Social historians, correspondingly, work to develop new sources of information and to use familiar sources in new ways, in order to sustain this redefinition of what history is all about.

Social history does more, however, than simply add to the list of major historical topics. It also tends to examine and present the past in distinctive ways. Because social historians believe in the importance of groupings of people and concentrate on large forces—like population growth—as causes of change, they spend relatively little time on individual biography. Because they look at patterns of behavior, they present their findings in terms of social processes more than single events. Major events such as wars or revolutions of course reflect social change and cause additional social change; but smaller developments, such as a change in political administration or the advent of a new king or president, do not necessarily have deep impact on the social fabric. Often, more general social processes are more important. The massive reduction in birth rates, for example, that occurred in the United States and Western Europe in the 19th century resulted from literally millions of individual events—decisions by individual families in various social classes to have fewer children than their parents had had. Social historians thus do not trace the individual events but rather their cummulative effect in a radically different popu-

lation pattern. Explaining the shift in pattern, and its impact on other social behaviors, provides the key focus—which means an attention to processes more than sharply defined events like laws or elections. It also means a definition of change in terms of often decades-long transitions, rather than tidy chronological packages marked by a new monarch or a major battle. Periodization and the designation of change in social history march to their own drummer, not to the more measured beat of textbook history.

Social history, in sum, has a distinctive analytical style and distinctive problems of presentation that are different from more familiar historical genres.

Constructing the Encyclopedia: How Selections Were Made

Social history's topical expansion and its analytical styles form the basis of this *Encyclopedia*. The largest entries focus on the new topics that social historians have particularly explored—topics such as social mobility and slavery. Many entries also derive from social historians' need to consider new sources, new analytical issues, and new forms of teaching and presentation. Correspondingly, types of entries that dominate more conventional historical lists—notable people and leading events—figure little in these pages.

This said, two important complications also reflect the selections made in the pages that follow. First, social history consists not only of new topics but of new interpretations of more familiar items. And second, social historians pay a great deal of attention to geographical specificity—they talk of family history not in the abstract, but in terms of American, or Chinese, or Muslim patterns.

Social historians, while emphasizing such characteristic subjects as social structure and gender relations, also ply their trade in dealing with religion and war, politics and culture. They partially reinterpret the spread of Christianity or Islam to include the religious role of ordinary people and the impact of religious change upon them—often modifying conventional interpretations substantially. They increasingly attend to the interaction between the state and society, urging a somewhat novel kind of political history that will include the pressures and demands of various groups of people and also the effective (not just the announced) functions of the state in dealing with these same groups. The social history of military institutions and of wars has become a growing subject area.

A manageable encyclopedic work on social history cannot list all the events, institutions, and intellectual movements open to new sociohistorical data and analysis. This volume contains a significant sampling, however, plus additional references (under headings such as "State and Society" and "Culture of Poverty") that permit further inquiry.

Social history has been applied to all major parts of the world, by scholars in the United States and, of course, internationally. Like other historians, social historians regard geographical specificity as an essential precondition of their craft. They do work on redefining certain geographical staples. Some of the more ambitious family historians, for example, have developed regional typologies of family structure that divide Europe into distinctive patterns, or that link European and Asian family forms. Similarly, some research on popular culture finds unexpected links among basic beliefs in otherwise distinctive parts of the world. Finally, a flourishing brand of comparative history has been applied to some key social history topics, such as slavery, which offers another variation on familiar geographical models. These innovations, including comparative history, are covered under appropriate rubrics in this *Encyclopedia*.

Still the geographical contours remain vital, and for the most part they also remain fairly familiar. Social historians define themselves primarily as Americanists, Europeanists, Chinese specialists, and the like. This regional concentration has produced not only distinctive specific coverage but also some distinctions in the balance of topics emphasized: thus the social history of the United States and Western Europe has emphasized family history somewhat more than Asian, African, and Latin American history has, while peasant and protest history looms larger in the overall sociohistorical picture of Asia and Latin America than where Europe or the United States are concerned. Nevertheless, the basic topics, methods, and sources are similar,

and social historians, whatever their own speciality limitations, readily conceive of their enterprise as an approach applicable to world history in general. The fact remains, however, that for any time period regional specificity adds greatly to the detailed treatment of social history. It is vital to remember that findings in European family history are not necessarily applicable to Africa or Asia and vice versa.

Here, too, a single volume cannot do full justice to the social history of every major region. This *Encyclopedia* makes no effort to deal with national social histories across the board, particularly for regions such as Europe or Latin America, which are characterized by a multitude of nations. Even larger regions are sampled, rather than covered exhaustively. Entries under regional headings such as China, the Middle East, South Asia, Africa, and Latin America convey some of the special social history features of those areas. Larger articles on major social history topics, such as artisans or crime, cite examples from several regional cases. The *Encyclopedia* clearly establishes social history's international range and provides mechanisms for further exploration of specific civilizations and areas.

In sum, this *Encyclopedia* emphasizes extensive coverage of the major social history topics and methods, thus defining the most characteristic features and issues in the field. It offers a more selective introduction to social history approaches to history more generally and, without pretending to cover each regional social history thoroughly, presents basic features of social history geographically defined. Social history, a growing and dynamic field, inevitably escapes any effort at tidy definition or even encyclopedic coverage. This volume nevertheless captures many of social history's essential ingredients, including its continued striving.

Each entry is followed by one or more references, offering opportunities for more extensive reading. Some reference lists include obvious classics, but most emphasize the latest and/or the most comprehensive work. Many important works are not listed, however, and sometimes additional authors are mentioned in the entries themselves. By consulting bibliographies in the references cited and by following up the supplementary suggestions, users of the *Encyclopedia* can easily construct a vigorous reading list on each of the topics covered.

The editors of the *Encyclopedia* wish to acknowledge the enthusiastic assistance of the many contributors, without whose expertise this range of topics would obviously have been impossibly ambitious. Special thanks are due to the scholars associated with the Pittsburgh Center for Social History, whose suggestions as well as contributions were invaluable. Special thanks also to Gary Kuris and Garland Publishing, for the initial good idea and for much encouragement along the way. Ria David provided indispensable administrative service and scholarly judgment; her knowledge and efficiency were impressive. Donna Scheuble kept the operation together as ideas moved into manuscript, overseeing the complex coordination among many contributors and many production phases. Clio Stearns did some masterful copyediting. Thanks also to Scarlett Townsend, Jennifer Geller, and Karen Callas for help in manuscript preparation.

List of Entries

Topical Contents

Contributors

W. Andrew Achenbaum is currently at the University of Michigan, Institute of Gerontology and has written widely on the history of old age.

Thomas M. Adams is the author of *Bureaucrats and Beggars: French Social Policy in the Age of the Enlightenment* (New York: Oxford University Press, 1990) and is a program officer at the National Endowment for the Humanities.

Michael Adas is a Professor of History at Rutgers University.

Jeffrey S. Adler teaches U.S. urban history and the history of crime at the University of Florida and is the author of *Yankee Merchants and the Making of the Urban West: The Rise and Fall of Antebellum St. Louis* (New York: Cambridge University Press, 1991). He has also written on vagrancy, poverty, and prostitution in the nineteenth-century American city, and his current research examines street violence in the industrial city.

Margo Anderson is a Professor of History at University of Wisconsin, Milwaukee.

George Reid Andrews is Professor of Latin American History at the University of Pittsburgh.

Luis Leobardo Arroyo earned a PhD in United States History at UCLA and is a Professor of Ethnic Studies at Humboldt State University. He has written articles on Chicano labor history, Mexican demographic history, and a (co-authored) book on the celebration of Cinco de Mayo. He is researching race relations in the Los Angeles furniture industry, 1900 to the present.

Rod Aya works at the Department of Anthropology, University of Amsterdam, the Netherlands, and wrote *Rethinking Revolutions and Collective Violence: Studies on Concept, Theory, and Method* (Amsterdam: Spinhuis, 1990).

Kristin S. Bailey is an Assistant Professor in the Department of History at the University of North Carolina at Wilmington. She received a PhD in History from Carnegie Mellon University in 1988.

Peter Bailey teaches Social History and Cultural Studies at the University of Manitoba and is author of *Leisure and Class in Victorian England* (1987).

Victor Bailey is Associate Professor of Modern British History at the University of Kansas. He is the author of *Policing and Punishment in Nineteenth-Century Britain* (1981) and *Delinquency and Citizenship: Reclaiming the Young Offender, 1914–1948*.

Samuel L. Baily, Professor of History at Rutgers University, is a specialist in comparative migration and in Latin American social history. In addition to various books and articles on Argentina and Latin America, his publications include "The Adjustment of Italian Immigrants in Buenos Aires and New York, 1870–1914," *American Historical Review* 88:2 (April 1983); *One Family, Two Worlds, An Italian Family's Correspondence Across the Atlantic, 1901-1922* (New Brunswick, NJ: Rutgers University Press, 1987); and a forthcoming book (to be published by Cornell University Press) on Italian immigrants in Buenos Aires and New York.

Jean Baker is a Professor of History at Goucher College. Her books include *The Politics of Continuity; Mary Todd Lincoln, and Affairs of Party*. She is working currently on a family biography of the Adlai Stevensons.

Peter Bakewell is a Professor of History at Emory University.

Lois W. Banner is Professor of History and of the Program for the Study of Women and Men in Society at the University of Southern California. She is the author of *American Beauty* (1983) and *In Full Flower: Aging Women, Power, and Sexuality* (1992).

Andrew E. Barnes is Associate Professor of History at Carnegie Mellon University.

Steven M. Beaudoin, a graduate student at Carnegie Mellon University, is doing research on French Associations.

Seymour Becker is Professor of History at Rutgers University and is the author of two books on 19th-century Russian history.

Jonathan Beecher is Professor of History at the University of California, Santa Cruz. He has written a major biography of the French utopian socialist Charles Fourier and is now completing a book entitled *Victor Considerant and the Rise and Fall of French Romantic Socialism*.

William Beik, a specialist in early modern French history, is Associate Professor of History at Emory University.

Robert J. Bezucha is Andrew W. Mellon Professor in the Humanities and Professor of History at Amherst College. He is at work on a study of animals and Western culture since the 18th century.

Terry D. Bilhartz is an Associate Professor of History at Sam Houston State University. His major publications include *Francis Asbury's America* (1984), *Urban Religion and the Second Great Awakening* (1986), and *Constructing the American Past* (1991).

Martin Blatt, a practicing public historian, is Supervisory Historian at Lowell National Historical Park, National Park Service.

Stuart M. Blumin is Professor of American History at Cornell University. His books include *The Emergence of the Middle Class: So-cial Experience in the American City, 1760–1900* (Cambridge, 1989).

John Bohstedt teaches history at the University of Tennessee, Knoxville. He has written *Riots and Community Politics in England and Wales, 1790–1810* (Harvard, 1983), and articles on women in riots and the diffusion of riots.

James Borchert is a social historian and has written on urban and suburban life and historical methods. He teaches at Cleveland State University.

Constance B. Bouchard is Professor of Medieval History at the University of Akron, specializing in social and ecclesiastical history of high medieval France.

Joseph Bradley is the author of *Muzhik and Muscovite: Urbanization in Late-Imperial Russia* and *Guns for the Tsar: American Technology and the Small Arms Industry in Nineteenth-Century Russia*. He is currently Professor of History at the University of Tulsa.

Warren Breckman is an advanced PhD candidate in modern German history at the University of California, Berkeley.

Margaret Brindle holds her PhD from Carnegie Mellon University. Her studies focus on medical history and health policy, and her thesis is a study of indigent care policy as it has evolved in Pittsburgh over the 20th century.

Liping Bu is a doctoral student in the History Department, Carnegie Mellon University.

Richard W. Bulliet is Professor of History at Columbia University. His work concentrates on the history of Islamic society and the history of technology. He has written *The Patricians of Nishapur: A Study in Medieval Islamic Social History* (1972), *The Camel and the Wheel* (1975), and *Conversion to Islam in the Medieval Period: An Essay in Quantitative History* (1979).

Orville Vernon Burton is Professor of History and Sociology and University Scholar at the University of Illinois, Urbana-Champaign. He is the author of *In My Father's House Are Many Mansions: Family and Community in Edgefield, South Carolina*.

Jon Butler is the William Robertson Coe Professor of American History at Yale University.

Leon G. Campbell is Visiting Professor of History at Stanford University.

Ronald C. Carlisle is currently Director of the Cultural Resources Section, Michael Baker Jr., Inc., Pittsburgh, Pennsylvania, and is Adjunct Associate Professor in the Department of History and the Department of Anthropology at the University of Pittsburgh. Dr. Carlisle's primary research interests include historical archaeology and the use of documents in archaeological research, material culture studies, and vernacular architecture.

Mark C. Carnes is author of *Secret Ritual and Manhood in Victorian America* (New Haven: Yale University Press, 1989) and editor, with Clyde Griffen, of *Meanings for Manhood: Constructions of Masculinity in Victorian America* (Chicago: University of Chicago Press, 1990). He also co-edited the *Dictionary of American Biography* (Supplement VIII) and is managing editor of the 20-volume *American National Biography* (New York: Oxford University Press, forthcoming.)

Carolyn Leonard Carson is a PhD candidate at Carnegie Mellon University. Her focus is women's medical history and health care policy, and her dissertation is an exploration of American gynecological practice following World War I.

Jack R. Censer, Professor of History at George Mason University, specializes in the history of the Old Regime and the French Revolution.

Lee Chambers-Schiller is an Associate Professor, President's Teaching Scholar, and Chair of the Department of History at the University of Colorado, Boulder. She is author of *Liberty, A Better Husband. Single Women in America. Three Generations 1780–1840.* She is currently working on a biography of abolitionist Maria Weston Chapman.

Herrick Chapman is an Associate Professor of History at New York University. He is the author of *State Capitalism and Working-Class Radicalism in the French Aircraft Industry* (1991), and with Peter N. Stearns, *European Society in Upheaval: Social History Since 1750,* Third Edition (1992).

William Chase, an Associate Professor of History at the University of Pittsburgh, is the author of *Workers, Society and the Soviet State: Labor and Life in Moscow, 1918–1929.*

George Chauncey teaches history at the University of Chicago. He is the co-editor of *Hidden from History: Reclaiming the Gay and Lesbian Past* (Chicago: University of Chicago Press, 1989) and author of *Gay New York: Gender, Urban Culture, and the Making of the Gay Male Worlds of New York City, 1890–1970* (New York: Basic Books, 1994).

David Christian, BA, PhD (Oxford University), is Associate Professor in the Department of History, Macquarie University, Sydney, Australia. His research interests are 19th- and early 20th-century administrative and social history of Russia, food and drink in Russian village life, prohibition in Russia (1914–1923), and history of the Eurasian plain. His teaching interests include Russian history, large-scale history of the Eurasian plain, and world history.

Christopher Clark teaches American history at the University of York, England. His book *The Roots of Rural Capitalism: Western Massachusetts, 1780–1860* was published by Cornell University Press in 1990.

Paul F. Clark is Associate Professor of Labor Studies and Industrial Relations at Pennsylvania State University. He has published books on the United Mine Workers and the United Steel Workers of America unions.

Richard Cleary is an Associate Professor in the Department of Architecture at Carnegie Mellon University.

Lisa Cody, a doctoral student at University of California, Berkeley, is writing a dissertation on the history of reproduction and gender in 18th-century Britain.

David Cohen teaches in the Department of Rhetoric and the Department of Classics at the University of California, Berkeley. He is the author of *Law, Sexuality, and Society: The Enforcement of Morals in Classical Athens* (Cambridge, 1991) and numerous other publications on Greek and Roman legal and social history.

Lizabeth Cohen, Associate Professor of History at New York University, is the author of *Making a New Deal: Industrial Workers in Chicago, 1919–1939* (New York: Cambridge University Press, 1990). She is now writing a book, tentatively entitled *A Consumer's Republic: The Politics of Consumption in Postwar America,* about how Americans have carried out their struggles over class, race, and gender during the post–World War II era through their power as consumers more than producers.

Samuel K. Cohn, Jr. is Professor of History at Brandeis University. He has written several books and articles on the Italian Middle Ages, including the forthcoming *Cult of Remembrance and the Black Death: Six Cities in Central Italy.*

Alon Confino is Assistant Professor of German History at the University of Virginia. He has recently completed his PhD dissertation about the Heimat (homeland) idea and the construction of regional and national memo-

ries in the German Empire between 1871 and 1918.

Harold J. Cook, Associate Professor, Department of the History of Medicine, University of Wisconsin, Madison, teaches the history of European medicine specializing in the early modern period.

Frederick Cooper is Professor of African History at the University of Michigan and author of *From Slaves to Squatters: Plantation Labor and Agriculture in Zanzibar and Coastal Kenya, 1890–1925* (1980) and *On the African Waterfront: Urban Disorder and the Transformation of Work in Colonial Mombasa* (1987). He is currently completing a book on "Decolonization and African Society: The Labor Question in French and British Africa."

Alain Corbin is Professor of Nineteenth-Century History at the Université de Paris I, Panthéon-Sorbonne.

Timothy J. Crimmins teaches historic preservation and American urban history at Georgia State University.

James E. Cronin is Professor of History at Boston College. He has been on the editorial board of the *Journal of Social History* for many years and is the author of *Industrial Conflict in Modern Britain* (1979); *Labour and Society in Britain, 1918–1979* (1984); and *The Politics of State Expansion: War, State and Society in Twentieth-Century Britain* (1991).

Gary Cross, author of *A Quest for Time: The Reduction of Work in Britain and France, 1840–1940* and *Time and Money: The Making of Consumerist Modernity,* is Professor of History at the Pennsylvania State University.

Ria David, a social historian of United States immigration and cultural history, is currently researching second-generation Japanese and Jewish Americans in business. Her interests lie in the transformation of cultural values, mobility change, and ethnic identity. She is an advanced PhD candidate at Carnegie Mellon University.

C.R. Day is Professor of History at Simon Fraser University in Vancouver, British Columbia. He is the author of numerous articles on French education and of the book *Education for the Industrial World: The Ecole d'Arts et Métiers and the Rise of French Industrial Engineering* (Cambridge: MIT Press, 1987), which was published in France as *Les Ecoles d'Arts et Métiers, l'enseignment technique en France XIXe–XXe siècle*, Jean Pierre Bardos, translator (Belin, 1991).

Jared Day is a graduate student at Carnegie Mellon University. He has done research on Ohio's juvenile corrections system and is currently researching landlord activism in New York City from 1904 to 1933.

Carolyn Dean is Assistant Professor of History at Brown University. She is the author of *The Self and Its Pleasures: Bataille, Lacan, and the History of the Decentered Subject* (Ithaca: Cornell University Press, 1992).

Brian M. Downing teaches social science at Northwestern University.

Seymour Drescher is University Professor of History at the University of Pittsburgh and has published social studies on antislavery campaigns and the processes of emancipation.

Laura F. Edwards is Visiting Assistant Professor in U.S. History at the University of Chicago. She currently is working on her book, *The Politics of Womanhood and Manhood: Reconstruction in North Carolina.*

Paul Edwards is Deputy Director of the Industrial Relations Research Unit, University of Warwick, Coventry, England. He has written widely on conflict and workplace relations in the United States and Britain.

James Epstein, Associate Professor of History, Vanderbilt University, is author of *The Lion of Freedom: Feargus O'Connor and the Chartist Movement* (1982) and co-editor of *The Chartist Experience* (1982).

Anthony Esler, Professor of History at the College of William and Mary, is the author of several books on generational conflict, including *The Aspiring Mind of the Elizabethan Younger Generation* (1966); *Bombs, Beards and Barricades: 150 Years of Youth in Revolt* (1971); and *Generations in History: An Introduction to the Concept* (1982).

Alessandro Falassi, a cultural anthropologist, is the Academic Director of the University for Foreigners in Siena, Italy. Once a year he teaches at UCLA.

Toyin Falola is Professor of African History at the University of Texas, Austin. He is the author or editor of over a dozen books.

James R. Farr is an Associate Professor of History at Purdue University.

John Ferling is a Professor of History at West Georgia College, Carrollton.

Bruce Fetter is Professor of History at the University of Wisconsin, Milwaukee. His latest book is *Demography from Scanty Evidence: Central Africa in the Colonial Era.*

Geraldine Forbes, author of *Positivism in Bengal,* editor of Shudha Mazumdar's *Memoirs of an Indian Woman,* and general editor of the new series of memoirs and autobiographies *Foremother Legacies,* is a Professor of History at the State University of New York, Oswego. She currently is working on *A History of Women in Modern India* for the series New Cambridge History of India and a book entitled *Photography and the History of Indian Women.*

Stephen P. Frank teaches at the University of California, Riverside.

Sandria B. Freitag has worked on the intersection of popular culture, collective violence, community identification, and the formation of a public in the civic society of the modern nation state. Her work on South Asia is placed within a comparative social history context necessitated by the influence of imperialism. She is the editor of several collections of essays on these subjects and the author of *Collective Action and Community: Public Arenas in the Emergence of Communalism in North India* (Berkeley: University of California Press, 1990).

William E. French is Professor of History at the University of British Columbia.

Nancy E. Gallagher, Professor of Middle Eastern and North African History, University of California, Santa Barbara, is a specialist in the social history of medicine in the early modern and modern preiods in the Middle East and North Africa. Her publications include *Medicine and Power in Tunisia, 1780–1900* (New York: Cambridge University Press, 1983) and *Egypt's Other Wars: Epidemics and the Politics of Public Health* (Syracuse, NY: Syracuse University Press, 1990).

Dee Garrison, Professor of History, Rutgers University, is a specialist in the history of professions, American reform, and women's history.

Steven M. Gelber is a professor of American social history at Santa Clara University. He has published on employment integration, New Deal art, and new American religion and currently is writing on the historical relationship between work and hobbies.

David A. Gerber is a member of the History Department at the State University of New York, Buffalo. His writings as a social historian have been on marginal social groups in the American past and on the character and formation of American pluralism.

He is the author of *Black Ohio and the Color Line* (1976) and *The Making of an American Pluralism: Buffalo, New York, 1825–1860* (1989), and the editor of *Anti-Semitism in American History* (1986).

Mary Gibson teaches history at John Jay College of Criminal Justice, City University of New York and is the author of *Prostitution and the State in Italy, 1860–1915* (New Brunswick, NJ: Rutgers University Press, 1986).

James A. Gilchrist is a graduate student at Carnegie Mellon University.

David Gilmartin is Associate Professor of History at North Carolina State University. He is the author of *Empire and Islam: Punjab and the Making of Pakistan* (1988).

Kees Gispen is Associate Professor of History at the University of Mississippi. He received his PhD from the University of California, Berkeley (1981).

Richard Godbeer is Assistant Professor of History at the University of California, Riverside. He is author of *The Devil's Dominion: Magic and Religion in Early New England* (New York: Cambridge University Press, 1992).

Barbara K. Gold is Professor and Chair of Classics at Hamilton College. She is the author of two books on patronage, *Literary and Artistic Patronage in Ancient Rome* (Austin, TX: 1982) and *Literary Patronage in Greece and Rome* (Chapel Hill, NC, 1987).

Wendy Goldman is Professor of History at Carnegie Mellon University in Pittsburgh.

Paul Gootenberg is a specialist on Andean economic and social history at the State University of New York, Stony Brook.

William Graebner is Professor of History at the State University of New York, Fredonia. He is the author of *Coming of Age in Buffalo: Youth and Authority in the Postwar Era* (Philadelphia: Temple University Press, 1990).

Richard Graham is Frances Higginbotham Nalle Professor of History at the University of Texas, Austin. He is author of *Patronage and Politics in Nineteenth-Century Brazil* (Stanford, 1990), *Independence in Latin America* (New York, 1972), and several articles on slavery, as well as on other social and economic topics.

Gerald Michael Greenfield is a Professor of History at University of Wisconsin, Parkside.

James Grehan is a doctoral student in the History Department at the University of Texas, Austin.

Erwin P. Grieshaber is Professor of History at Mankato State University.

James S. Grubb is Associate Professor of History at the University of Maryland, Baltimore County.

Myron P. Gutmann is Professor of History and Research Associate at the Population Research Center of the University of Texas, Austin. He is author of *War and Rural Life in the Early Modern Low Countries* (1980) and *Towards the Modern Economy: Early Industry in Europe 1500–1800* (1988).

Jane I. Guyer is Associate Professor of Anthropology at Boston University and has carried out research in West and Equatorial Africa.

Louis Haas is Assistant Professor of Medieval and Early Modern History at Duquesne University. He specializes in the study of family and ritual in the premodern era.

David L. Haberman is a historian of religions who specializes in the cultures of South Asia. He received his PhD from the University of Chicago in 1984 and has taught religion at the University of Arizona and Williams College.

Timothy J. Haggerty is a PhD candidate at Carnegie Mellon University. His dissertation examines the effect of the Civil War on community structures.

Michael R. Haines is Banfi Vintners Professor of Economics, Colgate University; Research Associate, National Bureau of Economic Research; and Research Affiliate, Population Studies Center, University of Michigan.

John R. Hall, Professor of Sociology at the University of California, Davis, is author of *Gone from the Promised Land: Jonestown in American Cultural History* (Transaction Books, 1987). He currently is writing a book on the methodology of sociohistorical inquiry.

Linda B. Hall is Professor of History at the University of New Mexico and has authored or co-authored three books on the Mexican Revolution.

Gina Hames is a doctoral student in the History Department at Carnegie Mellon University.

Michael P. Hanagan is a Visiting Associate Professor of History at the New School for Social Research in New York City. He is the author of *The Logic of Solidarity* (1980) and *Nascent Proletarians* (1989) and is currently engaged in a collaborative study of the origins and development of the welfare state in England, France, and the United States.

Julie Hardwick is Assistant Professor of History at Gettysburg College.

Stephen Hardy coordinates the Sport Studies Program at the University of New Hampshire. He has written extensively on the growth of sport in America.

Tamara K. Hareven is Unidel Professor of Family Studies and History at the University of Delaware, Adjunct Professor of Population Sciences at Harvard University, and editor of the *Journal of Family History*.

Ralph S. Hattox received his PhD in Near Eastern studies from

Princeton University in 1982. He is currently Associate Professor of History at Hampden-Sydney College.

David Henige teaches history at University of Wisconsin, Madison.

Kathleen C. Hilton is an Assistant Professor of History at Pembroke State University. Her primary research interest is the relationship between adult female reform movements and the socialization patterns of adolescent females.

John Hinshaw is a PhD candidate at Carnegie Mellon University. His dissertation is on black and white Pittsburgh-area steelworkers between 1945 and 1973. The dissertation focuses on work and community, particularly churches and bars.

Elizabeth Hitz is Adjunct Professor of History at the University of Wisconsin, Milwaukee. She has spent most of her working life in museums.

Steven J. Hoffman is a doctoral candidate at Carnegie Mellon University and author of "'A Plan of Quality': The Development of Mt. Lebanon, a 1920's Automobile Suburb" in the *Journal of Urban History* 18 (1992), 141–81. He completed his dissertation on the role of race, class, and gender in the city building process in Richmond, Virginia (1870–1920).

David G. Hogan is an Assistant Professor of History at Heidelberg College.

Jan Hogendorn is the Grossman Professor of Economics at Colby College. He has written widely on African indigenous moneys.

Daniel Holbrook is a PhD candidate in Applied History at Carnegie Mellon University.

Elliott Horowitz is a historian at the University of Bar Ilan, Ramat-Gan, Israel, specializing in Jewish history and the study of ritual.

Allen M. Howard is an Associate Professor of History at Rutgers University and has written on West African economic, urban, and ethnic history.

Cho-yun Hsu received his doctorate at the University of Chicago. He is a Professor of History at the University of Pittsburgh and a member of Academia Sinica.

William B. Husband is an Associate Professor in the Department of History at Oregon State University. He is the author of *Revolution in the Factory: The Birth of the Soviet Textile Industry, 1917–1920* (New York: Oxford University Press, 1990) and is currently writing a social history of atheism in the USSR (1917–1945).

Allen Isaacman is Professor of African History at the University of Minnesota and Director of the University of Minnesota's MacArthur Program of Peace and International Cooperation.

Robert H. Jackson is Assistant Professor of History at Texas Southern University, Houston. His research interests include the economic and social history of Bolivia, and the economic, social, and demographic history of the missions in northern Mexico.

Ann Bowman Jannetta is Assistant Professor of History at the University of Pittsburgh. She is interested in the comparative history of disease and the history of disease and public health in Japan.

Julie Roy Jeffrey is a Professor of History at Goucher College.

Mary Ann Jimenez is a Professor at California State University, Long Beach. She has written on the history of madness in colonial America and on psychiatric conceptions of mental disorder in immigrants and women.

Colin Jones is Professor of History at Exeter University, Great Britain. He specializes in the social history of France between the 17th and 19th centuries.

Nicholas F. Jones teaches in the Classics Department at the University of Pittsburgh.

Ibrahim M. Jumare teaches at York University, Ontario.

Hartmut Kaelble is a Professor of History at Humbolt University, Germany.

Daniel H. Kaiser is Professor of History and Joseph F. Rosenfield Professor of Social Studies at Grinnell College.

Peter Karsten, Professor of History and Sociology at the University of Pittsburgh, is the author of *Naval Aristocracy: The Golden Age of Annapolis and the Emergence of Modern American Navalism* (Free Press, 1972); *Soldiers and Society: The Effects of Military Service and War on American Life* (Greenwood Press, 1978); *Law, Soldiers and Combat* (Greenwood Press, 1979), and the editor of *The Military in America from Colonial Times to the Present*, Second Edition (Free Press, 1986).

Michael Khodarkovsky is an Assistant Professor of Russian History at Loyola University of Chicago.

Dina Rizk Khoury is Assistant Professor of Middle Eastern History at George Washington University.

John E. Kicza, Professor of History at Washington State University, has published extensively on Latin American merchants and other occupational groups. He is composing a comparative study of the Spanish overseas conquests.

Alan Kimball, Chairman of the Department of Russian Languages and Literature and member of the History Department, University of Oregon, is completing a book-length study to be titled "To Make a Better Life: The Mobilization and Defeat of Russian Civil Society in the Middle of the Nineteenth Century."

W. Dean Kinzley is Associate Professor in the Department of History at the University of South Carolina. He is the author of *Industrial Harmony in Modern Japan: The Invention of a Tradition* and other studies of Japanese and social history.

Peter F. Klarén is Professor of History and International Affairs and Director of the Latin American Studies Program in the Elliott School of International Affairs at George Washington University.

Mark T. Knapp is a PhD candidate in legal history at Carnegie Mellon University. He also holds a JD from the University of Pittsburgh School of Law.

John Komlos is Associate Professor of History and of Economics at the University of Pittsburgh.

Kenneth E. Koons is Professor of History at Virginia Military Institute.

Rudy Koshar is Associate Professor of History at the University of Wisconsin, Madison. In addition to articles on modern German and European social and cultural history, he has published *Social Life, Local Politics, and Nazism: Marburg, 1880–1935* (1986) and edited *Splintered Classes: Politics and the Lower Middle Classes in Interwar Europe* (1990).

Bruce Kraig is Professor of History at Roosevelt University. His publications and teaching are in prehistory and early history with a special interest in the history of food.

Richard Lachmann, Associate Professor of Sociology at the State University of New York, Albany, is the author of *From Manor to Market: Structural Change in England, 1536–1640* (Wisconsin, 1987), and *Capitalist Class and State Formation in Feudal Europe* (Oxford, forthcoming).

Richard Landes is a Professor of Medieval History at Boston University. His primary research concerns the Peace of God and other popular religious movements at the turn of the first Christian millennium.

Erick D. Langer is Associate Professor of History at Carnegie Mellon University.

William Lavely is Associate Professor of Sociology and International Studies at the University of Washington.

Lynn Hollen Lees is Professor of History at the University of Pennsylvania.

Susan H. Lees is Professor of Anthropology at Hunter College and the Graduate Center of the City University of New York. She has done research on the relationship between irrigation and society in Latin America and the Middle East and has published numerous articles and book chapters on this subject. She co-edits an interdisciplinary journal, *Human Ecology*.

Helena Waddy Lepovitz is an Associate Professor of History with the State University of New York, Geneseo, and the author of *Images of Faith* (Athens: University of Georgia Press, 1991). Her research focuses on the culture and economy of Alpine Bavaria with particular reference to religious traditions.

David Levine teaches in the Department of History and Philosophy at the Ontario Institute for Studies in Education in Toronto. He received his PhD from Cambridge University in 1975. In addition to a number of articles in scholarly journals, he has authored *Family Formation in an Age of Nascent Capitalism* (1977) and *Reproducing Families* (1987); he has co-authored *Poverty and Piety in an English Village* (1979) and *The Making of an Industrial Society* (1991); and he has edited *Proletarianization and Family History* (1984) and co-edited *The European Experience of Declining Fertility, 1850–1970* (1992). Professor Levine currently is preparing a new manuscript, provisionally entitled *Forget the Family: The Social History of the World We Have Made*.

Carl Lindahl is an Associate Professor in the Department of English, University of Houston.

Mary Lindemann is Associate Professor in the Department of History at Carnegie Mellon University.

Tessie P. Liu teaches European history at Northwestern University.

Paul K. Longmore is a Visiting Assistant Professor of History at Stanford University who specializes in U.S. history.

Paul E. Lovejoy is a Professor at York University, Ontario.

Nancy Lubin has been an Associate Professor, Departments of History and Engineering and Public Policy, Carnegie Mellon University. She is the author of *Labor and Nationality in Soviet Central Asia: An Uneasy Compromise*, and numerous scholarly articles and congressional reports on Soviet and post-Soviet affairs.

Katherine A. Lynch is a social historian working in the fields of family history and historical demography of modern Europe.

Theresa McBride is Professor of History at Holy Cross College and the author of *The Domestic Revolution* (London, 1977).

Robert McCaa, Professor of History at the University of Minnesota, edits the *Latin American Population History Bulletin*.

Sean D.M. McConville is a Professor in the Department of Criminal Justice at the University of Illinois, Chicago. He recently has published a second volume of *A History of English Prison Administration* (London, New York, 1993).

Lawrence T. McDonnell is Assistant Professor of History at the University of Saskatchewan. His research focuses upon 19th-century America—specifically, social contradictions within the antebellum South and the African-American slave community.

Thomas A.J. McGinn teaches at Vanderbilt University.

Frank McGlynn is Associate Professor of Anthropology, University of Pittsburgh, Greensburg. He has edited *Health Care in the Caribbean and Central America* (1985); *The Anthropology of Political Behavior*, with A. Tuden (1991); and *The Meaning of Freedom: Economics, Politics and Culture after Slavery*, with S. Drescher (1992). His interests are political economy, anthropology, history, and the Caribbean.

Constance M. McGovern (PhD, University of Massachusetts, Amherst, 1976) is an Associate Professor of History at the University of Vermont, where she currently serves as Vice Provost. Her research focuses on the confluence of race, gender, and class in American psychiatric practices in the 19th and 20th centuries.

James McLachlan is the author of a prosopographical work, *Princetonians, 1748–1768: A Biographical Dictionary* (Princeton, N.J.: 1976) and a work in collective biography, "American Colleges and the Transmission of Culture: The Case of the Mugwumps," in Stanley Elkins and Eric McKitrick (eds.), *The Hofstadter Aegis: A Memorial* (New York: Knopf, 1977).

Angus McLaren, Professor of History at the University of Victoria, British Columbia, is the author of several studies of birth control.

John R. McNeill is the author of *The Mountains of the Mediterranean: An Environmental History* (New York: Cambridge University Press, 1992) and presently is working on a global environmental history of the 20th century. He teaches history at Georgetown University.

Abraham Marcus is an Associate Professor of History and Middle Eastern Studies at the University of Texas, Austin.

John Markoff is Professor of Sociology and History at the University of Pittsburgh

James W. Martens is an Instructor of History at Red Deer College.

Scott C. Martin received his PhD in history from the University of Pittsburgh in 1990. He currently is working on a book on the emergence of leisure in southwestern Pennsylvania in the first half of the 19th century.

Alan Mayne teaches comparative urban history at the University of Melbourne, Australia.

Mary Jo Maynes is a Professor of History at the University of Minnesota. Her current research is on working-class life course and autobiography in 19th-century Europe.

Edgar Melton is Associate Professor of History at Wright State University. He has published articles on serfdom in Russia and Eastern Europe.

Stephen Meyer is a Professor of History at the University of Wisconsin, Parkside, a co-editor of *On the Line: Essays in the History of Auto Work*, and author of *The Five Dollar Day: Labor Management and Social Control at the Ford Motor Company* and *"Stalin over Wisconsin": The Making and Unmaking of Militant Unionism, 1900–1950*.

Anne Meyering is Associate Professor of History at Michigan State University. She is the author of articles in the *Journal of Economic History* and in *Annales de Démographie Historique* and of chapters in *Research in the History of Economic Thought and Methodology*, Vol. 8 (1990) and in *Women's Work and the Family Economy in Historical Perspective* (Manchester, 1990).

Peter V. Meyers is Professor and Chairman of the History Department at North Carolina Agricultural and Technical State University.

David W. Miller, Professor of History at Carnegie Mellon University and author of *Church, State and Nation in Ireland, 1898–1921* and *Queen's Rebels: Ulster Loyalism in Historical Perspective*, currently is working on an analysis of pre-famine Irish society in spatial perspective.

Montserrat Martí Miller is a graduate student in the History Department at Carnegie Mellon University.

Leslie Page Moch teaches European history at the University of Michigan, Flint. She is the author of *Paths to the City: Regional Migration in Nineteenth-Century France* (1983) and *Moving Europeans: Migration in Western Europe since 1650* (1992).

John Modell is Professor of History at Carnegie Mellon University. A social historian of the United States, he has spent the past decade emphasizing studies of the life course of youth. His most recent book on this theme is *Into One's Own: From Youth to Adulthoood in the United States, 1920–1975* (Berkeley: University of California Press, 1988).

Richard H. Moore is an Associate Professor in the Department of Anthropology at Ohio State University and author of *Japanese Agriculture: Patterns of Rural Development* (Westview Press, 1990).

Shirley Ann Moore, Assistant Professor of History at California State University, Sacramento, is completing her first book, *To Place Our Deeds: The Black Community in Richmond, California, 1910–1963*.

Ewa Morawska is Associate Professor of Sociology and History at the University of Pennsylvania. She specializes in historical sociology of immigration and ethnicity in the United States, American Jewish social history, and East European studies (historical and contemporary).

Bernard H. Moss teaches French history and European community studies at the University of Aston in the UK. He is the author of several studies of French labor, socialism, and industrial relations.

Edward Muir, who teaches at Louisiana State University, is the author of *Civic Ritual in Renaissance Venice and Mad Blood Stirring: Vendetta and Factions in Friuli During the Renaissance* (1981).

Robert A. Nye is a Professor of European history at the University of Oklahoma.

Karen Offen is a historian and independent scholar affiliated with the Institute for Research on Women and Gender, Stanford University.

Max J. Okenfuss (PhD, Harvard, 1971) is Associate Professor of History at Washington University and the American editor of the *Jahrbuecher fuer Geschichte Osteuropas*. He studies the history of education in early modern Russia.

Peter S. Onuf teaches at the University of Virginia.

Robert L. Paquette is an Associate Professor of History at Hamilton College.

Jane L. Parpart is a Professor of History at Dalhousie University in Halifax, Nova Scotia. She studies labor and women in Africa and is particularly interested in the development of a global theoretical approach to the study of women.

Cynthia Patterson is Assistant Professor of History at Emory University. She has published a monograph on Athenian citizenship law, articles on marriage, bastardy, and infanticide in ancient Greece, and currently is working on a project entitled "Family and Household in the Greek Polis."

Linda Penkower is an Assistant Professor in the Department of Religious Studies at the University of Pittsburgh. She completed her PhD at Columbia University in 1992. Her area of concentration is East Asian Buddhism. She

has lived and studied in Tokyo, Japan, for seven years.

Marifeli Pérez-Stable is an Associate Professor of Sociology at the State University of New York, Old Westbury. During 1991–1992, she held a National Science Foundation Visiting Professorship for Women at the New School for Social Research in New York City.

Andrejs Plakans is Professor of History at Iowa State University and associate editor of the *Journal of Family History*.

Anne Marie Pois (History PhD) is an instructor for the History Department and Women Studies Program at the University of Colorado, Boulder. Her main area of research deals with U.S. women and peace, with a particular focus upon the Women's International League for Peace and Freedom during the interwar years.

William E. Pomeranz received his PhD from the School of Slavonic and East European Studies, University of London in 1990. He is currently a Visiting Assistant Professor at the Catholic University of America.

Steven W. Pope (PhD, University of Maine, 1992) is revising his dissertation on American sport, tradition, and national identity for publication.

G. Robina Quale, (BA, MA, PhD, University of Michigan) has taught in the Albion College History Department since 1957. Her latest book is *Families in Context* (Westport, CT: Greenwood, 1992).

Donald Quataert is Professor of History and Director of the Southwest Asian and North African Program, State University of New York, Binghamton.

Howard N. Rabinowitz is Professor of History at the University of New Mexico. He is the author of *Race Relations in the Urban South, 1865–1890* (1978, 1980) and *The First New South, 1865–*

1920 (1992) and the editor of *Southern Black Leaders of the Reconstruction Era* (1982).

Pamela Radcliff is Assistant Professor of History at the University of California, San Diego. She is working on a manuscript entitled *Class and Community in Twentieth Century Spain: The Growth of Urban Radicalism in Gijon, 1900–1937*.

Gloria Goodwin Raheja received a PhD in anthropology from the University of Chicago and currently is Associate Professor of Anthropology at the University of Minnesota. She is the author of a monograph on caste, ritual, and exchange in a north Indian village, and co-author of a forthcoming book on gender and oral traditions in India.

Evelyn S. Rawski is Professor of History at the University of Pittsburgh.

James A. Reilly, a specialist on Ottoman Syria, teaches modern history in the Department of Middle East and Islamic Studies, University of Toronto.

Katherine Reist is a Professor of History at University of Pittsburgh Johnstown.

Daniel P. Resnick, an applied historian, is a Professor at Carnegie Mellon University.

Heather Cox Richardson graduated from Harvard University's Program in the History of American Civilization in 1992.

Jaime E. Rodríguez is a Professor of History at the University of California, Irvine.

Herman Roodenburg is a Professor at the P.J. Meertens-Instituut, Amsterdam, Netherlands.

Sonya O. Rose is Associate Professor of Sociology at Colby College. She is the author of *Limited Livelihoods: Gender and Class in Nineteenth Century England* (Berkeley: University of California Press, 1992).

Linda W. Rosenzweig is Associate Professor of History and Education at Chatham College. Her most recent research has focused on the social history of mother-daughter relationships.

Gilbert Rozman is the Musgrave Professor of Sociology at Princeton University. His publications compare China, Japan, and Russia and examine their mutual perceptions, past and present.

Guido Ruggiero is Professor of Italian Renaissance History at the University of Connecticut. He has published extensively on the social history of Venice and the history of sex and gender, including, among other works, *The Boundaries of Eros: Sex Crime and Sexuality in Renaissance Venice* (New York: Oxford University Press, 1985); *Sex and Gender in Historical Perspective: Selections from Quaderni Storici*, edited with Edward Muir (Baltimore: John Hopkins University Press, 1990); and *Binding Passions: Tales of Magic, Marriage, and Power from the End of the Renaissance* (New York: Oxford University Press, 1994).

Harry Sanabria teaches economic anthropology at the Department of Anthropology, University of Pittsburgh. He has carried out field research in Bolivia and New York City.

Lillian Schlissel is Director, American Studies Program, Brooklyn College. She presently is working on a history of the women of vaudeville from 1860 to 1960, with the working title *Bawdy Women*.

Robert A. Schneider is Associate Professor at the Catholic University of America and author of *Public Life in Toulouse, 1463–1789: From Municipal Republic to Cosmopolitan City* (Ithaca: Cornell University Press).

Joseph E. Schwartzberg received his PhD in geography from the University of Wisconsin in 1960. His principal academic specialization is South Asia. He is the editor and principal author of *A Historical Atlas of South Asia*, origi-

nally published by the University of Chicago Press (1978) and revised in an updated edition by Oxford University Press (1992).

Robert W. Scribner is a Fellow of Clare College, Cambridge, England, and works on the social history of the German Reformation, especially its impact on popular belief.

James Searing is Assistant Professor, University of Illinois, Chicago.

Carole Shammas is Professor of History and Women's Studies at the University of California, Riverside, and specializes in economic history.

Stuart Shapiro is a Research Fellow at the Centre for Research into Innovation, Culture, and Technology at Brunel University, England.

Marshall S. Shatz is Professor of History at the University of Massachusetts, Boston. He has published books, articles, and translations on Russian intellectual and political history.

Sarah Shields received her PhD in history from the University of Chicago. She studies the economy and society of the Middle East.

Leo K. Shin, a native of Hong Kong, is pursuing his doctorate degree in Chinese history at Princeton University. He is interested in the social history of the later imperial period.

Nancy Shoemaker is Assistant Professor of History at Texas Christian University

Lisa Z. Sigel is a graduate student at Carnegie Mellon University.

Richard W. Slatta is Professor of History at North Carolina State University and author of *Cowboys of the Americas* (1990), *Bandidos* (1987), and *Gauchos and the Vanishing Frontier* (1983).

Richard J. Smethurst is Research Professor at the University Center for International Studies, University of Pittsburgh. He is the

author of two books and a number of articles on twentieth-century Japanese agriculture and militarism.

Alison A. Smith, a social historian of Renaissance Italian elites, teaches at Vassar College.

Bonnie Smith is a Professor of History at Rutgers University.

Daniel Scott Smith, Professor of History at the University of Illinois, Chicago, has written a number of essays in American family, demographic, and social history. During the 1980s he was the editor of *Historical Methods*.

Harvey Smith is Associate Professor of History, and Acting Director of the Social Science Research Institute, at Northern Illinois University.

Woodruff D. Smith is Professor of History at the University of Texas at San Antonio. He has published books on the German colonial empire, Nazi imperialist ideology, modern European imperialism, and 19th-century German cultural science, and now is working on a book on the demand for overseas products in Europe (1600–1750).

Denise A. Spellberg is a Professor of History at the University of Texas, Austin.

Joe Spillane, an advanced graduate student at Carnegie Mellon University, is teaching the history of drug policy at Indiana University.

John C. Spurlock, Assistant Professor of History at Seton Hill College, is the author of *Free Love: Marriage and Middle Class Radicalism in America, 1825–1860* (1988).

Peter N. Stearns is Heinz Professor of History, Carnegie Mellon University, and editor-in-chief of the *Journal of Social History*. He has written and edited over 40 books, mainly in the field of social history, with recent work focusing on the history of emotion and on issues of humanities education.

Mark D. Steinberg teaches the history of 19th- and 20th-century Russia at Yale University. He is the author of *Moral Communities: The Culture of Class Relations in the Russian Printing Industry, 1867–1907* (Berkeley: University of California Press, 1992), and presently is working on a study of worker intellectuals in Russia from 1900 to 1927.

Theodore Steinberg is an Assistant Professor at the New Jersey Institute of Technology.

Traian Stoianovich is author of *A Study in Balkan Civilization* (New York: Knopf, 1967), *French Historical Method: The "Annales" Paradigm* (Ithaca: Cornell University Press, 1976), and *Between East and West: The Balkan and Mediterranean Worlds* (New Rochelle, NY: Aristide D. Caratzas, Publisher, 1992). Traian Stoianovich is Professor of History Emeritus at Rutgers University, where he was a teacher.

Tyler Stovall is an Associate Professor of History at the University of California, Santa Cruz. He is the author of *The Rise of the Paris Red Belt* (Berkeley: University of California Press, 1990), as well as several articles on urban and French history. He currently is working on a study of working-class protest in Paris at the end of World War I.

David Strand, an Associate Professor of Political Science at Dickinson College, is the author of *Rickshaw Beijing: City People and Politics in the Twenties*.

Carl Strikwerda teaches at the University of Kansas.

Donald S. Sutton has written a book on provincial militarism in 20th-century China (1980) and articles on local religion in the *Journal of Asian Studies*, the *Journal of Ritual Studies*, and other publications. His current work combines textual research, anthropological theory, and ethnographic fieldwork in Taiwan.

Thomas Szendrey, PhD, is Professor and Chairman of the Department of History at Gannon University. His area of specialization is historiography and the philosophy of history, in which he has edited two books and written several dozen articles.

Amy M. Thomas teaches in the English Department at Montana State University.

John B. Thomas is a PhD candidate at Carnegie Mellon University. His dissertation examines the dynamics of the consumer culture emerging around automobile ownership in the United States.

Micheál Thompson is a social historian of modern Europe with interests in identity formation, language issues, the politics of small nations, and the European Community. His current research concerns the evolution of regionalism and European integration with a particular focus on Italy and the British Isles.

Robert J. Thompson is an Associate Professor at the Newhouse School of Public Communication at Syracuse University. He has written or edited four books on American television.

Robert W. Thurston, Associate Professor of History at Miami University, Oxford, Ohio, is author of *Liberal City, Conservative State: Moscow and Russia's Urban Crisis, 1906–1914* (New York: Oxford University Press, 1987) and articles on the social history of the Soviet Union in the 1930s.

Charles Tilly is Professor of History at the New School for Social Research, New York City.

Michael Timberlake is a Professor of Sociology at Kansas State University. His research has explored the global context of Third World urbanization, international dependency and internal repression, and contemporary rural poverty in the Mississippi Delta region of the southern United States.

Steve Tripp teaches social history at Grand Valley State University.

He received his PhD in social history at Carnegie Mellon University in 1990.

Joe William Trotter, Professor of History at Carnegie Mellon University, is the author of *Coal, Class, and Color: Blacks in Southern West Virginia, 1915–32* and *Black Milwaukee: The Making of an Industrial Proletariat, 1915–45*. He currently is working on a comparative study of blacks in three Alabama cities during the 20th century.

Judith E. Tucker is an Associate Professor of History at Georgetown University. Author of *Women in Nineteenth Century Egypt* (New York: Cambridge University Press, 1985) and editor of *Women and Arab Society: Old Boundaries, New Frontiers* (Indiana University Press, 1992).

David Turley, Senior Lecturer in History, University of Kent, Canterbury, England, specializes in the history of reform and radicalism in Britain and the United States and the comparative history of slavery. He is the author of *The Culture of English Antislavery, 1780–1860* and essays and articles on American and British abolitionists and social commentators.

Robert D. Ubraico, Jr. is Professor of History at Webster University, specializing in various facets of American social history.

Bruce Vandervort teaches modern European history at Virginia Military Institute.

Eric Van Young is Professor of History at the University of California, San Diego. His work is currently the social and economic history of colonial Mexico.

Steven Béla Várdy, PhD, is Professor of History at Duquesne University; Director of Duquesne University's History Forum; Adjunct Professor of East European History at the University of Pittsburgh; and a frequent Visiting Scholar at the University of Budapest and at the Institute of History of the Hungarian Academy of Sciences. Professor Várdy is the author or co-author of 250 articles and essays and over a dozen books, among them *Modern Hungarian Historiography* (1976), *The Hungarian-Americans* (1985), *Clio's Art in Hungary and Hungarian-America* (1986), and *The Austro-Hungarian Mind* (1989).

James H. Vaughan is Professor Emeritus of Anthropology at Indiana University. Since 1959 he has conducted field research in the Mandara Mountains, which form the northeastern border of Nigeria and Cameroon.

K. Steven Vincent is Professor of History at North Carolina State University and the author of *Pierre-Joseph Proudhon and the Rise of French Republican Socialism* (1984) and *Between Marxism and Anarchism: Benoit Malon and French Reformist Socialism* (1992).

Lynne Viola is Associate Professor of History at the University of Toronto. She is the author of *The Best Sons of the Fatherland* (New York: Oxford University Press, 1987) and co-editor (with Sheila Fitzpatrick) of *A Researcher's Guide to Sources on Soviet Social History in the 1930s* (Armonk, NY: Sharpe, 1990).

John O. Voll is Professor of History at the University of New Hampshire. He is president (1993) of the Middle East Studies Association of North America.

Theodore H. Von Laue, Hiatt Professor of European History (emeritus), Clark University. An immigrant from Germany (1937) and a cultural insider-outsider, Professor Von Laue moved as a historian from Europe into Russian/Soviet affairs, with a side trip into West Africa. His chief conviction: the Westernization of the world has opened an unprecedented new age in human experience, still uncomprehended by observers imprisoned in the limited cultural envelopes of the past.

John K. Walton, BA (Oxford), PhD (Lancaster), is Reader in Modern Social History, University of Lancaster, UK. He is the author of *The English Seaside Resort: A Social History, 1750–1914*, and other books and articles on leisure, holidays, and resorts in England.

Joan Wang is currently a PhD candidate in the History Department of Carnegie Mellon University.

David Weber is Professor of History at Southern Methodist University.

William Weber (California State University, Long Beach) has written on musical subjects found variously in England, France, Austria, and Germany in the 18th and 19th centuries.

J. Robert Wegs is Professor of Modern European History at the University of Notre Dame.

Robert Weinberg teaches Russian and European history at Swarthmore College and has written on the 1905 Revolution in Odessa and anti-Jewish pogroms in late imperial Russia. He now is working on a history of Birobidzhan, the Jewish Autonomous Region in Russia.

Robert Weisbrot, Professor of American History at Colby College, is the author of *Freedom Bound: A History of America's Civil Rights Movement* (New York: Penguin, 1991).

Lee Shai Weissbach received his PhD at Harvard University in 1975 and is currently Professor of History at the University of Louisville. He has published widely on topics in French and American social history and in modern Jewish history.

Robert V. Wells is the Washington Irving Professor of Modern Literary and Historical Studies at Union College. He has written extensively on American demographic history.

Merry E. Wiesner-Hanks is an Associate Professor of History and the Director for Women's Studies at the University of Wisconsin, Milwaukee. She is the author of *Working Women in Renaissance Germany* (New Brunswick, NJ: Rutgers University Press, 1986), *Women and Gender in Early Modern Europe, 1500–1750* (Cambridge, 1993) and a number of articles on women and the Reformation, the relationship between work and gender, and other aspects of early modern German social history.

Jacqueline S. Wilkie is an Associate Professor of History at Luther College.

Phillip Wilkin is a PhD in European and African history, Indiana University (1981). His current position is Social Sciences Bibliographer in the University Library System at the University of Pittsburgh. He currently is writing *Christianity and Islam in Sub-Saharan Africa: An Annotated Bibliography* for Greenwood Press.

J.M. Winter is University Lecturer in History and Fellow of Pembroke College, Cambridge, England. He is the author of *The Great War and the British People* (1986) and *The Experience of World War I* (1989).

Richard S. Wortman is Professor of History at Columbia University. He is the author of *The Crisis of Russian Populism* (Cambridge, 1967) and *The Development of a Russian Legal Consciousness* (Chicago, 1976).

Cas Wouters, a sociologist, is Lecturer at the Department of General Social Sciences of the State University of Utrecht, the Netherlands.

Anand A. Yang teaches at the University of Utah.

Sandra L. Zimdars-Swartz is Professor of Religious Studies at the University of Kansas.

Marilyn Zoidis, a former director of two local historical societies, is studying for a PhD in American history at Carnegie Mellon University.

The Encyclopedia

Abolition of Slavery

See Emancipation

Abortion

Women seeking to control their fertility have had recourse, as far back as it is possible to trace, to abortion. Such a backup method of fertility control was essential given that until the 20th century coitus interruptus was the main method of contraception. In the ancient world inducement of miscarriage did not pose a major moral problem; human life was not thought to exist until late in the gestation cycle. In the Christian era churchmen condemned abortion practices, associating them with magic and promiscuity, but even clerics held that "ensoulment" or quickening only occurred sometime in the second trimester. Criminalization of abortion took place in the United States and Britain in the 19th century and was not so much the result of older religious concerns for, or new scientific investigations of, fetal development as it was of doctors' success in asserting that they alone could determine when induction of miscarriage was justified.

Who aborted? The evidence suggests that in the past most were wives attempting to limit family size. Only in the 20th century, as the married took advantage of the wider provision of contraceptives, would the single woman seeking to avoid a first birth become the typical case. How many aborted? Some historians have spoken of an abortion "epidemic" occurring in the late 19th century. Given the increased desire to limit family size it is probable that rates of abortion went up, perhaps accounting for one-sixth of all pregnancies in the United States. But opponents of fertility control tended to attribute to abortion the entire decline in the fertility rate; in the 1890s French commentators spoke of hundreds of thousands of abortions per year. Hard figures are difficult to come by given that few attempts at inducement of miscarriage, aside from those that ended in the death of the mother, were thoroughly investigated.

What methods were employed? Ancient Greek abortion exercises, herbal remedies, and instruments were still being employed in the 19th century. But in addition to these traditional abortifacients, such as savin, ergot of rye, and pennyroyal, the expansion of the newspaper press brought advertisements for a vast range of patent medicines that claimed to "remove obstacles." Most probably did not work, and recourse then had to be made to the assistance offered by a friend, midwife, or medical practitioner.

Women continued to hold to the notion that until quickening they had the right to take whatever measures were necessary to make themselves "regular" (an alternate term used instead of the medical term "abortion"). They often viewed inducement of miscarriage not as distinctly different from contraception, but rather as simply one technique among many located along a fertility control continuum. Although dangerous, abortion had its advantages. In allowing a postponement of the decision of controlling fertility until a late date in the reproductive cycle it gave women living at a subsistence level time to assess whether they could support an additional child. Abortion was, for those whose husbands would not cooperate in contracepting, often the only alternative against unwanted pregnancy. Ironically, the most determined attempts to contrast sharply abortion and contraception were made in the early 20th century by birth control advocates who believed that by publicly condemning the inducement of miscarriage they could win contraception the support of the respectable. The decriminalization of abortion in the 1960s represented a return to the notion that in the first months of a pregnancy the woman's interests were paramount; however, doctors now policed the abortion decision. The investigation of the history of abortion, in revealing the tenacity with which women in past centuries sought to control their fertility, has played a crucial role in undermining the stereotyped notion of the "passive" female. It also reveals an important series of changes in dominant attitudes and policies toward abortion. (*See also* Birth Control; Infanticide; Women's History)

Angus McLaren

REFERENCES

Brookes, Barbara. *Abortion in England, 1900–1967.* London: Croom Helm, 1988.

McLaren, Angus. *A History of Contraception: From Antiquity to the Present Day.* Oxford: Blackwell, 1990.

Mohr, James. *Abortion in America: The Origins and Evolution of a National Policy, 1800–1900.* New York: Oxford University Press, 1978.

Abuse

Family abuse is an obvious topic for social historians, and because of the increased attention to abuse in recent years several American historians have ventured serious histories. The topic is fascinating, because some of the information that historians would most like to have is so elusive: it is probably impossible to gain a firm sense of abuse rates in the past, which means that exact assessments of the relationship between present rates (themselves difficult to determine precisely) and any previous trends are questionable. Claims by nonhistorians that rates have soared are dubious, save in the very short run, but more definite statements have not yet emerged. Considering this, abuse is rather like rape or suicide—a vital topic, open to historical inquiry, but not fully understandable.

Without pretending exactitude on rates, historians have contributed to discussions of abuse in several ways. First, they have discussed general frameworks. Some historians of childhood argue that abuse was commonplace before the 20th century, because parents and other adults so commonly used physical punishments and other harsh measures. Abuse, in other words, was almost routine. More recent work questions this approach, noting that societies (as in colonial America) did distinguish between abuse and normal punishment. They might have been harsh in their normalcy, by our standards, but they were not usually abusive. One historian has indeed argued that abuse went up in the United States in the 19th and 20th centuries, because of decreased community supervision of families and increased tensions on the part of parents, who might take out their work and other frustrations on their children. Obviously, a focus on overall framework is thus far inconclusive, but it does raise important issues.

Several historians have done their best with available abuse rates for the 19th and 20th centuries. One argues that, because of the pressures of early industrial life, working-class wife abuse went up in Britain in the early 19th century but then declined partly because of disapproval by middle-class observers but mostly because wives learned to be more cautious. Other recent work deals with family abuse as a function of hard economic times, which relates to contemporary findings that emphasize the same correlations. No systematic study has yet been generated, and 20th-century trends have not been historically investigated. Family abuse by women has also not been explored, since in recent years abuse has most commonly been studied as part of larger examinations of male family power.

A third approach to abuse involves attention to societal reactions. In the United States, attention to abuse has been sporadic, peaking in periods when larger reform movements have died down (after Reconstruction, for example, or after the 1960s); regulatory efforts bear little clear relationship to actual abuse trends. To date, most regulatory efforts have waned after a time, because of a desire to assume that families should be left alone to take care of themselves. Even in this policy area, a great deal of work remains to be done.

Finally, changing definitions of abuse demand attention. As with other crime categories, such as juvenile delinquency, abuse standards have changed at different points in history. Recent expansion of definitions of abuse, to include more types of sexual abuse, for example, or inadequate attention in addition to physical beatings, complicate the historical study of abuse rates but invite more systematic study of changes in rigor and the reasons for such changes. Here too, historical inquiry is just beginning, and social historians will surely learn more about abuse in the future despite the inherent problems with data.

Peter N. Stearns

REFERENCES

Gordon, Linda. *Heroes of Their Own: The Politics and History of Family Violence.* New York: Viking Press, 1988.

Haag, Pamela. "The 'Ill-Use of a Wife': Violence in Domestic and Public New York City, 1860–1880," *Journal of Social History* 25 (1992): 447–477.

Pleck, Elizabeth H. *Domestic Tyranny: The Making of Social Policy Against Family Violence from Colonial Times to the Present.* New York: Oxford University Press, 1987.

Tomes, Nancy. "A Torrent of Abuse: Crimes of Violence Between Working-Class Men and Women in London, 1840–1875," *Journal of Social History* 11 (1978): 328–345.

African American Society

The origins and development of African American society are deeply rooted in the rise of slavery, industrialization, and the recent deindustrialization of American society. Although the struggle to record systematically and to interpret the black experience emerged during the late 19th and early 20th centuries, prevailing scholarship has either ignored blacks or treated them as objects of forces beyond their control. Thus, during the first half of the 20th century, African American history received little recognition within academia. Over the past two decades, however, under the impact of the modern civil rights and black power movements, the new social history, and increasing efforts to study American society from the bottom up, African American history emerged and developed as a vital field of scholarship within U.S. history. Recent scholarship suggests the outlines of a fuller and more satisfactory portrait of African American society from slavery to recent times. The same scholarship has constituted a major focus of social history, contributing greatly to the definition and momentum of the field.

An understanding of the African American experience is nonetheless complicated by contradictory and often misleading historiographical traditions. Until World War II and its aftermath, historians treated the black experience with little concern for the views of African Americans. With the exception of pioneering black scholars like W.E.B. Du Bois and Carter G. Woodson, and a small number of sympathetic white allies, few scholars placed African Americans at the center of their analyses. Whatever the chronological or topical focus—slavery, emancipation, Reconstruction, or 20th-century migration and urbanization—professional historians invariably emphasized race relations, usually defined as white attitudes and actions toward blacks.

As late as World War II white historians continued to cite U.B. Phillips's *American Negro Slavery* (1918) as the principal authority on black life under bondage. Relying primarily upon plantation records and the words and deeds of planters, Phillips portrayed slavery as a paternalistic institution, which, though marked by the use of force, introduced "backward Africans" to the blessings of Western civilization. Although studies by Kenneth Stampp (1956) and Stanley Elkins (1959) overturned the racist portrait, only since the early 1970s have scholars fundamentally reshaped our understanding of slaves and slavery in the United States. Studies by John Blassingame (*The Slave Community*, 1972), Eugene Genovese (*Roll, Jordan, Roll*, 1976), and the late Herbert Gutman (*The Black Family in Slavery and Freedom*, 1976) all illuminate the emergence of a vibrant African American community and cultural life under bondage.

Moving beyond the records left by planters to a variety of sources left by slaves, the recent scholarship shows how Africans created a new African American culture. Antebellum slaves created new religious and family practices, songs, dances, folktales, oral traditions, and a variety of customs and beliefs. The slaves' culture alleviated the burden of oppression, promoted group solidarity, built self-esteem, and supported subtle and sometimes overt forms of resistance to bondage itself. As one scholar put it, "However oppressive or dehumanizing the plantation was, the struggle for survival was not severe enough to crush all of the slave's creative instincts."

New scholarship on emancipation and Reconstruction also stress the creative role of African Americans in shaping their own experience. Emancipation studies by Thomas Holt, Leon Litwack, Armstead Robinson, Eric Foner, Nell Painter, and Barbara Fields emphasize the role blacks played in giving meaning to their own freedom. Black politicians were not merely pawns of their northern and southern Republican allies; they often broke ranks and pushed for measures in their own interests. Sharecropping was not unilaterally imposed upon ex-slaves by ex-masters; it represented intense bargaining between white landowners and black laborers, who insisted on access to land and a measure of independence in its cultivation. And, far from waiting for whites to help shepherd their transition to freedom, African Americans struck out on their own, building a plethora of institutions—churches, fraternal orders, and social clubs, as well as business, professional, political, and civil rights organizations. Moreover, the black working class had poorly voiced socioeconomic goals and aspirations that were often at variance with the political aims of nascent black elites.

Similar to research on slavery and the first years of freedom, scholars, until recently, approached the Great Migration of blacks to the North during World War I and its aftermath in highly mechanistic terms. Blacks were not so much actors as they were reactors to impersonal social forces beyond their control; they were simultaneously pushed out of the South—by declining economic conditions, segregation, disfranchisement, and racial violence—and pulled into the urban North—by the labor demands of wartime production, the decline of European immigration, and the lure of better social conditions and full citizenship rights. Recent studies by Earl Lewis, James Grossman, Peter Gottlieb, and others are reversing this static image of black migration to the urban North and South. They show how African Americans developed elaborate kin and friendship networks, shared information and resources, and organized their own movement into the rapidly industrializing cities.

In relation to the migration of blacks to American cities, scholars of American and African American social history are also reshaping our understanding of the transformation of black urban life itself. From the mid-1960s to the mid-1970s scholars like Gilbert Osofsky, Allan Spear, and Kenneth Kusmer documented the making of black urban ghettos—emphasizing the impact of white hostility on virtually every facet of black life in the modern city. Driven by the desire to prove that blacks were not simply another immigrant group, these scholars portrayed the black urban community as a uniquely racial and spatial phenomenon. Recent studies by Dennis Dickerson, Robin D.G. Kelley, and Joe W. Trotter among others emphasize the emergence of new classes and social relations within the African American community. They suggest that the process of class formation or proletarianization is as critical to understanding the black urban experience as is the process of ghettoization.

Despite recent strides in African American history scholars are only now beginning to approach the complicated interplay of gender, race, culture, and power in the development of black life. Until more studies like those of Darlene Clark Hine, Deborah Gray White, Jacqueline Jones, Dolores Janiewski, Lawrence Levine, and Earl Lewis are conducted, our understanding of African American society will remain incomplete. Still, based upon the recent scholarship, a fuller and more satisfactory portrait of African American society from slavery to the present is now possible. Recent scholarship suggests that the interrelated processes of migration, work, and class formation underlay the development of African American society, shaping its persistent search for social justice, freedom, and full citizenship in a democratic but hostile polity.

Unlike European and Asian immigrants, Africans entered the New World as slaves. Beginning in the 17th century, 1½ million blacks reached the United States via the international slave trade. They came primarily from the west coast of Africa, and, through natural increase, rose to an estimated 4 million by 1860. In the wake of the American Revolution, the center of the black population moved from the Upper South tobacco-growing region of Virginia and Maryland to the cotton-growing areas of the Deep South. Despite their enslavement and forced movement from one region to another, slaves acted on their own behalf by running away, planning rebellions, and, as suggested above, deepening their efforts to build a viable slave community. Their resistance to bondage gave rise to an estimated half-million free blacks by 1860. Free blacks established the first independent black institutions like the African Methodist Episcopal Church, the Prince Hall Masonic lodges, and numerous local mutual aid societies. Black resistance to bondage, however, gained its greatest expression during the Civil War, when slaves deserted the plantation in growing numbers and joined federal forces as they moved deeper into the Confederacy. Slaves "voted for freedom with their feet" as well as with their muskets in the Union Army. African American society was radically transformed under the impact of the Civil War and Reconstruction. As W.E.B. Du Bois noted in his classic study *Black Reconstruction* (1935), "Easily the most dramatic episode in American history was the sudden move to free four million black slaves in an effort to stop a great civil war, to end forty years of bitter controversy, and to appease the moral sense of civilization." Spurred by the presence of federal troops, the ending of chattel slavery, and the enactment of full citizenship legislation, the legal status of African Americans began to converge with that of the larger white working class. Through the early efforts of the Freedmen's Bureau and later through their own agency, ex-slaves entered new contractual relations with white employers and landowners. Along with sharecropping, a new black wage-earning proletariat expanded in the rural and urban South. Closely intertwined with the rise of this new black working class, a new black middle class also slowly expanded; black landownership rose to about 12 million acres by 1910, and urban black business and professional people extended their services to an increasingly all-black clientele.

Despite the freedmen and women's optimism, hope, enthusiasm, and determination to make freedom real, white resistance soon marred their dreams. As historian Joel Williamson suggests, American society experienced "a great changeover" of white elites from a pragmatic engagement with the welfare of blacks, through the institution of slavery and the abolitionist movement, to a new alliance with the white masses. By the early 20th century, whites had developed a consensus on the race question, perceiving and treating blacks as distinctly inferior members of American culture, society, and polity. Lynchings, disfranchisement, segregation, and innumerable forms of social injustice emerged in the South. As racial barriers hardened in the South, a de facto system of racial segregation developed in the North. One historian called this period the "nadir" in African American history. "The United States had emerged as a 'world power,' but at home it was faithless to its own basic principles as far as nine million black citizens were concerned."

Black Americans were by no means passive as the system of racial subordination consolidated. Black elites like Booker T. Washington used black colleges like Tuskegee Institute to develop a program of racial self-help. Others, like W.E.B. Du Bois, used Atlanta University to conduct a series of social scientific studies, designed to fight racism through education. Still other elites joined a small coterie of white allies and pushed for full citizenship rights through the formation in 1909 of the National Association for the Advancement of Colored People. Black workers formed segregated all-black unions and fought racial inequality among employers and white workers alike, while others where possible joined white workers in biracial or interracial unions like the International Longshoremen's Association and the United Mine Workers of America, for example. Most importantly, however, the black working class and masses used their traditional religious and folk culture to forge new bonds, strengthen their own resolve to survive, and buttress the larger institutional, political, and civil rights activities of the black community. For their part, black women formed the National Association of Colored Women's Clubs, adopted the motto "Lifting as we climb," and protested against gender inequality within and without the black community.

Although southern blacks resisted racial, class, and gender inequality, they nonetheless migrated from the rural South in growing numbers. Under the impact of World War I, an estimated 700,000 to 1 million blacks left the South. Another 800,000 left during the 1920s. Although the number of blacks moving to cities dropped during the Great Depression, during World War II and its aftermath a variety of forces completed the long run transformation of blacks from a predominantly rural to a predominantly urban proletariat. The African American population rose from 13 million in 1940 to over 22 million in 1970, while the number of blacks in the labor force increased from less than 5.7 million to nearly 9 million. At the same time, the percentage of black farm workers dropped from over one-third of gainfully employed blacks to less than 4 percent; the proportion of black men in operative jobs rose from less than 15 percent to over 25 percent; and the percentage of black women in domestic and personal service jobs dropped from 60 percent to less than 20 percent. While African Americans also slowly moved into white collar professional, business, and clerical positions, they remained disproportionately concentrated in low-wage jobs in the service sector (unprotected by tenure and seniority provisions) and in vulnerable goods-producing industries in the central cities.

As the black urban proletariat expanded during World War II and its aftermath, blacks faced increasing residential segregation, economic discrimination, and political inequality. In order to counteract the debilitating impact of class and racial discrimination on their communities (including the gerrymandering of electoral districts), black workers and black elites developed vigorous cross-class alliances and launched the militant civil rights and Black Power movements of the 1950s, 1960s, and 1970s. Their efforts destroyed the legal foundations of the segregationist system and instituted government-led affirmative action programs, designed to attack racial discrimination in jobs, housing, and education.

In the wake of conservative reactions against the gains of the civil rights movement, black America faced new challenges during the during the 1980s and early 1990s. Deindustrialization compounded their difficulties. As jobs and resources moved from central cities to suburban and overseas locations, poverty, crime, and a sense of hopelessness increased within black urban communities. Still, black America tried to "keep hope alive" by strengthening their institutions and rallying behind Jesse Jackson's bid for the Democratic Party's nomination for President in 1984 and again in 1988. Speaking to black America and other distressed groups, Jackson exclaimed, "Our time has come. From freedom to equality, from charity to parity. . . . From aid to trade, from welfare to our share, from slave ship to companionship."

Although blacks had entered freedom as the most rural of Americans, they had become the most urbanized. By redistributing the black population throughout the urban North, West, and South, the great migration had nationalized the interrelationship between class, race, and ethnicity in American society. Today, however, the city no longer holds the attraction that it once did. Indeed, African Americans living in the North and West are returning South in growing numbers. After declining for more than a century, the proportion of blacks living in the South increased during the late 1980s. African American society is again in the throes of change, but its future, like its past and present, is deeply rooted in the processes of migration, class formation, and the ongoing quest for social justice in a democratic nation.

While social historians have touched on most facets of African American historical experience, there have been a series of shifts in emphasis. These include, of course, growing concern with gender and with social class structure. Initial concern with slavery, while still lively, has yielded to a new round of research on the Great Migration and on urban and work experience from Reconstruction onward. This new surge of scholarship has also suggested the many facets of African American social history still to be probed. (See also Civil Rights Movement, Emancipation, Slavery)

Joe William Trotter

REFERENCES

Harris, Robert L., Jr. "Coming of Age: The Transformation of Afro-American Historiography," *Journal of Negro History* 57, 2 (1982): 107–121.

Hine, Darlene Clark, ed. *The State of Afro-American History: Past, Present and Future.* Baton Rouge: Louisiana State University Press, 1986.

Meier, August, and Elliott Rudwick. *Black History and the Historical Profession, 1915–1980.* Urbana: University of Illinois Press, 1986.

Trotter, Joe William, Jr., ed. *The Great Migration in Historical Perspective: New Dimensions of Race, Class, and Gender.* Bloomington: Indiana University Press, 1991.

Wilson, William J. *The Truly Disadvantaged: The Inner City, the Underclass, and Public Policy.* Chicago: University of Chicago Press, 1987.

African American Women

African Americans have been subjected to and have fought against an economic, political, and social system that, from its inception, attempted to devalue their humanity and deny them the fruits of their labor. African American women have labored under a double yoke of race and gender oppression. Recent scholarship shows that African American women have had a "clear understanding that race issues and women's issues were inextricably linked, that one could not separate women's struggle from race struggle." Thus, the history of African American women has been informed by this duality, and this has triggered an increasing output of sociohistorical research focused on the parameters of race combined with gender.

The first Africans experienced treatment different from indentured whites. Unlike whites, blacks were listed in census records by first name only or, more commonly, as "Negro Man," "Negro Women 5," or "Negro woman and young Child of hers." An African-born woman who arrived in Jamestown, Virginia, in 1619 was listed in the census of 1624 as "Isabell Negro." She married "Antoney Negro" in 1625. The couple had a son, William, who was baptized in Jamestown's Church of England in 1625, and apparently they were freed.

Elizabeth Key, born in 1636 to a black woman and a white Virginia politician, also experienced distinctive treatment. At age five or six her father sold her for a period of nine years to another planter. She then "passed into the possession" of another owner, who died in 1655. Key sued for freedom in the Northumberland County Court, arguing that English common law guaranteed that all children inherit their father's condition of servitude. She also claimed that her conversion to Christianity precluded lifelong bondage and that her nine-year period of original indenture had expired. After a reversal, the court eventually freed Elizabeth Key.

Such disparate treatment of blacks was created by the demands of tobacco, rice, indigo, and, in the 19th century, cotton cultivation. Those staple crops produced great wealth for white planters but were extremely labor intensive. The limited bondage of white indentured servants could not meet the rising demands for labor. As planters turned to Africa for a seemingly inexhaustible store of human beings, white lawmakers developed slave codes that enslaved blacks based on the condition of the mother. Historian Lerone Bennett has noted that slave codes made a "sharp distinction in law between white women and Black women." They redefined the status of African American women as chattel property and appropriated "the issue of their reproductive organs." Unborn generations were consigned to perpetual, hereditary bondage. Free black women "though permitted to enjoy their freedom" would not be "admitted to a full fruition of the exemptions and impunities of . . . English women."

On the eve of the Civil War, there were 4 million African American slaves; slightly over 2 million were women. Free blacks numbered almost 500,000, with women representing about half that number. African American women confronted an entrenched system that exploited them because they were black and female. Slave women were exploited by white men who "bred" them for economic gain or used them for personal sexual gratification. Although ties of affection sometimes did develop between slave and master, such unions rested on and were maintained by unequal, coercive power. A Georgia slave explained that when her master "make me follow him into de bush, what use me tell him no? He have strength to make me." Despite the imbalance of power, the historical record is replete with instances of African American slave women who resisted unwanted sexual advances at great risk to themselves and their families.

In addition to sexual exploitation, slave women faced labor exploitation. Historian Elizabeth Fox-Genovese estimates that approximately 25 percent of female slaves lived on plantations with 25 to 50 slaves, while 25 percent lived on plantations with 50 or more slaves. For those and the majority of the other 50 percent, "their gender played an important role in their daily experience." In the large plantation regions like South Carolina and Georgia, virtually all black women worked in the fields, performing every task of cultivation. Most female field slaves performed household labor as well. Working as a house servant, however, did not ensure slave women an easier life. Indeed, house servants were on call around the clock; they often became the targets of sexual advances of white males in the household; they frequently found themselves caught in the middle of family disputes; and they often experienced isolation from the rest of the slave community.

Recent scholarship has emphasized slave women's "freedom from the control of slave men as a foundation for [their] self-reliance and sense of autonomy." In fact, slaveowners, having an economic interest in diminishing the influence of African American men as husbands and fathers, did not permit male slaves any rights over their wives or children and gave no legal status to slave marriages. Owners' financial reverses or deaths often meant sales that tore apart slave families. Generally, however, a mother and children were sold as a unit. Thus, African American women were central to the maintenance of family continuity. They developed and relied on extended kinship and friendship networks that served the supportive functions of family within an environment hostile to black family cohesiveness.

African American women emerged as leaders and shapers of their communities despite the racial and gender restrictions placed on them. Slave women served as midwives, religious and community leaders, and revolutionaries. Indeed, approximately one out of every four escapees on the Underground Railroad was a woman, and Harriet Tubman, an escaped slave from Maryland, became the most celebrated and fearless "conductor" on the line. Although men were the acknowledged leaders in free African American communities in the North, racism and segregation relegated most blacks, men and women, to second-class citizenship and menial employment. Therefore, free African American women were vital to the financial stability and social cohesiveness of their communities. Their efforts produced numerous mutual aid, religious, and educational institutions. For example, an 1830 study of Philadelphia's black mutual benefit societies identified 27 female societies that disbursed almost $4,000. The Daughters of Africa was comprised of some 200 working-class women who "pooled their pennies to pay sick and death benefits to needy members." The women of Philadelphia's Mother Bethel Church organized a Contraband Committee to aid freed black slaves during the Civil War. The New York–based Colored Ladies' Literary Society maintained branches in virtually all the major cities in the Northeast.

African American women also stood at the forefront of the antislavery movement. Charlotte Forten was an "excellent motherly wife" who presided over a large household "with ease and grace, brought up five children" and still found time to establish and participate in the Philadelphia Female Anti-Slavery Society. Her granddaughter and namesake, Charlotte Forten Grimké, influenced by her grandmother's abolitionist commitment, became a teacher in the newly established Freedmen's Bureau schools in Port Royal, South Carolina. Former slave Sojourner Truth became one of the most tireless abolitionists in the antebellum era. Drawing upon her own experiences as a slave, she attacked the racist and sexist foundations upon which slavery and sexual discrimination rested. Black female abolitionists quickly learned that many of their white female counterparts in the movement were not untainted by racial prejudice. The presence of black women in northern antislavery organizations caused whites to relegate them to segregated seating at some meetings and incited threats of racial violence at national conventions.

Boston abolitionist Maria W. Stewart, a leading antislavery advocate, found inspiration in David Walker's *Appeal to the Colored Citizens of the World,* which called for armed rebellion in the South. Despite encountering racial prejudice from whites and sexual prejudice from a significant portion of Boston's black male leadership, who found the messages of racial self-help, antislavery militancy, and women's empowerment unacceptable coming from a female, Stewart became the first African American woman to deliver a public lecture in the country. In her 1832 address she urged, "Daughters of Africa, awake! arise! distinguish yourselves." She challenged African American men to "throw off your fearfulness and come forth." The male hostility her speeches aroused compelled her to leave Boston and eventually to settle in Washington, DC, where she continued to lecture until her death in 1879.

The self-reliance that characterized African American women in the antebellum years, continued through Reconstruction and into the twentieth century. The realities of Jim Crow, sharecropping, and urban industrialization made the rigidly defined Victorian model of femininity unattainable and undesirable for most African American women. More broadly, African American women were far more likely to be employed, even after marriage, than their white counterparts; their work and their fertility experience form distinct paths in 19th- and 20th-century American history. Public and private life intersected for African American women who struggled against sexual and racial discrimination. Thus, the National Association of Colored Women (NACW) flowered at the turn of the century under the leadership of women such as Josephine St. Pierre Ruffin, Mary Church Terrell, Mary McLeod Bethune, and Nannie Burroughs. The black women's club movement was responsible for the establishment of schools, child care centers, homes for the elderly, orphanages, and savings banks. Moreover, the club movement advocated women's suffrage and fought for a national antilynch law. The antilynching campaign of crusading black journalist Ida B. Wells enjoyed its strongest support from African American women's clubs. Historian Paula Giddings has noted that Ida B. Wells's meticulous documentation of lynchings was a "call to arms for the race, but for women specifically" because it undermined the stereotype of the sexually unrestrained black man and challenged "presumptions of the immorality of Black women."

Two world wars thrust African American women into the spotlight of national and global affairs. The duality of race and gender continued to characterize their experiences throughout the 20th century. The civil rights movement of the 1950s and 1960s was a product of heightened expectations and tireless agitation by African American women who worked alongside African American men to overturn the barriers of segregation and discrimination. The 1954 *Brown* v. *Board of Education* Supreme Court decision banning public school segregation followed years of antisegregation struggle in which women were key players. Irene Morgan's refusal to move to the back of a Greyhound bus traveling from Virginia to Baltimore in 1945 resulted in the Supreme Court's 1946 ruling *Morgan* v. *Commonwealth of Virginia,* which outlawed segregation in interstate commerce. Ada Sipuel's challenge to the University of Oklahoma's law school resulted in a precedent-setting desegregation ruling in 1949.

Rosa Parks's refusal to relinquish her bus seat in Montgomery, Alabama, in 1955 became the symbol of the civil rights movement. Montgomery's Black Women's Political Council, under the leadership of Jo Anne Robinson, transformed Parks's singular act of defiance into a citywide demonstration with national consequences. Jo Anne Robinson remarked, "we knew if the women supported it, the men would go along." African American women like Fannie Lou Hamer of the Student Nonviolent Coordinating Committee (SNCC), Daisy Bates of the National Association for the Advancement of Colored People (NAACP), Ella Baker of the Southern Christian Leadership Conference (SCLC) and SNCC, and countless others were vital to the leadership, strategies, and operations of the civil rights movement. However, Stokely Carmichael's infamous pronouncement that the "only position for women in SNCC is prone" highlighted the degree to which sexism permeated the movement.

African American women remained ambivalent about the women's movement that emerged in the 1970s, perceiving it to be irrelevant, alien, and at times hostile to the aspirations of black women. Their concerns were confirmed by census data of the 1980s and 1990s, which revealed that the face of poverty was becoming increasingly female and black, particularly through an increase of female-headed households. African American women remained a marginal group in the labor force with an unemployment rate exceeding that of white women or white men. Thus, the 1980s and 1990s have found African American women struggling to create a movement that does not delimit their commitment to racial, or gender, issues. Indeed, some women, like writer Alice Walker, have begun to employ the term "womanist" to describe an emerging philosophy of black female activism that recognizes the inseparability of gender and race. This linkage has characterized the "unique nature of feminism among Afro-American women" and has informed their history. (*See also* African American Society; Women's History)

Shirley Ann Moore

REFERENCES

DuBois, Ellen Carol, and Vicki L. Ruiz, eds. *Unequal Sisters: A Multicultural Reader in U.S. Women's History.* New York: Routledge, 1990.

Giddings, Paula. *When and Where I Enter: The Impact of Black Women on Race and Sex in America.* New York: Bantam Books, 1984.

Jones, Jacqueline. *Labor of Love, Labor of Sorrow: Black Women, Work and the Family from Slavery to Present.* New York: Basic Books, 1985.

Sterling, Dorothy, ed. *We Are Your Sisters: Black Women in the Nineteenth Century.* New York: Norton, 1984.

White, Deborah Gray. *Ar'n't I A Woman? Female Slaves in the Plantation South.* New York: Norton, 1985.

African Lineage

The African lineage is a descent group which claims to be able to trace its ancestry to a known ancestor. Because of the actual and fictive ties which connect the living members of the lineage (community ties, in fact, may apply in addition to blood and marriage relationships in African lineage), the kin groups signify the real and symbolic continuity of African society. Through the roles of lineage exogamy, or outmarriage, African lineages become linked to each other through involved ties of alliance and mutual support. Even in those African societies where corporate lineages are absent or are present in only a muted form, persons still focus about an extended family. The principles which are felt to guide these kin groupings are defined by respect, loyalty, and reciprocity. Lineage groups play a major role in African social history comparable to social class categories in some other societies, providing, for example, the framework for merchant activities in premodern Africa.

The social functions of African kin groups, particularly in respect to property and decisionmaking, have provoked major debates. African lineages were often depicted as a political statement. In this regard lineage members act through a cultural model of political and social relations which anthropologists represent as an abstract model. The social representation of a lineage mirrors political and territorial structures. Hence the corporate nature of the lineage is in its unity and apposition to like groupings. This is expressed in the following structural assumptions: (a) joint equality founded upon collective responsibility, (b) lineage genealogies are pseudo-histories which contain both constitutional considerations with reflections of the power status quo, and (c) the prevailing divisions within and between lineages are manifested by the fissioning of kin groups along factional lines and fissioning due to external threat or internal differentiation. This usage of lineage theory presupposes a stateless political formation where politics and power are imbedded within kinship. These kinship conventions are enterprises which meld genealogical charters with rights to, or control over, dependents and resources.

Beginning in the 1960s this structural functional understanding of lineage theory gave way to criticism emanating from research not in Africa but in New Guinea. It was duly noted that genealogical kinship relations are reserved for social reproduction. It is not sufficient therefore to consider the official story of kinship without juxtaposing that model with the multileveled and bivocal expressions of kin ties. Forms of cooperation or competition are expressed in kin terms which represent masculine, feminine, age, and mixed divisions of labor. The lineage then is a continually changing mixture of various mobilized kin units. Although the lineage appears equalitarian, there are tendencies to concentrate power in the hands of elders who have capitalized upon matrimonial ties and dependents to buttress their effective control of viable land and livestock. External exchange and alliances may allow the elders to promote further their own interests. This poses the question of the transformative nature of lineage societies. Why in some ethnographic instances are there generation-type kin groupings and in others lineage groups? How do social segments have access to common resources while other segments consolidate their control over social resources? This process may be grounded upon two tendencies which are sometimes contradictory, incompatible, and, in other cases, merely the opposite side of the same coin. First, certain strategically placed kin segments may represent themselves as coterminous with common lineage interests as they increasingly gain control over the collective property, leading to a chiefdom or to true social

stratification. Second, however, in other cases lineages, particularly their African ethnographic representatives, are responses to frontier conditions whereby alliances and cooperation are products of the insecurities of pioneering conditions of social life. (*See also* Genealogy; Kinship)

Frank McGlynn

REFERENCES

Fortes, Meyer. *Kinship & the Social Order*. Chicago: Aldine , 1969.
——— and E.E. Evans-Pritchard, eds. *African Political Systems*. Oxford: Oxford University Press, 1946.
Godelier, Maurice. *Perspectives in Marxist Anthropology*. Cambridge: Cambridge University Press, 1977.
Kopytoff, Igor, ed. *The African Frontier*. Bloomington: University of Indiana Press, 1987.
Radcliffe-Brown, A.R., and D. Forde, eds. *African Systems of Kinship & Marriage*. London: Kegan Paul, 1950.

African Marriage and Family

In sub-Saharan Africa the singular importance of social groupings such as the family is a consequence of demography and economy. With characteristic high mortality rates, the survival of individuals in this area is problematic, and reliance upon individual initiative and achievement are dangerous values. In addition, labor intensive agriculture, which typifies African subsistence systems, places particular importance upon cooperative work. Thus, the group rather than the individual becomes the fundamental unit of society, and the family is the most basic of social groups. Consequently, despite variety in the vast reaches of sub-Saharan Africa, African families tend to be larger, more structured, and generally more important than those found in societies strongly influenced by scientific medicine and industrial production.

Because the family is so important to the survival of African societies marriage is less an impulsive act of two individuals than a strategic act of two families. Hence, it is best to think of marriage as an alliance of groups through the union of a female from one group to a male of another. Without the cooperation of the couple, however, the marriage will not last. In most cases the affection between spouses is at least as great as that found in other societies.

African marriage is almost universally legitimized by the transferral of wealth—in money, services, or valuables—from the family of the groom to the family of the bride. This transaction is called bride wealth, or bride-price. (The term "bride-price" has been criticized because it implies that the bride is being bought, and though that may be close to the case in some societies, it is inaccurate for the vast majority.) Bride wealth is best understood as compensation for the loss of the woman's production, including the production of her womb. So closely is bride wealth tied to children that typically it must be returned in proportion to the number of children born in the marriage, up to some number, such as three, at which point the bride wealth is considered amortized.

In approximately 97 percent of African societies, polygyny is traditionally the preferred form of marriage, that is, a man may be married to two or more women at the same time. Polygyny maximizes the size of the family, which meets the need for labor in unmechanized subsistence systems. It also happens that on average women in polygynous marriages have fewer children than women in monogamous marriages; consequently, births are spaced farther apart, which is beneficial for the mother's health.

Typically, a young man will have one wife. Then as he accumulates wealth and prestige he will become polygynous. Finally, with advanced age, unless he is a person of high status, he may lose his younger wives and once again become monogamous. Thus, although the incidence of polygyny in a society is usually only 30 to 35 percent at any given time, almost all individuals are in polygynous marriages at some time during their lives.

The determination of where the couple resides seems closely tied to which sex plays the dominant role in the economy. For example, in pastoral societies, where mobility of the herd is important and it is necessary for herders to be away from the home for substantial periods of time, the wife moves to her husband's homestead, or virilocal residence. On the other hand, in societies that rely upon agricultural subsistence, which characterizes about three-quarters

of African societies, the determining factor seems to be heritability of land. And since patrilineal inheritance is more prevalent, the virilocal residence prevails. In matrilineal societies, however, where there is female inheritance of land (only about 2 percent), husbands move to their wives' estates, or the matrilocal residence.

The size of the African family is influenced by polygyny, fertility, and familial organization. Since the end of the 19th century African mortality rates have gradually declined, resulting in increased household sizes. At the present time in rural West Africa a typical husband-wife/wives household numbers approximately 10 persons. In addition, approximately 50 percent of societies prefer a form of familial organization wherein several nuclear families are lodged in the same household. Such an extended family may include an aging patriarch, his wives, and unmarried children; his sons, their wives, and unmarried children; and even his grandsons and their budding families. Obviously, these families may comprise very large and effective working groups with obvious advantages, but it would be unrealistic to view these extended families as collections of persons happily cooperating for the good of all. In fact, they are often characterized by intense rivalry and jealousy among the sections. To minimize and control such conflict, African families are more organized than is typical of small nuclear families. Such organization is based upon age and order of birth among males and seniority among wives. In about 75 percent of African societies each wife and her children live in a separate dwelling within the larger household, an arrangement that also helps to reduce conflict by giving each wife her own area of authority.

Approximately 75 percent of African societies are patrilineal, 90 percent of which are virilocal with a general tendency to patriarchal organization. Women, however, have a great deal of initiative, particularly with regard to the family, and their importance is widely recognized. Further, in the give and take of life, rules and customs may be ignored; even though a society may practice virilocal marital residence, if there is good reason for a man to move to his wife's village, he may do so.

Divorce statistics for individual African societies are difficult to obtain. Based on available data, however, divorce is common. In 20 African societies in which data are available, the divorce rate is from 25 percent to 85.9 percent; the median is approximately 60 percent. In large families, however, there are surrogate parents, and the disorganization typically associated with divorce is not characteristic. The best predictor of divorce is relative infertility: the fewer children, the more likely there is to be a divorce. It also should be noted that in many African societies women initiate divorce more often than men.

When marriage is terminated by the death of a husband, often there is a practice that supports our earlier observation that marriage is an agreement between groups rather than between individuals. In a very large percentage of African societies, when a husband dies, his kinsmen are obligated to accept his wives and children into their households—a custom called the levirate.

The African family has proven resilient and has not changed much in the 20th century. As mortality rates improve and the economy becomes more mechanized and urbanized, however, it seems likely that the African family will develop new patterns, perhaps more nearly like those in industrialized societies. Already many urban Africans report tensions with traditional extended family obligations, preferring to concentrate on a more separate, nuclear family. Birth rate reductions also often accompany urbanization.

Social historians have not traced patterns of change in African families in great detail, except for examining the impact of commercialization and urbanization on family life and gender patterns during the past century. Major features of the African family, in terms of both structure and values, figure in other kinds of sociohistorical work on Africa in earlier periods, particularly where kinship relations and family-based economic specialization are concerned. The de facto importance of African women, for example, works into assessments of market activity or the impact of Islam in the great African kingdoms from the 10th century onward.

James H. Vaughan

REFERENCES

Bohannan, Paul, and Philip Curtin. "African Families," in Paul Bohannan and Philip Curtin, eds., *Africa and Africans.* Prospect Heights, IL: Waveland Press, 1988.

Lesthaeghe, Ron J., ed. *Reproduction and Social Organization in Sub-Saharan Africa.* Berkeley: University of California Press, 1989.

Mair, Lucy. *African Marriage and Social Change.* London: Frank Cass, 1969.

Vaughan, James H. "Population and Social Organization," in Phyllis Martin and Patrick O'Meara, eds., *Africa* (2nd ed.). Bloomington: Indiana University Press, 1985.

African Peasantry

During the past two decades historians, anthropologists, geographers, and developmental economists have explored both the complex web of relationships which links rural producers to the world economy and the internal dynamics of peasant communities. This increasing attention to peasants in Africa has produced important new findings on agrarian change but has failed to produce a consensus on how to define the term "peasants" or on what constitutes the essence of a peasant society.

Although the issue is broader than definition, that the concept is elusive helps explain why peasants were rendered invisible in much of the earlier literature. Until the 1970s Africanists encapsulated rural societies in a series of paradigms (structural functionalism, modernization theory, underdevelopment theory, modes of production analysis) that ignored or marginalized peasants as historical actors. This reinforced the dominant view that the concept had little analytical value.

In the early 1970s a small group of radical political economists dissented, arguing peasants existed as an exploited class which emerged in the colonial and, in some cases, postcolonial periods. By the end of that decade this broad political economy approach predominated. Most Africanists agreed that the term "peasant" referred to an agriculturalist who controls the land he/she works either as a tenant or small holder, is organized largely in a household that meets most of his/her subsistence needs, and is ruled by other classes who extract a surplus directly or through control of state power. This consensus, however, did not obviate the inherent problem of capturing the diverse range of peasant relationships and experiences within a single construct.

During the 1980s a new generation of Africanists, mainly social historians, have attempted to resolve this conceptual dilemma by considering the development of peasantries rather than a homogeneous African peasantry. Much of the critical rethinking came from scholars who had remained outside the prior debates. (Feminist scholars, for example, argued what the literature portrayed as the peasant reality was, in fact, an undifferentiated male reality shaped, in turn, by rarefied anthropological assumptions about the sexual division of labor.) Collectively, these Africanists stress micro-analysis and the importance of appreciating differences among and within rural communities. They contend uneven population densities, varying property relations, and the different ways that labor was organized and work obligations were secured through political-legal institutions all combined, over time and space, to produce different peasantries.

By unpacking the term "peasant," scholars have sharpened the distinctions among petty commodity producers, independent household producers, sharecroppers, labor tenants, and oscillating peasants, each enmeshed in different labor regimes and property arrangements varying, additionally, by gender and generation. Petty commodity producers, such as cocoa growers of Ghana, who controlled their own labor and means of production but rarely the terms of exchange, stand in sharp contrast to peasants, such as cotton cultivators of colonial Mozambique, forced to grow specific crops under a highly regulated labor and marketing system. The daily lives of each were quite different from independent household producers who sought to resist or minimize commodity production in favor of food production for use. These, in turn, experienced a different reality from labor tenants or squatters in settler-dominated Kenya or Rhodesia who gained only conditional access to land by giving up a portion of their labor. Conversely, South African sharecroppers guarded their labor jealously and instead yielded a percentage of their crops for temporary access to land. Finally, peasant households in which members periodically worked in towns or on estates experienced quite a different reality from domestic units which remained intact.

Just as new research has exploded the notion of a homogeneous peasantry, so has it challenged the assumption that peasants were a phenomenon of colonialism. Scholars had explained the lack of a precolonial peasantry in terms of a weak market economy, harsh environmental conditions, conservative production strategy, and state systems lacking power to organize and appropriate free rural labor. Until recently, most Africanists presumed that captives were the primary producers of agricultural commodities in the precolonial period and that peasants were inconsequential. Two quite different conclusions flow from more recent literature. First, in many parts of precolonial Africa peasants were neither invisible nor marginal, figuring prominently in the agricultural and political history of Nigeria, Ethiopia, Madagascar, the Congo, Rwanda, and Burundi, among other countries. Second, precolonial peasant regimes were more varied than previously assumed, evidencing, in addition to those producing agricultural commodities to satisfy tribute, tax, or rent obligations, sharecropping and labor tenancy systems throughout the continent. Moreover, there is evidence that many slaves in 19th-century West Africa actually lived as part-time peasants, producing for the market and accumulating a certain amount of wealth.

The ways scholars conceptualized peasantries over time and space are inextricably tied to the types of data they used. It is not by chance that the literature of the 1960s and 1970s, which had rendered peasants invisible or had reduced them to the status of hopeless victims, was also excessively and uncritically dependent on written sources focusing on the colonial period. Also, archival data tended to emphasize exchange relations over production and production over social production, thereby ignoring critical dimensions of peasant village and household life. Only since the late 1980s have Africanists begun to pay greater attention to the variety of peasants—old and young, women and men, sharecroppers and prospering commodity producers. Carefully collected and critically analyzed oral testimonies provide important historical data on the organization of work, crop-management systems, and famine strategies, as well as indigenous notions of property, justice, and struggle—essential for a new social history of the countryside.

Thinking about and listening to the voices of peasantries rather than peasants has opened up new areas of investigation and has exposed many myths about rural societies. There is, for example, growing recognition of the value of peasant science and of the creative ways rural Africans developed intercropping systems, promoted soil conservation, and controlled plant diseases. These interpretations stand in opposition to previous approaches characterizing African agricultural practices as "backward" and "unproductive." Students of agrarian politics have also challenged prior notions of peasant quietism, conservatism, and low levels of political consciousness, arguing convincingly that evidence of the day-to-day forms of struggle, and the critical role peasants played in social movements, demonstrate much greater peasant agency than previously had been assumed.

The seemingly intractable agrarian crisis in Africa has propelled the field of peasant studies to new prominence. Two decades of drought, famine, declining agricultural production, and increased food imports all demand new agendas for thought as well as for action. At the very least, the work of social historians has suggested the need to extend the discussion of agrarian change beyond excessively narrow formulations focusing on market organizing strategies of the dominant classes and the state while ignoring the ways different peasantries helped to make their own history. (*See also* Peasantry)

Allen Isaacman

REFERENCES

Faller, L.A. "Are African Cultivators to Be Called 'PEASANTS'," *Current Anthropology* 2 (1961): 108–110.

Isaacman, Allen. "Peasants and Rural Social Protest," *African Studies Review* 33 (1990): 1–120.

Klein, Martin, ed. *Peasants in Africa*. Beverly Hills: Sage, 1980.

Woods, Saul J. and R. "African Peasantries," in T. Shanin, ed., *Peasants and Peasant Societies*. London: Penguin, 1971.

African Regions

Geography

Africa is a huge continent of 30.2 million square kilometers of mostly plateau, with a regular coastline, a limited number of bays and peninsulas or inlets that merge with the sea, and ancient rocks rich in metals and precious stones. There are over 1,000 languages spoken, including such widely used ones as Arabic, Swahili, Fula, and Hausa and foreign ones like English, French, and Portuguese that have spread with recent colonialism. Africa's long history is influenced by the ingenuity of its people, the environment, and contacts with the outside world.

In the northeastern part of the continent are the Nile River and the Ethiopian highlands. This area is distinct for its rich soil and congenial climate. Lying between this highland and the Indian Ocean is the dry and torrid Somalian plain.

In the northern part of the continent is the Mediterranean region, with a climate similar to but warmer than that of southern Europe and a long narrow coastal strip. To the northwest is the fertile Maghrib area, with the Atlas Mountains.

South of the Maghrib's Atlas Mountains is a contrast—the Sahara, the largest desert in the world. It does not, however, constitute a barrier to relations between the regions. Indeed, the trans-Saharan trade has become one of the greatest in world history. Scattered oases provided water while the Tibesti, Aïr, and Ahaggar mountains in the central and western Sahara attract enough rain to make it possible to farm and rear animals.

In western Africa, there is a long Sudanic belt, a savanna stretching across the continent. Here, the vegetation is well nourished. To the south of the savanna is the rainforest, which adds to the Zaire forests to make the world's, largest tropical forests. The savanna-forest pattern is broken by the Atlantic Ocean to the south, Lake Chad in the east, and rivers like the Niger and Benue. In the southern part is an extensive plateau, with a spine at its highest peaks in the Ruwenzori Mountains. West of the spine is the Zaire-Kasai rivers system, which is dominated by a forest that gives way in the south to a savanna and a plateau. East of the spine are the Shire Highlands, the slopes of Mount Kilimanjaro, and the Great Lakes (Victoria, Tanganyika, and Malawi), and the interlacustrine region (part of modern Uganda)—the cool area between Lakes Victoria, Kyoga, and Kivu.

In the southernmost region is a prolonged plateau surrounded by a coastal strip. The plateau is a dry savanna, with abundant grass and a mid-year cold winter. This region is cherished by nomads for its grass and lack of the tsetse fly, which kills cattle and causes malaria in humans, the number-one disease south of the equator.

Peoples and Societies

Africans can be classified into four physical types. Those in the north, the Caucasoids, are light skinned. South of the Sahara are three Negroid groups, comprising the Negroid proper (with black skin and curly hair), the Pygmoid of the Zaire forest and the Capoids, with short stature, peppercorn hair, and a yellowish-reddish skin.

The Nile valley witnessed ancient civilizations at Egypt, Kush, and Axum. Egypt was a leading civilization, with a dependence on the Nile River, a mastery of irrigation, and a kingship ideology that had emerged by 3000 BC. The king, priests, and others associated with power lived a life of comfort and promoted culture. In many ways, the history of Ethiopia was connected with that of the upper Nile valley, with additional ties with South Arabia. The foundation of the Ethiopian Empire was laid at Axum. Here, a national language, the Geez, evolved, and large-scale temples and monuments were built for the gods. Success in Red Sea trade enhanced the prestige of Ethiopia as a world power. Contacts were established with the Greeks, and Christianity became an official religion until as recently as 1974. In the rest of North Africa, the Berbers were predominant. Those who lived in the Sahara or its fringes were nomadic, while their counterparts in fertile areas of the mountains and the coast took to large-scale farming. As elsewhere, there is also a history of external contacts and invasions. Between the 8th and the 19th centuries, there was the migration to the Maghrib of nomadic Bedouin Arabs, who spread from Tunisia to Morocco. The Bedouin were instrumental to the spread of Arabic culture, to the extent of assimilating the Berbers, except in the Atlas hills in Morocco and the Kabylia regions in Algeria, where the Kabyle Berbers have been able to retain their old culture and language.

South of the Sahara is occupied by the Negroes. The opening up of this great sub-continent to agriculture and urbanization is attributed to the Bantu-speaking peoples. In West Africa successful agriculture and trade led in part to the emergence of complex civilizations and kingdoms in the Sudanic belt (e.g., Ghana, Mali, Songhai, and Kanem-Bornu) and in the forest belt (e.g., Oyo, Benin, Dahomey, Fante, Asante). Further south were such other kingdoms as the Kongo, Lunda, and Kuba in the Zaire area. On the East African coast, where extensive trade developed between Africans and the Arabs and Persians, a Swahili language came into being, as a combination of Bantu and Arabic languages. In the interlacustrine area, there is a history of kingdoms, like the legendary Kitwara to the more recent ones of Bunyoro, Nkore, Buganda, Tor, and Busoga. The well-known empire of Mwene Mutapa emerged to the south of the Zambezi River.

External Factors

Islam spread to different parts of Africa after the 7th century. The greater part of North Africa became Islamic and the religion spread to many other parts of the continent.

The major European contacts began in the 15th century, with voyages by the Portuguese, who established two white communities in Mozambique and Angola, introduced a number of new crops, and began the notorious Atlantic slave trade. In the 19th century the slave trade was replaced by trade in raw materials, and Christianity spread to many places.

In the last years of the 19th century the continent was partitioned by several European countries, leading to the creation of the modern African countries. Some of the impacts and events of colonial rule were economic and political domination, population increase and urbanization, and expansion in agriculture, communication, and education. Colonial rule came to an end in most of Africa by 1980. Today, the continent grapples with the challenge of underdevelopment and political instability.

Sociohistorical research on Africa must keep the complex framework of regions and peoples at the forefront. While many history programs teach African or sub-Saharan African history courses covering most of the regions and peoples, the bulk of social history research on Africa focuses on specific regions. Only a few very general social and cultural characteristics can be extended more widely.

Toyin Falola

REFERENCES

Ajayi, J.F.A., and Crowder, M., eds. *Historical Atlas of Africa*. London: Longman, 1985.

Greenberg, J.H. *The Languages of Africa*. Bloomington: Indiana University Press, 1966.

Murdock, G.P. *Africa: Its Peoples and Their Culture History*. New York: McGraw-Hill, 1959.

African Slave Trade

Research on the social history of the slave trade developed from efforts to quantify the export trade in slaves and assess its impact on African societies. Three topics have dominated research. The dominant role of warriors and military states in much of Africa has been linked to the export trade in slaves and the expansion of African slavery. The merchant networks that purchased, transported, and resold slaves within Africa played an equally vital role in the history of the slave trade. Finally, historians have examined the history of the slaves in transit, the mortality caused by malnutrition and disease, incidences of flight and rebellion, and the factors that led some slaves to be purchased in Africa and destined others for the export trade. Historical developments related to the slave trade have also inspired research. The regular movement of large numbers of slaves along established trade routes led to the emergence of new towns and the expansion of commerce in provisions produced to feed slaves in transit. Many of the laborers whose work sustained the trade in slaves were slaves themselves. In all these areas the history of the slave trade is inseparable from the history of slavery in Africa.

Warrior predation flourished during the era of the slave trade. Warlordism and slave raiding played a crucial role in a political economy based on slavery and the slave trade. In the most striking cases warlords and slave warriors who served them as loyal henchmen reshaped the political order. The *ceddo* of the Wolof states, the *tonjon* of the Bambara states, and many of the armies of West Central Africa were warrior societies in which slaves provided the bulk of the new recruits and sometimes overturned the old order they had been called to serve. These specialists in violence relied on other slaves, mainly women, to supply them with food and domestic labor. Although the rise of warrior states in the 17th and 18th centuries is well established, there has been debate about the extent to which warfare and enslavement were tied to internal and external demand for slaves. The debate has centered on the division of profits between warriors and merchants, the responsiveness of slave supply to market incentives, and the causes of warfare within Africa. The relative importance of large-scale military campaigns versus small-scale banditry and kidnapping in supplying the slave trade has also provoked debate. In many regions expanding military states provided fewer slaves to the market than states experiencing dynastic crisis and civil war or states too weak to control the predation of warriors and nobles.

A second topic crucial to an understanding of the slave trade is the history of the merchant groups that organized the trade within Africa. The economic role of the merchants was to transport slaves from the point of their initial sale to a distant market where there was a demand for their labor. Merchants had to prevent runaways, protect their merchandise from marauders, pay transit taxes to the states through which they passed, and feed and care for the slaves in transit. Most slave traders were professional merchants who combined the transport of slaves with trade in other commodities, frequently using slaves as porters to carry trade goods as well as the provisions required by caravans. In West Africa *juula* merchants exchanged cotton cloth, grain, gold, leather goods, and slaves from the savanna for salt, horses, and manufactured goods brought by Arab merchants crossing the Sahara Desert and for European imports sold at ports in Senegambia and the Gold Coast. The Niger, Senegal, and Gambia rivers were linked by caravan traffic to establish trade links that connected much of West Africa with the Islamic and the Atlantic worlds. Many merchants were large slaveowners as well as slave traders. The Maraka merchants of the middle Niger employed slaves to produce grain and cotton cloth in towns that provided a permanent base for the organization of annual long distance caravans that transported slaves, cloth, and gold. Merchants played a fundamental role in the slave trade by gathering together the victims of warfare, kidnapping, and famine, and those condemned to slavery for crimes or debt.

The slave trade called into being important new merchant groups, particularly along the Atlantic coast and major rivers. Some of these merchants had mixed origins, as witnessed by the growth of Afro-Portuguese communities on the upper Guinea coast and in the ports of West Central Africa, particularly Luanda. Similar communities were found in the coastal ports of Senegambia, the Gold Coast, and the Slave Coast. The most successful coastal merchants played a major role in the overseas slave trade. The *habitants* of Saint Louis and Goree used riverboats and coasting vessels to link the Atlantic coast of Senegambia and the Senegal River valley to merchant networks in the middle and upper Niger River. They employed slaves as sailors on their vessels, while women slaves in the coastal cities processed food to feed the slaves on their way to slavery in the Americas. New merchant groups arose along major African rivers to take advantage of the export trade in slaves. The Bobangi traders of the Zaire River used canoe traffic, military force, and the cataracts on the Zaire to impose a monopoly on trade. The Bobangi became large slaveowners, employing slaves as paddlers and soldiers, while their wives and female slaves prepared food to sustain the river traffic in slaves and other goods.

The social history of the slave trade included the experience of the slaves in transit and social and economic transformations indirectly linked to the slave trade. The journey of slaves to the coast was a human drama. Mortality rates and the relationship between famine and the slave trade have been used to assess the demographic impact of the slave trade, but can be redirected to encompass the experience of slaves in transit and to expand our knowledge of the economics of the slave trade. Use of quantitative methods relevant to these topics has been substantial. The great famine that struck West Africa in the 1750s had a dramatic impact on the slave trade from Senegambia. Mortality rates skyrocketed, and the geography of enslavement was turned upside down. Slave exports from the interior declined, while exports from regions near the coast reached levels never seen before. The changes all stemmed from the scarcity of grain. This one example points to the importance of understanding how large numbers of slaves were fed along all the major trade routes. In the Senegal River valley slavery expanded because slaves produced the grain required to sustain the export trade in slaves. The export trade in slaves was therefore linked to the expansion of slavery within Africa. New attention to economic activities and labor demands generated within Africa by the slave trade should produce a clearer understanding of why women slaves outnumbered men in many societies.

James Searing

REFERENCES

Klein, Martin A. "Women and Slavery in the Western Sudan," in Claire C. Robertson and Martin A. Klein, eds., *Women and Slavery in Africa*. Madison: University of Wisconsin Press, 1983.

Lovejoy, Paul E. *Transformations in Slavery: A History of Slavery in Africa*. Cambridge: Cambridge University Press, 1983.

Miller, Joseph. *Way of Death: Merchant Capitalism and the Angolan Slave Trade, 1730–1830*. Madison: University of Wisconsin Press, 1988.

Roberts, Richard L. *Warriors, Merchants and Slaves: The State and Economy in the Middle Niger Valley, 1700–1914*. Stanford: Stanford University Press, 1987.

Searing, James. *West African Slavery and Atlantic Commerce: The Senegal River Valley, 1700–1860*. Cambridge: Cambridge University Press, 1993.

Thornton, John. *Africa and Africans in the Making of the Atlantic World, 1400–1680*. Cambridge: Cambridge University Press, 1992.

African Slavery

The attempt to understand the institution of

African slavery is an old one. The varieties of interpretations over the past several centuries have vacillated between European reports of an institution brutal and horrific during the era of the slave trade, and then paternalistic if not actually benign during the era of colonialism. Beyond the need to separate historical reality from the self-justifying reporting of the Europeans it is necessary to disentangle African slavery as an ensemble of practices with variously defined roles and ideologies not always mutually compatible and subject to fundamental transformations due to the excesses of the slave trade, state formation, and the altering of social stratification. Despite importunate debates, there is no question of the importance of slavery in African social history from early societies into the modern era.

Miers and Kopytoff (1977) understand African slavery as one form of dependency in societies organized on the basis of kinship, where "rights in persons" is glossed in various contexts within the kinship domain. Individuals in African societies had to be assimilated to a kin group and/or a section. Therefore, according to Miers and Kopytoff, it is the assimilation of the slave which creates the social problem of slavery in African societies. Although their argument clearly distinguishes traditional African slavery from classical or New World chattel slavery it leaves undefined the property basis of the slaves' status and condition. Slaves were acquired within African kinship domains by capture or purchase, and they entered a social situation where elders and chiefs were authoritarian, with power over their persons. While slaves, including women, could have significant control over resources and some authority, their ownership by a master was never in doubt. Women indeed predominated in the internal market and exchange transactions of African kinship slavery, valued for their reproduction of dependents and production of domestic, craft, and agricultural factors.

Claude Meillassoux (1991) links the issue of the slave as property in precolonial West Africa to the transformations between kinship slavery and emerging polities, which both expanded and developed slavery. Military states of the Sudan and the coast gave rise to a predatory aristocratic class which inevitably linked nobiliary and state slavery with the demands of an export slave market, first trans-Saharan (with destinations in North Africa and the Middle East, where some trade persisted into the 20th century) and then transatlantic (with destinations in the Americas and the Caribbean, where trade began in the 16th century and ended in the 19th). In those instances where the slave trade intensified internal exchange and social differentiation linking predation to internal surplus extraction there emerged mercantile, or chattel, slavery. Meillassoux's simple typology is a nuanced and complex reading of the contradictions and conflicts inherent in this model of transformation of African slavery. It addresses the important issue of relating African slavery per se to the changes involved when slaves were captured for sale to other areas.

Lovejoy (1983) and Manning (1990) have attempted to chart a periodization and mapping of African slavery during the era of the Atlantic trade (1400–ca.1880). Employing arguments generally consonant with Meillassoux, their contributions show the gradual but piecemeal penetration of merchants and warlords that spread mercantile slavery into every area of the continent by the end of the 19th century. One of the manifold effects of the trade on African society, though a matter of debate, is on demographic patterns in Africa itself. Changes in the international demand for slaves with its commodification of strangers, enemies, and even kin affected the militarization of social groups, authority patterns, and gender relations, each exaggerated by population losses, new settlement patterns, and new disease vectors. The demographic loss to the African continent during the centuries of slave trade must allow for the demographic variation of the various catchment regions such as the highly generalized zones of the west coast, east coast, and the Sudanic belt/Horn of Africa. Each of these zones had its own population issues affected by the timing of their absorption in high-volume trade and the destination and uses of the human cargo. Manning estimates that West African slave exports grew at an average of 2 percent per year until the mid-1700s and then balanced off to approximately 70,000. This does not take into account the disruption to fertility and rate of mortality resulting from the trade. And of course cultural loss and human pain are impossible to measure. Lovejoy claims that there were more slaves in Africa than in the New World in the 19th century. For students of slavery as a most ancient form of human exploitation, or as an institution inseparable from the making of the modern world, continuing studies of African slavery and its instances will prove invaluable. (*See also* African Slave Trade)

Frank McGlynn

REFERENCES

Lovejoy, Paul. *Transformations in Slavery, A History of Slavery in Africa.* Cambridge: Cambridge University Press, 1983.

Manning, Patrick. *Slavery and African Life: Occidental, Oriental and African Slave Trades.* Cambridge: Cambridge University Press, 1990.

Meillassoux, Claude. *The Anthropology of Slavery: The Womb of Iron and Gold.* Chicago: University of Chicago Press, 1991.

Miers, S., and F. Kopytoff, eds. *Slavery in Africa: Historical and Anthropological Perspectives.* Madison: University of Wisconsin Press, 1977.

Miller, Joseph. *Way of Death: Merchant Capitalism and the Angolan Slave Trade 1730–1830.* Madison: University of Wisconsin Press, 1988.

Robertson, Claire, and Martin Klein. *Women and Slavery in Africa.* Madison: University of Wisconsin Press, 1983.

African Urbanization

Cities in Africa have grown explosively since World War II, propelled by growing commercial, government, and industrial employment and by an even larger tide of people waiting for the elusive job. Between 1950 and 1980, Lagos grew from 250,000 people to 3 million; Kinshasa, from 220,000 people to 2.7 million; and Nairobi, from 130,000 to 900,000.

African urbanization, however, has a much older history. Early cities were centers of power—where kings mobilized forces and distributed goods—and nodal points in commercial networks. By the 1st century AD, entrepôt cities dotted the coast of the Indian Ocean—linked by trade routes to Arabia, India, and Southeast Asia. Later, cities grew along the southern edge of the Sahara Desert, connected by camel caravans to North Africa and the Mediterranean world. In both areas wealth brought impressive building projects, while connections to the Middle East brought in Islam.

The cities of the early colonial era were also loci of power, the administrative and military headquarters of the European conquerors of the late 19th and early 20th centuries. These were bastion cities in a symbolic as well as a material sense: their self-consciously European architecture marked them as a space Europeans could claim to dominate, set apart from the mysterious and dangerous bush. In fact (to paraphrase Marx), Africans did as much to ruralize the city as Europeans did to urbanize the countryside. Africans would try to mold urban life in their own ways and in their own neighborhoods, while colonial regimes at times tolerated these low-cost settlements and at times bulldozed them in the name of sanitation or order. In West Africa, African families with long experience in coastal trade and new migrants imposed to a significant extent their own spatial, social, and religious patterns upon the city, while market women pioneered new branches of commerce that neither colonial officials nor the patriarchal authorities of African kinship groups could easily dominate. Large-scale capital and the state exercised a more thorough domination in South Africa, but even there could not determine the texture of life in the townships. The word "syncretism" hardly does justice to the patterns of cultural inventiveness and reinterpretation found in African cities.

Whatever their early illusions, European officials were soon claiming that Africans were inherently rural people and should not be allowed to become detribalized. Officials figured out that the preservation of village life and the development of migrancy between village and city allowed urban employers to pay wages too low to support families. For a time, Europe made a virtue of what it could not transform, although the traditional societies they saw as intrinsically African now reflected the exercise of colonial power. The continued circulation of labor migrants depended on the stagnation of populous regions of Africa, in part the consequence of colonial action or inaction.

Yet by the late 1930s, colonial regimes began to doubt the desirability of this low-cost symbiosis. The urban infrastructure and the commercial pathways linking regions remained so constricted that small labor forces in ports, railways, and mines held the colonial economy in their unsteady hands. During the post-1929 Depression, colonial regimes could slough off excess labor onto the countryside, but with the recovery, labor returned to the same (or reduced) miserable wages, miserable housing conditions, and miserable support services. As prices rose and urban wages did not, a strike wave, starting in the copper-mining zone of British Central Africa, began.

In a wartime and postwar climate where Great Britain and later France needed reliable production to rebuild imperial economies and where governments were anxious to set forth a coherent political and ideological basis for colonial rule, the need to reassert control was acute. Officials began to rethink the African city. The urban mass, moving into and out of jobs, had to give way to a stabilized labor force, and a new generation of workers and other urbanites had to be born, socialized, and acculturated away from the contagion of African backwardness.

The late 1940s and 1950s brought a wave of modernist projects to African cities funded by new colonial development plans: housing construction, improved water supplies, expansion of the prestige city centers, and efforts—including hesitant moves to pay urban workers enough to support a family—to create a work force attached to their jobs and to their urban futures.

This turned out to be a contradictory process. A slum clearance project might rehabilitate an area of squalor and hardship, but it also destroyed communities, commercial networks, and cultural institutions. Colonial policy assigned a domestic role to urban women which most families lacked the means to sustain, but distrusted and hampered their more autonomous activities in marketing. As urban infrastructures proved unable to handle the resources being poured through them, a cycle of high costs and high wages relative to rural incomes left the development process unbalanced and inadequate.

As European powers, unable to engineer the kind of social change they dreamed off, pulled back from direct control, the kernel of the reformed economy remained small. For many Africans, seeking a regular urban job became more

like a lottery than a smoothly functioning market. People gambled on the low odds of finding a job and mobilized rural-urban networks to survive while making the try. Even as governments tried to clean up colonial cities, squatter settlements mushroomed around them. Colonial regimes—having set out to tame the urban mass— had created a more differentiated urban population, but had not ended urban poverty or the diverse economic and social strategies of African men and women seeking to make their lives.

Fear of urban disorder became a major impetus behind government efforts to stabilize the working class and to cultivate a respectable political class. Nationalist leaders like Kwame Nkrumah in the Gold Coast succeeded in mobilizing portions of the urban population—including unemployed school dropouts and at times the unionized working class—in their movements. Eventually, European leaders convinced themselves that only African political leaders could control the forces colonization had unleashed.

In South Africa, a massive bureaucracy, intensive police control, and the strong political will of the majority of the white population led to massive expulsions of black citydwellers in the 1950s (and again in the 1970s). This still did not prevent extensive squatting, massive violation of regulations, and the growth of urban subcultures and urban political movements. South African cities by the 1970s were the crucibles of revolt.

In independent Africa, cities remain something of a bastion of state power and modernist architecture, now surrounded by squatter settlements made from scraps of metal, wood, and cardboard. Social scientists and policymakers use terms like "overurbanized" and "urban informal sector" to convey the fact that social change has not followed any Western blueprint. They have not been able to remedy the extreme unevenness of African urbanization; they have only been able to label it.

Frederick Cooper

REFERENCES

Cooper, Frederick, ed. *Struggle for the City: Migrant Labor, Capital, and the State in Urban Africa.* Beverly Hills, CA.: Sage, 1983.

Coquery-Vidrovitch, Catherine. "The Process of Urbanization in Africa: From the Origins to the Beginning to Independence," *African Studies Review* 33, 1 (1991): 1–98.

Agricultural Systems

Because agriculture provided the economic and social framework of life for so many people during much of human history, understanding the agricultural systems of the peoples under study is essential for social history. The most basic distinctions among agricultural systems include sedentary agriculture, swidden (or slash-and-burn) agriculture, and hunting and gathering. Generally speaking, sedentary agriculture produces the greatest surplus, whereas swidden agriculture, the hacking of brush or forest and the planting of field for only a few seasons before abandoning the site, is less productive. In turn, after Neolithic times most hunting and gathering societies also maintained some rudimentary agriculture essential to the maintenance of the group, most often the exclusive providence of women. The type of agriculture that developed in different regions of the world depended on a mixture of rainfall, technology, geographic conditions, and culture. Some factors are more important than others. Until northern Europeans adopted a deep plow that could penetrate the soil of northern Europe in the Middle Ages, little intensive agriculture existed. In turn, the hunting and gathering cultures of the Amerindians of the Midwest and California, which could survive perfectly well without intensive agriculture, mitigated against the use of this rich land for farming.

The most intensive exploitation of the land occurred where irrigation was possible, giving rise to some of the earliest civilizations, such as in Mesopotamia, Egypt, and China. Because of the need for careful regulation of the water supply over relatively large areas, irrigation has fostered the growth of complex regulations and a state. Moreover, since irrigation is an especially productive system, sufficient surplus is produced to create relatively extensive social specialization beyond farming, monumental structures, and sufficient leisure time for the elite—all features that we associate with the rise of civilizations.

Unlike their Eurasian counterparts, Ameri-can civilizations such as the Maya, central Mexican, and Andean cultures may have relied much less on irrigation systems. The Maya in particular were primarily swidden farmers who were able to create enough surplus to build extremely impressive monumental structures and a sophisticated high culture. Nevertheless, new evidence from the Maya lowlands suggests that irrigation systems in fact did exist; similarly, research near Tiahuanaco in the high Andes shows that the Tiahuanaco culture used control of lake water to prevent the freezing of potato plants, making the fields much more productive.

Another important distinction in agricultural systems is whether farming is primarily for the market (commercial agriculture) or whether it is oriented to produce enough for consumption to ensure the survival of the household (subsistence agriculture). These two polar ideal types in practice rarely exclude one another, since most subsistence-oriented producers (which is one definition of the peasant) also usually produced something for the market (if only to buy salt and pay taxes). Likewise, highly commercialized sugar plantations in the Caribbean and Brazil in the 19th century often gave their slave populations plots of marginal lands to farm and so supplement their diets. Although highly commercialized agricultural systems are often associated with large holdings and subsistence agriculture with small holdings, this is not always the case. The vast estates of 17th-century northern Mexico, for example, were oriented mainly toward subsistence, whereas the often very small family farms in present-day Europe are highly commercialized.

Labor systems are important components of agricultural systems, for they determine in large part the living conditions of the rural population and the relationship between landowners and the rest of the population. One can distinguish five principal types of labor systems: slavery, serfdom, tenantry and sharecropping, reliance on family labor, and free wage labor. Whereas it was previously believed that there was a progression, at least during the modern era, from various forms of unfree labor to "modern" wage labor, recent research has shown that this is not necessarily the case. In many ways, the slave systems of highly commercialized plantations in the

Americas of the 18th and 19th centuries were more exploitative and brutal than those of the Roman Empire many centuries before. Serfdom, similarly, can become harsher over time (as in Russia), rather than looser (as in late-medieval western Europe). Often, there is a mixture of various forms of labor, as in the 20th-century hacienda regimes in Latin America. While much of the day-to-day labor was accomplished by hacienda tenants for free in return for rights to land, during the harvest season landowners might have hired peasants from nearby villages and paid them daily wages.

The reliance on family labor, a characteristic of subsistence-oriented peasant economies, merits special consideration. According to A.V. Chayanov (1986), a Russian economist, because of this reliance on family labor peasant economic behavior often appears to contradict rational economic behavior. Sheer attachment to land may cause peasants to bypass other opportunities that would provide for higher earnings. As a result, when prices of goods drop to levels that appear to make their production uneconomical, peasants may produce more of this good rather than stop producing it. This is because peasants do not count their labor as a factor, but instead, in Chayanovian terms, may overexploit their own family's labor. The objective of the peasants often is to acquire a certain amount of cash (thus selling more of their produce when prices are low) rather than to get the highest profit. Thus, peasant economic behavior may appear irrational at times and can often undercut prices of highly commercialized and more efficient enterprises. This overexploitation of family labor combined with overpopulation can lead to agricultural involution. This has occurred in Indonesia and in early 20th-century Romania, where the increasing fragmentation of landholdings led to widespread rural poverty.

Indeed, a similar process was at work in the protoindustrialization phase of European manufacturing. In order to make ends meet due to overpopulation or poverty, peasants engaged in manufacturing at home. While this system, called putting-out or domestic manufacturing, existed since the Middle Ages, it became especially extensive in the 18th and 19th centuries. This system featured peasants who had a spinning wheel or loom who produced thread or cloth at home with materials provided by an urban merchant and who generally purchased the finished product. Often the roles within the peasant households were rigidly defined by gender, an important topic that only recently has begun to receive some attention. In any case, while the putting-out system helped preserve the peasant economies in the medium term, in the long run it made the peasantry increasingly dependent on the urban economy and thus led to a weakening of the peasant economy.

Agricultural systems vary greatly according to land tenure and inheritance. Some systems emphasize village smallholding, with widely distributed property. This was characteristic of much of western Europe by the 19th century. In other areas large estates predominated. Inheritance patterns are related to land tenure patterns. Primogeniture preserves holdings (both large and small) by passing on to the eldest son, whereas partible inheritance among many children fragments land property. Both landholding or inheritance systems may change over time, as in the rise of estate agriculture in Russia from the 16th through the mid-19th centuries.

Exploring the implications of agricultural systems has provided some of the most fertile ground for social historians. The typologies of agricultural systems are numerous, when landholding, extent of commerce, geography, types of crops, labor systems, and other variables are assessed. The emphasis on nonelites in agriculture has brought about a much more profound understanding of the way in which the vast majority of the people lived until very recently and has clarified some of the great turning points in human history, such as the basis of civilizations and the rural origins of the industrial revolution. Much still needs to be done; the recent conjuncture of social history and anthropology appears to be particularly promising in elucidating issues that have received inadequate attention. (*See also* Manorialism, Peasantry, Protoindustrialization)

Erick D. Langer and Peter N. Stearns

REFERENCES

Chayanov, A.V. *The Theory of Peasant Economy,* Daniel Thorner, Basile Kerblay, R.E.F. Smith, eds. Madison: University of Wisconsin Press, 1986.

Geertz, Clifford. *Agricultural Involution: The Processes of Ecological Change in Indonesia.* Berkeley: University of California Press, 1963.

Grigg, David B. *Population Growth and Agrarian Change: An Historical Perspective.* Cambridge: Cambridge University Press, 1980.

Hodges, Richard. *Primitive and Peasant Markets.* New York: Basil Blackwell, 1988.

Alienation

The concept of alienation is frequently used by social historians dealing with work and the working class, particularly in the modern period. The word means hostility or estrangement from some activity or experience. Karl Marx, in *Capital,* applied the term particularly to the work processes of industrial capitalism. Because workers no longer owned any producing property and because their formal training often declined, Marx argued that they were alienated from the products of their work, feeling no real stake in the manufacturing process. His claim made good theoretical sense, though historians and social scientists have had problems finding actual clear measures of alienation. Do alienated workers lead in labor protest, because of their estrangement? Or is the disorientation so great that protest goals cannot be found—meaning that alienated workers are less likely to strike or join unions than workers who find some partial meaning in their jobs? Though many labor historians refer to alienation, most social histories have found working-class groups rather divided in their degree of estrangement, with many able to make some partial accommodations.

For 20th-century social history, some sociologists have added a concept of white-collar alienation, referring to clerks or middle managers whose careers do not meet their middle-class mobility expectations. Again, alienation is hard to measure, but early retirements, frequent illness, plus expressions of extreme frustration may capture the concept. In sum, alienation in its major theoretical statements forms an important but elusive concept, which helps orient modern social history while also provoking extensive debate and empirical confusion.

Peter N. Stearns

REFERENCES

Koditschek, Theodore. *Class Formation and Urban Industrial Society: Bradford, 1750–1850.* New York: Cambridge University Press, 1990.

Stearns, Peter N. *Lives of Labor: Work in Maturing Industrial Society.* London: Croom, Helm, 1975.

Allied Occupation of Japan

The Allied occupation of Japan took place between Japan's surrender on August 14, 1945, and the enforcement of the San Francisco Peace Treaty on April 28, 1952. The occupation can be divided into two parts: 1945 to 1947/1948, when SCAP (Supreme Commander for Allied Powers, which refers to both the military commander General Douglas MacArthur and the U.S. Government) carried out extensive reforms to demilitarize and democratize Japan; and 1948 to 1952, the so-called reverse course period, when the United States under the impact of the Cold War emphasized Japan's economic and eventual military rehabilitation.

In 1945–1947, SCAP, which was essentially an American military government that allowed no separate zones of occupation for other Allies, demilitarized Japan by abolishing Japan's military; repatriating over 6 million Japanese soldiers and civilians from the overseas empire; trying over 4,000 war criminals (including 28 class A war criminals for conspiring to fight aggressive war); and purging 200,000 officers and politicians from public office.

SCAP democratized Japan by imposing a constitution that established the basic freedoms: gave suffrage to women; separated religion and state; set up an independent judiciary; took sovereignty away from the emperor and made him a symbol of the state; and renounced the right to fight wars or maintain military forces. SCAP carried out a land reform that increased owner-farmed land from 56 to 89 percent of all arable; a labor reform that led to unions with 4.8 million union members by 1947; began the dissolution of the *zaibatsu,* or prewar business combines; and established an educational system that broadened educational opportunity. The extent to which Japan needed democratization and the extent to which the reforms of 1945–1947 were the outgrowth of prewar trends rather than radical changes are much debated scholarly issues. They raise important questions about the relationship of recent social trends to past Japanese social history, and also provide a context in which to analyze the connection between policy and society.

In 1947–1948 the Cold War and the instability of the Nationalist government in China led SCAP to stress Japan's economic recovery from its wartime destruction and postwar stagnation. Accordingly, SCAP slowed its efforts to break up the *zaibatsu*, discouraged left-wing labor unions, balanced government budgets, and stabilized the foreign exchange rate. These reforms set the stage for Japan's rapid economic growth after the outbreak of the Korean War in 1950. During the Korean War, SCAP allowed the creation of the National Police Force, the forerunner of Japan's Self Defense Forces. Scholars have debated whether there was a reverse course that reconsolidated the power of Japan's prewar elites or whether SCAP's post-1948 policies were a natural extension of its earlier ones.

Richard J. Smethurst

REFERENCE

Ward, Robert E., ed. *Democratizing Japan: The Allied Occupation.* Honolulu: University of Hawaii Press, 1986.

Alltagsgeschichte

Alltagsgeschichte, the history of everyday life, is the West German version of Anglo-American and French "history from below," that is, history from the standpoint of the lower classes. A heterogeneous phenomenon, *Alltagsgeschichte* originated since the 1970s in lay and professional circles: the meeting of history and anthropology, which generated studies on rural society and the working class, influenced by ethnology and folklore; working-class social history based on oral history; grass-roots activity of the semiprofessional milieux who wanted to take history to the public; strong interest in the Third Reich among the young generation, who embraced *Alltagsgeschichte* as a means to understand the Nazi past.

As a new departure in German historiography, *Alltagsgeschichte* has sought to develop a new understanding of ordinary people's lives by looking at their subjective experiences and mentalities in the production of daily existence and in the world of popular culture, in the family, the workshop, and the community. *Alltagsgeschichte* includes, therefore, such diverse topics as crime, leisure, eating habits, and social protest. By exploring social history in its experiential dimensions, *Alltagsgeschichte* aims at capturing the relationship between daily experience and social structures, popular consciousness and formal politics, and everyday politics and the politics and domination of society and the state.

Critics have argued that by centering on daily life *Alltagsgeschichte* overemphasizes details of secondary importance, idealizes romantically the world of "small people," banishes from social history theoretical and methodological guidelines, proposes a history with politics left out, and, most important, obscures the Nazi regime's uniqueness and the distinctions between its supporters and opponents, thus dissolving clear value judgments. However, *Alltagsgeschichte* at its best has provided new perspectives on German history, for example, histories by Alf Lüdtke on workers' everyday life and Detlev Peukert on racism, popular consciousness, and Nazi politics. The spread of basic concepts in *Alltagsgeschichte*, thanks to recent translations, is beginning to have some impact on sociohistorical work outside of Germany.

Alon Confino

REFERENCES

Eley, Geoff. "Labor History, Social History, *Alltagsgeschichte*: Experience, Culture, and the Politics of the Everyday—a New Direction for German Social History?" *Journal of Modern History* 61 (June 1989): 297–343.

Peukert, Detlev. *Inside Nazi Germany: Conformity, Opposition, and Racism in Everyday Life.* New Haven: Yale University Press, 1987.

American Exceptionalism

American exceptionalism involves an approach to American history that assumes that the United States is different from societies elsewhere in the world, and particularly different from those of western Europe, which it in some ways resembles. Exceptionalists assume that the United States formed a civilization of its own, that American social structures, values, and political institutions are all distinctive (and, some imply, often better). Exceptionalists do not necessarily explore what caused the United States to be different, but causation sometimes involves the impact of the frontier, the mixing of varied peoples, or unusual social mobility.

Exceptionalism helped organize the presentation of American history well before the rise of social history. It helped justify history teaching that inculcated patriotism, and it often derived particular power from beliefs about the unusual virtues of American politics. Exceptionalist assumptions were often untested by real comparative analysis. The exceptionalist framework involved a number of social history topics, however—such as the idea of unusual mobility or of a particularly pragmatic popular culture. Not surprisingly, many social historians dealing with the United States, even as they generated new subjects and new methods, maintained exceptionalist assumptions. Social history did not overturn many beliefs about American distinctiveness, and it could indeed add to them. On the other hand, comparative analysis, still more the exception than the rule, did modify some exceptionalist assumptions, both by showing common social patterns in the United States and elsewhere (as in the timing and impact of the industrial revolution) and by refuting or modifying some common assumptions. Thus social historians have shown that American mobility rates were not as different from those of industrializing Europe as was commonly assumed, though American beliefs about mobility were somewhat unusual.

The problem of grappling with exceptionalist assumptions (that is, the need to test them carefully) has been extended to a new range of historical subjects but it has not yielded to consistent improvements in analytical sophistication under the spur of social history. Exceptionalist beliefs are often correct, but they are less often tested. Social history, particularly in its comparative thrust, invites more careful statements about the relationship of American trends to those of other societies, but there are many assessments yet to complete.

Peter N. Stearns

REFERENCE

Shafer, Byron E., ed. *Is America Different? A New Look at American Exceptionalism.* New York: Oxford University Press, 1991.

American Revolution

The American Revolution grew out of a colonial protest against Great Britain's new imperial policies, especially the government's repeated attempts after 1763 to impose taxes without representation and to enforce previously ignored commercial regulations. While this upheaval did not arise from a rebellion by an underclass against a ruling elite, the ideas and events unleashed by the American resistance transformed the colonists' view of their traditional institutions and society. The protest gradually mutated into a struggle to redesign American politics and society upon a republican conception of liberty and equality. Furthermore, while social historians have not transformed the picture of the Revolution itself in terms of grand class conflict, they have established important social dimensions in terms of working-class political grievances, generational tensions, and even changing family values that contributed to new challenges to establish hierarchy.

In some respects American society at the end of the war in 1783 resembled that which had existed in 1763. Society had not been leveled; class lines remained quite visible. Yet change had begun.

Colonial society, like premodern England and the medieval world from which it arose, had been hierarchical and bound by webs of personal attachments and obligations. No one had been truly independent; subordination had been customary, especially for women, children, servants, slaves, and tenants, but even for artisans and ordinary yeomen, who had been thought to differ physically and emotionally from society's patricians. This social system was called into question during the American Revolution by republicans who sought to create a new society devoid of the old servile dependencies.

The Revolutionary republican ideology that all men were equal and that all possessed the fundamental natural rights of "life, liberty, and the pursuit of happiness" had a corrosive effect on the traditional pattern of rigid class lines and distinct class privileges. A spirit of egalitarianism, especially a belief in equality of opportunity and an untempered opposition to inherited prerogative, took hold. Profound modifications came slowly, but by early in the 19th century ordinary people had achieved respectability, even dominance, prompting Alexis de Tocqueville, a Frenchman traveling in America in 1831, to conclude that in the United States "men are nearer equality than in any other country."

Other significant social changes also occurred. The first Americans whose lives were changed significantly by the events of the Revolution were those who adhered to the Crown, the Loyalists. Approximately 20 percent of America's population of 2.5 million remained loyal to Great Britain. Occupation and social class cannot explain their decision. Loyalism was strongest where the economy was tied to Atlantic markets, in areas controlled by the British army, among those who dreamed of the potential power and wealth of Anglo-America, and among those who feared Revolutionary republicanism.

Faced with severe persecution, including fines, surveillance, social ostracism, physical violence, incarceration, and the confiscation of their property, perhaps 80,000 Loyalists eventually fled into exile. Their displacement had social implications, for not only did their land and offices pass to others, but their emigration removed well-to-do gentry who often had controlled extraordinary local power and patronage.

The Revolution meant social mobility for many Americans. As the availability of cheap land decreased during the half-century after the 1720s, economic opportunities declined for many colonists. Many people moved to new frontiers—to the Wyoming Valley in Pennsylvania, northern New York and New England, the southern backcountry—but land prices skyrocketed so that many were unable to afford land. Victory in the War of Independence brought change, for in the Treaty of Paris the United States acquired all territory between the Appalachians and the Mississippi River, save for Florida. By 1790 more than 100,000 easterners had moved into Kentucky and Tennessee alone, and others relocated in Ohio, western Virginia, and Pennsylvania. Moreover, Congress and the states awarded land

bounties to thousands of veterans of the late war, enabling countless Americans to become property-owning farmers.

Military exigencies, as well as the Revolutionary ideology, also transformed the lives of numerous enslaved African Americans. Wartime necessity led both sides to promise freedom to slaves in return for their service; nearly 20,000 persons were liberated in this manner, primarily in the northern states. In addition, prompted by the spirit of the Enlightenment and the Declaration of Independence's ringing assertion of natural rights, many Americans for the first time contemplated the evils of slavery. By the 1790s the foreign slave trade was abolished, private manumissions in the South had been legalized, and every northern state had provided for eventual emancipation. By 1810 three-quarters of the black population in the northern states was free, while in the South the number of free blacks had nearly quadrupled since 1770.

Female patriots were active during the Revolution. Like men, women participated in the various boycotts, published their sentiments, and supported the war in numerous ways, including manufacturing bullets and organizing fund drives to assist soldiers. This unprecedented feminine involvement in public affairs provoked restiveness among some women with their assigned feminine sphere. Some seminal changes resulted. By 1800 women had more control of their destiny than had been true of their grandmothers; women were freer to select their husbands or to choose not to marry at all, and one profession—teaching—had begun to open to females. If most Americans still thought it improper for females to be politically active, the new republican society did assign new duties to women. After the Revolution most Americans presumed that women had a public role to play in their domestic duties, though this vision was fraught with tension and conflicting interpretation. Women now were charged with responsibility both for creating a reassuring home life for their spouses and raising republican sons committed to the preservation of Revolutionary virtues.

Americans had not fought for independence alone. During their struggle with the parent state the colonists sought to alter their traditional social and political systems. In place of an old order based upon manmade privilege, they erected a new order modeled upon a republican ideology that proclaimed that all men were born free and equal. Not all Americans were free by war's end, nor had a genderless and classless society been established. Nevertheless, by 1800 most Americans lived in a society substantively different from that of 1750. Social historians have added to the understanding of the causes of the Revolution and the groups that participated. They are also extending our grasp of the results of revolutionary ideals in subsequent decades, as they affected relations among classes, men and women, and key age groups.

John Ferling

REFERENCES

Maier, Pauline. *From Resistance to Revolution: Colonial Radicals and the Development of Opposition to Britain, 1765–1776.* New York: Norton, 1992.

Wood, Gordon. *The Radicalism of the American Revolution.* New York: Knopf, 1992.

Anarchism

Anarchism refers both to a doctrine and a series of activist groups and individuals. The term, of Greek origin, literally means without a chief or head, and this accurately reflects the doctrine, which is based on the idea that justice requires the abolition of the state and of all other authoritarian institutions not based on some form of cooperative agreement among autonomous individuals. Central to the doctrine is the belief that human beings possess a moral sentiment powerful enough to hold society together; institutions like the state are viewed as artificial, unnatural, and oppressive.

While the theoretical roots of anarchism can be traced back to the ancient Greek philosopher Zeno of Citium (ca. 335–ca. 263 BC) and followed through utopian and millenarian religious movements like the Brethren of the Free Spirit of the 13th century and the Anabaptists of the 16th century, modern anarchism is rooted in the doctrines of William Godwin (1756–1836), Max Stirner (1806–1856), Pierre-Joseph Proudhon (1809–1865), Mikhail Bakunin (1814–1876), and Pyotr Kropotkin (1842–1921).

From the beginning there were fundamental disagreements concerning the appropriate means necessary to move society toward anarchism and whether this means should be violent or nonviolent. Most of the original proponents advocated peaceful change. Bakunin, however, argued that the explosive destruction of present political institutions was a creative and necessary first act which would prepare for the emergence of the natural solidarity of humanity. Others—Proudhon, for example—rejected violent revolution and even suggested that full-blown anarchism could never be attained, but that it was an exemplary ideal toward which humanity should strive.

It is difficult to summarize the historical development of practical anarchism because it seldom assumed the form of an organized mass movement. Indeed, the very essence of anarchist doctrine—based on the primacy of individuals and of loose confederations and impermanent groups—would seem to preclude organization. Correspondingly, anarchism has far more often been studied from an intellectual perspective than in terms of social history. But while generalizations are risky, a few patterns are reasonably clear. Geographically, the anarchist movement in Europe was more socially significant in France, Italy, Spain, the Swiss Jura, and the Ukraine than in Germany, England, Scandinavia, or the Low Countries. In Latin America it was important in Argentina and Mexico, with less significant movements also present in Cuba, Brazil, Peru, Uruguay, and Chile. We know less about anarchist movements in other parts of the world. Some scholars suggest that anarchism exerted an important intellectual influence in China during the early 20th century.

It is difficult to explain this geographical pattern. Some social historians have suggested that anarchist strength has corresponded with varying levels of industrial development, and that more advanced industry naturally fostered Marxist or reformist movements on the left. There does seem to be a rough correspondence with levels of economic development, with the greatest mass following of anarchism occurring in areas where a majority of the working class (including a rural segment) has remained near subsistence level, where people have seen their standard of living eroding, or where groups of traditional producers (like artisans), have seen themselves excluded from an ascending curve of economic progress. Many analysts, however, have objected to explanations based solely on socioeconomic characteristics, noting such factors as the weight of centralized administrations and pseudo-constitutional systems that have frustrated hopes for change through politics; the importance of individual militants; a variety of indigenous historical variables like revolutionary traditions, types of industries, or the character of local elites.

The development of an anarchist movement was often accompanied by the emergence of a more politically oriented movement on the left, and the opposition between these left-wing groups seemed to stimulate doctrinal examination and clarification. The 1870s division between Marxists and nonauthoritarians in Europe, for example, which led to the split in the International Workingmen's Association in 1872, produced more finely articulated doctrines among those anarchists who were willing to support Bakunin's violent agenda as well as among those who were committed to peaceful change through associative action. Chronologically, the largest following of anarchism occurred in the 70 years following this split, when anarcho-syndicalist labor movements sporadically erupted with considerable force in parts of Europe and Latin America.

Anarchism has received its greatest public attention neither through its theoretical works nor through the mass movements in places like Spain or Mexico, but through the spectacular gestures of individual terrorists who claimed to be anarchists, such as Leon Czolgosz, the assassin of President William McKinley of the United States, in 1901. Such violent acts often led to legal proscriptions against all anarchists (and often against socialists as well) but in fact they had little in common with the theoretical doctrine of anarchism or with mass movements in either Europe or Latin America. [See also: Anarchism (Russia)]

K. Steven Vincent

REFERENCES

Guerin, Daniel. *Anarchism*. Translated by Mary Klopper. New York: Monthly Review Press, 1970.

Joll, James. *The Anarchists*. New York: Grosset & Dunlap, 1964.

Woodcock, George. *Anarchism: A History of Libertarian Ideas and Movements*. Cleveland: World Publishing Company, 1962.

Anarchism (Russia)

Russian anarchism arose from the ideas of two noblemen, Mikhail Bakunin and Pyotr Kropotkin. (The writer Leo Tolstoy, also a nobleman, created a kind of Christian anarchism, but it did not become a social movement.) It has usually been studied in terms of intellectual or labor-movement history but relates to the social history of Russian protest as well.

Unlike other Russian radical movements, anarchism sought not just to overthrow the tsarist political and economic system but to abolish the state altogether. It would be replaced by grassroots associations of producers, consumers, and other like-minded individuals, which would voluntarily federate into larger networks as needed. The hierarchy and oppression of the state, organized "from above downward," would be replaced by a society organized naturally and spontaneously "from below upward"—what Kropotkin called "anarchist communism."

Bakunin and Kropotkin spent most of their lives as political exiles in western Europe, so implementation of their ideal was left to their followers inside Russia. The first anarchist groups arose in the early 20th century. Their members came mostly from the intelligentsia, the educated and semi-educated stratum. They found their strongest support among the Jewish artisans of the western and southern regions of the Russian Empire. Belostok, Ekaterinoslav, and Odessa were principal anarchist centers, although groups formed also in St. Petersburg and Moscow.

These first anarchists adhered to anarchist communism, but unlike Kropotkin they adopted terrorism as the way to achieve it. During the 1905 revolution, anarchists carried out numerous acts of violence, hoping thereby to incite a popular insurrection or at least to publicize their aims. Other anarchists began to question these tactics. They turned from anarchist communism to anarcho-syndicalism, which regarded trade unions as the nucleus of the new anarchist society, and began recruiting factory workers to their cause. Anarchists refused on principle to form a political party, so local groups jealously preserved their ideological and organizational independence.

Anarchist activity declined after 1905 but revived during the 1917 revolution and ensuing civil war. Petrograd and especially Moscow were now the main centers. Anarchism had its greatest success in the peasant partisan movement led by Nestor Makhno in the Ukraine. Makhno, a peasant-born anarchist, used guerrilla tactics to fight first the Whites and then the Bolsheviks, but the latter finally defeated him. Makhno's peasant followers may have had only a superficial understanding of anarchism, but their traditional desire for communal autonomy harmonized easily with anarchist objectives. Anarchism also made itself felt in the revolt of the Kronstadt Naval Base against the Bolshevik dictatorship in March 1921. Direct anarchist influence among the sailors was limited, but anarchist principles of local freedom and self-rule coincided with their aspirations.

Pyotr Kropotkin's funeral in February 1921 brought some 20,000 anarchist sympathizers into the streets of Moscow. But repression of anarchists, which had begun in 1918, intensified after Kronstadt, and Kropotkin's funeral proved to be Russian anarchism's last public demonstration. (*See also* Anarchism)

Marshall S. Shatz

REFERENCES

Avrich, Paul. *The Russian Anarchists.* Princeton, NJ: Princeton University Press, 1967.

Bakunin, Mikhail *Statism and Anarchy.* Translated and edited by Marshall S. Shatz. Cambridge: Cambridge University Press, 1990.

Miller, Martin A. *Kropotkin.* Chicago: University of Chicago Press, 1976.

Ancestor Veneration (Africa)

Ancestor veneration, as part of African indigenous religion, is common in societies where value is placed on unilineal descent. Ancestor veneration goes hand in hand with the worship of the High God and other minor gods or spirits. By including the ancestor in the religious complex, the motive is to establish a strong linkage between the present and the past, that is, the previous generations and the living. Ancestors must have been respectable and worthy persons in their lifetimes, with contributions that are well known and preserved in the oral traditions of their lineages or communities. It is unusual to venerate people who died young or who had an evil reputation when alive. Both men and women could acquire the prestige of veneration.

Ancestors have power and influence on those who venerate them. The ancestor acts as the custodian of customs and laws, and visits offenders with misfortunes and sickness. The ancestor is the "police" of the living, watching carefully and calling upon them at death to account for their deeds. The ancestor rewards those who respect traditions and maintain good relations with the supernatural.

A town or state may have its ancestor, usually the person associated with the foundation of the place or the dynasty. Veneration in this case becomes part of the people's identity. Present rulers are accountable to the ancestor while new rules and regulations must receive the ancestor's sanctions.

Veneration takes three major forms: prayers, offerings, and sacrifice. Prayers are addressed to the ancestor for any reason and for blessings. Offerings are regular presentation of food and drinks, as part of the rituals of prayers. In sacrifice, the worshipper kills an animal as a presentation. In all three forms the living person maintains regular communication with the ancestor and shows love, respect, and care. Sacrifice is the limit of communication, especially in the distant past when it involved human sacrifice. Then and now, the reasons for sacrifice are to thank, petition, combat evil spirits, propitiate, render gifts, and commune.

Veneration that involves an entire community is the most elaborate. It comes at harvest period, with plenty of food to eat and time to play. Religion mixes with socials, like public dancing, marriage celebrations, and exchange of gifts by individuals, and public display of generosity by the rulers. In a number of communities, the public is allowed the pleasure of criticizing their rulers through songs and poems.

One reason for ancestor veneration is to use the dead to build and maintain cohesion in the lineage and society. Land, the most prized possession, belongs both to the ancestor and the living, which makes parting with it abominable. Another reason is to use ancestors as regulators of social relations: individuals are related to one another and must show love because they have a common ancestor. Where an ancestor serves as a collective symbol of a group or dynasty, the motive is not only to ensure solidarity but also to accept the rulers as legitimate inheritors of power, in respect for authority and the laws that receive the blessing of ancestors.

Social historians use the characteristics of ancestor veneration in studying various aspects of African social history, including not only mentalities but also commercial and political patterns where kinship links play a great role. Obviously, recent African history, under the impact of colonialism and economic change, raises questions about how traditions of ancestor worship are adapted or preserved. Social historians have not worked extensively on ancestor worship per se, if only because of limited evidence concerning major changes in the premodern past. Existing knowledge derives mainly from anthropological and oral history research. (*See also* Ancester Worship)

Toyin Falola

REFERENCES

Idowu, E.B. *African Traditional Religion: A Definition*. London: S.C.M., 1974.

Mbiti, J.S. *An Introduction to African Religion*. London: Heinemann, 1969.

Parrinder, G. *African Traditional Religion*. London: Hutchinson, 1954.

Ray, B.C. *African Religions: Symbol, Ritual and Community*. Englewood Cliffs, NJ: Prentice-Hall, 1976.

Ancestor Worship

In traditional China the people believed in spirits. Each person had many souls, some of which separated from the body upon death. If a body did not receive proper burial the unhappy spirit roamed the earth causing disease or misfortune for his family. Food and other goods that the person enjoyed in life were sacrificed to the spirit

of the deceased in order to placate his/her spirit. Here was the basis for a belief system that undergirded Chinese culture in various social groups during much of the society's history.

During the Shang Dynasty (1750–1100 BC) the royal house was divided into clans; the clan heads directed family worship. Direct ancestors, especially those who had ruled or held high office, were accorded sacrifices. Since the afterlife was believed to be structured in accord with life on earth, high rank in life would translate into positions of influence in the hereafter. Therefore, those who had held positions of power would be able to use their influence to intercede for their families. Also, as on earth, there was a supreme arbiter of power who guaranteed order among the other spirits. This supreme spirit was Shang Ti. The Shang justified their political power through this cult of ancestor worship, which assigned their family founder with supreme power in the next world. A hereditary hierarchical social structure in this life also translated into the next; all honors acquired would be maintained and venerated by one's descendants. The greater the lineage, positions held, and honors in life, the stronger the soul after death. The afterlife of honored souls revolved around an emperor; that of ghosts or unhappy spirits, around a king of ghosts.

Common people at this time had no ancestors or funerary ceremonies. Only after a proscribed period of mourning did the deceased become ancestors. Each new ancestor became the family protector, and power weakened as each new generation died. After three generations all power was lost; sacrifices were no longer made to those without power. The only exceptions were clan founders and those who had achieved status in their lifetimes.

The Chinese philosopher Confucius (Kung Fu-tzu, 551–479 BC) shifted the focus of this practice by advocating visible signs of respect for one's parents and, by extension, their parents. Confucius believed that the family was the basis of stability and order. Since his teachings had as their goal the effecting of stability and social order, in place of the constant civil war of his era, the role of the family in creating this order was emphasized. Ceremonies of respect for family would instill in the young, and serve as a reminder to adults, of their place and responsibility in the natural order. These ceremonies could also reinforce the common interests of the extended family, particularly during such festivals as Ching Ming, in which the graves of the deceased were tended and offerings to ancestors made by the entire family.

A visible symbol of this respect was the family altar, upon which was displayed name tablets of the recently deceased. Incense and other gifts were symbolically offered. New family members presented their respects, thereby becoming part of the family. Clan temples served the extended family in much the same manner. These temples and altars served as the home of the spirits, rather than, in the Western sense, a place of worship.

The living expected to be remembered properly in their turn. In order for proper ceremonies to be conducted, it was necessary for each generation to produce at least one son. Daughters married outside of the family and became members of the husband's family. They were not able to sacrifice to their own parents.

For the Chinese to adopt foreign religions (primarily Buddhism) a concept of respect for family and ancestors had to be present. Once Buddhism became Sinicized, from about 300 AD onward, its doctrines were accepted by many Chinese. In order to gain acceptance for the idea of monastacism, which removed a son from his family and prevented him, in turn, from producing sons, a method of reconciling this practice with the need for sons to perform ceremonies of respect for their parents was needed. In Chinese Buddhism, a son joining a monastery is an act of filial piety in that he can then spend his life praying for his parents and family. Later, Christian missionaries had more of a problem with this practice. While some believed that demonstrations of respect for an ancestor were one way of obeying the commandment to honor one's parents, others found this practice akin to idolatry, or at least incompatible with Christian beliefs and practices. Buddhism became one of the major Chinese religions; Christianity was frequently proscribed.

Ancestor worship has been most extensively studied for its durable role in Chinese sociocultural history. Ancestor worship formed part of the religious practice in some other cultures as well, particularly in Africa, where it also served to bind family and kinship ties. The phenomenon is open to further comparative analysis in social history. The veneration of ancestors remained a part of Chinese culture into the 20th century.

Katherine Reist

REFERENCES

Confucius. *The Analects*. New York: Penguin, 1983.
Gernet, Jacques. *A History of Chinese Civilization*. New York: Cambridge University Press, 1982.
Maspero, Henri. *China in Antiquity*. Amherst: University of Massachusetts Press, 1965.

Animals

"Many animals have the power of memory and can be trained," stated Aristotle (384–322 BC), "but the only one which can recall past events is man." The history of the relationship between animals and society originated long before classical antiquity with two as yet unexplained events: the genetic change in the human brain which made language and writing possible, and the domestication of a small number of other species that began about 10,000 years ago. From the Lascaux cave drawings to the photographs of William Wegman, animals, the mysterious Other, have been represented as totems, gods, and symbols of ourselves (anthropomorphism). They are present in the foundation myths of the world's religions, like the Garden of Eden, where humankind is given "dominion . . . over every living thing that moves upon the earth" (Genesis 1), and animals are often cited as natural correlatives in theories of government, as when Thomas Aquinas (1225–1274) noted that "cranes follow their leader, and bees obey their queen." From the prehistoric to the start of the modern era, animals were also hunted and sacrificed, captured and observed; they provided a source of food, clothing, shelter, companionship, tools, and weapons; and they supplemented wind, water, and human energy in the development of farming, transportation, and warfare. Animals are, in sum, central to human social history in hunting and in agricultural societies. Many basic social features depend on available animals—for example, civilizations in Central America before the arrival of Columbus lacked draft animals, and their social achievements must be assessed accordingly.

In recent decades, social historians have also dealt with change in human relations with and ideas about animals as part of the emergence of industrial society. Westernization, the great cultural watershed of the past 500 years, profoundly altered perceptions of the natural world. Europe's global expansion; its agricultural, industrial, and political revolutions; capitalism; science; and technology have transformed our interaction with other living creatures in complex ways. As historian Keith Thomas (1983) observes, the conflict between material expectations and new sensibilities "is one of the contradictions upon which modern civilization may be said to rest."

While Linnaeus's (1707–1778) classification of humankind still stands (Genus Mammals, Order Primates, Species Homo Sapiens), even before Charles Darwin's (1809–1882) theory of natural selection our imagined position as the supreme link in a Great Chain of Being, nearer to God than to other animals, was brought into question by a growing recognition that the earth is not the center of the universe and does not exist for us alone. Beginning with a late 18th-century concern for the treatment of slaves, women, and children, a humanitarian reform movement swept Western society in the 19th century, including the establishment of a network of voluntary societies (as well as laws) for the protection of domesticated animals, and also smaller groups devoted to antivivisection and the rights of animals. Related to this new attitude was a Victorian cult of affection for household pets, complete with cemeteries for dogs and cats, which has grown into a multibillion dollar service industry. The late 20th-century dispute between science and sentiment is a product of these changes. When protesters besiege a laboratory where human and animal genes are spliced in experiments to combat cancer or AIDS, each party is likely to maintain that it is acting in the best interest of society.

Domesticated and wild animals have both been used to measure the trajectory of social progress since the 18th century, although different species followed separate paths. The equine population of Britain grew from 1.3 million to 3.3 million between 1811 and 1901, over 18 million working horses served a human population of 76 million in the United States in 1900 (a ratio of 1:4), and approximately 8 million horses were killed in the Great War of 1914–1918. That they were reduced to instruments of sport and leisure, or became a sign of backwardness, once their labor could be replaced should not obscure the fact that 19th-century industrial and urban growth occurred in what was essentially a horse-based economy where a considerable portion of arable land was devoted to feed production and their excrement an unavoidable feature of city life. The jobs of millions of persons (breeders, traders, stableboys, blacksmiths, etc.) were eliminated worldwide by the introduction of internal combustion engines.

Economist Adam Smith doubted "whether butchers meat is any where a necessity of life" in 1776, whereas Lord Beveridge (the welfare reformer) reported that "meat, next to bread," was "in popular estimation the most important article of food" in 1944. A mass carnivorous diet is one of the principal achievements of capitalist democratic society. The English midlands shifted from grain to livestock production in the 18th century, while ranching (extensive commercial grazing) emerged as a major agricultural system in areas of recent European settlement (the American West, Australia) in the 19th century and continues to expand in Latin America and Africa today. Global distribution became possible through new technologies (refrigeration, the steamship) and facilities like the Union Stock Yards of Chicago (1865) that employ thousands of workers. The relationship between class and meat consumption has changed during the past century. In Great Britain, for example, members of the upper class, who ate three times more meat than factory workers in 1902, now eat less of it than the wage earners who frequent fast food restaurants.

A resolution adopted at the 1869 International Congress on Animal Protection opposed "abuses" of wildlife "without ignoring the difficulty of assuring the triumph of these principles among hunters and persons of the elevated class." Market hunting played a significant role in empire building (the fur trade) and made a range of luxury items (women's feathered hats) and inexpensive commodities available to consumers: the slaughter of 2 million elephants between 1880 and 1910 reduced the price of ivory to the point where it was used for shaving brushes, and hydrogenation, the process by which soap and margarine are manufactured from animal fat, increased production of whale oil to 800,000 barrels by 1914. The sporting ethos of elites, by contrast, favored restricted hunting (a privilege of the French nobility until 1789) through poaching laws, conserved vermin (the fox in England), and maintained private estates on which to display their power by killing deer and rabbits. These atavistic institutions were forerunners of the nature reserves visited by tourists in the postcolonial age. Recent environmental concerns about animal survival should be interpreted in the larger perspective of modern human/animal history.

Robert J. Bezucha

REFERENCES

MacKenzie, John. *The Empire of Nature*. Manchester: Manchester University Press, 1988.

Ritvo, Harriet. *The Animal Estate*. Cambridge, MA: Harvard University Press, 1987.

Salt, Henry. *Animal Rights Considered in Relation to Social Progress* (1892). Preface by Peter Singer. Clarks Summit, PA: Society for Animal Rights, 1980.

Thomas, Keith. *Man and the Natural World*. New York: Pantheon Books, 1983.

Thompson, F.L.M., ed. *Horses in European Economic History*. Reading: British Agricultural History Society, 1983.

Animism

Animism is a term once used to designate religious systems which function on the premise that the unseen, or supernatural, world is controlled by spiritual beings who also influence events in the seen, or natural, world. Scholarly use of the term has become increasingly cautious, primarily because the religious beliefs of no cultural group have been shown to operate in the ways animism assumed.

The term was first introduced into anthropological discourse by E.B. Tylor (1832–1917) to describe the religious beliefs characteristic of what he believed to be the lowest or simplest human cultures. Nineteenth-century western European civilization held that human consciousness had evolved through stages, from primitive to civilized, the chief barometer of this development being technology. Aboriginal populations which continued to practice technologies which appeared hopelessly outdated to more highly civilized populations—hunter/gatherers and slash-and-burn agriculturalists—were assumed by Europeans to have similarly anachronistic religious ideas. Tylor insisted to the contrary that the beliefs of such cultural groups were actually the building blocks of all religious systems.

Tylor identified as the simplest and most essential religious cognition the thought that whatever animated the human body continued to exist after that body ceased to function. This thought, that living organisms are possessed by spirits (*anima*), led to the thought that other spirits exist, and that those spirits could manipulate phenomena in the seen world, could reside in objects, and so on in a cognitive progression which culminated, for Tylor at least, in the Christian God.

A student of Tylor, R.R. Marrett (1866–1943), added to the argument the idea that, previous even to the identification of spirits, human consciousness grasped the operation within the natural world of an undifferentiated supernatural power. For Marrett, the original religious impulse was the effort to identify "what is out there?"; an effort rewarded with "a force beyond human comprehension." This preanimistic stage was left behind once supernatural power was perceived as being differentiated into types and as emanating from different sources.

The evolutionist assumptions of Tylor and Marrett led to the conclusion that monotheism, the belief in the all encompassing power of one central high god, could only occur toward the end of the progression of religious understanding. Andrew Lang (1844–1912) was the first of many scholars to call attention to the fact that high gods appear in the belief systems of many peoples at the bottom of the evolutionist's scale. The fatal blow to Tylor's arguments, however, is the appearance of numerous anthropological, art, and religion studies which illustrated just how sophisticated the belief systems of so-called primitive peoples actually were. For example, studies of the Yoruba (Nigeria) indicate that their traditional belief system, Ifa, consists of an estimated 400 to 2,600 *orisa*, or gods. Yet the system possesses a high deity, Olodumare (also known as Odumare, Olorun, Eleda, Eleemi), both the ultimate source of all creation and the determinant of every destiny. Olodumare lacks sexual identity and generally remains removed from the affairs of both divine and worldly beings.

In short, animism does not exist and has never existed as a phenomenom or evolutionary step in religious consciousness. The term was an intellectual blind alley, down which anthropology turned at a time when it sought to be the cutting edge of positivism. The adjective "animistic" retains some limited descriptive value as a label for religious systems which celebrate the continued presence of spiritual beings in earthly objects and living organisms. The noun "animism" must be recognized to be a reification.

These things said, from a broader perspective the concept of animism can be appreciated as a step forward in the European understanding of the world beyond Europe's borders. Europe's own past had predisposed its intellectuals to condemn all belief systems other than their own. Animism was one of the first breaks with that tradition. Since the time of Augustine of Hippo (AD 354–430), Christian intellectuals have perceived the various types of spirits that, according to popular imagination, populate the unseen world as the devil's minions. Such preconceptions influenced elite thinking during the witch craze (1550–1650) when thousands, perhaps hundreds of thousands, of Europeans were put to death as "servants of Satan." Previous to the witch craze, a popular culture featuring oral traditions concerning a multitude of different pre-Christian spiritual entities held its own against efforts at suppression by the literate elite. During the witch craze, the elite gained a cultural hegemony it has never relinquished. The medicinal and curative remnants of the older popular culture the elite dismissed as "old wives tales." Continued belief in the existence of pre-Christian supernatural beings the elite explained away as the result of superstition.

During the 18th century, a split developed within Europe's cultural elite. Discoveries during previous centuries in the fields of what would become astronomy, physics, and chemistry, coupled with the technological advances which permitted the expansion of European capitalism across the globe, motivated part of the intelligentsia to repudiate the cultivation of Christian understanding and to embrace the pursuit of reason as its ultimate goal. The old Christian intelligentsia continued to exist, though now it spent a significant amount of time battling the new secular elite for the hearts and minds of the political authorities. The former also found its interpretations of cultural phenomena challenged. For Christian intellectuals, pre-Christian spiritual entities remained evil. Secularists, for whom only the rational was real, dismissed these entities as the product of irrational superstition.

The expansion of literacy during the Renaissance continued during the Reformation/Counter-Reformation and concluded with the late 19th-century secularization of national school systems. This expansion extended literate sensibilities deeper into European society and thus helped broaden the distance western Europe's literate classes perceived between themselves and believers in the old oral traditions. Both halves of the cultural elite agreed that believers in the old traditions were ignorant. The only debate was the source of that ignorance; Christians maintained the case for Satan, and secularists identified an on going popular indulgence with irrationality. Stories of pre-Christian entities were acknowledged only in the form of fairy tales, written down to entertain or to frighten children.

Systematic contact between Europeans and Africans, Asians and Native Americans began in the 16th century. Yet Europeans became technologically advanced only enough to impose political control over these regions toward the end of the 19th century. In Europe many explanations were put forward to account for European expansion. Boosted by the scientific evidence supplied by Charles Darwin in his *On the Origin of Species by Means of Natural Selection* (1859), explanations that proceeded from the conclusion that Europeans were the most evolved race of humans on earth gained the greatest currency, especially among secular intellectuals.

Three centuries of frustration followed because of non-Europeans' insistence that their gods continued to satisfy, coupled with the failure of European cultures to make many inroads where European political authority did not hold sway, predisposing European cultural elites to see native religious systems from the harshest perspective possible. Secular intellectuals, seduced by evolutionary theories, read continued adherence to indigenous belief systems as a resistance to reason, a trait of less-evolved races. Christian intellectuals, less infatuated, yet still convinced that Europe presented the one spiritually mature civilization on earth, dismissed native religions as fetishist, that is, fixated on the worship of images and idols. Behind both arguments was a conviction that non-Europeans continued to believe in shibboleths Europeans themselves had discarded.

Tylor presented an argument which permitted European intellectuals to see non-European belief systems not as evil, superstitious, or irrational, but as comprehensible according to a certain cognitive progression. In retrospect his passive speculations may appear hopelessly chauvinistic. But his effort to identify the universal principles underlying religious experiences can still prompt admiration. It must also be acknowledged that early on animism lost its scientific value and became yet another prop of a Eurocentric worldview. As the *Encyclopedia of Religion and Ethics* (1912) proclaims in its article on the topic, animism is the religion of all the "un-civilized" peoples of the world. But as the starting point of an intellectual effort to understand the world outside a narrow cultural tradition, animism was, and should be, considered a breakthrough. Social historians who deal with the persistence of animistic elements in the popular versions of Christianity or Islam, or who study religious change in animistic cultures in modern centuries, share a broad definition, though they also agree with their anthropologist colleagues—that each particular belief system must be studied carefully on its own. (*See also* Religion)

Andrew E. Barnes

REFERENCES

Drewal, H.J., et al. *Yoruba, Nine Centuries of African Art and Thought.* New York: Center for African Art in association with H.N. Abrams, 1989.

Murphy, J.M. *Santeria.* Boston: Beacon Press, 1988.
Sharpe, E.J. *Comparative Religion. A History.* New York: Scribner, 1975.

Annales School

The *Annales* school of thought has been one of the leading influences in modern social history. One should differentiate between two historical conjunctures, the appearance of an *Annales* school of history and the affirmation of an *Annales* paradigm; both have been important in the development of social history. Embracing the ideas of whole cultures, culture areas, and of a multiplicity of temporal rhythms of historical evolution, the object of the *Annales* paradigm is to lay a foundation for a world-historical framework of analysis even when its focus is a small space. Placing as much emphasis on factors of disruption as on factors of continuity, the paradigm strives to uncover the unconscious meanings present in material objects and symbols. It embraces a history of events but differentiates between events that are ephemeral and events that can be ordered as part of a cycle of events, as part of a social structure or cultural mind-set, or as part of a structure of very long duration.

The chief protagonists of the paradigm were the founders of the French review *Annales d'histoire économique et sociale*, the second generation of *Annales* scholars, and for a time the third generation. Founded in 1929 by Lucien Febvre and Marc Bloch, the *Annales d'histoire économique et sociale* reflected the orientations of scholars from France's eastern territories. These thinkers were inspired in part by two new directions in German historical scholarship prior to World War I, namely, Gustav Schmoller's *Vierteljahrschrift für Sozial- und Wirtschaftsgeschichte* and Karl Lamprecht's conception of *Kulturgeschichte* as a succession of long waves of diverse sociopsychological experience. The new directions represented a reaction against a narrative history of individuals and political events, against the kind of history that had evolved since the mid-19th century as a result of the imperfect imitation of the model set by Leopold von Ranke. The object of the founders of the *Annales* review was to combat the protagonists of the older German model in favor of the newer German models in improved form, without abstract philosophizing and without concentration on the recent phenomenon of the nation state as the appropriate unit of study.

The improvement came from suggestions by France's other social sciences. The *Annales* paradigm thus was formed under the impact of the views of philosopher mathematician Antoine-Augustin Cournot that events can be set in a "regular series" and that a century may constitute a distinctive unit of experience. It further benefited from the regionalist and possibilist geography of Paul Vidal de la Blache and from François Simiand's studies of cyclical change. It drew on the ideas of Paul Lacombe that facts of repetition are no less important than facts of succession and that history represents the deployment of psychology in space and time. Inspired by the science of linguistics and by Henri Berr's goal of a unifying social science of historical psychology, it embraced Émile Durkheim's sociology of "collective representations," Lucien Lévy-Bruhl's anthropology of the whole mental fact, and Marcel Mauss's anthropology of the mobile total social fact and of "unconscious categories" in magic, religion, and language.

Febvre and Bloch combined many of the foregoing ideas. One of Febvre's contributions was the definition of a fact as an operational construct. Adopting the concept of social structure, Bloch also emphasized the usefulness of comparison. A developed initial *Annales* paradigm did not fall into place, however, until the completion by Fernand Braudel, the leader of the second generation, of the first version of his *Méditerranée* (1949), much of which he wrote as a prisoner of war in Germany, especially the part on geography and geohistory, for which his main sources were works in German. Superficially influencing his work may be Friedrich Ratzel's determinist geography. Braudel himself, however, disclaimed that he was a determinist. To retain people on the scene, a way in which his work differs from Ratzel's, he embraced the idea of three temporal dimensions, in two of which people were present: long duration, a middling time, and the time of events.

The second edition of Braudel's *Méditerranée* (1966), a study of socioeconomies, continues to emphasize the role of cities and communication

and provides a better measure of cyclical movements. It differs from the first by giving more attention to factors of production and to the rural sector. What he most neglects is the role of the family, household, and other small groups.

The major significance of his work on capitalism and material culture stems from his emphasis on the meanings that one may derive from material goods, from quantity, and from different ways of combining material goods; from his use of location theory; and from his distinction between capitalism (always aspiring to privilege) and market economy. He does not distinguish clearly, however, between market economy and an economy of marketplaces.

The success and failure alike of the *Annales* movement were the result of institutionalization. An early establishment phase included the appointment of the two founders to the University of Strasbourg, the founding of the *Annales* itself, Febvre's appointment to the Collége de France and Bloch's to the chair of economic history at the Sorbonne in Paris, and Febvre's charge of a topical *Encyclopédie Française*. Then came World War II and Bloch's engagement in the resistance movement, culminating in his execution.

The second and most important phase of institutionalization, henceforth under the name *Annales: Économies, Sociétés, Civilisations*, extended from 1946 to 1968. It included the building of the research group known as the Sixième Section at the École Pratique des Hautes Études, Braudel's succession to Lucien Febvre at the Collège de France, his designation to chair the history section of national teacher certification, his inspection tour of American area studies programs, and the establishment under his direction of a Maison des Sciences de l'Homme to coordinate nondegree research in the human or social sciences.

Between 1946 and 1968 *Annales* conceptions spread to countries and regions with traditions amenable to French culture. *Annales* ideas found a modest welcome in the Anglo-American cultures only after 1968, that is, only after, as the result of overexpansion, *Annales* scholars themselves started to question many aspects of the paradigm, rejecting the holism or total history (*histoire globale*) that one associates mainly with Braudel.

Most *Annales* scholars, including Fernand Braudel, disclaim that there is as any such thing as an *Annales* school. They mean thereby that they lack a common philosophy of history or political ideology, that they do not pursue a uniform methodology, or that they disavow the paradigm's holistic tendencies.

The rejection of total history by some *Annalistes* followed soon after the student rebellion of May 1968. Among the consequences of the rebellion was the entry of third-generation scholars into positions of leadership; a predilection for a problem-solving history instead of total history; a growing inclination to attribute totalitarian underpinnings to total history; a new respect for narrative history, political history, and "immediate" or contemporary history; a turning away from deconstruction aiming to improve one's understanding of a totality (as in the science of linguistics) toward deconstruction as an intellectual exercise (as in literature).

The turning away from total history was in part a response to American models. Following the rebellion against the "father" (de Gaulle at the national level, Braudel at the level of the discipline of history), in 1968, French historians identified increasingly with liberal ideas, reacted vigorously against every kind of determinism, and turned their attention to "marginal" groups (heresies, Jews, immigrants, women) and ideological superstructures. After 1968, the way of the third generation was the way of an identity crisis, marked by a narrowing professionalization, a growing influence of American models, and a predilection for marginal groups and for fragmentation (*éclatement, émiettement*). In reaction against excessive forms of the foregoing trend and in an effort to reaffirm his own peasant roots and France's identity (unity in diversity), Braudel wrote an unfinished posthumous book entitled *The Identity of France*, which some persons may regard as a return to the nation-state as the appropriate unit of study. During the 1990s, the fourth generation of *Annales* scholars will have to resolve the same and other problems: how to integrate Europe while maintaining ancient autonomies and diversities; how to respond to the demise of the Soviet Union, the refueling of nationalist and provincialist sentiments, and the affirmation of Muslim and other fundamentalisms; how to reorganize the world's state systems and economic regions; and, above all, how to resolve the contradictory demands of economy and ecology. (*See also* Anthropology; Civilization; Comparative History; Environment; European Regions; Geography; Islam; *Longue Durée;* Marxist Historiography; Quantification; Time; World History)

Traian Stoianovich

REFERENCES

Braudel, Fernand. *Civilization and Capitalism, 15th–18th Century*, 3 vols. Translated by Siân Reynolds. London: William Collins Sons; New York: Harper & Row, 1981–1984.

————. *The Identity of France*, Vol. I. *History and Environment*. Translated by Siân Reynolds. New York: Harper & Row, reprinted by arrangement with William Collins Sons, London, 1988.

————. *The Mediterranean and the Mediterranean World in the Age of Philip II*, 2 vols. Translated by Siân Reynolds. London: William Collins Sons; New York: Harper & Row, 1972–1973.

Burke, Peter. *The French Historical Revolution: The "Annales" School, 1929–89*. Stanford, CA: Stanford University Press, 1990.

Stoianovich, Traian. *French Historical Method: The "Annales" Paradigm*, with a foreword by Fernand Braudel. Ithaca, NY: Cornell University Press, 1976.

Anthropology

Anthropology has been separated from history by barriers higher than those usually erected around disciplines. It was partly a geographic division of labor: historians did the West and the classical Orient, and anthropologists, the smaller societies in the rest of the world—those presumed to have no history, or at least none that could be detected. It was partly that historians found the prevailing views of anthropologists uncongenial, in fact, ahistorical. In its heyday until the 1960s, functionalism (strictly speaking, British structural-functionalism) posited a sociocultural equilibrium. It looked at underlying patterns but was blind to change. Structuralism seemed still more repellent. Not only did Claude Lévi-Strauss and his followers neglect change in their concern for common human structures of thought, but they often ignored social and historical context. Oddly, though social history has long widened its scope to include many topics of concern to anthropology, and anthropologists have turned their attention to larger societies and the modern West, this aversion has persisted among many historians.

Three groups of historians did, however, come early under the spell of anthropology. When some historians associated with the *Annales* School in Paris turned to mentalities in the 1970s, they found themselves on the same terrain as anthropologists, but perhaps because structuralism—then reigning in Paris—was difficult to adapt to historical study, it was in localized studies—like E. Le Roy Ladurie's "ethnographic history" of the 14th-century Cathar village *Montaillou*—that that discipline's influence was most strongly felt. Anthropology also affected Le Roy Ladurie's *Carnival in Romans* (English trans., New York, 1979) and Mona Ozouf's *Festivals of the French Revolution* (Cambridge, MA, 1988).

Slightly later, some historians at Princeton University began to look to anthropology, falling under the influence of Clifford Geertz, who had done fieldwork in Indonesia and Morocco and took a semiotic view of culture, espousing "thick description" of key cultural practices or incidents that could be deciphered like texts. Natalie Davis wrote on carnival inversions and rites of violence in 16th-century France and, in the manner of many ethnographers, turned to the medium of film, as advisor to *The Return of Martin Guerre* (1982), about a bigamous peasant couple, the subject of her subsequent book of the same title (Cambridge, MA, 1983). Robert Darnton included in his collection *The Great Cat Massacre* (New York, 1984) another microstudy resembling Geertz's famous Balinese cockfight, about a puzzling 18th-century incident in which printing apprentices killed cats in a symbolic attack on their master, whose wife's beautiful grey cat was the first victim. He also drew on symbolic anthropology and structuralism in decoding cultural symbols in European folktales. The value of anthropology for these scholars—one could add American historians like David Sabean (*Power in the Blood* [Cambridge, 1984])—was its systematic concern with culture and its ability to deal with alien societies, some of them

surprisingly similar to medieval and early modern Europe.

In England, the group of scholars that gathered around the journal *Past and Present*, notably Keith Thomas, E.J. Hobsbawm, and Peter Burke, was no less receptive to anthropology, but unlike the Princeton historians, these writers have tried to account for change. Thomas used a largely functionalist perspective at community level to explain the decline of witchcraft in his massive *Religion and the Decline of Magic* (New York, 1971). Hobsbawm, a Marxist, edited with anthropologist Terence Ranger a collection that could be regarded as a disproof of functionalism. Entitled *The Invention of Tradition*, it underlined the social and political importance of symbols and rituals, but demonstrated that the modern state was capable of manufacturing them. Burke has fruitfully turned an anthropological lens to post-Reformation Italy.

These influences, passed on to numerous younger scholars, have been curiously delayed and selective. Though Bronislaw Malinowski and the early Geertz have long fallen out of favor among anthropologists, current approaches like practice theory, and most brands of postmodernism have not as yet had an impact on published sociohistorical research. Anthropology, meanwhile, has not only changed its favored theories, but also its view of history. As if animated by E.E. Evans-Pritchard's dictum that "anthropology must choose between being history and being nothing" (*Anthropology and History* [Manchester, 1961], p. 20), scholars in a number of areas have done noteworthy historical-anthropological work: Renato Rosaldo on Ilongot headhunting, Jean Comaroff on South Africa rituals of resistance, Maurice Bloch on royal Madagascar ritual, Sidney Mintz on sugar and the West Indies, and Marshall Sahlins on Captain Cook's reception in Hawaii. Many other anthropologists have also explored their informants' notion of history and the contemporary role of the past, supplemented fieldwork with written materials, and abandoned the convention of the "ethnographic present," which gave a static feel to so many ethnographies. Anthropologists have become conscious of the dependence of classical ethnographers on European colonial power. Nowadays they are inclined to be very critical of their sources (which historians should applaud) and aware, indeed to the point of narcissism, of their effects on informants. Additionally, intellectual trends from other disciplines have entered both disciplines, notably Marxism (or "post-Marxism"), semiology, and theories of discourse. These common influences have laid the groundwork for closer contact with historians. The first fruits of collaboration have already appeared, in co-authored works and in conference volumes sponsored by various North American institutions on western Europe, Oceania, and China. A new journal, *Anthropology and History*, is published at Cambridge University in England.

Convergence should not be exaggerated. The two disciplines do not define history in the same way. Often anthropologists theorize in the vein of the philosophy of history, or perversely (like Robert Netting in *Balancing on an Alp* [Cambridge, Eng., 1981]) look for change in unchanging communities, or take "history" in the sense of myth—a powerful belief bearing little relationship to past events. Have anthropology and history been converging, as Peter Burke has suggested half-seriously, like express trains on parallel tracks, only to pass each other and exchange positions, with historians returning to political history and narrative, just as anthropologists reach back into the past? In any case, it is unlikely that many historians will be inclined to reverse Evans-Pritchard's dictum, as he himself suggested, and admit that "history must choose between being social anthropology or being nothing" (1961:20). Yet for those who would make social history more aware of theory, more systematic in treating culture, and more broadly and explicitly comparative, that suggestion bears thinking about.

Donald S. Sutton

REFERENCES

Biersack, Aletta, ed. *Clio in Oceania: Toward a Historical Anthropology*. Washington and London: Smithsonian Institution Press, 1991.

Burke, Peter. *The Historical Anthropology of Early Modern Italy: Essays on Perception and Communication*. New York: Cambridge University Press, 1987.

Davis, Natalie. *Society and Culture in Early Modern France*. Stanford, CA: Stanford University Press, 1975.

Geertz, Clifford. *The Interpretation of Cultures*. New York: Basic Books, 1973.

Hunt, Lynn. *The New Cultural History*. Berkeley: University of California Press, 1989.

Anthropometric History

One can think of the average height reached at a particular age or of the adult height attained by a population as a historical record of the nutritional experience of the individuals composing that population. This line of reasoning is based on medical research, which has established beyond doubt that the cumulative nutritional intake of a population has a major influence on its average height, with the epidemiological environment also playing a part. Therefore, both physical stature and the biomass index can be used as indicators of how well the human organism thrived in its socioeconomic environment prior to reaching adulthood. (The biomass index is calculated by dividing the weight of an individual by his height squared, both in metric units.) In contrast, weight for height is an indicator of current nutritional status.

More specifically, nutritional status is a measure of nutrient intake minus the claims of basal metabolism, disease, and physical exertion on those nutrients. Nutritional status—and thus height—is related to food consumption and therefore to real family income, and thus to wages and prices, and consequently to the biological standard of living broadly conceived. Thus, physical stature can also be used as a rough measure for these economic variables.

Anthropometric history was born in the mid-1970s in conjunction with efforts to quantify changes in the standard of living during the course of the last 200 years in economies for which conventional measures of welfare such as GNP per capita were either not available or were controversial. In contrast to evidence on real wages, anthropometric data is plentiful and has the additional advantage of being available for groups that did not work for a money wage. Richard Steckel's (1979) work on American slaves might be considered the manifesto of the discipline. He demonstrated that slaves attained adult heights that were indicative of a reasonably high nutritional status. In fact, their physical stature was closer to that of European aristocrats than to that of European peasants.

Other research into the history of physical stature revealed the existence of cycles in human height, which were previously unknown. Research is underway to explain the relationship between the turning points in these cycles and economic, demographic, and epidemiological changes. It has been demonstrated with remarkable consistency that during the second half of the 18th century the European societies experienced a decline in nutritional status and physical stature, brought about by a rapid rise in population. A similar downturn was found among both American and British military men born in the 1830s. The height of the upper classes was less affected by external circumstances; even in America, upper-class men were taller than lower-class men. Urban populations were invariably shorter than rural ones in the preindustrial era. In fact, until the end of the 19th century, the farther one lived from urban markets, the taller one was likely to be.

John Komlos

REFERENCES

Floud, Roderick, Kenneth Wachter, and Annabel Gregory. *Height, Health and History.* Cambridge: Cambridge University Press, 1990.

Fogel, Robert W. "Nutrition and the Decline in Mortality Since 1700; Some Preliminary Findings," in Stanley Engerman and Robert Gallman, eds., *Long Term Factors in American Economic Growth.* Chicago: University of Chicago Press. National Bureau of Economic Research, Studies in Income and Wealth, Vol. 51, pp. 439–555.

Komlos, John. *Nutrition and Economic Development in the Eighteenth-Century Habsburg Monarchy: An Anthropometric History.* Princeton, NJ: Princeton University Press, 1989.

Steckel, Richard H. "Slave Height Profiles from Coastwise Manifests," *Explorations in Economic History* 16 (1979): 86–114.

Tanner, J.M. *Foetus into Man. Physical Growth from Conception to Maturity.* Cambridge, MA: Harvard University Press, 1990; first ed. 1978.

Antimilitarism

France's *Grand Larousse* dictionary (1963) defines antimilitarism as opposition to the "preponderance of the military element in a nation."

Antimilitarism first emerged as an organized movement among republicans and socialists in France during the Second Empire. Its European heyday came during the two decades before World War I, when resistance to the influence of the military in politics and the onset of war became major preoccupations of left liberals, social-democrats, syndicalists, and anarchists throughout Europe. Never a majority movement, and most often studied in political terms, antimilitarism warrants sociohistorical attention as well.

American and British antimilitarists generally have focused on military threats to civilian government, including control of the armed forces. Antimilitarism was equivalent to "civilianism," wrote the American historian of militarism Alfred Vagts. In the Anglo-Saxon world, militarism was presumed to have been held in check by the constitutional arrangements of 1688–1689, which limited standing armies in Britain and by the restraints on the military written into the U.S. Constitution. Confidence on this score has been eroded in recent years, however, by the emergence of the military-industrial complex in the United States. While sharing the Anglo-Saxon concern about military influence in government, antimilitarists in Continental Europe, where the persistence of conscription has meant large standing armies in peacetime, have been more apt to decry the infusion of military values into civilian society and the perceived symbiotic relationship between militarism and capitalism.

Before the advent of fascism in the 1920s, there was a tendency, especially among liberals, to equate militarism with a semifeudal warrior aristocracy whose influence would wane with the growth of modern industry and representative democracy. Socialists, particularly Marxists, disagreed (except in Japan, where antimilitarists of all stripes view their nation's potent pre-1945 militarism as a corollary of economic backwardness). Marxists saw the military as the handmaiden of capitalism. At home, troops were used to repress strikes, while abroad they carved out colonies for capitalists to exploit. In countries that had conscription, leftists also condemned the impact of military training upon working-class conscripts, conditioning them to reactionary politics, low pay, regimentation, and strict obedience to commands. In Germany and especially France, where antimilitarism was strong before World War I, militants lobbied for reductions in military budgets, highlighted military brutalities at home and abroad, passed out tracts encouraging recruits to resist military indoctrination, and distributed money to enable servicemen to continue to attend union meetings.

Antimilitarism should not be confused with antipatriotism, which opposes the exaltation of the nation-state, although the two sentiments have often coexisted in the same movements or individuals. Many prominent antimilitarists, such as the pre-1914 French socialist leader Jean Jaurès, were also strong patriots. But others, for example Jaurès's contemporaries, the leading German antimilitarists, left social democrats Karl Liebknecht and Rosa Luxemburg, were equally fervent antipatriots. Nor should antimilitarism be equated with pacifism, which seeks to eliminate war through universal disarmament. Most antimilitarists did not favor the abolition of the military. Jaurès, for example, wanted to retain a French military capability, but advocated replacement of the standing army with a Swiss-style militia. (*See also* Military and Society; World Wars)

Bruce Vandervort

REFERENCES

Berghahn, Volker. *Militarism: The History of an International Debate, 1861–1979*. New York: St. Martin's, 1982.

Bond, Brian. *War and Society in Europe, 1870–1970*. New York: St. Martin's, 1984.

Chickering, Roger. *Imperial Germany and a World Without War: The Peace Movement and German Society, 1892–1914*. Princeton, NJ: Princeton University Press, 1976.

Vagts, Alfred. *A History of Militarism*. New York: Free Press, 1967.

Anti-Semitism

See Scapegoating

Apartheid

Apartheid (Afrikaner word meaning separateness) is the term for the legal and political system of racial segregation which whites imposed on blacks in South Africa from the late 1940s until 1991. Segregation began soon after the first whites landed at what is now Cape Town in 1652, and was easy to maintain in an agrarian economy. South Africa's industrial revolution, sparked by the discovery of diamonds (1867) and gold (1886), created an ever-increasing need for black labor. As blacks were absorbed into the economy, increasingly in urban areas, white governments sought barriers to political and social integration.

The theory supporting apartheid was a mixture of Calvinist theology, a genetically based theory of racial superiority, and the concepts that culture was genetically determined and that race mixing was evil. The term "apartheid" had been used during the 1930s as a synonym for segregation, but it came into common use during the 1948 general election campaign. The National Party came to power and, in the next two decades, constructed the legal system known as apartheid. The National Party was dominated by the Afrikaners (approximately 55 percent of the white population), descendants of the original Dutch settlers. They owned most of the land and controlled the government, military, judiciary, and police. Fearful of losing their racial identity, the Afrikaners were an intransigent ruling class with a siege mentality.

In one sense apartheid was merely a more extreme application of segregationist principles that had been followed by all South African governments during the 20th century; by mid-century there was already a strict color bar, based on legislation and public opinion. Social historians have studied these principles as part of comparative work on racism and social structure. But in another sense 1948 began a distinct new period; by 1970 apartheid was the most comprehensive form of government-sanctioned segregation on a racial basis in the modern world. The entire population was divided into racial categories; one's access to housing, employment, legal rights, and so on was determined on a racial basis. The government established a number of Bantustans, or "homelands," which were given political independence. These Bantustans constituted about 13 percent of the total land area (blacks currently constitute about 87 percent of the total population), and few were economically viable. All blacks were to be citizens of one of these areas. Blacks were forbidden to enter white areas except for specific purposes, usually employment; their movement into such areas was regulated by passbooks, which they were forced to carry at all times. Marriage and sexual relations between blacks and whites were outlawed. The educational system was rigidly segregated.

During the 1980s apartheid came under increased domestic and foreign pressure. The African National Congress led a virtual guerrilla war against the state. Strikes and boycotts hampered economic activity. Internationally, South Africa became a pariah nation and was the target of trade and financial sanctions by many nations. Under these pressures and the leadership of President F.W. de Klerk, the South African government revoked all of the major apartheid legislation in 1990 and 1991. But most of the economic and social barriers remained, and blacks were still excluded from the democratic political process.

In conclusion, apartheid drew so much attention in the international arena largely because of timing and the race of the parties involved. In the postwar period there was a universal mood toward condemnation of racism and the concept of inferior peoples. While European empires were crumbling, the South African government created a comprehensive legal framework for an already oppressive system in which race was the central organizing principle. (*See also* Racial Segregation; Racism)

Phillip Wilkin

REFERENCES

Berger, Peter L., and Bobby Godsell, eds. *A Future South Africa: Visions, Strategies, and Realities.* Boulder, CO: Westview Press, 1988.

Debroey, Steven. *South Africa to the Sources of Apartheid.* Lanham, MD: University Press of America, 1989.

———. *South Africa Under the Curse of Apartheid.* Lanham, MD: University Press of America, 1989.

Lewis, Stephen R. *The Economics of Apartheid.* New York: Council on Foreign Relations Press, 1990.

Price, Robert M. *The Apartheid State in Crisis: Political Transformation in South Africa.* Oxford: Oxford University Press, 1991.

Archaeology

Archaeology, like the fields of anthropology of which it is one of four subfields, and history, traces its roots to the Renaissance and to the rediscovery of classical cultures and forms, particularly in architecture and in the artifacts that populated Greek and Roman daily life. Expanded European interest in and familiarity with the physical artifacts of classical antiquity was later supplemented by exposure to the material culture of the native inhabitants of the New World. The worldwide expansion of European culture after the 15th century revealed tremendous diversity in human cultural adaptations, not only the different ways people provided for life's necessities but also how they organized themselves socially, and what their ideologies and beliefs were. Categorization, study, and attempts to understand and interpret this cultural diversity were further spurred by the intellectual inquisitiveness of the 18th-century Enlightenment, by the development of the concepts of geological time and biological and social evolution, by an increasing awareness of the great span of human history, and by developments in the method and theory of the natural sciences.

Archaeology as an academic field of study, however, is a phenomenon of the 19th century, a trait that it shares with the discipline of history. Most archaeological work during the second half of the 19th century and the early decades of the 20th was predicated upon the collection of artifacts and the development of artifact and culture chronologies among North America's native cultures. Particular attention was focused on the Southwest, where surviving traditional cultures were at first presumed to represent "arrested," or fossilized, stages in human cultural development. Detailed ethnographies of the economy, social organization, ideology, religion, myth, among other aspects of these peoples propelled early anthropological (ethnographic) research. As the stone, wood, bone, and other tools utilized by these people resembled those from archaeological sites, a direct interpretive and historical connection was often drawn between present and past. Furthermore, since Europeans had been in contact with these and other native peoples for some centuries, the writings of earlier European travelers, explorers, and priests (ethnohistorical accounts) provided additional information on native cultures that was used to interpret, by analogy, the archaeological artifacts for which no living descendants could be identified and for whom no historical documents existed. The interplay between material and historical lines of evidence and a reasoning from present to past conditions (the "direct historical approach") is thus a venerable one in the development of American archaeology.

Predicated upon late 19th century European concepts of science, American archaeological research during the first four decades of the 20th century was preoccupied with time-space systematics, the importance of obtaining facts, presumed objectivity in observation, the working out of detailed regional and area chronologies, the development of artifact types, and the identification of archaeological cultures based upon similarities in the attributes of stone tools, ceramics, and other artifacts. This preoccupation helped to legitimize both anthropology and archaeology as disciplines but forestalled their crisis in theory that history experienced somewhat earlier.

Beginning in 1948 with the publication of Walter W. Taylor's *Study of Archaeology*, some American archaeologists began to examine critically the limitations of these traditional approaches and goals. Taylor's work was a logical positivist call to arms for archaeologists aggressively to pursue greater meaning in the archaeological record through a conjunctive approach that shifted the emphasis from the artifact to the study of the human behaviors that lay behind a now expanded concept of what constituted the archaeological record. The methodology was to be interdisciplinary and was to focus not only on artifacts but processes by which artifacts were (or were not) incorporated within and preserved in archaeological contexts in a patterned, nonrandom way that was subject to explanation. Taylor and the New Archaeology school of the 1960s, to which his work gave rise, emphasized the importance of theory and an expanded range

of methodologies as the driving forces behind the new agenda, the scientific study of the processes of culture itself.

This new emphasis on archaeology as a processual science of the long-term human past promoted expansive, eclectic thinking and the adoption of methods and theories from geology, biology, materials science, mathematics, engineering, history, geography, sociology, and many other natural and social sciences. New models of past human behavior were articulated, tested, and subjected to statistical proofs. In the mid-1960s, the subdiscipline of historical archaeology emerged and explored the interface of history and archaeology and human behavior in the more recent past. Similarly, social archaeology emerged as a subfield within prehistoric archaeology and undertook the study of significant long-term processes in the history of humankind, for example, the environmental and social factors that resulted in the shift from hunting and gathering economies to agriculture, the forces behind the emergence of cities, states, complex societies, and civilization. Prehistoric archaeology's study of these and other themes in the lengthy process of prehistoric human cultural development parallels the examination of long-term historical trends advocated in the approach (*longue durée*) of, among others, Fernand Braudel.

Many contemporary archaeologists (at least those who find the time to read outside their own discipline) also share the perspectives articulated clearly by the *Annales* historical school in promoting both a problem orientation to their work as well as the use of rigorous and multiple methodologies designed to elicit new information about the human past by cutting the data in innovative ways to get at recurring patterns. Frequently, the data set for historical archaeologists is, in part, similar to or the same as that employed by social historians. Census data, probate inventories, military records, labor statistics, farm production data, diaries, account books, demographic data, and other historical sources that are common grist for the social historian's mill are also utilized by historical archaeologists. Such historical data are not viewed as correctives to the archaeological data nor strictly as supplements but as data on an equal footing with the material culture evidence provided by archaeology. This evidence can include not only artifacts per se but also such diverse information as the plant and animal remains of meals, fragments of cloth and leather, the remains of microorganisms within the digestive tracts of human burials, and the geological and pedological (soil) contexts of archaeological sites. When taken together, these data can permit a fuller and more detailed reconstruction of the daily lives of humans in the past.

Archaeologists today, whether prehistorians or historical archaeologists, share many subjects of interest with their counterparts in social history. These topics include gender studies, the transfer of power and status, social inequality, the factors underlying consumer choices, ethnic studies, classism, the organization of labor and production, the social impacts of technological change, ecological studies, the social and economic effects of capitalism, and studies of the sexual division of labor, among many others.

Almost inevitably, the idealism and naiveté of the 1960s New Archaeology could not be sustained. Its practitioners fell prey largely to the questioning, skepticism, and self-doubt produced, ironically, by the very successes of archaeological projects undertaken during the 1960s and 1970s that demonstrated the enormous complexity and diversity of culture, past and present, to say nothing of the difficulty of constructing a science that purported to study it. Beginning in the 1980s, therefore, a portion of archaeological theory was spun off into a postmodern, postprocessual orbit characterized at one extreme by a position of ultimate pluralism, nihilism, and relativism that in its logical conclusion denies that the past is knowable through a study of material culture. Other archaeologists returned to hyperempiricism. As a counter argument to both postprocessual extremes, Lewis Binford, himself the chief proponent of the New Archaeology of the early 1960s, has advocated (and operationalized) the concept of middle-range research, by which static archaeological data are related to the dynamic cultural processes that produced them and caused them to be deposited when and where they were. This approach continues to emphasize the holism and interconnectedness of human life while remaining cognizant that the past is a construct,

that there are many pasts, and that archaeology (like history) does not discover the past so much as it creates it by developing various analytical frames of reference "... that living, breathing persons have in fact never directly experienced" (Binford 1986: 474). (*See also* Ethnography/Ethnohistory)

Ronald C. Carlisle

REFERENCES

Binford, Lewis R. "In Pursuit of the Future," in David J. Meltzer, Don D. Fowler, and Jeremy A. Sabloff, eds. *American Archaeology Past and Future; A Celebration of the Society for American Archaeology 1935–1985.* Washington and London: Smithsonian Institution Press, 1986, pp. 459–479.

Bintliff, John L. *The Annales School and Archaeology.* Leicester: Leicester University Press, 1991.

Little, Barbara J. *Text-Aided Archaeology.* Boca Raton, FL: CRC Press, 1992.

Preucel, Robert W. *Processual and Post-Processual Archaeologies: Multiple Ways of Knowing the Past.* Carbondale, IL: Occasional Paper No. 10, Center for Archaeological Investigations, Southern Illinois University at Carbondale, 1991.

Renfrew, Colin, and Paul Bahn. *Archaeology; Theories, Methods, and Practice.* New York: Thames and Hudson, 1991.

Architecture

Architecture is the art and practice of designing and building settings for human activities. Its scope embraces shepherds' huts and skyscrapers, farmsteads and cities, fast-food restaurants and cathedrals. Its aspirations range from providing utilitarian solutions for basic human needs to representing society's highest ideals. Architectural studies address patterns of use, the shaping of form and space, the aesthetic and technical properties of materials and structural systems, intended and acquired meanings, and processes of planning, financing, and construction.

There are many models for organizing architectural practice. It can be a communal activity shared by all members of a social group, such as the Tamberma in Africa, or a specialization delegating responsibility for design and construction to a master builder, such as the masons of Europe's medieval cathedrals, or dividing it between designers and craft workers, as in the contemporary United States. Modern industrial societies have tended to disperse the vast scope of architecture among a number of related professions including civil engineering, landscape architecture, city and regional planning, and interior design. Although the boundaries between these professions are often fluid, the architect's realm today is usually focused on the design of individual or grouped buildings. Architects generally play a supervisory role in construction but, typically, are not builders. Construction is organized and conducted by separate networks of contractors, workers, and suppliers whose histories for the most part have yet to be written.

The division between design and construction in contemporary practice was codified during the Italian Renaissance when theoreticians such as Leone Battista Alberti (1404–1472) sought to elevate the status of art and architecture from that of manual trades to professions. Alberti made the case in neoplatonic terms arguing that the essence of architecture was an intellectual product, that is, the concept, which was invariably compromised in the built work. Longstanding consequences of this position, which has profoundly colored the writing of architectural history and criticism, include the glorification of the architect as the primary figure in the building process and the ranking of buildings according to the relationships their underlying concepts have with the accepted principles of high art. Both consequences have obscured our understanding of the full range of architectural practice. The former has cast shadows over the essential and often creative roles of clients, financiers, and craft workers; the latter has slighted the achievements of popular and folk cultures. They have also contributed to an emphasis on the study of architecture in terms of isolated artifacts rather than as locuses of human activity.

All architecture is achieved at some economic cost. It can be the few hours Eskimos required to build an igloo, or the significant drain on the royal treasury occasioned by the thousands of workers and expensive materials necessary to create Louis XIV's palace at Versailles. Societies have varied greatly in the way they have allocated economic resources among private and public interests. In many, such as that of 17th-century France, the ability to undertake large-scale works is an attribute of power and high status readily exercised by political and religious leaders and echoed by private individuals eager to advertise their own success. The notion of "keeping up with the Joneses" embedded in the culture of suburban neighborhoods of the United States has its counterparts in the palaces of the Russian court in Leningrad and the plank houses of the American Indians living along Pacific Northwest coast.

The use of architecture for rhetorical purposes issues from a fundamental human trait of projecting an image of the self on one's immediate environment. It is through this projection, for example, that a house or other residential unit becomes the psychologically secure haven we refer to as a home. To this end the Tamberma of western Africa (Togo) conceive their houses in terms of human anatomy, and in China, cosmology ordered the organization of houses and cities alike. Meaningful architecture accommodates and reinforces such transformations, thereby creating settings that endow the great and modest rituals of human activity with a distinct sense of place.

Architecture conveys meaning through a variety of devices. It can provide a framework for inscriptions, paintings, and sculpture that describe or illustrate its purpose. On its own terms, it can generate impressions through manipulations of scale, relationships to the natural or urban context, and the quality and craftsmanship of its materials. It can also offer associations with other places and times by incorporating suggestive motifs in plan, elevation, and detail. The Latin cross plan, for example, is an iconic image of the Christian church, and the triumphal arch, a motif from ancient Roman architecture, has been a symbol in Western culture of victory and enduring fame. Such associations are often specific to a particular culture or subculture, and the meanings intended by one group may not be those received by others with different values and symbolic languages, who, in turn, will ascribe new meanings to existing forms. Architecture, thus, can be multivalent, and the historian's challenge in attempting to recover intended or received meanings is to develop, as fully as possible, an understanding of the people who created them.

Of all the art forms, architecture may be the most useful to social historians. Buildings, because of their cost, require social support and are therefore indices of a society's or group's values. Idiosyncrasy is more difficult than with music or painting. Social historians thus use architecture in dealing with material culture and what it reveals about social structure, beliefs, and family and community norms. Research on changes in home design, for example, is central to our understanding of the evolution of the middle-class family in the 19th and 20th centuries. The elimination of a separate room for the husband and father in the later 19th century and the rise of multiple bathrooms in the 20th century are the kinds of changes that are open to sociohistorical analysis. Change, then, as well as differences among groups and societies revealed by the built environment makes architecture a key focus in many forms of social history.

Richard Cleary

REFERENCES

Blier, Suzanne Preston. *The Anatomy of Architecture: Ontology and Metaphor in Batammaliba Architectural Expression.* New York: Cambridge University Press, 1987.

Goldthwaite, Richard. *The Building of Renaissance Florence.* Baltimore: Johns Hopkins University Press, 1980.

Kostof, Spiro. *A History of Architecture: Settings and Rituals.* New York: Oxford University Press, 1985.

Wright, Gwendolyn. *Building the Dream: A Social History of Housing in America.* New York: Pantheon Press, 1981.

Aristocracy

The literal definition of aristocracy, "rule by the best," does not require that the privileged group exercise sole authority. Formalized elites have generally shared power, sometimes (the Greek city-state, republican Rome) with broadly based magistracies, but more frequently with monarchy. By the core definition, however, aristocracy cannot be detached from public performance: structured inequality confers obligation as well as privilege. Social rank rests upon prerogative, which must be exercised lest it be withdrawn. Whether the power to command derives from an original share in administration or integration into a centralized regime, once-independent aristocrats have had to reconstitute themselves as officials or risk marginalization. The Confucian ideal of dutiful service to the state and its Western equivalents of stoicism and *noblesse oblige* do not allow categorical retirement into epicurean idleness.

Aristocracies exist in most agricultural societies, as the top power group, but they vary widely. Their importance and their complexity have commanded great attention in social history. Usually, aristocrats are also landholders. Almost always they have defined legal privileges. Almost always they define a common culture and seek to limit contacts with outsiders. Almost always they claim special political rights, though relationships with the state range from hostility to subservience. The size of a definable aristocracy varies; usually, the group averages around 3 percent of total population, but in exceptional circumstances like Hungary and Poland, the percentage is much larger. Many aristocracies are internally divided, between wealthy, powerful magnates and a larger number of rural, often quite unsophisticated gentry. In some instances a lower group of aristocrats is impoverished, like a group in 18th-century France, proudly claiming legal status and wearing swords while plowing their own meager fields themselves. The sizes, divisions, roles, and cultures of aristocrats also change over time, providing another research angle for social historians.

Aristocratic ideals look back to fierce independence but acknowledge assimilation. Roman histories, medieval *chansons de geste,* and chivalric romances celebrated heroes who had, in fact, found second vocations in their rulers' armies and civil services. The *bushido* literature which enshrined the Japanese samurai ethos appeared after Tokugawa shoguns (1603–1868) obliged samurai to live in castle towns rather than on ancestral lands, fed and housed by stipends rather than private incomes. But ideology is not altogether anachronistic: all texts stress faithful service to superiors as the hallmark of the aristocrat. The true knight or samurai or courtier is a functionary, called upon to make war but no longer a warlord.

Performance Elite

The best (*aristoi*) are those who claim they are distinguished from the mass of the populace by some quality of excellence or prowess (*arete*). Aristocracies usually traced their eminence to past status as elite fighters, and they retained a martial vocation even as warfare shifted toward mass formations such as hoplite phalanxes, mercenary bands, or conscript levies. Japanese and European aristocracies were disproportionately represented in officer corps well into the 20th century, long after the right to command was dissolved. The image of the noble as warrior has been enhanced, as well, by ethical codes—chivalry and *bushido*—which revere those whose duty it was to protect the weak.

But as the primary occupation of aristocrats changed from war to administration, martial displays presented artifacts and symbols rather than indicators of ongoing careers: arms and armor became beautifully elaborate when used only in ceremony. Mature aristocracies, in fact, reduce martial prowess to a secondary and purely formalized qualification. Even the Homeric chariot elite needed skill in counsel to demonstrate rounded excellence; Greek and Roman generalships were a consequence, not a cause, of patricians' preeminence in rhetoric and statecraft in assemblies and law courts. The samurai would never have survived as a privileged group if fit only for war, given the long peace of the Tokugawa period.

Indeed, prowess is frequently defined in terms which are unconnected with excellence in battle. This is a key area in which aristocratic cultures vary greatly. Chinese emperors gave priority to scholarship, with office conferred almost exclusively on the basis of examinations in the Confucian classics. Aristotle's *aristoi* and Plato's Guardians were distinguished by the capacity to discern and apply principles of truth and justice; those responsible for physical protection received low rank. Even the fractious Russian boyars were assimilated with the "service gentry," and by the Table of Ranks in 1722 the composite nobility (*dvorianstvo*) was defined strictly in terms of service to the tsar. Battle enhanced prestige, but renown itself was commonly won off the field.

Archaic cultures primarily reward expertise in interpreting the divine will or the cosmic order, hence their priestly elites. The rise of complex states and sacerdotal specialists has not, however, canceled association of the aristocratic with the sacred. Greek and Roman patricians held top religious offices even under democracy and, like Japanese and Chinese counterparts, directed cults of ancestor veneration. The longest-lived of world aristocracies, the brahmans of India, is theoretically characterized by a priestly vocation. In Hinduism's four *varnas,* which broadly define social hierarchy, brahmans' spiritual purity is stained by violence or worldly engagement, and so military and political command rests with the second-tier *kshatriya.* And the notion that the best should seek the most profound sorts of excellence has been everywhere compelling: not a few aristocrats have abandoned arms and office for the monastery.

The most martial elite must demonstrate skill in manners and command of higher culture. Homeric heroes, samurai, and Arab, Byzantine, and Chinese courtiers were notable for mastery of intricate etiquette, while courtly love demanded that Europe's knights woo, recite, and counsel in a courteous style. Poetry, dance, song, and conversation are the universal currencies of aristocracy, no less than swords and office; East Asian elites added calligraphy and tea drinking to the list of requirements.

Hereditary Base

Aristocracy as performance elite has nowhere canceled the principle of hereditary aristocracy. Common understanding of inheritance, that moral and intellectual as well as physical qualities passed from parent to child, held that ancestral eminence was transmissible. Confucians and Greek philosophers assumed that the masses lacked the innate capacity to develop excellence, and that the wellborn alone would receive requisite training to achieve superiority. Birthright set two corollaries: the limited pool of talent should be conserved through endogamy, and the inherently superior should prevent contamination by resisting the upward mobility of inferiors.

The claim of blood has received mixed treatment, however. Greeks, Romans, and Renaissance humanists thought that heredity provided a general but often fallible indicator of worth:

ancestral *virtus* easily degenerated into vice and indolence, and true nobility was found in personal ethical qualities alone. The Judeo-Christian heritage was ambivalent: "the good tree brings forth good fruit," said the Gospels; still, the Hebrew God spoke through shepherds, and Jesus's disciples were fishermen. Confucians believed in natural hierarchy, but held that standing should be based on individual character and education.

If these objections could not sway aristocratic instincts for family perpetuation, they prevented caste closure. In China competitive examinations gradually triumphed in recruitment to imperial service; though the gentry usually did best, if only because they could afford the best education, others could also pass the tests. Gradual establishment of provincial and local schools created a large pool of applicants. Only 55 to 60 percent of top officials in the Tang Dynasty (AD 618–907) came from the great clans that received official genealogies, and the proportion then sank to negligible levels.

Practical factors also blocked closure. Though many aristocracies are protected by laws forbidding others to claim titles, new recruitment is vital. Aristocracies were periodically decimated by war and dynastic upheaval. The whim of rulers broke many houses; sterility, early death, and incompetence took others. Extinction rates were always high. Of 50 Roman *gentes* in the 5th century BC, for example, only 14 survived the republic; some 30 to 50 percent of noble families disappeared in any given century of late medieval Europe. A cycle of 4 to 6 generations from obscurity to prominence and back to obscurity (or extinction) was the norm in Europe, and it was scarcely longer in China, where polygamy and concubinage produced a greater pool of heirs. Only brahmans were partially protected, owing to relative detachment from worldly strife. But many brahmans were kings and landlords, in fact, and prosopography shows that the top caste required constant renewal.

The imperative of survival mandates inclusion; everywhere save Japan, elites reluctantly allowed hypergamy (recruitment of brides from lower strata). Aristocrats were forced to admit newcomers, as well, when sovereigns ennobled commoners in order to reward supporters and legal or talented individuals to the bureaucracy, dilute opposition, and raise money. France in the 17th century sold some titles to win funds for the state. The Russian tsar regularly enrobed some commoner bureaucrats. Modernizing states raised baseborn specialists in the fields of law and finance, where aristocrats were never numerous, and those invested with real power (*noblesse de robe*) were not long denied a share in nobility. Thus, endemic carping at the vulgarity of *nouveaux* is a rearguard action, aimed against too-easy admission of outsiders rather than at absolute exclusion. The caste demands of apologetic tracts represent a high ideal only.

Inherited rank produced a specific social ordering. As individuals claimed rank from worthy forebears, the lineage became the primary vehicle for transmitting status and property. The entire descent group is too amorphous to sustain personal identity, however, and aristocracies have focused on the direct male line and so weakened earlier clan loyalties. Patrilineal succession triumphed over (though never eliminated) matrilineal descent: as an Arab poet put it, "The mothers of men are but vessels; the fathers account for nobility." Women were not thereby excluded from aristocracy. They shared good blood, forged marital links between lineages, provided biological continuity, and brought honor to the family through sexual purity and refined manners. But they were secondary members of natal patrilines, and never completely joined marital lineages. They seldom claimed a full share in the patrimony.

Legal Privilege

Favored legal status (like separate courts or exclusive hunting rights) and exemption from civil obligations (taxes and labor services) are the natural privileges of status. Functional specialization demanded, as well, that the aristocrat be detached from subsistence activities. Rank was conjoined with occupational purity: quotidian labor was both source and symptom of a lesser state. Both the *varnas* and the Confucian systems of China and Japan, for example, placed merchants near the bottom of the social hierarchy; traders could not sit for Chinese civil service examinations until the Ming Dynasty (1368–1644). Aristotle and medieval scholastics deprecated speculative commerce as unstable, sterile, and morally damaging; rising bourgeois in the West abandoned trade and bought estates. At best, European aristocrats and younger sons in Tokugawa Japan might invest in commerce, but they were advised against direct management. This is one reason that growing commercialism (16th-century Europe, 19th-century Japan) often put aristocrats at an increasing disadvantage.

Rarely could premodern states afford to pay for administration; China and Ottoman Turkey are the only consistent exceptions. Most fund governing cadres through land, either allowing nobles to amass wholly owned estates or granting holdings which, though nominally precarious, became heritable (as in western European feudalism). Property then reinforced privilege: since national well-being was identified with terrain rather than commerce, those with property claimed to hold the major stake in the community and so demanded predominance in government. High culture then cemented the nexus of rank and land through themes of landscape and pastoralism which contrasted the exalting influence of the countryside with the sordid effects of the marketplace. Shintoism even raised veneration of nature to a spiritual principle. Only in India, where classical texts placed ownership in the mid-level *vaishya* caste, and China and Ottoman Turkey, where great landowners often did not enter government, was control of land dissociated from the highest rank.

Land presented challenges as it conferred honor and sustenance. A family's demographic success fractioned its patrimony, jeopardizing an appropriate standard of living. In response, many elites adopted conservation mechanisms such as entail, unigeniture, and limited marriage to reduce the claims of extra sons and those daughters not needed for alliances. But restrictive strategies are dangerous: if land is closely constricted, it cannot be fully exploited; if too many children are unmarried or consigned to monasteries, the family risks extinction. Excess offspring could not be jettisoned altogether, and always retained a claim to maintenance. Many societies—Russia, China, Poland, and medieval Japan—resisted tampering with partible inheritance. Yet agricultural yields were largely static, save for brief periods of topographic expansion or intensified

cultivation and new crops. Aristocratic families thus faced recurrent downward economic pressures, and neither state service nor hypergamy could supply a general remedy.

Status Signs

Public acknowledgment of nobility rests upon marks of superiority such as behavior, customs, and insignia as much as upon ancestral title and land. Recent study of mores, however, tends to blur rather than clarify social boundaries, since habits associated with aristocrats were seldom exclusive to the aristocracy. The middle ranks established networks of patronage and clientage; the poor had notions of honor, deference, etiquette, ritual exchange, and status display which, in the abstract, resembled those of the mighty. Manners and fashions trickled down quickly, especially when printing brought them to a mass audience. Western burghers soon learned to use forks and napkins, and merchants excelled in the Japanese tea ceremony. The difference between aristocratic and non-aristocratic behavior is usually a matter of degree.

All aristocracies aspire to codify markers of precedence. The sword hunts that disarmed Japanese cultivators after 1588 reserved martial display for the samurai, much as the European aristocracy monopolized war substitutes such as hunting, duelling, and jousting. The color-coded caps and robes which proclaimed gradations in the Chinese bureaucratic hierarchy find parallel in the kimonos of Japanese lords (*daimyo*), the purple-hemmed togas of Roman magistrates, and the precisely defined styles of Byzantine court dress. Arab pleasure palaces, Ottoman villas, and country houses in Europe match the mansions of Edo (present-day Tokyo). More honorable punishment—nobles decapitated or allowed to commit suicide, commoners roughly dispatched—was universal. Even practical limits on legislation recur: in Ching China (1644–1911), late Tokugawa Japan, and early modern Europe, sumptuary laws against lavish expenditure by commoners were issued so frequently that they were evident failures. Exceptional only as an extreme are the minute prescriptions of Indian caste law, safeguarding grades of purity by determining which *jati* could touch certain objects or persons, prepare and serve food for brahmans, or approach within specified distances of superiors.

But hierarchies of insignia largely collapsed in Europe after the Middle Ages, as the commercial revolution produced a bourgeoisie able to buy education and manners and monarchs recruited specialist officials from the third estate. Noble attire one day was everyone's attire the next, forcing aristocrats into extravagant and fruitless quest for novelty. With the rise of land markets, commoners' share of estates and seigneurial rights rose constantly. Newcomers concocted genealogies or purchased royal patents, and schools of fencing, dance, and equitation supplied other credentials. In the interest of status protection, colleges of heralds and special tribunals weeded out proliferating claims to nobility—a French court in 1666 canceled the rank of 4,000 would-be aristocrats—but both were as ineffective as sumptuary laws.

No single indicator could divide indelibly aristocrat from commoner. Upper ranks could claim precedence only by multiplying the signs of distinction: vast shrines and country houses, endless entertainments, rococo gowns and hairstyles, armies of liveried retainers. Indeed, the sheer scale of consumption is a distinctive feature of later European aristocrats. Unprotected by a caste system or the strictures which isolated samurai and *daimyo* and Chinese degree-holders from lower strata, they could not accept the sort of personal constraints imposed by the more austere Eastern religions. Relative social insecurity led to status competition, and so the aristocratic artifacts of the West are more ostentatious than their exquisitely refined counterparts in Asia.

Universally, the pursuit of honor and recognition cost heavily in time, energy, and money, but it was not as irrational as its critics have claimed. Generosity, literally the defining feature of a noble house (*gens*), calculated outlay against expectation of respect and favors from above, acceptance from equals and deference from below. Cultivating the good will of superiors and supporters was a form of capital investment, and to refrain from that investment was to risk isolation and eventual marginalization.

But inflation in the status economy put pressure on aristocrats to invest more heavily than inelastic resources would allow. Later samurai, *daimyo*, Chinese scholar-bureaucrats, and European nobles were chronically in arrears. This gave leverage to monarchs, as an elite pinned down by etiquette and debt posed less of a threat to central authority. So Tokugawa shoguns formalized the *sankin kotai* system which required *daimyo* to reside in Edo in alternate years: *daimyo* endured surveillance and the expenses of dual households and processions between homeland and capital. In ancient Rome and Constantinople and later Istanbul, Versailles, and St. Petersburg, favors were distributed at the capital, virtually forcing attendance, while residence brought higher costs and distracting ritual. Court society celebrates aristocratic standing while draining aristocratic vitality.

Decline

With the Enlightenment, denial of inherited transmission of excellence ended the automatic nexus of blood and talent which had justified inherited privilege. Social historians have amplified the new ideas and military and economic pressures that gradually led to the decline of aristocracy in modern society. Later assertions of natural inequality—from social Darwinism, liberal elitism, or natural law—seldom ascribed unequal distribution of ability to birth. The aristocrat's claim of occupational superiority, compelling when social priorities were martial, agrarian, or sacral, declined as the focus shifted to profit: commercialization spreads wealth, validates quotidian work, and devalues the skills which were once an aristocratic preserve. Mass access to high culture and material goods destroys another monopoly. Professionalized states require merit, not pedigree. Armies became more specialized, less open to aristocratic generalship.

Cancellation of innate privilege has not ended the eminence of great families, which have proven remarkably adaptive and willing to compete in business and party politics. But survival of aristocrats is not the same as survival of aristocracy. The latter is based upon cumulative inequalities: a single body holds simultaneous, innate prerogative in the political, economic, and social sectors. The modern age, in contrast, is characterized by dispersed inequalities in which the components of aristocracy are separated into distinct arenas. Amidst plural and open elites, superiority in one sector cannot guarantee superiority in another. In each, good background assists access to careers but cannot assure long-term success, and the offspring of the advantaged are everywhere exposed to competition.

At the Restoration in 1815, European nobilities at least for a time regained their titles but lost exemption from civil obligations and the right to special treatment under the law. Japanese golf clubs, Communist Party dachas, and gentry estates demonstrate that property and its entertainments still exercise inordinate attraction on the social imagination, but wealth and office must be earned anew in every generation. Superior training, patrimonies, and personal contacts still propel the wellborn to the forefront of finance and traditional vocations of public service, diplomacy, and the military, but these are careers rather than entitlements, and the old guard's share of economic and vocational eminence is vestigial. Descent associations keep genealogists busy, but proof of good breeding confers little more than personal satisfaction. Finally, material display and eccentric behavior still proclaim social distinction, but they are detached from considerations of lineage. The gossip media celebrate self-made celebrities, while Boston brahmans and European bluebloods generally shun the limelight. (*See also* Elites; Feudalism; Inheritance Systems)

James S. Grubb

REFERENCES

Beteille, André. *Castes: Old and New*. New York: Asia Publishing House, 1966.

Bush, M.L. *Noble Privilege*. Manchester: Manchester University Press, 1983.

Hall, John Whitney. *Government and Local Power in Japan, 500–1700*. Princeton, NJ: Princeton University Press, 1966.

Ho, Ping-Ti. *The Ladder of Success in Imperial China*. New York: Columbia University Press, 1962.

Starr, Chester G. *The Aristocratic Temper of Greek Civilization*. New York: Oxford University Press, 1992.

Art

All artistic production takes place in a social context that particularizes the meaning of images. This is true whether an artist draws from contemporary stylistic and narrative elements, from

the society's cultural heritage, or from foreign artistic traditions. For example, a modern painting using classical stylistic devices and describing a classical scene would nevertheless reflect the influence of contemporary concerns; it might even combine current and inherited references, as does a Nazi painting of the Judgment of Paris where a Stormtrooper replaces the Greek hero Paris. Social history's contribution to the interpretation of art is to reconnect images with their original range of meaning for contemporaries; once made meaningful, such images become useful as visual documents similar to other material sources like clothing or farming implements. Reconstructing the social context of images is an approach employed by historians and practitioners of the new art history. It approximates the method made popular by anthropologist Clifford Geertz (1973) as "thick description," which through contextualizing symbolic communication allows us to enter the minds of social actors.

For example, we encounter the particular mentality of a Tyrolean family, the Alpöggers, in an 1831 painting. There, two receding rows of this peasant family kneel in an Alpine meadow; above them float several cloud-borne saints whose protection the family invokes with their fixed skyward gaze. The father, Jakob, heads the male row, marked by the blue coat traditionally worn by local patriarchs; his wife Agnes heads the female ranks. In front lie two dead swaddled infants. To understand the original meaning of these familial and religious relationships, a social historian could begin by researching the actual roles of patriarchs and housewives in Tyrolean peasant society; the painting suggests that they were complementary yet provides the authoritative symbolism of Jakob's blue coat. The swaddled infants point to research into local infant mortality and its linkage with child-rearing habits, while the Alpöggers' engagement of supernatural forces in human affairs merits study of local religious attitudes toward Catholic saints.

Researching the famous Isenheim Altarpiece, art historian Andrée Hayum (1989) appreciated the value of recontextualizing images in their contemporary social setting. She reunited this complex iconographical work with its original church setting beside the Isenheim monks' hospital, where it complemented their physical healing efforts with spiritual comfort. In particular, she found that the Isenheim monks' role as healers explains symbols in the Altarpiece such as the Hebrew script decorating a chamber pot, which expresses a contemporary belief in the occult's medical efficacy.

Visual documents like the Alpöggers' painting or the Isenheim Altarpiece encourage historians to ask questions of the historical record; they can even reveal social attitudes never committed to writing. Anthropologist Anthony Forge (1973) adds the possibility that some forms of artistic symbolism in the New Guinea Abelam art he studies operate on the subconscious level, since their full meaning is never verbalized. One would, therefore, have to grow up in Abelam society to understand completely the messages expressed in local art works. As historians seek to raise imaginative questions about past societies, they can adopt Forge's awareness of the unspoken messages that art communicates to contemporaries. Since it is also true that art may vary in its importance as an expressive outlet, depending on the particular culture or period, this is another topic for social historians to explore.

Visual documents can also aid historians once their research agendas are in place, since art, like other material sources, provides evidence that either complements or adds to the written record. Nonverbal sources are particularly valuable for researching questions about illiterate social groups. For example, historians have used paintings like that of the Alpöggers as a statistical database to analyze changing attitudes toward supernatural powers; they quantify the relative sizes of saints and humans in the picture space to reveal shifts in perceived power between them. Public and popular art is most important in these connections. However, visual documents can also illuminate the private lives of those literate groups whose public affairs are well covered in written documents. Philippe Ariès's pioneering social history of childhood, for example, relied heavily on presentations in painting, though his use of art seems unsophisticated by current standards.

Art and social history combine most profitably in the microhistorical approach known as historical anthropology. Certainly, visual documents sometimes provide enough comparable data to permit statistical analysis of either temporal changes or regional variations in mentality. But art's particular usefulness for reconstructing the history of illiterate groups often leads historians to very local contexts like the Tyrolean setting of the Alpögger painting. In that intimate communal matrix they can act as anthropologists who travel in time as well as space to restore the immediacy of social meaning to once-mute historical records. (*See also* Anthropology; Family; Local History; Material Culture; Microhistory)

Helena Waddy Lepovitz

REFERENCES

Ariès, Philippe, and Georges Duby, eds. *A History of Private Life*. 5 vols. Cambridge: Harvard University Press, 1987–1991.

Carrier, David. *Art Writing*. Philadelphia: University of Pennsylvania Press, 1991.

Forge, Anthony. *Primitive Art and Society*. London: Oxford University Press, 1973.

Geertz, Clifford. *The Interpretation of Cultures*. New York: Harper, 1973.

Hayum, Andrée. *The Isenheim Altarpiece*. Princeton, NJ: Princeton University Press, 1989.

Artisans

The *Oxford English Dictionary* defines the word "artisan" as: "One who is employed in any of the industrial arts; a mechanic, handicraftsman, artificer." By that definition there have been artisans in human societies since smiths began forming jewelry and tools in the Bronze Age, and there are still many artisans found in all countries of the world today. When social historians use the word "artisan," however, they generally have a more restricted meaning; for them, artisans are not all those who transformed raw materials into commodities, but only those who also sold these commodities and owned their own tools. The slaves or servants of the ancient world who produced goods for their masters or employers are therefore not usually termed artisans, nor are the workers in modern factories. People did not have to call themselves artisans to be described as such in modern scholarship, however, for that label is also given to those who called themselves craftsmen, tradesmen, or mechanics, or who spoke of themselves simply by occupation, such as shoemakers or butchers.

Some historians include those who were learning a craft in their discussions of artisans, while others who see the ownership of the tools of the trade as the key factor in being an artisan make distinctions between true artisans and their journeymen and apprentices. These debates about who was and who was not a true artisan are found not only among modern historians but also among artisanal groups in the past as they tried to define and protect their status compared to other population groups, particularly industrial workers. In this article we will use a broad definition to include those in training, and will discuss artisans in three stages of economic development: the preindustrial, largely precapitalist period, stretching from the 12th century to, in some areas, the 18th; the beginnings of large-scale capitalist investment in production, often termed "protoindustrialization" or "the putting-out system," which stretched from the 16th century to, in some areas, the 19th; the period of industrialization, stretching from the 18th century in some areas to the present. In the first of these stages we will focus on Europe; in the second, on Europe and North America; and in the third, on these areas and the rest of the world, for historians are now beginning to investigate the history of artisans in the non-Western world. These three periods overlap chronologically because economic development proceeded at a different pace throughout various parts of the world, so that artisans confronted similar problems at different times in different places.

Because of the long duration of an artisanal economy in every urban society, and because of the key importance of artisans in many protest movements into our own day, artisans have drawn a great deal of attention from social historians. Many artisans have proved relatively articulate, leaving good records and evidence of ritual traditions. Here is another reason they have served as an entry point for social historians dealing with many societies and periods.

The Preindustrial Period

Social historians generally use the word "artisan" first when discussing urban development in Europe in the Middle Ages. In the 11th and 12th centuries, cities began to grow in Europe, initially as the result of a reinvigoration of long-distance trade. Cities quickly became centers of production as well; the wealth of the merchants encouraged the production of luxury goods such as fine cloth and jewelry, and the growing populations attracted food and clothing producers. These producers recognized the benefits of banding together, and the 12th century in many parts of Europe witnessed the birth of craft guilds which regulated most aspects of production. A craft guild was an organization of all the producers of one particular item in any town, such as shoemakers or blacksmiths. Each guild set standards of quality for its products and regulated the conduct of its members; the number of assistants, hours of operation, and amount of raw materials available to each master were all limited, thus preventing any one master from dominating the market and assuring every master that his household-workshop would be able to support itself. In most cities individual guilds achieved a monopoly in the production of their product, forbidding nonmembers to work at their trade. In some towns each craft formed its own guild, so that by the 13th and 14th centuries more than 100 separate craft guilds had been formed in many cities throughout Europe; in other towns related crafts were combined within larger guilds. The members of these craft guilds are the first workers in Europe who were without dispute termed "artisans."

Each guild set the pattern by which its members were trained. To become a shoemaker, for instance, it was necessary to spend about seven years as an apprentice and then at least that long as a journeyman working in the shop of a master shoemaker. Apprentices or their parents normally paid the master for their training, and remained with one master the entire period. Journeymen received room and board and sometimes a small wage, and often traveled from master to master gaining skill and experience until ready to make their *masterpiece*. If the masterpiece was approved by the other master shoemakers, and if they thought the market for shoes large enough in their town to accommodate another shoemaker, the journeyman became a master and opened his own shop. Though the time required to be an apprentice and journeyman varied slightly from craft to craft, all guilds followed this same three-stage process.

Apprentices and journeymen usually lived with the master and his family and were often forbidden to marry. Conversely, most guilds required that masters be married, as they believed a wife was absolutely essential to the running of the shop and household and, moreover, that married men were more likely to be stable and dependable. Artisans in medieval cities were thus set off from unskilled laborers and the poor not only by their skill and training but also by the fact that they were often homeowners and the heads of rather large households. As guilds grew in economic power they began to demand a share of the political power in their cities and came into conflict with the city councils, which were often dominated by merchants. In some cities, the guilds were unsuccessful, and artisans were excluded from political power, while in others they became members of city councils and other governing bodies.

Craft guilds were not simply economic organizations but also systems of social support for artisans. They supported elderly masters who could no longer work as well as widows and orphans. Guilds maintained an altar at a city church, paid for the funerals of their members and the baptisms of their children, and often set up religious confraternities separate from the guild itself for devotional purposes. Guild members marched together in city parades, reinforcing their feelings of solidarity by special ceremonies and distinctive dress. Guild workshops provided an important means of socialization and education for young men, especially before the introduction of compulsory schooling, and really created an identifiable artisan culture, proud of the traditions of the workshop and often hostile to outsiders. At times these outsiders included women, as formal membership in craft guilds was limited to men. Masters' daughters and wives worked in guild shops alongside the apprentices and journeymen, and a master's widow could generally keep operating a shop for a short time after the death of her husband, but women could never vote or hold office in craft guilds, except for a few all-female guilds in a handful of European cities. Craft guilds thus reinforced links among men, and, though women

worked in many craft shops, the preindustrial artisan was depicted and conceptualized as male.

Though in many European cities almost all production was regulated by guilds, in smaller towns and in the rural areas guilds were often not established until the 17th century, or never established at all. There were still people in these areas who we would clearly label artisans, such as blacksmiths, carpenters, masons, wheelwrights, and others who produced goods needed by the rural population. It is often more difficult to find information about how such people learned their skills, how they regarded themselves or were regarded by their neighbors, and how they responded to economic change than it is to find information about urban guild members, but in sheer numbers these rural artisans often outweighed their more organized urban counterparts. This is an area that historians are only beginning to investigate, and one which should yield important information about work patterns in the past.

The Period of Protoindustrialization

Beginning in the 14th century in a few areas of Europe, and in many more areas by the 16th century, individuals who had made money in trade and banking began to invest in production. They wanted to make products on a larger scale than guilds would allow, and so set up workshops in the country or in small villages, often hiring many households, each of which performed only one step of the process. This production process is called cottage industry or the putting-out system, and by the 16th century it was in open competition with urban guild production in many areas, particularly cloth production. These new industries could produce goods much more inexpensively than the guilds, and those who set them up were able to persuade cities to allow their cheaper products to be sold; in cities where guild artisans had no political voice, city governments also took away guild monopolies on production and allowed the new industries to establish themselves within cities themselves.

Though most guilds fought this trend, more enterprising or wealthier masters recognized the benefits of the putting-out system and began to hire other households to work for them, promoting a greater division within the guild between wealthier masters and the poorer masters and journeymen they hired. Some masters became so wealthy that they no longer had to work in a shop themselves, nor did their wives and family members. Instead of being artisans, they became capitalist investors, though they still generally belonged to the craft guild. This stage of economic development—in which the investor provided the raw materials and, in some cases, the tools, and paid households or individuals for their work but did not perform any of the actual labor himself—is often termed "protoindustrial capitalism."

While protoindustrial capitalism provided opportunities for some artisans to become investors and entrepreneurs, for many it led to a decrease in income and status. Guilds often responded to competition by limiting membership to existing guild families, which meant that journeymen who were not masters' sons or who could not find a master's widow or daughter to marry could never become masters themselves. They remained journeymen their entire lives, losing their sense of solidarity with the masters of their craft and in some cities forming separate journeymen's guilds—termed *compagnonnages* in France, where they were most common—in the 16th, 17th, and 18th centuries. These journeymen's guilds developed elaborate rituals and oaths of initiation, requiring members to travel around more extensively than they had before, a practice known as "tramping" in England and the "tour de France" in France; this practice spread to crafts that did not have organized journeymen's guilds in the 18th century. Journeymen tried to prevent anyone who was not a member of a guild or who had not traveled from working in any craft shop, enforcing their aims with boycotts; this worked against women working as artisans, for women were only very rarely accepted into journeymen's guilds and could not travel alone without a loss of honor.

As their actual status and economic prospects declined and their work became proletarianized, journeymen and poorer masters emphasized skill and honor as the qualities that set them apart from the less skilled workers hired by capitalist investors. They thus continued to regard themselves as artisans, no longer viewing ownership of the means of production as important in achieving this status, though wealthier master craftsmen (and some more recent historians) often began to view themselves as the only true artisans.

Though protoindustrialization had significant positive and negative effects on the artisans in some trades, such as weavers in Europe and shoemakers in North America, in many other trades production continued to be carried out in small workshops run by a master craftsman well into the 19th or even 20th centuries. In London in 1830, for example, there were over 2,500 adult practitioners in each of the trades of shoemaking, cabinetmaking, printing, clockmaking, jewelrymaking, and baking. In New York City, 50 to 60 percent of the city's occupational force in 1800 was labeled "mechanic" (this number included journeymen and apprentices), with cartmen, carpenters, shoemakers, tailors, masons, butchers, shipwrights, blacksmiths, and coopers each numbering over 100. In this more recent period the word "guild" is used less often to describe artisanal organizations (indeed they were outlawed in many places), and instead historians use simply "crafts," "skilled trades," or, in France, "corporations."

Along with their trade organizations, which regulated training and production, artisans in European and American cities in the 18th and 19th centuries often formed fraternal benevolent associations, such as the General Society of Mechanics and Tradesmen in New York, which lobbied for their economic interests, supported the opening of schools for members' children, and fostered a sense of community. Such associations continued the tradition of craft-based social and philanthropic activities begun by medieval craft guilds. Later artisans also continued the medieval tradition of demanding a share in political power; the role of artisans in the American Revolution, especially in the cities of Philadelphia and New York, and in pushing for a broadening of the electoral base in the Jeffersonian and Jacksonian periods, has been very well documented. In France, artisans were generally strong supporters of the French Revolution, the backbone of the group who became known as the *sans-culottes* ("without knee-breeches," a title which they gained because they wore long pants instead of the knee breeches of the nobility and wealthier middle class). They were involved in the events which began the revolution in 1789 and pushed for the more radical changes which began in 1793.

The Period of Industrialization

In many ways, artisans responded to the industrial revolution in the same ways they had to protoindustrialization, by stressing their skill and traditions and differentiating themselves from unskilled or semiskilled factory workers. For example, a new journal titled *The American Artisan,* designed for tinsmiths, coppersmiths, and other sheet-metal craftsmen, began publication in 1880, just at the point that much sheet-metal work in America was being transferred to factories. Artisans also often led crowds who smashed machinery and destroyed new types of tools in unsuccessful attempts to stop larger-scale production, such as the Luddites in northern England in the early 19th century.

Though artisans in some areas of production did lose their jobs or at least their independence with industrialization, mass production also created new opportunities for skilled crafts. For example, though iron production in Britain by 1850 was completely dominated by large-scale firms, creating small metal goods out of iron, such as nails, tools, tableware, or toys, continued to be carried out by small workshops with apprentices, journeymen, and a master; because much more iron was available through mass production, the number of these workshops was greater than it had been before industrialization. In addition, skilled factory workers such as carpenters and machinists began to set up unions in the 19th century, modeling these on the organizations of independent artisans; artisanal pride in skill thus carried over into the new factories, for these unions generally prohibited unskilled workers (which included most women) from joining. Artisans of this sort became a key segment of what has been called the "aristocracy of labor," better educated and better paid than the mass of industrial workers. The combined effects of industrialization on artisanal production are hard to measure and have been the subject of much debate among historians and economists; this debate has current political relevance as indus-

trialization spreads to parts of the world such as India, where small workshops are still the most important centers of production.

Large-scale industrialization in many countries led artisans to define their interests more specifically and organize politically to promote them, or follow leaders who appealed to their interests. In some cases, such as artisan support for the Chartist movement in 19th-century Britain, this political activity promoted greater democracy, while in others, such as widespread artisan support for the Nazi party in Germany or the Vichy government in France, it encouraged antimodernist extremism. Many analysts see contemporary artisans, especially in Europe, as forming the backbone of conservative political parties such as the Tories in England or the Christian Democrats in Germany, uniting in these with business interests in opposition to political parties designed to promote the interests of labor. In the United States it is hard to identify a particular artisanal political stance, for a plumber in Chicago and a jewelry-maker in San Francisco might support widely divergent political candidates. For this reason, and because the apprenticeship system is much less organized in the United States than in Europe, the word "artisan" is rarely used to describe any contemporary American worker, but is reserved for discussions of Europe and developing nations.

Research on artisans lends itself to comparative analysis, which is beginning to gain ground. Differences in artisanal protest traditions, while reflecting some common beliefs in the importance of skill, training, and creativity in work, can be crucial in defining larger political differences among societies, and these can be understood only through sociohistorical analysis. Increasing research on artisan and guild traditions outside the West—for example, in Japan, where until the industrial revolution artisans were exceptionally independent—will further enrich this vital focus in social history. (*See also* Guilds; Protoindustrialization)

Merry E. Wiesner-Hanks

REFERENCES

Farr, James R. *Hands of Honor: Artisans and Their World in Dijon, 1500–1650.* Ithaca, NY: Cornell University Press, 1988.

Leeson, R.A. *Travelling Brothers: The Six Centuries' Road from Craft Fellowship to Trade Unionism.* London: Allen and Unwin, 1979.

Mackenney, Richard. *Tradesmen and Traders: The World of Guilds in Venice and Europe, c. 1250– c. 1650.* Totowa, NJ: Barnes and Noble, 1987.

Rock, Howard B. *Artisans of the New Republic: The Tradesmen of New York City in the Age of Jefferson.* New York: New York University Press, 1979.

Thompson, E.P. *The Making of the English Working Class.* New York: Vintage, 1963.

Zdatny, Steven M. *The Politics of Survival: Artisans in Twentieth-Century France.* New York: Oxford University Press, 1990.

Asian Americans

Asians have lived in the United States for over 150 years, yet it was not until the late 19th century that the Asian Americans became numerically significant and their society and role attracted much attention. There is an increasing interest in various aspects of Asian experience in the United States in the past two decades. Nevertheless, there is a growing need for tracking the diversity and complexity of the historical experiences of Asian Americans or any of the subgroups. The social history of Asian Americans is just beginning to attain the richness of other immigrant history, with attention to the experiences of the immigrants as well as reactions from American society.

The first great impetus for Asian immigration to the United States in the 19th century was the need for cheap labor on Hawaiian plantations and amid the gold rush of 1848–1849 in California. Most of the Chinese, however, did not arrive in time to make the lucrative rush. Instead, they worked on the railroad and, later, with the Japanese and Filipinos, drifted into such jobs as market gardeners, storekeepers, fishers, and laundrymen, spreading along the coast from Los Angeles to Seattle.

Because the hostility toward the Asian settlers was complex and profound, their processes of settlement were not easy. Around the turn of the 20th century, many Asians were recruited as laborers, but laws discouraged them from staying. For example, the Chinese Exclusion Act of 1882 barred the entry of Chinese laborers for ten years and prohibited the naturalization of Chinese immigrants as U.S. citizens. The law was not revoked until 1924. Starting from the 1890s, the influx of Japanese began almost immediately after Chinese immigration had been halted. Yet, in order to curb the rapid penetration of the Japanese into the agricultural economy, the California legislature passed the Alien Land Act in 1913 to make those noncitizen aliens ineligible to own agricultural property. Before the early 20th century, Chinese, Japanese, and Filipinos in many states were not allowed to testify against whites in court and were forbidden to hold public-service jobs. Most had to struggle for even basic educational opportunities. One reason for prejudice against Asian immigrants lay in their work habits, dress styles, and social customs. There was a common belief among white workers that the Asians would always work harder and longer and would seize whatever opportunities presented themselves, a bias sustained by the occasions when employers used the Chinese as strikebreakers.

Under these circumstances, many Asian immigrants made no attempt to assimilate. Because they often had no family in the United States, many Asian Americans, particularly the male Chinese and Filipino immigrants, were sojourners who lived mentally in their home country while working in this land. Male Japanese Americans, however, married (sometimes by sending for so-called picture brides) and began to raise families and form community networks.

Furthermore, Asians in the United States tended to cling together according to dialect and locality groups. The anti-Asian discriminatory legislation only reinforced the segregation of Asians into separate neighborhoods variously called Chinatowns, Little Tokyos, and Little Manilas. The crowding of these ethnic enclaves, compounded by scarce housing and the loneliness of thousands of single males, led to an explosive social situation, sexual frustrations, and the prevalence of disease. For example, rival Chinese groups became involved in associations like *tongs*, which provided protection systems but created battles between gangs.

Women among the earlier immigrants experienced some special circumstances. A very large percentage of the Asian women by the turn of the 20th century worked as prostitutes, laundresses, farm women, cooks, seamstresses, and helpers in the stores, even after they gave birth. While many wives of Japanese farmers lived under harsh conditions and did heavy "men's work," many of the few Chinese immigrant women were not allowed to appear in public and thus lived extremely isolated lives.

The outbreak of World War II brought new forces into play for Asians in the United States. On the eve of World War II, the second generation of Asian Americans was increasingly mature. Due to racial barriers in the labor market, they remained economically dependent on their fathers or grandfathers, and socially confined to the ethnic enclaves. The war had a dramatic impact on the various Asian American communities. On the one hand, Japanese Americans were evacuated to internment camps due primarily to the Japanese bombing of Pearl Harbor and to general wartime hysteria. On the other hand, the Chinese and Filipinos in this country had improved their image and were allowed access to the general labor market.

Asian Americans have been a fast-growing ethnic minority group since 1965. With the abolition of the racist national origins quota system, enacted in 1924, Pacific migration has steadily changed the character and composition of U.S. immigration. The 1965 Immigration Act also favored reunification of families and focused on specific labor skills and professional capabilities. During the decade 1960–1970, the Asian population in the United States almost doubled, largely through immigration. In addition, the second wave immigration since 1965 included Asians who were not represented in the groups of first wave immigration in the 19th century. Thus, Koreans, Asian Indians, and particularly Southeast Asian refugees (Vietnamese, Laotians, and Cambodians) since the end of the Vietnam War in 1975 have joined Chinese, Japanese, and Filipinos in America. While their total number in relation to the entire U.S. population (1.5 percent) is small, this percentage is increasing fast because of substantial immigration.

The occupational status of Asian Americans has become more diverse over the years. In the first half of the 20th century, although still mainly active in such enterprises as farming, gardening, and service jobs like restaurants and laundries,

some Asian Americans had moved into new careers in retailing and manufacturing, and also spread out of the old ethnic enclaves on the West Coast into other parts of the country. Asian value systems and culture (e.g., work hard, study diligently, respect authority, emphasize the family and the supportive organizations of the community, and provide mutual credit) enabled Asian Americans to operate small businesses or gain technical jobs and thus achieve some socioeconomic mobility.

By the late 20th century different subgroups of Asian Americans varied in their representation in the work force. Japanese, Asian Indians, and Filipinos were overrepresented in the professions, technical occupations, clerical jobs, and the service area. They were underrepresented in the blue-collar occupations. Korean and Southeast Asian refugees maintained a high percentage of small businesses. Low wages and large families put many refugee households well below the poverty level, and this helped to drive refugee women into the job market. Chinese Americans were marked by a paradox: a large number of professionals but an even larger number of individuals in unskilled, low-paid occupations.

Asian Americans, especially foreign-born Asian immigrants, had a distinct demographic profile. They displayed high marriage rates and few divorces in comparison with the overall U.S. population. However, both the households and family size were larger than the U.S. norms because they tended to include relatives other than nuclear family members. While the median income of a full-time Asian American worker in 1980 was lower than that for a comparable American worker, the household income of Asian Americans was higher because of the fact that Asian households had more employed persons per unit.

Many Asian Americans continue to face a number of hardships. A large majority of Asian American groups, with the exception of Japanese Americans, are foreign-born. Uprooted from their homelands, they have to cope with language barriers, cultural differences, and isolation. Asian Americans who own small businesses tend to have strong community ties and solid ethnic solidarity. In many cases, radical change in social status creates crises in self-esteem and makes adjustment even more difficult. Under-employment and unemployment plague the ethnic communities, and among the less well educated, problems like delinquency are severe.

Asian Americans vary greatly in the cultures from which they come and the circumstances impelling their exodus from their homelands. The immigrants exhibit different economic backgrounds and religious traditions. As social historical research on these groups gains in sophistication, the immense internal diversities pose important challenges. (*See also* Assimilation/Acculturation; Immigration)

Joan Wang

REFERENCES

Daniels, Roger. *Asian America: Chinese and Japanese in the United States Since 1850.* Seattle: University of Washington Press, 1988.

Takaki, Ronald. *Strangers from a Different Shore: A History of Asian Americans.* Boston: Little, Brown, 1989.

Asian Disease History

Disease represents a fundamental threat to human life and by extension to society at large, and the nature of this threat has differed from place to place and over time. The social history of disease is concerned with three major areas of inquiry. The first examines how changes in the demographic structure of human communities have altered the incidence and the kinds of disease that afflict those communities; the second considers how changes in the activities of man have influenced and have been influenced by disease; and the third is concerned with how man has responded—individually and collectively—to the changing threat of disease. These questions have long occupied a central place in the economic and social history of the West. By contrast, the history of disease in Asia has only recently attracted the attention of social historians, and there is still much that is unknown in all three areas of inquiry.

Research on the history of Asian diseases has benefited from Western scholarship, because research approaches and techniques are already well established. These approaches and techniques are varied and include both time-honored methods and relatively new scientific techniques. For example, written records that tell of severe epidemics, high mortality, and population decline are found almost universally in historical sources. Historians typically use such contemporary accounts to construct disease chronologies which provide clues to the history of important epidemic diseases in different parts of the world. Current knowledge about disease processes also provides important information about the history of human diseases. For example, scientists use carbon-dating techniques and the methods of paleopathology to study skeletal remains, which are dated and examined for traces of disease. Diseases such as tuberculosis and syphilis deform human bones, and these dating techniques tell us when and where such diseases were prevalent. In addition, the techniques of epidemiology—the study of the characteristics of different pathogenic agents (viruses, bacteria, etc.) and their modes and patterns of transmission—also help historians to reconstruct the histories of different diseases. Finally, when useful death data are available, statistical techniques can be used to measure changes in causes of death and age- and sex-specific death rates, and to determine the impact of political, economic, and social change on disease. All of these techniques are now being used to study the disease histories of Asian countries.

The advent of disease as an important factor in human history is associated with the Neolithic revolution, a technological transformation that changed the demographic structure of human communities. The successes of early agriculture encouraged people to stay in one place, to cultivate the land, and to establish permanent communities. These permanent human settlements provided an environment that encouraged disease-causing organisms to establish parasitic relationships dependent on man and the domestic animals he tended. In Asia, early civilizations based on intensive cultivation of the land developed in the Indus and Ganges valleys of India, and the Yellow River valley of northern China. These Asian civilizations provided high concentrations of human hosts and a favorable environment in which disease parasites could multiply and flourish.

The ancient civilizations of India and China also supported large cities, which became the disease centers of Asia. These centers of density became foci of infection from which disease-causing organisms radiated outward to the peripheral regions that were within the range of human contact. Disease centers, where high-density populations gained immunity to the diseases to which they were frequently exposed, had a distinct advantage over the hinterlands, where low-density populations had infrequent exposure with little or no immunity, and where severe epidemics caused a great loss of human life. An important political consequence of this biological response to new disease-causing agents was the domination of peripheral regions by the center.

There are, however, exceptions to this pattern. An interesting case in which the people of the periphery used knowledge of immunity to a specific disease to their advantage comes from Chinese history. The case concerns the Manchu invasions of China in the 17th century. The Manchus were a semipastoral people who lived in the steppelands north of the Great Wall of China. They were especially vulnerable to the "civilized" diseases of China, to which they were not often exposed. The Manchus were especially fearful of smallpox, which they knew from experience could infect their troops and bring defeat. They chose, therefore, leaders and troops who had been exposed to and had survived smallpox. K'ang Hsi, the second Manchu emperor of China, was chosen over his older brothers because he had contracted the disease as a child. Similar policies continued under Manchu, or Ch'ing, rule, and Manchus were selected for government positions in China only if they had survived smallpox.

Differences in exposure and immunity to important human diseases also cause great catastrophe when two developed civilizations come into contact with one another for the first time. The most celebrated case occurred in the late 15th century when the European transatlantic explorations established contact for the first time between European and Amerindian populations. This set off an exchange of diseases between the populations of Europe, the Americas, Africa, and Asia, which resulted in the introduction of small-pox, measles, plague, and other Old World diseases to the Americas, and the introduction of venereal syphilis to Eurasia. The Amerindian populations never recovered from the combination of disease and conquest.

Examples from East Asian history are not well known, but similar disease exchanges must have occurred much earlier when contacts were first established between the populous civilizations of South and East Asia about 2,000 years ago. India and China are separated by the high Tibetan Plateau and the Himalayan Range, by the mountainous terrain of southwest China, and by the jungles of Southeast Asia—barriers that made contact between the peoples of these two regions difficult. However, the expansion of the Han Empire and the spread of Buddhism in the 1st centuries BC and AD brought these two civilizations into contact with one another. Buddhist missionaries traveled by land from northern India through central Asia to northern China, and by sea to southern China. Chinese scholars journeyed to India to study at Buddhist monasteries, and then returned to spread word of this foreign religion throughout China.

Chinese sources suggest that these activities initiated an exchange of foreign diseases as well as foreign philosophies. The first known reports of smallpox in China come from this period. Smallpox was known in India well before this time, and it is most likely that it came to China from India. Independent evidence from the Middle East (where smallpox lesions have been found on Egyptian mummies embalmed 2,000 years ago), India, China, and Japan suggests that smallpox spread from west to east over a long period of many centuries.

If smallpox was first introduced to China during the Han Dynasty, we can be certain that it caused a demographic crisis of considerable magnitude, because smallpox had a high mortality rate, particularly in virgin populations. Given the size of China's population around the 1st century BC and the well-developed links between the many centers of density in China at that time, smallpox would have killed many people within a relatively short period of time. While little is known about the demographic consequences of early epidemic diseases in China, early Japanese records document severe epidemics which were said to have come from China. The Japanese records leave no doubt about the catastrophic effect of smallpox on a population with little or no immunity. A detailed description of a devastating smallpox epidemic in western Japan in AD 735–737 is among the earliest clear descriptions of smallpox in the world. Severe epidemics continued to ravage Japanese society, and one interpretation of Japanese history holds that the decline of central government and the rise of the warrior class was a consequence of population decline caused by frequent and severe epidemics.

These few examples demonstrate the antiquity and richness of Asian sources on the history of disease. At present our understanding of disease history is based on the experience and the viewpoint of western Europeans who, for most of their history, inhabited a very small part of the world. New research on the history of disease in Asia, which has long supported much of the world's population, will add not only new information but new perspectives to the history and geography of human disease. (*See also* Demography; Native Americans)

Ann Bowman Jannetta

REFERENCES

Farris, William Wayne. *Population, Disease, and Land in Early Japan, 645–900.* Cambridge, MA: Harvard University Press, 1985.

Hopkins, Donald H. *Princes and Peasants: Smallpox in History.* Chicago: Chicago University Press, 1983.

Jannetta, Ann B. *Epidemics and Mortality in Early Modern Japan.* Princeton, NJ: Princeton University Press, 1987.

McNeill, William H. *Plagues and Peoples.* Garden City, NY: Anchor Press/Doubleday, 1977.

Asian Peasantry

Asia is home to much of the world's peasant population today. Throughout most of South Asia, Southeast Asia, and East Asia (excluding Japan), peasants comprise as much as 70 percent or more of the inhabitants.

The first systematic studies of the peasantry, including that of Asia, were carried out by anthropologists. Using a community study approach, scholars in the 1930s and 1940s investigated villages as embodiments of the larger agrarian economy, society, and culture they sought to portray. In much of the early literature, "peasant" was a term applied more descriptively than analytically to refer to villagers or folk people. As an analytical concept, it did not acquire sophistication until the 1950s and 1960s, when the field of peasant studies took off, its growth fostered by Western concerns regarding modernization in newly emerging nations as well as by apprehensions about "peasant wars" and agrarian unrest. The rise of the new social history with its emphasis on reconstructing the experiences of ordinary people also enhanced scholarly interest in the peasant world.

The boom in peasant studies, however, represented a rediscovery of the peasantry, although it was not an entirely novel enterprise because peasants have long figured in the historical literature. They have also been at the center of political and policy considerations. Note that Mao Zedong's 1920s remarks about the revolutionary potential of the peasantry constituted an intervention in an ongoing debate initiated by Marx himself and sustained by later Marxists.

The resurgence of peasant studies produced works focusing primarily on the political, economic, and social aspects of peasants; their cultural characteristics received far less coverage. This imbalance is reflected in the seemingly endless debates over definitions of peasants, with controversy issuing from the varying emphases placed on these different aspects. In the classic anthropological definition, peasants are said to constitute part of a larger system, rural populations whose surpluses are used by dominant ruling groups to underwrite the standard of living of elites and of service groups generally located elsewhere in urban centers. Peasants are typically organized as household units of agricultural production that is predominantly oriented toward household consumption. And when their culturally distinct characteristics have been recognized—not all definitions highlight these traits—they have generally been typologized as "traditional."

Until the 1970s most historical studies of the Asian peasantry concentrated on the materialist aspects of peasant experience. Central concerns in this literature were the relation of peasants to power holders and those connected to them, to processes and institutions tied to administrative power, to credit resources and the market, to surplus capital, to technology, and to religious, kin, caste, and class networks. These relationships were generally fleshed out by examining their workings in specific events (time and place) and/or historical contexts. Drawing on community study methodology, a common technique in these studies was to restrict the site of investigation to well-defined localities and regions.

Although cultivators remained at the center of peasant studies, refinements generated by this initial wave of systematic scholarship brought into focus the full roster of actors on the rural stage, including landless laborers and artisans. The category of "peasant" itself furthermore was disaggregated to reflect peasant differentiation, differentiation that Mao Zedong had anticipated when he had classified peasants as rich, middle, and poor.

Similar in many respects, studies of Asian peasantry also diverged considerably, particularly along geographical lines, because research on each region of the continent was shaped partly by its own peculiar historical realities and historiographical traditions. Contrast, for example, the preoccupation of modern South and Southeast Asian history with assessing the effects of colonialism on agrarian society with that of Chinese history with interpreting the effects of imperialism and explaining the causes and conditions of rebellions and revolutions.

The recent development of global history may move peasant history beyond national boundaries by turning attention to generic issues such as the impact of the modern capitalist world economy on peasant life. Certainly, one result has been a branching out into comparative history and macrohistory; another, the reworking of microhistory so as to contextualize local experiences in global terms. Nor can the standard political periodizations withstand this new advance. Instead of historical periodizations organized by political markers, new time frames are being devised that are more consonant with peasant life in which considerable stability and occasional crises combine with long-term and gradual changes in society and economy, a *longue durée* conceptualization of history that fits in well with the concerns of the new social history.

These new approaches have prompted a much needed interrogation of the Eurocentric assumption that the encounter with the West produced modernization. Thus, especially Chinese but also Indian historians have taken the lead in looking into the indigenous roots of change, tracing transformations (e.g., capitalism) back to premodern times. By not conceptualizing the transition from old to new as being determined by the contact with the West, the new scholarship endows the peasant with more agency because rural society is not seen as merely reacting to changes set in motion by external forces.

An enlarged notion of peasants as historical actors is also emerging in studies analyzing their behavior. Particularly influential in this regard has been the moral economy debate about whether peasant society is to be viewed as a moral economy of shared moral values or as a rational and political economy in which peasants operate as self-interested economic maximizers. Developed to explain peasant rebellion in Southeast Asia, this literature has also sparked interest in more routine forms of peasant actions, that is, everyday forms of peasant resistance that include the gamut from foot dragging to theft, arson, and sabotage. A more complete portrait of peasants is also emerging from the current focus on peasant culture and ideology, work whose findings on peasant consciousness, discourse, and symbolic modes of expression has rendered untenable earlier conceptions of peasants as inherently traditional. The Asian peasantry, long a presence in history, has now finally returned to occupy its rightful place as historical agent.

Anand A. Yang

REFERENCES

Mencher, Joan P. *Social Anthropology of Peasantry.* Bombay: Somaiya Publications, 1983.

Popkin, Samuel L. *The Rational Peasant.* Berkeley: University of California Press, 1979.

Scott, James C. *The Moral Economy of the Peasant: Subsistence and Rebellion in Southeast Asia.* New Haven: Yale University Press, 1976.

Assembly Line

The assembly line is usually associated with Henry Ford and automobile assembly in the 20th century. However, the assembly line is better seen as continuing earlier technological and organizational changes. It continued the trend toward worker deskilling, replacing many previously skilled positions with machine tenders and operatives. The assembly line also enhanced management's control over workers and the production process. From an even larger perspective in social history, the assembly line tests the impact of major technological and organizational change on work and workers.

The 19th century saw the introduction of continuous-flow production processes. In the production of textiles, oil, iron, and steel, as well as the processing of food, sequentially ordered production steps increased outputs. This demanded close coordination and control.

The development of interchangeable parts, another essential prerequisite for the assembly line, was first achieved by armsmakers. Interchangeability required new developments in metalworking technologies. Precise, special-purpose machine tools, combined with the use of accurate fixtures, jigs, and gages ensured the precise and consistent shaping of parts.

Manufacturers pursued efficiency in production through the division of labor, decomposing production tasks into simpler subtasks. Simplifying production tasks made it easier to construct machines that could perform them. Thus, the manual and intellectual skills of the workman could be transferred to machines, reducing manufacturers' previous dependence on the availability and tractability of a skilled work force. Deskilling of workers brought control of production into the hands of management, rather than remaining with the skilled workers. Increasingly, technical skills were required only by machine designers, creating a relatively small class of skilled designers and engineers.

The autonomy that workers' skills granted them was corroded by these technological and organizational changes. Workers resisted alterations in the nature and organization of work. This resistance took the forms of absenteeism, strikes, restrictions of production, and the formation of labor organizations.

As the size and scope of industrial enterprises grew, the need for control and coordination increased. New management ideas, the aim of which was to rationalize the organization of pro-

duction, gained ground. Perhaps the most thoroughly developed were those of Frederick W. Taylor. Invoking scientific management, Taylor's adherents from 1911 onward sought the "one best way" to perform tasks and organize the flow of work. Through time and motion studies, experts set strict standards for the performance of each task. These organizational changes further reduced the need for skilled workers, as the "one best way" frequently entailed the extreme division of productive tasks.

The earliest, and best known, example of a moving assembly line was installed at the Ford Motor Company in 1913–1914. The Model T's standardized design, and the demand for it, allowed Ford to pursue new, more efficient production methods. Previously, teams of men assembled the cars in one place, completing one car before beginning the next. Ford production engineers analyzed the assembly process. Beginning with subassemblies, they broke assembly down into small, discrete steps. One man was assigned to perform each step, then push the part on to the next man, who would perform the next step, and so forth until assembly was complete. Expanded to other subassemblies and to the assembly of the complete car, and with the addition of conveyer belts and other devices to move the workpieces past the workers, the time and skill required to assemble the final product were greatly reduced.

The assembly line required coordination of unprecedented scale. The supply of parts to the assembly line was crucial; the nature of the system demanded near perfection, for a failure at any one place halted the whole process. Likewise, the failure of any worker to perform the assigned task disturbed the flow of production; as the "weak link" in the production system, that worker was then closely controlled by an increased number of supervisors, inspectors, and other management personnel.

Work on the assembly line was marked by monotony and its demanding pace. Workers on the assembly line responded to this with high rates of lateness, absenteeism, and quitting. The initial solution in addressing these labor problems—higher pay—soon gave way to more coercive means of control, such as shopfloor spies and induced competitiveness between the workers. Restricting production, a traditional form of worker protest against the imposition of strict work discipline, was difficult, if not impossible, because the pace of work was controlled by management through the assembly line's speed, not by the workers themselves.

The assembly line restructured factory work routines, introduced new occupational groups on the shopfloor, and enhanced management control of the production process. The assembly line's success at Ford accelerated its adoption by other industries, in Japan, Europe, the Soviet Union, as well as the United States.

Social historians have studied the impact of the introduction and initial dissemination of the assembly line particularly, but later developments also warrant attention. Growing worker dissatisfaction with repetitive jobs played a role in worker unrest in the 1960s and, particularly outside the United States, generated some movement away from assembly line operations. (*See also* Industrialization; Scientific Management; Technology; Working Class)

Daniel Holbrook

REFERENCES

Chandler, Alfred D. *The Visible Hand.* Cambridge, MA: Harvard University Press, 1977.

Hounshell, David A. *From the American System to Mass Production, 1800–1932.* Baltimore: Johns Hopkins University Press, 1984.

Meyer, Stephen, III. *The Five Dollar Day.* Albany: The State University of New York Press, 1981.

Montgomery, David. *The Fall of the House of Labor.* Cambridge: Cambridge University Press, 1987.

Assimilation/Acculturation

Assimilation and acculturation are two different concepts applied to studies relating immigrants to their new society. The concepts have been used particularly in United States social history but are potentially applicable elsewhere. *Assimilation* is the process whereby a person or group exchanges the original culture for the values, behaviors, and attitudes of another culture. Traditionally, historians focused on the political and economic aspects of migration rather than on the migrants. Further, historians assumed that permanent migrants fully assimilate into the host culture. Social historians, however, are more interested in the immigrants themselves, and in the cultural and social structures they create in their new environment. In fact, social history holds that immigrants *acculturate*, rather than assimilate, to a new society: they retain key aspects of their original culture, as well as acquiring cultural values and behavior patterns from their new host society.

Cultural pluralism, the theory of acculturation in vogue since the 1970s, strives to identify and explain the cultural diversity of a society comprised of large numbers of immigrants. This theory of acculturation differs from the assimilation model by recognizing that immigrant groups will inevitably retain certain cultural and structural patterns from the premigration culture while incorporating many attributes from the surrounding host culture. Unlike the melting pot theory of assimilation (popular in the early 20th century), which held that the various ethnic groups would all contribute some cultural traits to the common cauldron of society from which would emerge a new culture, cultural pluralism recognizes the commonalities and differences in each ethnic segment that make up a patchwork society.

According to the assimilation model, the process of integration into the host society is linear, and therefore complete assimilation is inevitable. Milton Gordon, refining the assimilation theory in his book *Assimilation in American Life* (1964), described two kinds of assimilation, cultural and structural, of which cultural was the easier and more common. To completely assimilate, immigrants would have to go through seven stages of adaptation, from changing their cultural patterns to those of the host society, to having the same values and power status of the native born. Oscar Handlin's *The Uprooted* (1954) was the first study to concern itself with these changes and their effects on immigrants. He portrayed the alienation and upheaval experienced by eastern European immigrants whose culture and foreign language ill prepared them for the industrialized American cities of the late 19th and early 20th centuries. Despite concluding that assimilation was not immediate, both Gordon and Handlin believed that at some future point it was inevitable.

Social historians moved away from this linear assimilationist model when studies in the 1960s showed that even the second and third generation native-born children of immigrants retained aspects of their parents' Old World culture. Rudolph Vecoli, studying Italian immigrants and their communities, argued that premigration social structures did not disappear but reemerged and played an important role in the immigrants' adaptation and integration into American society. Immigrants tended to concentrate in areas where fellow countrymen had already settled, thus creating ethnic communities from this form of chain migration. These communities provided important support systems and functions, such as finding work for new arrivals. Familiar community institutions, such as churches, helped alleviate alienation and eased the transition into American life. In addition, these ethnic communities ensured ethnic cultural perpetuation through the children who were exposed to this subculture as well as to American society. As a result of such studies, historians realized that immigrants were active participants in the process of acculturation, rather than helpless victims of assimilation.

Historically, concerns about assimilability of permanent migrants have focused on the race, class, and religion of immigrants. The United States, a country founded by immigrants, only became concerned with immigrant assimilation from the mid-19th century onward, when the type of immigrant changed from farmers and middle-class professionals. Between the 1880s and the 1927 National Origins Act (which completed the 1924 Immigration Act's halt to most European and other immigration, the 1882 ban on Chinese immigration, and the 1907 ban on Japanese, and set an exclusionary policy not reversed until the 1965 Nationality Act removed biased quotas), immigrants were predominantly poor, unskilled or semiskilled eastern and southern Europeans, or of Asian origin. Americans worried about assimilation, fearing that these immigrants, who were unused to a democratic society and believed to be culturally and racially inferior, would weaken the dominant Anglo-Saxon values and undermine American democracy.

These concerns led Americans to focus on assimilating immigrant children to ensure the democratic nature of these future citizens and to encourage the assimilation of their parents. This goal was promoted primarily through the public schools, where American culture, behavior, and values were stressed at the expense of the immigrants' culture, though programs such as the Americanization scheme sponsored by Henry Ford worked to the same end. Even those immigrants who viewed Americanization favorably found the emphasis on American values, to the exclusion of ethnic values, troubling. Studies of the immigrant children and native-born second generation show that they often experienced cultural identity conflicts arising from the demands of a combined American and ethnic lifestyle. For some immigrants, Americanization and educational advancement promised rewards of social mobility for themselves and their children. Others resisted their children's acculturation, and sought actively to restrain it through parochial schools. Still others sought to adjust aspects of their ethnic culture to accommodate American society.

The workplace was the first place adult immigrants encountered the host culture and were forced to adapt. Most immigrants in the United States during the late 1800s and early 1900s worked primarily in industry, where they often needed to learn some English, although those who worked for co-ethnics could manage to avoid this onerous task. Although many immigrants had been exposed to some form of mechanized industry in Europe, almost all had to adjust to more rigid work patterns in an automated manufacturing system. The workplace, however, did not necessarily guarantee acculturation. Immigrant groups who tended to concentrate in selective industries limited their need to interact with other groups, further helping to maintain ethnic insularity. Those immigrants, particularly women, who worked in the home, had even less incentive to acculturate as they functioned mostly within the ethnic community. Often, their primary source of contact with their new society was through their children.

On the surface it appeared that immigrants could most easily control the degree of assimilation in their families and community. Language in the home, food, religious practices, interfamilial relationships, and child-rearing practices have always been less influenced by the host culture. The social circles and community institutions immigrants formed and identified with retained a heavy ethnic influence. These combined to provide the immigrants with a strong sense of ethnic cohesion and identity. Thus, immigrants could monitor and maintain certain cultural habits and values, which eased their transition into the foreign host culture.

Yet even within the family the influence of acculturation was felt, particularly in generation conflicts between parents and children; immigrant parents accustomed to a different, usually stricter, form of child/parent relationship were often confronted with the more relaxed American expectation of their acculturated children, who demanded freedoms and exhibited behavior the parents found foreign. Thus, even in the relative privacy of the home and family, immigrants felt the stress of adapting to a new culture. In the process of adapting, immigrants learned that they could not always preserve cultural aspects they valued and wished to preserve.

Some immigrants, planning on returning to their homeland, had little incentive to acculturate actively into American society beyond the workplace. Yet eastern and southern European immigrants could integrate fairly rapidly into American society once they recognized that the United States was their permanent home. For immigrants of a different race or religion, acceptance was less rapid due to continued discrimination in such areas as housing and work. This was particularly the case for Asian and Jewish immigrants, who, despite achieving high educational goals, faced professional discrimination in many sectors of the economy. The most striking example of outsider status resulted during World War II when basic citizens' rights of Japanese immigrants and their native-born children were overridden as these people were relocated to internment camps. Thus, structural assimilation could be hampered as much by the host culture's discrimination as through the active resistance of the immigrants. Different initial value systems also affected the speed and manner of acculturation, however, in such areas as birth rates and education.

Social historians in other countries have also begun to focus on the effects of acculturation in their societies. In England historians concentrate on the experience of the predominantly black and Indian immigrants who came from the British Empire to settle during the past half-century. In Europe the focal point is more on the migrant workers, especially from northern Africa, the Middle East, and Asia, who remained rather than returning home. In South America, Australia, and Canada, questions of assimilation and acculturation point to the different ways in which societies can incorporate their immigrants. Unfortunately, the insights from these countries have yet to be compared seriously by social historians, and no broad based model of acculturation has been ventured.

Since the early 1960s social historians have greatly expanded their understanding about the nature of immigrant acculturation. While some patterns, such as declining fertility rates, have occurred fairly uniformly, others, such as changes in family relationships and ethnic identity, have taken different forms for each group. The question therefore remains whether the acculturation experience of each immigrant group is a unique phenomenon, with some commonalities, or whether there is a general acculturation experience with similar patterns, but occurring at different rates and in varying degrees. Part of the answer perhaps could be found by comparing the acculturation experience of similar immigrant groups in different countries or the general acculturation patterns across countries. As the studies of each immigrant group's experience become more specific, social historians need to combine their findings to form a broader view of acculturation. (*See also* Asian Americans; Ethnicity; Immigration; Migration; Subcultures)

Ria David

REFERENCES

Bodnar, J. *The Transplanted. A History of Immigrants in Urban America.* Bloomington: Indiana University Press, 1985.

Daniels, R. *Asian America: Chinese and Japanese in the United States Since 1850.* Seattle: University of Washington Press, 1988.

Higham, J. *Strangers in the Land: Patterns of American Nativism, 1860–1925* (2nd ed.). New Brunswick, NJ: Rutgers University Press, 1988.

Morawska, E. *For Bread with Butter: The Life-Worlds of East Central Europeans in Johnstown, Pennsylvania, 1890–1940.* Cambridge: Cambridge University Press, 1985.

Rabinowitz, H.N. "Race, Ethnicity, and Cultural Pluralism in American History," in J.B. Gardner and G.R. Adams, eds., *Ordinary People and Everyday Life, Perspectives on the New Social History.* Nashville: The American Association for State and Local History, 1982, pp. 23–49.

Takaki, R. *Strangers from a Different Shore: A History of Asian Americans.* Boston: Little, Brown, 1989.

Asylums

In the premodern world, Europeans and Americans believed either that the devil drove people to madness or that God tested insane persons' piety or punished their sins. Furthermore, madness was placed within a divine scheme that fostered inculpability for the insane. The mad roamed freely as long as they did no harm to themselves or others.

Seventeenth-century Enlightenment thought, mercantilism, and emerging capitalism began to change the world of the mad and other dependent poor people. In this secular world of commerce, work, and individualism, irrationality and dependency took on a new meaning. Less tightly knit communities became less willing to care for dependent members directly. As societal values shifted responsibility for behavior to the individual and as communities became increasingly stratified, almshouses, poor farms, workhouses, and general hospitals for the poor appeared in the large cities of Europe. Later, separate quarters within these institutions were used to confine the mad. In 17th-century America there were some constraints on the legal rights of the insane, but few confinement measures. By the mid-18th century, America had its almshouses, jails, and hospital wards housing the insane.

Enlightenment philosophy also gave birth to scientific medicine which placed a particular emphasis on active intervention in the course of disease. As madness became disassociated from the supernatural, doctors applied their explanations for physical illness to madness. The optimism endemic to Enlightenment Europe led to the belief that insanity was reversible and intervention essential. Simultaneously, a growing sentiment emerged against the indiscriminate confinement of the insane with criminals, vagabonds, and others. Reformers never questioned the concept of confinement itself, but worked only to alter the conditions of confinement.

Incarceration of the mad shackled in cells without heat or light, with gruel for food, flew in the face of new ideas about insanity. Philippe Pinel of France, William Tuke in Britain, Vincenzo Chiarugi of Italy, Maximilian Jacobi in Germany, Benjamin Rush in the United States, and others were at the forefront of the reform movement in the early 19th century. They differed in their beliefs about the nature of insanity, but agreed about the need for a number of active therapeutic interventions that became known as moral treatment.

Moral treatment called for the isolation of the patient from family and community by incarceration in an asylum. Patients received medical treatment, but emphasis was on a regime of religious, recreational, educational, and occupational therapy. The doctors who administered the asylums and practiced moral treatment claimed successes in curing the insane.

Many of the early asylums were privately supported, but the enthusiastic claims of the asylum doctors contributed to the rapid involvement of the state. In the United States, in 1833, Massachusetts set such a strong pattern for public support with the funding of the Worcester Asylum that by 1880 every state had built at least one asylum, and by 1940, 98 percent of the insane hospitalized in the United States were in public institutions. European nations moved toward public funding as well. England maintained its long tradition of private madhouses and charitable asylums, but called for the establishment of publicly supported county asylums in 1808. France established a system of asylums in 1838 that combined care provided by the provinces with state surveillance. Germany emulated the French model. In the Eastern world and in much of Latin America, the asylum movement arose a half-century later. In some areas, such as China and India, the asylum was imposed by Western influences or existed for the treatment of European colonizers.

In the late 19th-century Western world, patient populations grew exponentially; state support for staff and upgraded facilities did not. In the optimism that had driven the asylum movement, the public had lost sight of the dual nature of the asylum. The number of insane who could not be cured, but who needed humane care, filled the wards and overwhelmed the ability of the asylum to respond. By the 1890s, across the world, asylums built for hundreds of patients housed thousands, most therapy disappeared, and even attempts at decent custodial care failed.

Growing dissatisfaction with asylum conditions in the early 20th century produced a spate of exposés. The mental health movement and the rise of psychopathic hospitals and outpatient clinics were harbingers of a change delayed by the outbreak of World War II. In the postwar years, shifting intellectual and social arguments brought about a crusade for deinstitutionalization. The new emphasis on psychodynamic therapies, community-based treatment centers and prevention-oriented clinics, and the development of psychotropic drugs all played a role, as did civil rights defenders, antipsychiatry intellectuals, and patient advocates, who took up the cause of the institutionalized. The population of asylums plummeted as patients were discharged to nursing homes, community mental health centers, or the streets. By the 1990s the problems of inadequate resources and therapeutic failures plagued the deinstitutionalized as they had the hospitalized in earlier times. Societies still had not found a way to combine decent and humane care for the chronically ill with the availability of therapeutic services for the less seriously stricken.

The most common approach to the writing of the history of asylums before the rise of the new social history in the 1960s was that of historians who interpreted all developments as an uninterrupted march of progress. Antipsychiatry interpreters and social control theorists have seen asylums as places of incarceration and repression. More orthodox social historians accept insanity as illness and asylums as therapeutic, and they also study the reasons ordinary people chose asylums for family members. These historians attribute the asylum's decline to society's failure to address fully the complexity of issues that underlie the interplay of the state, institution, family, community, medical profession, race, class,

and gender. (*See also* Mental Illness; Social Control)

Constance M. McGovern

REFERENCES

Foucault, Michel. *Madness and Civilization*. New York: Pantheon, 1965.
Grob, Gerald N. *From Asylum to Community*. Princeton, NJ: Princeton University Press, 1991.
———. *Mental Institutions in America*. New York: The Free Press, 1973.
———. *Mental Illness and American Society*. Princeton, NJ: Princeton University Press, 1983.
Scull, Andrew. "Psychiatry and Its Historians," in *History of Psychiatry* 2 (1991): 239–250.

Athenian Democracy

Democracy at Athens, Greece, was the outgrowth of more than 100 years of internal turmoil characterized by competition among aristocratic factions. Although the Athenians themselves frequently traced the roots of democracy to an early phase of this process, it was Clisthenes of Athens who, locked in struggle with the extreme oligarch Isagoras, put into effect the reforms of Solon and established the new government near the end of the 6th century BC. Except for two brief oligarchical revolutions occasioned by the Peloponnesian War, the democracy remained intact down to the Macedonian overthrow in 322 BC.

Over time certain elements of the democracy's fabric became more and more egalitarian. Thus, unlike the practice of more restrictive regimes, citizenship, rather than being tied, say, to the ownership of a minimum of property, was conferred universally on the legitimate offspring of citizen parents. True, the so-called census class system inaugurated by Solon, whereby the extent of one's eligibility to participate in the constitution was determined by the amount of annual income, remained in existence under the classical democracy, but there are clear signs that the standards were either relaxed or abandoned altogether. To ensure that even the poorest citizen not be prevented by his poverty from participating in government, pay for service was introduced. Amounts between one-half and one and one-half drachmas are attested for the Assembly, Council of 500, the courts, the archons, and the governor of Salamis; one scholar has calculated that a family of four could be supported on less than one-half drachma per day, so the very poor will have found the payments attractive, though evidence is lacking that citizens actually managed to sustain themselves there on a continuing basis. Equity in the distribution of governmental offices was probably the object of another practice, the use of a lottery for the selection of the archons (beginning in 487) and probably of all other magistrates except military and financial officers, who continued to be elected. Finally, a nonrepeat rule for all but the military posts (to which a citizen might be returned consecutively an unlimited number of times) and the Council of 500 (on which a citizen might serve twice in his lifetime), in combination with the fact that tenure in all offices was restricted to one year, guaranteed that a high percentage of citizens would hold public office at some time, probably in many cases repeatedly over a lifetime.

Given these inducements to participation, are socially significant patterns nonetheless discernible? Basic political structures have been explored by historians for a long time, but the actual social meaning and involvement have gained new attention with the rise of social history. The citizenship was of course confined to adult males to the exclusion of women, minors, resident aliens, foreigners, and slaves. But even within the eligible minority barriers to participation existed. Foremost among these was the factor of wealth. Only the wealthy could afford the sort of education in rhetoric that would make possible a leadership role in the democracy. Wealth might be converted to political influence through bribery or legitimate gift-giving with a view to future support in elections (or trials). Wealth made possible the ownership of slaves, providing leisure time for attendance or service as an officer. Good birth, too, might have helped the realization of political ambitions early in the democracy, but later the trend is toward specialization as a basis for political leadership. Still another factor was place of residence. Since the seat of government was physically situated in the urban center, rural dwellers might experience great difficulty in traveling to town, not to mention the interference of

agricultural schedules. Taken together, these considerations point to domination of the government by the urban population, with the lion's share of the elective offices filled by the educated wealthy.

Nicholas F. Jones

REFERENCES

Aristotle. *The Athenian Constitution.* Translated with introduction and notes by P.J. Rhodes. London: Penguin, 1984.

Hignett, C. *A History of the Athenian Constitution to the End of the Fifth Century BC.* Oxford: Clarendon Press, 1952.

Sinclair, R.K. *Democracy and Participation in Athens.* Cambridge and New York: Cambridge University Press, 1988.

Automobile

It is possible to argue that no single item of technology has had a more far-reaching impact on the course of the 20th century than the automobile and allied forms of individualized transportation. Certainly by the second decade of the 20th century, the automobile was established symbolically, if not entirely functionally, as what the world viewed as the central prerequisite for a modern society. This commodity and its effects intersect structures and events of the past century in myriad ways—from economic patterns, labor movements, and spatial patterns, to recent foreign policy. Scholarly discussion of the automobile itself runs a wide and disparate gamut. Some of the central issues covered by a range of social scientists include (listed roughly in order of quantity of study) business, labor, and industrial analysis; technological and stylistic development; sociological and environmental effect; economic impact and centrality to industrial economies; and social and cultural meaning. Historical works, both popular and scholarly, long were dominated by rather traditional studies of the auto industry and the great men who controlled them. This pattern held true until relatively recently, when the automobile began to be examined in terms of gender identity, leisure use, and cultural meanings. The basic periodization of automobile history, primarily though not entirely based on the United States example, unfolds as follows.

Genesis and Industrial Foundation, 1890–1912

Although independent, self-propelled transportation can be traced back to the late 18th century (and as a concept much further), the actual beginnings of organized production of automobiles materialized in the last decade of the 19th century. Building on technologies used in bicycles, wagons, carriages, and gas and steam combustion engines, the earliest experimenters and manufacturers gradually developed various formulations of horseless carriages. The first murmurs of an embryonic auto industry were heard in France and Germany by 1890 and in the United States and Britain a few years afterward. These early producers quickly multiplied so that, by 1900, scores of manufacturers were producing cars that ran on steam, electricity, and, the eventual preference, gasoline. These early car builders produced high-priced vehicles for a strictly upper-class market, using production methods still rooted in the techniques of 19th-century skilled labor. Other factors severely limited auto ownership; roads were dreadful, distribution systems and repair facilities were inadequate, and the vehicles themselves were difficult to operate and far from dependable. Further, governments in many countries did little to encourage auto use. In the case of England, government regulation so severely limited use of automobiles that it crippled their fledgling industries. Still, by the end of this period, the auto had progressed from being a novelty item to a very lucrative and attractive, if not widely dispersed, consumer commodity.

Mass Diffusion Stage One, 1913–1945

This period is best known for the rise to preeminence of Henry Ford and the Model T. By utilizing the assembly line and perfecting methods of mass production, Ford was able to produce tremendous numbers of automobiles at prices increasingly affordable throughout the 1920s, to an ever-expanding portion of the population. By transferring production skills from the worker to the machine, Ford was able to hire a largely unskilled (and frequently immigrant or rural migrant) labor force and maximize specialization on the assembly line. This resulted in tremendous increases in production and, taking advantage of economies of scale, dramatically lower costs per unit. Ford transformed the U.S. and, to a lesser degree, the European automobile markets then to include those never before considered as potential owners. Prerequisite to widespread ownership were several structural factors: widespread public acceptance of individualized transport, settlement of legal constraints (particularly patent controls on basic technology), and especially roads, bridges, and other infrastructure. Mass automobility in the United States spread first to the better-off rural areas of the Midwest and West, then to towns and younger cities.

In the late teens and 1920s, General Motors (GM) followed Ford into the mass market, developing critical internal and external characteristics of automobile production and marketing. Under William (Billy) Durant and Alfred Sloan, GM developed the model for modern organizational structure of the corporation. Perhaps more importantly, GM also innovated methods of stratifying the auto market, perpetuating demand by a yearly model change, and raising styling to be the preeminent feature of vehicles. In Europe, a different model held sway; auto producers implemented Ford's production techniques, but to a much lesser degree. Most importantly, European producers continued to focus mainly on elite markets. In the United States, mass production of cars brought about a proliferation of other industries such as petroleum, glass, and rubber, to name a few. With over 20 million vehicles on the road, a full 56 percent of the families in the United States owned cars by 1927. Further, as evidenced in film, popular literature, and in sport and other leisure activities, the auto was fully integrated into the cultural landscape.

Automobile production dropped considerably in the early years of the Depression, with resulting unemployment and dislocation for much of the industry. The market for new cars reached saturation point in the late 1920s and a huge quantity of used cars quenched much of the demand for low ticket vehicles. The auto industry rebounded slowly in the 1930s, but many companies had disappeared; signs of recovery were evident prior to World War II, however. During the war, auto production was discontinued, but auto industries played important roles in both the Allied and Axis war efforts.

Mass Diffusion Stage Two, 1946–1973

Using savings built up during the war, Americans in the late 1940s and early 1950s purchased autos at a rate not seen since the 1920s. By now, the Big Three (GM, Ford, and Chrysler) still dominated world auto production and reaped tremendous profits. Postwar prosperity brought even wider diffusion of the auto to include more of the working class and more women. Widespread ownership accelerated the process of suburbanization, which came to symbolize postwar America. In Europe mass diffusion was occurring for the first time, though still to a smaller extent than in the United States The emergence of a suburban culture manifested itself in tract housing, shopping malls, and drive-in restaurants and theaters. This auto-based society drew widespread criticism decrying the abandonment of urban centers and decline in traditional communities and values. For the auto industry, some indications of trouble were present by the 1960s. These took the form of allegations of technological stagnation and complacency, important struggles over safety and environmental control, as well as some loss of market share to West Germany and Japan.

Crisis and Disenchantment, 1973–1984

Symbolic of the last leg of the periodization were crises brought about by the OPEC (Organization of Petroleum Exporting Countries) boycott in 1973 and the later shortage of 1979. The resulting shortages of oil awakened America to the limitation of petroleum-based transport and the finite supply of world energy. Further, Detroit's slow response in the development of fuel-efficient vehicles over the past decade had reached a climax point in the 1970s and resulted in German and Japanese ascendance to new heights of market penetration. This slow response sharpened the focus on the American auto deficiencies, prompting consumers at home and abroad to purchase cars from the European and, especially, Japanese upstarts. Perhaps the final straw was the $1.5 billion bailout of Chrysler in 1979 by the federal government, signifying the decline and near collapse of the U.S. auto industry. This decline played a large part in the deindustrialization of the United States occurring at this time. Concerns about the environmental impact of the auto further raised questions about this form of transportation. Smog continued to plague metropolitan areas, despite the utilization of catalytic converters. Increasingly, critics assailed the wisdom of individualized transportation for both its damage to the environment and extreme squander of resources. This cacophony of problems merged to jeopardize seriously the future of this form of transportation and the resultant culture.

The spread of sociohistorical studies of the automobile, using the framework of automobile diffusion, has focused on impacts and meanings. Growth of women's interest in automobiles, reflected in significant changes in manufacturer's sales and marketing techniques, car advertising campaigns, and design, began during the 1920s. The importance of automobiles in greater youth independence from family is a vital topic for the postwar United States. The role of cars in crime (and as focus for theft) is another topic just being explored.

John B. Thomas

REFERENCES

Flink, James J. *The Automobile Age.* Cambridge: MIT Press, 1988.

Moorhouse, H.F. *Driving Ambitions: An Analysis of the American Hot Rod Enthusiasm.* New York: St. Martin's, 1991.

Rae, John B. *The American Automobile.* Chicago: University of Chicago Press, 1965.

Scharff, Virginia. *Taking the Wheel, Women and the Coming of the Motor Age.* New York: The Free Press, 1991.

B

Baby Boom

The baby boom, at its height in the 1950s, focuses a number of themes in recent social and demographic history, for western Europe and the United States. Quite generally, population experts in the second quarter of the 20th century, in western Europe no less than in the English-speaking world, believed that population size in the economically advanced nations would shortly cease to grow, eventually shrinking unless increased immigration was permitted. There was solid reason to believe this: in some parts of the world (France and the United States are the clearest examples), the fertility rate had been declining for a century or more, and would shortly reach the level of population replacement, if these long-term trends simply continued. And in the rest of the economically advanced world, the same trend had been in operation, if for somewhat shorter periods. The reasons for the fertility decline—urbanization, the hope of economic betterment of each child through extended education or other pre-employment preparation, the awakening of ambitions in women that were in-

compatible with frequent pregnancy, and the spirit of individualism—were clear enough and were quite general.

When, at the conclusion of World War II, fertility rates increased sharply in most of these same nations, experts were not very surprised: just such an increase had been experienced quite generally after World War I, a natural response to the release of tensions and to the postponement for the duration of the conflict of many aspects of normal life, including marital sexuality and family life. But when, in nation after nation, fertility began to rise again, soon after the brief postwar burst had receded, and population growth began to exceed all prior estimates, surprised experts began to wonder if a new era had been entered—an era in which one of the central defining characteristics of the transition to the modern was reversed.

By about 1960, however, the baby boom was over in most countries, and fertility resumed its historic decline. Mortality had become somewhat lower in the interim, and immigration had increased, so that few national populations had actually declined in the subsequent decades. Even so, the period of startling fertility growth, about a decade in duration, can be seen in time series and in current population age structures—a "blip" in a trend toward continued downward fertility rates, a period that deviates from the modern in its demographic pattern, fascinatingly.

The demographic components of the baby boom, in most of the societies in which it occurred, were the same. They did not include, on the level of the individual family, a return to the traditional large family. Few couples had more than three children: the boom occurred in a regime in which fertility was generally controlled, usually by mechanical contraception or by natural devices of fertility avoidance. But most couples elected to avoid the fertility strategies that had become especially common at the tail end of the prewar fertility decline, that is, childlessness or the single-child family. Most families now had two or three children, and, moreover, they had them earlier in their marriages than previously. And, in fact, in most countries a "marriage boom" accompanied and to some extent explained the baby boom in a demographic sense. The marriage boom did not so much affect the proportions of people ever marrying as the age at which people married. With couples marrying earlier and having their children earlier within the marriage, the time between generations was reduced, and the birth rate thereby increased.

The baby boom must be understood, first of all, in its economic context. By the time fertility began to rise (apart from the brief, immediate post–World War II spurt), economic recovery and/or growth were occurring, and there was reason for economic optimism on the part of young couples contemplating forming a family. Jobs were relatively plentiful and relatively remunerative. Families would not need to go childless, or to have only a single child, to protect their standard of living. In the optimism that economic growth encouraged, one might well hope to gather resources enough to prepare well three children for their lives as adults.

Most young couples during the baby boom shared the values about the centrality of family to their lives and the centrality of children to family that they believed their parents had expressed but could not carry out, on account of economic insecurity. They did not have to choose between a family of two to three and the opportunities for material well-being for themselves and economic mobility for their children; and they did not choose. Themes of modernity—feminism is a very prominent and a very relevant one of these—that had been widely discussed in the 1920s and probably influenced a certain amount of the late marriage and childlessness present in the demographic patterns of that decade did not so often press on the consciousness of young couples in the postwar expansion.

Ultimately, the familistic focus would be challenged by other orientations and economic security would again prove fleeting for many families, and the baby boom would be a thing of the past. But its consequences linger on. The vastly enlarged number of children that it engendered encouraged the building of schools and of new housing designed for such families, often in new suburbs. As the large baby boom generation has aged, they have confronted a labor market that was at first accommodating, but, beginning in the mid-1970s, far less so. The children of the baby boom are numerous enough that, even at post–baby boom fertility rates, an "echo effect" of increased numbers (but not rates) of births can be seen in the population. But the largest echo effect of the baby boom can be expected early in the 21st century, as the physical robustness of this large group begins to fade, and medical demands and then retirement funds become required by them in large quantities.

John Modell

REFERENCE

Westoff, Charles F., Robert G. Potter, Jr., and Philip C. Sagi. *The Third Child*. Princeton, NJ: Princeton University Press, 1963.

Banditry

Banditry is the taking of property by force or by the threat of force. The act is as old as private property itself. Bandits operate in the shadows, often on the fringes of society or in geographically isolated areas. Their lives and actions are shrouded in mystery and legend. They have been lionized by romanticizers and vilified by government officials. Bandits, however, are more varied and complex figures than either popularizers or detractors allow.

Banditry often involves violent acts by common criminals for whom theft is simply a job. Such "ignoble robbers" find few defenders. Such bandits, like the *haiduks* described by Eric J. Hobsbawm (1981), robbed simply for profit. They robbed the rich more often than the poor, because the rich had more booty. In most cases, gangs formed ties with rural elites, not with humble peasant society. Bandits could aid local elites as hired thugs. Ties to local elites provided political protection and a degree of legitimacy to the bandits.

Some bandits gained fame, Robin Hood reputations, and popular adulation. Hobsbawm describes such figures as "social bandits." These men made themselves admired by flaunting authority and championing the interests of the folk masses against elite oppression. In exchange, peasants protected and aided such bandits. Figures like Diego Corrientes (Spain), Antônio Silvino (Brazil), Pío Romero (Bolivia), and Manuel García (Cuba) became symbols of popular resistance.

Some bandits declared a political agenda simply to cloak their activities with a measure of legitimacy. For Latin America, historian Christon Archer calls such men "guerrilla-bandits"—opportunists who used the banners of warfare to pillage. Guerrilla-bandits in Venezuela, Mexico, Cuba, and elsewhere showed no political or class loyalties. They changed sides if they perceived that it would increase the spoils.

Political bandits, in contrast, developed loyalties to larger political movements. They did not shift sides merely for monetary gain. They sometimes took up arms for a partisan or regional agenda, which overrode class allegiances. Political banditry emerged in parts of early-20th century Balkan and Latin American societies and during the Colombian *Violencia* of the 1950s. Hobsbawm agrees that, in the Colombian case, banditry was "in essence more political than social."

Banditry and its social context vary widely. Analysis of traditional, peasant communities yields one set of conclusions. Research on remote, sparsely populated frontier regions yields

another. Social marginals, like Australian bushrangers, Venezuelan *llaneros*, or Argentine *gauchos*, do not exhibit ties to the peasantry.

Adulation in myth and folklore on the one side and official condemnation on the other have generated conflicting visions of bandits. These problematic sources make banditry a subtle, intriguing challenge for social historians. Hobsbawm's research is based primarily on fictional literature (often elite lore) and folk sources. Folktales often overlook the brutality and indiscriminate terror and killing of flesh-and-blood bandits. The bandit's cowardice disappears when he gains the mythical status of class champion. Elite lore reflects mostly the (often urban) writer's imagination and the reading public's taste for blood and gore.

Recently, scholars have scoured official police and judicial archives for clues to the behavior of real bandits. But the true incidence of criminal acts ("the dark figure") is impossible to determine. The political and class motives of government officials constrain the historical record. Officials often labeled political dissidents as "bandits" to discredit them.

Social historians are attacking the complex problems of sources and methodology in a variety of ways. Ranajit Guha and other advocates of "subaltern studies" seek to "decode" peasant consciousness and thereby balance the biases of the "official mind." Gilbert Joseph and others suggest placing banditry into the context of other forms of "everyday peasant resistance," along lines suggested by James Scott (1985). Richard W. Slatta (1987) urges further comparative analysis, both within and across cultures. The social history of banditry has focused on a variety of geographical areas, including southern Asia as well as southern and eastern Europe and Latin America.

Historians still face many questions about banditry. Literary scholars and historians must continue comparing and contrasting evidence from official historical documents with literary and folk imagery of banditry. The existence and roles of women bandits need examination. The relationship between the types and incidence of banditry and levels of integration into world markets should be explored. Clearer relationships between banditry and other forms of peasant resistance and rebellion must be established. Further comparative studies, especially cross-cultural, should reveal the relative influences of structural and cultural variables in bandit behavior.

"Bad apples," or common criminals, exist in every society. But even if few bonafide social bandits actually existed, banditry itself can represent widespread popular discontent. It can be one adaptation by the rural poor to an elite-constrained world of limited, legitimate opportunity. Banditry can serve as one weapon of oppressed people seeking legitimate means of survival and political participation. (*See also* African Peasantry; Asian Peasantry; Chinese Social Protest; Comparative History; Crime; Elites; Folklore/Oral Traditions; *Gauchos, Llaneros;* Peasant Rebellion; Protest)

Richard W. Slatta

REFERENCES

Crummey, Donald, ed. *Banditry, Rebellion and Social Protest in Africa.* Portsmouth, NH: Heinemann Educational Books, 1986.
Hobsbawm, Eric J. *Bandits* (rev. ed.). New York: Pantheon, 1981.
Latin American Research Review 25, 3 (1990); 26, 1 (1991).
Scott, James C. *Weapons of the Weak: Everyday Forms of Peasant Resistance.* New Haven: Yale University Press, 1985.
Slatta, Richard W., ed. *Bandidos: The Varieties of Latin American Banditry.* Westport, CT: Greenwood Press, 1987.

Begging

See Poor Relief

Birth Control

The term "birth control" was coined in America by Margaret Sanger in 1913 as part of her campaign to present family limitation, viewed by most Victorians as a taboo subject, in a positive light. Many historical studies of fertility control followed Sanger's lead in assuming that until the late 19th century fertility restriction was rarely present in the Western world. Such studies of birth control accordingly focused on the pioneers

who brought the good news of contraception to the masses in the 20th century. Women, so the story goes, once subjected to repeated unwanted pregnancies, were now enlightened and finally able to control their bodies. Was it that simple? Fertility rates obviously did fall sharply in the late 19th and early 20th centuries, but social historians have pointed out that North America and Europe never experienced the extraordinarily high fertility levels of Africa and Asia. As far back as one looks evidence can be found that in the West some people were in one way or another seeking to "control" births; in the 4th century St. Augustine referred to women resorting to means "against nature" to prevent pregnancy. Social historians' work on birth control has expanded our understanding of its premodern forms, while also looking at the wider causes and implications of the more modern patterns.

Today we tend to equate "controlled" fertility with small family size, but in the past vigorous attempts were often made, by way of rituals or diet, to avoid sterility, ensure conceptions, determine a baby's sex, avoid miscarriage, guarantee successful labor, and produce large families. The popular herbal texts which carried such information remind us that, for centuries in rural communities with a demand for labor, fruitful marriages were esteemed. But those same herbals also hinted that some on occasion might seek ways of limiting births. How? Demographic historians have noted that in past centuries Western families were relatively modest in size in the first instance because women traditionally did not marry until their mid-twenties. Births were widely spaced. Lengthy nursing provided many mothers with a margin of protection against a subsequent pregnancy. In the 20th century contraception is the main way in which marital fertility is controlled, but the great decline in the fertility of the Western world between 1850 and 1920 took place before the mass employment of any of the modern barrier forms of birth control such as the condom and diaphragm. The Pill was, of course, only available from the 1960s onward.

To look for evidence of birth control in past cultures accordingly necessitates a widening of the term's definition. "Natural means" of birth control included abstinence, reliance upon the sterile period in the woman's ovulation cycle (sought for centuries but only definitely established in 1929), and extended nursing. The "artificial methods" of fertility restriction resorted to since the time of the Greeks ranged from the use of herbal potions to prevent conceptions to the employment of instruments to induce miscarriages. By the 18th century mention was made by libertines in France and England to condoms and sponges, but coitus interruptus, or withdrawal, would remain until the 20th century the single most important method of contraception. Abortion was always, in the absence of any completely reliable contraceptive, turned to by the married as a backup method of fertility control.

Demographic data make it clear that by the early 1700s segments of the upper classes in both France and Britain were not only controlling but reducing their fertility. At the end of the 18th century Robert Malthus, although himself an opponent of the artificial restriction of fertility, popularized the notion that the poor could only hope to prosper by limiting their numbers. The small band of 19th-century birth control activists (or neo-Malthusians as they were called from the 1880s in Britain and America) wedded Malthusian population concerns to a secularist morality. Hostile public opposition to birth control was voiced by almost every social faction: by doctors for being physically debilitating, by churchmen for being immoral, by socialists for being antisocial, by nationalists for threatening their nation with "race suicide." It says something of the tenacity of ordinary men and women that birth rates were brought down despite the dire predictions of the "respectable."

Such hostility was in part sparked because of the fear expressed by eugenicists and pronatalists that the educated and ambitious would be first to curb family size with the result that ultimately the "unfit" would outbreed the "fit." When fertility rates began to decline precipitously class differentials did emerge. The 1911 English census revealed that the births per thousand married males in the upper and middle classes was about one-half those of unskilled workmen. In the next few decades this gap was closed. Some historians have asserted that the middle classes restricted their fertility in the latter 19th century to protect their recently achieved standards of gentility and that in the early 20th century the working classes followed the lead of the middle classes as both their innovative birth control devices and norms regarding family size diffused downward into laboring districts and outward into rural areas. But such a diffusionist argument has its weaknesses. France provides the classic case of a country which, though slowly industrializing and retaining a large farming population, reduced its fertility far earlier than its more advanced neighbors. This reduction was attributed by 19th-century commentators to the Napoleonic inheritance law that insisted on an equal division of property among all children, but the fertility decline in fact predated it. In England some segments of the working class— particularly in textile areas where many women worked—already had very low fertility rates in the late 1800s, which suggests that their family size was dictated primarily by economic and social pressures, not middle-class models. There was moreover little evidence among workers either in Europe or the United States (where fertility rates began their long-term decline in 1800) of the mass employment of new contraceptives; what was clearly crucial was the resolution to control fertility with whatever methods were already at hand.

By the time of the Great Depression of the 1930s public morality began to catch up to social reality and the defense of birth control became respectable. The propagandizing campaigns of advocates such as Margaret Sanger in the United States and Marie Stopes in England who argued that uncontrolled fertility could blight otherwise happy marriages were important. Sanger was particularly concerned about providing female-controlled and medically approved contraceptives such as the diaphragm. But major social changes, not the sudden turn of heart of a few individuals, was what provided these campaigners with large, receptive audiences. Industrializing early 20th-century states were already actively policing the health and welfare of their work forces. As education was made compulsory, child labor restricted, and the paid employment of women expanded, the definition of marriage and family necessarily changed. The cost of children, now dependents rather than wage earners, increased dramatically. At the same time the growing division between the home and workplace fostered the cult of domesticity. The financial and emotional investments parents were now obliged to make in the care and attention of their children could only be given if their numbers were restricted. In this changing social context the shrinking of average family size from the six children of the mid-19th century to the two children of the 1930s was not only understandable but necessary. Increasing numbers of couples were turning from coitus interruptus to some more effective appliance methods; only a small minority attended the clinics birth controllers established in the 1920s and 1930s as part of the campaign to show that contraception now had medical support. Although the defenders of birth control insisted that contraceptives were only meant for the married, the late 19th- and early 20th-century decline in the illegitimacy rate suggests that the single also took advantage of them. A dwindling number of vocal opponents continued to claim that birth control was both a cause and an effect of whatever threat to the family they most feared—urbanization, alien immigration, materialism, feminism, promiscuity. The reality was that birth control, far from undermining the family, allowed it to respond to the new social environment in which it found itself. The birth control pill of the 1960s was also greeted with predictions that it would "free" women, but there is little evidence that it seriously threatened traditional gender relationships. The history of birth control is much more than the account of contraceptive technologies; social historians are only beginning to unpack the full account of its cultural, economic, and moral ramifications. (*See also* Abortion; Body; Demographic Transition; European-Style Family; Fertility; Infanticide; Women's History)

Angus McLaren

REFERENCES

Banks, Joseph. *Prosperity and Parenthood: A Study of Family Planning Among the Victorian Middle Class.* London: Routledge and K. Paul, 1954.

Gittens, Diana. *Fair Sex: Family Size and Structure, 1900–1939.* London: Hutchinson, 1982.

Gordon, Linda. *Woman's Body, Woman's Right: Birth Control in America.* New York: Grossman, 1976.

McLaren, Angus. *A History of Contraception: From Antiquity to the Present Day.* Oxford: Blackwell, 1990.

Woycke, James. *Birth Control in Germany, 1871–1933.* London: Routledge, 1988.

Body

Over recent decades social historians have turned their attention to several themes that might at first glance seem completely ahistorical or, at the very least, especially impervious to change over time. Many historians have recently placed biological realities, such as sex, death, and the body, under the historical microscope for a closer look. Scholarly work has revealed these topics to possess a history all their own as well as a peculiar ability to contribute in multifarious ways to a deeper understanding of broader historical issues. Social histories of the body most clearly expand on topics in gender relations and sexual politics, but current research on culture and social policy has suggested a corporeal imperative here as well. Work on the body has been done principally, it is true, by historians of gender investigating sexual politics, and by medical historians interested in the "social construction of illness." More recently, however, historians of *mentalité* have also turned their attention to the body, focusing on the perception and representation of physicality in a myriad of arenas.

Historians of gender have been drawn to the history of the body in terms of how bodies—especially female bodies—were perceived, policed, and even shaped. Early work was often unnecessarily reductionist, attributing the policing of women's bodies, through medical practice and social conventions, to the misogynist attempts of males to control the inherently "out-of-control" female body. Others have used evidence from advice manuals, especially those directed toward child-rearing practices, to demonstrate how parents and authorities sought to regulate the child's body, sometimes physically—using braces and supports—but more often through psychological and moral pressures. Toward the end of the 18th century in Western society, this was more forcefully expressed in extravagant fears of the bodily harm done by masturbation and in vigorous efforts to suppress this "vice." Historians of the body, moving along these axes of interpretation, have found some of their richest material in the late 18th and 19th centuries. The Victorian image of the passionless woman, the discovery of new links between mind and body in the form of diseases or pseudo-diseases like neurasthenia and hysteria, and issues of race have all received scholarly attention.

Closely linked to these medicalized and gendered studies of the body are works dealing with the perception and representation of physicality. Like studies of the "social construction of illness," this research pursues questions such as how people perceive their own bodies and understand the physical envelope they inhabit. Barbara Duden, in her fascinating book *The Woman Beneath the Skin* (1991), exploited the records of an 18th-century physician on his female patients to construct a picture of how these women viewed the functioning of their own bodies (mostly in terms of oozing fluidity), "felt" their very fleshiness, and comprehended their illnesses viscerally. Attention to increasingly mechanistic conceptions of the body, after the late 18th century, may have altered popular beliefs about body as well as illness. The idea of the body as a machine rather than a vessel for fluids and humors, had important implications just beginning to be fully explored.

Body has also loomed large in historical examinations of the "civilizing process." According to Norbert Elias (*The Civilizing Process,* 1978) and his disciples, in the early modern period people gradually began to acquire manners, concealing bodily functions, such as urination and defecation, once freely exposed. There developed simultaneously with the use of knife, fork, and spoon at table, new forms of etiquette regarding spitting, sneezing, and farting. At the same time there was a growing sense of the inviolability of another human being's "personal space." The result was a growth of civility, a decline of aggressive behavior, and—more broadly—a significant elevation of the power of the modern state. More recently, gestures—such as the handshake—have been integrated into this history of the body and of civility.

But the field of historical research on the body has not been left to the medical historians, to the historians of gender, or even to those inter-ested in the civilizing process. The body has also moved to center stage in the realm of a new political history, one equally informed by anthropology, cultural studies, and linguistic theory. Michel Foucault has also written extensively on sexuality and the body. His volumes on sexuality are, of course, inherently body-linked. Perhaps more influential has been his perception that the body formed an exhibition site where state power was (and is) acted out. Foucault, for example, discussed executions in just these terms. The significance of executions, as well as the many other ways in which the state sought to "discipline and punish" the socially marginal or those defined as deviant, turned on the centrality of body control in the enhancement of state power. Likewise, military and educational discipline was intimately linked to body management as any examination of drill manuals, for example, clearly shows. Foucault also demonstrated how the body was subjected to the authority of physicians in a long-term process of medicalization. This line of thought has nurtured a series of works in "body politics," or rather stimulated investigations that are concerned with political culture but which locate significant expressions and representations of that culture in physicality. Historian Lynn Hunt, for example, in her study of the political culture of the French Revolution, focused on the "body symbols" of the Revolution. Dorinda Outram (1989) went further and claimed that the body "is the most basic political resource."

Even the definition of "biological sex," which appears to most of us a given (one seems irreducibly either male or female), has been brought under closer scrutiny by the new "body historians." Thomas Laqueur (1990) suggested that gender, not sex, is the immutable reality. Whereas historians of gender have often argued that gender roles (masculinity and femininity) are historically constructed, Laqueur turned this around and insisted that sex itself has a history. Western society has moved from accepting a one-sex model where the genitalia of men and women were essentially seen as inverted forms of the same organs, and which conceived of individual males and females as merely different points on the spectrum of sex ranging from "perfect" male to "perfect" female, to the two-sex model that, particularly in the 18th and 19th centuries, created the "biological" differences between the sexes.

Thus, there are several provocative agendas driving body history today. Unfortunately, too much of the evidence we have about physicality still relies on elite impressions or prescriptive literature. Most historians have worked with advice manuals, medical theory, physicians, and the literati. Even Duden's provocative work depends on the speech of women filtered through a male voice. The history of the body, therefore, needs to reach out to examine class differences, although admittedly here the problem of sources is immense. (*See also* Cleanliness; Mentalities; Sexuality)

Mary Lindemann

REFERENCES

Duden, Barbara. *The Woman Beneath the Skin: A Doctor's Patients in Eighteenth-Century Germany.* Translated by Thomas Dunlap. Cambridge: Harvard University Press, 1991.

Gallagher, Catherine, and Thomas Laqueur, eds. *The Making of the Modern Body: Sexuality and Society in the Nineteenth Century.* Berkeley and Los Angeles: University of California Press, 1987.

Laqueur, Thomas. *Making Sex: Body and Gender from the Greeks to Freud.* Cambridge: Harvard University Press, 1990.

Outram, Dorinda. *The Body and the French Revolution: Sex, Class, and Political Culture.* New Haven: Yale University Press, 1989.

Porter, Roy. "History of the Body," in Peter Burke, ed. *New Perspectives on Historical Writing.* University Park: Pennsylvania State University Press, 1991, pp. 206–32.

Schiebinger, Londa. *The Mind Has No Sex? Women in the Origins of Modern Science.* Cambridge: Harvard University Press, 1989.

Bolshevism

Bolshevism was a radical Russian Marxist movement that began in 1903. Its end might best be dated around 1934, when the Stalinist regime adopted conservative social policies. Vladimir Il'ich Lenin (real name Ulianov, 1870–1924), led bolshevism from its inception through the Russian Revolution and Civil War.

Bolshevism began as a wing of the Russian Social Democratic Labor Party (RSDLP), a Marxist group created in 1898. The term "bol-shevism" comes from the Russian *bol'shinstvo*, or majority. This referred to a crucial vote in Lenin's favor at a party congress. The losers then formed a political faction labeled Mensheviks, or people of the minority. The Bolsheviks were "harder": they pointed more toward inciting a revolution rather than waiting for Marx's laws of social development to unfold. They were much less inclined to work with the liberals. Before 1917 both wings of the RSDLP were dedicated to political and social democracy, based on the elimination of classes.

After the February Revolution of 1917 overthrew the tsarist autocracy, the two factions split irrevocably. The Mensheviks believed that Russia would be ripe for socialist revolution only after an unspecified period of capitalist development. Meanwhile, liberals had to lead.

Lenin, however, urged his followers to radicalism. He advocated all power to the soviets, as the councils of workers', soldiers', and peasants' deputies were called. By October, workers and soldiers in the major cities supported the Bolsheviks, who seized power in an almost bloodless revolution. Lenin then guided his party in the creation of a one-party state.

The Western "liberal" tradition argues that from the start intellectuals led the Bolshevik Party for their own personal and political goals. Workers joined only to gain a chance for education, and relations between the two groups were hostile. Lenin, a power-hungry elitist who believed that he possessed the correct political understanding ("consciousness") needed to make a revolution, misled workers in 1917 with promises of power and wealth. Ignorance and greed caused workers to fall for this line. Backward workers chose the Leninists, but more conscious factory hands supported the Mensheviks' gradualist approach. Once in power, the Bolsheviks imposed a system of harsh coercion on the hapless populace.

Other Western writers, the "revisionists," have challenged these views; and their work has reflected the emergence of a more sophisticated social history of bolshevism. Workers and intellectuals experienced some mutual antagonism in the early stages of bolshevism but also realized that they needed each other. Intellectuals supplied broad perspectives and articulateness that few workers could muster. Lenin was an elitist, but in that he fit squarely into a long Russian tradition that included the Mensheviks and many others.

If some highly literate workers became Mensheviks, other skilled hands often became Bolsheviks. During 1917 workers turned to Lenin because of specific incidents. As the economy declined under the provisional government and factories closed, workers moved to take over plants in order to protect their jobs. Workers began to believe that only a radical, socialist solution could end what they deemed the capitalists' sabotage of industry and workers' rights. Only strong government control of factories could keep them open and protect jobs. The Bolsheviks were the sole party to advocate such a program.

Revisionist social historians maintain that "the Bolsheviks" cannot be contrasted with "the people" in the creation of a coercive state after 1917. The Bolsheviks shot down protesting workers and peasants at times, but other ordinary people carried out these actions in support of the new government. There were always workers who favored firm state control in view of the devastated economy and the grave threat from counter-revolutionary forces. The Bolsheviks may have had little active support, but their opponents had even less. (*See also* Revolutions; Russian Industrialization; Russian Revolution; Russian Working Class; Stalinism)

Robert W. Thurston

REFERENCES

Lenin, V.I. *What Is to Be Done? Burning Questions of Our Movement.* New York: International Publishers, 1929. Originally published in Russian in 1902.

Pipes, Richard. *Social Democracy and the St. Petersburg Labor Movement, 1885–1987.* Cambridge, MA: Harvard University Press, 1963.

Rabinowitch, Alexander. *The Bolsheviks Come to Power: The Revolution of 1917 in Petrograd.* New York: Norton, 1976.

Wildman, Allan. *The Making of a Workers' Revolution: Russian Social Democracy, 1891–1903.* Chicago: University of Chicago Press, 1967.

Bourbon Reform

A program of administrative and economic reforms affecting Spain and its empire during the 18th century, these new reform policies were instituted by the Bourbon Dynasty, which assumed the Spanish Crown following the death of the last Spanish Hapsburg, Charles II, in 1700. Inspired by the absolutist policies of the French Bourbons, the reforms sought to reinforce central monarchical control over Spain and its empire, stimulate economic growth, and increase tax revenues.

Given the size and wealth of Spain's American empire, many of these new policies were aimed specifically at the colonies, where their economic and social impacts were strongly felt. Particularly during the reign of Charles III (1759–1788), the colonial reforms produced substantial increases in silver production, transatlantic commerce, and tax revenues. The creation of new viceroyalties, royal appellate courts, militia units, and the intendants, a new corps of province-level administrators, increased the royal presence in areas of the empire where it had previously been weak. The Bourbons also reduced the participation of American-born Creoles in the colonial bureaucracy, replacing many of them with professional administrators from Spain.

While the reforms achieved many of their stated goals, research by social and economic historians has revealed their destabilizing effects on Spanish rule in the colonies. Here is an important case where state-society connections reveal more than the history of policy alone can. The increased tax burden weighed heavily on the nonelite population, as did expanded demand for forced Indian labor in the Andean silver mines and for African slave labor on the plantations of the Spanish Caribbean. Despite the economic growth registered during this period, living standards seem to have declined in many parts of the empire, producing a wave of popular rebellions—most notably the Tupac Amaru uprising in Peru and Bolivia and the Comunero revolt in Colombia—which swept the region from the 1750s through the 1790s.

Creole elites benefited from economic growth, but were discomfited both by new taxes and by Bourbon efforts to reduce the Creoles' role in colonial administration. These elites remained loyal to Spain during the uprisings of the late

1700s. But when the Spanish Bourbons were deposed by Napoleon in 1808, Creoles in Argentina, Chile, Colombia, Venezuela, and elsewhere moved to seize power, and by 1824 every Spanish American colony except for Cuba and Puerto Rico had won its independence. Thus, reforms intended to fortify Spanish rule in the Americas actually contributed to the eventual undoing of that rule. [*See also* Independence Wars (Spanish American); Tupac Amaru/Tupac Katari]

George Reid Andrews

REFERENCES

Fisher, John R., et al., eds. *Reform and Insurrection in Bourbon New Granada and Peru.* Baton Rouge: Louisiana State University Press, 1990.

Jacobson, Nils, and Hans-Jürgen Puhle, eds. *The Economies of Mexico and Peru During the Late Colonial Period, 1760–1810.* Berlin: Colloquium Verlag, 1986.

Lynch, John. *Bourbon Spain, 1700–1808.* Oxford: Oxford University Press, 1989.

Phelan, John L. *The People and the King: The Comunero Revolution in Colombia, 1781.* Madison: University of Wisconsin Press, 1978.

Bourgeoisie

See Middle Class

Brideprice

Brideprice refers to payments made by the groom's to the bride's kin that establish the groom's family's rights to her children. Often the goods received by the bride's family are then used, in turn, to acquire a wife for one of their men. Such payments vary from one society to another, and brideprice payment of some sort has been practiced in societies otherwise as different as those of central Asia, ancient northern Europe, and Africa. Brideprice can also vary historically within the same society. The payments may be made in installments over many years or all at once; they may be given and received by a single person from each side or they may consist of numerous separate transactions among group members; the payments may be in currency or include stipulated valuable items; they may fluctuate relative to economic forces or remain stable.

It is the contrast with dowry that encourages scholars to retain a single concept for such a variable phenomenon. Dowry is a payment, sometimes in land or other real property, made by the bride's family to the couple, and is characteristic of South Asia, the Middle East, and medieval and early modern Europe. Although similar in that both bridewealth and dowry establish the public acceptability of a marriage and both may be returned in case of divorce, the two payments differ in social context: brideprice circulates wealth to recruit people to groups, whereas dowry usually establishes funds of property for permanent family use and inheritance.

Records of marriage payments have provided invaluable data on the meaning of marriage, transactions in landed property, conceptions of wealth, and gender relations. Their variability has provided the basis for comparative studies of entire civilizations, and their intricacy has allowed increasing conceptual precision about family change.

The term "brideprice," however, has provoked controversy because it implies sale. In 1926 the League of Nations ruled that brideprice payment was equivalent to enslavement. Anthropologists argued that a wife retained membership in her own kinship group and was terminologically distinguished from a slave. Consequently, from 1931 onward scholars increasingly adopted "bridewealth" instead, and in many modern African legal systems bridewealth is an accepted part of customary marriage. There have been government and popular efforts to control levels of payment and/or to diminish the importance of marriage payments altogether. (*See also* Marriage/Remarriage)

Jane I. Guyer

REFERENCES

Goody, J. *The Development of the Family and Marriage in Europe.* Cambridge: Cambridge University Press, 1983.

Goody, J., and S.J. Tambiah. *Bridewealth and Dowry.* Cambridge: Cambridge University Press, 1973.

Hughes, D.O. "From Bridewealth to Dowry in Mediterranean Europe," *Journal of Family History* 3: 262–296.

Miers, Suzanne, and Igor I. Kopytoff. *Slavery in Africa.* Madison: University of Wisconsin Press, 1977.

Tambiah, S.J. "Bridewealth and Dowry Revisited," *Current Anthropology* 30 (1989): 413–435.

Buddhism

Buddhism, along with Christianity and Islam, is one of the three great religions of the world. With roots in India and a historical founding dating back some 2,500 years to Siddhārtha Gautama, who became known as the Buddha, or the Enlightened One (ca. 563–ca. 483 BC), it has expanded its borders throughout Asia and has made inroads in Europe and North America. Today, Buddhism claims more than 500 million followers and remains the dominant tradition of Sri Lanka, Burma, Thailand, Laos, Cambodia, Vietnam, Bhutan, and Japan. Historically, it played a decisive role in India, Indonesia, Nepal, Tibet, Mongolia, China, and Korea, and continues to influence the religious, social, ethical, artistic, and political views and behaviors of those societies. Thus, Buddhism has changed and developed over time and place. Adapting to and being adapted by, influencing and being influenced by, a diverse number of individuals, cultures, and political structures, Buddhism encompasses a wide variety of monastic, sectarian, lay, and popular beliefs and practices.

Buddhism is broadly divided into three major traditions: Theravāda (way of the elders) or, more pejoratively, Hīnayāna (small vehicle); Mahāyāna (great vehicle); and Vajrayāna (diamond, or esoteric, vehicle). Versions of the Buddhist canon are preserved in Pali, Sanskrit, Chinese, and Tibetan; represent sectarian variants; and include the purported sermons of the Buddha, the monastic rules of discipline, and scholastic treatises. Mahāyāna and Vajrayāna also accept texts that advocate doctrinal and cosmological developments not found in the earlier literature.

What then defines Buddhism as a single tradition? According to the Buddhist worldview, life is suffering due to the transitory nature inherent in all human existence. Suffering is caused by the human desire to cling to that which, in reality, has no substantial substratum—one's own life and material possessions. More specifically, suffering is the product of karma, the moral agent defined as one's intentional thoughts, words, and actions, fueled by ignorance of the mutually dependent nature of reality. One's present existence is the result of karma accrued in the past and present; one's future depends upon actions taken in the present. Despite the relative circumstances of each individual, however, all are subject to the fundamental disease of the human condition, played out in an infinite number of rebirths (in human and other forms), until and unless stopped by corrective measures. Both the cause and cessation of suffering are thus located within the individual, not within the natural or sociopolitical environment, nor attributable to supernatural forces—devotional Buddhism being a later sectarian and popular development.

At the heart of Buddhist ethics is the principle of nonattachment. This nonattached orientation specifies an attitude to be cultivated through moral discipline (refusal to lie or steal, commit violence against others, or engage in sexual misconduct), meditative introspection, and insight; a life lived in accord with the true nature of the self and of reality free from any notion of personal aggrandizement. This middle way between self-indulgence and self-mortification, self and other, brings salvation.

For early Buddhism, salvation is a transcendence outside and above the world in which we live. In the later traditions, an enlightenment identical to that of the Buddha is open to all and attainable in the present life. The *bodhisattva* ideal, the compassionate activities of enlightened beings who live in this world but are not of it, present in early Buddhism, is accentuated.

Thus, while Buddhists have always considered the monastic lifestyle to be most conducive to spiritual development, it is not a radical renunciation of the mundane world. While the primary function of monks and nuns is to lend spiritual support to the laity, Buddhist doctrinal and ethical principles insist upon involvement in education, social welfare and reform, and matters of good governance, peace, and the environment. Popular Buddhist tales and life-cycle and annual rituals reinforce moral and political ideals, filiality, and ancestor worship. The laity, for its part, provides material support to the monastic community and honors it through pilgrimage, in art, architecture, and literature. Further, the principle of nonattachment is operative in the administration of family and career responsibilities and in service to the community and state. A society characterized by spiritual and material reciprocity and in accord with the interpersonal and societal values of its members works in tandem with the pursuit of salvation. While ultimately unreal, it reflects the ideal of selfless altruism, is consistent with the idea of karma, results in a greater harmony with reality, and provides the ground for salvation. The transformation of Buddhism over time and place further accords with its universal ethos, its concern not only with the truth but with the particular communication of that reality, and the idea of the middle way.

Thus, on the popular level, Buddhist principles and cosmological orientations have been absorbed, both consciously and unconsciously, into the social fabric of the cultures in which Buddhism flourished and continues to flourish. An understanding of changing Buddhist beliefs and practices is therefore a vital component of grappling with popular mentalities in many parts of Asia. Doctrinal, monastic, and institutional histories of Buddhism are only half the picture. Of equal importance is attention to the popular expression and uses of Buddhism and the religion's impact on family, and on political and economic views in individual cultures and during specific periods of history.

Most histories of Buddhism have stressed its doctrinal aspects, though important studies also deal with monasticism. An understanding of changing Buddhist beliefs is also a vital component of grappling with popular mentalities in many parts of Asia. Opportunities for further work on popular uses of Buddhism and the religion's impact on family and economic behaviors, in major regions and major periods of the past, remain considerable. (*See also* Ancestor Worship; Charity; Chinese State and Society; Monasteries/Nunneries; Religion)

Linda Penkower

REFERENCES

Chen, Kenneth K.S. *The Chinese Transformation of Buddhism.* Princeton, NJ: Princeton University Press, 1973.

Corless, Roger J. *The Vision of Buddhism: The Space Under the Tree.* New York: Paragon House, 1989.

Dumoulin, Heinrich, and John C. Maraldo, eds. *Buddhism in the Modern World.* New York: Collier Books, 1976.

Robinson, Richard H., and Willard L. Johnson. *The Buddhist Religion: A Historical Introduction* (3rd ed.). Belmont, CA: Wadsworth Publishing Company, 1982.

Sizemore, Russell F., and Donald K. Swearer, eds. *Ethics, Wealth, and Salvation: A Study in Buddhist Social Ethics.* Columbia: University of South Carolina, 1990.

Bureaucracy

The term "bureaucracy" has different meanings. Perhaps most prevalent is the pejorative one of "red tape," that is, unnecessary complication, waste, inertia, and so on. Bureaucracy can also mean a form of government characterized by high-handed decision making by unaccountable officials, or it can refer to professional administrators as a distinct social group.

These meanings must be distinguished from the term "bureaucracy" used in a technical sense. Social scientists and historians employ the term to designate a special system of administration carried out continuously by salaried experts in accordance with written regulations. In this technical sense, the meaning of bureaucracy stems from the German sociologist Max Weber (1864–1920).

Max Weber on Bureaucracy

According to Weber (see Gerth and Mills, 1946, for a convenient summary), bureaucracy perfects administrative efficiency because it possesses the following, machinelike characteristics: (1) *Rules and records.* Bureaucracy operates in accordance with written laws or regulations and keeps records of its activities, which it performs on an impersonal basis according to the rules—professionally and routinely, without arbitrariness or favoritism. (2) *Defined responsibility.* Bureaucracy is concerned only with official business and obeys the principle of clearly defined jurisdictional and hierarchical competency (different areas of responsibility, a chain of command). Bureaucrats execute but do not formulate policy. (3) *Continuous operation.* Bureaucratic activity goes on indefinitely and provides officials with full-time, salaried careers and opportunities for regular advancement in exchange for loyalty to their office. (4) *Expert knowledge.* To be employed in a position of responsibility requires expert knowledge of the rules, a professional skill, or a combination of the two; it is typically demonstrated by examination.

Weber's definition of bureaucracy has endured to become the benchmark for two reasons. First, it is an abstract model rather than a description of any actual system of administration. Weber constructed this and other models, which he called "ideal types," roughly as one might draw a map or caricature—by consciously accentuating those features of a given subject that are relevant for purposes of orientation and interpretation. Thus, Weber's model is a device for creating conceptual clarity in light of certain values or goals, and serves to measure the discrepancy between norm and empirical reality. While methodologically controversial, this technique builds a bridge between sociology and history and has become a cornerstone of modern social history and historical sociology.

The second reason for the abiding relevance of Weber's definition is the world-historical interpretation to which his model relates. In as much as he considered it the ultimate human machine, Weber viewed fully developed bureaucracy as humankind's greatest organizational achievement and simultaneously as the attainment of complete dehumanization. Weber's fundamental preoccupation was his vision of the relentless bureaucratization and formal rationalization of all spheres of life in modern society, maximizing administrative efficiency but also threatening to result in a petrified social order without personal liberty or individual initiative. If not checked by some countervailing force, bureaucracy was liable to produce, in Weber's words, the "iron cage of future serfdom."

Weber conceived of world history as an eternal struggle between two principles of dynamism. One was charismatic innovation, exemplified best by great religious figures such as Buddha or Jesus. This type of visionary leader effects a fundamental reorientation of values, producing revolutionary power that challenges everyday reality and inspires new patterns of social organization. The other principle was the process of institutionalization and rationalization that results

when, for example, an organized priesthood begins to systematize the doctrines of a religious movement after the founder's death and sets itself up as the exclusive authority in doctrinal matters. In time this impulse produces a bureaucratic system of organization and a body of knowledge taught in schools, interpreted and developed in a consistent, rational manner by designated intellectual and administrative experts (e.g., the doctrines and hierarchy of the Roman Catholic church). The fundamental tendency of this impulse, especially in modern industrial society, is to eliminate all remaining sources of irrationality or unpredictability by extending the system's grasp evermore. Operating with mechanical perfection and tirelessness, bureaucracy also stifles freedom and creativity and fosters submissiveness. With regard to his own time, Weber conceded the theoretical possibility of new charismatic breakthroughs but feared bureaucracy was about to triumph permanently.

Weber's model and his apocalyptic vision of the world's fate spawned tremendous scholarly interest. To test the validity of his hypotheses, subsequent writers have investigated all imaginable aspects of bureaucracy. Despite new findings and broad agreement that his views need modification, Weber remains the starting point for studying the problems of bureaucracy. For the purposes of this discussion those problems may be divided into three parts: (1) the development of bureaucracy in Western society, (2) the limitations of Weber's model, and (3) the ethical and political problems of bureaucracy.

Historical Development of Bureaucracy

While bureaucracy in the private sector is a recent phenomenon, bureaucracy in government has a long history. The empires of ancient and medieval China and the Babylonian, Egyptian, Roman, Byzantine, and Ottoman empires all possessed administrative structures that included many features of bureaucracy. Appointment of the Chinese officials known as mandarins, for example, depended on examinations to prove qualification and followed a chain of command.

In Europe, bureaucracy goes back to attempts by early medieval kings to organize the duties of their household, which included the ruler's immediate military followers as well as family and servants, at a time when there was no clear distinction between personal and public service. Rulers appointed retainers to manage tasks such as procuring supplies, dealing with weapons, horses, among others. As the royal household grew larger and more complex and the king's territory increased in size, a separation occurred between the immediate household and the various governmental functions. This division of labor and the emergence of a distinction between public and personal functions is one of the two roots of modern bureaucracy.

The second root sprang from the problem of controlling administrative officials and maintaining power at the center. Royal service bestowed honor on officials, who in time developed into a lower nobility. Territorial expansion and functional specialization meant that officials frequently lived at a distance from the king, causing them to increase their independence. The absence of a money economy, the practice of rewarding service with hereditary grants of land, and difficult communications magnified this tendency toward autonomy and resulted in the growth of a landholding aristocracy that appropriated public duties for private gain. The ruler's consequent loss of authority prompted him to recruit new, more dependent and reliable officials, who in time followed in the footsteps of their predecessors. This resulted in alternating cycles of tightening and loosening royal control, the formation of different groups of officialdom and nobility, and fragmentation of sovereignty.

Rulers managed only gradually and imperfectly to overcome the problem. Sometimes they employed church officials, whose celibacy protected against the dynastic and territorial ambitions of the landholding aristocracy. Clerics' duty to the prince, however, conflicted with their loyalty to the church, which limited the usefulness of this administrative technique. Once the economy had become money based, kings sometimes delegated authority by selling governmental functions. This too was an imperfect solution, as it ended up creating a hereditary class of higher officeholders, such as the French *noblesse de robe* ("nobility of the robe"), a judicial aristocracy organized in *parlements* (provincial courts) that emerged in the 18th century as the most powerful opposition to royal absolutism.

The decisive step in the emergence of modern bureaucracy took place only when kings in their quest for loyal and dependent officials began to employ university-trained laymen on salary and subject to instant dismissal in positions of great power (e.g., the French *intendants*, or the Prussian *kommissarische Beamte*). The widespread use of such "commissars" evolved on the European continent between the 16th and 18th centuries. Since the late 18th century, this new type of administrative official managed once again to establish a degree of autonomy, through regularization of employment conditions, acquisition of tenure, civil-service regulations, fixed administrative procedures, and other devices to safeguard impartiality and curb the arbitrary powers of the king.

Despite a somewhat different lineage of bureaucracy in England and the United States, the 20th-century outcome in all Western societies is roughly the same. Everywhere, bureaucratization has produced social systems characterized by the power of centralized government, separation of public and private spheres, and government in accordance with written rules and laws. Public officials are in charge of administering the various tasks of government, such as defense, currency, social services, legal disputes, education, taxation, and so on.

Since the late 19th century, there has been an explosion of bureaucracy. This was the result of the industrial and technological revolutions, the spread of egalitarian-democratic values, and the emergence of mass society. The rise of business corporations after 1870 meant the growth of huge private-sector bureaucracies to invent, produce, market, and service products, while armies of bookkeepers and accountants keep track of costs and profits, and other business bureaucracies coordinate relations with government and labor. The latter in turn established new bureaucracies to respond to the numerous social, political, technical, and educational challenges associated with the rise of modern society and organized capitalism. Socialist experiments since World War I and the welfare state's takeoff after World War II have produced further massive waves of bureaucracy.

Limitations of Weber's Model

Modern scholarship on bureaucracy has identified a number of discrepancies between reality and Weber's model, two of which may be mentioned here. One pertains to Weber's thesis of bureaucracy's administrative efficiency. Empirical analysis of complex organizations suggests that adherence to the formal organizational structure may impede rather than promote efficiency. Strict hierarchy can restrict the flow of information from below, literal interpretation of the rules can produce rigidity, and tenure and seniority can cause stagnation. Conversely, it is often the existence of informal networks of communication within the system that eliminate friction, and personal relations between functionaries that permit smooth functioning.

A second problem concerns bureaucracy in private industry as opposed to government. Weber believed there was no difference between them in principle. Research has shown that bureaucracy in the private sector is primarily a system for the provision of goods and services, rather than the hierarchical system of domination that Weber emphasized. Private property, ownership, and survival in a competitive market also prevent private bureaucracies from developing secure tenure, appointment on the basis of educational certification, and promotion by seniority that Weber viewed as typical. These findings suggest that a single administrative model may not be appropriate for all organizations.

Ethical and Political Problems of Bureaucracy

The most intriguing question about bureaucracy relates to Weber's specter of modern society's relentless rationalization and the morally paralyzing consequences of that development. To what extent, if any, does bureaucratic administration engender a dehumanized system of formal rationality (a fully calculable, predictable, and routinized legal order), leading to a society of obedient subjects dominated by a privileged class of omnipotent but visionless officeholders? Scholars do not agree, and there is evidence both for and against Weber's scenario.

On one side, authors point to the numerous instances of bureaucratic petrification, arrogance of bureaucrats, and enslaving powers of bureaucracy to prove the validity of Weber's interpretation. A crucial economic problem of contemporary Western society, for example, is the seemingly iron logic with which small firms led by charismatic inventor-entrepreneurs gradually become huge, stagnating bureaucracies that fall behind technologically and can no longer provide leadership. Another major problem of contemporary civilization is the authority of unaccountable professional experts and administrators, against which lay supervision often stands powerless, as in the impenetrability and substantive irrationalities of bureaucratized medical care in the modern welfare state. As for the morally debilitating consequences of bureaucracy, it may be noted that treatments of the Jewish Holocaust in World War II often center on the dehumanizing effects of bureaucratic administration. With its twin corollaries of specialization and division of labor bureaucracy created the obedience, the psychological and physical distancing, and the attenuation of individual responsibility that made genocide possible.

On the other side, social historians and other scholars point to the fact that bureaucracy is not the monolithic automaton Weber claimed. Modern society has many different and conflicting bureaucracies that engage in mutual bargaining with unpredictable outcome. Bureaucrats can develop conflicting professional, political, and class loyalties that create freedom of choice and affect the policies of their employing organizations. There are also various ways of securing political control over bureaucracy, such as the system of dual political and bureaucratic appointments in the former Soviet Union, and the political appointment of top bureaucrats, open-access policies, and citizen participation in democratic societies. In the end, this argument goes, the rational calculability of modern bureaucratic society as a whole is no greater than it was in the prebureaucratic age, and Weber's iron cage has never materialized.

In conclusion, bureaucracy is a more equivocal phenomenon than Weber maintained. Weber's views were influenced both by the authoritarian context of imperial Germany and by the prevailing mechanical metaphors of technology of his time, and he overemphasized the machinelike qualities of bureaucracy. Although he overrated bureaucracy's dangers and lack of flexibility, Weber correctly identified many of its inherent tendencies, and his pairing of charisma and bureaucracy as alternating sources of dynamism in society has universal applicability. (*See also* Elites; Modernization; State and Society)

Kees Gispen

REFERENCES

Gerth, H.H., and C. Wright Mills, eds, trans., intr. *From Max Weber: Essays in Sociology.* New York: Oxford University Press, 1946.

Mommsen, Wolfgang J. *The Political and Social Theory of Max Weber.* Chicago: University of Chicago Press, 1989.

Rosenberg, Hans. *Bureaucracy, Aristocracy, and Autocracy: The Prussian Experience, 1660–1815.* Boston: Beacon Press, 1958.

Torstendahl, Rolf. *Bureaucratisation in Northwestern Europe, 1880–1985.* London and New York: Routledge, 1991.

Capitalism

The study of the social history of capitalism has produced an uneven, often wildly clashing scholarship rooted in theoretical disagreement over what capitalism is. Following Werner Sombart and sociologist Max Weber, two seminal German scholars of the late 19th century, one school has traced the growth of the capitalist "spirit" of economic rationality, enterprise, and profit seeking. A second group has shifted emphasis from business attitudes to commercial organization, identifying capitalism as a process of money-based trade for the purpose of profit. A third camp, working in the tradition of Karl Marx, focuses upon social relations of production as defining or specifically viewing capitalism as a mode of production in which labor power itself becomes a commodity, purchased for the purpose of creating surplus value.

The distinctive features of these three definitions—profit-mindedness, markets, or exploitation—tailor the time span and geographic range historians of capitalism might examine in sharply contrasting forms. Ultimately, too, Weberian analysts have tended to subsume the study of capitalism under the rubric of intellectual and cultural history, while the market approach claims the subject for economic history. Although most closely boundaried in terms of time and space, the Marxist perspective has understood capitalism most clearly as social history. In practice, however, these sharp distinctions have blurred considerably. Variant political agendas and moral assumptions have added complexity and confusion. In recent decades, also, scholars have often blithely mixed and matched elements of these warring perspectives, often in the name of progressive "synthesis," with widely variant individual results. Collectively, the upshot has been either the generation of a rich variety of innovative studies, or, depending on one's perspective, a mongrelized muddle.

Certainly nothing like a broad interpretation of capitalism's social history has gained wide acceptance. Scholars have even failed to agree on the proper focus for study: individual, household, community, class, nation, or world–system. Since the 1940s, however, historians have concentrated attention on several broad questions concerning capitalism: its social origins, its effects upon material well-being and consciousness, its relations with other modes of production within a social formation, and the response of communities and classes to its rise and triumph.

Until the mid-1970s, the basic features of capitalism's emergence, describing an "industrial revolution" that grew up first in England and France, then swept across North America and western Europe, gained general assent. The material changes that the coming of this factory system wrought focused debate. On one hand, Eric Hobsbawm and others suggested that Marx and Friedrich Engels had been correct to denounce a falling standard of living among British laboring families. Marshaling variant statistics, the economic historian T.S. Ashton led the charge to refute these claims, without great success. This standoff among British historians was replicated in the work of Americanist Stephan Thernstrom, whose pioneering quantitative study of a late 19th-century Massachusetts town found native-born workers achieving tangible material progress, especially home ownership, while immigrants seemed stuck in poverty after years of labor. A host of ethnicity-oriented case studies has refined but essentially confirmed this native/immigrant split, though antebellum studies, led by Edward Pessen, have tended to paint a darker picture of capitalism's benefits to American workers. With publication of Edward Thompson's seminal *The Making of the English Working Class* in 1963, emphasis among British and North American scholars shifted toward understanding workers not as passive objects—beneficiaries or victims of capitalism—but as actors exerting some control over their own collective destiny; theoretically shielded from the empiricist assumptions of this tendency, Continental European historians have been slower to adopt its voluntarist perspective.

Beginning in the early 1960s, a pair of debates over capitalism's origins diverted attention from the increasingly technical wrangling over its material effects. In contrast to industrial revolution analysis, these debates focused on earlier periods of capitalism. In a mostly intramural contest among Marxists aligned with Maurice Dobb (1947) and Paul Sweezy, respectively, historians and political economists argued past each other for more than two decades over whether shifts in productive relations or in exchange—particularly long-distance trade—played the dominant role in unleashing capitalism. The outcome was both pregnant and exhausting. A theoretically broader argument over the causes and character of the so-called crisis of the 17th century, which Hobsbawm, Christopher Hill, and others claimed laid the foundations for capitalist expansion, replicated the older claims of the causal power of profit-mindedness, market expansion, and exploitative production. Most recently, Eugene Genovese and Elizabeth Fox-Genovese (1983), and Robert Brenner have attempted to redress the balance between these tendencies, deepening analysis of the peculiar nature and power of merchant capital, at which Marx and Dobb had only hinted. Several detailed studies on the origins of 18th- and 19th-century industrial capitalists in England contribute some specifics on the emergence of capitalism—its leaders and its culture—from a social history standpoint.

In his stimulating 1944 study *Capitalism and Slavery*, Caribbeanist Eric Williams opened the door to these widening arguments, claiming that New World slavery had provided the financial and productive basis for Old World capitalism. Eurocentric scholars battered Williams's sometimes reckless assertions, but in broad outline a toned-down version of his thesis has survived. Bolstered by the impressive quantitative research of Jacob Price, Jan de Vries, and Philip Curtin, among others, an "Atlantic perspective" on capitalist growth gained strength in the 1970s. Just how best to examine this expanding capitalist sphere, however, remained in doubt. Fernand Braudel's celebrated *Civilization and Capitalism* ranged even beyond the Atlantic, delineating the structure of capitalism's rise and early development in *pointilliste* fashion across three centuries; his perspective virtually annihilated the concept of social class, however, and tended to obscure whatever the general dynamic of expansion might have been. Viewing this world from the other end of the telescope, Pierre and Huguette Chaunu's daunting multi-volume study of Seville and the Atlantic achieved surprisingly similar results. Emphasizing exchange over production relations, sociologist Immanuel Wallerstein's "world–systems" approach (1980) has found capitalists and proletarians in the most far-flung corners of the globe, tied into an increasingly integrated web of trade. Case studies by Philip McMichael, among others, have edged this perspective back toward more traditionally Marxist ground. Most successful, perhaps, has been anthropologist Eric Wolf's *Europe and the People Without History*, a synthetic, elliptical vindication of the Marxian approach, without its Eurocentric emphasis.

At the same time that British, French, and American scholars were widening the scope of study, however, central European historians tightened the focus in their search of capitalism's origins. Concentrating on demographic and capital shifts, technological changes, and alterations in productive relations at the state, community, and even household level, Hans Medick, Franklin Mendels, and others (1981) described a complex process called "protoindustrialization." Capitalism's growth, it turned out, was not a progressive, linear tale of industrialization, urbanization, and the rise of a waged working class. As research charting regional depopulation, deindustrialization, and more complicated transition to proletarian status has piled up, the classic English model of capitalist growth has come to seem increasingly atypical, if not downright mistaken. Among North American scholars, the protoindustrialist argument has had little impact, though Joan Jensen, Christopher Clark, and others have sketched case studies congenial to this viewpoint, minus the theory and most of the quantitative research.

The problem of social and economic linkage or "articulation" between capitalist and noncapitalist modes of production had also generated considerable controversy. Although scholars such as Wallerstein and André Gunder Frank have tended to collapse these distinctions at the point of exchange, anthropological studies like Pierre-Phillipe Rey's *Les alliances de classes* have sketched out dynamics and structural permutations in ways social historians are only beginning to explore, a host of young Latin Americanists leading the way. Perhaps the most

vigorous recent debate over the question of linkage, however, has centered on the slave economy of the antebellum American South. Focusing on productive relations and cultural achievements, by 1918 Ulrich Phillips analyzed a noncapitalist South bound to clash with the capitalist North sooner or later; agricultural historian Lewis Gray countered with a portrait of a rationalized, profit-minded plantation society essentially at peace with the rest of the nation and the industrializing world. By the mid-1970s, the cliometricians Robert Fogel and Stanley Engerman had taken Gray's argument seemingly as far as it could go, even describing slaves as imbued with a close-calculating Protestant work ethic. Steven Hahn and others, however, countered just as oddly, asserting that antebellum southern small farmers were actually market-fearing noncapitalist yeomen. Amid a growing body of local case studies with surprising claims, the central question of articulation has become virtually lost, except in the work of Genovese and Fox-Genovese. Similar difficulties have arisen in other areas of American, Canadian, and European social history examining agricultural change and its implications for rural capitalist practices and attitudes at the community level. Greater attention to the debates between such rural sociologists as Weberian Patrick Mooney and Marxists Susan Mann and James Dickinson, or among agricultural economists weighing A.V. Chayanov's ideas against those of V.I. Lenin on the character of peasant economy may help resolve these problems.

All of these important issues, however, have been largely neglected by social historians over the past two decades—even and especially those of a leftist persuasion. Overwhelmingly, scholarship has focused on rewriting the history of those who lived under capitalism, recapturing individual and community experience, restoring human agency, celebrating the worlds working people made for themselves within industrial society. Building upon the work of Thompson in England and Herbert Gutman (1976) in the United States, "radical" historians have redrawn Marx's concept of class along subjectivist lines, discovering a proud heritage of struggle in virtually all corners of culture and community. By 1976, Fox-Genovese and Genovese had pronounced this literature a "bourgeois swindle" and denounced it for creating a "political crisis of social history." This scholarship, they charged, routinely sidestepped or shortchanged what they saw as the central question of social history: "who rides who and how." Their critique availed little, however, and the flood of case studies has continued unabated. While social historians of capitalism have guided their readers through every imaginable aspect of working- and middle-class culture and community from sports to foodways to fashion to shoplifting, even the minority who have focused on social relations at the point of production have tended to deflect attention from capitalism's great punch line, that the working classes have always made their own lives within parameters capital's overwhelming power has self-servingly permitted, and that their puny wriggling has done little to reshape those parameters objectively or extricate them from its grip. Patrick Joyce, Bryan Palmer, David Montgomery, and Walter Rodney are among labor historians who have intermittently resisted this tendency. The recent success of the American Social History Project's textbook and video series *Who Built America?* suggests that the celebration of culture and community will remain in vogue, if toned down, for the foreseeable future.

Despite its misplaced emphasis, this new literature has undeniably added a wealth of information—some trivial, some vital—to our understanding of what shaped capitalism and what capitalism shaped. Recent work on demography, fertility, and social relations of reproduction by David Levine and others (1989) seems especially valuable. Yet combining these disparate shards of experience into a synthetic history of capitalism remains difficult. We know now, for example, far less about bosses than about workers, far more about those who defended community than those who sold it out for individual benefits. Not only are Anglo-American, French, and central European scholars addressing different questions, using different methods, under different assumptions, but most are proceeding cross-culturally blinkered and with outmoded interdisciplinary techniques. As we grope forward, questions become smaller, methods become "softer." Greater attention needs to be paid to the stimulating literature focusing on capitalism in Third World countries, especially India, southern Africa, Oceana, and Latin America, which has profitably transcended internecine squabbles over imperialism, underdevelopment, and dependency theory. Increased dialogue across the social sciences may also provide greater theoretical clarity and rigor. Like capitalism itself, such developments will be painful, crisis ridden, but highly productive. (*See also* Protoindustrialization; Slavery; Standard of Living)

Lawrence T. McDonnell

REFERENCES

Dobb, Maurice. *Studies in the Development of Capitalism.* New York: International Publishers, 1947.

Fox-Genovese, Elizabeth, and Eugene D. Genovese. *Fruits of Merchant Capital: Slavery and Bourgeois Property in the Rise and Expansion of Capitalism.* New York: Oxford University Press, 1983.

Gutman, Herbert G. *Work, Culture, and Society in Industrializing America: Essays in American Working-Class and Social History.* New York: Pantheon Books, 1976.

Kriedte, Peter, Hans Medick, and Jurgen Schlumbohm. *Industrialization Before Industrialization: Rural Industry in the Genesis of Capitalism.* Cambridge: Cambridge University Press, 1981.

Wallerstein, Immanuel. *The Modern World-System,* 2 vols. New York: Academic Press, 1974, 1980.

Caste System

In general usage, caste system refers to a rigid social hierarchy in which members of a caste are born by birth and from which individuals and families cannot move up because of tight legal and social restrictions. It can be compared with other systems of social inequality, particularly those marked by legal barriers among social groups. A number of social systems have approximated the characteristics of caste, in several periods and areas. The system is most clearly applied to the social history of India, however, where social history and anthropology have revealed a number of complications in any overrigid definition.

"Caste" is the word (derived from the Portuguese *casta*) used in Western writing to describe several kinds of social categories in Hindu South Asia. The term sometimes appears as a translation of *varna.* The earliest Indian religious texts, composed approximately 1000 BC, spoke of four varnas, that is, four categories of people generated from the sacrifice of Purusa, the primal man. *Brahmins,* generated from the mouth of Purusa, are the highest varna, whose *dharma,* or inborn moral code, is to teach the religious texts (the *Vedas*) and to perform sacrifices for and receive gifts from the two varnas ranking just below them. *Kshatriyas* were said to be born from the arms of Purusa. As warriors and kings, possessors of royal power, their dharma is to protect the kingdom and the people within it, and to give gifts to Brahmins. *Vaishyas,* born from the thighs of Purusa and ranking below the Kshatriya, were enjoined to produce wealth for their own enjoyment and for that of the kingdom as a whole. The lowest varna in this textual formulation was the *Shudra,* whose dharma is to serve the three highest varnas. These varnas are ranked, with Brahmins at the apex of the hierarchy, yet the ritual and political centrality of the royal caste, at the level of the kingdom in pre-British India, or the dominant landholding Kshatriya castes at the level of the village, is an equally significant aspect of southern Asian social thought and social practices. As givers of ritual gifts and sponsors of ritual events, king and dominant caste *jajmans* (sacrificers) are seen as protectors of the well-being and prosperity of the kingdom or village. Both the hierarchical superiority of the Brahman priest and the ritual role of the king or village jajman are important aspects of the indigenous conceptualization of caste society; historians and anthropologists are currently debating the relative significance of hierarchy and royal power in caste systems.

While this varna classification continued to provide a fundamental template for thinking about the social and moral bases of society, social categories termed *jatis* (for which the term "caste" is also used) provided the most immediate and compelling social and moral identities. Discussions of jati (from the Sanskrit word for birth) first appeared in Hindu texts dating from approximately 200 BC. The thousands of jatis existing at that time and in contemporary South Asia were seen in those texts as resulting from intermarriages among men and women of different varnas.

Like the duties incumbent upon the four varnas, jati obligations too are generally seen as a matter of one's dharma, or inborn code for conduct. Individual jatis are frequently named in terms of specific caste occupations. In most Indian villages, for example, one finds such jatis as Barber, Sweeper, Carpenter, Brahmin Priest, Ironsmith, Washerman, Leatherworker, and, frequently, a landholding agricultural caste held to be representative of the Kshatriya varna and wielding political and economic power in the village. These traditional occupations are hereditary, though people of many castes in the village may in fact work primarily as agricultural laborers. Hereditary occupational tasks are frequently performed by the various castes for the dominant landholders of the village, in return for which they typically receive some share of the landholder's harvest yields, as well as payments for specific caste-related ritual services throughout the year. Prior to British rule in India, such a system of exchange of goods and services for a share of the harvest extended far beyond the village, including even a share of the harvest paid to the king. The introduction of a market in land, widespread cash-cropping, and increasing urban orientation has led to a decline in the significance of these exchange relationships among castes in contemporary India, though in many villages significant remnants remain as important aspects of everyday village life.

Jati identity is maintained by very potent rules concerning endogamy and food etiquette. Marriages are almost always arranged within the caste, and a complex set of restrictions concerning the giving and receiving of food ensures that meals are shared either within the caste or from higher-ranking castes. These considerations are grounded in the fundamental Hindu assumption that moral, social, and cosmic order are all dependent on the maintenance of dharma, the specific inborn code for conduct appropriate to one's caste. Because dharma is viewed as inherent in the bodily nature of the various castes, transformations in that bodily nature brought about by intermarriage and intercaste sharing of food may be viewed as a threat to the moral order of society. Lower castes, however, frequently seek to improve their moral natures, and their caste standing, by modifying their dietary practices, marriage patterns, and ritual practices to conform more closely to higher caste practices.

Western historical, Indological, and anthropological writing, and the British imperial writings from which later academic views took shape, frequently depict caste as an unchanging and essential feature of the Indian landscape, as an institution that has endured as an unquestioned foundation of southern Asian Hindu society. Such a formulation is problematic for several reasons. First, social historians are now concerned with the issue of how British rule profoundly altered the nature of caste ideology and intercaste relations, arguing that much of what social scientists have characterized as "traditional" India is in fact an artifact of colonial rule. And second, though the relationship between caste and dharma has indeed been a fundamental aspect of Hindu social thought, caste ideology has been subject to intense indigenous scrutiny and critique throughout history. As they are documented from the late 19th and early 20th centuries, myths of the origin of caste told by people of lower castes, unlike those told by upper castes, frequently contest the moral basis of the hierarchical order of caste society. And as early as AD 1000 in southern India, and a few centuries later in northern India, poets of the *bhakti* devotional movements of Hinduism saw dharma not in terms of an inborn and caste-based moral order, but in terms of a devotional relationship with god. Their poetry rejected the orthodox ritual forms of Hinduism and frequently questioned the caste divisions that underlie them. Some of this poetry, such as that of Ravidas, a 15th-century low caste (untouchable) Leatherworker poet, has found a place in contemporary demands for social reform.

Demands for legal, educational, and social reforms have been widespread since the mid-19th century. Under British rule in the mid-20th century, a certain percentage of seats in legislative bodies were to be reserved for untouchables, those people of jatis ranking below even the *Shudras*. The constitution of India, passed in 1950, made illegal any public discrimination against untouchables. Legislation since then has extended the policy of reservations, and widespread and sometimes violent public debate in 1990 about the extension of reservations to many other low castes indicates both the legacy of colonial policy and the uncertainty of the course of future change. While the ritual, occupational, and commensal aspects of caste are becoming somewhat less salient in contemporary village India and considerably weakened in urban India, caste-based political associations continue to exist both as vehicles for the assertion of low caste rights and as voting blocs and political interest groups for the higher castes in both rural and urban areas. (*See also* South Asian Colonialism, Stratification and Inequality)

Gloria Goodwin Raheja

REFERENCES

Dirks, Nicholas B. *The Hollow Crown: Ethnohistory of an Indian Kingdom.* Cambridge: Cambridge University Press, 1988.

Dumont, Louis. *Homo Hierarchicus.* Chicago: University of Chicago Press, 1970.

Hawley, John Stratton, and Mark Juergensmeyer. *Songs of the Saints of India.* New York and Oxford: Oxford University Press, 1988.

Prakash, Gyan. "Becoming a Bhuinya: Oral Traditions and Contested Domination in Eastern India," in Douglas Haynes and Gyan Prakash, eds., *Contesting Power: Resistance and Everyday Social Relations in South Asia.* Berkeley: University of California Press, 1991, pp. 145–174.

Raheja, Gloria Goodwin. *The Poison in the Gift: Ritual, Prestation, and the Dominant Caste in a North Indian Village.* Chicago: University of Chicago Press, 1988.

Caudillismo

The term "caudillismo," in the broadest sense, refers to the early 19th-century Latin American experience of militarist and regionalist political strife. Caudillismo erupted between the breakdown of the Spanish Colonial Empire in the 1820s and the consolidation of stable elite nation-states by the 1870s. Sometimes, the term is taken to mean this half-century historical period itself or (in adjectival form, "caudillistic") to describe varied social or political aspects of 19th-century instability. With varying intensity and timing, all the new republics suffered stretches of caudillistic internal warfare, with the important exceptions of Chile and Brazil. Yet unlike the massively destructive U.S. Civil War, caudillismo was generally an intermittent and low-level form of armed conflict.

The term derives from "caudillo," the era's dominant form of political leadership. The caudillos were military strongmen, who raised irregular or provincial armies on the basis of personal charisma or personalistic rewards to followers. In terms of political style, machismo and authoritative personality appear more typical of caudillo politics than finely articulated political ideals, aims, or constituencies. In fact, the majority of caudillo takeovers were simple barracks revolts or *golpes de estado* (coups). The eruption of caudillo struggles in the 1820s foiled early attempts to instill parliamentary rule or rule of law in the initial Latin American republics. Instead, countless infamous and obscure military chiefs stamped the era's turbulent political history. Notable figures include Juan Manuel de Rosas (Argentina's ruthless general of gauchos), Antonio López de Santa Anna (who irregularly served as Mexican executive some 11 times between 1821 and 1855), Agustín Gamarra (the conservative from Andean Peru), and José Antonio Paez (Venezuela's powerful initial strongman).

Recent work, however, veers from misleadingly general psychological, individual, or cultural definitions of caudillismo. This work relates the phenomenon more loosely to sociohistorical findings on Latin America. First, literally thousands of caudillo types emerged across 19th-century America, ranging from august members of the professional officer corps (loyal to centralized bodies and interests such as the church) to extremely ephemeral and localized political bosses, militia chiefs, and bandits—social or otherwise. Such diversity defies general analysis of caudillos as social type. Second, overgeneralization breeds ahistorical usage; thus, while journalistic reference to 20th-century populist or military politicians as "caudillos" is common, these men on horseback draw power from quite modern political ideologies or party organizations. Historians prefer a systemic view of caudillismo, but limited to specific 19th-century conditions and time frames.

Social history research on caudillismo remains in its infancy, for the chaotic postindependence era is the least studied in Latin American history. Several approaches or models exist, however, to explain caudillismo in clearer terms than the traditional "Latin inability to rule themselves." Most generally, historians suppose that caudillismo somehow reflected the ruralization of many Latin American societies as aftermath of political independence, or reflected their violent assertion of new forms of regional and ethnic identity. Others stress the postcolonial ruling elites' feeble civil hegemony, unity, and vision; the consequent breakdown of initial constitutionalist formulas left the power vacuum filled by multifarious military chiefs. A more precise model by anthropologist Eric Wolf links caudillismo to the individualistic and anarchic character of emerging *mestizo* (mixed-race) cultures. Caudillos were highly competitive mobilizers of rootless mestizos, able to forge a lucrative redistributive economy of plunder until the advent of more stabilizing export economies after 1850. Historian William Beezley, on the other hand, depicts caudillismo as an outgrowth of colonial corporate authority principles. In the absence of a unifying foreign king, caudillos arose as the most legitimate political actors for mediating the disparate group interests of Spanish American society. In short, there is no social scientific consensus on the causes and nature of caudillismo, nor should there be, given its remarkable variety.

Recent social history sheds light on many facets of caudillismo. Some historians have explored the popular roots, affinities, or mobilizations of caudillos—for example, their ties to various peasantries, dubbing some as quasi-democratic "folk" politicians. Others trace the origins of caudillismo in the novel late-imperial militarization of previously unmilitarized colonies, and the rapid expansion and fragmentation of these militias during the region's prolonged independence struggles of 1808–1824. A few historians challenge the apolitical image of caudillos, by piecing together their ruling projects and regional or social constituents, for example, in the regional struggles between protectionist and free trade parties. Quantitative studies computerize the frequency and composition of revolts, using these data to test broader theories about Latin American instability. A major new concern is the social impact of instability—for instance, the effects upon traditional agrarian or caste structures. Caudillismo tended to weaken colonial social barriers. Finally, social historians are focusing increasingly on the eclipse of caudillismo after 1850. They are probing the social coalitions behind the region's new centralizing states and how these worked to absorb or suppress the free-wheeling caudillo heritage. For later "order and progress" regimes, reacting against caudillismo though not necessarily its authoritarian strain, became the lasting legacy of Latin America's troubled postcolonial experience.

Paul Gootenberg

REFERENCES

Callcott, Wilfrid. *Santa Anna: The Story of an Enigma Who Once Was Mexico.* Tulsa: University of Oklahoma Press, 1936.

Gootenberg, Paul. *Between Silver and Guano: Commercial Policy and the State in Postindependence Peru.* Princeton, NJ: Princeton University Press, 1989.

Lynch, John. *Argentine Dictator: Juan Manuel de Rosas, 1829–1852.* Oxford: Clarendon Press, 1981.

Sarmiento, Domingo F. *Life in the Argentine Republic in the Days of the Tyrants, or Civilization and Barbarism.* New York: Hafner, 1960.

Stevens, Donald. *Origins of Instability in Early Republican Mexico.* Durham: Duke University Press, 1991.

Causation

Historians dealt with issues of causation long before the rise of social history. Social history adds certain emphases concerning causation, but there is no single sociohistorical approach. Exploring what causes change can indeed join social and other historians in creating new syntheses about the past and about periodization. At the same time—and again like historians generally—many social historians concentrate on describing phenomena in the past, even in tracing changes, without directly exploring causation. Often, causes are handled implicitly or incompletely, which further prevents any claims to a sociohistorical mode of causal analysis.

Determining causation in history is inherently imprecise. In contrast to the physical sciences, where causation can be proved through repeated experiments in which a given cause uniformly yields a given result, social changes are never exactly repeated. Each instance of change has some factors unique to itself. Hence, absolutely proving historical causation is impossible, as opposed to identifying the causes most probably involved. The sources of information that demonstrate change from protest manifestoes to material artifacts do not directly show why the changes were occurring. Despite the limitations, analytical historians usually deal with causation. When they define distinct time periods, they point to the causes of breaks in patterns; they try to "tease" explanations of change from their source materials. To the extent that this use of social history has encouraged a more analytical approach to the past, it has advanced attention to problems of causation. Many social historians try to figure out why new trends develop—why birth rates drop in the modern demographic transition, for example—and also why some behavior patterns persist even amid other change. Particularly after the first phase of social history, in which basic descriptive patterns were set forth concerning protest, or mobility, or demography, interest in causation has grown.

Social historians characteristically downplay certain possible causes. They do not assume that a new king or a new president causes major social change, which is why, increasingly, social history periods differ from the most conventional political markers. New regimes may promote new social patterns, but the causation issues must be investigated, not assumed.

Neither do social historians give great weight to individual great men or great thinkers as causing major social change. One of the key problems in relating fields such as diplomatic history to social history results from the clash over causation. Most diplomatic historians, looking to events, assess the actions and motives of individual statesmen or, at most, elite groups such as the diplomatic corps. Social historians are only beginning to venture a sense of social and cultural patterns that offer alternative causation for basic diplomatic initiatives, including willingness to go to war or policies that treat certain foreign countries as particularly inferior.

If social historians play down the importance of individuals in causing major change, they play up the causal role of various social groups. While a few social historians see a group as totally victimized by the power of an elite or by elite-dominated social structures, most social historians see even theoretically powerless groups, like slaves, as helping to shape their social environment and even causing some of the behaviors of more powerful groups—like slaveowners. Interactive causation, in which social patterns emerge from the efforts and beliefs of many groups, forms social history's most distinctive contribution to the analysis of historical change. Most efforts to argue that an upper-class group simply caused a new behavior—such as new treatment of children in 18th-century Europe—that then gradually trickles down to cause comparable innovations on the lower classes ultimately runs afoul of more sophisticated social historical analysis. Thus, similar kinds of family changes may reflect not only upper-class influence but also distinct lower-class traditions and motivations.

Multigroup causation definitely applies to the impact of new laws, like the child labor laws of the 19th century. Social historians agree that laws are usually administered differently from professed intent, according to class and gender factors, and that subordinate groups usually affect the ways laws are applied to them. Laws may play an important role in causation, but they are mediated by the interactions among the various social groups involved.

Besides attention to multigroup causation, social historians grapple with priorities among various structures that might cause change. How important is the state? Social historians are now more interested in assessing the state's role in causing change than they were in recent decades, but only some social historians routinely look to political factors first. Many would also argue that the state's role in causing social change varies greatly according to time and place, and according to the group and behavior involved. Economic structures are usually given great attention in explaining social changes, including behaviors seemingly as distant from economics as treatment of children or the elderly. One bold historian-sociologist, Charles Tilly, has argued that all major social trends in western Europe since about 1600 can be traced to two major structural changes: the rise of commercial capitalism and the emergence of the nation-state.

Since 1980 attention to cultural causation has gained ground. Changes in beliefs prepare new economics or political habits. Growth of literacy and new kinds of dissemination of ideas help explain the nature and force of cultural change. By the 1990s the new cultural history school might argue that language and culture alone determined (or "constructed") social patterns, though this view was contested by other social historians on grounds of the importance of power structures (including physical force) or the normal interplay among various kinds of causation in generating significant social change.

Many social historians continue to debate the relationship between cultural causation and structural causation of other sorts. Did a new interest in consumerism or a new sense of time result from the economic and technological changes of the industrial revolution or, as many British social historians have argued in dealing with the earlier 18th century, were they initially shaped by new beliefs and values that helped prepare the industrial revolution itself?

Social historians have long sought to look beneath the pronouncements of policymakers in exploring changes such as the rise of asylums for the mentally ill or attacks on the slave trade around 1800. Social historians believe that real causation is usually more complex than the proposed motives of humanitarians or others reformers. Some look simply to structural change: the decline of community and the growth rate of state power required new institutions to deal with deviance. The rise of industrial wage labor revealed the unprofitability of slavery and so brought movements to end the slave trade. Other social historians, however, argue for cultural factors as well. Various groups developed a new sensitivity to the afflictions of others—a new humanitarianism—and also saw in antislavery campaigns a new means of gaining greater political voice. Middle-class culture, gaining an increased stake in beliefs about rationalism and self-control, saw in institutionalization a genuine means of curing some unfortunates but also an essential removal of the unfortunate from normal social intercourse. In debates over the causes of antislavery or the asylum movement, social historians continue to disagree fiercely. They do, however, urge that pronouncements of individual leaders cannot be taken at face value in explaining change. Even when new beliefs are involved, they are more complex than the justifications officially, sometimes perhaps sincerely, offered at the time.

Social historians have not theorized very generally about causation. They leave the most systematic issues to philosophy or social theory. They characteristically reject or complicate some kinds of causation, used earlier by many historians—such as the "great man" approach to explanation. A few have opted for a single, determining kind of cause—like technology, economic structure, or, more recently, cultural discourse—but most have preferred a mixture of causation in exploring development of new demographic patterns (change in the economic roles of children but also new beliefs about family goals) or new protest forms (changes in expectations about the state, but also traditional values juxtaposed to a new organization of work). In exploring complex causation, interaction among groups and insistence on looking beneath the surface of policy claims constitute characteristic sociohistorical impulses in causation analysis. Beyond this, concerning a host of specific social changes in every society and period, debate and dispute continue, and at best help sharpen the quest for the most probable causation combinations in social history. (*See also* Asylums; Cultural History; Emancipation)

Peter N. Stearns

REFERENCES

Bryan, Palmer. *Descent into Discourse.* Philadelphia: Temple University Press, 1990.

Genovese, Eugene D. *Roll Jordan Roll: The World the Slaves Made.* New York: Random House, 1976.

Rothman, David. *Discovery of the Asylum: Social Order and Disorder in the New Republic,* Vol. 1. Boston: Little, Brown, 1990.

Tilly, Charles. *Big Structures, Large Processes, Huge Comparisons.* New York: Russel Sage, 1985.

Cemeteries

Cemeteries constitute one of the kinds of physical constructions that social historians use to interpret a major facet of society—in this case, the values and behaviors associated with death. Cemeteries, studied both in western Europe and the United States, have changed considerably over time. In the European Middle Ages they were located close to churches where people would pass by as part of everyday life. This pattern, implying acceptance but also a constant reminder of death, continued in colonial America. Early in the 19th century, however, a garden cemetery movement began. Cemeteries were not so centrally located, and they were rendered less stark by lush plantings. Death, still accepted, was now supposed to be surrounded by evocative sentiment and a kind of bittersweet grief; cemeteries, reflecting this feeling, were places to visit recurrently, though no longer part of daily life. Later in the 19th century, along with other changes such as lifelike embalming of dead bodies, cemeteries were located still farther from urban centers, and by the 20th century they were sometimes supplemented or even displaced by crematoria. Death was becoming a facet of life largely to shun.

Along with the location of cemeteries, the styles of funeral monuments indicate beliefs about death, religion, and the individual self. In the 19th century, middle-class monuments became increasingly grandiose. This reflected growing affluence and a desire to impress one's neighbors, as well as the new emphasis on public grief. Death, still common before old age, now evoked a new guilt, as people worried that they had somehow failed a family member who died; striking monuments reflected this as well. In the 20th century new controversies arose about this kind of emotion and expense, and monuments were on the whole scaled down—or in the case of cremations, eliminated. Again, material culture provides an entry into the dramatically changing approach to an inevitable human experience. (*See also* Architecture; Death; Material Culture)

Peter N. Stearns

REFERENCES

Ariès, Philippe. *The Hour of Our Death.* New York: Random House, 1981.

Farrell, James J. *Inventing the American Way of Death 1830-1920.* Philadelphia: Temple University Press, 1980.

Houlbrooke, Ralph. *Death, Ritual, and Bereavement.* London: Routledge in Association with the Social History Society of the United Kingdom, 1989.

Stannard, David, ed. *The American Way of Death.* Philadelphia: University of Pennsylvania Press, 1975.

Census

A census is a complete count of a population, most commonly of people in some political entity—for example, a nation-state, province, or local government jurisdiction. The term is currently used in contrast to "sample," which connotes a count of representative elements of a population—either through the use of a probability or a judgment sample.

The term "census" originated in Roman times, and then implied a count of a population liable for taxation or military conscription. Such censuses were generally limited to a count of adult male citizens, or economically active members of a community. The modern complete count census of all persons of a population dates from the late 18th and early 19th centuries and begins in the nation-states in western Europe and North America.

Over time, these efforts have become more elaborate. Early censuses were rather simple counts of the numbers of people in each household of a political jurisdictions, classified by sex and age cohorts. Currently, censuses collect information of dozens of individual characteristics and tabulate and publish the results in multivolume government reports, computer tapes, and CD-ROM disks. In recent years, governments have made available machine readable samples of the censuses for private researchers to use for further analysis.

The uses of censuses vary by political jurisdiction. In the United States, for example, the 1787 Constitution mandated a decennial population count to apportion membership in the House of Representatives among the states. Theoretically, political authority was seen to derive from the people and hence required a population count. Many nations have adopted this one-person, one-vote principle, as it has come to be named. Other governments have used censuses to allocate the tax burden among the population or, more recently, grants-in-aid from one unit of government to another—particularly from the central to the local.

Censuses also form the baseline data used worldwide by social scientific researchers, including social historians studying economic and demographic growth and change, political mobilization, and stratification. Much of this research is historical and comparative. At the turn of the 20th century, about 43 percent of the world's population could be accounted from data in about 68 separate censuses. Since World War II about 150 to 180 censuses are taken each decade, encompassing about two-thirds of the world's population.

Enumeration methods vary by country and include house-to-house enumerations conducted by government-appointed officials, or self-enumeration—for example, with a mail census. In recent years, a large technical literature has developed evaluating census accuracy, analyzing coverage and data quality, considering data confidentiality, and recommending methods for data improvement. Issues of data adequacy affect social historians' use of censuses, but the great value of this source for modern periods remains uncontested.

Margo Anderson

REFERENCES

Alonso, William, and Paul Starr, eds. *The Politics of Numbers.* New York: Russell Sage, 1987.

Anderson, Margo J. *The American Census: A Social History.* New Haven: Yale University Press, 1988.

Higgs, Edward. *Making Sense of the Census: The Manuscript Returns for England and Wales, 1801–1901.* London: Her Majesty's Stationery Office, 1989.

Taeuber, Conrad. "Census," in David Sills, ed., *International Encyclopedia of the Social Sciences,* Vol. 2. New York: Macmillan and The Free Press, 1968, pp. 360–365.

Central Place Theory

Central place theory seeks to explain the relative location on the earth's surface of human settlements of differing size and complexity. In the classic formulation of the theory in the 1930s, geographer Walter Christaller predicted that, given a flat, featureless plain of uniform population density, settlements would array themselves in a hexagonal pattern implied by mathematical packing theory and that the location of various retail activities within this honeycomb would be determined by a hierarchical ordering of settlements. Demand for certain goods and services (e.g., groceries) would ensure that vendors of such items would locate in every settlement, while higher order goods and services (e.g., banking) would appear only in higher levels of central places that were spaced farther apart. Every lower-level center would be equidistant from two higher-level centers that would compete with each other to service the needs of smaller towns. The ratios between the numbers of towns at successive levels would be determined by whether the system optimized marketing efficiency, traffic efficiency, or administrative efficiency. Christaller conducted a study of the towns of southern Germany in the 1930s and, using somewhat crude measures of centrality, found patterns consistent with his theory in a system dominated by the "marketing principle." (A more rigorous but less influential contribution by August Lösch does not make Christaller's assumption of uniform population density.)

All real-world urban systems differ from the pattern predicted by Christaller, often for reasons other than violations of his assumptions (e.g., by rugged topography). These divergences from the theory can be of great interest to social historians, though the most ambitious application of the theory so far to a society in the past, late imperial China, is by anthropologist G. William Skinner (1965). Introducing a temporal dimension into the model, Skinner suggests, for example, that modernizing forces can affect the ratios between the number of centers at different levels, and thus seriously impact the boundaries of community in peasant society.

Critics of Christaller observe that the urban systems of many societies fit the classic model much more awkwardly than do those of southern Germany in the 1930s and of late imperial China. For example, in 19th-century America, very large areas of the South and Midwest were devoid of substantial cities, in apparent violation of Christaller's prediction that higher-order centers would be placed interstitially among the lower-level centers. James Vance (1970) argues that this fact illustrates a fundamental flaw in Christaller's thinking. Few consumers, according to Vance, ever travel very far to obtain goods

not available locally, and merchants meet their needs, by various devices, from *entrepôts,* or "unraveling points," which they establish on the perimeter of agrarian regions. The entrepreneurial decisions of wholesalers, not the consumer's journey to shop at retail establishments, is what really drives the system. Vance speculates that the regular and interstitial placement of centers of different orders in southern Germany may have been a legacy of feudalism, but he believes that his wholesaling model accounts more satisfactorily for the structure of urban systems that have developed in modern times. (Some scholars refer, rather confusingly, to Vance's alternative to the classic model as "network theory" rather than central place theory.)

Many Third World societies also appear to deviate from the Christallerian model. E.A.J. Johnson (1970) observes that developing countries typically have a much higher ratio of villages to towns than do more developed societies. Carol Smith (1976) formalizes and extends this observation by proposing several alternative central place models. In her view, the interlocking central place model of Christaller is appropriate to only a fully commercialized society with a highly competitive market economy. For partially commercialized societies, where exchange is often controlled, Smith proposes two alternatives—the dendritic and solar central place hierarchies.

Where exchange is controlled by the local resident elites of major towns, as in the case of many parts of Latin America under Spanish rule, all lower-order centers in a region may be focused on a single sunlike regional capital, whose elite uses its administrative power to shield itself from competition with its counterparts in adjacent regions. Smith retains the hexagonal lattice to diagram this solar model, but she utilizes a treelike diagram to represent the dendritic model, which she associates with a society in which exchange is controlled in the interests of external powers and of an ethnically distinct elite living outside the area of peasant cultivation. In a dendritic system each lower-order center is oriented toward only one higher-order center which exercises a monopoly over its custom. Finally, Smith proposes two simpler models to represent uncommercialized societies such as feudal Europe and the tribal communities of lowland South America.

So far the use of central place theory by historians has seldom been informed by an awareness of the extensions of and alternatives to the classic model which have been provided especially by anthropologists. These developments open rich possibilities for understanding societies in the past, but they also raise empirical difficulties. In operationalizing central place models, geographers and anthropologists depend upon fieldwork—an option that is generally unavailable to the historian—to delineate journeys to shop and other exchange patterns. Moreover, a common method for comparing central place systems, the analysis of ratios between the number of markets operating at different levels, will seldom distinguish conclusively among different central place models. All of Smith's alternatives to the classic model, for example, as well as one of Christaller's own alternatives (the "administrative principle") imply "bottom-heavy" hierarchies. Thus, to take full advantage of this body of theory, social historians must exercise resourcefulness and empirical ingenuity. (*See also* Cities)

David W. Miller

REFERENCES

Johnson, E.A.J. *The Organization of Space in Developing Countries*. Cambridge, MA: Harvard University Press, 1970.

Marshall, J.U. *The Structure of Urban Systems*. Toronto: University of Toronto Press, 1989.

Skinner, G.W. "Marketing and Social Structure in Rural China," *Journal of Asian Studies* xxiv (1964): 363–399; xxv (1965): 195–228, 363–399.

Smith, C.A., ed. *Regional Analysis*, 2 vols. New York: Academic Press, 1976.

Vance, J.E. *The Merchant's World: The Geography of Wholesaling*. Englewood Cliffs, NJ: Prentice-Hall, 1970.

Charity

Although often viewed as a marker for social and economic history, charity forms part of the wider history of giving and receiving, and abuts on broad sociopolitical questions. Historians of charity have to fight their way through a veritable swamp of conceptual and methodological problems. It is essential, first of all, to historicize a social practice which is often viewed as an ahistoric psychological propensity: just as the poor are always with us, so, it is held, will the wish to alleviate want through charitable activity be constant over time. Social and economic historians have endeavored to measure the charitable performance of different societies by studying the long-term development of certain charitable acts, such as testamentary donations. W.K. Jordan's (1959) pioneering analysis of English philanthropy based on this approach has been criticized, however, for failing to take into account inflationary trends, and also for assuming that formal charitable acts offer a reliable guide to the total charitable performance of a given society. Certainly it would seem unquestionable that formal charitable acts have always been outweighed by private and informal acts of giving in face-to-face situations (this includes charity *within* lower-class groups, an important topic for the urban working class). The social history of charity thus involves sensitivity to limits of evidence, beyond formal acts, as well as insistence that charity can vary greatly according to social and cultural context.

There is a problem too, in any impulse to view charity as a preeminently and quintessentially Christian virtue, which can be counterpoised against alleged non-Christian indifference to charitable activity. It is certainly true that Christianity has always been associated with a high prioritization of charitable rhetoric and values and with an impressive range of caring activities. The idea that the story of charity is thus the chronicle of Christian piety, however, is erroneous as well as ethnocentric. Medieval hospitals, for example, which are habitually viewed as an archetypal institutional expression of a Christian "Age of Faith," were paralleled by similar institutions in Islamic society, and indeed the Islamic hospital tradition may have influenced Christian institutions. Moreover, charitable institutions have habitually had social as well as religious objectives. Hospitals, the most enduring institutional form of religiously motivated charity, have also been a means whereby the wealthy could give to—and thereby control and dominate—the poor. Correspondingly, responses of the poor *to* charity form a vital, if difficult, aspect of the topic.

The social control features of charity raise another problem that has bedeviled histories of charity, namely the assumption that changes in charitable performance of different societies are directly linked to pressure "from below." Popular turbulence and revolt have often triggered a charitable response, it is true: urban crime and misery of the sort chronicled by Friedrich Engels, Henry Mayhew, and others were important determinants of the charitable enthusiasm of the ruling classes of Victorian England, for example. However, charity has also been the locus of struggles within the dominant classes. As Sandra Cavallo's recent work (1991) on early modern Italy has suggested, new forms of charitable provision were often sponsored by emerging factions of the elite—notably the mercantile classes—who saw in poor relief a means of symbolically marking their own raised social status, establishing patronage networks, and shaping provision to benefit their own material and political interests. Charity is often an arena for power struggles between rival factions of the elite, and new poor relief policies have often been as much about dispute between charitable donors as about pressure from below.

A further putative dichotomy historians have often detected in the history of charity relates to the alleged contrast between Christian voluntarism on one hand and modern policy responses on the other. It is held that the habits of voluntary giving so strong within the Christian—and particularly Orthodox and Roman Catholic—traditions contrast with a degree of state-driven compulsion in modern welfare states, with the latter predicated upon the alleged drying up of the charitable impulse. However, in the confessional states prevalent in medieval and early modern Europe, for example, where the spiritual and temporal influence of the church was strong, there was often a kind of "charitable imperative" in place, which imposed significant pressures of social and moral conformity as well as religious orthodoxy on the faithful and impelled them toward charitable activity. Similarly, though many historians assume a long-term linear passage from charity to state welfare in modern history, recent research has underlined the vitality of the charitable impulse in industrial and postindustrial societies. Even formal welfare policies have often utilized charitable impulses.

Overall, the considerable amount of research conducted since the 1960s on the history of charity has highlighted the several misleading features of the traditional framework for the subject. Social history research has emphasized the need for subtler and more nuanced conceptual approaches which take account of the full complexity of the social, economic, political, and cultural contexts in which the giving and the receiving of charity takes place. (*See also* Hospitals; Medicine; Patronage; Poor Relief; Poverty; Welfare State)

Colin Jones

REFERENCES

Amundsen, D.W., and R.L. Numbers, eds. *Caring and Curing, Health and Medicine in the Western Medical Traditions*. New York: Macmillan, 1986.

Barry, J., and C. Jones, eds. *Medicine and Charity Before the Welfare State*. London: Routledge, 1991.

Cavallo, S. "The Motivations of Benefactors: An Overview of Approaches to the Study of Charity," in J. Barry, and C. Jones, eds., *Medicine and Charity Before the Welfare State*. London: Routledge, 1991.

Granshaw, L., and R. Porter, eds. *The Hospital in History*. London: Routledge, 1989.

Jones, C. *The Charitable Imperative, Hospitals and Nursing in Ancien Régime and Revolutionary France*. London: Routledge, 1989.

Jordan, W.K. *Philanthropy in England, 1480–1660*. London: G. Allen and Unwin, 1959.

Chartism

Chartism was a mass movement for democratic rights that flourished throughout England, Wales, and Scotland from 1838 to 1848. As studied in recent years, it forms a major stage in the social history of protest. Chartism revealed the emergence of new political demands and gave new industrial workers important protest experience.

In the wake of the 1832 Reform Act, which extended the franchise predominantly to the urban middle class, there was widespread radical feeling that the majority of people had been politically betrayed. There was also intense resentment to the harshness of the 1834 Poor Law

Amendment Act, which made poor relief more degrading and difficult to acquire. Chartism harnessed such resentments, building on a well-established tradition of popular democratic politics. Chartism was distinguished by its large scale, its national character, and its predominantly working-class support.

Chartism took its name from the "People's Charter," a document drawn up by the cabinet-maker William Lovett and published in May 1838 by the London Working Men's Association. The famous six points of the Charter included universal male adult suffrage, vote by secret ballot, the abolition of property qualifications for Members of Parliament, the payment of salaries to Members, equal electoral districts, and annual parliaments. Chartism made no formal demands for female suffrage, although many Chartists favored votes for unmarried women and widows; many women took an active but generally subordinate role in the movement.

Early Chartism (1838–1839) focused on mobilizing a National Petition to Parliament, demanding universal male suffrage. At mass demonstrations Chartists elected members to a General Convention that met in London to superintend the Petition's presentation and sought to devise a strategy to attain their goals following the rejection of their demands. In 1842, and again in 1848, Chartists launched massive agitations. The Petition of 1842, the largest, collected over 3 million signatures. Chartists sometimes moved beyond constitutional agitation. Abortive insurrections occurred in 1839–1840 and 1848. In summer 1842, activists transformed a series of industrial strikes into a general strike demanding the Charter be made law. In 1839–1840, 1842, and 1848, the movement suffered arrests and the imprisonment of many local and national leaders. The two most striking innovations of the 1840s were the formation of the National Charter Association, often regarded as the world's first working-class political party, and the Chartist Land Plan, which settled urban workers on small plots of land. By the late 1840s Chartism had fragmented, although the movement maintained a national presence into the early 1850s.

James Epstein

REFERENCES

Epstein, James, and Dorothy Thompson, eds. *The Chartist Experience*. London: Macmillan, 1982.

Jones, David. *Chartism and the Chartists*. London: Allen Lane, 1975.

Thompson, Dorothy. *The Chartists*. New York: Pantheon, 1984.

Child Abuse

See Abuse

Child Labor

In traditional societies all over the world, the use of children in productive labor has always been accepted as a practice essential for the economic maintenance of the family. Even very young children could be expected to fetch water, herd animals, glean in the fields, or help their parents in handicraft production. Only the most exceptional families could provide their children with a prolonged period of nurturing, leisure, and schooling.

The history of child labor in traditional settings has been incompletely explored. Children did not always work assiduously, and they mixed play with work in many settings. Youths, particularly when assigned to apprenticeship, were frequently subject to much more rigorous regimens. Children were often sent to work for other families, both to supply extra labor needed in other households and to relieve the strain of an overlarge brood on their own family's resources. Finally, gender distinctions marked children's work, and so work formed a major component of gender socialization through direct contact with same-sex adults.

Much sociohistorical research on child labor focuses on the industrial era. The employment of children came to be questioned only at the turn of the 19th century, as those who dominated society and politics began to recognize the importance of protecting and educating children, and as industrialization brought new attention to child labor. Many opinion leaders in early industrial society came to consider employment in mining and manufacturing a far greater threat to children than traditional labor in agriculture and handicrafts had been. They noted that, unlike children working under the guidance of parents or master craftsmen, those who worked in mines and factories were forced to do monotonous tasks under conditions of strict discipline in environments where little attention was paid to their physical needs, their moral conduct, or their educational development. For this reason the earliest objections to child labor were attacks on the employment of children in industry. Only toward the end of the 19th century were some attempts made to limit the work of children in small shops, in services, and in street trades such as peddling and acrobatics. Child labor in agriculture is still largely unregulated, even in the most economically advanced countries of the world.

As England was the first country to industrialize, it was also the first country to confront the problem of industrial child labor. As early as 1802 some restrictions were imposed on the employment of pauper children placed in factories, and in 1819 Parliament enacted a child labor law applicable to all children working in textile mills. The Factory Act of 1819 made 9 the minimum age for employment and allowed a workday of no more than 12 hours for children under age 16. In 1833 England's factory legislation was further strengthened as the workday was reduced to 9 hours for textile workers under age 13 (of which there were then some 56,000) and as an effective system of factory inspection was introduced for the first time. England's legislation was revised and extended several more times during the 19th century, most notably in 1878, when the minimum age for employment was raised to 10 and the workday of children under age 14 was limited to 6 hours.

England's early factory acts set the tone for child labor legislation in other countries, as they too wrestled with the problem of child labor abuse. By the turn of the 20th century, all the industrialized countries of Europe and many American states had some sort of child labor legislation. In general, this legislation stipulated a minimum age for employment in industrial establishments, set limits on the hours youngsters could work, prohibited work at night and on Sundays and holidays, and barred children from certain jobs deemed to be especially hazardous. In the United States, federal legislation on child labor, initiated in 1916, was fully accepted by the courts only in 1938.

The early child labor laws of countries such as England, France, and the United States were often enacted because of pressure put on the government by reformers from the middle and upper classes, who were concerned not only that child labor was harmful to young people, but also that it might render them unfit for military service and for adult labor later in their lives. Those most affected by factory laws often resisted them, however. Working-class families and individual entrepreneurs generally believed that the employment of children was a necessity. Parents relied on the income their children provided, and factory owners considered young employees to be essential both because they were paid less than adults and because they were thought to be better suited for certain jobs (tying broken threads in textile mills, for example). Some opponents of child labor reform argued that factory work kept youngsters from idleness and taught them valuable skills, and that, in any case, government should not infringe on the rights of parents and employers. Opposition to child labor legislation diminished only as industrial operations became too complex for children, as factory owners became convinced that controls would affect all manufacturers equally, as adults began to earn wages that could support their entire families, and as both the value of an extended childhood and the propriety of government interventionism became widely accepted.

The problem of child labor is closely associated with the issue of education, and many early child labor laws, such as the English Factory Act of 1833 and the French Child Labor Law of 1841, carried some minimal provisions for the schooling of factory children. It was always difficult to enforce the education provisions of these laws, however, and only generalized compulsory education legislation eventually guaranteed that working-class children would abandon the factory and go to school. In the non-Western world, still today it is generally those countries that have enacted compulsory education laws, or at least made a substantial investment in primary schools, that have the lowest rates of child labor.

Child labor restrictions are far fewer and far less likely to be enforced in developing countries than in the West. In India, for example, even primary education is not compulsory, and only child labor in factories is illegal. Because the dominant classes in India accept the existence of a highly stratified society, they continue to countenance the employment of millions of poor children in cottage industries, in domestic service, in shops and restaurants, in street trades, and in agriculture. In the Indian town of Sivakasi, for instance, some 45,000 children under age 15 work in the local match and fireworks industry.

International efforts to coordinate limits on child labor can be traced to the International Labor Conference held in Berlin in 1890. The International Labor Organization, established after World War I, continues the work of promoting restrictions on child labor all over the world. The ILO now advocates that all countries adopt 13 as a minimum age for light employment, and 15 as the minimum age for most work. However, there is some disagreement in the international community over whether more attention should be paid to abolishing child labor or to improving the conditions of children who must work. (*See also* Abuse; Child Rearing; Childhood; Education; Household Economy; Industrialization; Public Schools; Social Control; Youth/Adolescence)

Lee Shai Weissbach

REFERENCES

Nardinelli, Clark. *Child Labor and the Industrial Revolution*. Bloomington: Indiana University Press, 1990.

Trattner, Walter I. *Crusade for the Children: A History of the National Child Labor Committee and Child Labor Reform in America*. Chicago: Quadrangle Books, 1970.

Ward, J.T. *The Factory Movement: 1830–1855*. London: Macmillan, 1962.

Weiner, Myron. *The Child and the State in India: Child Labor and Education Policy in Comparative Perspective*. Princeton, NJ: Princeton University Press, 1991.

Weissbach, Lee Shai. *Child Labor Reform in Nineteenth-Century France: Assuring the Future Harvest*. Baton Rouge: Louisiana State University Press, 1989.

Child Rearing

The history of childhood, while never completely ignored, first became the subject of sustained scholarly interest with the publication in 1962 of Philippe Ariès's *Centuries of Childhood*. This work, with its controversial claim that children were only "discovered" in the 17th century, set the topic of debate in terms of adult attitudes toward children. Consequently, much of this debate has focused on child rearing and its psychological implications rather than childhood per se, relying heavily on Freudian and, later, Eriksonian concepts. Indeed, one researcher, psychohistorian Lloyd de Mause, viewed the entirety of the history of childhood through what he termed the psychogenic model. Focusing only on child rearing, this model began with an infanticidal mode in the antiquity and ended with the helping mode by the mid-20th century (in which parents merely assisted their children to grow without demanding compliance to a rigid behavioral model). Largely found within historical studies of childhood or the family, the history of child rearing has thus revolved around questions of family structure and discipline, changing relations within the family, and, occasionally, the impact of child rearing on later adult behavior.

Family structure plays a determining role in child rearing practices, and as such, remains a principal subject of analysis. Early agricultural societies established strong, patriarchal family structures in which the father's power was in principle absolute. Religious, political, and economic systems all combined to strengthen paternal authority, especially rules of inheritance. Perhaps the best example of such families emerged in Confucian China, where fathers commanded profound respect from all family members through a deeply rooted sense of honor and duty taught from an early age. Expressive emotional systems in some societies, such as classical India and the Islamic Middle East, tempered this structure slightly, however, by stressing sentimental bonds between family members. In all agricultural societies, birth control for the vast majority of population was limited, though prolonged lactation and sexual abstinence did allow some child spacing, as in early modern western Europe and colonial America. Families were large, with all members involved in the maintenance of the whole. Mothers swaddled their infants in order to decrease the demand on their time. Usually by age five, children began working alongside adults in the fields or workshop until the addition of younger siblings provided excess labor, making it more economical to hire out the older children to younger families.

This method of child rearing prompted some historians like Ariès to claim that parents considered children little more than mini adults requiring little special attention. Subsequent work has called this thesis into question, but legitimizes the view that childhood has had different meanings and child rearing has had different purposes in distinct historical periods. In this early stage of history, when life was precarious and child mortality rates were high, parents placed little emotional value on children. Indeed, Christianity held that children were born with Original Sin that could only be countered by breaking their will at an early age. Parents placed value instead on economic worth, accenting discipline and work. Infanticide was common, especially for girls and the handicapped; parents would not preserve the lives of those who could not help provide for the family later in life. The amount of physical discipline varied, with European parents stricter than parents in some other cultures (including Africa and American Indian groups). Affection for children was also muted among the upper classes, those who could better afford their children, by the practice of wet nursing, separating parents from children until weaned. Male children spent little of this subsequent time at home, however, as parents soon sent them away to school in order to prepare them for a career. Girls, on the other hand, remained at home, preparing for their lives as wives and mothers by helping their own mothers.

The patriarchal family structure continued for centuries, coming under attack in Western societies only in the 17th century. Predictably, historians have documented changes in child rearing practices slowly developing at the same time, although the causes for such changes remain vague and difficult to support. Lawrence Stone (1977), for example, depicts the development of

stronger emotional ties in middle-class English families, resulting in the rise of the nuclear family. Within this new family children were treated as malleable, neither good nor bad at birth, and parents adopted a new loving and permissive attitude that allowed children greater freedom (demonstrated by the gradual end of swaddling and wet nursing, and, for older children, a greater say in choosing their own spouses). Stone attributes these changes to a rise in the spirit of individualism, which spread, along with changes in child rearing, to the aristocracy and then the lower classes. Some historians also link the demographic transition to changes in the value of children and child rearing practices. Specifically, they claim that the drop in birth rates occurring in most Western societies in the late 18th and early 19th centuries indicates a new attitude of concern. Parents cared enough to have fewer children, maximizing interest and emotion in those children as individuals. It is important to note, however, that these changes in child rearing occurred gradually, combining with the impact of industrialization to affect lower-class families mainly in the 19th and 20th centuries.

Although no work has effectively discounted this notion of a distinct change in the child rearing patterns prevalent in early modern Western societies, the view has not been immune to attack and nuance. Linda Pollock (1983), relying upon a sociobiological approach, disputes the claim that parents before the 17th century did not care about their children and treated them cruelly. She claims, rather, that human nature entails a natural bond between parent and child. Using diaries as evidence, she finds little change in child rearing between the 16th and 19th centuries. Philip Greven (1977), meanwhile, nuances the singular nature of Stone's approach by identifying three different modes of child rearing in colonial America, not in different classes, as Stone would have it, but in different regions (although each region had at least minor representations of each mode). The bases for these differences were religious conviction and family background, producing evangelical, moderate, and genteel temperaments. Perhaps most interesting, however, is Greven's claim that differences in child rearing help explain revolutionary action in the late 18th century. His is one of the only works to link the history of child rearing to larger historical issues apart from the development of the family and childhood. Lately, scholars have also challenged Stone's interpretation for its emphasis on prescriptive literature (printed material such as advice manuals on how to raise children) rather than "real" behavior, a recurring problem in the history of child rearing. While subsequent works have thus cast doubt on Stone's orderly progression in child rearing and family life, few historians dispute that important changes did occur in the 17th century.

These changes seem minor in comparison, however, to those observed in the wake of industrialization. The growth of factories moved manufacturing outside of the home, removing the father as well. It also shut middle-class mothers and children out of their past roles in production. This process greatly increased the role of the mother in child rearing, a function strengthened by the cult of domesticity (a philosophy highlighting the mother's role in maintaining moral purity in her home). Thus, while fathers retained their legal authority over their families, de facto power began to flow to the ever-present mother, particularly in the middle classes. This change also created a new emphasis on the gendered nature of child rearing. Previously mothers prepared their daughters for their futures as wives and mothers while fathers spent their time focusing on their sons. With fathers removed from the daily routine of the home, boys now came under more careful scrutiny from their mothers. This resulted in the creation of what one historian, Anthony Rotundo, has termed an independent boyhood culture emphasizing traits deemed more manly. Education also grew in importance for the middle classes as a means of removing boys from too much feminizing attention from their mothers. Girls, however, were deemed better taught at home, where mothers could continue to prepare them for their future domestic lives. The growing concern over education was also fundamental in the creation of a new stage of life, adolescence. Middle-class interest in lengthening childhood stemmed both from the necessity of more education to compete effectively in a complicated economy and the desire to control a potentially unruly force (less of a problem in early modern Europe, when community traditions restrained youthful energy in various festivals). For children generally new standards of cleanliness and toilet training promoted new rules, even as adults glorified childhood and provided a new array of children's toys and books. One American historian, John Demos, noting the decline of physical punishments, argues that the 19th century witnessed the replacement of shame with guilt as a primary disciplinary mode. Finally, industrialization also spurred interest among the middle classes in forging a working class more like themselves, especially in matters of family structure and relations. Thus began a growing demand for states to play a role in working-class family life, including control over children's behavior.

For the working class, industrialization also translated into a loss of paternal authority. First, the ability of most children to find gainful employment, a godsend for most families when the child was young and contributed to family income, became a window to independence. Young adults no longer had to wait until their late twenties to marry, when normally they would have inherited their family farm. They could now marry when they wanted, leaving their family at great pains to replace the lost income (though, in fact, many working children stayed home for a while). The greatest attack on paternal authority, however, came from the state in the form of middle-class reforms. Middle-class concern for the working-class family developed in response to general anxiety over the impact of industrialization. By the mid-19th century, many members of the middle classes were denouncing the prevalence of child labor. They insisted upon on a working-class family modeled on their own image—fewer children, better education, and a distinct separation between childhood and adult life. They saw child labor as a physical, intellectual, and moral danger. By the end of the century, most societies enforced child labor regulations for all children under age 13, replacing factory work with mandatory attendance in school. In many societies, of course, schools did not bring the classes together. Often, schools not only separated the working class from the middle classes, but also boys from girls. Each group was trained for a different adult life.

These changes were not limited to Western societies, of course. As other societies began to feel the impact of industrialization, they experienced similar transformations. In Africa, for example, 20th-century urbanization also weakened paternal authority; many fathers went to the cities in search of employment while mothers remained with the children in the villages. Like their Western counterparts, they began to experience more de facto power within the family.

Meanwhile, in Western societies, the growing role of state institutions in the socialization of children, brought to an extreme by certain fascist and communist regimes in the 20th century, caused middle-class and working-class expectations to converge. Child labor became abhorrent as adults labeled childhood and adolescence a separate stage in the life course demanding affection, nurturing, and guidance. In the United States, one related change in the 20th century involved increased parental monitoring of young children, manifested in new concern about emotional displays such as sibling rivalry—another way in which child rearing modes might be redefined and adult standards rigidified. Furthermore, John Modell (1989) has observed that, as the need and acceptability of child labor has decreased, youth life course decisions such as courtship and marriage have become individual decisions, no longer based upon the needs of the family. The individualization of such transitions has also increased the role of institutional certification, like licenses and diplomas, in delineating movement from youth to adulthood. In brief, while one cannot discount parents' predominant role in raising their own children, state institutions and laws now ensure that many child rearing decisions are monitored and controlled.

The history of child rearing has clearly generated much scholarly work, for it is in many respects the ideal social history topic. Historians have used it to explore issues related to the private, daily lives of ordinary people, as a means of understanding how they experienced life. This should not, of course, lead one to conclude that little work remains to be done. Up to this point, most of the attention to child rearing has focused upon prescriptive literature, a readily available source. Historians must work, however, to attain more insight into actual methods of child rearing, on which the sources are limited. Furthermore, picking up on recent research on the socialization of children to certain emotional standards, more research should be conducted on the means parents have adopted in the past to socialize their children to other standards of behavior. Finally, while the sources are again difficult to find, historians should resist the temptation to discuss children as passive recipients of child rearing and delve into the impact of child rearing patterns on later adult behavior, examining how children have responded to their own upbringing. Overall, the history of child rearing continues to offer historians many avenues to understanding the past.

Steven M. Beaudoin

REFERENCES

Ariès, Philippe. *Centuries of Childhood: A Social History of Family Life*. Translated by Robert Baldick. New York: McGraw, 1962.

Greven, Philip. *The Protestant Temperament: Patterns of Child-Rearing, Religious Experience and the Self in Early America*. New York: Knopf, 1977.

Modell, John. *Into One's Own: From Youth to Adulthood in the United States, 1920–1975*. Berkeley: University of California Press, 1989.

Pollock, Linda. *Forgotten Children: Parent-Child Relations from 1500 to 1900*. Cambridge: Cambridge University Press, 1983.

Stone, Lawrence. *The Family, Sex and Marriage in England, 1500–1800*. New York: Harper, 1977.

Childbirth

Early studies of childbirth focused on the progression of scientific advances suggesting that as childbirth changed from a social to a medical phenomenon medical progress was made. Since the 1960s greater attention has been paid to childbirth as a social phenomenon and as an aspect of women's lives, rather than just as medical history.

Childbirth today is a medical-centered hospital event, but in the past it was a woman-centered home event, although specific customs varied in different cultures. Until the 19th century childbirth was a major focus of most women's lives. Many women functioned within a 20- to 30-month cycle of conception, pregnancy, birth, nursing, and weaning, giving birth to an average of 8 babies through their fertile years. Before the late 19th century, childbirth occurred at home. Friends, relatives, and a female midwife assisted the mother with delivery while offering emotional support. Women delivered in a standing, squatting, or kneeling position, sitting on someone's lap, or on a birthing stool. Neighbors and kin did household chores and minded other children during the "lying-in" period, sometimes lasting three to four weeks. Male barber-surgeons or physicians attended emergencies only when either the baby or mother had to be sacrificed for the life of the other, utilizing tools to destroy and remove the fetus or, less frequently, performing caesarean sections on dead mothers.

Prenatal care was nonexistent. Before the 16th century, women took precautions of a magical nature, reflecting the widespread belief in the supernatural. People believed if the mother swore or was blasphemous, she would give birth to a monster. If she looked at the moon, her child would be a lunatic. Pregnant women practiced venesection and wet cupping (used to draw blood to the body's surface), believing their health would be improved.

Destitute women began to have physician- or midwife-assisted births in the hospital in 16th-century France. This afforded the opportunity for physicians, who previously were called in only for abnormal deliveries, to view normal births. Influenced by Enlightenment ideology, physicians, seeking rational explanations, systematically observed, measured, and recorded births, relating the body to a machine, describing the uterus as a mechanical pump that expelled the fetus. Doctors devised manual manipulations to ease passage and pelvic measurement techniques to predict birth difficulties. Although the French found few new methods, they eliminated magical and religious explanations of the birth process and proved the ineffectiveness of old practices.

In England, barber-surgeons, who desperately struggled to save infants and mothers, devised new techniques to reduce mortality. The English midwife Peter Chamberlen, the Elder, developed obstetrical forceps (ca. 1630) enabling him to extract the fetus without destroying it. By the early 18th century forceps were widely used, although improper usage resulted in maternal injuries.

As physicians began to view obstetrics as a science, patients began to seek their assistance in normal deliveries. French and English upper classes gradually began to employ male midwives in the 17th century. By 1800, American middle- and upper-class women frequently chose a physician instead of a midwife, although births continued to occur at home.

Historians have suggested several reasons why women began to employ physicians, in addition to physicians' efforts to increase their clientele. Coinciding with the declining impact of religion and beliefs in acceptance of God's plan, women, no longer resigned to their fate and believing in the promise of science, began to seek improvements in childbirth. New family values encouraged attention to women's fears of pain and death in childhood. Nineteenth-century physicians offered ergot to hasten deliveries and, after mid-century, anesthesia. In addition, they utilized forceps, which midwives, for unexplained reasons, did not. Birth, being less frequent, became special instead of a central focus of women's lives. Historians have suggested that middle- and upper-class women, desiring not to be associated with lower classes who utilized uneducated midwives, chose educated male physicians, which enhanced their own social status.

Childbirth in the 20th century is marked by an increase in medicalization and hospitalization. Whereas in previous centuries only destitute women were delivered in hospitals, in the 20th century, middle- and upper-class women also made the move to hospitals, another subject of historical debate. Physicians encouraged mothers to move to the hospitals in order to raise their status professionally, enjoy the financial benefits of practicing obstetrics, and gain control over their patients. They have been portrayed as misogynists attempting to control women, reflecting gender relations of the period. Doctors argued that they could guarantee a safer delivery with improved technology at their fingertips. Other historians have argued that women themselves desired to move to the hospital. Social reformers and physicians of the early 20th century, concerned over alarmingly high infant and maternal mortality rates, asserted that medical attention would promise a safer outcome, so women felt safer in the hospital. Further, women actively sought anesthetics, which doctors claimed were easier to administer in the hospital. Changes in the urban environment literally destroyed the female networks so essential to social childbirth within the home setting.

Another issue of debate is whether or not women actually controlled childbirth. It has been argued that women relinquished control when they moved to the hospital. Prior to that, they shared in any decision-making process regarding interference from the physician. Some claim that women never really controlled their own deliveries but were subject to custom and community regulations which decreased mothers' choices.

Other controversial issues have revolved around which women were the active agents of change in childbirth. Upper- and middle-class women were the first to employ physicians instead of midwives for their deliveries, but lower-class women were the first to utilize hospitals and, therefore, it has been argued, were first to direct the doctor-patient relationship. There are still gaps in historical works with little sociohistorical research having been done on minority groups, urban blacks, class differentials, or customs of various ethnic groups. (*See also* Abortion; Birth Control; Health; Hospitals; Medicine; Midwifery; Motherhood; Women's History)

Carolyn Leonard Carson

REFERENCES

Leavitt, Judith Walzer. *Brought to Bed, Childbearing in America, 1750–1950.* New York: Oxford University Press, 1986.

Shorter, Edward. *A History of Women's Bodies.* New York: Basic Books, 1982.

Wertz, Richard W., and Dorothy C. Wertz. *Lying-In, A History of Childbirth in America.* New Haven: Yale University Press, 1977.

Childhood

If the adage "the child is parent to the adult" is true, then a historical understanding of what childhood meant through the ages is essential for our understanding of both the past and our-

selves. In a work drawing broad conclusions about childhood and family life in the past Philippe Ariès in his *Centuries of Childhood* (1962) argued that the premodern world had no concept of childhood, which he defined as an interest in children as children. If anything, children were seen as little adults. At best their special needs were ignored; at worst these children were brutalized. The development of a concept of childhood occurred only in the modern world, beginning in the 17th century, with its emphasis on education.

Ariès's book has been tremendously successful and influential in opening childhood as a topic in social history based on a search for changes in conditions and adult outlook. Other historians have argued for progression over time from a nonaffective, almost dysfunctional family that ignored or physically and emotionally brutalized its members, including the children, to a close, loving family that respected and supported each other emotionally, including the children.

These arguments have created a "black legend" of premodern childhood, with the premodern era seen as a dismal time for children. The high infant mortality rates of the era (some 25 percent to 30 percent of all children born in premodern Europe died by their first birthday) forced parents to devote less emotional time to their children. This lack of emotion led parents to feel distanced from their children, which could even prompt them to brutalize them. Distance and cruelty toward children were common, as evidenced by premodern practices such as infanticide, abandonment, swaddling, wet-nursing, and harsh apprenticeship. With the advent of industrial society (and its attendant conquest of disease and declining infant mortality rates) childhood and attitudes toward children became more humane, and these cruel practices ceased.

A necessary aspect of this black legend of childhood is that the Middle Ages was a true dark age for children, a point many medievalists have accepted. Some medievalists, however, rejected this, and have fashioned a revisionist school of family history. Too many works had accepted the black legend uncritically and even tailored evidence to fit it. When more intimate and personal sources are used systematically (like letters and diaries), a more humane, more intimate, and even familiar picture of premodern family life and childhood emerges. Adult attitudes toward children, in particular, proved less destructive than Ariès had claimed.

Linda Pollock (1983) noted a curious phenomenon. Historians who argued for change in the era they were most familiar with had done very little research on the era prior to their own and had little proof, therefore, to substantiate that a change had really occurred. A closer observation of the historical record punctures much of this evolutionary theory. Historians have relied heavily on the cessation of wet-nursing in the modern era as proof of more positive attitudes toward children; yet recent work has shown that aristocratic English women continued to send children out to the wet-nurse well into the 19th century and that wet-nursing was a feature of French artisan family life up to the end of World War I.

Any attempt to show that the premodern world was devoid of affection crumbles on close examination as well. In late medieval England people believed that parental affection was normal, expected, and natural. The consistent depiction of the holy family throughout the Middle Ages at least implied that the Western church favored a child-centered family. Many premodern stories assume parental and familial affection toward children. Fathers in premodern England seemed very pleased at the birth of their children, and sent out congratulatory letters.

Nevertheless, historians have continued to pursue the advent of modern attitudes toward children. Virtually every historical era has been cited as the time when modern attitudes toward children have developed. Many historians date this dramatic change in attitudes toward children to the late 18th and 19th centuries and see it as the result of modernization. Others have found the greatest change occurring in the early 18th century—before industrialization—as the result of capitalism. Some have seen the change occurring during the Reformation era, especially with its heightened sense of Christianity. Some scholars have seen a change in attitudes toward family and especially children occurring during the Renaissance, especially in the 15th century. Lifelike paintings of the Madonna and Child are used as evidence that the Renaissance ushered in a new attitude toward motherhood and childhood, though it is also true that all Renaissance paintings emphasized lifelike portrayals regardless of subject.

Discipline for children was harsh in the premodern world, according to most historians, especially psychohistorians. Accounts, for instance, by Renaissance humanists or Reformation theologians of their own childhood or what they witnessed can be horrifying, at least on the surface. A schoolmaster beat young Johannes Butzbach bloody for not studying—shocking, and, as some insist, demonstrable evidence that the premodern world treated its charges cruelly. On the other hand, the schoolmaster was fired for this act: discipline has changed over time, but extreme brutality was reproved in the past as well. Indeed, historians currently debate whether child abuse has not in fact increased in the past two centuries, with greater stress and less community control.

Historians must be very careful defining attitudes from practices, especially when they do not understand the proper context of those practices. Abandonment, for instance, while on the surface appearing to support the idea that the past was both distant and cruel toward its children, even infanticidal, takes on new meaning when we discover that people who abandoned their children expected someone to take them up, someone more capable of raising them themselves. In a sense abandonment was a mechanism for premodern adoption. Apprenticeship, where a child would be sent to live with another family to learn a trade, does not so much imply neglect and distance as it does an attempt to take advantage of a particular premodern education system.

Again, our inability to understand the dimensions and context of certain premodern child rearing practices contributes to an often exaggerated belief that premodern parents were neglectful. Wet-nursing surely must signify neglect—or so most historians tell us. Yet recent studies of wet-nursing in the premodern and modern world that describe it as a form of premodern child care should caution historians to be careful attributing motives to practices without understanding their context. In an era without adequate artificial means of feeding infants, where animal milk was not pasteurized, how else could working mothers combine their work and child rearing? Although a child might be with a wet-nurse for years, Pollock found from the diary evidence she used that parents would frequently visit their children there. She concluded that within these constraints children did develop significant and lasting emotional bonds with their parents.

Compared to the modern Western world, high mortality rates were standard for all age groups and sexes in the premodern world, though especially high for infants. Although numbers vary and the demographic conclusions can be debated, one fact is clear: a high proportion of children died in the premodern world. Many historians have recounted one consistent premodern reaction to this high infant mortality rate. Some parents exhibited a curious lack of grief at the death of their children, curious until one realizes that this must have been a defensive mechanism against the high infant mortality rate. Even other children learned not to invest emotional time in others, such as playmates and siblings, who would probably die off rather quickly. Yet many parents, like Martin Luther, were emotionally shattered by the death of their children.

Historians of childhood have also dealt with children's toys and games. Here as with many aspects of the history of childhood is a window into children's own activities and into adult attitudes as well. The wider introduction of children's toys and books in 18th-century Europe denotes not only new adult attention to children but also new efforts at control. United States historians identify the early 20th century as another period when adults attempted to gain new control over children's games—for example, in reducing the autonomy of middle-class boys' play. Interpretation of changes of these sorts involves sometimes skeptical assessment of benevolent rhetoric, as well as analysis of the results of adult efforts on different age groups and social classes of children. The interpretation also moves away from the simplistic kind of premodern/modern dichotomy that Ariès's formulation encouraged.

At the present time, most social historians have moved from the black legend approach, though it continues to stimulate debate and re-sourceful scholarship. Many modern historians deal not with some triumph of enlightenment but with more specific topics such as the shifts in children's functions that accompanied the industrial revolution, as children moved from work to schooling. They discuss changes in attitudes that were involved in reducing the birth rate, which could include placing heightened emotional importance on individual children. A few historians, again particularly for the modern era, venture into assessments of children's own culture, apart from parents and other adults, though this is a difficult area to research. Childhood history lacks an overarching model at this point, but it remains a vital topic in social history, and a challenge to sound interpretation. (*See also* Abuse; Child Rearing; Childbirth; Demography; European-Style Family; Family; Greek and Roman Family; Industrialization; Infanticide; Modernization; Renaissance Italy; Siblings; Wet-Nursing)

Louis Haas

REFERENCES

Ariès, Philippe. *Centuries of Childhood: A Social History of Family Life.* New York: McGraw, 1962.

Golden, Mark. *Children and Childhood in Classical Athens.* Baltimore: Johns Hopkins University Press, 1990.

Pollock, Linda. *Forgotten Children: Parent-Child Relations from 1500 to 1900.* Cambridge: Cambridge University Press, 1983.

Stone, Lawrence. *The Family, Sex and Marriage in England, 1500–1800.* New York: Harper & Row, 1977.

Wiedemann, Thomas. *Adults and Children in the Roman Empire.* New Haven: Yale University Press, 1989.

Chinese Communist Revolution

The Chinese Communist Revolution lasted nearly three decades, from the founding of the Communist Party in Shanghai in 1921 to unification of the mainland under Communist rule in 1949. At different moments in this long revolution, the party took in iconoclastic intellectuals, insurgent proletarians, parochial peasants, deserting soldiers, and city people displaced by war, producing a complex, sometimes unstable, sedimentation of revolutionary generations and experiences. The physical expanse of China contributed to the revolution's protracted nature, both in the sense of tremendous distances to be traversed by cadres seeding the Communist message and method and in the sense of extreme differences in social context from city to village and community to community. The duration and nature of the revolution, as well as its importance in Chinese and world history, target extensive studies from a social history vantage point.

Chinese communism began in the city, moved to the countryside, and returned, in victory, to its urban points of origin. The first Chinese Communists emerged from literary and political societies in Beijing and Shanghai. The avowedly anarchistic tenor of these loose networks of teachers and students, fellow provincials, friends, and lovers supported a culture of radicalism pitched toward personal and national salvation. "Missionaries" from the Soviet Comintern found converts to Leninism within these circles, but progress toward a truly disciplined party took time. Patron-client ties centering on slightly older figures like librarian and editor Li Dazhao and university administrator and publicist Chen Duxiu lent a measure of order, as well an enduring factional tendency, to Communist Party life. Personal loyalties and betrayals traced out a pattern of heartfelt, but incomplete, rebellion against a Confucian model of family and familylike relationships.

The party prospered in the 1920s by joining a rush of nationalist sentiment in the cities, organizing support among urban workers and forging an alliance with the non-Communist Nationalist Party. Patriotic feeling sustained a politics of community-based protest against imperialism that made radicalism of the nationalistic sort close to a mainstream value. Communists as nationalists allied with a broad spectrum of urban compatriots including workers, businessmen, students, and intellectuals. In addition to being responsive to patriotic appeals, workers were ripe for unionization following the rapid advance of industry in coastal cities. The Communists succeeded in this endeavor by learning to be sensitive to the social nuances of workplaces divided by class, but also fractured by status hierarchies, place of origin, and gender. For example, many female workers eventually entered the Communist labor movement in Shanghai through traditional "sisterhoods." In 1924 the Communists parlayed their growing social influence and organizational skills into a political alliance or "United Front" with the Nationalist Party. In some ways, this was a logical extension of their earlier experiences of allying locally with diverse social groups over patriotic issues. But ties with the Nationalists that the Comintern insisted would allow them to ride the "national bourgeoisie" to power in fact placed the mostly unarmed Communists in the hands of well-armed military figures like Chiang Kai-shek. This misalliance ended in 1927 with a bloody purge of the Communists by Chiang and retreat to remote rural areas.

Conversion of these often desolate redoubts into "soviets," or rural Communist political units, allowed the Communists to survive Nationalist repression. Relocation to the countryside gave the party a village and peasant base, and the resulting movements play a vital role in 20th-century peasant history. However, rural society was more complex than a myriad of villages, polarized into rich and poor classes. Sometimes small landlords joined the Communists in opposing bigger landlords. Declassé elites might preserve their status by joining or supporting the party. Some peasants remained stubbornly loyal to local notables and resisted the Communists. Villages themselves were normally part of a cluster of communities sharing marketing and other social functions. Communists often began their organizing work in market towns and then moved "down" to smaller communities or "across" to neighboring villages and finally "up" to higher administrative centers. Like rebels of old, the Communists fought to seize walled county seats. Depending on the geopolitical circumstances, this kind of military strike might follow weeks or months of organizing at a more local level or in a more remote area. Alternatively, such a battle could clear the way, in chess (or weiqi)-like fashion, for mobilizing a previously untouched county.

Without outside help peasants were hard put to build the "little politics" of rent or tax resistance into revolution. And their direct interest in such wild projects was limited at best. As an initially weak political and military force, the

Communists allowed themselves to be shaped by peasant concerns and expectations. They took blood oaths, listened carefully (difficult in many cases where local dialects were impenetrable to outsiders), and were keen to avoid offending local customs. But the Communists also moved as quickly as possible to mold peasants into suitable material for the construction of ever-larger and more expensive state structures. Through "struggle meetings" and peasant participation in numerous associations, cadres turned tensions over everything from interest rates to the crimes of local bullies into class conflict. Revenge, rough justice, and Marxian dialectics mingled in a new, often violent politics of retribution and redistribution, or "small chickens pecking another's cabbage" as some peasants less enthusiastically described these rural Bastille stormings and microrevolutions.

Populist and moral economy renditions of this process have stressed peasant autonomy and willfulness. Other studies have emphasized the ability of Communists to "make" revolution when and where they pleased. Judgments on these questions require a degree of social and spatial depth perception suitable for looking down at and sorting out both the "localizing" effects of organizing at the village level and also the higher scales of regimentation that emerged once taxes, recruits, and moral support were pried out of these little communities and sent on their way to the Communist state-in-the-making hovering at some remove.

The breakthrough for the Communists came with the Japanese invasion in 1937. At mid-decade, the Communists had just completed another long retreat, from soviets in central China collapsing under the weight of Nationalist military pressure to the momentary safety of the northwest. During this Long March, the Communists had taken 90 percent casualties and accepted Mao Zedong as leader. The Japanese invasion dislodged the Nationalists from most of their rich urban base and made further military attacks on the Communists seem unpatriotic. With foreign armies in or near some rural communities, applying at times a "kill all, burn all, destroy all" policy, the Communists could more easily add nationalism to their earlier, rural repertoire of socioeconomic appeals. Peasant na-

tionalism, though not an oxymoron, did require a significant victory over the by now familiar forces of localism and parochial thinking. It was not unknown for villagers to welcome Japanese troops as better disciplined than predatory warlord armies. In fact, Red Army soldiers on at least one occasion were mistaken for Japanese. Turning "peasants into Chinese," to borrow Eugen Weber's formula for comparable changes in French rural political attitudes, became a high priority for the party. Success helped the Communists consolidate their position in the countryside and improve their image among city people long concerned about the fate of the nation.

After Japan's defeat, the final civil war between the Communists and Nationalists was a race between the growth of the former and the collapse of the latter. The weaknesses of the Communists were real enough. But factionalism, political persecution, and a barely restrained impulse to ram the center's policies down local throats were largely concealed by the cumulative impact of party-led political and military mobilization. The Nationalists, in addition to having to concede the countryside to the Communists, bungled their chance to reestablish control in the cities through the corrupt activities of their politicians and a wild, inflationary binge of printing money to pay the government's bills. Poor generalship finished the job, leaving the Communists with the novel (for them) problem of absorbing whole provinces rather than counties into their area of control. (*See also* Peasant Rebellion)

David Strand

REFERENCES

Chen, Yung-fa. *Making Revolution: The Communist Movement in Eastern and Central China, 1937–1945.* Berkeley: University of California, 1986.

Dirlik, Arif. *The Origins of Chinese Communism.* New York: Oxford University Press, 1989.

Esherick, Joseph W., and Mary Rankin, eds. *Chinese Local Elites and Patterns of Dominance.* Berkeley: University of California Press, 1990.

Fairbank, John, and Albert Feuerwerker, eds. *The Cambridge History of China*, vol. 13; *Republican China 1912–1949*, parts 1 and 2. New York: Cambridge University Press, 1983, 1986.

Honig, Emily. *Sisters and Strangers: Women in the Shanghai Cotton Mills, 1919–1949.* Stanford, CA: Stanford University Press, 1986.

Chinese Deviance

Based on the Confucian ethic, there has been established a code of conduct which permeated Chinese society since at least the Han Dynasty. Each person was to know his place and act accordingly. The rules governing social intercourse were to be leavened by compassion and concern for others. Thus, human attributes made the established norms less rigid. Any deviation from these norms was attributed first to failure of the family to instill them properly; second, to failure of the education system to produce a properly motivated person; or third, to illness, which might be either the causative agent or the result of improper behavior. Anyone whose actions or attitudes could not be so understood was simply outside of the system. These attitudes were prevalent in traditional China, and are still found, with some modifications, in the People's Republic. In the latter, people's attitudes were to be guided by Marxism-Leninism, Mao Zedong Thought. The most noticeable difference is that traditionally one was to put the interests of the family first. As recent events have demonstrated, however, the former attitude has not disappeared.

The nature of the Confucian ethic means that deviance forms a particularly important window into the actual workings of Chinese society. Various social historians have looked at criminals, brigands, magicians, and other marginal people as an indication of diversities and tensions in Chinese history. The Confucian ethic was often confirmed by harsh penalties meted out to unrepentant deviants—an important instance of the broader proposition that deviance helps understand the accepted values of mainstream society. Confucian definitions of deviance also changed at certain points: shamans and magicians were newly attacked in the 17th and 18th centuries, as definitions of proper behavior rigidified. New issues of deviance define important features of the social history of modern China.

Opium smoking developed in China in the 18th century. It was banned by the imperial government; importation of the drug was illegal. In the 1830s Western traders introduced large quantities of the drug into China, with the connivance of corrupt officials. Problems of crime, as well as health, resulted.

Other instances of deviant behavior are linked to the secret societies collectively known as Triads. Organized gangs were active, particularly in large cities. They were allegedly engaged in extortion, prostitution, theft, and smuggling.

In the People's Republic of China (PRC) delinquent youth are generally dealt with at the community level. This care is both effective and efficient in that it utilizes existing community resources. Prior to the establishment of the PRC, crime among youth was high, including gang wars, gambling, and misdemeanors; the most serious crimes were based on differences between social classes or those with differing political beliefs. By the early 1960s these problems seemed to be under control. New problems began with the transfers of large numbers of urban youth to the countryside. Some drifted back to the cities, without work or residence permits. They turned to gambling, robbery, or prostitution to support themselves. The years of the Great Proletarian Cultural Revolution witnessed much disruption in social structures and the acceptance of some deviant behavior such as destruction of property (of capitalists) and public punishment of those whose thinking deviated from those temporarily in control. Many of that generation are confused, disillusioned, lack education or training, and do not fit well into a society that has reestablished behavioral norms. Serious offenses became more numerous—armed robbery, murder, and rape.

Crime is viewed as resulting from wrong ideology, bad influences, and bad attitudes or from family problems, broken families, or improper training. Rapid social change has been blamed for the recent rise in crime statistics. There has been an increasing problem with school dropouts, who leave school to make money but find few jobs available and turn to crime.

Traditionally, the Chinese used punishments such as exile, wearing the cangue (a wooden yoke), or other public humiliation, incarceration, and beatings. Since deviant behavior was viewed as a failure of family and community to instill proper social values, problems in this area were handled at the local level. Statistics are difficult to obtain. Research methodology parallel to that of the West has been adopted comparatively recently.

The Chinese attitude toward mental illness incorporated an ideological and humanistic approach. Emphasis is placed on early preventive strategy through the use of informal social groups and exercises in self-discipline. In 1980 an insanity defense was incorporated in the revision of China's law code, but the defendant may not initiate such a defense. The most severe mental problems reported are in the areas of schizophrenia or psychotic cases. These cases require hospitalization. Neurotic disorders can be treated within the community and workplace. As is the case with criminal deviance, group therapy encourages a realization of correct behavior. Thus, both criminal and mental behavior aberrations are dealt with in familiar surroundings and with family and community support unless those exhibiting such deviance are a danger to themselves or society.

Katherine Reist

REFERENCES

Mok Bong-ho. "Community Care For Delinquent Youth: The Chinese Approach of Rehabilitating the Young Offenders," *Journal of Offender Counseling* 15 (1990): 5–20.

Troyer, Ronald J., ed. *Social Control in the People's Republic of China.* New York: Praeger, 1989.

Tseng Wen-shing, ed. *Chinese Culture and Mental Health.* New York: Academic Press, 1985.

Chinese Family/Demography

If the family is a fundamental institution in any society, in China it is even more so. The Confucian tradition, the guiding ideology of the Chinese state for over two millennia, made the family an essential metaphor of the social order. It was not merely that state officials assumed a paternal role. A well-ordered empire required that individual families observe the rituals and norms prescribed in ancient texts, amplified in sophisticated guides to etiquette, and distilled in peasant homilies. Western influence and Communist revolution in the 20th century have altered the Chinese family, certainly, but strong Confucian elements persist, and the contemporary Chinese state continues to intervene in the family and to assign it important functions.

Confucianization of the family did not occur overnight. Only gradually did commoners and barbarians adopt Confucian practice, but by the Qing Dynasty (1644–1911), most ordinary Chinese observed marriage and burial customs akin to those practiced by elites 20 centuries earlier. The family in late imperial times was patriarchal and patrilineal. It was imbued with a religious ethos of reverence for ancestors and a belief in their continuing influence on the affairs of the living, which made it imperative to secure a male heir to carry on the family sacrifices. Marriage, a family matter, was arranged by elders, and a new bride would join the household of her husband after marriage. The fate of virtually all women was to marry and be subsumed by her husband's family and the broader circle of patrilineal kin. The cultural ideal was a grand family, a household containing a patriarch, his married sons, and their married sons, for as many generations as possible.

The Confucian tradition glorified the grand family and fertility, but the ideal multigeneration family with many children was mainly attained by elites, whose property provided incentives for family unity and the financial clout to bring in wives and concubines. Sons of smallholders and the landless had to delay their marriages, and were sooner to divide family property and establish new households through the process of family division. Grand families may have been the minority, but most Chinese lived with parents in an extended household for at least some period after marriage, and most older people resided with a son if one was available. This remains true today. As for fertility, all evidence suggests that traditional Chinese had moderate levels of marital fertility, probably the result of lengthy breast-feeding that led to longer periods of temporary sterility, although this low marital fertility was offset by high rates of marriage among females. In this respect, China was the polar opposite of traditional northwestern Europe, where late marriage and high rates of celibacy were offset by high levels of fertility within marriage. Despite the Malthusian view that fertility in China was high and unconstrained (and a traditional government policy of favoring large population), between 1550 and 1850, vital rates and the population growth rate were probably quite similar in Europe and China, though earlier expansion meant that total Chinese population was considerably larger. China did not, however, undergo a demographic transition in the 19th century, so growth rates persisted.

Beneath the Confucian stereotypes lurk remarkably varied marriage and family forms. In Taiwan Arthur Wolf and Chieh-shan Huang (1980) have described an area where the preferred marriage form was for a boy to marry his adopted sister. In southern mainland China Burton Pasternak has described a locale where it was the norm for a man to marry into his wife's family. In the Guangdong region were locales where women formed sisterhoods and refused to marry, and others where it was customary to delay co-residence with the husband for years after the wedding. Whether responses to local ecology or remnants of local cultures, these phenomena were somehow both tolerated and ignored by the guardians of Confucian tradition.

The late 19th and 20th centuries brought a series of shocks to the Chinese social order. Western family models, brought by missionaries and merchants, seduced urban elites. By the 1920s, the revolutionary republican government had codified the new thinking in family laws that gave women new rights to choose their spouse, to hold property, and to divorce. But the reform movement was mainly limited to cities, and except for the ubiquitous decline of footbinding, rural families remained little changed. The family agenda of the Communist revolutionaries after 1949 was only somewhat more radical than that of the republican reformers, but the Communists did attempt to bring the revolution to rural areas. Women were brought into the labor force, divorce was legalized, and arranged marriages were banned, along with ancestor worship and other feudal customs. But resistance from peasants, including local Communist cadres, forced the party to downplay the family revolution. Rural collectivization beginning in 1955 influenced the family, but the effects were contradictory. Deprived of a property base, there was little incentive for the formation of grand families, but the collectives also reinforced the role of the family as an economic and welfare unit. Although it is difficult to gauge the tenor of relationships within families, Chinese family customs seemed to emerge from the collective era in 1980 remarkably little changed from what they had been three decades before, and with the family restored as a center of entrepreneurship, there are signs of a renaissance of traditional religious observance, child marriage, and extended households.

The most revolutionary force affecting the modern Chinese family has been the policy to limit births. In the 1970s in rural areas, marriage and childbearing were gradually brought under bureaucratic surveillance and control. Marriage ages rose rapidly in the 1970s in response to the policy, and the total fertility rate dropped 50 percent in under a decade, the fastest fertility decline on record for a large population. The One-Child Policy, in force since 1979, has been quite effective in cities, although de facto policy in most rural areas permits two children. The sudden contraction in fertility will have far-reaching effects on family composition and values. Many families face a future without a male heir, and a generation of urbanites will grow up as only children. With the decline in siblings, a rising proportion of married couples will reside with a parent, while a rising proportion of the elderly will find themselves living without the support of a son or daughter. The implications of the birth control policy for the family are still unfolding. (*See also* Chinese Communist Revolution; Chinese Gender Relations; Chinese State and Society; Confucianism)

William Lavely

REFERENCES

Baker, Hugh D.R. *Chinese Family and Kinship*. New York: Columbia University Press, 1980.

Ebrey, Patricia Buckley. *Confucianism and Family Rituals in Imperial China*. Princeton, NJ: Princeton University Press, 1991.

Hanley, Susan B., and Arthur P. Wolf, eds. *Family and Population in East Asian History*. Stanford, CA: Stanford University Press, 1985.

Lang, Olga. *Chinese Family and Society*. New Haven: Yale University Press, 1946.

Parish, William, and Martin King Whyte. *Village and Family in Contemporary China*. Chicago: Chicago University Press, 1978.

Wolf, Arthur, and Chieh-shan Huang. *Marriage and Adoption in China, 1845–1945.* Stanford, CA: Stanford University Press, 1980.

Zeng, Yi. *Family Dynamics in China.* Madison: University of Wisconsin Press, 1991.

Chinese Gender Relations

Gender relations involve both the actual interactions and the perceptions of men and women. Studies on gender patterns are playing an increasingly important role in Chinese social history. Due to limited sources on peasant lives, research on Chinese gender relations generally deals with the elite until the modern period.

Since ancient Chinese society, perceptions of men and women have been closely linked with the *yin/yang* philosophy, which viewed the cosmos in the unity of opposites. Men were associated with *yang*—the heaven—and women with *yin*—the earth. Hence, men were strong, active, and rigid, and women were gentle, passive, and yielding. The male-female relationship was viewed as the *yin/yang* complementarity and harmony. Women's subordination was justified by the assumption that *yin* dominance signified disorder.

Family has been the most important social institution to shape gender roles and gender relations in China. The ancient *Li ji* (*Record of Rites*), which was codified in the Zhou Dynasty (ca. 1100 BC–256 BC), explained rules for proper conduct and upheld the ideas that parents dominated children and males dominated females. A woman, confined to domestic sphere, was supposed to subordinate herself to her father and to her husband, and to her son after the death of her husband. Marriage, viewed as an obligation to ancestors for the continuation of family line, was arranged by parents and conducted in ritualized ceremonies. The husband-wife relationships, though characterized as controlling-serving, were to be maintained, in accordance with the *li*, by mutual respect. A woman reinforced her ties with her husband's family by bearing a son. Monogamy was the conventional norm, but polygyny existed as a show of status and from the desire for many sons. The Chinese form of polygyny guaranteed the wife privileges and legal protection not available to concubines, who were purchased and resalable. The inheritance of family line through the male, not the female, left woman as a child-bearing vehicle to perpetuate her husband's family. Moreover, women had no inheritance right to family property except in special cases. These conditions devalued woman as a human being in family and society. From birth, daughters were regarded as inferior and sons superior.

During the Han Dynasty (206 BC–AD 220), when Confucianism was adopted as state ideology to promote the ancient values and the *li*, higher moral standards began to be imposed on women than on men. Two books spelled out criteria for proper conduct and social expectations of women: *Biographies of Virtuous Women* (*Lienu zhuan*) by Liu Xiang (male) praised motherhood, wisdom, faithfulness, and purity, and *Admonitions to Women* (*Nu jie*) by Ban Zhao (female) emphasized submission, diligence, manners, and devotion. While elaborating the ancient notion of husband-wife relationship, Ban Zhao stressed domestic learning for daughters and wife's devotion to husband. Although Ban Zhao was most frequently cited in later dynasties to regulate women's behavior, she seems to have had limited contemporary influence. Remarriage during the Han was a common practice, and remarried women were not looked down upon. Women who actively influenced their husbands were much respected. The mother-son relationship seldom conformed to the gender patterns of the *li*. A mother identified herself with the success of her sons, who elevated her status and respected her will.

The T'ang Dynasty (AD 618–907) enacted the first Chinese laws for women to keep their dowries as their own property, though women still could not inherit family property in general. The T'ang elite continued the fashion started around the 6th century to marry daughters of eminent ancestry so that grandchildren would carry the social status the mother brought into the marriage. This admiration for aristocratic pedigrees inflated the value of betrothal gifts, which became so exorbitant that the emperor had to take measures to curb the trend. The highly urbanized T'ang also witnessed the association between literati and urban prostitutes who were well trained in music, dance, literature, and art. Some historians have suggested that this interaction contributed to the flourishing of T'ang poetry. Meanwhile, emphasis on women's beauty shifted from simplicity to flamboyance. Garments appeared seductive with bright colors and floral designs; makeup and decorative hairstyles created more sensual appeal. These changes in the T'ang suggested a relatively relaxed environment for women and the recognition of a female gender.

Strong reaction against this trend toward freer social life arose with the formation of Neo-Confucianism in the 12th century. Emphasis on women's chastity extended to virginity. A man faced social stigma if he married a widow or a divorcée. But Neo-Confucianism did not take a strong hold on people's daily life until later time. Some historians have indicated that remarriage during the Sung Dynasty (AD 960–1279) was not condemned and that the male-female relationship was romantic. The shifting customs in marriage finance, however, required families to give large dowries to marry out their daughters. This dowry crisis, which became a burden for many families, encouraged female infanticide and the new practice of adopting child daughters-in-law (*tongyangxi*) later in certain areas. Meanwhile, foot-binding began to be fashionable as a standard for feminine attractiveness and spread from elite to peasant families. Foot-binding, achieved by tightly wrapping a girl's feet to break bones for the prevention of normal growth and walk, was considered as important to daughters as schooling was to sons.

The promotion of Neo-Confucianism in the Ch'ing Dynasty (AD 1644–1911) reduced women's status. Women were expected to look weak and sick to arouse men's pity easily. This perception of women enhanced the *yang* aspect of gender relations. A woman's chastity was supposed to be more precious than her own life. To discourage remarriage, the Ch'ing laws, following those of Yuan and Ming Dynasties (AD 1271–1644), stated that women could not take their dowries with them if they remarried.

Men have shown sympathy toward women's suffering on different occasions. Some of the Ch'ing literati openly criticized foot-binding and the double moral standards oppressing women. Li Ruzhen's satirical novel *Flowers in the Mirror*

(*Jing hua yuan*) attacked the injustices imposed upon women, such as foot-binding, polygyny, and coerced chastity.

The effort to liberate women did not start until the late 19th century, when China began reform. Chinese reformers and revolutionaries alike regarded the liberation of women as an essential element in making China strong. They believed that a nation could not be strong with half of its population weak. Western missionaries also promoted women's education and attacked foot-binding. The May Fourth Movement of 1919, which produced an enormous literature on women's issues, disseminated ideas of freedom of marriage and equal education. In the following decades, many women, urban and rural, joined revolutionary activities.

The effective implementation of the 1950 Marriage Law changed the lives of many Chinese women. Monogamy and free choice of partners have become the basis of the new marriage system. The husband-wife relationship is defined as a full and equal partnership with women's equal right to knowledge and independence and full participation in economic, social, and political life. The general acceptance of women's equality with the expectation of their submissive gentleness today demonstrates the coexistence of new gender roles with old beliefs. Although a woman's ability is recognized and respected, she is usually expected not to surpass her husband in public achievement. In general, seniority takes priority in Chinese gender relations. In rural areas, marriage is still largely arranged by parents, but children's consent is sought. The emphasis on economic development since the late 1970s has given rise to increasing discrimination against women. In response to the population control policy, female infanticide has increased since the 1970s. To protect women, the government enacted a Women's Rights Law in early 1992.

Studies on Chinese women's issues have shed much light on gender patterns, though little has been written historically on Chinese gender relations. While Western feminist theories exert increasing influence on studies in this area, Western feminist interpreters, like Tani Barlow, are attempting to "engender" China in a theoretical framework. In China itself, gender as a subject of study has just begun to be conducted by some specialists such as Li Xiaojiang.

Liping Bu

REFERENCES

Barlow, Tani E. *Imagining Woman: Ding Ling and the Gendering of Chinese Modernity*. Durham, NC: Duke University Press, forthcoming.

Croll, Elisabeth J. *Feminism and Socialism in China*. London, Boston: Routledge & Kegan Paul, 1978.

Hershatter, Gail, et al., eds. *Engendering China*. Cambridge: Harvard University Press, 1994.

Guisso, Richard W., and Stanley Johannesen, eds. *Women in China*. Youngstown, NY: Philo Press, 1981.

Li Yu-ning, ed. *Chinese Women Through Chinese Eyes*. New York: An East Gate Book, 1992.

Watson, Rubie S., and Patricia B. Ebrey, eds. *Marriage and Inequality in Chinese Society*. Berkeley: University of California Press, 1991.

Chinese Gentry

The English term "gentry" in Chinese social history refers not to a land-based subaristocracy (the common meaning for gentry in European history) but to the *shenshi*, the social elite produced by the Confucian civil service examinations. This elite is peculiar to late imperial China, gradually succeeding the aristocracy of the 7th century and before, and entirely monopolizing the 10,000 to 20,000 official civil positions only by the Ming Dynasty (1368–1644). Such was its dominance in town and country that Ming and Ch'ing (1644–1911) China is often described as a "gentry society." In the 19th century the number of gentry—including irregular gentry with purchased titles—reached over 1 million, constituting with their family members between 1 percent and 1.5 percent of the population. Eighty thousand to 100,000 were upper gentry qualified to serve as officials by virtue of earning the provincial or metropolitan degrees.

Gentry status was much sought after, not only by gentry sons but by any young male whose family could spare him from farm work or trade. Each of the three stages of the civil service examinations (district, province, and metropolitan, at Peking) was highly competitive, and one or more decades of arduous preparation and several failed attempts normally preceded success. But even families that grew prosperous in trade or money lending or brokerage would sponsor an examination candidate from among younger relatives for the sake of the prestige and connections and official protection a degree holder could bring. For those upper gentry who became officials, posts in various provinces yielded considerable income in salaries, gifts, and customary extralegal surcharges. Once invested in land at home such earnings as gentry property could escape taxation by a variety of strategems. While the far more numerous lower degree holders often owned no land, these made a good living with teaching and public services in their home area.

The Chinese gentry was perhaps the most open of all elites in traditional societies. Upward mobility was facilitated by the absence of qualifications of birth or property in the examination system and by the presence of private and public schools, at least in well-off areas. Downward mobility tended to result from the repartition of property among all sons, unlike the customary primogeniture of northwestern Europe. Yet those of modest means or lacking connections could scarcely hope to step on the first rung of the ladder of success, let alone enter officialdom at its top. It is true that among men awarded metropolitan degrees in 48 of the Ming and Ch'ing triennial examinations as many as 30 percent had no relatives who had succeeded in examinations at any level for the preceding three generations. But the proportion of new men dropped sharply from Ming to Ch'ing, and if more than three generations are counted the proportion is considerably lower overall. Having relatives, even distant ancestors, who were gentry was clearly helpful to an aspiring candidate.

The lineage system prevailing over southeastern China and present in some central and northern provinces was a key institution for the maintenance of gentry influence. Because its corporate property escaped the rule of partible inheritance, the lineage accumulated wealth that could be used to school its male children to be future degree holders and to reinforce through ritual the sense of loyalty to lineage interests. Strong lineages dominated not only land but every aspect of their localities; at the same time they incorporated poorer nongentry branches whose sons might rise through the lineage school and examination to gentry status.

In the mid-19th century the gentry rallied to the Ch'ing Empire and suppressed a series of rebellions of unprecedented scope and violence, but their identification with the foreign Manchu rulers was soon to weaken. In the last decades of the Ch'ing, helped by indiscriminate official sales of titles and offices, the Chinese gentry were gradually merging into a composite merchant-gentry elite, and when the dynasty in belated recognition of the need for drastic reform abolished the Confucian civil examinations in 1905, the gentry ceased to exist as a class dependent on the expectation of official employment. The collapse of the imperial dynasty six years later may be attributed in part to this sacrifice of its strongest bulwark. The gentry in the Republican period (1911–1949) shared many social and cultural characteristics with their predecessors, except for some crucial weaknesses: a sundered link with officialdom, more crudely exploitative relations with tenants, and an inability to protect localities from bandits and warlords. These changes made the gentry vulnerable to the first sweeping challenge to their rural power when—redefined as a much larger class, namely landowners who did not work their own land—they became the Chinese Communist Party's main domestic enemy and the target of revolutionary land reform at the hands of former tenants, poor farming neighbors, and the landless. In the People's Republic (since 1949) the gentry survive only as an epithet, and until recently their children and grandchildren have borne a life-long stigma.

Gentry culture was permeated with Confucian values, for the examinations were heavily based on the Confucian classics and Neo-Confucian commentaries. This system of thought was profoundly conservative. In myriad ways it rationalized the emperor and his bureaucracy, the patriarchal family, and the gentry's position as moral exemplars and rightful leaders, as well as reinforcing their neglect of scientific experiment and disparagement of technological achievement. That is why Confucianism has been anathema to Chinese Communists. Yet Chinese written culture, in its rich and ever-changing variety, is undeniably the product of the gentry

tradition. Besides their skills as classicists and drafters of official documents and historical records, the gentry perfected such arts as ritual performance, divination, calligraphy, poetry, textual criticism, local history, painting, antique collection, belles lettres, and landscape gardening; Chinese libraries and museum collections in China and abroad stand as monuments to their achievement. Life under gentry society, however, should not be idealized. The seamy side of gentry households, in particular the sufferings of maids and concubines, is widely portrayed in fiction—for example, in two famous autobiographical novels, Cao Xueqin's *Dream of the Red Chamber* (1792) and Ba Jin's *Family* (1931), and the Republican gentry are pilloried, sometimes caricatured, in countless socialist-realist works of the 1950s and 1960s for their maltreatment of the poor and weak. (*See also* Aristocracy)

Donald S. Sutton

REFERENCES

Chang, Chung-li. *The Chinese Gentry: Studies on Their Role in Nineteenth-Century Chinese Society.* Seattle: University of Washington Press, 1955.

Duara, Prasenjit. *Culture, Power, and the State: Rural North China, 1900–1942.* Stanford, CA: Stanford University Press, 1988.

Ebrey, Patricia Buckley, and James L. Watson, eds. *Kinship Organization in Late Imperial China, 1000–1940.* Berkeley: University of California Press, 1986.

Ho, Ping-ti. *The Ladder of Success in Imperial China: Aspects of Social Mobility, 1368–1911.* New York: Columbia University Press, 1962.

Kong, Demao, and Lan Ke. *In the Mansion of Confucius' Descendants.* Peking: New World Press, 1984.

Chinese Periodization

In Chinese conventional historiography, history is arranged by the sequence of dynasties. Dynasties, however, are differentiated into major ones that lasted a long time and unified China, while the minor ones usually clustered in the intermediate periods between major dynasties. The typical arrangement of dynastic history is reflected by the curriculum for history majors in Chinese universities, as shown in the table on page 124. Such divisions according to the changes of sovereign court, of course, are of relatively little sig-

Major Dynasties	Intermediate Periods
Shang (ca. 16th century–ca. 11th century BC) and Western Chou (ca. 11th century–770 BC)	
	Spring and Autumn (770–476 BC)
	Warring States (476–221 BC)
Ch'in (221–206 BC) and Han (206 BC–AD 220)	
	Three Kingdoms (AD 220–265)
	Chin (AD 265–420)
	Southern and Northern Dynasties (AD 420–581)
S'ui (AD 581–618) and T'ang (AD 618–907)	
	Five Dynasties (AD 907–979)
Sung (AD 960–1279)	
	Liao (AD 916–1125)
Chin (AD 1115–1234)	
Yuan (AD 1271–1368)	
Ming (AD 1368–1644)	
Ch'ing (AD 1644–1911)	

nificance to nonpolitical historical concerns, and they have been variously rethought in connection with growing interest in social history.

Since the 1930s, Marxist historians tried to apply their periodization on Chinese history. At that time, the "Asiatic mode of production" was adopted by some as an excuse for not rigidly periodizing Chinese history into the five standard stages: primitive communism, slavery, feudalism, capitalism, and socialism. During the 1950s periodization of these five stages became a major focus for historians in mainland China as a means of interpreting Chinese history. It is difficult, however, to define 2,000 years of development in China, after the obvious feudalism was over in the 3rd century BC, until capitalism was introduced by Western powers in the recent centuries. There is virtually no way to reconcile the deviations between the Marxist theoretical frame and historical reality in China, other than by labeling ancient feudalism as slavery and the entire span of imperial bureaucratic society as feudalism. This irony, after another round of discussions in the late 1970s, still remains to be settled.

The tripartition of ancient, medieval, and modern periods was borrowed from Western historiography as early as the 1920s. This approach coexists conveniently with dynastic periodizations. College courses that cover a prolonged span often are described in tripartition. There are still different opinions among histori-

ans about the respective beginnings and endings of these three stages. Some historians would include the Ch'in-Han period in the ancient era, obviously a counterpart of the Western concept of including the Roman Empire in the classical era. Other scholars, however, would take the Ch'in-Han unified empire as a fresh departure from the era of ancient feudalism and, therefore, make it the beginning of the middle ages.

Likewise, the beginning point of the modern era is also a problem. A theory attributed to T. Naito of Japan, which has had great impact upon Western sinology, suggests that the history of the Sung Dynasty already exhibited many modern features. Nevertheless, Chinese historians are still debating whether any sign of budding capitalism ever could be detected in the Ming-Ch'ing period. Furthermore, the obvious departure of Chinese history taking place in mid-19th century, as the Western powers forced China to open treaty ports, might be more legitimately assigned as the starting point of a new era in Chinese history. Yet the question of the beginning of the modern era is far from being settled.

It can be suggested that Chinese history need not strictly follow the tripartition of Western history. However, Chinese history, just as those of other civilizations, should be treated as part of the common history of humankind. In its long history, China changes constantly. As its status evolves along the course from having local states, then an empire, and finally to being a member of international communities, its socioeconomic elements and composition change accordingly. The following scheme represents an effort to chart the development of Chinese history in cultural and socioeconomic dimensions. A new periodization of this kind is probably more meaningful than the old dynastic one or the conventional tripartition divisions. A scheme is therefore suggested as follows:

I. Late Neolithic to bronze cultures (ca. 4000 BC–ca. 1200 BC). In this stage, people have already adapted to their natural surroundings. The state is formed while village communities remain fundamental social units.

II. Foundation of a nation of Chinese as well as a cultural definition (ca. 1200 BC–250 BC). A coalition of peoples forms a common identity in the world. A Chinese pattern of thinking, advanced by Confucianism, Taoism, and other schools of thought, is taking shape. This period also witnesses the rise and fall of feudalism and drastic social changes thereof related. Kinship units replace tribes and village community as primary social groups.

III. Universal empire and cultural universalism in the Ch'in-Han period (250 BC–AD 300). A Chinese territory is defined, and its cultural characteristics are fully recognized. State authority monopolizes social resources. Confucianism is established as orthodoxy. A bureaucracy staffed by Confucian scholars takes shape. Intensification of farming coincides with formation of a nationwide marketing network. Social structure gradually is settled with kinship organization as the most crucial building block.

IV. Breakdown and transformation (AD 300–1000). China is invaded by people from the steppe lands, and masses of Chinese move to the south. Classes are formed due to differentiation of the conquerors and the conquered. A cultural transformation takes place due to the movement of population. The state declines while lineages formed by local magnates dominate society. Confucian orthodoxy is challenged by Buddhism and Taoism.

V. Multistate systems in East Asia (AD 1000–1550). Although China remains a domi-

nant power, other states are formed as major powers around China. Commercialization and urbanization have impacts on social structures that result in greater social complexity of society. Advancement of technology is witnessed. A symbiosis of imperial state and gentry-led society is formed.

VI. China enters the global system (AD 1550–1950). A worldwide interdependence emerges due to continuous interactions and exchanges among the major cultural entities. China must deal with others in the same world. Deterioration of urban-rural continuum gradually leads to their mutual alienation. Intellectuals' leadership role decreases. Gaps between the rich and the poor widen. Social reorganization takes place, triggered by the impact of Western culture and modern capitalism.

VII. China redefines its role (1950 to present). This is a stage of reintegration of individual cultural entities into a global system. Two Chinas are coexisting, both with new political and economic elites. The People's Republic adopts nationalism and socialism, while the Republic of China (Taiwan) tries the road of capitalistic industrialization. A world economic system has enormous impact on China, in which new Westernized political and social institutions replace the traditional ones. (*See also* Periodization/Sequences)

Cho-yun Hsu

REFERENCES

Dirlik, Arif. *Revolutions and History.* Berkeley: University of California Press, 1978.
Huang, Ray. *China: A Macro-History.* New York: M.E. Sharpe Inc., 1988.
Meskill, John. *The Pattern of Chinese History.* New York: D.C. Heath, 1965.

Chinese Printing

East Asian printing precedes the use of printing in Europe by about 700 years. The Chinese are believed to have invented printing, although the earliest printed text that survives (dated from the middle of the 8th century) was found in Korea. As in Europe, the first printed Asian texts were religious in nature, prompted by the Buddhist belief in acquiring merit through the copying of Buddhist charms (*dharani*). In supplanting the laborious process of hand copying, printing was not only a timesaving technology; its ability to reproduce exactly the same text, without variation, was a decided asset in the propagation of texts where there was a concern for the preservation of orthodoxy. Government encouragement of authorized editions of the Confucian classics led to the rapid expansion of printing in Sung (AD 960–1279) times. From the Ming Dynasty (1368–1644) on, private literati and commercial publishers joined official printing bureaux to create a varied and voluminous body of printed materials of all kinds.

Although movable type was known in China, the nonalphabetic nature of the written language did not encourage its adoption; instead, Chinese printing technology was dominated by the simple and inexpensive method of wood-block printing, or xylography. Chinese printing technology, by contrast with European printing, permitted easy entry into publishing. Unlike movable type, this printing technology required virtually no capital and no capital equipment. The major costs were the raw materials (paper, ink, and woodblocks) and labor. The carver did not need to be literate, since the texts, written on thin sheets of paper, were pasted onto the blocks. Although a woodblock made of the standard pear or jujube wood could be used to print 16,000 to 26,000 copies, since the blocks could be stored for future printings, no minimum volume of imprints was required.

Printing obviously influenced the historical evolution of Chinese society. The new technology enabled Confucian texts to be disseminated more effectively and more accurately. One wonders whether it would have been possible, without printing, to recruit officials on the basis of written examinations, as was done in China for at least the last millennium. But printed materials were not monopolized by the rich and powerful. Although the educated elite dominated publishing both as creators and consumers, the 16th-century commercial expansion linked with the onset of maritime trade with Europe supported an expansion of education which itself increased the demand for books. In artifacts of popular culture such as the almanac or religious print, we can see the extent to which even peasants participated in the literate culture. Printing was thus one of the keys to cultural integration in Chinese society.

Evelyn S. Rawski

REFERENCES

Miller, Constance R. *Technical and Cultural Prerequisites for the Invention of Printing in China and the West.* San Francisco: Chinese Materials Center, 1983.

Twitchett, Denis. *Printing and Publishing in Medieval China.* New York: Frederic C. Beil, 1983.

Chinese Social Protest

Social protest in China is based on the premise that the government is moral, that its individuals set a moral example for the people, and that its purpose is to care for their interests and well-being. If in fact the government has failed to be moral in itself, or worse, to care for the people, protests serve as a warning to reform, or as a collective expression of dissatisfaction, which if further organized or not answered by reform could overthrow the government. All Chinese governments are established to ensure order. Protests disturb this order, threatening chaos. If the government cannot deal with these disturbances, then it has outlived its function. The social history of protest in China works within this destructive cultural political context.

Social protests were usually instituted by peasants, in traditional China; such protests dealt with lack of peasant ownership of land or high taxes. Other protests were begun by intellectuals. They protested social conditions and the need for reforms, social, political, and/or economic. Peasants organized through secret societies, such as the Heaven and Earth Society or the Elder Brother Society (1850), at various points in Chinese history. Some such groups were associated with religious sects of the Taoists, such as the Five Pecks of Rice Movement (AD 184), or Buddhists, such as the White Lotus Society Uprisings (1352–1368; 1796–1804). The Taiping rebellion of the mid-19th century began with the antigovernment God Worshipper Society, whose appeal was, for the peasants, land, communal sharing of wealth, and an end to the status of the landed gentry. Some intellectuals were attracted by an alternative philosophy of government. Although the rebellion was suppressed with the help of Chinese officials, danger to the existing order occurred when the peasants and intellectuals joined forces.

Banditry in China was perhaps an informal form of social protest. Disbanded soldiers, dispossessed farmers, and others displaced from the system could only exist outside of it by preying on those successful within established social niches. Kidnapping and robberies were endemic examples of the attempts of displaced persons to cope with being outside of the system and protesting their lack of remedy within it.

In the 20th century protests were conducted against opium usage, foot-binding, and female infanticide. These protests were most effective in urban areas. Demonstrations were held for increased access to education, education for females, and for the teaching of modern subjects such as science, health sciences, Western languages, and international law. Additional protests for reform of the political system, particularly for success in preventing the expansion of foreign rights in China, and for modernization in order to answer foreign military challenges, led to the overthrow of the crumbling imperial system in 1912.

Protests following the Versailles Conference of 1919 were directed at the lack of assertiveness of the Chinese delegation in protecting Chinese interests. This May Fourth Movement was begun by professors, students, and journalists and spread throughout much of Chinese society. In attempting to make China strong and respected, the intellectuals searched for a new organizing philosophy to replace the discredited Confucianism, along with a new system of government, economic, and social organization.

Simultaneously, protests against foreign rights in China, a result of the unequal treaty system, began to gather momentum. Demonstrations were many; riots occurred on more than a few occasions. Some foreign concession areas devolved to China as a result. However, the most effective protest technique was the boycott. Workers would not enter foreign-owned factories; foreign shops and products were ignored;

ships were neither loaded nor unloaded; foreign commerce in China slowed or went out of business. Such economic demonstrations were difficult to maintain, but they were often effective, at least in the short term. They were most prevalent in the 1920s and 1930s, and as a result, foreign privileges were reduced or modified.

After 1919 some protests became more fully organized along class lines. Workers protested factory or other work conditions; peasants objected to taxes and land manipulation by landlords. Political organizations began to identify with the interests of particular groups. For the remainder of the 20th century, social protests have had more pronounced political and economic components. Examples range from the Communist-organized, peasant-based Autumn Harvest Uprisings of 1927 to the student demonstrations in the major cities in the 1970s and 1980s. The best known of these were the demonstrations organized in Tiananmen Square in 1989.

As with many of its predecessors, the Tiananmen demonstrations began with students. They protested corruption on the part of the government and preferential appointments for the families of officials, the so-called princes' clique. Demands for reform included conditions at Chinese universities and job assignments after graduation. When these issues were ignored, the students were joined by others protesting inflation, discriminatory economic policy, which affected negatively urban workers' standard of living, and lack of demonstrable concern by the government. Many wished for political reform akin to those instituted in the economic sphere.

The use of force against these protesters was to demonstrate to the world, the country, and possibly themselves, that the government was still in control and demonstrably so. The government had to prove that it could deal with disturbances, that it had not, in fact, outlived its function.

Research on protest history is generally centered around one major event such as the Boxer Uprising, or one province or city of China in a particular period. Except for comparative studies of the Chinese Revolution, comparing it with those of Russia and France, comparative research on social protests has not been a major area of scholarship, though it invites further attention.

Katherine Reist

REFERENCES

Chesneaux, Jean. *The Chinese Labor Movement, 1919–1927*. Stanford, CA: Stanford University Press, 1968.

Chow Tse-Tsung. *The May Fourth Movement, Intellectual Revolution In Modern China*. Cambridge: Cambridge University Press, 1960.

Wakeman, Frederic, Jr. "Rebellion and Revolution: The Study of Popular Movements in Chinese History," *Journal of Asian Studies* 36, 2 (Feb. 1977): 201–37.

Chinese State and Society

"State and society" is an 18th-century European term applied by Enlightenment thinkers to the difficult relations between the growing power of the central state and hereditary interests represented in deliberative bodies. But it can also be applied to agrarian states' relations with their elites. Thus, the Chinese Empire sustained central government by controlling the rural economy at arm's length, sharing the surplus with land-based elites. By the 15th century, state linkage with these elites can be described as symbiotic, with the result that some Western scholars hyphenate the term "state-and-society."

How was such a symbiosis achieved? Notwithstanding a highly developed lineage system in the south especially, and some powerful families that boasted generations of officials, China in late imperial times lacked the hereditary aristocratic class that hamstrung the medieval and Renaissance state in Western Europe. Instead, the scholar-gentry bestrode state and society, serving the former as officials and belonging to the latter as landowners or their relatives.

The scholar-gentry's loyalty and cooperation were assured by numerous incentives and prohibitions. Its "ladder of success," in Ho Ping-ti's term (1962), was an official statewide civil service examination system. Both private and public education prepared male candidates for the examinations. The unquestioned prestige of the civil service among careers, and its ability to confer wealth and security on officials, channeled the interests of most ambitious males in Chinese communities. Since the content of the examinations, and therefore of education, was closely based on the Confucian classics, future state employees along with other local leaders were in effect indoctrinated with a common conservative ideology. This local elite saw itself as an ally of the state, not its rival.

Should indoctrination fail, important customary checks weakened local interests. Property was divided among all sons to inhibit the growth of huge personal fortunes, and as each new dynasty began old noble titles were terminated. Officials were pried away from their native provinces and shuffled regularly from post to post. Merchants were co-opted and restrained as official supervisors of trade and of monopolies on salt and other commodities. Nor did the state rely exclusively on the gentry. Extra-official, nongentry guarantors and headmen collected taxes and oversaw local order.

In understanding the prominence of the scholar-gentry, the power of the state, and the importance of the connection between them, we must stress that civil bureaucracy had no competitors in China. For example, religious institutions were scattered and disunited; merchant organizations (*huiguan*) existed for the convenience of traders far from home, never for self-government; voluntary associations existed underground, as secret societies or illegal scholarly associations; and the military was weak, decentralized and disparaged as a career. Chinese law, which might have served to strengthen the rights of local vested interests or individuals, was designed instead as an instrument for preserving state order.

These institutional patterns were buttressed by the entire symbolic-ideological system of orthodoxy centered upon the political concept of the heavenly mandate. According to this, the emperor and the dynasty to which he belonged presided as an intermediary between heaven and earth, maintaining order and harmony in the universe through Confucian scholar-officials. An elaborate system of ritual worship, which was conducted on specified days from the capital down to the walled cities that oversaw each county, reaffirmed the emperor's centrality and the agency of his officials. Educated people might argue about politics or philosophy, but none challenged the basic principle that they were participating actively in a universal moral order. Its assumptions were linked with the ancient ideas of yin/yang—unequal, alternating, and mutually necessary principles like male and female, or day and night—and embodied in the very language and the world it described. No wonder foreign conquerors adopted the same system once they settled down to rule China.

One should not follow some Enlightenment thinkers in simplifying and idealizing China. The state-and-society was established late and never worked perfectly. For much of the Six Dynasties period (4th to 6th centuries) and into the reunified S'ui/T'ang period, there were enduring aristocratic clans in northern and southern China. The T'ang Dynasty (618–907) did not demean military status, and in its middle centuries contended with powerful Taoist and Buddhist establishments. During the Sung Dynasty (960–1279), the government tried to put its own representatives into the villages, and came to base its taxation more on commerce than on land. The Mongols forsook for a time the system of examinations. In the late Ming, the elite took more interest in philosophy and poetry and factional politics than in a governmental career, and local order collapsed in a series of vast peasant rebellions. Even at its apogee in the 18th century, the Ch'ing rulers found their formal and informal controls of administration fell short, and could not draw enough revenues from the land to keep pace with population growth.

In the 19th century the symbiotic Chinese state-and-society began to break down irremediably, as a series of humiliations at Western hands undercut political authority. The abolition of the Confucian classics–based examination system in 1905 strained the bond of educated men with the state. The replacement of the Manchu Empire by a theoretically Republican Chinese system in 1911 and 1912 finally severed that bond entirely, and neither of the two great political parties under the Republic (1912–1949) tried to reconstruct it. The Nationalist Party (Guomindang) wanted to govern directly, but the rural elite, no longer dependent on any government, frustrated its efforts, and Nanjing finally ceded the land tax to local rulers. The Communist Party leadership blamed land-

lords and their allies for China's rural ills and mobilized a land reform movement of poorer peasants to destroy their authority. They were even more adamant than modernizing elites elsewhere that state power should not be compromised. Ideologically and politically, there was no "society" on the mainland in the decades after 1949: theoretically, the state, or rather the party, embodying proletarian values and serving the interests of the people, ruled supreme.

Donald S. Sutton

REFERENCES

Eastman, Lloyd. *Family, Field, and Ancestors.* New York and Oxford: Oxford University Press, 1988.

Ho Ping-ti. *The Ladder of Success in Imperial China: Aspects of Social Mobility, 1368–1911.* New York: Wiley, 1962.

Hsiao, Kung-ch'üan. *Rural China: Imperial Control in the Nineteenth Century.* Seattle: University of Washington Press, 1960.

Mann, Susan. *Local Merchants and the Chinese Bureaucracy, 1750–1950.* Stanford, CA: Stanford University Press, 1986.

Naquin, Susan, and Evelyn Rawski. *Chinese Society in the Eighteenth Century.* New Haven: Yale University Press, 1987.

Chinese Urbanization

China has a long, continuous, and substantial urban tradition. Its first walled settlements can be dated back almost 4,000 years, and its largest cities were until the 19th century almost always among the world's largest. It is estimated that prior to 1800 over one-third of the population that had lived in cities lived in China.

Urban development in China can be divided into six stages: (1) The emergence of walled settlements in northern China no later than 1800 BC; (2) The transformation of cities (*ch'eng*) from fortresses of nobles into hierarchical administrative centers between the 2nd and 6th centuries BC; (3) The relaxation of urban regulations and the flourishing of market towns and coastal ports in the T'ang and Sung periods (AD 618–1279); (4) The intensification of urban development in the Ming and Ch'ing periods (AD 1368–1911) as a result of population increase and commercial development; (5) The establishment of "treaty-ports" between about 1842 and 1937; and

(6) the implementation of strict urban policies in contemporary China.

The strategic locations (protected by natural barricades) and the physical layouts (including rectangular city walls and centrally located ancestral temples) of China's earliest walled settlements indicated that their establishment was an important component of the political process through which the ruling lineages exerted their authority. As the feudal order gradually gave way to the multistate (*kuo*) order between the 8th and 3rd centuries BC, cities expanded (to having two layers of city walls), multiplied (to the order of hundreds), and became centers of production and commerce, as well as of administration and military functions.

Under the unified but short-lived kingdom of Ch'in (221–206 BC), numerous cities were destroyed. The Han regime restored many of the destroyed cities and established 1,180 county seats throughout the empire. These walled cities were to form the backbone of urban development for the next 2,000 years. During the period of disorder between the 3rd and 6th centuries, capital cities maintained a population of over one million each, and the southern region, especially the Yangtze River region, witnessed extensive urban growth.

Between the 8th and 13th centuries, China underwent what some scholars have termed the Chinese Commercial Revolution in which cities and market towns flourished. Facilitated by trade and by the relaxation of government regulations, cities no longer consisted of closed quarters and controlled markets. Of the 27 cities yielding the highest tax levels in the 11th century, 12 were connected to the Grand Canal linking northern and southern China, 4 were coastal ports, and 9 were associated with border defense. K'ai-feng, the capital of northern Sung, is estimated to have housed between 800,000 and one million residents, about 10 percent of the country's urban dwellers.

During the Ming and Ch'ing periods, the population growth (approximately 150 percent over the 17th and 18th centuries) and the development of agricultural and handicraft production led to more intensive long-distance trade and development of commercial centers. In the early 1600s, approximately 5 million people lived in over 100 cities of at least 10,000 inhabitants. By the 1840s, about 15 million lived in 306 cities, compared to western Europe around 1800, with 12.2 million in 364 cities. The greater concentration of population and wealth, especially in the lower Yangtze region, brought about immense social change, characterized by relatively high physical and social mobility and the establishment of new types of urban organizations such as commercial guilds and charity halls.

The introduction of modern communication and transportation systems in "treaty ports"—foreign-dominated trading ports—altered the traditional urban pattern by focusing development in a handful of coastal cities and inland ports and by linking the chief cities more closely together. The treaty ports were influential both economically, chiefly through international trade, and culturally, as exemplified by the introduction of the modern press.

Urban population in China increased almost twice as fast as the total population from 1950 to 1980 despite tight restrictions on migration into cities imposed by the communist government. The growth was particularly significant in the early 1950s before China entered a radical phase. As a result of the government's defense-oriented policy of "equalization of development," the percentage growth of urban population was higher in inland and border cities than in coastal cities. This trend was reversed in the 1980s with the implementation of the "open-door" policy.

Several noteworthy patterns characterize China's urban experience and relate it to several wider issues in social history. First, China's particular administrative structure, especially the 1,200-odd county seats dating from the 2nd century BC, provided the foundation for more than 2,000 years of urban development. Second, since the mid-T'ang period, the Chinese urban hierarchy has developed into functionally distinct administrative and commercial networks with most cities playing a role in both. Third, southward migration and the natural resources of the southern region (fertile soil, a crisscross of waterways) led from the 8th century on to more intensive urban developments in that region. Fourth, the city wall in China possessed only defensive functions; it did not entitle the residents within it to any significant legal rights or privileges over rural residents. Fifth, traditional Chinese cities did not experience a marked culture distinct from that of the countryside. City residents, at least until the last two centuries of the imperial period, displayed no distinctly urban attitude or mode of living. Sixth, Chinese cities were strikingly lacking in monuments. For a culture that places special emphasis on its literate tradition, cities are memorialized in words more than in stones. Though Chinese cities in this century share many commonalities with their Western counterparts, their development has exhibited, and will continue to exhibit, unique characteristics. (*See also* Chinese State and Society; Cities; Urbanization)

Leo K. Shin

REFERENCES

Kirkby, R.J.R. *Urbanization in China.* New York: Columbia University Press, 1985.

Rowe, W.T. *Hankow: Conflict and Community in a Chinese City, 1796–1895.* Stanford, CA: Stanford University Press, 1989.

Rozman, G. *Urban Networks in Ch'ing China and Tokugawa Japan.* Princeton, NJ: Princeton University Press, 1973.

Schinz, A. *Cities in China.* Berlin and Stuttgart: Gebrüder der Borntraeger, 1989.

Skinner, G.W., ed. *The City in Late Imperial China.* Stanford, CA: Stanford University Press, 1977.

Christianity

Christianity is the name given to the beliefs of those who accept Jesus Christ as their spiritual savior. Until the 16th century the major division within Christianity was between Eastern Orthodoxy and those who accepted the authority of the pope (bishop) of Rome (Roman Catholic). In the 16th century most nation-states in northern Europe created national churches independent of Roman authority. The authority of these national churches was in turn challenged by sectarian movements which rejected any formal ties between church and state. Both participants in national churches and sectaries are commonly known as Protestants.

Sociohistorical research on western European Christianity long focused on the influence of Protestant Christianity on the development of modern Western society, though there is important work on the impact of Christianity on popular beliefs during the Middle Ages, and on the gender implications of various Christian forms. The German scholar Max Weber (1864–1920) in his *The Protestant Ethic and the Spirit of Capitalism* (1904–1905) postulated that adherence to the teaching of the Protestant theologian John Calvin (1509–1564) had the unintended result of rationalizing capitalist accumulation. Catholicism, and earlier forms of Protestantism such as Lutheranism, allowed for the release of religious anxieties through the performance of devotional acts which repudiated the material world. Calvinism, through the creation of what Weber labeled "this-world asceticism" identified the material world as a venue for devotional expression. For the Calvinist, and the followers of Protestant creeds Weber saw as inspired by Calvin, engagement in the transformation of the material world was the one path to spiritual release.

The Weber thesis launched a sociohistorical approach to Christianity early, amid more conventional studies of theology and church politics. Weber's argument was reinforced by the scholarship of his friend and colleague Ernst Troeltsch (1865–1923). In *Protestantism and Progress* (1906) Troeltsch also called attention to the degree to which Calvinism underlaid the "modern Protestantism" which emerged in 18th-century western Europe. Troeltsch's real contribution, however, was the typology of possible institutional frameworks for the expression of Christian belief he provides in *The Social Teachings of the Christian Churches* (1912). Christianity as a system of social ethics has implicit in it three responses to the corruption of the secular world. A social ethos of accommodation permits an institutionalization of Christianity as an extension of the community, of the state. The resulting *church* identifies sanctity as transcendent in the society. It also demands, however, that access to this sanctity be monopolized by a professional clergy, who can then dispense it as a curative salve.

Those who out of faith chose to reject the corruption of the world coalesce around two alternatives. *Mysticism* provides an individualistic solution, each mystic following his or her unique approach to the avoidance of moral compromise.

The *sect* offers a collective, yet voluntary means of rejection. Its doctrines not only affirm the impurity of the state and the community, but provide a way of living which avoids that impurity. In analyzing the dynamics of interaction between the three institutional forms of Christian religious expression, Troeltsch created a paradigm of the formalization of an idea into a social institution still accepted as valid. His analysis lent support to Weber's contention that it was in the process of evolving from sects into churches that Protestant religious groups effected their greatest influence over the development of Western society.

Ideologically conservative, both Weber and Troeltsch presented their theses as alternatives to Marxist explanations of the course of European history. In his *Religion and the Rise of Capitalism* (1926) the British historian R.H. Tawney (1880–1962) took the step of wedding their ideas with post-Marxian analysis based on social class. Tawney saw Calvinsm as providing European (English) society with the crucial intellectual justification for jettisoning the outdated medieval condemnation of commercial activity as ethically anti-Christian. Calvinism, according to him, "liberated" the economic energies of the "rising bourgeoisie" and allowed it to establish the pursuit of profit as a moral imperative.

The most general impact of what is collectively known as the "Weber thesis" has been a regrettable tendency among social scientists to dichotomize between Calvinist/sectarian influences as in some way "modern" and Catholic/Lutheran influences as in some way "traditional," in their analysis of Western societies, and Western/Protestant as "modern" and non-Western/non-Protestant as "traditional" in their analysis of other societies. Beyond that, the generalization most often extracted from reading the works of these three scholars, that Calvinism is the ultimate source for all that is uniquely modern in 20th-century Western civilization, continues, as Adrian Furnham's (1990) work illustrates, to influence thinkers in almost every area of social scientific research.

Stimulated by Tawney, and the more recent rise of social history, historians have systematically studied the social impact of English Puritanism in the Old World and New World. Christopher Hill, in *Society and Puritanism in Pre-Revolutionary England* (1964), has continued to emphasize Tawney's association between the Protestant ethic and the English bourgeoisie. Tawney's student Lawrence Stone, in *The Family, Sex and Marriage in England, 1500-1800* (1977), broadened the impact of Puritanism and argued it to be the stimulus to the emergence of the nuclear family as the center of the socialization process in early modern England. Carl Degler, in *At Odds: Women and the American Family from the Revolution to the Present* (1980), has taken up and expanded upon Stone's argument, identifying Protestantism as the impetus behind the particular directions feminism has taken in the United States. Philip Greven in *The Protestant Temperament* (1977) and other historians have examined Protestant forms of family and child rearing. Mention should also be made of R.K. Merton's *Science, Technology and Society in Seventeenth Century England*, which granted Puritanism a primary impetus in the rise of modern science. The Merton variation on the Weber thesis remains a point of contention among sociologists and historians of science (e.g., I. Bernard Cohen, *Puritanism and the Rise of Modern Science*).

Already by the 1930s intellectual historians such as Perry Miller (*The New England Mind*) were tracing Calvinist social ethics back to the writings of Saint Augustine of Hippo. Miller's student Edmund Morgan used his insights in *The Puritan Family* (1944). Moving forward from that point, A.D. Wright (*The Counter-Reformation*) has characterized the early modern centuries in Europe as a period of Augustinian "renaissance" during which Augustinian puritanism influenced Catholic as well as Protestant social attitudes. Historians such as John Bossy (*Christianity and the West, 1400–1700* [1985]) and Philip Hoffmann (*Church and Community: The Diocese of Lyon, 1500–1789*) have validated the impact of Augustinianism on Catholic social thought. Margo Todd (*Christian Humanism and the Puritan Social Order*) has followed the trend toward looking at Puritanism in the broader context of intellectual change among early modern elites. The understanding of clerical interaction with popular religion, clerical influence on family practices has steadily advanced, including important findings about changes in Catholic efforts to regulate popular mentalities in the early modern centuries.

On the plus side, the work of Weber, Troeltsch, and Tawney can be credited with providing social scientists with a model of how cultural values determine social behavior, which continues to stimulate new hypotheses. On the negative, their work must be recognized as having stimulated an unbalanced approach to the study of the relationship between doctrinal change within Western Christianity and the emergence of modern Western society. More recent mentalities studies, though less sweeping than the Weberian models, have added new subtlety and a more complex periodization to the social analysis of Christianity in the West. These have been matched by a growing number of attempts to assess modifications in popular Christianity, including a decline of classic Calvinist beliefs, under the impact of 19th-century industrialization. The impact of Christian missions on non-Western peoples is another subject of growing social historical interest. (*See also* Mariology; Missions; Reformation/Popular Religion)

Andrew E. Barnes

REFERENCES

Bossy, John. *Christianity and the West, 1400–1700.* New York: Oxford University Press, 1985.

Eisenstadt, S.N., ed. *The Protestant Work Ethic and Modernization: A Comparative View.* New York: Basic Books, 1968.

Furnham, Adrian. *The Protestant Work Ethic: The Psychology of Work-Related Beliefs and Behaviours.* New York/London: Routledge, 1990.

Greven, Philip. *The Protestant Temperament: Patterns of Child-Rearing, Religious Experience, and the Self in Early America.* New York: Knopf, 1977.

Hill, Christopher. *Society and Puritanism in Pre-Revolutionary England.* New York: Secker & Warburg, 1964.

Stone, Lawrence. *The Family, Sex and Marriage in England, 1500–1800.* New York: Harper & Row, 1977.

Cities

Cities can be defined in several ways. The simplest approach stresses demography or population size. A city is a relatively dense, concentrated settlement which houses more than a certain number of people. Since the advent of the modern census, many Western nations have selected a threshold of approximately 2,000 people to distinguish rural and urban places, but a much lower number would be appropriate for cities in ancient or medieval times. This demographic definition, however, neglects important urban structures and functions; it therefore needs to be supplemented. Cities are places where goods, services, and information are exchanged. Many important theorists, among them Max Weber, have in fact defined cities as markets. Urban residents tend to specialize in the production and distribution of goods, services, and ideas which circulate in a society through commercial and transportation networks centered in cities. Cities also can be defined through legal criteria, through charters and laws which define their rights of self-government, their local functions, and their relationships with outside powers. In medieval Europe, cities were places whose citizens had documents from kings, emperors, or other feudal princes outlining the rights of the community to elect, to tax, to sell, and to judge. Citizenship in a city was a legal status, minutely regulated and defensible in a court of law. The Spanish government used legislation to define and to organize the cities of colonial Latin America; court authorities specified cities' functions, government, layouts, and relations with other settlements through "The Laws of the Indies."

In the 20th century, scholars have also identified cities through normative qualities of urban life. Cities have been said to foster specific sets of values and to spread urban lifestyles. Anthropologist Robert Redfield identified cities with the disintegration of local cultures and the forging of new modes of thought, producing reform and progress. Other theorists see increased alienation and deviance being produced by the relatively greater freedom and impersonality of cites. For the social historian, normative definitions of cities are particularly useful because they draw attention to the social characteristics of urban communities. By the same token, urban history with attention to urban residents and values has long constituted a vital focus for social history research.

Early cities reveal themselves through archaeological evidence; carbon dating of artifacts places the origins of Jericho around 7800 BC and that of Çatal Hüyük in Anatolia at around 6500 BC. City-centered civilizations flourished in the area of the Tigris and Euphrates river valleys and along the Nile, in Egypt by 3000 BC and somewhat later in the Indian subcontinent near the Indus River. The development of cities came later in other parts of the world. Early cities in China, which scholars estimate originated around 1500 BC, have been found in the Yellow River valley. In Meso-America, the Mayan civilization and that of Zapotecs, the Mixtecs, and the Aztecs developed major urban communities more than a thousand years later, Teotihuacan being one of the earliest and largest sites.

Cities originated when sufficient surplus from a farming population was available to support nonfood-producing activities—worship, war, art, handicrafts—on a major scale. Priests would trade appeals for divine protection in return for tribute. Potters and weavers would exchange their wares for grain. In areas where the land could not produce sufficient food, residents had to trade goods and services in order to survive. When they prospered, the resulting market settlements became towns. Early cities, therefore, were closely linked to the development of agriculture in a region. They also encouraged the specialization of occupations and the diversification of functions within a society.

Some of the earliest city functions were defense and government. Cities sheltered literate elites, who administered empires from their urban strongholds. Priest-kings and their soldiers and servants lived in the cities of Ur, Babylon, and Thebes. In ancient times, the city-states of Greece developed sophisticated methods of self-government, which they exported to their colonies throughout the Mediterranean world. Islamic cities before the advent of nation-states housed military governors, who extracted food and money from residents of the region and who directed the territory in the name of a distant sultan or caliph. In Europe, many of the cities of central and eastern regions developed from a *cité,* or citadel—the fortified dwelling of a religious or warrior lord. He ruled the surrounding territory from his protected site. Then the demand

for goods and services of the lord, his soldiers, and his servants drew artisans and other migrants to the settlement, which soon acquired a market and a merchant quarter, the *portus,* outside the castle's walls. In the longer run, the site became a town offering a variety of religious, political, and economic services to the region. Its walls sheltered the population in wartime, while their churches and squares provided the sites for important ceremonies and festivals. In the city, courts dispensed justice and regulated trade.

This function of government, which European urban populations sought to exercise on their own behalf, extended also to territory outside the walls. Through both ownership and conquest, land in the immediate vicinity was often ruled by a city's government. Kings and other rulers used cities as the sites through which to govern rural territory, smaller towns, and villages. Functions like tax collection, justice, and army recruitment extend to all the citizens of a region but tend to be located in towns. As kingdoms and empires developed, administrative services were commonly divided among a hierarchy of different sized cities from county and provincial centers up through the capital, each higher level center controlling more and more functions for a larger area. At the top of the system in cities like Washington, DC, Moscow, or Nairobi are to be found the institutions of the central government—ministries, legislatures, party organizations, the residents of presidents and bureaucrats. The largest of these places, cities like London, Tokyo, and Mexico City, have become metropolises, international cities whose influence stretches far beyond a country's borders. When such places dwarf the other towns of their country, they are called primate cities because of their domination of a national urban hierarchy.

Cities, which may well have begun as fortresses, trading centers, or religious sites, over time acquired many other functions. Their concentration of literate, wealthy people drew into them craftsmen of luxury goods. Cities through the ages have served as sites for the most complex forms of manufacturing. Urban artisans have produced the silks, the jewelry, the sculptures, and the paintings that we identify with "civilization." Cities are also educational centers, their populations both demanding advanced training and supplying it for others. Whether in palaces, temples, or universities, cities house the cultural and intellectual capital of a culture. The vast resources of human capital, when combined with the massive cultural investments of past and present, make cities the home of a commercial culture. Their orchestras, museums, dance troupes, and entertainers of all sorts make them the creators and custodians of the many forms of culture, which the combination of state and marketplace support. But cities do more than keep alive the past; they are centers of innovation. New technologies, new institutions, and new ideas spread from urban centers because of the concentration there of governments and social elites. City dwellers were the first to enjoy paved streets, electric lighting, and public supplies of purified water. Through inventions like the printing press and movable type, which were adopted by urban printers, cities became the sites of a vast information industry that has spread the values of literate elites and standardized languages.

Cities, almost by definition, are multifunctional. Still, many have specialized in one or another service sufficiently to be identified as a particular type of town. Many of the earliest cities in the Mediterranean region were ports, flourishing through the long-distance trading connections of their merchants. Port cities can be found all over the world, their dominance secure in eras of water-born commerce. Hong Kong and Singapore were founded as ports to foster trade between the British, the Chinese, and the Malays. The coastal sites and fine harbors of Buenos Aires and Rio de Janeiro helped them to serve as gateway cities for the commerce and culture of Spanish and Portuguese rulers after their conquest of South America. Another important type of specialized city is the resort or the spa. Romans vacationed in nearby Ostia. Today Russians visit Sochi, and an international set periodically descends upon Acapulco. In such places, employment in hotels, restaurants, and the service sector dominates. In contrast, jobs in manufacturing dominate in industrial cities, which grew up around factories and coal mines starting in the 19th century. Although they began with few urban institutions and amenities, over time their service sectors grew and their

political machinery became more complex. Like most specialized cities, in the longer run they became multifunctional.

Cities create distinctive societies. Not only is the array of occupations represented among their citizens relatively large and varied, but they attract large numbers of immigrants. Because cities grow through migration as well as (and sometimes instead of such increase, when urban death rates are high) through natural increase, their residents include whatever ethnic and religious groups have traveled into them. Although cities in medieval Europe tightly controlled residence and citizenship, the relative lack of control today over internal migration and the opportunities for international resettlement have produced heterogeneous urban populations. In proportion to a city's size, residents form subcultures that set themselves apart from the majority of residents. Village or family of origin, religion, language, and sometimes tribe or caste are only a few of the lines of division separating city dwellers; add to these differences the important distinctions of social status, income, education, age, gender, and political affiliation. Urban society is a mosaic of separate groups, some of whom join together in larger units to exercise power or to struggle for rights. These primary affiliations have not been constant over time and space, and they also shift according to the issue at hand. Adult male merchants representing the most important religious and ethnic group dominated most of the cities of medieval and early modern Europe. In Muslim cities in earlier centuries, however, particular family groups and religious leaders have held disproportionate influence. Wealthy industrialists constituted the elite in many of the newer manufacturing towns of North America and Great Britain. Racial, religious, and ethnic identities have mobilized people in the cities of the United States during the 19th and 20th centuries, but these same people have also redivided themselves into neighborhood groups to defend themselves against outsiders. The question of how urban societies operate has been one of the major issues discussed by social historians. When studying the cities of the last three centuries, many have stressed the primary influence of social class, seeing fundamental divisions among patricians, capitalists, and workers. But these categories work less well for non-European societies and for times when religion, ethnicity, or language are divisive issues. Everywhere, however, income levels and occupations constitute important social divisions. Industrialization has brought a degree of homogenization to the cities of the world, most of whose populations now dress in a similar manner, work in similar industries, and respond to a mass culture spread by television and newspapers. Cities themselves have been forces for social homogenization. Through their schools, mass media, and relentless merchandising of the latest in consumer goods, they spread both national and international standards among populations who can no longer escape the influence of cities.

Before the rise of social history, urban historians defined their field in terms of city governments and systems such as transportation or sanitation. They advanced typologies of cities, including periodization distinctions (for example, among early cities, commercial but preindustrial centers, and industrial types). With social history, emphasis has shifted to the groups composing city populations (including in-migration), popular pressures on city institutions, and urban ceremonies, behaviors, and mentalities. A tension persists between urban history as a distinct field and a temptation to treat it simply as a topical branch of social history, and urban historians are actively debating their identity. (*See also* African Urbanization; Central Place Theory; Chinese Urbanization; Ghetto; Houses and Housing; Latin American Urbanization; Lower Middle Classes; Merchants; Middle Class; Middle Eastern Urbanization and Cities; Neighborhoods; Street Life; United States Urbanization)

Lynn Hollen Lees

REFERENCES

Hohenberg, Paul M., and Lynn Hollen Lees. *The Making of Urban Europe, 1000–1950.* Cambridge: Harvard University Press, 1985.

Konvitz, J.W. *Cities and the Sea.* Baltimore: Johns Hopkins University Press, 1978.

Mumford, Lewis. *The City in History.* New York: Harcourt Brace and World, 1961.

Sjoberg, Gideon. *The Preindustrial City.* New York: The Free Press, 1960.

Civil Rights Movement

The modern civil rights movement began with the ratification of the Thirteenth Amendment, which abolished slavery in 1865. The newly freed southern blacks asserted their rights in ways ranging from participation in electoral politics, as voters and public officials, to nonviolent protests against segregated horsecars. The rise of Jim Crow laws throughout the South, following the withdrawal of federal troops in 1877, revived black nonviolent resistance. By the early 1900s, however, these protests had succumbed to white racial violence, the disfranchisement of most southern blacks, and a national resurgence of racism, symbolized by the Supreme Court's validation of a state segregation law, in *Plessy* v. *Ferguson* (1896), on the grounds that it afforded blacks "separate but equal" facilities.

The intense race prejudice in American society during the early 20th century largely excluded blacks from the benefits of "Progressive" reforms to aid urban workers and farmers. In 1910, however, some white Progressives joined black activists in a new civil rights group, the National Association for the Advancement of Colored People (NAACP), which sought to extend democratic reforms to issues of race. The NAACP helped prod the House of Representatives to pass federal antilynching bills in 1937 and in 1940, though these yielded to southern filibusters in the Senate. In 1941 the black union leader A. Philip Randolph escalated black activism by threatening a march on Washington against discrimination in defense plants. President Franklin Roosevelt averted a confrontation by creating an advisory committee to promote fair employment practices in munitions factories. A limited step, it was also the first executive order for civil rights since Reconstruction, and the first intended to quiet an emerging black mass movement.

Civil rights progress quickened in the wake of World War II, during which Americans had denounced the Nazis as vicious racists, making it harder to justify Jim Crow at home. Jackie Robinson's performance as the first black baseball player in the major leagues in 1947 headed a parade of black "firsts" in many areas of American society. The registration of over 2 million blacks by the late 1940s, many of them southern migrants to northern cities, further undermined the racial status quo, as did the Cold War competition between the United States and the Soviet Union for support from emerging nonwhite nations, which made evidence of racism a damaging national embarrassment.

In March 1947 President Harry Truman endorsed a report by his committee to investigate violations of black rights, which prescribed a comprehensive federal assault on Jim Crow. Two years later he began desegregation of the armed forces, in part to heighten military efficiency in the Korean War. In 1954 attorneys for the NAACP persuaded a unanimous Supreme Court, in *Brown* v. *Board of Education*, to declare that "the doctrine of 'separate but equal' has no place" in public education. Southern white resistance pressed the Court to retreat a year later with a ruling that asked only that school districts move "with all deliberate speed." When President Dwight D. Eisenhower sent troops to Little Rock, Arkansas, in 1957, to guard black students at a formerly all-white high school, the resulting racial furor further discouraged national intervention for black rights.

Despite its scant immediate impact *Brown* emboldened black activists in the South. In December 1955 blacks in Montgomery, Alabama, organized a bus boycott after a woman named Rosa Parks was arrested for refusing to yield her seat on a segregated bus to a white man. The boycott leader was a northern-educated minister originally from Atlanta, Dr. Martin Luther King, Jr. King gained national attention by linking the protest to Christian morality, American ideals of liberty, and the ethic of nonviolent resistance in order to expose injustice and impel those in power to end it. In November 1956 the boycott triumphed with aid from the NAACP, which secured a Supreme Court decision that voided Montgomery's laws enforcing bus segregation. In 1957 Congress passed the first Civil Rights Act since Reconstruction, which created a commission to monitor civil rights violations and allowed the Justice Department to sue discriminatory registrars.

Black impatience with the lax enforcement of federal civil rights edicts increasingly spurred nonviolent demonstrations. On February 1, 1960, a sit-in by four black students at the Woolworth's lunch counter in Greensboro, North Carolina, triggered similar protests, which desegregated many public accommodations throughout the South. In May 1961 James Farmer, who had cofounded the Congress of Racial Equality nearly two decades earlier, led white and black volunteers on a "Freedom Ride" to desegregate interstate bus terminal facilities. As these rides proliferated amid episodes of white violence, President John F. Kennedy, a Democrat elected with heavy black support, quietly secured southern white compliance. In October 1962 the President sent troops to quell mob violence after a black student, James Meredith, registered at the all-white University of Mississippi at Oxford. Growing racial tensions in Birmingham and other southern cities impelled Kennedy to propose a sweeping civil rights bill in June 1963.

At an interracial March on Washington on August 28, 1963, black leaders urged passage of the civil rights bill, and Martin Luther King, Jr., spoke of his "dream" of racial brotherhood. When Lyndon B. Johnson became President on November 22, 1963, he made passage of the civil rights bill his top priority, and in July 1964 he signed a Civil Rights Act that barred discrimination in public accommodations, employment, and voting rights, and ended federal aid to segregated institutions. On March 7, 1965, blacks setting out from Selma toward Montgomery, Alabama, to petition for voting rights were assaulted by state and local police. The televised violence boosted national support to safeguard blacks seeking the ballot. On August 6, 1965, Johnson signed a Voting Rights Act that authorized the Attorney General to send federal examiners to supersede local registrars and regulations wherever discrimination occurred.

After 1965 Black Power militants challenged the integrationist civil rights movement, while ghetto riots weakened the movement by harming its nonviolent image and by shifting its focus from legal rights to problems of poverty, for which no reform consensus existed. On April 4, 1968, the assassination of Martin Luther King, Jr., in Memphis, Tennessee, further polarized race relations, though Congress passed the Civil Rights Act of 1968, which banned discrimination in the sale and rental of most housing.

The 1970s witnessed the emergence of race-conscious government programs to redress the legacy of discrimination, including busing to desegregate schools and "affirmative action" to give minorities preference in school admissions and employment. During the 1980s, however, a conservative shift in national politics reversed many civil rights gains, symbolized by President Ronald Reagan's directive in 1982 that restored federal tax exemptions for segregated private schools. In the late 1980s the Supreme Court weakened key federal safeguards against discrimination in employment. Congress countered this in 1990 with a civil rights bill that restored these curbs, but President George Bush vetoed it; a year later he signed a milder version of the bill.

The civil rights movement remains far from achieving its central goal of full equality between blacks and whites. De facto segregation of homes, churches, social centers, and private schools remains routine throughout the nation, while blacks in 1990 were still three times as likely as whites to be poor. Civil rights campaigns have nonetheless transformed race relations, most visibly by desegregating southern public accommodations and most southern public schools. Also, the federal government has checked hate groups like the Ku Klux Klan through infiltration and indictments. The Voting Rights Act has had an especially great impact: between 1965 and 1989 the number of black Americans holding elective office rose from around 100 to more than 7,200, two-thirds of them in the South. The black minister Jesse Jackson spurred this growing participation in electoral politics by twice campaigning for the Democratic presidential nomination, finishing third in delegates in 1984 and second in 1988. Jackson drew attention, in fiery campaign speeches, to the continuing effects of discrimination on African Americans, even as his strong showings in northern and southern primaries underscored the distance blacks had traveled since the era of Jim Crow.

Historians and others have studied the civil rights movement mainly from the standpoint of individual leadership and politics. It becomes increasingly clear, however, that the movement involved important changes among many black Americans, in expectations and outlook, and that its causes as well as its results form a vital part of ongoing research on modern United States social history.

Robert Weisbrot

REFERENCES

Bloom, Jack M. *Class, Race, and the Civil Rights Movement.* Bloomington: Indiana University Press, 1987.

King, Martin Luther, Jr. *Why We Can't Wait.* New York: Mentor, 1964.

Sitkoff, Harvard. *The Struggle for Black Equality, 1954–1980.* New York: Hill and Wang, 1981.

Civil War, United States (1861–1865)

Even before independence, colonists realized that the different economic systems and philosophies of government that separated them could lead to disunion. The American Civil War pitted an industrializing North against an agrarian South. As the nation expanded westward, sectional grievances were exacerbated by a political and moral debate over the proper use of new lands. Central to this conflict was the importance of slavery to southern agriculture. Due to its demands on labor and land, the southern economy could expand its markets only by expanding geographically.

After the Mexican War (1846–1848), the North began to block slavery's expansion into western territories, first through the Wilmot Proviso that stipulated which territories would enter the Union as "free soil," and then the Compromise of 1850, which admitted California as a free state but allowed the governments of Utah and New Mexico to decide the issue themselves.

As the issues of slavery, union, and states' rights came to the forefront of political debate, the Whig and Democratic parties disintegrated. The Whig Party, losing influence in the elections of the 1850s, became a basis of southern political unity after the the Kansas-Nebraska Act. Disaffected northern Whigs founded the American (or Know-Nothing) Party; other Whigs, along with "free-soilers," helped to found the Republican Party.

Slavery's impact went beyond politics. In 1853 Harriet Beecher Stowe wrote *Uncle Tom's Cabin,* dramatizing slavery's moral dilemmas. The enforcement of the Fugitive Slave Act heightened a militant response to slavery by abolitionists, who helped to populate the Kansas territories after 1855. The Supreme Court decision in *Dred Scott* v. *Sanford* (1856) affirmed the rights of slaveowners to bring their slaves into free territories and thus questioned the constitutionality of barring slavery in the free states.

Organized violence erupted in Kansas. In 1856 proslavery forces attacked Lawrence, the provisional capital. In retribution, John Brown massacred five proslavery farmers at Pottawatomie Creek. This set off violence in the territory that foreshadowed and legitimated the use of force over the issue of slavery.

In defense of their "peculiar institution," southerners viewed themselves as heirs to a republican tradition of states' rights and denied an increasing federal role in local economies. As the region lost its political parity with the North due to expansion and immigration, political rhetoric turned to succession. In leading a raid on Harper's Ferry (1859) John Brown failed in bringing about a slave revolt, but succeeded in bringing the polarized conflict to the end of compromise.

In a divided nation, Abraham Lincoln won the presidency in a four-way contest with 40 percent of the vote and virtually no southern support. On December 20, 1860, South Carolina became the first state to secede from the Union, followed by the Deep South and several Border States. By the time of Lincoln's inaugural, they had formed the Confederate States of America. On April 12, Confederate forces began shelling Fort Sumter in Charleston Harbor.

More than 2 million men fought for the Union; approximately 900,000 men served the Confederacy. After the initial flush of volunteers, both governments drafted conscripts, initiating a federal power that has continued to this day. Particularly in the North, the practice of substitution or commutation heightened existing class and race divisions, occasionally leading to violence. In service, about 360,000 men died for the Union; approximately 258,000 died for the South, comprising 6 and 18 percent of the draft-age men, respectively.

The Civil War was the only war totally fought in the United States. Because of new developments in firepower and strategy, the war's dev-

astation was felt by belligerents and civilians alike. Early victories proved indecisive, and strategies shifted from direct battle to attrition. The sieges of Vicksburg and Atlanta were made possible by the North's superior armaments, rail capacity, and provisions. General William T. Sherman's "March to the Sea" through Georgia and South Carolina again changed warfare; attrition turned to retribution, with the civilians, crops, and supplies of the South the object of conquest.

The war's effect on women was widespread. With the dearth of men, middle-class women entered the market economy in increasing numbers. Women provided aid in administrative and support capacities, as well, turning previously domesticated talents into professional skills, particularly in the development of the United States Sanitary Commission and through nursing.

Lincoln's issue of the Emancipation Proclamation on January 1, 1863, altered the war's meanings. For white southerners, the war's loss would mean the discontinuance of their social structure; for the North, it changed the meaning of the war from one of preservation of the Union to the insurance of personal freedom. For African Americans, it meant the end of bondage and the possibility of full citizenship, a promise that remained unfulfilled after the war.

On April 9, 1865, Robert E. Lee surrendered the Confederate forces to Ulysses S. Grant. As a social revolution, the Civil War had touched every person in "The United States of America," as the Union came to be called after the war. By engaging the nation in single conflict, as well as expanding and rationalizing the roles of the federal government, the war created a single unified nation rather than a federation of interdependent states.

The Civil War constitutes one of those great events that challenge social historians. Social history has by no means transformed understandings of the Civil War, which continue to depend heavily on political developments. By deepening analysis of the social patterns of North and South, including not only an industrial contrasted with a slave economy but also widely different popular mentalities, social historians have improved understanding of the war's causation. Recent work has focused also on the social experiences of the war itself, as they prepared further changes in outlook and behavior not only in the defeated South, but in northern communities as well. (*See also* African American Society; Emancipation; Reconstruction; Revolutions; State and Society)

Timothy J. Haggerty

REFERENCES

Linderman, Gerald F. *Embattled Courage: The Experience of Combat in the American Civil War.* New York: The Free Press, 1987.

McPherson, James M. *Battle Cry of Freedom: The Civil War Era.* New York: Oxford University Press, 1988.

Sutherland, Daniel E. *The Expansion of Everyday Life, 1860–1876.* New York: Harper & Row, 1989.

Vinovskis, Maris. *Towards a Social History of the American Civil War: Exploratory Essays.* Cambridge and New York: Cambridge University Press, 1990.

Civilization

The word "civilization" is derived from the Latin *civilis* meaning "of the citizens." The term was coined by the Romans to distinguish between themselves as citizens of a cosmopolitan, urban-focused empire and peoples that they regarded as inferior who lived in the forests and deserts beyond the boundaries of their imperium. For the Romans—or the Greeks, Chinese, and city-dwelling Amerindians who made similar distinctions between civilized and "barbaric" peoples—cultural attributes (language, dress, manners, etc.) were the key markers of civilized status. Beginning in the 17th century, social thinkers in western Europe sought not only to define more systematically the differences between civilized and noncivilized, they strove to identify a series of stages in human development that ranged from what were regarded as the lowliest savage bands to the highest forms of civilized expression. Largely on the basis of the historical experience of the peoples of the Mediterranean and western Europe, a number of key cultural attainments came to be seen as essential ingredients of civilization. These included systems of writing, the development of cities, social stratification and the emergence of specialized elites, centralized political institutions, and high levels of technological innovation and monumental architecture.

Depending on the writer doing the ranking, candidates for civilization varied somewhat, but they invariably included Egypt, Greece, Rome, and (not surprisingly) Europe of the 17th (and later 18th and 19th) century. Most of the other peoples of the globe, whose "discovery" by the Europeans since the 15th century had prompted the efforts to classify them in the first place, were ranked in increasingly complex hierarchies. The Chinese and Arabs, for example, who had created expansive empires, great cities, large buildings, and extensive literary corpora, usually won a place along with the Europeans near these hypothetical ladders of human achievement. Pastoral peoples, such as the Mongols and Turks, were usually classified as barbarians. Civilized and barbarian were in turn pitted against various sorts of savages. These ranged from the hunters and gatherers who inhabited much of North America and Australia before the arrival of the Europeans to the slash-and-burn or migratory cultivators in the hill and forest zones of South and Southeast Asia and southern China.

Beginning in the late 18th century, these classificatory schemes of human societal development took on an added dimension. In keeping with a growing emphasis in European thinking and social interaction on racial or biological differences, modes of human social organization and cultural production were increasingly linked to what were alleged to be the innate capacities of each human race. Though no one could agree on what a race was or how many races there were, numerous European writers argued that some races were more inventive, more moral, more courageous, more artistic—and thus more capable of building civilization—than others. The hierarchy from savage to civilized took on a color dimension from white at the top, where the civilized peoples clustered, to yellow, brown, red, and black in descending order.

Though the association between race and capacity for civilization has been discarded by virtually all social scientists in the post–World War II decades, the early, highly Eurocentric gauges of civilized development have shown surprising staying power in the 20th century. In some of the most influential works, such as those by Carleton Coon and V. Gordon Childe (1950), on the rise of civilization, cities, and writing remain essential to the attainment of that exalted status. The retention of these standards means that the societies of most of sub-Saharan Africa and much of the Americas have traditionally been classified as other than "civilized," though "primitive" or "tribal" have tended to be substituted for earlier, cruder designations like "barbarism" and "savagery." One consequence of the proliferation of area specialist studies in recent decades and consequent advances in the sophistication of our understanding of the processes of human social evolution has been the gradual abandonment of rigid and self-serving 17th–19th-century definitions of civilization. The prevailing trend is to view civilization as one of a number of human approaches to social organization, rather than attempting to identify specific kinds of cultural achievement that are unique to civilized societies. In this view, all peoples from small bands of hunters and gatherers to farmers and factory workers live in societies. All societies in turn produce cultures—combinations of the ideas, objects, and patterns of behavior that result from human social interaction. But all societies and cultures do not generate the surplus production that permits the levels of occupational specialization, scale, and complexity that distinguish civilizations from other modes of social organization. All peoples are seen as intrinsically capable of building civilizations. But many have lacked the resource base, historical circumstances, or, quite simply, the motivation for doing so. Thus, rather than specific cultural productions, civilization has come to be associated with more general patterns of production and social organization. This shift has freed the concept of civilization from the ethnocentric and racist assumptions that were strongly associated with its early formulations and applications. (*See also* Hunting and Gathering; Neolithic Revolution; Pastoralism; Racism)

Michael Adas

REFERENCES

Childe, V. Gordon. *What Happened in History.* Harmondsworth, Eng.: Penguin, 1950.

Hodgson, G.S. Marshall. *The Venture of Islam.* Chicago: University of Chicago Press, 1974.

Mellaart, James. *The Neolithic of the Near East.* London: Thames and Hudson, 1975.

Stearns, Peter, Michael Adas, and Stuart Schwartz. *World Civilizations: The Global Experience.* New York: Harper Collins, 1992.

Class

Social class is a fundamental focus of research in social history. Although specialized definitions abound, and many students of social class have drawn heavily on Max Weber, the most common usages have their roots in Karl Marx. Three separate elements of class can be distinguished: first, class as an objective category, as a location within the relationships of production; second, class as a subjective category, as class consciousness; and, third, class as a reproductive order, as an enduring, multigenerational system of social relationships.

As an objective economic category, class can be defined as a position of an individual within the structure of production relations, including their effective rights and duties. Marx, in *Capital,* claimed that classes have existed throughout most of recorded history and as examples included patricians, plebians, slaves, lords, serfs, guildmasters, and journeymen. In the society of his day, Marx distinguished the existence of capitalists, artisans, proletarians, petit bourgeoisie, and peasantry. Much recent debate among Marxists and others has centered about the rise of new classes, with considerable attention given to college-educated, white-collar employees, who have been identified as a "new working class," "new middle class," "intelligentsia," "managerial elite," and "new bureaucrats." But debates over the existence of new social classes, sooner or later, touch on questions of consciousness, and "objective" class criteria are inseparably bound up with subjective factors.

While debate still swirls about the objective, economic category of class, the greatest debates have doubtless centered over its subjective elements. In its fuller sense, class consciousness did not emerge until the 19th century, when, first, many capitalists and, later, large numbers of workers began to identify themselves as sharing common interests based on their location within the relations of production. Different forms of class consciousness have appeared in earlier times. At one time or the other, groups of slaves, nobles, and peasants all have recognized themselves as sharing similar interests, but such interests have seldom been construed as economically based or endemic to an entire social order. Other bases for social hierarchy, like castes or legal orders, might predominate over class structure at least officially, which is another reason social class is a particular preoccupation in modern social history. In early modern times, European nobles were often conscious of themselves as part of an international ruling class, but they were reluctant to define themselves as a group that lived off revenues from the land; honor, race, and lifestyle were their characteristic marks of self-identification. Class consciousness in modern-day societies almost invariably demarcates itself within the bounds of individual nation-states.

Since the 19th century, the most important elements of class consciousness rest less on the personal identity of individual members of classes and more on participation in class-based formal and informal social networks. In general, the more exclusive and extensive, the more likely they are to promote a sense of class. Class consciousness founded on lifestyles that span a great part of the social life of a particular class yield one elementary type of consciousness. Among capitalists, participation in high society, kin ties, or school or religious background may all give rise to a sense of identity. Similarly, among workers, concentrated residence within urban neighborhoods, or factory villages or mining communities may yield a sense of common destiny. Nationally organized private clubs, cartels, or company directorships have all been crucial agents in politically organizing capitalist-class action. Membership in national, often industrial, trade unions and participation in mass socialist and labor parties have been key in structuring class dispositions among workers. Some economic classes, such as the petit bourgeoisie (lower middle class) have had great difficulty in building informal social networks within their own class while other economic classes, such as the peasantry, have trouble maintaining class-based formal organizations over wide areas. This inability has often proved a great limitation on their class consciousness.

No matter whether we discuss class consciousness as a product of formal or informal organization, all societies possess social options that do not involve class consciousness. Religious solidarities, patriotic societies, and racial or cultural organizations can all link members of different social classes together and reject class identification. Much American social history is written in terms of ethnic groups more than classes, though many social historians emphasize class analysis in the United States as well. The strength of class consciousness as embodied in formal and informal structures has ebbed and flowed in all industrial societies. In some industrial societies, such as France, Germany, and Russia, class cleavages have loomed for long periods as the most important social divisions, while in others, such as the United States, they have figured less significantly.

Whether class consciousness has been a salient social division or not, some basic elements of consciousness must exist in all societies to ensure the reproduction of economic classes over time or from one generation to another. Class reproduction is not automatic. Even without legal repression or abolition, peasantries, proletarians, nobles, and capitalists have all disappeared from individual societies because of their inability to reproduce their class. Colonialism has frequently decimated native capitalists, while the availability of free land has occasionally led to the disappearance of working classes. In the modern world, proletarianization may deprive individuals of their property and make their skills obsolescent, without in any way providing them with the education or ability to find work.

As a reproductive system, class formation may require schools, neighborhoods, families, religious organizations, charitable societies, or government welfare. Class membership is often passed on through family and kin. Children learn skills, have expectations, and develop ties with peers which sustain their own class identity. Working-class neighborhoods may provide valuable information about job opportunities and ways of making due on an inadequate income as well as providing help in difficult times. Education is also of key importance. It also may be as important in acquiring a peer group of friends as in providing skills and job training. Finally, in most industrial countries the state is directly involved in perpetuating class locations. Social insurance plans which are based on employment and financed by payroll deductions are only one of the most obvious ways in which states foster class reproduction. (*See also* Aristocracy; Artisans; Lower Middle Classes; Middle Class; Peasantry; Proletarianization; Reproduction and Class Formation; Underclass; Working Class)

Michael P. Hanagan

REFERENCES

Cohen, G.A. *Karl Marx's Theory of History: A Defence.* Princeton, NJ: Princeton University Press, 1978.

Giddens, Anthony, and David Held, eds. *Classes, Power and Conflict: Classical and Contemporary Debates.* Berkeley: University of California Press, 1982.

Katznelson, Ira, and Ari Zolberg, eds. *Working-Class Formation: Nineteenth-Century Patterns in Western Europe and the United States.* Princeton, NJ: Princeton University Press, 1986.

Thompson, E.P. *The Making of the English Working Class.* New York: Vintage, 1966.

Wright, Erik Olin, ed. *The Debate on Classes.* London: Verso, 1989.

Classical Athletics

Non-Greek Minoans engaged in boxing and in a poorly understood form of "bull-leaping," but the actual progenitors of classical athletics are not recognizable until Homer's depiction of supposedly Mycenaean practice in the funeral games of Patroclus (*Iliad,* book 23) and the games of the Phaeacians (*Odyssey,* book 8). Historically, our earliest date is 776 BC, when the Olympic Games were reportedly first held; later times saw the foundation of similar Panhellenic festivals at Delphi (the Pythian Games), Isthmia, and Nemea. Games were also regularly staged by certain of the Greek city-states in various periods; and, on a less organized basis, Greeks always enjoyed competition in athletics, particularly in the gymnasium and its *palaestra,* or wrestling hall.

The principal events of the panhellenic games were running (races ranging in length from a single *stadion,* or about 200 meters, to 24 *stadia*), boxing, a no-holds-barred contest called the *pankration,* a pentathlon (*stadion,* javelin, discus, long jump, and wrestling), and various horse and chariot races. These were all individual contests; no team competition or scoring is recorded. Such individualism stands in striking contrast with the corporate cohesiveness of the classical city-state—not to mention the national team organization of the modern Olympic Games.

Beginning with Cylon, an Olympic champion who failed in an attempt to overthrow the aristocratic government of Athens, successful competitors endeavored to convert their popularity into political influence. The city itself, if the Athens case is typical, might reward its panhellenic victors with lifetime civic privileges. Later, however, the bond with the city was weakened with the emergence of the professional athlete touring the Greco-Roman world in pursuit of an international—and lucrative—career.

Athletics followed class lines to the extent that they, and the equestrian events in particular, given the expenses involved, were predictably dominated by the rich, above all by the aristocratic rich. But wrestling, as presumably running, jumping, and the like, came close to being a universal sport among the Greek men. We do not know enough about ball games and other popular pastimes to identify any as narrowly class specific.

Did women participate? At Olympia, beginning in the 5th century BC with a victory in horse racing by the daughter of a Spartan king, female competition is attested; here, too, the so-called Sixteen Women are recorded to have sponsored foot races for girls of different ages. But as late as the 2nd century AD a literary source implies that married women, unlike virgins, were prohibited from viewing the games. Elsewhere, victories by women in the *stadion* and the chariot race in armor (as well as in music) are recorded in an inscription of the early Christian era.

The Romans, exposed to Hellenic athletics and maintaining the festivals in imperial Greece, themselves inclined to the chariot events. Possibly under Etruscan influence, they also adopted in Rome, and later throughout the empire, gladiatorial and other gruesome spectacles, reflecting a shift in emphasis from the Greek ideal of competition among individuals to the gratification of the lusts of the stadium audience.

Nicholas F. Jones

REFERENCES

Gardiner, E. Norman. *Athletics of the Ancient World.* Chicago: Ares, 1978.

Harris, H.A. *Sport in Greece and Rome.* Ithaca, NY: Cornell University Press, 1972.

Cleanliness

Standards of cleanliness seem to most people to be solely a matter of personal choice. Nonetheless, our outlook on how clean our bodies, homes, clothing, and material possessions should be is frequently the result of deeply rooted social codes. Therefore, to social historians, standards of cleanliness and their evolution reveal information not simply about the way we live our everyday lives, but also about the way we see ourselves and our world.

In the recent past most people did not keep their bodies, homes, or clothing as pristine as 20th-century Americans have come to expect. Preindustrial peoples in western Europe and colonial America were probably not concerned that homes were cluttered and dirty, clothing soiled, and bodies unwashed. Technology played an important part in these lower expectations. When it is difficult to clean, people do not expect things to be clean. Conversely, recent studies of household technology demonstrate that technological innovations such as vacuum cleaners and washing machines increased middle-class expectations about how clean homes and material possessions should be. And if homes were to be dust free and clothing to be spotless, cleaning had to be done more frequently.

In recent years standards and methods of personal hygiene have received considerable attention from historians of Western society. This research strongly illustrates the interaction between technology and rising standards of cleanliness. We know that bathing facilities have been available to at least some people in western European society from ancient times. Archaeological digs have revealed elaborate plumbing in Minoan palaces on the island of Crete. Ancient Middle Eastern societies established public baths partially as a result of religious injunctions. The ancient Greeks and Romans similarly provided public bathing facilities for male citizens. The Roman Empire and Islamic invasions spread this tradition into western and northern Europe, where it persisted until the introduction of syphilis in the late 15th century. But these services met the needs of only a small number of people. Before the industrial revolution most people who wanted to bathe relied on natural waters or manually carried water to portable basins and tubs (as do many people in less developed regions today). Under these circumstances even the elite, who could rely on servants, bathed infrequently. Beliefs supplemented practice, as frequent bathing was considered dangerous to health.

Development of private plumbing technology beginning in the early 19th century altered personal hygiene. The gradual introduction of water closets, sinks, portable and fixed tubs and showers, running water, and attached drains led to the acceptance of the standard bath cell as a prominent part of the proper middle-class home. The advent of urban water and sewage systems supported even more rapid adoption of these technologies in the late 19th and early 20th centuries. This trend led to the development of class-related standards of personal and household cleanliness. For the economically comfortable white middle class, laundered clothing, pristine homes, and frequent bathing became the norm; standards of social as well as visual appearance escalated. For the economically hard-pressed older patterns of cleanliness persisted. After World War I these differences in cleanliness standards declined in the United States, as the urban working classes and rural people were able to obtain homes which included the new mechanisms.

In contrast to the rapid adoption of private household technologies for bathing or cleaning, movements to establish public facilities were generally unsuccessful. For example, American urban reformers had difficulty generating sufficient demand for public baths. The few public baths that were built in the United States were rarely used to capacity. European, especially British, public bath advocates were more successful, but in the United States the immigrant working class for whom public baths were established rejected this method in favor of waiting until they could afford private facilities.

Social historians observing these phenomena see two related questions: why did standards of cleanliness rise, and why were methods of cleaning privatized? Some answers seem fairly obvious—technology allowed greater cleanliness, which led to greater comfort and health. But these same levels of comfort and health could have been obtained through public baths, cooperative laundries, and so on. And the degree of concern about cleanliness, particularly within the United States, exceeds the requirements for comfort and health. In fact the American penchant for daily bathing may in harsh winter climates produce health problems related to dry skin conditions.

Therefore, many social historians attribute this trend to more than technological change. Some assert that norms for cleanliness were created by reformers who exaggerated the health benefits of cleanliness in order to obtain public acceptance of sanitary reform and the germ theory. Others discuss the importance of advertising, which associated personal hygiene and household cleanliness with social acceptability and self-worth. Certainly the emphasis in advertising on what others might think of a mother who did not properly clean her house or children supports this contention. Other researchers conclude that reformers and advertisers simply used social and psychological concerns that were already a part of industrial society. These historians attribute the adoption of high standards of cleanliness to an emphasis on external appearance as a sign of individual worth in a socially mobile society. Still others identify psychological impulses, such as rejection of the perceived dirtiness of industrial society.

There is still much we do not know about the social history of cleanliness. One of the most glaring inadequacies is the paucity of attention to preindustrial and early industrial household technology. Similarly, historians have insufficiently explored cross-cultural comparisons such as changes in Japanese use of public baths. Broadening the base of the questions historians ask may help us gain greater understanding of culturally determined attitudes which can become unrecognized sources of ethnocentrism and contemporary culture conflict. (*See also* Domesticity; Health; Houses and Housing; Housework; Industrialization; Manners; Mass Culture; Modernization; Motherhood; Standard of Living;

United States Reform Movements; Urbanization; Working Class)

Jacqueline S. Wilkie

REFERENCES

Cayleff, Susan. *Wash and Be Healed: The Water Cure Movement and Women's Health.* Philadelphia: Temple University Press, 1987.

Cowan, Ruth Schwartz. *More Work for Mother: The Ironies of Household Technology from the Open Hearth to the Microwave.* New York: Basic Books, 1983.

Williams, Marilyn Thornton. *Washing "The Great Unwashed": Public Baths in Urban America, 1840–1920.* Columbus: Ohio State University Press, 1991.

Wright, Lawrence. *Clean and Decent: The Fascinating History of the Bathroom and the Water Closet.* London and Boston: Routledge and Kegan Paul, 1966.

Cleric

See Ulama

Clientage

Clientage implies action from below, from people seeking some kind of protection from a patron or sponsor. A client is one who seeks aid or advantage from another person who is wealthier, more powerful, or better connected. *Webster's Dictionary* traces the word to the Latin *clinare*, meaning "to lean." A client has someone to lean on. A client might seek from his or her patron a job, land, housing, money, information, aid in a legal matter, or other things. In return, the client might give political backing, labor, or other forms of support. The relationship is dyadic (two-sided), between unequals, contains an expectation of reciprocity, and is private rather than public. Historically, in many farming areas of the world, poor peasants and the landless have been bound to better-off landholders. In pastoral societies, the receipt of cattle or other animals has afforded clients with subsistence and the well-to-do with political loyalty. Chains of patron-client ties have connected villages and towns to national centers, while clientelist politics have typified both ancient and modern cities and states. Clientage has existed in diverse forms in many cultures and time periods. But the concept is drained of its meaning if it is equated with all vertical social linkages. Thus, it is useful to exclude situations where such relations are legal and contractual, as in feudal Europe, or are governed by fixed rules, as in highly bureaucratic organizations. Increasingly precise understanding of clientage plays a growing role in the social history of many agricultural societies and in urban settings as well.

Until the late 1960s, scholars tended to treat clientage in a static, system-sustaining manner, or subsume it under patronage, as if the dominant party were the only actor. Influenced by structural-functionalist theory, researchers emphasized patterns of patron-client relations and how they helped to maintain a social order. Since then, actor-oriented studies have focused upon why people enter clientage relations, how the ties change over time, what causes conflicts, and why people sever bonds.

Clientage appears to have been an especially pervasive and enduring institution in the Mediterranean, Islamic Near East, Latin America, and Southeast Asia. S.N. Eisenstadt and L. Roniger (1984) have argued that in such places patron-client relations have constituted part of the central institutional arrangements of society, or in other words, they structured exchange generally. This approach can slip back into structural-functionalism. However, it has also helped to identify certain characteristics that tend to be present when clientage is core: relatively weak corporate kin groups, a weak national government, and decentralized control of valued services and goods. Through patrons, clients gain access to needed resources unavailable by other means.

One form of clientage, *compadrazgo*, or godparentship, has been particularly important in the Mediterranean and Latin America. Typically, parents have chosen godparents who are of higher social status and who could provide material aid and connections that might enhance their children's lives. Upon marriage in Andalusian Spain, a couple often would select an elder brother of the groom and his wife as godparents; the latter would contribute to the costs of the ceremony and the welfare of the first-born child. In other countries, the *compadres,* or godparents, would not be close relatives, and the special bond of friendship would complement kin ties. Recent studies have shown how

clients negotiate multilateral relationships. In the Peruvian Central Highlands during the middle 19th century people established multiple sets of compadrazgo ties, which ideally were relationships of mutual respect and affection. The poor looked to wealthier compadres to aid them with land disputes, debt, food and labor shortages, and other problems. By establishing networks beyond their own communities, they spread their farming over different environments and reduced risk.

Historically, clientage ties have existed in many parts of the world and often cut across cultural lines. Within Africa interregional commerce was facilitated by hosts who regularly provided traveling traders with lodging, food, translation services, brokerage, and other cross-cultural exchange assistance. Rulers and commercial "landlords" on the African coast served European traders arriving by ship, and comparable arrangements existed in ports around the Mediterranean Sea, Indian Ocean, and China Sea. Worldwide, "strangers" have found patrons among local rulers. Such relationships often have been dynamic, and the initial power balance could be reversed. For instance, prestigious migrants in precolonial Africa who intermarried with their patrons, gained legitimacy, and built up power not infrequently took over existing states or formed new ones.

Scholars once tended to view clientage as typical of an agrarian or premodern "stage in development." This pseudo-evolutionist approach has now been rejected. Clientage has been strong in cities not because it represents a continuity from the rural past but because it has been one means by which migrants have created urban life. Newcomers seeking scarce resources learn whom to contact and how to forge bonds. In the cities of the United States, Latin America, Africa, and elsewhere, clients oftentimes have found patrons within ethnic organizations, which control such resources as jobs and housing. Given the mutability of ethnic boundaries and identities, migrants have taken on new cultural symbols and leaders have mobilized ethnic sentiments to strengthen clientage ties and to justify exchanges. It has often been said that shared values provide for the trust and reciprocity upon which compadrazgo and other patron-client ties depend; however, urban studies from Lagos, Nigeria, and other cities demonstrate that a common, all-encompassing value system is not needed. Urban clientage often draws diverse people together and helps to generate a new cultural unity.

Personal and private clientage ties have operated alongside formal urban and national political systems or in some cases virtually replaced them. During the era of city machine politics in the United States, supporters gained food, jobs, and business deals from party leaders in return for votes. The Tammany Hall machine, for example, controlled city hall in New York for 70 of the 80 years between 1854 and 1933, dispensing aid to indigent immigrants as well as contracts to prominent friends. On the national level, clientelist politics in the United States have excluded from decision making the poor and others who have little to reciprocate. In postindependence African and Asian countries where the state has been weak, clientage has become a critical element in the governmental process. Entrepreneurial leaders hold key positions by heading patron-client pyramids. Scholarships, jobs, contracts, and other benefits have been made available to their clients in exchange for support. Through clientelism individuals may rise into the dominant class, and many sectors of society may gain some participation in the system. On the other hand, as in the United States, the larger national good may not be served by politicians providing favors and contracts to local or foreign corporations and business people whose strength and influence is so great that they cannot be considered clients in the sense used here. Politicians themselves may become clients of such interests.

Much debate has focused on whether or not a moral economy—a commonly accepted, determining set of values and beliefs—limited the extraction by rulers and other elites in the era before the impact of modern capitalism and colonial domination. Proponents of the moral economy viewpoint argue, for example, that in precolonial Southeast Asia religious ritual, oral literature, and other carriers of custom prescribed what share of labor, crops, and taxes should be fairly demanded and given. This evaluation also focuses attention on popular reaction to attacks on clientage from capitalists or colonial governments interested, for example, in more standardized taxation systems; people at times protested new tax and labor systems because they contradicted clientage standards. Opponents of the moral economy perspective emphasize that in the past extraction was circumscribed by inefficient bureaucracies, interelite competition, and the nature of elite-peasant interaction. Chains of patron-client clusters helped patrons dominate those under them but also provided clients with buffers against excessive demands. They could shift their loyalty away from tyrannical or ineffectual patrons to those who demanded less and shielded them better against royal levies. Similarly, in the Peruvian Highlands, although patrons exacted taxes, labor, and obedience from peasants, the latter resisted by playing elite factions off against one another. The two-way, double-cutting nature of patron-client relations is one of its distinguishing features.

Nonetheless, clientage has often been coercive and has prevented those at the lower levels of society from becoming a class acting for themselves. Powerful landowners have suppressed dissent in rural villages. Officials and politicians have used patronage to control and split poor urban communities. However, when patrons abuse their positions to extract heavy rents and taxes, supply laborers to mines or plantations, or make other excessive demands, clients may become radicalized or the system may break down. Those processes have been hastened in the 20th century, when colonial authorities have co-opted elites and economies have become commercialized. In Latin America, urban squatters have organized to defend their neighborhoods and challenge clientelist governments. In Asia a disintegration of clientage has helped open the way for rebellion and revolution. (*See also* Patronage; Peasant Rebellion; Rural Labor and Agricultural Protest; Stratification and Inequality)

Allen M. Howard

REFERENCES

Barnes, Sandra T. *Patrons and Power. Creating a Political Community in Metropolitan Lagos.* Bloomington: Indiana University Press, 1986.

Clapham, Christopher, ed. *Private Patronage and Public Power. Political Clientelism in the Modern State.* New York: St Martin's Press, 1982.

Eisenstadt, S.N., and L. Roninger. *Patrons, Clients and Friends. Interpersonal Relations and the Structure of Trust in Society.* Cambridge: Cambridge University Press, 1984.

Mallon, Florencia E. *The Defense of Community in Peru's Central Highlands.* Princeton, NJ: Princeton University Press, 1984.

Schmidt, Steffen W., Laura Guasti, Carl H. Lande, and James C. Scott, eds. *Friends, Followers, and Factions. A Reader in Political Clientelism.* Berkeley: University of California Press, 1977.

Coffeehouses

Coffee (Turkish *kahve*; Arabic *qahwa*) and the coffeehouse appeared almost concurrently in the Islamic Near East at the beginning of the 16th century. The coffeehouse quickly became an important social institution in the Middle East. Coffee was introduced to the Yemen, probably from Ethiopia, prior to the late 15th century, and thence spread north through the Arabian Peninsula. By 1511, coffee was being drunk at Mecca in shops that an early source describes as "similar to taverns," and within a short time coffee had reached Cairo and Damascus. The coffeehouse was a convenient marketing device: Istanbul learned of coffee through the efforts of two Syrian merchants who opened a coffeehouse in the 1550s to introduce potential customers to the new Arabian drink.

Controversy accompanied coffee from the beginning. While Muslim scholars argued at length about the legality of the drink itself, many of the pious were scandalized by the activities of coffeehouse patrons, some of which, such as occasional use of drugs, gambling, and prostitution, were bald violations of Holy Law, while others merely suggested indolence or frivolity. The potential of coffeehouses as centers of political discussion and possible sedition caused anxiety among the authorities. Debate over the legality of coffee itself was soon settled in favor of the drink, but even in the 1630s Murad IV tried to suppress coffeehouses at Istanbul.

European writers such as Prosper Alpinus and Rauwolff had acquainted their public with coffee by the end of the 16th century, but it was scarcely used in the West before the mid-17th century. The tale of the Viennese adopting the drink when they looted sacks of beans from the abandoned Ottoman camp after the unsuccessful siege of 1683 is perhaps apocryphal; coffee appeared in several European cities simultaneously around mid-century, first in the salons of travelers returning from the Orient, soon thereafter in coffeehouses, usually opened by Levantine Christians. European rulers were as aware as their Near Eastern counterparts of the seditious potential of such places: within decades of their opening, Charles II attempted to shut down cafés in England. Louis XIV, in France, apparently had similar misgivings in the 1680s.

In spite of such official opposition, both coffee and the coffeehouse became fixtures in European cities. They never entirely supplanted the social functions of wine or ale houses, but by the 18th century they had become, particularly for the middle classes, fashionable centers of social and intellectual exchange. In some regions the function of the coffeehouse ultimately merged with that of the older alcohol-serving establishments; in French and Italian cafés, where there is a two-tier pricing system, many now prefer the economy of drinking coffee standing at the bar to the leisure—and expense—of drinking it at a table. Elsewhere, the coffeehouse has retained a bit more of its separation from the alcohol-serving establishments, often merging with the on-premises consumption of confections at the *Konditorei*. In the Near East, the coffeehouse still exists as a center of male social life, although in some places, such as Turkey, prohibitively expensive imported coffee has been replaced with domestic tea.

Ralph S. Hattox

REFERENCES

Hattox, Ralph S. *Coffee and Coffeehouses.* Seattle: University of Washington Press, 1985.

Leclant, Jean. "Coffee and Cafés in Paris, 1644–1693," in Robert Forster and Orest Ranum, eds., *Food and Drink in History: Selections from the Annales Economies, Sociétés, Civilisations,* translated by Patricia M. Ranum. Baltimore: Johns Hopkins University Press, 1979, pp. 86–97.

Von Hünersdorff, Richard, and Holger G. Hasenkamp. *Bibliography of Coffee.* London, forthcoming.

Collective Biography

See Prosopography

Collective Memory

The construction of collective memory dominates all human societies. Collective memory—what a social group, be it a family, a class, or a nation, remembers of the past—is not a metaphor but a social reality transmitted and sustained through the conscious efforts of a social group.

A latecomer in social historical studies, the notion of memory appeared only in the last 15 years or so. Historians were preceded by psychoanalysts (Sigmund Freud), philosophers (Henri-Louis Bergson), and writers (Marcel Proust), who, unlike historians, regarded memory as a resource of the individual psyche; by anthropologists, who found memory a more suitable concept than history for the reality of "savage" societies; and by sociologists.

The sociologist Maurice Halbwachs (1980) laid the theoretical groundwork for the study of memory by establishing both the nexus between memory and a social group, and the necessity of a social foundation for all recollections. Even the most intimate memory is connected to society's past, symbols, language, and landscapes. The social function of memory is to construct a past to explain the present; memory always starts, therefore, from the present and goes back in time through a selective process of invention, manipulation, and appropriation.

Collective memory is also constructed via historical forgetfulness; historical memory and amnesia are complementary, not contradictory. For example, after the unification of 1871, German regions had to obliterate the memory of the civil war of 1866 to construct a unifying national memory. What is remembered is often an object of political struggle, for in a single society coexist several memories that often contradict and oppose each other.

The history of memory traces the evolution of social practices whose purpose or effect is to represent the past and perpetuate its memory within a particular group or the society as a whole. A study of memory can focus on the history of a particular group (e.g., regional, political, religious) or on the manipulation by collective memory of a key event. To explain how memory is created, transmitted, and sustained, historians have often located vehicles of memory and analyzed their forms, mechanisms, and functions in the lives of social groups. The magisterial study edited by Pierre Nora (1984) on France's national memory includes "sites of memory" such as symbols (flag, hymn), commemorations, monuments, museums, legends, and landscapes. Concerning the orally transmitted memory of mostly illiterate groups, (e.g., popular classes in early modern Europe), historians have to rely on noninscriptive components of memorylike rituals and images.

The recent historical interest in memory results from the decline of the historian's traditional role as a delegate of a singular national identity; from the proliferation of countermemories (feminist, working class) by groups determined to discover their roots; and from the essential expansion and multiplication of modern memory as mass media fabricate and commercialize an ever-growing number of collective memories turning the past into a commodity for mass consumption. Thus, modern memory is dominated by its most popular, accessible, and inexpensive source, namely cinematographic and televised images. Historical interest in memory is also connected to the new studies of oral history—where memory is submitted, like any historical document, to critical analysis.

Collective memory both differs from, and converges with, history. Memory is different because it is a malleable guide to the past while history is a discipline built on evidence; they converge because at times the historian's story becomes an integral part of the collective memory (Julius Caesar's *De Bello gallico*), and because the historian is never totally disconnected from the image of the past shared by society. The historian's task is to explain the connections between memory and history without blurring their differences. In this analysis memory is one of several cognitive understandings that people have of the past—along with history, historical consciousness, and so on—that are interconnected, but not identical. The interplay of these representations of the past, whose relations are not inherently contradictory or concurring but depend on the period and the society, is at the heart of the relations between memory and history—for example, Yosef Hayim Yerushalmi's (1982) study about Jewish history and memory.

Scholars have debated the relations between memory and history in premodern and modern societies and in terms of the shift from oral to written transmission of memory. Halbwachs saw malleable memory and scientific history as antinomies, but his rigid opposition between memory as belonging to premodern society and precritical historiography, and history as belonging to modern society and scientific discipline now seems questionable. For Nora history and memory were united before the development of scientific history in the 19th century and have been split since. But his consequent distinction between a premodern memory as a social practice (a milieu of memory) and a modern memory as voluntary and deliberate should be rethought, because deliberateness is a matter of degree, and no memory is spontaneous. Modern memory seems a kind of social practice that fundamentally differs from premodern memory due to commercialization and the mass media. Recent work on how traditions are invented in human societies indeed opens new research areas in the social history of collective memory. As this debate continues the historian of collective memory, perhaps more than other historians, is caught between contemporary images of the past and the historian's craft. This is the challenge and the fascination of this topic. (*See also* Oral History)

Alon Confino

REFERENCES

Halbwachs, Maurice. *The Collective Memory.* New York: Harper & Row, 1980.

Hobsbawm, Eric, and Terence Ranger. *Invention of Tradition.* Cambridge: Cambridge University Press, 1984.

Nora, Pierre, ed. *Les lieux de mémoire.* Paris: Gallimard, 1984 et seq.

Wachtel, Nathan. "Memory and History: An Introduction," *History and Anthropology* 2 (1986): 207–224.

Yerushalmi, Yosef Hayim. *Zakhor.* Seattle: University of Washington Press, 1982.

Collectivization

Collectivization was an integral part of the USSR's First Five-Year Plan (1928–1932), which was intended to socialize agriculture. Collective forms of ownership replaced communal and private land tenure, and joint cultivation supplanted family farming. Collective farmers earned "labor-days" (pay units based on quantity and quality of work) and theoretically shared in farm profits after the compulsory delivery of grain and other produce to the state. Collectivization radically altered the lives of the USSR's 25 million peasant families and was accomplished at great human and material cost.

Although the formation of a large-scale socialized agriculture had long been a tenet in the Communist Party program, collectivization was shaped less by ideology than by the specific political, social, and economic context that gave rise to the Stalin Revolution. By the end of the 1920s, the USSR had entered into crisis. In the midst of a war scare, leadership struggles, and fears of counterrevolution from within, the USSR began experiencing difficulties in grain procurement. Reacting to state-imposed low grain prices, high industrial goods prices, and a manufactured goods famine, many peasants withheld their grain or diverted it to other agricultural concerns. The Stalin faction in the leadership responded with "extraordinary measures"—forcible grain seizures, market closures, and other coercive measures. This intemperate response derived from a refusal to raise agricultural prices at the expense of capital accumulation for the ongoing industrialization program as well as the crisis atmosphere of the times, which promoted extreme radicalism.

Collectivization grew out of extraordinary measures as a method of extracting grain from peasants. The policy of "wholesale" collectivization was proclaimed at the November 1929 Party Plenum. Collectivization was scheduled for completion in major grain-producing regions by fall 1930, spring 1931 at the latest, and in grain-consuming regions by fall 1931, spring 1932 at the latest.

The actual pace of collectivization far exceeded the already radical schedule announced in Moscow. The party mobilized tens of thousands of urban party members and industrial workers to implement policy. Although the party expected its cadres to participate in a rural class struggle between poor and rich peasants (the *kulaks*), most peasants defied Marxist categorization and united against the outsiders in defense of their common interests as petty producers. The small minority of peasants supporting collectivization was drawn from migrant laborers, poor peasants, party and Komsomol members, and Red Army veterans. Mainly, however, the policy was forced upon the peasantry, often at gunpoint. The peasantry's violent reaction led Stalin to call a temporary retreat in March 1930 with the publication of his article "Dizzyness from Success," in which he blamed the cadres while renouncing central responsibility for the campaign's violence. Collectivization was resumed the following fall at a slightly less breakneck pace, but nonetheless with continued use of coercive means. Collectivization was completed in major grain-producing regions by 1932 and elsewhere by the mid- to late 1930s.

Collectivization was accompanied by the elimination of the kulak as a class. Peasants labeled as kulaks were subject to varying forms of repression, ranging from expropriation and resettlement within their districts to deportation beyond their regions to internment in concentration camps, according to a differential hierarchy of kulakdom. Over one million peasant families were affected by this policy. The policy was carried out brutally, uprooting peasants from their homes and placing them in subhuman conditions. Because of the difficulties of applying Marxist categories to the peasantry, the term "kulak" was used arbitrarily and frequently became a political axe wielded against peasant critics of collectivization.

Peasants responded to collectivization with all the methods of resistance at their disposal. Assassinations and assaults of officials, arson, slaughter of livestock, women's riots, and village uprisings accompanied the early phase of collectivization. Active forms of peasant resistance were crushed mercilessly. Peasants therefore also had recourse, especially in later years, to more passive forms of resistance, such as flight to the cities, poor work performance, theft, and breakages.

Collectivization was a disaster. The short-term consequence of the campaign was the 1932–1933 famine, claiming as many as 5 million lives. The long-term consequences have included massive rural out-migration, endemic food supply difficulties, and unproductive agriculture. The collectivization campaign established the foundations for contemporary Soviet agriculture as well as serving as a model for collectivization in Eastern Europe, China, and elsewhere.

Scholarship on collectivization is meager and mainly follows a cold war approach to understanding Soviet historical development, stressing politics and ideology at the expense of social factors. Consequently, scholars have only recently begun to explore the social context of Stalinist policies. The crisis of the late 1920s, popular participation in collectivization by urban cadres, peasant resistance, and peasant support for collectivization are topics requiring further investigation. (*See also* Land Tenure and Reform; Peasant Rebellion; Peasantry; Russian Industrialization)

Lynne Viola

REFERENCES

Davies, R.W. *The Socialist Offensive.* Cambridge, MA: Harvard University Press, 1980.

Lewin, M. *Russian Peasants and Soviet Power.* New York: Norton, 1975.

Viola, Lynne. *The Best Sons of the Fatherland.* New York: Oxford University Press, 1987.

Colonialism

The word "colonialism," like "imperialism," was coined in the 19th century to give a name to a set of social phenomena, some of them as old as recorded history, that had taken on a collective ideological meaning in European and American politics. In their primary senses, both words referred to the motives which led states to extend their control over distant lands and over peoples of different ethnicity, and to the political frameworks through which control was established and maintained. "Colonialism" tended to be applied to situations in which a formal system of political dependency was constructed, whereas "imperialism" was a broader term including many different forms of hegemony. Neither word was, however, clearly defined, and the distinction between them remains fuzzy. The notion that colonialism and imperialism usually involved European domination of non-Europeans overseas dissolved when Japan and the United States became colonial powers and Lenin wrote of capitalist "imperialism" in Russia. In its secondary senses, "colonialism" also came to refer to direct exploitation of the labor and trade of a country by an elite of resident foreigners, and to the settlement of European communities overseas.

Despite continuing problems of definition, many social historians have treated colonialism as a coherent object of study. They have examined it in roughly four contexts: in searching for the causes of overseas expansion, in examining relationships between colonies and their "home" countries or larger economic systems, in explaining the structures and dynamics of colonial societies, and in exploring the reasons for the collapse of colonial authority. Recently some social historians have also explored cultural contexts for colonialism, including gender as well as racial imagery.

Many studies of the origins of particular cases of colonial expansion have emphasized social factors. The establishment of Greek colonies throughout the ancient Mediterranean and Near East has been traced to demographic pressures, subsistence crises, and class conflict in the mainland Hellenic states. Similar factors have been cited as causes of the Viking explosion of the Middle Ages, the Arab conquests, and the Crusades. But the greatest amount of research has been done on the social origins of the European overseas expansion which commenced in the 15th century. Social historians from Karl Marx to Immanuel Wallerstein have seen a correlation between the emergence of a capitalist economy in western Europe and a complex set of changes which altered society in such a way that colonialism became a continuous aspect of European life. The expansion of internal European trade and local market economies produced an aggressive class of investors capable of organizing colonial ventures and exploiting new commodities. Among the landed elites of Spain and England, those fortunate enough to benefit from market capitalism contributed to colonialism with their money and their political support. If additional motives asserted themselves, as in the case of the Puritanism of New England's leaders, such people might also venture themselves and their dependents. Losers in the process of socioeconomic change also found reasons to become colonialists. The elite of the conquistadores who presented Spain with its overseas empire was recruited from the impecunious sons of the declining lesser nobility. The same held true for many colonial administrations in the 19th century, drawn from aristrocrats (including Japanese Samurai) losing ground at home. Throughout western Europe, humbler emigrants often derived from social groups, like craftsmen in the 19th century put at a disadvantage by economic change and the development of capitalism.

In recent years, increasing attention has been paid to less obvious social factors underlying preindustrial European colonialism. Some historians have argued that the dynamic societies of western Europe in the 17th and 18th centuries produced consumer behavior patterns that vastly expanded demand for overseas textiles and food products by encouraging the widespread emulation of elite fashions. Some of the most important elements of preindustrial European colonialism (the Atlantic slave and sugar trades, for example, with their bases in West Indian colonies) were built around consumption of this type. Such behavior became more general in the 19th century as incomes increased and as cultural modes that signified a person's respectability through material lifestyle became more prevalent.

The social origins of the remarkable resurgence of European colonialism in the late 19th century which led, among other things, to the partition of Africa has also been a subject of major research. Supplementing the more standard diplomatic, economic, Marxist, and psychoanalytical interpretations, social historians have developed approaches emphasizing class conflict and modernization. In one view, late 19th-century European expansionism was an attempt by traditional elites to retain control of their governments by advertising colonies and other forms of imperialism as a way of protecting the jobs of workers and the markets of industrialists and merchants against foreign competition. By espousing colonial expansion, conservative elites could undercut the bourgeois support base of anticolonial liberals and try to seduce workers from the socialists. Other historians portray colonialism and imperialism as ideologies often adopted (especially in Germany) by radically nationalist bourgeois groups to expression resentment against the domination of society by industrial and traditional elites. Before 1914 these elites were typically accused of being too passive in the international competition for colonies.

Studies of the "imperial relationship" between colonies and metropolitan centers abound. Most focus on administrative arrangements and economic exploitation, but social historians have also examined the ways in which colonies extended the European social order abroad, placing non-European subject peoples into the lower ranks of hierarchies of which the upper ranges were fixed in Europe. The development of dependency theory to explain peculiarities in the economic modernization of formerly colonial countries has focused attention on the crucial role of colonial elites as intermediaries in the imperial relationship. Such elites (especially in Latin America) often led movements toward independence, but they also shaped political and economic systems afterward which perpetuated domination by Europe and the United States. The cultural element of elite dependency has also been studied—both because it helped to legitimate colonial control and because in some cases (such as British North America) it produced part of the ideological basis of a demand for political independence. Images of colonial people as effeminate resulted from European gender ideologies in the 19th century but also affected independence struggles bent on reasserting masculinity.

Social historians have had a great deal to say about the structures of colonial societies and about how they operated. Most studied have been the British colonies in North America. American colonial historians have shown how local social tensions in the colonies intersected with imperial disputes with Great Britain and led to revolt. Considerable work in other fields such as family history has also been done on colonial America. Such research is now being undertaken by historians of colonial societies throughout the world. Colonial social history has become particularly sophisticated through the study of societies that contained both a substantial European population which replicated European social phenomena and an indigenous non-European population. Studies such as David Prochaska's on French Algeria (1990) have helped to erase boundaries between social and cultural history.

As many of the preceding examples suggest, one of the motivating forces behind research in colonial social history has been the desire to explain the collapse of traditional colonial authority in modern times and the bewildering array of social, cultural, economic, and political consequences of national liberation. Historians have tried to determine the extent to which the kind of society that emerged in many African countries under colonial rule was responsible for chaotic politics and continuing economic subordination after independence. Understanding of how independence was achieved in, for example, India has been extended beyond the rather narrow political and ideological context within which the subject was at first examined by considering the ways in which a wide array of social groups and organizations were mobilized for political action.

Because of the enormous variety of the subject matter that can be considered in the field and because of its continued political relevance, colonial social history is a thriving and growing enterprise. It has attained particular importance as a result of the recent explosion of interest in global history. (*See also* Dependency Theory; Imperialism)

Woodruff D. Smith

REFERENCES

Fieldhouse, D.K. *The Colonial Empires: A Comparative Survey from the Eighteenth Century.* New York: Delta, 1966.

Katz, Stanley N., and John M. Murrin, eds. *Colonial America: Essays in Politics and Social Development* (3rd ed.). New York: Knopf, 1983.

Kennedy, Paul M. *The Rise of the Anglo-German Antagonism, 1860–1914.* Atlantic Highlands, NJ: Humanities, 1987.

Prochaska, David. *Making Algeria French: Colonialism in Bone, 1870–1920.* Cambridge: Cambridge University Press, 1990.

Wallerstein, Immanuel. *The Modern World System*, 3 volumes. New York: Academic Press, 1977–1988.

Columbian Exchange

When all of the emotional rhetoric that surrounds the quincentenary celebration of the arrival of Columbus to the New World is removed, the Columbian consequences, the changes brought about by the union of the Old and New Worlds, describes one of the most important events in the history of the world. The Columbian exchange describes the social consequences of the exchange of pathogens, cultigens, and animals between the Americas, Europe, Asia, and Africa.

The introduction of draft animals to the New World, for example, revolutionized the lives of many Indian tribes. The horse provided greater mobility, making it easier to hunt. Many tribes which had lived on the edges of the Great Plains began to live full time on the plains, following herds of buffalo. Tribes such as the Sioux, Apache, Comanche, among others, developed superb equestrian skills, and slowed the advance of white settlement in the 19th century. Competition in the 18th and 19th centuries over hunting grounds in the southern plains between Apaches and Comanches resulted in increased warfare along the northern frontier of Mexico that did not end until the surrender in the 1880s of the last Apache bands to the United States Army. Other tribes in the Americas modified their social and political organization and economy with the acquisition of horses. Examples include the Araucanians of southern Chile and tribes of the Pampas, who resisted white settlement until the 1870s.

The acquisition of livestock modified the economy of many tribes. Cattle provided meat otherwise obtained through hunting. Sheep provided wool used in textile production. For example, the Navajo of Arizona and Aymara peasants of Bolivia earn money through the sale of woolen textiles, especially for a lively tourist trade.

The exchange of cultigens modified both the Old and New Worlds. Plant foods introduced into the Old World from the New included corn and potatoes, now cultivated throughout the world. Potatoes introduced into Europe from the Andes revolutionized the economy and society of northern Europe, particularly Ireland. Potatoes were ideally suited for the heavy damp soils of northern Germany and Ireland, providing a cheap supply of food for peasant families that led to rapid population growth. Then the destruction of the potato crop in Ireland in the 1840s by a fungus caused a severe famine and considerable loss of life. Thousands of Irish peasants migrated to the United States following the famine, where many settled in and changed life in such cities as Boston. Another crop, corn, changed life in the Old World. Corn gives a higher return of seed harvest, and supplemented the Old World grains traditionally grown in many areas.

Perhaps the most important consequence of the union of the Old and New Worlds was the exchange of pathogens, or disease organisms, previously unknown in the Americas. Diseases such as smallpox, measles, typhus, typhoid fever, bubonic plague, pneumonia, and others reached lethal proportions in epidemics that swept across the Americas. Indian populations experienced frightful mortality, frequently in excess of 90 percent from precontact population levels.

Indian depopulation changed the development of the Americas. In what is today the United States, epidemics literally paved the way for Anglo-American settlement. For example, epidemics decimated the population of New England in the years prior to the arrival of the pilgrims and Puritans. In the more densely settled areas of America, such as Mesoamerica and the Andes, Indian population decline modified the development of Spanish colonial society and economy. Depopulation left abundant land and little labor, leading to the growth in importance of ranching. Moreover, as the Indian population declined, the Spanish colonial government rationed labor through labor drafts such as the Mexican *repartimiento* and the Andean *mita*. Other colonial policies related to Indian population decline included *congregacion* (Mexico) or *reduccion* (Andes), the resettlement of Indians into compact settlements that facilitated the collection of tribute, exaction of labor, and evangelization. The congregacion policy was the model for the frontier missions on the fringes of Spanish America and Brazil.

Overall, as a worldwide exchange of foods, animals, and diseases, the Columbian exchange affected population structures and food habits on every continent, while the resulting weakening of the American Indian (and later, Pacific Island) societies paved the way for European conquest.

Robert H. Jackson

REFERENCES

Crosby, Alfred. *The Columbian Exchange: Biological and Cultural Consequences of 1492.* Westport, CT: Greenwood Press, 1972.

Dobyns, Henry. *Their Numbers Become Thinned: Native American Population Dynamics in Eastern North America.* Knoxville: University of Tennessee Press, 1983.

Gibson, Charles. *The Aztecs Under Spanish Rule.* Stanford, CA: Stanford University Press, 1964.

McNeill, William. *Plagues and Peoples.* New York: Anchor/Doubleday, 1976.

Sanchez-Albornoz, Nicolas. *The Population of Latin America: A History.* Translated by W.A.R. Richardson. Berkeley and Los Angeles: University of California Press, 1974.

Combination Acts

The Combination Acts defined the British law's attitude toward labor organization before the modern era. The acts played some role in territory labor unrest during the crucial early phases of industrialization (similar laws existed in other industrializing countries later on). The term "combination" refers to trade associations of journeymen artisans; the term "union" gradually replaced "combination" during the 19th century. The legal status of workers' combinations was complex because of the overlapping of English common and statute law, but particularly important was the application of the law of conspiracy to combinations which might be ruled as operating in restraint of trade and thus as being liable to punishment as felonies. During the 18th century statutes were passed curbing the activities of specific trade societies, although workers also remained liable to prosecution under a range of preexisting laws. At the end of the 18th century the first general combination acts were adopted. The term "Combination Acts," therefore, usually refers to the act passed in 1799 (39 Geo. 3, c. 81) and to the act which repealed and replaced it in 1800 (39 and 40 Geo. 3, c. 106). These acts aimed at consolidating, generalizing, and simplifying the law. The Combination Act of 1800 created no new crime but insured speedier, cheaper, less complicated and surer means of prosecution and conviction. Under this act two justices of the peace decided the issue of guilt or innocence, as opposed to a common law action for conspiracy, which required a jury trial. The extent to which this act represented a change of policy or effectively curbed trade societies, which often continued under the guise of friendly societies, remains a controversial question. In 1824–1825, in a celebrated utilitarian maneuver, social reformer Francis Place arranged the repeal of the old and new combination laws in the name of laissez faire economic policy. Unionists, however, remained vulnerable to legal action, particularly on charges of breach of contract.

James Epstein

REFERENCES

Orth, John. "English Combination Acts of the Eighteenth Century," *Law and History Review* 5 (1987).

Rule, John, ed. *British Trade Unionism, 1750–1850.* New York: Longman, 1988.

Thompson, E.P. *The Making of the English Working Class.* New York: Viking, 1963.

Commercial Diaspora

The term "commercial diaspora" refers to a network of merchants engaged in interstate and cross-cultural trade, usually over long distances across land and/or sea and most often involving the movement of luxury goods. Throughout history and in virtually all societies, there have been pockets of foreigners, religious minorities, and outsiders who have performed vital economic functions for the larger societies in which they lived. One notable example of such communities was the Jewish ghettos that dotted Europe and the Mediterranean world in the medieval and early modern eras. These Jewish communities monopolized key economic activities that depended upon links among the dispersed settlements. There have been many other such commercial diasporas, including Armenian communities in eastern Europe and the Middle East, Chinese settlements in Southeast Asia, the Hausa merchants of West Africa; the Swahili along the East African coast; Lebanese and Syrian merchants in Africa and elsewhere; Afro-Portuguese along the western coast of Africa during the period of transatlantic slave trade; and the métis fur traders of 17th- and 18th-century North America. The phenomenon was common in the ancient world and in the Americas before European contact.

Commercial diasporas filled an economic niche in the widely scattered and imperfectly integrated economies of the preindustrial world. Merchants who formed such a dispersed network recognized a shared ethnic, religious, and linguistic identity that was essential in bridging the cultural and economic gaps between different states and societies. In some cases, ethnic identity evolved from interethnic marriage and hence was mixed, and in other cases ethnic purity was emphasized as a distinguishing feature of identity. Religion has played an important role in maintaining identities. Judaism, Islam, and Christianity have been equally important in the maintenance of diaspora cultures, and in some cases other religions have been used as well. Commercial languages associated with diasporas have often emerged as lingua franca over wide areas where linguistic diversity was common. Intermarriage among diaspora inhabitants and kinship connections over great distances helped to strengthen these commercial associations. In many cases, educational institutions, usually connected with religious teaching, developed in these communities as a mechanism to reinforce cultural exclusiveness and to train children in accounting, law, and other practical subjects of business. Apprenticeship for the relatives of community members was a common means of limiting access to commercial knowledge.

The common cultural features of commercial diasporas made it possible for resident merchants along trade routes to fulfill two important commercial needs—brokerage and agency. Resident merchants who shared a diaspora culture served as brokers in the purchase and sale of goods, and they acted as agents for traveling merchants.

Common cultural identity, kinship, marriage, and religion were useful in reducing the risks of trade, particularly in situations where credit mechanisms, insurance, currency exchange, banking, storage, and legal protection were poorly developed. In times of poor communication and difficult transportation, diaspora merchants shared information on prices, the demand for commodities, and the sources of local products in a manner that encouraged oligopoly and monopoly. Price-fixing and the manipulation of weights and measures were not uncommon.

Participants in commercial diasporas can be divided into two groups—the resident brokers and landlords who provided accommodation and services, and the itinerant merchants who traveled among the communities of the diaspora. The resident merchants, of course, might travel sometimes, and they maintained connections with distant communities. Their principal tasks, however, involved the provision of services that required knowledge of local markets, access to food and supplies, and political and legal protection. These merchants often provided accommodation and food and therefore doubled as hotel keepers and landlords. The itinerant merchants usually traveled in caravans overland and in armed vessels on sea because trade routes were frequently infested with bandits and pirates and because they often crossed political frontiers where legal protection was nonexistent. Caravan organization and ocean shipping each required a high degree of specialization and investment.

Relations between diaspora communities and their host societies have often been tense, precisely because commercial diasporas monopolized foreign trade and because they insisted on maintaining their cultural distinctions. Host societies, in turn, frequently intensified suspicions about commerce with hostility to foreigners in their midst. Whether or not diaspora communities were required to live in ghettos, as in the case of most Jewish communities, or choose to establish "twin towns" some distance for local political centers, the separation of communities from their host societies was a common feature. The economic importance of these communities usually meant that they were adjacent to central markets and fairs, or they were located in the heart of commercial districts. Often diaspora communities developed at strategic caravan stops, river crossings, or coastal ports. The importance of diaspora communities in social history is obvious, though the phenomenon warrants further comparative study. (*See also* Merchants)

Paul E. Lovejoy

REFERENCES

Chaudhuri, K.N. *The Trading World of Asia and the English East India Company,* Cambridge: Cambridge University Press, 1978.

Curtin, Philip D. *Cross-Cultural Trade in World History.* New York: Cambridge University Press, 1984.

Innis, Harold. *The Fur Trade in Canada.* Toronto: University of Toronto Press, 1956.

Lovejoy, Paul E. *Caravans of Kola. The Hausa Kola Trade, 1700–1900.* Zaria and Ibadan: Ahamdu Bello University Press and Oxford University Press, 1980.

Meillassoux, Claude, ed. *The Development of Indigenous Trade and Markets in West Africa.* London: Oxford University Press, 1971.

Commercialization

From the vantage point of consumer societies in the late 20th century, wage labor, mass consumption, and mass production constitute the foundation of our daily lives. Although historians differ radically in how they interpret the causes and significance of these developments, most agree that any satisfactory account must explain such basic transformations as the changing status of money-making, new conceptions of property and contract, the commodification of labor (that is, the selling of work for a wage), and the rise in productivity as a result of technological changes in manufacturing and agriculture. The term "commercialization" is often used to summarize all these developments. It is a convenient way to refer to these complex and unwieldy historical processes without suggesting any particular explanation or set of interpretations. From this perspective, commercialization tends to be the ever-present backdrop for modern economic and social history. Taken for granted, it is rarely the main focus of inquiry.

While the impulse of professional historians is to dissect the phenomenon into smaller, more easily researchable topics, the popular understanding of the term moves in the opposite direction. Defined loosely as the process whereby a vast array of productive activities and services, including leisurely pursuits, become drawn inexorably into the net of market relations and monetary exchanges, this representation of commercialization articulates how many people experience change as consumers. The story is often marked by a sense of loss. For the 19th and 20th centuries, one standard plot describes the power of markets and money-making to replace the "things we used to make for ourselves" with "things made by others." It laments the fact that services once rendered out of love or neighborliness are now available for pay. Thus, commercialization, as it is popularly understood, is infused with our moral quandaries about what ought and ought not be bought and sold. It names our unresolved anxieties about the relation between people and their things and between the people who make things and the people who buy them. These two strands—commercialization as a neutral description of a set of historical changes and as a reflection of unease about the nature of social relations in the present—have intertwined in the writing about commercialization from the 18th century to the present. The popular discussion of commercialization, however, has been far more consequential in shaping the development of social history. This connection is especially evident in how social historians have studied preindustrial societies and the transition to capitalism.

In the postwar generation, intellectuals who are critical of market society are profoundly influenced by the work of Karl Polanyi, who formulated his analysis of self-regulating markets at a moment when Europe was blighted by depression, fascism, and war. In *The Great Transformation* (1957), Polanyi argued that self-regulating markets were incompatible with human social life. The attempts by various groups to shelter themselves from the consequences of self-regulating markets, as instituted in the 19th century, ultimately destroyed liberal society and opened the way to authoritarian regimes. The fundamental problem, for Polanyi, was that capitalist market relations invert human priorities: instead of embedding the economy in social relationships, social relationships are embedded in the economic system. As a result a narrow calculus of profit and risk dictate social life.

In order to conceive of better alternatives, Polanyi thought that we must surmount the habits of our market mentality. For commercialization to stand out as a social phenomenon, one must be able to imagine other ways to organize the relationship between economy and society. Accordingly, Polanyi and his students situate their studies of particular historical contexts within a broader comparative framework. Only by understanding how people in other societies reason about exchange, particularly their notions of gift and reciprocity, can we combat the tendency, encouraged by the first political economists, to project "the propensity to truck, barter, and exchange" onto human nature itself.

Enlisting the aid of archeology, history, and ethnography to displace the familiar and to broaden our sense of possible alternatives has become standard practice. This rhetorical strategy was important in defining a research agenda for social history, and for cultural and economic anthropology in the past generation. Many of the most influential studies of peasants and artisans in preindustrial society, and of workers in early industrial societies, whether in preindustrial Europe or in worlds colonized by Europeans, have implicitly adopted this comparative method. The mutual influences of cultural anthropology and social history are thus especially prominent in these studies.

For example, James C. Scott (1976), in his study of peasant rebellions in Southeast Asia in the 20th century, confirms his notion of a rural subsistence ethic as a general characteristic of rural society by drawing on E.P. Thompson's (1971) "moral economy of the poor," developed in Thompson's study of popular justice in the bread riots in 18th-century England. Similarly, Thompson relies on Evans-Pritchard's study of concepts of time among the Nuer in eastern Africa to underscore his contrast between the "task orientation" of preindustrial labor and the "time orientation" of capitalist discipline. In his essay "Time, Work-Discipline and Industrial Capitalism," Thompson (1967) explains that, in order for human labor to be measured by time and money, it must be turned into an abstract potential and separated from the social experience of

work as concrete activities which fulfill tangible needs. In doing so, Thompson retrieves a vision of work which is lost to industrial society. Following in the spirit of Thompson's analysis of alienation, anthropologists like Michael Taussig (1980) argue that the "exotic" beliefs and "quaint" practices of people whose contact with capitalism is recent can also reveal truths about the capitalist social relations of exchange and production which we can no longer perceive. For example, in the Cauca Valley of Colombia, godparents are sometimes accused of slipping a *peso* under the child during a baptism so that the money is baptized and not the child. Such a bill is said to return continually to enrich its owner. This practice is a literal rendering of how "money makes money." But unlike our own understanding of profit and capital, this understanding conveys a moral judgment about the nature of capital accumulation. The wealth gained from the baptized note is illegitimate because money has no power of its own, it gains its vitality by robbing the child whose baptism it had usurped.

These studies thus present compelling images of precapitalist societies, images that set the dominant values of our own capitalist society in relief. Analytically, these works rely on a sharp contrast, examined most explicitly by Taussig, between production subordinated to use-value and social relationships dominated by exchange-value. In the former, the goal of exchange is to make visible the social connections between the actors, while in the latter, typical of capitalist relations of exchange, the social relationship within which the exchange occurs is veiled by the seeming primacy of the transaction itself.

The opposition between use-value and exchange-value is effective in conveying a moral message. Precommercial societies are used to highlight presumably dubious features and assumptions of modern societies. However, this didactic purpose, no matter how vital politically, is served at the cost of romanticizing our understanding of precapitalist social relations of exchange and production. The source of the problem is the role that peasants, artisans, and workers are assigned in the rhetorical structure of this inquiry. Casting them as exemplars of alternative social relations, they become repositories of our forgotten values. As heros of our lost battles, we compel them, in our analysis, to be communities unified in resistance. Such representations homogenize these groups both by presenting them as internally undifferentiated and by erasing the distinctions between different phases of capitalist development.

A new self-reflectiveness has led cultural anthropologists and social historians to examine consequences of this rhetoric. The growing importance of feminist scholarship has introduced a new awareness of power and hierarchy, especially in the most idealized of harmonious communities. As William Roseberry (1989) reminds us, whether we are studying sharecroppers in 18th-century France, weavers in industrializing England, or tin miners in 20th-century Bolivia, peasants, artisans, and workers have histories and social existences far more complex than oppositions between use-value and exchange-value are able to capture. Their lives and aspirations are not just overwhelmed by capitalist relations of production. Rather, they are active in the creation of capitalist society. Their resistance, acquiescence, and at times, the common cause that they make with capitalist merchants or producers are part of the struggles that shape the particular patterns of capitalist development in various regions around the world.

Awareness of the romanticism in earlier studies does not invalidate the insights that we have gained about ourselves from the contrast. The work of scholars like Polanyi, Thompson, and Taussig, just to name a few, continue to offer important critiques of capitalist society. That rhetorically they have more in common with the popular discourse on commercialization should remind us that intellectuals are also situated actors, engaged in the moral and political issues of their own times. Just as current critical studies of commercialization are revealing about our own anxieties about identities in an age of mass consumption, similar discussions from earlier eras are equally revealing about the concerns of their own times. For example, in the 17th and 18th centuries, critics feared that the new fashionable garment trades encouraged a democratization of consumption. Disassociating styles of dress and adornment from aristocratic privilege destabilized society, critics argued. It confused identities by rendering meaningless the outward symbols of power and social hierarchy—symbols such as distinctive clothing. When middle-class consumption was a novelty, commercialization was criticized for leveling the social classes. Ironically, in an age when workers can realize their dreams by shopping on credit, critics now fear that the abundance offered to consumers veils the true hierarchical nature of society. For these skeptics, consumption diverts discontent by encouraging people to rush after ephemeral images of well-being rather than fight for true participation and equality.

Commercialization has been used by social historians also to denote a period in which rapid economic change, including increasing production for sale and growing use of money, develops but in advance of outright technological revolution or industrialization. Western Europe from the 16th to the 18th century is thus described as a commercializing society. New England around 1800 was rapidly commercializing, moving away from locally subsistent agriculture, amid considerable anxiety. During the past century many societies in Africa and Asia have commercialized, under the impact of Western trade, without necessarily industrializing. Commercialization can affect social class structure (leading to growing divisions between property owners and wage earners in the countryside as well as in cities), family functions, and gender roles, even the nature of friendships as more competitive relationships enter in. While this use of commercialization is somewhat more specific than the more sweeping judgments of scholars like Polanyi, it may carry some of the same moral connotations about a shift from a simpler, "purer" society to one more tainted.

As this brief survey of the concept indicates, neutral discussions of commercialization are rare. The term is used frequently to invoke powerful moral and political anxieties. What contemporaries in a society report about the consequences of commerce for social life offers us insight into the tensions and the ideals of that society. Students of social and economic change must keep in mind, however, that our knowledge about markets, production, and consumption in the past is structured rhetorically by these discussions of commercialization. (*See also* Capitalism;

Consumerism; Market Economy; Moral Economy)

Tessie P. Liu

REFERENCES

Polanyi, Karl. *The Great Transformation: The Political and Economic Origins of Our Time.* Boston: Beacon Press, 1957.

Roseberry, William. *Anthropologies and Histories: Essays in Culture, History, and Political Economy.* New Brunswick, NJ; Rutgers University Press, 1989.

Scott, James C. *The Moral Economy of the Peasant: Rebellion and Subsistence in Southeast Asia.* New Haven: Yale University Press, 1976.

Taussig, Michael T. *The Devil and Commodity Fetishism in South America.* Chapel Hill: University of North Carolina Press, 1980.

Thompson, E.P. "The Moral Economy of the English Crowd in the Eighteenth Century," *Past and Present* 50 (1971): 76–136.

———. "Time, Work-Discipline and Industrial Capitalism," *Past and Present* 38 (1967): 56–97.

Community

Social historians of Europe first expressed their interest in community through studies of collective protest activities (from food riots to working-class political mobilization); more recently they have focused on popular culture and leisure activities. For many authors, "community" in Europe equaled the village, parish, or other bounded unit of premodern society. What characterized these bounded units were social bonds: Sabean (1984) has described these as "a series of mediated relationships," or, in other words, a "relational" form of community. While this form of community is often buttressed by ideas of overarching connection—notably, kinship models or hierarchies relating to social order—it refers fundamentally to personalized connections among participants. Such connections, transacted through face-to-face relationships, reflected geographical proximity, economic and political ties, and the like.

Other studies have isolated ideologically based identities, in which "community" has operated in broad terms, encompassing participants through inclusive but abstracted ideological appeals and terms of reference. Significantly, the ideologically constructed form of European community has been demonstrated in the premodern period only for towns. Indeed, it is striking to note the extent to which European historiography clusters on each side of the great divide of 1800. The clear implication is that no single narrative can unite the preindustrial and industrialized constructions of community.

Applied to the post-1800 period, "community" has related primarily to the ideological expressions of social organization, with the relational elements attenuated or treated as objects of nostalgic longing. For Europeanists, preconditioned by the impact of the industrial revolution, ideological community has generally translated into expressions of class interests, particularly as they were reflected in the antagonisms between an emerging working class and the alliance forged between the state and emerging middle class.

Historians of the United States operate in a somewhat similar framework, often discussing tight-knit village communities in New England and then tracing the decline of community cohesion after about 1800. The rise of new institutions like the police and new habits such as an emphasis on individual guilt rather than community-based shame to guide proper conduct follow from this community decline. It is also true, however, that American historians frequently cite community decline at later dates, and sometimes note the ability of certain groups—such as immigrants—to formulate community structures in the industrial period. Here is a slight variant on the European emphasis on class interests, as opposed to bounded community relationships, in the modern period.

By contrast, the scholarly discussion for other parts of the world—particularly the Third World areas subject to imperialism—has focused on other forms of social organization as the basis of premodern community, most notably caste or tribe or—reflecting the vast agrarian societies these imperial structures ruled—villages. (Analysts are only now beginning to delineate the extent to which these ostensibly ethnographic categories were, in fact, colonial constructions that served central political purposes in the ideology of rule.) For historians of India, for instance, the concept of community has provided a fundamental mode of analysis. Conditioned by anthropologists and 19th-century administrators alike, community in the South Asian context has continued to refer to village or caste or to their urban equivalents, such as identities relating to region of origin (and, hence, linguistic identity), caste status, or religious belief. More recent studies have broadened their horizons, examining popular protest and cultural activities in terms similar to those used by scholars of Europe, but often still focusing on caste, region, and religion. Marxist scholars have attempted, without great success, to interpolate class identity into this array of community identities. To date, only a handful of studies have moved beyond caste and religion to discuss other forms of local organization and identity that could constitute the basis for community, such as neighborhood or voluntary association. Indeed, the most dramatic event of recent history—the division of the subcontinent in 1947 into two separate postcolonial states ostensibly along lines of religious identity—has often, if implicitly, dominated these analyses.

Implied in much of the social history of community has been the assumption that a linear progression characterized the evolution of community: that is, the general pattern was a movement from localized, relational community to more broadly based ideological definitions of community, culminating in the identification of the individual with fellow citizens of the same "community"—the nation-state. At least two elements proved important in the European shift of popular identification from local community to that of the nation-state: (1) participation in collective rituals that were informed by an ideological framework that came to equate the terms "community" and "nation" and (2) creation of a public sphere in which participants of the nation helped shape it through the exercise of informed public opinion.

The 18th century in England, for instance, witnessed a consolidation of power by new local elites and members of the "middling sort." Several studies have documented the efforts by many "middling sorts" to suppress local community rituals such as church sales, and to replace these local rituals with ones that explicitly connected the individual participant to the larger ideological community, the state. An increased polit-

icization accompanied this broadened frame of reference, fostered especially by the development of print capitalism, which ensured a shared basis of information accessible to significantly larger numbers of people. Benedict Anderson (1983) has argued that "the nation" constructed by the public opinion that emerged from this process resulted in an "imagined political community."

This underlying assumption—in which the presumed historical experience of western Europe has become an implicit norm against which other historical developments have been measured—shaped much social history of colonized areas as searches into why particular community formations seemed to short circuit or undermine the linear development toward nation. In places as unlike as Lebanon, Ireland, and South Asia, an exotic "other" was probed to explain these supposed shortcomings in historical development.

The unraveling of the Communist imperial structure in Eastern Europe has served as a great corrective for this presumption of linear progression toward national definitions of community. Viewed from the perspective of the early 1990s, it seems likely that social historians will return to renewed study of community, preoccupied with explaining how other forms of identity—based on ethnic, linguistic, and religious definitions of community (or what is now often labeled "cultural nationalism")—can be pitted against the nation in contests for claims to legitimacy and authority. Indeed, the process by which community is imagined and constructed may lie at the heart of social history itself. (*See also* Caste System; Central Place Theory; Ethnicity; Festivals; Middle Eastern Village Life; Public Sphere; Street Life; Subcultures)

Sandria B. Freitag

REFERENCES

Anderson, Benedict. *Imagined Communities: Reflections on the Origin and Spread of Nationalism.* London: Verso, 1983.

Freitag, Sandria B. *Collective Action and Community: The Emergence of Communalism in North India.* Berkeley and Los Angeles: University of California Press, 1990.

Sabean, David. *Power in the Blood: Popular Culture and Village Discourse in Early Modern Germany.* Cambridge: Cambridge University Press, 1984.

Underdown, David. *Revel, Riot and Rebellion: Popular Politics and Culture in England, 1603–1660.* Oxford: Clarendon Press, 1985.

Yang, Anand Y. *The Limited Raj.* Berkeley and Los Angeles: University of California Press, 1989.

Comparative History

As its label suggests, comparative history is the systematic comparing and contrasting of two or more historical cases in order to identify and explain their important similarities and differences. Such comparison has two primary goals. First, by examining more than one instance of historical change, comparative historians try to identify significant aspects or features of each instance which might have escaped the notice of historians focused on a single case. Second, in the process of identifying those features and comparing their presence or absence across cases, comparative historians hypothesize and test generalizable theories or principles of historical change.

Comparison seems to be an innate characteristic of human cognition. In daily life we are constantly noting similarities and differences among the people, places, and events, among other things, that we encounter; in so doing we are engaging in comparative analysis and drawing comparative judgments. Whenever we assert that something is unique or exceptional, we are noting its difference from others of its type; conversely, when we note that something is typical or representative of the broader category to which it belongs—for example, a "typical" midwesterner, or the "usual kind" of rock concert—we are asserting its similarity to others of its kind. When we draw generalizations—"all politicians are corrupt"—we are asserting similarity; and when we find exceptions to that generalization—"Mayor X, however, is honest"—we are both reaffirming the previously asserted general trend while noting a case that differs from it.

The difference between these everyday acts of comparison and the work of comparative historians is that the latter compare and contrast complex processes of historical change taking place over extended periods of time, with the goal of identifying and explaining the causes of those changes. In carrying out this task, most comparativists follow the methods first proposed by philosopher John Stuart Mill in *A System of Logic* (1843). Mill prescribed two basic means by which observers of several instances of the same phenomenon—say, the outbreak of social revolution—could arrive at a determination of the general causes of that phenomenon. The first was the Method of Agreement, in which the historian examines a number of cases of social revolution and, after determining the apparent causes of each case, eliminates all causes which do not appear in every case. The remaining cause or causes—that is, those which do appear in every case—are those which have the general effect of producing revolution.

Mill's second method, and the one which he regarded as more conclusive, was the Method of Difference. Here, instead of gathering cases with the same outcome, the historian seeks cases with similar preconditions and *different* outcomes. To continue the example of social revolution, one might examine two nations with similar characteristics, in one of which revolution eventually occurred and in the other of which it did not. After determining the relevant causes and preconditions in each case, the historian would eliminate those which appeared in both instances, concluding that the remaining causative factor or factors—those present in one case but not the other—are the general cause(s) either of revolution or, in the contrasting case, of stability.

As Mill himself recognized, these principles of comparative analysis are better suited to experiments in the natural sciences than to the study of human society. Even the most carefully selected historical cases seldom offer the precise mix of variables (present in some cases, absent in others) required by these two methods. As a result, few if any comparative historians have achieved the level of scientific rigor which Mill proposed. Nevertheless, despite the shortcomings of the data and cases with which they must work, historians since World War II have become increasingly aware of the analytical possibilities offered by comparative analysis.

One such possibility is the identification of generalizable characteristics of historical change.

Historians studying a single instance of such change—for example, the expansion of suffrage in the United States—will be able to identify a number of factors which appear to have caused that particular event or trend. But a historian studying the expansion of suffrage in a number of countries would be able to identify causes operating in more than one instance, and thus to construct a general explanation or theory for the expansion of voting rights in modern societies.

Theory building of this sort is an area of comparative inquiry that has tended to attract sociologists (prominent examples include Reinhard Bendix, Shmuel Eisenstadt, Barrington Moore, Orlando Patterson, Theda Skocpol, Immanuel Wallerstein, and others) rather than historians. This reflects the differences in the nature of the two disciplines. While sociology places great emphasis on the construction and testing of theories of human society, historians tend to be less concerned with questions of theory and more focused on acquiring deep, detailed knowledge of the specific time and place on which they are working. This knowledge is usually obtained through extensive research in primary sources and documents, often requiring years to carry out. While historians do make use of sociological and other social scientific theories to help them organize their research and eventually construct a causal explanation of the changes they have documented, relatively few are interested in designing such theories themselves. To the contrary, most historians are highly skeptical of the broad generalizations of the historical sociologists, which they view as insufficiently sensitive to the enormous variety and complexity of historical experience in different times and places.

In questioning the generalizing tendencies of historical sociology, historians have exploited a second potential benefit of the comparative method—its utility for testing hypotheses. Comparative analysis is equally suited for testing both the theoretical pronouncements of historical sociology and assertions of causation based on a single case. Such analysis has served to alert historians, not just to the dangers of excessive generalization, but to the limitations as well of what we might call "one-case" history.

One such limitation is the error of attributing historical change to what French historian Marc Bloch termed "local pseudo-causes"—factors which appear to be causing events or developments in the time and place which one is examining, but which do not appear in other times and places where the same or similar developments were taking place. Bloch cites the case of a historian using purely local factors to explain the expansion of landed estates in a 15th-century French province. That historian failed to note, however, that agricultural estates were expanding not just in that province but in much of western Europe as well. This suggests that there were historical forces at work which transcended the boundaries of that province, as indeed there were; but those forces were not visible to a historian focused on a single locality.

"One-case" historians also run the risk of mistaking the degree to which the conditions and events they are examining are typical of, or different from, similar conditions or events elsewhere. Frederick Jackson Turner's celebrated "frontier thesis" argued that much of the distinctiveness of American society and culture could be traced to the formative experience of conquering and settling the western frontier. This interpretation enjoyed considerable popularity among American historians during the first half of the 1900s. It fell from favor, however, as comparative analysis of frontiers in Australia, Canada, Latin America, and South Africa showed that the American West was not as distinctive a historical experience as Turner had thought, nor were the impacts of the frontier experience on the broader society as direct and straightforward as Turner had painted them.

The pitfalls of "one-case" history thus seem clear. Focusing on a single geographical and temporal area of specialization can lead historians to neglect or ignore broader processes of historical change. The result is partial or inaccurate explanations of the events they are analyzing, as well as erroneous judgments of how unique or representative the phenomena under investigation really are. The recognition of these pitfalls, and the hope of avoiding them, have led a growing number of historians in recent years to become increasingly comparative in their work.

In the United States much of the impulse behind the rise of comparative history came from debates and controversies surrounding the institution of slavery. One of the first important works of cross-cultural comparative history produced in this country was Frank Tannenbaum's *Slave and Citizen* (1946), which argued that legal and religious protections available to slaves in Latin America led to a more humane form of slavery than in the United States, where such protections did not exist. *Slave and Citizen* helped stimulate a wave of new research which has enormously deepened our understanding of slavery in the Americas and in the process has refuted Tannenbaum's original argument. That research has also formed the basis for more recent comparative works: for some examples, see Herbert Klein, *Slavery in the Americas: A Comparative Study of Cuba and Virginia* (1967); Carl Degler, *Neither Black nor White: Slavery and Race Relations in the United States and Brazil* (1971); George Fredrickson, *White Supremacy: A Comparative Study in American and South African History* (1981); Orlando Patterson, *Slavery and Social Death* (1982); Peter Kolchin, *Unfree Labor: American Slavery and Russian Serfdom* (1987). On the period after slavery, see John Cell, *The Highest Stage of White Supremacy: The Origins of Segregation in South Africa and the American South* (1982).

Social class has formed another major focus of comparative work. William Reddy, *Money and Liberty in Modern Europe* (1987), uses comparative analysis to critique concepts of class. Peter Stearns, *Lives of Labor: Work in Maturing Industrial Society* (1975), and Charles Tilly et al., *The Rebellious Century, 1830–1930* (1975), contrast the experiences of workers in western European countries; Charles Bergquist, *Labor in Latin America: Comparative Essays on Chile, Argentina, Venezuela, and Colombia* (1986), does the same for Latin America. On the middle class, see Jurgen Kocka, *White-Collar Workers in America, 1890–1940: A Social-Political History in International Perspective* (1980), and Fritz Ringer, *Fields of Knowledge: French Academic Culture, 1890–1920, in Comparative Perspective* (1991). Two studies of urban elites which suggest the possibilities for comparison within a single country are E. Digby Baltzell, *Puritan Boston and Quaker Philadelphia* (1979), and Frederic Jaher, *The Urban Establishment: Upper Strata in Boston, New York, Charleston, Chicago, and Los Angeles* (1982).

One could cite additional comparative titles within social history, as well as in economic, political, and other subfields of history. Nevertheless, the number of genuinely comparative monographs remains extremely low—almost infinitesimal, in fact—in relation to the total number of historical works published in any given year. This reflects a number of obstacles which stand in the way of comparative research and writing. In part those obstacles are the direct result of the current organization of history as a discipline and its fairly rigid division into nationally or regionally defined specializations (African history, American history, Chinese history, etc.). Such divisions provide little incentive for attempting cross-cultural comparison; and when historians do try to move on from their original specialization into completely new areas—say, from American history into Latin American or East Asian— they face formidable challenges of learning new languages, new historiographies, and new archival sources.

As a result, the number of historians who write the kinds of comparative monographs cited above is quite small in relation to the discipline as a whole. Nevertheless, even when they stop short of attempting full-fledged comparative history, many historians are by now well aware of the shortcomings of "one-case" history and are seeking to overcome those shortcomings in two ways, both of which are clearly visible in social historical research of the last 20 years. The first is, while continuing to focus one's research on a particular time and place, to ask questions about that time and place that are derived from comparative work on similar phenomena in other historical settings. This approach is particularly appealing to social historians, who tend to define themselves as much by their thematic concerns (e.g., as historians of the family, or women's historians, or historians of slavery) as by their regional and chronological specialization. Historians working on Japanese or Latin American family history, for example, are likely to pay as much attention to the historical literature on family structure in western Europe and the United States as to the standard historiographies on their countries of specialization. And when they prepare to carry out research using local sources, they often design that research around questions and hypotheses taken from the family history literature on other parts of the world. In western Europe and the United States, for example, age at marriage tended to fall with the onset of industrialization; did this happen in the developing world as well? Is the relationship between urbanization and family size similar to or different from that observed elsewhere? What about birth rates?

In research and writing of this sort, historians continue to carry out research on a single episode of historical change. But they do so by asking explicitly comparative questions, looking for the presence or absence of historical causes and outcomes observed in other settings. As a result, their conclusions will be comparative in character and will be addressed directly to debates on general historical processes of family structure, or class formation, or gender roles, or whatever the topic may be.

A second way of deriving the benefits of a comparative approach while continuing to focus on one's original area of specialization is to meet with other historians and social scientists in conventions, working groups, or informal gatherings to discuss the results of research on a given phenomenon in different times and places. Discussions and meetings of this sort are a relatively efficient way for historians to learn about related work being done on other parts of the world. Not infrequently such gatherings result in edited volumes of essays addressing a central topic or question in a variety of historical settings. A number of these publications fall squarely within the boundaries of social history. As might be expected, slavery is well represented: see, for example, David W. Cohen and Jack P. Greene, eds., *Neither Slave nor Free: The Freedmen of African Descent in the Slave Societies of the New World* (1972); Suzanne Miers and Igor Kopytoff, eds., *Slavery in Africa* (1977); and James L. Watson, ed., *Asian and African Systems of Slavery* (1980). Workers and their unions form the subject of Ira Katznelson and Aristide Zolberg, eds., *Working-Class Formation: Nineteenth-Century Patterns in Western Europe and the United States* (1986), and Edward Epstein, ed., *Labor, Autonomy and the State in Latin America* (1989). For an exceptionally coherent and stimulating example of this kind of collective comparative publication, see

Nicholas Canny and Anthony Pagden, eds., *Colonial Identity in the Atlantic World, 1500–1800* (1987).

We might close by noting the possibilities for applying the comparative method to the field of comparative history itself, as several prominent historians and sociologists have in fact done (see References). In identifying significant convergences and divergences within the comparative literature, these analysts have found that comparativists can be mapped on a spectrum defined by Mill's two methods. At one end are those comparativists who use the Method of Agreement to identify similarities among cases and to present those similarities as generalizable theories of historical change. Not surprisingly, these "universalizers," to use Charles Tilly's term, tend to be historical sociologists. At the other end of the spectrum are the "contrasters" and "individualizers," who stress the irreducible uniqueness of the various cases they examine, rely on the Method of Difference to identify the sources of that uniqueness, and in so doing reject general theories of historical change. Again not surprisingly, these "contrasters" are almost exclusively historians. Intermediate positions on the spectrum are occupied by a mixed group of sociologists and historians who are trying to understand how large-scale structural variables—economic forces, demography, the state—operate in different historical settings. These "macro-analysts," to use Skocpol and Somers's (1980) term for them, are interested in constructing theoretical explanations of historical change; but at the same time they are alert to, and indeed are actively searching for, significant differences in the operation of those variables from case to case.

Each of these variants of comparative history is dependent on, and to a significant degree presupposes the existence of, the others. General theories of historical change provide hypotheses to be tested by the "contrasters" and "macro-analysts," whose findings in turn set limits on those theories by showing the cases in which they accurately describe historical change and the cases in which they do not. Conversely, as the "contrasters" and "macro-analysts" identify variables which appear to be of key importance in determining different outcomes in different cases, they alert "universalizers" to the possibility of modifying and refining their theories in such a way as to make them more accurate, or constructing entirely new ones. This creative tension or complementarity among the various "logics" of comparative history gives the subdiscipline a particularly dynamic quality and helps account for the substantial impact which it has had on historical research and writing during the last 30 years. (*See also* Frontier Thesis; Revolutions; Slavery; Sociology)

George Reid Andrews

REFERENCES

Fredrickson, George. "Comparative History," in Michael Kammen, ed., *The Past Before Us: Contemporary Historical Writing in the United States.* Ithaca, NY: Cornell University Press, 1980.

Skocpol, Theda, ed. *Vision and Method in Historical Sociology.* Cambridge and New York: Cambridge University Press, 1984.

Skocpol, Theda, and Margaret Somers. "The Uses of Comparative History in Macrosocial Inquiry," *Comparative Studies in Society and History* 22, 2 (1980): 174–197.

Tilly, Charles. *Big Structures, Large Processes, Huge Comparisons.* New York: Russell Sage, 1984.

Van den Braembussche, A.A. "Historical Explanation and Comparative Method: Towards a Theory of the History of Society," *History and Theory* 28, 1 (1989): 1–24.

Concubinage

Concubinage was one of the social features of slavery which existed concurrently with the institution of marriage in both Muslim and non-Muslim societies in Africa and the Middle East. A concubine is neither a wife nor a mistress. A concubine is regarded as a legal category in Muslim societies because her children occupy the same status with the children of wives. In non-Muslim societies, concubines may not occupy any legal status. This is, however, subject to debate because no serious study of concubinage has been done in non-Muslim societies. The system in Muslim societies was an arrangement in which a slave woman lived with a man as his wife without being married to him in a civil or the normal way. This affiliation was only considered lawful if the woman was a slave who was captured in a holy war (*jihad*) or born to slave

parents. Slave status is fundamental to the phenomenon of concubinage.

Different classes of people keep concubines in their homes in addition to their legal wives. However, keeping and using concubines is legal though strictly on social and economic conditions. Anyone who keeps concubines must be capable of providing them with all the etiquette of life in return for their procreative and domestic services. Under no circumstances can a concubine be unfairly treated. Should a concubine be maltreated by her master, the Islamic law grants her freedom automatically. In Muslim societies, for example, once a concubine delivers a child, she becomes undeniably free for the rest of her life. On the other hand, if a concubine is barren she may remain in slavery unless she gets resources to pay for her freedom.

Historical studies and gender analysis have shown how women suffered from total exploitation of their sexuality and labor under the system of concubinage. As a matter of fact, concubinage is a kind of socially forcible dependency in a family structure in which a concubine woman does not participate in daily decision making in a household. Rather, she takes orders from both her master and his wives in a polygamous household or wife in a monogamous situation. In this position, a concubine provides sexual satisfaction to her master and does most of the hard work in a household, which may include cleaning, cooking, supply of water, spinning, nurturing children, threshing of grain, and hairdressing, all at the behest of her master or his wives.

In the theory and practice of concubinage, children of concubines enjoy equal status, rights, and privileges with other children born by a wife or wives because of having the same biological father. They are recognized by both the law and the society because of this biological truth. To this extent, therefore, concubine offspring are eligible for equal and equitable share of inheritance in Muslim societies. The Islamic law does not allow the status of their mother to inhibit their rights to equal and equitable share of inheritance of all kinds of property.

In most slave societies, concubinage was used to facilitate demographic growth and settling of male slaves in agricultural estates. Concubines attracted higher prices than male slaves because of their role in reproduction of human beings and production of goods and services. Age and sensual attractions were some of the important determinants of the prices of concubines. Finally, concubinage declined dramatically after the *jihad* wars in Muslim societies around 1900. The establishment of colonial rule in Africa and the Middle East also encouraged decline. (*See also* Slavery)

Ibrahim M. Jumare

REFERENCES

Fisher, Allan G.B., and Humphry J. Fisher. *Slavery and Muslim Society in Africa.* London: C. Hurst, 1970.

Lovejoy, Paul E. "Concubinage in the Sokoto Caliphate 1804–1903, Slavery and Abolition," *Journal of Comparative Studies* 11, 2 (September 1990).

———, ed. *The Ideology of Slavery in Africa.* Beverly Hills: Sage Publications, 1981.

Willis, John Ralph, ed. *Slaves and Slavery in Muslim Africa.* London: F. Cass, 1985.

Confraternities

Confraternities were Catholic lay associations that met regularly to perform collective devotions. Those devotions often included charity toward the poor. Some confraternities served as burial and mutual aid societies. Almost all provided their members with a recreational outlet, confraternal feasts being legendary for their debauchery. They have attracted considerable social historical interest as a means of dealing with popular Christianity and the religion's changing social role.

Historically, confraternities were a vehicle of evangelization for religious orders. The term "confraternity" signals more a type of institutional relationship between a clerical entity and a group of lay people than it does an actual social organization. In pursuit of access to the grace or sanctity possessed by a religious order, a group of laymen would agree to participate in devotions sponsored by members of that order. Laymen would often take their commitment to the extent of confessing and receiving communion from the members of the religious order, while seeking to be buried in the order's burial grounds.

The great age of confraternities was the later European Middle Ages, when religious orders such as the Franciscans and Dominicans utilized them to evangelize the new urban laity. Tension developed between religious orders and bishops, the latter feeling that the religious orders were leading the laity away from the parish churches. The Council of Trent (1545–1562) placed all lay organizations, even those housed in monasteries, under the supervision of the local bishop, a move in part designed to limit the ability of religious orders to recruit the allegiances of lay people away from parish priests. The Jesuits followed the medieval orders in creating a network of lay associations. While the Jesuits were popular (16th and 17th centuries), these confraternities were successful. The 18th-century decline of the Jesuits, however, spelled the end of confraternities as a preferred vehicle of lay evangelization. Confraternities continued to be created, but they lost place to parish-based lay social organizations.

The study of confraternities evolved differently in different European nations. H.F. Westlake (*The Parish Gilds of Medieval England* [London, 1919]) initiated the British approach of looking at confraternities from the perspective of their role in charity and poor relief, an approach continued by W.K. Jordan (*The Charities of London, 1480–1660; The Aspirations and Achievements of the Urban Society* [London, 1960]), Brian Pullan (*Rich and Poor in Renaissance Venice: The Social Institutions of a Catholic State, to 1620* [Cambridge, MA, 1971]), and most recently Christopher Black (1989).

In late 19th-century France local historians, concerned to depict local religious and festive life before the French Revolution, scoured local archives to unearth details about the confraternities in which their ancestors participated. Their research became in turn the source material for church historians in the early 20th century, eager to demonstrate Europe's Christian past. In the 1960s Maurice Agulhon (*Pénitents et Francs-Maçons de l'ancienne Provence* [Paris, 1968]) redirected French energies toward evaluating the role confraternities played in the maintenance of social networks. In the 1980s Marie Froeschle-Chopard (*La Religion Populaire en Provence Orientale au XVIII siècle*, [Paris, 1980]), and Louis

Chatellier (*L'Europe des Devots* [Paris, 1987]) turned research in the direction of assessing confraternities as agents of Counter-Reformation (post-Tridentine) sensibilities.

Only in Italy did historians concentrate on the evolution of confraternities as religious associations, an approach best illustrated by the collected essays of G.G. Meerseman (*Ordo Fraternitatis: confraternite e pieta dei laici nel medievo* [Rome, 1977]). In the United States, study has been influenced by European schools, the one exception being Ronald Weissman's quantitative analysis of male participation in the flagellant confraternities of Florence (*Ritual Brotherhood in Renaissance Florence* [New York, 1982]).

Andrew E. Barnes

REFERENCES

Barnes, Andrew. *The Social Dimensions of Piety: Associative Life and Devotional Change in the Penitent Confraternaties of Marseilles (1499–1752).* Mahweh, NJ: Paulist Press, 1993.

Black, Christopher. Italian *Confraternities in the Sixteenth Century.* New York: Cambridge University Press, 1989.

Confucianism

The term "Confucianist," or "Confucian scholar," is an English misnomer of the Chinese term "*ju-chia,*" which refers originally to the literati who were experts on rites, history, music, and literature related to rituals. In many cultures there are such groups of literary elites, such as the Brahmans of the Hindu tradition. The forefathers of Chinese *ju* probably were scribe-diviners of the Shang-Chou period who served at the court as prototype bureaucrats.

The English term "Confucianism" is named after Confucius (551–479 BC), a scholar whose interpretations provided these old materials with new meanings. Confucius, born to a poor scion of an old aristocratic lineage, received an education that was to prepare for the career as a member of the ruling class. However, he had to earn a living by working as bookkeeper, ranch-master, and other functions. This life experience in a period of drastic social changes gave Confucius opportunities to reinterpret the ethical codes of the elite into universal moral standards.

The centerpiece of the Confucian moral system is the concept *jen* (or *ren*), which has been variously rendered in English as "love," "compassion," "humane," and the like. Etymologically, jen was the essential characteristic of a gentleman. It also is sometimes found to depict the essence of life, Confucius tried to define jen as the most fundamental essence attributed to human life, both as an individual and as a member of a collective society. A rough translation of the concept of jen, therefore, is "humanness," or human nature. The cardinal rules of personal conduct consist of, at best, two attitudes: to be sincere to oneself, including sincerely fulfilling one's very humanness, and to share the feelings of others by putting oneself into the position of others, that is, one should not do unto others what one does not like others doing unto oneself.

Confucian sayings were collected in a small book titled *Confucius' Analects.* The concept of jen, nevertheless, needed to be expanded to apply to the social dimensions of human life. Thus, another Confucian master, Mencius (372–289 BC) added onto the teaching of the Master by defining the term "*i*" (or "*yi*"), roughly rendered in English as "justice," which served as a fundamental guarantee of a just order of the group, as well as an appropriate relationship between individuals.

Later Confucian scholars added other interpretations while sharing in an esteem for learning as a major approach toward reaching full comprehension of human ethics. Two classics, the *Great Learning* and *The Principle of Means,* both emphasized the gradual advancement of the ethical conscience via reflection and learning, cultivating a perfect personality toward the goal of taking a fruitful part in various levels of social groups—household, community, the state, and the world.

By the Han period, Confucianism further developed by absorbing issues on metaphysics, cosmology, and statecraft, which concerned other schools of thought. In the 2nd century BC, Confucianism was established as orthodoxy.

The Confucian impacts on Chinese society are profound particularly but not exclusively among intellectuals and the bureaucratic elite. The emphasis on moral achievement through learning has prevented Chinese intellectuals from pursuing knowledge purely for knowledge's sake. Thus, the Chinese did not develop sciences in its modern definition. Emphasis on social relationship on a continuum from individual to various social entities to the universal humankind has conditioned Chinese to emphasize the importance of social networks, including family. Here Confucian values repeat widely in Chinese culture, supporting the social and encouraging ritual and self-control.

The Confucian scholars who, from the Han period onward, took roles of intellectual and communal leadership as well as that of civil servants dominated Chinese society and helped shape China as a Confucian state for two millennia. They, on the one hand, created an authoritarian society, and on the other hand, kept alive an idealized Confucian society as a utopia for Chinese to strive for.

Many aspects of Confucianism have long been studied in Chinese history, and social history adds little to the basic definition. Social historians have emphasized Confucianism's culture. They have also emphasized stresses between the somewhat rigidified Confucianism among 19th-century Chinese elites, and pressures for change (this is a topic of interest in Japan and Korea as well, as they are societies under considerable Confucian influence). Research on Chinese protest and revolution has also focused on attacks on Confucian restraints—a facet, for example, of the communist surge in the 20th century.

Cho-yun Hsu

REFERENCES

Lau, D.C., trans. *The Analects (Lun yu)*. Dorset, 1988.
———. *Mencius*. Beijing: Chinese University Press, 1984.
Schwartz, Benjamine I. *The World of Thought in Ancient China*. Cambridge: Harvard University Press, 1985.
Watson, Burton, trans. *Hsun-tzu*. New York: Columbia University Press, 1963.

Conquest Dynasties

State formation has often been identified with conquest. This is a theory which has proved attractive in the easy identifiability of subordinate and dominant strata after conquest. The theory relates to larger considerations in relating state formulation to social structure—part of the concern for juxtaposing social and political developments historically. However anthropological considerations of pristine state formation or state evolution due to largely endogenous conditions stress a multiprocessual and gradualist account of state formation from egalitarian to ranked to stratified to state system.

Anthropologists have utilized archeology and ethnohistory to test various theories of explanation of the emergence of the state. Carneiro presents the most sophisticated theory of war and conquest as prime movers in state formation when coupled with population pressure under certain ecological conditions. These conditions were environmental, when a population with the potential for intensified production found itself in an environmentally confined area. Social circumscription occurs when hostile neighbors preclude an expansion of the increasingly pressurized population. This crisis leads to internal differentiation and the creation of mobilizing and redistributive mechanisms which lead to dominant and subordinate relations internally (a version of a protection racket) but also provide the means of conquest externally. Certainly the role of violence in the transition to the state is an essential consideration but only if seen as concomitant with tensions around stratification, property, and authority.

Whatever role warfare played in the emergence of the state there is little doubt that militarism was an accepted and fundamental representation of historical states from the ancient Near East, China, Mesoamerica, and Peru to the present world.

The great expansionary epochs of historical states and empires, whether in China, the Middle East, Highland Mesoamerica, or the Central Asian steppes, were directed by an armed aristocracy which was in a position to direct a large military apparatus which was itself superimposed upon a productive and reproductive base. This coercive-intensive mode (Tilly 1990) involves the state apparatus not only in an exploitative extraction from the peasantry but in predation, trade, and tribute from peripheries to the state core. Literally, trade follows the flag. For these trade and tribute relations with the periphery to lead to expansionary conquest, a number of variables must exist: The target of conquest must (1) exhibit vulnerability by being reduced to a client status; (2) exhibit a flexible tribal or civil society to allow incorporation; (3) provide opportunities through land, office, and plunder to support a conquering aristocracy and its administrative apparatus; and (4) present a logistical system which allows incorporation.

The rise and fall of conquest tributary states have dominated world history. Once the emperor or monarch loses the ability to deploy the internal/external means of coercion the empire disintegrates. Border marches, satraps, and armed landlords may become strong enough to challenge the strategic heights of the dynasty, setting in motion new regimes both internal and external to the old core and its periphery.

Frank McGlynn

REFERENCES

Gledhill, J., B. Bender, and M. Larsen. *State and Society: The Emergence of Social Hierarchy and Political Centralization.* London: Unwin and Hyman, 1988.

Kautsky, John. *The Politics of Aristocratic Empires.* Chapel Hill: University of North Carolina Press, 1982.

Khazanov, A.M. *Nomads and the Outside World.* Cambridge: Cambridge University Press, 1984.

Mann, M. *The Sources of Social Power.* Volume I. *A History of Power from the Beginnings to A.D. 1760.* Cambridge: Cambridge University Press, 1986.

Tilly, C. *Coercion, Capital and European States, A.D. 990–1990.* Oxford: Blackwell, 1990.

Consumerism

Any attempt to define consumerism must distinguish between its narrower and broader meanings. Consumerism can refer to the organized advocacy or protection of consumer interests. It also describes the doctrine that general economic growth depends on consumer spending. However, in a broader usage which incorporates both these narrower meanings and frequently implies a moral judgment, the term has come to denote the development of "consumer culture" in the industrialized West. It is primarily in this sense that consumerism has interested historians as the product of profound economic, social, and cultural transformations.

The development of consumerism must be understood as a transformation not only of supply but of demand as well. To take the former, a vast increase in the variety of consumer goods was made possible first by foreign trade, as in the late 17th-century English craze for colorful Indian calico cottons, and then by the introduction of the factory system and mechanized production which began in England after 1750 and later expanded to the Continent and America. The nature and meaning of this first explosion of consumerism has found considerable attention among social historians, many of whom argue that fundamental shifts in outlook and self-definition were involved in the widespread interest in fashionable clothing and other consumer items.

The industrial revolution dramatically increased the supply of cheap goods, and it initiated a dynamic process of technological innovation and expansion of production which has ensured a steady stream of new consumer goods up to the present. The effects of mass production were far-reaching for the consumer. Handmade goods were passed over in preference for mass-produced goods, as in the shift from wooden tablewares to factory-made porcelain. Far from marking a decline, as some critics charged, mass production improved the quality of many familiar household items. Moreover, many hitherto inaccessible goods became affordable to poorer consumers, thereby contributing to what contemporaries after the mid-19th century called the "democratization of luxury."

The growing complexity and capital intensity of manufacturing during the 19th century led to vertical integration in some cases, and in others, an increasingly sharp separation of production from retailing. Retailers themselves faced new challenges and opportunities posed by the flood of consumer goods. Great urban department stores emerging after the 1860s met new problems of marketing and distributing by assembling a dazzling array of goods under one roof. They greatly stimulated the development of the advertising industry, which served as a creative intermediary between retailers and the new mass media, themselves products of the consumer age.

Some stores also established financial services whereby credit could be offered to customers, thereby anticipating the great consumer credit institutions which have become so crucial to 20th-century consumerism. The growth of department stores appeared to be at the expense of smaller specialized retail. Not surprisingly, this frequently provoked hostility among shopkeepers who sought to restrict large retail by legislative means, pleas to consumers, or polemical attacks on the monopolistic trends of modern retailing, including the wrongful blame of Jews. Subsequent history has shown that small shops and boutiques retain an important place in consumer culture, but the department stores were and remain the greatest institution of mass consumerism.

It is perhaps easier to explain the increase in the supply of consumer goods than changes in consumer demand. Certainly, by creating more goods and concentrating populations in cities, economic forces made an increase of consumption on the market inevitable. Moreover, whereas investment in heavy industry, transportation, and communication infrastructure absorbed capital in the 19th century, in the 20th, the emergence of consumer durables as a new leading sector, the appearance of inflation (which caused a disjunction between nominal and real returns on investments), demographic changes, and the development of welfare state social security often made immediate consumption both preferable to the acquisition of capital assets and indispensable to economic growth. Advertising was also undoubtedly important, but the actual relationship between advertising and consumer demand is the subject of much controversy; at the very least, like any single cause, it is an inadequate explanation. Indeed, if economic factors go far in explaining the rise of consumer demand, they do not account for the particular shape that increasing demand would take; nor is a strictly economic explanation sufficiently sensitive to the cultural obstacles which had to be overcome or revised before consumer demands could expand so dynamically. For although the roots of the consumer revolution have been traced as far back as Holland in the 17th century, a social and religious ethic of restraint and conservation remained influential in the 19th century. In sharp contrast, the multiplication of new consumer desires and acquisitiveness, far from being vices, are today considered to be the measure of personal success and the very engine of economic growth.

This profound change in social values and practices is best understood as part of the larger transformation of Western societies in the 19th and 20th centuries. The rapid growth of industrial cities after 1800 created enormous populations dependent upon the commodity market. Cultural factors helped to shape consumption patterns among these new city dwellers. Where ethnic or racial groups maintained separate enclaves within the larger city, traditional practices or constraints could continue to influence the consumer behavior of members. Nonetheless, commercialized entertainments, leisure pursuits, and new goods did attract many, particularly the young. Removed from rural pastimes and practices, these people were not only relatively open to novelty, but leisure itself became more central to their lives, for industrial labor introduced a sharp distinction between work and free time. Moreover, a steady, if not unbroken, rise in the real wages of workers, and the emergence of a new white-collar middle class, meant increases in discretionary income. Rising wages stimulated rising expectations; but again, other cultural determinants were at play as well. The belief in progress, a generalized romantic ideal of self-fulfillment, improvements in educational standards, and a widespread sense of social flux all might have contributed to the weakening of traditional constraints on personal expectations. The conspicuous consumption and social mobility of the new middle class produced an observable consumer class by 1900, although the arrival of mass consumer culture dates to the 1920s in America and the post–World War II years in Europe. Such generalizations, however, must be attentive to variations in the development of consumerism. Comparative studies would reveal the extent to which consumerism interacts with, and is part of, specific regional or national cultures.

Crucial to the development of consumerism is the issue of gender. Historians have traced the sharpening opposition during the 19th century between the male-dominated public sphere of commerce and politics and the private sphere of the family, in which women found their "natural" place. Within the private sphere, a woman's role was defined in part by her management of the household economy, including the responsibility of using her husband's income to provision the family from the consumer market. Not surprisingly, then, women were described as the vanguard of the consumer revolution. This observation prompted anxieties among men that wives would squander family earnings on the allurements of the new department stores. But it also led retailers and advertisers to recognize early the importance of women as customers and the family as a unit of consumption. Marketing messages often reinforced traditional gender roles and the ideal of comfort and convenience within the private sphere of the family. However, an important tension has persisted in consumerism between its appeal to the patriarchal family and its promise of personal liberation through consumer choice. For women in the 20th century have gained new roles, and their activities as consumers have extended well beyond the confines of the family. Finding access to work as clerks and secretaries after 1900, young women patronized the expanding fashion industries and commercialized forms of leisure and entertainment. New forms of women's consumerism have both reflected and helped to shape their changing lifestyles and claims for individual freedom and equality. Still, even though consumerism has proven flexible enough to bend traditional gender categories, consumer culture nevertheless remains dominated by familiar divisions of masculine and feminine.

Interpretations of the social and political impact of consumerism have differed among historians. Until the 1980s, many social historians accepted the argument that consumerism had transformed people from active participants in the satisfaction of their own physical and intellectual demands into passive consumers. In this view, consumer gratification has replaced demands for genuine social and political justice, while a banal, leveling, and depoliticized mass culture has replaced older, more "authentic" cultures. Few historians would entirely discard the idea of mass culture as a descriptive and critical term for late 20th-century Europe and America. However, new research has greatly nuanced our understanding of the relationship between consumerism and political and social activism.

Inspired in part by anthropological insights into the "expressive" or symbolic functions of material objects in human societies, historians have recognized consumption itself as a site of symbolic struggles in which different groups attempt to express their social values or identity. For example, in Germany from 1890 to World War I, rather than emulating the middle class, many well-paid workers embraced the idea of austere and orderly proletarian respectability in distinction to extravagant bourgeois decadence. Poorer workers often engaged in hand-to-mouth consumption, including payday binges, that expressed not only their precarious lives eked out on low wages but also their rejection of an ethic of temperance urged upon them by moralizing bourgeois and respectable proletarians alike. Such findings suggest ways in which consumer behavior has dramatized important social and cultural tensions, while the study of such phenomena as "taste" and "lifestyle" ideals reveals both the self-image and aspirations of groups or classes in society.

Consumerism has been politicized in more direct ways, as different groups and institutions have sought to control consumption. With the vast increase of new products on the market, states and publics have actively sought to supervise product quality, leading to new bureaucracies and interactions between state and society. At a broader level, the order and legitimacy of political and economic systems have come to rest largely on their capacity to guarantee the conditions within which citizens can satisfy their demands as consumers. The promise of fulfillment offered by consumer culture has proven capable of stimulating militancy when reality failed to conform to rising expectations. The political power of consumer expectations was revealed most dramatically in the failed communist systems of Eastern Europe. Because consumption was controlled by the political state, consumer frustration contributed directly to the politicization of society against the state.

Consumerism was politicized around conciliatory goals in the Consumers' League founded in New York in 1891 and its parallel organizations in Belgium, France, and Germany. Middle-class women pledged themselves to the task of improving the social, aesthetic, and ethical conditions of shopping. Members vowed not to treat store workers unfairly. They also undertook to educate themselves and others on the usefulness and quality of products. Underlying the program of the Consumers' Leagues was a belief that women must become conscious of their economic role as consumers, and by acting ethically within that capacity, they could contribute to the reconciliation of tensions in modern industrial society.

The period after 1890 also witnessed the proliferation of consumer cooperatives in Europe and America. The cooperative movement represented the most important attempt by consumers to reduce their dependency upon market forces by reasserting control over their needs. In Germany, for example, around 1 million people belonged to co-ops in 1905. Despite initial antagonisms, working-class consumer co-ops allied with trade unions and the Social Democratic Party, thereby creating a broad front representing the interests of working people as both producers and consumers. Historians have identified a persistent tension in the history of the consumer co-op movement between utopian aspirations and consumer neutrality. That is, co-ops were perceived either as an alternative and eventual successors to the capitalist market, or as adaptive organizations that could at best secure more equitable prices within the market.

The ethical aims of the Consumers' Leagues and the tensions of the cooperative movement are two examples of the moralizing discourse that must be considered part of consumer culture's history, for consumerism strikes deep at traditional misgivings about wealth, egotism, and worldliness. A judgmental stance has characterized critics of consumer culture from late 19th-century conservatives and socialists to the New Left of the 1960s, environmentalists, and many in developing nations, who believe that consumerism epitomizes the West's willingness to perpetuate foreign poverty and domestic extravagance. With good reason, social historians have not ignored these misgivings, but they have found promising paths of inquiry into the dimensions of self-expression, expanding personal horizons, and political action, which have also been part

of consumer culture. Research in consumerism has become one of the liveliest branches of modern social history. (*See also* Commercialization; Embourgeoisement; Household; Household Economy; Industrialization; Leisure; Lower Middle Classes; Market Economy; Mass Culture; Mass Media; Material Culture; Mobility; Modernization; Popular Culture; Standard of Living; State and Society; Urbanization; Women and Work; Women's History; Work Ethic; Working Class)

Warren Breckman

REFERENCES

Breckman, Warren. "Disciplining Consumption: The Debate About Luxury in Wilhelmine Germany, 1890–1914," *Journal of Social History* 24, 3 (1991).

Brewer, J., N. McKendrick, and J.H. Plumb. *The Birth of a Consumer Society: The Commercialization of Eighteenth-Century England*. Bloomington: Indiana University Press, 1985.

Campbell, Colin. *The Romantic Ethic and the Spirit of Modern Consumerism*. London: Basil Blackwell, 1989.

Fox, R.W., and T.J. Lears, eds. *The Culture of Consumption: Critical Essays in American History, 1880–1980*. New York: Pantheon, 1983.

McCracken, Grant. *Culture and Consumption: New Approaches to the Symbolic Character of Consumer Goods and Activities*. Bloomington: Indiana University Press, 1988.

Williams, Rosalind. *Dream Worlds. Mass Consumption in Late Nineteenth Century France*. Berkeley: University of California Press, 1982.

Copperbelt

The Central African Copperbelt lies along the border between Zaire and Zambia on the divide between the Congo and Zambezi basins. Africans mined and smelted copper oxide deposits for a thousand years before colonial conquest at the turn of the 20th century, but the processing of copper sulfide required the importation of Western technology and transport facilities for large-scale export. The roles and conditions of African miners have focused considerable research in social history.

The first European company to produce copper was an Anglo-Belgian enterprise. The Belgians, who feared a British takeover of both their colony and the company, pushed foreigners out of the management and the work force between 1917 and 1926. British entrepreneurs turned their attention to copper sulfide deposits in what was then Northern Rhodesia, forming two companies. Development there was delayed by the Great Depression, but by 1940, British output had outstripped Belgian.

All three firms depended on a combination of large capitalization and cheap labor. At first the Belgians followed the South African labor policy of high turnover of unskilled workers. A labor shortage developed in the 1920s because of heavy demand by other employers and high death rates in the mining camps. The Belgians thereupon turned to a policy previously rejected by the settler government of South Africa, the stabilization of African labor. The company recruited workers for three-year contracts, encouraging them to settle in company camps with their wives and children. As an incentive, it offered the best living conditions available to Africans in the entire region, with nutritious food, brick houses, and medical care. By 1945 both British companies had also adopted stabilization. Some social historians see the workers as exploited proletarians created by colonial dependency; others see them as relatively well-off members of African society.

Parallel to each mine site urban centers developed for commerce and administration, leading to the urbanization of many additional Africans. Nonminers had less good physical conditions but greater freedom. Since independence (1960–1964), both mines and towns have continued to operate, but the Copperbelt has not grown as rapidly as the national capitals. Copper miners continue to enjoy a high standard of living but have been far surpassed by government officials. (*See also* African Urbanization; Dependency Theory; Miners; Proletarianization)

Bruce Fetter

REFERENCES

Fetter, Bruce. *The Creation of Elisabethville, 1910–1940*. Stanford, CA: Hoover Institution, 1976.

Higginson, John. *A Working Class in the Making*. Madison: University of Wisconsin Press, 1989.

Parpart, Jane. *Labor and Capital on the African Copperbelt*. Philadelphia: Temple University Press, 1983.

Perrings, Charles. *Black Mineworkers in Central Africa*. New York: Africana, 1979.

Coronations

A coronation consists of symbolic and ritual acts that legitimate the accession of a new monarch to the throne. In the essential ritual of a coronation, a crown is placed on the ruler's head, but the term can also refer to other acts accompanying the coronation, such as the investiture of royal insignia, administering an oath, anointment, enthronement, a feast, a progress before the populace, and entrances into the capital or subject cities.

Coronations have traditionally been seen as a form of communication employing gestures and symbols in a highly regulated theatrical presentation of the ideas of the political elite. The most important of these ideas in the premodern period was the "king's two bodies," a principle most clearly developed in France and England. One body was that of the incumbent and the other the institution of kingship, which was sometimes represented by the crown. The central function of the coronation ritual in these kingdoms was to distinguish between the king's mortal, fallible self and the eternal, perfect character of kingship. This function helped society compensate for the failings of individual kings by representing the political community as a divinely created, incorruptible body and by building social solidarity for the status quo.

A more recent view places less emphasis on coronations as encoded messages and more on the active ways in which such rituals construct, preserve, and modify the structures, definitions, borders, and hierarchies that constitute society. From this point of view, a coronation is both an open-ended dialogue about government among various social groups and an event that creates the institution of kingship, an institution that stands above the workings of mundane society and yet still interacts with it. Rather than concentrating on decoding symbols, scholars pay careful attention to the immediate context of individual coronations, showing that subtle variations in traditional gestures or in the programmatic decorations and pageants that surround the coronation can alter the meaning of the whole performance. The coronation thus becomes an important moment in the working out of social and political conflicts.

Throughout history coronations have brought about political change as well as reinforced the status quo. Modern coronations have typically created at least temporary social solidarity even in the absence of a political consensus or a body of shared beliefs. Such coronations can generate mass enthusiasm, inculcating loyalty by focusing the attention of subjects on what are presented as sacred traditions but without requiring adherence to a particular political creed. [*See also* Emotion (Emotionology); Feasts and Celebrations; Ritual]

Edward Muir

REFERENCES

Bak, János M., ed. *Coronations: Medieval and Early Modern Monarchic Ritual.* Berkeley: University of California Press, 1990.

Jackson, Richard A. *Vive le Roi: A History of the French Coronation from Charles V to Charles X.* Chapel Hill: University of North Carolina Press, 1984.

Kantorowicz, Ernst H. *The King's Two Bodies: A Study in Medieval Political Theology.* Princeton, NJ: Princeton University Press, 1957.

Kertzer, David I. *Ritual, Politics, and Power.* New Haven: Yale University Press, 1988.

Corvée Labor

The term "corvée labor" comes from a Latin phrase for "works collected." It describes labor rendered as a tax applied by the state and its agents or (more commonly) as a form of rent when applied by a land/labor lord. Corvée labor played an important role in peasant life and power relations in many rural societies. Changes in labor requirements and protest over these figure prominently in historical periodization in preindustrial societies.

In the first instance, involving state corvées, the appropriational demands of many agrarian states made the corvée one of several methods to mobilize and expropriate surplus. The imperial state in China thus required road construction and maintenance work from peasants. Often these various measures of surplus extraction were not clearly defined. Corvée was often applied directly to immense tasks of labor mobilization as in the irrigation works of China, while in other instances the year-to-year infrastructures of large

state systems were dependent upon corvée drafts, such as the social systems of the Inca, or the maintenance for the Great Wall and the Grand Canal of China. Labor conscription for the Grand Canal involved millions of peasants, including the conscription of all able bodied men between ages 15 and 20. Children, women, and the aged were utilized in various support capacities. The administrative and logistical personnel and material must have been proportionally immense. Corvée was also often applied in the construction and maintenance of ceremonial/administrative centers. Examples are universal, but a telling instance is the Yoruba (West Africa) allocation of building and maintenance of cult centers and palaces to assigned communalities. The Inca Empire merged an extraordinary complex mixture of corvée based upon rotational services in both agricultural/craft production and monumental/infrastructural labor.

Corvée is a form of surplus labor extraction in nonmarket or noncapitalist social formations that satisfied requirements for large volumes of labor on concentrated tasks. Corvée often commingled with other forms of coerced labor and unfree labor situations. Peasant attacks on corvée labor figured in many rebellions, including the French Revolution of 1789.

Corvée has been applied to various forms of direct appropriation of peasant surplus in the form of labor expanded on the landlord domains in instances as varied as Aztec Mexico and feudal Europe. Eastern Europe witnessed an increase in corvée and dues on estates from the 16th century to the 19th century, suggesting how peasants' coerced labor could be utilized on the periphery to a market economy in seigniorial estate domains; required labor was expanded to generate grain production for sale in western European markets.

Anthropologists have recorded the high use of corvée in colonial economies in Africa, South America, and Southeast Asia. Pressed labor has been used by colonial authorities to build fortifications, roads, and other public works as well as mining, export production, and simple industrial activities. The Spanish applied *repartimiendos,* whereby Indian communities of the ex-Aztec and Inca domains were compelled to give up labor to the demands of the authorities. This last case shows the vagaries of the residual term "corvée labor" in a setting where so-called corvée covered labor demands and property relationships as fundamentally different as those of the Incas and the viceroyalty of Peru.

Frank McGlynn

REFERENCES

Claessen, H., and P Skalnick. *The Early State.* The Hague: Mouton, 1978.

Stavenhagen, R. *Social Classes in Agrarian Societies.* New York: Doubleday, 1975.

Stover, L. *The Cultural Ecology of Chinese Civilizations: Peasants and Elites in the Last of the Agrarian States.* New York: PICA, 1974.

Wallerstein, I. *The Modern World System II: Mercantilism and the Consolidation of the European World-Economy, 1600–1750.* New York: Academic, 1986.

Wheatley, P. *The Pivot of the Four Quarters.* Chicago: University of Chicago Press, 1971.

Cossacks

The Cossacks were a product of the frontier between Russia and the Ottoman Empire. They figure strongly in the social history of Russian expansion, and their development can figure in the comparative study of frontier societies. The word "Cossack" is commonly derived from the Turkic "kazak" and means a freebooter, a vagabond. The first Cossack settlements appeared in the Lower Don River in the late 15th century and consisted of Russian, Ukrainian, and other fugitives. The Cossack society was a military democracy. Local military commanders (*ataman*) as well as the chief commander (*voiskovoi ataman*) were elected in a public gathering (*krug*). The Cossacks sustained themselves by booty captured in the raids against the neighboring peoples and by fishing. With the increased population in the Don, the Cossacks emerged as an important military and political force in the area. In 1695 there were 125 permanent settlements along the Don with an administrative center in Cherkassk. With the beginning of the peasant colonization of the area in the 18th century, the Don Cossack settlements become united into a *stanitsa*—a constellation of two or three villages. The smallest settlement was a *khutor*—a hamlet with no church. In the early 19th century there were 114 *stanitsa* with a new administrative center at Novocherkassk. The population of a *stanitsa* varied from 700 to 10,000 people. While retaining their political and administrative autonomy, the Cossacks grew more dependent on Moscow economically and militarily. Until the 18th century the Don Cossacks did not practice farming, and their military commanders specifically banned such an activity. Instead, they received annual supplies of grain, gunpowder, bullets, liquor, and cash from Moscow in exchange for their military service. By the end of the 18th century, the frontier moved further south, and the military significance of the Cossacks diminished. They eventually became a part of the Russian irregular military and were identified by their area of residence. The Don Cossack Host was the most numerous and the earliest known in Russia. Second largest and most significant was the Zaporozhian Host formed in the borderlands of Poland and the Ottoman Empire in the Lower Dnepr River in the middle of the 16th century. The Tersk Cossack Host was founded in the Lower Terek River in the North Caucasus in the late 16th century, and the Iaik Host was founded in the Lower Iaik River (now known as the Ural River). With the expansion of the Russian state and the government's encouragement the Cossack Hosts proliferated, forming a defensive belt along the borders of the empire. By the late 19th century, in addition to the earlier ones, there were the Amur, the Baikal, the Kuban, the Orenburg, the Semirechensk, the Siberia, the Volga, and the Ussuriisk Cossack Hosts. In prerevolutionary Russia the Don Cossacks enjoyed an administrative and territorial autonomy. With the creation of the Soviet Union the lands of the Don Cossacks were incorporated into the Rostov, Volgograd, Voronezh, and Lugansk regions. The dissipation of the USSR in 1992 led to the reemergence of the regional Cossack identities.

Michael Khodarkovsky

REFERENCES

Glazkow, W.G. *History of the Cossacks.* New York: Robert Spuler & Sons Press, 1972.

Great Soviet Encyclopedia, a translation of the third edition, vol. 8. New York and London: Collier Macmillan Publishers, 1975, pp. 366–367.

Longworth, Philip. *The Cossacks.* New York, 1969.

Courtship

Social historians have studied courtship as part of family history and the history of youth. As with many of the more subjective aspects of family history, courtship has been particularly studied in modern western European and American societies. In many cultures, arranged marriages, handled by parents perhaps aided by marriage brokers, precluded much formal courtship; sometimes early marriage age further limited participation by a couple though something like a courting period might be encouraged after marriage or co-residence to allow a couple to commit to each other. Thus traditional Hinduism urged a three-day period between marriage and first sexual intercourse.

By the 17th and 18th centuries in Western society, despite the persistence of arranged marriages, courtship also occurred. In the lower classes, with little property to settle on a marriage, freer courtship may have developed particularly early. Among peasants and farmers, courting activities were part of youth entertainment, though formal courtship between two people—as opposed to flirtation in a large group setting—awaited parental arrangement and occurred over a fairly brief span of time. Here the idea was to allow a couple to be sure of mutual interest before the bargain was definitely sealed.

By the 19th century courtship had become more involved, for young people were supposed to choose their marriage partner by personal inclination. Adult supervision existed, but at least in Britain and the United States couples had considerable freedom. Working-class courtship was particularly informal and often involved sexual intercourse. Middle-class courtship occurred at a later age, and involved tensions between romance and sexual restraint. By 1920, headed by the United States, courtship practices gave way to dating, which involved more varied entertainment and more sexual emphases. Dating also began at an earlier age than middle-class courtship had done.

The history of courtship thus involves study of marriage selection procedures and criteria. It has focused on cases where adult-arranged marriage declined, but also reflects distinctions by social class, changes in marriage age, and shifts in youth entertainment. Courtship also enters the study of social ritual, and uses ethnographic evidence particularly for courtship customs before 1800.

Peter N. Stearns

REFERENCES

Bailey, Beth. *From Front Porch to Back Seat: Courtship in Twentieth Century America.* Baltimore: John Hopkins University Press, 1989.

Gillis, John. *For Better, For Worse: British Marriages, 1600 to the Present.* New York: Oxford University Press, 1988.

Modell, John. *Into One's Own: From Youth to Adulthood in America, 1920–1975.* Berkeley: University of California Press, 1989.

Rothman, Ellen K. *Hands & Hearts: A History of Courtship in America.* Cambridge: Harvard University Press, 1987.

Cowries as Money

The cowrie shells of the Indian Ocean were an important primitive money. Their greatest use was in West Africa and Bengal, while their major production center was the Maldive Islands near India, where the Maldive sultan enforced a monopoly.

Money cowries, *Cypraea moneta,* are white shells about three-quarters of an inch long. They can stand hard usage, and those found in Africa today were shipped at least a century ago. Their original attraction was religious and magical, but their attractiveness, durability, smallness, difficulty in counterfeiting, and easy handling made them an effective money. Cheap at their source, they were used as ballast in ocean shipping, so their transport cost was also low. These traits explain their employment not only in West Africa and Bengal, but also in China and parts of Southeast Asia. The African case has been most closely studied.

Money cowries were originally shipped to West Africa by Arab traders moving them to the North African coast and then south across the Sahara. Later, in the 16th century, the Portuguese shipped them around the Cape of Good Hope to Lisbon, whence they came back to West Africa. In the 17th century, Portuguese dominance was broken by the English and Dutch, who shared the trade until the Dutch dropped out at the end of the 18th century. In the 1840s,

German traders sent trial shipments of a related shell, *Cypraea annulus,* from Tanzanian coastal islands to West Africa. African willingness to accept *annulus,* distinguished by a reddish-orange ring around the crown, led to major inflation as traders flooded the market with the East African shells.

Western Africa's cowries, entering mostly along the coast from Ardra and Ouidah to Lagos, were purchased as any other import with payment mostly in the form of slaves until the 19th century. They were used in a zone that at its maximum encompassed some or all of modern Mali, Burkina Faso, Côte d'Ivoire, Togo, Bénin, Niger, Nigeria, Cameroon, and Chad. Having entered Africa, the shells remained, because Europeans would not accept them for other goods. In Africa their use expanded well into the 19th century; at century's end the imported shells numbered at least 1 hundred billion. Innovative counting systems were developed, facilitating the handling of vast numbers. The shells' acquisition required substantial investment, which was lost from 1900 to 1920 as the colonial authorities demonetized cowries and substituted colonial currencies. Yet in scattered African locations near borders, cowries still find use locally, allowing avoidance of foreign exchange costs. In the Maldives, they are still fished and exported to India, not for money but for decoration and, after crushing, as a medicine.

Jan Hogendorn

REFERENCES

Hogendorn, Jan S., and Marion Johnson. *The Shell Money of the Slave Trade.* Cambridge, 1986.

Johnson, Marion. "The Cowrie Currencies of West Africa," *Journal of African History* (Part 1) 11, 1 (1970): 17–49; (Part 2) 11, 3 (1970): 331–353.

Crime

Although general histories have begun to incorporate some topics of the new social history, few have acknowledged the vibrant field of the history of crime. This is especially surprising as state-building—a fundamental process of historical development since the Middle Ages—rested on two main pillars: the assertion of control over the army in order to provide national defense, and the centralization of the legal system to ensure internal justice. For the last 15 years, European and American historians have pioneered a variety of approaches to studying the centralization of justice, often drawing on theories from other social sciences such as sociology, anthropology, and psychology. While earlier research on the legal system was not entirely lacking, it had been carried out almost exclusively by legal historians whose narrow and traditional approach separated the development of law from that of society. The hallmark of the new "criminal justice history" is its emphasis on the interdependence of changes in crime and the criminal justice system on the one hand and broad developments in society, economy, and politics on the other.

Research on the history of crime in Europe and the United States has defined two broad types of categorization. Geographically, the Anglo-American experience has diverged significantly from continental Europe in the development of law, courts, and the police. Based on the tradition of the unified Roman law of Justinian, the states of continental Europe have evolved toward a highly centralized legal system with national law codes, court systems, police, and standards of punishment. Great Britain and the United States, while differing in many ways, have both built more local control into their criminal justice systems. The United States represents the most extreme case of decentralization, with states or cities responsible both for devising most penal legislation and administering the police, courts, and prisons.

A second type of categorization is chronological, with a definite shift in crime and criminal justice occurring in the late 18th and early 19th centuries. In the earlier period, the nation-state had not yet asserted a monopoly over the legal system, so that it shared power over dispensing justice with other institutions like the church and the nobility. By the 19th century, most states claimed a unique right to make and enforce the law, whether at the national level on the Continent or at the local level according to the Anglo-American model. Simultaneously, the transition from feudalism to capitalism affected crime rates, which became increasingly high in urban areas swelled by rural migrants looking for work. With these geographical and chronological categorizations as a framework, the rest of this article will survey both crime and the criminal justice system. Historians have found the interaction between the two to be so great that research on one is meaningless without reference to the other.

Rates and Nature of Crime

As the field of criminal justice history developed in the 1970s, researchers first sought to determine patterns of crime as part of the everyday life of the lower classes. Like other practitioners of social history, they hoped that quantitative data would produce a more reliable and universal picture of crime in past societies than anecdotal evidence. Statistics offered a way to get beyond the pronouncements of elites about the "problem of crime" and discover what social groups were committing crime and why. The reconstruction of crime rates requires laborious work, especially those preceding the 19th century, when nations began to collect and publish their own statistics. For premodern Europe and colonial America, historians usually had to limit their geographical scope since data had to be collected from voluminous, handwritten records of court proceedings. They also tended to focus only on felonies, or more serious crime, while ignoring misdemeanors, which were petty but more numerous and therefore more typical of everyday life.

Because of these difficulties, we still do not have reliable, long-term crime rates for either Europe or the United States. Several hypotheses have emerged, although none of them is clearly proven. French researchers, for example, initially posited what is called the *violence/vol* thesis, that is, that the majority of crimes shifted from those against persons in premodern society to those against property in industrial society. Other studies have argued that the total amount of violent crime has decreased steadily since the Middle Ages, with the only significant upsurge occurring after World War II. Within this pattern of decline, however, short-term variations have been evident. Historians of sex crimes have found a temporary increase of prosecutions for adultery, infanticide, prostitution, and homosexuality during the era of the Reformation in the 16th and 17th centuries. Perhaps the most notorious example of mass trials grouped together in one era was evidenced during the same period when tens of thousands of people—mostly women—were condemned to death for witchcraft, a charge no longer in our criminal codes.

As historians compiled statistics on crime, however, they came across some fundamental problems that put this entire approach into question. Most basically, how should they define crime? As the example of witchcraft illustrates, certain behaviors have been considered illegal in some societies but not in others. Most historians have chosen to define crime as those acts that could lead to prosecution and punishment by a court during the period of their study. This of course complicates the task of compiling long-term crime rates, since certain crimes are periodically added or dropped from penal laws. Indeed, a key subfield in crime history involves the "invention" of new crimes, as in the criminalization of minor vandalism under the heading of juvenile delinquency around 1900. Researchers have also questioned whether official statistics themselves really measure crime. They have long recognized the difficulty of estimating the "dark figure" of crime composed of both reported and unreported crime. This may be less of a problem for a serious crime like homicide, where the difficulty of disposing of a dead body makes concealment unlikely. But underreporting may be rampant where the loss is not significant, like pickpocketing; where victims are culturally stigmatized, such as rape; or where citizens have little faith in getting justice, as has been the case with African Americans.

Finally, historians recognized that the criminal justice system itself distorts crime rates by its very activity. Courts indict and finally convict many fewer defendants than are initially arrested by police, sometimes simply because of lack of evidence or plea bargaining. Therefore, researchers have preferred quantitative data not yet modified by the courts such as statistics on complaints to police or arrests. Yet police also affect crime rates, since campaigns to tighten enforcement against, for example, drugs or prostitution cause an immediate increase in arrest rates. Thus, apparent increases in crime might simply be the result of moral panics or control waves.

The various difficulties in quantifying crime rates have not prevented important advances in the understanding of the role crime played for various social groups. Slave crimes in the United States, for example, form part of a study of feasible protest. Boundaries between essentially professional criminals and others can be traced as they changed over time. Social historians have also dealt with changes among professional criminals themselves, and their methods, as in the rise of confidence men in the 19th-century United States. Attention to changes in the definition of crime yields information on a variety of social groups and on gender issues, and on labeling certain acts criminal. Thus, in the 20th-century West, certain sexual practices were decriminalized. Early in the 20th century, however, a variety of youthful vandalisms were converted into crimes (under the new rubric of juvenile delinquency).

Criminal Justice System

As historians debate the meaning of crime statistics and crime definitions, they have come to acknowledge that crime is not an autonomous category but is intimately related to the functioning of the criminal justice system. Focus has thus shifted from the bottom to the top, that is, from interest in the social characteristics of criminals to the elites who make and administer penal law. Historians of crime now admit that they must learn from traditional, legal history, although they insist that study of the criminal justice system must always be placed within broader social developments. Research has focused on three phases in the processing of criminals: law enforcement, criminal trials, and punishment.

Law enforcement, or what we commonly call police, is a rather new activity for the state. Until the early 19th century, citizens often had to raise the "hue and cry" in order to attract attention to crimes and their perpetrators. Courts had their own constables to bring in wanted persons, nobles employed their own thugs for protection, and cities usually appointed night watchmen to provide security. But this type of law enforcement was not uniform even within nations, and personnel was amateur and often volunteer. Of course, the need for police was not great in premodern Europe, where most people lived in rural villages, everyone knew their neighbors, and criminals could be easily identified. By the early 19th century, however, fear of popular political protest and increased urban crime led to the establishment of modern police forces. The earliest ones in Continental Europe were usually centralized, organized along military lines, and used by national governments for political spying as well as crime control. Fearing that such a force would encroach on personal liberties, England and the United States relied on the ideal of a civilian police that would be local and dedicated to serving citizens rather than enforcing the will of a certain politician. The London "bobbies," organized in 1829 by Robert Peel, came closest to this ideal and became the model for urban police throughout the world. By the turn of the 20th century, police in all nations began to adopt the techniques of scientific policing, such as fingerprinting, photography, and forensic laboratory techniques, to improve their ability to identify criminals.

After arrest, suspects passed through the appropriate court system for indictment and trial. In premodern Europe, every powerful group had its own court so that political struggles often involved disputes over legal jurisdiction. Most courts were local, like the feudal courts for nobles, manorial courts for peasants, and municipal or commercial courts for townspeople. On the other hand, the courts of the Catholic church were transnational and applied a uniform Code of Canon Law; the regular ecclesiastical courts were under the direct control of provincial bishops, while the notorious Inquisition was a series of special courts responsible to the Pope. Only royal justice was national in scale, and kings had to struggle for centuries to enlarge their legal jurisdiction. The era of the French Revolution finally swept away the local and religious courts leaving the new, powerful nation-states with full control over the judiciary.

The revolution in the courts in the late 18th and early 19th centuries was accompanied by the writing of new, liberal law codes whether national in nature as on the Continent or local as in the United States. These new codes incorporated many Enlightenment principles, most clearly enunciated in the famous book by Cesare Beccaria, *On Crimes and Punishments*, published in 1764. Beccaria taught that all citizens should be equal before the law (at least white men), should be considered innocent until proven guilty, and should not be subjected to inhumane punishment. While many states did not fully implement these principles, defendants began to have the right to demand due process during criminal trials.

The standard punishment for those convicted has evolved dramatically since the Middle Ages. Prisons were unusual in premodern Europe and the United States, being reserved for debtors and those convicted by ecclesiastical courts. Authors of less serious crimes either paid restitution to the victim through fines or underwent a ritual of shaming by being put in stocks or on the dunking stool. When most people lived in small, face-to-face communities, the fear of shaming provided a significant deterrent and adequate punishment for many crimes. For felonies, courts might decree banishment or physical torture such as branding or mutilating various body parts. Sea powers like France sentenced many convicts to rowing the galleys. The most severe punishment in church courts was excommunication, although heretics and witches were usually turned over to the state, which carried out the death penalty by burning, hanging, or decapitation.

By the early 19th century, prison became the standard punishment for both misdemeanors and felonies. Lively debate developed over the most effective organization and architecture of penitentiaries, with some reformers advocating the "Philadelphia system" of complete separation in individual cells and others preferring the "Auburn system" where prisoners, although pledged to silence, were allowed to congregate for daily work. In both cases, experts predicted that long periods of quiet reflection would lead to repentance and reform among inmates. By the end of the 19th century, rising rates of recidivism seemed to contradict the prison's promise of reform. Criminologists theorized the existence of a hard-core group of irredeemable delinquents, labeled first the "dangerous class" and later "born criminals." Believing women and children to be more amenable to redemption, many nations began building reformatories meant to separate these groups from the hardened adult males in penitentiaries and to provide for education and training consonant with their special natures. New policies of suspended sentences and parole promised to offer reformable offenders, whether male or female, the chance to avoid prisons, increasingly seen as "schools of crime." Despite disillusionment with prisons, however, they have remained the major type of punishment until the present day.

Historiographical Debates

Historians have advanced various theories to explain how crime is linked to society and why such a major shift in criminal justice policy occurred between the 18th and 19th centuries. The earliest studies, including most legal history, adopted a liberal, Whig interpretation that saw changes in criminal justice reflecting the general progress in society. They characterized the legal and prison reformers of the turn of the 19th century as idealists who were dedicated to eradicating the oppressive, irrational, and inefficient system of feudal Europe. Typical of the barbarity of the Old Regime, in their eyes, was England's "Bloody Code" that prescribed capital punishment for over 200 crimes. Instead, they sought to erect a new system predicated on the Enlightenment values of reason, equality, and humanitarianism.

Most recent historians have disputed the Whig interpretation, chiding its authors for naively accepting the words of reformers at face value. Some critics have tried to employ Marxist theory to tie changes in criminal justice to the transition from feudalism to capitalism with its accompanying shift of power from the aristocracy to the bourgeoisie. Eric Hobsbawm, for example, has argued that certain categories of criminals were "primitive rebels" or "social criminals," whose defiance of law was part of a larger political revolt against oppression by the capitalist ruling class. Others have compared the prison to the factory, pointing out that they emerged simultaneously as institutions dedicated to molding docile factory workers out of the urban poor. Contributors to the path-breaking collection of essays entitled *Albion's Fatal Tree* (Hay, 1975) showed how capitalist landowners in the 18th century criminalized many activities that had previously been permitted to feudal peasants such as chopping wood, hunting, and gleaning on common lands. Edward Thompson (1963), in perhaps the most nuanced Marxist analysis, has argued that while the rule of law has always been wielded by the elites, its claim of neutrality has also offered a tool for the lower classes to defend their rights.

The theory of social control loosely unites a second group of critics of the traditional Whig argument. Michel Foucault's brilliant book *Discipline and Punish* (1977) refuted the Whig argument that Enlightenment reforms were progressive and instead argued that industrial society simply replaced one type of control, based on corporal punishment, with the even more repressive system of surveillance and discipline typical of the modern penitentiary. He differs with the Marxists, however, in locating the power to punish as dispersed and pervading all aspects of society rather than centralized in the capitalist economic system. From this point of view, several studies have renamed the legal reformers of the early 19th century as "moral entrepreneurs" and see them as promoting change in the criminal justice system not from idealism but in the pursuit of power. Social control theory has recently been faulted for assigning too much power to the ruling classes while ignoring the ability of subordinate groups to evade, resist, or renegotiate programs to normalize them.

These three approaches in no way capture the richness and variety of current research in criminal justice history. Many studies have even questioned the validity of positing a sharp break between premodern and industrial society and devaluing the former. Before the 19th century, it appears that prisons were more widespread, constables and night watchmen more efficient, and courts more professional than previously thought. In his important contribution to *Albion's Fatal Tree*, Douglas Hay has persuasively argued that capital punishment was rare in 18th-century England despite the Bloody Code, and that its erratic enforcement was not a sign of irrationality but a strategy for keeping the lower classes deferential and dependent on the good will of the local gentry who served as judges. Feudal justice, far from having been ruthless, now appears to have offered perhaps more access to litigation for the lower classes than the modern system dominated by public prosecutors and expensive lawyers.

Some of the most current approaches to criminal justice history point to a research agenda for the future. The study of female crime and juvenile delinquency has shown that most generalizations about crime rates apply only to adult males, since women and children commit fewer and less serious crimes. Similarly, the criminal justice system has often processed these groups differently, sometimes segregating them from the typical criminal. General historiographical theories must begin to reckon with these insights. New directions for research are also emerging from the application of Norbert Elias's theory of the "civilizing" influence of state-building to crime. Most popular in Europe, these studies are looking at general changes in comportment and interpersonal relations to explain, for example, the dramatic drop in violent crime between the 17th and 19th centuries. This approach places crime within the "history of mentalities," and will encourage researchers to look at crime and criminal justice as just one of many types of dispute resolution employed in past societies.

Other topics have been almost entirely neglected. Except for Nicole Rafter's (1985) excellent history of black and white female prisoners in the United States, almost all studies have ignored race as a variable. More research in non-Western countries will help to fill this gap, but American and even European researchers must go beyond class to integrate race and ethnicity in their paradigms. Other possible directions for the future include white-collar crime, crime under totalitarian regimes, and historical victimology. (*See also* Deviance; Juvenile Delinquency; Law/Legal History; Police)

Mary Gibson

REFERENCES

Foucault, Michel. *Discipline and Punish: The Birth of the Prison*. London: Allen Lane, 1977.

Hay, Douglas, et al. *Albion's Fatal Tree*. London: Allen Lane, 1975.

Johnson, David. *American Law Enforcement: A History*. St. Louis: Forum Press, 1981.

Rafter, Nicole Hahn. *Partial Justice: Women in State Prisons, 1800–1935*. Boston: Northeastern University Press, 1985.

Zehr, Howard. *Crime and the Development of Modern Society.* Totawa, NJ: Barnes and Noble, 1978.

Cuban Revolution

On January 1, 1959, the Cuban Revolution came to power. Why Cuba had a radical revolution is a central question in recent social history. Some contend the relatively high levels of socioeconomic development before 1959 underscored the appropriateness of reforms. Others argue that only radical revolution could have redressed a history of national subjugation and social inequality. Neither unnecessary nor inevitable, the revolution originated in a rather unique interaction of factors: late 19th-century independence from Spain; a protectorate relationship with the United States until 1934, including military interventions in 1906–1909 and 1917; dependence on U.S. capital and markets; high levels of social mobilization; sugar monoculture; widespread wage labor; uneven modernization; weak and divided upper classes; a defused revolutionary situation during the 1930s; frustrated representative democracy during the 1940s; and military dictatorship during the 1950s. The catalyst against the old order, however, was the politico-military opposition which Fidel Castro, the Rebel Army, and the July 26th Movement mounted against Fulgencio Batista.

The revolution upheld national sovereignty and pursued social justice. The new government quickly established measures like agrarian and rent reforms, wage increases, job expansion, and full access to education and health services, which significantly redistributed income. Struggles against the upper class buttressed popular dignity; confrontation with the United States prompted national pride. Whether the revolutionary government could have struck a compromise with the United States without sacrificing its goals is another central question. From their reading of Cuban historical experience, the revolutionary leadership concluded such a compromise impossible and radicalized the revolution in favor of the popular classes. On the eve of the U.S.-sponsored Bay of Pigs invasion in 1961, Castro proclaimed the revolution socialist and, subsequently, steered Cuba into a tacit alliance with the Soviet Union.

With Soviet aid, trade, credits, and military assistance, the Cuban government consolidated the revolution and institutionalized socialism. After 1961, Cuba achieved its independence from the United States in exchange for a new dependence on the Soviet Union. Dependent socialism achieved impressive levels of social equality without, however, significantly diversifying the economy or establishing meaningful forms of democracy. The collapse of the Soviet Union in the early 1990s bared the vulnerability of Cuban socialism and the likelihood that Cuba would also undergo some form of capitalist restoration. An important question about the transition appears to be how an opposition movement capable of constituting a credible alternative to the leadership which brought the 1959 revolution to power would develop. (*See also* Mexican Revolution; Modernization; Revolutions; Socialism)

Marifeli Pérez-Stable

REFERENCE

Pérez, Louis A., Jr. *Cuba: Between Reform and Revolution.* New York: Oxford University Press, 1988.

Cultural Hegemony

The essence of this concept is that a fundamental class and its allies exercise political, intellectual, and moral leadership and control over larger society through a complex network of ideas and meanings. Contemporary social historical application of "cultural hegemony" derives from Antonio Gramsci's (1971) thesis that subordinate classes appear to consent to the rule of more powerful classes because they successfully adopt and integrate the fundamental values, perceptions, beliefs, and prejudices that define and legitimate the dominant social order. Hegemony denotes consent to the dominant values without explicit physical coercion. Such hegemonic values are not merely abstract, but as experienced in the workplace, legal system, schools, churches, government bureaucracies, family, and media (the network of institutions which Gramsci termed "civil society"), they appear as reciprocally confirming.

Social historians have primarily employed cultural hegemony to study the relationship between dominant and subordinate identities. Eugene

Genovese's pioneering *Roll, Jordan, Roll* (1976) emphasized the pervasiveness of paternalism in American slave culture—an ideology used by slaveowners to justify oppression and also appropriated by slaves to create a limited set of rights for themselves. Slaves were by no means reduced to passive tools (as previous historians had argued); their conduct revealed a complex combination of accommodation and resistance to the dominant power structure and accompanying ideology.

The concept of cultural hegemony has been most extensively applied to popular culture as a way of discerning how power relations writ large throughout society manifest themselves in common experiences. Popular culture is one of the sites where the struggle for and against a culture of the powerful is engaged. Social historians have challenged earlier interpretations that social practices can be assigned an essential class-belongingness, emphasizing instead the complex and changing ways in which class, gender, race, and ethnicity may overlap each other in different historical circumstances. Although most historians agree that popular cultural activities have sustained specific sets of capitalist relationships, many have also echoed Raymond Williams's (1977) conviction that a lived hegemony is always a fluid process. Historians have utilized the concept of "cultural hegemony" to demonstrate, for instance, the contradictory nature of modern consumer culture. Subordinate groups both accommodated and resisted new cultural forms and values, without necessarily repudiating working-class, ethnic, and racial identities. Recent works that perceptively analyze the struggle for hegemony in popular culture include: Susan Davis, *Parades and Power* (1986); Roy Rosenzweig, *Eight Hours for What We Will* (1983); Kathy Peiss, *Cheap Amusements* (1986); Lizabeth Cohen, *Making a New Deal* (1990); and George Lipsitz, *Time Passages* (1990).

Historians employing the concept have illuminated that popular culture is never merely a history of producers and consumers, it is also a history of intellectuals whose business it is to define what is popular and legitimate. Steven Watts, *Republic Reborn* (1987) studied the role of middle-class and elite intellectuals whose writings legitimated the shift from republican to liberal values—which underlaid the emergent "culture of capitalism" during the early 19th century. Kerby Miller, *Emigrants and Exiles* (1985) astutely illuminates the critical role played by bourgeois Irish American intellectuals in adapting Irish traditions and American experiences to both the hegemonic imperatives of the Irish American bourgeoisie and the assimilable notions of their social inferiors. According to Miller, identifications with Catholicism, nationalism, and transatlantic family ties linked middle-class Irish Americans to Ireland and its hegemonic culture, while simultaneously enabling them to assert that they were "good Americans" as well.

Future research should emphasize the relationships between the state and civil society in the struggle for cultural hegemony. Eric Hobsbawm and Terence Ranger, *The Invention of Tradition* (1983), explored the myriad ways elites have solidified bonds between themselves and the "people nation" through nationalistic rituals, symbols, and rhetoric. Hobsbawm's writing prompts further analysis of nationalism as a principal arena for cultural hegemony in the modern state. Victoria De Grazia's analysis of the relation between the Italian fascist state and popular leisure, *The Culture of Consent* (1981), is suggestive of such a direction. Italian political elites invented a "national" identity through state-sponsored sport and leisure, which prompted the people to embrace shared cultural goals, rather than those defined by class, gender, racial, and ethnic differences.

The basic assumptions of research on cultural hegemony allow for important changes over time—some periods see heightened efforts at cultural dominance (the 17th century in Europe was one such point, for example), others see greater freedom to various popular subcultures. The importance of the rise of the middle class and accompanying changes in media, including the mass press and mass political parties, focus attention to new forms of cultural hegemony in the 19th and 20th centuries. (*See also* Subcultures)

Steven W. Pope

References

De Grazia, Victoria. *The Culture of Consent.* New York: Cambridge, 1981.

Genovese, Eugene. *Roll, Jordan, Roll*. New York: Vintage, 1976.

Gramsci, Antonio. *Selections from the Prison Notebooks*. New York: International, 1971.

Hargreaves, John. *Sport, Power and Culture*. New York: St. Martin's, 1986.

Miller, Kerby. *Emigrants and Exiles*. New York: Oxford University Press, 1985.

Williams, Raymond. *Marxism and Literature*. New York: Oxford University Press, 1977.

Cultural History

The most famous work of cultural history no doubt is German sociologist Max Weber's 1905 study *The Protestant Ethic and the Spirit of Capitalism*. The still controversial book wears well as an exemplar, especially today, when developments in social history, cultural studies, and postmodern thought raise questions about how to practice cultural history. Essentially, Weber argued that a particular form of individual self-discipline originated out of early modern Protestant concerns over salvation. This self-discipline, which Weber called "inner-worldly asceticism," influenced how early Protestants conducted themselves in work and business dealings, and thereby reinforced the "spirit of capitalism" that promoted a rationalistic capitalist industrial order. Weber's study is a good exemplar of specifically cultural history because he traced (1) the origins of a particular cultural complex of ideas (about the relation of self-discipline to concerns about salvation); (2) the interaction over time between those ideas and both elites and rank-and-file people (Protestant ministers and their congregations), so that ideas are traced in terms of social resonance; and (3) the historical consequences of the socially affirmed and practiced culture. There are a number of important approaches to cultural history. However, in the last two decades, the rise of poststructuralist and postmodern thought and the consolidation of interdisciplinary cultural studies have brought most approaches around to practices that look remarkably similar to Weber's.

At its most basic, cultural history is the historical study of culture. But how is culture to be defined? And what does it encompass? An inclusive working definition might include: (1) *ideas, knowledge* (correct, wrong, or unverifiable belief) and *recipes* for doing things; (2) humanly fabricated *tools* (such as shovels, sewing machines, and computers); and (3) the *products* of action that may be drawn upon in the further conduct of social life (a dwelling, clothing, a transportation vehicle). Using this definition, cultural historians can identify discrete packages or cultural objects and study their history as a series of more or less similar replications of form and content (e.g., in a play, a piece of music, a technique of food processing, a genre of art, or a set of etiquette rules). Such cultural objects sometimes endure, other times shift—gradually or suddenly—to new meanings, forms, practices, and the like. In these terms, cultural history encompasses a wide range of topics—the histories of art, music, popular culture, dance, histories of technology and of production, of fashion, design, and so on. Emphasis on knowledge, ideas, and practices opens onto intellectual history, histories of ideas, ideology, religion, sexuality, privacy, and freedom, to name some possibilities. Indeed, since all social life has its cultural aspect, culture could (and should) be a dimension of analysis in any historical account.

An important category of cultural history, of great importance in social history, involves political culture—the ideas and expectations people have of the state and the political process. These can vary and they began to change greatly, well before the rise of parliaments and widespread suffrage. They affect behaviors ranging from family relationships to protest, as well as (in modern societies) voting patterns. Social historians are interested also in relationships between political culture and other aspects of popular belief, including beliefs about risk plus fatalism and about hierarchy.

The topics of cultural history are so diverse that the study of cultural history ought to be defined by approach rather than by any coherent content. The question of approach, however, is contentious. It can be traced briefly via three issues—the controversy over universal history, the problem of elite versus popular culture, and the relation of culture to other analytic dimensions such as economic and social patterns.

To take up the first issue, universal (or sometimes, philosophical) histories are encompassing, holistic approaches based on the idea that history has overall coherence, direction, and meaning, which can be captured with either the proper historical methodology or a sound sociological theory about the dynamics of change. In either case, researchers would strive to uncover a grand narrative amid the multitude of historical events. One approach to culture mirrors universal history: structural-functional social theory similarly posits culture as a relatively coherent system of norms and values that guide all kinds of conduct in a society. Together, holistic ideas about history and culture warrant topics such as the character of the Renaissance (Jacob Burckhardt) or the consequences of individualism as an ideology in the United States (Robert Bellah and his associates). But today, claims about general cultural and historical coherence are subject to postmodern skepticism, and cultural histories have become focused on more discrete—and more conflicted—cultures.

The second debate concerns the significance of elite, or high, culture versus popular culture. Culture conceived holistically was conventionally based on a high-culture aesthetic concerned with identifying the great works of artists, musicians, persons of letters, and so on. Sociologists and anthropologists increasingly regard culture as more differentiated, however, and they question the primacy of high culture in fundamental social processes. Moreover, they argue that there are a variety of parallels in the dynamics of high- and popular-culture processes. Finally, cultural historians like Peter Burke (*Popular Culture in Early Modern Europe*) have demonstrated that the supposed distinction between high and popular culture obscures fascinating and important movements of culture across social and geographic boundaries. In these terms, it no longer makes sense to make any arbitrary distinction between types of culture. Instead, the task is to understand cultural materials of diverse aesthetics and status origins.

Third, researchers have become increasingly sophisticated about tracing the connections of cultural phenomena to concrete groups and social actors. No longer can culture be isolated from the social and economic conditions of its production, its audiences, its reception, and its role in the life practices of concrete individuals. There are diverse fruitful analyses of such sociological relationships. For example, researchers have shown how specific cultural objects (ranging from Shakespeare's plays to cultural themes such as the vision of a "promised land") become reinterpreted, consciously or unconsciously, by various social groups in different historical circumstances. As Weber suggested by his panoramic comparisons of world religions, cultures establish the frameworks through which social life is organized and made meaningful. Even world-historical events like the Cold War are affected by cultural constructs that frame them. Cultural history potentially revolutionizes the practice of all history by showing that the past is an artifact of cultural practices that are themselves historically located.

The relationship between social and cultural history is both fruitful and tense. In the 1960s, many early social historians tended to downplay culture, looking for more objective factors in discussions of class, mobility, and protest. Unquestionably, cultural interests have surged since the 1970s, with social historians tracing the nature of popular beliefs or mentalities as a fundamental feature of their work, though arguing about the degree to which culture caused or reflected other social developments. Since the late 1980s, and in association with postmodernism, this cultural interest has been complicated by the rise of new cultural historians, some of whom rely on single cultural statements carefully decoded (rather than seeking, social-history fashion, a wider variety of cultural expressions) or even formal intellectual doctrines simply assumed to have wide social resonance without, however, being relevantly traced. This renewed tension between social and cultural history, however, is incomplete. Many new cultural historians seem (though often without acknowledging the relationship) to continue the interest in tracing and interpreting cultural change as part of understanding society. (*See also* Mentalities; Reproduction and Class Formation)

John R. Hall

REFERENCES

Chartier, Roger. *Cultural History: Between Practices and Representations.* Cambridge, Eng.: Polity Press, 1988.

Darnton, Robert. "Intellectual and Cultural History," in Michael Kammen, ed., *The Past Before Us.* Ithaca, NY: Cornell University Press, 1980, pp. 327–354.

Hall, John R. "Social Interaction, Culture, and Historical Studies," in Howard S. Becker and Michal McCall, eds., *Symbolic Interaction and Cultural Studies.* Chicago: University of Chicago Press, 1990, pp. 16–45.

———, and Mary Jo Neitz. *Culture: Sociological Perspectives.* Englewood Cliffs, NJ: Prentice-Hall, 1993.

Hunt, Lynn, ed. *The New Cultural History.* Berkeley: University of California Press, 1989.

LaCapra, Dominick, and Steven L. Kaplan, eds. *Modern European Intellectual History.* Ithaca, NY: Cornell University Press, 1982.

Culture of Poverty

Anthropologist Oscar Lewis (1966) developed the culture of poverty concept based on his extensive field research in the 1950s and 1960s with poor families in Mexico, Puerto Rico, and New York City. It refers to the appearance of a distinct subculture among the poor in both rural and urban areas and across national boundaries. According to Lewis the culture of poverty appeared where poor people suffered from very limited resources, difficult living conditions, and isolation from the socioeconomic and political institutions of the larger society. Those who developed a culture of poverty adopted a series of traits unlike the more affluent: few formal organizations, broken families, provinciality, a present orientation, and a sense of helplessness and alienation. Lewis emphasized positive adaptations that permitted the poor to survive their often desperate circumstances, but the culture of poverty was also self-perpetuating as children quickly adopted these values which ensured that they would remain poor.

Although his work lacked a historical base, Lewis traced the culture of poverty to "the early free-enterprise stage of capitalism" and colonialism; it tended to decline in socialist and highly developed capitalist societies with a welfare state. However, not all poor people developed a culture of poverty. Landless rural migrants to cities tended to do so while migrants with well-organized traditional culture were more likely to move

out of poverty. Lewis estimated that only about 20 percent of the U.S. poor in the 1960s lived in a culture of poverty.

During the 1960s, liberal writers and policymakers in the United States drew on Lewis's concept for the War on Poverty. Despite Lewis's emphasis on the adaptive and positive aspects of the culture of poverty and the potential for change as in the U.S. civil rights movement or revolutionary activities elsewhere, policymakers focused on the concept's many negative aspects, including poor people's apparent inadequacies, dependency, and apathy. By the 1970s, conservatives used the concept to justify cutting support for the poor.

Drawing on earlier social theory on urban breakdown, some U.S. social historians anticipated aspects of the culture of poverty; others initially adopted the concept into their work on migration history. In either case historians claimed urban conditions caused the disintegration of migrants' traditional cultures, producing social disorganization such as broken families and crime.

More recently most social historians have taken exception to both notions. During the mid-1960s and early 1970s, scholars interested in social mobility directly attacked the culture of poverty thesis. To determine the extent to which poverty became intergenerational as hypothesized by culture of poverty theory, Stephan Thernstrom (*The Other Bostonians* 1973) traced the occupations of unskilled workers from 1880 to 1970. He found that, for the past century, "the evidence suggests that there has been a fairly high and relatively constant rate of upward intergenerational mobility, . . . [the] clear majority of youths born into what has sometimes been taken as a 'culture of poverty' finding their way into either a skilled trade or a white-collar post."

Thernstrom does note that not everyone experienced upward mobility, that pockets of continuous poverty did persist, and that historical sources make it impossible to say whether or not a culture of poverty emerged in such areas. Recently, historians of the homeless have pointed out that Thernstrom's sources, city directories and manuscript censuses, omitted many of the poorest Americans. This does not substantiate the presence of poverty culture but does indicate that intergenerational poverty did exist after 1865.

More recently, scholars of U.S. migration history have focused on the inner world of those who made up a large part of the country's poor since 1865. Their studies, largely of a single ethnic or racial group, demonstrated that migrants maintained and adapted their traditional cultures in U.S. cities. In contrast to earlier social historians and culture of poverty theory, they concluded that migrants, including the poorest (Borchert 1980), developed thick networks of informal groups of kin, friends, and neighbors. Similarly, scholars also reported that migrants founded a wide variety of formal organizations including religious, fraternal, benevolent, cultural, civic and social groups. While few studies speak directly to Lewis's thesis, their findings refute his view that the poor in American cities developed a low level of organization.

Utilizing methods and concepts adopted from anthropology, many migration historians also failed to find the emergence of a universal poverty culture. In contrast, each migrant group maintained and adopted its own culture to changed circumstances; each response was specific by group and location. Sociologists and anthropologists have also challenged the culture of poverty formulation for similar reasons.

In contrast, other students of migration history have looked more closely at intergroup relations among different migrant groups. They report that many children of migrants assimilated into U.S. life and culture. This assimilation helped undermine the isolation that Lewis found important in poverty culture formation. Moreover, because migrant enclaves contained diverse social class groupings, from unskilled workers to professionals and owners of small businesses, the very poor were never fully isolated from the more affluent or community institutions in the way Lewis postulated.

Many social scientists have also questioned poverty culture research and theory. They attacked Lewis's broad conclusions about culture based on research that focused narrowly on family; they also found the poverty culture concept overgeneralized and vague. Finally, as social historian Michael Katz (1989) pointed out, while the term "culture of poverty" reflected the neutral language of social science, it fit a long tradition of stigmatizing the poor from the "undeserving poor" of 19th-century America to the "disreputable poor" of more recent times.

James Borchert

REFERENCES

Borchert, James. *Alley Life in Washington*. Urbana: University of Illinois Press, 1980.

Katz, Michael. *The Undeserving Poor*. New York: Pantheon Books, 1989.

Lewis, Oscar. *La Vida*. New York: Vintage Books, 1966.

Thernstrom, Stephan. *The Other Bostonians*. Cambridge: Harvard University Press, 1973.

Valentine, Charles. *Culture and Poverty*. Chicago: University of Chicago Press, 1968.

D

Death

Until the 20th century, most of the world's population lived in the shadow of very high mortality rates. Virtually everywhere death was close and familiar. Even in the United States the average life expectancy in 1900 stood at 47 years, a reminder that it was in this century that Americans made the greatest advances in the struggle against death's dominion, adding some 25 extra years to their lives. During that period many of the less developed countries also made dramatic gains, bringing their death rates down from annual levels of 4 to 4.5 percent to 1 to 2 percent.

The modern demographic revolution, with its resultant blessings as well as population pressures, forms but one recent development in the long and varied human experience with death. The array of issues relevant to a fuller understanding of that experience—issues that have now been explored in smaller or larger measure for different cultures and periods—is broad indeed. It includes such matters as the causes of death, the social patterns of mortality, the responses to deadly epidemics, old age, death rituals and customs, deathbed scenes, the funeral industry, grief and mourning, death laments, wills, tombs and sepulchral art, epitaphs, cemeteries, notions of the afterlife, widows and orphans, the relationships of the living with the dead, the worship of saints' tombs, executions and capital punishment, blood feuds and violent crime, and the portrayal of death in literature and art. The scholarship on these topics, which has tended to be weighted toward Western societies and the more contemporary period, is the work of researchers in many fields, including history, demography, anthropology, sociology, psychology, medicine, philosophy, religion, law, art, folklore, literature, and archeology.

In recent decades social historians have entered this area of inquiry with bold attempts to recover the approaches to death in past societies and the shifts in attitudes and practices over time. The French historian Philippe Ariès (1981) led the way with a series of pioneering studies that provided a detailed outline of the changing approaches to death in Western society in the last millennium. A subsequent survey of Western attitudes and realities during roughly the same period by the historian Michel Vovelle (*La mort et l'Occident de 1300 à nos jours,* Paris, 1983) added another monumental piece to the historical study of death, refining aspects of Ariès's work and integrating into the picture social and demographic developments that help to explain why attitudes and realities took the forms they did. These broad overviews as well as specialized case studies establish how the approaches to death in Western society varied among classes and changed over time. Through the prism of death they also cast new light on a host of other issues in social history, from health and property to religious faith and family relations.

One of the more intriguing phases in this recovered history has been the Western approach to death in the 20th century. A large body of writing has now described, often critically, the inhibitions and taboos that have come to surround death in the United States and Western Europe. It identifies several characteristic patterns of this new way of death which stand in contrast with past realities and attitudes: most people (over 80 percent) die in institutions rather than at home; they often spend their last hours in a depersonalized environment, connected to machines, drugged, attended by professionals, and largely isolated from family and friends; many of them face death without a consoling belief in the afterlife; the strong faith in science and medicine built into the culture creates exaggerated expectations of defeating death and makes death harder to accept; mourning for the dead is a private, family affair, not a communal event; mourners are expected to control their emotions, repress open expressions of grief, and get on with their lives; mourning clothes are not considered in good taste; burial and ritual are handled almost exclusively by professionals hired on a commercial basis; children are often sheltered from the dying and from death; and cemeteries are solemn and forbidding places in which people often feel uneasy.

The fascination with this modern Western phenomenon helped originally to spark interest in the larger history of death. The vibrant research on the subject has now extended to non-Western cultures, promising to enrich this fertile field of study still further. As more patterns become known they point to cross-cultural parallels and differences, and these in turn suggest possible clues to the question most challenging to historians: what is it about societies in different places and periods that causes them to approach death in their particular ways? That in the Middle East or rural Greece, for instance, people have traditionally died at home, often in the presence of family, and their departure occasioned unrepressed expressions of grief and mourning, active communal participation and support, and extended commemoration, including routine visiting of cemeteries by young and old, juxtaposes immediately the very different approaches to death in the eastern Mediterranean and in contemporary America. The search for explanations of such differences, and of the particular patterns current in any society, leads into various underlying factors such as the demographic regime, the social organization, the structure of the family, the level of technology, the economic conditions, the place of religion in society, the system of values, and the level of individualism. For the way of death of a society is ultimately a reflection of its way of life, and can be understood best in relation to it. (*See also* Cemeteries; Demography; Health; Life Course/ Life Cycle; Mortality Decline; Old Age; Plague; Ritual; Suicide; Widows)

Abraham Marcus

REFERENCES

Ariès, Philippe. *The Hour of Our Death.* New York: Random House, 1981.

Cohn, Samuel. *Death and Property in Siena, 1205–1800.* Baltimore: Johns Hopkins University Press, 1988.

Farrell, James. *Inventing the American Way of Death, 1830–1920.* Philadelphia: Temple University Press, 1980.

Marcus, Abraham. *Death in the Middle East: Realities and Attitudes, 1700–1920.* New York: Columbia University Press, forthcoming.

McManners, John. *Death and the Enlightenment: Changing Attitudes to Death in Eighteenth-Century France.* Oxford: Oxford University Press, 1981.

Deconstruction

"Deconstruction" is a term and an approach borrowed from contemporary literary criticism. In literary criticism, deconstructionists often approached literature in quite ahistorical ways, seeking meanings regardless of historical context. Historians who use deconstruction seek techniques of analysis that will develop the new cultural history and that may relate to social history as well. Historians "deconstructing" a text may intensely analyze and seek hidden implications from their source—an account of ritual, for example, or a popular protest document, or even a formal policy statement by a middle-class reformer—finding meanings that the document did not overtly intend to convey. Implications about gender, or the human body, are often "teased out" of a document by deconstruction of this sort. Critics of these techniques sometimes find that deconstructionists devote too much attention to individual documents that may or may not be representative, rather than seeking the broadest evidence. Critics also worry that deconstructionists become so enmeshed in getting beneath the surface of cultural appearances, assuming that everything is cultural and subjective, that they downplay objective factors such as economic trends or power relationships.

Social historians are, however, widely interested in using documents to gain understandings about a broad range of topics. Some social historians are also attempting to combine deconstructionist techniques with substantial cultural evidence and with parallel consideration of economic and technological trends. They seek in other words the benefits of deconstructionist insights while obviating potential limitations. Deconstruction does not yet have a secure place among social historians, reflecting ambiguities between the newest cultural and social history, but some practical combinations already exist. (*See also* Cultural History)

Peter N. Stearns

REFERENCES

Bourdieu, Pierre, and Jean-Claude Passeron. *Reproduction in Education, Society and Culture.* London: Routledge, 1977.

Eagleton, Terry. *Literary Theory: An Introduction.* Minneapolis: University of Minnesota Press, 1983.

Kelly, Joseph, and Timothy Kelly. "Searching the Dark Alley: New Historicism and Social History," *Journal of Social History* 25 (1992): 677–94.

Deindustrialization

Deindustrialization refers to a process whereby industrial activities, such as mining and manufacturing, significantly decline over several decades so that the portion of a region's or a society's income that comes from industrial activities also significantly decreases. The process has received increasing attention from social historians, who deal not only with the impacts of loss of modernity but with the values and social relationships of groups who try to preserve key traditions in the face of industrial decline. The classic cases of deindustrialization in early modern European history are northern Italy and Flanders (present-day northern Belgium) during the 17th century. Milan in 1640, for example, produced 3,000 wool cloths; in 1705, it produced only 100. Since the industrial revolution, no country as a whole, with the possible exception of Britain, can be said to have deindustrialized, but certain regions clearly have. Some historians would consider the decline of rural or cottage industry as part of deindustrialization. During the 19th century, rural or proto-industry in Ireland, Brittany, and parts of the rural Northeast in the United States all declined as factories in other areas took away the work done in these regions. Older coal mining areas are the clearest cases of modern deindustrialization. These areas declined as newer, more easily worked coalfields and new fuel sources, such as oil, undercut the old fields. In 1913, South Wales produced 57 million tons of coal. In 1937, it produced only 34 million tons. Similar declines have occurred in Scotland, Appalachia in the United States, Belgium, and France. In Great Britain as a whole, including Wales and Scotland, the number of coalminers fell 75 percent between 1948 and 1984, from 716,000 to only 181,000. Although less dramatic, the decline of older textile, automobile, and iron and steel regions can be considered as cases of deindustrialization. The consequences of severe deindustrialization, especially in the coalfields, have been unemployment, out-migration, and human tragedy.

Deindustrialization is intended to refer to more than temporary unemployment or industries hit by a recession. Although observers sometimes describe unemployed workers in depressed industries as suffering the effects of deindustrialization, the industries may actually be producing their products more efficiently, that is, producing the same amount with fewer workers. Similarly, certain industries may decline or disappear, but new ones may replace them. Industrial activities as a whole, in other words, could still produce the same amount of income as before. Carriage making, gas lamp production, and the construction of steam engines are all activities which have virtually disappeared without necessarily lowering the level of industrialization overall. In earlier periods of deindustrialization, agriculture grew as urban or rural industry declined. Italy and Flanders at the end of the 17th century, and Ireland and Brittany at the end of the 19th century, were more dependent on agriculture than they had been 50 years earlier. In contemporary economies as a whole, service industries and white-collar occupations appear to have taken up at least some of the unemployment produced by deindustrialized regions.

Some economists and historians do not see deindustrialization as a process similar to industrialization. Instead, they see industrialization itself as containing many costs and periods of uneven growth in which old firms and technologies are constantly being replaced by new ones. Thus, some would argue that regions before the industrial revolution which produced manufactured goods at higher costs or with less efficiency were continually being replaced by newer regions until full-scale, factory-based industrialization finally took off. Similarly, as hard hit as certain older manufacturing and coal regions have been in the 20th century, this school of economists and historians argues that societies as a whole, over the long run, have been able to generate enough jobs in other industrial areas or in service and white-collar occupations to offset declining areas. The task for older industrial countries, in this view, is continually to foster new, innovative industries. Other observers are less optimistic. During the 1970s and 1980s, these observers coined the term "deindustrialization" because they believed that expanding sectors did not make up for the decline of older ones. A sizable portion of those put out of work by declining industries were not absorbed elsewhere or were forced to take jobs in service industries, which paid less. The costs of deindustrialization,

according to this view, are not only the human pain and suffering of those unemployed. A potential lowering of the standard of living of the whole society may occur, since it is feared that service industries will not contribute as much to the national economy as did industrial activities. As of the late 20th century, little of this debate has taken account of the world outside of Western Europe and North America. As industrialization continues, however, the same debate over deindustrialization will certainly include other areas of the globe.

Carl Strikwerda

REFERENCES

Blockaly, Frank, ed. *De-industrialization.* National Institute of Economic and Social Research, Economic Policy Papers 2. London: Heinemann Educational Books, 1978.

Gutmann, Myron. *Toward the Modern Economy. Early Industry in Europe, 1500–1800.* New York: Knopf, 1988.

Piore, Michael, and Charles Sabel. *The Second Industrial Divide: Possibilities for Prosperity.* New York: Basic Books, 1984.

Reid, Donald. *The Miners of Decazeville. A Genealogy of Deindustrialization.* Cambridge, MA: Harvard University Press, 1985.

Rowthorn, Bob, and J.R. Wells, eds. *De-industrialization and Foreign Trade.* New York: Cambridge University Press, 1987.

Sella, Dominico. *Crisis and Continuity: The Economy of Spanish Lombardy in the Seventeenth Century.* Cambridge, MA: Harvard University Press, 1979.

Demographic Transition

The demographic transition refers to a process in which a society's demographic system changes from one with high death and birth rates to one with much lower birth and death rates. This transition is generally thought to begin with a decline in mortality rates, which leads to a temporary rise in rates of population growth. After members of a society become conscious of declining mortality, however, they try to find ways to limit the number of children born.

Nations of western Europe and their former colonies with largely European populations were the first to experience this transition. With the exception of France, which began its demographic transition before the Revolution of 1789,

European countries began their transitions in the 1880s and 1890s. From 1890 to 1920 nearly all nations of Europe had begun to experience sharp declines in their rates of fertility and mortality.

How and why mortality declined in 19th-century Europe has been less well examined in recent years than the fertility decline. Most population historians point to declines in mortality rates from infectious diseases such as typhoid and tuberculosis. Arguments occur, however, over why these rates declined. Thomas McKeown (1976) dismissed the importance of medical advances and ascribed mortality declines to improved levels of nutrition in the latter part of the 19th century, which he believed led to greater resistance to infectious disease. More recent analysts, however, have once again suggested the importance of public health improvements such as sanitation and pure water and milk supplies as factors underlying the mortality decline, especially in the cities. While the mortality of children over age one experienced a gradual decrease in the 19th century, oftentimes before substantial declines in fertility, there is little evidence of declines in the mortality of infants under age one on the eve of the demographic transition, except in Norway and Sweden. In other words, in most European nations, declines in infant mortality appear to have accompanied or succeeded substantial reductions in fertility, not preceded them.

Research on European populations reveals that birth rates declined because married women began to stop childbearing earlier in their lives and after fewer pregnancies than had been the case previously. The best evidence now shows that coitus interruptus—the withdrawal method—and/or sexual abstinence were the main behavioral changes causing the decline of fertility. While illegal abortions became more available to women in larger cities at the end of the 19th century, the massive decline in fertility during the demographic transition cannot be accounted for by recourse to what were dangerous and unlawful procedures. The mass of European women and men who cooperated to limit the number of their offspring did so by adopting a consistent set of constraints on their sexual lives.

Contraception was not new to Europeans of the 19th century. Urban elites, such as the middle classes of Geneva, and large proportions of the populations of northern French cities had practiced birth control within marriage since the late 17th century. What was new to late 19th-century Europe and America was the *mass* adoption of contraceptive behavior. The middle classes were in the avant-garde of family limitation. But by the end of the 19th century, all social groups—including lower white-collar workers and manual workers—had begun to reduce their fertility.

Since World War II, the demographic transition has sometimes been called a theory or a model, since it not only describes a transition from one demographic system to another, but also tries to explain it. The theory of the demographic transition developed since the 1940s argues that changes in mortality and fertility were somehow caused by the advent of modern urban, industrial society. Europe experienced the transition first, so the theory goes, because it was more modern, more urban and industrial than other places in the world. This orthodoxy, however, has recently been challenged as historical demographers probe more deeply into the European experience. Research shows, for example, that European nations at radically different levels of economic development (say England and Bulgaria) began to experience the demographic transition around the same time. Recent scholarship has also emphasized the importance of cultural factors such as levels of religious belief in explaining why some people began to experience fertility declines earlier than their close neighbors who lived on the other side of linguistic and cultural borders. Currently, economic arguments seem inadequate to explaining the timing of demographic transitions in Europe.

This finding is also relevant to the demographic transition in less developed countries today. Here, the mortality part of the story has been quite different from Europe's experience. Whereas Europe's mortality rates declined in rather gradual fashion, mortality rates in the less developed world were often reduced nearly overnight as a result of the application of Western medical and public health knowledge that was particularly aggressive following World War II. The very rapid population growth that followed led to vigorous efforts on the part of both Western authorities and some indigenous leaders to encourage corresponding declines in fertility. These efforts appear increasingly important given findings that economic growth, by itself, seems insufficient to trigger the adoption of fertility control. The continuing vitality of family systems that encourage high fertility and that subject wives to husbands and their kin help to explain much resistance to efforts to spread the practice of birth control. Changes in social and cultural practices such as the adoption of Western-style family norms that include delayed marriage (and a corresponding growth in education, particularly of women), a diminished participation of kin in arranging marriages, and a growing concentration of parental wealth on their own children rather than their larger lineage appear most likely to encourage family limitation, thus completing the process of demographic transition. (*See also* Birth Control; Childbirth; Fertility; Household Economy; Modernization; Mortality Decline; Motherhood; Sexuality; United States Demography; Westernization)

Katherine A. Lynch

REFERENCES

Beaver, Steven. *Demographic Transition Theory Reinterpreted.* Lexington, MA: Lexington Books, 1975.

Caldwell, John C. *Theory of Fertility Decline.* London: Academic Press, 1983.

Coale, Ansley J., and Susan Cotts Watkins, eds. *The Decline of Fertility in Europe.* Princeton, NJ: Princeton University Press, 1986.

McKeown, Thomas. *The Modern Rise of Population.* New York: Academic Press, 1976.

Menard, Scott W., and Elizabeth W. Moen, *Perspectives on Population.* New York: Oxford University Press, 1987.

Demography

Demography is the scientific study of population. Almost all demography is historical, because while the modern science of demography is frequently concerned with the projection of future populations, the discipline is mostly involved in the analysis of existing data about populations. Within the larger discipline of demography, one subdiscipline is called *historical demography*; this subdiscipline makes use of a particular group of sources and special methods for the study of past populations.

The study of population is based on the analysis of a number of kinds of sources. The important sources for demographic research are censuses, which are lists of all the inhabitants of a territory at some time, and vital event registers, which are lists of births, marriages, deaths, and sometimes migration. The fundamental method of demographic analysis makes use of both census and vital events, to calculate a demographic rate, which is the number of events divided by the population said to be "at risk" of experiencing that event. The basic demographic rate is the crude birth or death rate, in which the population used in the calculation is the total population. The crude birth rate for the United States in 1990 was 16.9 per 1,000 people; the crude death rate was 8.3 per 1,000 people.

Although there are earlier local or regional censuses, the earliest systematic national censuses were taken in the Scandinavian countries in the mid-18th century. The first modern English census was taken in 1801, and the first American census was conducted in 1790. Until 1850, American censuses only enumerated the head of each household, and therefore cannot be used to study the complete population. The earliest vital event registration was done by churches, which recorded the baptisms, marriages, and burials performed by their clergy. Governmental vital registration began to be collected in Europe around 1800, beginning in France at the time of the French Revolution, and in England in 1838. The United States was slow to require vital registration, although many cities and some states began to register deaths and later births in the 19th century. Vital registration was not complete for all the states of the United States until 1933.

In addition to censuses and vital event registration, the sources for historical demographic research include continuous registers of population, which combine elements of both the census and the vital event register, and lists of taxpayers. A large quantity of historical demographic research has been done on the basis of privately compiled genealogies, especially those for whole communities. For more recent times, sources for demographic research also include sample surveys conducted by governments and private research organizations.

Demographic researchers prefer to make use of the original census or registration document, or a photographic or microfilm copy, rather than consulting tabulations of data prepared at the time of the census. This preference arises from the fact that contemporary tabulations may have been inaccurate, and they almost certainly did not ask the kinds of questions which would be asked by demographers today. Governments, registration officials, and archivists are sensitive to the privacy of those who were enumerated in a census or whose vital events were registered, so many original documents are not available, especially if they took place less than 72 years ago in the United States, or less than 100 years ago in the United Kingdom. An increasing volume of demographic information has been converted to computerized form, and many samples drawn from censuses and surveys are available. These computerized data are an effective replacement for the original manuscript data, and can be made available relatively quickly because names can be removed in order to preserve confidentiality.

The modern science of demography has its origins in the 17th century, when the Londoner John Graunt (1620–1674) studied the lists of persons who died in that city and in 1662 proposed a series of conclusions. His research struck a chord with contemporary Dutch and English mathematicians and actuaries, who developed further the concept of forecasting the length of life of members of a group, based on the lifetimes of other members of the group. By 1693, the polymath Edmund Halley (1656–1742; he also predicted the return of Halley's comet) had developed this approach nearly to its modern form. The method of Graunt and Halley, the calculation of a *life table,* tells us the average number of years of life left to the members of a group of people, after they had lived a certain number of years. This calculation was important then as now because it can be used by insurers and the sellers of annuities to determine the cost and value of their products. The average expectation of life at birth (age zero) has become a common expression of the likelihood of death among the members of a population. In the United States in 1988, the average expectation of life at birth

for males was 72.3 years, while for females it was 78.9 years.

During the 18th and 19th centuries the methods for calculating the elements of the life table were perfected, and the science of demography advanced in a variety of ways. Perhaps most important, in the work best characterized by Thomas Robert Malthus (1766–1834), an English minister and moralist, the relationships between population characteristics, economic change, and social conditions were argued, and the path was set for further study in the 20th century of the relationships between births, deaths, marriages and migration, and between these four fundamental aspects of population change and the rest of the social and economic environment. Malthus argued in his *Essay on the Principle of Population* (1798) that left unchecked the population would grow faster than the supply of resources, and that two kinds of checks were possible: a "preventive" check that limited population growth by delaying or avoiding marriages and consequently births, and a "positive" check that limited population growth by raising the death rate. The Malthusian concern with the relationship between population and resources, and the possibility of shaping the size of the population through the timing of marriages and the numbers of children, has persisted over time and remains one of the building blocks of our understanding of both historical and present-day populations.

In the 20th century improvements in the understanding of mathematics and statistics, and the development of high-speed computers, have increased the quantity and accuracy of demographic research. It is now possible and desirable to analyze many thousands of individuals enumerated in a census, making use of sophisticated statistics. One of the great theoretical advances in demography in the 20th century has been the concept of a *demographic transition.* The theory of the demographic transition asserts that, prior to some time (different in each population), fertility and mortality were high and in relative equilibrium. The transition reduced fertility and mortality to low levels and kept them in balance.

A great revolution in the study of historical demography has taken place since 1950, spurred first by innovations by French demographers, which have been taken up by demographers elsewhere. The first great innovation in historical demography was the discovery by Louis Henry (1911–1991), in the early 1950s, of a way to study the fertility of a population when one only had parish registers of baptisms, marriages, and burials, and no census. He did this by creating a history of a population's experiences from parish registers organized to look like a genealogy, and then by calculating birth, death, and marriage rates. This innovation, called *family reconstitution*, revolutionized historical demography by making it possible to study the large number of communities that existed before 1800, for which there are parish registers but no censuses. The research undertaken by Henry and others using his methods have shown that the demographic transition began with a reduction in fertility in France (and possibly also the United States) in the early 19th century and spread elsewhere; mortality declined somewhat later, although the largest declines in mortality in the developed world took place during the 20th century.

Another great theoretical discovery made in the second half of the 20th century is the persistent importance of what Malthus called the "preventive check." Especially in northern Europe, and at least from 1500 until 1850 or later, men and women married relatively late (men aged 25 to 28, women aged 23 to 25), and a large proportion (as many as 15 or 20 percent) never married. This European marriage pattern was first reported by the demographer John Hajnal in 1965, and it, together with the demographic transition, has shaped demographers' understanding of historical populations. Most children in Europe were born to married couples; when marriage was delayed, fewer children were born. Even before couples began to limit the number of children in their families, communities were capable of limiting the rate at which they grew by discouraging marriage when economic conditions were poor. Recent work by E.A. Wrigley and Roger Schofield has confirmed this conclusion for England in the 17th century.

The study of the demography of Asia, Africa, and Latin America has developed more slowly than that of Europe and North America, but exciting work is underway. Western concepts of the family and of authority seldom held sway in these other cultures, and they have produced different results. Age, for example, has a different meaning in Japan than in Europe, and marriage can have a different meaning in Africa and South America than in North America. Research is now underway to explore the meaning of these differences for demographic history, and their results will surely overturn our understanding of many issues.

Because of its specific sources and methods, demographic history sometimes stands a bit apart from other branches of social history. Increasingly, however, discussion of cause and methods of changes in birth rates links to other facets of social history, including social class characteristics, gender issues, and shifts in cultural values. At the same time, knowledge of population trends and also age structure (another outcome of birth and death rates) provides fundamental frameworks for periodization in social history. (*See also* Demographic Transition)

Myron P. Gutmann

REFERENCES

Hanley, Susan B., and Arthur P. Wolf. *Family and Population in East Asian History*. Stanford, CA: Stanford University Press, 1985.

Wells, Robert V. *Uncle Sam's Family: Issues in and Perspectives on American Demographic History*. Albany: State University of New York Press, 1985.

Willigan, J. Dennis, and Katherine A. Lynch. *Sources and Methods of Historical Demography*. New York: Academic Press, 1982.

Wrigley, E.A. *Population and History*. New York: McGraw-Hill, 1969.

———, and Roger Schofield. *The Population History of England, 1541–1871: A Reconstruction*. Cambridge, MA: Harvard University Press, 1981.

Dependency Theory

Dependency theory emerged in the 1960s as a distinctly Latin American analysis of the causes and prescription for the region's chronic, historical underdevelopment. Though focused on economic performance, dependency theory has also been used to explain important social structures in Latin America; though the theory's popularity crested in the 1970s, it is still used in sociohistorical analysis of Latin America.

Previously, the region's underdevelopment had been largely attributed to endogenous or internal causes. In the 19th century racist notions of Indian backwardness and a supposedly nefarious Spanish Catholic colonial legacy were widely believed to be at the root of Latin America's general impoverishment.

A more empirical explanation appeared in the United States after World War II in what came to be called modernization theory. It held that Latin American backwardness was also endogenous, caused mainly by a feudal system of institutions and values derived from the region's conquest and colonization by Spain and Portugal in the 15th and 16th centuries. These mainly cultural elements retarded the region's assimilation of a modern, entrepreneurial, mainly capitalist spirit and ethos that had emerged in the West's earlier transformation to modernity. To become developed, the "modernizationists," as they were called, argued that Latin Americans had to discard their archaic and traditional cultural attitudes and embrace modern, Western values and beliefs, capital, technology, and democratic institutions. These were precisely the elements that many believed had led Europe and North America to become societal models of economic growth, social equity, and democratic government.

In the 1960s Latin American social scientists countered this seemingly one-sided, Eurocentric explanation which focused exclusively on endogenous causes for the region's chronic backwardness. They proposed instead that exogenous or external factors had bound Latin America into an intricate web of dependent relationships with a world economy centered in the West and controlled, dominated, and manipulated by the Western powers, including the United States. They drew on two main sources for their theoretical response: (1) an economic analysis by the United Nations Commission on Latin America (ECLA) in 1951, which attributed Latin America's slow growth to excessive dependence on primary export products; and (2) Marxist-Leninist ideas about imperialism, capitalist transformation, and revolution.

Dependentistas rejected the Modernizationists' contention that traditional Latin American cultural and institutional features were the princi-

pal causes for Latin America's underdevelopment. Rather they argued that external, primarily economic factors related to the history of imperialism from the 16th to the 20th centuries had forged a dependency that was at the root of the region's backwardness. In their view, a developing, metropolitan center in the West had expanded by conquest and colonization into the peripheral regions of the world to impose, to its advantage, a global world economic order which systematically drained wealth to the center to sustain the continuing development of the West. Andre Gunder Frank, a leading dependentista, dubbed this process the "development of Underdevelopment" in Latin America.

It was not only the peripheral economies, however, that were conditioned by the dominant center. Fernando Henrique Cardoso, perhaps the most important dependency analyst, carefully showed in his path-breaking book *Dependencia y Desarrollo en America Latina* (Dependency and Development in Latin America, 1979, with Enzo Faletto) how the internal social and political structures of Latin America were also shaped so as to reinforce the primary nature of the export economy. What was crucial to him was how and under what circumstances each dependent economy was linked to the world market. In other words, the key question was one of political power—how class alliances were formed and political decisions taken in each Latin American country in a given historical circumstance.

To this end, Cardoso and Faletto sketched a primarily historical rather than a theoretical model which described the evolution of Latin American economic and political dependency beginning with colonialism (Spain and Portugal, 1492–1824) and followed by neo-colonialism (British domination in the 19th century and United States preeminence from World War I). They also introduced various stages within their historical model. These included the rise of enclave economies at the end of the 19th century; the emergence of import substituting industrialization (ISI) as both a consequence of the two world wars and the Depression of the 1930s and as a way for populist regimes to break out of dependency; and the spread of multinational companies (MNC) into the incipient manufacturing process in Latin America during the 1960s and 1970s after the apparent exhaustion of the ISI model.

The dependency analysis of Latin American underdevelopment was favorably received ("consumed" in Cardoso's words) in the United States during the 1960s when it seemed to dovetail with the intellectual climate of the times. Among other things, it coincided at that time with a rising critique of U.S. foreign policy engendered by the generally adverse public reaction to American intervention in Vietnam. (*See also* Modernization; World Economy/Dependency Theory)

Peter F. Klarén

REFERENCES

Cardoso, Fernando Henrique, and Enzo Faletto. *Dependency and Development in Latin America.* Translated by Marjorie Urquidi. Berkeley: University of California Press, 1979.

Klarén, Peter F., and Thomas J. Bossert. *Promise of Development: Theories of Change in Latin America.* Boulder, CO: Westview Press, 1986.

Depression, 1930s

The Great Depression threw much of the world, and especially Europe and North America, into the worst economic crisis of modern times. Millions of people lost jobs, farms, and homes, and saw their savings disappear. Banks, factories, and commercial companies of all sorts collapsed. Wages dropped, markets shrunk, and a sense of insecurity became pervasive even among people who stayed employed. In Germany and the United States, the countries hardest hit by the Depression, economic activity declined by as much as one third. These conditions had profound political effects. Radical movements grew, fascism spread through much of Europe, and governments assumed new roles. The Depression contributed in a variety of ways to the causes of World War II. The psychological and cultural effects of economic trauma were profound as well, since the Depression prompted people to reassess much of what they had taken for granted about society, the economy, and themselves.

Social historians have written a good deal about the effects of the Depression on particular social groups, and especially on their political behavior. Historians have looked at how economic fear, even more than joblessness itself, helped inspire middle-class voters to support fascist parties in Europe. Specialists in working-class history have found economic hardship at work in every industrialized country in prompting workers to find better ways to defend their collective interests. Early in the 1930s movements for the defense of the unemployed gained momentum through much of North America and Europe. In countries spared the repressive grip of fascist regimes left-wing parties and trade union movements grew enormously by the middle of the 1930s. Class experiences varied in subtle ways, too. American historians, for example, have found evidence for attitudinal differences across class lines: middle-class employees were more inclined to blame themselves and suffer shame for losing their jobs than were their working-class counterparts.

Historians have also investigated the diverse experiences of racial and ethnic groups. In Europe immigrant groups often suffered inordinately from job loss and even deportation as labor markets shrunk. Many Polish and Italian workers in France, for example, having served a French economy in the 1920s when labor was scarce, were forced to leave in the 1930s. Xenophobic and anti-Semitic propaganda spread throughout Europe and indeed became a central feature of government policy in the case of Nazi Germany. In the United States Mexican workers also suffered forced repatriation. By contrast, former European immigrant workers and their families became more integrated into American life in the 1930s through labor unions and the successful efforts of the Democratic Party to appeal to white ethnic voters. Likewise, African Americans, who bore an especially heavy burden of under- and unemployment in northern industrial cities and in the severely depressed agricultural South, became more visible in national political life as trade unionists and as part of an important voting block for the Democratic Party.

The Great Depression also had an impact on gender relations and the family. High rates of male unemployment forced many women and children into the work force, reversing long-term trends. Many employers encouraged this shift, since they could pay women and teenage workers lower wages. Little changed, however, in popular attitudes about gender roles. Trade unions in Europe and the United States generally fought to restore and protect jobs for men and to secure seniority rights for long-term employees. New welfare provisions tended to reinforce conventional notions of the husband as primary breadwinner, though government policies varied internationally to some extent in this respect. World War II was to have a greater impact on gender relations than did the Depression.

Governments tried a wide variety of measures to cope with the social havoc and to restore economic stability. Virtually everywhere, from Nazi Germany to conservative Britain to New Deal America, the role of government expanded in the course of the decade. Historians have examined many facets of this shift in the relationship between state and society, including changes in business-state relations, the rise of new forms of social provisioning such as government-financed pensions and family allowances, and the gradual emergence of Keynesian policies of state economic management. Scholarship on these issues has focused more on how policies were made than on their consequences.

To understand the Great Depression as a significant era in social history, historians still need to do more work comparing its effects across social groups as well as across countries. More research could be done, too, on how people interpreted their experiences, especially during the early phases of the crisis before parties and organizations came to assume prominence and claimed the authority to speak for people in distress. Finally, experiences outside Europe and North America need much more attention. Little has been written to put local and national experiences in a truly global perspective. [*See also* African American Society; Class; Economics (Economic and Social History); Ethnicity; Family; Fascism; Gender Division of Labor (Africa); Immigration; Middle Class; Racism; State and Society; Unions; United States Labor Movement; Welfare State; Women and Work; Working Class; World Wars]

Herrick Chapman

REFERENCES

Cohen, Lizabeth. *Making a New Deal: Industrial Workers in Chicago, 1919–1939*. New York: Cambridge University Press, 1990.

Hamilton, Richard F. *Who Voted for Hitler?* Princeton, NJ: Princeton University Press, 1982.

Kindleberger, Charles P. *The World in Depression, 1929–1939*. Berkeley: University of California Press, 1973.

Orwell, George. *The Road to Wigan Pier*. New York: Harcourt, Brace, 1958.

Sitkoff, Harvard. *A New Deal for Blacks: The Emergence of Civil Rights as a National Issue*. New York: Oxford University Press, 1978.

Deviance

Deviance is behavior that violates or challenges social norms, and historians studying deviance usually focus their attention on either the process through which deviance is defined or those individuals or groups considered to be outcasts from society. Depending on the particular historical setting, strangers, beggars, prostitutes, unattached women, witches, tramps, religious and political dissenters, lepers, or any number of others might be termed "deviant." Moreover, behavior considered to be "normal" during one era might be identified as "deviant" during another era. In short, no behavior is intrinsically deviant. Rather, such a label is conferred upon activities or individuals by the community or by elements of the community. When society changes, definitions of deviance often change as well. Thus, historians study deviance in order to understand social, political, and cultural development, including accepted norms as well as the mechanisms set up to handle reproved behaviors. Records associated with deviance can be widely revealing in social history, particularly in premodern periods.

Many social historians have studied deviance as a form of criminal behavior. In early modern Europe and 17th-century America, for example, heresy was often considered to be deviant, and legal sanctions were imposed through the criminal justice system. Law enforcers, therefore, identified and punished those convicted of such deviant behavior.

But not all behavior considered to be deviant has been criminal behavior. In many settings, for example, a sexual relationship between an older man and a young girl would be viewed as deviant but not illegal. Similarly, violations of racial taboos in the 19th-century American South challenged social norms but often entailed no violation of the law. In such instances, members of the community relied on informal mechanisms to identify behavior as deviant and to punish the offender. Southerners sometimes tarred and feathered those considered to be deviant. In other settings, gossip might have been employed to stigmatize a deviant, neighbors might have paraded around the home of the transgressor chanting and banging pots against one another (a ritual known as "charivari"), or self-appointed guardians of community standards might have physically assaulted and even mutilated those considered to be deviant. In these settings, the process of defining particular activities as aberrant and the methods used to identify the deviant provide social historians with a guide to collective or community sentiment.

Because deviant behavior is that which departs from the norm, communities often respond to social change by reemphasizing old standards of conduct. Many historians, drawing from the work of the French sociologist Emile Durkheim, have argued that the process of defining deviant behavior and of punishing deviants serves a crucial function for societies in times of flux. Influential residents often lead the charge to preserve or to sharpen the boundaries between good and evil. Thus, by identifying deviants, they remind members of the limits of acceptable conduct. Isolating outcasts serves to bolster old values and to generate internal cohesion. Those who fear social change might reaffirm their bonds to one another and their commitment to the values of racial solidarity, for example, by punishing individuals who engage in interracial relationships or who conduct business transactions across racial lines.

Kai Erikson (1966) has used this conceptual framework to analyze witchcraft prosecutions in 17th-century New England. Erikson asks why particular societies define deviance in distinctive ways. He concludes that because Puritans belonged to a society in which religious belief girded community values, settlers in 17th-century New England defined deviance in religious terms. Societies that placed special value on particular political views often defined deviance in political terms. More important, according to Erikson, the process of defining and punishing deviants served an extremely important function for society. When Puritans seemed to stray from their original commitment to religious principles, guardians of the old values used the prosecution (and persecution) of deviants to punish those who threatened the traditional standards of conduct. Erikson argues that by generating community indignation against religious dissenters and witches, Puritan leaders strengthened an older definition of acceptable conduct. Those who shared in the condemnation of witchcraft simultaneously purged society of outcasts and reaffirmed their sense of religious and social unity. Thus, defining particular behavior as deviant preserved and bolstered a particular set of values.

For Erikson, the Salem witch trials of 1692 provide telling clues about the function of deviance and about the development of Puritan society. During the late 17th century, according to Erikson, the "unique identity," or distinctive features, of Puritan society began to wane. He argues that the sense of religious and communal mission that had generated internal cohesion during the early years of the settlement seemed to fade. But just as the old spiritual and communal identity began to disappear, Puritans, particularly in Salem, Massachusetts, felt besieged by the agents of Satan.

By responding to the threat from a deviant group (witches), Puritan ministers, according to Erikson, reestablished old boundaries between good and evil. Moreover, the crusade to safeguard communal ideals generated group cohesion; Puritans were drawn together in the brief war to protect their godly commonwealth against witches. Identifying deviant behavior (in this case witchcraft), therefore, helped to reemphasize religious values. With each new crisis in Puritan society, Erikson argues, deviance assumed a different form, though the crusade to eliminate the threat served the same function.

Although other scholars examining witchcraft in America, such as John Demos (1982), have devoted less attention to the Salem trials and draw less directly on Durkheim's model, they have also argued that witchcraft prosecutions, by reaffirming the boundaries between proper and dangerous conduct, represented a "conservative" effort to "renew the inner bonds of community." Similarly, Carol Karlsen (1987), a leading scholar of witchcraft in colonial New England, has discovered that women who deviated from traditional gender roles were often charged with witchcraft. Thus, many historians of 17th-century New England have concluded that Puritans defined deviance in ways that reflected an effort to preserve older notions of "acceptable" behavior.

Other historians have argued that changing assumptions about deviance represented a struggle to establish new standards of conduct. In these instances, behavior that had long been considered acceptable was recast and considered to be deviant. For example, during the 19th century very rapid social, economic, and demographic changes challenged long-held attitudes toward proper conduct. Increasing migration and heterogeneity often shattered any collective or communal consensus. Traditional mechanisms of regulating conduct in small towns became ineffective in large, diverse urban centers. Different groups with distinctive cultural traditions held alternate and often conflicting assumptions concerning the limits of acceptable behavior. The religious and sexual practices of some ethnic groups seemed deviant to other groups. Native-born residents of mid-19th-century American cities, for example, viewed Irish immigrants and their cultural traditions with contempt and fear. Thus, segments of the diverse urban population battled for the power to define deviance. By controlling the definition of proper behavior, the elite, for example, tried to extend their values over all of society and to punish, often through the use of the criminal justice system, those who did not conform.

The growth of large cities sparked particularly explosive battles for the ability to define deviance. Working-class traditions concerning alcohol consumption, for example, came into conflict with middle-class assumptions, which emphasized self-discipline, sobriety, and the restraint of passionate or impulsive behavior. Members of the middle class, such as Protestant reformers in American cities, attempted to gain control of municipal government, including the police, in order redraw the limits of acceptable public behavior. They instructed law enforcers to arrest deviants—those who held alternate views, such as workers who often spent their leisure time in saloons.

John Merriman (1991), in his study of French cities during the early 19th century, argues that municipal officials struggled to bring beggars, prostitutes, rebellious workers, and other "outcasts" into conformity with bourgeois standards of conduct. According to Merriman, large numbers of such outcasts lived at the physical edges of French cities (faubourgs), where they seemed to reject urban culture. Beggars and prostitutes appeared particularly frightening because they lived in a physical and cultural setting that was beyond the reach of orderly, bourgeois society; they appeared irrational, reckless, and uncontrollable. Such marginal groups comprised the "dangerous classes" of the 19th-century city. By defining deviance in ways that reflected the fears of bourgeois society and by directing the police to apprehend these outcasts, urban policymakers attempted to force those who lived at the margins of urban society to conform to bourgeois standards of conduct. Shifts in the boundaries of proper behavior represented an effort to forge—even if through coercive means—a new cultural consensus in the 19th-century city.

Historians interested in gender relations in 19th-century America have studied a similar process. As middle-class culture, which emphasized domesticity and sexual restraint, expanded its influence, policymakers recast assumptions about deviance. According to some social historians, such as Estelle Freedman (1981), public officials and intellectuals began to argue that women who resisted middle-class notions of sexual purity and restraint were deviant and dangerous. Freedman notes that many middle-class writers believed that "fallen women" not only challenged family life but also contributed significantly to male criminality. By using their sexual wiles to corrupt virtuous men, fallen women lured their victims into lives of debauchery and crime, destroying the self-discipline that preserved social order.

Historians have also explored the ways in which this view of deviance shaped—or reshaped—public policy. In mid-19th-century St. Louis, for example, law enforcers devoted particular attention to drunken and homeless women. Neither homelessness nor drunkenness among women was a new phenomenon. The emergence of middle-class culture, however, emphasized new standards of behavior and made these women seem deviant. To municipal officials, such women, because they were inebriated or lived in desperate circumstances, were likely to engage in uncontrollable and reckless behavior; they possessed the ability to seduce and, therefore, to corrupt unsuspecting men. Ironically, local policymakers did not view prostitutes residing in brothels in the same terms. Full-time brothel "inmates," according to the police, did not threaten middle-class society. City law enforcers regulated the activities of prostitutes in brothels, confining houses of prostitution to one section of the city and persuading brothel keepers to operate relatively orderly "businesses." Thus, the police felt confident that most prostitutes, unlike degraded outcasts, conformed to well-established rules regarding when and where to engage in sexual relationships. Like their French counterparts, St. Louis officials feared those who seemed to live beyond the reach of proper society and used the criminal justice system to redefine deviance, to establish new standards of acceptable behavior, and to support middle-class views of domestic relations and sexual virtue.

In short, deviance is more revealing about the society or culture that defines it than it is about the individuals considered to be deviant. Historians of deviance, therefore, have focused their analyses on two basic issues. First, scholars have attempted to determine who (or what groups) defined deviance. Did the community at large shape standards of acceptable behavior? If so, deviance provides important clues about collective sentiments. Many social historians, particularly those writing from a Marxist perspective, have emphasized the battle between different elements of society for the ability to define proper conduct. From this view, social and cultural power can be understood by examining the process through which deviance is defined.

Second, social historians have analyzed the significance of specific definitions of deviance and treatments of deviants. Why did perceptions of particular kinds of conduct change? Were

attitudes toward deviance part of an effort to expand the influence of formal institutions, such as a dominant church or municipal government? Were attempts to stigmatize homeless women, for example, directed at redefining gender relations? In sum, because deviance is a reflection of the society that defines it, historians have studied deviance in order to understand the nature of power, the establishment or maintenance of cultural values, the application and function of the law, and the role and status of outsiders. (*See also* Crime; Prostitution; Social Control; Subcultures; Witchcraft)

Jeffrey S. Adler

REFERENCES

Demos, John Putnam. *Entertaining Satan: Witchcraft and the Culture of Early New England.* New York: Oxford University Press, 1982.

Erikson, Kai T. *Wayward Puritans: A Study in the Sociology of Deviance.* New York: Macmillan, 1966.

Freedman, Estelle B. *Their Sisters' Keepers: Women's Prison Reform in America, 1830–1930.* Ann Arbor: University of Michigan Press, 1981.

Karlsen, Carol F. *The Devil in the Shape of a Woman: Witchcraft in Colonial New England.* New York: Random House, 1987.

Merriman, John H. *The Margins of City Life: Explorations on the French Urban Frontier, 1815–1851.* New York: Oxford University Press, 1991.

Disabilities

Recent estimates reckon that 20 percent of the world's population has disabilities significantly affecting daily activities. The proportion was undoubtedly as high in the past. Because the history of handicapped people is just beginning to be reconstructed, this article can only suggest its probable contours. This is one of the frontier areas of sociohistorical research in which significant findings are only starting to emerge. Disabled persons' social identities and experience, especially in modern times, have largely been determined by the ideologies shaping policies and institutions.

Most premodern societies seem to have stigmatized or venerated handicapped individuals as divinely punished or purified moral deviants. Contemporary versions of this moral model still prescribe social perceptions of physically or mentally different persons. Some popular cultural images (telethon poster children, horror-film villains) portray them as the embodiment of disorder and disintegration and thus of social abnormality and moral failure. Counterimages of those who have overcome their handicaps present them as exemplars of mythic individualism, the capacity to mold oneself regardless of circumstance.

In the 18th century an emerging medical model redefined disability as any of a series of disease states. Only correction of physical deviance could make social assimilation possible. This paradigm remained predominant in late 20th-century medicine, education, and social welfare. While it ostensibly abolished moral stigma, it relegated disabled persons to a patient or client role, a status of social defectiveness and enforced dependency, unless they could be rendered normal.

The medical model was institutionalized in western Europe and America by medical and educational reformers who aimed both to control potential threats to social order and to facilitate human capacities. For instance, recognition of Sign as the natural language of deaf people led to establishment of manualist residential schools in France and the United States (1750s–1850s). Competing oralist schools in Britain and parts of Europe insisted that deaf children must learn speech. Apart from this disagreement over language, most hearing benefactors saw deafness as an affliction and believed deaf people should be assimilated into hearing society to prevent their becoming a deviant minority.

Despite that aim, the manualist schools became the seedbeds and centers of a signing subculture. Graduates of the U.S. schools formed local and state clubs, including in 1880 the National Association of the Deaf to advocate deaf interests. Emergence of this linguistic and cultural minority evoked a virulent response. For the first time oralism gained ground in American deaf education with calls for suppressing Sign and dispersing the deaf subculture. Since hearing people still largely controlled deaf education, by 1900 oralists took over virtually all the schools.

The oralist triumph coincided with intensified bias against people with other handicaps. For example, American schools to educate men-

tally retarded people had been founded in the 1840s and 1850s with high hopes for their ultimate social assimilation. By the 1880s professionals concluded that most not only could never fit into the new industrial society but posed a threat to its well-being. People with various disabilities were lumped among the "defective classes." New testing procedures claimed to ascertain disability, particularly mental retardation, more rigorously and to find its incidence more prevalent. Society must protect itself by segregating such people. Some youngsters were permanently institutionalized. Others were regulated in special education to keep them from disrupting instruction of normal peers.

The social-welfare system fashioned in the late 19th and early 20th centuries also promoted segregation by defining disability as inability to engage in productive labor. Though the stated goal was to limit access to relief and keep able-bodied workers in the labor market, these policies simultaneously restricted access of handicapped people to jobs and society. The welfare state thus placed most disabled adults in a state of economically dependent, stigmatized and segregated clientage, under permanent oversight by medical and social-service professionals.

In the late 20th century, social movements of disabled persons worldwide opposed institutionalized stigma and segregation. They and some social scientists developed a social environmental/minority-group model of disability. It explained limitations in social and vocational functioning not as the inevitable result of medical conditions, but as a product of the interaction of handicapped individuals with the social and built environments. It also described cultural devaluation of mentally or physically different persons as a primary component of most historic environments.

The social history of handicapped people and the ways they have responded to cultural definitions of disability needs more study. Some groups apparently adopted a minority view. Late 19th-century U.S. deaf leaders spoke of deafness as an "affliction" but saw their chief problem as hearing prejudice. Late 20th-century activists went farther, redefining deafness as not pathology, but primarily linguistic difference. Historical self-definitions of other disability groups require study. (*See also* Body; Deviance; Health; Social Control)

Paul K. Longmore

REFERENCES

Tyor, Peter L., and Leland V. Bell. *Caring for the Retarded in America*. Westport, CT: Greenwood, 1984.

Van Cleve, John, and Barry Crouch. *A Place of Their Own: Making the Deaf Community in America*. Washington, DC: Gallaudet, 1989.

Discourse

The concept of discourse was first elaborated in the 1960s by the French historian Michel Foucault. He published a series of works between 1961 and 1969 on the history of madness, psychiatry, and the natural sciences, all of which diverged considerably from positivist and Marxist historiography by taking as their object what he termed "discursive practices." In his 1969 theoretical essay *The Archaeology of Knowledge* (1981), Foucault defined in clear terms the meaning and relevance of discourse and distinguished his use of the word from its conventional meaning as "verbal exchange in speech or writing." The historian who analyzed discourses, he said, performed a "task that consists of not—of no longer—treating discourses as groups of signs (signifying elements referring to contents or representations) but as practices that systematically form the objects of which they speak."

Foucault thus made an important distinction between language conceived as a vehicle for communication ("signifying elements referring to contents or representations") and language conceived as a system of meaning production ("practices that systematically form objects"). He did not conceive language as a reflection of material reality, a tool individuals used as a means of self-expression. Instead, Foucault insisted that language produced material reality, and hence constructed individual subjects. In so doing, he challenged the distinction presumed by historians of various ideological persuasions between discourse and material reality. This was particularly vexing to many social historians, who conceive language primarily as an epiphenomenon of social relations. At the same time, other social historians, especially those interested in workers' and women's culture, have found discourse a useful concept.

Though discourse was Foucault's invention, he drew on other important work, and without some understanding of this work it is impossible to grasp the full import of the concept for social historians. Two generations of French thinkers known as structuralists and post-structuralists (with whom Foucault's work was identified) emerged in the 1950s and 1960s and are still highly influential in both American and French avant-garde circles. These include the anthropologist Claude Levi-Strauss, the psychoanalyst Jacques Lacan, and the philosopher Jacques Derrida, to name only the most prominent.

In spite of their different disciplines, all in varying ways conceive social systems in terms of socially constructed symbols ordered and patterned after the laws of language. All believe language constitutes rather than reflects material reality, and all insist on the primacy of language over the individual, since the individual does not exist prior to the meaning systems within which he or she is mired. These thinkers consequently analyze cultural phenomena as if they were "texts"—as if they could be read and deciphered like the formal linguistic structures of literary narratives. In so doing, they efface the conceptual boundaries between texts (literary works) and contexts (cultural and social relations) as well as between different kinds of texts (archival documents, canonized literary works, a legal decree). For example, Foucault once argued that the historian's task was not to uncover what men and women said or thought in the past but to analyze the "rules proper to discursive practices."

Foucault's work was most immediately relevant to historians. But the challenge his thought presents cannot be distinguished from this broader structuralist and poststructuralist attention to language and its implicit critique of two fundamental assumptions that underlay most social historical work: the concept of an accessible historical "truth," and the concept of agency—that individuals, to paraphrase Karl Marx, make their own history.

Because Foucault and others insisted that language constituted rather than reflected reality, they argued that there was no "truth" prior to language or interpretation—a truth the historian conventionally deemed it his or her task to uncover. Furthermore, if language was not simply a means by which individuals communicated but actually produced those individuals, historians could no longer refer uncritically to experience and consciousness as the so-called motor of history.

Historians like R.G. Collingwood assumed it was their job both to assess how texts approximated or distorted reality, and then, through cautious interpretation, to approximate (and hence recover) that reality themselves. This method presupposed an objective interpreter able to situate him or herself "outside" the documents at hand. It thus also presumed that documents reflected the intentions, thoughts, or feelings of individuals in the past—their experience—which could be recovered and used to explain the meaning of an event.

Other Marxist historians, many of whom populated the growing ranks of social historians in the United States during the late 1960s and 1970s, were more suspicious of such claims to objectivity. Yet they also presumed historical truth could be arrived at using the analytical tools of historical materialism, which focuses on the way in which the mode of production determines social relations. They analyzed how ideology fixes and naturalizes meaning in the interests of the ruling class by demonstrating precisely how it does so—by restoring, as it were, the "truth" to history. In so doing, they sought above all to recover the experiences of populations of workers, peasants, ethnic and racial minorities, women, and others long considered marginal by an older generation of political and intellectual historians. The social historians' task was thus to demystify bourgeois ideology—to reveal the truth beneath its distortions—in order to delineate and identify oppression and its workings and therefore to liberate the voices of silenced groups and individuals, to permit them to "speak."

This emphasis on lived experience in the interest of liberation characterized much social history after 1968, which rebelled against the sociological determinism—the exclusive focus on modes of production and the state, in short, on

structures rather than individuals—of traditional Marxist historians. But these explorations of (mostly workers' and peasants') culture, modeled after Edward Thompson's now classic *The Making of the English Working Class* (1963), did not always challenge the fundamental premises of sociological determinism. Instead, many scholars continued to explain the nuanced expression of workers' culture in relation to determinant social relations shaped by the mode of production.

Not surprisingly, social historians were slow to respond to Foucault's work and to "discourse" more generally, since it challenged the founding assumptions of most historical scholarship. To those on the left, furthermore, it appeared to repudiate the political agenda that had drawn them to social history in the first place. For by questioning the possibility of an accessible historical truth, Foucault's work dispenses with a normative framework capable of analyzing and defining oppression. This tendency became increasingly pronounced in his concept of "power," which, like discourse, produced rather than reflected or repressed material reality. And Foucault's privileging of the constitutive power of symbolic systems over individuals seemed simply to reiterate in other terms the traditional Marxist stress on determinant structures—shifting modes of production—over the lived experience of workers and others.

Nevertheless, by the early 1980s, some social historians began to use "discourse" to criticize and rethink what they now deemed the unacceptable orthodoxies of social history scholarship. Foucault's most receptive audience was among feminist historians and social historians of France, both of whom used the concept of discourse in different ways to attack professional and intellectual hierarchies. Feminists used discourse to question the marginalization of women's experience within social history in a more systematic and theoretical fashion than had yet been undertaken. French historians found in Foucault an ally against the ossified Marxism of historiography on the French Revolution and on labor movements.

The turn to discourse, as it were, is thus primarily (though not exclusively) rooted in a left-wing critique of the established historical profession and its disciplinary certainties. It is most powerful in North America, where feminists have made some inroads into the profession and feminist scholarship is more theoretically sophisticated and less marginal than in Europe. It is equally powerful in France, where official Marxism both within and outside of the academy generally discouraged innovative scholarship.

Two of the most influential attempts to use discourse to rewrite the premises of social history are Joan Scott's (1988) work on gender and labor history and Jacques Rancière's (1989) poststructuralist history of 19th-century French workers. Lynn Hunt (1984) and François Furet have also written important new cultural histories of the French Revolution, both of which turn away from what Hunt calls an analysis of "origins and outcomes"—long-term structural developments—to focus on politics conceived in terms of discursive practices. Countless others have written Foucault-inspired histories, but Scott and Rancière have perhaps most dramatically dispensed with the conventional conceptual apparatus of the social historian.

Scott's and Rancière's works are very different, but they have several methodological premises and aims in common. First, both invoke Foucault and Jacques Derrida to argue that language constitutes the very categories of experience most social historians presume to be the objective ground of analysis. Historians, they argue, assume an essential working-class and female experience they then proceed to uncover, begging the question of how that experience was constituted in the first place.

For example, as Rancière sees it, social historians conceive working-class consciousness as a goal which workers achieve or fail to achieve. The historian thus analyzes the reasons for the success or failure of the working class to fulfill a preordained historical role, without interrogating the concept of a working-class consciousness itself. Labor historians conceive the worker's pride in work as fundamental to worker identity and in so doing are blind to the worker's more complicated, ambivalent relationship to his or her labor: "What exactly," he asks, "is this 'his own thing' about which the worker should be excited but cannot bring himself to be? What exactly is at stake in this [historian's] strange effort to reconstruct the world around a center that its inhabitants dream only of fleeing?"

Similarly, Scott insists that feminist historians must attend to how discourses of gender construct female experience. She argues that social historians of women have thus far exposed gender inequality (for example, by identifying hierarchical, gendered distinctions between private and public, nature and culture) without explaining how specific cultural attributes are associated with women in the first place. They thus assume that women organize around their identity and experience as women and do not ask how that identity is constituted.

Scott and Rancière argue that social history must thus emphasize how working-class and women's identity or experience is itself constructed instead of seeking to recover its "truth." They claim that identity is not a unitary, given "thing," but always constructed relationally—by reference to an "other." The worker defines his or her identity in relation to the bourgeois, women to men, and so forth. "Worker" and "woman" are thus never essential identities, but always divided and precarious ones torn between class, gender, and other loyalties. As Rancière sees it, the "making" of the working-class can only be conceived paradoxically in terms of its unmaking, in terms of the fundamental instability of any working-class identity.

These kinds of challenges to the methodological norms of social history are compelling. But they too pose a series of problems their advocates have not yet addressed persuasively. If we question all historical objectivity or truth, how can we explain oppression? How can we speak with knowledge about historical developments and give them meaning? Second and related, if dominant discourse constitutes experience, then any account of marginal people only reiterates cultural norms about their experience. Is it possible to account for their experience in terms that do not presume it as an objective ground of analysis but also do not deny the specificity of so-called marginal experience altogether? For many social historians, these questions constitute a new point of departure.

Debates about discourse continue to burn brightly in social history; this is not a resolved category. Challenges to objective history involve the entire discipline, of course, and not social history alone, but social historians are particularly affected because of their previous claims about research methods on nonelite groups and of their frequent political alignment with older kinds of radical politics. Discourse analysis mixes challenges to history writing with new methods of handling written and other sources. Many social historians are very interested in paying greater attention to forms of discourse and cultural construction in the past, without necessarily buying into the full discussion of the discipline's truth claims. (*See also* Cultural History)

Carolyn Dean

REFERENCES

Foucault, Michel. *The Archaeology of Knowledge and the Discourse on Language.* New York: Pantheon, 1981.

Hunt, Lynn. *The New Cultural History.* Berkeley: University of California Press, 1984.

Palmer, Bryan. *Descent into Discourse: The Reification of Language and the Writing of Social History.* Philadelphia: Temple University Press, 1990.

Rancière, Jacques. *The Nights of Labor: The Worker's Dream in Nineteenth-Century France.* Philadelphia: Temple University Press, 1989.

Scott, Joan. *Gender and the Politics of History.* New York: Columbia University Press, 1988.

Divorce

Divorce disturbs most societies. Governments, religions, and social institutions quake at something which threatens the most basic of all institutions—the family unit. It has scared most Western societies in the past century. Ever since divorce rates began to climb in the late 19th century, and to skyrocket since the early 1970s, policymakers have tried to fend off this specter and have tried to figure out its causes in modern society.

The answers to questions about this phenomenon require historical research, particularly that type provided by social history. In fact, it could be argued that one initial thrust of social history research was motivated in large part by the need to answer questions regarding family instability. Clearly, work in the social history of women and men, gender relations, emotions, the family, marriage, sexuality, and even crime can trace

some of their intellectual roots to concerns over the rising divorce rates in the past century.

To be sure, historical research designed to answer these questions did not begin with social historians. Traditional historical research with its focus on intellectual debates and elite manipulations primarily through laws traces back to the early 20th century. S.B. Kitchin's *History of Divorce* (1912) is an example of this work. Later, William L. O'Neill's *Divorce in the Progressive Era* (1967) carried on this tradition.

However, the impact of social history after the early 1970s has changed not only the focus of inquiry but has more clearly forced the issue of causation by connecting the recent trends to broader historical influences. Recent research has postulated many probable causes of the rising divorce rate, including secularization, changing morality, changing roles of women and men both within and without the marriage, the rise of affection as an important factor in marriage, greater expectations of marriage, individuality, military conflict, urbanization, and of course industrialization.

Moreover, as social historians look at these questions, it becomes clear that what is important is not divorce, but rather marriage breakdown. Divorce, as a legally sanctioned dissolution of a valid marriage, may tell us something about legal change and societal attitudes toward the legitimacy of legal institutions, but it only is an indicator (and maybe a poor one at that) of the real issue of marital breakdown.

Roderick Phillips effectively argues this point in his seminal work *Putting Asunder: A History of Divorce in Western Society* (1988). He paints a very long and broad picture of divorce, while at the same time focusing on some of the debates over the evidence. Phillips explores the evidence of alternatives to divorce, such as desertion, suicide, or even murder, as well as the pressures, both economic and social, against separation in earlier times. He recounts the theoretical and evidentiary problems associated with the demographic data.

By contrast, the periodization of changes in the legal availability of divorce has been less problematic. In the long expanse of Western history, historians have detected three significant points of transition in divorce. First, divorce became legal with the Protestant Reformation, although not widely popular. Next, the French Revolution brought more liberal legislation concerning the availability of divorce, which precipitated broad legal changes throughout the 19th century. New grounds, like mental cruelty, reflected important changes in family values. The final point of transition is the rapid rise in the incidence of legal divorce since the late 19th century, especially in the past 25 years with the advent of no-fault legislation.

Within this framework, social historians have explored issues of race, class, and gender distinctions regarding the incidence of divorce and the impact of material conditions and social context upon marriage breakdown. As in other areas of social history, the middle class of the 19th century receives considerable attention. Little work has been done to expand the time frame and focus of inquiry. However, research on immigrant cultures shows promise of at least giving insight into the working class. Here, however, the impact of the immigration process may be a primary cause of marital stability or breakdown among these groups. Other work has been comparative in exploring the reasons for France's divorce rate lead over England in 1900, or the United States' consistent lead over Europe.

Gender-based study of divorce has placed characteristic emphasis on women and their involvement in initiating divorce. For the 20th century, the effects of divorce and marital breakdown on women has remained the focus of attention, but at the expense of men's history. Divorce's impact on men is a topic ripe for sociohistorical research.

Another area open to social historians is divorce in non-Western cultures. Here, the work of anthropologists, such as Jack Goody's *The Oriental, the Ancient and the Primitive: Systems of Marriage and the Family in the Pre-Industrial Societies of Eurasia* (1990) serves as a useful starting point, with much more to be learned. We have some indication of cultures where divorce has long been legal, yet is granted only to males. For example, the T'ang Code of ancient China allowed males divorce, and not until the Marriage Law of 1950 under communism was the right equalized by sex. The social history of these laws has not been widely explored, which is also true of the social workings of Islamic law on divorce, to say nothing of African cultures.

The problem of divorce in the modern era has been the spur to diverse areas of social history. The challenge continues to involve addressing current problems by better understanding the past.

Mark T. Knapp

REFERENCES

Griswold, Robert. *Family and Divorce in California, 1850–1890: Victorian Illusions and Everday Realities.* New York: New York University Press, 1983.

May, Elaine Tyler. *Great Expectations: Marriage and Divorce in Post-Victorian America.* Chicago: University of Chicago Press, 1980.

Phillips, Roderick. *Putting Asunder: A History of Divorce in Western Society.* Cambridge, Eng.: Cambridge University Press, 1988.

Stone, Lawrence, *Road To Divorce: England.* Oxford: Oxford University Press, 1990.

Domestic Service

See Servants

Domesticity

Domesticity, a constellation of skills and responsibilities associated with competently managing a household, also names an ideology equating these tasks with traits and realms of activity considered distinctively female. Middle-class norms for the competencies and the ideology itself have exerted forceful pressures on class and gender relations in modern society. Both uses of the term are relevant to social historians' efforts to reconstruct the fabric of life. Reflecting middle-class praxis, the tasks and ideology have become inextricably linked in a historical paradigm of separate spheres that is widely employed to analyze gendered relations in industrial society, in the United States and Europe particularly, but also in other regions such as Japan.

Domesticity, as a descriptive term identifying women's provision for the physical, emotional, and social needs of their families and communities, requires historical definition. Colonial women, 19th century pioneers, and suburban housewives of the 1950s all considered cooking an important domestic task but accomplished it in widely diverse manners. Similarly, health care may have meant personally nursing the ill or arranging for professional medical attention. Christine Stansell's (1987) working-class mothers in New York City sent children out to scavenge and developed patterns of pawning to stretch family resources. Scholars, looking beyond prescriptive literature to women's experiences, have found that all analytical categories—class, ethnicity, race, region, and age—nuanced the practice of domesticity.

Historical trends associated with modernization redefined domesticity in other ways as well. Shifts from a barter to a cash economy, and from an artisan to a wage-labor system, distanced domestic tasks from major economic patterns. Professionalization and specialization also left their mark. Home economics, gradually defined by female scientists as an academic specialty, gave scholars positions from which to promote scientific housekeeping practices. Historians have reconstructed the changing imperatives of domesticity by combing prescriptive literature, household inventories, diaries, correspondence, photographs, and artifacts.

The ideology of domesticity, however, demanded more than successfully accomplishing the tasks of domesticity. The antebellum ethos that Barbara Welter named "the cult of true womanhood": piety, purity, submissiveness, and domesticity has provided the primary framework for analyzing U.S. gender relations for over 25 years. Whether social historians have interpreted the virtues women were to practice within their private homes as a form of oppression or base of agency, the fact that women and men inhabited "separate spheres" within industrial society has been an uncontested convention of U.S. gender history until very recently. European scholars also examine domesticity, but the phenomenon of separate spheres has been a less central analytical preoccupation.

According to the tenets of the ideology of separate spheres, men occupied the public spaces of business and political activity and women, by remaining free of the skills and attitudes that tainted both forms of exchange, gained moral superiority within the private home. Nancy Cott (1977) described the emergence of a distinctively "woman's sphere" in New England between 1780 and 1830 and identified opportunities it created for participants. Mary Ryan, in *Cradle of the Middle Class*, analyzed the process by which former artisan households arrived at this arrangement between 1790 and 1865. Many excellent studies have explored the implications of the phenomenon.

Participants, at minimum, recognized the paradigm. In fact, Catharine Beecher and other 19th-century authors popularized the dichotomy among their contemporaries. The ideology of domesticity influenced female employment opportunities, limiting acceptable occupations and legitimizing inequitable wages. When 19th- and 20th-century women ventured into the public sphere successfully, they often did so in the name of domesticity. Reformers who advocated temperance outside saloons, founded settlement houses, and sought protective labor legislation and suffrage claimed they were not overstepping their bounds because "municipal housekeeping" simply extended their distinctively female responsibilities. Whether women shared an urban middle-class lifestyle or not, they experienced the prescriptive implications of the ideology of domesticity.

By 1850 the ideology of domesticity encapsulated urban middle-class females' understanding of their social roles and described an enduring normative context for evaluating female behavior. However, contemporary scholarship suggests that the paradigm of separate spheres has obscured the experiences of many women. Recent work on minority and rural communities documents shared productive labor and a mutuality of interests as central to women's understanding of their lived experience. One remaining challenge is establishing more pluralistic descriptive boundaries for domesticity which will, in turn, reconfigure the private/public framework for discussing gendered roles in shaping the productive and reproductive work of society. Twentieth-century redefinitions of domesticity also invite further research. (*See also* Feminism; Gender Socialization; Housework; United States Reform Movements; Women's History)

Kathleen C. Hilton

REFERENCES

Cott, Nancy. *The Bonds of Womanhood: "Woman's Sphere" in New England, 1780–1830.* New Haven: Yale University Press, 1977.

Kerber, Linda K. "Separate Spheres, Female Worlds, Woman's Place: The Rhetoric of Women's History," *Journal of American History* 75 (June 1988): 9–39.

Matthews, Glenna. *"Just a Housewife": The Rise and Fall of Domesticity in America.* New York: Oxford University Press, 1987.

Osterud, Nancy Grey. *Bonds of Community: The Lives of Farm Women in Nineteenth-Century New York.* Ithaca, NY: Cornell University Press, 1991.

Stansell, Christine. *City of Women: Sex and Class in New York, 1789–1860.* Urbana: University of Illinois Press, 1987.

Dress

The history of dress or clothing has an ambivalent place in social history. Traditional accounts of fashion were regarded as antiquarian (and often elitist) by social historians, and clothing was as a result long neglected save as part of standard of living debates. Recently, however, the serious analysis of changes in clothing, as they relate to issues of gender, personal identity, consumerism, and other basic topics has propelled this branch of material culture into a much more prominent place in social history.

Dress, as clothing, involves body covering or adornment in the form of garments constructed of, for example, grass, plant fibers, animal skins, fur, or synthetic material. It can also involve decoration applied to the skin through painting, tattooing, or scarification, the latter characteristic of prestate, tribal groupings. In traditional societies, regular dress tends to be unchanging, as in the Japanese kimono or the Indian sari. Many societies, however, differentiate styles of clothing by class, occupation, status, or ceremonial function, as in soldiers' uniforms, priests' or kings' robes, or costumes designed for the stage. Dress may also indicate gender difference, as in the encompassing chador, a cloak from head to toe, worn by Muslim women but not by men. Yet class, rather than gender, may predominate: in traditional China both men and women of the elite wore long robes, while commoners of both genders wore trousers and jackets.

In modern, especially Western, societies, dress has been associated with fashion, or the regular changing of the most favored clothing designs. Historians of dress trace the origins of Western fashion to the emergence of mercantile capitalism in the late Middle Ages, although European elites displayed an interest in up-to-date style as early as Charlemagne's 9th-century court.

Regular changes in fashionable Western dress have occurred over time in shapes of skirts and trousers and thus of body silhouette and in decorative features like sleeve size, color, and head covering. Yet certain features have been constant. The first has been class differentiation, with a drive on the part of the aristocracy and the wealthy toward luxury in fabric and design. The second has been gender differentiation, with men wearing trousers and women skirts. The third has been sexualization. Low cut dresses, for example, have periodically been fashionable for women, while male sexuality was emphasized in, for example, the codpiece, a sheath enclosing the penis, in vogue from the late 15th century through the 16th century.

The analysis of clothing and fashion is never simple. The often tight-laced corsets worn by women from the 16th century to the 20th century displayed both status and sexuality: by hampering the body for farm or domestic work, the corset indicated a leisured social position, while by reducing the size of the waist and thus accentuating bosom and hips, it indicated sexuality. Military and medical as well as sexual motives produced the codpiece: these motives included the desire to protect the penis during battle and to prevent the staining of expensive fabrics by the mercury ointment applied to the male organ to treat syphilis, which was epidemic in Europe by the late 15th century. Moreover, despite differences between men's and women's clothing, both genders wore sumptuous clothing through the 18th century, while they mirrored each other in such style details as high heels and neck ruffs in the 16th century and elaborate hats in the 17th century.

During the 19th century, however, occurred a radical disjuncture between women's and men's clothing, in line with impacts from the French Revolution and the development of high capitalism. By mid-century men abandoned the decorated clothing they had worn for centuries to take up the trouser suit style still in vogue today. Women continued to dress in variations of the older constricting styles for nearly a century longer, in line with their conservatizing Victorian position as exemplars of domesticity and spirituality. In the first decades of the 20th century they, too, began to dress more simply and comfortably.

Activities like soldiering and sports have periodically influenced fashion. The short tights and tunics worn by men in the 14th century were probably modeled after a newly designed flexible and shortened mesh armor. The simplified 19th-century male dress was partly related to modernizing states' adoption of uniforms for soldiers and government officials. The sports tradition of the 18th-century English country gentleman was also significant in generating the 19th-century simplicity in male dress. Women's 20th-century adoption of more simplified dress was also related to the importance of sports among them, beginning with the popularity of the bicycle in the 1890s and of tennis in the 1900s.

The Euro-American fashion system in dress has extended across regional and national boundaries, and the state dominant in world politics has usually held fashion hegemony. Thus, the black, constricting fashions of 16th-century conservative, Catholic Spain during its ascendancy were worn throughout Europe. Male fashions in the 19th century originated in England, the day's leading power. French domination over female fashion from the 18th century through the mid-20th century, however, seems related as much to French cosmopolitanism, its position as an intellectual and style center, as to any political preeminence.

Social upheavals like the 17th-century English Puritan Revolution and the 18th-century French Revolution produced distinctive dress. International involvement also produced new vogues, as in the 19th-century popularity of cashmere shawls brought from the East by Napoleon or in the orientalism popular in dress styles in the early 20th century. Commercial motives influenced dress: in the 1850s Empress Eugenie of France inspired a vogue for huge, bell-shaped skirts held in place by hoops, partly to insure business for the French silk industry.

In Europe and the United States, the elites have played a major role in determining the mode. Yet the fashion system has never been static, even in tradition-bound medieval and early modern Europe. Although as early as the 15th century European governments issued sumptuary laws establishing dress codes by class and status, these laws were decreed in reaction to middle-class adoption of aristocratic dress and were indifferently enforced. Moreover, styles often have originated in groups outside the elites, as in the 16th-century male fashion of slashing sleeves and pants, originally devised by Swiss mercenary soldiers to celebrate success in battle. In the 20th century, Levis denim jeans were originally designed as rugged work clothing long before they became a general vogue. Still, in traditional European societies, the popular classes often wore out-of-date clothing discarded by the elites, thus maintaining observable class distinctions. But, beginning in the early 19th century, the advent of mass-produced clothing and institutions like department stores brought general access to the latest fashion look and thus more subtle distinctions in dress.

Growing popular appetite for more fashionable clothing was a fundamental part of the rise of new forms of consumerism in places like 18th-century England, where it was accompanied by a great increase in clothing thefts. Exploring the new meanings of clothing in this period, and into the industrial revolution, is a growing research area in social history.

Changes in dress styles are related to advances in the cutting and fitting of clothes, as in the discovery of goring in the 19th century and the bias cut in the 20th century. Beginning in the late 18th century, with the widespread distribution of fashion magazines and fashion illustrations, individual designers, like Charles Worth in the 19th century or Paul Poiret and Gabrielle Chanel in the 20th century, also became major arbiters of styles in dress. And, fashion seems to have its own dynamic, with styles often extending to an extreme before the occurrence of an abrupt shift. Thus, for example, the bell-shaped skirts worn by women in the 19th century slowly gained such width that women had difficulty walking. In the 1860s they were deflated into a silhouette moulded to the body with a gathering of fabric over the buttocks. This bulge, eventually draped over a metal frame, was known as the bustle; it remained fashionable through the 1890s.

Dress reform, or the attempt to eliminate constricting or elaborate features of dress, first appeared in the 19th century, as one of the reform movements of that age. In 1850, in the United States, women's rights advocates Elizabeth Cady Stanton, Elizabeth Smith Miller, and Amelia Bloomer designed the so-called bloomer dress, consisting of an uncorseted, mid-calf, modestly adorned dress over pantaloons. In England in the 1880s, rational dress societies appeared, calling for simplified styles, while the pre-Raphaelite painters inspired a trend toward "esthetic" dress, based on draped Greek and medieval models. Although none of these reform tentatives gained widespread success, it is probable that each played a role in the early 20th-century impetus toward simplified dress for women.

Dressing, like eating, is a basic human activity, and fashion is a protean force. Many analytic systems have been applied to understanding it. Marxists have stressed economic and status motivations, and Freudians have focused on sexuality. Semiologists have viewed fashion as a structure of signs signifying social meanings or as akin to a language, with a grammar and word order. Anthropological theories of boundary maintenance, of drawing distinctions between the forbidden and the permissible, have also been employed. Some analysts have asserted that fashion is irrational; others, that it is an expression of the spirit of the times, of the zeitgeist of an age. Fashion has been seen as part of the civilizing process which brought manners and etiquette to modern nations. Feminists have accused fashion in dress of serving as a major enforcer of patriarchal hierarchies of gender, class, and ethnicity. Its supporters contend that it functions as a means of individual expression and thus of democracy within mass society. Or, relating it to both fine and popular art, apologists view it in terms of basic aesthetic drives or as a kind of individualized performance art.

Dress and the attendant system of fashion have been associated with features other than clothing, including hairstyles and cosmetics. Fashions in both of the latter have varied over time, with the use of wigs and face paint periodically in vogue. Although a trend toward simplicity has characterized clothing styles in the 20th century, such fashions as fingernail and face paint and curling hair through chemicals have remained in fashion since the 1920s. Indeed, the past decade has witnessed the growing popularity (among both women and men) of a wide variety of plastic surgeries to maintain a voguish youthful look. These techniques include face lifts, breast implants, and liposuction, or the removal of the body's fatty deposits through a suction technique. (*See also* Body; Consumerism)

Lois W. Banner

REFERENCES

Banner, Lois W. *American Beauty*. New York: Knopf, 1983.

———. "The Fashionable Sex, 1100–1600," *History Today* 42 (April 1992): 37–44.

Boucher, Francois. *20,000 Years of Fashion: The History of Costume and Personal Adornment*. New York: Harry N. Abrams, 1987.

Steele, Valerie. *Fashion and Eroticism: Ideals of Feminine Beauty from the Victorian Era to the Jazz Age*. New York: Oxford University Press, 1985.

Wilson, Elizabeth. *Adorned in Dreams*. Berkeley: University of California Press, 1987.

Drinking

Drinking customs and practices are woven intricately into the fabric of many societies and reveal much about shared meanings, contested values, and the construction of social identities. The symbolic dimension of drinking makes it an especially useful window on social processes and group dynamics. The act of sharing a drink with an acquaintance, buying someone a drink or allowing oneself to be treated, or offering a toast at a public gathering may have enormous social significance. Depending upon the circumstances, drinking can affirm patterns of deference, promote feelings of equality or group solidarity, or reinforce reciprocal social obligations like generosity and hospitality. Conversely, refusing to drink can be a powerful symbolic rejection of an existing or proposed social relationship.

Social historians have approached drinking by examining its contexts—occasions, settings, and traditions. One focus has been the relationship of drinking to work and leisure. In preindustrial societies, for instance, work and leisure were often intertwined, and drinking punctuated periods of labor and rest. For agricultural workers, the alcoholic beverages provided by landowners served as both a necessary respite from work and an expected accompaniment to long hours of labor in the fields. Drinking also regulated the work rhythms and labor relations of preindustrial urban artisans. Craft workers paused several times during the day for alcoholic refreshment, and an elaborate system of obligation and reciprocity governed the purchase of drinks by employers and fellow workers. Weekends and the conclusion of intense labor provided another occasion for artisans to drink for relaxation and celebration. So prevalent was this pattern of drinking on weekends that labor often did not resume until Tuesday because workers needed an extra day to recover from their recent excesses. "Saint Monday," an unofficial weekly holiday forced upon employers by workers unwilling to give up their customary weekend celebrations, was only one example of how drinking influenced preindustrial patterns of work and leisure.

The social settings of drinking also reveal much about a society's interpersonal dynamics and collective values. Solitary alcohol use has often been viewed with suspicion, as a sign of misanthropy or moral decay, while social drinking with friends has signified amiability and egalitarianism. Setting has also influenced how drinking fosters socially desirable qualities: a planter of the Old South, for example, offered guests a welcoming drink as a sign of hospitality and gentility, just as an industrial worker bought a round of drinks for friends and co-workers to show generosity and fraternity. For working people, bars, pubs, and taverns have frequently assumed an importance which transcended their role as settings for socializing and relaxing. Drinking places provided sources of news and employment information, links in transportation networks, and affordable meeting places for social and civic organizations. In Europe and the United States, drinking establishments have been particularly important as hotbeds of working-class political radicalism. Whether Boston taverns, London pubs, or Parisian cafés, drinking places have provided settings for organizing causes ranging from reform to revolution.

Also central are the traditions and customs which organize and define those who engage in drinking. Historians have described a variety of drinking patterns and traditions based on ethnicity, class, and gender, all embodying systems of meaning and notions of identity. To celebrate and perpetuate their common heritage, ethnic groups may consume specific beverages, preserve unique customs and drinking traditions, or designate special occasions as appropriate for drinking. Workers promote a shared identity through the camaraderie, solidarity, and equality generated by social drinking. By drinking and socializing together, workers gain a sense of their own group identity as well as their differences from other classes. Drinking has helped to define gender roles as well: in many societies, public drinking is considered an activity appropriate only for males. Drinking and the male sociability associated with it have thus contributed to notions of masculinity based on alcoholic consumption and capacity, promoted gender solidarity, and helped define notions of sexual difference.

Attempts to regulate drinking both reflect and shape societal values and meanings. Not all societies perceive drinking, even heavy drinking, as a problem, if it is contained within a framework of customs and norms which mitigate or control the consequences of excessive consumption. Historically, drinking becomes problematic when social or economic developments produce a marked change in the volume or pattern of alcohol consumption. The introduction or increased availability of spirituous liquors to a society accustomed to beer and wine has often produced deleterious social consequences. In early 18th-century England, for example, the combination of surplus grain and improved distillation techniques led to the widespread production and use of gin plus intensification of its alcoholic content. Rapid increase in gin consumption resulted in a gin "epidemic" among London's lower classes, prompting government action to curtail the production and drinking of hard liquor. Attempts to decrease or control drinking do not always proceed from objective problems, however. Some efforts to reduce alcohol consumption have been directed more at specific groups of drinkers than at drinking per se. As early as the 18th century, especially in England and France, middle- and upper-class groups viewed lower-class drinking with suspicion and alarm, seeing it as confirmation of the idleness, dissipation, and criminality already attributed to the poor. By emphasizing the variety of social settings and contexts of drinking and by assessing changes in drinking, drinking's functions, and perceptions of drinking, social historians have illuminated the dynamics of particular societies and provided a necessary historical component for current discussions of drinking as a social phenomenon. Ongoing historical work should move beyond a focus on Western drinking (though a few outstanding treatments already deal with other areas), and explore drinking patterns and practices in a wide range of geographic and cultural areas, making cross-cultural as well as temporal comparisons possible. (*See also* Russian Drinking; Saloons; Temperance)

Scott C. Martin

REFERENCES

Austin, Gregory A. *Alcohol in Western Society from Antiquity to 1800: A Chronological History.* Santa Barbara, CA: ABC-Clio Information Services, 1985.

Barrows, Susanna, and Robin Room, eds. *Drinking: Behavior and Belief in Modern History.* Berkeley: University of California Press, 1991.

Rorabaugh, W.J. *The Alcoholic Republic: An American Tradition.* New York: Oxford University Press, 1979.

Taylor, William B. *Drinking, Homicide and Rebellion in Colonial Mexican Villages.* Stanford, CA: Stanford University Press, 1979.

Drugs

The social history of drugs could be broadly defined to include all manner of drugs used for therapeutic reasons. The revolution in the development of drugs such as penicillin in the past century contributed to important shifts in social values and daily life: people live longer, views of disease have changed, even our sense of control over our world has grown, raising expectations about the quality of life and health. Likewise, even a narrowed definition of "drugs" might include a variety of substances, such as alcohol or tobacco, not normally thought of in this context. In the minds of most, however, the term "drugs" holds associations which are of comparatively recent origin. These include drug taking as an intellectual voyage of discovery, a symbol of a break with social conventions, a sign of societal breakdown, a cause of urban violence and breakdown, or as evidence of individual failure. The drug issue in this narrow sense is receiving growing attention from social historians, though important gaps remain.

Drug taking for pleasure has a long history, although the origins are rather obscure. Historians know, for example, that opium was used in Europe many centuries ago. The Andean Indians of South America chewed coca leaves before any contact with Europeans. Plants were the source of these drugs, and their use in many cases was limited to areas where these plants grew.

Moreover, ancient cultures endowed drug use with a different sort of meaning from that in contemporary Western society. People took drugs for relief of pain, disease, fatigue, and so on. Although cultures recognized the mood-altering properties of these drugs, these effects do not seem to have been regarded as by themselves reasons for drug taking. While Andean cultures endowed the coca leaf with tremendous status, the stimulant effects were valued for their ability to sustain the labors of its users and to maintain healthy balance in both body and mind. Origins of contemporary drug use in the West may also be found in the use of drugs as a therapeutic agent, although there were no important distinctions between medicine, health, and pleasure. Opium came to take its place not only as the central drug in 19th-century medicine but also the broader culture of drug taking.

Changes in trade and technology have changed the face of drug use nearly everywhere. In the West, standardized medicines became available to the consumer. Laudanum, developed in the 17th century, provided an easy-to-use, standardized form of opium—and the development of Dover's Powder in early 18th-century England provided a form of opium popular through the early 20th century. Another critical step was the isolation of chemical alkaloids from the plants themselves. In the 19th century, morphine and cocaine provided physicians and drug consumers powerful new drugs. Since then, the introduction of new drugs of abuse (heroin, amphetamines, barbituates, LSD, Quaalude, PCP) created in the research laboratories of pharmaceutical companies have frustrated those who would "solve" the drug problem.

With increased exposure to these drugs came the problem of addiction. Some of this was so-called accidental addiction stemming from its overuse, such as in the administration of large amounts of opiate-containing soothing syrups to children and the overuse of hypodermic injections of morphine by physicians in treating all manner of ailments. In fact, there was little acknowledgment of the concept of addiction before the 19th century. Even with the existence of addiction established, the exact nature and meaning of addiction remained a source of much contention. This uncertainty inevitably caused disagreement over how to treat the addict. If the addicted person was a victim of a drug, then sympathy and assistance were in order. If the addiction was simply the satisfaction of unnatural cravings for the drugs, then a more repressive approach might be taken.

The concerns raised by the awareness of addiction were multiplied by the fear of a newer type of user—the recreational drug user. These users self-consciously took a certain drug for its pleasurable physical and emotional effects. One group of recreational users were intellectuals and elites who found inspiration in the use of opiates. Another group was a lower class group, who turned to drug taking as a social activity in much the same way as their consumption of alcohol. These users might have been found in opium dens or sniffing cocaine. In the early 20th century, heroin took its place as the social drug of choice among young urban youths. Later users of marijuana, LSD, and other drugs endowed their drug use with many of the same meanings as the 19th-century intellectual opium users. Crack cocaine, on the other hand, has generated the same fears about its users and their behavior that heroin had.

Spurred by a dual concern over the physical effects of drug abuse and social threat of the recreational drug users' subculture, Western governments began their efforts to restrict the public's access to certain drugs. In the United

States, the landmark event was the passage of the Harrison Anti-Narcotic Act in 1914, which drastically limited the legal use of opium, morphine, and cocaine. Since then, there have been cycles of drug toleration among the population as a whole, but the governmental position has retained a basic continuity in its prohibition policy.

The worldwide market for drugs has had convulsive effect on the producing and using countries. The development of an opium market in China in the 19th century created enormous social and political problems. The demand for coca has made several Latin American countries economically dependent to coca growing, while their governments struggle to maintain an independence from the drug economy. Large-scale population shifts, wealth redistribution, and cultural transformations follow cocaine. Most recently, producer nations have found their own people increasingly attracted by drug consumption, creating new problems around the world.

The historian's effort at recapturing the historical context of drug use comes at a time when the public concern over current drug use looms large. The historical debate inevitably attempts to link itself to present-day policy. This is particularly true in the attempt to explain the success or failure of drug policy by searching for its beginnings. But for social historians, there is an additional goal—to re-create the world of the drug user. This involves writing a history of persons often ignored or misunderstood in their own time. Without a thorough history of drugs and their users, the history of the War on Drugs remains incomplete.

Joe Spillane

REFERENCES

Berridge, Virginia, and Griffith Edwards. *Opium and the People: Opiate Use in Nineteenth Century England.* New Haven: Yale University Press, 1987.

Courtwright, David T. *Dark Paradise: Opiate Addiction in America Before 1940.* Cambridge: Harvard University Press, 1982.

Morales, Edmundo. *Cocaine: White Gold Rush in Peru.* Tucson: University of Arizona Press, 1987.

Musto, David F. *The American Disease: The Origins of Narcotic Control.* New York: Oxford University Press, 1987 (expanded ed.).

Duels

It is probable that every society has exhibited violent behavior that can be likened to dueling. Indeed, a range of contentious rites, from vendettas and gang warfare to jousting and other violent sport, partake of elements of the duel. But the duel itself signifies something rather specific, both structurally and historically.

The structure of the duel distinguishes it from other sorts of contentious behavior. In theory, at least, the duel in western European and American society was a highly ritualized combat between gentlemen over questions of honor. That duels often degenerated into mass brawls did not devalue it in the minds of noblemen as a civilized form of combat, reserved for them alone. As a violent but accepted ritual, the duel was bounded by a fairly well-known set of rules governing the choice of participants, arena, weaponry, and the etiquette of its enactment. Rules governed the process leading up to the duel as well, for the issuing of a challenge, upon one's suffering an insult worthy of satisfaction in blood, was a rite in itself, practiced by some adepts with literary aplomb. Once the challenge was accepted, the combatants would meet at the designated time and place, accompanied by seconds (supporters/witnesses), known in some countries as "godparents," and square off. A fight to the death was common, though historians have noted other instances where dueling ritual encouraged the spectators to intervene earlier.

European noblemen understood the duel as a class prerogative, emblematic of their privileged position which, where honor was concerned, placed them above the law. But it is important to note that by the mid-16th century the duel was a crime virtually everywhere in western Europe. And it was categorically condemned by the Council of Trent (1545–1564) as well. Thus, one feature of the duel which undoubtedly endowed it with added appeal was its central place in the nobility's understanding of its privileged status, especially in the face of efforts by state and church to wean it away from such violent practices. Indeed, one reason the duel has attracted the attention of historians is that it illustrates precisely those problems and dynamics that grew out of the centralized monarchy's confrontation with its nobility, a confrontation that was perhaps the most crucial aspect of early modern statemaking.

The high point of the duel in Europe was in the late 16th and 17th centuries, when it was a major form of bloodletting among the nobility. One late 16th-century French critic claimed that more young nobles had perished dueling than in actual combat during the recent religious wars. Several factors were responsible for the duel's rise: the civil and religious wars themselves, which created a general climate of internecine violence breeding rivalries and vendettas; the so-called military revolution which, in denying the nobility its traditional role as warriors, prompted many to seek an outlet for their heroic impulses in the duel; and the pullulation of new nobles and the inflation of noble titles which fostered increased competition for scarcer resources among noblemen. And one factor explains the duel's increased deadliness: the invention in the 16th century of the needlepoint, lightweight rapier, which endowed every armed encounter with a lethal potential. But more than anything else it was the code of honor, developed in Renaissance Italy, which instilled in noblemen a heightened sensitivity to insult, leading to the drawing of swords at the slightest imprecation. Only when this code waned as the cornerstone of the nobility's self-definition did the duel decline. By the 19th century it had gone out of fashion, save in special settings such as German university clubs. The decline is an important index of historical change in modern European and American society. (*See also* Aristocracy)

Robert A. Schneider

REFERENCES

Billacois, François. *Le Duel dans la société française des XVIe–XVIIe siècles. Essai de psychologie historique.* Paris: Editions de L'Ecole des Haute etudes en Sciences Sociales, 1986.

Kiernan, V.G. *The Duel in European History.* Oxford: Oxford University Press, 1986.

Schneider, Robert A. "Statemaking Versus Swordplay: Aspects of the Campaign Against the Duel in Early Modern France," in C. Bright and S. Harding, eds., *Statemaking and Social Movements.* Ann Arbor: University of Michigan Press, 1984.

Stone, Lawrence. *The Crisis of the English Aristocracy, 1558–1641.* Oxford: Clarendon Press, 1965.

E

Economic Development

Economic development occurs when jobs become more specialized, productivity rises, living standards go up, and the transportation network improves. The term is most frequently used as a substitute for "industrialization" and the subsequent increasing economic complexity and capacity to produce greater wealth. The idea of economic development in its modern sense has emerged as an important concern only after World War II. As the industrialized powers began to relinquish their colonial empires in the 1940s, they became concerned with the process of how agrarian economies could industrialize.

Three major explanations have been offered for understanding the process of economic development. One is the technological explanation, which sees the improvement of technology, such as the inventions of steam engines, railroads, or computers, as the reasons for economic development. As these technologies improve productivity, economic development occurs. Another, more complex explanation is modernization theory, which uses the Western European case as the model. Economies industrialize according to certain stages of economic growth that Europe (and the United States) first experienced, after a while creating a snowball effect where one innovation leads to improvements in other areas. Thus, the establishment of a textile factory provides a need for better roads to market its cloths. These better roads make it possible to establish a machine shop in a different town, in turn creating the need for iron goods, and so on. Key to many modernization theorists are the "modern" attitudes of the entrepreneurs who help to change the system. Without these visionaries who are willing to risk their capital on new ventures, modernization would not occur.

The third explanation is the world economy model. Pioneered by Immanuel Wallerstein (1974–86), this model is based largely on trade relations. The political centralization of nation-states in Western Europe in the early modern period made it possible for these countries to expand politically and economically. Not only did they acquire colonies, but they also began to dominate other regions of the world through the control of shipping and trade. Later, Western Europe used capital siphoned off from these regions to establish manufacturing and exchanging expensive manufactured goods for cheap raw materials. In this fashion Western Europe was able to garner resources from what Wallerstein calls peripheries and become the economic "core" of the world. The only way that the elites in the peripheral regions were able to make money despite helping drain capital from their own areas was to repress labor and pay them less than the true market value.

All three theories have profound implications for social history. Social historians have been very much interested in the way that new technology has affected workers' lives. For example, the factory imposed a different perception of time on peoples used to the less precise rhythms of the agrarian cycle. How people adjusted to these new divisions of their day has been a subject of serious research.

In turn, modernization theory has spurred much research on attitudes to determine how and why a region did or did not industrialize. Thus, the unification of France into one national entity, the improvement of roads, and the diffusion of factories and the concomitant attitudes throughout the country in the 19th century have been informed by modernization theory. Likewise, the presence of British merchants in the major cities in Brazil served to stimulate attitudinal changes among the Brazilian elites, making possible nascent industrialization in that country.

World economy theory and, its close relative, dependency theory show most powerfully why certain countries did not experience economic development. The exploitation through trade imbalances, which siphoned off capital, made it virtually impossible for most of the world outside of the already industrialized North Atlantic nations to industrialize. At best, what occurred was "dependent development" (in dependency terminology), which meant that an underdeveloped country would be yoked even more closely to the industrialized North. The exploitation of the Third World was only possible with the connivance of the Third World elites who had to pay their workers little to make money. Thus, why these regions often had very exploitative labor systems, such as debt peonage and slavery, can be explained in part to reference to the larger capitalist system. In addition, the persistent poverty and lagging economic development of regions blessed with large quantities of raw materials, such as Latin America, is a powerful argument for this paradigm.

Despite the explanatory power of the above explanations to help understand the economic development of a particular region and its social consequences, none of these theories can explain all facets. The technological argument lacks sophistication, for it fails to take into account the richness of human behavior and experience that help explain economic changes. In turn, modernization theory is too wedded to the Western European model and may not be applicable to the rest of the world. Moreover, it is profoundly ethnocentric and does not define what modernity actually consists of, other than defining it as the state of the North Atlantic countries and Japan. In turn, world economy theory and similar paradigms based on trade cannot account for the industrialization of former colonial areas such as the United States and, more recently, the Pacific Rim countries such as Taiwan and Korea. The actual world history of economic development, particularly in the past half-century, is richer than most models allow.

Thus, while we realize that economic development is intimately tied to many areas of social history, such as perceptions of time, labor relations, mentalities, and class structure as well as standards of living, we have not come up with completely adequate explanations of how or why economic development occurs as it does. Even charting economic development according to any single measurement presents difficulties, particularly when significant changes in agriculture or light industry play a primary role. (*See also* Industrialization; Modernization; World Economy/Dependency Theory)

Erick D. Langer

REFERENCES

Rostow, Walt W. *The Stages of Economic Growth.* New York: Cambridge University Press, 1960.

Stern, Steve J. "Feudalism, Capitalism, and the World-System in the Perspective of Latin America and the Caribbean," *American Historical Review* 93, 4 (Oct. 1988): 829–872.

Thompson, E.P. *The Making of the English Working Class.* New York: Vintage Books, 1966.

Wallerstein, Immanuel. *The Modern World System,* 3 vols. New York: Academic Press, 1974–1986.

Weber, Eugen. *Peasants into Frenchmen.* Berkeley: University of California Press, 1976.

Economics (Economic and Social History)

In common with anthropologists, economists, and sociologists, social historians are deeply divided over the relationship between economies and societies. Social history developed in close relationship to economic history, in studying topics such as industrialization and material conditions. Yet the relationship between social history and economics is complex, and as economics has become more theoretical and quantitative this complexity has increased. Social and economic historians interact less now than they did two decades ago. Because econometric models leave out human variables, they pick up little from social history (and, social historians would add, suffer in accuracy as a result). Yet, important relationships and potentials between economics and social history persist, and one key link follows from an understanding of theoretical positions. Three basic positions can be identified: a "formalist," or "neoclassical," position; a "substantivist" position; and a "structuralist" position.

The formalist, or neoclassical tradition, originates with Adam Smith (*Wealth of Nations*, 1776) and defines economics as choosing among alternatives in order to maximize output or profit within a general context of scarce resources. Basically, it argues that economic logic obtains everywhere. Such principles as diminishing marginal utility, diminishing returns to scale, and economic rationality have an ahistorical validity and apply in all times and places. Following this perspective, an anthropological study of New Guinea tribesmen claimed to find there an American capitalism in miniature, lacking only sophisticated economic institutions and suitable measures for making economic calculations.

The most valuable contribution of the formalist perspective to history has undoubtedly been its discovery of vigorous markets in times and places where political and religious institutions were generally unfavorable to market principles. For instance, William G. Skinner's (1977) analysis of urban hierarchies in 19th-century China forcefully argues and provides important evidence that trade patterns exerted a determining influence on Chinese urban structure long before the entrance of foreign capitalists.

Most social historians have been skeptical of such an approach, and as an alternative, some have embraced the "substantivist" economics of Karl Polanyi (1957), who emphasized the extreme degree to which modern capitalist society has separated economic motivations from other aspects of society. The existence of an autonomous economic rationality is seen as a distinguishing characteristic of modern capitalist societies. In contrast, in preindustrial societies, the economy is embedded in a larger social context to which economic calculations are subordinated. One of the most important trademarks of this perspective is its sharp differentiation between modern market societies seen as beginning in the 19th century and a variety of nonmarket societies portrayed as dominating most of human history and most regions of the modern world. Thus, in contrast with the neoclassical approach, substantivists assert the historical character of market principles and the existence of a crucial distinction between market and nonmarket societies.

As alternatives to market society, Polanyi emphasized the importance of "reciprocity," "redistribution," and "householding." Reciprocity refers to the obligatory exchange of gifts. Redistribution indicates the flow of payments such as taxes, tribute, and dues to a central authority and its allocation by the central authority toward its supporters or to those who followed its commands. Householding, a vague term indicating the largely self-contained character of production and consumption of the household unit, is characteristic of peasant subsistence agriculture.

Polanyi and others who have argued along similar lines, such as the American economist Thorstein Veblen, have stressed the extent to which important and extensive limitations were placed on market expansion in most societies.

Polanyi emphasized the importance of "ports of trade" that were carefully controlled locations in which cultures based on different economic institutions exchanged important goods. He further argued that economists misunderstood the use of economic instruments in preindustrial societies. Although classical economists themselves agreed that money could be used for a variety of different purposes, as a medium of exchange, as a standard of value, and as a means of payment, they were sometimes too quick to assume that because money served one purpose it served them all. Supporting Polanyi, a recent study of farmers in upstate New York in the early 19th century suggests that the money was used as a standard of value while most economic activity took the form of barter or reciprocity.

Polanyi himself maintained that it was not until the 19th century that market society became dominant in Western Europe and that its hold was already failing by the end of the first third of the 20th century. In his classic study, *The Great Transformation*, Polanyi argued that the convergence of a balance of power state system, an international gold standard, a self-regulating market, and the liberal state were necessary to create a true market society. But market mechanisms produced social disorganization and invariably brought about a general reaction within society to defend itself against market anarchy. Both the left and the right in late 19th-century Europe were seen as part of the general reaction to the liberal triumph of the market.

Structuralists influenced by theorists such as George Herbert Meade and Karl Marx provide a third major interpretation. Social relationships, the pivot of structural analyses, are viewed as far less encompassing than those societywide mores lauded by substantivists but as larger than the individualism presupposed by formalists. Social relationships refer to networks of individuals who interact with one another on a routine basis. Such interaction creates the preconditions for the formation of identities which can give meaning and direction to individual actions. To the extent that they are sustained by routine interactions, networks based on family, class, religion, or race can all underlie conceptions of self-interest. Structuralists such as Marc Granovetter (1985) emphasize that almost all societies contain both market and nonmarket structures. These relationships provide the basis for social identity from which interest can be calculated. Network-based social identities provide cohesion for political and economic actions designed to secure the benefits of nonmarket loyalties for one's own groups while subjecting others to market principles. Groups as diverse as guilds, organized employers, craft unionists, farm lobbyists, and noble landowners attempt to use private or public force in order to secure monopolies and oligopolies for themselves while inflicting the market on others.

An important feature of social networks that needs to be underlined is their historical character. In common with substantivists, structuralists accept that those units responsible for the shaping of individual actions are subject to historical change, and thus, what might seem in the interest of historical actors in the 12th century might seem utterly irrational to historical actors in the 20th. In common with the formalists, however, structuralists emphasize the workings of common principles, such as the crucial character of social relationships, in all societies.

Debates over the appropriate posture for relating economic conditions and changes with social history continue to inform interdisciplinary research. Social historians of various sorts must make important decisions about the kind of economic overview that most suits their findings and about the extent to which economic development causes or results from other kinds of social change. (*See also* Capitalism; Clientage; Commercialization)

Michael P. Hanagan

REFERENCES

Granovetter, Marc. "Economic Action and Social Structure: The Problem of Embeddedness," *American Journal of Sociology* 91 (November 1985): 481–510.

Hechter, Michael. "Karl Polanyi's Social Theory: A Critique," *Politics and Society* 10, 4 (1981): 399–429.

Humphrey, S.C. "History, Economics and Anthropology: The Work of Karl Polanyi," *History and Theory* 8, 2 (1960): 165–212.

Polanyi, Karl. *The Great Transformation.* Boston: Beacon Press, 1957.

Skinner, G. William. "Cities and the Hierarchy of Local Systems," in William G. Skinner, ed., *The*

City in Late Imperial China. Stanford, CA: Stanford University Press, 1977.

Education

Few fields have profited as much from social history research as the history of education. Prior to the 1960s, most publications on the history of education were studies either of particular schools by devoted alumni or of education legislation. Since then, however, scholars have increasingly delved into the complicated relationships between schools and society, examining education's contributions to social transformation, its response to societal change, and the social forces at work in the development of educational systems. Most of that research, however, has concentrated on the last two centuries, particularly in Europe and the United States. This article focuses mainly on the insights of that scholarship.

Prior to the late 18th and early 19th centuries, education had few social functions in either Europe or America. In both, the major determinant of social status and opportunity was family background. Schooling had little bearing on adult prestige or life chances, though it embellished the culture of elites. Moreover, schools were relatively few, and those that existed were usually tied to religious bodies and functioned primarily to perpetuate religious conformity. Thus, since very few students attended school at all, formal classroom education played only a minor part in most children's lives. Young people generally acquired necessary occupational skills through training within the family or through apprenticeships. To be sure, schools were an avenue of social mobility for those few lower-class men able to train for clerical careers. In addition, the smattering of classical languages and literature taught to those few who enrolled in higher education helped brighten the social luster of those who were already aristocratic by birth and, thus, buttressed assertions of their "natural" superiority. Generally, though, the schools were simply not an important factor in either the preservation or alteration of the social structure.

The shock waves released by the American and French revolutions, often compounded by the disruptiveness of industrialization and population growth, produced massive social unrest over most of Europe and the United States from the 1770s to the 1830s. The lower and middle classes were mobilized behind new, often contradictory, political and social doctrines, while, in Europe, revolutionary outbursts overwhelmed the elite of the old regime, replacing it with an amalgam of old aristocratic families and recruits from the upper bourgeoisie. Revolutionary chaos swept away the older props of social prestige, especially the legal privileges attached to high birth, and largely discredited the family as an agency of social training.

It was in the midst of this turmoil that the availability of formal education—particularly for boys—suddenly began to increase dramatically. Prior to the rise of social history most historians of education, assuming that the extension of schooling to the masses was beneficial and progressive, studied this development in terms of pedagogical theory and the political actions that were responsible for it.

When social historians began to examine this period, they adopted a fundamentally different focus, trying to determine which groups, and what motives, were behind the creation of these new schools. Some of these new scholars, in keeping with a continuing strand of social historical research, examined the expansion of schooling from the perspective of the lower classes and concluded that it was the result of rising popular demand for skills and that government actions merely rode that wave. Most social historians, however, have found that governing groups in both Europe and the United States initiated the reforms—often contrary to the wishes of parents—in order to bring education under public control so that schools could be used to discipline and control the newly aroused working populations. Education, therefore, became a battleground in the evolving contest for societal power, and schools were transformed into indispensable underpinnings of rigidly stratified societies.

Once governments became involved in the process of education, the stage was set for a whole new relationship between the schools and the society at large. In marked contrast to the premodern situation, classroom instruction gradually ceased to be a minor and easily forgotten aspect of a person's life. Instead, schools began to share with parents the important function of instilling values in children, fundamentally altering customary child-rearing practices. Furthermore, in contrast to premodern arrangements, educational practices and the social structure as a whole developed in tandem rather than in isolation.

The new interaction between schools and the broader social structure has resulted in education being pulled in opposing directions over the past two centuries. At first, schooling was used to preserve the existing social and political order, teaching docility to the masses and elitist values to the upper classes. Gradually, though, schooling replaced apprenticeships as the vehicle for training people in the new skills required by government and industry, making it possible for those with new abilities to rise in society and, perhaps, challenge the traditional social hierarchy. But the tension between the two tasks, of helping to keep order while assuring progress, continues to this day.

In the early 19th century, it fell to elementary education, rapidly expanded on both sides of the Atlantic, to instill proper character traits in the laboring classes. Elite groups deliberately limited the scholastic content of the primary school curriculum to little more than the three R's and religion. Christian dictates and morality were woven into a consistent political and social ideology, which stressed self-control, humble resignation, and social tranquility. Leaders tried to use classroom instruction and the school environment to compel children from the lower and lower middle classes to view obedience to their superiors as one of their duties in life. Also, personal ambition was constantly attacked, since man was to find his reward in heaven, not on earth. Finally, the dreary boredom, penal discipline, and unhealthy conditions of the schools were praised as tonics which "habituated" the low born to their destined toil in shops, factories, and fields. Thus, primary schools became central instruments of social control, committed to restoring social peace and to channeling popular aspirations and energies toward socially acceptable goals.

With the elementary schools engaged in teaching students the virtues of remaining in their ranks, the higher schools—mainly meant for boys in the early 19th century—became bastions of elitism by preparing mainly middle- and upper-class children to fill high-status posts. Secondary institutions and universities ceased to be merely finishing schools for the wellborn; instead they were newly cast as indispensable defenders of social privilege.

To preserve secondary and university education as scarce and valuable social commodities, enrollments were kept quite small, stabilizing in western Europe prior to 1850 at only 3 to 5 percent of all school-aged children. American data, though fragmentary and scattered, seem to indicate a somewhat less elitist orientation, particularly in less prestigious schools, which apparently allowed more social mixing than was commonly found in Europe. That secondary education was not only entirely separate from the elementary system, but, in fact, even had its own primary grades to educate young boys, further underlined its elitist orientation. Moreover, entrance to the secondary school was largely based on the ability to pay high tuition fees, thus assuring that the students would be drawn mainly from a self-perpetuating clique of the wellborn and well-to-do. However, a small number of students from various levels of the middle class gained admittance either through great parental sacrifices or with the aid of a very limited number of scholarships, a form of support which was both more common and extended to somewhat lower levels within the middle classes in the United States than elsewhere. Thus, secondary schools both defended existing privilege and recruited some fresh blood from socially ambitious families.

The higher schools protected and renewed elite strength through their educational programs, too. Schools used the intensive study of Greco-Roman languages and literature to prepare students for leadership roles. The ancient heroic sagas, for instance, were freely used as vehicles for handing on, especially to those students from nonaristocratic households, the traditional gentlemanly virtues of honor, duty, public service, self-confidence, and courage. In fact, the whole upper-class school setting was designed to prepare children for command positions; in England, older students had considerable power over younger ones to give them a taste of authority. Sports became important school activities because of their supposed contributions to leadership development. Particularly in Europe, successful completion of the rigorous secondary school program became a prerequisite for upper-class careers in government bureaucracies and admission to the universities, which provided training for the professions.

By the mid-19th century, education had clearly adopted a host of new social functions. With few exceptions, school policies worked to limit adults to the positions determined at birth. Social historians have frequently tried to assess whether this massive task of social engineering was successful. Some have examined teachers to see if they actually transmitted to students all the social messages that school leaders mandated. Trying to determine what instructors actually did in the classroom, however, has proved to be quite difficult and merits more effort. Others have examined teachers to see if their needs and goals were consistent with the educational plans of policymakers. Significantly, social historical studies of teachers at all levels of education and in all Western countries has revealed that, as a group, they were much more interested in increasing their own status than in serving as models of social satisfaction. This perhaps means they did a better job of teaching the elite how to rule than of teaching the poor how to follow.

Other social historians have examined adult attitudes, particularly of those who attended elementary schools. Universally, this research has found that the 19th-century faith that schools could counteract all parental and peer influences was very naive. Schools did not eliminate all lower-class ambitions or criticisms of the status quo. Moreover, morality lessons could be brushed aside. One major dispute, found in both American and European research, examines whether, or the extent to which, education resulted in the lower classes adopting middle-class outlooks, allowing the middle classes to establish social hegemony in the evolving urban industrial society. No resolution of the scholarly disagreements on this issue has yet been reached, and it remains a fruitful area of research, for it involves close scrutiny of one crucial aspect of the linkages between education and both the class structure and class relationships.

By the late 19th century, it was becoming increasingly difficult, in the midst of accelerating industrialization, to maintain the social conservatism and elitism that had dominated educational practices for so long. In Europe, moreover, popular demands for equality of educational opportunity could no longer be so easily ignored after suffrage was extended to the masses. And in the United States, massive immigration prior to World War I also was highly destabilizing. In addition, government and business leaders on both sides of the Atlantic realized that restricting the education available to most lower-class and many middle-class children deprived the nation of potential talent and expertise that was sorely needed as international economic and diplomatic rivalries intensified. Women, too, were demanding increased educational opportunities. In the pre–World War I decades, therefore, educational reforms marked a shift toward a new variation in the connections between the classroom and the social structure. Education no longer just stifled or took the sting out of social change, but actually initiated it. After being a major force in the perpetuation of existing social relationships, education gradually became a source of their modification.

One set of changes, hesitantly begun not long after mid-century in parts of western Europe, involved the creation of a variety of new educational branches for boys and, increasingly, for girls—higher primary schools, technical and vocational courses, even nonclassical secondary schools and universities—that were designed to teach new skills which were clearly more advanced than primary studies but in no way competitive with the elite classical secondary and university systems. By no means were these new branches designed to foster unlimited mobility through the creation of an educational ladder up which any aspiring parents could push their child. Instead, each new unit was designed to fix a new group in its appropriate educational slot.

Even the elite secondary schools and universities, however, were forced to make some adjustment to the new social realities of the second half of the century. The first step in this adjustment, dating from the 1870s, involved the entrance of the sons of newly enriched factory owners and upper-level managers whose parents had found that wealth alone was an insufficient source of social prestige. These schools, in fact, became one of the most important means of absorbing industrial magnates into the upper classes. Lest this restructuring at the top damage the position and prestige of older elites, children of the nouveaux riches could gain social acceptance only by adopting the cultural attitudes of older social groups, which were the very attitudes taught at the elite schools. Thus, elite secondary schools and universities, particularly in Europe, did not change to reflect the growing importance of industrial leaders and their values, but became bastions of groups hostile to the economic and cultural forces unleashed by industrialization.

By the turn of the 20th century, elite European schools made another adjustment to outside pressures with the creation of tuition-free places for qualified students who at age 11 would transfer from the elementary system to the lower grades of a secondary school. By 1914, 5 percent of all secondary school students in England were from primary schools, reaching 9.7 percent by 1921. France and Germany followed similar policies, but transfer students formed a much smaller segment of the secondary school student body. Even the universities, by opening their doors to women, furthered the new effort to use schools as limited agents of social change rather than stability.

Only in the United States did a new educational institution—the public high school—emerge that fundamentally challenged, but did not replace, the high status private academies. High schools were not simply extensions of the existing primary institutions, but real secondary schools that formed an intermediate rung of an academic ladder that drew its students from the elementary schools and propelled a favored few up to university study. In fact, these schools mixed children of nearly all social classes in the same institutions.

Although the political supporters of public high schools touted them as socially democratic, social historians in recent decades have penetrated the rhetorical fog and found that they were far from purely meritocratic institutions. Instead,

students were carefully tracked by newly developed intelligence tests that masked with the cloak of scientific impartiality the preferential placement of middle-class children in the academic program, the track that led to university study. Most others were relegated to the general or vocational classrooms as the educational decision makers molded a system that balanced between serving the manpower needs of the economy without unduly disturbing the social status quo. Nonetheless, compared to Europe at the time, the development of the public high school was a socially progressive institution that attracted students by leaps and bounds, requiring the construction of an average of one new high school every day from 1890 to 1920 and enrolling 28 percent of American youth between the ages of 14 and 17 in 1920.

It should be stressed that efforts to equalize educational opportunities were just beginning by 1914. A child still had no inherent right to an education commensurate with his abilities. Nonetheless, individualistic criteria of intelligence and educational achievement, as opposed to accidents of birth such as family wealth and status, became increasingly important determinants of social position.

Further reforms made after World War II were much more consciously meritocratic than those taken early in the 20th century. Most importantly, in Europe the barriers to universal enrollment in secondary schools have been largely dismantled, and these institutions ceased to be part of a separate system and became a widely accessible next level of schooling. In both Europe and the United States, university education has been greatly expanded and opened to much larger segments of society so that women and, to a lesser extent, minorities are now much more heavily represented than ever before. Only the United States, however, has experimented with mass higher education, sending 58 percent of all high school graduates on to some form of postsecondary education in 1985.

And yet, social realities continue to mute the meritocratic tendencies of the system. Throughout the Western world, there is a strong relationship between social background and postsecondary enrollment and an even higher correlation with graduation rates. Moreover, especially in Europe, lower-class children become proportionately less well represented as one moves up the ladder of prestige toward the most renowned higher educational institutions in the society. As social historians have continuously found, social background still counts.

Sociohistorical research on education continues, ranging from work on student backgrounds and subsequent mobility or immobility to assessment of curricula, discipline, and extracurricular activities. The role of education in various cultures receives increasing attention, as does the relationship between education and labor force formation. In these and other areas comparative possibilities remain considerable, both within the Western European–North American context and elsewhere. The social history of Russian and also of Japanese schooling is gaining momentum, and with the spread of educational systems patterned on Western models in other parts of the world during the past century, the larger social history agenda offers many possibilities. (*See also* Childhood; Literacy; Stratification and Inequality; Youth/Adolescence.)

Peter V. Meyers

REFERENCES

Maynes, Mary Jo. *Schooling in Western Europe: A Social History*. Albany: State University of New York Press, 1985.

Ringer, Fritz. *Education and Society in Modern Europe*. Bloomington: Indiana University Press, 1979.

Spring, Joel. *The American School, 1642–1985*. New York: Longman, 1986.

Elites

The term "elite" is used very loosely in much sociology and social history. The best definition involves a focus on the group holding primary power within an institution or in society at large. This definition distinguishes elites from upper classes, for while elites in society at large are generally drawn disproportionately from the upper class (though this may change from one time period to the next, as in revolutions), not all upper-class people are in the elite (for example, the top government bureaucracy), while elites also exist in institutions, like peasant villages, run by lower classes. The term "elite" also has a mean-

ing as a group setting standards of taste and culture, again within an institution or in society at large.

Since a certain hierarchy is evident in all organized groups, elites can be found in all walks of life, and they can be compared in terms of functions, values, and social composition. From the ruling elite of a governmental bureaucracy to the most notorious criminal in a federal penitentiary, any individual that possesses a considerable amount of wealth or the ability to exert control, shape events, and command respect, or who has achieved a certain degree of excellence in a chosen profession can be classified as a member of an elite. These individuals, who occupy a place of preeminence in either community, regional, or national affairs, serve as reference groups for the remaining population. They are largely responsible for establishing acceptable codes of behavior and externalizing value systems, and they monopolize existing political, cultural, economic, and military leadership positions.

The study of elites centers around the question of hegemony and influence. Some theorists argue that contemporary elites abuse their power by forming multifunctional oligarchies. Composed of leaders from the corporate boardroom, the armed forces, universities, and the political arena, these individuals, or power elites, manipulate affairs in order to protect the interests of the privileged few. Other scholars, who view elites from a pluralist perspective, maintain that power and authority tends to be more decentralized and diffused among conflicting special interest groups, thus undermining the institutionalization of a power elite. Sociologist Ralf Dahrendorf (1959) argues that, whereas in preindustrial societies social elites came disproportionately from the upper classes, to dominate the state, the military, the churches, in advanced industrial societies multiple elites prevail, some of them (like the diplomatic service) recruiting heavily from the upper class, but others (like the media or trade unions) open to more social mobility from below. Yet despite these competing and diametrically opposed paradigms, few would disagree that elites continue to play a critical role in our understanding of social history.

Although elites reside within every social class, very few individuals have an impact on an entire society. Status, wealth, and family background largely determine the composition of elites in the upper socioeconomic stratum, and these individuals have the means to control the outcome of affairs on a national level. Often referred to as strategic elites, this group tends to control the leadership roles in government, business, the military, and the entertainment industry. Middle-class elites tend to be local community leaders, scholars, athletes, and others who have excelled in their professions. They often serve as a society's heroes and role models, but they lack the material resources and the scope of power shared by the upper echelon. Lower-class elites also command respect and serve in authoritative roles. They tend to be community politicians, ethnic group spokespersons, and community businesspeople, but their influence is usually localized and diminishes considerably outside the borders of their own neighborhoods.

Elite studies tend to rely on three perspectives, or models, of analysis. By posing the question of what constitutes an elite, the compositional approach emphasizes the importance of descriptive traits and is primarily concerned with issues of identification and in the construction of social profiles. This method examines the role of the family, kinship ties, wealth, and ethnicity, and it is extremely valuable in measuring the persistence rates and the geographical mobility of a particular group of elites such as the Boston Brahmins, the Philadelphia gentlemen, or the New York knickerbocker families. More specifically though, the compositional approach helps identify the changes in elite structure due to factors like immigration, urbanization, and the emergence of industrial capitalism. Peter Decker's study of 19th-century San Francisco (1978) has shown how these variables affected the growth of a "pioneer merchant" class of elites. For instance, Claus Spreckels, a German immigrant who settled in Charleston, South Carolina, in the 1850s and became a local grocer, eventually developed into a powerful business elite member by relocating in California during the formative stage of urbanization and gaining control over the sugar market. The second approach, the operational technique, accentuates

the primacy of behavior. It focuses on the functions, lifestyles, achievements, leisure activities, and taboos of various elite groups, and it enables social historians to differentiate, separate, and rank group activity. Finally, the intellectual model diagnoses the significance of ideas, ideology, and belief systems. This not only enhances the ability to recognize social values, it helps determine whether or not a particular group of elites intended to form a multifunctional oligarchy. It should be noted, however, that none of these perspectives is mutually exclusive; in fact, they are interdependent in character and every credible study utilizes all three perspectives before formulating its conclusions.

Elite studies have improved dramatically with the advent of quantitative history. Social historians are now able to construct more sophisticated collective biographies from the data obtained through local property and tax records, city directories, and social registers. With the aid of computers and statistical software, scholars can now simultaneously juggle several variables at once, and this in turn enhances the possibilities for insightful interurban and interclass comparisons. More formidable conclusions can now be made regarding social mobility, persistence rates, residential patterns, party affiliation, and class divisions. For instance, multivariate analysis, or the impact one variable has on several others, has recently been used to highlight the relationship between religion, occupation, educational background, and age among elites in various midwestern cities. Consequently, computers are now allowing students of elite studies to store previously unheard of data samples, and this is providing researchers with the ability to ask questions and formulate theses that were once beyond the reach of many of the early theorists like Vilfredo Pareto, Karl Mannheim, and C. Wright Mills.

A successful survey of elite literature must begin with the classics. Claude Henri de Saint-Simon, *Oeuvres choisis* (1807); Pareto, *Les systèmes socialistes* (1902–1903); and Mannheim, *Man and Society in the Age of Reconstruction* (1935), represent the early seminal attempts to classify and group elites into separate and comprehensive categories such as academicians, business planners, religious clergy, and military leaders. Gaetano

Mosca, *The Ruling Class* (1896), emphasized the fundamental differences between elites who are recruited into positions of strategic importance and those who obtain them through inherited privileges. Every elite study must also consider Mills's perceptive argument in *The Power Elite* (1956). This book is not only still considered to be the standard work on the concept of multifunctional oligarchies, it has set the tone of the historiographical debate ever since.

Other recent works have attempted to build upon these theories by approaching elite studies from a more localized perspective. Nathaniel Burt, *Perennial Philadelphians* (1965); Jackson Turner Main, *The Social Structure of Revolutionary America* (1965); and Lawrence Stone, *The Crisis of the Aristocracy* (1965), provide much needed historical perspective. Robert Dahl, *Who Governs? Democracy and Power in an American City* (1961), addresses the issue of elite growth and change. Frederic Jaher, ed., *The Rich the Well Born, and the Powerful* (1973), not only contains several methodological and quantitative masterpieces, it covers a wide range of topics both geographically and historically, and the bibliography serves as a resourceful guide to the early literature. Peter Decker, *Fortunes and Failures: White-Collar Mobility in Nineteenth-Century San Francisco* (1978), underscores how industrial and urban growth affected elites, and it explores the "rags to riches" myth in American history. One of the most comprehensive manuscripts on this topic is Jaher, *The Urban Establishment* (1982). In his comparison of 19th-century elites in Boston, Charleston, New York, and Chicago he explores the power elite thesis and stresses the relationship between modernization and changes in elite composition.

Elite studies can sometimes be overlooked among social historians who are overly concerned with history from the bottom up. Yet we must be reminded of the fact that those on the lower rungs of the socioeconomic ladder not only had their own elites, but that they often looked to upper-class elites for models of acceptable behavior. Thus, without a proper recognition of the importance of elites, social history can never achieve a holistic picture of organized social life.

Robert D. Ubraico, Jr.

REFERENCES

Jaher, Frederic Cople. *The Urban Establishment.* Urbana: University of Illinois Press, 1982.

Dahrendorf, Ralf. *Class and Class Conflict in Industrial Society.* Stanford, CA: Stanford University Press, 1959.

Emancipation

For more than two millennia most societies regarded the existence of some slavery as part of the natural social order. By contrast, the destruction of slavery in the New World was relatively rapid. Between the late 18th and the late 19th centuries, an institution which had been legally sanctioned from Canada to Argentina was abolished in one area after another. In some societies hundreds of thousands of slaves were liberated on a single day. Once conceived primarily in terms of Whiggish framework of linear human progress, abolition has come to be viewed as a complex process in which a dynamic and highly profitable system of labor and capital was destroyed by varying combinations of religious, ideological, and political mobilization.

Major historiographical debates have arisen over the causal nexus that best accounts for the general timing of the abolition process, as well as the divergent paths to emancipation. Perhaps the most exhaustive discussion to date, and an important one in terms of cooperative social history, has centered upon the putative relationship between the ending of slavery and the acceleration of Anglo-American capitalist industrialization in the century following the war of American Independence. First rigorously articulated by Eric Williams in *Capitalism and Slavery* (1944), historians have since proposed various combinations of economic and ideological changes to develop market and class hegemonic models of the rise and triumph of antislavery.

Other historians seek to identify the emergence of social actors more distinctly related to the rise of mass politics. Some scholars stress abolition as a reflection of the empowerment of new social groups and the democratization of the free labor sector of the Atlantic economy. Others have focused attention upon the transformation and extension of slave resistance in the Americas. Because it has become one of the more controversial objects of historiographical attention, comparative and international perspectives have been invoked with increasing frequency and the range of relevant variables has been extended to incorporate the findings of historical demography, economics, ideology, political economy, class, religion, race, and gender.

Almost all histories of slavery differentiate modern plantation slavery in the Americas from the slave societies of antiquity and most systems of slavery in the Eastern Hemisphere. The ancient and medieval Mediterranean slaves tended to be widely distributed among the affluent and more powerful members of a society near the major centers of wealth and culture. Modern American slavery was correspondingly characterized from the outset by a number of distinguishing features. It was concentrated at the geographical and political periphery. It was unevenly distributed among the political and economic elites, to a degree unprecedented in the Eastern Hemisphere. New World slavery's survival and development were also dependent upon an unusually complex chain of labor, credit, technology, and consumption outside the slave societies themselves. Slavery in the Americas was therefore potentially vulnerable to even low-intensity external political and social attacks. Moreover, demographic, epidemiological, economic, and cultural constraints insured that by the 17th century slaves in the Americas were overwhelmingly of African descent, while the masters were overwhelmingly of European ancestry. The problem of slave discipline in the New World was compounded by perceptions of collective racial threat. This additional fault line in the structure of slaveholder power developed even where some free people of color were themselves owners of slaves.

Before the mid-18th century, however, expansions and contractions of slavery occurred in the absence of any widespread ideological or collective assault on the institution as such. The great religious movements of Christianity and Islam placed some constraints on the enslavability of believers without creating sanctions against acquiring pagans or infidels as bondsmen. In the Mediterranean slavery maintained an unbroken continuity from antiquity to the 19th century,

expanding or contracting in response to political, economic, and demographic opportunities. Mediterranean modes of sugar production also provided ready-made models for the transference of slavery across the Atlantic. Thus, despite the system's political, demographic, and commercial dependency upon the Old World, plantation slavery became the basis of a vast economic system in the Americas. For every European who reached the New World before the 19th century four or five enslaved Africans were landed. In all, the Atlantic slave trade accounted for the landing of perhaps 10 to 12 million Africans in the Americas between about 1500 and the late 1860s. Only the Islamic African slave trade, over 12 centuries, may have exceeded the number of Africans transported to the Americas.

Just as slavery in the Americas displayed certain distinguishing features, its termination differed from the more gradual declines and displacements of previous forms of servitude. The modern abolition process was enormously uneven. Some plantation zones were experiencing their most rapid period of expansion at the same time contiguous areas were being subjected to severe limits on their capacities for expansion, or dramatic mass emancipations. Slavery boomed in British Guiana and Trinidad while it was being ended violently in Haiti (St. Domingue) at the end of the 18th century. In the early 19th century it flourished in Cuba and Brazil while it was constricted and abolished in the British colonies. It was eliminated in the northern United States just as it was expanding at an unprecedented rate in the U.S. South, Cuba, and Brazil.

Abolitionism first emerged in late-18th-century northwestern Europe, and in parts of North America where free labor was the norm. Earlier attempts to introduce African slaves into northwestern Europe produced legal friction and constraints upon master behavior. During the 18th century the expansion of towns, commerce, and wage labor reinforced the legal norms opposed to enslavement with contractual and humanitarian notions of ethics. Certain characteristics of overseas slavery, such as its recruitment by violent uprooting and family destruction, its public acceptance of sexual exploitation, mass sales, the whip, and gang labor, were sources of intermittent condemnation long before the emergence of political abolitionism.

Anglo-American abolition emerged as a collective movement in the 1780s. It found a fertile ideological milieu among expanding groups of voluntarist religious dissenters—Quakers, evangelical Anglicans, Unitarians, Congregationalists, Methodists, and Baptists. The religious congregations eventually constituted a primary organizational network for the development of antislavery movements. Abolitionism arose in what was to remain its heartland—the rapidly industrializing zones of Great Britain and the United States north of the Chesapeake. These two areas became the zones of the most extensive and durable antislavery movements during the century following the War of American Independence.

Anglo-American abolitionism also coincided with the birth of national social movements in Britain. From its inception in the 1780s mass abolitionism adopted the characteristics of the modern pressure group: public meetings, petitioning, newspaper campaigns, local organizations, boycotts, electoral pledging, and specialized organs of propaganda. Anglo-American abolitionism also exhibited a broad but differential social appeal. It was stronger among artisans, tradesmen, and professionals than among the rural gentry; among skilled wage-earners than among unskilled laborers, factory owners, and proprietors; among Protestant dissenters than among High Anglicans and Catholics.

Leadership of abolitionism was drawn largely from the educated middle classes, but antislavery also appealed to a rank and file who were politically excluded or marginalized by reason of poverty, gender, religion, or race. Workingmen formed a significant proportion of abolitionist petitioners, from the very first stages of mass abolitionism. Women entered the movement as public debaters, electoral canvassers, petitioners, and delegates to antislavery conventions. Non-Protestants were invited to participate in both local and international gatherings. Generations of urban blacks and free people of color initiated freedom suits, wrote autobiographical propaganda, and spoke on the antislavery circuit. While humanitarianism was the most universal component of Anglo-American abolitionist rhetoric, U.S. antislavery also utilized racial and economic fears to mobilize opinion against the transatlantic slave trade and the expansion of southern slave labor.

Abolition followed a different course outside Anglo-America. With rare exceptions, Continental European antislavery lacked both a mass base and a supporting religious network. The established Catholic churches of southern Europe and their northern Protestant counterparts offered little institutional or ideological encouragement to abolitionists. Leaders of minuscule abolitionist movements were usually heavily dependent upon British political or financial support. Such support was frequently a source of nationalist resentment against Anglo-Protestant hegemony. Mass associations and public agitation were long illegal on the Continent and were rarely desired by abolitionist notables. With the exception of France's emancipation in 1794, engendered by the Haitian slave uprising, British initiatives rather than domestic movements occasioned Continental moves to restrict the slave trade and to form emancipation societies.

The special demographic conditions of New World plantations also played a major role in the abolition process. Except in the United States, plantation systems required a constant influx of African slaves for their maintenance and expansion. In all cases ending transatlantic African recruitment produced relative declines of slavery's economic significance. Even U.S. slavery could not match the growth of free labor after the abolition of the U.S. African slave trade in 1808.

Eliminating the flow of African slaves also hastened the process of creolization within each slave system. The trend toward native-born and acculturated slave populations expanded the possibilities of systemwide communication for collective resistance or flight. Mass Caribbean slave uprisings during the French Revolution were followed by less spectacular revolts or mass flights in Jamaica, prior to British emancipation, in the U.S. South during the Civil War, in the Cuban wars of independence, and finally in Brazil in 1887–1888. The most dramatic mass emancipations included those in the French Caribbean in 1793–1794 (ca. 600,000), the British Empire in

1834 (770,000), the United States in 1863–1865 (4,000,000), and Brazil in 1888 (750,000).

Abolition also encountered formidable opposition. Every slaveholding class in the Americas was linked to a powerful institutional complex in the free labor zones of the North Atlantic, involving established religious hierarchies, imperial military corps, and an imposing network of economic interests. The attack on the slave interest was frequently begun when slave-based production accounted for a significant share of the economic activity or wealth of the free labor zone. Slaveholders were usually able to invoke the inviolability of private property, sanctioned by law, to great effect. Except in the case of the first French emancipation, European-initiated abolition entailed an indemnity for slaveowners and/or a transitional system of labor obligations for the ex-slaves.

In some instances the planters possessed sufficient leverage to incorporate temporarily a recognition of slaveholding into the creation of the largest new nations in the Americas (Brazil and the United States). Anti-abolitionists also appealed to antipathy toward abolitionists on nationalist or religious grounds. Anti-black sentiment and racism offered potent ideological weapons with which to blunt abolitionism in the United States.

Given this countervailing power, emancipation proceeded along a variety of paths. In areas where chattel slavery was relatively less important, policies of gradual emancipation were most successful. From Pennsylvania in 1780 to New Jersey in 1804 the entire northern United States took steps to end slavery within their borders. In Spanish America the emancipation process extended over more than seven decades, beginning with Miguel Hidalgo's unsuccessful Mexican rebellion in 1810, and Simon Bolívar's liberation of Venezuelan slave recruits in 1816, to Spain's ending of Cuba's *patronato* system of apprenticeship in 1886. Massive slave flights were probably decisive in the final phase of Brazilian emancipation and of some significance in the case of the United States. Defeat by a superior military power was of crucial influence in forcing emancipation on the U.S. southern planters.

In Africa itself slavery continued to expand into the late 19th century, in response both to the ending of the transatlantic slave trade and to world economic expansion. In the mid-19th century there were probably more slaves in Africa than in the Americas, and toward the end of that century as much as one-half to two-thirds of the African population was enslaved. Increased European domination at the end of the century was accompanied by further slave emancipations, usually with considerable accommodation to the existing African social and political structure. In Central and Eastern Europe there was a parallel dismantling of serfdom from the late 18th century onward, culminating with the emancipations of the serfs in the Habsburg (1848–1853) and Russian empires (1861).

In plantation societies the existence of large areas of undeveloped arable land at the time of emancipation created serious problems of labor organization and replacement. Ex-slaves, especially women, frequently withdrew from field labor. Where no alternative labor force was available emancipation could entail stagnation or even a serious decline in production for export. Production levels recovered where replacement expedients were successful. These included the introduction of indentured Asian migrants into the Caribbean, subsidizing European migrations to Brazil and the movement of white farmers into cotton production in the postbellum South.

Just as forced labor seemed to be receding into insignificance in tropical agriculture, Eurasia itself became a major new zone of coerced labor in areas of Nazi and Soviet Communist domination. For a brief period in the early 1940s the uprooted and coerced labor force within Germany alone was greater in magnitude than the total slave population of the Americas a century before. By the 1970s the world was considered to be relatively free of legally sanctioned slavery. Although semi-clandestine forms of coercion such as debt bondage and child labor continued to be widespread, the pre-19th century preponderance of servile forms of labor had ended. (*See also* African Slave Trade; Emancipation of Serfs; Humanitarianism; Slavery)

Seymour Drescher

REFERENCES

Davis, David Brion. *Slavery and Human Progress.* New York: Oxford University Press, 1984.

Drescher, Seymour. *Capitalism and Antislavery: British Mobilization in Comparative Perspective*. New York: Oxford University Press, 1986.

Eltis, David. *Economic Growth and the Ending of the Transatlantic Slave Trade*. New York: Oxford University Press, 1987.

Fogel, Robert William. *Without Consent or Contract: The Rise and Fall of American Slavery*. New York: Norton, 1989.

———. *Technical Papers*, edited by Robert W. Fogel and Stanley L. Engerman. New York: Norton, 1992.

Genovese, Eugene D. *From Rebellion to Revolution: Afro-American Slave Revolts in the Making of the Modern World*. Baton Rouge: Louisiana State University Press, 1979.

Emancipation of Serfs

In medieval Europe central authority was relatively weak, because of the small tax base and the high transaction costs of governing distant lands in an underdeveloped economy. The low level of commercialization and the limited quantity of money in circulation had to be overcome in order to provide for defense, given a significant external threat. This complex problem was solved by delegating authority to local lords to tax and administer the peasants who lived on their estates.

To provide the lords a captive labor force, the peasants, as serfs, were denied freedom of movement. The tithe, a tax, was paid by the serfs in kind—a tenth of their gross produce to the lords and an additional tenth to the church. In addition, the serfs paid rents for the land they held by working on the demesne, the portion of the estate the lord kept for himself. For instance, in 19th-century Hungary the average serf paid annually about 26 days of labor service without, or 13 days with, animals for the right to cultivate about 5 hectares of land.

With the development of the European economies, and with the growth of state power, the need for the maintenance of this system diminished, inasmuch as it no longer minimized transaction costs. Rents and taxes were changed into monetary units. In northwestern Europe the system had waned or even died out for the most part by the end of the Middle Ages, though in many regions noble privileges persisted, in prerevolutionary France, for instance. In most other parts of Europe, particularly in eastern Europe, serfdom persisted in its original form well into the 19th century, and its end was more formal and abrupt. Emancipation replaced the system by granting the peasants property rights in the lands they cultivated and freedom of movement without the lord's permission. In turn, peasants paid taxes to a central government in lieu of their prior obligations, and politically, they came under state authority instead of that of the local lords. The lords were usually compensated for their lost income by both the peasants and the government (the latter often paid with bonds of various maturation dates). Land and labor thereby became freely tradeable commodities. In the Habsburg monarchy the emancipation took place in two steps: in 1781 the peasants were allowed to leave the estate, and in 1848 their service obligations to the lords were commuted. The last European countries to undergo such institutional transformation were Russia (1861) and Romania (1864). Russia's emancipation, in 1861, is one of the major developments in modern political and social history.

Social historians study emancipations in terms of causation—the mixture of peasant pressure, reassessments by nobles and the state, and shifts in economic structure that prompt such a fundamental change in labor systems. They also examine the often ambiguous results of emancipation, which see some peasants often more burdened by land hunger and high taxes than under serfdom.

John Komlos

REFERENCES

Blum, Jerome. *The End of the Old Order in Rural Europe*. Princeton, NJ: Princeton University Press, 1978.

Komlos, John. *The Habsburg Monarchy as a Customs Union: Economic Development in Austria-Hungary in the Nineteenth Century*. Princeton, NJ: Princeton University Press, 1983.

North, Douglass. *Structure and Change in Economic History*. New York: Norton, 1981.

Embourgeoisement

"Embourgeoisement" is a term of essentially Marxist provenance, indicating the process by which a group or class comes to resemble in outlook and behavior the bourgeoisie. It has been applied primarily to the working class, though it has also been used to describe the aristocracy or the peasantry. The concept is premised on the notion that classes exist, hold relatively consistent and distinct outlooks, and display characteristic forms of behavior. Each of these assumptions can be challenged, and recent scholarship has tended to avoid overly deterministic uses. Still, there would seem to be sufficient evidence from diverse societies and different eras to suggest some validity to the notion and its value as a rough guide to what to expect from people who share similar social locations.

The theory of embourgeoisement has been deployed more specifically to explain how and why people who are not themselves bourgeois nevertheless come at various times to exhibit values and behaviors considered bourgeois. It is, of course, no simple matter to specify what is typically bourgeois, but most social historians would probably agree that the bourgeoisie—or, in Freidrich Engels's phrase, the "class of great capitalists"—is more likely than other groups to hold to an ethos of individualism; to believe in the virtues of competition, hard work, self-denial, piety, respectability, and the nuclear family; and to give allegiance to parties that espouse these values and are committed to such classically bourgeois shibboleths as laissez-faire, free trade, frugal government, and the career open to talent (meritocracy). In fact, none of these ideas has been the exclusive property of the bourgeoisie. It is a commonplace, for example, that the landed classes in England were engaged in commercial agriculture long before the rise of manufacturing industry in the 18th century, and in their pursuit of profits acted thoroughly bourgeois. Likewise, peasants have frequently shown themselves as capable of calculating their self-interest—and acting upon it—as any middle-class devotee of the liberal economist Adam Smith. Hence the occasional use of the term to explain such cases.

It is, however, when the industrial working class expresses bourgeois beliefs or supports bourgeois politics that scholars are most likely to employ the concept of embourgeoisement. The reason is that bourgeois behavior on the part of workers runs so counter to what is regarded as the proper or expected pattern. Marxists, for example, feel that workers not only have an interest in rejecting bourgeois values and behaviors but also that the circumstances of their daily lives encourage more collectivist views and practices. Many non-Marxist social scientists hold comparable views. Workers have often disappointed these expectations, prompting the search for an explanation. Many possible explanations have been preferred—for example, false consciousness (Lukacs), bourgeois hegemony in the sphere of ideology or in the institutions of civil society (Gramsci), or embourgeoisement. The process of embourgeoisement, in this use, is a way of linking these cultural and political facts to changes in economy and social structure. The most important social changes are the steady increases in material well-being that have occurred for all or part of the working class and the parallel transformations in occupational structure—in particular, the growth of white-collar jobs and the shift from manufacturing to services—that have blurred the stark contrasts between bourgeois and proletarian typical of the early stages of industrialization. Scholars are far from agreement on the extent or even the direction of these changes, and they are more ambivalent still on their political and cultural consequences. Nevertheless, there is a growing consensus that changes in living standards and class structure in the advanced societies in recent years have made it ever more likely that workers will act and think in ways that were once considered anomalous and for which the label "bourgeois" is not unreasonable.

James E. Cronin

REFERENCES

Giddens, Anthony. *The Class Structure of the Advanced Societies*. London: Hutchinson, 1973.

Goldthorpe, John, et al. *The Affluent Worker in the Class Structure*. Cambridge: Cambridge University Press, 1969.

Jacques, Martin, and Francis Mulhern, eds. *The Forward March of Labour Halted?* London: New Left Books, 1981.

Wright, Erik. *Classes*. London: Verso, 1985.

Emotion (Emotionology)

The focus of social historical research on emotion is straightforward: it deals with changes in emotional standards and experience and the interaction between emotion and other shifts in historical context. Social historians and sociologists dealing with emotions have conclusively demonstrated that emotional reactions can change in significant ways, in response to new cultural climates (such as the advent of Protestantism) and new economic frameworks. Change in demography, similarly, can generate and express new emotional expectations; substantial reductions in average birthrates often produce or result from new emotional attachments to individual children, as in the United States and western Europe around 1800.

Explicit historical research on emotion is relatively recent, though the great French social history pioneer Lucien Febvre called early on for a "historical psychology" that would "give up psychological anachronism" and "establish a detailed inventory of the mental equipment of the time." Many social historians were long bent on dealing with lower-class groups as rational actors, in protest situations, for example, which prompted them to shy away from emotional ingredients. Growing interest in family history, however, ultimately stimulated attention to the emotional components of family relationships. Similarly, work on mentalities or popular belief systems, encouraged attention to rituals and other evidence that expressed emotional impulses and were susceptible to change. Interest in psychohistory, though mainly focused on individual biography and based in Freudian theory, could generate attention to collective emotional standards and a less rigid theoretical framework.

In various ways, analysis of emotional change and its impact had become an inescapable challenge in social history. Historians dealing with the Western family in the 18th century pointed to new emphasis on love and affection in courtship and between parents and children, and a new hostility to anger within the family. Mentalities historians argued that elites attempted to reduce popular emotional spontaneity in festivals and other manifestations, during the 17th and 18th centuries in western Europe. One French historian also pointed to a marked decline of fear of the outside world by the 18th century, accompanied by a reduction of the use of fear in child rearing. Finally, several social historians and sociologists revived the work of Norbert Elias who had argued for a growing "civilized" restraint in habits and manners in the 18th century, beginning with the western European upper classes, that urged new control over physical outbursts, such as spitting and nose-wiping, and over emotional outbursts as well.

During the 1980s, an explicit social history field dealing with emotions and emotional change emerged. The social history of emotions continued to point to significant change, though not always in such stark terms as earlier statements had implied. New forms of love did indeed emerge in the 18th century, involving greater privacy, more romance, and less robust physicality, but earlier western European families had expressed love concerns as well. Many social historians urged distinctions between "emotionology"—the standards promoted within a society or group concerning good and bad emotions and how to express each category suitably—and actual emotional experience. Emotionological change affects emotional experience and also laws and other institutional arrangements that depend on emotional standards. Emphasis on marital love, for example, helped generate mental cruelty as legal grounds for divorce in the 19th-century United States. Changes in actual emotional life can also be traced: strong prohibitions on expressions of anger as "unfeminine" among middle-class women in the 19th century help account for psychological disorders such as paralytic hysteria and anorexia nervosa, which allowed women to sublimate their anger without becoming overtly unfeminine. Real emotional change is, however, more difficult to probe, and it may occur less frequently and less completely (given, among other factors, unchanging biological components of emotional response) than shifts in emotionology.

Sociohistorical research on emotion has been applied to premodern Europe, including eastern Europe, and to China, while work by anthropologists on other emotional cultures, such as that of Tahiti, sometimes includes a solid historical component. The richest literature on emotions history continues to apply to modern history in western Europe and the United States. It covers a wide variety of emotions, including grief, jealousy, shame, and guilt as well as anger, love, and fear. Focused particularly on middle- and upper-class experience, emotions history works increasingly to deal with lower-class standards and experience as well. Evidence from prescriptive literature, diaries, and autobiographies increasingly combines with ethnographic sources, including accounts of ritual, as the basis for this branch of social history. Substantial interchange of research findings and of theoretical formulations between social historians and sociologists enlivens the field considerably. More than some other disciplines concerned with emotions research, social historians pay substantial attention to the causes of emotional and emotionological patterns and to the results of new emotional contexts, in behaviors ranging from family to law to social protest.

Three periods of European and American history concentrate the most extensive findings in the social history of emotions thus far. The idea of a fundamental emotionological transformation in the 17th and 18th centuries continues to apply. In addition to redefining love and developing new concern about anger—the word "tantrum" was coined in English to delineate unacceptable, childish outbursts—this early modern transition involved growing disapproval of sadness or melancholia, which had been traditionally accepted as an appropriate sign of humility. Emphasis on guilt began to replace primary reliance on shame as a disciplinary tool, both for children and for criminal offenders. New kinds of disgust, particularly directed against offensive odors, added to the emotional experience in another respect.

During the 19th century this new emotional framework was elaborated, disseminated to some new social groups, but also adjusted to the increasingly industrial, urban context. Love between man and woman became virtually a religious ideal, involving self-abnegation and worshipful devotion. In other areas gender features were emphasized, to suit the new division between men's and women's roles. While anger was unfeminine, American men were urged to channel anger toward competition and social reform. Another new word, "sissy," came to denote men who could not muster up aggressiveness or control fear.

Innovation in the 20th century has been formulated in two overlapping ways (in addition to a simple modernization formula, used in the past by some sociologists, that interpreted the 20th century simply in terms of increasingly free individual expressiveness; this formula is now discredited). One approach sees 20th-century standards in terms of growing spontaneity and informality, as against the controls stressed during the previous centuries, but against a backdrop of careful management. Restraint of violence and unwanted sexuality has been widely internalized by this point, according to this interpretation, which in turn allows some informal emotional idiosyncrasy. It is permissible to talk about being angry, for example, without expecting some massive explosion to follow. The second interpretation focuses on a new division between negative and positive emotions, associated with the consumerist mentality and the "people skills" required in a managerial and service economy. Manipulation of emotion, by encouraging people to talk out unacceptable feelings and by providing symbolic outlets for violence and excitement through spectator sports, films, and popular concerts, gains new sophistication. Intense emotion is downplayed. Thus, in the 19th century, as a function of deep love, grief was widely indulged and won elaborate expression through lavish funerals and cemetery monuments plus extensive mourning. In the 20th century the acceptability of grief diminished, and its intensity was often concealed.

As a new field, emotions history raises many unresolved questions. The need to develop the field in a wider range of cultures, subcultures, and time periods is obvious and increasingly recognized. Debates about causation need further attention. Some emotions historians, and sociological theories, emphasize a functional approach, that sees emotional change as the result of shifts in economic or organizational context, while others urge fuller recognition of cultural factors such as religion. The timing of change raises problems. Many of the redefinitions of emotionology that have been explored clearly extend over many decades, with results such as new laws or new institutional arrangements often coming far later than might be expected; but there are as yet no convincing theoretical formulations in this area.

The same open-endedness, however, makes the history of emotions an exciting field. It has added important dimensions to social history, and it has contributed a vital new vantage point to other social research on emotion. The social history of emotions adds complexity to the study of emotion by introducing the factor of change as a central ingredient. It also provides many of the tools necessary to deal with the issue of change and to use it toward fuller understanding of the ways emotions develop and function. (*See also* Family; Mentalities; Prescriptive Literature)

Peter N. Stearns

REFERENCES

Corbin, Alain. *The Foul and the Fragrant: Odor and the French Imagination.* Cambridge: Harvard University Press, 1986.

Gillis, John. *For Better, For Worse: British Marriages, 1600 to the Present.* New York: Oxford University Press, 1985.

Lystra, Karen. *Searching the Heart: Women, Men and Romantic Love in Nineteenth-Century America.* New York: Oxford University Press, 1989.

Stearns, Carol Z., and Peter N. Stearns, eds. *Emotion and Social Change: Toward a New Psychohistory.* New York: Holmes and Meier, 1988.

Stearns, Peter N. *Jealousy: The Evolution of an Emotion in American History.* New York: New York University Press, 1989.

Enclosure

See Land Tenure and Reform

English Revolution and Civil War

The English Revolution and Civil War are the names given to a sequence of conflicts which spanned the years 1640 to 1649. Those events were unprecedented for three reasons. First, while many European monarchs had been overthrown and killed, in all previous instances (except for geographically small city-states) they had been succeeded by other hereditary rulers. English King Charles I was replaced for more than a decade by a republican government. Second, all previous rebellions against European kings had been mounted by either noble pretenders to the throne, aggrieved peasants, or foreign powers. The principal challengers to the Crown during the Revolution and Civil War were wealthy London merchants, gentry and yeomen commercial farmers, small merchants, and artisans. These social groups became decisive agents of national political change for the first time during the English Civil War. Third, the ideology of the newly active social groups was Puritan. Their victory over the Crown made a procapitalist, rationalist, and scientist Protestant ethic the dominant mode of thought in England, while the egalitarian and republican ideology of a radical minority of the Puritans (the Levellers) gained an enduring place in the discourse of English politics and religion.

Social historians have been concerned with understanding why members of different social groups supported the Royalist and/or Parliamentary sides during the various phases of conflict, and with tracing shifts in the ideological orientations of factions on each side and their relationship to wider social beliefs. As with other revolutions, social historians have moved away from political narrative and primarily political causation in dealing with the Civil War. A principal reason for the lack of consensus among historians is that the bases of conflict changed over time, and therefore, the factors accounting for divisions within the body politic changed as well. Continued debate includes a recent renewal of essentially political stories that dispute the analytic approach of social history.

The Revolution began as a broad-based elite-led challenge to a monarch who sought to reassert ancient royal privileges against elites whose wealth had come to be based upon landownership and commercial activity rather than feudal office and royal patronage. The enduring achievements of the Parliamentary side were those which were endorsed by this broad elite coalition: (1) the abolition of feudal privileges, the guarantee of property rights (including rights to former royal and monastic lands) and broad access to markets; (2) Parliamentary primacy over state finances, including taxes to finance the military in peace and war; and (3) religious freedom and pluralism alongside a state-sponsored Church of England.

The coalition splintered over the demands of Levellers on the Parliamentary side, mainly yeomen and artisans, for a broadened franchise, redistribution of land, and other egalitarian measures. The allegiances of nonelites and of the emergent London capitalists can be understood in class terms. The complex divisions among rural gentry are not amenable to a class analysis. Gentry and aristocratic loyalties were consequences of long-standing patronage links within counties and to the Crown, and of more recent loyalties to religious factions (Catholic, Anglican, or Puritan) cemented by control over clerical offices in localities.

The radicals' main base of power was in the New Model Army, the force created by Oliver Cromwell to counter the armed forces under the control of the king and those aristocrats who had returned to his side in the Civil War in an effort to block some of the Parliamentary reforms. Ultimately, the interests of London merchants and rural gentry proved decisive. Most of them supported the Parliamentary side, providing the financial backing crucial to the New Model Army's victories, but then allied with the surviving great landowners in England and Scotland to form a government capable of resisting further radical demands and eventually disbanding the popular army. A limited monarchy was restored in 1660, which respected the power of a Parliament elected by wealthy landowners and urban merchants secure in their property rights and in their access to markets.

Richard Lachmann

REFERENCES

Hill, Christopher. *The World Turned Upside Down.* Harmondsworth, Eng.: Penguin, 1975.

Hunt, William. *The Puritan Moment.* Cambridge: Harvard University Press, 1983.

Stone, Lawrence. "The English Revolution," in Robert Forster and Jack P. Greene, eds., *Preconditions of Revolution in Early Modern Europe.* Baltimore: Johns Hopkins University Press, 1970, pp. 55–108.

Environment

It is only recently that historians have begun to study the relationship between social and environmental change. Although an interest in the environment can be traced back as far as the work of Frederick Jackson Turner and other his-

torians, most notably Walter Prescott Webb and James Malin, it was not until the 1970s that scholars began exploring the social history of human relations with nature. Much of this present interest can in turn be traced to the emergence of environmental history.

Environmental history is an interdisciplinary field of study that combines aspects of social history, ecology, historical geography, and ecological anthropology. Social history, in particular, has exerted a very strong influence on the field. The historians of the *Annales* school in France, people such as Marc Bloch, Lucien Febvre, and Fernand Braudel, for example, showed an interest in the role of the environment in history. Braudel's monumental work on the Mediterranean begins with a detailed consideration of the way the environment—the region's land and water—worked as a backdrop to long-term historical change. Emmanuel Le Roy Ladurie's *Times of Feast, Times of Famine* (1967) explores the history of climate, and his classic work *The Peasants of Languedoc* (1966) has an important concern with agriculture and land use.

Building on such work and insights from other disciplines, environmental historians have explored the relationship between social and ecological change. Their concern has been with the place of nature in the historical process, with understanding how the natural world has influenced and shaped history. Thus, they have focused in particular on the environmental consequences of historical change. But it is rare that ecological change itself does not have important social and cultural impact. Analyzing the interrelated effects of ecological and social transformation is thus a main concern for environmental historians.

Social historians have had a long-standing concern with the struggles in the workplace, the family, and the church, to mention just a few examples. But until recently there has been little consideration of the conflict over nature, a point that some environmental historians have been trying to address.

The European colonization of North America has been an important area of study in this regard. Alfred Crosby's *The Columbian Exchange* (1972) explores the biological consequences of Columbus's fabled journey to North America, detailing the important changes in fauna, flora, and disease patterns that resulted from European colonization. William Cronon's *Changes in the Land* (1983) and Carolyn Merchant's *Ecological Revolutions* (1989) have traced the story of European settlement through the colonial period. Focusing on New England, both Cronon and Merchant examine the important ecological shifts that accompanied European settlement of the continent. The economic culture of capitalism that the colonists brought with them—founded on markets and private property—completely transformed New England's ecology, reworking the landscape and destroying what remained of Native American culture.

The conflict between Native Americans and whites over the environment did not end with the colonial period. As white settlers pushed their way across North America, they undermined Native American subsistence patterns, restructuring the Indians' relationship with the land. That point is driven home in Richard White's *Roots of Dependency* (1983), which traces Indian and white struggles over land use in the 19th and 20th centuries. Capitalism ultimately conquered the Native Americans by destabilizing their relationship with the natural world and making it impossible for them to survive on the land.

That same capitalist economic culture also proved destabilizing for the whites themselves as Donald Worster shows in his book *Dust Bowl* (1979). In Worster's view, the dust storms of the 1930s were not the product of drought or technological failure, but of the capitalist will to subdue both people and nature. Worster's book, now a classic in environmental history, was one of the earliest efforts to examine how culture and nature came together in history. It has thus had enormous influence for those concerned with studying the social history of human relations with nature.

As capitalism evolved along industrial lines, with its emphasis on wage labor and its more insistent demands on nature, the ecological consequences became even more apparent. A number of historians have explored the role of water in industrial and urban growth, notably Joel Tarr, who has examined the shifting impact of sewage disposal in American cities, and Jean-Pierre Goubert, who has explored the place of water in French urban development during the 19th century. Theodore Steinberg's *Nature Incorporated* (1991) looks at New England's industrial revolution from an ecological perspective, focusing on the struggle to control and master water.

Indeed water has remained an important focus for environmental historians. As a common resource not easily privatized and owned, water has emerged as a particular source of conflict and struggle. In *Rivers of Empire* (1985), Donald Worster examines how the effort to control water in the American West has resulted in ecological devastation and the concentration of power in the hands of a corporate elite, as dedicated to dominating nature as it was to dominating people. Of related interest is Arthur McEvoy's *The Fisherman's Problem* (1986), which looks at the history of California's fisheries, exploring the relationship between nature, law, and economics.

Environmental history is still in its early stages as a field of study. A number of extensive environmental histories, dealing with various parts of the world, are currently in preparation. But thus far, the field has had some important insights to offer social historians, particularly in focusing their attention on the interaction between nature and society. At the very least, the work produced suggests that the attempt to control nature does not benefit everyone equally and that social history both informs, and profits from, an understanding of environmental change in the past. (*See also Annales* School; Colonialism; Environmentalism)

Theodore Steinberg

REFERENCES

Steinberg, Theodore. *Nature Incorporated*. New York: Cambridge University Press, 1991.

White, Richard. "American Environmental History: The Development of a New Historical Field," *Pacific Historical Review* 54 (1985): 297–335.

Worster, Donald, ed. *The Ends of the Earth*. New York: Cambridge University Press, 1988.

Worster, Donald. "History as Natural History: An Essay on Theory and Method," *Pacific Historical Review* 53 (1984): 1–19.

Environmentalism

Environmentalism is both an intellectual tradition arising in the 19th century and a popular movement of the 20th. As an intellectual tradition it seeks to situate human experience in its fullest global context. As a popular movement it aims to preserve, protect, and, in places, restore nature, and to limit the degradation that human actions bring to water, air, soils, and living things.

As an intellectual tradition it has flourished most conspicuously in Europe and North America, where it brought together ideas from the science of ecology (which emerged in Europe, particularly Germany) in the mid- to late 19th century and ideas from the field of energy economics, which emerged in the United States. These currents fused around 1970, and drew strength from concern generated by mounting ecological difficulties, ranging from local pollution to global population growth. Environmentalism acquired global focus in the 1970s; prior exponents generally had local or national concerns, sometimes associated with agendas that were frankly nationalist or autarkic in nature.

As a popular movement, environmentalism became significant only in the late 1960s. In the Western world it emerged as part of the general cultural criticism of the 1960s and early 1970s, although it has outlasted most of the other movements with which it was once associated. It acquired a following in North America, Western Europe, and Japan, where several prominent legal cases arose from lethal toxic pollution incidents between 1965 and 1975. The most famous, a methyl mercury poisoning episode, known as Minimata disease after the town where it happened, sparked one of the more successful grass-roots movements in Japanese political history. In Western Europe and North America environmentalism attracted followers concerned about pollution problems, about the energy shortage of 1973-1974, and additionally about global concerns such as population pressure, made vivid by famines in the African Sahel that were often interpreted in newspapers and on television as consequences of overpopulation.

In Europe, environmentalism became an explicitly political movement in many countries, most notably West Germany, with the creation and modest electoral success of "green" parties. Their fullest success came when the established mainstream parties found it necessary to appropriate much of the agenda from the greens in order to protect their electoral positions. Thus, green politics became mainstream politics in Germany, Scandinavia, Britain, and elsewhere. Normally, rhetoric has exceeded commitment, however.

Outside of the richer parts of the world environmentalism made little headway, as most accepted the view that ecological degradation was a necessary and acceptable price for economic expansion. This view began to change in the 1980s, as the agenda of environmentalism became more global. Environmental movements grew in Brazil, in Kenya, in India, and elsewhere in the tropical world, spurred by local and global concerns. In Eastern Europe and Russia environmental protests became commonplace by the mid-1980s, driven by dissatisfaction with extreme levels of air and water pollution, and played a role in the demise of communism there. Meanwhile, in the West and Japan environmentalism has tilted toward global issues, including deforestation, depletion of the ozone layer, and the possibility of rapid human-induced climate change. To date the effect of environmentalism as a popular movement has been notable chiefly on industrial pollution; governments have found it prudent to finance cleanups and regulate pollution.

Historical studies of environmentalism are not overabundant and tend to focus on institutional and intellectual more than social history. The surge of environmental protest as a serious social movement and the decline of some other forms of modern protest, however, invites sociohistorical assessment as part of contemporary, international social history.

John R. McNeill

REFERENCES

Bramwell, Anna. *Ecology in the Twentieth Century.* New Haven: Yale University Press, 1989.

McKean, Margaret A. *Environmental Protest and Citizen Politics in Japan.* Berkeley: University of California Press, 1981.

Pepper, David. *The Roots of Modern Environmentalism.* New York: Routledge, Chapman & Hall 1986.

Estate Agriculture

Agricultural production on more or less large landed properties first existed in the ancient world, was a dominant feature of medieval and early modern Europe, and has played a major role in the colonial and postcolonial lands of Asia, Africa, and Latin America. Estate agriculture has historically shared much in common with the family farm, but can be distinguished from the latter in several ways. Unlike the family farm, which draws primarily on family labor (plus hired hands), the landed estate has generally operated on a larger scale; the estate owner and his family do not work the land directly, but depend instead on labor drawn primarily from an indigenous peasantry that has often been dependent on, and subordinate to, the estate owner.

This dependence and subordination have taken many forms. The manorial system in Europe, for example, rested in large part on customary or statutory laws that subordinated the peasant tenants to the lord of the manor. In late 19th-century Indonesia (to cite a very different case), the imposition of a system in which many Indonesian peasants had to work part of the year on Dutch-owned estates, was the direct result of colonial domination. In some cases, like the great estates (*Latifundia*) in southern Italy in the late 19th century, subordination of the estate labor force rested on a less formal system that mixed paternalism, violence, and the desperate economic dependence of the rural labor force. Whatever the specific mechanisms of subordination, however, the position of the estate was the same—it symbolized the social and political dominance of the estate-owning elite, while providing the latter with much of its livelihood.

This elite has varied immensely; in medieval and early modern Europe, for example, most of the estates were owned either by the nobility or by religious foundations (monasteries and bishoprics). In the colonial world of the 19th and early 20th centuries, estates might belong to European colonists, or they might belong to the colonial government. In the postcolonial period, many estates have passed into the hands of indigenous elites or corporations. Despite these variations, all estate owners have had one thing in common—their income depended largely on the agricultural wealth produced on their estates by the estate labor force.

The incomes derived from estate agriculture (whether in cash or kind) have depended in turn on two basic factors: first, the specific crops or goods produced on the estate, and, second, the organization and control of the labor force. The types of agricultural goods produced on landed estates have varied immensely, with climate, land, and market conditions the decisive factors. In medieval and early modern Europe, household consumption needs of the estate owners themselves have also helped determine the choice of crops and goods produced.

We see all these factors at work on Elton, a 13th century English manor belonging to Ramsey Abbey. The main cereals grown on Elton manor were barley, wheat, and oats; these three, along with rye, were the staples that did best in the damp, temperate lands of northwestern Europe, where their cultivation was usually combined with dairy farming. On Elton, large quantities of butter and cheese were also produced. Most cereal and dairy products went for the consumption needs of the clerical and lay inhabitants of Ramsey Abbey, although part of the butter was sold on the market.

Such diversified estate agriculture was typical of the medieval manor, since the market economy was still relatively primitive, and most production went for the direct consumption of the estate owner's household. In eastern Europe, however, where a market-oriented estate agriculture arose in the 16th century and flourished well into the 19th, estate agriculture tended toward greater specialization: many 17th-century Hungarian estates, for example, specialized in cattle, while estate agriculture in Poland specialized in rye and wheat. This tendency to specialization should not be exaggerated, however. Throughout eastern Europe there were estates with a highly diversified agricultural production that often supported estate-owned industries like glassmaking, distilling, and textile production. This was especially true in the Czech lands of Bohemia and Moravia, where fisheries and beer brewing often provided the estate owner with much of his revenue. The major difference between medieval manors in western Europe and landed estates in early modern eastern Europe lies in the fact that the latter were much more oriented toward production for the market.

Organization and control of the labor force, the second major factor in estate agriculture, is a more complex problem, and has been of major interest for social historians. Estate agriculture has depended on a mix of free and unfree (forced) labor. The classic type of unfree laborer was the peasant tenant who held a small farm from the estate owner, for which he had to work a specified number of days on the latter's estate. The classic free laborer was landless, or semilandless, and worked on the estate as a hired hand or day laborer. In practice, however, labor organization was much more complex, and the distinction between free and unfree labor was often blurred. In eastern Europe, for example, in the early modern period, peasant tenants on noble estates were, to a greater or lesser extent, unfree, and had to provide heavy labor services on their lords' estates. Often, however, the tenant did not personally work on the estate, but sent his own hired hands to do the work. On the same estates, moreover, there were often free laborers who worked, not for cash wages, but for a small allotment of land. In both cases, free and unfree labor were intermingled in a complex system of land tenure and labor organization. In the contemporary world, where estate agriculture is largely confined to lands and countries in the postcolonial world, these complexities remain, despite the growing importance of wage labor.

Historians and social scientists are currently engaged in a lively debate over the social, economic, and political implications of estate agriculture. At issue is the role of estate agriculture in social and economic development. Many scholars have argued that estate agriculture, whether in the European or colonial context, encourages (if it does not require) social, economic, and technological backwardness. These scholars also suggest that such backwardness is difficult, if not impossible, to overcome because the estate-owning elite usually enjoys political power as well. While this is the dominant interpretation of estate agriculture, it has been challenged by research showing that estate agriculture has often played a progressive—and pioneering—role in the economic development of lands and regions in England, Russia, eastern Europe, and southern Italy, to cite only a few of the areas that are currently the subject of such research. (*See also* Corvée Labor; *Haciendas/Encomiendas;* Land Tenure and Reform)

Edgar Melton

REFERENCES

Duby, Georges. *Rural Economy and Country Life in the Medieval West.* Columbia: University of South Carolina Press, 1968.

Geertz, Clifford. *Agricultural Involution. The Processes of Technological Change in Indonesia.* Berkeley: University of California Press, 1963.

Gies, Francis and Joseph. *Life in a Medieval Village.* New York: Harper Collins, 1990.

Hoch, Steven. *Serfdom and Social Control.* Chicago: University of Chicago Press, 1986.

Melton, Edgar. "Gutsherrschaft in East Elbian Germany and Livonia, 1500–1800," *Central European History* 21 (December 1988): 315–349.

Ethnicity

The immense diversity and vitality of ethnic groups and processes in the contemporary world preclude a comprehensive treatment here of the multiple and complex problems of studying ethnicity. This overview of different conceptualizations of ethnicity is, therefore, by design highly selective and limited to what can serve the more immediate research interests of American readers. Namely, it focuses primarily on the major approaches used by historians and sociologists studying the incorporation of ethnic groups into Western urban-industrial societies in the modern era and, specifically, the adaptation of immigrants and their offspring in the United States. Not surprisingly, ethnicity has been a dominant analytical category in American social history, often eclipsing social class.

From the European Enlightenment until recently, the prevailing view of social theorists was that modern society promotes universalist, encompassing bases of social integration and senses of identity generated primarily by individual accomplishments, as opposed to particularistic, divisive kinds of solidarity based on localism, religion, or ethnic origin and the collective identities derived therefrom. In the United States, on the basis of the same underlying vision of general societal modernization, combined with a notion of American exceptionalism, the dominant interpretation in American historiography and social-scientific theories as well as nationalist ideology, was for a long time that of assimilation—that is, of the progressive weakening and ultimate disappearance of the ethnic attachments and distinct characteristics as succeeding generations adopt the general society's unitary system of cultural values and become absorbed into economic, social, and political networks that are blind to ethnicity. Consequently, the major concern of students of ethnicity and ethnic groups was the degree of compatibility the sidestream ethnocultures and social patterns the mainstream—in the U.S. case, American, or dominant Anglo-Protestant, rather—equivalents.

Over the past two and a half decades, social-historical studies of ethnically plural urban-industrial societies have called into question both the theoretical assumptions of the straight-line assimilation paradigm and the resulting agenda for empirical research. Scholars, particularly in the United States, where the problematic of immigration and ethnicity has naturally always attracted considerable attention, have increasingly emphasized the determination with which immigrants and their descendants supported their communities against dissolution into all-Americanist, and the often stubborn persistence, or even intensification, of distinctive ethnic identities and group cultural practices.

In a somewhat differently conceptualized critique of the conventional assimilation model, several studies have argued that, while enduring, these traditional Old World cultures and social arrangements do not remain unchanged. Rather, as immigrants and their children are increasingly incorporated over time into the different realms of the larger American society, the Old and New (American) World self-conceptions, cultural outlooks, pursuits of life goals, and forms of social interaction become mixed, blended, or brought to coexistence in complex, often contradictory patterns. This process of combination has been called *ethnicization*, and the people and communities emerging in the course thereof are called *ethnic* American.

As the straight-line assimilation model has been abandoned in view of the unexpected persistence and vitality of ethnicity as a source of group identity and solidarity demonstrated by the rise of ethnic movements in the United States and throughout the world, from the 1970s on ethnicity has become a key concept in the social-historical analyses of processes of adaptation to the dominant society of immigrants and their descendants. As a result, an enormous amount of research and writing followed on the nature of ethnicity as a form of peoples' collective existence and an important aspect of their self-consciousness.

Two basic understandings of ethnicity can be distinguished in Western social sciences, each of which can be conceptualized as a form of protest against or adjustment to the dominant culture and society. One, originally derived from the Greeks, presumes ethnic identity and commitment to be (1) inherent in group membership and shared cultural traditions (such as language and collective memory of common ancestry, religion and other values, social norms, and customary behavioral patterns); and (2) experienced primarily affectively as a primordial attachment, expressing a natural, instinctive almost human need for belonging.

The other conception of ethnicity originated in opposition to the primordialist interpretation, which was criticized for a static view of social relationships and an inability to account for cultural change. This alternative approach, known as circumstantialism, gained popularity among students of ethnicity during the 1970s, and has since undergone significant transformations. Basically, in this conception ethnic identity and group solidarity are seen not as givens but as acquired or resulting from historical configurations of social circumstances, both inside and outside the ethnic groups in question. Variants of this general approach differ from each other by the causal importance ascribed to human agency and, in consequence, the place granted to cultural mediation and voluntarism in the explanations of social becoming of ethnicity.

The earliest and most emphatically structuralist—probably as an (over)reaction to the then dominant primordialist paradigm, but more fundamentally as a reflection of a general, *marxisant* perspective on the social world shared by many Western social scientists in that period—was a conception of so-called emergent ethnicity. The term referred to the development of group ethnic institutions and a shared sense of belonging as the result, to take the United States as an illustration, of the combined effects of social-structural conditions such as residential proximity, occupational concentration, and mutual economic dependence of the immigrants.

Also derived from social circumstances rather than natural impulse, but focused on the effects of purposeful human actions generated by these conditions rather than on those structural opportunities alone, has been the notion of ethnicity as a means of mobilizing a particular group behind issues relevant to its collective interests, particularly those related to its socioeconomic position and political influence in the larger society (this approach is also called "instrumentalist" or "mobilizationist").

Another conception in the same general category of contextual rather than primordialist interpretations has emphasized even more strongly the voluntaristic element in the emergence of ethnicity or, more accurately, granted a more autonomous, and causally significant, role in this process to human agency. This is the notion of so-called situational or optional ethnicity, whereby the emergence of ethnic identity and group solidarity are seen as the outcome of individual or collective choices made toward instrumental and/or expressive or affective purposes. M. Hansen's early (1938) conception of the third generation's "return to ethnicity," and H. Gans's more recent (1979) conception of "symbolic ethnicity," both designed to account for the voluntary and subjective nature of ethnic identity and cultural participation among later generations of American descendants of the immigrants, are based on premises similar to those informing the circumstantial-optional view. A more recently formulated conceptualization, currently quite popular among students of ethnic processes in the United States and western Europe, of ethnicity as a continuous cultural construction or (re)invention accomplished over time by participating actors can, too, be seen as a variant of a circumstantialist approach to ethnic phenomena. Lastly, some recent efforts should be mentioned—in this author's opinion the most promising for future theory-building and research in the field of ethnic studies—at bringing together different conceptions and interpretative frameworks relating to the meanings and expressions of ethnicity, and its psychological, cultural, and social correlates. And so, on the one hand, there have recently appeared in sociohistorical analyses of the phenomenon of ethnicity attempts at combining elements from different approaches—primordialist as well as circumstantialist, both structural and agentic. Such a theoretical "synthesis," as some of its advocates have called their approach, allows for flexible and dialectical interpretations of ethnic phenomena, contingent on historical contexts.

A similar reconciliation—rather than "synthetic," "historical" seems a more apt label for the underlying methodological directive that postulates the treatment of all social phenomena as inherently time- and place-specific—was also recently proposed between the ethnicization and assimilation models. It is not, according to this view, that assimilation has not been taking place. On the contrary, there exists solid empirical evidence of this process in several areas of life: residential (decreasing residential segregation), social (increased intergroup contacts, including intermarriage), cultural (both in outward behavior such as language and customs, and in values and attitudes), and psychological (identification with American national symbols and a sense of civic-political membership). The reason why the classical assimilation theory of linear progression toward a common American amalgamate of lifestyles has proven inadequate is that it was precisely what it was originally designed to be—simple and general. In order, then, to make bridging between the ethnicization and the assimilation models possible, ways must be found to historicize the latter and thus make it usable for dialectical analyses of flexible, and changeable, ethnicities. (*See also* Assimilation/Acculturation)

Ewa Morawska

REFERENCES

Gans, Herbert. "Symbolic Ethnicity: The Future of Ethnic Groups and Cultures in America," in H. Gans et al., eds., *On the Making of Americans: Essays in Honor of David Riesman.* Philadelphia: University of Pennsylvania Press, 1979.

Sarna, Jonathan. "From Immigrants to Ethnics: Toward a New Theory of 'Ethnicization,'" *Ethnicity* 5 (1978): 370–378.

Scott, George. "A Resynthesis of the Primordial and Circumstantial Approaches to Ethnic Group Solidarity: Towards an Explanatory Model," *Ethnic and Racial Studies* 13 (April 1990): 147–171.

Smith, Anthony. *The Ethnic Revival in the Modern World*. Cambridge: Cambridge University Press, 1981.

Thompson, Richard. *Theories of Ethnicity. A Critical Appraisal.* New York: Greenwood Press, 1989.

Yancey, William, et al. "Emergent Ethnicity: A Review and Reformulation," *American Sociological Review* 41 (June 1976): 391–402.

Ethnography/Ethnohistory

Ethnography, or the study of a people, is the primary research strategy of anthropology and the provider of its data and wellspring of its theory. This definition raises fundamental issues concerning the nature of social science observation and the role of critical theory. What is the purpose of ethnographic research? How and by whom is the research conducted? Whose truths are being conveyed and under what authority?

Ethnography, participant observation plus census and hard data collection, was early perceived as a corrective to the distortions and biases implicit in the highly ethnocentric reporting of the lifeways, customs, and beliefs of non-Western societies provided by missionaries, explorers, government agents, and so on. This issue of data reliability within the context of radical change among the so-called primitives as they experienced the trauma of colonialism presented the discipline of anthropology with the quandary of meaning, representation, change, and comparability which have proven to be enduring epistemological and theoretical issues in the discipline. The early ethnographers, with few exceptions, reflected the inexperience of cultural interlocutors and interpreters plus the haste with recording ways of life understood to be in the process of being fundamentally altered. This reflected a form of ethnographic reporting which contributed to a salvage approach and was likely to be highly functional and static. This program led to a reconstruction or invention of a cultural experience presumed to have existed in some pristine and autonomous past enshrined in the phrase "the ethnographic present." These studies are easily criticized for their lack of dynamics and systemic analysis, but if the researchers provided rich data and situated themselves within the fieldwork experience, contemporary and future researchers should be able to read that study with discriminations and questions not apparently obvious to the ethnographic researcher of that era.

Of critical importance in the conducting of fieldwork is the nature of the researchers' participation and the perceptions to which this gives rise within the culture being observed. The ethnographer alters the social space of his hosts and by so doing inevitably becomes a player in the actions which unfold. How and in what manner the ethnographer arrives at a point where an acceptable role with workable relations occurs is a key issue of trust, acceptance, and accountability in the ethnographic endeavor. The key to acquiring ethnographic reporting that conveys the sense of structure versus chaos, norm versus ambiguity, and order versus contradiction, which constitute culture, is through the relationship with key informants. It is they who can provide the researcher with the experiences, challenges, and perspectives through which that culture's subsequent interpretation is filtered, processed, and made testamentary. Developing numerous such relations from various statuses and roles is necessary so as to minimalize involvement with too narrow a sample of individuals in too small an arena. Besides the wide variety of research techniques and devices which may be employed in participant observation, the contemporary ethnographer is compelled to situate the social unit under study in the necessary context of multiple social fields created by historical forces which are international, national, or regional in their layering. Government records, archival data, business logs, and primary and secondary histories require consultation. Rarely is the social unit under scrutiny an actual bounded and autonomous ethnounit, as the ethnographic present implied. Instead units are defined by some criterion of cultural ecology, demographic profile, or type of social identity either externally and/or internally defined, which manifests issues of culture history. It is the ethnographer's responsibility to identify the criterion being utilized and the research problem which is being addressed.

According to Marcus and Fisher (1986) the practice of ethnography requires the following considerations: (1) Feelings and cultural expressions can never be known directly, much less comparatively, without attention to their mediating roles of expression. (2) Careful attention must be paid to the categories, metaphors, and rhetoric employed in informants' accounts and the contexts in which they are conveyed. (3) The ethnographer must be prepared to explore the philosophical and political problems of translation and interpretation. There must be textual space for the informants to present their views, understandings, confusions, and doubts in their own voices. (4) The researcher should question the degree of coherence in the culture. (5) Interpretation requires that the ethnographer takes into account history and power relations within the lives of their hosts and informants within political economy. These systemic power domains are part and parcel of the culture's internal and external representations.

Ethnography and culture history have always had to wrestle with important epistemological issues of interpretive conceit, simple empiricism and philosophical naivete. These issues will always bedevil social analysis if the tension between "data" and "values" remains a creative tension. One can be doing ethnography in the archives and history in the ethnographic field study. E.E. Evans-Pritchard, a pioneer ethnographer with all of the attributes and deficiencies of the pioneer, understood clearly that anthropology is history or it is nothing.

While ethnography remains rooted in anthropology, social historians share its interests in terms of the basic cultural issues raised. They also use ethnographic work and materials from the past—as in folklore—and attempt to apply ethnographic methods to such materials. Finally, in dealing with recent social patterns social historians often apply ethnographic methods directly. (*See also* Anthropology; Cultural History)

Frank McGlynn

REFERENCES

Auge, Marc. *The Anthropological Circle: Symbol, Function, History.* Cambridge: Cambridge University Press, 1979.

Comaroff, John and Jean. *Ethnography and the Historical Imagination.* Boulder: Westview Press, 1992.

Fox, Richard, ed. *Recapturing Anthropology: Working in the Present.* Seattle: University of Washington Press, 1991.

Marcus, George, and Michael Fisher. *Anthropology as Cultural Critique: An Experimental Moment in the Human Sciences.* Chicago: University of Chicago Press, 1986.

Roseberry, William. *Anthropologies and Histories: Essays in Culture, History and Political Economy.* New Brunswick: Rutgers University Press, 1989.

European Migration

Migration—defined simply as departure from village or town of birth—historically has been a routine part of European life, embedded in patterns of family formation and inheritance. Because exogamous marriage has been the norm, marriage partners often have been from different villages, hamlets, or parishes, and brides have usually moved at marriage. Systems of impartible inheritance have determined that while one or two children were able to remain in their home, the others moved to other plots of land, neighboring villages, or nearby towns, if not farther from home.

Migration forms an essential component of European labor practices. The period of years between physical maturity and marriage gave young men and women time to be mobile and to train for work; whether peasant farmhands, apprentices, or domestic servants, historical forms of premarital labor allowed young people to work away from home. Although adult landowning peasants were attached to property holdings, the historical record shows that even peasant families moved and that rural proletarian individuals and families were even more mobile. Both rural and urban labor encouraged mobility; large-scale farming around 17th-century London, Paris, and Amsterdam, for example, gave rise to teams of migrant harvest workers. As centers of economic activity and cultural life, cities and towns historically attracted newcomers from beggars and unskilled workers to the highest levels of the bourgeoisie; indeed, urban death rates were so high that few cities or towns could maintain their populations before the 19th century without the intrepid migrant. Preindustrial societies were not sessile: in southern and midland England, for example, 63 percent of men and 67 percent of women left their home parish in the 1660–1730 period.

It is useful to distinguish historical migrations by distance traveled and the extent of a break with home. Most migrations occurred in systems built from contacts among family and compatriots. In the early modern period, *local migration* was most significant, as cities and towns drew on regional populations, young people annually moved for agricultural service work, and marriages joined people from nearby villages. Teams of harvest laborers and temporary urban workers moved in systems of *circular migration* (movement with a routine return home) that focused on destinations in Spain, Holland, East Anglia, and the Paris basin. *Chain migration* (movement within a set of social relations from home that greet and aid newcomers at destination) moved men and women to join compatriots at destination and settle in a new place, be it a city or a new town such as Versailles. Employees of church, state, and corporate bureaucracies took paths of *career migration* (movement along the employer's trajectory). *Colonizing migration* (settlement on a distant frontier) took Europeans to Siberia, southeastern Europe, and the American Plains. Finally, *coerced migration* (forced movement from home), came in the wake of religious intolerance and war.

These patterns of migration in early modern Europe shifted with changing patterns of population expansion, land ownership, labor force demand, movements of capital, and changing state policies. In the 18th century, migration changed with the proliferation of rural industry and population expansion. On one hand, population pressure expanded systems of circular and chain migration; on the other hand, widespread rural industry enabled many villages and towns effectively to support expanded numbers, reducing emigration from industrial rural areas.

As population expansion intensified in the 19th century, markets for rural-produced goods declined; eventually urban production, commerce, and services came to demand an expanded labor force. Europeans moved farther than ever before: men and women left home provinces that could no longer support them, migration to and from cities expanded, and some 52 million Europeans emigrated from the Continent between 1840 and 1930. Systems of local and circular migration increasingly gave way to chain migration and, with the expansion of national state bureaucracies, career migration; colonizing migrations in Australia, New Zealand, and the Americas reached unprecedented importance. In the years before World War I, Europeans moved as part of a global labor force, building not only the cities of the Continent, but those of the Americas as well.

World War I depressed this global movement, inaugurating a period in which the state dramatically increased attempts to control international migration. Wartime governments regulated the movements of nationals, munitions workers, and prisoners of war. Subsequently, the United States restricted the entry of southeastern Europeans. In the 1930s, European governments increased supervised border crossings with the Great Depression and the rising tide of refugees from Spain, Germany, and central Europe. World War II inaugurated unprecedented coerced migration on the Continent as labor was forced into German territories, people were displaced behind Soviet lines, prisoners of war were incarcerated, and enemies of the Third Reich were pulled into concentration camps and death camps. The war created over 11 million displaced persons.

By the prosperous 1950s and 1960s, low birth rates and war deaths had reduced the labor force of western Europe—a labor force overeducated for the many unskilled jobs available in this prolonged economic boom. Through bilateral agreements, the nations of western Europe recruited immigrant workers from former colonies, southern Europe, and the Mediterranean basin to perform tasks that rural migrants had performed a century before. By the early 1970s, over 7.9 million migrants from Italy, Spain, Portugal, Turkey, Yugoslavia, Greece, Algeria, and Morocco lived on the Continent in Belgium, France, Germany, the Netherlands, and Switzerland; over a million migrants, primarily from the Commonwealth, lived in Britain. With the economic slowdown after the 1973 oil crisis, further immigration was discouraged, and migrant laborers settled into permanent ethnic minorities. As the European Economic Community consolidates its policies in the early 1990s, workers may move within EEC nations; with the political changes in central and eastern Europe after 1989, the future of migration into Europe from the south and east as well as Europe's ability to control immigration remain uncertain. (*See also* Migration)

Leslie Page Moch

REFERENCES

De Vries, Jan. *European Urbanization, 1500–1800.* Cambridge: Harvard University Press, 1984.

Lucassen, Jan. *Migrant Labour in Europe, 1600–1900.* London: Croom Helm, 1987.

Moch, Leslie Page. *Moving Europeans: Migration in Western Europe Since 1650.* Bloomington: Indiana University Press, 1992.

European Regions

The regions of Europe represent an intermediary level between that of the commune or county and that of the nation-state. They serve to bring together microlevel data and yet avoid generalizations found in national-level studies. The regions of Europe came into existence for a variety of reasons: physical geography, areas of common language, traditional feudal units, and past administrative or economic demands. While some contemporary regions are relatively new creations amalgamating older regional distinctions (e.g., the Mezzogiorno in Italy), the majority reflect a long-standing reality and lay claim to the allegiance and loyalty of those who live there. The importance of regions is also widely recognized in European social history. French social historians, particularly, have used the regional unit as a basis for analyzing the relationship among wide-ranging facets of social structure and behavior. While this article cannot survey the total diversity of the regions of Europe, by highlighting their vitality and some key features, their importance for an understanding of Europe should become clear.

The continued strength of the German Länder is matched by the resurgence of the regions in Spain (Galicia or Valencia) and Italy (Friulia or Lombardy). Regions represent continuing focii for political mobilization and group loyalty. This vitality is demonstrated in the growth of Europe-wide regional organizations and in the increasing role of regions in the European Community. As an important part of identity formation, regions are of significance to social historians and are important keys to understanding past and contemporary Europe. While the specific origins of individual regions vary, what sets one region apart from another are cultural differences. Like culture itself, these differences extend to many aspects of everyday life. Within this wide range the most commonly encountered are those concerning language, religion, political adherence, land tenure, and family practices.

The boundaries between the regions of Europe are frequently associated with distinct languages or dialects. In some cases these boundaries have changed over time leaving a regional border which no longer reflects a linguistic reality (as in Brittany or Wales) or where a language community has been divided for so long that its parts have developed their own regional identity (as in Catalunya on both sides of the Franco-Spanish border). In other cases (Gascony or Languedoc) the regional linguistic difference has become largely one of dialect, while in others (Cornwall or the Channel Islands) a language has virtually disappeared while regional identity has been maintained. The persistence of dialect differences is a reflection partly of the relative newness of consistent efforts to eradicate them and partly of deliberate efforts to promote them. The social value attached to certain regional linguistic differences (Piedmontese in Turin or dialect in Vienna or Zurich) reflects a conscious cultivation of a local identity. Some dialect differences even serve to distinguish religious groups (Rhaeto-Romontsch). The significance of linguistic differences as regional markers applies in both rural and urban areas and can still lead to political separatism (Canton Jura). Whatever connotations particular linguistic distinctions may have, they are significant markers of regional difference and one of the most widely used means of establishing one's own identity and that of others in contemporary Europe.

While the number of individuals who regularly practice a religion in a formal sense has declined, traditional adherence to religious practice still serves to differentiate regions, as does the variety of formal religion observed there. The relatively high level of church attendance in Brittany contrasts with the low level of Bas Languedoc. The importance of Catholicism in Bavarian regional identity contrasts with Protestantism in Schleswig-Holstein. The reasons for this regional variation in religion stem from a variety of factors: the post-Reformation state religion, the Catholic Reformation, or resistance to centralized authority and political change. Within adherence to a formal religion, a rich variety of traditional religious practices (including pilgrimages and local cults) differentiate one region from another. The general validity of the idea that knowing the regional identity of a person will indicate both religious preference and practice can be verified on any map of church attendance in Europe.

If the regions of Europe have a religious dimension, they also have a political one. This can take the shape of regional parties or of a pattern of political allegiance which sets the region apart. Many of these differences date from the beginning of modern politics after the French Revolution, when regions such as the Auvergne or Savoie were noted for their distinctiveness. Regional political patterns have also remained largely constant in other countries. Specifically regionalist parties are a more recent development. Their strength in regions such as Wales and the recent development of new regionalist parties (Veneto or Andalucia) underlines the importance of politics in regional identity. In some cases (Sud Tirol) regionalist politics have achieved a change in status for the region, which appears to be a phenomenon which will recur (Scotland). In only a few instances has this led to the formation of new nation-states (Faeroes).

While these factors serve to delineate European regions, a whole range of cultural and social practices are also significant. Family structure is a reflection of land tenure arrangements and the economic and physical constraints which dictate agricultural and other production. These generally resulted in simple or nuclear families, but in many regions (Emilia-Romagna or the Loire) co-residence or extended families could be found. Sharecropping especially favored co-residence. Related to residence and tenure, the European Marriage Pattern was common. There were, however, variations even in this pattern. A few European regions also featured scattered farms instead of the more standard village unit. The presence or absence of neolocalism also varied between regions being strong in some cases (southern England) and weak in others (Austria).

The variety of regions also led to a range of traditions and cultural practices. Differences between regions are reflected in things as various as traditional costume, music, sports and diet. While many regional customs have been abandoned, such as Veillees in Occitania (winter gatherings for communal meetings, work, and singing), others continue with renewed vigor, such as Eistedfoddau in Wales (music and cultural meetings). The diversity of European regions remains striking, and it also remains at the center of the sense of identity of many contemporary Europeans. (*See also* European-Style Family; Land Tenure and Reform)

Micheál Thompson

REFERENCES

Christian, William. *Person and God in a Spanish Valley*. New York: Seminar Press, 1977.

Kertzer, David. *Family Life in Central Italy 1880–1910*. New Brunswick, NJ: Rutgers University Press, 1984.

Sahlins, Peter. *Boundaries*. Berkeley: University of California, 1989.

European-Style Family

The European-style family has been defined by a set of characteristics that have apparently existed at least since the 16th century, particularly in northwestern Europe.

The European-style family was generally residentially nuclear rather than extended in form, consisting of parents and children, and in many cases, of unmarried servants or employees of the household head. While the nuclear family form predominated, many families went through a stage in which extended kin—especially a grandparent—lived in the household. The European-style family almost never included more than one married couple.

Other features of this family type that distinguish it from family systems in other regions of the world include the practice of relatively late marriage (age 26–28 for men, age 24–25 for women) and a relatively small age gap between spouses. These features were particularly evident among the common people. A relatively high age at marriage and small age gap between spouses have led scholars to hypothesize a relatively companionate sort of marriage system among the masses of Europeans. Social elites, however, often married at much lower ages, a practice associated with the greater participation of parents and other kin in choosing spouses and arranging matches. Among all social classes, marriage in the early modern period was based primarily on practical considerations of similar background and material advantage. It was among the highest classes that questions of personal attraction gave way most obviously to those of wealth and power to be gained by a match.

Marriage ages among Europeans were higher than in other parts of the world because of values that associated marriage with setting up a new household. Men and women could not marry until they had accumulated the material resources (in land, tools, household goods) that they would need to support a family. Young women and men who were not given such property by their kin needed to earn resources through their own labor. Difficulties in doing so delayed legitimate marriage or made it impossible. These factors led to another characteristic of what has been called the European Marriage Pattern— the existence of a relatively high percentage (8–15 percent) of persons who never married.

After their marriages, European women could expect to give birth to a child approximately every two and a half years, as long as she breastfed her child. Since breastfeeding provides some physiological protection against pregnancy, the failure to breastfeed—for example, by hiring a paid wet nurse—could result in even shorter intervals between successive childbirths. The average European woman could thus expect to bear approximately seven children in her lifetime if she and her husband both remained alive until she reached menopause. It should be noted, however, that high mortality rates for adults meant that many couples did not survive to the end of the woman's childbearing years together and that only approximately half of the children a woman

bore would themselves reach the age of reproduction and marry.

The family characteristics described so far apply mainly to northwestern Europe, that is, England, northern France, Germany, and Scandinavia, in the period from the 16th to the 19th centuries. The family systems of Mediterranean Europe and eastern Europe seem to have deviated from them in several ways. In southern and central Europe, the marriage age of women seems to have been somewhat lower than in the north, and the corresponding age gap between spouses correspondingly greater, yielding what has been seen as a more patriarchal kind of family. In both central and southern Europe, more complex forms of family residential systems coexisted alongside the nuclear. Extended family types such as the Yugoslav *zadruga* were based on the need for large supplies of agricultural labor. Whereas landowning families in large parts of northwestern Europe relied on hired labor, families in southern and central Europe appear to have relied more on labor resources drawn from extensive kin relations.

While the basic outlines of these family systems seem to have existed for centuries, there have been some variations over time and important changes beginning in the late 19th century. There is some evidence that extended families (including collateral kind such as brothers, sisters-in-law) may have become more prevalent in many parts of northwestern Europe in the 19th century as the result of declining adult mortality, which made more kin available; the rise of a wage-based family economy that could make use of the labor resources of resident kin; and values that increasingly sentimentalized family life and bonds as sources of personal fulfillment. In some instances, marriage ages fell and rates rose, which are other departures from the classic European-style family. Furthermore, historians have noted the growing importance of considerations of personal happiness in marriage across time. Beginning with the Protestant Reformation of the 16th century, notions of the need for shared values of piety as the basis of domestic intimacy flourished. Gradually, however, by the 18th century, the search for personal happiness in marriage was shedding some of its religious trappings and had become increasingly secularized, legitimizing young people's right to choose their spouses on grounds of emotional attraction rather than material considerations. It should be noted, however, that such values did not lead to high levels of intermarriage across social classes, since young people from different milieus still led largely segregated lives. A major change in the European family came at the end of the 19th century, with the onset of the demographic transition, which entailed sharp reductions in the number of children women bore. The control of fertility within marriage was perhaps the most important force for change in the European-style family.

Katherine A. Lynch

REFERENCES

Flandrin, Jean-Louis. *Families in Former Times.* Cambridge: Cambridge University Press, 1979.

Hajnal, J. "European Marriage Patterns in Perspective," in D.V. Glass and D.E.C. Eversley, eds., *Population in History.* Chicago: Aldine, 1965.

Hajnal, John. "Two Kinds of Preindustrial Household Formation System," *Population and Development Review* 8, 3 (1982): 449–493.

Journal of Family History, Special Issue, 16, 1 (1991).

Laslett, Peter, with Richard Wall, eds. *Household and Family in Past Time.* Cambridge: Cambridge University Press, 1972.

European University

European universities originated in the intellectual revival of the high Middle Ages, appearing before 1200 in Italy and then in France, where the University of Paris became a center of northern intellectual life. A group of dissident students from Paris founded Oxford University in England around 1200, followed soon after by Cambridge. The first university in Germany was established at Heidelberg in 1385. By 1300 there were a dozen universities in Europe, by 1500 almost a hundred.

Organized as self-governing corporations, the universities were bodies of men interested in learning and were normally organized into faculties of theology, law, and medicine. They offered instruction in Latin, held examinations, and awarded degrees (bachelor of arts, master of arts, and doctorate), recognized throughout the Latin West. As centers of scholarly enquiry, the universities facilitated the rediscovery of the heritage of ancient Greece, which formed the basis for the high-medieval synthesis of Greek and Arabic philosophy and the Christian faith known as Scholasticism.

During the Renaissance and Reformation, universities continued to be established in France, Germany, Scandinavia, Scotland, and Spain, but the Protestant Reformation, the Catholic Counter-Reformation, and the religious wars that followed led to religious sectarianism and general decline. In England and France most of the intellectual advances of the 17th and 18th centuries took place in royal societies and scientific academies, outside of, and often in opposition to, the universities. In contrast, Holland, Scandanavia, Scotland, and, somewhat later, Germany reformed their universities. Beginning in 1810, Prussia, defeated by Napoleon, reorganized secondary education and created the University of Berlin modeled on *Bildungsbürgertum,* a humanistic ideal designed for an educated class drawn from the aristocracy and bourgeoisie. As the century progressed general culture gave way to *Wissenschaft,* or scientific research, and the universities competed with each other for outstanding scholars. The 19th century saw the flowering of German higher education, based on the freedom to learn and to teach, but weaknesses existed also in the guildlike power of the professors, who resisted the creation of new fields and disciplines. Moreover, universities in Germany and in other European countries emphasized pure knowledge to the exclusion of new applied fields such as agriculture, engineering, clinical medicine, and some of the social sciences, which continued to be relegated to specialized schools and/or to apprenticeship. Consequently, governments had to intervene in order to upgrade professional schools to university level and to establish research institutes to provide for new fields not covered by the universities.

Faced with rapid strides in German research during the second half of the 19th century, the French reorganized their universities in the reform of 1896, and the English abolished religious tests for graduation at Oxford and Cambridge and gradually improved their science programs. The University of London was established in 1827, followed by other civic universities—Manchester, Leeds, among others—which opened higher education to new fields of research and to the applied and social sciences.

American universities originated with the creation of Harvard College in 1643. Between 1850 and 1920 they introduced the department and the graduate school and established professional schools on campus. Departmental organization made possible the creation of chairs in new fields and subfields, as opposed to Germany, where a single professor covered a broad range of disciplines, or France, where bureaucrats in Paris governed virtually every aspect of university life. English universities also had departments, though these were smaller and more hierarchically organized. The flexible and decentralized American system allowed competition between public and private sectors and catered to a variety of interests, to teaching, research, and professional functions, and to business and community. American universities have been widely imitated in Europe since World War II, especially since the years of explosive growth beginning in the 1960s.

First created 800 years ago, European universities are among the most adaptable and successful of Western institutions. Their history contributes to an understanding of the organization and diffusion of knowledge, the recruitment and placement of elites, and issues of social mobility, cultural reproduction, and professionalization. Universities existed traditionally to transmit culture and to train elites in the fields of law, medicine, theology, and, later, letters and sciences. The rapid expansion of the universities since World War II was justified on democratic and economic grounds, for there was a need to meet increasing demands for scientists, engineers, teachers, executives, and medical researchers. Sociologists have found, however, that universities continue to recruit among the professional and executive classes and that working-class and minority groups and women are seriously underrepresented among students and faculty, especially in graduate and professional schools. High expectations, rapid growth, a growing awareness of the failure of the universities to achieve their democratic objectives, combined with increasing concern over colonial wars and environmental and social issues, have caused confrontation on university campuses through-

out the world. This not only has led to attempts to reform university recruitment policies and structures but also has led to political interference on the part of governments and a tendency to turn universities into professional schools. Despite the serious problems that face universities today, one must emphasize their many successes—longevity, contributions to learning, scientific accomplishments, defense of individual liberties, and pursuit of knowledge.

Universities have been of interest for many years to intellectual historians of the Middle Ages and Renaissance. Social historians have shifted focus, dealing particularly with changes in social recruitment, curriculum, student groups, and the admission of women since the 19th century. The social history of universities involves more comparative analysis, on university-channeled social mobility and the adequacy of technical training. (*See also* Cultural History; Education; Intelligentsia; Mobility; Professionalism; Science)

C.R. Day

REFERENCES

McClelland, Charles E. *State, Society and University in Germany, 1700 to 1914.* Cambridge: Cambridge University Press, 1980.

Ringer, Fritz. *The Decline of the German Mandarins: The German Academic Community, 1890–1933.* Cambridge, MA: Harvard University Press, 1969.

Sanderson, Michael. *The Universities and British Industry, 1850–1970.* London: Routledge and Kegan Paul, 1972.

Stone, Lawrence, ed. *The University in Society,* 2 vols. Princeton, NJ: Princeton University Press, 1974.

Weisz, George. *The Emergence of Modern Universities in France, 1863–1914.* Princeton, NJ: Princeton University Press, 1983.

Evangelicalism (Awakenings)

Most denominational bodies within Christendom are "evangelical" in the literal sense of the word, that is, they espouse the religious teachings contained in the New Testament and consider propagating this message a basic religious obligation. Following the Reformation, however, the term "evangelical" became associated more narrowly with a particular theological school within the Protestant tradition. This school held that the essence of Christianity is contained in the doctrine of salvation by faith in the atoning death of Christ, denied that either good works or the sacraments of the church have any saving efficacy, and insisted that the Bible was the ultimate authority for both doctrine and discipline. Like most other Christians of the era, evangelicals asserted that humans are sinful by nature and in need of "conversion," or spiritual regeneration. Yet, unlike many of their Christian contemporaries, evangelicals also insisted upon a special kind of religious conversion—an instantaneous experience of faith, preceded by a strong sense of personal guilt and followed by a joyous assurance of forgiveness. For evangelicals, a datable, instantaneous, and often emotional conversion followed by the pursuit of a rigorous moralism was considered the normative Christian experience. For their critics, such behavior often was viewed as religious fanaticism and drab puritanism.

Evangelicals and, subsequently, historians of evangelicalism refer to periods of extraordinarily religious excitement as "awakenings." This term, an abbreviated form of Paul's admonition to the Ephesians, "Awake thou, that sleepest, and arise from the dead," connotes special seasons of spiritual attentiveness within a population, which often are evidenced by heightened piety and an increase in the number of evangelical conversions. Such periods of religious renewal have occurred at frequent intervals in Protestant nations since the Reformation. Modern examples of Anglo-American awakenings include the mid-18th-century Wesleyan, or Methodist, revival in England and its North American counterpart known as the Great Awakening; the so-called Second Great Awakening of early 19th-century America, characterized in the West by large and emotional outdoor camp meeting services and in the East by the creation of moral reform and missionary associations; the Dwight Moody/Ira Sankey evangelical campaigns in England and the United States of the late 19th century; the Holiness and Pentecostal revivals which flourished in American cities around the turn of the 20th century; the post–World War II resurgence of evangelical piety within mainstream American Protestant denominations; and the interdenominational charismatic movement and the rise of the New Religious Right during the 1970s

and 1980s.

Traditionally, church historians have attempted to explain the ebb and flow of evangelical impulses in terms of the theology of the various denominations and the leadership and charisma of their clerical leaders. At least since the publication of Whitney Cross's *The Burned-Over District* (1950), however, social historians have sought to interpret revivalistic activity, which, they note, generally occurs during eras of dramatic social change, as a product of socioeconomic conditions. Armed with a variety of theoretical models and quantitative methodologies taken from the social sciences, these scholars have attempted to identify the specific circumstances which make individuals in a given time and place more susceptible to evangelical proselytizing than individuals of other eras and locales. While no consensus has emerged, scholars such as Paul Johnson (1978), who associates 19th-century evangelical success with the rapid advancement of the capitalistic market, and Mary Ryan (*Cradle of the Middle Class,* 1983), who links this awakening with the movement from farm to city and the corresponding breakup in the intergenerational patriarchal family unit, have produced a number of intriguing hypotheses concerning the interconnections between evangelicalism and economic development.

In recent years a number of social historians, among them Jon Butler, Nathan Hatch, Harry Stout, and Terry Bilhartz, have questioned the primacy of economic influences upon American religious development and have attributed changes in the forms and popularity of evangelical Christianity to national political forces, to the marketing strategies of voluntary churches, and to innovations in the techniques of mass communication. The ongoing dialogue between those who look for explanations from both the "demand side" and the "supply side" of the equation has made the study of evangelicalism a fertile area of sociohistorical interest. Also important, particularly in American history, is the impact of evangelicalism on this wider society, in areas ranging from child-rearing patterns to political behavior. (*See also* Christianity; Missionaries; Reformation/Popular Religion; United States Politics and Society)

Terry D. Bilhartz

REFERENCES

Bilhartz, Terry. *Urban Religion and the Second Great Awakening.* Rutherford, NJ: Fairleigh Dickinson University Press, 1986.

Hatch, Nathan. *The Democratization of American Christianity.* New Haven: Yale University Press, 1989.

Johnson, Paul. *A Shopkeepers Millennium.* New York: Hill and Wang, 1978.

McLoughlin, William. *Revivals, Awakenings and Reform.* Chicago: University of Illinois Press, 1978.

Vandermeer, Philip R., and Robert P. Swierenga. *Belief and Behavior: Essays in the New Religious History.* New Brunswick, NJ: Rutgers University Press, 1991.

Events

Unlike more traditional kinds of history, social history does not focus on events as primary units of description and analysis. This is one of the key sources of disjuncture between social history and political history, one of the key problems in integrating social history into conventional, event-based textbooks. From the early *Annales* school onward, social historians have grappled with the relationship between events and social processes. The problems involved are not insuperable, but they affect style of presentation and coherence within the wider discipline of history.

Certain kinds of events clearly attract social historians' attention. Much Anglo-American social history in the 1960s and 1970s focused on describing and interpreting protest, that is, riots and revolutions. These events involved extensive lower-class participation, and they generated abundant source materials through which the conditions and aspirations of the lower classes could be assessed. Correspondingly, a sociohistorical interpretation of events such as the French Revolution of 1789 or the revolutions of 1848 gained ground, focusing on the political power, rational selectivity of goals, and intense grievances of lower-class actors, as opposed simply to the machinations of leaders or the impulse of formal ideologies, on the one hand, or totally impersonal economic forces on the other. On the whole, however, social historians were more interested using the events to explore lower-class lives or larger protest patterns than in exploring the events per se.

Social historians have also delighted in analyzing unfamiliar, seemingly obscure events, such as a massacre by Paris artisans of several hundred cats in the late 1730s (Darnton 1985). The fact that the exact date is not known and does not matter is characteristic. For here the event is only a revealing episode, again providing unusual documentation, not significant in itself. On the other hand, certain kinds of events do not particularly interest social historians because they neither cause nor reflect substantial social change. Many modern elections do not signify noteworthy changes in popular beliefs or modifications of government impact on society. Many diplomatic alignments, once lovingly explored as part of foreign policy history, do not matter much in social terms.

Rather than using events as their principal research category, social historians more commonly focus on processes. A shift in birth rates reflects hundreds of thousands of individual events—family decisions about sex, children, and contraceptive devices—but the events cannot be probed one by one. A change in birth rate levels sums them up, and this is what the social historian tries to convey and to analyze. New efforts to regulate personal habits, such as table manners, involves events—such as the publication of new kinds of etiquette books, and possibly some exemplary social gatherings. Clearly, however, events do not capture the real change, which is conveyed by assessing alterations in standards over usually an extensive period of time. Even social protest is typically handled by categorizing different kinds of protest (in terms of goals, methods, nature of participants) rather than by narrating one event after another, though events may be described at points for purposes of illustration. Major revolutions themselves, in this approach, may appear as part of an evolutionary trend in popular protest, rather than as a direct target of historical inquiry. By the same token, social historians do not feel compelled to reinterpret every familiar event, as opposed to redefining the place of such events among other research priorities.

Social historians tend to argue, then, that event-based histories often miss the main point. The industrial revolution is not mainly a series of events such as new laws about trade, the foundation of new banks, and the introduction of new inventions; though these do play a role, the industrial revolution, rather, consists of the installation of new work systems (the "events" here being the formation of countless new factories and the hiring and indoctrination of thousands of foremen), the impact of new products, and the separation of production from the household. Developments of this sort take shape gradually, and are best described as processes rather than discrete occurrences.

Social historians do not always agree about the role of events. Some avoid events altogether, while others continue to target social history toward the interpretation of causes and impacts of such events as the French Revolution or the U.S. Civil War.

Integrating social history with more familiar kinds of history clearly requires a reassessment of events, and while this has not fully transpired, some of the ingredients are clear. Some events have massive social importance, and social historians will eagerly examine them in terms of the forces that brought them about and in terms of the changes the events themselves made in subsequent society. World War II, thus, is routinely seen as a major factor in social history as in other kinds of history, causing, among other things, a significant breach in previous gender role divisions as women gained new access to factory and clerical work. The challenge of dealing with big events brings social historians and other historians onto a common terrain, though it does not automatically unify their methods or their explanations.

Other events may interest social historians as illustrations of wider processes—like accounts of particular festivals that happen to provide unusually rich data concerning ritual behavior and purposes. Events that produce little impact on social institutions or behaviors and involve only a handful of individuals, however officially important, will continue to be downplayed by social historians. Branches of history, like traditional diplomatic history, that rely particularly on narratives of events will continue to pose the greatest barriers to integration with social history—which is one reason diplomatic history has declined in vigor in the discipline more generally. Here a real challenge remains—to combine a selective focus on events with other kinds of analysis; this is increasingly occurring in military history, with a downplaying of battle stories in favor of wider features of the military experience. Finally, social historians' insistence on dealing with phenomena that cannot be conveyed in terms of events will also remain strong. How quickly and to what extent remaining gaps can be closed between historians who insist that their work must revolve around events, on the one hand, and virtually every variety of social historian on the other, cannot be predicted. (See also *Annales* School)

Peter N. Stearns

REFERENCES

Darnton, Robert. *The Great Cat Massacre and Other Episodes in French Cultural History.* New York: Random House, 1985.

Hunt, Lynn. *Politics, Culture and Class in the French Revolution.* Berkeley: University of California Press, 1984.

Stearns, Peter N., ed. *Expanding the Past; A Reader in Social History.* New York: New York University Press, 1988.

Stone, Lawrence. *Past and Present.* London: Routledge, Chapman and Hall, 1987 (rev. ed.).

Tilly, Charles. *The Contentious French: Four Centuries of Popular Struggle.* Cambridge: Harvard University Press, 1986.

Extended Family

The inclusion of the family in social history research has meant that historians have had to find concepts to refer to familial groupings larger than the family household. In all periods of the past, family members kept ties alive, even when they did not live together, for a variety of purposes. They assisted each other by lending money, by helping to find jobs and to recruit spouses, and by coming together in work teams when such mutual aid was required. They enhanced their economic and political power through networks of relatives and maintained it by ensuring that property was transmitted over generations in the family line. Without a thorough understanding of these relationships, an important aspect of the social past would escape attention, and description of historical family life would be too simple. Although *anthropologists* have devised dozens of conceptual categories to focus on these extra-household social groups and activities, *social historians* have generally used relatively few terms, such as "extended family" and "lineage."

In usage by historians these terms have remained imprecise, perhaps by intent, because primary sources do not contain pure examples of any categorical type of family structure. "Extended family" usually refers to all those living persons who, regardless of residence, understand themselves to be linked by kinship (sometimes loosely understood) and who use these links when the need arises. In a somewhat more specialized sense, the term can refer to a group of co-residing relatives that includes more than a husband, wife, and their children—perhaps a widowed parent, married or unmarried siblings, or even married or unmarried cousins. The term "extended family" is intended to be contrastive: it is brought into play when social description requires a contrast with the terms "nuclear family" or "simple family household." Household historians use the term "extended" in an even more specialized sense, however: for them, an "extended family household" is a category standing between the "simple family household" (head and spouse the sole married couple) and the "multiple family household" (the head, spouse, and married relatives of the head). Extended families tend not to have a reproducible principle of kin recruitment, perhaps because they emerge in the face of external challenges and harsh conditions in order to reduce expenses and pool resources, to help with child care and child rearing, to provide a haven for older people, or to create a larger group for self-defense. Under those conditions, survival of the family as a group appears to be more important than strict observation of kinship rules.

In a lineage, however, precisely defined kin relations are very important. When historians use the term in the anthropological sense of a "descent group," it refers to a group of living persons who, regardless of residence, understand themselves to be linked by descent from a common ancestor. In some societies the common ancestor may be fictitious; in those most frequently studied by historians using written sources the ancestor is more than likely to have been a real individual. In a more specialized sense, the term has also been used to refer to all those persons, living and dead, who belong to a single line of descent. The important point is that those who use this grouping principle for social activities understand themselves as having descended from the same individual and understand also that they have special obligations toward each other because of this fact. It is entirely possible for an extended family to define itself restrictively in terms of a common line of descent, and in such cases the lineage becomes a specialized form of the extended family.

Although family historians have now confirmed the overwhelming significance of the nuclear family in the past of Western societies, historical sources abound with information about the presence and activities of non-nuclear forms as well. Both the extended family and the lineage (or descent group) were important, but their relative significance at the given point in past time and their changing significance over long stretches of time in any society are very difficult to document, particularly in quantitative terms. An accurate record of the patrilineage was important for those social strata in which titles and property were to be bequeathed over generations. In the *zadruga* (joint family household) of the South Slav areas of the European Continent, one can observe an excellent example of the descent group assembled by reference of patrilineal descent. The history of the Great Depression of the 1930s contains many examples of the formation of extended family households in the United States and on the European Continent in response to harsh economic conditions. The familial history of English industrialization suggests that family members assisted each other in migrations to industrial cities, exemplifying in that process the benefits flowing from family relationships extended over space.

In the social history of the family the least described domain of action is precisely the one in which such configurations as the extended family and lineage fall. The deficiency is informational (the internal dynamics of such groups), geographical (what their incidence was in the Western world), and chronological (how their importance changed over the long run). The current state of research suggests at least this much: the extended family as a functioning family form has had a continuous social existence from the earliest times to the present, whereas the lineage, at least in Western societies, has become an increasingly weaker principle of group organization. This is so because the extended family appears most frequently in times of familial stress and requires fewer kin to become viable, whereas the lineage (or descent group) in the past served functions no longer deemed important and because it requires recognition of kin obligations that individualism renders onerous. (*See also* Anthropology; Demography; European-Style Family; Greek and Roman Family; Household; Inheritance Systems; Kinship; Modernization; Parish Records; Russian Family, Demography)

Andrejs Plakans

REFERENCES

Anderson, Michael. *Family Structure in Nineteenth Century Lancashire*. Cambridge: Cambridge University Press, 1971.

Plakans, Andrejs. *Kinship in the Past: An Anthropology of European Family Life, 1500–1900*. Oxford and New York: Basil Blackwell, 1984.

Segalen, Martine. *Historical Anthropology of the Family*. Cambridge: Cambridge University Press, 1986.

F

Family

Family history has become a central aspect of social history. Particularly well developed for western Europe and the United States, historical research on the family has also been conducted for Russia, Latin America, Japan, and other parts of Asia. A relatively new field, the uniqueness of historical research on the family lies both in its providing a perspective on change over time, as well as in its examining family behavior within specific social and cultural contexts. The historical study of the family has thus contributed not only to examinations of diachronic changes but to investigations of synchronic patterns within distinct time periods as well. The cumulative impact of studies on the history of the family has been to revise a simplistic view of family behavior over time and of social change.

As the field of family history developed since the 1970s, historians expanded their inquiry from the classification of households and family structures to a broad range of subjects encompassing marriage and sexual behavior, child rearing, gen-erational relations, and interaction of individuals and members of the nuclear family with extended kin; from a narrow examination of the family as a household unit at one point in time to a view of it as a process over the entire lives of its members; and from a study of discrete domestic family or household structure to a study of the nuclear family's interaction with the wider kinship group. Their inquiry has also been expanded with the worlds of work, education, correctional and welfare institutions (where expectations about what a family should be play a significant role) and with the larger social and economic processes, notably with industrialization and urbanization.

Efforts to explore internal decision-making processes within the family have led to an investigation of the strategies and choices that individual family members and family groups make. Finally, the life course approach, which has greatly influenced historical research on the family in recent years, has added an important developmental dimension to the history of the family by focusing on age and cohort comparisons in ways that link individual family time to historical change.

The history of the family has thus served to generate a realistic view of the complexities in the relationship between the family and other institutions confronting historical change. Beyond the specific topic of the family, an understanding of how individuals and families have responded to historical change and how they, in turn, have affected such change has considerably broadened our understanding of the process of change itself.

The family is one of the most complex social institutions. It is affected by biological processes; psychological dynamics; cultural values; market conditions; demographic changes; the institutions of industrial capitalism, churches, government, and welfare agencies; and long-term historical changes. Internally, the family contains different age and sex configurations, depending on its members' stages of life and household arrangements. In addition to husbands, wives, and children, families contain grandparents and grandchildren, and various other kin, real or fictive, bound to one another by blood ties as well as by social, emotional, and moral bonds.

The roles and status of each family member in relationship to other members, and in relation to the collective family unit, are defined differently in various cultural and historical contexts. The meaning of "family" and the expectations differ even among various members of the same family. Individual and family life transitions, such as leaving home, getting married, and forming a new family, are timed and synchronized differently. An understanding of the family in past time, as in the present, is linked to courtship, marriage, childhood, adolescence, youth, adulthood, and old age. Family behavior is further connected to gender roles, sexuality, emotions, and human development.

Since the family interacts with various institutions and social and economic processes, historical changes in the family can be best understood in the context of institutional changes, such as education and welfare, and in relation to larger processes such as the commercial revolution of the 17th century, industrialization, and urbanization. An examination of family behavior in the past has contributed, therefore, to a deeper understanding of social change.

The historical study of the family as it is practiced now originated from several systematic approaches developed in the 1960s. One impetus came from demography and a concern for family structure with strong reliance on quantitative data. The French demographers, particularly those of the *Annales* school, provided historians with the techniques of family reconstitution that were essential for reconstructing patterns of migration, fertility, mortality, and nuptiality. Using nominal individual and family data, the family reconstitution technique has enabled historians to reconstruct the family patterns of vast numbers of people in the past, to trace them over several generations, and to relate their demographic behavior to family organization and household structure and to economic behavior in preindustrial populations. While the French demographers focused primarily on demographic patterns, the historical demographers of the Cambridge Group for the History of Population and Social Structure in England and, subsequently, historians of colonial American society reconstructed household and family patterns in relation to demographic behavior. When interpreted in the context of economic and social institutions, such as landholdings, inheritance, religion, and community structure, demographic patterns served as the backbone for a rich family and community analysis.

A parallel major impetus for family history came from the publication of Philippe Ariès's *Centuries of Childhood* (1960; English translation 1962). Ariès argued that childhood as we know it emerged in western Europe in the early modern period and that its discovery was closely linked to the emergence of the modern conjugal family, which was child-centered and separated itself from the community as a private entity. While Ariès's thesis was to be criticized, it established the importance of using cultural evidence along with demographic data in the study of the family and in emphasizing the relationship between the history of childhood and the family. Following Ariès's approach and influenced by anthropology and the French social history tradition, a group of French historians integrated demographic analyses with patterns of family and sexuality, linking community, social, and cultural variables with *mentalité*.

The third impetus came from analyses of 19th-century urban patterns in the United States and England, which utilized nominal household census schedules for the analysis of family and household patterns in urban communities. Linking census data with a rich array of other sources, these studies went beyond their original purpose, and reconstructed patterns of household and family membership in relation to labor force participation, education, and geographic and social mobility.

While no single grand theory now predominates in family history, an attempt to evaluate significant change and to subject social science concepts about the family to careful historical scrutiny continues to inform this growing field.

This article discusses historical changes in the family, primarily in Europe and North America—the areas where research on the history of the family has concentrated in depth over the past two and a half decades, since the emergence of this field.

Revision of Myths

Before systematic historical study of the family began, other social science disciplines had generated their own myths and grand theories about continuity and change in family behavior historically. These notions claimed that modern family and population behavior such as nuclear households, family limitation, and the spacing of children were innovations introduced by industrialization, and that in preindustrial society the dominant household form had been extended, involving three co-resident generations. It was the prevailing assumption that industrialization destroyed a three-generation family structure and led to the emergence of the isolated nuclear family—a type thought more compatible with the demands of the modern industrial system. Industrialization was thus considered a major watershed in family structure and demographic behavior.

Research in the history of the family in the 1960s has demolished some of these myths and has led to the revision of a simplistic linear view of historical change. The demographic analyses for France and England, and later for Germany and Sweden, revealed that in the preindustrial period couples practiced some form of family limitation and child spacing as early as the 17th century; age at marriage was later than had been generally assumed; and that contrary to prevailing myths, households were predominantly nuclear rather than extended. In the late 1960s Peter Laslett and many other demographic historians staked out new findings about the continuity of nuclear households in Western society well before the modern era. Through family reconstitutions of parish records, French and English demographers found, for example, that in the 17th and 18th centuries rural births and marriages responded sensitively to changing economic conditions. As E.A. Wrigley put it, the key change involved in the demographic transition was "from a system of control through social institution and custom to one in which the private choice of individual couples played a major part in governing the fertility rate." A later age at marriage served as a method of family limitation, by leading to the postponement of childbearing. Marriage was contingent on a couple's ability to support their families of orientation and to accumulate resources in order to establish a self-supporting family. Late marriage was thus linked to the nuclearity of the household.

Households and Kin

Households in preindustrial western Europe and in the American colonies were nuclear in their structure. Nuclear households were common in parts of Italy as early as the 12th century and in England in the 14th century. Members of the nuclear family were enmeshed, however, in close ties with extended kin. Aging parents did not reside in the same household with their adult children, but lived in the vicinity, often on the same land. The most important conclusion emerging from these patterns was that industrialization did not break down a "great" extended family and did not lead to the emergence of an isolated nuclear family type. To the contrary, in some cases industrialization and urbanization may have led to an increase in the proportion of households containing extended kin because of the need to share housing in urban, industrial centers. (A *nuclear family* is defined as a unit consisting of parents and their children, or of a childless couple, or of one parent and his or her children. In this definition, it is necessary to distinguish between *family* and *household*. A nuclear *family* is not identical with a nuclear *household*, as the domestic group may have included nonrelatives as well.)

In eastern Europe and in parts of central Europe (Austria), and in southern Europe (Italy), more complex patterns of household organization persisted. These involved a *stem* family system, where the inheriting son and his spouse and children co-resided with the parents. These varieties of household structure were closely related to land ownership or tenure and to inheritance customs. Even in western Europe and in the United States and Canada, where a nuclear household pattern persisted over time, there were considerable variations in the composition of the household over the life course of the family members. As people aged, they were more prone to live in extended households.

Nuclear families of the past were different, however, from contemporary ones in their age configurations and in their composition. Because of higher fertility children were spread over a larger age spectrum within the family. Older children often took charge of their younger siblings; sisters in particular acted as surrogate mothers. Because of the multiplicity of functions which the family carried, the household contained nonrelatives as well. Preindustrial households included life cycle servants—young people who were placed in other people's households by their own parents—and dependent members in the community of various ages. In the 19th and early 20th centuries nonrelatives residing in the household were usually servants, boarders, and lodgers.

The household was the basic residential unit of the family as well as the locus of various aspects of economic and social activity. Households formed the cells that joined in making up the fiber of neighborhoods and entire communities. Prior to the early 20th century, solitary residence was almost unknown. Almost all men and women expected to live out their lives in familial or surrogate familial settings. In preindustrial society, the household was also the basic site of production, vocational training, and welfare. Through its control of housing space, the family engaged in economic exchange relations with kin as well as with nonrelatives. As a flexible unit, the household expanded and contracted in accordance with the family's needs and over the life course of its members. Household composition was responsive to changes in the age configurations and membership of the family, to economic need or opportunities, and to changing historical conditions.

The distinguishing historical feature in the organization of the household in Western society was not its extension through the presence of other kin, but its augmentation by nonrelatives, such as boarders and lodgers. Boarding and lodging was part of young people's transition to adulthood, but it was also related to migration, particularly for young men and women in the transitional period between departure from their parents' households and marriage. For migrants and immigrants, boarding represented a creative use of the household as a means of access to jobs and sociability. The overall tendency and the inferred preference in western Europe and North America was thus to include nonrelatives in the household rather than kin, at the same time engaging in mutual assistance with kin outside the household.

Kin fulfilled a central role in mediating between the nuclear family and other institutions. They were crucial in organizing migration, in facilitating settlement, in finding employment for newly arrived relatives, and in cushioning the shock of migrants' adaptation to new conditions. The migration of individuals or family groups to new areas was directed, organized, and supported by kin. In the absence of a public welfare system, kin served as the major source of assistance and social security. They provided assistance in daily living, as well as in critical life situations.

Among immigrants or migrants, the salient role of kin extended beyond the immediate community to encompass long-distance functions as well. Kinship networks stretched over several communities and were most useful during crises in the local community. The overall pattern of historical change, however, has been one of an increasing shift from family collectivity to individual goals and aspirations. These changes have led to a decline in the integration of individuals with extended kin. The pace and nature of these changes has varied considerably, however, among various classes and cultural groups.

The Family's Relation to the Process of Industrialization

Recent research in the history of the family has had a profound impact on our understanding of the family's response to changing social and economic conditions. Because the family has served as mediator between individuals and the social forces and institutions affecting them, it has both facilitated the adaptation to change and initiated change. In negotiating such larger processes as migration, urbanization, and industrialization, the family was an active agent, engaged in interaction with various social institutions rather than a passive unit, as it had been previously depicted. Depending on the circumstances, the family planned, initiated, or resisted change; it did not just respond blindly.

Until recently, sociologists have argued that the family broke down under the impact of industrialization; that throughout the history of industrial development, migration from rural to urban centers uprooted people from their kinship networks and stripped them of their traditional culture; and that the pressures of industrial work and urban life have caused a disintegration of the family unit. Historical research has led to the rejection of these simplistic models of social and economic change. Industrial capitalism in itself did not cause a breakdown of the family. This is exemplified in the family's active role in the process of industrialization, and in the phases that preceded it, most notably in protoindustrialization.

Protoindustrialization rested on household production for a capitalist employer who sold the products in external markets. It preceded the factory system or overlapped with it in the countryside and in some urban areas of England, France, Belgium, Switzerland, and Austria. In some areas, various forms of family labor coexisted in a protoindustrial system with large-scale factories; in other areas, artisans continued to make traditional products in a cottage industry, by using new technology and by reorganizing their family labor configurations accordingly.

While following their own priorities, families facilitated the process of industrialization in several ways: rural families released members to migrate to and work in urban factories, or took in machinery and transformed their own households into a cottage industry; protoindustrial families as well as those of factory workers helped stabilize migration by providing housing, employment, and training for new migrants in their households; families of traditional artisans sent some members to work in new industries, while maintaining a crafts production system in their own households. It was families' response to economic opportunity or necessity that led them to cope with innovations in production and with changing markets, by directing their members' know-how and resources into new directions.

In the early phases of industrialization families functioned as crucial intermediaries in recruiting workers from the countryside. The very success of the industrial system depended on a continuous flow of labor from the countryside to the newly industrializing centers. Most of the recruitment and migration of workers was carried out under the auspices of kin. Kinship ties with the workers' communities of origin were reinforced by the back-and-forth migration of individuals and the transfer of resources.

Thus, the family type most "fit" to interact with the modern factory was not the isolated nuclear type, but a nuclear family embedded in an extended kinship network. The family and wider kin groups were brokers between individuals and the institutions of industrial capitalism and facilitated their members' adaptation. The family and the kin group interacted with the industrial employer in influencing the placement and transfer of workers to desirable jobs, socializing novices, and, at times, manipulating work schedules and procedures. Rather than simply carrying over premigration traditions, the family addressed the factory system on its own terms.

In doing so, families followed their own strategies while drawing on their own culture and traditions. In response to the ups and downs caused by business cycles, the family devised new responses to cope with the insecurities resulting from unemployment and strikes. Different social classes, correspondingly, generated somewhat different family forms, and followed different patterns in their adjustment to new opportunities and constraints.

Emergence of Domesticity

Industrialization has had an indirect impact on changes in the functions, values, and division of labor in the family. Many of these changes were not linked directly to industrialization but emerged as consequences of the restructuring of the economy and of rapid urbanization following industrial development. One of the most crucial changes wrought by these processes was the transfer of functions from the family to other social institutions. The preindustrial family and household served as a workshop, a church, a reformatory, a school, and an asylum. Following industrialization and urbanization, these functions have become, in large part, the responsibility of other institutions. The household has been transformed from a place of production to a place of consumption and child rearing. Accompanying these changes was the separation of the spheres with women being in charge of the domestic and men of the public sphere. The family has become specialized, and has withdrawn from the public world, upholding privacy and intimacy as its major sources of strength.

The home has been viewed increasingly as a retreat from the outside world, enshrining the family in the domestic sphere. The commitment to the domesticity of the family is itself the outcome of a historical process, which commenced in the early modern period in western Europe, a process characterized by Philippe Ariès in his *Centuries of Childhood* (p. 404) as follows: "The modern family . . . cuts itself off from the world and opposes to society the isolated groups of parents and children. All the energy of the group is expended in helping the children to rise in the world, individually and without any collective ambition, the children rather than the family." By contrast, the premodern family was identified by its sociability and interconnectedness with the community. Ariès concluded that the privatization of the family weakened its adaptability and deprived children of the opportunity to grow up in a flexible environment with a variety of role models to follow.

Emergence of the Modern Family

Since change in the family is slower than in other social institutions, and since the family does not simply respond to change but also generates it, it has been difficult for historians to develop a typology of change in the family over time. Lawrence Stone, Philippe Ariès, and Edward Shorter have identified the rise of "affective individualism" as the major criterion of the modern family. They have generally agreed that the modern family (at least in Western society) is private, nuclear, domestic, and child-centered, and that the sentimental bond between husbands and wives and parents and children is the crucial base of family relations. Marriages are based on emotional bonding between husband and wife and are a result of personal and sexual attraction rather than alliances between sets of parents or lineages. Ariès and Stone have singled out the late 17th and early 18th centuries, whereas Shorter (*Making of the Modern Family*, 1974) has dated its emergence as being in the late 18th and early 19th centuries.

There has also been some disagreement and some lack of clarity about which social class first experienced these changes. Ariès and Stone have viewed the bourgeoisie and the gentry as the vanguard, whereas Shorter has assigned a crucial role to peasants and workers. For American society, Carl Degler (1980) has placed the origins of the modern family in the middle class. Still absent from historical studies of long-term changes in the family are more systematic distinctions between social classes and a more detailed understanding of the historical process by which modes of middle-class family behavior were adopted by other classes, if indeed that was the case; and conversely, what class differences have survived.

There is also a greater need to know how long-term changes in the family took place and what the nature of the interaction among these different factors was. The main dissatisfaction with the studies of grand changes in the family over time has been their linearity, and their venturing of generalizations based on the experience of one class for the entire society. This is the area where the critique that social historians have made against modernization theory applies as well.

While the history of the family is particularly well developed for the early modern and industrial periods (17th–early 20th centuries), social historians are also realizing the need to develop an approach to subsequent, 20th-century changes. Specific data are abundant: the increasing removal of older parents from the nuclear family and isolation of the elderly, loosening control over adolescents, the baby boom and subsequent birth rate reductions, rising divorce rates, cohabitation, impact of new patterns of women's work. But a historical synthesis that combines these and other developments and relates them to previous family history remains a challenge.

The concept of "modern" family in itself needs to be subjected, therefore, to scrutiny. The broad pattern of historical change that was based primarily on the experience of the upper and middle classes has tended to obscure the persistence of earlier forms of behavior among other classes. In working-class and ethnic families, some preindustrial family characteristics persisted, although in modified form. Even if all members did not work in the same place, the family experienced a continuity between work outside the home and household production, especially in women's work. The family continued to be a major economic decision-making unit, organizing the careers of its members and plotting collective strategies.

The intense focus on family history in Europe and in North America has left similar questions about historical changes in the family in other parts of the world unanswered. Even a cursory comparison between the United States and Japan suggests how profoundly different internal family relations are in the two societies, even though on the surface changes in the Japanese family are presumably heading in the direction of the American family.

The realization that historical changes in the family have not taken place uniformly throughout society has challenged simplistic, linear interpretations of change. Instead, historical research is now being carried out on a synchronic level, examining family interaction with societal processes and institutions within specific community contexts. Although such work has already contributed to a revision of earlier generalizations, historians still have to face the challenge of welding ongoing research into a more systematic pattern ranging over a longer historical period. We still need to develop a comprehensive model of change in family behavior that does justice to the complexities of social change. A final challenge involves relating changes and varieties in family history back to the wider society. (*See also* Demographic Transition; Middle Class; Modernization; Urbanization; Working Class)

Tamara K. Hareven

REFERENCES

Degler, Carl. *At Odds.* New York: Oxford University Press, 1980.

Demos, John. *A Little Commonwealth.* New York: Oxford University Press, 1970.

Hareven, Tamara K. *Family Time and Industrial Time.* New York: Cambridge University Press, 1982.

———, and Andrejs Plakans, eds. *Family History at the Crossroads.* Princeton, NJ: Princeton University Press, 1988.

Laslett, Peter. *Family Life and Illicit Love in Earlier Generations.* Cambridge: Cambridge University Press, 1977.

Stone, Lawrence. *The Family, Sex and Marriage in England, 1500–1800.* New York: Harper & Row, 1977.

Family Reconstitution

Family reconstitution is a method for reconstructing the demographic history of individual couples, and eventually the histories of entire parishes which they composed. The method was refined and systematized by the French demographer Louis Henry in the 1950s and has since that time been adapted and used by scholars in other countries which have parish registers appropriate for its implementation. Henry and his collaborators developed the method primarily to study fertility patterns of French women before the 19th century, when French people began consciously to limit the size of their families. The method of family reconstitution, however, yields information on many more subjects than simply the number of children ever born to couples. It illuminates patterns of nuptiality and mortality as well, and has played a major role in social history research, particularly on early modern Europe.

The method is an example of nominal record linkage (i.e., linking together pieces of information on named individuals) and entails culling information about each couple from parish register records of marriage, baptism, and burial. Researchers begin with a couple's marriage record and put the names of the wife and husband, along with information about their ages, dates of birth, and their parents, on a printed form, called a family reconstitution form, which resembles those used by genealogists to record family trees. The difference, however, is that the family reconstitution form contains spaces for noting demographic information on one particular couple.

After recording information about the couple's marriage, the researcher searches registers of baptism and burial to find the baptisms and burials of the couple's children, and the deaths of the couple themselves. After reconstructing the life of each couple, the researcher creates parish-level demographic rates by aggregating information from all of the reconstitution forms. (*See also* Genealogy; Latin American Demography; Life Course/Life Cycle; Marriage/Remarriage; Parish Records)

Katherine A. Lynch

REFERENCES

Accampo, Elinor. *Industrialization, Family Life, and Class Relations*. Berkeley: University of California Press, 1989.

Levine, David. *Family Formation in an Age of Nascent Capitalism*. New York: Academic Press, 1977.

Willigan, J. Dennis, and Katherine A. Lynch. *Sources and Methods of Historical Demography*. New York: Academic Press, 1982.

Wrigley, E. Anthony. *An Introduction to English Historical Demography*. New York: Basic Books, 1966.

Famine

Famine refers to mass starvation stemming from a failure of food entitlements. Starvation is a combination of reduced energy and food consumption that, continued long enough, leads to death. Neither preharvest hunger, characteristic of many peasant economies, nor the various dietary deficiency diseases are properly classified as famine. Famine has occurred often enough in all historical periods, including the present, to command serious attention from social historians, seeking to both explain causes and wider social effects.

Following Amartya Sen (*Poverty and Famine*, 1981), recent work has seen famine less as a product of per capita decline in the availability of food and more as the result of the failure of entitlements to food. While much attention has been given to fluctuations in food supply and their underlying causes, far too little consideration has been given to decline in wages, to wartime conditions, and to failures in social welfare institutions, which usually play an important role, sometimes the main role, in the outbreak of famine.

Famines may be seen as the product of both short- and long-term factors. In the short term, they are produced by cyclical changes or external shocks. Starvation among those who combined farming or cattle raising with domestic industry in northwestern England in the late 16th and early 17th centuries was at least as much due to the declining prices for woolen goods and cattle as it was to harvest failure. Starvation in Germany in 1918–1919 was caused by the maintenance of the Allied blockade, even after the armistice. From the perspective of the entire United Kingdom, where food was not lacking, the Great Irish Famine of 1846–1850 is probably best viewed as the failure of entitlement relationships in regard to welfare. The refusal of the British state to extend to its Irish subjects similar social entitlements to those available to its English, Scotch, and Welsh subjects was responsible for the famine when the potato crop failed successively at a time when the Irish population was still readjusting to declining agricultural opportunities after 1815.

Long-term changes in economic and political structures, however, underlie the short-term factors that expose populations to famine. By forcing large portions of populations to depend on markets for access to food, proletarianization increases the possibilities for famine in societies with insufficient resources or political will to provide state aid. In expanding their power to extract resources from local populations, state organizations have also increased the possibilities for famine in cases where the state's need for food supplies conflicts with that of local residents.

The social effects of famine are uneven. Because of their greater need for protein and calories, children are most susceptible to starvation, and the effects of serious malnutrition in youth can persist throughout life even among survivors. Further, famine forces large populations to disperse to other regions in search of food, which usually leads to the spread of epidemic diseases, in turn compounding the mortality effects of famine. The close relationship between starvation and epidemic disease often makes it difficult to estimate or even to identify the effects of famine on mortality. (*See also* Agricultural Systems; Demographic Transition; Potato)

Michael P. Hanagan

REFERENCES

Arnold, David. *Famine: Social Crisis and Historical Change*. Oxford: Basil Blackwell, 1988.

Newman, Lucille F., et al., eds. *Hunger in History: Food Shortage, Poverty, and Deprivation*. Oxford: Basil Blackwell, 1990.

O'Gráda, Cormac. *The Great Irish Famine*. London: Macmillan, 1989.

Post, John D. *The Last Great Subsistence Crisis in the Western World*. Baltimore: Johns Hopkins University Press, 1977.

Walter, John, and Roger Schofield. *Famine, Disease and the Social Order in Early Modern Society*. Cambridge: Cambridge University Press, 1989.

Farm Protest/Populism

The first wave of U.S. agrarian protest began in the late 1860s in the West and then the South. The protest movement has long been understood as a link between political and wider social history. Social historians have honed our grasp of the type of farmers involved in the movement, and therefore its underlying goals.

In 1867 the Patrons of Husbandry, whose local organizations were called Granges (the name for feudal farms), began as a social and educational group in response to the isolation of rural life. Men and women alike founded and were active in the local Granges, which were family-oriented, neighborhood groups, and which were initially recognized by the U.S. Department of Agriculture.

Granges soon moved beyond social activities and farming techniques, recognizing that outside forces limited their ability to improve, or even to maintain, their economic status quo. When the Granges began cooperative buying and selling enterprises and calling for regulation of railroad and grain elevator fees, however, corporations immediately sued them. The courts ruled against "Granger Laws," so the Granges reverted to farmers' social clubs. Nevertheless, they had laid the foundation for the Farmers' Alliances.

The second wave of agrarian protest began in the late 1870s with two groups: the Farmers' Alliance and Industrial Union, known as the Southern Alliance, and the Northwestern Farmers' Alliance. The Southern Alliance, formed on the frontier of Texas in 1875, was the real vanguard of populism. The smaller Northwestern Farmers' Alliance initially grew out of a New York State farmers' organization that became a national farmers' alliance in Chicago in 1880. In addition, the Colored Farmers' National Alliance originated in Texas in 1886 and recruited African Americans in a counterpart to the all-white Southern Alliance in the South. African American farmers were heavily involved in the movement; by the 1890s the Colored Farmers' National Alliance had over a million members. Some white Southern Alliance and Populist leaders, although eschewing social equality, called for cooperation and argued that black and white farmers were fighting the same monopolies and money power. Many of the Farmers' Alliance and Populist movements crossed class lines, but racial barriers remained.

The Farmers' Alliance surged forward in the South, the Midwest, and the Plains States in the late 1880s, coinciding with crop failures. Building upon the foundation of the Granges and continuing the emphasis on cooperatives and education, the Farmers' Alliance spread its message with traveling lecturers, and sometimes meetings carried the religious fervor of a community revival. In 1889 at St. Louis, an effort to merge the Southern and the Northwestern Alliances failed. Although the two resembled one another in their cooperative ventures and social and educational activities, the Northwestern Alliance disapproved of the Southern's secrecy, centralized control, and segregation of African Americans into separate organizations. Moreover, farmers in the Northwestern Alliance were more diversified than the single-crop (cotton) farmers in the Southern Alliance. In fact, the single-crop (wheat) state alliances of Kansas and North and South Dakota withdrew from the Northwestern Alliance and joined the Southern Alliance.

Farmers joined alliances to address real grievances about land, transportation, and money, and to fight against discriminatory railroad rates, monopoly prices for fertilizer and farm machinery, high tariffs, an unfair tax structure, the urban-controlled banking system, and the deflationary monetary gold standard. To tackle a major problem faced by farmers, that is, a lack of cash and a desperate need for credit, and to counter merchant control and the pervasive crop lien system, the alliances developed a subtreasury proposal. Adapted from Russian and French examples, subtreasuries would have allowed farmers to store their harvests in anticipation of better prices. Farmers then would have been able to draw notes on the subtreasury of up to 80 percent of the current market value of their stored harvests and use these subtreasury notes in lieu of cash.

To get their agenda accepted, the alliances shifted naturally into politics, lobbying for favorable legislation. In the South the Alliance endorsed friendly Democratic Party candidates, and in the West (Kansas, Nebraska, and South Dakota) successfully fielded candidates under third-party banners. In Omaha in 1892, the alliances joined with reform groups (and some labor support) to form the People's Party. The 1892 Omaha platform was an amazing reform document. The inveterate Minnesota reformer Ignatius Donnelly eloquently penned the preamble which proclaimed that "wealth belongs to him that creates it." Calling for expanded government powers of regulation, the Populists called for the abolition of poverty! The Populists' first national political convention advocated the Subtreasury plan; free and unlimited coinage of silver at the ratio of 16 to 1; a graduated federal income tax; a postal savings bank; public ownership of railroads, telegraphs, and telephones; prohibition of alien landownership, recovery of lands "illegally" held by railroads; im-

migration restriction; an eight-hour workday for industrial workers; and the prohibition of private armies used against strikers. Because elected and appointed government officials could do something about their problems, the Populists also focused on unrepresentative political institutions and political corruption.

Although the rhetoric of the People's Party denounced a conspiracy of monopolies, the Populists were not psychically paranoid (as some historians have suggested). Neither were they any more anti-Semitic, antiblack, or antiforeign than any other group in American society at that time; some evidence shows that they were less so.

The basis of farmer unrest was economic hardship and a feeling that government was not protecting agrarian interests. Farmers were trapped in a vicious cycle; when more money was needed to pay for increasing costs of seed, fertilizer, manufactured goods, and transportation, the farmers grew more crops—which in turn meant even lower prices. As farmers increased the amount of land under cultivation, mechanization also increased productivity. A bushel of wheat sold for $1.45 in 1866, 80¢ in 1885, and only 49¢ in 1895. Cotton moved downward to its lowest price, yet banks and merchants insisted southern farmers grow cotton or lose their credit for needed supplies.

Not all farmers joined the Populist crusade, not even all those living in the cotton and wheat states most affected by the agrarian protest movement. Most of its members were middling or yeoman farmers who worked family farms. In Kansas the wheat farmers most likely to become Populists were yeomen who were trying to hold onto their land and make gradual improvements. In Alabama, Populists drew heavily on farmers who had just lost ownership of land or who were living on the margin between land ownership and tenantry. Populism was the political protest of a downwardly mobile social group, a group of farmers left behind in the process of industrialization.

The Populist Party launched a broad reform leftist third-party movement and in 1892 held 20 percent of the popular vote. With obvious political success, the Populist Party took more moderate stands and narrowed its reform demands in order to broaden support, so that the single issue of free coinage of silver dominated. The Populist Party faced a dilemma in 1896 when the Democratic Party nominated a strong advocate of the silver standard, William Jennings Bryan, from the strongly Populist state of Nebraska. If they endorsed the Democrats and Bryan, the Populists risked party loyalty; if they ran their own slate, Populists ensured the defeat of any reform candidate. They chose the former and fused with the Democratic Party. Alliance with the conservative Democratic Party and their defeat in 1896 resulted in the demise of the Populist Party, but many populist ideas were later institutionalized under different auspices.

The Populists may be understood as part of a yeoman class who protested the growing centralization of economic power and decision making. They sought to extend the personal, virtuous, face-to-face social relations they grew up with as rural, evangelical Protestants. Consequently, while radical and forward looking in many of their programs, they were conservative in their ultimate goals. The Populists spoke in terms of their yeoman class, sanctioned by Jeffersonian ideals. Outsiders, they were nonetheless in tune with American democratic traditions.

Orville Vernon Burton

REFERENCES

Goodwyn, Lawrence. *Democratic Promise: The Populist Moment in America.* New York: Oxford University Press, 1976.

Hackney, Sheldon. *Populism to Progressivism in Alabama.* Princeton, NJ: Princeton University Press, 1969.

Hahn, Steven. *The Roots of Southern Populism: Yeomen Farmers and the Transformation of the Georgia Upcountry, 1850–1880.* New York: Oxford University Press, 1983.

McMath, Robert C., Jr. *Populist Vanguard: A History of the Southern Tenant Farmers' Alliance.* Chapel Hill: University of North Carolina Press, 1975.

Palmer, Bruce. *"Man Over Money": The Southern Populist Critique of American Capitalism.* Chapel Hill: University of North Carolina Press, 1980.

Farmers

Farmers produce food and fiber through the practice of agriculture. They till the soil and work the land to manage the growth of plants which, when harvested, serve as foodstuffs for human and animal consumption, or as sources of fiber for the production of textiles. In many cultures, farmers incorporate a pastoral component into the basic activity of plant production, by husbanding livestock which convert grasses, grains, and other vegetable matter into meat and milk for consumption by humans.

Food, of course, is fundamental to human existence. In preagricultural societies, humans met food requirements by hunting and gathering. With the shift from food gathering to food production that occurred during the Neolithic Revolution, agriculture became a required and paramount economic activity, and farmers, therefore, became a critically important social and economic group. Past methods of farming were sufficiently primitive and inefficient that production of enough food for the subsistence of all required the work of many hands. From the Neolithic Revolution until the modern era, agriculturalists have dominated numerically in the occupational structures of Western societies. Historians estimate their number to have comprised about 90 percent of the populations of premodern societies.

In western Europe and the United States during the modern period, industrialization and urbanization and a host of related social and economic changes led ultimately to a phenomenon unprecedented in the human experience, and no less profound than the Neolithic Revolution itself. In the late 18th century, the historic primacy of the agricultural sectors of Western developing economies began gradually to give way to the increasing dominance of industrial manufacturing. The long-term effect of this shift was a vast reduction in the proportion of farmers and farmworkers in the labor forces of the various countries affected by these changes. In France, for example, by 1850 about 50 percent of the labor force engaged in agriculture, and by 1970, only 13 percent. In England and in the United States, where these changes manifested themselves earliest and most strongly, only about 3 percent of the work force engaged in agriculture by 1970.

The causes of this epochal shift in the composition of the work forces of Western countries were many, but a prime factor which made it possible was the ever greater and ultimately spectacular increases in production of agricultural commodities achieved by farmers. Through practices associated with the agricultural revolution of the 18th century—enclosure and consolidation of landholdings, the introduction of legumes into crop rotations, and increased use of livestock manures to restore essential nutrients to the soil—farmers produced agricultural commodities at dramatically higher levels and with greater efficiency than ever before. Subsequent revolutionary changes in agricultural practices—mechanization, increased use of artificial fertilizers, and select breeding of animals and hybridization of plants—contributed further to this trend. Thus, even as their own numbers dwindled during the modern period, first relatively then absolutely, farmers produced with sufficient abundance to supply food for a rapidly growing population.

In its broadest usage farmers are agriculturalists. The term "farmer," however, is also used in a more restrictive sense to denote European or American agriculturalists who produced mainly for commerce. This usage of the term serves to distinguish profit-oriented agriculturalists who produced for the market, from agriculturalists (called peasants) who produced mainly for subsistence. Thus, social historians who study the shift to capitalistic agriculture in European society apply the term "farmer" to entrepreneurially spirited agriculturalists who had broken away from the tradition of subsistence farming and the legacy of seignorialism. Some social historians, dealing with countries like France, have traced the shift from peasantry to farmers as recently as the mid-20th century.

In an American context, the term "farmer" usually implies an agriculturalist of the northern United States. Often referred to as a yeoman farmer to suggest a middling socio-economic status in rural society, this type of agriculturalist relied on family members as a source of labor and, if possible, produced for the market. Much of what is known about American farmers from a sociohistorical point of view results from work in the "new rural history." In exploring the nature of past rural populations of the United States, these historians examine the usual variety of top-ics and processes that draw the attention of social historians, from social structure to patterns of work and leisure, from the family as an economic, emotional, and reproductive unit, to patterns of geographic mobility.

As with sociohistorical work on European rural life of the 19th and 20th centuries, a central issue in the study of American farm communities has been the transition to capitalist agriculture and its impact on the lives of farmers and their families. Another standard research thrust of the new rural history has been the study of the economic dimensions of farming. What were the determinants of success in attempts to secure livelihood through farming? Inheritance arrangements among farm families have also attracted considerable attention from rural historians. Land is the basic resource necessary for the conduct of agriculture. Accordingly, its bequeathal to a younger generation represents a critical juncture in the formation, evolution, and dispersal of farm families. A related area of inquiry has been to determine the extent to which farm families reduced their fertility as a response to declining availability of land. Other subjects examined by new rural historians include kinship networks in rural communities, the roles and status of women in farm society, and the family cycles and life courses of rural dwellers, with particular attention given to demographic patterns and household structures. (*See also* Agricultural Systems; Animals; Capitalism; Civilization; Commercialization; Food; Industrialization; Manorialism; Market Economy; Neolithic Revolution; Nomadism; Pastoralism; Peasantry; Urbanization)

Kenneth E. Koons

REFERENCES

Atack, Jeremy, and Fred Bateman. *To Their Own Soil: Agriculture in the Antebellum North.* Ames: Iowa State University Press, 1987.

Hahn, Steven, and Jonathan Prude, eds. *The Countryside in the Age of Capitalist Transformation: Essays in the Social History of Rural America.* Chapel Hill: University of North Carolina Press, 1985.

Huggett, Frank E. *The Land Question in European Society Since 1650.* London: Thames and Hudson, 1975.

Montmarquet, James A. *The Idea of Agrarianism: From Hunter-Gatherer to Agrarian Radical in West-*

ern Culture. Moscow: University of Idaho Press, 1989.

Osterud, Nancy. *Bonds of Community: The Lives of Farm Women in Nineteenth-Century New York*. Ithaca, NY: Cornell University Press, 1991.

Fascism

Fascism refers to a group of ultranationalist ideologies, sociopolitical movements, and regimes that emerged primarily in Europe between 1914 and 1945. The two most important examples are the Italian National Fascist Party, led to power in 1922 by Benito Mussolini, and the German National Socialist Workers' Party (Nazism), which gained power in 1933. Based on the bundle of rods with projecting axe carried before a Roman magistrate as a symbol of authority (*fasces*), the term was first used by an antisocialist militia, the Fascio di Combattimento, in Milan in March 1919.

In general, fascism was a product of Europe's uneven and often violent transformation from a largely rural into a capitalist, urban-industrial society. But it emerged specifically as a reaction to the sociopolitical disruptions of World War I and the interwar years, which included the collapse of the German, Austro-Hungarian, and Russian empires; the Bolshevik Revolution in 1917; intense political unrest based partly on the mobilization of the left in Italy, Germany, and Spain; and the economic and political crises associated with the Great Depression of 1929. Some fascist movements, such as those in Italy and Germany, had broad, multiclass followings that enabled their leaders to gain political power, whereas others, such as the Arrow Cross in Hungary, the Iron Guard in Romania, or the Falange in Spain, had some popular support but could gain power only under the conditions of World War II (Hungary and Romania) or as subordinates to authoritarian nationalism (the regime of Francisco Franco in Spain). In addition, there were small, imitative movements with little social backing such as the British Union of Fascists or Danish National Socialist Party, as well as the so-called Quisling regimes, named after the Norwegian traitor Vidkun Quisling, which the Germans put in place in occupied countries in World War II. Since 1945 there have been marginal fascistlike movements in Europe, the United States, and South Africa, and some fascist trappings in parts of Latin America.

Although fascist movements varied tremendously in terms of size, organization, and influence, they shared several common features. They defined themselves in vociferous opposition to previous ideologies, emphasizing anticommunism, antisocialism, antiliberalism, and a selective anticonservativism. They aimed for authoritarian or totalitarian states, hypernationalist political cultures, heavily regulated and protected national economic systems in which capitalist principles generally still had significant influence, and aggressive and often revisionist foreign policies. They used a style of politics and organization that was unprecedented for the time, featuring mass meetings, charismatic speakers, and (especially in Germany) the original use of modern communications technologies including film and radio. They were militaristic, idealistic, activist, misogynist, and homophobic, and they were often fascinated with technology, speed, modernity, and violent death. Most fascists aimed for national order based on ethnic purity, although only in Germany did hatred of Jews, Poles, Slavs, and Sinti and Roma (Gypsies) reach a level whereby nearly 6 million Jews and millions from other groups were systematically exterminated in concentration camps in World War II. Anti-Semitism's centrality to the German case has led some scholars to argue that Nazism was a unique case based on German peculiarities. Although fascist regimes in Italy and Germany modernized some parts of their economies and social structures, the balance of their rule was total war, political and racial persecution, massive disruption of social life, and unprecedented destruction.

For much of the post–World War II period, scholars considered fascism's social following to have been rooted mainly in the petite bourgeoisie, or lower middle classes, who consisted generally of small-scale artisans and retailers, low-level service personnel in commerce and administration, and small farmers. (Social factors have long drawn attention, though sometimes they have been subordinated to intellectual or political approaches.) Based on research first undertaken by Italian scholars in the early 1920s, fascism was identified with a "little man's" radical-ism motivated by hatred of the left, fear of mod-ernization, inability to compete successfully in capitalist markets, collective anxieties over social status, resentment of elites, and authoritarian personality structures. Whereas sociological and historical research of the first quarter century after World War II supported this view, schol-arly work of recent decades has stressed the so-cial heterogeneity of fascist movements. Detailed scholarship on Germany has demonstrated that voting support and party membership fluctuated tremendously, including not only the lower middle classes but also substantial groups of uni-versity students, former military officers and ser-vicemen, farmers, manual workers, and the up-per middle classes. Substantively and potentially, fascist movements of the interwar period ap-pealed to a broader range of collective interests than other parties on the right or the left, mak-ing their claim of being both comprehensively "social" and "national" convincing to many of their supporters. Sociohistorical scholarship has focused a great deal of attention on the social roots and consequences of fascism, particularly in the German case. Current research aims for an ever more complex and differentiated view of the phenomenon. (*See also* Depression, 1930s; Jews; Lower Middle Classes; Middle Class; Nationalism; Racism; World Wars)

Rudy Koshar

REFERENCES

Childers, Thomas, ed. *The Formation of the Nazi Constituency, 1919–1933*. London: Croom Helm, 1986.

Payne, Stanley. *Fascism: Comparison and Definition*. Madison: University of Wisconsin, 1980.

Mühlberger, Detlef, ed. *The Social Basis of European Fascist Movements*. London: Croom Helm, 1987.

Feasts and Celebrations

A celebration (from the Latin *celeber*, meaning "famous") is a solemn event, occasional or peri-odical, intended to honor, praise, or extoll pub-licly a person worthy of acclaim, or to commemo-rate the anniversary of a socially important event (e.g., a battle, the Fourth of July, or the birthday of a President, or a season of the year, a solstice, or an equinox). The observances that form a cel-ebration include appropriate rites or ceremonies and special objects and paraphernalia (e.g., as games, parades, processions, theatrical or musi-cal performances, special food, costumes, and masks) that acquire a special meaning for the occasion.

The word "feast" derives from the Latin *festum*, meaning originally "public joy," "merri-ment," and "revelry." *Feria* instead meant "absti-nence from work in honor of the Gods." From *festum* derive the Italian *festa*, the Spanish *fiesta*, the Portuguese *festa*, the French *Fête*, the Middle English *feste* as well as the French and English *festival*, at first an adjective connotating social events and later a noun denoting them. In con-temporary usage, a feast is an elaborate abun-dant ritual meal or a convivial occasion accom-panied by ceremonies and entertainment. A secondary meaning of the word feast is some-thing that gives great joy, or an outstanding or unusual pleasure.

The Feast of Fools, widely celebrated in me-dieval Europe, was the counterpart of Roman pre-Christian festivities, such as the *festum stultorum* and the *Saturnalia*, both carnivalesque in character, occurring at the beginning of the year cycle. In these, the daily world was repre-sented in burlesque reverse: masters served their slaves, social classes and sex roles were reversed, official hierarchies were ridiculed, chaos replaced order, and nonsense replaced daily common sense. The Feast of Fools lasted through Re-naissance times, until the Council of Trent (1545–1553) condemned them. The religious powers played a central role in these Christian-ized *Saturnalia*: a pope of fools (or a bishop) was nominated and ordained in a burlesque cer-emony; then a procession of masked prelates, often dressed in women's clothes, performed a symbolic "profanation of the temple" singing in church "*carmina turpia atque luxuriosa,*" obscene and vile songs, then danced, played dice and other games on the altars, while they ate pudding and blood sausages, censed the holy books with cen-sers where they burned garbage and old shoes; then paraded the streets in carts, giving mock blessings and throwing garbage to the crowds, with the accompaniment of obscene gestures and postures. A similar ceremony was the one of the

Boy Bishop, chosen among the altar boys to perform caricatures of religious ceremonies.

Fast and feast have been studied together, for instance in the ritual complex Carnival-Lent, as complementary aspects of ritual behavior dramatizing cultural attitudes toward foodways and their social, religious, and symbolic value (e.g., fasting to attain ritual cleanliness or public attention, or to summon the Gods; feasting as thanksgiving for harvest and as a prayer for abundant fruits of the earth).

Feasting, the ritual and ceremonial assumption of food and drinks with an explicit symbolic value, especially prepared for a festive occasion, is part of many celebrations: the *convivium* (literally "living together"), the *symposium* (literally "drinking together"), as well as the refreshments served on festivities are contemporary counterparts of older ceremonial occasions originally centering on the solemn consumption of food and drinks. Feasts range from the sharing of first fruits and killed game to ritual offerings of edibles to the gods. Special parts of the game killed (such as the heart, the brains, or the genitals) may be reserved to the hunter who killed the animal or to the gods. Feasting is often considered as a means to communicate with the gods; for instance, the Christians believe in the presence of Christ at the symbolic sacred meal of Holy Communion, held in celebration of the Last Supper, an important episode in the life of Christ. Similarly, in classical Greece it was believed that Zeus was invisibly present at the ritual feast being held in his honor during the Olympic Games. The *potlatch* is the most widely known example of ritual and spectacular consumption and destruction of food and other items of special value with the purpose of representing and propitiating prosperity, abundance, fertility, and power.

In some cases, the terms "feast," and "celebration," or "Feast and Celebrations" are used as synonyms for "festival," in the sense of periodic observances commemorating and honoring publicly an event, a person, a god, or a thing. In the social sciences, such festivities are usually intended as periodically recurrent social occasions in which, through a multiplicity of forms and a series of coordinated ritual events, all members of a community participate directly or indirectly and with various degrees of involvement and are united by ethnic, linguistic, religious, historical bonds, and sharing a world view. The social functions and symbolic meaning of such festivities and their component parts are closely relevant to the explicit and implicit values that the group organizing and participating in the celebration of the festive events considers essential. Festive events enact and celebrate the worldview, social identity, historical roots, and ultimately the psychical survival of the celebrating and feasting group.

Feasts and celebrations have been studied, as part of festival history more generally, for what they reveal about the values and community ties of various societies and periods—not only Europe, but Asia, Latin America, and Africa. Anthropological methods for deriving meaning from celebrations form an important tool in this social history, with work of Clifford Geertz and Victor Turner often cited. The study of celebrations can be carried into modern history as well, and many social historians work on rituals such as the Fourth of July in the wider terms of celebration history. Feasts, in their traditional communal sense, declined in Western society after the 17th century—as in the conversion of Thanksgiving from community to family feast—and this process too forms a target for sociohistorical analysis of historical change. (*See also* Festivals; Food; Greco-Roman Festivals; Ritual; South Asian Festivals)

Alessandro Falassi

REFERENCES

Falassi, Alessandro. *Time Out of Time. Essays on the Festival.* Albuquerque: University of New Mexico Press, 1987.

Feminism

The term "feminism" and its derivatives originated in France during the late 19th century. *Féminisme* was then commonly used as a synonym for "women's emancipation." French dictionaries have erroneously attributed the invention of the word "féminisme" to Charles Fourier in the 1830s, but in fact its origins remain uncertain. The first self-proclaimed *féministe* was the French women's suffrage advocate Hubertine Auclert, who from 1882 on used the term in her periodical, *La Citoyenne,* to describe herself and her associates. The words gained currency following discussion in the French press of the first "feminist" congress in Paris, sponsored in May 1892 by Eugénie Potonie-Pierre and her colleagues from the women's group *Solidarité*.

By 1894–1895 the terms "feminism" and "feminist" had crossed the English Channel to Great Britain, and before 1900, they were appearing in Belgian, French, Spanish, Italian, German, Greek, and Russian publications. By the late 1890s the words had jumped the Atlantic to Argentina, Cuba, and the United States, though they were not commonly used in the United States much before 1910. During the 20th century, the words also entered non-Western languages.

Much historical work on feminism focuses on intellectual or political aspects. The social bases of feminism have been explored, however; many feminist movements have drawn primarily from middle-class women (and some men), and explanations for the lesser involvement of other social groups reach deep into social history. Feminism has also roused responses, both favorable and hostile, that must be part of any gender history of Western society since the later 19th century. The expansion of feminist activism, though linked to ideological and political change, also relates to the the massive social changes in gender roles and individual opportunity brought by the industrial revolution and subsequent developments—again, a fundamental social link. Though tensions between sociohistorical and other approaches to the history of feminism remain, the subject has a larger place in modern Western social history.

The concept of feminism (viewed historically and comparatively) encompasses both a system of ideas and a movement for sociopolitical change based on a critical analysis of male privilege and women's subordination within any given society. It addresses imbalances of power between the sexes that disadvantage women. Feminism posits the notion of gender, or the differential social construction of the behavior of the sexes, based on their physiological differences, as the primary category of analysis. By so doing, feminism raises issues concerning personal autonomy or freedom but not without constant reference to basic issues of societal organization. In West-

ern societies, these issues have centered on the long-standing debate over the family and its relationship to the state, and underlying this debate, on the historically inequitable distribution of political, social, and economic power between the sexes. Feminism opposes women's subordination to men in the family and society, along with men's claims to define what is best for women without consulting them; it thereby offers a frontal challenge to patriarchal thought, social organization, and control mechanisms. It seeks to destroy masculinist hierarchy but not sexual dualism as such.

Feminism is necessarily pro-woman. However, it does not follow that it must be anti-man; indeed, in time past, some of the most important advocates of women's cause have been men. Feminism makes claims for a rebalancing between women and men of the social, economic, and political power within a given society, on behalf of both sexes in the name of their common humanity, but with respect for their differences. As a historical movement in the Western world, open to penetrating comparative study, the fortunes of feminism have varied widely from one society to another, depending on the possibilities available within a given society for the expression of dissent through word or deed. Feminist protest, which can be documented as early as the 15th century in Europe, erupted in sporadic collective action during the French Revolution, followed by much larger and better organized movements around 1900. Feminism experienced some decline between the world wars and a new surge of organizational activity since the 1960s. Feminism can be viewed as a rapidly developing major critical ideology, or system of ideas, in its own right. As an ideology, feminism incorporates a broad spectrum of ideas and possesses an international scope, one whose developmental stages have historically been dependent on and in tension with male-centered political and intellectual discourse but whose more recent manifestations transcend the latter. Feminism must be viewed as not intrinsically a subset of any other Western religious or secular ideology, whether Catholic or Protestant Christian, Judaic, liberal, socialist, or Marxist (although historically a feminist critique has emerged within each of these Western traditions by initially posing the question "And what about women?"). In order to comprehend fully the historical range and possibilities of feminism, however, the origins and growth of these ideas must be located within a variety of cultural traditions, and situated in terms of the historical experiences of different social groups of women and men.

The specific claims that have been made by feminists at particular times and in specific places in European, Australian/New Zealand, Canadian, and United States history range from arguments for ending the maligning of women in print, for educational opportunity, for changes in man-made laws governing marriage, for control of property and one's own person, and for valuation of women's unpaid labor along with opportunities for economic self-reliance; to demands for admission to the liberal professions, for readjustment of inequitable sexual mores and ending prostitution and other forms of sexual exploitation, for control over women's health, birthing, and child-rearing practices, for state financial aid to mothers, and for representation in political and religious organizations (symbolized in Western societies not only by the vote but also by access to public office). Such claims can all be seen as culturally specific subsets of a broader challenge to male pretensions to monopolize societal authority, that is, to patriarchy or male rule. At the same time, each of these claims addresses a structural issue, a problematic practice with political dimensions, which transcends the boundaries of the Western world and has applicability to the experience of women in other societies. Goals that are particular to specific cultural settings, such as rights equal to those granted men and gaining the vote for women, or short-range issues of strategy and tactics, such as combatting legalized prostitution or opposing cliterodectomy, should not be seen as coterminous with the phenomenon of feminism understood as a historical whole.

Based on such a broad cross-cultural understanding of feminism, feminists can be identified as any persons, female or male, whose ideas and actions (insofar as they can be documented) show them to meet three criteria: (1) they recognize the validity of women's own interpretations of their lived experience and needs and acknowledge the values women claim publicly

as their own (as distinct from an aesthetic ideal of womanhood invented by men) in assessing their status in society relative to men; (2) they exhibit consciousness of, discomfort at, or even anger over institutionalized injustice (or inequity) toward women as a group by men as a group in a given society; and (3) they advocate the elimination of that injustice by challenging, through efforts to alter prevailing ideas and/or social institutions and practices, the coercive power, force, or authority that upholds male prerogatives in that particular culture. Thus, to be a feminist is necessarily to be at odds with male domination in culture and society, in whatever geographical location or situation in historic time. [*See also* Divorce; Economics (Economic and Social History); Education; Feminist Theory; Law/Legal History; Marriage/Remarriage; Motherhood; Sense of Self/Individualism; Women's History]

Karen Offen

REFERENCES

Black, Naomi. *Social Feminism.* Ithaca, NY: Cornell University Press, 1989.

Cott, Nancy F. *The Grounding of Modern Feminism.* New Haven: Yale University Press, 1987.

Dyhouse, Carol. *Feminism and the Family in England, 1880–1939.* Oxford: Blackwell, 1989.

Miller, Francesca. *Latin American Women and the Search for Social Justice.* Hanover, NH: University Press of New England, 1991.

Offen, Karen. "Defining Feminism: A Comparative Historical Perspective," *Signs: Journal of Women in Culture and Society* 14:1 (1988).

Rendall, Jane. *The Origins of Modern Feminism: Women in Britain, France and the United States, 1780–1860.* New York: Schocken Books, 1984.

Sievers, Sharon L. *Flowers in Salt: The Beginnings of Feminist Consciousness in Modern Japan.* Stanford, CA: Stanford University Press, 1983.

Feminist Theory

Feminist theories developed in conjunction with the women's movement of the 1970s as scholars and activists attempted to understand and explain the positions of women in society. These combined developments led an ever growing number of social historians to make women's experiences central to their scholarship. Feminist scholars focused on women's social, political, and cultural subordination, and also studied how women were active contributors to the societies in which they lived. They introduced the concept of "gender" in order to indicate that women's positions in society were the consequence of social constructions, and were not due to their "sex," meaning their biological differences from men.

Feminist theorists of the 1970s focused particularly on the concept of "patriarchy," by which they meant the structures of social relations through which women are subordinated to men, and they directed their attention to understanding women's family relationships and their positions in society at large, especially in the economic sphere. Some feminist theorists, known as radical feminists, argued that patriarchy, especially as it controlled and dominated women's sexuality, was the primary or basic means by which women were subordinated. Others maintained that capitalism, the economic system based on private property and the accumulation of profits that produced class inequalities, was crucial to understanding women's inequality. Some of these scholars were known as Marxist feminists because they developed their ideas about society from the writings of Karl Marx and Friedrich Engels, and argued that changing gender relations were a consequence of the development of capitalism. Others who were known as socialist feminists developed what became known as "dual systems theory," and argued that patriarchy and capitalism interacted to produce the division of labor by gender and women's subordination.

Marxist feminists and socialist feminists have had a major impact on social history by stimulating historical studies of women's work and labor activism, the connections between women's family lives and economic contributions, and the differences between men's and women's work. These historical studies have challenged the work of labor, family, working-class, and middle-class historians who either left women out of their analyses or who assumed that gender was not relevant to the phenomena with which they were concerned.

As a consequence of both such scholarship in social history and further developments in feminist theory, the idea that gender is important to understanding all areas of social life has become increasingly accepted. Social historians now focus not only on women, or the differences in women's and men's family and work lives, but also on men as men. Increasingly, historians are investigating how men's lives are shaped by gender relations, and how the meanings of manhood have changed over time. In addition, scholars are examining the ways that gender has been central to areas of social life formerly believed to be the province of men, or thought to have nothing to do with gender. A major focus of study since the mid-1980s, for example, has been on gender and the state. A growing interest, especially among European social historians, concerns gender and the nature of citizenship.

While the concept "gender" was becoming the centerpiece of much feminist social history in the 1980s, developments in feminist theory were being influenced by critiques of European and Euro-American feminism by Third World and nonwhite feminist theorists, and the ideas of postmodernist literary theorists and Continental philosophers. In different ways they have led feminist scholars to make heterogeneity and difference central to their theories.

Third World and nonwhite feminist theorists had persistently challenged those feminists who argued that women share a common experience of oppression. They argue that race, ethnicity, and nationality as well as class shape women's life experiences. Their critiques have contributed to feminist theorizing that questions how theories can be about "women" when the term does not refer to people with the same experiences.

This question is also being raised by theorists who are known as postmodernist feminists. They are called postmodernist theorists because they reject scholarship that claims to provide a neutral, objective, universally applicable, and all-knowing view of the world. While there are many different and competing varieties of postmodernist theories, those that have most relevance for social history insist that discourse, or the meanings created by language, should be a primary object of study. Such theorists challenge the idea that women's and men's *experiences* are the appropriate object of historical investigation. Instead, they suggest that historians study the discursive categories "woman" and "man" to reveal how these categories are contested, are unstable, and how they mask difference, multiplicity, and heterogeneity. Social historians influenced by these new feminist theorists are paying increasing attention to visual representations of gender as well as to language as they study such topics as sexuality and the body, as well as how discourses about gender shape class, politics, and national identity.

Critics of postmodernist feminist theory are concerned that its application to social history will deflect attention away from how gender relations and other forms of inequality have affected peoples' lives. In addition, feminist historians who are interested in the relevance of social and economic factors for gender relations are unhappy about what they perceive as the tendency of postmodernist feminism to view language or discourse as determining social life.

We may expect that future theoretical developments and their applications to social history will resolve some points of contention by moving beyond thinking dichotomously about social and economic relations on the one hand and discursive constructions on the other. In any case, social history will continue its dialogue with feminist theories. (*See also* Cultural History; Women's History)

Sonya O. Rose

REFERENCES

Moraga, Cherrie, and Gloria Anzaldua, eds. *This Bridge Called My Back: Writings by Radical Women of Color*, 2nd ed. New York: Kitchen Table, 1983.

Nicholson, Linda J., ed. *Feminism/Postmodernism*. New York: Routledge, 1990.

Sargent, Lydia, ed. *Women and Revolution: A Discussion of the Unhappy Marriage of Marxism and Feminism*. Boston: South End Press, 1981.

Scott, Joan Wallach, *Gender and the Politics of History*. New York: Columbia University Press, 1988.

Tong, Rosemarie. *Feminist Thought: A Comprehensive Introduction*. Boulder, CO, and London: Westview Press, 1989.

Fertility

Fertility is one of three major forces that shapes populations, along with mortality and migration. Not only the size and growth of a population but also characteristics such as age composition, sex ratios, and racial and ethnic balance are determined by these three factors. Fertility is defined as the actual extent of childbearing achieved by a population. This is different from fecundity and sterility, which refer to whether or not people are capable of bearing chilren. Demographic historians have often referred to "natural fertility," which means childbearing in a population in which no actions are consciously taken to limit births. Levels of natural fertility can be quite different because of circumstances that limit births, but are not intended to do so.

Fertility is studied by two types of measures. Period measures study fertility in a particular year or set of years. The most common period measure is the crude birthrate, determined by dividing births in a year by the total population. Historical studies often use a period rate known as the child/woman ratio. This measure uses census data, in the absence of vital statistics registration, and calculates the ratio of children under some age, often five, to women of childbearing age, generally fifteen to forty-five or fifty. The second type of measure is of cohort fertility. A cohort is a group who experiences some event at the same time—for example, birth or marriage—which allows demographers to follow them for the rest of their lives. One measure of cohort fertility is to calculate the average number of children ever born to couples or women born or married at the same time. A very refined fertility measure is the net reproduction rate, which refers to the number of daughters a cohort of women will have. This is a measure of generational replacement, in which a net reproduction rate (NRR) of more than one means growth, and less than one, decline. Studies of fertility change have often used the experience of a small religious group in the United States, the Hutterites, as a standard for measuring the level of fertility. The Princeton University study of fertility decline in Europe constructed several indices which use Hutterite fertility as the basis of comparison, assuming few populations will ever exceed their fertility.

Levels of fertility in past and present populations vary greatly. Fertility is determined by three factors: exposure to sexual intercourse, probability of conception, and the chance of giving birth to a living child. Exposure to sexual intercourse is generally controlled in societies, often by the age at first marriage or the proportion ever marrying. In the context of world history, Europeans have married relatively late and infrequently over the last four centuries, and thus have had relatively low fertility. Sexual intercourse, and hence fertility, outside of marriage has sometimes been extensive and sometimes not. War, business journey, and religious customs can also limit the amount of sexual activity. The probability of conception is determined by involuntary causes such as nutrition, or marriage at ages when sterility is high. Venereal diseases can also prevent pregnancy. Conception can also be controlled voluntarily by techniques such as mechanical or chemical contraceptive devices, or by surgical sterilization. Prolonged nursing will often delay, but will not ultimately prevent another conception. The chances of giving birth to a living child are determined partly by the health of the mother, and are partly affected by acceptance of abortion as a means of family limitation. Obviously, social factors that affect the health and well-being of a population, and customs related to the forming of sexual unions and the appropriateness of sexual behavior, influence the level of fertility.

Social historians have been interested in fertility for several reasons. Of concern to both European and American historians is the remarkable decline in birth rates that has occurred since 1800. This decline began in France, and in parts of the United States, by 1800, and has spread to the rest of Europe and the U.S. population since then. As part of the demographic transition, the average number of children ever born fell from seven or eight in 18th-century America, to about two today. European fertility was not as high in the 18th century, but is as low today. Of great interest is whether this decline will occur in parts of the world which still have high birth rates. Thus the motives for controlling fertility are of great interest. Factors such as urbanization, industrialization, and the increasing scarcity of economic goods have been pointed to as reasons for limiting fertility. Often overlooked is the fact that birth control techniques in the past were generally determined by the women, and so explanations for fertility decline must recognize women's interests in having fewer children.

Differential fertility is another issue of concern. Not all groups in society have children at the same rate. Fertility has been shown to vary according to racial or ethnic background, religion, occupation, and language. Some such differences reflect only faster or slower adaptation to change, but others are more lasting. When differences exist, they can be matters of public debate. In the early part of the 20th century, some Americans expressed the fear that established groups in the population were committing "race suicide" by having fewer children in the face of massive influxes of high-fertility immigrants from southern and eastern Europe. In Europe, governments have adopted policies to encourage births among desired groups, and to build up military manpower in the face of external threats, often with little effect.

Recently, historians of the family and of women have demonstrated how declines in fertility have had reciprocal patterns of cause and effect with new family structures and new roles for women. (*See also* Abortion; Baby Boom; Birth Control; Childbirth; Demographic Transition; Family Reconstitution; Illegitimacy; Menarche; Midwifery; Sexuality)

Robert V. Wells

REFERENCES

Coale, Ansley J., and Susan Cotts Watkins, eds. *The Decline of Fertility in Europe.* Princeton, NJ: Princeton University Press, 1986.

Forster, Colin, and G.S.L. Tucker. *Economic Opportunity and White American Fertility Ratios: 1800–1860.* New Haven: Yale University Press, 1972.

Haines, Michael. *Fertility and Occupation: Population Patterns in Industrialization.* New York: Academic Press, 1979.

Tilly, Charles, ed. *Historical Studies of Changing Fertility.* Princeton, NJ: Princeton University Press, 1978.

Vinovskis, Maris A. *Fertility in Massachusetts from the Revolution to the Civil War.* New York: Academic Press, 1981.

Festivals

Festivals may perhaps best be defined as days or periods set aside for the commemoration or ritual celebration, often through traditional observances, of events or seasons that hold particular importance for an individual and his community. They may commemorate events in the distant past or celebrate those occurring in the present; they may be observed within a single village or around the world. They may, as in the case of court festivals, involve elaborate and costly spectacles, or center around simple folk customs, as in the case of most rural agricultural festivals. Their observance frequently involves special foods, household utensils, or types of clothing that mark the time of the festival as being different from other times, whether an account of its solemn or joyous character. Festival occasions may also involve various degrees of ritualized violence and licentiousness, both being especially characteristic of festivals of inversion such as the Roman Saturnalia, the pre-Lenten Carnival, and the Jewish Purim. The sociologist R. Caillois has suggested that in traditional societies man lives "in remembrance of one festival and in expectation of the next."

Festivals have been widely studied by historians and anthropologists, as they formed a vital part of the life of ordinary people, often combined elites and ordinary people in common rituals and values, and served a host of functions ranging from controlling youth (by giving them special festival roles) to supporting the cohesion of villages or artisan guilds. Festivals developed in every agricultural society, and anthropologists have studied them widely. Historical study has thus far focused particularly on western Europe. Social historians also deal with the decline of festivals and their ultimate displacement by other possibly less meaningful leisure forms, during the past several centuries.

The ancient Athenian calendar included more than 50 days on which all business, including the administration of justice, was suspended by order of the magistrates. Some of these commemorated historical events, but most were nature related, linking themselves particularly with the phenomena of the seasons, the equinoxes, and the solstices. The fullest list of ancient Hebrew holidays occurs in Leviticus 23, where the three pilgrimage festivals, linked also with seasonal changes, appear together with the more solemn "days of awe," Rosh ha–Shana and Yom Kippur. Sabbaths and days of the new moon were also festive occasions. Hannukah, the eight-day winter festival of lights, and Purim, falling, like the later Carnival, during the transition from winter to spring, were also added in ancient times, thus forming the classical cycle of the Jewish year.

The Roman calendar included more than 100 feast days, dedicated mostly to various gods and goddesses, of which a relatively high number fell during the months of December and February. The Saturnalia, one of the oldest of Roman festivals, was celebrated around the time of the winter solstice, on December 17, and sometimes extended for as many as seven days. Seneca claimed that in his day all Rome seemed to go mad on this holiday. Its perhaps best known feature was the social inversion of slaves being waited on by their masters and treated in every respect as their equals. This sort of role inversion had also been characteristic of various festivals among the ancient Greeks and Babylonians and was later to characterize others, such as Shrove Tuesday in England. Another feature of the Saturnalia, stressed especially by the anthropologist James G. Frazer, was that of the mock king, the ancient Lord of Misrule, who would issue commands of a playful nature to his temporary subjects, and who would be required, in some variations of the festival, to die or be killed in effigy at its end.

The Roman Lupercalia, a fertility festival that fell on February 15, was, like many other pagan festivals, eventually Christianized, being transformed in the late 5th century by Pope Gelagius I into the Purification of the Virgin Mary. Similarly the ancient festival of the summer solstice (midsummer) eventually became Feast of St. John (June 24), traditionally celebrated in Europe with the lighting of bonfires. These too were given Christian meaning, and were later incorporated in local festivals held in honor of John the Baptist in those cities (such as Florence) in which he served as patron saint. Frazer and others have argued that "on the whole the evidence goes to show that the great Christian festivals were arbitrarily timed by the church so as to coincide with previously existing pagan festivals for the sake of weaning the heathen from their old faith and bringing them over to the new religion." In the case of Christmas, however, this was not quite arbitrary, for the midwinter festivals traditionally included ritual reversal, and as Burke (1978) has recently noted, "the birth of the son of God in a manger was a spectacular example of the world turned upside down."

Moreover, the debt of Christianity to the festivals of ancient Judaism must also be taken account of, chiefly in the case of Easter, which linked the rebirth of spring with the resurrection of Christ and Pentecost (Whitsunday), which commemorated the descent of the Holy Spirit on the disciples. These were closely modeled upon Passover and Shavuot in the Jewish calendar, which were also seven weeks apart, and which marked, respectively, the arrival of spring and of the summer harvest. Passover was seen in the Hebrew Bible as commemorating also the Exodus from Egypt, but Shavuot, the feast of the first fruits, came only later, in Rabbinic tradition, to be celebrated as the commemoration of the central event—the giving of the Law to Moses on Mount Sinai. In early modern times, especially after the widespread dissemination of coffee, the custom of maintaining nightlong study vigils on Shavuot became increasingly popular. These two holidays, together with that of Sukkot (Tabernacles), which marked the conclusion of the harvest season, had constituted the three festivals of pilgrimage to Jerusalem. Relatedly, these were also the occasions upon which, according to classical Jewish law, public executions would be performed.

Other festivals of major importance in the early Christian centuries included Epiphany (January 6), originally celebrating the baptism of Jesus and later associated with his appearance to the Magi, and Ascension Day, observed on the fortieth day (sixth Thursday) after Easter. Both were widely celebrated earlier than was Christmas, which from medieval times inaugurated the 12 winter holiday days culminating in the festivities of Twelfth Night. These activities traditionally included the lighting of fires and the carrying of torches in the fields, another fertility practice ("everywhere primarily intended," according to Frazer, "to burn the witches and other maleficent beings swarming invisible in the mischief-laden air") that came to be Christianized. Also customary for many centuries on Twelfth Night (and also eventually Christianized) was the election of a king and/or queen of the bean,

a member of the household who received a bean (or more precious object) that had been baked into their holiday cake, and who would reign festively during the holiday. In 19th-century England the Twelfth Day was recognized in some places as an opportunity for clearing up old grudges and back reckonings, "all of which," according to an 1840 source, "can be done with impunity."

The festive activities of the Feast of Fools, observed also around Christmastime, centered around various forms of ritual inversion, including those of a sexual nature, and were in the Middle Ages and early modern times often presided over by "joyous companies" (of which there were some 20 in 16th-century Lyons) led by young Lords of Misrule. A traditional observance was also the election of a mock bishop who would ride an ass backward. In the urban Feast of Fools in France, Davis (1975) has noted, "the fertility function of transvestism was overshadowed by its carnivalesque derision of the celibate priestly hierarchy." The double role of inversion as a form of popular festivity and of social and political criticism was also characteristic of the pre-Lenten Carnival at winter's end. Although some have seen these carnivalesque forms of festivity as prepolitical "safety valves" intended to deflect attention from social reality, Davis has argued persuasively that they could serve "both to reinforce order and to suggest alternatives to the existing order."

The state, for its part, could also make use of traditional festivals for purposes of self-legitimation. Thus in Venice, from medieval times, the rites of Ascension came to be the center of a vast spring festival complete with public entertainments, featuring the Doge's annual espousal of the sea "as a sign of true and perpetual dominion." The marriage of the sea may have been seen (Muir 1981) as a Venetian version of a spring fertility festival, in which the traditional agrarian goals of such rites were transformed to serve the maritime and mercantile needs of the state. In Elizabethan England the Accession Day of the monarch was promulgated as an official holy day of the Established Church, its festivities, historian Roy Strong has argued (1984), replacing those of the medieval saints' days. In his view, throughout Renaissance Europe "the art of festival was harnessed," with the aid of humanistic ideas, "to the emergent state as an instrument of rule."

The tensions between order and disorder central to many festive occasions made these especially ripe for ritualized violence, whether planned or spontaneous. In early modern France, it has been noted, quarrels, brawls, and murders were more numerous in such times of revelry as saints' days and Carnival week than in normal times, and in Italy the Carnival season was a time of licence, "not only to overeat and drink and indulge sexually before the abstinence of Lent," but also, as Peter Burke (1978) has stressed, "to engage in acts of ritualized aggression." These could include, as in the case of Renaissance Rome, the cudgeling of minor offenders and the execution of criminals.

Relatedly, festivals, especially those of inversion, could be associated with various forms of riot and rebellion. In late 12th-century northern France the Jews of Brie (or possibly Bray) chose Purim as the day for executing a Christian who had killed a Jew—and later paid a heavy price for their festive violence. Noteworthy also are the massacre in Basel on Fastnacht (Shrove Tuesday) of 1376 and the peasant revolt in Bern during Carnival of 1513. During the wars of religion in France, festivals were particularly likely to turn violent, the most famous instances being the 1572 St. Bartholomew's Day Massacre in Paris and the insurrectional 1580 Carnival at Romans in the Dauphiné. The Masaniello revolt in Naples during the summer of 1647 was closely linked with Ascension and with two major local feasts of the Virgin Mary. Revolt was often seen by the European populace as a legitimate form of festive rejoicing. In England it was common for festive events to serve as convenient opportunities for individuals to settle their grievances with others.

In early modern times, however, there emerged a powerful tendency from above to delegitimize various forms of traditional popular festivity, a tendency in which the twin forces of Protestantism and the Catholic Reform played an important role. Although the medieval Christian calendar, from the 12th century on, mandated 125 days or more in the year (including Sundays) of enforced leisure, this changed radi-

cally with the rise of Protestantism. Erasmus in a letter of 1519 argued that the festivals of the Church robbed laborers of regular earnings that would otherwise have been theirs. In England the Puritan Order of 1536, abrogating all festivals, claimed that they were the occasion of much sloth and idleness, riot and superfluity, and led to the decay of industrial crafts. The Church of Scotland, in 1645, banned all holidays except for Sundays. Although in Catholic countries festivals continued, during the 16th century, to punctuate the calendar quite regularly, the trend in the following century was to cut down on their number, and to purify of their more profane elements those which were allowed to survive. The number of obligatory feast days in the Paris region declined from 55 early in the 17th century to 21 in 1666. Throughout France, it has been argued, religious feasts were turned into moments of piety rather than pleasure, and the major urban festivities were transformed into spectacles in which the populace were no longer real participants. This occurred elsewhere in 17th- and 18th-century Europe with regard to the Carnival, and in many Jewish communities, too, efforts were made to limit or prohibit various festive observances (such as Purim masquerade), which had long been deemed acceptable.

In the late 18th century new festivals, drawing often on older models, emerged in connection with the American and, more extensively, the French revolutions. The American colonists siezed Pope Day (November 17), by then an antipapal festival that had previously been observed as Queen Elizabeth's Day, and turned it against the English Monarchy itself. The festivals of the French Revolution, it has been argued, sought to transfer sacrality from the religious feast days of the old regime to the values of a modern, secular, liberal world. They numbered more than 20, including the Festival of the Federation (the very first to be instituted) and the Festival of the Supreme Being, designed by the revolutionary leader Robespierre to demonstrate the difference between the god of nature and the god of the clergy. These festivals were often quite syncretistic in character, borrowing liberally from the Greco-Roman heritage, but also from the Christian one.

The Muslim calendar contains only two real festivals known by the name *'id*, the Great Festival, or Festival of the Sacrifice (*id al–adha*), associated with the sacrifice of Ishmael by Abraham, and the Little Festival, or Festival of Fast-breaking (*id al–fitr*), which concludes the month-long fast of Ramadan. However, as E.W. Lane observed in early 19th-century Egypt and many others have noted, "in most respects, what is called the Minor Festival is generally observed with more rejoicing than that which is termed the Great Festival." Traditional observances of both included the wearing of new clothes, prayers in the mosque, and visits to friends and to the cemeteries, which were temporarily transformed into sites of festive activity. R.F. Burton, another 19th-century observer, commented on the "scene of jollity," which obtained at one of Cairo's cemeteries during the "little" festival. ("Tents and ambulant coffee-houses were full of men equipped in their . . . Sunday best, listening to singers and musicians, smoking and chatting, and looking at jugglers, buffoons, snake-charmers, Darwayshes, ape-leaders, and dancing boys habited in women's attire.") The same observer noted that "even on this solemn occasion there is . . . not a little flirtation and love-making; parties of policemen are posted, with orders to interrupt all such irregularities, with a long cane; but their vigilance is notoriously unequal to the task."

During the nights of Ramadan, too, a particularly festive atmosphere generally obtained, with abundant food and diverse entertainments being enjoyed after the traditional cannon blast concluding each day's fast. In medieval Egypt considerable efforts were made to suppress some of the more transgressive and carnivalesque features of these 40 nights, but some were still apparent to 19th-century observers. "Night is turned into day," wrote Lane, and Burton observed somewhat later that on the nights of Ramadan the streets were "crowded with a good-humoured throng of strollers; the many bent on pleasure, the few wending their way to Mosque." Many would saunter about shopping until the late hours of the night or sit at the coffeehouse entrances, smoking waterpipes, chatting, and listening to storytellers, singers, or itinerant preachers. Lane was particularly struck by the wandering criers who would, after receiving a coin, recite the opening chapter of the Qur'an followed by tales "of a grossly indecent nature," which were nonetheless listened to "by females in houses of good repute." The latter was moved to remark: "How incongruous are such sequels," but our current understanding of the nature of festive time and festive observance, whether Greco-Roman, Christian, Jewish, or Islamic, has allowed us to make somewhat better sense of such apparent incongruities.

The rise of industrialism and growing concerns about public order further dented the festival tradition in the West, with newly-formed police forces spending a great deal of time preventing traditional festival rowdiness during the 19th century. This change became a vital part of the social history of modern leisure. Festivals, and attacks on them amid growing pressure for labor efficiency in the 19th century, have also been studied in Latin America and in southern and eastern Asia, though the festival tradition, major changes in festival types, and comparative features also generate extensive opportunities for further analysis. (*See also* Feasts and Celebrations; Leisure)

Elliott Horowitz

REFERENCES

Burke, Peter. *Popular Culture in Early Modern Europe*. New York: Harper & Row, 1978.

Davis, Natalie Z. *Society and Culture in Early Modern France*. Stanford, CA: Stanford University Press, 1975.

Malcolmson, Robert W. *Popular Recreations in English Society, 1700–1850*. Cambridge: Cambridge University Press, 1973.

Muchembled, Robert. *Popular Culture and Elite Culture in France: 1400–1750*. Baton Rogue: Louisiana State University Press, 1985.

Muir, Edward. *Civic Ritual in Renaissance Venice*. Princeton, NJ: Princeton University Press, 1981.

Feudalism

The term "feudalism" is used by social historians in two different senses. Broadly conceived (and sometimes referred to as "feudal society"), it designates a distinctive type of social system that prevailed in medieval Europe and perhaps elsewhere. In a narrower, more legalistic sense, medieval historians use the term to refer to a system of relationships between lords and vassals that developed in Europe between the 10th and the 12th centuries. This narrower definition can also be applied to Japanese society from about the 12th to the 16th centuries.

The original concept emerged in the 18th century. While social critics like Montesquieu and Voltaire began to criticize "feudal" aspects of their society, Adam Smith's *Wealth of Nations* (1776) referred to the "feudal system" as a system of production relying on coercion and regulation instead of market forces as incentives. Thus, the idea of feudalism emerged as the antithesis of the individualistic, market-oriented values that reformers were hoping to promote. It was in this sense that the French revolutionaries declared, on August 4, 1789, that "the National Assembly completely abolishes the feudal regime," thereby lumping together an entire complex of manorial rights, legal privileges, and ecclesiastical advantages into one systemic concept. This tradition was perpetuated by the liberal historians and economists of the 19th century. In the 1850s and 1860s Karl Marx added a critical twist to the same ideas by developing a more rigorous method of analyzing the essential characteristics of any society and a theory of historical change based on the concept of developing productive forces and the struggle of conflicting classes. Marx concentrated his attention on capitalism, but since feudalism was the system out of which capitalism arose, the nature of the transition from feudalism to capitalism has become a central analytical problem for Marxist historians.

At the core of the analysis is the idea of a low-yield, relatively localized agricultural economy in which a class of lords (knights, later the nobility) extracted labor from a class of farmers (serfs, later dependent peasants) by virtue of their immediate control over the attributes of public power (justice, economic regulations, law enforcement). The peasants were forced to pay the lords manorial (seignorial) dues in the form of labor in the lords' fields (corvée) or payments in kind or money. These payments enabled the ruling class not only to live without doing agricultural labor but to devote its energies to military exploits and, since ecclesiastics also lived off feudal rents, to religious activities. Unlike slaves,

these serfs or peasants owned their plots and tools and disposed of their own persons and their free time; but unlike modern farmers their property rights were limited by the overlord's capacity to intervene, monitor, and collect unearned payments.

Thus feudal society was built around the concept of the innate superiority of certain groups and a system of mutual but unequal obligations, in a situation where the relative scarcity of money and trade made control of food production a primary concern. There have been fascinating discussions about this concept of feudalism and its implications in western Europe. Issues such as the role of towns and trade, the place of Catholic ideology, the link between the dictates of the manorial economy and the nature of knightly culture, the reasons for the rise of feudal monarchies, the crisis of the 14th century, and the place of the rise of absolutism have all been hotly debated. Since many of the same conditions prevailed in Japan during the "feudal" period (12th–16th centuries) and societies with some of the same characteristics can be found in other parts of the world in key periods (including the Middle East, Russia, and Latin America), possibilities exist for interesting cross-cultural analysis.

The second, narrower definition of feudalism avoids making the connection between economic production and social arrangements. For many social historians of medieval Europe and Japan, *feudalism* is simply a system of personal ties between lords and vassals, all of whom belonged to the superior military class. It is to be sharply distinguished from *manorialism* (or seignorialism), the system of ties between landlords and tenants on the manor. In the feudal system a lord delegated land and power to followers (vassals) who promised in return to provide military services when called, to pay tribute on specific occasions such as the knighting of the lord's son, and to provide the lord with advice and counsel. The vassal received a fief, which was a grant of land from which to draw his support (in effect, one or more manors with authority over peasants), and the lord was thereby able to maintain a group of supporters who had the means to equip themselves to fight an aggressor. As the system developed, lords became vassals of higher lords, and vassals subinfeudated their lands to lesser vassals, creating a pyramid of relationships. Fiefs became hereditary and feudal rights became established in law. Power became extremely decentralized. This situation emerged in the 9th century as the Carolingian Empire disintegrated and gradually disappeared in the late Middle Ages as monarchs began recentralizing power. It was a response to a society in which the primitive nature of production and distribution made it necessary to position followers close to the lands that supported them rather than accumulating supplies and soldiers in one central location. This narrower feudalism is also controversial. Historians debate whether it really existed in England and in southern Europe. Some argue that it is nothing more than an artificial construct.

The two meanings of feudalism have in common an emphasis on personal, reciprocal relationships rather than bureaucratic structures and a concept of shared ownership of property. The narrower definition can be seen as an aspect of the broader definition, but their different implications should not be overlooked and the precise meaning of the term needs careful attention in any sociohistorical work. By the narrow definition, for example, feudalism was never fully developed in Russia and eastern Europe; by the broader definition, feudalism based on serfdom intensified in eastern Europe from the 16th to the 19th centuries. (*See also* Aristocracy; Manorialism)

William Beik

REFERENCES

Anderson, Perry. *Passages from Antiquity to Feudalism.* London: NLB, 1974.

Bloch, Marc. *Feudal Society.* Translated by L.A. Manyon. Chicago: University of Chicago, 1961.

Critchley, John. *Feudalism.* London: Allen & Unwin, 1978.

Ganshof, F.L. *Feudalism.* Translated by Philip Grierson. New York: Harper & Row, 1961.

Herlihy, David, ed. *The History of Feudalism.* New York: Harper & Row, 1970.

Hilton, Rodney, ed. *The Transition from Feudalism to Capitalism.* London: Verso, 1978.

Folklore/Oral Traditions

"Folklore" is the term that designates the traditional, unofficial culture of communities (folk groups) and the academic discipline that studies such culture. When British antiquarian William John Thoms coined the word "folklore" in 1846, he was seeking a new name for "popular antiquities"—the customs, beliefs, stories, and artifacts that composed the communal legacy of the old-fashioned and poorer segments of society.

To early folklorists, folklore was above all an item—a proverb, riddle, song, tale, dance, custom, ritual, design, tool, or building. Items of folklore were assumed to be of great antiquity, passed down from generation to generation with little change. A second trait of early definitions was folklore's strong association with certain groups—ethnic (such as Italian Americans), religious (Pentecostals), occupational (sailors), regional (Ozark mountaineers), or national (Americans).

Recently, folklorists have stressed a third trait: folklore is a community-based process, usually involving word-of-mouth and face-to-face communication in close-knit groups, through which people express and negotiate their shared understandings, beliefs, and concerns. Folklore is constantly changing to reflect the changing circumstances of those who share it. Thus, contemporary folklorists reject the old assumption that lore is a fossil, passed on unaltered for centuries. Any vital folk group will refashion old stories to address current needs.

Today's folklorists view folklore as the unofficial culture of any group, not just the product of the poor or old-fashioned. Whatever their social background, such groups as families share beliefs, attitudes, gestures, and behaviors—as well as such material traditions as cooking and crafts—which they create and reshape as unofficial expressions of group identity.

The folklore process is both conservative and dynamic. Because such folk performers as storytellers must meet the expectations of a live audience, they present their hearers with familiar time-tested plots, themes, and styles, ensuring that each performance owes much to the norms established by past performers and audiences. Yet, because no two storytelling sessions are identical, each performance is also a newborn expression of its present context.

According to modern formulations, folklore

is the day-to-day unofficial community process on which most other culture is based. Because its influence on society is so pervasive, folklore does not exist simply in oral documents, but also permeates many written sources from which scholars reconstruct the lifestyles and value systems of past societies. Historians of unofficial culture, some identifying themselves as folklorists and some not, have used various written records and archaeological evidence to supplement or substitute for oral traditions. In *Montaillou* (1978), Emmanuel Le Roy Ladurie artfully rereads testimony from the trials of accused heretics and finds beneath the official veneer of these documents a wealth of evidence allowing him to describe the home life, sexual practices, funeral customs, and folk religion of a 13th-century French village. In *Earnest Games* (1987), Carl Lindahl employs slander records, courtesy books, coroners rolls, and Chaucer's poetry to reconstruct folk techniques of indirect insult employed in 14th-century England. In *Black Culture and Black Consciousness* (1977), Lawrence W. Levine uses oral folktales and slave narratives collected in the 20th century to supplement 19th-century writings and produce a thorough study of the value systems of American slave societies.

Items of folklore are available to the social historian in many extensive collections, such as the Folktales of the World Series (University of Chicago Press), Francis J. Child's *The English and Scottish Popular Ballads* (5 volumes, 1882–1898) and Newman I. White's *The Frank C. Brown Collection of North Carolina Folklore* (7 volumes, 1952–1961). The most useful collections include notes describing the communities, tellers, and contexts that created the lore. But social historians best benefit from such sources by first considering some of the premises and methods of folklorists.

1. Because folklore combines stable, long-lived patterns with the needs and nuances of its immediate context, such forms as folktales present an excellent medium for studying intercultural variation and change over time. For example, certain English and American stories of outlaw heroes spanned a period of nine centuries, during which they told of the Anglo-Saxon resister Hereward (11th-century England), the legendary yeoman Robin Hood (15th-century England), and the bank robber Jesse James (19th-century America). One of the Robin Hood tales is recast as a story about Jesse James: the outlaw provides money to a virtuous victim (a knight in the Robin Hood tale; a widow in the Jesse James version) threatened with poverty by a cruel landlord (the church, for Robin Hood; a banker, for Jesse James); after the landlord collects his rent, the hero sets an ambush for the villain and steals back the money.

The traits shared by all groups of stories reveal something about the function of outlaw legends in general. In all three cases, the stories arose in the midst of domestic unrest, and the outlaw hero emerged to represent the values of groups alienated from the dominant power structure. By aiding the oppressed at the expense of the oppressors, the outlaw hero rejects the dominant culture and asserts the moral superiority of the underdog.

Yet, more specifically, the differences between the various outlaw heroes express something of the social climate in which each emerged. Hereward was an Anglo-Saxon earl allied with Anglo-Saxon peasants against the Norman occupation; his stories show the English side of an ethnic conflict with the new French-speaking rulers. Robin Hood unites yeomen and dispossessed nobles against church leaders and corrupt barons, thus revealing the shared concerns of minor landowners and tradesmen threatened by the interests of powerful landlords and lawmakers. Jesse James—defending widows, children, and poor farmers against predatory bankers and lawmen—represents a largely rural and southern subculture dominated by northern urban interests. As similar as the three groups of legends are, each can be located in a specific social context, a context which is "truer" than the events of the story. Hereward and Jesse James were flesh-and-blood outlaws; Robin Hood probably was not. The legends just discussed almost certainly do not represent actual events in the lives of these outlaws. Like so much folklore, these tales are older than the events portrayed; their "truth" lies in the ways in which they reflect the tellers' values.

Historians using tales to document social contexts should know as many intercultural versions of a tale as possible; that knowledge will help them discover what is unique to the region or period under study. Such catalogues as Antti Aarne's and Stith Thompson's *The Types of the Folktale* (1961) and Thompson's *Motif-Index of Folk-Literature* (1955–1958) help researchers find variants of internationally distributed narratives.

2. In conducting intercultural studies, folklorists find that the more similar two items of lore, the more significant the differences between them. For example, most items of folklore possess at least three kinds of style: generic, cultural, and individual (John Ball, "Style in the Folktale," *Folklore* 65 [1954]: 170–172). "Generic style" refers to the fact that different folklore forms are told according to different rules. For example, *Märchen* (called "fairy tales" by nonfolklorists) emphasize magic, fantasy, and an optimistic, wish-fulfilling worldview. By contrast, legends feature supernatural beings—such as ghosts and witches in American culture—that are part of the belief system of many of its tellers and hearers. Unlike *Märchen,* legends emphasize frightening aspects of the unknown. Thus, to compare German *Märchen* and American legends is to compare apples and oranges—generic differences are too great to reveal valid cultural distinctions. Robert Darnton's *The Great Cat Massacre* (1984) commits a similar error in trying to reveal differences between French and English folk cultures by comparing French *Märchen* with English nursery rhymes.

To find real cultural differences embedded in folklore, one must compare items of the same genre, and items that—to the greatest extent possible—share the same plots and themes. Furthermore, one should compare as many plots and variants as possible, because every taleteller has an individual style. Cultural style becomes apparent only after one examines the styles of many tellers within a group.

3. Folklore combines two types of truth: actual fact and social truth. Both types are valuable for different purposes, but they are often difficult to separate. For example, William Camden's *Britannia* (1586) records an oral tradition about a giant named Jul Laber buried in a mound in southern England. Camden discovered that the mound was probably the burial place of the Ro-

man tribune Laberius Durus, killed in Julius Caesar's invasion of Britain. If so, a tenacious oral tradition preserved the tribune's name for more than 1,600 years. Yet this *actual fact* was combined with the *social fact* that the tribune had been converted to a giant—through the English folk tradition of ascribing ancient Roman ruins to the work of giants.

To separate social truth from actual fact, social historians should consult all the sources at their disposal. Archeology has helped substantiate Paiute Indian tales that describe the migrations, lifestyle, and physical stature of a vanished tribe they called the *Mukwitch.* The discovery of pots, dwellings, and skeletons belonging to an 800-year-old civilization in Utah confirms that the area was once occupied by a tribe greatly resembling the *Mukwitch* as described by present-day Paiutes.

Even when only oral evidence is available, a great number and variety of sources will help establish the probability of certain claims. In *The Saga of Coe Ridge* (1970), William Montell consulted both blacks and whites to assemble an oral history of a 19th-century African American community in Kentucky. The two groups were in conflict and did not share their stories with each other. Although the two groups differed greatly in evaluating the motives underlying their conflicts, blacks and whites agreed remarkably in their chronologies and descriptions of events. Montell's extensive collecting allowed him to separate probable fact from two different versions of social fact.

4. Folklore—though a strong indicator of the teller's worldview—may provide a very skewed version of someone else's reality. For example, legends told in the Renaissance and summarized in such documents as the *Malleus Maleficarum* (c. 1485) claim to describe the actual practices of witches, but are in large part retellings of older stories once used by monks to stereotype Jews and heretics. These stories tell us little about the folklore of accused witches, but they reveal much about the fears and folk beliefs of the accusers. Only a thorough knowledge of earlier and international legends about witches can help separate the inquisitors' claims from the victims' reality. Carlo Ginzburg's *Night Battles* (1983) applies such knowledge to transcripts from the witch-

craft trials of Renaissance Italy, peeling away the outsiders' lore and discovering the actual folk magical practices buried in surviving records.

5. As ancient as much folklore appears, the fact that it changes over time makes it a much better indicator of the present than the past. For example, American ballads collected in the 20th century contain very little evidence of supernatural belief, except for occasional references to the Christian god and devil. Such evidence may lead us to conclude that the British folk groups that brought the ballads to America possessed few non-Christian supernatural beliefs. Yet British ballads from the 18th century often mention elves, fairies, and giants. Studying the two groups of ballads can reveal many differences between 18th-century British and 20th-century American folk culture, but will also demonstrate that recent folklore does not necessarily reflect ancient belief. This last point deserves special stress, because some of the greatest early folklore studies were based on the premise that folklore embeds the worldviews of long-dead peoples. Historians should use caution in applying these early studies. It is also true that use of folklore to determine cultural change is less well developed than other aspects of folklore's role in social history, including its service in comparing different popular-cultural tradition. (*See also* Cultural History; Ethnography/Ethnohistory; Popular Culture)

Carl Lindahl

REFERENCES

Cocchiara, Giuseppe. *The History of Folklore in Europe.* Philadelphia: ISHI Press, 1981.

Dégh, Linda. *Folktales and Society.* Bloomington: Indiana University Press, 1969.

Dorson, Richard M., ed. *Handbook of American Folklore.* Bloomington: Indiana University Press, 1983.

Kaplan, Steven L., ed. *Understanding Popular Culture.* Berlin: Mouton, 1984.

Toelken, J. Barre. *The Dynamics of Folklore.* Boston: Houghton-Mifflin, 1979.

Food

Food is the basic source of the nutrients that the human body converts into energy to grow and maintain itself. Attitudes toward what is considered edible vary by culture and by class. Offal (the innards of animals) provides one example of this variation; so does consumption of (or distaste for) dog meat. All cultures have some prohibitions and ceremonial functions related to eating, and changes in food etiquette (as in 19th-century America) are of great interest in social history.

Social historians have studied food in many different contexts, including diet in the past; the culture of food consumption; quantities of food consumed by different social groups and the results of known deficiencies; the demographic implications, and effect on subsistence crises, of the scarcity or abundance of food; and the politics of food production and distribution. Until about 10,000 years ago, when humans learned to cultivate food and domesticate livestock, food was obtained by hunting and gathering. The Neolithic agricultural revolution, by providing a reliable source of sustenance, enabled human populations to grow from about 6 million to 400 million by AD 1200.

The industrial revolution of the 18th and 19th centuries enabled European societies to escape from the Malthusian demographic regime, which had constrained population growth until then. The procurement of food was the most important task of most households until well into the 19th century. Even at the turn of the 20th century British workers in Europe consumed a mere 2,000 calories a day, well below recommended standards, and well below American levels of the time. Until recently the European diet was composed essentially of carbohydrates obtained from bread. (Vegetables provided 80 percent of calories consumed.) However, compared with those living in Asian societies, Europeans have had a diversified diet, and the availability of some animal stock has always provided somewhat of a buffer against harvest failures.

Social historical work on food has branched out from standard of living debates to considerations of food's cultural meanings on the one hand and implications of changing nutrition on the other. Food history provides a number of important topics in social history, where exploration is by no means complete.

John Komlos

REFERENCES

Appleby, A.B. *Famine in Tudor and Stuart England.* Stanford, CA: Stanford University Press, 1978.

Kaplan, Steven L. "The State and the Problem of Dearth in Eighteenth-Century France: The Crisis of 1738–41 in Paris," *Food and Foodways* 4 (1990): 111–141.

Levenstein, Harvey. *Paradox of Plenty: A Social History of Eating in Modern America.* New York: Oxford University Press, 1993.

Livi-Bacci, Massimo. *Population and Nutrition. An Essay on European Demographic History.* Cambridge: Cambridge University Press, 1991.

Mennell, Stephen. *All Manners of Food: Eating and Taste in England and France from the Middle Ages to the Present.* Oxford: Blackwell, 1985.

Mintz, Sidney W. *Sweetness and Power: The Place of Sugar in Modern History.* New York: Viking Penguin, 1985.

Oddy, Derek, and Derek Miller, eds. *The Making of the Modern British Diet.* London: Croom Helm, 1976.

Food Riots

Food riots were the predominant form of grassroots politics in societies undergoing industrialization and state growth, especially between 1750 and 1850 in Britain, France, and Germany. Analysis of these riots plays a prominent role in sociohistorical research and resultant protest theory. Critical periods witnessed 300 riots in France's "Flour War" in 1775, and hundreds more in 1847; 400 food riots in 1790–1801 in Britain; 200 food riots in Prussian Germany in 1847. Food riots were touched off by harvest failures and high prices. Rioters followed familiar rituals. Crowds took over marketplaces and sold grain at moderate prices; they intercepted shipments on canals or roads; they forced farmers to sign agreements to lower prices; sometimes they broke into warehouses or punished dealers. But they usually acted in orderly fashion so as to retain legitimacy and avoid capital prosecution for theft.

Food riots resulted from economic, cultural, political, and social factors. Plebeian households spent half to two-thirds of their budgets on food. While production and transportation remained relatively primitive, European societies were vulnerable to harvest failure. With early industrialization and regional economic specialization, more consumers came to depend on markets for their food. Nevertheless, food riots did not simply occur where prices were highest or people poorest, for rioters acted on the basis of beliefs and social networks.

Rioters and elites shared beliefs in a moral economy that justified controlling food supplies and prices in emergencies. They had political expectations in assuming that governments should actively counter food crisis. Often, prompted by the threat of riot, local officials encouraged farmers to supply the markets at reasonable prices and organized subscription funds to buy relief supplies. But national policies on food marketing in France and Britain shifted from paternalist control to laissez faire in the period 1760–1800, as governments became persuaded that only free trade would supply growing cities.

Riots also depended on local social networks. Rioters did not threaten local officials but tried to press them to use their wealth and power to improve prices and supplies. Food riots were the main form of local politics in which women participated, alongside men; it seems that their roles in household production flowed into joint defense of family living standards. Riots were most successful in stable medium-sized communities where rioters and officials had multiple ties through work, politics, and patronage (q.v.) that permitted effective negotiation. In English agrarian villages social controls were too tight for riot, though French peasants might riot after their own stocks gave out. By 1800 officials in big cities ceased to tolerate riots, and they were rare in Paris and London because governments ensured their supplies. Food riots declined with urbanization and the creation of police forces; with the triumph of laissez faire economic theory; with improvements in food production and transportation; and with the shift of popular campaigns toward wages, poor relief, and voting rights.

In recent times food riots have occurred in Eastern Europe, the Sudan, Egypt, Zambia, Venezuela, and Tashkent, in protest over the lifting of government price ceilings on food.

John Bohstedt

REFERENCES

Charlesworth, Andrew, ed. *An Atlas of Rural Protest in Britain, 1548–1900.* London: Croom Helm, 1983.

Thompson, E.P. *Customs in Common.* London: Merlin, 1991.

Wells, Roger A.E. *Wretched Faces: Famine in Wartime England, 1793–1801.* New York: St. Martin's, 1988.

French Revolution

The French Revolution has proven so complex that even now after an extraordinary torrent of scholarship that began almost simultaneously with the revolution itself, scholars disagree on important issues—a disagreement that also involves the extent to which a social history approach suffices. Still the basic outline may be told. The crisis that would change France forever, though one may locate deep roots, began with the calling of the Assembly of the Notables early in 1787. At that moment the government had outstripped its ability to borrow and hoped to raise taxes and reduce expenses. To legislate such would require structural change and concurrence by the Parlement of Paris, the chief court in the land. The government believed it impossible to get this type of compliance; consequently the king, Louis XVI, tried to put together an alternate elite to ratify these changes.

Not only did the Assembly of the Notables not enact the program submitted to it, it exacerbated problems by asking for a meeting of the States-General before any decision on new taxes. Convening this ancient elected body, which had not met for almost 175 years, portended no good for the monarchy because in the circumstances of the late 18th century it would almost certainly have led to a serious diminution of royal authority. But in the end as the king could not resist, it was eventually gathered in Versailles in May 1789.

The political controversy had so widened in the course of the elections and discussion of the States-General that by the spring of 1789 the entire country was to some extent involved. Assessment of causation here formed one of the early instances of sociohistorical research. The most aggressive of the participants were the representatives of the commoners. Although composing one-half the body, they were unsure whether the king would decree vote by head or, as tradition dictated, one vote for each order: the nobility, the clergy dominated by noble members, and the commoners. But the commoners had no intention of letting things drift to what they believed would be regrettable results, and they unilaterally converted themselves into a Constituent Assembly with a claim to rule on behalf of the nation. When the king tried to disband them, a riot in Paris and the seizure of the Bastille on July 14, 1789, thwarted him. A revolution had transpired.

The revolutionaries, or patriots as they were called, were not entirely certain about how to take advantage of their victory. Nonetheless, in a series of actions including the August 4th decrees (1789), the Declaration of the Rights of Man and Citizen (1789), and the Constitution of 1791, the Constituent Assembly obliterated much of the old regime and set up instead of a nation of subjects a polity of citizens equal before the law. Although the king survived, he became a public functionary, deprived of claims to sovereignty.

In France, the revolution, at first widely hailed, became increasingly disliked because of an unpopular reorganization of the church, disappointment over what were seen to be the revolution's unfulfilled material and political promises, and a European-wide conflict that led to a military draft as well as many battlefield catastrophes. Enemies emerged on left and right with the former increasingly capturing power and the latter increasingly disaffected. By mid-1793, matters had so deteriorated that the working people of Paris (the *sans-culottes*), who continued to push for greater change, had installed their Jacobin allies in power in the legislature while the countryside remained often restive and in much of western France even actively rebellious. To subdue the opposition and quell the civil war as well as prosecute the foreign conflict, the Jacobins, having delegated executive authority to the Committee of Public Safety, set up the Terror. It worked.

With the war going well and counterrevolution increasingly subdued, the rationale for the Terror dissipated and undermined the support for the Committee of Public Safety. An internal split among the leadership there gave the legislature an opportunity to disband the institutions and practice of arbitrary justice. Wishing to change course, the deputies arranged a new government, characterized by divided responsibilities that they planned would be less problematic than the last. Unfortunately for them, enough of the difficulties that had led to the Terror continued and afflicted this fledgling government. More and more, those in power turned to the army in general and Napoleon Bonaparte in particular to protect them. He capitalized on their dependence in late 1799 by seizing, with help from disaffected members of the administration, the reins of power. Finally, it was he who accomplished what various governments could not. He preserved many of the social results of the revolution, but at the very high price of completely undermining its political achievements.

Social history has had much to say about the revolution. Even this narrative, focused on major events, could not evade discussing social groups as collective actors. But while it is virtually impossible to ignore social history when considering the revolution, the former's import has declined considerably in recent historiography. Only two decades ago the debate on the causes of the revolution consisted largely of a quarrel between Marxists and their detractors over whether it was the bourgeoisie or other social groups that caused the revolution and over the extent to which the bourgeoisie foreshadowed a modern middle class. More specific social history arguments included the issue of whether the Committee of Public Safety fell because it practiced bourgeois economics and alienated the artisanal *sans-culottes*, who possessed fundamentally different economic goals, or whether more specifically political explanations would suffice. Moreover, scholars believed that the revolution had extraordinarily significant social effects as the decade instituted a legal system that freed capitalism and the bourgeoisie from the dominance of the then collapsed feudal, noble order.

While social explanations still have adherents, they have been widely challenged. For example, in discussions of the causes of the revolution, intellectual historians who emphasize the role of Rousseau and early constitutional developments occupy center stage. Perhaps the most persuasive critique of this analysis no longer originates from social historians dealing with class analysis but from those studying culture who work on ideas but those of the society at large instead of those of the intellectual elite (which may be judged part of a new cultural history or an extension of social history itself). As for the social effects of the revolution, most scholars tend, though conceding some change, to downplay their significance, focusing on the long-term evolution of social forms. One scholar has recently asserted that the social effect, such as it was, may have been ironic as the nobility emphasized its exclusiveness more after the revolution than before. All in all, the scholarly evaluation of the revolution has apparently moved toward the view that more than anything it was a political event with political results. (*See also* Revolutions)

Jack R. Censer

REFERENCES

Chartier, Roger. *The Cultural Origins of the French Revolution*. Translated by Lydia G. Cochrane. Durham, NC, and London: Duke University Press, 1991.

Doyle, William. *Origins of the French Revolution*. Oxford: Oxford University Press, 1980.

Furet, François. *Interpreting the French Revolution*. Translated by Elborg Forster. Cambridge: Cambridge University Press, 1981.

Lefebvre, Georges. *The Coming of the French Revolution*. Translated by R.R. Palmer. Princeton, NJ: Princeton University Press, 1947.

Palmer, R.R. *Twelve Who Ruled: The Year of the Terror in the French Revolution*. Princeton, NJ: Princeton University Press, 1941.

Friendship

Friendship is a marvelous topic that has to date attracted relatively little attention by social historians. Friendship is an important facet of personal and social life, and it surely has a history in that its contours can change; but social historians have, with a few important exceptions, not yet gotten around to it. The subject stands then as an exciting invitation to innovative research.

Some general arguments have developed concerning changes in male friendship as part of other shifts in western European society in the 16th and 17th centuries. Several scholars have argued that, with growing commerce, male friendships weakened as men became more competitive. One result was that men transferred more emotional attachments to family, explaining part of the increased importance attributed to friendship and sexual compatibility between husbands and wives. This is a fascinating theory, but it has not yet been fleshed out by much specific research.

The most focused studies of friendship to date have addressed the 19th century, particularly in the United States. Carroll Smith Rosenberg (1975) probed intense friendship ties among women, which she argued developed because women needed strong emotional bonds but could not find them with their "superior" business-distracted husbands. This and other inquiries into the powerful emotive language of women friends in the 19th-century middle class have raised questions about changes, at least in language, among friends in the 20th century.

Several studies of working-class communities have stressed the bonds women formed among their neighbors, as women grouped together to attempt to regulate abusive behavior by husbands and to counter loneliness and material problems as families became more removed from work.

A recent article on 19th-century male friendship in the United States finds that young middle-class men grouped together in intense, physically demonstrative friendships much as women did, to tide them through a long period between school and marriage. Unlike women, however, men seem to have closed down these friendships when they did decide on lifetime careers and marriage. This pattern of friendship changed in the early 20th century, when fears about homosexuality gained ground. The resultant changes in friendship patterns have not, however, been explored.

The social history of friendship stands at a tantalizing point. Enough has been done to demonstrate the feasibility and importance of the topic, for, clearly, different historical periods see different forms and functions of friendship. But the great, pioneering work has yet to emerge.

Peter N. Stearns

REFERENCES

Leites, Edmund. *The Puritan Conscience and Modern Sexuality.* New Haven: Yale University Press, 1986.

Rotundo, Anthony E. "Romantic Friendship: Male Intimacy and Middle Class Youth in the Northern United States, 1800–1900," *Journal of Social History* 23 (1989): 1–26.

Smith-Rosenberg, Carroll. "The Female World of Love and Ritual: Relations Between Women in Nineteenth-Century America," *Signs* 1 (1975): 1–29.

Frontier Societies

Frontiers are regions that cannot be made subject to a state's routine administrative patterns but which a state may temporarily or partially penetrate with military force. As contexts for social life, frontiers are likely to have certain common characteristics. First of all, they are probably poor in the sort of resources that nearby states are able to seize; states therefore find it extremely difficult to extract enough resources from such regions for administering them closely to be very attractive, particularly prior to the development of cheap forms of transportation and communication, which make it less costly to equip local administrators from distant centers. Second, they are likely to have populations with the capacity to resist successfully a state's tendency to establish such stable administrative patterns; a region whose resources might make it barely worth governing sinks below the threshold of governability if those who dwell there can put up a good fight. Third, frontiers will be rural. Towns and cities are concentrations of capital that can support externally imposed administrative structures or that could develop their own. Fourth, economic life is unlikely to be based on settled agriculture. Rooted populations—especially if agricultural yields permit high population densities—are relatively easy to tax compared to herders.

Frontier societies are likely, then, to be mountainous, desert, thickly forested, or uncultivated grassland. Such zones are sometimes legendary for their populations that have resisted states and their administrative routines for decades or centuries (in the case of the Eurasian steppe, for millennia). Some examples would include the

Scythians, Parthians, and Bactrians of antiquity; the desert peoples of Arabia; the Mongols; the warring tribes of northern New Spain; the cattle hunters (and later cattle herders) of Iberoamerica.

The relationship of states and frontiers can be quite complex. The war-making capacities of some frontier populations has encouraged states to attempt to employ them in their battles with other states; at other times states have attempted to recruit one nomadic frontier people to defend its boundaries against others. One may find examples of both processes in the histories of European expansion in the Western Hemisphere and Chinese relations with the northern "barbarians."

The general lack of effective, centrally controlled policing makes smuggling a secure livelihood. Those fleeing established authority may find refuge in the frontier, where they intermingle with those already living there. To central authorities, frontier populations are likely to be seen as violent, criminal, dangerous, culturally remote, and, where such concepts exist, ethnically alien. When the frontier terrain is grassland and horses have been acquired, their mobility, cultivation of martial skills, and access to protein (made possible by their pastoral economies) may make them an extremely formidable cavalry.

The social ecology of frontier societies can be created. The Iberian introduction of diseases and heavy animals into the Western Hemisphere radically reduced population densities and turned potential cropland into waste. But the frontier ecology can also be ended.

In the 19th and 20th centuries the major grassland frontier societies were effectively incorporated into states, although there are still a few mountain or forest areas where administrative routines are very hard to enforce. This was brought about both by virtue of changes in productive activities that made frontiers the site of new profits and because the evolution of states made it easier to administer zones previously not worth the costs. Advances in agricultural technology made the profitable exploitation of previously hard-to-farm land possible. This entailed the development of settled agriculture, dense populations, and profitable tax collection. Modern plows revolutionized Argentina, for example, and it is with good reason that a staple of Hollywood westerns is the struggle of established cattle barons and new would-be farmers. Within the pastoral economy itself, moreover, refrigeration meant that newer breeds were highly profitable in world markets, starting in the late 19th century, and free mobility across trackless wastes gave way to demarcated properties, fencing, roads, and railroads.

On the state side, improvements in transportation and communication made it cheaper to administer remote areas; developments in military technology destroyed the capacity of frontier people to defend themselves (even the cavalries of grassland frontiers could not triumph over repeating rifles, let alone machine guns and tanks); interstate rivalries that, since the French Revolution, took on the form of national mobilizations, led competing states to seek effective control right up to their borders; and national educational systems and nationwide mass media promulgated cultural models that positively valued the ways of being of idealized members of centrally located peoples and devalued the ways of peripheral peoples. Increasingly effective state controls insured that frontier regions would participate in national and international economies.

The decline of the frontier in the United States generated an important theory, the Turner thesis, relevant to social history though devised before its surge. The Turner thesis argued that the frontier had provided an outlet that reduced social tensions in the settled areas of the United States before the 1890s, as discontented individuals could seek opportunity westward. This mold of simple before-and-after consequences of the frontier has largely been discredited.

Since social historians have been extremely interested in studying the ways in which ordinary people have evaded or have resisted the will of the powerful, there are several other aspects of frontier societies that have received the particular attention of recent historical research. The endemic banditry has been a central preoccupation, with a lively discussion of the ways in which bandits do or do not represent some broader form of social rebellion. The ways in which frontiers in a number of national contexts became imaginatively represented in national historical mythologies as places of freedom tragically eradicated by economic and political change has been an important theme as well. An important line of research now would be to explore why this frontier mythology is so much more prevalent in some places (United States, Argentina) than others with similarly extensive historical interaction with frontier zones. One recent theme that might be emerging in the historical literature is the ways in which frontier peoples interacted with state-making administrators to forge a sense of nationality, an encounter in which the peripheral regions may have been more than zones invaded and penetrated by the state's agents, ultimately to be culturally subdued; it may be, rather, that local groups have sometimes invited the distant central authorities in. The comparative possibilities in frontier history, for example, for Russia, North and South America, and Australia in the 18th and 19th centuries, provide a set of significant research opportunities—an analytical frontier for social history. (*See also* Banditry; Commercialization; Cossacks; *Gauchos, Llaneros;* Latin American Frontiers; Nomadism; Pastoralism; State and Society; Taxation and State Formation)

John Markoff

REFERENCES

Hall, Thomas. *Social Change in the Southwest, 1350–1880.* Lawrence: University of Kansas Press, 1989.

Hobsbawm, E.J. *Bandits.* New York: Delacorte Press, 1969.

McNeill, William H. *Europe's Steppe Frontier, 1500–1800.* Chicago: University of Chicago Press, 1964.

Sahlins, Peter. *Boundaries: The Making of France and Spain in the Pyrenees.* Berkeley: University of California Press, 1989.

Slatta, Richard W. *Cowboys of the Americas.* New Haven: Yale University Press, 1990.

Frontier Thesis

In a paper that he delivered to the American Historical Association in 1893, Frederick Jackson Turner argued that two social processes intrinsic to the American frontier explained "American development." First, the availability of "free land" (by which he meant land free of rents and not of people), provided opportunity for upward social mobility not enjoyed by Europeans. Second, the struggle for survival on the frontier required that Europeans simplify their lives (what he termed "a return to the primitive"), and thus gave westering peoples a chance to rebuild their societies afresh. Those twin social processes shaped American character and institutions, quickening the assimilation of immigrants of different ethnic groups, "consolidating" and "nationalizing" young America, and promoting social and political democracy. Moreover, Turner wrote, "to the frontier the American intellect owes its striking characteristics": inventiveness, practicality, inquisitiveness, restlessness, optimism, and individualism.

This overarching explanation of the formation of American society rejected the school of academic wisdom that American institutions and character had been transplanted unchanged from Europe, but Turner's ideas, crafted in rhetorically compelling prose, resonated with a deep strain of belief in American exceptionalism. Insofar as it gave national significance to local experience and made ordinary men and women the agents of change, the frontier thesis represented a pioneering argument for writing history from the bottom up.

Turner's frontier thesis (later expanded in a book) came to be regarded as the single most useful concept for understanding the distinctive features of American civilization. It enjoyed widespread public acceptance (counting Theodore Roosevelt and Woodrow Wilson among its supporters), and spawned numerous scholarly elaborations before coming under attack in the 1930s and 1940s. Much of the criticism was well-founded. Turner had overstated his case and failed to define terms carefully, including the word "frontier" (a place, a process, or a condition?). He later acknowledged the error of his assertion that the frontier served as a "safety valve," draining displaced and potentially radical factory workers from the East, and he also revised his view that the frontier had developed in orderly, linear evolutionary stages as represented by archetypal Indians, trappers and hunters, cattlemen, miners, farmers, and town dwellers.

Turner's thesis survived these criticisms due in large part to its restatement and modification in several books by Ray Allen Billington, published between 1949 and 1973. By then the thesis had lost its preeminence as the sole explanation for the uniqueness of national institutions and culture, but Billington's influential work positioned it as the central paradigm for understanding the history of the American frontier if not the nation itself.

Although often pronounced dead, the thesis has refused to expire. In the 1950s and 1960s, for example, scholars tested the Turner thesis by contrasting the American frontier to its counterparts in Canada, South Africa, even the Roman Empire. Results were mixed, with some historians seeing support for Turner's ideas and others seeing little to confirm the Turner thesis. In the 1970s, social historians began to compensate for Turner's neglect of women and nonwhite groups, and some of this work bore imprint of Turner's ideas. But in the 1980s and early 1990s, the thesis came under further attack from some frontier historians, who saw it as Eurocentric, imperialistic, sexist, racist, presentist, triumphalist, romantic, and of little use for understanding the West after 1890 when, Turner said, the era of frontier expansion had

ended. Although many historians still refer to Turner's ideas, his thesis has lost much of its influence. New definitions of the frontier and attention to race, gender, and class have transformed the research on the frontier and the West.

Julie Roy Jeffrey and David Weber

REFERENCES

Billington, Ray Allen. *Frederick Jackson Turner: Historian, Scholar, Teacher.* New York: Oxford University Press, 1973.

Cronon, William. "Turner's First Stand: The Significance of Significance in American History," in Richard W. Etulain, ed., *Writing Western History: Essays on Major Western Historians.* Albuquerque: University of New Mexico Press, 1991, pp. 73–101.

Hofstadter, Richard, and Seymour Martin Lipset, eds. *Turner and the Sociology of the Frontier,* New York: Basic Books, 1968.

Ridge, Martin. "The Life of an Idea: The Significance of Frederick Jackson Turner's Frontier Thesis," *Montana* 41 (Winter 1991): 2–13.

Turner, Frederick Jackson. *The Frontier in American History.* New York: Holt, 1921.

G

Games

Games are a form of play, yet two classic analysts of the genre fail to distinguish them explicitly. Johan Huizinga (1950) describes play as being separate from ordinary life, unproductive, and operating in its own time and space according to its own rules. He further believes that play defines social groups and is both the source of culture and the means by which it is perpetuated.

Huizinga does not differentiate games as a subset of play. Roger Caillois (1958) refines Huizinga's definition, but uses play and games synonymously. In addition to being separate, unproductive, and self-ruled, Caillois says games have to be voluntary and have an uncertain outcome. Any game that does not meet all these criteria is some other form of amusement.

The Huizinga-Caillois approach to play and games is descriptive and thus useful for categorizing a culture's games, but it ignores both the distinction between games and play and the social meaning of games. It may also omit some differences between the nature and function of games in industrial societies and those charac-teristics of more traditional societies, though historians disagree on the extent to which the nature (as opposed to the form) of games has changed over time. Anthropologists Brian Sutton-Smith and John M. Roberts (1970) rectify the basic definitional problems by explaining that both play and games share a variety of qualities but that games differ from play because they are systematically controlled by rules that create a rigid structure and lead to a predictable outcome. Sutton-Smith and Roberts, among others, argue that games are expressive models through which individuals learn and practice the culturally accepted methods of dealing with the inevitable conflicts of life related to obedience, achievement, and responsibility. Viewed from this perspective, games become metaphoric microcosms of social relationships and values. They exist on the margin between unstructured free play and totally structured work, integrating elements of each into the other.

Athletic contests or sports, which require physical prowess, are the most studied form of games, but gambling, board games, and children's games have also received some attention from scholars. Wagering can take place on any event whose outcome is unknown, but many cultures have games in which chance is more important than skill. There are, for example, American Indian games requiring players to guess the location of hidden objects, and a variety of ancient and modern games in which the players guess the random result of a particular act such as throwing marked objects like sticks or dice. Gambling games have been linked by some observers to societies, or individuals within societies, that believe that they do not have much control over the forces that determine success or failure.

On the other hand, games that depend heavily on strategy (rather than on chance or physical skill) are found most widely in complex societies where success and failure depend on learning how to obey (and manipulate) rules. While some card games, like bridge, require complex strategy, it is in board games that strategy becomes preeminent. Most board games of strategy involve some element of chance, although a few, such as chess, go, and checkers, are purely strategic. H.J.R. Murray (1952) has divided board games into five categories: (1) alignment—in which the players attempt to put their pieces into a particular configuration (e.g., tic-tac-toe); (2) war—in which each player attempts to capture the pieces or territory of the other (e.g., chess); (3) hunt—played with unbalanced sides in which the larger group attempts to hunt down the smaller (e.g., fox and geese); (4) race—in which each player attempts to be the first to move pieces along a track to reach a goal (e.g., snakes and ladders); (5) mancala—a form of game popular in Africa and Asia in which a number of pieces are moved one at a time into a series of parallel holes.

Board games have been played for at least 4,000 years, and there is some slight knowledge of games played in ancient Egypt, Mesopotamia, Assyria, Cyprus, and Crete. The rules of most ancient games remain unknown, however, and the first systematic description of games and their rules is a report ordered by King Alfonso X of Castile in 1283. Various sources over the next 100 years indicate that both board games and card games were widespread enough in Europe

to prompt governments to try to control them. Thus, in the Western tradition at least, games were viewed with ambivalence because at best they wasted time and at worst they presented opportunities for gambling.

Because children are particularly fond of games, adults have always attempted to invent games for them that would be uplifting. As early as the 15th century educational playing cards were produced in both Germany and England. Instructional cards were joined in the 1760s by educational jigsaw puzzles (which may or may not be a game) and educational board games. The Mansion of Happiness, produced in 1843 by Anne W. Abbott, was the first American board game. It used a teetotum or spinner (dice were too closely linked to gambling) to determine which player would avoid the vices of the world and reach paradise. The city of Salem, Massachusetts, became the center for several major producers of board games that dominated formal children's play until the mass distribution of home video games after 1978.

Folklorists have been gathering a large body of descriptive information on informal children's games for over 100 years. Unlike board games, which are controlled by adults, children's games are passed on informally from generation to generation and reflect a uniquely spontaneous source of sociohistorical information. Here, as with many kinds of adult games, extensive research opportunities remain, as well as a need for historical syntheses. (*See also* Childhood; Sport)

Steven M. Gelber

REFERENCES

Caillois, Roger. *Man, Play, and Games*. New York: The Free Press, 1958.

Huizinga, J. *Homo Ludens*. Boston: Beacon, 1950.

Murray, H.J.R. *A History of Board-Games Other Than Chess*. New York: Hacker Books, 1978, 1952.

Opie, Iona and Peter. *Children's Games in Street and Playground*. London: Oxford University Press, 1969.

Sutton-Smith, Brian, and John M. Roberts. "The Cross-Cultural and Psychological Study of Games," in Gunther Luschen, ed., *The Cross Cultural Analysis of Sport and Games*. Champaign, IL: Stipes, 1970.

Gauchos, Llaneros

The *gaucho* of the Río de la Plata and the *llanero*

of Venezuela and Colombia are horsemen who played important historical and cultural roles in South America. As colonial wild cattle hunters, they slaughtered animals for hides, tallow, and jerked beef. As cavalrymen, they fought in Latin American independence, civil, and Indian wars. By the 20th century, both gauchos and llaneros had achieved cultural and political significance in several countries.

These horsemen shared many values. They believed in free, unfettered access to land, water, and wild livestock. They harbored a burning desire to work and play on horseback. Government officials and outsiders often viewed them as barbarians. Like other frontiersmen, these horsemen resorted to flight, violent resistance, and banditry to fend off official attempts to control them. Both groups blended elements of Hispanic equestrian culture with Amerindian language and material culture. Machismo pervaded their values. Both enjoyed singing and dancing and developed lively oral cultures. Because both groups remained illiterate and marginal, they pose challenging and interesting research subjects for the social historian.

During the 18th century and later as seasonal ranch hands, the horsemen helped build major plains livestock industries. As wild cattle herds diminished in the 19th century, gauchos took jobs on (*estancias*) ranches of the temperate plains (*pampas*), tending and branding cattle. Llaneros labored on *hatos* (ranches) of the tropical plains (*lanos*). Some riders became especially skilled at breaking wild horses or at scouting. All enjoyed wild, dangerous equestrian games. Gauchos played a rough-and-tumble game of mounted keep-away called *pato*. Llaneros enjoyed grabbing the tails of running bulls and pulling them to the ground.

As cavalry conscripts, gauchos fought against frontier Indians, British invaders (1806 and 1807), and Spanish Royalist forces during the independence wars. José Gervasio Artigas ably led a gaucho army in Uruguay. Llaneros fought for Royalist forces behind José Tomás Boves until his death in 1814. After that time, the charismatic José Antonio Páez drew llaneros into the independence camp. Military service somewhat improved the horsemen's coarse image and im-

bued them, in the minds of some, with an aura of valor and patriotism.

During the late 19th century, rapid socioeconomic change radically altered the pampas. Massive European immigration, new technology (notably fencing and refrigeration), agriculture, sheep raising, and new livestock breeds altered traditional ranch life. Old gaucho ways were pushed deep into remote regions of the plains. In contrast, the llaneros remained a static, marginal frontier producing traditional jerked beef and hides. Very little outside change impinged on traditional llanero life. The decline of the jerked-beef trade and the rise of oil and coffee production doomed the llaneros as an economic backwater during the first decades of the 20th century.

Like Cossacks and pastoralists in other societies, gauchos and llaneros gained prominent positions in folklore and literature. Writers in Argentina, Uruguay, and southern Brazil (home of the culturally similar *gaúcho*) have idealized rural and ranch life in their creative works. The Argentine writer Ricardo Güiraldes provides a memorable literary portrait of a gaucho bronco buster (*domador*) in his novel *Don Segundo Sombra* (1926). Venezuelan writer and one-time president Rómulo Gallegos depicts the danger, power, and mystery of life on the llaneros in his novel, *Doña Bárbara* (1929). Dozens of writers in the Río de la Plata created a vast corpus of "gauchesque" literature. Works by Bartolomé Hidalgo, Domingo F. Sarmiento, José Hernández, Benito Lynch, Leopoldo Lugones, Ezequiel Martínez Estrada, and many others enrich the Spanish literary world. Today the llanero remains an important regional symbol in Venezuela and Colombia. For Argentina and Uruguay, the gaucho is a compelling national symbol. Calling someone or something "very gaucho" remains a high compliment. (*See also* Cossacks; Duels; Frontier Societies; Landless Laborers; Latin American Frontiers; Machismo; Pastoralism)

Richard W. Slatta

REFERENCES

Mayer, John. "El llanero," *Atlantic Monthly* (February 1859).

Rausch, Jane M. *A Tropical Plains Frontier: The Llanos of Colombia, 1511–1831*. Albuquerque: University of New Mexico Press, 1984.

Slatta, Richard W. *Gauchos and the Vanishing Frontier*. Lincoln: University of Nebraska Press, 1983.

Slatta, Richard W. *Cowboys of the Americas*. New Haven: Yale University Press, 1990.

Slatta, Richard W., ed. *Bandidos: The Varieties of Latin American Banditry*. Westport: Greenwood Press, 1987 (chapters 3 and 4).

Gay Rights Movement

The term "gay rights" describes the activity of those advocating the legal rights of gay men and/or lesbians. These groups have as their goal the repeal of laws that discriminate on the basis of sexual preference and the encouragement of mores that allow sexual minorities a participatory role in society. Historical evaluations of this movement fit growing sociohistorical research on homosexuality.

Despite early homophile associations in the late 19th and early 20th centuries, a gay movement did not get underway until after World War II in the United States and elsewhere. The movement benefited from the migrations engendered by war mobilization, the adoption of a medical model of homosexual behavior, and the popular dissemination of information concerning human sexual behavior by Alfred Kinsey and others. First in the United States, then in other industrialized nations, the movement took its organizational and strategic cues from other groups seeking to redress social grievance, notably the black civil rights and women's movements. Rejecting a legalistic approach, the movement has striven to portray lesbians and gay men as a minority with a separate past and oppression.

The Stonewall Riots of June 1969, protesting the closing of a bar in New York City, marked the beginning of a radical period where a rejection of familial norms was voiced over a dominant integrationist discourse. The lasting contribution of a separatist movement was the emergence of an urban subculture for gay men and lesbians in the 1970s and 1980s. While the organized political activity of gay men and lesbians has focused heavily on local advocacy politics, the existence of a subculture has altered the way that lesbians and gay men are perceived, and perceive themselves, in Western culture today. (*See also* Homosexuality; Subcultures)

Timothy J. Haggerty

REFERENCES

Adam, Barry. *The Rise of a Gay and Lesbian Movement*. Boston: Twayne Publishers, 1987.

D'Emilio, John. *Sexual Politics, Sexual Communities*. Chicago: University of Chicago Press, 1983.

Duberman, Martin Bauml, Martha Vicinus, and George Chauncey, Jr., eds. *Hidden from History*. New York: New American Library, 1989.

Gender

See Masculinity; Women's History

Gender Division of Labor (Africa)

The gender division of labor in Africa has been neither static nor monolithic; it has responded to changing economic, political, and social circumstances. In precolonial Africa (before 1884), most African peoples were farmers or pastoralists, although some engaged in long-distance trade. Among the agriculturalists, women often performed much of the agricultural labor, but this was not always the case. Culture made a difference. For example, among the Beti people of Cameroon, in West Africa, women dominated food production, while the neighboring Yoruba peoples assigned women to trade and left most farm work to men. Among the pastoral cattlekeepers, men and boys generally tended the cattle while women and girls gathered or grew food. Long-distance trade, often dangerous and time consuming, generally remained a male preserve. But, here again, exceptions abound. However, most societies assigned food preparation, child care, and general domestic labor to females.

Of course, the gender division of labor often varied by class and ethnicity as well. The royal daughters and wives of the Baganda aristocracy, in Uganda, had little to do with food production. The queen mother and other royal women in pastoral societies often led privileged lives, very different from those of their peasant sisters.

Minority women, such as the Hutu in Rwanda, worked much harder than aristocratic Tutsi women.

Colonial rule, and the introduction of colonial capitalism, altered the gender division of labor in Africa. In the rural areas, cash crop production increased, and colonial officials, adopting Western gender stereotypes, assumed African men, as household heads, should control that production. As a result, rural women increasingly lost control over the products of their own labor. They worked harder, for less reward, particularly in areas with large-scale male out-migration.

Colonial officials argued that Africans were basically rural and that urban employment should thus be primarily for males, who were expected to return to their tribal homes after earning some money in town. As a result, men outnumbered women in the colonial towns, and this demographic imbalance enabled some women to survive in town through prostitution, beer brewing, and other forms of domestic labor. A stabilized urban population grew up in the towns as well, however, and the wives and daughters of these men tried to fulfill colonial expectations that they be "proper" wives and mothers. These women sometimes managed to obtain the education needed to enter teaching, nursing, or social work, the few professions considered respectable enough for women. Whatever their class position, however, urban women remained largely responsible for raising children and caring for the home.

Since independence (which began in 1957 in Ghana and has since gradually moved down the continent), educational and employment opportunities have increased for African men and women. However, women lag behind men on both counts. They still have difficulty owning land, inheriting property, and obtaining well-paying jobs. And, as in the past, reproductive labor remains largely a woman's responsibility. Thus, African women are still burdened by a double day, which has intensified during the current economic crisis and the imposition of structural adjustment packages that have reduced educational and health facilities. Women more than men find themselves having to fill in for reduced social services, as they are the ones who must balance their own career goals with family and community responsibilities. (See also Women and Work)

Jane L. Parpart

REFERENCES

Bay, Edna, ed. *Women and Work in Africa*. Boulder, CO: Westview Press, 1982.

Creevey, Lucy, ed. *Women Farmers in Africa: Rural Development in Mali and the Sahel*. Syracuse, NY: Syracuse University Press, 1986.

Guyer, Jane. *Family and Farm in Southern Cameroon*. African Research Studies No. 15. Boston: Boston University Press, 1984.

Hafkin, Nancy, and Edna Bay, eds. *Women in Africa*. Stanford, CA: Stanford University Press, 1976.

Hay, Margaret Jean, and Sharon Stichter, eds. *African Women South of the Sahara*. London: Longman, 1984.

Gender Socialization

Gender socialization, the process through which a society inculcates boys and girls to proper (and often different) standards of conduct for men and women, has become a fascinating new topic in social history. Not only is it valuable in understanding the lives of ordinary people—an early goal of social history—but it also provides insights into the relatively new history of mentalities, the study of how people approach and understand their world. Scholars have not always recognized the importance of gender socialization. Rather, early researchers sought to understand gender differences in attitudes and actions through physical difference alone—a vein of research often reinforced by religious beliefs. Even more recent, scientific approaches have relied upon biological causation. Sigmund Freud, for example, explained developmental differences between men and women by asserting that without castration anxiety women could not fully develop the superego and conscience. Consequently, they could never attain the level of independence that men do, causing differences in the way they approach abstract notions like justice. More recently, sociobiologists have returned to biological explanation for gender differences in sexuality or school performance. While many women in the 19th and 20th centuries used views of this sort to justify greater involvement in the public sphere (highlighting their supposed moral superiority), others have questioned this reliance on physical difference. It is only recently, however, that theorists like Carol Gilligan and Nancy Chodorow have stressed the different socialization processes boys and girls undergo as children. But socialization does not end with childhood. The characteristics boys and girls acquire as children are reinforced and questioned as youths and adults in a number of different settings. As a new social history topic, gender socialization remains an open field, but already early research (focused primarily on the middle classes in Western societies) highlights certain arenas in which this important process is most evident.

Families, of course, remain a central focus for study. In agricultural societies, men prepared boys for their futures while women were responsible for raising girls. Beginning at an early age, the sexual division of labor and traditions of single-sex sociability greatly facilitated this process. By removing middle-class women and children from manufacturing, however, industrialization forced great changes in gender socialization. First, the meanings of gender changed as domesticity took on new importance in women's lives. Bonnie Smith (1981), in her study of bourgeois women in northern France, demonstrates how women who were forced out of industry developed a system of domestic symbols that underscored their ties to nature. They acknowledged their sole social role as mothers by creating a domestic symbolic system through fashion and housekeeping habits that glorified that role—aiming, along the way, to inculcate their daughters to such a worldview. The removal of fathers from the daily routine of home life also had a dramatic impact on the gender socialization of boys. Historian Anthony Rotundo (1993) cites, for example, the creation in Victorian America of an independent boyhood culture, developed to counteract the feminizing result of too much attention from their mothers. Through games and secret pacts, this culture constituted a masculine atmosphere deemed lacking at home. Gender socialization need not always highlight the differences between boys and girls, however. Peter Stearns (1993) reveals a convergence in gendered emotional standards for children in the United States after 1920. While Victorian parents had stressed differences in the ways boys and girls were supposed to deal with emotions (they taught boys to channel the energy from anger, for example, while simultaneously scolding girls for their unladylike tempers), their 20th-century counterparts applied similar standards for both sexes. In brief, families, the prime force in child rearing, played a significant role in teaching boys and girls what would be expected of them as men and women, regardless of how those terms changed in definition.

As education has grown in importance during the last few centuries, it too has become a significant arena of gender socialization. Long the preserve of elite men, attendance in educational institutions gradually became in 19th- and 20th-century Western societies a state-mandated prerequisite to adult life. The organization of schools in different national contexts contributed, however, to very different results in gender socialization. In France, for example, a strict policy of single-sexed education produced an educational system that tailored subjects to the sex of the students. In science class, girls learned *puericulture*, the science of child care, while boys covered more general scientific principles of the sort followed up, for a few, at university. Great Britain, meanwhile, grew infamous for its schoolboy culture. While public education remained relatively weak, a strong system of private schools for elite and middle-class boys developed a reputation for strict discipline and a deep sense of school loyalty (often through sport), defining masculinity for many in British culture. In the United States, however, education took on a less gendered appearance. Due to local control over education and the small size of many communities, American educators found it more economical to support co-educational institutions. While American teachers did not ignore gender ideologies in the classroom, they did not tailor academic subjects to their pupils' sexes. It would be incorrect, however, to portray American education as the great equalizer. Feminists have demonstrated for years the subtle ways all schools have perpetuated certain gender ideologies through the promotion of cultural norms.

Related to the socialization acquired at school, literature has also come under the scrutiny of historians interested in gender socialization. Using textual theories, one scholar has explored how English children employed popular juvenile literature to organize contradictory experiences. In brief, Kirsten Drotner (1988) argues that popular magazines allowed children to cope emotionally with the contradiction of being trained for adult life while increasingly isolated from it. As the problems of adolescent life changed with time, so too did popular literature—as consumers, the young readers shaped what publishers offered. Mid-19th-century middle-class boys, for example, accepted subdued images of masculinity in their magazines because their futures as male providers was secure. Working-class boys in the 20th century, however, demanded more aggressive symbols to compensate for a future of subordination in some factory. This work is interesting not only for its discussion of how gender socialization has changed but also for its emphasis on the role of children as active participants in the process. Similar attention to this role in other aspects of children's lives awaits serious attention.

Of course, the influence of popular culture is not limited to children. The process of gender socialization is also an important factor in adult lives. In early modern Europe, for example, villagers often used traditional festivals like *charivaris* to upbraid a member of the community who had transgressed proper gendered conduct (although others have argued that such festivals could also challenge certain gender ideologies). Religion played a similar role: both the Qur'an and the Bible convey proper codes of behavior for men and women. As science came to surpass religion in the West, medical discourse, especially as it was popularized in prescriptive literature (printed material such as advice manuals), often replaced scripture as a code of proper gender behavior. Finally, American historians have also demonstrated how associational life for both men and women served as institutions of gender socialization, spurring members to question earlier assumptions or providing them a means of addressing an aspect of masculinity or femininity missing in daily life.

Current research leaves many questions unanswered. Much work on gender socialization remains to be done. Historians need to examine the process among the working class (done to a certain extent in the realm of sports history) and non-Western civilizations, for they offer interesting opportunities for comparison. Moreover, findings on the 19th century need comparison with earlier socialization, while 20th-century changes are only partially understood. As in the field of child rearing, the problems involved in gauging impact on actual boys and girls must also be overcome; prescriptive literature, while useful, can only tell us so much. Finally, just as gender is being increasingly linked to other ideologies, particularly politics, so historians could benefit by exploring the links between gender socialization and socialization to other standards of behavior (as has been done in the field of emotionology). The topic of gender socialization beckons many social historians, for the rewards are great for those who would work through difficult theoretical problems and the challenge of elusive sources. [*See also* Childhood; Emotion (Emotionology); Masculinity; Women's History]

Steven M. Beaudoin

REFERENCES

Carnes, Mark C., and Clyde Griffen, eds. *Meanings for Manhood: Construction of Masculinity in Victorian America*. Chicago: University of Chicago Press, 1990.

Clark, Linda. *Schooling the Daughters of Marianne: Textbooks and the Socialization of Girls in Modern French Primary Schools*. Albany: State University of New York Press, 1984.

Drotner, Kirsten. *English Children and Their Magazines, 1751–1945*. New Haven: Yale University Press, 1988.

Gilligan, Carol. *In a Different Voice: Psychological Theory and Women's Development*. Cambridge, MA: Harvard University Press, 1982.

Smith, Bonnie. *Ladies of the Leisure Class: The Bourgeoises of Northern France in the Nineteenth Century*. Princeton, NJ: Princeton University Press, 1981.

Stearns, Peter N. "Girls, Boys and Emotions: Redefinition and Historical Change," *Journal of American History* 80 (1993): 36–74.

Genealogy

Simply put, genealogy is the study of ancestry and of descent—the search for origins through bloodlines. Typically, it consists of tracing the lineage of individuals back for as many generations as possible with the purpose of positioning the individual with respect to his or her contemporaries and kin. During recent decades the study of genealogy has become popular with the onset of leisure time and with easier access to birth and death records, passenger lists, and immigration data. Using these materials, thousands of people have conducted research into their own ancestry and that of others.

Genealogy has a complex relationship with social history. Its focus on individual family patterns may have little bearing on the major analytical interests of social historians. On the other hand, accumulated genealogical data provide major sources of understanding of larger developments in family and society. Genealogical archive collections, like those assembled by the Church of Latter Day Saints, are vital social history repositories.

Compiling genealogies is one of the most ancient forms of inquiry. Some of the earliest records from Egypt and the ancient Near East consist of the pedigrees of rulers, workmen, and traders. It was recognized early that one of the principal requirements for achieving and maintaining authority was correct descent, and these records were designed to proclaim the legitimacy of those who constructed them. The practice of maintaining genealogies continued in the Greek and Roman worlds and even more so in medieval and early modern Europe, again confined largely to preserving information intended to legitimate dynastic and other hierarchical structures. Elsewhere in the world similar patterns have existed and continue to exist. For ancient, medieval, and modern India hundreds of long and short royal genealogies exist, which have been used by historians to create, often unjustifiably, a large and comprehensive dynastic structure for the area.

Among the most famous genealogies are those in the Bible, beginning with attempts in Genesis to link the Israelites with the first biblical man and woman, Adam and Eve. Other books of the Bible carry the genealogies forward through the royal houses of Israel and Judah, while some of the Gospels trace the ancestry of Jesus Christ back to King David in order to provide secular justification for his ministry.

Perhaps the most elaborate known genealogies are those constructed by the Polynesians.

Some of these comprise thousands of names and purport to trace certain families back more than a millennium to the original settlers of various island groups. Their purpose, as usual, was to establish the hierarchical refinements that became necessary as the Pacific islands became more populous and state systems began to emerge. In many places in Africa elaborate genealogies exist as well, both in areas where states existed and in those where states did not but where genealogies were needed to differentiate clans and other groups for purposes of intermarriage and resource sharing. Using genealogical information to determine distance between people as well as closeness reflects the universal need to position individuals as precisely (if not necessarily as accurately) as possible in terms of blood descent.

The widespread political and social importance of genealogies has inevitably led to their being invented and manipulated frequently for partisan purposes. Most of the royal houses of early modern Europe—to cite just one example—had genealogies devised which connected them with Troy, Egypt, and other ancient civilizations. In India and Africa colonial policies of seeking legitimate traditional rulers resulted in great numbers of new genealogies sprouting up on demand. Even in the contemporary world family genealogies are often embellished to demonstrate exalted status as measured by alleged descent from ancestors who came to England in 1066 or to America in 1607 or 1620. In the circumstances it is unwise to accept any genealogy that cannot be documented independently.

Commoner genealogies are now widely used for historical demography, for instance, to trace migration, marriage patterns, life expectancies, and disease transmission. The application of sophisticated statistical techniques to these data enables demographers and others to develop models of population growth, decline, and movement. In addition they have proved useful in social history for tracing occupational mobility, wealth accumulation, and the like. The genealogies used for these purposes are more stable and more accurate than those retrospectively created for openly political purposes. Even so, they serve to emphasize that genealogical information continues to have value as an important means of penetrating and understanding the past.

David Henige

REFERENCES

Dyke, Bennett, and Warren T. Morrill, eds. *Genealogical Demography*. New York: Academic Press, 1980.

FitzHugh, Terrick V.H. *Dictionary of Genealogy*. Totowa, NJ: Barnes and Noble, 1985.

Henige, David. *The Chronology of Oral Tradition*. Oxford: Clarendon Press, 1974.

Wagner, Anthony. *Pedigree and Progress*. London: Phillimore, 1975.

Generations

Conflict between generations—between young people and their elders—has occurred in many societies, ancient and modern. Clashes between younger and older factions often divided ancient Greek city-states, and rambunctious students and guild apprentices repeatedly shattered the peace of medieval towns. Youthful dissidents defied the governments of tsarist Russia in the 19th century, of China in the 20th century, and of the United States in the 1960s. Younger generations swelled the waves of political revolution which swept much of Europe in 1848, reached around the world in the 1960s, and toppled many communist governments as recently as 1989. Youthful rejection of society has also produced unconventional countercultures—groups who develop a different lifestyle from that of the majority—like the so-called bohemian artists and writers of the 19th century and the long-haired hippies of the 20th.

Attempts to explain the generational phenomenon have in recent times produced the theory of social generations. Generational theory tries to analyze the causes, characteristics, and consequences of generational conflict in society and history. The concept "generation" has not become a primary focus in social history, but it has surfaced recurrently and some important findings are available. Most recently, life-course studies have linked to work on generations historically.

Conflict between the generations is most common in periods of rapid social change, such as the 19th and 20th centuries. These youth revolts, in turn, stimulate attempts to define and explain the generational phenomenon. Among 19th-century commentators on the conflict of generations were such social thinkers as Auguste Comte, the French founder of modern sociology; Leopold von Ranke, the German father of modern professional history; such statistically oriented analysts as Justin Dromel in France and Giuseppe Ferrari in Italy; and the German cultural historian Wilhelm Dilthey. These early analysts began to see young rebels or rebellious artists not as disturbed individuals, but as important contributors to modern social history. For many of them, social generations were groups of people of the same age who, like social classes, shared ideas and attitudes which made them a force for change in history.

The volume of generational analysis grew denser in the 20th century. The period of the "lost generation" of the 1920s and the youthful left-wing militants of the 1930s produced classic works of generational theory by the Spanish philosopher Jose Ortega y Gasset and the German sociologist Karl Mannheim. Ortega's popular essays on the subject, published in *Man and Crisis* (1923) and *The Modern Theme* (1933), suggested that 4 separate generations coexist at any one time: children (through age 15), youth (ages 15 to 30), those at the stage of initiation into social leadership (30 to 45), and those with real power (45 to 60). The interaction of these four age groups, Ortega believed, plays an important part in making history happen as it does. Mannheim's key essay "The Problem of Generations" (1928) defined the social generation more concretely as a birth cohort, a group born during a particular span of years. Mannheim explored the generational phenomenon in terms of social influences, masses and elites, and subgroups, or "generation units," which react in different ways to the common circumstances which shape the generation as a whole.

An important new wave of generational studies finally grew out of the epidemic of generational unrest of the 1960s. Centered in the United States, this approach drew upon the techniques of modern social history, sociology, political science, social psychology, and related disciplines. Such scholars as Vern L. Bengtson, Richard and

Margaret Braungart, Lewis S. Feuer, Robert S. Laufer, Marvin Rintala, Norman Ryder, Alan B. Spitzer, Lillian Troll, and Robert Wohl contributed significantly. These researches added to our empirical knowledge of past generational revolts and of contemporary youth movements concerned with civil rights, poverty, and the Vietnam War. These scholars also developed and elaborated theoretical models to explain the inner dynamics of generational conflict.

From all this work has evolved a coherent and sophisticated body of theory about the conflict of generations in modern society. Social generations are defined as birth cohorts, people born during the same brief span of years and shaped by growing up in the same culture, class, and period of history. Family structure, child rearing methods, education, and the social and cultural trends of the times all influence the emerging generation, as do traumatic historical events such as wars, economic depressions, and revolutions. Generationists assert that these common factors, impacting on a social generation during the formative years of childhood and youth, have a lasting influence on the age group. A generation may thus be predisposed toward certain political policies, social practices, ideas, or lifestyles. Furthermore, because different generations are shaped by different periods of history, older and younger generations often have different views of politics, society, and culture. The result is generational conflict. This is especially likely to happen during times of rapid change, when the formative periods of successive cohorts may be drastically different, generating radically different worldviews in successive generations.

Social historians differ on the part played by generational conflict in history. Such learned authorities as Lewis S. Feuer (1969) have seen generational revolt as rooted in the irrational rebellion of children against parents and as a pathological factor in history. Other scholars, like Herbert Moller, view dissenting generations as instruments for social change. Whether rebellious younger generations are socially destructive or are forces for positive change in society, one thing seems sure. Generational conflict is a real and potentially powerful factor in modern history. (*See also* Civil Rights Movement; Life Course/Life Cycle; Peace Movement; Subcultures; Youth/Adolescence; Youth Movements)

Anthony Esler

REFERENCES

Bengtson, Vern L., and Robert S. Laufer, eds. "Youth, Generation, and Social Change," *Journal of Social Issues* 30, 2 & 3 (1974).

Braungart, Richard and Margaret. "Generational Politics," *Annual Review of Political Science* 2 (1987): 34–83.

Esler, Anthony, ed. *The Youth Revolution: The Conflict of Generations in Modern History.* Lexington, MA: Heath, 1974.

Feuer, Lewis S. *The Conflict of Generations: The Character and Significance of Student Movements.* New York: Basic Books, 1969.

Mannheim, Karl. "The Problem of Generations," in Paul Kecskemeti, ed., *Essays in the Sociology of Knowledge.* New York: Oxford University Press, 1952.

Geography

Geography is the study of the earth's surface as the locus of human society. The answers geographers have offered to three broad questions may be helpful to social historians: Why have human beings chosen particular *locations* for their settlements and institutions? What patterns are there in the *movement* of goods, persons and messages? and How can we discern and take into account spatial *structures* analogous to the social, economic, and political structures which historians are accustomed to thinking about? Around these questions a certain amount of interdisciplinary effort between geographers and social historians is beginning to take shape.

Location theory has its origins in the work of three German social scientists: J.H. von Thunen (fl. 1820) on the location of different types of agricultural production, Alfred Weber (fl. 1910) on the location of industrial plants, and Walter Christaller (fl. 1930) on the location of settlements based on commercial activity. Each of these three students posited the rational economic man of classical economic theory and made severe simplifying assumptions about the initial physiographic and social conditions of the space in which locational processes would take place. Von Thunen suggested that differences in locational rent (the farmer's revenue for a crop minus his production and transport costs) should lead to concentric zones of different crops around cities. Weber offered a method for predicting factory locations based on the location of sources of raw materials, of markets, and of labor, as well as on transport costs of raw material and products. Christaller proposed a hierarchy of evenly spaced "central places," each of which would provide the most basic retail functions, but smaller subsets of which—also evenly spaced—would provide progressively more specialized functions.

Each of the theories fails to account satisfactorily for important cases, but historians can learn a great deal by trying to understand why real-world systems differ in particular ways from these classic models. (For criticisms and revisions of Christaller's theory, see "Central Place Theory" on p. 101). Another body of theory associated with the so-called Chicago school of sociology offers models for understanding the location of functions within major cities.

Although classic locational theorists were attentive to the costs of the movement of bulky goods, they tended to regard the movement of persons as unproblematic. Allan Pred (1990) has shown how changing patterns of routine movement may reflect the most fundamental social transformations. Can a locational theory that assumes weekly journeys to shop or daily journeys to work, for example, make sense of settlement hierarchies in a transhumance society in which movement from place to place tends to be seasonal? Classical economics' picture of human nature as invariant offers no adequate model of human movement prior to the market. Social history may, therefore, by clarifying the character and periodicity of human movement in the past, contribute significantly to our understanding of the location of religious, military, and administrative functions that classic locational theories tend to neglect but whose prior existence is clearly relevant to what they seek to explain.

Not only routine movement, but also infrequent movement of persons, such as migration, can sometimes be usefully explored by means of the geographer's adaptation of Newton's law of gravitation. This theory predicts that migration (or some other measure of interaction) between two towns will be proportional to the product of the populations (or some other measure of size) of the two towns divided by the distance between them squared (or raised to some other power). Investigators try to estimate empirically the constant of proportionality and exponent, and then seek to interpret differences between observed and expected values.

The movement of ideas through space is usually conceptualized as a diffusion process. The work of Torsten Hägerstrand suggests that diffusion includes both a hierarchical component (diffusion from the top city in a central place hierarchy to the cities in the next level, etc.) and a neighborhood component (diffusion from individual adopters of an innovation to those with whom they are in frequent contact). Diffusion processes are probably of most interest to social historians in the study of such phenomena as popular disturbances, where it may be important to control for diffusion effects so as to evaluate other causal variables. Social historians using geographical variables are thus tracing why rural protests fan out spatially as they do, embracing certain areas but omitting others in the same political unit.

The concept of spatial structure is perhaps most familiar to social historians in the form of the differentiation of territory into affluent core and poorer periphery. World systems theory (q.v.) applies that concept to the modern world as a whole, but geographers more commonly use it to specify the spatial structure of a single society and/or its component regions. For the period prior to the introduction of mechanized overland transport, dependence on navigable waterways for the movement of bulky goods meant that fertile river basins containing major urban centers often constituted regional cores, while surrounding mountainous watersheds delimited regions. Even for the period when technology has rendered these physiographic features less salient, such delineation of "nodal" or "functional" regions is the usual method of describing spatial structure. (It is not to be confused with an alternative type of regionalization: the specification of homogeneous regions, each of which is intended not to be internally differentiated but rather to be uniform with respect to some variable such as predominant crop or major ethnic group.)

It is important to delineate spatial structure for reasons analogous to those which prompt historians to reflect carefully on periodization; one should cut space, as well as time, at the joints. It is possible that very different social processes are occurring simultaneously in different regions of the same society, and only the "definition" of space allows appropriate analysis. Moreover, it is also possible that controlling for those variables that most clearly differentiate core and periphery will reveal crosscutting spatial structures of great interpretive interest. (*See also* Central Place Theory; World Economy/Dependency Theory)

David W. Miller

REFERENCES

Bradford, M.G., and W.A. Kent. *Human Geography: Theories and Their Applications.* Oxford: Oxford University Press, 1977.

Braudel, Fernand. *The Identity of France.* Volume I. *History and Environment.* Translated by Siân Reynolds. New York: Harper & Row, 1988.

Meinig, D.W. *The Shaping of America: A Geographical Perspective on 500 Years of History.* Volume 1. *Atlantic America, 1492–1800.* New Haven: Yale University Press, 1986.

Pred, Allan. *Making Histories and Constructing Human Geographies: The Local Transformation of Practice, Power Relations, and Consciousness.* Boulder, CO: Westview Press, 1990.

Gestures

The study of gestures deals with ephemeral acts, and involves the work of sociologists, social psychologists, and anthropologists, all of whom are able to note down, draw, photograph, or film the gestures of the people they study. Historians (like art historians), however, have a much harder time. They can work only with representations of gestures—textual or figural—the clues of which are often scattered over a wide range of sources, demanding from the social historian of gesture not only a thorough knowledge of the culture in question but also an interdisciplinary approach. He or she needs the skills of a social, a literary, and an art historian all at the same time. Even though the new social history has stressed

the place of symbolism in everyday life and has concentrated on apparently trivial routines and rituals in reconstructing the rules implicit in a given culture, gestures have hardly been studied, probably because of the difficulties just described.

It will be helpful to define the concept rather loosely, drawing no rigid lines between "gesture" (of the hands and limbs) and "posture" (the whole carriage and deportment of the body). The range of sources is considerable. There are treatises that are entirely devoted to the subject, such as *L'arte de' cenni* (1616) by the Italian lawyer Giovanni Bonifacio. There are the many treatises on manners, beginning more or less with Castiglione's *The Courtier* (1528) or Erasmus's *De civilitate morum puerilium* (1530). No less important is the vast literature on public eloquence (going back to Aristotle, Cicero, and Quintilian), on clothing, dancing, acting, fencing, and the like. On actual behavior much is to be gleaned from such personal sources as letters, diaries, and memoirs, and from such administrative sources as judicial, notarial, and church records. These sources can inform us concerning the social aspects of gesture (class, gender, ethnicity, and the like) and on moral aspects such as honor and shame. So may paintings, prints, sculpture, or painted ceramics (for example, Greek and Roman vases). Though mostly overlooked by iconologists, much of this material contains valuable information on the routines and rituals of everyday life, including gesture and posture.

Inevitably the social (or cultural) history of gesture is an interdisciplinary discipline. Its practitioners can learn from sociologists, such as Erving Goffman and his "dramaturgical approach," from anthropologists, sociolinguists, and semiologists. No less important is the work done on nonverbal communication, in particular on kinesics (the study of communicative body movements). Being to a large extent dependent on visual material the history of gesture blends into iconology as well. A very new branch of social history, research on gestures is beginning to generate important findings.

Herman Roodenburg

REFERENCES

Bremmer, Jan, and Herman Roodenburg, eds. *A Cultural History of Gesture from Antiquity to the*

Present Day. Cambridge: Cambridge University Press, 1991.

Mauss, Marcel. "Les techniques du corps," *Journal de psychologie normale et pathologique* 39 (1935): 271–293, reprinted in his *Sociology and Psychology* (London 1979), pp. 97–123.

Schmitt, Jean-Claude. *La raison des gestes dans l'Occident médiéval.* Paris 1990.

Ghetto

Contemporary ghettos—nearly all-black areas within American cities—are the product of several interrelated developments in American and African American history. It reflects the impact of white racial hostility in the wake of the Great Migration; the African Americans' quest for freedom, work, and social justice; and, perhaps most importantly, the rise of new classes and social relations within the black community. Yet, the "ghetto" as a theoretical construct had its roots in the Jewish experience in urban America and Europe. Social historians have studied ghetto segregation as part of the immigrant experience, sometimes finding less rigid community boundaries than the term implies, and the development in the 20th century of ghettoization for blacks.

As early as the 1920s, however, the sociologist Lewis Wirth suggested the ghetto as a way to study other ethnic and racial groups, including blacks. Social scientists St. Clair Drake and Horace R. Cayton followed Wirth's lead. In their classic study of blacks in Chicago, *Black Metropolis* (1944), they used the notion of a ghetto to highlight the strongest visual evidence of a color line in the city's social, economic, and political life. During the 1960s and early 1970s, historians elaborated upon the ghetto model, making it the dominant conceptualization of black urban life and history. In recent years, however, new scholarship—emphasizing patterns of class, culture, and power—has moved to the fore, demonstrating fundamental limitations in the use of ghetto as a framework for fully understanding black urban history. Still, as a way of describing patterns of residential segregation along color lines, the ghetto retains utility.

Unlike Europeans and other nonwhite immigrants, blacks first encountered urban America

as slaves. Beginning with negligible numbers during the 17th century, the number of urban slaves and free blacks reached sizable proportions by the eve of the Civil War. Confined primarily to domestic service, common labor, and, to some extent, artisan jobs in white households, antebellum blacks, slave and free, were dispersed widely over the urban landscape. More importantly, as late as 1910, nearly 90 percent of the nation's black population lived in the South, and less than 22 percent of southern blacks lived in cities. The percentage of northern blacks living in cities had increased to over 60 percent in 1890, but blacks made up little more than 2 percent of the total. Under the impact of World War I, an estimated 700,000 to one million blacks left the South. Another 800,000 to one million left during the 1920s. Although blacks would face increasing residential segregation in the urban South, the ghetto would gain its sharpest expression in northern cities.

Beginning with relatively small numbers on the eve of World War I, the black urban population in certain cities of the West, Midwest, and Great Lakes region increased even more dramatically than that of the old Northeast. Detroit's black population increased by 611 percent during the war years and by nearly 200 percent during the 1920s, rising from less than 6,000 to over 120,000. Cleveland, St. Louis, and Los Angeles also registered huge increases. Nonetheless, as in the prewar era, New York City, Chicago, and Philadelphia continued to absorb disproportionately large numbers of black newcomers. Between 1910 and 1930, Chicago's black population increased more than 5-fold, from 44,000 to 234,000; New York City's trebled, from about 100,000 to 328,000; and Philadelphia's grew from 84,500 to an estimated 220,600.

As the black urban population increased, residential segregation accelerated in all major cities. The index of dissimilarity (a statistical device for measuring the extent of residential segregation) rose from 66.8 to 85.2 percent in Chicago; 60.6 to 85.0 percent in Cleveland; 64.1 to 77.9 percent in Boston; and from 46.0 to 63.0 percent in Philadelphia. In Chicago, the number of census tracts of over 50 percent black rose from 4 in 1910 to 16 in 1920; 35 percent of the city's blacks lived in census tracts that were over 75 percent black. By 1920, two-thirds of Manhattan's black population lived in Harlem; the area bordered by 130th Street on the south, 145th Street on the north and west of Fifth to Eighth Avenue was predominantly black. In Cleveland, no census tract was more than 25 percent black in 1910; ten years later two census tracts were more than 50 percent black. By 1930, 90 percent of the city's blacks lived in a restricted area: bounded by Euclid Avenue on the north, East 105th Street on the east, and Woodland Avenue on the south. Likewise, although the black population in Milwaukee remained small by comparison to other cities, 4 wards contained over 93 percent of the city's 7,500 blacks.

In cities with large black populations like New York and Chicago, the World War I migration intensified a pattern of housing discrimination that was already well underway. Planned as an exclusive, stable, upper- and upper middle-class white community, Harlem represented a desirable location to the city's expanding black population. Although an economic depression undercut the flow of whites into Harlem, the Harlem Property Owners' Improvement Corporation waged a vigorous fight to keep blacks out. It launched a vigorous restrictive covenant campaign, informing black realtors that houses in the area were off limits to black buyers. Although the movement failed to keep Harlem white, the poor economic position of most migrants, discriminatory prices, and the dearth of necessary repairs all undermined housing quality during the 1920s.

In Chicago and elsewhere, North and South, blacks faced similar restrictions in the housing market. As early as 1909, Chicago's Hyde Park Improvement Protective Club called for a concerted ban on the selling of real estate to blacks. When such practices failed, whites resorted to violence. From July 1917 through February 1921, blacks in Chicago experienced 58 home bombings, which killed 2 persons, injured others, and resulted in over $100,000 in property damage. Racial antagonism culminated in riots in East St. Louis, Pittsburgh, and Philadelphia, as well as Chicago. Racial violence reinforced residential segregation in northern cities and highlighted

the growing spatial expression of the "race problem" in American society.

Under the impact of the Great Depression and World War II, a variety of factors reinforced the segregation of urban blacks. Although some realtors lowered racial barriers in the wake of hard times, such measures did little to reverse the pattern of ghettoization. Facing disproportionately high rates of unemployment, few blacks could take advantage of lower rents and housing prices. More importantly, the emergence of New Deal housing programs like the Federal Housing Administration and the Works Projects Administration helped to deepen established patterns of spatial separation. Until the U.S. Supreme Court outlawed restrictive covenants in 1948, the official FHA *Underwriting Manual* stated that "the presence of incompatible racial elements results in a lowering of the rating, often to the point of rejection." Accordingly, in Milwaukee, Chicago, Cleveland, and other cities, the federal government funded segregated housing units.

The ghetto, however, was not only a problem of racial segregation, it was also an expression of shifting class relations in the urban environment. As the ghetto expanded and consolidated, it stratified internally. Not all African Americans shared the same space. As the new black middle class expanded during the 1920s, it slowly moved into better housing vacated by whites, leaving the black poor concentrated in certain sections. During the 1930s, in his studies of Chicago and New York, sociologist E. Franklin Frazier demonstrated the division of the black urban community along socioeconomic lines. In Chicago, poor and working-class blacks concentrated in the northernmost zones of the South Side black ghetto, while the higher socioeconomic groups lived on the extreme South Side. In Harlem, middle- and upper-class blacks lived on the periphery, while working-class and poor blacks clustered in the center. According to Frazier, the center of Harlem was "essentially a non-family area," an area of "the emancipated from all classes and elements." While each city contained significant areas of interclass mixing, poverty increasingly characterized specific sections of the ghetto.

African Americans were by no means passive recipients of externally imposed residential segregation. They played a dynamic role in giving shape to spatial patterns in the urban environment. Misunderstandings, cleavages, and conflicts along class and status lines would often hamper their efforts. Nonetheless, in order to combat racial discrimination and to make the black community more livable, blacks developed cross-class alliances and built their own churches, fraternal orders, social clubs, newspapers, real estate firms, and a plethora of social welfare, civil rights, and political organizations. Deeply rooted in black kin and friendship networks, these organizations not only played a role in the migration of southern blacks into the city, but they mediated the rise of nearly all-black communities in American cities. If whites played a determining role in confining blacks to certain portions of the city, blacks determined the specific shape of their own community life.

As the nation entered the postwar years, a variety of factors, new and old, reinforced the segregation of urban blacks. The African American population increased from 13 million in 1940 to over 22 million in 1970. The proportion of blacks living in cities rose to over 80 percent, 10 percent higher than the country at large. Beginning as the most rural of Americans, blacks had become the most urbanized. Distributed almost equally between regions, by the late 1970s the black urban migration had completed its familiar 20th-century course.

Southern-born blacks from the North and West returned home in rising numbers. During the 1980s, the proportion of African Americans living in the South increased for the first time in more than a century. Some returnees point to deteriorating conditions in their neighborhoods—crime, drugs, unemployment, welfare dependency—as the prime motives for their return home. Although it is impossible to predict the outcome of current housing patterns, residential segregation will no doubt continue to reflect a complicated mixture of African American activism, interracial animosities, and internal conflicts along class lines. Thus, as a descriptive device for highlighting the color line in American cities, the concept of the ghetto will likely continue to facilitate social analysis.

Joe William Trotter

REFERENCES

Harris, Robert L., Jr. "Coming of Age: The Transformation of Afro-American Historiography," *Journal of Negro History* 57, 2 (1982): 107–121.

Kusmer, Kenneth L. "The Black Urban Experience in American History," in Darlene Clark Hine, ed., *The State of Afro-American History: Past, Present and Future.* Baton Rouge: Louisiana State University Press, 1986.

Meier, August, and Elliott Rudwick. *Black History and the Historical Profession, 1915–1980.* Urbana: University of Illinois Press, 1986.

Trotter, Joe William, Jr. "Afro-American Urban History: A Critique of the Literature," in Joe William Trotter, Jr., ed., *Black Milwaukee: The Making of an Industrial Proletariat, 1915–1945.* Urbana: University of Illinois Press, 1985.

———. *The Great Migration in Historical Perspective: New Dimensions of Race, Class, and Gender.* Bloomington: Indiana University Press, 1991.

Wilson, William J. *The Truly Disadvantaged: The Inner City, the Underclass, and Public Policy.* Chicago: University of Chicago Press, 1987.

Godparenting

Baptism does more than just introduce another member into the Christian community. During the ritual, by virtue of its spiritual nature, the sponsors, the godchild, and the godchild's parents are bound together for life in a web of religious and social obligations and honors. They become spiritual relatives in this web, commonly known as godparenting. Individuals within the godparenting web should cultivate a heightened degree of friendship with one another, which can initiate the exchange of gifts. Godparents in particular have the social duty of naming their godchild and providing the godchild's religious education. Because of this particular relationship between godparents and their godchild, godparents sometimes provide for their orphaned godchild.

Most Christian cultures have had some form of godparenting, but the specific practice has varied by time, place, and sect. The Catholic church today, for instance, officially recognizes only a religious bond between the godparents and the godchild. Catholics in Latin America, however, also recognize a religious and social bond between the godparents and the parents, which is called *compadrazgo*. In the European past, before Reformation era theologians narrowed the scope of the religious bonds, godparenting paralleled the modern Latin American version.

Anthropologists have long known the significance of godparenting for various cultures in premodern and modern Latin America. There, godparenting has provided for the education of children, eased the tension of social conflict, and established economic, political, and psychological support networks for people. Recently, anthropologists and social historians have begun investigating the significance of godparenting in premodern Europe. Their studies indicate that premodern European godparenting performed many of the same social and religious functions that premodern and modern Latin American baptismal kinship has performed. Godparenting provides an important key to larger family relationships in premodern history. (*See also* Anthropology; Child Rearing; Christianity; Kinship; Latin American Religion; Naming Practices; Ritual)

Louis Haas

REFERENCES

Lynch, Joseph. *Godparents and Kinship in Early Medieval Europe.* Princeton, NJ: Princeton University Press, 1986.

Nutini, Hugo G., and Betty Bell. *Ritual Kinship: The Structure and Historical Development of the Compadrazgo System in Rural Tlaxcala.* 2 vols. Princeton, NJ: Princeton University Press, 1980 and 1984.

Greco-Roman Festivals

Greco-Roman festivals were sacred rites repeated at periodic intervals, sometimes accompanied by cessation of work. Although many of these rites did not originally involve a specific deity, most eventually came to do so in time. The central fixture was the sacrifice, with less prominent roles often played by prayers, feasts, processions, and other activities. Over time, urbanization, while it did not entirely eradicate the original agrarian orientation, did result in the organization of the festivals under the auspices of the state and its officers. Even so, participation did not thereby parallel the state's narrow restriction of the franchise to the citizen segment of the population, for the festivals remained in several instances remarkably inclusive.

Thus in Athens, the Kronia was in the classical period a day of rest for slaves when they were allowed to dine with their masters; similarly, during the Anthesteria slaves were permitted to join the remainder of the household in celebration. For the Panathenaia, a shroud for the cult statue of Athena was woven by girls chosen from aristocratic families; and the procession included still other girls, *metics* (resident aliens), freed slaves, and non-Greeks. The Mysteries of Eleusis observed no distinction between male and female, and slaves as well as free people could be initiated, though a prohibition against "barbarians" was relaxed only for the Romans. Males were totally excluded from the Thesmophoria, Stenia, Haloa, and Skira, while females played prominent roles on the sixth of Munichion, and at the Brauronia, Oschophoria, Arrephoria, and Plynteria. At the Dionysia, metics processed and, along with foreigners and possibly women, observed the dramatic productions in the theater; they were also assigned an appreciable share of the sacrificial meats at the Prometheia.

At Rome, slaves participated in a number of festivals, notably the Saturnalia, during which by a kind of role reversal they were waited upon by their masters; other instances are provided by the cults of Fortuna, Hercules, Diana (like the Saturnalia, a holiday for slaves), and the Compitalia. The rite of Bona Dea, observed only by women, was performed, not in a sanctuary, but in the house of a high magistrate whose wife, attended by vestals, officiated. (The festival of the vestals themselves, charged with the maintenance of the sacred hearth, is not recorded to have been confined to women.) Additional women-centered festivals are the Matralia, the Veneralia (of Venus), the Carmentalia, and the festivals of Juno Lucina and of Fortuna Virilis.

The study of festivals forms an important part of the social history of the classical world, particularly in terms of the values and rituals of ordinary people vis-à-vis officially sponsored culture. Linkage to the later festival tradition and comparison with festivals in other ancient societies have not been widely attempted to date. (*See also* Festivals)

Nicholas F. Jones

REFERENCES

Parke, H.W. *Festivals of the Athenians.* Ithaca, NY: Cornell University Press, 1977.

Scullard, H.H. *Festivals and Ceremonies of the Roman Republic.* Ithaca, NY: Cornell University Press, 1981.

Greco-Roman Sexuality

In recent decades, there has been an explosion of scholarship on sexuality and the family in classical antiquity. Employing a variety of approaches, these studies have sought to uncover norms and attitudes relating to sexuality in the art, literature, law, medicine, religion, and social and economic relations of societies spanning almost 1,500 years and ranging across the Mediterranean. The result clearly establishes this topic in the social history of the classical Mediterranean, though sources inevitably bias the study toward the practice of the upper and urban classes rather than the peasant majority. Surveying this varied landscape, from the pre-literate heroic society depicted in the Homeric epics to the complex urban Christian culture of the late Roman Empire, a number of central themes stand out:

1. Greco-Roman societies were slave societies. Slaves, described by Aristotle as "animate tools," were a form of property that could be used or marketed by their masters for sexual purposes. The ubiquity of domestic slaves and slave-prostitutes clearly had a powerful impact on attitudes and values concerning sexual relations.

2. Greco-Roman sexual relations were characterized by a fundamental asymmetry. First, sexual relations were often conceptualized as taking place between unequal participants and, hence, involving the dominance of one partner and the submission of the other. The most extreme case, of course, is intercourse between free persons and slaves. In marriage the element of asymmetry was buttressed by the disparity in ages between partners (the man was typically much older), the legal disabilities of women, and the freedom of men to pursue sexual relations outside of marriage. On the other hand, this asym-metry in marriage was to some extent tempered by the notion of marriage as a sexual, economic, social, and spiritual partnership. Further, though always more constrained than men, the relative sexual and marital freedom of women varied greatly across societies, epochs, and social classes.

3. Sexual relations were permeated by the larger normative system associated with values of honor and shame. Here, too, asymmetry played a central role: Men were dishonored by being thought feminine or passive instead of dominant and aggressive, both in their pursuit of women and boys as well as in the sexual act. On the other hand, they were dishonored if they did not successfully guard their own wives, daughters, and sisters against the predatory attentions of other males. For women, honor, in this male-centered scheme, consisted in virginity prior to marriage and sexual submission to, and only to, their husbands. Needless to say, ideology stood in considerable tension with social practices.

4. Whereas it was regarded as the natural social role of a man to marry and have children, it was also thought natural that many men sexually pursued both women and boys. Asymmetry also characterized homoerotic relations, in which an adult male pursued a boy. In such relations, the boy was seen as adopting the passive sexual role of a woman, submitting to penetration by the active male partner.

The rise of Christianity, of course, had a significant impact upon conceptualizations of sexuality. Peter Brown's (1988) work on the complex transition away from classical sexual codes highlights the importance of these codes in the long classical period itself.

David Cohen

REFERENCES

Brown, P. *The Body and Society.* New York: Columbia University Press, 1988.

Cohen, D. *Law, Sexuality and Society.* New York: Cambridge University Press, 1991.

Dover, K. *Greek Homosexuality.* Cambridge, MA: Harvard University Press, 1978.

Halperin, D., J. Winkler, and F. Zeitlin, eds. *Before Sexuality.* Princeton, NJ: Princeton University Press, 1991.

Rousselle, A. *Porneia: On Disease and the Body in Antiquity.* Oxford: Basil Blackwell, 1988.

Greco-Roman Stratification

Among the more than 1,000 Greek city-states, the social systems of only 2 are known in any detail, and one of them, Sparta, was idiosyncratic. Here we confine ourselves to classical Athens, of which we can speak with some confidence about the various strata of both citizen and noncitizen society.

Citizenship, originally extended to all whose fathers were citizens, came to be more narrowly confined beginning in 450 BC to those of legitimate birth both whose father and mother were of citizen status. Furthermore, over the 200-year history of the democracy, grants of citizenship to outsiders are recorded only rarely. Thus, the citizen class came to approximate an exclusive caste, closed to even the most successful and deserving aliens.

Citizens enjoyed an absolute monopoly over government, though, somewhat surprisingly, not over military service, open as it was to *metics* (resident aliens) and occasionally even to slaves. Within the citizen class, however, gradations of privilege were formally imposed under Solon, according to whose "census class" system, based on annual income, individuals were differentially granted access to the various organs of government. But by Aristotle's day late in the 4th century BC there are clear signs that the system, though still in existence, was no longer enforced, so, constitutionally speaking, the citizen class had become virtually monolithic.

Nonetheless, distinctions within the citizen class persisted. Lower-class Athenians, corresponding more or less to the lowest Solonian category, the *thetes*, were often landless citizens who inhabited the densely populated urban center and presumably drew payment for government service and, especially under the Empire, found regular employment as rowers in the fleet (hence forming the core of the radical prowar imperialist faction). Another recognizable group is the *hoplites*, or heavy-armed infantry. Traditionally recruited from the smallholding farming population, the hoplites constituted a class to the extent that they necessarily possessed the minimum wealth needed to outfit themselves with armor; politically, they, like the farmers generally, opposed the Empire and war with Sparta, longing instead for the bygone era of harmonious cooperation against the national enemy, Persia. Aristocrats, typically associated with landed wealth, defined themselves by their persistent efforts to respond to the leveling tendencies represented by the adoption of hoplite armor and tactics and by the triumph of democracy, although, politically, one can distinguish from the conservatives another group—among them, for example, Pericles—devoted to the championing of the radical poor.

Below the citizens, metics, approximately one-third of the free population, were subject to a number of disabilities, including a poll tax, a prohibition against the ownership of land and houses, and service in the military in separate units. While discriminated against, however, they did find an important niche, serving as merchants, traders, bankers, and the like, though success could not normally bring with it the coveted award of citizenship.

Occupying the lowest level of the Athenian stratification system were the slaves. In contrast to Sparta, where the slaves (called *helots*) were owned by the state, Athenian slaves were with few exceptions privately owned chattels. Mobility was made possible through manumission, though ex-slaves joined the metics and typically rose no higher.

Roman social stratification from at least the early Republic was founded upon the division between the patricians and plebeians. The former, as the term itself (connected with the Latin *pater*, "father," and so implying social superiority) suggests, were a privileged class, originally enjoying a monopoly over magistracies, certain priestly offices, and perhaps membership in the Senate. The latter, comprising the remainder of the citizen population, were, among other disadvantages, prohibited from intermarriage with patricians and in many cases played the subordinate role of client to a patrician patron. As a consequence of the so-called Struggle of the Orders, ending in 287 BC, however, the plebeians were able to achieve a measure of equality in constitutional, if not social, affairs.

With the incorporation within the expanded oligarchy of numerous political and wealthy plebeian clans, new distinctions came to the fore, particularly with reference to participation in

Republican political offices. "Nobility" denoted at first simply the "known" members of the oligarchy, but later acquired greater specificity when it came to be limited to those families whose members included a holder of the consulate, a high elective office and the goal of the Republican political career. Due to upper-class exclusiveness, however, outsiders only rarely penetrated the circle of the nobility, and a special term, New Man, eventually designated the first man of a family to attain the consulate—thereby, importantly, ennobling his descendants. More broadly, the Senatorial class embraced those (and their descendants) who, after Sulla (d. 78 BC), had entered the Senate automatically through election to the (relatively low) public office of quaestor.

Within the upper classes but outside the Senatorial order was another group, the equestrians, literally (but no longer in fact) the "cavalry." The equestrians preferred business and the cultivation of private interests to the pursuit of elective office and so did not under most circumstances become involved in Roman political affairs, the chief exception being their control of the courts under the late Republic. Although subjected to attempts at political manipulation, the equestrians survived the civil wars, to emerge as an important component in Augustus's new imperial administration.

The growth of the Empire witnessed the development of a new stratification overlying the (now) transformed Republican orders. Replacing the increasingly antiquated dichotomy of citizen and noncitizen was a largely social distinction between the *honestiores* (upper class), embracing the old aristocratic orders and the veterans, and the *humiliores* (lower class), including all others. Although not legally defined, the distinction was nonetheless meaningful in that humiliores were subject to appreciably severer criminal penalties. Alongside the Senatorials and equestrians, the *decuriones*, the local councillors of the Roman municipal cities and colonies, constituted a third order. Each, furthermore, was characterized by internal divisions and was cut across by gradations of status often not commensurate with the order itself.

Roman slaves, like their Greek counterparts, might achieve mobility through manumission, though, again like their Greek counterparts, as a condition of their liberation they were often obligated to perform certain services for their former owners. But, unlike the Athenian case, freed slaves were not excluded from the citizenship, and especially under the early Empire were able to obtain positions of great power and responsibility in the imperial administration, despite social rejection by the upper classes. (*See also* Athenian Democracy; Sparta)

Nicholas F. Jones

REFERENCES

Boren, Henry C. *Roman Society. A Social, Economic, and Cultural History*, 2nd ed. Lexington, MA, and Toronto: D.C. Heath, 1992.

Frost, Frank J. *Greek Society*, 4th ed. Lexington, MA, and Toronto: D.C. Heath, 1992.

Greek and Roman Family

The formal structures of the Greek and Roman family (or families—for although the two can and should be compared they can not be equated), for example, marriage, inheritance, kinship, and legal power and responsibility, have been systematically studied since the 19th century, when the ancient family played a major role in the intellectual debate over the evolution of the modern European family (See Kuper 1988). A with the debates over whether the original form of the family was matriarchal or patriarchal, the 19th-century analysis attempted to identify the primitive forms of family institutions and trace their development through the classical period. Fustel de Coulanges's derivation of Roman patriarchal power (*patria potestas*) from the father's (*paterfamilias*) role in family religion—the cult of the hearth and of the male ancestors—may be taken as representative of the character of this scholarship. Although his analysis of the ancient family is now read more as an intellectual tour de force than a historical account, its emphasis on patriarchy and patrilinearity and its evolutionary viewpoint have remained paradigmatic until recent times.

After a half-century of productive conversation, the disciplines of classics and anthropology parted company in the early 20th century. The result for the study of the ancient family was a turn toward descriptive treatises based on ancient texts (and sometimes art and artifacts) that classified "family" under "private life." This approach has been remarkably persistent through at least the first half of the 20th century, and its fruits can be seen quite clearly in the work of W.K. Lacey (1968) and J.P.V.D. Balson (1969). The attempt of Philip Slater (1971) to use Athenian tragedy to psychoanalyze the Greek family is provocative but flawed, and should be used with caution.

In recent years, historians of the ancient family have begun to look once again to the work of social anthropologists, particularly those working in Mediterranean contexts and on issues of gender. One productive result has been a heightened awareness of the inadequacy of the public/private dichotomy and of the essential public importance of family identity and behavior in ancient society. Further, the emergence of women's history and family history as innovative fields of social historical research has prompted classical historians to ask new questions of old evidence. An appreciation of the demographic realities of ancient Rome, for example, leads one to the question: How often did fathers live long enough to continue to assert *patria potestas* over adult sons (or daughters)? With numerous books and articles appearing each year on a broad array of questions, the study of the Greek and Roman families can be said to be currently experiencing a renaissance (see, e.g., Humphreys 1983; Rawson 1986). This relates to the large trend of integrating ancient history with social history more generally. (*See also* Family; Women's History)

Cynthia Patterson

REFERENCES

Balson, J.P.V.D. *Life and Leisure in Ancient Rome.* New York: McGraw-Hill, 1969.

Humphreys, S.C. *The Family, Women and Death: Comparative Studies.* London: Routledge, 1983.

Kuper, A. *The Invention of Primitive Society.* London: Routledge, 1988.

Lacey, W.K. *The Family in Classical Greece.* Ithaca, NY: Cornell University Press, 1968.

Rawson, B., ed. *The Family in Ancient Rome: New Perspectives.* Ithaca, NY: Cornell University Press, 1986.

Guilds

Guilds as urban institutions have existed in many cultures, but nowhere more importantly than in Europe between 1200 and 1900. Guilds were associations of skilled artisans of the same trade or craft. They had legal, economic, social, political, and religious aspects.

Guilds originated in the 13th century, supposedly declined in the 16th and 17th centuries and were abolished in the 18th and 19th centuries. In the European experience, guild membership usually was restricted to masters, but in some places journeymen (skilled laborers working for masters) and apprentices (youths in training to become skilled craftsmen) had partial membership privileges.

Guildsmen insisted upon legal protection of their municipal monopoly on the manufacture and sale of their product, leading most historians to depict them as obstacles to economic growth and opponents of capitalism, doomed to be abolished as free trade and industrialization took hold. This thesis has been forcefully challenged by Mackenney (1987). He argues that entrepreneurial guildsmen can be found in many early modern European cities actively engaged in expansive, if small-scale, commercial activities, in freer enterprise than previously recognized, precisely when guildsmen were supposedly millstones around the neck of the European economy.

From the perspective of their members, guilds were first and foremost social entities, sites of interaction that helped organize and give meaning to their lives. Guild activities often proclaimed solidarity among its members. This was accomplished, for example, by coordinated public display on ceremonial occasions like processions, and could be sealed by oaths and other rituals securing membership and a sense of belonging.

Guilds also promoted the collective welfare of the membership. Guild statutes legally restricted competition and regulated prices, wages, and the labor supply. The political welfare of guild members was often secured by guildsmen serving on town councils where they wielded real political power, notably, for example, in the German free imperial cities.

Everywhere in Europe guilds were formally associated with confraternities, religious brotherhoods that satisfied the spiritual welfare of its members. These associations collected dues and then provided members such things as funeral expenses, masses for the dead, and charity. Through their confraternities, guildsmen participated in banquets and festivals, usually in honor of the guild's patron saint, which functioned to secure even tighter the sense of community among guildsmen.

Social interaction among guild members had a communitarian and implicitly egalitarian emphasis, but it would be a mistake to assume that this was the sole organizational principle active in their lives. Guild membership, for example, contributed to the honor and respectability of the craftsman, notably in the German "Home Towns," and membership placed the guildsman in the appropriate rank of the social hierarchy.

The world of the guild was no less affected by the principle of hierarchy than the society of which it was an essential part. Though hierarchy among and within guilds was not rigidly defined nor uniform across Europe, there were gradations in status among and within guilds. Although the contours of a middle class of masters can be glimpsed in many towns, distribution of wealth among and within guilds was usually uneven.

Elements of hierarchy beyond the economic are also evident. Within guilds during the 16th and 17th centuries, for example, there was a drift toward oligarchy among officeholders. Furthermore, hierarchy within guilds that included journeymen in their ranks can be seen clearly in the relations between masters and journeymen. This unequal relationship became increasingly acute as opportunities for journeymen to advance to mastership were reduced in the early modern period throughout Europe. This development mirrored the ossification of society at large, and likely accounted for the formation of separate journeymen guilds in 16th-century London.

Hierarchy was also pronounced in gender relations, owing much to paternalism. Many guilds permitted female membership (although in such mixed guilds everywhere they were categorically excluded from officeholding). The women in guilds were usually but not always widows of masters, and were permitted to continue to practice their husband's trade if they remained single or married someone in the trade. Exclusively female guilds were much rarer than mixed guilds, and invariably of lower social and legal status. The linen and hemp producers of Paris, the wool packers of Southampton, and the silkwomen of London were such examples.

Guilds were essential institutions in the social life of Europeans, and they have counterparts in some other cultures. In the Ottoman Empire craft guilds of skilled artisans were closely associated with religious brotherhoods, and provided a sense of belonging in a world where currents of migration depersonalized social relations.

In Japan and China, in contrast, guilds of skilled craftsmen (*za* and *hong*, respectively) served commercial functions but not religious ones. The *za* were abolished early in the Tokugawa period (1603–1868), while the *hong* survived into the 19th century.

In North America apprenticeship and mastership took hold in the American colonies and survived into the antebellum United States, but guilds did not. During the colonial period, this was due primarily to shortages of skilled labor, inadequate mechanisms of legal enforcement, and a lack of articulated municipal governments.

In addition to dealing with guilds during the medieval and early modern period in Europe and elsewhere, and changes that occurred including growing gender rigidity and, often, growing master-journeymen tension, social historians have dealt with the decline of guilds under the impact of new laws and new capitalistic principles on the eve of the industrial revolution (1780s–1840s). They have also examined the longer run impact of guilds on later labor union goals and organizations, artisanal protest, and other modern survivals.

A full appreciation of the social history of guilds requires viewing them in a broad context and focusing on them as groups of people rather than as institutional abstractions. This will, in turn, force our eye toward social and cultural relationships beyond the guild itself. Although guilds no doubt were a locus of community, they were only one of many in the lives of the men and women of guilds. If we peer behind the institutional facade, glimpses of solidarities that span guilds can be caught. (*See also* Artisans; Women and Work)

James R. Farr

REFERENCES

Farr, James R. *Hands of Honor: Artisans and Their World in Dijon, 1550–1650.* Ithaca, NY: Cornell University Press, 1988.

Mackenney, Richard. *Tradesmen and Traders: The World of the Guilds in Venice and Europe, c. 1250–c. 1650.* Totowa, NJ: Barnes and Noble, 1987.

Ménétra, Jacques-Louis. *Journal of My Life.* Translated by Arthur Goldhammer. New York: Columbia University Press, 1986.

Rorabaugh, W.J. *The Craft Apprentice from Franklin to the Machine Age in America.* New York: Oxford University Press, 1986.

Walker, Mack. *German Home Towns: Community, State, and General Estate, 1648–1871.* Ithaca, NY: Cornell University Press, 1971.

H

Haciendas/Encomiendas

The countryside and urban-rural relationships in Latin America have traditionally been dominated by large landed estates called variously *latifundios* (from the Latin), *fazendas* (in Brazil), *estancias* (in Argentina), or *haciendas* (Spanish America generally), as well as by a variety of other local terms. Although the economic, social, and political importance of these agrosocial units has tended to diminish under the impact of political change, urbanization, and industrialization, they are still key features in the social landscape of many areas. Large estates may in the future even experience a resurgence in some countries, as for example in Mexico, where the system of collective landholdings (*ejidos*) initiated by the land reforms of the Mexican Revolution (1910–1920) is being dismantled during the 1990s under the influence of revived neoliberal economic policies. In most areas of Latin America labor relations, patterns of social deference, elite social aspirations, attitudes about wealth, the terms upon which the Latin American economies were integrated into the world

economy, and other key elements of the social constitution were formed or strongly influenced by the dominance of large estates in the countryside. Unresolved political and academic debates still swirl around the nature and history of this institution. Many observers have characterized the societies of Latin America as feudal in their main social outlines until fairly recent times because of the supposedly hierarchical and non-profit-oriented nature of rural estates there, while others would see the Latin American great estate as capitalist (or at least market-oriented and economically rational) from its beginnings, even in those cases in which it relied heavily on slavery and other forms of coerced labor.

Generally speaking, the hacienda and its attendant social forms did not arrive full-blown on the New World scene immediately with the main Iberian conquests (1492–ca. 1535), but rather evolved from related forms over the first century and more of European colonization. For several decades immediately following the major European eruptions into the New World,

315

native populations remained dense and in control of a variety of economic resources, most notably land, so that the major economic problem for the European conquerors boiled down to extracting labor and other resources from the indigenous populations in a parasitic fashion while not themselves directly engaging in the demeaning task of production. To achieve this the Spanish colonizers implanted the *encomienda* (not set up in Brazil, a Portuguese colony), an institution developed in the Iberian realms during the medieval Christian reconquest of the peninsula from the Moslems. Under the New World encomienda, the Spanish Crown granted to preferred conquerors and colonists (an ad hoc settler aristocracy) the right to collect labor and tribute from specified Indian populations, theoretically in return for the *encomendero's* military fealty to the Crown, and his efforts to Christianize the Indians under his control and see to their material welfare. Such grants explicitly did not include property rights to indigenous lands, but over the course of time often formed the basis for private landholdings. Aside from the direct collection of tributes in money and kind, encomenderos employed Indian labor in mining, urban construction, farming, textile manufacture, and myriad other economic activities. As indigenous population melted away in Ibero-America with the great pandemics of the 16th century, and as church and Crown sought to protect dwindling populations and assert control over the turbulent New World settlers by emasculating the encomienda, Indian labor naturally became less available and access to land and other productive resources easier. Although the encomienda survived in some areas of Spanish America (e.g., Paraguay) nearly until the end of the colonial period, its heyday had lasted until 1550–1560 in Mexico, and somewhat later in the Andes.

Up until the 1960s scholars often confused the encomienda with the hacienda, since the encomendero's hacienda often seemed to arise in the same territory in which the encomendero had his encomienda: the hacienda system stressed landed estates, not government grants of labor. The new research in colonial Latin American social history laid this confusion to rest, as historians examined new sources, such as contracts

and wills. While some encomenderos used their power over their charges to acquire land, most of the haciendas did not arise in this fashion. Instead, rentals of community lands, outright usurpations, and some land sales by indigenous peoples who had little concept of land as individual property explains the initial expansion of the hacienda in Latin America. Moreover, as the Indian population declined, the Crown or the community itself sold off land not cultivated by the villages. Indians fleeing the tribute and labor requirements of the Indian communities often went to work on the Spanish estates, forming a group of laborers called hacienda peons.

As the encomienda declined, private Spanish landholdings—always on the New World scene—increased in social and economic importance as the colonists took an active interest in acquiring land and organizing production. Iberian models also existed for large landed estates, dating from the slave-worked *latifundia* of Roman times, and though these forms were adapted to New World conditions there is little doubt that large-scale landownership and its associated social ideas formed part of the cultural baggage of Europeans in the colonies. Although there was certainly a far from perfect overlap between encomienda and hacienda, many of the latter found their origins in the labor practices and unofficial land acquisitions of the former, evolving over time from institutions of labor and tribute extraction into private landed estates.

Haciendas (with equivalent units in the Caribbean colonies and in Brazil) existed all over Spanish America during the centuries of colonial domination (to about 1825), developing essential forms that, though they adapted themselves to the entry of Latin American societies into the modern export-economy era (after about 1850), remained nonetheless recognizable over time. Less characterized by large size per se than by forms of labor relationships and productive organization, haciendas could vary in extent from the hundreds of thousands of acres some embraced in northern Mexico and the Argentine pampas, to estates of a few hundred intensely farmed acres in the vicinity of major cities like Santiago de Chile, Lima, or Mexico City. Land was acquired through a variety of means, including the occupation of barren lands, royal (subsequently republican) land grants, purchase, and outright usurpation from Indian peasant communities, the latter creating endemic and often violent conflict between *hacendados* (hacienda owners) and indigenous farmers as population pressures on land increased from the 18th century or so. Farming technologies tended to remain simple, since hacienda profitability and the wide availability of plentiful and cheap labor generally did not justify heavy expenditures on labor-saving machinery, expensive fertilizers, or irrigation systems. At certain places and times, however, such investments were made, as in the central valleys of 19th-century Chile under the impact of a growing international demand for wheat, or on the north coast of Peru in the production of sugar, even during colonial times a capital-intensive industry. With certain exceptions markets for hacienda products tended to remain local or regional in scope, the traditional hacienda demonstrating a notable ability to contract its production and investment levels in response to periodically worsening economic conditions.

What most distinguished haciendas from other agrosocial forms, however, even up until recent times, was its use of labor and the patriarchal flavor of its social relations. A bewildering array of labor systems, typically in combined forms and employing some degree of legal or informal coercion, characterized hacienda labor regimes depending upon local ecological and demographic conditions, product mix, proximity to markets, and so forth. These types ranged from African and occasionally Indian slavery, through forms of debt peonage both mild and harsh, to tenancy and sharecropping arrangements, and finally to free and highly mobile temporary wage labor. Yet haciendas were also social units, often sizable communities of as many as several thousand people living under the personal domination of a resident manager or landlord, on which laborers and managerial personnel might be born, marry, live, and die, and in which the strains of class and ethnic conflict between owner and laborers were often tempered by ties of patronage and personal acquaintance. Their physical arrangement often reflected this, with the house of the owner's family dominating a central plaza on which might be found the

laborers' huts, storage and processing buildings, and even estate churches and schools. (*See also* Estate Agriculture; Feudalism; Latin American Indian Communities; Peonage; Plantation Economy; World Economy/Dependency Theory)

Eric Van Young

REFERENCES

Bauer, Arnold J. *Chilean Rural Society from the Spanish Conquest to 1930.* Cambridge: Cambridge University Press, 1975.

Bauer, Arnold J. "Rural Workers in Spanish America: Problems of Peonage and Oppression," *Hispanic American Historical Review* 59, 1 (Feb. 1979): 1–33.

Keith, Robert G. "Encomienda, Hacienda, and Corregimiento in Spanish America: A Structural Analysis," *Hispanic American Historical Review* 51, 3 (August 1971): 431–446.

Schell, William, Jr. *Medieval Iberian Tradition and the Development of the Mexican Hacienda.* Syracuse, NY: Maxwell School of Citizenship and Public Affairs, 1986.

Van Young, Eric. *Hacienda and Market in Eighteenth-Century Mexico.* Berkeley: University of California Press, 1981.

Handicapped

See Disabilities

Health

The social history of health addresses the material conditions and the encompassing belief systems of social life in the past. An enormous array of materials—printed texts, manuscripts, and material artifacts, from government health agencies, professional associations, reform societies, and the popular media—attests to an enduring preoccupation with health and ill health. Yet the field has been relatively neglected by historians. Most commonly, historians have studied medical history rather than the broader social well-being of families and communities.

The reasons are not hard to find. First, historians have been intimidated because of the medical training which the field seemed to require. Second, they discounted the historical relevance of health because of the crudeness of existing scholarship. This consisted of narrow biographies of famous medical pioneers and celebratory interpretations of medical history in terms of progress from ignorance to enlightened modernity. One of the triumphs of social history, however, has been its ability to revolutionize the frameworks of historical significance by demonstrating how seemingly unpromising subjects can open revealing windows upon past social life. This is now being achieved in the social history of health in two main areas.

The first of these areas is concerned with environmental health. Social historians argue that community health is anchored in the material conditions of living, which in turn are determined by social variables such as class structure and demographic change. One application of this interest is to be found in the study of infectious diseases. The catastrophic incidence of disease, and its correlation with socioeconomic disadvantage, have been used to reconstruct the very different life chances of the winners and losers in evolving capitalist societies during the 19th and 20th centuries. Death rates in Europe and its New World offshoots substantially declined from the end of the 19th century, in tandem with gradual improvements in real wages, a reduction in family size, and the catch-up by government regulators in key areas of social legislation. This social transformation is highlighted in a second application of environmental health history—the growth of cities. The course of urbanization in the 19th and early 20th centuries is in large part a history of endemic community ill health, rooted in the low-wage economy and laissez faire spirit of early capitalism, and exacerbated by the flow-on effects of inadequate and overcrowded housing and hospital care, by malnutrition, primitive water supply systems, and ineffective waste removal. The resultant health problems were worsened by the displacement of working-class neighborhoods as a consequence of railroad construction and street widening, and of the building of specialized central business districts in city cores.

Rigorous additional scholarship is needed to consolidate these applications of sociohistory inquiry, for this branch of the discipline remains excitingly open. Historians have hitherto concentrated upon major epidemics of cholera, smallpox, plague, and yellow fever, at the expense of endemic infections which were present at lower levels of intensity, but which were more protracted and ultimately of more social significance. Other areas which await full recognition include occupational, maternal, infant, and school health, physical disabilities, and aging. Attention to rural health—for example, famines and the poverty-related nutritional disease of pellagra—is needed to complement the attention given to cities. Moreover, the histories of both rural and city health must be linked to broader economic regions, in order to assist understanding of the historical relationships between dominant (or core) and dependent (or peripheral) regions in the widening sphere of free-market capitalism. This is evident, for example, in the concerns by migrant-receiving societies such as the United States, Canada, and Australia, with migrants as carriers of typhus, trachoma, and favus from supposedly socially and economically primitive regions in Europe and Asia. It is also evident in the disastrous demographic and social consequences of European colonialization upon indigenous peoples.

A related expansion of the concern about environmental health, just underway, involves attention to serious health issues that were not, however, life threatening. Much health history to date has involved diseases that caused death. This is particularly true with the important attention to the impact of plagues in human society from early times into the 20th century, but it also affects attention to the modern history of children's health or old age. Work on historical changes in mental illness also fits in this category, and here there is a substantial social historical literature. Efforts to find out about broader health issues, and their results in social behavior, constitute a vital new frontier.

The second main area of sociohistory significance addresses the cultural context of health. Social attitudes to health reflect the prevailing values and priorities of a society. The preoccupation with health in 19th- and 20th-century public policymaking mirrored bourgeois rationalizations for inequality and the determination to maintain order in the face of rapid and unpredictable change. Health therefore highlights the hegemony of bourgeois discourse in forming common-sense opinion. Public health policy functioned as a tool of social control.

There have been three important applications of these interests. The first consists of case studies of epidemics. Scholars argue that communities in times of crisis reveal their core values in response to the tensions and contradictions posed by the emergency. The second application addresses the health reform movement. Sanitarians explained urban ill health and poverty in terms of working-class deviance and moral debasement. They argued that unhealthy slums threatened respectable suburban society with epidemics of immorality, criminality, and feeble-mindedness, as well as of disease. The public health movement thus formed the core of broader social-reform initiatives, which were gradually subsumed by professionalization and state growth. Medical professionalization and government intervention form the third important area of social-history specialization.

The effectiveness of these applications has been constrained by class and geographic exclusiveness. Insufficient attention has been given to the different common-sense horizons of social groups other than the bourgeoisie. Thus, working-class and women's attitudes toward health have been overlooked or trivialized. Historians are only now beginning to address the subject of ethnicity and health, in order to revise the demeaning stereotypes of peasant backwardness that have colored New World immigration. Scholarly attention has recently broadened its traditional focus upon Europe and North America to consider Africa, the Pacific, Australasia, and Asia, where disease and medicine are being dramatically reinterpreted as tools of imperialism. Finally, the several promising projects that are beginning to address health issues in relation to work and family experience, dealing with problems short of life-threatening experiences, requires attention to the way different subcultures defined sickness and to how concepts of being sick or well could change. Sickness (including, of course, psychosomatic distress) may reflect family roles or reactions to work, and may vary or shift on these bases. Further, the results of routine illnesses or other life experiences and institutions need careful historical attention and exploration of records such as

hospital and insurance archives. Here too, important new directions are just taking shape. (*See also* Hospitals; Medicine; Mortality Decline; Plague)

Alan Mayne

REFERENCES

Arnold, David, ed. *Imperial Medicine and Indigenous Societies.* Manchester: Manchester University Press, 1988.

Duffy, John. *The Sanitarians. A History of American Public Health.* Urbana: University of Illinois Press, 1990.

MacLeod, Roy, and Milton Lewis, eds. *Disease, Medicine, and Empire: Perspectives on Western Medicine and the Experience of European Expansion.* London: Routledge, 1988.

Smith, F.B. *The People's Health, 1830–1910.* London: Croom Helm, 1979.

Wohl, Anthony S. *Endangered Lives. Public Health in Victorian Britain.* London: J.M. Dent, 1983.

Hellenistic Society

Alexander the Great's conquest of the East in the 4th century BC brought about the introduction of Greek civilization to a vast population and eventually the creation of a new civilization that we call Hellenistic. This was no crude mixture of Greek and indigenous societies, certainly not in the East; Alexander's attempts at ethnic fusion were soon abandoned, not to be heard of again. Rather, on Walbank's (1982) reconstruction, the Greek element constituted an exclusive ruling elite that amounted to no more than 2.5 percent of the population of a typical city, while the great mass of the local peoples continued to retain their former character. What is new is the homogeneity, both internally within a given city and from city to city, of the so-called common Greek culture of the elite, in contrast to the city-state particularism of the classical era of Old Greece. Agents of this leveling process, besides the soldiers brought and left by Alexander, were various itinerant envoys, athletes, teachers, pilgrims, and so on, whose movements made impossible the insularity previously typical of the city-state. Homogeneity, in turn, made for greater solidarity (in spite of varied origins and social status) and inhibited entry into the elite by outsiders.

Hellenistic societies have been studied particularly in terms of formal culture, including scientific work, and to a lesser extent political organization. Some social changes also formed part of the Hellenistic period (4th–2nd centuries BC).

For Greece proper, some demographic indications are available. The Greek historian Polybius ascribed a decrease in population to an unwillingness of people to marry or, if married, to raise the children that were born to them. The latter cause presumably refers to exposure or infanticide, practices attested sporadically from early times but now in the Hellenistic age evidently on the rise. Tarn (1952), working from contemporary inscriptions, concluded that families were small, with a decided preference for two sons (the second insurance against the loss of the first in war), while more than one daughter was hardly ever raised. Obviously, given the high rate of mortality in antiquity, families of such size will soon have led to the depopulation claimed by Polybius. Nonetheless, the decline was not general, and Tarn (1952) may have been correct in positing an influx of aliens—slaves, freed people, and foreigners—into the Greek cities.

Of the various classes of Hellenistic society, the greatest advances were probably enjoyed by women, that is, at least upper-class free women. Pomeroy (1975) suggested that the increased power and visibility of Hellenistic queens served by a sort of trickle-down effect to enhance the prestige of nonroyal women as well. But the explanation for any such gains is more likely economic. Since women were now enjoying increased financial power, as witnessed, for example, by the ownership of land, it is arguable that the honors now conferred upon them for the first time—such as citizenship and access to public offices—were ultimately motivated by a desire to tap these new sources of wealth. (*See also* Greek and Roman Family; Sparta)

Nicholas F. Jones

REFERENCES

Pomeroy, Sarah B. *Goddesses, Whores, Wives, and Slaves. Women in Classical Antiquity*. New York: Schocken Books, 1975.

Tarn, W.W. *Hellenistic Civilization*, 3rd. ed. Cleveland and New York: World Publishing Company, 1952.

Walbank, F.W. *The Hellenistic World*. Cambridge, MA: Harvard University Press, 1982.

Hinduism

Hinduism is the predominate religion of India, followed by approximately 80 percent of the nation's 800 million people. It has had a large following in many other regions of South Asia, including what are now Pakistan, Bangladesh, Sri Lanka, Nepal, and Sikkim; it has spread with the movement of South Asians into East Africa and Southeast Asia, and is now moving into Europe and North America.

Scholars have had great difficulty defining Hinduism; it lacks a central book and founding figure that lends definitional precision to other religions. At the same time they recognized Hinduism's central importance in Indian social history. Traditional Hinduism involves a doctrine of the transmigration of souls, typically linked with the belief that all souls are essentially one, and complex theological reflections on a pantheon of deities, often related as different aspects of a nondual reality. Many scholars conclude that Hinduism is best defined as simply the "way of life" followed by the majority of people in South Asia. As a social system, Hinduism has been associated with the *varnashrama-dharma*, an organizational scheme that divides human life into social categories (*varnas*) and stages of life (*ashramas*). The *varnashrama* system reveals two of the most distinctive features of Hindu society—caste and the creative tension between the householder and the renouncer.

Hinduism developed from an early synthesis of the religions of the indigenous peoples of South Asia with the sacrificial cults of the invading nomadic Aryan warriors, who brought with them organizational concepts that determined the social principles which became associated with Hindu civilization. Although all people were viewed ultimately as one in essence (*purusha*), they were functionally divided into hierarchical categories deemed necessary for the maintenance of social order (*dharma*) and the spiritual development of all. Society was divided into three functional categories: the priests (*brahmanas*), responsible for maintaining sacred knowledge and performing the rituals; the warriors (*kshatriyas*), responsible for protecting society; and the cultivators and craftsmen (*vaishyas*), responsible for the production of materials necessary for the sustenance of society. The indigenous populations formed a fourth category of servants (*shudras*).

The social structure of the *varnashrama* system was most fully worked out in a collection of texts known as the *Dharma Shastras*. These texts established norms for all social interaction and mapped out an ideal pattern of life in terms of the four stages: one begins as a celibate student (*brahmacari*), then marries and takes up the life of a householder (*grihasthi*), producing children and fulfilling social duties. When one's children are established with children of their own, one can enter the third stage, that of a forest-dwelling (*vanapratha*) ascetic, and finally one gives up everything to be a wandering renouncer (*sannyasi*) and pursue ultimate liberation (*moksha*). This ideal was probably never followed by more than a small minority, but it set a norm which provided developmental direction and attempted to ameliorate the threatening impact of the renouncer, whose goal of ultimate liberation undermined the established values of society. This ideal schema hides the fact that the conflict between the household and the renouncer, with their respective goals of social duty and ultimate liberation, defines one of the most important creative tensions in Hindu society.

In addition to being challenged by other religions of South Asia, such as Buddhism, the hierarchical view of Hindu society has been challenged in significant ways from within Hinduism itself by such movements as devotional *bhakti*, which frequently insisted that divine grace was not limited by caste boundaries, and by the more peripheral *tantric* groups, who challenged the Brahmanic concepts of hierarchy and purity from a philosophical position of radical nondualism. Hindu reformers from the 19th century, many directly influenced by Christian missionaries, questioned the validity of the *varnashrama* system, and in more recent times, this social arrangement has been challenged by modern law. The Indian constitution abolished

caste "untouchability" and forbids restrictions from public facilities on the grounds of caste membership. (*See also* Caste System)

David L. Haberman

REFERENCES

Dumont, Louis. *Homo Hierarchicus: The Caste System and its Implications*. Complete revised English edition, translated by Basia Gulati. Chicago: University of Chicago Press, 1981.

Hopkins, Thomas. *The Hindu Tradition*. Encino, CA: Dickenson Publishing, 1971.

Hispanic Americans

Many Americans assume that Hispanic Americans constitute one ethnic group, presumably sharing a common culture, language, and heritage. However, not all Hispanics speak Spanish, in fact many are not of Spanish descent, but come from other European, African, or Native American ancestry. The term "Hispanic American" actually encompasses many distinct ethnic groups, drawn from more than 20 Spanish American countries and Spain, each with its own national origins, cultural traditions, and racial and ethnic makeup. Each ethnic group's acculturation has been determined largely by the era and circumstances of its entry into the United States. The term "Hispanic American" is thus an umbrella label, applied inclusively to long-time Americans, such as Mexican Americans who trace their roots to the era before the Mexican American War, and as well to recent immigrants, such as most Nicaraguans and Salvadorans who arrived after 1970.

Hispanic population growth has been impressive in recent decades. In 1950, they numbered only 4 million, a mere 2.7 percent of the nation's population of 151.3 million. Drawn from three distinct ethnic groups concentrated largely in several areas, the label "Hispanic American" was seldom used, if at all, as an umbrella term. Several million Mexican Americans lived in the Southwest. Several hundred thousand Puerto Ricans and about 30,000 Cubans lived in New York City, Florida, and California. As of the 1960s, however, changes in America's immigration laws and worsening political and economic conditions in many Latin American countries induced millions of persons to immigrate, legally or illegally, to the United States. By 1990, Hispanic numbers had increased more than 5-fold to 21.1 million, or 8.5 percent of the total population. Mexican Americans accounted for 60 percent of the Hispanic population; Puerto Ricans, 14 percent; Cubans, 6 percent; and immigrants from over 17 countries, including war-torn Central America, 20 percent. Hispanics now live throughout the United States. Projecting present population trends, demographers predict that Hispanic Americans will supplant black Americans as the nation's second largest minority by the year 2010.

Sizable waves of newcomers speaking Spanish and practicing different customs complicated America's racial and ethnic mosaics. But public policymakers, scholars, and the national media chose not to scrutinize the impact of each ethnic group on American society. Instead, they found it convenient to treat all the ethnic groups as members of one group, the Hispanic Americans. The term caught on, and by the late 1970s, "Hispanic American" was widely accepted as the appropriate label for all Latin Americans in the United States. On the other hand, not all so-called Hispanics accepted the term. Some objected to the obliteration of their national identities and favored terms reflecting identification with the homeland, such as Chilean Americans and Nicaraguan Americans. Others favored terms reflecting their distinct cultural adaptation to the United States, such as Chicanos for Mexican Americans and Nuyricans for New York City's Puerto Ricans. Still others found the term "Hispanic American" too narrow, excluding Latin Americans who are not of Spanish descent. This last perspective is increasingly gaining converts, and as of the early 1990s, "Latino" seems the unifying term of choice.

The social history of Hispanic Americans or Latinos is in an embryonic state. Much is known about Mexican Americans and to a lesser extent Puerto Ricans, but the same is not true for Cuban Americans and other Hispanic groups. Only now are social historians developing a comparative approach for writing an inclusive history of all the ethnic groups subsumed under Hispanic Americans. Only now is the range of research—on culture, demography, work, gender, discrimi-

nation, and other topics—moving toward the levels achieved for groups of European immigrant and African origin. (*See also* United States Ethnic Diversity)

Luis Leobardo Arroyo

REFERENCE

Bean, Frank D., and Marta Tienda. *The Hispanic Population of the United States.* New York: Russell Sage, 1987.

Historic Preservation

Historic preservation is a movement concerned with the retention and interpretation of structures, places, and physical remnants from the past. It can trace its origins in the United States to the 1840s when Ann Pamela Cunningham formed the Mount Vernon Ladies' Association of the Union to acquire and preserve the home of George Washington. The rationale for the Mount Vernon movement is the associative value of buildings and grounds with the first President, whom preservationists sought to elevate to a symbol of national unity in a time of sectional strife.

The effort to save Mount Vernon became a prototype of preservation: citizens who saw a historical association with the home of an important American leader joined together, raised the purchase price of the property, and opened the home to the public.

In England, the preservation movement grew out of a renewed interest in antiquity and from an admiration of historical architecture promoted by John Ruskin. Similar interests in the United States prompted the founding in 1910 of the Society for the Preservation of New England Antiquities by William Sumner Appleton. The method of preservation was similar to that pioneered by Cunningham, but the rationale was different: buildings were acquired because of their distinctive architectural qualities.

While private groups were formed for preservation purposes in the 19th and early 20th centuries, government was also beginning to take a role. Conservationists sought to convince the federal government to protect the spectacular beauty of such natural wonders as Niagara Falls.

Three major pieces of legislation have established a role for the federal government in historic preservation. The Antiquities Act of 1906 required that archaeological sites be identified and protected on federal lands. The Historic Sites Act of 1935 gave the Department of the Interior the responsibility of identifying sites associated with national history. The National Historic Preservation Act of 1966 established the National Register of Historic Places to identify structures and areas of national, state, or local importance based on architectural, historical, or archaeological merit. The act also set forth a process requiring review of all federally funded and licensed projects that might have an effect on National Register properties. In the 1970s and 1980s the federal government established a group of financial subsidies for the restoration of historic properties through the passage of income tax credits and deductions.

The preservation movement has broadened its focus in the late 20th century. The conservation of urban neighborhoods and rural areas began to share the spotlight with the preservation of monuments of great architecture and national history. The protective mechanism established to save buildings and neighborhoods is historic zoning. A historic preservation ordinance was first established in Charleston, South Carolina, in 1931, requiring an approval by an appointed board for all exterior changes to the oldest section of the city. By 1990 over 1,800 communities throughout the United States had passed preservation legislation.

The preserved sites of national and local history present the social historian with an interpretive challenge—to describe the associative historical value in complex, not simple, terms. At Mount Vernon this means analyzing the role of slaves and women, as well as the presidential affairs of George Washington. The rise of social history has played a role in extending the definitions of what buildings to preserve, away from strictly elite associations, and has amplified the training needed to interpret preserved sites for the general public. (*See also* Public History)

Timothy J. Crimmins

REFERENCES

Benson, S.E. *Presenting the Past: Essays on History of the Public.* Philadelphia: Temple University Press, 1986.

Stipe, R.E. *The American Mosaic: Preserving a Nation's Heritage.* Washington, DC: US/ICOMOS, 1987.

Homosexuality

Many historians of homosexuality have advanced a remarkable claim: no homosexuals—or heterosexuals, for that matter—existed before the late 19th century. Drawing variously on the theoretical insights of French post-structuralists (especially Michel Foucault) and Anglo-American sociologists of deviance and symbolic interactionism (especially Erving Goffman), these historians have argued that such identities are socially constructed, culturally variable, and historically specific. While people in all societies have engaged in behavior that modern observers might classify as homosexual or heterosexual, they argue, such behavior usually did not have the same meaning for its practitioners or implications for their identities that it does in the contemporary West. In particular, the idea that homosexual behavior is engaged in only by "the homosexual," a distinct kind of human being for whom "homosexuality" is a characteristic, defining an involuntary condition of some indeterminant psychological or physiological origin, is a relatively new and unusual historical development. While other historians have argued that sexual identities are essential or transhistorical, even most of them agree that such identities have taken markedly different forms in different societies.

Most historical studies developing this argument have focused on western Europe and North America, particularly ancient Greece, Renaissance Italy, Victorian England, and the 20th-century United States, although other European societies (notably Holland, France, and Germany) and a few non-Western societies (notably China, Japan, and Brazil) have also received attention.

Historians have joined anthropologists in identifying three major patterns in the social organization of homosexual relations and in arguing that a distinct identity and social role have not always been assumed by the participants in such relations. These are very broadly defined patterns, though, and the social context and cultural meaning of same-sex relations vary widely within them.

The first and apparently oldest pattern consists of age-asymmetrical relations between adults and youths, often in an initiatory context. A number of historians, for instance, have studied the love of students for teachers, or of younger students for older students, in girls' boarding schools and women's colleges in the 19th century: such "smashes" were considered a normal part of a girl's maturation, and only came under suspicion with the development of new models of homosexuality. Historians of ancient Greek society have discerned a sexual culture at even greater variance from our own, in which it was thought that all adult men were capable of desiring sexual contact with both women and boys and that such sexual relations, so long as decorously conducted, were an unobjectionable part of a boy's education and socialization. (In our own time, by contrast, most people believe that a man interested in sex with boys is a distinct kind of person, a pederast, who has no sexual interest in women or girls, and that his youthful partners are psychologically scarred by the experience.)

In a second and more widespread pattern same-sex relations are organized along lines of an asserted gender difference—between persons who abide by their culture's gender conventions and persons who assume the cultural status of the other gender or of an "intermediate" gender, with only the latter usually considered abnormal. In 18th-century London, for instance, "molly houses" existed in which men dressed as women and enacted marriage ceremonies; in early 20th-century American seaports, sailors often had sex with men called "queers" or "inverts" without being labeled abnormal themselves; and at mid-century many masculine (or "butch") lesbians were involved in relationships with conventionally feminine women (called "fems") who were not considered lesbian. Indeed, the general shift from this paradigm to the third broad pattern, the one more familiar today, in which both partners are of the same gender and age status and both identify themselves and are labeled by others as "gay," appears to have been one of the major transitions in the history of gender and sexuality in Western cultures in the 19th and 20th centuries.

Historians have just begun to investigate the distinctive meeting places, argot, folk traditions, and cultural styles of the men and women known as inverts, gay men, and lesbians. They have usually had to rely on the records of the courts, medical authorities, and other policing agencies that sought to regulate public sociability; such documents must be interpreted with special care and, unfortunately, illuminate only certain aspects of gay life. Nonetheless, they have allowed historians to trace the emergence of certain social clubs, restaurants, bars, streets, parks, and other sites as gay meeting places; the development of distinctive subcultural styles of dress and demeanor that allowed people to identify each other surreptitiously or to announce their presence boldly; and the elaboration of an extensive "grapevine" that informed people of new meeting places, special social events, periodic police crackdowns, and the like at a time when no gay newspapers or other guides existed.

Most historians have tied the emergence of distinctive gay and lesbian subcultures to the rise of cities in which relatively anonymous participation in gay society became possible, the emergence of medico-legal authorities who sought to classify and regulate (and thus, inadvertently, helped constitute) new urban sexual "types," the breakdown of the family economy (which had required people to marry or otherwise subordinate themselves to the supervision of a household-based workshop or farm), and, in the case of women in particular, the development of new economic opportunities in the late 19th century that made it possible for the first time for large numbers of them to be economically independent of families.

Differences in lesbian and gay male history point to broader differences in the social history of women and men. Gay men developed more extensive and visible subcultures than lesbians did in most societies, for instance, primarily because men had access to higher wages and thus to greater economic independence from family life. They also enjoyed greater freedom of movement: the public spaces where gay men met, from street corners to bars, were culturally defined as male spaces. At the same time, the common presumption in the 18th and 19th centuries that women had relatively little sexual interest sometimes enabled them to develop closer relationships than men could, because observers were less likely to suspect such relationships had a sexual component. As a result, a number of college-educated women with independent financial means lived together in the 19th century in "Boston marriages," which enjoyed considerable social respect.

Analyzing "Boston marriages" and the emergence of gay identities has directed historians' attention to the homosocial character of many premodern societies (and, indeed, of many societies before the 1920s), in which many people's primary emotional and social ties centered on people of the same sex, their marriages notwithstanding, and in which women and men alike often developed passionate attachments (or "romantic friendships") with people of the same gender. The emergence of the more heterosocial culture associated with the development of urban commercial amusements at the turn of the century, and the new emphasis on dating among youths in the 1920s, both reflected and contributed to that era's increased self-consciousness about and stigmatization of homosexuality.

Historians originally focused on the marked category of the homosexual, but have recently begun to ask questions about the presumed universality of heterosexuality as well, suggesting that if one is a historically specific social construct, then so, too, is the other. Thus, while some historians have claimed that the many romantic friends who expressed passionate love for each other in the 19th century could not have been homosexual since no concept of the homosexual existed in their culture, others have pointed out that they could not have been heterosexual either, since the one category is dependent on the other. In any case, they note, men who expressed passionate love for other men were certainly not heterosexual in the same sense in which men are heterosexual today.

The social history of homosexuality, its definitions and its relationship to gender constructions and sexuality generally, continues to develop rapidly, spurred by its power to reveal important facets of various patterns and changes in the past and by the growing awareness of gay groups in the present. Opportunities for additional research, for example, on additional periods in the history of of lesbianism, are considerable. (*See also* Sexuality)

George Chauncey

REFERENCES

Boswell, John. *Christianity, Social Tolerance, and Homosexuality: Gay People in Western Europe from the Beginning of the Christian Era to the Fourteenth Century.* Chicago: University of Chicago Press, 1980.

Duberman, Martin, Martha Vicinus, and George Chauncey, eds. *Hidden from History: Reclaiming the Gay and Lesbian Past.* New York: New American Library, 1989.

Faderman, Lillian. *Odd Girls and Twilight Lovers: A History of Lesbian Life in Twentieth-Century America.* New York: Columbia University Press, 1991.

Honor Codes

Honor codes are studied by social historians as part of an inquiry into key value systems that affect behavior and also link deeply held beliefs to law and politics. Honor codes often differentiate between men and women and among social groups. Modern history, with its major changes in values, often sees a decline in the centrality of honor, and tracing this change is a developing facet of social history.

The history of honor has been most fully explored in European society. Honor also figures prominently in Japanese and Middle Eastern history; some historians identify a Mediterranean emphasis on honor that indeed links the Middle East, North Africa, and southern Europe. Some research on the United States South has also emphasized the importance of honor codes.

Though the concept of honor is as old as Greek civilization, the golden age of honor codes in European societies began in the early Middle Ages and lasted until the eve of World War I. From Spain to the Balkans, anthropologists are still able to find evidence of the persistence of the social and cultural practices typical of honor societies in the rural Mediterranean, and chivalric organizations such as the Knights of Malta, which can trace their lineage to the Crusades, continue to employ ancient honorific formulas to exploit the cachet of an aristocratic ambiance.

As these modern vestiges suggest, honor codes have operated at different levels of society throughout the European past. For the topmost layers of feudal society, honor codes regulated relations between nobles jealous of power and precedence. With varying degrees of specificity, the codes prescribed the rules for the entire range of behavior between the manners required at court and the rituals governing personal combat. The coherence of the noble code of honor was such that the bloody exigency of the duel was believed to be the only solution when the personal comportment of gentlemen fell short in trivial things. For the noble classes in the old regime, honor codes served not only to govern the relations between gentlemen, but demarcate effectively the lines between noble and ignoble.

At the lower levels of society honor codes were perhaps less exacting in their forms, but artisans and rural smallholders alike in old regime society defended their honor with vigor to avoid being excluded from the mainstream of social and economic life. Though they have left fewer traces for the historian than the affairs of honor of the elite, judicial archives contain ample proof that disputes and violence among the humble of society over property, betrothals, and local precedence often took the form of a defense of personal or corporate honor. The *vendetta* of rural Corsica or Sardinia was thus part of a family of social practices that included the sword duel between nobles.

What these socially diverse expressions of honor shared in common was a deep concern about precedence based on kinship, heirship, and marriage alliances. In the dominant system of patrilineal heirship of European society, the male leaders of a family or clan were responsible for the assets of their primary group. Along with real property, children were also assets in this system, the sons as heirs and dowry winners and the daughters for the links they forged in marital alliances. Honor was the concept that covered the rights and obligations embedded in these webs of kin relations, for which the patriarch was the symbol and guarantor. As the chief player in this game of assets, the patriarch was responsible for the integrity of all its elements, perhaps especially that of a wife or daughter, whose illegitimate child could dishonor him and bring damaging claims against his patrimony.

We know less about the evolution of honor codes in rural or artisanal milieux than about the fortunes of honor in upper-class society. In the course of the 16th and 17th centuries, the ethos of the old feudal code began to give way to a far more nuanced code of personal "honnêteté," reflecting the qualities of personal character and moral integrity pertinent to the new middle-class domain of commerce and law. But the inclusion of "bourgeois" values in honor codes did not automatically mean the older military virtues were automatically excluded. Except in Great Britain, where dueling disappeared by the 1840s, the civilian duel continued to prosper until 1914; the *point d'honneur* remained throughout much of Europe a legal or tolerated method at private law for defending reputation and personal character. Though national variations are important, men of property and standing could lay claim to the possession of honor virtually everywhere in Europe by the mid-19th century.

By examining dueling manuals, court cases, and the publicity surrounding affairs of honor, we may determine that honor was not an ontological essence that men possessed by nature, but the product of an attribution process consisting of successive judgments by contemporaries about the consistency of a man's public behavior. Sincerity, candor, and loyalty were highly prized in both feudal and modern society; in the course of the 19th century, honesty, sexual self-restraint, and other bourgeois qualities gained in importance. The clear moral component in honor allows us to understand how the codes could serve as the foundation for professional ethics in medicine, law, and engineering as well as provide the inspiration for the ideal of disinterested sportive amateurism that emerged near the end of the 19th century, culminating in the modern olympic movement.

Until the late 19th century, women figured in the system of honor only as wards of husbands and fathers. Though they were obliged to defend their sexual honor, women's dependency on men disqualified them—in the terms of the honor code—from public life on the grounds that since they had no honor to lose they could not be responsible or independent actors in the public sphere. Much of the resistance to the legal and political demands of women and ethnic and religious minorities in 19th- and 20th-century Europe has been motivated by such considerations. (*See also* Aristocracy; Duels; Middle Classes)

Robert A. Nye

REFERENCES

Billacois, François. *Le duel dans la société française des xvi–xviie siècles. Essai de psychosociologie historique.* Paris: Editions de L'Ecole des Hautes etudes en Sciences Sociales, 1986.

Castan, Yves. *Honnêteté et relations sociales en Languedoc (1715–1780).* Paris: Presses Universitaires de France, 1974.

Neuschel, Kristin. *Word of Honor, Interpreting Noble Culture in Sixteenth-Century France.* Ithaca, NY: Cornell University Press, 1989.

Nye, Robert A. *Masculinity and Male Codes of Honor in Modern France.* New York: Oxford University Press, 1993.

Hospitals

The social history of hospitals has been developed mainly in the context of European and United States/Canadian history. In this tradition, the origin of the hospital institution dates to medieval Europe. However, the medieval institutions were preceded by the Greeks who had established several hundred temples between 500 BC and AD 400 to the god Asclepios, reflecting the Greek esteem for health and by the Judaic tradition of sheltering fellow Jews. Hospitals as social asylums were founded in the 4th century, according to the Christian command of providing charity to the infirm. Initially known in Greek as *xenodochia* (*xenos* meaning "stranger") or *hospitalium* (from the Latin word *hospes* for "host"), the first public hospitals were meant to provide shelter and care for the poor and infirm, rather than medical treatment. And, when Christianity was legalized, the first Ecumenical Council of Nicea ordered every bishop to build a xenodochia in his diocese. Thus, the early social asylums or xenodochia spread rapidly throughout the towns of northern and western Europe. It is also vital to note that, in advance of Europe,

hospitals developed in various parts of the Middle East and in India.

In the European Middle Ages, hospitals were established primarily by the church and were intended to meet diverse social needs, primarily of the poor whose welfare was in the hands of the church. Most monasteries set up hospital pauperum to care for the ill and infirm poor and leproseries to care for people suffering from contagious diseases. In addition, by the high Middle Ages, most towns had developed various institutions for caring for the needy, whose numbers increased, due, in part to the Crusades. There were parish hospitals, pauper hospitals, the asylums, and foundling homes, staffed by the religious, apothecaries, midwives, and barber-surgeons. In short, medieval towns established a relatively comprehensive system of caring for the poor and infirm, and this form remained basically stable for many centuries. The hospital served largely as a place for the very poor, lacking family resources, to go to die. It was not a preferred location for dealing with diseases.

The Enlightenment brought about a fundamental change in the way that sickness was perceived—away from divine providence and toward the secular ideology that man could exercise control over his environment, including eradicating disease. The rise of hospitals as institutions for scientific treatment soon followed. The French Revolution had a cataclysmic effect on hospitals, as well, transforming them from centuries of religious control toward institutions dominated by medical doctors. These doctors began to apply scientific principles toward patient treatment such as observation, physical examination, anatomy, and autopsy, fueling the notion that the hospital was the most suitable place for the new medical training. As medical expertise advanced, the French were followed by the Germans, who applied scientific principles to diagnosis and treatment; hospitals were transformed into institutions to promote the goals of the practitioners as well as patients. And, by the second half of the 18th century, specialty hospitals such as lying-in and psychiatric institutions were on the rise.

Throughout the 18th and 19th centuries, therapy remained limited as doctors practiced more visible than effectual treatments, such as bloodletting, and strong emetics surgery consisted most frequently of amputations. Hospitals were frequented by the lower classes, while the upper classes obtained physicians' services in their homes. Aside from basic nursing care focusing on cleanliness and nutrition, drugs were the most frequently applied therapeutics in the hospitals. This was a transition period in the hospitals' social history, in which new medical uses combined with popular suspicion.

In the United States, hospitals were founded primarily by voluntary rather than religious organizations, copying the English rather than European model. However, American medicine lagged behind, and doctors, along with other perceived aristocrats, were long disdained. The rural environment, lowly status of physicians, and individualism fueled the peculiarly American phenomenon of eclectic medicine. The "irregulars" disdained hospital-based treatment. The poor status of physicians, unorganized medical education, and lack of state support retarded the proliferation of American hospitals, and by 1873, the United States boasted only 120 general hospitals.

Widespread industrialization, immigration, and resultant urbanization during the late 19th century spurred hospital development, and by 1920, there were 2,000 general hospitals in America. The proliferation was aided by advances in medical science, such as the discovery of antisepsis, which reduced the menacing reality of "hospitalism," that is, hospital acquired disease. Sterilization procedures began to reduce hospital death rates on both sides of the Atlantic. Anesthesia led to advances in surgery best suited to the hospital environment and developments such as the x-ray increased the doctor's ability to objectively diagnose disease. Simultaneously, improved organization among physicians led to improved standards in medical education and the need for hospital-based training. Finally, increased interest in scientific medicine caused growing use of hospitals for contingencies such as childbirth, while change in family functions, particularly in crowded cites, produced a growing interest in hospitals as centers for care of the sick.

By the 20th century, the middle class were increasingly supportive of the hospital, causing the hospital to change from being a refuge for the "deserving" poor to conform to middle-class needs for privacy and comfort. By the mid-20th century, European and British hospitals had become state institutions, whereas American hospitals faced new tensions as they struggled to maintain financial solvency while accommodating their original charitable mission. Increasing levels of controversy surround them as costs spiral, while they are unique in receiving a combination of voluntary, private, and public funds. The social history of 20th-century hospitals has mainly focused on changing policies and rising costs; it is less rich than the works done on hospitals during their 19th-century transitions. Social historians have debated the trajectory of hospitals during the past two centuries from several vantage points, some stressing their growing array of functions, others lamenting their increasing displacement of familial and other personalized care, particularly for the dying. (*See also* Asylums; Health; Medicine)

Margaret Brindle

REFERENCES

Ackernecht, Erwin. *Medicine at the Paris Hospital, 1794–1848.* Baltimore: Johns Hopkins University Press, 1967.

Rosenberg, Charles. *The Care of Strangers: The Rise of America's Hospital System.* New York: Basic Books, 1987.

Shryock, R.H. *The Development of Modern Medicine.* Philadelphia: University of Pennsylvania Press, 1936.

Starr, Paul. *The Social Transformation of American Medicine.* New York: Basic Books, 1982.

Household

Sociohistorical research on the household became systematic and comparative from the early 1970s onward, as the result of the work of scholars associated with the Cambridge (England) Group for the History of Population and Social Structure. While earlier historians had not wholly neglected past social life at the household level, their generalizations tended to be questionable because they were based largely on individual case studies. The Cambridge Group, by contrast, argued that a large class of historical evidence—census-type household listings—had been overlooked by earlier work, and that this evidence, quantitatively analyzed, could form the basis of general statements about small-group life in the past and its changes over historical time. Subsequent historical research on the household in fact has maintained the quantitative thrust, challenging earlier characterizations of domestic life and opening a host of new questions that still need answers.

The new direction in historical household research moved three problems to center stage: (1) the average size of households (or domestic groups) in the past and their composition; (2) internal household dynamics accounting for changes in size and composition; and (3) the relationship between the household and its varied socioeconomic contexts. While the importance of some of these problems—such as numerical size—have diminished as a result of continuing research, others are as open now as they were when first broached.

Size and composition. In the early phases of the new research, one important measure—mean household size (MHS)—allowed researchers to bring many communities scattered in space and time into a comparative framework. The statistic was obtained by dividing all persons in a given community who were residing in households by the number of household units. Surprisingly, this measure suggested that in some Western societies, such as England, there had been very little change in MHS (4–5 persons) over the centuries from the 16th to the 20th. This finding, together with supporting analyses, called into question the broad generalization (derived from 19th-century evolutionary sociology) that industrialization, urbanization, and other large-scale socioeconomic changes had reduced the allegedly large traditional household to a smaller modern one. Moreover, careful scrutiny of pre-20th-century household listings revealed that domestic groups frequently had porous boundaries and involved, as co-residents with the head's family, people who were not the spouse and children of the head—for example, other relatives of the head (especially retired parents), servants, lodgers, retired people, and the like. The proportion of such persons in an average household varied according to many factors, including the household's social class and geographical location. In northwestern Europe wealthy households tended to have more such people than poor ones; in the eastern parts of Europe, however, peasant households almost always included them, sometimes in numbers that exceeded the size of the head's own nuclear family. The societies of the European northwest tended to have households that were smaller, had simpler composition, and contained fewer generations; measures of size and complexity tended to become higher, however, as one moved across the European map into the Mediterranean areas and the eastern parts of the European Continent. The poles appear to have been England (and the United States) and Russia, with the nuclear family household predominating in the former and complex households in the latter.

Dynamics. Not only were household boundaries remarkably porous in earlier times, but the size and composition of households responded to various dynamics of internal development. The proportion of household members who were not related to the head was often linked to how many grown children the head had: when the head had offspring who could perform household tasks, the number of external people was small; as the head's offspring grew up and left, the number of servants (farmhands, etc.) could go up because of the household's continuing labor needs. Size and composition were frequently related also to the age at which a married couple formed a new household: the later the age of household formation, the smaller the number of surviving children (the age of childbearing for the wife having been shortened); the later the age, the less likely were retired parents to be living with their married children (the years between the formation of children's household and average age at parents' death having been reduced). The interplay of individual lives (life-course analysis) in the household context remains an important area of future work. Variations in size and structure over the lifetime of even a single household, and the different ways individual household members experienced life in the household, mean that researchers have had to interpret static measurements (such as MHS) with much greater care.

Socioeconomic contexts. Household size and composition varied as well because of different local and regional socioeconomic practices. Inheritance systems (partible: holding divided between heirs; impartible: holding goes to single heir) appear to have been significant determinants of whether or not a stem family household (one married offspring residing with parents) ever emerged in a locality. Obligatory labor services owed by peasant households to the estate (as in areas of rural serfdom) led to complex family households as a solution to the added labor demand. The regional cultural imperative that a new marriage had to result in a new household simplified household composition; the practice of placing adolescent children for some years in other households as apprentices or servants (life-cycle servitude) created another compositional variant. Some historians have also suggested that different occupations (viticulture, shepherding) and locations of communities (mountains, valleys) had an impact on both household size and composition. Contextual information of this kind has required a retreat from the idea that pre-20th-century social life at the household level was so uniform as to have experienced only one mode of adaptation to the arrival of the urban, industrial world. (*See also* Extended Family; Household Economy; Inheritance Systems; Kinship; Urbanization)

Andrejs Plakans

REFERENCES

Laslett, Peter, and Richard Wall, eds. *Household and Family in Past Time.* Cambridge: Cambridge University Press, 1972.

Netting, Robert McC., Richard R. Wilk, and Eric J. Arnould, eds. *Households: Comparative and Historical Studies of the Domestic Group.* Berkeley and Los Angeles: University of California Press, 1984.

Wall, Richard, Jean Robin, and Peter Laslett, eds. *Family Forms in Historic Europe.* Cambridge: Cambridge University Press, 1983.

Household Economy

As a unit of social and economic analysis the household has become increasingly important to historians. The word "economy" itself derives from the Greek *oikos*, for "house," and until the 18th century the term "economic" often referred to household management. A "household" can be defined as a group which shares resources and income. It can be coterminous with a nuclear family and occupy a single dwelling, but it might also include kin, servants, apprentices, slaves, or others. According to circumstances a household might control a farm, a workshop, or an urban residence. Historians employ the concept of household economy to explore links between everyday life and broader patterns of economic change.

In many periods and cultures households have been the main institutions influencing production, labor, and consumption, sometimes as the owners of property, often as dependents of elites. The decline of demesne farming in medieval western Europe, for example, left much land in the hands of peasant households. Scholars once associated household economies with self-sufficiency and separation from markets. They distinguished them from those dominated by large estates, or capitalist commerce and industry, regarding household economies as "traditional" or "preindustrial," largely superseded by "modern" institutions. Recent research, however, has modified this view and accorded households greater historical significance.

The protoindustrialization debate has stressed the importance of household structures and economic strategies. In early modern Europe and America, family size and wealth, farming practices, inheritance systems, age and gender divisions of labor in the household, and seasonal unemployment all influenced the growth of rural cottage industry and were, in turn, altered by its presence. They helped determine whether manufacture was controlled by households themselves (*Kaufsystem*) or by urban merchants (the putting-out system, or *Verlagssystem*). Men, women, and children worked to contribute to the household's livelihood. When cottage industry declined in the 19th century, household strategies helped determine which rural regions became centers of urban growth and large-scale industry and which remained specialized in agriculture. Rural households remained an important source of migrant labor for industry.

Social historians have also recognized the significance of household organization and strategies to the lives of the growing industrial working class itself. Industrialization certainly entailed the growth of wage work and the separation of "work" from "home," but this transformation was never total. Skilled male workers claimed the right to a family wage sufficient to support all members of their households, but others had to pool the incomes and efforts of men, women, and children to make ends meet. In all households women made vital and substantial contributions in the form of unpaid domestic work, and this has continued to be the case in modern societies. In 1980 French women's unwaged household work was estimated to contribute 25 or 30 percent of France's total national production.

Household economy has also been an important analytical concept in the study of agricultural societies in the modern world. The opening up of new grain supply regions, in 19th-century North and South America, Australasia, and elsewhere, on which industrial populations depended for food, relied to a considerable extent on household-based farming; in Canada, for instance, farmers and their families made up 77 percent of the agricultural work force in 1871 and 84 percent by 1921. Farm households were closely tied to the international markets they supplied, becoming increasingly dependent on markets even for their own food supplies, and their importance is a reminder that household-based economies were not merely a facet of traditional societies. To the contrary, social historians of the world-systems school would argue that households have played a distinctive and vital role in modern capitalist development, providing labor, food, and other products as well as reproductive functions.

The concept of household economy will continue to be important to historians. First, perhaps four-fifths of all the world's farms are still family run, and analysis of household organization and strategies has become central to studies of Africa, Asia, and Latin America and their connections with world economic patterns. Second, analysis at the household level is leading to a better understanding of issues such as gender, the division of labor, power, and morality, which are central to the social historian's task. As many scholars have warned, however, it is crucial not to treat the household as a fixed or romanticized

category. Household economies have been important in many different periods and cultures, but have differed according to context and circumstance. Studies must always take account of the broader social and economic patterns of which households formed a part. (*See also* Child Labor; Domesticity; Family; Gender Division of Labor (Africa); Household; Protoindustrialization; Women and Work)

Christopher Clark

REFERENCES

Berg, Maxine, ed. *Markets and Manufacture in Early Industrial Europe.* London: Routledge, 1991.

Fox-Genovese, Elizabeth. *Within the Plantation Household.* Chapel Hill: University of North Carolina Press, 1988.

Smith, Joan, et al., eds. *Households and the World-Economy.* Beverly Hills: Sage Publications, 1984.

Tilly, Louise A., and Joan W. Scott. *Women, Work and Family.* New York: Holt, Rinehart and Winston, 1978.

Houses and Housing

The house is a building used as a dwelling by one or more families. It shelters individuals or families as they engage in social and economic activities. Sleeping, eating, washing, procreation, religious worship, child care, education, recreational activities, and the processing of food and animal products are among the activities that take place or have taken place in the home. Housing and housing conditions have been central to sociohistorical research on changing living standards and, more recently, material culture.

Houses vary widely in size and style, ranging from one-room huts to multiple-room mansions. Houses are also categorized according to the materials used in construction. Social historians also deal with change and variations in the meanings of houses, including how much time people spend in them, whether they are production or leisure centers, and what symbolic meanings they have.

Housing is associated with architecture, law, economics, health, city planning, and politics. An individual's housing choices are affected by climate, the availability of building techniques and materials, economic and social class standing, race, gender, ethnicity, religion, and occupation.

Working people throughout the world have constantly struggled to obtain quality housing. Rural housing, sometimes idealized in nostalgic images of the countryside, offered many limitations in preindustrial societies, as many peasant historians make clear. Much production equipment filled preindustrial houses as well. Industrialization and the growth of the market economy did not end the difficulties working people faced finding affordable housing. During the late 18th, 19th, and early 20th centuries, industrialists in the United States, Great Britain, France, and Germany constructed housing developments for their employees. Company housing developed in part as a result of a shortage of worker housing. Another reason why companies built housing was the desire to control or supervise employees. For example, textile workers in the Piedmont region of the southeastern United States reported that during the 1920s and 1930s, company officials knocked on the doors of workers' homes to determine why their lights were on after 10:00 PM.

In the industrialized nations, only a small percentage of all workers lived in housing rented or purchased from their employers. Most workers rented or purchased a home on the private real estate market. Home ownership was a goal of most working-class families in the United States, not only for economic reasons, but for social reasons as well. Working-class families purchased homes often at a tremendous economic and social cost. Workers deprived their families of education, clothing, and even food in order to purchase a home, which clearly had meaning beyond place of residence.

As industrialization altered the character and composition of cities during the 19th century, concern was expressed about the conditions under which laboring people lived and worked. Housing reformers argued that poor housing conditions created social problems such as crime, disease, and infant mortality. Many housing reformers argued that the construction of model working-class housing and building codes would improve housing conditions.

Resistance to the intervention of the government in the housing market was greater in the United States than in other industrialized nations. The banking, real estate, and home-building industries opposed the public housing programs initiated in the United States during World War I, the Great Depression, and World War II, and supported housing programs that helped the private housing industry. These programs stimulated home ownership, subsidized housing costs for low-income families, opposed racial discrimination, and encouraged neighborhood revitalization.

Europe and Japan also suffered from a housing shortage after World War II. Instead of relying solely on the private home-building industry to supply the needed housing, governmental programs were initiated. In Great Britain, public funds were used to construct housing and entire planned residential communities called New Towns. In Germany and the Scandinavian countries, housing was constructed by housing cooperatives, labor unions, and other private associations, often with the use of government loans or grants. In Japan, governmental housing agencies provided financing, assembled development sites, and helped offset the high cost of land.

The former Communist nations of Eastern Europe initiated ambitious postwar housing programs after World War II. The Soviet government established policy concerning construction standards, supply, location, financing, consumer costs, and tenure. Despite the Soviet Union's attempts to address its housing problems, acute shortages persisted.

In developing countries, housing shortages exist in both rural and urban areas. Housing is especially scarce in cities that experience infusions of migrants from the countryside. Governments in certain Asian, African, and South American nations have undertaken housing construction programs, but thus far have been unable to meet the demand for housing. Informal housing production networks still supply the bulk of necessary housing.

Housing problems have existed in both urban and rural areas for centuries. Both developed and developing countries have yet to solve their housing problems. The social history of housing includes research on housing problems and standards, on changing policies used to address housing issues, and on changes in the material arrangements of houses (including apartments, which have been understudied) including the allocation of space, privacy, and other features. (*See also* Architecture; Cities; Historic Preservation)

Kristin S. Bailey

REFERENCES

Andrusz, Gregory D. *Housing and Urban Development in the USSR.* Albany: State University of New York, 1985.

Ball, M., et al. *Housing and Social Change in Europe and the USA.* New York: Routledge Press, 1988.

Morrison, Minion K., and Peter C. Gutkind, eds. *Housing the Poor in Africa.* Syracuse, NY: Syracuse University Press, 1982.

Housework

Housework is the kind of prosaic, everyday activity that should have received more attention from social historians than has thus far been the case. Some may assume that housework presents little change or variety—merely a constant drudgery. Certainly it has normally been a woman's sphere either through her labors or her direction of servants. Recommendations for "good women" as far back as Han China stress maintaining a well-ordered household, with responsibilities for cleaning, clothing, and cooking. Yet many women's historians, bent on stressing other areas of endeavor more to feminist taste, have played down housework as a significant topic.

Yet housework has changed and varied, depending on physical layout of a household, other activities for women, even pervasive cooking style; it depends also on cultural standards. Some aspects of household tasks emerge from social histories of domestic service. Changing middle-class standards of household care formed one of the tensions between servants and their mistresses in 19th-century England or the United States.

More specific studies of housework, though rare, are suggestive. Increased household goods and more attention to family meals encouraged women in western Europe and colonial North America to spend more time on housework and less on productive labor in many social groups from the 17th century onward. A subsequent increase in household standards—particularly cleanliness—kept middle-class women devoted to hours of chores well into the 20th century, for definitions of a respectable home associated even as labor-saving devices (sewing machines, vacuum cleaners) might otherwise have lightened tasks. Only in the 1960s was there some widespread rebellion against housework. These findings may encourage other social historians to deal more elaborately with housework and its changes over time, in various societies and in earlier historical periods. (*See also* Servants; Women's History)

Peter N. Stearns

REFERENCES

Branca, Patricia. *Silent Sisterhood: Middle Class Women in the Victorian Home.* Pittsburgh: Carnegie Mellon University Press, 1975.

Cowan, Ruth S. *More Work for Mother: The Ironies of Household Technology from the Open Hearth to the Microwave.* New York: Basic Books, 1985.

Shammas, Carole. *The Pre-Industrial Consumer in England and America.* New York: Oxford University Press, 1990.

Humanitarianism

"Humanitarianism" as a current term is usually applied to organized, frequently international, efforts to combat human misery on a large scale, when produced by natural disasters, war, or the breakdown of government and the institutions of civil society. But in the historical literature it has a more limited reference to a mainly Anglo-American "religion of humanity," which emerged in the later 18th century and eventually became absorbed into a more secular, professionalized and bureaucratic mode of dealing with social problems that developed from the mid-19th century. Often treated as part of the intellectual history of the Enlightenment, humanitarianism also has been explored as a topic in social class in mentalities history.

Although American and British humanitarianism displayed some divergent features which reflected cultural and social differences between the United States and Britain, with some justice humanitarians saw their activities as part of a transatlantic phenomenon. American and British reformers often developed strong links with each other and even when they did not were involved in a similar spectrum of humanitarian reform. Typically, humanitarians were engaged in one or more of antislavery, temperance, agitation for international peace, penal reform, lunacy reform, education, and regulation of the adult and child poor. Activists constructed a similar pattern of humanitarian organization in both countries. They mobilized support through a structure of local and national associations and conventions as in antislavery and temperance. In other cases like lunacy reform they relied on applying pressure to legislators and political notables in the community. Humanitarian activity was also characterized by extensive publication and distribution of books, pamphlets, and newspapers exposing moral and social evils and proposing remedies, since reformers were able to take advantage of the wider distribution of printing presses and technical advances in the printing and paper-making trades to produce propaganda materials cheaply and in bulk.

The idiom of humanitarianism was predominantly religious; those active in the various causes stressed the personal moral inadequacy of the deviant or dependent individuals and groups whom they attempted to redeem. Slaveholders and drunkards were seen in this light. But reformers also acknowledged environmental influences, both physical and moral, as contributing to the situation of the powerless and aberrant such as slaves, the insane, criminals, paupers, and children of the laboring poor.

The humanitarian outlook drew no clear distinction between moral and social problems because the zeal of reformers to tackle them both came from their powerful religious connections and the strong sense among some social groups of what was required for community and social harmony. These concerns were not simply indicative of moral and social conservatism but did arise from the inevitably disorienting experiences of living through the decades of major industrialization in Britain and the equally destabilizing years of democratization, expansion, and initial industrial development in the United States. The moral fervor of middle-class humanitarians has been reassessed as a form of social control by some social historians, as it led to rigorous prison

rehabilitation schemes or new asylums for the insane.

Most humanitarians in both countries embodied the surging evangelical impulse of popular Protestantism, which ignored denominational lines and in Britain gained sufficient influence within the established Church of England to allow limited humanitarian collaboration between Anglicans and nonconformists until sectarian lines hardened again from the 1830s onward. Although numerically much weaker in both countries than evangelicals, Quakers, Rational Dissenters (in late 18th century Britain), and, later, Unitarians were active in humanitarian causes; in Britain they were disproportionately influential because of their wealth, social position, and education in a sharply stratified society. All groups were united in the fundamental conviction of their "religion of humanity" that humankind was one family under God. It was their duty to encourage moral change in those whose deficiencies contributed to social evils and radically alter or establish new model penitentiaries, asylums, and reformatories as purified environments which aided individual reformation. In the early phase of modern humanitarianism the initiative in institution building often lay with private individuals or voluntary societies, as with the York Retreat asylum in England (1796) and the New York House of Refuge for juvenile delinquents (1825); public authorities usually later intervened to establish inspectorates to guarantee standards and to provide funding.

Almost universally, humanitarians took as the mark of moral and social health, as well as a necessity in a changing economy, the achievement of self-motivating and consistent labor on the part of the victims of the social evils they were attacking, whether remedied within institutions or mainly by moral suasion and law. In theory and practice humanitarians had different views about how much discipline of the deviant and the dependent was necessary in institutions and in society. In the more democratic and socially open United States a perfectionist strain in humanitarianism, evident in antislavery and peace activities, promised social transformation as a result of moral revolution without need of institutional or legal constraint; this had no parallel in Britain. The mainstream of humanitarianism in both countries, however, drew less on elites fearful of disorder or loss of social leadership than middle-class elements, including manufacturers, aspirant artisans, and, for secondary tasks, many middle-class women, all of whom translated religious commitment into a search for harmony in societies which they believed could achieve a dynamic equilibrium. At the community level in both countries the search for harmony, since it was to be based on moral homogeneity, provoked some class and ethnic tensions, yet in many cases it was established elites as well as recalcitrant deviants who resisted the disruptions of humanitarian endeavor. The fading of this kind of humanitarianism in both Britain and the United States by the 1850s resulted from evidence of failure of social improvement through moral change both inside and outside the new social institutions. It was replaced by patterns of social policy more dependent on legal regulation and bureaucratic management of institutions less evidently aspiring to moral redemption.

Clarification of the history of humanitarianism is most likely to arise from future systematic comparative study of American and British humanitarianism and from detailed community studies. (*See also* Emancipation; Middle Classes)

David Turley

REFERENCES

Davis, David B., ed. *Ante-Bellum Reform.* New York: Harper, 1967.
Turley, David M. *The Culture of English Antislavery, 1780–1860.* London and New York: Routledge, 1991.
Walters, Ronald. *American Reformers, 1815–1860.* New York: Hill and Wang, 1978.
Wiener, Martin, ed. "Humanitarianism or Control?" *Rice University Studies* 67, 1 (1981).

Hunting and Gathering

Since the emergence of our species, one that researchers can identify as clearly *homo,* human societies survived by hunting and gathering. There are three senses in which this phrase is used. One is economic, meaning specifically the acquisition of food by organized hunting of game animals, and gathering of many varieties of plants. The term "hunting-gathering" also implies certain social organizations and lifeways, that is, small bands numbering perhaps 25 to 30 people that moved from place to place in search of food. The third meaning is chronological, denoting the huge span of time called the Paleolithic Age (Old Stone Age) that ran from about 1.5 million years ago to about 10,000 to 9,000 BC. However, hunter-gatherers are still found in some parts of the world today. Peoples such as those commonly known as Bushmen in Africa's Kalahari Desert and some Aborigines of the Australian desert regions follow life patterns that mirror those of our very distant ancestors. Like those long dead peoples, the lives of modern hunter-gatherers depend entirely upon the environments in which they live.

Earliest evidence for the hunting-gathering pattern may date to the emergence of ancestral *homo erectus* in a broad band of semitropics running from Africa to Southeast Asia. With chipped stone hand axes (the Acheulean tradition) and knowing the use of fire, these early peoples pursued large game animals across wide stretches of the Old World. At Terra Amata, in southern France and other sites, temporary huts with hearths have been found dating from 300 to 200,000 years ago. As yet we cannot tell the exact nature of social organization in this early period, but there must have been a differentiation of activities: men hunted large game; women gathered plants and had primary responsibility for the care of the group's children. Modern hunter-gatherers arrange their societies this way.

Environmental change played a crucial role in the development of all early societies, and in fact, apparently on the development of the human species itself. For the last million years the earth has been subjected to severe climatic fluctuations known as ice ages and interglacial periods. Some scholars think that modern humans (*homo sapiens sapiens* and our close relatives *homo neanderthalis*) with their larger brains and more complex cultures developed in response to having to live in harsher climates. Neanderthals evolved in Europe, the Middle East, and North Africa about 120,000 years ago. They had complex tool kits used mainly for processing the game animals upon which they lived. Neanderthals also built open air huts, though most of the evidence for them comes from cave shelters. Burials of the dead with grave offerings or in special places in the caves imply both a sense of afterlife and family linkages both in this world and a world of the spirits. The short life spans of these people, on average in the later twenties to thirties, may have contributed to these ideas. Their successors, fully modern people, shared these economic and religious concepts.

Fully modern humans seem to have evolved in the same areas as the original *homo* types, perhaps as early as 90,000 years ago. By about 40,000 to 30,000 years ago (the Upper Paleolithic) bands of people had colonized all the habitable continents, from the Americas to Australia. All had sophisticated tool-making and craft traditions including carving of wood and bone, leather working, and production of jewelry from bone and shell. The bow and arrow, harpoons, fish hooks and nets all were invented in this age, some 18,000 years ago. In Europe, now in the grip of the last great glaciation, humans built open air shelters from wood and the skin and bones of the great mammoths and reindeer that they hunted. In eastern Europe, some of these were reused year after year and some have yielded figurines of animals and women both carved and made of baked clay. These are evidence of territoriality among bands and a distinctive role for women as keepers of the home and hearth and, perhaps, as central in the religious life of most groups.

The best known Upper Paleolithic sites are the spectacular painted caves of southern France and northern Spain. Ancient artists placed highly colored pictures of the animals that were hunted deep inside the caves. At Altimira in Spain, a ceiling is covered in red bison, while at Lascaux in France a great procession of horses and reindeer in multiple colors covers a whole wall. All are realistic depictions of the animals as they appeared to the hunters. No one can tell the exact meaning of these pictures, though clearly they have to do with food animals and likely have religious qualities. The art does tell us that the hunters of the last ice age, living in their small social groups, told stories and probably had a developed mythology. In this, they are very much like hunter-gatherers today.

In the late Paleolithic era new economic trends appeared that prefigured the more permanent settlements of later centuries and the skills needed to gather and prepare more food. On the banks of the Nile some 17,000 years ago, hunter-gatherers collected large seeded grasses and ground them on flat stones into meal. In Europe people became specialists in hunting one animal, the reindeer, with ever more sophisticated methods, and gathered plants more intensively. On this basis, individual groups began to settle into specific lands, social territories, and to use all the resources they found there. Indeed, figurines, painted caves, and burials in them show a people that had developed a sense of home, a center for the family or group. Small-scale trade networks arose, but there is evidence from Egypt of fighting, probably over scarce resources. In short, the elements of settled village life existed in the last centuries of the ice age. It took only environmental change to convert hunter-gatherers all over the world to settled farmers.

Past hunting and gathering societies are studied mainly by archaeologists, and present-day groups, by anthropologists. Social historians need to keep the hunting and gathering tradition in mind dealing with the transition to agricultural societies (the Neolithic revolution); it provides a baseline for assessing later social patterns including gender relationships. (*See also* Archaeology; Environment)

Bruce Kraig

REFERENCES

Bordes, Francois. *The Old Stone Age.* New York: McGraw-Hill, 1968.

Gowlett, John A.J. *Ascent to Civilization.* New York: Knopf, 1984.

I

Illegitimacy

The history of illegitimacy plays a significant role in social history in two respects. First, its definition reveals much about standards applied to sexuality, marriage, and gender. Second, where known, actual rates of illegitimacy help social historians understand varieties and changes in sexual behavior. Some of the most important debates over modern sexuality have been associated with the interpretation of changes in illegitimate birthrates.

The infraculture of Western Christianity was revolutionized when the Council of Rome in 1069 created the justification and the methods of clerical supervision of daily life. Marriage was subjected to ecclesiastical control and definition. In establishing the centrality of consent in the making of a Christian marriage, the canon law of marriage made the marital union easy to create, but endowed it with serious consequences— exactly the opposite of the situation prevailing in both Roman and barbarian law. The administration of the sexual economy both disciplined and regulated entry into marriage—by clarifying

the meaning and intention of consent. It also policed marital relations by demanding that its parish clergy report notorious adulterers and fornicators to the proper courts. This represented a continuity with ancient systems in which marriage was required for the purpose of social reproduction between unequal partners; but it also represented a deviation from antiquity in terms of the esteem with which marriage was held in comparison with any other intimate relationship. If sexuality was the problem, then, for most men and women, marriage was to be the solution which ended concubinage. Illegitimacy, then, developed in tandem with the legitimation of clerically sanctioned marriages.

The church was not able to exert a totalitarian hegemony over either the minds or the bodies of the population; rather, it tried to police those individuals and groups who ignored, abused, or ridiculed its edicts. Seigneurial rights dovetailed with the moral discipline urged on the feudal classes by the priesthood. When unfree villains were indicted in the manorial court for having been convicted by the ecclesiastical court for moral lapses, they were subject to another fine for alienating the lord's property. This form of double jeopardy could only be avoided if the hapless peasant allowed himself/herself to be bodily whipped rather than paying the fine. Lords were less concerned with the moral discipline of their tenants than with watching them (and especially their coins) slip from seigneurial control. But that is not to say that feudal lords did not interest themselves in the moral conduct of their subject population; in fact, women who were caught in illicit premarital relations were required to pay a special fine, *legerwite*, to compensate for the devaluation of their sexual purity. Courts were more concerned with maintaining social stability—based on the sexual honor of families—than in righting wrongs. Abandoned women of low social status were given short shrift; their pain was usually ignored. Their virginity was beneath valuation; its loss was of no social importance. Prenuptial intercourse called into question the proper moment of marriage and, in particular, the uncertainty surrounding the operational definition of consent; adultery—not infrequently initiated by women and, thus, so alarming to judicial patriarchs and their notions of sexual decorum—introduced passion into customary regime of family life. There can be no question about the prescriptive vision that animated the courts—female sexuality was to be encapsulated: for the higher social classes, virginity at marriage and subservience thereafter was the ideal; for the rest births in wedlock were sufficient. Women's sexual property in their own bodies was only valued if they were propertied, and penalties were finely calibrated to reflect the extent that their behavior had dishonored or discounted that value. The lower classes, in contrast, were the objects of policy only insofar as their disorderly conduct made their behavior and self-image problematic.

A new marriage re-formed another basic unit of social life. In a very real sense, the public culture of licit sexuality was collapsed into this system of social reproduction and defined by its relationship to the reproductive family. Acceptable female sexuality was channeled into marriage and defined by its relation to reproduction.

The stereotypical female role—a virgin marrying at puberty and thereafter closeted in the privacy of her home at the bidding of her lord and master—frayed in the crucible of daily life. While it is evident that female chastity was demanded among the elite for whom bloodlines and lineage were of paramount interest, it could be guaranteed only by marrying off their daughters just after puberty. Among the popular classes, marriage took place later and female age was higher; these young women were not subject to the same surveillance. Nonetheless, the culture of sexual purity reached down to the lowest ranks of the population among whom it was considered a sign of honor to marry off a youthful daughter with a small dowry; reputation was jealously guarded, and sexual slander was vigorously rebuked.

If the first 500 years of our millennium were concerned with the creation of a definition of a legitimate marriage, then during the last 500 years those births that took place outside clerically sanctioned wedlock were technically illegitimate. Before the advent of parish registers in the 16th century, it is methodologically impossible to quantify the extent of illegitimate births. (The feudal *legerwite* was not a fine for illegitimacy so much as an exaction on peasant women who devalued their own bodies and their lord's property in their bodies.) English parish registers, which provide the longest series of continuous vital statistics, have been examined in detail. Between 1538 and 1837 there were two peaks in English illegitimacy—the periods 1590–1609 and 1780–1837. The first period is rather obscure, but it seems that a significant factor was the joint result of declining living standards and downward social mobility. Thus, many couples discovered that their anticipated marriages could not be celebrated because they lost the wherewithal to finance an independent household. Because many had begun sexual relations immediately after their public betrothal, an unexpected social crisis resulted in broken engagements and rising levels of illegitimate births—averaging about 6 percent for the whole country and peaking at triple that level in some villages. The widespread sexual anticipation of marriage by betrothed couples has been underscored by detailed family reconstitution studies that have indicated nearly 40 percent of 16th-century brides bore their first child within eight months of marriage.

This high level of bridal pregnancy and illegitimacy did not continue for long after 1600; indeed, a series of social adjustments—stabilization of wage rates, an end to rapid population growth and downward social mobility, and declining geographical mobility and tighter supervision of betrothals by political authorities—combined to create a new, controlled climate in which marriages took place. The second rise in illegitimate births was a pan-European phenomenon, also affecting North America. It was again accompanied by rising levels of bridal pregnancy. Moreover, when we consider the fact that the age at first marriage for women was earlier after 1750, then it becomes apparent that not only was the *ratio* of illegitimate births rising but the *rate* of illegitimate fertility was rising even faster. These illegitimate births were occurring among a relatively smaller number of single women who were at risk for a relatively shorter time between puberty and marriage. The highest ratios of illegitimate births occurred in parts of Germany where there were restrictive marriage laws.

Historians have been sharply divided in explaining this second rise in illegitimacy, which accounted for between under 1 percent (in Ireland) and almost 25 percent (in Bavaria) of all live births. One school of thought has suggested that there was a general relaxation of control over young women who took advantage of their freedom to engage in expressive sexual relationships. The other side argues that most illegitimate births took place to proletarian women who, far from being sexually liberated, were socially dependent and economically powerless. These young unmarried mothers were attempting to pursue traditional courtship strategies in the vastly changed circumstances of the industrial and commercial city. Such women—frequently employed as domestic servants or mill operatives—found themselves alone, deserted by their intended spouse when the unpredictable economic cycle exacerbated their lack of control over their own destiny. Supporting this latter argument is the fact that when proletarians' living standards rose in the second half of the 19th century, illegitimacy rates and ratios began to drop in tandem.

Illegitimacy, then, accompanied the transition from peasant to proletarian in conditions of population growth, declining real wages, and widespread downward social mobility. The growing stabilization of capitalist society and the creation of stable neighborhoods in the new cities was accompanied by a culture of domesticity and respectability which grew up in working-class communities, partly as a result of the missionary activity of middle-class moralizers and partly as a result of regendered identities among the common people. The rise of the breadwinner economy not only marginalized female workers by shunting them into job-ghettos and/or confining them to the role of homemakers but also stressed the femininity of young women who could only realize their biological destiny in motherhood. In contrast to their peasant and plebeian forebears, proletarians' courtships were more private affairs, which were in part a response to age grading in social life (the discovery of adolescence) and in part a reflection of the growth of new facilities that catered to this expanding market—music halls, dance halls, and cinemas being the most popular gathering places for young unmarrieds. These courtships may also have been accompanied by the sexual anticipation of marriage, but the immense spread of abortion in the period after 1870 makes inference from demographic statistics less reliable.

Was the second wave of illegitimacy the product of widespread promiscuity? Our answer is negative. Most children born out of wedlock were the product of frustrated marital unions.

The history of illegitimacy has been utilized mainly by social historians of western Europe and the United States. They have also attended to the most recent rise in illegitimate birth rates, associated with the "sexual revolution" of the 1960s and also new social class and age group differences in sexual behavior.

Illegitimacy standards have also been examined in Middle Eastern and Latin American history, as part of exploring the sexual regulation of women. Until recently, illegitimacy rates in non-Western societies (where at all known) have been relatively low, because of widespread early marriages, and so less useful for discussing the history of sexuality. Current research identifies significant increases in Russian illegitimacy rates in the later 19th century, associated with wider social changes at that point. The subject invites additional research and comparison. (*See also* Family; Gender Socialization; Marriage/Remarriage; Sexuality; Women and Work; Working Class)

David Levine

REFERENCES

Knodel, John. "Law, Marriage, and Illegitimacy in Nineteenth Century Germany," *Population Studies* 20 (1967): 279–294.

North, Tim. "Legerwite in the Thirteenth and Fourteenth Centuries," *Past and Present* 111 (1986): 3–16.

Shorter, Edward. *The Making of the Modern Family.* New York: Basic Books, 1975.

Tilly, Louise A., Joan W. Scott, and Miriam Cohen. "Women's Work and European Fertility Patterns," *Journal of Interdisciplinary History* 6 (1976): 447–476.

Wrightson, Keith, and David Levine. "The Social Context of Illegitimacy in Early Modern England," in Peter Laslett, Karla Oosterveen, and R.M. Smith, eds. *Bastardy and Its Comparative History.* Cambridge: Cambridge University Press, 1980, pp. 158–175.

Immigration

Although migration—people moving from one place to another—is a universal process that has taken place since the beginning of human life on earth, by far the greatest number of those who have migrated did so within the last 500 years. Beginning in the 16th century, and especially since the early 19th century, a number of economic, social, and political conditions led to the dramatic growth of migration nearly everywhere. Population growth, unequally distributed resources, natural catastrophes, political and religious upheavals, and improved types of transportation led millions of individuals to move from their place of birth to other locations which seemed to offer greater opportunities for a meaningful existence.

It is difficult to determine the precise number of individuals who have migrated because in many parts of the world no one recorded such moves. Even in the areas where governments attempted to keep records, significant numbers of migrants eluded the record keepers. Nevertheless, sufficient data exist to enable us to estimate the general dimensions of migration in many areas of the world. During the past five centuries approximately 68 million people left Europe, and of those more than four-fifths went to various destinations in the Americas. From the 16th to the 19th century 9.5 million forced migrants left Africa as slaves for the Americas. There are fewer data to document the great Asian migrations, but we know the numbers are similarly large. For example, scholars estimate that during the 19th and 20th centuries alone between 31 and 45 million Indians migrated to destinations in Southeast Asia, East Africa, and the Caribbean; probably a similar number of Chinese moved throughout Southeast Asia, to Africa, and to the Americas; and perhaps 4 million or 5 million Japanese migrated primarily to areas of Southeast Asia, the United States, and Brazil.

Scholars make a distinction between voluntary migration—those who chose to move—and forced migration—where, as with African slaves, people had no choice in the matter. Most of the great migrations during the past 500 years have been voluntary, and the outcomes of this process have varied. Some individuals chose to migrate to a given destination and to settle there permanently. Others chose to return home—the so-called sojourner immigrants, more common from some cultures of origin than others—and perhaps to remigrate a second or third time to the same or to a different location. Still others moved directly from a destination in one country to another in a different country. Voluntary migrants were motivated by self-interest, in most cases economic self-interest, but some moved for political and religious reasons as well.

Immigration is that phase of the migration process during which individuals arrive and settle in a new host society. It is preceded and integrally linked to the emigration phase, during which the individuals make the decision to migrate from their homelands and travel to their destinations of choice. Because immigration is part of the larger process of migration, immigration historians have come to analyze the potential migrant in the society of origin, the auspices under which the migrant moved from origin to destination, the initial incorporation into the receiving society, and the subsequent sociocultural adjustment.

Among the best documented areas of greatest immigration during the past 500 years are the continents of North and South America. In 1492 there were approximately 57 million people living in the Americas. During the first century after contact, disease, exploitation, and warfare created one of the greatest demographic catastrophes in history, reducing the population to less than 5 million people by 1600. In order to exploit the natural resources (land and minerals) of the Americas, the Europeans needed labor. With the Native Americans reduced to a fraction of their former number, millions of forced and voluntary immigrants arrived to meet the growing demand for workers.

During the 17th and 18th centuries thousands of Spaniards and Portuguese immigrated to South America, the Caribbean, Central America, and Mexico. The English, Dutch, and French went to the Caribbean and the eastern parts of North America. At the same time the Europeans brought in millions of forced migrants—black African slaves to work the plantations of Brazil, the Caribbean, and the southern English colonies of North America.

The volume and diversity of immigration to the Americas was much greater during the 19th and 20th centuries. Approximately 50 million immigrants arrived during the century preceding the Great Depression of the 1930s. At first northern Europeans (those from the British Isles, Ireland, Germany, and Scandinavia) and then central and southern Europeans (Jews, Italians, Poles, Slovaks, and Hungarians, among others) migrated in large numbers to the United States, but significant numbers also went to South America (Jews, Italians, Poles, Spaniards, and Portuguese) and Canada (from the British Isles, France, and Italy). During this period 35 million people arrived in the United States; 6 million, in Argentina; 5 million, in Canada; and 4 million, in Brazil. The forced migration of Africans to the Americas was phased out during the early 19th century with the abolition of slavery. Asian immigration, in part to replace the loss of plantation slaves, increased dramatically in the second half of the 19th and the 20th centuries: Indians went to British Guiana and Trinidad;

Japanese, to Brazil and the United States; and Chinese, to Peru, Cuba, and the United States. Between 25 percent and 35 percent of these immigrants returned to their countries of origin.

The impact of immigration during the 19th and 20th centuries on population growth has been of major significance in many countries. Approximately 60 percent of the Argentine and Uruguayan populations of 1960 were attributable to immigration within the preceding century; just under half the population of the United States in 1970 was attributable to immigration since 1790; Canada, Brazil, Australia, New Zealand, and in the 20th century western Europe have also depended heavily on immigration.

Although immigration has been an important influence in world history, until the 1970s scholars for the most part ignored it. The few historians who wrote about immigration during the immediate post–World War II period were influenced by the then dominant consensus school of history and based their analyses on the classical assimilationist model of immigration. This model posited an inevitable linear progression of immigrant culture toward complete absorption within the so-called melting pot of the receiving society's national culture. For these scholars, the immigration process began when an individual, uprooted from his culture of origin and socially disorganized, got off the boat and came under the influence of the all-pervasive host environment. The migrant was, for the most part, a pawn whose fate was determined by the impersonal push and pull of demographic and economic conditions that shunted him/her from place to place. Success depended on the migrant's own personal attributes, especially those which fostered individual achievement. The process ended with complete assimilation.

Beginning in the mid-1960s and emerging more vigorously during the 1970s and 1980s, a new generation of immigrant historians increasingly rejected some and modified other aspects of the classical assimilationist model. The new work formed a vital facet of the rise of social history. The assimilationist model was too simplistic and therefore unable to explain the increasing manifestations of ethnic resiliency and pluralism of the 1960s, 1970s, and 1980s. How, these scholars asked, can we account for the tremendous variation and the multiple outcomes of the migration process?

Influenced by the new social history—like their colleagues in labor and women's history—the new immigration historians focused on giving voice to the working classes and other nonelites previously considered to be inarticulate and unimportant. As they moved in this direction, they redefined the parameters of immigration, shifted their assumptions about the migration process, and developed new analytical approaches to the subject.

The new immigration historians set forth a pluralist model that reconceptualized immigration as a complex, multicausal, multidimensional, dynamic, and open-ended process that began in the village or town of origin and continued with migration, incorporation into the host society, and sociocultural adjustment. They no longer assumed that there was one outcome—such as complete assimilation—to the process, that it necessarily terminated after any given period of time, or that any specific pattern of interaction was inevitable or irreversible. The economic and social structures and the culture of the country of origin became crucial to an understanding of what happened to the immigrant in the new society. Understanding the initial setting of migrants allows exploration of the varying values and behaviors different groups might bring to new settings. The sending and receiving societies were linked together in a dialectical framework of analysis that enabled these scholars to conceptualize the simultaneous influence of cultural persistence and change. And the immigrant was viewed as an active participant who made meaningful choices about his/her fate and who influenced the host society as well as being influenced by it.

The pluralist model which emerged in the 1970s and early 1980s provided the basis for the more recent development of several additional conceptual approaches. Some immigrant historians are now emphasizing the structural determinants of the process, focusing on the collectivist strategies used by migrants, locating their subjects in a global context, and analyzing the relationship of ethnicity with gender and class.

The time- and place-specific economic, so-cial, and political structures—both of the sending and receiving societies—are increasingly recognized by many immigrant historians as establishing significant parameters within which migrants lived and made decisions. There is, nevertheless, disagreement over the relative importance of these structural factors in relation to cultural attributes in explaining the differences in immigration and ethnic patterns. Future studies will need to clarify the relationship between structure and culture.

Along with an increased emphasis on structure, some immigrant historians are concentrating on the collective strategies immigrants developed to negotiate their relocations. Individuals experienced the migration process as members of various collective entities: families, kinship and community networks, ethnic institutions, and host society institutions. These groups provided social structures which in turn significantly influenced the individual migrant.

Prominent among these socially embedded and group-sustained structures were social networks, or what is frequently referred to as migration chains. Set forth initially by the post–World War II generation of New Zealand and Australian scholars, the concept has been used extensively by others interested in migration to all parts of the world. Originally, the concept referred to the family, kinship, and community-based networks which personally linked potential immigrants and those who had already migrated. The migrants abroad, by providing information and assistance, influenced more recent migrants' decisions regarding destination, settlement, occupations, and social relations. Presently, some scholars are exploring such issues as how networks operated specifically to inform and assist members, who was actually and potentially in a network, the overlapping of networks in places of origin and destination, and how these networks were renegotiated over time. Even though we do not have complete answers to these questions, most immigration historians now view social networks as an important part of the explanation of immigrant behavior.

Some immigration historians have also become increasingly interested in the relationship of ethnicity to class and gender. Formerly, scholars who focused on ethnicity and labor historians who focused on class ignored, for the most part, the findings of the other. Now, however, a number are incorporating the perspectives of both in their studies of immigration. Because most immigrants were of the working class and because much of the behavior of immigrant workers can be understood as working-class behavior, this is an essential step toward deepening our understanding of the migration process. A number of recent studies also explore the roles of immigrant women. The important issue is not whether ethnicity, class, or gender alone explains the behavior of migrants, but how the simultaneous interaction of all three influences the actions of individuals and groups. Some scholars are now exploring the specific situations and conditions in which one variable was more important than the others and why.

Finally, some immigration historians have recently studied immigration in a global and comparative context. Traditional interpretations assumed the primacy of the nation-state and the predominantly one-way movement of individuals between two such political entities. A few scholars now reject the nation-state as the effective unit of analysis and replace it with a unified global system involving exchanges of technology, capital, and labor. Immigrants from a particular village or region frequently migrated to different destinations within a receiving country and to different countries. Many returned only to migrate to a different destination. And still others migrated directly from one destination abroad to another. To understand these moves such historians view the migration process in a global perspective.

Along with this shift from the nation-state to a global system of interaction is the emergence of a village-outward approach to the study of migration. This approach, which takes as its starting point the village of origin where potential migrants are located and follows them to all of their multiple destinations over time, better conforms to the conceptualization of migration as a global phenomenon. It enables us to understand the options available to individual migrants, the decisions they made, and the subsequent forward and backward linkages between the village of origin and all of the multiple destinations in which its inhabitants temporarily or permanently resided.

The global perspective and village-outward approach also supported a multinational comparative analysis of immigration to various destinations. International comparison is not a new idea to immigration historians. A few pioneers as early as 1960 called for such comparisons of the United States with Argentina, Brazil, Canada, Australia, and the other major receiving countries of the past several centuries, but until recently almost nothing was done to heed this call. Now, a few are making these comparisons and providing fresh new insights into the significance of differing host societies on immigration.

In addition, such an approach provides an essential corrective to the assumption of exceptionalism on the part of the receiving society. For example, for many years American immigration historians assumed that the United States was the exceptional attraction to immigrants and that its society provided a unique assimilating environment for the newcomers. Yet, in fact, many immigrants went to other destinations.

There have been significant changes in the way immigration historians approached their subject over the past four decades. The assimilationist model of the 1950s gave way in the 1970s and 1980s to a pluralist paradigm emphasizing the causes of ethnic persistence and the diversity of the immigration experience. In recent years some scholars have incorporated structural constraints, collectivist responses, the interaction of ethnicity with class and gender, and a global and comparative perspective into their analyses. The future paradigm of immigration history will very likely be based on these most recently developed themes. As a result of the changing conceptions, we have gained a better understanding of how to explain the immigration process in all its complexity and variation. (See *also* Assimilation/Acculturation; Ethnicity; Migration; Social History)

Samuel L. Baily

REFERENCES

Bodnar, John. *The Transplanted, A History of Immigrants in Urban America*. Bloomington: Indiana University Press, 1985.

Hoerder, Dirk, ed. *Labor Migration in the Atlantic Economies.* Westport, CT: Greenwood Press, 1985.

Pozzetta, George E., ed. *American Immigration and Ethnicity,* Vol. 1, *Themes in Immigration History.* New York: Garland, 1991.

Yans-McLaughlin, Virginia, ed. *Immigration Reconsidered, History, Sociology, and Politics.* New York: Oxford University Press, 1990.

Imperialism

The very narrow original meaning of the term "imperialism," which was coined in the late 1840s with reference to the military adventurism and foreign intrigues of the French emperor Louis Napoleon, contrasts sharply with the broad and often overly loose usage of the term in the century and a half since it was first employed. From the outset, "imperialism" and "imperialist" had decidedly negative connotations. They also suggested strong linkages between foreign policy and domestic social issues that would be central to the early 20th-century authors who broadened the meaning of the terms and devised the interpretations of imperialism that are still heatedly debated in the present day. Ironically, J.A. Hobson, whose 1902 work *Imperialism: A Study* recast the term as it has been generally employed in the 20th century, was concerned not with the domination of African or Asian peoples by the European colonial powers, but with British attempts in the 1880s and 1890s to control the economies, shape the social policies, and curtail the foreign relations of the white settler enclaves of the Transvaal and the Orange Free State in South Africa. Since the first decades of the 19th century, the Afrikaner founders of these republics had struggled against what Hobson argued were imperialistic British advances that were prompted first by strategic considerations and more recently by lucrative investments in the diamond and gold mines of the region.

Though he produced little evidence to back up his claims, Hobson argued that in South Africa and elsewhere British imperialism was driven primarily by financiers anxious to protect investment outlets. Hobson linked the intense concern of the British financiers for overseas investment opportunities to what he saw as serious, but reparable, flaws in economic organization and social class relations in Britain itself. Low wages paid to the working classes, he argued, resulted in low levels of consumer spending that in turn undercut the profits and domestic investment possibilities for Britain's capitalist class, thus forcing them to seek compensatory gains abroad, particularly in areas made "safe" by imperialist takeovers. Though Hobson believed that social reforms (higher wages, better working conditions, etc.) could remedy the domestic ills that were the key to imperialist expansion, V.I. Lenin argued vehemently that imperialist expansion was symptomatic of the fatal contradictions of capitalism and signified its impending collapse.

Lenin's *Imperialism: The Highest Stage of Capitalism* owed much to Hobson's earlier work, and like its predecessor was more concerned to elucidate the economic and social conditions within Europe that had led to overseas colonization than to deal with conditions in the subjugated areas. Writing in large part to explain the utter failure of socialist resistance to mobilization for World War I, Lenin—like Hobson with a notable paucity of reliable empirical data—blamed monopoly capitalism and its insatiable need for investment outlets for the great outburst of imperialist expansion that had dominated global history in the decades leading up to 1914. Lenin's seminal polemic was one of a number of works, including most notably those by Rudolph Hilferding and Rosa Luxemburg, written in the World War I era that both gave new meanings to the term "imperialism" and traced its origins to deep contradictions within the capitalist, industrialist economies and societies of Europe itself.

The basically Eurocentric and heavily economic conceptions of imperialism worked out in the first decades of the 20th century have subsequently proved to be the focus of much controversy and the stimulus for numerous efforts at reformulation. From the 1930s until the early 1960s, numerous questions and sustained assaults were raised regarding the economic interpretation of the origins of imperialism in its various guises. In this era political and strategic considerations were stressed in accounts devoted heavily to the motivations and actions of European politicians, diplomats, and colonial officials. These studies tended to focus on what became known as the "era of high imperialism," or the period between 1870 and 1914 in which most of Africa, the South Pacific, and what was left of Southeast Asia were divided among the European colonial powers. Those who wrote of this global scramble for colonies generally equated imperialism with military conquest and the establishment of direct European political control in overseas areas.

By the mid-1960s, the combined impact of area specialization in the academic realm and the process of decolonization in the real world resulted in yet another fundamental reassessment of our understandings of imperialism. New and more sophisticated arguments regarding the economic origins of the imperialist scramble were set forth that tended to play off economic crises and social tensions within European states against the preconquest breakdown of economic institutions and social systems in areas threatened with colonization. In the latter, the destabilizing effects of preconquest European penetration, such as that associated with the African slave trade, were stressed. This emphasis served to call into question earlier perceptions of the 1860s and 1870s as a watershed period in which imperialist expansion accelerated rapidly. It also underscored the importance of including the exercise of informal control—in the forms, for example, of gunboat diplomacy, market regulation, or the manipulation of nominally independent indigenous rulers—within the ambit of imperialism. This meant that imperialist dominance could be economic or cultural, every bit as much the exercise of political control that had so captivated the attention of earlier writers. Thus, the largely informal empire of the United States or the spheres of influence that the Western powers carved out in China in the late 19th century came fully within the purview of those studying the phenomenon of imperialism.

These shifts also brought increasing attention to the internal history of the societies and cultures that were brought under European colonial rule. The earlier Eurocentric perspective of writings on imperialism gave way to a decided emphasis on the fate of the colonized peoples in Africa, Asia, and Latin America. Within the colonies, the focus shifted away from collaborating princely elites and Western-educated nationalist leaders to peasants, urban workers, and eventually women. All of these shifts furthered the

full integration of studies of imperialism into the broader stream of social history, and they gave full voice—in many cases for the first time—to those who took advantage of, suffered under, or resisted European imperialist domination. (*See also* Colonialism)

Michael Adas

REFERENCES

Gallagher, John, and Ronald Robinson. "The Imperialism of Free Trade," *Economic History Review* 6, 1 (1953): 1–15.

Koebner, Richard, and H.D. Schmidt. *Imperialism: The Story and Significance of a Political Word, 1840–1960.* Cambridge, Eng.: Cambridge University Press, 1964.

Owen, Roger, and Bob Sutcliffe. *Studies in the History of Imperialism.* London: Longman, 1972.

Platt, D.C.M. *Finance, Trade and Politics in British Foreign Policy, 1815–1914.* London: Oxford University Press, 1968.

Independence Wars (Spanish American)

The Independence Wars have been studied in terms of political and military movements and in terms of the spread of liberal and nationalist ideas. The social history vantage point has long been recognized, explaining the groups involved in the independent movement and also those that remained on the sidelines. From this approach in turn, the widespread social and economic effects of the achievement of independence can be more fully understood.

The process of Spanish American independence may be best understood as a series of movements that erupted when Napoleon Bonaparte invaded Spain. The collapse of the Spanish monarchy precipitated a crisis that exacerbated socioeconomic and political tensions that had been building for several decades. Following the Seven Years' War, the Crown restructured the Empire in an effort to exercise greater control over its vast territories. It established a colonial army, reorganized administrative and territorial boundaries, introduced the intendancy system, restructured commerce, increased taxes, and abolished the sale of offices. These changes upset long-standing socioeconomic and political arrangements. The creation of the viceroyalty of the Río de la Plata (present-day Uruguay, Paraguay, and Bolivia) in 1776 and the relaxation of trade restrictions produced grave economic dislocations in Quito and Peru. Indeed, large areas of western South America entered a prolonged period of economic depression. Similarly, new trade policies undermined established commercial practices in New Spain (i.e., colonial Mexico).

Although these innovations were beneficial to some regions and groups and harmful for others, it is likely that in time adequate adjustments would have been made. But the onset of the French Revolution unleashed 20 years of war. To survive, the Spanish crown made extortionate demands on its American kingdoms, to no avail. The monarchy collapsed in 1808. The situation was complicated by a bourgeois revolution in the Spanish Peninsula.

The situation mystified the colonials. Who ruled Spain? Who, if anyone, should be obeyed? The political uncertainty provided the American elite (the *criollos*) the opportunity to press for home rule. Throughout the Empire, they attempted to form governing *juntas*. But the colonial authorities and the European Spaniards resident in America opposed such action. In Mexico they overthrew the viceroy to prevent the establishment of a local junta. In other areas, such as Quito, the authorities used military force to crush autonomist movements. As a result, many *criollos* sought mass support, appealing to urban and rural workers, many of whom were *mestizos,* Indians, blacks, and *mulattos.* The latter, in turn, took the opportunity to redress their own grievances, often to the detriment of the upper class. In New Spain, this resulted in the mass rural upheaval led by Father Miguel Hidalgo, which became a race and a class war. In Venezuela, the *castas* (the people of color) supported the royalists against the *criollo* elite. In Peru and Upper Peru (present-day Bolivia), some Indian communities in the highlands rose in rebellion, pressing their own demands. In many areas of the Spanish Empire, regional jealousies combined with race and class differences to provoke local civil wars. As a result, no unified Spanish American independence movement appeared.

New Spain, the wealthiest and most developed part of the Empire, endured 11 years of guerrilla warfare. Initially, all who had anything to lose, from wealthy miners and landowners to Indian villagers, opposed the mass insurgency of Hidalgo. But the brutal counterinsurgency alienated many groups. In 1811, Father José María Morelos continued the struggle while seeking to form a national government which would also attract the urban upper and middle classes. But his movement was undermined by the Spanish Constitution of 1812, which established representative government at three levels—the municipality, the province, and the Empire. It allowed towns with a thousand or more citizens (all men, except those with African ancestry) to form *ayuntamientos* (municipal councils). In ways we have yet to understand, political power was transferred from the center to the localities, as large numbers of people, including Indians and rural villagers, were incorporated into the political process. The virulence of the insurgency and counterinsurgency also contributed to the fragmentation of the viceroyalty and the emergence of regional *caudillos.* After Morelos's defeat and death in 1815, the insurgency fragmented into a series of local conflicts. Colonial Mexico broke into regions dominated either by insurgent or royalist warlords. In 1821, exhausted by 11 years of war, all sides accepted the Plan of Iguala, a compromise by which the royal army changed sides, declaring independence. But the long conflict had destroyed both the extensive, but fragile, infrastructure and the socioeconomic arrangements that had allowed New Spain to function. After independence, Mexico sank into nearly 50 years of economic decline, political instability, and social conflict.

In South America, unlike Mexico, the patriots defeated the Spanish militarily. There a military caste emerged from the plains of Venezuela (the *llanos*) and of Argentina (the *pampas*). The Creole elites of Caracas and Buenos Aires gained control of their regions early. In 1810, the *porteños* (the people of Buenos Aires) formed a local government and proceeded to establish their authority throughout the viceroyalty of the Río de la Plata. Subsequently rebuffed by local groups in peripheral areas of the former viceroyalty, the *porteños* formed new armies which, under the leadership of José de San Martín, continued the struggle in Chile. In New Granada (present-day Colombia), provincial groups organized local government, which fought against each other as much as against the royalists. The two patriot groups ultimately liberated all of South America. The struggle culminated at the end of 1824 in the decisive battles of Junín and Ayacucho in Peru and Bolivia.

Independence did not lead to unity and prosperity. The long struggle not only destroyed economic and political structures, it also engendered great social and regional divisions. North America divided into Mexico and Guatemala (the Central American union), while South America fragmented into many nations, whose overlapping territorial claims resulted in numerous boundary conflicts. The long, destructive struggle for independence also fostered the rise of regional military *caudillos* (bosses) who dominated their areas through force. Within each nation, significant divisions emerged as various groups struggled for control. Social, economic, and political conflict erupted between urban and rural groups, between the coast and the highlands, and among races—the white elite, the mestizo middle group, the blacks and people of color, and most of all the Indians. The native population suffered throughout the continent because with independence they lost the protection of the Spanish Crown, which had considered them its subjects, even if of lower status. Legal equality often meant that the Indians lost their lands and generally fell victim to the exploitation of urban groups.

The dismemberment of the Spanish Empire and the creation of new nations also resulted in new patterns of trade. Other western European countries, primarily England, sought to fill the economic void left by Spain. The Spanish American nations attempted to structure their economies so that they might benefit from increased trade. But, in general, such efforts proved ineffective. Most countries entered a prolonged period of economic decline coupled with political instability and social conflict. It would take many decades before the new nations overcame the trauma of their birth. (*See also Caudillismo;* Elites; Native Americans)

Jaime E. Rodríguez

REFERENCES

Bethell, Leslie, ed. *The Cambridge History of Latin America*, Vol. 3. Cambridge: Cambridge University Press, 1985.

Lynch, John. *The Spanish American Revolutions, 1808–1826,* 2nd. ed. New York: Norton, 1986.

Individualism

See Sense of Self/Individualism

Industrial Revolution

See Industrialization

Industrialization

Industrialization describes an increase in the proportion of the population involved in industrial production. Great Britain and, later, portions of the European Continent and the United States were leaders in the increase in industrial population characteristic of the modern period. Until recent decades, the period between 1760 and 1830 in Britain, that is, the industrial revolution, has been portrayed as the key moment in industrial transformation. Focusing on the introduction of steam power, the rise of the factory system in cotton textiles, and the development of new iron-making technologies that contributed to the appearance of the railroad, British developments have dominated the stage. But British industrial growth, now considered to have been slower than previously thought, depended on economic expansion in traditional sectors as well as technologically advanced sectors; and as late as 1840, less than 25 percent of the value of Britain's manufactures were in the modernized textiles, iron, and engineering triangle.

Historians often talk of industrialization as a revolution, and economic historian W.W. Rostow prompted the idea of an initial "take off" that signaled the beginning of rapid change. Yet the continuity of early 19th-century industrial development must be emphasized. Great Britain, which had 41 percent of its population in manufacture and mining in 1841, already had 30 percent of its population in this category in 1801, and Peter Lindert has argued persuasively that historians have underestimated seriously the extent to which the British population was engaged in industrial production even by the late 17th century. In France, the proportion of the population in industrial production in 1842 was 26 percent; in 1911, 30 percent. In Germany, industrialization was more rapid; the industrial population of Germany rose from 21 percent in 1800 to 40 percent in 1907, while the United States placed midway between France and Germany, from 20 percent of the population in 1860 to 32 percent in 1910. But in some smaller European countries, such as Portugal and Ireland, the proportion engaged in industrial production actually declined, or deindustrialized, during the 19th century; in Ireland the industrial population went from 30 percent in 1841 to 15 percent in 1926.

If industrialization was slower and more prolonged than once thought, it nonetheless had great impact on the lives of millions of people in Europe and the United States. Between the end of the 19th century and the mid-20th century, in many industrial regions, a large portion of the industrial work force was composed of a relatively new type of worker, the permanent year-round male proletarian, living with his family. At the same time, a particular form of industrial organization came to dominate industrial production—the large factory employing masses of unskilled and semiskilled workers, predominantly but not exclusively adult males, using single-purpose machines. Together, this new type of permanent proletarian, the new, power-driven machinery, and the new organization of work were to alter fundamentally the character of industrialization.

The growth of industrial regions in the years between 1760 and 1840 was a culmination of earlier developments. Industrial regions had long traditions of skilled artisans in city centers surrounded by large regions engaged in rural industry. By 1840 the northern counties in Great Britain (Lancashire and Yorkshire), the West Midlands, and South Wales emerged as regions with an exceptionally large proportion of their population involved in industrial production. On the Continent, central Belgium (with Charleroi, Liège, and Verviers), and the basin around Saint-Etienne were the leading industrializing regions.

The newly mechanized industrial regions evolved from preexisting protoindustrial regions, and the characteristics of the early industrial work force were not so very different from its predecessor. Birmingham, the city in which Matthew Boulton and James Watt produced the early steam engines, was for most of the 19th century dominated by skilled workers in an extraordinary variety of occupations, many working beside their masters in small shops and many families working on their own account at home. Outside Birmingham, to the north, toward the region called the Black Country, were many small forges in which domestic workers produced nails, bolts, and chains.

The importance of the labor of children and young women in many of the early textile factories and mines is further evidence of continuity. The labor of children and life-cycle employment of both men and women were characteristic of unskilled labor in the older European industrial tradition in which workers labored at home beside their parents or came to the city to work seasonally or for a number of years, until they had acquired enough money to acquire land or a dowry. The organization of mechanized industry also was considerably varied in the early 19th century and, in many areas, adapted to the forms of artisanal industry. Much metalworking was done in scattered small shops that specialized in a single mechanical process. Artisanal cooperatives were sometimes formed to employ machinery that was too expensive for a single small master. Even in the case of capitalist-owned factories, the distinction between factory and shop should not be exaggerated. In 1835, Andrew Ure, writing about the factory systems as a traveling observer with manufacturing experience of his own, calculated that the average cotton mill employed 175 people.

The partial exceptions here are miners in a few European coalfields, devoted to providing fuel for urban heating, for by the 18th or even the 17th century underground mining jobs were dominated by adult males and mining had become a lifetime occupation, passed on from father to son. Yet the position of mining was anomalous because, long after the urbanization of industry and its concentration into hierarchically organized factories with specialized machinery, mining's location in rural areas and the relatively decentralized and autonomous character of its organization retained strong ties to older forms of labor organization.

Those looking for a major reformation of the organization of production should look not to the beginning of the 19th century, but to its end, between 1880 and 1930, as large-scale capital accumulation and new disciplinary techniques developed. Originating in the late 18th and 19th centuries, one particular form of industrialization, that of mass production by single-purpose machines, grew so rapidly that by the end of the 19th century it dominated other paths. Domination did not mean replacement. In many industries, such as garments, mass production methods made advances while leaving older forms partially intact: in construction, mass production methods made limited headway; and, even in textiles, the area of their first successes, the economies of scale provided by mass production methods declined surprisingly quickly as factory size grew. Still, mass production methods transformed key industries in metal making and machine construction, where dramatic shifts were introduced in the character of the work force, organization of work, and, often, geographic location of work.

On the European Continent, the forward march of mass production methods was marked by the rise of relatively new industrial regions. The Briey Basin and Longwy in France, the Ruhr valley in Germany, and Upper Silesia in Germany and Poland witnessed the hitherto almost unknown phenomenon of great factories rising in the fields. Certainly, technological change played an important role. Epoch-making inventions such as the Bessemer convertor, the Thomas Gilchrist basic process, and the extension of the Siemens-Martin process opened up previously unusable coal and iron ore fields to steelmaking and made location next to ore fields economically advantageous.

But the new technologies could never have been used so effectively and so rapidly without the previous accumulation of large amounts of industrial capital. Few establishments could afford to buy the rights to new technologies, to build huge factories in the fields, and to recruit a work force from scratch. Building a new work force required a large-scale search for workers; recruitment was placed in the hands of private agencies and churchmen, and personnel offices gave employers new control over the work force. While the most skilled workers still had to be drawn from the existing supply, large-scale employers found it worthwhile to train their semi-skilled work force, whose numbers they expanded by placing greater reliance on single-purpose machines. The need to build houses and provide basic services to this new work force created the opportunities for industrial paternalism characteristic of these newly expanding industries.

Age, race, national origin, marital status, and gender figured more prominently in the new forms of industrial organization than in the old. Given their great industrial power, industrialists had considerable freedom to choose the kinds of workers they would employ. Most preferred to give the newly created stable semiskilled jobs to adult males who had families; women's and single migrants' participation in industry was limited to lower-paying, less-skilled jobs for which demand was often more fluctuating. (In the United States, however, racial prejudice often consigned adult black males to the same inferior status as women and foreign migrants.) Employers chose adult males partly because factory work was physically demanding and partly because they selected married males because they assumed that married males would form a stable work force, which insured year-round production over a long period. Manufacturers shared with working men the feeling that married women would and should stay home to take care of children.

The adult, primarily male, work force in the large factories differed from previous groups of unskilled and semiskilled workers by having its own identity. Working in the same industry, year after year, these men began to identify themselves as metalworkers, rubber workers, and automobile workers. Further, unlike the shifting and mobile casual labor force of the earlier period, these workers often remained in the same geographic area for most of their lives. Trained on relatively specialized machines in the large factories, the semiskilled workers had much less opportunity to move from place to place than the older artisanal workers. The gendered character of much industrial work also promoted an ethic of fraternalism that flourished in predominantly or exclusively male clubs, bars, and cafes. Thus, even when women entered into the workplace, they rarely participated in the outside-the-factory recreational life of the majority of male workers.

The working-class residential areas surrounding factories began to acquire distinctive class identities. Occupational identities, so dear to artisanal workers, declined, while a broader industrial identity crystalized. This new identity spread in residential neighborhoods, where young women performing poor-paying industrial labor became wives and mothers directing a family economy often under siege; these working-class homemakers frequently turned to networks of other working-class women for help and mutual protection. At work, the factory proletariat, both male and female, labored as part of a large mass of workers whose position was similar to their own; children grew up in an atmosphere that was saturated with class experiences.

The growth of a new brand of radicalism within the working-class communities created by the industrial revolution between the years 1850 and 1950 was one of the most important characteristics of political life in 20th-century Europe and the United States. Powerful industrial employers had considerable room for maneuver, and it was therefore only a matter of time before these new industrial workers, sharing their own industrial identity and possessing their own strong sense of solidarity, began to oppose these employers.

In many ways, the decline of the mass production form of industrialization after the mid-20th century provides vantage points to view the specificity and historical rootedness of Western industrial development. Much of the major industrial development since the 1960s has followed a different course, requiring, on the one hand, larger numbers of highly trained workers able to use multipurpose machines and ever-evolving computers and, on the other hand, larger numbers of totally unskilled workers to do basic assembly and maintenance work. Thus, jobs fled old industrial areas and moved to areas dominated by small and medium-sized establishments with large proportions of highly educated workers and also fled to foreign countries. Instead of providing firm industrial identities for workers and their families, modern industry has increased the number of its temporary employees even among the very skilled. The rising importance of formal education and training has also made substantial inroads into the gender division of industrial labor. Women's evolution into the service industry during the 20th century often provided them with a formal training that equipped them better for modern industrial work than males who went directly into factory work.

From the vantage point of the last years of the 20th century, the major outlines of the great industrial phase of economic development that occurred between 1850 and 1950 seems sharper and its distinctiveness clearer than it did to economic historians and social commentators of the 1960s and 1970s.

While focus on an early phase of factory industrialization has diminished, with greater attention to longer-term manufacturing growth and to a process with several phases, industrialization has been the framework for a host of topics in social history. The social consequences of industrialization into the 20th century has indeed stimulated many of the central findings in the field—on class formation, the nature of work and leisure, and the functions of the family, among numerous others. Much of the interpretation of the industrialization/industrial revolution transformation has indeed moved from a largely economic movement to the investigation of social causes and social impacts.

Industrialization has also stimulated comparative work on such subjects as differing roles for women. Different industrial characteristics affected several major European countries, with important ramifications in social history. Industrialization began to accelerate outside Europe and the United States by the later 19th century. Study of the social consequences of Russian and Japanese industrialization has shaped much of the modern social history applied to these areas. In all its locations to date (including most recently the Pacific Rim), industrialization has displayed not only some similar features, including radical new technology and the factory systems, but also major divergences, including the amounts of social protest it has elicited. [See *also*

Economics (Economic and Social History); Technology; Working Class]

Michael P. Hanagan

REFERENCES

Berg, Maxine. *The Age of Manufactures, 1700–1820.* Totowa, NJ: Barnes and Noble, 1985.

Hopkins, Eric. *Birmingham: The First Manufacturing Town in the World, 1760–1840.* London: Weidenfeld & Nicolson, 1989.

Landes, David S. *The Unbound Prometheus: Technological Change and Industrial Development in Western Europe from 1750 to the Present.* Cambridge: Cambridge University Press, 1970.

Piore, Michael, and Charles F. Sabel. *The Second Industrial Divide: Possibilities of Prosperity.* New York: Basic Books, 1984.

Stearns, Peter N. *The Industrial Revolution in World History.* Boulder, CO: Westview Press, 1993.

Inequality

See Stratification and Inequality

Infanticide

Infanticide is the deliberate killing of unwanted infants by parents, other family members, or even by the state. This is done either as a means of birth control for the nuclear family or for the family to conform to societal norms. For instance, modern China has stringent birth control laws that limit most families to one child. Since males are more desirable in rural society, families frequently drown their newborn infant daughters in order to have another chance at having a son. This is called colloquially "giving the baby a bath." In ancient Sparta, governmental officials examined each child and decided whether it was fit enough to live and become a Spartan. If not, they exposed it, that is, they left it outside, in an isolated area, usually to die. The Roman Law of the Twelve Tables (451 BC) stated that a father should quickly kill a deformed infant.

As a practice, infanticide has a long tradition in Western and other agricultural societies, where it seems to have been commonly used from antiquity to the modern era, when it tapered in frequency. Historians see this decline as proof of the beneficial effects of modernization on attitudes toward children. In fact, most historians see societal acceptance of infanticide as one of the hallmarks of premodern Western childhood. On the other hand, some ancient cultures forbade infanticide, including the religions of ancient Egypt and Israel. The German tribes did not practice infanticide, which astounded the Roman commentator Tacitus (56–120). Judaism's prohibition of infanticide influenced Christianity. Ecclesiastical regulations (and later civil law) have consistently forbade the practice in western Europe, though it has continued.

Although widespread infanticide is assumed for the premodern world, lack of evidence makes it difficult to establish actual rates. Overlaying, where a parent accidentally rolls over on and smothers a child that has been in bed with it, has been traditionally seen as proof of widespread infanticide, though camouflaged as an accident. Church law and civil law consistently forbade parents from taking children to bed with them to prevent this supposed form of infanticide. Yet these cases might not represent infanticide or even accidental deaths but may represent cases of crib death, which is mysterious enough to diagnose and explain for the modern age and would have been almost inexplicable to diagnose and explain for the premodern age.

Traditionally, scholars have interpreted abandonment, which was widespread in the past if stories about Moses, Oedipus, Cyrus the Great, Romulus and Remus, and others are any indication, as an infanticidal act. But recent research shows that was not always the case. Some people in the past, when circumstances forced them to abandon their children, expected that someone else would pick them up and rear them. It was a form of adoption. In ancient Greece there were known places where one could go either to abandon a child or recover one. Spartan children who were exposed by the state, would be picked up by Helots, the state serfs, to be brought up as Helots. Some scholars argue that widespread infanticide in the past is implausible since the premodern world had such high rates of infant mortality.

Though clearly a widespread practice, infanticide has varied considerably among agricultural societies depending on economic circumstances and on culture, and while precise rates are impossible to determine social historians are concerned with explaining the differences. Another important feature of infanticide in many cases, including ancient Greece as well as China, involves gender distinctions, with female babies killed far more often presumably because of their lesser worth, though in fact also as a means of further population control.

Certainly infanticide did occur—it occurs today—but there is no way to determine its scope. One of the proofs offered for society's acceptance of this crime, the frequent dismissal of infanticide cases by reason of insanity, probably shows that legally and socially infanticide was considered so horrible that only the insane would commit it. Proving widespread infanticide would not necessarily then prove the larger question of the lack of affection toward children in the premodern world. The Kalahari bush people in Africa, in times of societal stress, do practice infanticide, even today. Yet when given tests that measure parent to child affection, they consistently demonstrate scores comparable to those of modern Westerners.

In fact, all infanticide may represent is desperate reactions by people who find themselves in desperate situations, particularly before artificial birth control or abortions were widely available. Infanticide in the Middle Ages occurred primarily among those on the margins of society; and Regina Schulte's (1984) detailed study of infanticide in 19th-century Bavaria showed that the vast majority of those accused of infanticide were poor, uneducated, unmarried servant girls—in other words girls in trouble, which in the past meant destitution and even death for the mother. All infanticide may represent in most cases, horrible as it might seem, is an attempt at self-preservation. Maybe the leniency of premodern courts in these cases was even based on this humanitarian consideration. Infanticide remains an important facet of family history, and a challenge to sophisticated interpretations in social history generally. (*See also* Abuse; Birth Control; Chinese Family/Demography)

Louis Haas

REFERENCES

Boswell, John. *The Kindness of Strangers: The Abandonment of Children in Western Europe from Late Antiquity to the Renaissance.* New York: Pantheon Books, 1988.

Hoffer, Peter C., and N.E.H. Hull. *Murdering Mothers: Infanticide in England and New England, 1558–1803.* New York: New York University Press, 1981.

Schulte, Regina. "Infanticide in Rural Bavaria in the Nineteenth Century," in Hans Medick and David Warren Sabean, eds., *Interest and Emotion: Essays on the Study of Family and Kinship.* Cambridge: Cambridge University Press, 1984, pp. 77–102.

Inheritance Systems

The early work of social historians on the subject of material inheritance mainly concerned the distribution of a father's land among his sons and the effects of that distribution system on wealth concentration, agricultural production, fertility, and kinship relations. Social historians compared different inheritance patterns and also dealt with change over time. Did those peasant communities where primogeniture rules (eldest son inherits all land) prevailed experience greater inequality and did younger sons postpone marriages? Did partible division of land (all male heirs inherit) result in too many tiny holdings, early marriage, and greater numbers of people on the land than the land could support? Did the greater availability of land in America create a better situation for sons? These were the questions most often asked about the intergenerational transmission of wealth over time. Research on western Europe, the United States, and Canada showed, however, that seldom did all the propertied men of a locality adhere strictly to either an impartible or partible mode of wealth distribution, and that inheritance customs alone could not predict very efficiently the degree of wealth concentration, land parcelization, age at marriage, and fertility rate of a community. Only in the case of those members of the English aristocracy, who entailed their estates (gave heirs only a life interest) through a group of legal devices known as the strict family settlement, could one identify inheritance practices that clearly promoted greater and greater wealth inequality. Early American sons, in contrast to their counterparts in Europe and England, had greater access to land and could set up households earlier, before the death or retirement of the father. As the older settlements became more densely populated, however, sons had the choice of either postponing marriage, like European young men, or migrating to the frontier.

Recently, women's history and the kinship studies of anthropologists have broadened the scope of historical inheritance studies. Because women in Western societies more often inherited personalty (movable goods, livestock, money, financial assets) than land, devoting more attention to the fate of wives and daughters means also studying the transmission of a wider array of property types. It turns out that very little wealth of any kind was held by these women in previous centuries. The traditional legal codes of Europe greatly limited the ability of women to write wills and control the inheritances they received. It turns out that patriarchal family strategists wanting to preserve or enhance the status of the lineage relied much more on restricting the inheritances of widows, sometimes referred to as their dower, and the portions given to daughters, either as inter vivos dowries or upon the death of their father, than they did the portions of younger sons. Not until the latter part of the 19th century does one see much change in the women's situation. The creation of corporate forms of wealth, the resultant expansion in financial asset wealth, and the passage of laws giving married women the right to hold property and make wills encouraged more equal distribution of wealth between male and female heirs in the United States. Later, socialist governments in Europe and Asia instituted more gender-neutral inheritance provisions.

Cross-cultural studies by anthropologists remind social historians of the diversity of inheritance systems that have existed throughout the world. The descent of property in European societies was almost exclusively patrilineal (passed through the father's line). Many African and American Indian societies, however, practiced matrilineal descent, where daughters and sons inherit from their mother and her kin. Also in some societies there was a strict division between male and female types of property, fathers or mother's brothers transmitting masculine goods to sons and nephews, while feminine goods passed only between women. Opinions differ as to whether matrilineal descent confers greater power on women in a society, although there is general agreement that matrilineal descent should not be confused with matriarchy.

Historically, inheritance customs in most societies have allowed little room for individual initiative. Lineage groups act like corporate bodies and jealously guard the property of their members against alienation to outsiders. The considerable testamentary freedom that has characterized European inheritance, most particularly in England, since the medieval period is rather unusual. In England and in many of its former colonies, such as in the United States, there are intestacy statutes that set down the shares of wealth to be inherited by spouse, children, and, in the case of no immediate family, other relatives. These inheritance rules are simply the default arrangements. Most propertied individuals write wills in which they have the power to do what they want with their estate. They can even disinherit all their children, although in practice that seldom occurs. Historians have traced the development of wills in Europe to the Catholic church and its desire to encourage the propertied to make religious bequests. Wills have become a vital source for the study of changing attitudes toward family, community, and death.

In the first half of the 20th century, socialist governments sought to reduce wealth concentration by restricting the ownership of private property, while many capitalist countries dealt with the problem by levying stiff estate taxes on inherited wealth. The state in effect became a mandatory heir. The impact of these progressive taxes on inequality and capital formation are a very controversial yet under-researched part of the modern social history of inheritance. Although conservatives argue that savings have been greatly damaged by taxes on inherited wealth, liberals contend that the estate planning industry has managed to influence legislation and find loopholes, so that estate taxation has been no barrier to increasing wealth inequality. It is of some importance to investigate the relationship, because, at the end of the 20th century, many formerly socialist economies are privatizing capital once again, and many capitalist societies are reporting increases in wealth inequality. (*See also* Agricultural Systems; Family)

Carole Shammas

REFERENCES

Goody, Jack. *Production and Reproduction: A Comparative Study of the Domestic Domain.* Cambridge: Cambridge University Press, 1976.

————, Joan Thirsk, and E.P. Thompson, eds. *Family and Inheritance: Rural Society in Western Europe, 1200–1800.* Cambridge: Cambridge University Press, 1976.

Shammas, Carole, Marylynn Salmon, and Michel Dahlin. *Inheritance in America, Colonial Times to the Present.* New Brunswick, NJ: Rutgers University Press, 1987.

Sheehan, Michael. *The Will in Medieval England.* Toronto: Pontifical Institute of Mediaeval Studies and Texts, 1963.

Smith, James D., ed. *Modeling the Distribution and Intergenerational Transmission of Wealth.* Chicago: University of Chicago Press, 1980.

Instrumentalism

Instrumentalism describes an orientation of many modern workers toward their work. Instrumentalist workers disclaim significant control over their work and do not expect to find much regular satisfaction in it. They accept it, however, if it provides satisfactory, and often increasing, pay and material benefits including time off. Work becomes an instrument to what are now the principal emphases of a worker's life.

Instrumentalism has been described by contemporary sociologists. Historians have used the same concept to trace the origins of new work attitudes, as opposed to more traditional expectations about work's intrinsic satisfactions and noneconomic motivations; to help explain differences among different types of workers (some more instrumentalist than others); and to account for key patterns in many contemporary labor movements. The term has been explored particularly in terms of the history of workers in the United States and Western Europe, and it is certainly linked to the process of industrialization.

Instrumentalism, or as one historian puts it, acceptance of labor as a market commodity, became apparent first in Great Britain after about 1850, particularly among skilled workers who abandoned hopes of recapturing a traditional craft but realized that they had enough bargaining power to win significant improvements in their wages and hours. A classic instance of conversion to instrumentalism occurred among French printers shortly after 1900. Faced with a new machine that set type far more rapidly than skilled workers could do by hand, printers initially were inclined to resist. Fearing that resistance to the machine would be impossible, with union guidance they quickly changed their tune. They argued essentially that, while the quality of work would indeed deteriorate, they would accept the machines if their daily pay went up.

Considerable instrumentalism spread among many types of workers in the 20th century. Semiskilled workers, increasingly characteristic in factory industry where minute specialization reduced training demands, were particularly open to instrumentalist goals. Skilled workers more commonly hoped for a more elaborate array of work satisfactions, though instrumentalism entered in. As more workers accepted instrumentalist goals, labor unions turned to pay and hours demands as their common currency, reducing efforts at more fundamental restructuring of the workplace. On other occasions, as in the United States during the 1970s, many workers rejected brief attempts at reviving issues of work quality from a fear that their pay might suffer. Many critics of the 20th-century working-class and labor movement see instrumentalism as a key factor not in eliminating workplace conflict but in confining it to relatively restricted agendas. Whatever the verdict here, the process of adopting an increasingly instrumentalist stance is an important passage in the modern history of work, class relations, and value systems. (*See also* Industrialization; Working Class)

Peter N. Stearns

REFERENCES

Goldthorpe, John, et al. *The Affluent Worker in the Class Structure.* Cambridge: Cambridge University Press, 1969.

Hobsbawm, Eric. *Labouring Men.* New York: Basic Books, 1964.

Reddy, William. *Money and Liberty in Modern Europe.* Cambridge: Cambridge University Press, 1987.

Stearns, Peter N. *Lives of Labor: Work in Maturing Industrial Society.* New York: Holmes and Meier, 1975.

Intelligentsia

Intelligentsia, based on a word of Latin origin meaning "intelligence," has come into the modern global vocabulary from Russia. It relates to other social constructs including intellectuals and professionals, but emerged from Russia's destructive 19th-century social context. By the 1870s the word identified a particular type of publicly active Russian intellectual. The word supplied a taxonomic label for a distinct group of people whose professional identity or public function were no longer described by the traditional categories of the Russian social structure. These people might have been born into the customary *sosloviia* (formally defined and enforced social formations: the clergy, nobility, merchantry, middling urbanites, and peasantry). But education and pursuit of a livelihood moved them into realms of thought and behavior that bore little relationship to received categories of parental social existence. People of various ranks, or *raznochintsy,* also described them because their new identity was given by training or education, not by family background. The novelty of the intelligentsia was also signaled by the complications they faced when trying to reach out to more traditional social groups like the peasantry, who often distrusted theorizing.

The most famous *intelligenty* were revolutionists, but the revolutionary movement grew out of a more generalized situation in which most men and women of the creative professions and trained specializations found themselves. The Russian Empire was just then experiencing a decline of customary ways based on serf agriculture, hereditary social structure, and official Orthodoxy. At the same time Russia experienced an intrusion of modern ways based on market economies, industry, democracy, science, and technology. The Bolshevik Party, led by Vladimir Lenin, might best be thought of as an especially focused and narrowed political fraction of this novel class or stratum. In the Soviet period, the intelligentsia was identified as one of the three formal classes of revolutionary society, along with the workers and the peasants. The Communist Party of the Soviet Union, however, shunned close identity with the intelligentsia, and for its part the inelligentsia reciprocated. As early as 1909 a group of Russian thinkers brought out an influential book *Vekhi* (Signposts), which railed against the narrowly positivistic and political traditions of the Russian intelligentsia. In the Gorbachev era, the intelligentsia presented itself in an expanded or metamorphosed guise as a "civil society" and, throughout Eastern Europe, contributed to the fall of Lenin's focused and narrowed fraction.

The Russian experience over the half-century prior to the Soviet Revolution in 1917 foreshadowed the experience of many peoples over the whole globe in the half-century or so that followed 1917. History's first self-conscious intelligentsia in Russia provided a model that seemed particularly suited to the experience of African, Near Eastern, and Asiatic societies in the grip of European imperialist dominion and externally influenced modernization to overcome economic and social backwardness. Thus, it is no accident that a near universal phenomenon, the modernizing intellectual elite, should be labeled with national variations on the Russian word (e.g., *interigenchiya* in Japanese). (But the utility of the term in Western social history, where the relationship between intellectuals and the modern middle class is complex, is less well established.)

Yet the phenomenon has deep ancestry in many cultures where shamans, the priesthood, monasteries, or mandarin scholars play a central role, in or out of power. In *The Republic* Plato described the philosopher king and the role of "guardians" in the perfect society. In the years just after the French Revolution, the socialist theorist Henri de Saint-Simon defined the role of the *savant,* a technocratic elite of manufacturers, engineers, scientists, and creative intellectuals and artists. Later theorists, like Harold Lasswell, Edward Shils, Karl Mannheim, Antonio Gramsci, Zygmunt Bauman, Boris Kargarlitsky, Gyorgy Konrad, and Ivan Szeleny have explored the role of the modern intelligentsia. Some have praised and some have condemned these "symbol experts" and "managerial elites." The 19th-century German social critic

Wilhelm Riehl was fascinated and appalled by them. In our century Elie Halévy assumed an equally ambiguous position in his *Era of Tyrannies.* Jose Ortega-y-Gasset seemed to recommend them, while Julien Benda, Milovan Djilas, Waclaw Machaijski, and Max Weber warned against them. Many of these themes influence modern theorists of transnational corporations and the managerial executives of the global market economy.

Hundreds of studies of the intelligentsia have been written, but few of them might now be thought of as "social histories." In the English literature on the topic, the dominant theme has been philosophical or psychological. Mannheim's use of Alfred Weber's idea of "the socially unattached intelligentsia" has influenced many to deal with the intelligentsia outside of their precise social and economic setting. In this form we learn of intellectuals who sometimes seem like supermen or psychopaths. Biography, rather than prosopography (group biography) or aggregate analysis of cohorts, has been the preferred form.

In quite the opposite direction, in the original homeland of the intelligentsia, Russia, the study of the intelligentsia has been immersed in the study of larger and necessarily vaguer categories: for example, social classes as defined by Karl Marx. In the Soviet Union under Communist rule, the social history of the intelligentsia was constantly fragmented as a result of the enforced need to deny any independent social experience to that stratum. In this form, the intelligentsia was a dependent historical variable, always functioning as an expression of this or that class interest: thus, "bourgeois" or "aristocratic" intelligentsia. Thus also it was possible to explain how prerevolutionary elites were able to ally themselves with an alien social class. Lenin's father, for example, was a noble, elevated to that social position by state service, yet Lenin the radical *intelligent* was able to "choose" alliance with the working class. Lenin and his party, in this form, could not have its own independent "interests"; they pretended to serve the interests of supposedly more substantial reality, the proletariat.

Three larger tasks present themselves to social history. First, the intelligentsia must be re-attached to their precise social environment and described within their specific institutions and organizations. This task is being fulfilled by an increasing number of studies that distinguish many varieties of intellectual public activists among the intelligentsia: for example, economic managers, financial planners, liberal professions (especially journalists, teachers, lawyers, physicians), technical and scientific specialists, political ideologists, scholars, philosophers, theologians, and creative artists. Second, the particular interests of the various sectors of the intelligentsia must be given proper weight along with their ideologies. All too often intellectuals are treated as if they did not eat or shelter themselves, or as if they had no intrinsic and quotidian vested interests. What is "intellectual capital," what are the exchange value and social utility of knowledge or trained ability? Third, the rich interrelationship between the intelligentsia and other social formations must be described more closely, especially in the era of the electronic media. The time may come when the social history of the intelligentsia will help illuminate the social history of other aggregates, especially those, like the peasantry, who are too often thought to have nothing but grubby daily interests and very little spiritual or intellectual culture. (*See also* Anarchism; Bureaucracy; Chinese State and Society; Class; Elites; European University; Mentalities; Modernization; Professionalism; Revolutions; Socialism; Youth Movements)

Alan Kimball

REFERENCES

Coser, Lewis. *Men of Ideas: A Sociologist's View.* New York: The Free Press, 1985.

Gouldner, Alvin W. *The Future Intellectuals and the Rise of the New Class: A Frame of Reference, Theses, Conjectures, Arguments, and an Historical Prospective on the Role of Intellectuals and Intelligentsia in the International Class Contest of the Modern Era.* New York: The Seabury Press, 1979.

Kautsky, John H., ed. *Political Change in Underdeveloped Countries: Nationalism and Communism.* New York: Wiley, 1962.

Nahirny, Vladimir C. *The Russian Intelligentsia: From Torment to Silence.* New Brunswick, NJ: Transformation Books, 1983.

Pomper, Philip. *The Russian Revolutionary Intelligentsia.* New York: Crowell, 1970.

Irrigation Societies

The theory of "irrigation society" explains certain similarities in the form and development of social and political institutions in different societies as a consequence of their common dependence on irrigation. The theory, with sweeping implications, originated before the advances in social history research, but it has obvious implications for such research. The theory's fashionability has declined in recent decades, but it continues to inform some comparative works.

The principal social theorist of irrigation, Karl Wittfogel (1957), argued that the development of successful large-scale irrigation systems depended on the rise of a bureaucracy for the management of construction and maintenance of the physical infrastructure and the processes of irrigation. Such development enhanced the power of the bureaucracy, in turn, which became the core of state power in ancient agrarian societies such as China, India, and Egypt. The form of government that arose in societies dependent upon irrigation, he characterized as "agromanagerial totalitarianism," and the type of government, he labeled "Oriental Despotism." This was distinguished from European agrarian societies whose political economy was land-based rather than water-based, for in land-based societies, he claimed, there could arise a balance of power between great owners of land and other forces. In irrigation-based societies, of necessity, all was subordinated to the power of the irrigation bureaucracy.

Wittfogel's theory inspired controversy and further research among social scientists around two major issues: the importance of irrigation to the origin of the state in ancient times and the necessity for similarities among different contemporary societies dependent on irrigation.

Julian Steward (1955) argued that the great civilizations of the world, specifically their political structures, were "caused" by the need for a supralocal organization to construct and maintain large-scale irrigation systems. In the Old World, the location of the major early civilizations on watercourses in arid climates, and their known dependence upon large-scale hydraulic works, substantiated this idea. In the New World, similar arguments could be put forward.

However, prehistorians testing Steward's proposal found no clear evidence that large-scale irrigation systems preceded the formation of statehood in the archaeological sequences they examined. Most critics argued for a multicausal rather than a unicausal approach. They claimed that the state preceded the development of large-scale hydraulic works, which then contributed to the growth and development of the state. Other archaeologists accepted irrigation as a contributory factor along with other equally important material factors.

One interpretation of Wittfogel's theory concluded that irrigation would *always* be accompanied by state organization, by stratification, bureaucracy, or some other specific feature of statehood. Ethnologists set themselves to testing this generalization, finding no cross-cultural support for it, but a whole variety of exceptions. These studies resulted in a number of very fine ethnographies which illustrated the variability of ways of organizing irrigation and irrigators, particularly at the prestate or nonstate level (See Hunt and Hunt 1976).

Irrigation has been viewed as the creator of wealth through the taming or domestication of nature by humans, but also as a tool for manipulation of humans through the power of those who control the critical resource on which they depend. Managing a large irrigation system means that people must collaborate somehow on construction, maintenance, and allocation of water, because of the nature of the resource itself. Further, management of water resources requires technical expertise which, as exploitation of the resource becomes more complex, is limited to only a few. These few (or their employers) determine who will get water, and when, and how.

Though the potential for power differences seems inherent in large-scale irrigation because power through irrigation is so often vested in the state, it has in some cases been seen as a kind of antidote to other kinds of power, particularly that of propertied interest groups. Such an argument prevailed up to a century ago in the development of irrigation resources in the U.S. West (Worster 1985: 160–163). The belief in the power of the state to undermine economic differences through irrigation became embodied in laws regulating the amount of land that could be irrigated with federally financed projects; excess land was required to be sold off at pre-irrigation prices, so as to distribute land and opportunities more widely among the population. Thus irrigation was used as a democratizing device. However, many critics felt it had not achieved this objective; rather, irrigation gave rise to strong bureaucracies which, in conjunction with interest groups representing corporate power and wealthy capitalists, dominated the political economy of the West (Worster 1985). (*See also* Agricultural Systems; Chinese State and Society; Civilization)

Susan H. Lees

REFERENCES

Hunt, Eva, and Robert Hunt. "Canal Irrigation and Local Social Organization," *Current Anthropology* 17 (1976): 389–411.

Steward, Julian, ed. *Irrigation Civilizations: A Comparative Study*. Washington, DC: Pan American Union, 1955.

Wittfogel, Karl. *Oriental Despotism: A Comparative Study of Total Power*. New Haven: Yale University Press, 1957.

Worster, Donald. *Rivers of Empire: Water, Aridity and the Growth of the American West*. New York: Pantheon Books, 1985.

Islam

Today, some 800 million people affirm the fundamental creed of the Islamic religion, that there is one God (Allah in Arabic) and that Muhammad is the messenger of God. Beyond that affirmation, and an acceptance of the history of the *umma*, the universal community of Muslims (those who make *islam*, or "submission" to God's will), as their sacred history, there is little uniformity in the lived experience of the Islamic religion. Though most Muslim communities have mosques, and most Muslims recognize religious obligations to pray, fast, and abstain from alcohol and pork, there are individual, group, and regional exceptions even to these hallmarks of the faith, not to mention the myriad laws and expectations of the *shari'a*, the religious law of Islam. While practitioners of all religions vary in their performance of religious duties, Islam is marked by a historically evolved authority structure that sanctions diversity even while extolling adherence to legal norms.

Muhammad's death in AD 632, at a probable age of 62, left his community bereft of charismatic leadership but gifted with a corpus of rhymed prose that soon became organized and canonized as the Qur'an. The Qur'an was understood by Muhammad and his followers to have been revealed to Muhammad by God over the preceding 20-plus years. Since the revelations said that Muhammad was the last of God's prophets (literally "messengers"), the community could not hope for continuation of direct divine guidance. Moreover, Muhammad's singling out of his cousin and son-in-law Ali ibn Abi Talib as a leader was not generally understood to imply Ali's succession—though the Shi'ite sect that evolved over the next two generations to press the claims to spiritual leadership of Ali's family did understand it this way—so another successor, Muhammad's friend Abu Bakr, was chosen by a portion of the community, and then accepted by the rest as the first *khalifa*, or caliph. The institution of the caliphate lasted, in name, until the end of World War I, though it lost temporal power in the 10th century. It endured as the ideal political embodiment of Islam, but its definition, powers, and system of succession were long debated, with little correspondence at any given time between theory and practice. The community, represented by its religious scholars, never accorded the caliph the power to declare doctrine *ex cathedra*. Nor was any caliph able to construct an effective churchlike authority structure.

Throughout the initial period of caliphal strength, until the late 9th century, the empire was composed of a minority of Muslims and a majority of Christians, Jews, Zoroastrians, and others who had come under Muslim rule during the conquest period (AD 632–711), when the Arab followers of Muhammad, expanding from their original nucleus in Mecca and Medina in western Arabia, overpowered the Persian Sasanid Empire; stripped Syria, Egypt, and North Africa from the Byzantine Empire; and conquered Visigothic Spain. The Arabic language and Arab customs enjoyed a privileged role in the aftermath of the conquests even though other customary practices eventually acquired legitimacy within Islam upon the conversion of various non-Arab peoples; and Arabic persisted only as a liturgical and scholarly language east of Iraq while slowly being adopted as the language of daily interaction in Muslim lands to the west. The conversion of most of the conquered population took place over three to four centuries, depending upon the region. There is little evidence of planned conversion or organized missionary effort during the first two centuries, but as more and more non-Arabs became Muslims, they developed a more conscious goal of proselytizing their countrymen.

In search of a more fulfilling life as Muslims, and to escape ostracism by their former co-religionaries, many converts migrated to the Arab military and governing centers established by the first caliphs. These centers grew into bustling cities, most rapidly during the 9th and 10th centuries. This urbanization left an indelible mark on the evolving religion. The development of Islamic law, theology, and ethics, though prefigured by community practices of the prophet's time, reflects primarily the urban milieu of the 10th and 11th centuries. This environment also produced a body of religious learned men (called *ulama* in Arabic, *mullas* in Persian, *hojas* in Turkish) that morally dominated local Islamic society down to modern times. Controlling their own social boundaries, defining the content and standards of both education and law, and normally eschewing government service, these early ulama responded to local popular needs for religious leaders and moral exemplars and were more independent and less institutionalized than comparable clerical groups in other religions.

The period AD 1000–1400 witnessed intense political and social conflict, the latter marked by disagreements among the *ulama*. It was also a period of Islamic expansion into India, western Africa, southeastern Asia, and Anatolia (lost by the Byzantines in 1073). Out of this crucible of conflict and accompanying economic and demographic contraction emerged a set of religious institutions that emphasized social solidarity and mutual support. The college of higher Islamic learning (*madrasa*) standardized religious education and the credentialing of ulama. Young men's organizations (*futuwwa* in Arabic, *akhi* in Turkish, *javanmard* in Persian), brotherhoods centered on Sufi mystics, and artisan sodalities that crystallized into guilds at the end of the period characterize later Islamic society in the Middle East, along with the development of rural forms of Islam centered on local pilgrimages and, again, on Sufis. Outside the Middle East, the Sufi brotherhoods were the most important of these institutions, many of them playing a role in conversion.

Islamic social institutions of the early modern period made for social stability, which permitted the reemergence of strong centralized states in the 15th and 16th centuries (e.g., Ottomans, Safavids). The new empires coopted a portion of the religious elite into an official religious bureaucracy and recognized the theoretical supremacy of Islamic law and the unique position of the *ulama* as interpreters of the law. In the 19th and early 20th centuries, Middle Eastern governments, with European encouragement, instituted centralized autocracies, using Europe as a pattern. The institutional infrastructure of the religious elite withered in the face of Western-style law codes, secular state schools, and integration into the Europe-dominated world economy. The announced objective of the new autocracies was to reduce Islam to the status of a private religion. Yet the long history of populations looking to localized religious leadership, instead of the state, for moral guidance made possible a strong revival of Islam as a political force in the late 20th century (e.g., the Iranian Revolution of 1979) as many Muslims began to view autocratic nationalist governments as collaborators in the advance of Western cultural and economic hegemony. With this movement, Islam entered a new stage of its social history as thinkers, and organizations throughout the Muslim world sought to reinterpret Islamic values and institutions to fit modern conditions without pandering to Western social and political criteria.

Islam has posed a problem for historians because of the insistence of many scholars on using such terms as "Islamic society," "Islamic history," and "Islamic civilization." These usages have posed the question whether Islam is such a singularly distinctive religious tradition or force that it must always be taken as defining, or whether

Western historiography has created Islam as a special historical category. Most social historians see Islam in less absolute terms and acknowledge the wide range of diversity, including in doctrine, social structure, family patterns, and religious practice among Muslim peoples at different times and places. For social historians, Islamic social and family concepts form one of several factors to be considered in examining the actual social structure or gender relations in a particular period or region. At the same time, social historians are beginning to develop interests in popular religious concepts and medical practices in Islamic societies that will provide additional vantage points on the effective workings of Islam as a social force. (*See also Jihad;* Orientalism; Religion; Suffism)

Richard W. Bulliet

REFERENCES

Bulliet, Richard W. *Conversion to Islam in the Medieval Period.* Cambridge: Harvard University Press, 1979.

Marcus, Abraham. *The Middle East on the Eve of Modernity: Aleppo in the Eighteenth Century.* New York: Columbia University Press, 1990.

Lapidus, Ira. *A History of Islamic Societies.* Cambridge: Cambridge University Press, 1988.

Islam (Africa)

Islam first entered Africa with the Arab armies that crossed from Arabia into Egypt soon after the death of the Prophet Muhammed in AD 632. By AD 750, Muslims controlled most of northern Africa; virtually the entire population eventually converted. From the 8th century on, Islam was gradually carried by merchants south along the east coast of Africa as far as Mozambique (with little inland penetration); expansion was stopped only by 19th-century European colonialism. In East Africa, Islam remained basically an Arab religion; very little Africanization occurred. From the 8th or 9th century on, Islam was carried across the Sahara Desert into the Sudan of western and central Africa. During the period AD 1000–1750, Islam was adopted by the leaders and ruling classes of several Sudanic kingdoms, such as Ghana, Kanem, Mali, Songhai, and Wadai. But until the 18th century, Muslims constituted a small percentage of the population in west and central Africa.

Events in the Sudan in the last two centuries have transformed Islam into the predominant religion of the area. First, *jihads* (holy wars) erupted in the 18th and 19th centuries. Most were Muslim-led political revolutions against the leaders of established Islamic states, meant to purify Islam by sweeping away the traditional African beliefs, which had been absorbed over the centuries. Where the *jihads* were successful, Islam became the state religion, and society eventually became deeply Islamized. Second, in the late 19th century Europeans completed the colonization of virtually the entire continent. In general, Islam prospered under colonial rule—especially in West Africa, where Africans converted at an astonishing rate. European transportation and communications systems allowed Muslims to penetrate new areas, and Islam had a key advantage over missionary Christianity. Islam was seen as an indigenous religion, whereas Christianity had arrived simultaneously with, and was viewed as an adjunct of, imperial armies; it was highly syncretic, displaying more acceptance of traditional institutions than did virtually any Christian denomination. Social historians often emphasize the appeal of Islamic charismatic leaders (nearly all of whom were of the Sufi, a mystical religious brotherhood) during a series of profound social disruptions, caused by external factors such as the Atlantic slave trade and its abolition in the 19th century and the coming of European colonial rule.

In conclusion, Islam was spread in Africa mostly by the Sufi brotherhood. Nearly all African Muslims are Sunni, the majority sect in Islam. But African Islam is not monolithic; there are distinct geographical variations in doctrine and practice. Islam's major impact on Africa has been its conversion of the continent to Islam and all that that entails—the spread of literacy and state formation in West Africa. All of North Africa, Djibouti, Somalia, Gambia, Guinea, Senegal, Mali, and Niger are predominantly Muslim; there are majorities or significant minorities in Ghana, Togo, Benin, Nigeria, Chad,

Sudan, Ethiopia, Tanzania, and Mozambique; there are few Muslims elsewhere. (*See also* Islam; *Jihad;* Sufism)

Phillip Wilkin

REFERENCES

Abun-Nasr, Jamil M. *A History of the Maghrib in the Islamic Period.* Cambridge: Cambridge University Press, 1987.

Hiskett, Mervyn. *The Development of Islam in West Africa.* London: Longman, 1984.

Lewis, I.M., ed. *Islam in Tropical Africa,* 2nd ed. Bloomington: Indiana University Press, 1980.

Cruise O'Brien, Donal B., and Christian Coulon, eds. *Charisma and Brotherhood in African Islam.* Oxford: Clarendon Press, 1988.

Pouwels, Randall L. *Horn and Crescent: Cultural Change and Traditional Islam on the East African Coast, 800–1900.* Cambridge: Cambridge University Press, 1987.

J

Jacqueries

A major peasant uprising in the 14th century took its title from the generic name in rural France, Jacques, and this title, in turn, is often used for peasant risings more generally. The Jacquerie revolt of 1358 has become synonymous with peasant uprising, supposedly embodying the archetypal characteristics of peasant rebellion at least in Europe—extreme violence and hatred of the nobility. It was in fact the shortest and worst-organized of the peasant uprisings that swept through England, Flanders, France, Spain, and southern Italy during the 14th century. The popular movement itself was extensive, and though it included urban as well as rural risings, several general demands and grievances emerged. Other popular movements, such as the English rebellion of 1381, raised even clearer demands for social justice. A new current of unrest was developing that would periodically rage through Europe for several centuries. The rural risings, or jacqueries, that were part of this current featured peasant claims to the land and attacks on the houses, records, and occasionally landlords.

Though the Jacquerie was not the most important instance of these risings, its early date gave the name, and some of its targets suggested characteristic goals, for the subsequent rural "jacqueries" that would go beyond the most immediate subsistence demands.

The Jacquerie itself erupted on May 28, 1358, at Saint Leu d'Esserent, north of Paris, near Creil and Chantilly, and spread to neighboring villages, destroying manor houses and castles (as many as 5,000 according to the Chronicle of Jean de Venette), but failed in its attempt to enter the towns of Compiége and Senlis. Under leadership of Guillaume Cale, a prosperous peasant or member of the gentry, the peasants attacked the Marché de Meaux on May 9 and were brutally smashed the following day (two weeks exactly after its first surprise attack) by Picard noblemen led by Charles the Bad, King of Navarre.

The traditional view of the Jacquerie, derived largely from the contemporary chronicles of Jean Froissart, Jean de Venette, and the official

Grandes Chroniques, portrays a violent uprising of peasants against the nobility that sprung from conditions of misery in the wake of the Black Death. Historians since World War II, relying on new sources such as the acts of royal remissions issued after the uprising have modified this picture. First, the revolt arose in the most fertile region of France. It left the poorest areas of the Paris basin, southwest of the city, virtually untouched and instead spread through the prosperous villages north of Paris, where the commercial success of well-to-do cereal farmers was threatened by the breakdown of political and social order. Historians have even questioned whether this quintessential peasant revolt was indeed waged by peasants. The occupations found in letters of remission suggest instead a rural movement of artisans, petty officials, clergy, and even substantial proprietors.

Despite this revolt's quick demise, it is best understood in the context of longer-term economic and political events. During the yearlong truce between the English and the French that preceded the uprising, troops from both sides lived off the countryside. Instead of fulfilling their customary obligation of protecting the peasantry, the local nobility further enflamed the enmity of the rural population by seeking to profit from the breakdown of political order or by adding to traditional exactions. On the eve of the revolt, the nobility burdened the villagers and townsmen of the Paris basin with a new exaction—requisitions for victualizing the castles of the nobility. Political disputes and merchant hostility to the nobility added to the context in which peasants in some areas of France attacked castles and manor houses.

The Jacquerie and other rural risings of the late 14th century did show peasant hostility to landlord demands and produced statements of peasant rights, sometimes tinged with appeals to human equality. Risings of this sort, in reaction to landlord claims, in the name of peasant rights to the land, and in defense of a larger sense of justice, occurred periodically in France and other European countries into the 18th and 19th centuries. Hence, the idea of a jacquerie tradition outlasted the original event. (*See also* Peasant Rebellion)

Samuel K. Cohn, Jr.

REFERENCES

Cazelles, Raymond. "The Jacquerie," in *The English Rising of 1381.* Cambridge: Cambridge University Press, 1984, pp. 74–83.

Hilton, R.H. *Bond Men Made Free: Medieval Peasant Movements and the English Rising of 1381.* London: Temple Smith, 1973.

Luce, Simeon. *Histoire de la Jacquerie d'après des documents inédits,* 2nd ed. Paris: H. Champion, 1894; reprinted, Geneva: Slatkline Reprints, 1978.

Japanese Family/Demography

Social historians have approached the history of the Japanese family largely through research on population records. Japan's early population records are of unusually high quality, and they provide detailed information about family size and composition. The techniques used to study the family in preindustrial Japan are similar to those used to study the family in preindustrial western Europe. Historical households and villages are "reconstructed" from time series of population records—village population registers or censuses in the case of Japan and parish records in the case of Europe—that document how the family changed over time. European records have also been used to determine the timing of the modern demographic transition from high to low fertility and mortality rates.

Social history has also looked to the family for answers to questions related to the demographic history of Japan. Why did Japan's population—which doubled in size in the 17th century—stop growing in the 18th century? What changes in the behavior of Japanese families account for the different growth rates in these two periods? Such questions can also be designed to compare demographic trends in different parts of the world. For example, in most parts of the world, population began to grow more rapidly than ever before in the 18th century. Why was Japan different?

It is generally accepted that Japan's population grew in the 17th century because of an increase in the proportion of women who married and had children. Land reclamation projects doubled the amount of land under cultivation in the 1600s, and with more land available, more people married at an earlier age and formed new households. By the 18th century, opportunities for reclaiming additional land and for establishing new households were greatly reduced. Consequently, the 17th century witnessed a transition from large, extended families that typically included several generations and a number of unmarried siblings, to small, nuclear families in which one offspring inherited the property and siblings left the household to seek employment elsewhere. The consequences of this transition were a decline in the size of family holdings and in the size of the families that cultivated them.

Once this transition took place, average family size remained small and Japan's population stopped growing. But social historians do not agree on the reasons for this stationary, or stagnant, population. Some argue that war, famine, and disease produced mortality crises; others claim that Japanese families limited the size of their families—primarily through abortion and infanticide—to adjust to the shortage of cultivated land. The former claim that high and fluctuating mortality rates demonstrate Malthusian "positive" checks to population growth; the latter argue that low fertility—Malthusian "preventive" checks—prevented population growth in 18th-century Japan.

These different theories suggest two different prototypes for the preindustrial Japanese family. Positive checks suggest that the Japanese family was small and had great difficulty reproducing itself because it was poor and beset by periodic catastrophe. Preventive checks suggest that the small size of the Japanese family was a matter of choice: families limited the number of their offspring so as to maintain or improve their standard of living on smaller plots of land.

This controversy is unlikely to be resolved by further study of Japan's preindustrial population registers. Good vital statistics—birth and death records—are essential to show levels and trends of mortality and fertility. Buddhist temple death records suggest that both mortality and fertility were high in preindustrial Japan, and that child survival rates were as low as 500 per 1,000; but the records do not specify causation. These records also show that child mortality fell in the last quarter of the 19th century, allowing many more children to live to reproductive age.

Research on the demographic history of 20th-century Japan has been helpful in determining the timing of the demographic transition in Japan. National death data, available after 1899, and modern census data, available after 1920, show a long, slow decline in mortality rates after the beginning of the century. In the 1980s Japan achieved the world's longest life expectancy and the lowest infant and maternal mortality rates. These studies of family and demographic history make it clear that Japan's modern demographic transition—from high to low fertility and mortality rates—did not occur before the 20th century. Here, as in the case of the 18th century, Japan invites comparative analysis to the benefit of social history generally. (*See also* Demographic Transition; Demography; Extended Family; Family)

Ann Bowman Jannetta

REFERENCES

Hanley, Susan B., and Kozo Yamamura. *Economic and Demographic Change in Pre-industrial Japan, 1600–1868.* Princeton, NJ: Princeton University Press, 1977.

Jannetta, Ann Bowman. *Epidemics and Mortality in Early Modern Japan.* Princeton, NJ: Princeton University Press, 1987.

Jannetta, Ann B., and Samuel H. Preston. "Two Centuries of Mortality Change in Central Japan: The Evidence from a Temple Death Register," *Population Studies*, 45 (1991): 417-436.

Smith, Thomas C. *Nakahara: Family Farming and Population in a Japanese Village, 1717–1830.* Stanford, CA: Stanford University Press, 1977.

Taeuber, Irene. *The Population of Japan.* Princeton, NJ: Princeton University Press, 1958.

Japanese Industrialization

Industrialization began in Britain in the 18th century as a system of economic production that arose out of and harnessed new scientific knowledge and technical expertise to reduce real costs and increase output. Relying on new power-driven mechanical devices and increasingly specialized labor, Britain's economy grew dramatically, which quickly propelled it to a position of world leadership. Japan experienced industrialization later. It was not until the late 19th century that it would begin a process of sustained industrial development. Unlike Britain, which began to industrialize to meet internal needs, Japan's industrialization began substantially in response to external threats. First Britain and then other powers sought to expand into the Asian region in the middle of the 19th century. Following the Meiji Restoration of 1868, a new Japanese state sought to reshape Japanese life to meet this threat to the nation's economic and political independence.

The external impetus for Japanese industrialization has led to an important and continuing debate about the country's industrial development. On one side are those who take the position that Japanese industrialization was a state-led phenomenon. They point to vigorous state promotion of industry, the government role in establishing model plants in a variety of sectors of both light and heavy industry, and the essential task of acquiring new technology and skills by government hiring of foreign engineers and its sending Japanese abroad. On the other side are those who argue that despite the visibility of government activities in the early years of the Meiji period (1868–1912), it was not until the government sold off its model plants in the 1880s and took a back seat in the arena of economic development that industrialization truly began. Moreover, they say, in a number of key areas such as banking and mining the government role had always been negligible. Thus, the role of private capital, according to this line of argument, was most crucial in pushing Japan onto the path of sustained and sustainable industrialization.

Despite the vigor of this debate the fact remains that the role of the state was demonstrably more important in Japan than it had been in early developing nations such as Britain or the United States. It played the usual state role of establishing financial infrastructure by creating a sound national banking system and bringing into being stable, convertible currency. But, unlike the United States, for example, the Japanese government also took the early lead in establishing national transport and communication networks in the early 1870s. Moreover, the creation of numerous model plants, however unprofitable they may have been, brought important changes to the Japanese economy and society.

One of these changes was that they drew their employees from the rural countryside, transforming both the community and the meaning of work. Initially, firms sought workers from the immediate environs of the plants, but this soon proved impracticable. They began recruiting workers more widely, a pattern most prevalent in the textile industry, which from the 1880s onward recruited its young female work force mainly from among rural peasant families. Another role of the model plants as well as the later naval dockyards, military arsenals, and other government-controlled industries was that they acted as technological leaders. Machinery and techniques in these government enterprises were subsequently exploited by private capital, and in so doing served to dramatically expand the nation's industrial bases.

The emergence and growth of industries using modern technologies and systems of organization were crucial to the long-term development of Japan. Yet, up to about 1910 Japan's economy continued to be dominated by traditional forms of production; agriculture, traditional industry, and service all continued to be a major part of Japan's economic output. In the 1880s, for example, more than half of Japan's cotton yarn and raw silk were still being produced by farmers as agricultural by-employment. As late as 1910, 87 percent of cotton looms remained hand powered, and the bulk of cotton production continued to be a product of cottage industry. The same persistence of traditionalist methods could be found in the production of ceramics and paper as well as in more modern products such as matches and buttons.

As a result of this persistence, Japan's industrialization was characterized by economic dualism; both modern and traditionalist sectors grew together. The modern sector, built on the foundation of the model government plants (sold to private businessmen in the 1880s), was well financed and technologically sophisticated. By the 20th century, workers in this sector were the best educated and best paid. The modern sector came to be dominated by major financial cartels (*zaibatsu*), such as Mitsui, Mitsubishi, and Sumitomo, which wielded extraordinary economic and political influence. By contrast, the traditional sector was characterized by small-scale, poorly financed producers and extensive reliance on young, female workers. In this sector relative labor intensity rather than capital investment was the source of production growth. This dualism remained an important component of Japanese industrialization and in many ways is still felt in the relationship between major firms (e.g., Toyota) and the numerous small subcontracting companies dependent upon them.

Japan's industrialization, while beginning relatively late, developed rapidly. Within one generation the country transformed itself from a potential colonial holding of European imperialist powers to a great power itself. At the same time, the strategic importance given to industrialization and the very speed of industrial development brought marked divisions to Japanese economy and society. Fierce and persistent inequalities between large and small firms, the workers in those sectors, as well as between male and female workers or urban and rural communities were important features of Japanese industrial development. Thus, the goals of the Meiji state leaders were realized, but not without substantial social cost.

The social history of Japanese industrialization has not been studied as extensively as for Europe, Russia, or the United States. Considerable attention has been given to labor force development, including the employment of women, and to the emergence of distinctive labor policies in Japanese firms. Opportunities for additional study of protest, impact on family life, work values, and the like remain considerable. (*See also* Industrialization; Japanese Labor Relations)

W. Dean Kinzley

REFERENCES

Hirschmeier, Johannes, and Yui Tsunehiko. *The Development of Japanese Business, 1600–1980*. London: Allen & Unwin, 1981.

Gordon, Andrew. *The Evolution of Labor Relations in Japan*. Cambridge, MA: Harvard University Press, 1985.

Lockwood, William. *The Economic Development of Japan: Growth and Structural Change, 1868–1938*, expanded ed. Princeton, NJ: Princeton University Press, 1968.

Patrick, Hugh, ed. *Japanese Industrialization and Its Social Consequences*. Seattle: University of Washington Press, 1973.

Smith, Thomas C. *Political Change and Industrial Development in Japan: Governmental Enterprise, 1868–1880*. Stanford, CA: Stanford University Press, 1955.

Yamamura, Kozo. *A Study of Samurai Income and Entrepreneurship*. Cambridge: Harvard University Press, 1974.

Japanese Labor Relations

The main elements of the relationship between Japanese managers and workers are sufficiently distinctive that they are often referred to collectively as the Japanese Employment System. The central components of this system include, first, the idea of "permanent employment." Workers in Japanese firms enjoy an employment status characterized by an unusual degree of equality with management and considerable job security. Employers go to great lengths to avoid layoffs, and firing is not regarded as a legitimate option. Second, is the practice of so-called seniority-based wages and promotions. Pay reflects company-specific factors such as a worker's seniority and rank within the firm, features unconnected to skill levels or performance. The emphasis on seniority reinforces tendencies toward long-term employment. Such tendencies are encouraged still further by extensive, nontransferable, company welfare programs that include insurance benefits, subsidized housing or housing loans, and numerous company-sponsored leisure activities. Finally, Japan's labor-management relationship is notable for the presence of weak, company-based unions. In general, these unions are uninterested in conflict with management and prefer instead to work with it to insure long-term company stability. Behavior of this sort is rational when union members expect to remain with their employer over their working lives.

This system is not as generally practiced as it is often made to seem, and it did not develop immediately as Japan industrialized. Its emergence requires careful historical attention. The universe of workers eligible for permanent employment and the benefits it entails are limited to a narrowly constructed group of regular workers. Managers can, and frequently do, cut back on employment rolls and company welfare payments. But the victims of these cuts are nonregular, temporary workers or subcontractors. In addition, the system's elements have only come together in their current form in the years since World War II. The system is, indeed, a relatively recent creation.

During the early years of Japan's industrial development labor relations took one of two very different forms. The most notorious was found in the textile industry, the nation's most important through the 1930s. Textile mills hired in the main young girls from rural farm households on a short-term contract basis. Girls' salaries often were paid in advance to their families. This kind of employment by the 1880s had become little more than a form of indenture servitude. Conditions in the mills were dreadful, which encouraged the girls to flee in large numbers, leading textile companies to erect closed company dormitories, and to exercise close control over the girls, thereby worsening conditions still further. This employment pattern persisted through the 1920s, when it slowly began to give way. The other employment pattern emerged in heavier industries such as in the naval dockyards, arsenals, or steel mills. In such industries plant managers had only indirect control over the company's labor force. Direct control was in the hands of labor bosses, independent labor contractors who hired their work gangs out to specific companies. Company managers were held hostage to a labor market characterized by extreme shortages of workers with skills necessary for modern heavy industry. By the early years of the 20th century managers established internal skill training programs and bypassed labor bosses using newly established personnel departments. Therefore, as in the textile industry, managers moved to reduce labor mobility by seizing direct control over workers and their working lives.

Yet, still nothing like permanent employment or seniority wages existed. Managers dismissed workers with impunity when profit considerations demanded. Pay was most commonly determined by complex calculations of piecework or output wage formulae. However, companies did begin to establish a number of company-specific welfare programs as a means of retain-

ing skilled workers. As important, employers began to stress quasi-familial values in Japanese employment relationships. This emphasis on corporate paternalism was intended to justify managerial control as well as act as a defense against growing labor activism. Workers no less than managers were interested in stability and predictability. In numerous heavy industry plants workers and their representatives sought a greater emphasis on seniority and a commensurate reduction in efficiency-based wage calculations. During the depression years of the late 1920s and 1930s worker activism took the form of demands for employment security. It was only in the years after World War II, however, that these objectives gradually came to be achieved. Under the pressure of unions strengthened by United States occupation policy, most important Japanese firms began to move toward systems of permanent employment and seniority wages. Employers recognized that such a system had become the means to realize their long sought goal of reduced labor mobility and corporate stability.

Over the post–World War II period unions developed an increasingly symbiotic relationship with management as the Japanese Employment System became institutionalized. It is worth noting, however, that this system came into being and has been sustained during a period of extraordinary and continuous growth. As Japanese economic growth rates decline in the 1990s there is increasing pressure on the system. Japanese labor relations are entering a period of new uncertainty. (*See also* Japanese Industrialization)

W. Dean Kinzley

REFERENCES

Gordon, Andrew. *The Evolution of Labor Relations in Japan: Heavy Industry, 1853–1955.* Cambridge: Harvard East Asian Monographs, 1985.

Kinzley, W. Dean. *Industrial Harmony in Modern Japan: The Invention of a Tradition.* London and New York: Routledge Press, 1991.

Okochi, Kazuo, Bernard Karsh, and Solomon B. Levine, eds. *Workers and Employers in Japan: The Japanese Employment Relations System.* Princeton, NJ: Princeton University Press, 1974.

Taira, Koji. *Economic Development and the Labor Market in Japan.* New York: Columbia University Press, 1970.

Japanese Popular Protest

Japan has a long history of popular protest movements and uprisings, dating back at least six centuries to the *tsuchi ikki*, or land uprisings, of the 14th century and continuing in the 1990s with the farmers' league to protect its members' land by blocking expansion of Tokyo's new international airport. It is difficult to find common threads running through all these activities, but most historians think that the uprisings challenged the authority of the established powers of their time, and many believe that the participants, at least after 1750, showed protorevolutionary or revolutionary motives for their actions. Protest incidents and movements can be broadly divided into four periods: Muromachi and early Tokugawa (1350–1750), late Tokugawa–early Meiji (1750–1900), prewar modern (1900–1940), and post–World War II (1945–). While protests have been studied primarily as a leading feature of Japanese social history, Western and Japanese scholars have also related them to wider theories of protest and social change.

Muromachi–early Tokugawa Period. Between 1350 and 1500, a number of *tsuchi ikki* took place. One of them in 1441 enlisted tens of thousands of peasants, who demanded reductions of taxes or corvée or a cancellation of debts. In the late 15th and 16th centuries these were followed by the famous *ikkōikki*, or single-minded uprisings, of members of the True Pure Land Sect of Buddhism, who resisted the efforts of various *daimyō* generals to bring autonomous religious communities under warrior control. In 1637–1638, over-taxed peasants and masterless samurai in Shimabara, a domain near Nagasaki, inspired by an unorthodox Christian chiliasm, rose against the feudal authorities. The shogun sent massive forces against the rebels' stronghold and slaughtered 37,000 men, women, and children in the besieged castle. The Buddhist and Christian uprisings, because they challenged the idea of warrior rule, were particularly dangerous to the feudal authorities.

Late Tokugawa–Early Meiji Period. In the early Tokugawa period, a new form of uprising, *hyakushō ikki*, or farmers' uprisings, appeared. Although the *ikki* of the 1650–1750 period were initiated by the village elite, usually to protest some kind of samurai burden like high taxes or excessive forced labor, and were generally moderate in character, the post-1750 *ikki* took a new form. They were violent, involved thousands of peasants from many villages, and were instigated by poor peasants who challenged the authority of the local ruling elites. These *ikki* also tended to occur frequently and intensely in highly commercial districts. Marxist scholars see in these disputes the seeds of peasant class-consciousness, resistance to the spread of a market economy, and protorevolutionary motivations.

At the same time, urban riots, called *uchikowashi*, or destroyings, in which angry mobs attacked the storehouses of rice merchants and pawnbrokers, made their appearance. As the Tokugawa period ended, popular protests like the *yonaoshi ikki*, or world renewing uprisings, in the countryside and *eejanaika*, or "It's okay, isn't it?" mass outbreaks, in the city reached new heights. Although it is difficult to ascertain the importance of this rural and urban unrest in the samurai revolution that overthrew the Tokugawa regime in 1868, peasant uprisings did not end with the Meiji Restoration. In the 1870s, as the new government established conscription and introduced a new land tax system that eliminated regional inequities (thus lowering taxes in some areas, but raising them in others), anticonscription and antitax *ikki* erupted.

Prewar Modern Period. The 20th century introduced a new element to popular protest: an increasingly prosperous, educated, literate, cosmopolitan, and politically active public. The Hibiya Incident of 1905, a mass rally in Tokyo to protest Japan's acquiescence in the seemingly insulting terms of the treaty to end the Russo-Japanese War that turned into a riot, marks the first major protest by a public informed by mass media. The Rice Riots of July–September 1918, which took place during the rampant inflation of the closing years of World War I, lifted the scale of protest to a new level. Over one million people took part in violent outbreaks and the government mobilized 92,000 soldiers to suppress the riots. Japanese scholars see the Rice Riots as an indication of the revolutionary potential, unfortunately in 1918 unfocused, of the Japanese masses.

Thousands of strikes for better wages and working conditions and tenancy disputes for lower rents and better contract terms occurred in the 1920s and 1930s. To many Japanese scholars, these two movements were potentially revolutionary, but in the end were turned toward reformism and eventually fascism by the government's skillful use of "the carrot and the stick," that is, through inducement and repression. The debate over whether these strikes and disputes were revolutionary or not is complicated by the role of prewar left-wing intellectuals, the intellectual ancestors of the contemporary historians, in leading them. Revolutionary socialists and members of the fledgling Japan Communist Party often staffed the national offices of labor and tenant farmer unions. Thus, scholars debate whether the views of these national leaders were indicative of the views of the rank and file; whether or not the central leaders were revolutionaries while the local members were reformists using the unions to better their conditions bit by bit; whether the government subverted a revolutionary movement or recognized the reformist nature of the rank-and-file members and, by making concessions to them, divided them from the revolutionaries at the center.

Post–World War II Period. Whatever the role of the left in guiding interwar protest, it has played a leading part since World War II. The major protest movements—labor opposition to the occupation authorities and the Japanese government in the late 1940s, the opposition to the United States–Japan Security Treaty in 1959–1960, the student protests of 1968–1969, and more recently, the battle against the building and then the extension of Tokyo's airport at Narita—have all been violent and all received leadership or support from the Communist and Socialist parties, both of whom are out of power. Thus, although these protest movements were not successful in achieving their goals, they moderated the policies of the Liberal Democratic Party, the conservative party that ruled Japan since the 1950s. The confrontational unions of the occupation years were replaced by cooperative unions. The student protests of the late 1960s ended with factional infighting, and mounting public opposition. In sum, it seems that political protest in the 20th century was most successful

when it was nonviolent and aimed at achieving incremental rather than systemic changes.

Debate over the causes and significance of protest form a vigorous part of Japanese social history, as in interpreting the severity of riots in later Tokugawa Japan or in debating the degree to which early 20th-century food riots were spontaneous or planned and focused on some achievable goal. Some of these debates involve wider themes in protest analysis such as the moral economy concept, though historical writing about Japanese protest movements has not yet shown a significant comparative dimension. (*See also* Chinese Social Protest; Marxist Historiography; Moral Economy; Peasant Rebellion; Rural Labor and Agricultural Protest)

Richard J. Smethurst

REFERENCES

Gordon, Andrew. *Labor and Imperial Democracy in Prewar Japan.* Berkeley: University of California Press, 1991.

Nakamura, Masanori. *Workers and Farmers* (in Japanese). Tokyo: Shogakkan, 1976.

Smethurst, Richard J. *Agricultural Development and Tenancy Disputes in Japan, 1870–1940.* Princeton, NJ: Princeton University Press, 1986.

Vlastos, Stephen. *Peasant Protests and Uprisings in Tokugawa Japan.* Berkeley: University of California Press, 1986.

Japanese Religions, Mentalities

It is not uncommon to hear that Japanese are not religious and that religion no longer exists in Japan. When discussed along Western conceptional lines, where religion is defined as a belief-framed system wherein one tradition stands in sharp opposition to another, this assessment may have some merit. However, it inappropriately frames the issue, speaking neither to the Japanese worldview nor to behaviors stemming from it. Rather, the comfort level with which the Japanese speak in a collective voice itself reflects a Japanese worldview that is at the same time syncretic and nationalistic, and implies an attitude toward religion or, more rightly, religiosity, that is better expressed in actions that are consciously and unconsciously interwoven with the social, cultural, political, and personal fabric of the Japanese. Framed within the Japanese context, the question then becomes how the religious dimension, which works in tandem with the social dimension, is expressed in terms of actions and feelings.

In a society that tends to define people in terms of social and group identity, religious activities serve to instill a sense of belonging to the family, community, company or other organization, and nation. That is not to say that individual needs and aspirations are ignored, but rather that the ideals of social harmony and reciprocity, expressed through an exchange of obligation and gratitude, assume that self-benefit is best sought through socially responsible behavior—toward the living, the dead, and the supernatural.

Japanese religion then is oriented toward action, custom, and etiquette performed with a mind of sincerity. It emphasizes happiness in this life, and it is situational—providing psychological assistance through the stages of life and personal crisis, while integrating the individual into the social structure. In a world seen as fundamentally benevolent and infused with sacrality, and where such problems as discord, tragedy, physical and emotional illness, and unnatural and premature death are seen as consequences of neglect of one's obligations, purifying rituals and ceremonies are of utmost importance.

This syncretic worldview, which serves as the frame of reference for the various indigenous and imported religious traditions, results in a kind of religious division of labor, reflected in the expression "Born Shinto, die Buddhist," and borne out by the multiple nature of religious affiliations.

Thus Shinto, with its powers of renewal and deities that give life to and protect the Japanese and their land, presides over the celebratory experiences of life. In gratitude, newborns are introduced as members of the Japanese community to the indigenous Shinto tutelary deities. These ties are reestablished at various transitional periods during the life cycle and religious calendar year, such as on coming-of-age, marriage, and the seasonal renewal of the new year, when all over Japan, houses are cleaned, debts paid, old ties renewed, families united, and shrine visits made to pray for continued good fortune in the coming year. Even the well-known Japanese custom of gift-giving is rooted in the idea of the creation and repayment of obligations that characterizes the relationship between the Japanese and their deities, while reaffirming social cohesion and unity.

Buddhism, with its laws of causation and karmic retribution, primarily deals with the polluting elements of death, the memorialization of the dead, and ancestor worship, which presupposes a reciprocal relationship between the happiness of the dead as dependent upon actions taken by the living and the return of favors by the ancestors who continue to act as protectors and guardians of the family. In an ethical system based upon filial piety, malevolent spirits, souls of those who have no one to venerate them, and those who suffer untimely deaths, including aborted fetuses, are of particular concern. Buddhist rituals concerning the proper care of the dead include burial, periodic visits to ancestral graves, and placement of memorial tablets in the family altar. The near-universal participation in the mid-summer festival of the dead, when Japanese traditionally return to their ancestral villages and visit the family grave and temple, not only ensures the status of Buddhism within Japanese society but reaffirms the family as the primary religious unit.

Even the new religions and beliefs of the late 19th and 20th centuries, which uphold the traditional ideals of social harmony and reciprocity while empowering lay membership with healing abilities traditionally left to the clergy, often encourage participation in Shinto and Buddhist social and familial ritual.

On the popular level, religion takes on a kind of "try it and see" or "cover one's bets" pragmatism, equally rooted in the belief that physical and emotional well-being is contingent upon spiritual cooperation. Japanese pray for good fortune or turn to the new religions at specific times of personal and cyclical crisis and transition, buy amulets to ward off evil and talisman of good luck to guarantee safety on the road, tranquility at home, a safe childbirth, success at school, and the like, consult diviners and shaman, check almanacs to assure the most auspicious time to begin a new venture, avoid unlucky numbers and behaviors associated with death rituals, use salt, water, and *sake* as purifying agents, and participate in pilgrimages to holy sites and in local shrine and temple festivals. This animistic worldview also insists that one consecrate the ground before building a new structure, bless one's automobile, and hold memorial services for animals and inanimate things used in the service of humankind.

Examined over the course of Japanese social history, the various religious traditions, both individually and combined, have grown and changed and have contributed to the development of Japanese mentalities. Buddhism and other religious traditions, such as Confucianism, introduced into the Japanese court from the Asian continent in the 6th century AD and spreading through all strata of Japanese society by the medieval period played an important role in the development of Japanese political, group, and family organization. These ultimately provided the structure for feudal loyalties, the samurai code of ethics, and the apprenticeship system in Japan, and continued to influence the now famous Japanese work ethic and emphasis on education. Traditional folk and Shinto mythologies served as the basis for the rise of State Shinto in the early part of this century, and contributed to the attitudes of the Japanese during World War II. During the past century and a quarter, traditional folk, Shinto, Taoist, and Buddhist beliefs and practices have colored the Japanese approach to more modern beliefs, such as nationalism and science. This evolution of popular uses of basic beliefs, often with encouragement from above, sets a basic framework for Japanese social history.

Japanese religiosity, which has its roots in Japanese folk traditions, continues to be effective despite—and indeed because of—rapid contemporary social and demographic changes and the resulting "crisis in representation" inherent in the internationalization of Japan. It provides a social, ethical, cosmological, and national sense of identity from which the Japanese can then confidently move and function within a changing world, and finds expression in the recent "nostalgia boom," an idealized look back to and a periodic participation in a more simple, more "Japanese" way of life. (*See also* Ancestor Wor-ship; Animism; Buddhism; Festivals; Japanese Family/Demography; Magic)

Linda Penkower

REFERENCES

Davis, Winston. *Japanese Religion and Society: Paradigms of Structure and Change.* Albany: State University of New York Press, 1992.

Hori Ichiro. *Folk Religion in Japan: Continuity and Change.* Chicago: University of Chicago Press, 1968; Chicago: Midway reprint, 1983.

Kitagawa, Joseph M. *Religion in Japanese History.* New York: Columbia University Press, 1966.

Reader, Ian. *Religion in Contemporary Japan.* Honolulu: University of Hawaii Press, 1991.

Smith, Robert. *Ancestor Worship in Contemporary Japan.* Stanford, CA: Stanford University Press, 1974.

Japanese Wet Rice Economy

Japan's rice-based agriculture has been studied from several social history vantage points. It forms a significant illustration of links between agricultural specialization and both social class and family relationships, amid changes in larger social and economic structures.

The first records of "The Land of Abundant Rice" appear in the *Kojiki* and *Nihon Shoki*, which date to AD 712 and 720, respectively. These texts record the Shinto creation myth, which portrays the emperor as the embodiment of the God of the Ripened Rice Plant, a relative of the Sun Goddess. Each emperor annually plants and harvests by hand a small plot of rice. This rice is ritually offered to the gods at the Shinto shrine at festivals. This harvest ritual is celebrated at local shrines throughout Japan as farmers offer part of their autumn rice harvest to the gods. Despite the decrease in per capita rice consumption from over 160 kilograms per year in 1940 to only 71 kilograms in 1990, rice has maintained symbolic dominance in varied forms. These include drinking of rice wine *sake* in Shinto wedding ceremonies and eating of glutinous rice on ceremonial occasions such as New Year's.

Though rice dates to around 1000 BC and played a central role in the development of the first Japanese state, most research has focused on the recent feudal and modern periods. During the Tokugawa period (1600–1868) 276 feudal lords were ranked according to the rice production capacity of their fiefs. Retainers and samurai received earnings in both rice and money and oversaw land in the fiefs. At the beginning of this period the shogun took each lord's family hostage in Edo (now Tokyo), forcing these lords to maintain mansions for their families. In order to buy precious goods for these mansions, the lords had to exchange their tax rice for money, thus providing the opportunity for the Osaka merchant class to profit on the rice exchange. By the mid-1700s feudal lords had become heavily indebted to expanding capitalist institutions, which provided banking, coastal shipping, and mercantile trade services to the most remote parts of Japan.

Research on the feudal period has focused on the extent of economic growth and whether the lords were benevolent or oppressive to the peasants. Growth proponents have emphasized a total rice and economic production outpacing a limited population growth. The opposing view has concentrated on the moral and political economy of inequality by challenging the Confucian ideology of benevolence, consensus, and harmony and emphasizing forms of oppression and acts of resistance such as open protests, petitions, and flight. Such studies have revealed the need for a more critical description of usufruct and private property land rights and upstream-downstream water control. Also central to the debate is the extent local lords and peasants cooperated or whether lords coerced peasants into improving irrigation and drainage facilities and reclaiming swampland into paddies. Because of significant regional variation in both fief administration and cultural practices, only local case studies will be able to resolve these issues.

In the modern period, with the development of industry and wage labor, the above debate is further complicated by the question of whether the institution of the household (called *ie*) will collapse. A household traditionally preserved its collective resources such as rice paddies through a single heir who inherited these assets and took on the responsibility of maintaining the Buddhist altar in the home and grave site at the temple. This single heir became household head,

and through the 1898 Meiji Civil Code had authority over individuals recorded in a household registry system.

Western modernization theory predicted that the household would be a constraining factor in modernization, and that as Japan industrialized and individualized wage labor and market-oriented nuclear families became common, people would migrate to the cities for jobs and the *ie* as an institution would collapse. This idea was further strengthened by the 1873 Meiji Land Tax, which conferred land titles, land tax, and suffrage rights to individual males, and the 1948 Civil Code that abolished the title of household head and legalized equal heir inheritance.

Other researchers have stressed that the *ie* is more flexible and has merely changed form. These researchers caution that the trend toward fewer household members and nuclear families was not accompanied by a change in the succession or inheritance system. To the contrary, these scholars argue that the tax code waiver on the inheritance tax for single-heir succession and inheritance perpetuated the *ie*. They argue that the household resource base increased because the Land Reform of 1946 redistributed land to landless tenants and land prices skyrocketed due to the new demand created by the decentralization of industry into rural areas after 1970. Also, household members earned more off-farm than on-farm income because farm mechanization in the 1960s halved the time necessary to grow rice.

The ruling party maintained a rural power base through giving rural areas superior representation in the powerful lower house of the Diet and kept rural household income at parity with its urban counterpart. Over 15 percent of the population still farmed in 1990 as a result of the combined off-farm job opportunities, high rice price subsidies, rice import restrictions, and paddy infrastructural projects. (*See also* Japanese Family/Demography; Japanese Popular Protest)

Richard H. Moore

REFERENCES

Bix, Herbert. *Peasant Protest in Japan, 1590–1884.* New Haven: Yale University Press, 1986.

Fukutake, Tadashi. *Rural Society in Japan.* Tokyo: University of Tokyo Press, 1980.

Hanley, Susan, and Kozo Yamamura. *Economic and Demographic Change in Premodern Japan, 1600–*

1868. Princeton, NJ: Princeton University Press, 1977.

Smith, Thomas C. *Agrarian Origins of Modern Japan*. Stanford, CA: Stanford University Press, 1959.

Jews

Jewish history has a long pedigree. Before the rise of social history, the history of Jews focused heavily on issues of doctrine and political status. New facets of Jewish history have been explored in recent decades along with older themes and along with studies of the rise of modern anti-Semitism and the Nazi Holocaust. A social history of the Jews is developing concerning premodern patterns—finding some interesting parallels in ritual behaviors between Jews and non-Jews in early modern Europe, for example. Most social history of Jews explores their experiences in the modern period throughout Western and Eastern Europe as well as the United States.

One critical aspect of European Jewish history since the 18th century has been the encounter with modernity. Modernity confronted Jewry with the promise, if not the reality, of civil and political emancipation and challenged it to enter the social, cultural, economic, and political mainstream. The lure of participating on an equal footing with Gentiles as a minority group defined only in confessional terms in the emerging, centralizing nation-states of Europe helped undermine traditional Jewish society, which had been characterized by the domination of rabbinic Judaism and the right of Jewish communities to conduct their own affairs in accordance with Jewish law. The transformation of European Jewry entailed the reformulation of Jewish identity on both an individual and group basis, religious reform, and the adoption of new (generally non-Jewish) values and patterns of behavior in a Europe undergoing secularization, the collapse of corporate orders, the emergence of industrial society, and the spread of rights of citizenship.

Traditional historiography on the emancipation of European Jewry focuses on two key themes: the change in the legal and political status of Jews, a process begun in the late 18th century with the emancipation of French Jewry, and the intellectual response of Jews to modernity that sought to reassess the nature of Jewish life and Judaism (most commonly associated with Moses Mendelssohn and the *Haskalah*—Jewish Enlightenment—in German-speaking central Europe). By rooting out those practices and customs that they believed impeded the incorporation of Jews into European state and society, proponents of the *Haskalah* (known as *maskilim*) hoped to advance the cause of emancipation. Indeed, the German-Jewish experience has been accepted until recently as paradigmatic for the reception of modernity by European Jewry: self-imposed change in the religious, educational, and cultural ways of Jews was a conscious strategy of restructuring Jewish life in order to foster acceptance by non-Jewish states and societies.

In recent years many historians of European Jewry have begun to turn away from the emphasis on the ideological component of emancipation and have started addressing the importance of social change in understanding European Jewry's reaction to modernity. Rather than examine the intellectual reorientation of educated Jewish elites, these historians have concluded that the path toward emancipation as espoused by the *maskilim* was less typical of the European Jewish experience than was the process of acculturation, which frequently occurred before and sometimes in the absence of ideological justification and the granting of legal equality.

The case of English Jewry in the 18th century best illustrates how a social history methodology, with its emphasis on individuals and groups accommodating changing social and economic circumstances, can expand our understanding of the transformation of traditional Jewish society. Todd Endelman's *The Jews of Georgian England, 1714–1830: Tradition and Change in a Liberal Society* (Philadelphia, 1979) reveals that English Jewry adopted the manners and habits of English society and jettisoned much of Jewish tradition for reasons other than ideological commitment to the *Haskalah* or the granting of legal and political equality. Instead the acculturation and integration of English Jews, who became lax in religious practice, shaved their beards, and emulated the social and cultural trappings of Gentile society, occurred as a result of the Jewish-Gentile encounter and Anglo-Jewry's recognition of the benefits of non-Jewish culture and society. In England the *Haskalah* did not strike roots, and Anglo-Jewry thus put the cause of political equality on the back burner until it had achieved a high degree of acculturation and acceptance not found on the Continent.

According to Endelman and others who share his approach to the study of European Jewry, the complex and diverse history of traditional Jewry's response to modernity throughout Europe has been obscured by a focus on intellectual trends. While the *Haskalah* was undoubtedly an important phenomenon in many European Jewish communities, particularly in German-speaking Europe, it is not the only factor explaining the transformation of European Jewry. The singular experience of Anglo-Jewry holds the key to the further understanding of European Jewry's adjustment to the modern world, and the task of future historians is to study how acculturation occurred along with the intellectual reorientation that was taking root among many Jews outside England.

The social historical approach has prompted researchers to complement the traditional historiography with studies that probe a wealth of heretofore unmined statistical, journalistic, and other sources. Their purpose involves analyzing not only the articulated sentiments of the Jewish elite as it adjusted to the pressures of emancipation but also the response of once-ignored ordinary Jews to the broad socioeconomic and political changes that have occurred in Europe since the 18th century. The specific manner in which European Jews met the challenge of emancipation, secularization, urbanization, and industrialization varied from state to state and even from region to region within states, from one social class to another, and between men and women. The responses were shaped in large measure by the particular characteristics of the surrounding host society and the Jews themselves. These historians are concerned with understanding the new social and cultural interactions between Jews and Gentiles brought about by these changes and have been careful to underscore both the continuities and discontinuities within the Jewish community. They are providing the building blocks for a history of European Jewry that would

be comparative in scope, inclusive of all strata of Jewish society, attentive to the variable pace and timing of the transformation of traditional Jewish society, as well as focus on the internal development of the Jewish community. A social history of European Jewry can offer general insights into the processes of social, political, and economic change among ethnoreligious minorities.

The sociohistorical approach to Jewish history forms an important part also of United States immigration history, where issues of change in family patterns (for example, an early conversion of Jewish immigrants to low birth rates) as well as economic and religious outlook have great importance for the history of the Jewish experience and the United States more generally. (*See also* Assimilation/Acculturation; Ethnicity; Immigration)

Robert Weinberg

REFERENCES

Frankel, Jonathan, and Steven J. Zipperstein, eds. *Assimilation and Community: The Jews in Nineteenth-Century Europe.* New York: Cambridge University Press, 1991.

Hertz, Deborah. *Jewish High Society in Old Regime Berlin.* New Haven: Yale University Press, 1988.

Hyman, Paula. *The Emancipation of the Jews of Alsace: Acculturation and Tradition in the Nineteenth Century.* New Haven: Yale University Press, 1991.

Kaplan, Marion A. *The Making of the Jewish Middle Class: Women, Family, and Identity in Imperial Germany.* New York: Oxford University Press, 1991.

Rozenblit, Marsha J. *The Jews of Vienna, 1867–1914: Assimilation and Identity.* Albany: State University Press of New York, 1983.

Zipperstein, Steven J. *The Jews of Odessa: A Cultural History, 1794-1881.* Stanford, CA: Stanford University Press, 1985.

Jihad

Jihad is the Arabic noun meaning "striving" or "combatting" and is used by Muslims discussing efforts to support the good and oppose evil. Although jihad is used to refer to military combat, it also relates to personal struggles to live a righteous life. Ascetics and mystics, or Sufis, traditionally refer to the "greater jihad" as being the spiritual purification of personal and social life.

The foundations of the Islamic concept of jihad are in the Qur'an, where jihad primarily refers to armed struggle. Most references are from the verses revealed after the immigration of the Muslims from Mecca to Medina. In the Medinian period, Muslims created a community of their own and came into conflict with non-Muslim groups. Qur'anic references to jihad helped to define these relationships, with Muslims being obligated to strive "in the path of God." The goal was the expansion of the Muslim community, but non-Muslims who accepted Islamic rule were granted special protection within the Islamic world.

As Islamic law developed in the medieval era, the concept of jihad was part of the definition of the obligations of rulers and international relations. Jihad as armed struggle became defined as a communal rather than an individual obligation. Every individual Muslim was not required to engage in jihad except under extraordinary conditions. Although the ultimate goal was to spread Islam throughout the world, Muslim states could establish truce relationships with non-Muslim states. Scholars elaborated specifics regarding protection of noncombatants, treatment of prisoners of war, and conditions of combat. There was general agreement on most issues among the different schools of law and between Sunni and Shi'i Muslims.

After the first era of conquests, Islamic growth was increasingly the work of wandering teachers and merchants rather than military expansion. Jihad was the mobilizing call for defense of Islamic lands against attack from invaders like the Mongols or the European Crusaders. Jihad was also the rallying cry by radical reformers within Muslim society. Because Muslims are prohibited from fighting other Muslims, if this jihad involved armed struggle, the opponents had to be identified as unbelievers. As a result, labeling someone as an unbeliever became an important issue in the legitimization of jihad as a means for radical social transformation.

In the modern era, many movements of resistance to Western expansion took the form of jihads or were inspired by jihad traditions. In the late 20th century, jihad is an important part of the conceptual framework of Islamic revivalists. The Egyptian ideologue Sayyid Qutb developed an influential interpretation that Muslims were obligated as individuals to undertake jihad against their own governments if their rulers had become unbelievers. Other modern Muslim thinkers have emphasized the defensive character of jihad or have returned to the nonmilitary ideal of the spiritual jihad of individuals and groups.

From the perspective of social history, jihad is important as a major concept defining broad social boundaries. It developed as a societal rather than a state concept, defined by the religious thinkers rather than the political or military leaders. It helped to define appropriate behavior between Muslim and non-Muslim societies as a whole and, in the teachings of both pious mystics and puritanical reformers, is a part of the definition of the boundaries of proper behavior within Muslim societies. (*See also* Islam; Islam [Africa])

John O. Voll

REFERENCES

Khadduri, Majid. *War and Peace in the Law of Islam.* Baltimore: Johns Hopkins University Press, 1955.
Peters, Rudolph. *Jihad in Medieval and Modern Islam.* Leiden: Brill, 1977.

Jim Crow System

Although the term "Jim Crow" first came to public attention in "Jump Jim Crow," a song copyrighted by northern white minstrel performer Thomas "Daddy" Rice in 1828—"My name's Jim Crow, Weel about, and turn about, And do jis so"—by the end of the 19th century it was used to describe legally enforced racial discrimination against blacks.

Racially discriminatory laws were common in the antebellum and immediate post–Civil War North and South, but subsequently increased in number and breadth of coverage in the post-Reconstruction South. Most narrowly defined, Jim Crow laws were those that required segregation on public conveyances and in schools, public accommodations and all other areas where southern whites and blacks might come into contact. In *Plessy* v. *Ferguson* (1896) the United States Supreme Court held that such separation was constitutional as long as both races received equal treatment.

Recently, however, historians have broadened the term's usage to encompass a pattern of post-1890 racial discrimination that included not only legally enforced segregation (which, despite lip service, was inevitably unequal), but disfranchisement, exclusion from juries, antimiscegenation acts, and lynching. Social historians have demonstrated that much of the segregation legislation merely replaced long-standing de facto segregation (segregation by custom) or exclusion with *de jure* segregation (segregation by law), but the other examples of post-1890 discrimination introduced new restrictions on southern blacks. The actions were prompted by growing black assertiveness and political divisions among white southerners that led to race baiting, and facilitated by the withdrawal of northern support for federal intervention to defend black rights.

The Jim Crow system was never complete and therefore was less extensive than South Africa's apartheid system with which it is often simplistically identified. Some blacks retained the vote, legally enforced residential and workplace segregation proved elusive, and blacks and whites continued to mingle in some places of public accommodation.

Jim Crow dominated southern life until the civil rights movement of the 1950s, but it was already under piecemeal attack by the second decade of the 20th century. In *Bailey* v. *Alabama* (1911) the United States Supreme Court challenged the South's system of debt peonage aimed primarily at blacks and in *Buchanan* v. *Warley* (1917) declared unconstitutional legally enforced residential segregation. In *Smith* v. *Allwright* (1944) the Court struck down the white primary as a device to disfranchise black voters, and beginning in the 1940s a series of Court decisions struck at segregation and exclusion in higher education. Meanwhile, southern blacks protested against discrimination at the local level, though initially calling for equal treatment rather than the end of segregation per se.

With the *Brown* v. *Board of Education* decision in 1954, the civil rights movement entered a new phase. The federal government moved to guarantee blacks equal rights partly in response to demands for change from blacks and white

liberals and partly out of concern for world opinion. In the following years the Civil Rights Acts of 1957 and 1964, the Voting Rights Act of 1965 and the 24th Amendment banning the poll tax helped dismantle the South's Jim Crow system.

Racial segregation and discrimination remain serious problems in America today, but they are now de facto rather than *de jure,* and are ironically often more of a problem in the North than in the South.

Howard N. Rabinowitz

REFERENCES

Cell, John W. *The Highest Stage of White Supremacy: The Origins of Segregation in South Africa and the American South.* Cambridge: Cambridge University Press, 1982.

Rabinowitz, Howard N. *Race Relations in the Urban South, 1865–1890.* New York: Oxford University Press, 1978; Champaign: University of Illinois Press, 1980.

Woodward, C. Vann. *The Strange Career of Jim Crow.* New York: Oxford University Press, 1955, 1957, 1966, 1974.

Journals

Books continue to be a major medium for historians communicating their scholarship, in contrast to many social sciences, where journal articles are far more important. Social historians, however, use journals a lot, and several journals were instrumental in establishing the field in general and in identifying key topical segments. Many of these journals continue to provide excellent means of keeping up with the latest developments in social history, though by this point significant articles in social history also appear regularly in standard historical journals and also in outlets in sociology and other areas.

The granddaddy journal in social history was the French *Annales: Economies, sociétés, civilisations.* This was the journal that published basic definitions by Marc Bloch and Lucien Febvre and later the regional "total histories" of Fernand Braudel and his school. It continues to be a vital contributor to the field. Other European nations developed new journals specializing in social history in the decades after World War II, including the German *Vierteljahrshrift fuer Wirtschaft und Sozialgeschichte* and the Italian *Quaderni storici*.

Past and Present, in England, guided a great deal of sociohistorical research, publishing articles by E.P. Thompson, the leader of direct explorations of working-class culture, and Keith Thomas, who helped define the field of mentalities study. More recently, a journal simply called *Social History* has become significant.

Comparative Studies in Society and History led the move toward social history in the journals field in the United States, and it continues to flourish in areas such as peasant studies. The *Journal of Social History*, founded in 1967, claims a leading role in defining a number of topical branches of social history. The *Journal of Interdisciplinary History* and *Social Science History* also publish important works in social history, as does the Canadian *Histoire sociale/Social History*. Journals on special topics (the *Journal of Family History*, the *Journal of Sports History*, and others) also continue to play an important role. (*See also Annales* School)

Peter N. Stearns

Judiciary

Under the ancient Greeks, when popular assemblies guided by magistrates constituted the courts and defendants represented themselves, a few citizens made their political reputations by denouncing crimes and acting as prosecutors or preparing speeches for defendants to recite, but such legal activity was not refined in schools or through apprenticeships, and it did not result in lifelong careers.

Even under the Romans, until the end of the 2nd century AD, jurisprudence remained the province of the politically active nobility. A small number of jurisconsults functioned as the retainers of legal tradition. But with the extension of Roman rule over a vast hinterland, defendants needed representation by agents before distant courts. These procurators were the progenitors of the modern lawyer. Nonetheless, anyone could serve as a procurator for another party, and no professional group existed, though certain persons were appointed with regularity, and some of these came from the ranks of the common people. During the Empire, formal law schools emerged in major cities replacing jurisconsults. Fees were set for stipulated services and professional discipline was provided for. By at least AD 468, advocates had to be admitted to their practices, and the number of practitioners was restricted in some provinces.

Except for clerics, who benefited from receiving formal education and the codification of canon law, the independent practice of civil and criminal law largely disappeared during the Middle Ages. Lawyers reemerged as practitioners in England in the late 13th century; by the middle of the 15th century the English system of justice was fully organized into barristers and attorneys, with legal apprentices learning their craft under masters at the Inns of Court and Chancery. On the Continent, in the 12th century, universities began to teach Roman law, and its practice spread widely among lay courts. During that century, lawyers in Italy began to enter the upper ranks of government.

The total number of lawyers remained quite limited, and the membership was organized into guilds. About 200 civil and canon lawyers practiced in Florence between 1380 and 1530. A significant minority of lawyers in France and Italy came from traditional ruling families, often titled. These people brought status to the profession, which aspired to identification with the nobility and the monarchy throughout Europe. Most other lawyers came from prosperous, established families that usually had made their fortunes in commerce or estate ownership. Yet others were sons of professionals, commonly lawyers, notaries, or government officials. A few were the offspring of physicians. Like members of these other professions, lawyers have historically been urban oriented.

The practice of law does not seem to have been a primary avenue of social mobility in early modern Europe; rather, it provided dignified and useful employment to some sons of already well-to-do families. Most wealthy lawyers seem to have derived their money through inheritance or investments and not as a direct result of their professional activities. Prominent families did not direct their offspring into the legal profession in great numbers; most did not send even a single son; very few sent more than one. The lawyers of colonial Latin America had origins, careers, and wealth closely similar to those of their European counterparts.

Up until at least the 19th century, most lawyers did not aspire to independent practices. They sought instead to represent official agencies and important institutions and organizations. Only the least fortunate were not so affiliated. Legal firms and partnerships largely developed only over the last century and a half. A substantial fraction of trained lawyers have never practiced their profession even in the present day. Earlier, most of these nonpractitioners were children of the wealthy and powerful with an interest in the law but no need to earn a living from this knowledge. In more recent times, people have trained in the law as a path into certain business careers.

Since the emergence of the profession in the late Middle Ages, lawyers have sought to maintain some degree of exclusivity. Through at least the 18th century, they aspired to close association with the nobility and other members of the ruling class in their societies. The long duration and high cost of legal training eliminated many possible students. Further, children of prosperous artisans and shopkeepers who sought to enter the universities or inns faced social ostracism from their teachers and other students. Once graduated, lawyers have typically had to enter guilds or bar associations to obtain authorization to practice. These institutions commonly required letters from people of repute attesting to the applicant's high moral qualities. In Spain and Spanish America, descendants of Jews and Moors were explicitly excluded. In the latter, persons of mixed racial ancestry were also prohibited, though in practice some managed to join.

Over the past two centuries, much of this exclusivity has broken down. In the United States, until the early 20th century law schools had great difficulty establishing their preeminence over the rival tradition of legal apprenticeship. In most of the Western world, higher education, including law school, has become much more accessible to commoners. Social qualifications have been deleted with the result that substantial numbers of women and religious and ethnic minorities have entered the profession. In the United States in the first half of the 20th century, joining the bar constituted a primary avenue of upward mobility for immigrants and their children.

The tradition of independent legal representatives has been weak or nonexistent outside of the Western world. Lawyers emerged in the Middle East and Japan only in the mid-19th century. They have appeared only gradually in China even in the 20th century and developed in Africa as a consequence of European colonization.

In Western history, however, research on lawyers forms a vital facet of social history, particularly in illustrating changes in the nature of professions. Shifts in educational and examination requirements in the 19th century constitute an important case study of professional adaptation. Social historians have also worked on lawyers' reactions to alterations in conditions of practice, for example, the rise of corporate law firms in the United States before 1900, which reduced lawyers' freewheeling public image. (*See also* Professionalism)

John E. Kicza

REFERENCES

Abel, Richard L. *American Lawyers*. New York: Oxford University Press, 1989.

Berlanstein, Lenard R. *The Barristers of Toulouse in the Eighteenth Century (1740–1793)*. Baltimore: Johns Hopkins University Press, 1975.

Martines, Lauro. *Lawyers and Statecraft in Renaissance Florence*. Princeton, NJ: Princeton University Press, 1968.

Prest, Wilfrid R. *The Rise of the Barristers: A Social History of the English Bar, 1590–1640*. Oxford: Clarendon Press, 1986.

———, ed. *Lawyers in Early Modern Europe and America*. New York: Holmes & Meier Publishers, 1981.

Juvenile Delinquency

Young people have misbehaved throughout recorded history. But juvenile delinquency—the term and the concept—is a relatively recent phenomenon. The term "juvenile delinquency," first used in the 18th century, is primarily a legal one, referring not to specific behaviors (which differ widely over place and time), but to violations of the law by persons below the community's legal age of adulthood. The creation of a special legal category for juveniles was the product of several historical developments, including the inability of families and apprenticeship systems to deal effectively with juvenile misconduct amid the economic and social turmoil of the 16th, 17th, and 18th centuries, and a growing body of knowledge that suggested that children differed from adults and ought to be judged by different standards. The institutional separation of delinquent youth from adult criminals took place on a small scale at least as early as the 16th century in Rome, Amsterdam, and London and culminated in the 19th and early 20th centuries in municipal houses of refuge (the first in New York City in 1825), reform schools, and juvenile courts (the first in Illinois in 1899). These developments generally followed the path of industrialization and urbanization, eventually producing counterparts in virtually every modernized nation.

Some historians, among them Joseph Kett and Anthony M. Platt (on the United States) and John Gillis (on western Europe), have argued that the label "juvenile delinquent" has less to do with identifying young people who violate the law than with defining working class ways of life as inferior and criminal. Less controversial is the judgment that juvenile delinquents have generally been working class and, often, recent immigrants to large cities. For example, in 19th-century Chicago, the early delinquent populations were German and Irish, followed by Poles and Italians, and in the 20th century, by black and white working-class migrants from the southern states. For the "Chicago School" of sociologists, which dominated delinquency studies in the United States from the 1920s through the 1940s and remains influential, the keys to juvenile delinquency were the slums and poverty that were intrinsic to the modern city and destroyed family and community life, creating conditions conducive to the proliferation of predatory street gangs. While there is considerable truth in these analyses, they fail to explain why some urban, immigrant groups—notably Chinese Americans—have historically avoided official delinquency; why, even in the most economically depressed areas, most youth never become delinquent statistics; and why some large cities in, for example, Italy and Argentina have experienced either very low rates of juvenile delin-

quency or patterns of delinquent activity and gang behavior very different from those in large American cities.

Although low socioeconomic status remains the best overall explanation of juvenile delinquency, the Chicago School's emphasis on urban poverty has been supplemented and sharpened in the post–World War II era. In his 1955 study, sociologist Albert Cohen presented the delinquent gang as a powerful and attractive "delinquent subculture" of lower-class boys who, ill-equipped to compete in middle-class society, sought respect through participation in the gang's aggressive and destructive actions. In the relative affluence of the 1950s and 1960s, some scholars stressed the gap between the dream of success proffered by American society and the difficulty of fulfilling it, while others, like sociologist Edmund Vaz, found juvenile delinquency seeping into the middle class in the forms of drinking, gambling, and joyriding. For historian David Nasaw, turn-of-the-century police were active agents in the production of delinquency, harassing and arresting children for adventurous and victimless activities, many of which were socially sanctioned.

Other scholars found the family an important variable in delinquency. In her 1983 study of a 19th-century school for delinquent girls, historian Barbara Brenzel argued that the single most important factor in bringing girls to the facility was the absence in the home of the natural mother. In contrast, sociologist Talcott Parsons argued in 1949 that mother-centered child rearing, the norm in industrial societies, had encouraged delinquency by failing to provide male youths with sufficient opportunities to assert their masculinity. Social historians have also studied gender as a factor; around 1900, girls were less often termed "delinquent," but when convicted, mainly for "sexual" offenses, were treated more severely than boys.

Statistics on juvenile delinquency are neither highly reliable nor comparable from nation to nation. Nonetheless, it seems clear that delinquency rates have increased throughout the 20th century in developed and developing nations, receding during the Great Depression of the 1930s and amid the affluence of the mid-1950s and reaching temporary peaks during World War I,

World War II, and the late 1950s. By mid-century, most countries of the world had experienced problems with youth gangs. Although most scholars believe that rising rates of delinquency in the United States and other countries during and after World War II reflected serious new behavior problems among juveniles, historian James Gilbert (1986) believes the problem was exaggerated by contemporaries who misunderstood, feared, and disliked the emerging postwar youth culture. (*See also* Crime; Deviance; Punishment and Prisons; Youth/Adolescence; Youth Movements)

William Graebner

REFERENCES

Gilbert, James. *A Cycle of Outrage: America's Reaction to the Juvenile Delinquent in the 1950s.* New York: Oxford University Press, 1986.

Gillis, John. *Youth and History: Tradition and Change in European Age Relations, 1770–Present.* New York: Academic Press, 1974.

Hawes, Joseph M., and N. Ray Hiner, eds. *American Childhood: A Research Guide and Historical Handbook.* Westport, CT: Greenwood Press, 1985.

Lunden, Walter A. *Statistics on Delinquents and Delinquency.* Springfield, IL: Charles C. Thomas, 1964.

Mennel, Robert N. *Thorns & Thistles: Juvenile Delinquents in the United States, 1825–1940.* Hanover, NH: University Press of New England, 1973.

K

Kievan Rus' Period

Kievan Rus' refers to the period in Russian/ Ukrainian history when trade flourished between Scandinavia and the Byzantine Empire, when monarchy was first clearly established in the Russian political tradition, and when Christianization occurred. Centered in what is now western Russia, Belarus, and Ukraine, the Kievan Rus' period runs from AD 800–1200. Writing a social history of Kievan Rus' is not easy, given the character and scant quantity of the surviving evidence. In recent years, however, new evidence unearthed by archeologists and a fresh reexamination of some standard sources have helped inspire new, more convincing arguments about the kind of society which characterized Kievan Rus'.

Legal texts have proven especially revealing. The chief law code, the Pravda Rus'skaia, survives in two redactions: the Short version, which probably came together sometime in the 11th century; and the Expanded version, which took shape by the late 12th or early 13th centuries. These codes, far from legislating behavior, for the most part reflect customary practice. In doing so, they depict a society in which kinship played a more important role than did any impersonal state authority. For example, both versions begin by authorizing kin to avenge the deaths of their close relatives; the Expanded version adds a provision, thought to have originated in the 11th century, which authorizes kin to receive monetary compensation for homicide. In neither case does the law make any provision for a court or police. In this respect the society of Rus' resembled the so-called stateless societies documented by ethnographers of Africa, Asia, and the Americas.

A society in which kinship occupies such a pronounced place might be expected to evidence little social differentiation. To some extent that was true for Rus', where the main divisions of society seem to have been between free and unfree and between those who labored for the prince and those who did not. Kievan law devotes little attention to free labor, but allots substantial space to both slavery and indenture. Six of the 42 articles which make up the Short Pravda and 27 of the 121 articles of the Expanded Pravda, define and regulate slavery, making clear the central role of unfree labor in both elite administrative occupations as well as ordinary manual labor. In Kiev Rus' a person might become enslaved by virtue of military capture, purchase, bankruptcy, self-sale, or the fulfillment of certain duties, execution of which automatically enslaved the laborer. Indenture receives less attention from the law, but evidently did play a prominent role in society. Although unremarked in the older, Short Pravda, indenture is the focus of a seven-article section in the Expanded Pravda, which describes relations between the indentured laborer and his lord. Finally, the Expanded Pravda develops an entire unit devoted to commerce, credit, and interest rates, suggesting that these themes, to which the Short Pravda gave no attention whatsoever, had become more important or had become the source of increasing friction as social relations grew more heterogeneous late in the Kievan period.

Another distinction apparent in the law is the separation between those who served the prince and those who did not. The older Pravda Rus'skaia, for example, protects the life of the prince's overseer with a cash payment twice as large as that which protected an ordinary freeman, a principle which the later code generalized to apply to all the prince's servitors. Evidently, at exactly this moment the authority of the prince intruded into the traditional organization of Kievan society.

In Kievan Rus' gender was a significant index of social obligations and privileges. The precise lines of differentiation are difficult to make out, in part because of the bombast with which churchmen treated this issue, often hurling invective at "evil women" who shared in Eve's sin. That Rus' was patriarchal, however, cannot be doubted. The law protected a woman's life with a payment only half as large as that which defended a freeman. Inheritance law also privileged males; daughters might inherit only in the absence of sons, and widows could expect nothing more than a maintenance portion. Canon law, devoting special attention to protecting the sexual purity of women, confirms that in Kiev Rus' females were important primarily for their repro-

ductive contributions to their husbands' lineages. Consequently, canon law recognized a woman's adultery as good cause for divorce, but did not include a reciprocal provision enabling a woman to divorce her husband. All these measures are common in patriarchal, patrilineal societies.

Discussion about literacy in ancient societies is always hazardous, given the small and selective surviving source base. But since the end of World War II archaeologists have discovered in Russia much new evidence. Thorough examination of ancient buildings, primarily churches, has yielded an astonishing quantity of graffiti which, though often brief and undeveloped, gives reason to think that elementary literacy was not rare. Still more persuasive was the discovery of substantial quantities of birch bark charters, small strips of birch bark upon which various memos, letters, and agreements were scratched. To date investigators have discovered more than 600 of these, most of which originated in the city of Novgorod in the 12th century or later. The prosaic contents, the lexicon, and the identity of correspondents (which included women) indicate a widespread basic literacy, a view confirmed by the inexpensive materials used to store these communications.

The materials which assert basic literacy do not, however, supply any additional evidence on the mentalities of Kievan Rus'. The brief, businesslike character of the surviving material says little about embedded values. Other sources which have proven helpful elsewhere in reconstructing sentiments hardly existed in Rus'. Testaments, for example, survive in small numbers, and those which are extant belong almost exclusively to clergymen, who used this instrument to deliver one final sermon rather than reveal anything about their own psychology. Evidence on marriage, population movement, and other indexes of society is also wanting.

Daniel H. Kaiser

REFERENCES

Kaiser, Daniel H. *The Growth of the Law in Medieval Russia.* Princeton, NJ: Princeton University Press, 1980.

Kaiser, Daniel H. *The Laws of Rus'.* Salt Lake City: Charles Schlacks, Jr., Publisher, 1992.

Levin, Eve. *Sex and Society in the World of the Orthodox*

Slavs, 900–1700. Ithaca, NY: Cornell University Press, 1989.

Thompson, M.W. *Novgorod the Great.* New York: Praeger, 1967.

Kinship

The phenomenon of kinship began to loom large in the work of social historians when in the 1960s and 1970s their general interest turned to social microstructures such as families and households. It was readily apparent that, with computer-assisted data linkage, sources such as household listings and parish registers could be used to identify ties between persons living in different places and to open a new domain of structural connections that could be important in explanations of past behavior. This research direction was supported by influences from social anthropology, which from its founding as a discipline had viewed kinship relations as supremely important in the non-Western societies it studied; and by generally untested notions among social historians about the diminishing importance of extrafamilial kinship over the long history of Western societies, especially since the industrial revolution of the late 18th century. The main obstacle to a simple transferral of anthropological methods of kinship study into the past became apparent very quickly, however. Fine-grained anthropological descriptions of the importance of kinship depended heavily on observation of the behavior of and on interviews with living persons, whereas the most readily available historical sources in the main identified only the kinship tie but supplied virtually no information about the social meaning of the tie for the persons connected by it or for the community.

Thus, the study of historical kinship has progressed much more slowly than anticipated, but the accomplished research has led to a clearer understanding of the problems at issue. Researchers have learned the dangers of deducing statements about historical kinship from theories of long-term change and of making inferences to the kinship domain from changes that have occurred in other domains of social and economic life. The general proposition, for example, that the social importance of kinship has diminished over the past half-millennium of Western society is not tenable historically if stated in so simple a way. Structural, chronological, and geographical distinctions have to be made if such general statements about kinship are to have meaning by reference to known historical evidence.

Structural distinctions. An important difference affecting the validity of statements about historical kinship change is to be found in the distinction between kin as *corporate groups* and kin as components of *personal (ego-centered) networks.* The former had identity apart from any individual member, with the membership recruited by reference to some principle such as patrilineality; the latter were totally dependent on the recruitment preferences of the individual and did not have, because of that, continuous existence in time. Yet both kinds of structure were part of the history of kinship. Their historical manifestations still need considerable study. Though we know, for example, that in medieval Europe corporate kin groups—such as clans—played an active role in social life, we do not know what proportion of any given community's population they absorbed. Similarly, though ego-centered kin reckoning has evidently become more significant in recent centuries, we do not have a sufficiently diversified evidentiary record to describe how the network size and inclusiveness of individuals differed by reference to their other characteristics (such as class or ethnicity). The distinction between the two is made even more difficult to untangle in that an individual could belong to a corporate kin group *and* have a personal network comprising only some members of the primary group (uncles and their families, for example) and other relatives not of the group (spouses' kin, for example). Making use of the group for some social purposes and the network for others was perfectly acceptable and indeed perceived as necessary throughout all periods studied, but it can be hypothesized that at some point in historical time the importance of personal networks superseded that of group membership.

Chronological distinctions. An earlier view tightly linking changes in the history of Western kinship with significant increases in rates of migration, industrialization, urbanization, and with the demographic transition, appeared for a while to offer plausible explanations of long-term kinship change and to place the most significant changes in the very recent past. Accordingly, the importance of kinship groups and ties was supposed to have been diminished by people moving away, obtaining new sources of income, having fewer children and thus fewer kin in successive generations, and in the impersonal urban setting coming to value friends more than the kin left behind. Research at the community level, however, has demonstrated the tentativeness of such correlations. Migration rates appear in many Western societies to have been substantial already in the early modern period (16th to 18th centuries). The so-called protoindustrialization also is said to have modified relations between relatives. In the 19th century, during English industrialization, kin ties were evidently quite significant for easing the entry of migrants into industrial centers; and, in the 20th century, in older industrial centers, kin still served as the principal source of aid and assistance, especially for younger families and often for the very old. Finally, in European areas where patrilineal principle was particularly strong—southeastern Europe, for example—respondents born in the 20th century are able to describe growing up in and, after leaving, continuing relationships with patrilineal kin groups with a corporate identity. Repeated challenges to the general idea that the principal break in Western kinship history came with some postulated "modernization" in the recent past has reopened the twin questions of whether there was ever such a break and, if so, when it can plausibly be located in time in the national societies comprising the Western world.

Geographical distinctions. The reorientation among social historians toward microstructures—kinship among them—began in the western European historical professions and initially probed the historical records of English and French societies. Though there was concern with comparisons from the very beginning, they were drawn (within Europe, and between European societies and other parts of the world) at the level of kinship within the household rather than with respect to kin groups, kin networks, or other kin-based structures. As a result the social history of Western kinship remains uncompleted, insofar as we are unable to date the group/network transition in the different regions of the European Continent and in those overseas societies to which Europeans migrated in large numbers. The convention of linking major changes in family and kinship (as superstructures) to major changes in the economic base—especially to industrialization—now appears too simplified. At a minimum, this hypothesis will not have been tested completely until there is substantially more research on those European areas—eastern Europe, Russia, the Mediterranean littoral—where studies for both the pre- and post-industrialization periods have been very sparse.

Ascribing social significance to kin ties and using that information in social activities are both universals. Historians fully expect to find that in all societies and communities in the past kin ties beyond the immediate family were a part of social behavior. They also expect that in any given historical locality (1) the number of persons at risk of being related to each other will be determined by prevailing demographic rates; (2) the number of persons who can be ascertained *genealogically* to be related to each other will probably be larger than the number who actually recognized that relatedness; (3) the number of persons who can be demonstrated as having made use of the kin ties they recognized will be smaller still; and (4) sources from the locality, such as letters and third-person accounts, will probably contain descriptive terms for kin *roles* suggesting local recognition of certain relations. All these variables will play a role in weighing the importance of kinship at a particular time and place in the past. Since demographic rates, ascriptions of significance to particular ties, and the necessity for using kin relations are all themselves subject to change, demonstration of the persistence of a particular kind of kinship *system* over long periods of time requires that the same combination of evidence be assayed repeatedly at points in time after the baseline. Assertions that major kinship changes have taken place in populations numbering millions will remain weakly grounded unless future research continues to exploit the historical sources available for the level of human existence at which kinship ties were actually put to use. (*See also* Anthropology; Extended

Family; Genealogy; Godparenting; Inheritance Systems)

Andrejs Plakans

REFERENCES

Cordell, Linda S., and Stephen Beckerman, eds. *The Versatility of Kinship: Essays Presented to Harry W. Basehart*. New York: Academic Press, 1980.

Flandrin, Jean-Louis. *Families in Former Times: Kinship, Household and Sexuality*. Cambridge: Cambridge University Press, 1976.

Plakans, Andrejs. *Kinship in the Past: An Anthropology of European Family Life*. Oxford and New York: Basil Blackwell, 1984.

Schneider, David M. *American Kinship: A Cultural Account*, 2nd ed. Chicago: University of Chicago Press, 1980.

Smith, Richard M., ed. *Land, Kinship, and Life-Cycle*. Cambridge: Cambridge University Press, 1984.

L

Land Tenure and Reform

Land tenure (from the Latin *tenere* meaning "to hold") refers to those arrangements that define the rights of ownership in and use of agricultural land. Legal, contractual, or customary in nature, it embodies the complex relationships obtaining between people—as individuals or as groups—and the land, relationships reflecting a range of rights over the land—as landlords, tenants, share-croppers, or other categories of claimants. It also reflects the formal rules and procedures governing these relationships.

One of the early debates about land tenure in social history focused on the relationship between major landholding changes in 18th-century England, through the Enclosure movement, and industrialization. Enclosures involved landlords using acts of Parliament to require all owners in an area to fence or hedge in their lands; poorer farmers could not afford this and had to sell out, converting much of England to a large estate society. While earlier historical judgments that Enclosure forced landless workers to flee to the cities proved incorrect—the new estates hired tenants and wage workers—it is true that enclosed lands absorbed less population growth than peasant plots might have done, and so contributed indirectly to the formation of an available urban labor force. However, as with land tenure issues generally, Enclosure has receded as a primary historical focus, becoming part of broader evaluations of rural life.

Land reform is closely linked to land tenure because it denotes changes aimed at altering the system of tenure, that is, changing the patterns of access of people to land. Historically, land reform has involved revising the ownership structure of land, such as by expropriating the property of large landlords to redistribute to peasants and small cultivators; placing limits on the size of landholdings; abolishing or improving tenancy conditions by giving land to tenants or by imposing rent ceilings; and by granting fixity and security of tenure legally or contractually; and by the establishment of a record of rights. Although used interchangeably by some scholars, the term "agrarian reform" is generally used by researchers to refer to changes that are more radical in nature and that seek fundamental alterations in the rural political economy.

Much of the current literature relating specifically to land tenure and reform understandably focuses on predominantly rural areas, the so-called developing, or Third World, countries. Largely the work of social scientists, agronomists, administrators, and policymakers, this scholarship partly grew out of Cold War era concerns regarding the potential for and the possibility of rural unrest and revolution in many parts of Africa, Asia, and Latin America. A major impetus for the preoccupation with land reform—as a policy measure and as a subject of study—therefore was to identify and offer viable alternatives to the Leninist notion of "land to the tiller." But advocates of reform have a wide range of ideological stances, from those who consider reform as a means of securing political stability and establishing and enhancing democracy and economic development to those who criticize conventional reform efforts for their tendency to promote capitalism in agriculture.

Academics and officials alike recognize that the political nature of the debate about reform stems from the fact that changes in land tenure have the capacity of profoundly altering the structure and functioning of agrarian society and economy. Particularly in societies where land is the predominant source of wealth and power (most Third World countries), land and agrarian reform can result in fundamental shifts in existing patterns of income distribution, thus resulting in substantial political, social, and economic changes.

It is no wonder that reform efforts have historically encountered opposition from people in power. Indeed, the recent history of reform, analyzed in the social science literature in great detail through monographic treatments keying on specific countries or on multicountry comparisons, is a story of repeated failures. The rare exceptions are cases where changes were wrought by social revolutions or by the agency of the state. Recent success stories include the 20th-century revolutionary experiences of Russia, China, and Cuba on the one hand, and the government-directed changes instituted in Japan and Taiwan on the other hand. Contrast these few instances

with the record of any number of countries in Africa, Asia, and Latin America, however, where reforms have been either declaratory in nature or only partly implemented or undermined because they threatened to topple or undercut the existing power structure. Nor are examples lacking of countries where reforms have been instituted where the primary beneficiaries have been the dominant classes in society and not the rank-and-file peasants. Apparently, wherever and whenever attempted changes in tenure have not been accompanied by social structural changes, they have been blocked or neutralized by elites, whether national-level or regional and local elites, or some combination of the two. As a result, some observers have argued that agrarian reform cannot be attained through constitutional and democratic measures but require radical and violent measures.

For academics and officials alike, therefore, the subject of land and agrarian reform is tied to issues of equity, social justice, and, above all, economic development. How these interrelationships work theoretically and empirically are hotly debated in the literature. Can reform generate both equity and development? Or does the objective of equity and justice run counter to that of economic rationality and productivity?

A central concern in the literature is the relationship between reform and development, between reform and agricultural productivity and economic efficiency. Often implicit in such considerations is an assumption regarding the widespread applicability of the Western model of "agricultural revolution," whereby improvement in agriculture, fostered through changes in its institutional and technological arrangements, generated industrialization and modernization.

Although historians have taken the lead in analyzing and interpreting the "agricultural revolution"—in reconstructing the revolution in England and its variations in other parts of Europe in the 18th and 19th centuries and the virtual absence of comparable developments in most Third World countries in the 19th and 20th centuries—they are currently less concerned with specific issues relating to land tenure and reform. The recent "Brenner Debate" over the transition from feudalism to capitalism in western Europe is one illustration of the extent to which the focus is on other issues. Much of the controversy in this debate revolved around different interpretations of the relationship between agrarian structures and economic development in preindustrial Europe, scholars disagreeing with one another and with Robert Brenner over the significance of commercial, demographic, political, and social factors in patterning agricultural development. Earlier debates, as in the 18th-century enclosure movement in England that displaced small property owners, or the land tenure results of Russia's emancipation of the serfs, have receded, partly because earlier simplifications have been discarded and partly because of scholars, agreeing on land tenure changes themselves, moved in the wider topics about agriculture or rural protest.

In the literature on Third World countries where agrarian issues remain a central problematic, land tenure continues to receive coverage. It draws attention because its essential features in many regions and localities, particularly in the premodern periods, have yet to be fully delineated. Studies of Aztec or Mughal or precolonial African land tenures, for instance, continue to be conducted, although increasingly as stepping-stones to determining how, why, and in what ways did access to land define roles, statuses, and, most importantly, agrarian relations. A considerable body of work has sought answers to these questions for the colonial period, the emphasis in such writings focusing on assessing how colonial rule or contact with the West changed relations on the land, legally and contractually, as well as in actual practice.

Indeed, much of the best scholarship in all fields of agrarian history has gravitated toward addressing the big questions relating to the effects of world processes and systems (capitalism, imperialism, colonialism, etc.) on rural society. A major concern in such studies is to sort out how the internal dynamics of tenurial relations are transformed by the emergence of capitalism and by market forces that generate economic differentiation and commoditized production relations. In highlighting these processes, the central interest is in conceptualizing the development or nondevelopment of capitalism in the countryside.

Another major research trajectory, shaped by the emergence of the new social history and of peasant studies in the 1960s, aims at reconstructing specific aspects of peasant experience and behavior. The most striking characteristic of this new history is its portrayal of peasants as historical actors, as people endowed with consciousness and agency even as their experiences and actions are framed and constrained by larger structures and processes.

Such shifts in emphases mean that while an occasional work here and there may seek to reconstruct the system of tenures in this or that region or estate (even in the well-ploughed field of European history), particularly for earlier periods of history, the predominant concern is with other issues. To take a few landmark studies in European history as an illustration of the larger themes pursued by current research, consider Eugen Weber's analysis of the processes whereby peasants were made into Frenchmen or F.M.L. Thompson's examination of landed society in 19th-century England or Teodor Shanin's sociological/historical study of the "awkward class" of the Russian peasantry or Robert G. Moeller's investigation of peasant politics in 20th-century Germany. All these works also reflect the influence of social history and peasant studies, as do a plethora of works focusing on the lived experiences of ordinary rural folk themselves and their relationships to one another and to the larger systems which shaped their experiences. Recent British agrarian social history, for instance, has concentrated on reconstructing the experiences on the land of different groups such as farm servants, rural craftsmen, and harvesters—their living and working conditions and their involvement in collective action and protest. Such trends are mirrored by work conducted in agrarian history for other parts of the world.

By locating research interest in land reform and tenure within the field of agrarian social history, the new scholarship recognizes that considerations of systems of tenurial arrangements or changes in them have to take into account the larger structures and processes which shaped them. At the same time, the current tendency is to highlight the people themselves, particularly all the ordinary categories of people on the land whose lives were caught up in these developments. (*See also* Agricultural Systems; Aristocracy; Peasantry)

Anand A. Yang

REFERENCES

Aston, T.H., and C.H.E. Philpin, eds. *The Brenner Debate: Agrarian Class Structure and Economic Development in Pre-Industrial Europe.* Cambridge: Cambridge University Press, 1985.

Dorner, Peter. *Land Reform and Economic Development.* Baltimore: Penguin Books, 1972.

Lehmann, David, ed. *Agrarian Reform and Agrarian Reformism: Studies of Peru, Chile, China and India.* London: Faber and Faber, 1974.

Lowe, Philip, and Maryvonne Bodiguel, eds. *Rural Studies in Britain and France.* London: Belhaven Press, 1990.

Tai, Hung-chao. *Land Reform and Politics: A Comparative Analysis.* Berkeley: University of California Press, 1974.

Landless Laborers

Here we are only concerned with laborers who live in the countryside and possess no land, not urban workers. Landless laborers have been common throughout history, although they have often not left many records, since they tended to be the poorest sector of rural society and the state had little reason to take note of them because they had little capacity to contribute taxes.

There are many different types of landless laborers, some of whom shade into being landed peasants. It is perhaps more useful to think of a continuum between landless rural laborers and landed peasants, for the wide diversity of land tenure arrangements make landlessness a relative term. For example, on haciendas in the Andes, most peons were considered renters. However, since most estates lacked agricultural machinery, the more human labor, in this case renters, the hacienda possessed, the more it was worth. As a result, renters were in fact permanent peons in everything but name as long as they continued to pay a nominal fee for their land and contributed their labor. In turn, these renters had subtenants, called *arrimantes*. These perhaps were truly landless laborers, since they rented a subsection of the renter's plots and could be called on by the renter to perform tasks for himself and for the landowner as his substitute.

In fact, there were few truly landless laborers, since most people had access to land through relatives or other relations with landowners. Partly because of this problem, a long dispute has raged whether to consider landless laborers peasants or not. Most scholars agree that truly landless laborers are not peasants, but access to land is often difficult to determine.

Only in highly capitalized systems of agriculture is there a sharp distinction between those who own land and those who do not. The agribusinesses of California in the 20th century are perhaps the best examples of this case. These farmers (often large corporations) have a small core of permanent employees with no usufruct rights to the land. At harvest, they hire large numbers of migrant workers, often of Hispanic origin, who reside temporarily on the land while they work. Indeed, migrant workers constitute the purest example of the landless laborer, except that many migrant workers throughout the world have rights to plots of land in their places of origin.

However one defines the landless, the issue of landless laborers is particularly important for the transition from an agricultural to an industrial society. Population growth and changes in landownership make access to property more difficult. The rural workers without land tended to migrate to the cities and become the urban work force needed by factories, but for a long time a rural landless class, or proletariat, develops as well. The best-known case occurred in England, where during the 18th century the Enclosure Movement threw some peasants off the land and forced them into the cities.

The landless were important to industrialization even before they moved to the cities. They were crucial in the protoindustrialization phase prior to full industrialization. Thus, in France and in England, for example, landless laborers (both men and women) during the 18th and early 19th centuries participated heavily in textile piecework. In this system, textile merchants provided the workers with the raw materials and even sometimes the spindles and looms to make textiles and cloth at home at a certain predetermined price. Called the putting-out system, it was the precursor to textile factories in many parts of Europe. Landless laborers as well as impoverished peasants tended to participate heavily in this system, since it provided them with income independent of work in the fields.

Scholars since the 1960s have considered the landless an important group in rural rebellions. Some consider landless laborers who have become rural proletarians in plantation economies to be the most revolutionary of all rural groups, since they have the most to gain and the least to lose in a revolution. Others point out that the landless have virtually no independent resources and often only weak community ties, making it difficult for them to sustain armed resistance against the powerful landlords and the state; at best landless laborers sustain reformist movements. The debate over the revolutionary potential of the landless has not been fully resolved, but many social historians now analyze not so much the exceptional cases of revolution or even rebellion, but instead the everyday forms that the powerless in the countryside (of which the landless form the most numerous group) try to survive by resisting and taking from the more wealthy and powerful. The large historiography on everyday slave resistance has provided important insights that provide parallels to the actions taken by landless laborers. These actions include stealing crops, working as slowly as possible, or establishing special relationships with more powerful individuals.

When revolutions occurred, the landless laborers often received little. While living standards might have risen as a whole, in plantation societies the landless still did not receive land themselves, perhaps their greatest wish. This is especially the case in the 20th-century revolutions, where Marxist models have attempted to do away with private property. Thus, in Cuba, for example, after 1959 the large numbers of propertyless workers became members of agricultural cooperatives or of state-run plantations. Even in revolutions where private property was not abolished, the landless did not necessarily fare well. In Bolivia the land reform of 1953 parceled up the haciendas among the renters, leaving the *arrimantes* (who in this case can be considered the truly landless) without rights to land.

In the countryside, access to land, however defined, is one of the primary criteria dividing those who are relatively well off versus those who are not. Social historians need to improve their understanding of different types of land tenancy systems to distinguish the impact of access of land or their lack thereof on the rural poor. Most importantly, we are only beginning to understand how to find and analyze the more subtle ways beyond violent rebellion that the landless and the rural poor in general have used over the centuries to make ends meet, and how they have related to other groups in rural society. (*See also* Agricultural Systems; Land Tenure and Reform; Peasant Rebellion; Peasantry)

Erick D. Langer

REFERENCES

Paige, Jeffery M. *Agrarian Revolution: Social Movements and Export Agriculture in the Underdeveloped World*. New York: Free Press, 1975.

Scott, James C. *Weapons of the Weak: Everyday Forms of Peasant Resistance*. New Haven: Yale University Press, 1985.

Thompson, E.P. *The Making of the English Working Class*. New York: Vintage Books, 1966.

Latin American Demography

The peopling of Latin America is the outcome of four great transformations. In the first, a cataclysm begun five centuries ago, thriving Amerindians were afflicted by unremitting, demographically disastrous encounters with Europeans. Second came *mestizaje*, the intermingling of multi-ethnic and multiracial peoples with substantial admixtures of African, European, and even Asian stocks. Third, beginning in the 19th century, rising life expectancies and high, but largely stable, birth rates generated enormous demographic pressure. Finally, in recent decades, with birth control no longer limited to the wealthy and the ideal of the small family spreading throughout society, population growth rates are contracting and demographic pressures falling. As recently as 1810, the population of the entire region numbered only 17 million, now less than that of Mexico City alone. Over the 19th century the population of Latin America nearly quadrupled to 61 million, then surged almost 8-fold to 453 million in 1992. Historians, long spellbound by gross numbers, are now turning their attention to the demographic and social dynamics underlying these transformations.

The origins of Amerindian agricultural societies are found in south-central Mexico around 9,000 years ago. Over the ensuing three or four millennia, as agriculture spread and technology grew more sophisticated, urban settlements formed and a high-pressure demographic system—high fertility checked by high mortality—emerged. Greater densities did not lead to demographic paradise. Skeletal remains from the pre-Columbian era tell of omnipresent nutritional stress; life-sapping insults from vitamin, mineral, and protein deficiencies; tuberculosis; arthritis; syphilislike treponema; death-inflicting dental caries; debilitating parasites; famine; appalling infant mortality; and much more, but few of the crowd diseases common to medieval Europe. Life expectancy at birth averaged fewer than 20 years, with little to distinguish rulers from the ruled. (As in all agricultural societies, life expectancy at birth is somewhat misleading given high rates of infant mortality; survivors of childhood lived to age 35 or 40 on average.) Still by 1500 thickly settled populations emerged in central Mexico and along a swath of the Andean Highlands. Although social historians have shown little interest in pre-Columbian demographic conditions, our understanding of post-contact societies will be enhanced by carefully considering archaeological evidence as well as post-conquest narratives, tax records, and other written sources.

From 1492, sustained encounter with Europeans provoked demographic disaster. Subjected to wanton slaughter, forced labor, and environmental destruction, Amerindians were ravaged by the introduction of Eurasian/African diseases, including smallpox, measles, influenza, malaria, yellow fever, among others. Regarding the size of precontact populations, no consensus has emerged, even where the record is extensive, such as for the Mexican subcontinent. Whether the central Mexican basin numbered 30 or 3 million inhabitants when Spanish Christians first invaded is hotly debated, yet there is little doubt that by 1650 fewer than 1.5 million remained. Today, in all of Latin America, Amerindians, their culture and demography greatly transformed, exceed 25 million but account for less than 5 percent of the region's population. Survival was primarily a matter of ecology, not theology. In easily accessible, wet tropical lowlands or thinly peopled arid zones, extinction often resulted, while in temperate regions dense settlements surmounted enormous die-offs. Until well beyond the end of Iberian rule in the 19th century, recurrent famine and epidemics caused death rates among Amerindians to double or even quadruple, reaching 10 to 25 per cent per annum. Nonetheless, where indigenous language and culture survived, precontact Amerindian family patterns persisted in the form of early, universal coupling, moderate birth intervals (30–36 months), and timely remarriage.

Mestizaje, a natural, sometimes bitter fruit of Iberian colonialism, flourished thanks to greatly unbalanced sex ratios. While the conquered adopted the nuptial formalisms of Catholicism, the conquerors, with females of their own kind in short supply, eagerly embraced informal unions and the double standard. *Vale más bien amancebado que mal casado* ("better a good concubine than a bad marriage") became a cliché among men who sought "to make America." Clerics preached the sanctity of freely chosen marriage and sought to eradicate Amerindian polygamy. Meanwhile, wanton sexual intercourse, concubinage, seduction, and *rapto* (rape/theft) became as widespread in Latin America as they were rare in Latin Europe. Illegitimacy and child abandonment exceeded 50 percent or more in Europeanized towns and cities, compared with 10 percent or less among Indian villagers. Women who lacked family, community, or nuptial ties—Amerindian, African, and Euromestizo alike—sought shelter, sustenance, and employment in urban places, where sex was a readily commercialized, if rapidly depreciated, asset. One of the signal achievements of the new Latin American social history has been in the study of *mestizaje*—the role of the state, church, patriarchy, class, and more recently gender and the encounter between the sexes.

Ironically, there were fewer females among free European emigrants than among enslaved Africans. A constant of the intercontinental traffic in slaves, totaling some 10 million people from 1492 until its destruction in the 1870s, was that males outnumbered females two to one.

Among free emigrants, a much smaller group scarcely averaging 3,000 to 4,000 Spaniards and 1,000 Portuguese annually, the gender imbalance was twice as great, and its demographic impact was compounded by inequalities in wealth and privilege. As a rule the slaveholder's strategy was to buy slaves rather than breed them. On large tropical plantations, where the slave diet was often limited to manioc and putrid jerky, mothers were malnourished, nursing protracted, and children habitually weaned on protein-free pap. Low fecundity, long birth intervals, and life-sapping infant and childhood afflictions, including kwashiorkor, resulted. For slaves the odds of winning in the demographic lottery were halved again since death of either spouse or slaveholder meant the dismemberment of slave families. Yet, slave families survived and in peripheral regions thrived. Informal unions offered an escape hatch to freedom for mulatto offspring, and further weakened slavery.

Slavery, doomed by its peculiar demography, was destroyed in the 19th century, but its destruction did not signal the demise of a political economy forged in cheap labor. Instead, where labor was scarce, or made scarce by racism and peonage, the breach was filled sometimes by European immigration and often by pronatalism. The slogan "to govern is to populate," coined in the 1840s, retained its appeal into the 1970s. Some 9 million people immigrated to Latin America between 1880 and 1940. Their impact was greatest in Argentina, the Antilles, Cuba, Uruguay, and Brazil. Most immigrants settled in cities and, with each passing generation, fused with the native classes. Meanwhile, domestic policies, such as secularization of marriage and family law, weakened the position of women and children in the struggle for sustenance. Reform, whether liberal or conservative, extended greater license to fathers while secular courts proved unresponsive to female complaints about seduction, abuse, and abandonment. Female-headed households, once characteristic of the city, became common in the countryside as well. Household and headship structures were retooled by evolving labor demands of the great estate (*latifundio*), rancho, subsistence plot (*minifundio*), and native village. Historians, seemingly seduced by the enticements of the big house, where patriarchy ruled triumphant, have been slow to investigate the long-term evolution of matriarchy in the larger populace.

Beginning in the 19th century modest improvements in public health and nutrition raised life expectancy at birth from abysmal levels, from a regionwide average of 25 years in 1850 to 34 in 1930, 56 in 1960, and 67 by 1992. Women and children benefited more than men and the elderly, such that by 1960 deaths due to pregnancy and childbirth were reduced greatly while among males violence grew to 10 percent of all male deaths. The Latin American mortality transition began decades later than in Latin Europe, but here it progressed much more rapidly. To many experts it seemed that the fertility transition would never arrive, as annual growth rates topped 3 percent, yet when contraction finally began it was unexpectedly sharp. In Mexico, for example, the national fertility rate (TFR) drifted from 7 children at the beginning of the 20th century, to 6 in 1960, and 3.8 by 1990. Uruguay and Argentina, with large contingents of European immigrants, initiated the fertility transition almost a century ago (TFR = 2.9 in 1920), followed sluggishly by Cuba, then in the 1960s by Costa Rica, Chile, and Colombia, and recently Brazil as well as Mexico. At the beginning of the 20th century, the crude birth rate slipped below 40 per thousand in only one Latin American country. By 1992, in only one (Honduras) did it hover above 40, and the regional average fell below 30. Demographic pressure in Latin America is falling rapidly, but before it stabilizes in the middle of the 21st century, the population of the region is likely to surpass 700 million. Cities, demographic escape valves for much of the 20th century, no longer suffice for the enormous volume of migrants. Emigration within the region and beyond continues to rise, swollen by political strife, economic stagflation, or the allures of affluence elsewhere. (*See also* Columbian Exchange; Demography)

Robert McCaa

REFERENCES

Marcílio, Maria Luisa. "The Population of Colonial Brazil," in Leslie Bethell, ed., *The Cambridge History of Latin America*, Vol. 2. Cambridge: Cambridge University Press, 1984–1985, pp. 37–63.

Sánchez-Albornoz, Nicolás. "The Population of Colonial Spanish America," in Leslie Bethell, ed., *The Cambridge History of Latin America*, Vol. 2. Cambridge: Cambridge University Press, 1984–1985, pp. 3–35.

Sánchez-Albornoz, Nicolás. "The Population of Latin America, 1850–1930," in Leslie Bethell, ed., *The Cambridge History of Latin America*, Vol. 5. Cambridge: Cambridge University Press, 1984–1985, pp. 121–150.

Latin American Ethnicity

Patterns of ethnicity and ethnic identity in Latin America are the product of five centuries of cultural, social, and biological interaction among African, Amerindian, Asian, and European peoples.

Ethnic identities originating in Europe and Africa have proven to be those most subject to change over time, gradually melding into broader "racial" categories of white, black, and brown. At the time of their arrival in the New World, both Africans and Europeans were divided into a variety of ethnic identities. Spain did not exist as a full national entity until 1716, and colonial-period Spanish and Portuguese immigrants were most likely to identify themselves in terms of their regional origin. Economic and social competition among Andalusians, Basques, Catalans, Galicians, and other Iberian groups, erupting at times into armed violence, was a prominent feature of colonial life. However, as these immigrants produced American-born offspring, the importance of regional identities based in Europe tended to fade, to be replaced by new Creole identities defined in the Americas.

European-based ethnicity in the region was further diversified between 1880 and 1930, when several million immigrants from the Iberian countries, Italy, eastern Europe, and other European countries arrived in southern South America. This was also a period during which several hundred thousand Chinese contract laborers settled in Cuba, Mexico, and Peru, and Brazil became the recipient of the largest single stream of out-migration from Japan. Present-day descendants of those Asian migrants continue to form a distinctive ethnic community; but descendants of the turn-of-the-century European migrants are largely indistinguishable, save for their surnames or, in the case of Jews from eastern Europe, their religion, from the larger Euro-Latin American population.

Like Europeans, Africans were a far from homogeneous group at the time of their arrival in the Americas. Slaves from West, South, and East Africa were divided into over 100 tribal and national groups by barriers of language and culture; once in the New World, members of the different African nations relied on Spanish or Portuguese to communicate among themselves. As long as the slave trade continued, these African identities were constantly being reinforced by new arrivals. But as the trade wound down and was finally abolished in the 1850s and 1860s, African ethnicity declined in importance, to be replaced by such broader national and racial identities as Afro-Cuban, Afro-Brazilian, and Afro-Colombian.

Amerindian ethnic identities have proven to be more durable than their European and African counterparts. As in the European and African cases, these identities were numerous and well established at the time of the Europeans' arrival. Conflict and warfare among Indian peoples played a central role first in the creation and maintenance of the Aztec and Inca empires and then after 1500 in their destruction by the Spaniards, who enjoyed the invaluable assistance of the Amerindian enemies of both empires.

In the centuries following the Spanish and Portuguese conquests, several factors conspired to reduce the saliency of ethnic divisions among the Amerindians. One was the catastrophic decline in the Amerindian population produced by epidemic diseases, which wiped out some groups entirely and compressed others. Another was colonial law and practice, which consigned all Amerindian peoples to a single "Indian" legal and social category. And finally, as Amerindians became more Europeanized in language and culture, new "ladino" identities started to replace some elements of preconquest ethnicity.

Nevertheless, even in the face of these pressures, pre-Columbian tribal and national identities have displayed impressive staying power, and coexist down to the present with broader "Indian" identities. This is probably a function of the fact that, unlike Latin America's other "racial" groups, Amerindians have tended to remain in their regions of origin and have not experienced the homogenizing effects of transcontinental migration. Increased rural-to-urban migration by Indians during the 20th century may reduce the importance of these ethnic identities in the future; but that has not happened yet.

Further enriching and complicating patterns of ethnicity in Latin America is the extensive mixture, both biological and cultural, which has taken place over time among Europeans, Africans, Indians, and (to a somewhat lesser degree) Asians. Because of the scarcity of women in the first generations of European migrants to the New World, such racial mixture began during the conquest and continued on a broad scale throughout the colonial period. By 1800 racially mixed people—referred to as *pardos* or *castas* in both Portuguese and Spanish America—were the fastest growing racial group in the colonies, and the largest such group in a number of countries.

This high degree of racial mixture was interpreted by 20th century intellectuals such as José Vasconcelos, Fernando Ortiz, and Gilberto Freyre as evidence of the breakdown of Old World racial identities in the Americas and their replacement by a new, ethnically unified "cosmic race." Research by social historians and sociologists has made clear, however, the continuing preference throughout the region for white racial status and the correspondingly low social position occupied by nonwhites. Widely varying patterns of ethnic and racial diversity, inequality, and conflict in Latin America, and how those patterns were created over time, will continue to constitute subjects of social historical research into the foreseeable future. (*See also* African Slave Trade; Ethnicity; Spanish Conquest)

George Reid Andrews

REFERENCES

Lockhart, James, and Stuart B. Schwartz. *Early Latin America: A History of Colonial Spanish America and Brazil.* Cambridge and New York: Cambridge University Press, 1983.

Mörner, Magnus. *Race Mixture in the History of Latin America.* Boston: Little, Brown, 1967.

————, with Harold Sims. *Adventurers and Proletarians: The Story of Migrants in Latin America.* Pittsburgh: University of Pittsburgh Press, 1985.

Rout, Leslie B. *The African Experience in Spanish America: 1502 to the Present Day.* Cambridge and New York: Cambridge University Press, 1976.

Latin American Frontiers

In contrast to North America, where the frontier disappeared in the second half of the 19th century, in Latin America there are still a number of frontiers. Frontiers can be defined as areas where indigenous societies have not acknowledged the primacy of the nation-state. For much of the history of Latin America, this included wide swaths of territory, for the Spanish only attempted to settle and control areas where the Indian population was relatively dense or where certain natural resources—gold and silver in particular—were to be found. The rest of the territory was settled very lightly, including most of what is now the southwestern United States, the jungles of southern Mexico, the western fringes of the Amazon basin, the Gran Chaco, and the southern tip of South America (the pampas and Patagonia). Likewise, the Portuguese merchants settled only the coast of Brazil, except for the town of São Paulo, 100 kilometers in the interior, leaving most of the Amazon basin uncontrolled except for occasional expeditions to capture slaves. Thus, Latin America exhibited a pattern of multiple frontiers, in which many regions close to colonial settlements remained outside European control.

After the initial conquest of Latin America, in which Spanish and Portuguese explorers crisscrossed the Americas, conquering large indigenous societies in their path, the frontiers remained relatively stable. In the 18th century, under pressure from other European powers, both Spanish and Portuguese empires expanded into the frontiers. However, the independence wars in the Spanish Empire and the subsequent weakness of the state made possible a moderate expansion by indigenous groups. The Yaquis of northern Mexico, for example, achieved virtual independence as did the Chiriguanos in southeastern Bolivia. Only in the late 19th century did new technology (such as the repeating rifle), new economic incentives, and a consolidation of the state permit the Latin American governments to conquer most frontier areas. Most notable in this regard was the War of the Desert (1879–1880), when the Argentine government destroyed the power of the Araucanian Indians in central and southern Argentina. The penetration of the Amazon basin because of the rubber boom (1860–1912) by people from the various countries sharing the region also occurred in this period, but state control waned again when the boom turned to bust.

The frontier is very important in Latin America, for it is a prime area of racial mixture. Unlike the North American frontier, which was largely one of exclusion, the Spanish and Portuguese mixed easily with the native peoples. Rather than promoting democracy, as Frederick Jackson Turner has us believe for North America, on the Latin American frontier a kind of "conquest culture" continued to reign supreme. Indigenous peoples were usually incorporated into the frontier economy, but at best as agricultural laborers on the bottom rungs of society. Those who resisted were killed. A culture of violence, especially on cattle frontiers, appears to have been characteristic as well. The *encomienda,* in which Spanish landowners controlled the natives to the exclusion of the state, subsisted much longer on the frontier than in the core regions of the colonies. Vast landholdings, often using systems of debt peonage, kept the wealthy few in power and the rural laboring classes exploited. Only the Catholic missions sometimes mitigated the exploitation of the Indians, but also contributed to their demise by destroying indigenous culture and making possible the spread of European disease in densely settled populations. To most Latin American Indians the frontier meant an eventual death, whether physical or cultural. Other than those who were able to escape beyond the clutches of state, the frontier meant lack of freedom but for the few large landowners.

While this picture of the frontier is rather stark, new research has begun to change somewhat the image of the Latin American frontier. An ethnohistorical approach, taking the perspective of the indigenous peoples, has shown the ways in which peoples were able to resist for so long the onslaught from the Europeans. Ethnohistorical perspectives have also illuminated completely new facets of the frontier missions, showing, for example, that the Indians helped determine the way in which the missions specifically and frontier society in general was shaped. Comparative research is beginning to juxtapose insights about Latin American frontier history with that of other modern frontier societies, though additional analytical possibilities are considerable. (*See also* Missions; Ethnography/Ethnohistory; Frontier Thesis; *Haciendas/Encomiendas*)

Erick D. Langer

REFERENCES

Baretta, Silvio Duncan, and John Markoff. "Civilization and Barbarism: Cattle Frontiers in Latin America," *Comparative Studies in Society and History* 20, 4 (1978): 587–620.

Hennessy, Alistair. *The Frontier in Latin American History.* Albuquerque: University of New Mexico Press, 1978.

Latin American Indian Communities

A Latin American Indian community is a traditional social institution whose 500 to 1,500 inhabitants live a distinctive communal lifestyle within a specific territorial boundary. Stemming originally from pre-Columbian settlement patterns and located in portions of central and southern Mexico, Guatemala, El Salvador, Ecuador, Peru, and Bolivia, communal Indians number about 30 million presently. They rely, and have relied for centuries, on agriculture for their sustenance. Depending on regional topography and climate, Indian householders cultivate corn, beans, potatoes, and fruits. Controlling defined and inheritable parcels of land, often scattered about the community, family members use hoes, primitive plows, and animal power to prepare the soil, tend the plants, and harvest the crops. These same householders manufacture textiles and other handmade goods, which they carry to regional markets for both barter and sale. Through such traditional economic activities Indian householders have sustained themselves and produced small surpluses.

The community's cultural and political lives are marked by a number of annual celebrations, linked to planting, harvesting, or Roman Catholic religious holidays. Sponsors of celebrations, who provide food, drink, and music, earn the right to occupy positions of leadership. Officeholders adjudicate disputes, especially over the inheritance of land, and represent the community to outsiders. Although leaders change annually, giving opportunities to nearly all adult males to serve, the wealthier householders are expected to share their wealth via sponsorship. Reciprocity among households of unequal wealth is the chief cultural value of communal life.

While anthropologists have analyzed the contemporary social and economic relations among householders and the impact of the outside world, social historians have focused on demographic changes, as well as the community's relationship to ancient imperial organizations, to the Spanish colonial state and economy, and to the national export economies of the 19th and 20th centuries. Exploring the survival and importance of the communities has been an important contribution of social history to Latin American history more generally.

Before the Spanish conquest of the early 16th century, Indian communities were integral parts of indigenous imperial organizations, including the Inca and Aztec empires beginning in the 1400s. Regional lords collected tributes of food, wool, cotton cloth, and other goods, and enforced imperial rules. Villagers paid tribute regularly and generally accepted the rule of regional lords because the imperial government guaranteed access to land and distributed food in times of shortages. Reciprocity between the community and the empire was the basis of political legitimacy.

The Spanish conquest introduced significant changes. European disease decimated the Indian population so that the remnant Indian villages became vulnerable to Spanish control. The Spaniards destroyed the highest levels of indigenous government, assigned villages to influential men known as *encomenderos*, but retained the regional lords to keep the tribute system operating. By 1600 the colonial government imposed tribute in money (3 to 15 pesos per adult male), forcing the villagers to either sell their labor to Spanish enterprises, such as mines, or sell their goods in Spanish markets. Spaniards also occupied vacant lands and established agricultural and ranching *haciendas*. Some villagers became permanent hacienda residents, while others became temporary laborers to supplement their village income. As the villagers were forced into the colonial system, the regional lords, to the extent that they

cooperated with the Spanish officials, became as exploitive as Spanish lords. A measure of reciprocity remained, however. The colonial government guaranteed access to land by recognizing village boundaries and prohibiting the sale of communal land.

After gaining independence from Spain (1810–1825), the *Creole* elite in the second half of the 19th century abolished the legitimate corporate existence of Indian communities. Using European liberalism as a justification, Creoles distributed parcels to village householders. The transition to individual property rights legalized the sale of communal land to Creole landowners, who wanted village properties for coffee, sugar, or other commercial exports, or even as collateral for loans. Furthermore, vagrancy laws forced Indian laborers to the new export haciendas. Indian resistance to hacienda expansion and defense of communal life, in both the colonial and national periods, occupies a major place in contemporary social history.

Twentieth-century revolutionary governments, especially in Mexico, Peru, and Bolivia, recognized the surviving communities and sought to preserve them. But steady population growth on limited land has resulted in an exodus of villagers to the city and vastly increased contacts with the outside world. The social and cultural results of that contact constitute another major topic of research. (*See also* Communities; *Haciendas/Encomiendas*; Latin American Demography)

Erwin P. Greishaber

REFERENCES

Gibson, Charles. *The Aztecs Under Spanish Rule.* Stanford, CA: Stanford University Press, 1964.

Greenberg, James B. *Santiago's Sword: Chatino Peasant Religion and Economics.* Berkeley: University of California Press, 1981.

Katz, Friedrich. *The Ancient American Civilizations.* New York: Praeger, 1972.

Mallon, Florencia. *The Defense of Community in Peru's Central Highlands: Peasant Struggle and Capitalist Transition, 1860–1940.* Princeton, NJ: Princeton University Press, 1983.

Spalding, Karen. *Huarochiri: An Andean Society Under Inca and Spanish Rule.* Stanford, CA: Stanford University Press, 1984.

Latin American Merchants

The thriving mercantile firms of southern Spain, including numerous Genoese commercial houses, invested heavily in the initial 15th–16th-century voyages to the New World. The branches they soon set up in the early colonies in turn financed many of the expeditions that ventured across the Americas and also provided the settlements with African slaves. Merchants characteristically participated in the conquests and established businesses in the newly founded cities. Many prospered and their numbers expanded, as they provided vital services to the new societies, transferring precious metals—and later other profitable commodities—to Europe in exchange for items the colonists required to enjoy a comfortable, European-oriented way of life.

By the middle of the 15th century, the Genoese trading firms had been fully supplanted by Spanish businesses. During that century, Seville's commercial houses established a preeminence that would not be challenged until well into the 18th century. Their networks of associates extended from Spain to important colonial ports and cities and on to provincial centers. Kinship served as a vital bond in business affairs, as these employees operated with little supervision from their headquarters and the legal system could rarely be invoked successfully to control their behavior. At this early time, colonial merchants typically avoided marriage or significant investment in real property, as professional advancement ultimately entailed transfer back to Spain. They did, however, invest in mines from a very early date, for precious metals were both crucial to the prosperity of the colonies and coveted in Europe. Partnerships and company agreements, some of which endured for extended periods, characterized commercial associations throughout the colonial era.

By the beginning of the 17th century, merchants based in major colonial cities, such as Mexico City, had begun to attain autonomy from the Seville firms that had initially dispatched them. They frequently married into local elite families, but without abandoning commerce. In fact, their sons sometimes took over the firms.

Nonetheless, immigrants from Spain dominated wholesale trade until the end of the colonial period, though they might well be supervising long-established local firms. These immigrants were commonly impoverished relatives of the owners who came to the Americas while still adolescents. There they endured extended apprenticeships which might require travel to or postings in provincial settlements. Of the many who came to the colonies, only a fraction ever attained the directorship of a trading house. The others were retained as employees or were set up in smaller businesses which remained affiliated with the family's larger enterprise. The chosen successor to the firm's directorship often had his status ratified through marriage to a daughter of the current head of the business, thereby attaining control over her inheritance. Other heirs commonly turned over management of their shares to the successor. They appreciated that the value of their individual holdings benefited from the entire complex functioning as an integrated unit.

In important port cities such as Veracruz and Buenos Aires, merchants dominated the primary municipal positions. In interior cities, where estate and mine owners resided, they generally ceded most local posts to these interests.

Brazil's mercantile world operated in quite similar fashion. The process of intermarriage between successful merchants and local, generally landed, elite families was continual. Immigrants dominated the ranks of the profession. Successful merchants characteristically diversified into other lines of business, particularly commercial agriculture, without abandoning trade. They enjoyed heavy political representation in the colony's important port cities.

The coming of independence around 1820 after a decade of destructive warfare gravely weakened the position of Latin America's merchant community versus the enhanced international competition it faced at the same time. Here is another key passage drawing the attention of social historians of Latin America. The collapse of silver mining and credit systems within the societies and the prevalence of brigandage and political instability were the primary causes of merchant decline. While few immigrants came from Spain after independence, substantial numbers traveled from the other western European countries, and in the 20th century some came from the Middle East. A segment of these joined the contingent of locally born merchants who had endured through the difficult decades following independence and prospered in the improved economic and political climate that prevailed after roughly 1870.

As in the colonial period, these merchants generally diversified their investments after attaining a degree of wealth. In this new setting, however, some of them became among the first great industrialists in their societies, and with time their families transferred their interests out of commerce. (*See also* Capitalism; Commercialization; Market and Economy; Merchants)

John E. Kicza

REFERENCES

Brading, D.A. *Miners and Merchants in Bourbon Mexico, 1763–1810*. Cambridge: Cambridge University Press, 1971.

Hoberman, Louisa Schell. *Mexico's Merchant Elite, 1590–1660: Silver, State, and Society*. Durham, NC: Duke University Press, 1991.

Socolow, Susan Migden. *The Merchants of Buenos Aires, 1778–1810: Family and Commerce*. Cambridge: Cambridge University Press, 1978.

Walker, David W. *Kinship, Business, and Politics: The Martínez del Río Family in Mexico, 1823–1867*. Austin: University of Texas Press, 1986.

Latin American Racism

The belief in the superiority of one human group over another—groups that are often defined somatically—is perhaps as old as man himself. Certainly in Latin America prejudice toward Indians has been a constant since Europeans first met them, and blacks had been subject to discriminatory practices in Europe long before. Discrimination has not always taken the same form as in the English-speaking Americas, and this has sometimes led casual observers to allege that it does not exist. That is a false conclusion. Over many centuries Indians and blacks have remained at the bottom of Latin American social hierarchies, and this can only be the result of racism. Sophisticated statistical studies have shown that even when class position, educational level, regional disparities, and rural-versus-urban residence are taken into account (factors that are often alleged as the real source of the problem rather than racial discrimination), non-white populations have a shorter life span and a higher rate of infant mortality than do whites. Discrimination is rampant.

Why has anyone been led to believe otherwise? Because racism is often expressed in different ways in Latin America than in English America, not to mention the differences among the various Latin American cultures. In Brazil, for instance, color and not ancestry is the sole determinant of "race," so that the concept of "passing [for white]" is unknown and unnecessary. Racial mixture has been extensive and race prejudice and discrimination occur along a continuum: although to be whiter is to be considered superior, no sharp line divides distinct color groups. Furthermore, concepts of race are closely intertwined with concepts of class, so that a dark-skinned person of wealth and education will be thought of as superior to someone who is lighter-skinned, but poor and unschooled; in short, someone who is well off will be thought of and treated as if whiter than is objectively true. Nevertheless, as a person of color moves up the social scale, greater and greater obstacles are raised to any further social mobility, giving rise to the saying that "the more money whitens, the more money it takes to whiten."

Racialist concepts among educated opinion-makers have waxed and waned in Latin America as elsewhere. In European thought the identification of Africans with inferiority was already common at the time of the Renaissance. With the discovery of America, an intense debate erupted regarding whether Amerindians were truly human, with both sides appealing to the authority of Aristotle and the church fathers. Eighteenth-century developments in European science stimulated the impulse toward classifying all men according to some sort of uniform schema, and racial rankings derived from the theory of evolution prevailed in European and North American thought from the mid-19th century until the 1920s (and even to 1945). These concepts, especially "Social Darwinism," captured the allegiance of many Latin American writers. The spread of European colonialism and the rapid growth of the United States in the latter half of the 19th century brought additional and supposedly irrefutable scientific proof that so-called primitive Africans or Indians should be placed at the bottom of the scale and civilized white Europeans at its top. Many social policies regarding education, crime, health, and immigration were informed by these dominant racial theories.

Latin American thinkers then faced a difficult intellectual dilemma. On the one hand, racial heterogeneity characterized most of their societies. On the other, they and other elites aspired to an ever closer connection to Europe and sought to follow its leadership in every realm, whether in trade or finance, whether in politics or intellectual life. As the technological achievements of Europeans and North Americans clearly rested on science, its dictums took on a particular prestige. Scientific racism claimed to explain why some succeeded while others failed, seemed to make clear the reasons for contemporary realities in international relations, and justified the dominance domestically of the few (whites) over the many (colored). And the most eminent world scientists endorsed the view that the white race was superior and destined to triumph over blacks, Indians, mestizos, and mulattoes. Yet, with the racial composition of their societies clearly before them and a growing sense of national identity impelling consideration of national futures, these thinkers also hesitated. By the first decades of the 20th century they began elaborating a countervailing argument.

Mexican elites in the latter part of the 19th century had drawn on racialist theories to justify the disappropriation of Indian communities, as well as to legitimize their particular project for nation-building and economic development (benefiting white foreigners over mestizo or Indian nationals). The Revolution of 1910 sharply altered the course of that nation's history, and its leaders undertook to make a great range of drastic changes. They especially set themselves the task of opposing racist philosophy. José Vasconcellos was only one of the Mexican writers, albeit the most eloquent one, to claim the mestizo as the apotheosis of human development. Yet he and other spokesmen for *indigenismo* still failed to distinguish between race and ethnicity, allowing genetically inherited characteristics to play a role in their thought incon-

sistent with a non-racist approach. Revolutionaries thus perpetuated stereotypes and labels that justified or rationalized the treatment of Indians as objects of state intervention rather than historical actors in their own right.

Gilberto Freyre (1946), the Brazilian essayist, also failed to escape the racist paradigms of his time, despite his single-minded commitment to destroying them. His great masterpiece, *The Masters and the Slaves,* first published in 1933, set out to show that the heritage of slavery, not race, accounted for the sad condition of African Brazilians. Emphasizing culture rather than nature, and stressing slavery's importance in shaping the worldview of masters as well as slaves, he concluded by hailing race mixture as a national achievement for which Brazil should be proud, rather than a burden under which it suffered. Yet he too fell back upon categories of thought initially formulated by those whom he attacked, and frequently ended up attributing to inheritance qualities that are evidently learned. Nevertheless, he drove the last nail into the coffin of "scientific" racism in Brazil, and after the publication of his famous book, educated opinion no longer lived under the thrall of that spurious European doctrine.

Racial prejudice and discrimination still continue throughout Latin America, but at least such beliefs and action no longer draw sustenance from the work of intellectuals. The importance of race and its comparative complexity have served as important ingredients in Latin American social history and continue to inspire significant research. (*See also* Ethnicity; Latin American Ethnicity; Native Americans; Slavery)

Richard Graham

REFERENCES

Degler, Carl N. *Neither Black nor White.* New York: Macmillan, 1971.

Freyre, Gilberto. *The Masters and the Slaves.* Translated by Samuel Putnam. New York: Knopf, 1946.

Graham, Richard, ed. *The Idea of Race in Latin America, 1870–1940.* Austin: University of Texas Press, 1990.

Hanke, Lewis. *All Mankind Is One.* DeKalb: Northern Illinois University Press, 1974.

Latin American Regionalism

Much of the history of the Latin American nations may be understood as a struggle to replace strong regional identities and weak class identities with weak regional identities and strong class identities. This may be seen as key to the process of economic growth and modernization inasmuch as industrialization and urbanization, for example, imply a developing class structure (greater spatial and social concentration in the means of production and wealth). Strong regional differentiation in modern nations, on the other hand—the historical claims of large parts of a country to political, economic, and/or cultural autonomy from the center or the nation-state as a whole—are often seen as signs of archaism and backwardness, though what may be termed a "region" to a centralizing bureaucrat may be an ancient homeland to someone else. Regionalism and the centrifugal tendencies it represents are certainly not unique to Latin America; Basque and Catalan separatism in Spain, or the breakup of the Soviet Union in the early 1990s, represent European variations on the theme. Nor is Latin America marked by a uniform history in this regard; Mexico has on the whole been racked by regional conflict more often than Brazil, for example. Nonetheless, it seems fair to say that the creation and maintenance of viable nation-states and national identities in this area of the world has been made much more problematic than in some others by the survival and assertion of strong geographic and cultural regions and the political loyalties attached to them.

By the term "regionalism" is meant the more or less enduring cultural and/or political identification of substantial groups of people with geographic territories larger than cities but smaller than nation-states. This is not necessarily the same thing as regionality—the quality of "regionalness" or systemic integration, if you will, that inheres in geographic entities owing to the internal structures of population distribution, communication networks, location of economic activity, and so forth. The former is what may be called an "actor's" category, the latter an "observer's" category, though the two naturally tend to overlap.

Instances of regionalism and its influence on national political life in Latin America abound, nowhere more than in Mexico. During the 19th century and beyond, for example, the southeastern region of Yucatan, with its distinctive social structure and strong Maya cultural heritage, frequently tended to act as though it were a separate country from Mexico, even spawning plans for independence and mass collective political violence in opposition to the country's central government (e.g., the famous Caste War, 1847–1910). The great Mexican Revolution of 1910–1920 may itself be seen largely in regional terms. The country's northern region, steeped in cultural traditions quite different from the central parts of Mexico, among them its cowboy culture and love/hate relationship with the United States, produced many of the armies and leaders (e.g., Pancho Villa, Venustiano Carranza, Alvaro Obregon) which, while they may have fought each other, also dominated the national destiny and consummated the Revolution itself. The history of Argentina for much of the 19th century was dominated by violent interregional political struggle between Buenos Aires and its hinterland, and the interior provinces over the control of the nation. Similarly, Brazilian national life was long marked by conflict between the old sugar-producing northeast and the coffee-dominated, and later industrialized, central and southern regions; that of Peru by ongoing tensions pitting Lima and other coastal lowland regions against the Andean Highlands, and so forth. The relative muting of regionalism in the later 20th century, and of conflict either among regions or between them and national structures, owes much to the consolidation of modern state power, the expansion and thickening of national and international market relationships, and the advent of modern means of communication.

Certainly, though it would be simplistic to reduce the strength of regionalism to their effects alone, geography and other aspects of the natural environment in large parts of the New World have had something to do with the enduring force of subnational loyalties. Mexico, for example, is not well served internally with a navigable river system, and neither, for the most part, is the Andean area. Mountain ranges, aridity or tropical excesses of moisture, and the idiosyncratic distribution of fertile soils and other resources have strongly marked the land and are echoed in the evolution of strong regional identities. The absence of animal traction and therefore of wheeled transport among the great indigenous cultures helped cut deep the channels of regional character long before the Europeans arrived on the scene, while the newly introduced Old World technologies and animals could never fully overcome them.

Pre-Columbian cultural patterns and the heritage of colonial domination played their roles, too. As with much else in the history of Latin America, the association of enduring ethnic identities with specific territories has added complexity to the picture. But this was on the scene long before the Europeans arrived, as in the Inca empires of Cuzco, which sent out state-sponsored colonists to consolidate imperial control among restive ethnic groups newly conquered, or the Aztecs' practice of establishing military garrisons among their far-flung ethnic empire to insure the coherence of their tributary state. The commercial and administrative policies of the Iberian colonizers (particularly the Spanish) did much to compound the effects of already strongly entrenched regionality and regionalism. Interregional trade was heavily taxed, strictly regulated, or forbidden altogether, for example, so that each major region—sometimes corresponding to preconquest entities, sometimes (as with mining centers) not—tended to crystallize and develop around a dominant (primate) city, and to be linked to the metropolis (Spain) on its own. Lacking central cities, other types of regions nonetheless developed around plantation agriculture and exports (e.g., the sugar-producing regions of central Mexico, coastal Peru, and northeastern Brazil, or the coffee-centered ones of distinct zones of Brazil, Central America, or the northern Andes). (*See also* Caudillismo; Central Place Theory; Geography; Latin American Ethnicity; Native Americans)

Eric Van Young

REFERENCES

Cunha, Euclydes da. *Rebellion in the Backlands*, with Introduction and Notes by Samuel Putnam. Chicago: University of Chicago Press, 1944.

Smith, Carol A., ed. *Regional Analysis*, 2 vols. New York: Academic Press, 1976.

Van Young, Eric, ed. *Mexican Regions: Comparative History and Development*. La Jolla: Center for U.S.-Mexican Studies, University of California, San Diego, 1992.

Latin American Religion

Much of the literature on the history of religion in Latin America, particularly books and articles published prior to the 1960s, concerns itself with the institutional history of the Catholic church, or the role of clerics as movers in history. Examples include studies that focus on the priests who staffed the frontier missions throughout the region, or organized the early evangelization of the Indian populations in the core areas such as Mexico or Peru in the 16th century. A second topic that has received attention is the ideological content of the worldview of early Catholic missionaries in the Americas. Numerous books and articles are examples of church self-history, which generally lack objectivity.

Beginning in the 1960s, the study of the history of religion in Latin America changed. Historians drew upon the ethnohistoric/ethnographic record to gain greater insights on the exact nature of religion and religious change, and applied the techniques of ethnohistory, especially to the question of the evangelization of the Indians. Historians wrote social histories of religion, and refined the older institutional approach through the use of prosopography (collective biography).

This article focuses on three important themes in the religious history of Latin America: the evangelization of the Indian population, the social and economic role of *cofradias* (lay Catholic brotherhoods), and the recent surge in the popularity of evangelical Protestantism. These three topics do not cover the entire scope of religion in Latin America, but are representative of areas where scholarship has made great strides in recent years or are of such importance that they require scholarly attention.

In 1935, French historian Robert Ricard published a seminal book entitled *Conquête Spirituelle du Mexique* (published in English translation in 1966 by the University of California Press), which posited that despite considerable hardship and travail the early mendicant missionaries established the Mexican church and converted the Indians to Catholicism. Ricard's view of evangelization was overly optimistic because of his assumption that central Mexican Indians adopted Catholicism as taught by the missionaries, and relied almost exclusively on sources produced by the missionaries themselves. Moreover, Ricard presented missionary methods later applied to frontier regions in Mexico only in a positive light.

Social historians have since modified and rejected much of Ricard's characterization of the evangelization of the Indian populations. Stress is now placed on the ways in which Indians modified Catholic teachings for inclusion in their own worldview, and the use of coercion and violence in evangelization, particularly in anti-idolatry campaigns of the 16th and 17th centuries, which highlighted the shallowness of the conversions of the early 16th century. Recent scholarship has focused primarily on the core areas of Latin America (Mexico, the Andes). The impact of evangelization in the frontier missions in Spanish America and Brazil is a topic that still requires additional attention.

The *cofradias* were an important element of religious life in Latin America. Through the cofradia Catholics organized ritual fiestas for the patron saint of the community, or the patron of the brotherhood. Cofradias were also a useful mechanism for priests to earn additional income. Anthropologists first examined cofradias within the context of the cargo cult, a ritual system used for the redistribution of wealth in Indian communities. Cofradias also played an important role in the incorporation of Catholic beliefs into the Indian worldview. Other studies focus on the institutional organization of brotherhoods. Colonial-era cofradias were particularly important as sources of credit, especially to wealthy individuals and different church and government agencies. One area of needed research is the importance of cofradias in the day-to-day religious practices of common folk.

The most recent trend in Latin American religion is the growing importance of evangelical Protestantism, which claims as many as 50 million adherents. Disenchantment with the Catholic church, which historically has been a conservative force in Latin American society that supported the status quo, has resulted in the growth

in the number of conversions to evangelical Protestant sects. One attraction appears to be the more participatory nature of evangelicalism, which contrasts with the structured organization of Catholicism. However, the growth of Protestantism, especially in rural areas, has contributed to the decline of cargo cult practices and a redefinition of community relations. Important research questions which remain to be investigated include the class content of the evangelical Protestant movement. Historians and social scientists need to explore the attractions of evangelical Protestantism in Latin American societies experiencing rapid and profound changes. (*See also* Religion)

Robert H. Jackson

REFERENCES

Clendinnen, Inga. *Ambivalent Conquests: Maya and Spaniards in Yucatan, 1517–1570.* New York: Cambridge University Press, 1987.

Farriss, Nancy. *Maya Society Under Colonial Rule: The Collective Enterprise of Survival.* Princeton, NJ: Princeton University Press, 1984.

MacCormack, Sabine. *Religion in the Andes: Vision and Imagination in Early Colonial Peru.* Princeton, NJ: Princeton University Press, 1991.

Meyers, Albert, and Diane Hopkins, eds. *Manipulating the Saints: Religious Brotherhoods and Social Integration in Postconquest Latin America.* Hamburg: Wayasbah, 1988.

Serrat, Oscar (Associated Press). "Fertile Ground: Evangelicals Cultivate the Poor in Latin America," *The Houston Chronicle* (January 4, 1992).

Latin American Urbanization

Distinctive characteristics of Latin American urban patterns form a vital framework for the region's social history, including the recent high levels of urbanization and urban poverty.

A centuries-long indigenous urban tradition characterized portions of Latin America, especially the Central Valley of Mexico and the highland areas of South America, prior to the arrival of Europeans. The presence of urban-centered empires and of masses of sedentary Indian peoples profoundly affected initial Spanish settlement patterns. Thus, the Spaniards erected Mexico City as capital of the viceroyalty of New Spain directly on the ruins of the Aztec capital,

Tenochtitlán; founded many other settlements in order to pacify and control the labor of Indian peoples; and, in many instances, forcibly resettled Indians into towns. Although the precipitous decline in population of indigenous peoples, which began soon after the arrival of the Europeans and extended into the first half of the 17th century, increasingly minimized the economic rationale for regulating Indian labor, the pattern of cities functioning as administrative control centers and spearheads for settling land and organizing economic activity remained characteristic of the long colonial period.

This reflected not only New World conditions, but Spain's own enduring municipal tradition. When Columbus first touched down on the New World, virtually his first act (after giving thanks to God and claiming the land) was to formally establish a town and appoint officials. His behavior would be replicated throughout the period of Spanish conquest and exploration. Cities served as mining centers, as points of penetration and communication into the interior, and as fortified garrisons protecting Spanish interests against both indigenous peoples and European rivals. Within the Spanish imperial system, however, the administrative/bureaucratic function of cities assumed paramount importance. Whether great viceregal capitals like Mexico City or Lima, or more modest regional centers, colonial cities both symbolized Spain's authority and formed the sinews and nerves of the imperial system. The basic design of Spanish cities bespoke hierarchy and order. At the center stood a large square surrounded by the most significant public and ecclesiastical buildings. A grid pattern emanated out from the city center, with the homes of the wealthy enjoying the closest location to the central plaza. Today, despite urban sprawl and suburbanization, central city areas retain enormous vitality in Latin America and, to a great extent, remain a preferred residential location.

Spain rigidly controlled the flow of New World trade, establishing monopoly ports in both Spain and Latin America. Although 18th-century reforms eased this system, freedom of trade remained limited, even within Latin America. As a result, cities' most important economic relationships were with the overseas metropolises.

With this orientation, cities sparked relatively little development in their hinterlands, and the development of urban networks within Latin America was retarded. While urban merchants played a vital economic role, they generally failed to constitute an independent mercantile class, and concentrated instead on advancing family status interests. The export emphasis, when combined with both Spanish regulation and that nation's relatively underdeveloped state with regard to industry and technology further undermined Latin American economic development and retarded the development of manufacturing. In turn, this restricted employment opportunities within cities and helped forestall significant alterations in social class relationships. Indeed, for most of Latin America, the rise of substantial middle sectors and organized working classes did not occur until well into the 20th century.

The Brazilian colonial urban experience often is contrasted with that of Spanish Latin America. Portugal exercised far less control over its colony, and power in Brazil rested more in the countryside with the owners of great estates than in the cities. Furthermore, unlike the Spanish pattern, virtually every significant Brazilian city was located along the coast. Nonetheless, Brazil too had a hierarchical social structure, and the basis of its economy rested on overseas economic relationships. Like their Spanish counterparts, then, Brazilian cities offered relatively little opportunity for social mobility and sparked little development in their hinterlands.

If the colonial period bequeathed a pattern of urban enclaves whose most significant commercial relationships were overseas, and whose power largely rested on administrative functions, subsequent development in the 19th and 20th centuries reinforced these characteristics. Most of the nations of Latin America are characterized by pronounced urban primacy, a situation in which one city, usually the capital, houses an extraordinarily large percentage of the national population, has by far the best developed service infrastructure; serves as the chief financial, industrial, and commercial center; and by far dwarfs the nation's next largest urban place.

Primacy derives from multiple factors. During the 19th century, the trajectories of railroad systems, which largely were determined by national governments, reinforced the hegemony of capital cities, further advantaging them as commercial entrepôts. Works of urban beautification, typical especially of the later 19th and early 20th centuries, similarly enhanced the status of the national capital, which increasingly distanced itself from secondary cities and in the context of relatively underdeveloped countries assumed the status of a "modern" Western world metropolis. The presence of a higher quality and more extensive infrastructure proved attractive to both foreign businesses and domestic elites, further reinforcing the importance and influence of the primate city. And, as the overwhelming importance of access to government power continued to characterize Latin America, all major enterprises needed to maintain a presence in the national capital.

The growth of larger-scale capital intensive agriculture saw the expulsion of tenant farmers, sharecroppers, and smallholders, especially from the 1940s on, generating massive streams of rural-to-urban migration. The relative backwardness of all but the major metropolises, as well as the prevailing transportation networks, tended to funnel a disproportionate share of this migration to the primate city. Commensurate employment opportunities did not exist, nor did an adequate stock of housing. Squatter settlements grew up around the outskirts of the city, and land invasions, organized movements in which poor people take over municipal land and quickly erect dwellings, became common. Although in contrast to the social stratification of earlier days, the contemporary Latin American city does reflect the presence of a more powerful organized working class and an expanded middle group, underemployment, unemployment, and the increasing informal economy all testify to the enduring power of hierarchy. The Latin American city thus remains a site of massive inequalities and jarring contrasts between rich and poor. (*See also* Cities; Urbanization)

Gerald Michael Greenfield

REFERENCES

Gilbert, Alan. *Urbanization in Contemporary Latin America: Critical Approaches to the Analysis of Urban Issues.* Chicester, NY: Wiley, 1982.

Hardoy, Jorge Enrique. *Urban Planning in Pre-Columbian America.* New York: Braziller, 1968.

Hoberman, Louisa Schell, and Susan Migden Socolow, eds. *Cities and Society in Colonial Latin America.* Albuquerque: University of New Mexico Press, 1986.

Morse, Richard M., ed., with Michael L. Conniff and John Wibel. *The Urban Development of Latin America, 1750–1920.* Stanford, CA: Center for Latin American Studies, Stanford University, 1971.

Roberts, Bryan. *Cities of Peasants: The Political Economy of Urbanization in the Third World.* Beverly Hills: Sage, 1978.

Latin American Women

The social historical study of women in Latin America is a relatively new and growing field. Within the last 20 years the literature has multiplied from a few biographies of "great" women to analyses of gender relations in various arenas including women and the family, women and the state, and women and work.

Studies of women and the family have primarily concentrated on women's roles as wives and mothers, as well as on the changing influence of the church versus the family in women's lives. Over the 16th through the early 19th centuries, the church in New Spain lost its power to regulate marriage. When the church held the larger influence over marriage, young women exercised more personal choice. But with economic development, men in secular society gained more power, and economic security became the primary interest in marriage choice. Currently, female-headed households are the norm for many families in Latin America, and new definitions of family must be incorporated into future analysis.

Women's actual experiences have contrasted sharply with acceptable behavior regulated by family and the church. Colonial women had more economic power within the family than might be expected. Elite women sometimes owned their own businesses and property, inherited one-half their husband's estates (more than the one-third inherited by British colonial wives in New England) and had some say over the tutoring and upbringing of their offspring. Although fairly strict standards of behavior prevailed, the reality of women's lives did not always meet these expectations. The concept of "public virgin" stands out as an example. Women could be pregnant, and even mothers privately, but publicly still be considered virgins. This was, of course, to protect the honor of the males in the family and to keep the women marketable for marriage to other elites to cement important family ties. This does reflect, however, a marked difference between ideal and reality in women's behavior.

Gender has always played a role in state policies in Latin America. In precolonial and colonial Peru, for example, the state used gender to organize society. Under the Inca state, society was organized dually, though not equally. There were female and male gods, and women could own property and leave it to their daughters. With the Spanish conquest in the 16th century and the influx of Catholic and Spanish ideas of women's proper roles, women lost their property rights and their right to have a legitimate relationship to the state rather than through their husband. Agricultural reforms of the 19th and early 20th centuries, especially in Mexico, facilitated individual male ownership of land, which caused women to lose access to communal lands. In the 20th century state policies still discriminate against women. For example, the Peruvian state has blamed marketers, virtually all of whom are poor women, for food inflation. Through regulation, the state has attempted to force many women out of business; this has not been carried through, however, because of their integral role in the economy.

The nature of women's work, which has always been principally as domestic servants and marketers, has made them the most vulnerable sector of the working class. Competition from European factories cut into women's manufacturing for home use in the 19th century. Currently, sweatshop work, which is moving to Third World countries, employs primarily young single women. The nature of women's work differs from that of men because of the smaller amount of capital associated with women's work, so women, many of whom head families without male support, must use and manipulate scarce resources to maintain households.

While literature on women in Latin America has advanced considerably in a short period of time, some major problems as well as sizable gaps still exist. Most of the literature either concentrates on the colonial period or on the last 20 years. This leaves a sizable lacuna for the 19th and early 20th centuries. Second, much of the work has focused on elite women, particularly in the colonial period. Elite women were and are a small portion of society, and their lives differ dramatically from the majority of women in Latin America. Third, many studies have yet to focus on the importance of ethnicity and class for women's lives.

By grounding studies on gender within larger economic development and social issues in Latin America, we can gain an enhanced understanding not only of women's lives, but of Latin American social history more generally. (*See also* Women's History)

Gina Hames

REFERENCES

Babb, Florence. *Between Field and Cooking Pot: The Political Economy of Market Women in Peru.* Austin: University of Texas Press, 1989.

Nash, June, and Helen I. Safa. *Women and Change in Latin America: New Directions in Sex and Class.* Bergin and Garvey, 1985.

Seed, Patricia. *To Love, Honor, and Obey in Colonial Mexico: Conflicts over Marriage Choice, 1574–1821.* Stanford, CA: Stanford University Press, 1988.

Silverblatt, Irene. *Moon, Sun, and Witches: Gender Ideologies and Class in Inca and Colonial Peru.* Princeton, NJ: Princeton University Press, 1987.

Latin American Working Class, Strikes

As Latin America became increasingly incorporated into the world economy and wage labor grew in the 1880s, organizations composed mostly of skilled craftsmen, known as resistance societies, became prevalent. Their formation, as with the unionization of less skilled workers, generally took place during phases of economic expansion. One distinctive form of resistance society that emerged in the nitrate mining areas of northern Chile, known as *mancomunales*, brought together skilled and unskilled workers of diverse occupations on a regional basis. Across Latin America, these societies supplanted mutual aid societies, the first collective effort by artisans and, occasionally, wage earners to protect and improve their living and working conditions, that had emerged in most of the larger Latin American countries by the middle of the 19th century. While labor protest has not received as much sociohistorical attention for Latin America as Europe and the United States, a number of studies have emerged, some with important comparative dimensions.

As Latin American nations came to specialize in the export of primary commodities, regional differences in economic development and in the emergence of labor organizations and workers' tactics took place. A range of factors combined to encourage or inhibit working-class organization. These included geography, fluctuations in foreign capital and commodity markets, the nationality of owners and degree of concentration of ownership of the means of production, technology and the extent of capital-intensive production, the availability of labor, and the nationality or ethnic identity of workers. Whereas worker organizations remained weak in much of Central America and northern South America before World War I, Argentina, Chile, Brazil, and Mexico witnessed extensive labor activity. The strongest labor movement emerged in Argentina, where economic expansion encouraged skilled artisans organized along craft lines as masons, typographers, carpenters, tailors, tram conductors, and other professions, to form labor centrals and conduct solidarity strikes. Strikes begun over working conditions often spread beyond the initial group of workers to paralyze entire cities including Buenos Aires in 1904 and 1907.

Many participating in the general strikes in early 20th-century Argentina, the majority being immigrants from southern Europe, professed anarchist affiliations. While it is difficult to evaluate the influence of ideological currents such as anarchism, syndicalism, and socialism on working-class organization, workers in Argentina, as in the new industrial complexes and railways throughout Latin America, had no inherited ideals of the good industrial life to which they could appeal. They had to develop and absorb ideologies and experiment with new organizational forms and strategies. Whereas in certain times and places anarchism or syndicalism predominated, the dominant ideology of the working

class in Mexico remained liberalism. Throughout Latin America, workers formed unions to demand rights, privileges, or resources that they had not previously enjoyed and preferred to organize and strike rather than to engage in revolutionary violence. While increased wages and improved working conditions were their chief concerns, many also sought to assert their basic human dignity in the face of abuse and contempt. This was not easy as management clung to its prerogatives, the labor market was not conducive to unionization, and financial and logistical problems made association difficult. In most areas, as in northern Chile, where over a thousand nitrate workers and their families were killed in 1907, state repression impeded organization.

Strikes between 1917 and 1920, a period of unprecedented labor activity coinciding with increased industrialization and irregular economic expansion in some parts of Latin America, helped shape subsequent struggles and the response of states. In Cuba, Colombia, Ecuador, and Peru, areas with limited labor movements before the war, workers associated with export production organized and carried out general strikes. In Brazil and Chile, the expansion of union activity and a series of general strikes led to large-scale repression. The largest mobilizations took place in Argentina. A strike by metalworkers in Buenos Aires in 1919, in which police killed four workers, led to a massive general strike and battles in the streets pitting workers against the police and the army. New strategies to insure state domination of workers, including social reform legislation and cooptation (strategies that would be realized after 1930), began to emerge during this period.

Although a diminution of labor activity accompanied the economic downturn associated with the Great Depression, a new phase of import-substitution industrialization during the 1930s and export-led growth during World War II led to increased industrialization and labor activity. The number of strikes in Mexico, for example, rose in the late 1930s and culminated in a wave of strike activity in 1943–1944. In Argentina, the period between 1946 and 1951 witnessed both the extension of trade unionism and the emergence of the state as the ultimate arbiter of labor relations. In both countries, as in many others, corporatist control over workers meant the subordination of the union movement to the state. At the same time, however, the potential for working-class resistance was not eliminated. While workers were often asked to subordinate their interests for the supposed good of the nation, daily lived experience, especially the strike, led to the development of a strong oppositional culture. Through strikes, such as those mounted in the 1950s by Argentine workers, participants expressed the sense of unity and pride, even class, felt by workers. In Mexico, the emergence of independent unions in the automotive industry in the 1970s suggests that corporatist control over labor may be weaker than formerly thought.

The emergence of an oppositional culture has led workers to support revolutionary movements in some parts of Latin America. In Bolivia, for example, tin miners, organized early in the 20th century, developed a strong sense of identity as a community and a class in response to exploitation and repression. Employed in a key sector of the economy that has, at times, accounted for 90 percent of the country's exports, miners organized and struck in the late 1930s and 1940s. In 1952, they seized mines and took to the streets in support of the Movimiento Nacional Revolucionario and its leader Victor Paz Estenssoro. In Cuba, as well, a strike undertaken by bus drivers spread to almost all industry and helped to topple the government of Gerardo Machado in 1933. Workers also participated in the coalition supporting the Castro revolution that came to power in 1959. (*See also* Protest; Working Class)

William E. French

REFERENCES

Bergquist, Charles. *Labor in Latin America: Comparative Essays on Chile, Argentina, Venezuela, and Colombia.* Stanford, CA: Stanford University Press, 1986.

Hall, Michael M., and Hobart A. Spalding, Jr. "The Urban Working Class and Early Latin American Labour Movements, 1880–1930," in Leslie Bethell, ed., *The Cambridge History of Latin America*, Vol. 4. Cambridge: Cambridge University Press, 1986.

James, Daniel. *Resistance and Integration: Peronism and the Argentine Working Class, 1946–1976.* Cambridge: Cambridge University Press, 1988.

Roxborough, Ian. *Unions and Politics in Mexico: The Case of the Automobile Industry.* Cambridge: Cambridge University Press, 1984.

Law/Legal History

Interpretation of legal developments in light of broader social change, and use of such developments as evidence of social change, have gained ground in the past decade, as part of the more general outreach of social history. Even before this, social historians used evidence from court cases to determine a variety of social relationships among ordinary people, particularly before modern times. The social history of the law also gains focus, however, from evolution in the field of legal history itself, as debate about the position of the law in society began in the field soon after 1900.

For what was called "sociolegal history" stemmed from progressive era concerns about interpreting the law in socially useful ways. Sociolegal history grew out of a rejection by early 20th century scholars of sociological jurisprudence of internal, or doctrinal, legal history (the idea that law results from formal doctrine and legal precedent). Sociological history focuses on the historical interrelation of law and society and finds explanation for legal change primarily in social context. Since the 1950s, this inquiry has branched into two competing models for the driving force of legal change. One, best demonstrated in *A History of American Law* (1985) by Lawrence Friedman, says that the law expresses the dominant, primarily economic needs of a given society for a given period of time. As these needs change, so too does the law, form following function.

The other approach, advocated by Morton Horwitz in *The Transformation of American Law 1780–1860* (1977), rejects the implied politically neutral consensus advanced by Friedman, and claims that the law is really an instrument of hegemony by certain groups over others. The law, in this view, only legitimates and perpetuates a social structure wished by a few. In both these models, the law as a semi-autonomous institution either has very little or no salience.

In many respects, the social history of the law was initially the child of these two parents. It sought to document those groups, such as women, minorities, the working class, and the poor, who were in one respect the victims of Horwitz's law, and in another the seldom recognized contributors to Friedman's. One focus aims at the social effects of the law; the other, the social influences on its making. Thus, women, African Americans, and slavery dominate the early work and continue to form prominent areas of research. Joan Hoff-Wilson's *Law, Gender and Injustice: A Legal History of U.S. Women* (1991) and Kermit Hall's *Civil Rights in American History* (1987) are recent works that continue this tradition. The working class also finds recent coverage in *The Cold War Against Labor: An Anthology*, edited by Ann Fagan Ginger and David Christiano (1987).

In keeping with this early emphasis on the displaced, the criminal law was also an area of extensive research, although to a lesser extent in American history than in European social history. A collection of essays is found in *Crime and the Law: The Social History of Crime in Western Europe since 1500,* edited by V.A.C. Gatrell, Bruce Lenman, and Geoffrey Parker (1980). Other works have focused on the social history of specific areas of the law, such as prostitution. Peter Hoffer's *Murdering Mothers: Infanticide in England and New England, 1558–1803* (1981) bridges the gap, albeit for only the colonial period in American history. Much more needs to be done for the 20th century for both America and Europe, as well as the criminal law in other cultures and regions of the world.

These two focuses, the social effects of and the social influences on the law, remain the guiding themes of ongoing research in the field, but the models of the interaction have grown more complex as social historians uncover new dimensions of the legal institution. As social history in general has adopted new models of change and branched into new areas of research, so too has the social history of the law. For example, attention to cultural anthropology has inspired an attempt to detail and understand a "legal culture" in a given society. Here legal culture is taken to be the ideas and attitudes toward the law, and its legitimacy within society. Friedman's recent *The Republic of Choice; Law, Authority and Culture* (1990) explores this concept for 20th century

America and finds a "rights consciousness" driven by a peculiar and persistent American individualism as a dominant theme of modern American legal culture. In a similar vein, the work of Rhys Isaac, *The Transformation of Virginia, 1740–1790* (1982), details the close integration of the legal institution within the culture of the early Republic, an approach less fully developed for 17th-century America in David T. Konig's *Law and Society in Puritan Massachusetts: Essex County, 1629–1692* (1979).

Social history has also recently sought to define subcultures and groups, documenting how these groups retain the independence necessary for diversity within a society. It has shown how they react to larger forces of change or hegemony by other dominant groups. Lower-class families, for example, were often able to use juvenile delinquency law to help maintain their own family values. Especially for the 20th century in America, the law has been a realm of subcultural interaction, and its documents record the voices of some groups that left no other records. In many respects, legal documents are an evidentiary gold mine waiting to be tapped.

The growing emphasis on legal culture and subcultures has modified the competing paradigms of legal change. As a result, the older models no longer provide an exclusive explanation for legal change. For example, social historians have looked at the symbolic as well as the repressive roles of the law within a given legal culture, thus giving some credence to the view of at least a semi-autonomous institution. Even ideology has regained explanatory force for some legal developments, especially in the period of post–Revolutionary War Republicanism. Finally, Robert Steven's *Law School: Legal Education in America from 1859 to the 1980's* (1983) has detailed the extent to which professional ideology contributes to the content and direction of the law. Thus, the law does more for the civilized order than merely reflecting the functional needs or instrumental power of a few. Here, social history has shifted the balance of inquiry from the sociolegal history theories which saw law almost exclusively as a dependent variable to granting some autonomy to the law and ideology in interaction with various subcultures.

This focus on legal culture is part of a broader attempt to understand deeply held beliefs, or mentalities. As in the field of social history in general, this drive to understand mental attitude has pushed social historians to social psychological theory. Thus, Robert L. Griswold's *Family and Divorce in California, 1850–1890: Victorian Illusions and Everyday Realities* (1982), recounts the changes brought in divorce law, as people's beliefs about marriage changed. New work on emotionology, the study of emotional norms and their change over time, is beginning to reveal the interaction between massive shifts in social norms, and the formal legal rules affected by them. For example, the now familiar mental cruelty provision in divorce has been directly traced to changes in norms for love and anger near the turn of the century.

This same emphasis on mentalities has precipitated inquiry into the interaction between the law and other formal institutions, such as the family and marriage. Based on assumptions that the mentality of a culture for a given period is at least partially reflected in all of its social institutions, the comparative relationship between differing institutions becomes a subject of inquiry. Michael Grossberg's *Governing the Hearth: Law and the Family in Nineteenth-Century America* (1985) covers diverse areas of law affecting the family and its individual members, but mostly from a doctrinal survey viewpoint. Roderick Phillips's, *Putting Asunder: A History of Divorce in Western Society* (1988) incorporates the current research on the social history of divorce into a more formal cultural history of marital breakdown. Both these works are useful starts, but much more should be done to provide more detailed social histories of how the law of divorce worked in practice. Also, the interrelations between law and other institutions, such as religion and governmental structures, are areas of some research, with much more to be covered in terms of differing time periods and cultures.

Furthermore, social history has demonstrated that the law, if not in the books, then at least in practice, showed a penchant for regionalism, as in the American South. Since social history pushes beyond appellate cases or legislation to see the social effects and influences of the law, it also explores the law in practice. It is in practice that regionalism becomes most evident.

Kermit Hall's *The Magic Mirror* (1989) is the most recent attempt to evaluate the influence social history has had on the study of the law and to incorporate the conceptions of legal change. Allowing for some autonomy for the law, and detailing the social effects upon and influences of subcultures on the making of law, Hall demonstrates the utility sociohistorical research has had on legal history. No comparable synthesis on legal culture has developed within the European context, let alone for other regions and societies.

Outside the Euro-American histories, social history is just beginning to make inroads into legal history. An early work by Sybille Van Der Sprenkel, *Legal Institutions in Manchu China: A Sociological Analysis* (1977), adapted social anthropology theories to study commercial laws in late imperial China. A study of Russian women and the law in *Russia's Women: Accommodation, Resistance, Transformation,* Barbara Evans Clements, et al., eds. (1991), provides a nice comparative complement to much of the work done on women in Western cultures, as does that of Indu Prakash Singh's *Women, Law, and Social Change in India* (1989). Finally, Shlomo Deshen in *The Mellah Society Jewish Community Life in Sherifian Morocco* (1988) uses social history to trace the interaction between a small subculture within a Muslim legal structure. This type of comparative work is extremely useful to place current and ongoing research within a broader social context.

The influence of social history has extended into medieval legal scholarship, an area of recalcitrant "doctrinists" searching for the origins of legal rules. Thus, Robert Palmer's *The Whilton Dispute, 1264–1380: A Social-Legal Study of Dispute Settlement in Medieval England* (1984) and Stephen White's *Custom, Kinship, and Gifts to Saints: The Laudatio Parentum in Western France, 1050–1150* (1988) have presented a strong case for social history in areas of traditional legal scholarship.

The impact of social history upon the study of the law has been rewarding, while complicating the development of a full paradigm for legal change. With so many untapped areas as well as huge gaps in existing research, social history will continue to enliven and fundamentally change the direction of legal-historical research. (*See also* Judiciary; Mentalities; Popular Culture; Subcultures)

Mark T. Knapp

REFERENCES

Friedman, Lawrence. *A History of American Law,* 2nd ed. New York: Simon & Schuster, 1973.

Hall, Kermit. *The Magic Mirror: Law in American History.* New York: Oxford University Press, 1989.

Roderick Phillips. *Putting Asunder: A History of Divorce in Western Society.* New York: Cambridge University Press, 1988.

Leisure

Leisure is not a straightforward concept. It is not simply a state of not working, whether for a wage or on essential life-supporting activities. This kind of negative, residual definition offers little purchase for discussion. Significantly, dismay was expressed when research in southern Italy in 1958 found that one-third of the population used up its free time on working days in doing nothing at all. This was interesting, but unhelpful. Leisure as a subject of historical enquiry involves activities and practices undertaken in time which is not earmarked for making a living or sustaining basic personal and household needs: so-called free time, in the use of which people might be said to make choices and express preferences which help us to understand their culture and their wider social arrangements. So it is not just the activities themselves, but also the values which people bring to them and read off from them which are of interest to the social historian, as are the contexts of choice and constraint, economic, physical, and ideological, in which particular uses of leisure ebb, flow, and change their character and meaning.

Leisure can be difficult for historians studying modern societies because of the sheer range of phenomena which might be grouped together under the heading "anything from baseball to butterfly collecting, from dancing to knitting, from religious worship to the ill-defined aimlessness that British adolescents used to call 'mucking about'." Even a list like this involves potential controversy: for whom and under what circumstances should religious worship be defined as "leisure"? Obvious value judgments are inescapable. But it is possible to arrive at intermediate and relatively manageable generalizations by grouping together aspects of leisure which seem to have significant things in common, just as industries or occupations can be grouped. So historians write about competitive sport, or commercialized entertainment, or traditional enjoyments, though here again, the categories "commercial" and "traditional" are open to a variety of interpretations. Leisure can also be divided according to the moral calculus that contemporaries used—rational recreations against irrational amusements, respectable and unrespectable, amateur and professional in sporting and entertainment terms, to use a few sample dichotomies from Victorian Britain. But rather than sustain this focus on leisure as something discrete and apart from the rest of society, rather than pursue this classificatory theme, it is more useful to look at leisure in relation to the wider society and to see how it impinges on other historical concerns, and they on it.

Most obvious in a lot of the historiography is the relationship between leisure and work. Some, indeed, have almost taken the one as the reflex of the other. In fact, even in the classic factory industries of the later 19th century, the two cannot be kept apart in sealed containers. Thomas Wright, "the journeyman engineer," writing in 1867, commented that "such a monster as a working man who considered work, even during his working hours, to be his being's end and aim is happily for himself rarely to be met with in the flesh." Drink was smuggled in, and tobacco was smoked in hidden corners, while special occasions were marked with disruptive ceremonies. Matters were not much different in the German Rhineland. And Wright also pointed out that work could in its turn invade the drinking place, with many men having no other topic of conversation, and eagerly discussing skills, techniques, and ideas over a few beers. Moving on in time and jumping up a few steps, how should we categorize the game of golf whose true purpose is to clinch a business deal? Or, on the domestic front, is it work or leisure when a woman sits by the fireside knitting something which will contribute to the household economy? Where work ends and leisure begins is not as simple a matter as some sociologists suggest.

It is probably the case, however, that work and leisure have become more compartmentalized for more people during and since the first industrial revolution, although matters have become more complicated again in recent years. The decline of domestic manufacture, the separation of home and workplace, and above all the transition from what E.P. Thompson called "task-orientation" to "time-orientation" all helped to divide the week into "own time" and "boss's time." Instead of working until the task was completed, and then relaxing and enjoying oneself until the next one had to be started, the new regime of labor discipline imposed longer, regular hours and sought to punish the importation of leisure into the workplace, except on the employer's terms. This model works for those who moved from domestic manufacture into factory industries, despite continuing seepage from one compartment to the other; but it deals less effectively with the experience of those who continued to work on farms and in domestic workshops, and it fails to cope with those whose main occupation was housework, where work and leisure continued to be so intertwined as to be hardly separable. Nevertheless, the notion that for those below the level of the gentry the industrial revolution "invented" the distinction between work and leisure, especially for men, has considerable merit. Preindustrialized recreations, however, existed in abundance as in the festival traditions. A key task of historians of modern leisure is to trace breaks and continuities from preindustrial to industrial recreational forms and purposes.

There is no denying the growing economic, social, and perhaps political importance of leisure in the Western world over the last two centuries. Apart from the relationship between leisure and labor discipline, the most obvious economic theme has been the rise and spread of popular enjoyment as an item of consumption, in an enormous range of guises from reading matter and sheet music to seaside holidays and professional sport. Increasingly, the leisure industries—including domestic entertainment—have generated employment and attracted investment. Meanwhile, the leisure of the emer-gent working class, in particular, became a source of worry and controversy in ruling, religious, and philanthropic circles. Aspects of it were seen as immoral, disorderly, damaging to productivity and efficiency, threatening to life and property, and damaging to thrift and forethought in ways which might increase the cost of charity and poor relief. There was less concern about the pleasures of the propertied, although they were not neglected altogether: there was much middle-class introspection and discussion in mid-Victorian England over the proper role of pleasure in respectable life. Beyond all this is the overtly political agenda, developed more by subsequent historians than by contemporaries, although not absent from the concerns of (for example) socialists in Britain and Germany as the turn of the century and after. Did the growth of mass commercial leisure divert the working class from radical and revolutionary political activity by providing immediate satisfactions and excitement, alternative interests and loyalties to team, neighborhood and nation rather than class? More sophisticatedly, did it reinforce the legitimacy of the rulers of the industrializing world by winning the assent of the ruled to versions of "common sense" which emphasized the inevitability of existing economic and social arrangements and the pleasures they offered, while fostering patriotism, militarism, and a sense that, however unsatisfactory things might be, they might always be worse? Leisure as a defuser of discontent and prophylactic against revolution is a matter for serious discussion.

One of the strongest themes in the historiography, especially in Britain, is the relationship between leisure and class. Most basically, of course, different social strata with different economic resources were drawn into the leisure marketplace at different times; and generalizations can be made which differentiate between the experiences of the aristocracy and gentry, the middle classes and the wage earners, although the gap between the "labor aristocracy" and the unskilled and casual worker was very important. But there were also both "respectable" and "unrespectable" pursuits which cut across class and status lines in recruiting their devotees. In Victorian England popular science claimed the attention of small numbers of men from all social levels, although the lord seldom encountered the laborer. On the other hand, horse racing attracted men from all walks of life into the raffish freemasonry of "the turf", as the Liverpool journalist Hugh Shimmin pointed out in describing the merchants, doctors, and philanthropists who frequented the city's Aintree race meeting alongside aristocrats, prostitutes, farmers, "roughs," and a cross-section of manual workers. It would be wrong to regard all members of the Victorian, or any other, middle class as being uniformly in thrall to a narrow and restrictive code of bourgeois respectability. And where it was adopted at all, many were prepared to discard it when opportunity arose.

For the rich, an ostentatiously leisured and ceremonial lifestyle became almost a duty, extending beyond the charmed circle of the aristocracy in the 18th century and after. As the landed elite in England shared the formal enjoyments of the spas and county towns with people of inferior status, complex codes of manners and etiquette were devised to filter out those whose only claims to participation came from uncultivated wealth. As high society became superficially more accessible, so behavioral codes became more elaborate in public places of elite resort. In the 19th century, too, the tyranny of the visiting card, the afternoon "at home," and the mourning ritual penetrated the middle-class family. In effect, more and more people were having to work at their leisure, to cultivate their presentation of self. Among the lower orders, meanwhile, the survival of calendar customs and other social rituals into the industrial age was also a matter of duty as well as spontaneity. Customs had to be observed at times even though there was no pleasure and some discomfort in them, as in the wet and muddy gathering of rushes from distant moors to build the rushcarts for the Lancashire wakes. The power of custom to compel a fundamentally joyless use of leisure time was enduring, though the survival of the customs themselves was a patchy and complicated matter.

This theme is related to the most complex and widespread kind of interaction between class and leisure—the attempts of those with property and authority to constrain and mold the enjoyments of their social inferiors. This might be done through the coercive manipulation of law, police, and property rights, especially as an adjunct to labor discipline. Attempts to suppress popular fairs by these means were common in Britain and Germany, for example, in the 19th and early 20th centuries, but less in evidence in the Roman Catholic and less industrialized setting of Spain. In Germany, indeed, repression was more effective in new specialized industrial towns with elites dominated by Protestant big businessmen than in older-established towns with mixed economies and religiously divided rulers, such as Düsseldorf. The suppression of blood sports and the regulation of drinking outlets were also common themes, although in England the aristocracy's favored pastime and ritual of fox hunting survived unscathed while more plebeian activities like cockfighting (despite some aristocratic support) and dogfighting were driven underground.

On a broader front, attempts were made to channel working-class leisure into more acceptable spheres in a positive way, by providing and encouraging "rational recreations" to lure people away from the drinking place and the fairground or racecourse. Religious bodies offered fetes, excursions, classes, and reading rooms, especially from the 1830s, as did some large employers, and movements directed against alcoholic excess. Municipal intervention increased from the mid-19th century, with the provision of parks, libraries, and baths, often in partnership with private donors. Secular voluntary organizations, like the cooperative movement in Britain and settlement houses in Britain and the United States, also got involved. From the 1880s onward European socialist groups were also concerned to lead their members away from the distractions of the expanding commercial leisure market and sought to build an alternative, politically conscious leisure environment in which socialist values would be reinforced. But this was only attractive to a committed minority, and made it even more difficult to build a mass movement. The churches had similar problems. "Rational recreation" provisions did not languish unused, however, but a lot of people took what was an offer on their own terms and continued to enjoy themselves in other ways as well. Reformers of whatever stamp were rarely able to sustain the control they sought.

Sometimes traditional popular festivities were appropriated, and remade, by members or sections of the elite—a reminder that leisure practices and fashions do not always trickle down by emulation from top to bottom of the social order. Thus, at the turn of the century the pre-Lent Carnival in the Spanish resort and provincial capital of San Sebastián had its public face transformed by expensive floats and carefully orchestrated processions funded and put together by the recreational and political clubs of the better-off. The old informal street carnival of the "old town" continued, but more marginally and with less visibility. The reconstruction of football in mid-Victorian England, from encounters between whole villages, governed by customs rather than rules and with few constraints on space or time, to carefully regulated matches between nominated teams on pitches with strict time limits, is a more sweeping example. Muscular Christians from elite schools offered the new version under religious or educational auspices, extolling the virtues of health, competitiveness, team spirit, and above all chivalrous sportsmanship. The irony was that the new game, in its most popular variant, was within a generation being transformed again into a commercially run spectator sport which employed professionals, in contravention of the ideals of its original promoters.

Association football (soccer), with the limits its governing body imposed on dividends and its concern for playing as well as financial success, was not the most thoroughgoing example of the commercialization of leisure which gathered momentum rapidly, in Britain from the 1830s, and with varying time lags elsewhere. It is not an absolutely clear-cut concept, because payment for pleasures in association with alcohol and sex goes back a very long way. But the 18th century saw a marked development in the Western world of the luxury end of the pleasure market, from books and sporting prints to balls and assemblies. Specialized pleasure towns emerged, first spas, then seaside resorts, adding entertainment to their original and ostensible purpose of cure, and soon putting pleasure first. Then, as working-class living standards began to rise from

around the mid-19th century, music halls, dancing saloons, and cheap theaters for a plebeian audience became paying propositions. These in turn stimulated new fears of the corruption of morals, with economic and military implications; and problems arose when boisterous pleasure seekers of low status sought access to amenities and leisure space which had been the preserve of their "betters," whether at the racecourse or on the promenade and beach at the seaside. Here again, leisure generated conflict with overtones of class; and this posed further problems for municipalities, police, and entertainment entrepreneurs, as they sought to reconcile ideals of free trade and the pursuit of profit with conflicting ideas about morality, respectability, and decorum.

Women and young people were especially problematic when they entered the public (as opposed to the domestic) leisure market as consumers. Most women remained hidden from history in their leisure, insofar as they had any: it was invisible in the home to all but oral historians. When women chose to spend their wages in dance halls and music halls, they were severely criticized for flouting cultural expectations of demure domesticity, although female patronage of the cinema soon became acceptable. Adolescents, meanwhile, readily attracted the stigma of hooligans or *gamberros* as soon as they developed a leisure culture of their own, and especially when, in the 1950s and 1960s, they acquired spending power to go with it. Again, however, this applied much more to teenage boys than girls.

As leisure became more sharply differentiated from work, then, and as it ceased to be an elite preserve and became common property, though in many different forms, it became contentious in many ways which illustrated and contributed to wider social tensions in the West. Historians disagree about the implications and effects. Above all, battle lines are drawn between free-market liberals who argue that capitalism delivered the goods by providing a newly affluent working class with the commercial leisure that it wanted, and historians of a Marxist orientation who emphasize the efforts of the state and its dominant classes to control the working class through leisure, defining what is acceptable and discouraging what is threatening. Mass leisure would not work if it were not compatible with most people's perceived needs; but that does not mean that it need not exploit its workers and manipulate its customers. The debates will continue.

The social history of leisure continues to grow. Its analytical structure is richest for the 19th-century West. Work on the 20th century tends to be rather descriptive to date, though mass leisure organizes important research on movies and their audiences, while leisure has yet to figure as prominently in the social histories of areas other than Europe and the United States. The challenges for further work are obvious. (*See also* Festivals; Games; Sport; Working Class)

John K. Walton

REFERENCES

Abrams, Lynn. *Workers' Culture in Imperial Germany.* London: Routledge, 1992.

Bailey, Peter. *Leisure and Class in Victorian England.* London: Routledge, 1978.

Golby, J., and A.W. Purdue. *The Civilisation of the Crowd: Popular Culture in England, 1750–1900.* London: Batsford, 1984.

Peiss, K. *Cheap Amusements: Working Women and Leisure in Turn of the Century New York.* Philadelphia: Temple University Press, 1986.

Walton, J.K., and J. Walvin, eds. *Leisure in Britain, 1780–1939.* Manchester: Manchester University Press, 1983.

Liberalism

The term "liberalism" has two almost diametrically opposed meanings. In late 20th-century United States politics, it refers to individuals who are center-left in political orientation and who favor the intervention of the state to solve social problems. The original sense of the word, as used in the 19th century and even today in much of the rest of the world, is virtually the opposite. Liberalism in the original sense favors a reliance on the market to solve societal problems. The guiding idea is that if each individual is able to reach his or her own potential with minimal restraints by society, society will function best. Thus, liberals traditionally preferred a laissez faire economic approach, favoring, for example, free trade and few restrictions on internal markets.

The ideal of unfettering of human activity led many Latin American and European liberals into anticlericalism, particularly against the Catholic church. While often personally devout, many liberals saw monasticism and the holding of lands by the Catholic church as damaging to society, for monks and nuns were seen as unproductive members of society, restrained by their order from fully participating in life. The lands the Catholic church maintained could not, by tradition, be sold. According to liberal tenets, this greatly hindered the development of a land market and restricted agricultural growth. Village communal lands likewise were detrimental to full market development. Most liberals also favored a form of federalism, for this would diminish the power of the state to make excessive regulations.

Liberalism evolved from ideas first articulated during the Enlightenment in Europe during the 18th century. Hobbes, Adam Smith, and Ricardo can be seen as important liberal thinkers. The French and United States revolutions were also based on fundamentally liberal ideas. Although liberal ideas were exceedingly important in western and southern Europe, liberalism probably had its greatest effects in Latin America. In the early 19th century, liberalism was seen as a revolutionary doctrine that could undo the legacy of colonialism. In most Latin American countries liberals achieved power after the overthrow of the colonial regime. However, the liberal ideas were too utopian to be put in effect, and liberals almost uniformly were thrown out of power.

In the second half of the 19th century the liberals made a comeback, taking over governments throughout the region. They implemented numerous reforms, now in a much more authoritarian manner than before. Gone was the impulse toward decentralization and federalism. In any case, these reforms had a tremendous social impact. Free trade cemented Latin America's role as a raw materials exporter, making possible the full-scale integration of the region into the world economy. The abolition of the Indian communities and the sale of village lands made possible the expansion of the great estates at the expense of the Latin American peasants. Labor conditions in Latin America generally got worse, since the state permitted the land and factory owners to exploit workers almost at will or backed them up with armed force. The liberals also sold off the lands of the Catholic church, which again favored those who had large amounts of capital to purchase them. One of the best examples of these processes can be found in Mexico, during the period called La Reforma (1855–1876). Similar reform programs, in varying intensity, can be found in the rest of Latin America and southern Europe during this period.

By the last decade of the 19th century liberalism had become confounded with Positivism and Social Darwinism. Positivism, most strongly advocated by the French philosopher Auguste Comte, asserted that there were certain immutable social laws. Each society had to find these laws and implement legislation that complemented these laws; in this way society would run most smoothly. Advocates of Social Darwinism asserted that the European races were superior to all others and that the dark races, such as the Indians, were inferior and would soon die off as the fittest race would survive. These ideologies brought about untold suffering for the dark-skinned masses, since these ideologies justified the exploitation of the weaker members of society. In part because of this extreme exploitation, liberalism lost favor in the first few decades of the 20th century. It eventually brought about a backlash, as in the Mexican Revolution (1910–1920), when the peasants rose up to overthrow their exploitative masters.

Liberalism has made another comeback in the late 20th century. Virtually all of Latin America (and much of the rest of the world after the fall of the Iron Curtain) has reverted to laissez faire economics, monetarism, and free trade. It is not the same as the 19th-century version, since the anticlericalism and the racism, so important earlier, are largely gone. Critics have called this movement neoliberalism, trying to tar it with the detrimental policies of the past.

Much of the social history of liberalism still needs to be studied. Two agenda items are perhaps most important. One, we now have numerous studies of the social implications of liberalism for many parts of the world, but we lack a synthesis which will piece together the regional or national studies to comprehend the overall picture of the effects of 19th-century liberalism.

Two, the continued success of liberalism today makes necessary a comparison between the 19th- and the 20th-century versions.

Social historians have already, however, made important adjustments in the conventional history of liberalism as conveyed in standard intellectual or political histories. First, they have weakened the tendency to link liberalism with middle-class beliefs. Many middle-class people, in Europe and elsewhere, have been liberals, but other groups have shared liberal goals, and key middle-class elements have sometimes opposed or turned against liberalism. Here is an important instance of the complexity of the relationship between social groups and ideology. Change must also be studied from the standpoint of sociohistorical causation, when groups withdraw support from liberalism (as among some lower middle-class elements in Germany in the 1920s) or newly adhere. Second, social historians have highlighted the ambiguities of liberalism in practice, in genuinely advocating freedom but also frequently seeking to use the state or other institutions such as asylums or schools to try to compel change on the part of groups regarded as uncivilized or dangerous. (*See also* Asylums; Education; French Revolution; Latin American Religion; Mexican Revolution; Middle Class; Racism; Social Control)

Erick D. Langer

REFERENCES

Katz, Michael B. *Reconstructing American Education.* Cambridge: Harvard University Press, 1987.

———. *School Reform: Past and Present.* Boston: Little, Brown, 1971.

Love, Joseph L., and Nils Jacobsen, eds. *Guiding the Invisible Hand: Economic Liberalism and the State in Latin American History.* New York: Praeger, 1988.

Nord, Philip G. *Paris Shopkeepers and the Politics of Resentment.* Princeton, NJ: Princeton University Press, 1986.

Life Course/Life Cycle

The life course and the family life cycle, analytic concerns introduced into social history at about the same time and, in fact, by many of the same historians, are conceptually quite distinct. The life course refers essentially to a descriptive schema for understanding individual development within its social and cultural context; the life cycle is a considerably more normative notion designed to help make sense of diverse family behaviors. But aside from the similarity of the names of the two notions, there is also a conceptual commonality that explains why they appropriately are treated together in discussions of social history: they each have provided a way of understanding the intersection of development in the lives of individuals and development in the society in which they find themselves. Each permits in its own way the analysis, over a large number of cases, of "life and times." But whereas biography commonly seeks to display what is extraordinary about its subject, life course and life cycle analyses seek to understand the way in which a society (and the development of that society) directs and constrains individual development and family dynamics, while at the same time understanding how the rhythms of individuals' lives and families' characteristic patterns through time affect the operations of society.

The family life cycle entered social history from family sociology, and especially from those parts of that subject that focus on income and consumption. From this perspective, families were long ago recognized to be anything but static, even when neither geographical nor social mobility occurred. Rather, families (understood as being formed by marriages in those modern Western societies to which family life cycle analysis was applied) tended (among the working class, the most commonly examined instance) to go through stages. They were economically secure in their first stage, with two potential workers and no other mouths to feed. Shortly, after the birth of the first child, they would enter an economically tenuous stage, with one potential worker (the husband, not yet at the peak of his earnings), but with more than two mouths to feed. Only after some years in this stage, might the growth of the couple's children allow a second and perhaps a third worker to strengthen the family's economic security, and the family cycle to move to a third stage. In this stage, the family's economy might possibly be buttressed by a peaking of the family head's earnings from gainful employment, and perhaps, gradually, from some saved wealth, often in the form of a

house. The "empty nest" stage followed, a less prosperous phase, for the decline in mouths to feed rarely offset the dramatic loss in income with aging.

As will be recognized, the family life cycle is based on a set of a priori stages. Nonnormative families (for instance, in the above example, families that had children before marriage, or families where the wife was widowed while still caring for young children) are simply overlooked, unless a cumbersome typology be constructed in which the "stages" are not really stages, not really a sequence through which most families pass. If we leave this problem aside, the question is what is done with the stages, once established. And here the strength of the analytic scheme is revealed, for they permit the linkage to the environing social structure to be easily examined. In the first instance, owing to different demographic and economic patterns (timing of marriage, number and timing of childbirths, characteristic ages for entering and departing gainful employment, for husband and wife) the proportions of families in given stages will differ widely in different societies—with important consequences at both the family level and for the society as a whole. At the same time, because these are "stages" through which most families proceed, the life cycle schema raises questions about how families, and how social institutions, have at different times handled the characteristic stresses and opportunities through which families pass between formation and eventual dissolution. Must families squeeze the educational opportunities of the older children to support the younger? Are social welfare schemes necessary to handle the retirement phase of families because there are few children living to support the parents' households, and they typically are simultaneously engaged in supporting their own infants?

The life course examines transitions in the lives of individuals rather than in a priori stages of families. Such transitions—which commonly differ according to the analytic focus of the scholar—often but not always have to do with family connections: leaving parents' home, marriage, parenthood, divorce, widowhood. The life course looks at these from the point of view of the individual, seeking first to understand the extent of variation within a population in such timing, and the determinants of this variation. That women typically marry younger than men is a social fact with large implications both for the women themselves (women have less time than men to learn nonmarital social roles), for the couples (women typically will outlive their husbands, not only because women's life expectancy exceeds men's but because wives typically are younger than their husbands), and for the society as a whole (there has long been and probably even today continues to be a tension between women's tendency to marry earlier than men, and women's heightened wish for entry into prestigious professions by way of extended formal education).

As the life course approach has been employed within the discipline of history, it has typically served either to indicate the relationship of individuals to institutions, as in Tamara Hareven's *Family Time and Industrial Time* (1982), where the historian's effort is in extracting from the historical record how individuals' lives (transitions in and out of the factory labor force, for instance) were jointly structured by work and the family; or to focus attention upon the social construction of life-course transitions, as in Howard P. Chudacoff's (1989) examination of the social category of "age" in *How Old Are You?* In other than historians' accounts, however, two other emphases (quite adaptable to history, given adequate documentation) are also apparent. In some, an essentially demographic perspective is turned to an effort to explain statistically patterns of life-course timing, as in the work of David Kertzer and David Hogan (1989), together and separately. And, in the work of Glen F. Elder, Jr. (1974), and others, a more developmental eye is turned to psychological issues, examining emergent personality themes, response to stress, and the like.

The life cycle and life course notions, especially the latter in view of its greater reach and flexibility, would seem likely to continue to inform work in social history (whether formally or not), in view of how well they fit with social history's concern with systematically linking experience to changing social structure.

John Modell

REFERENCES

Chudacoff, Howard P. *How Old Are You?* Princeton, NJ: Princeton University Press, 1989.

Elder, Glen F., Jr. *Children of the Great Depression.* Chicago: University of Chicago Press, 1974.

Hareven, Tamara K. *Family Time and Industrial Time.* New York: Cambridge University Press, 1982.

Hill, Reuben. *Family Development in Three Generations.* Cambridge, MA: Schenckman, 1970.

Kertzer, David I., and Dennis P. Hogan. *Family, Political Economy, and Demographic Change: The Transformation of Life in Casalecchio, Italy, 1869–1921.* Madison: University of Wisconsin Press, 1989.

Literacy

Literacy, which may be defined as the ability to function in a given society through the use of written materials, is a term which cannot usefully be more precisely defined, even in societies using phonetic alphabetic scripts, where learning one's "abc's" can be a relatively simple task. What a society defines as the minimal standard depends on its level of economic and social development. The definition of literacy will change as a society develops.

Literacy is linked with societies that have writing. Some scholars have claimed that the invention of writing in the ancient Near East altered the structure of human thought. By creating permanent, fixed records, writing permitted individuals to study alternative explanations about the cosmos and stimulated the development of logic and specialization of knowledge. Writing seems to be critical to the development of bureaucratic states, which use written regulations to separate the office from individual officeholders, population registers to tax citizens, law codes to keep social order, written directives and reports to govern, and treaties to define their relations with foreign powers.

There were originally several alternatives to the alphabetic systems of writing adopted by many societies in the world. Hieroglyphic writing, used in ancient Egypt, and cuneiform writing, found in ancient Mesopotamia and Assyria, are no longer used, but "logosyllabic writing"—the use of signs for words, and signs for syllabic components of words, found in China—is one of the few ancient writing systems with a continuous history of use into the modern era. For the people of East Asia (China, Japan, and Korea) the adoption of Chinese characters imposed special barriers to the acquisition of literacy. Japan and Korea each eventually developed alternative scripts. Japan devised a phonetic syllabary in the 9th century, and Korea an alphabetic script in the 15th century. In China, however, the task of acquiring literacy was not eased by any such innovation. Only in the 20th century, when reformers introduced a phonetic system and, in the 1950s in the People's Republic of China (PRC), a system of simplified characters, was the traditional writing system modified. Under these circumstances, full literacy, defined as the mastery of the Confucian canons, was enjoyed by a very small minority of the total population; functional literacy, defined as the ability of a peasant to do simple accounts or a merchant to conduct his business transactions, was more widespread. In modern times, literacy has been defined in the PRC as the ability to read 1,500 (later 2,000) characters. Since the average newspaper includes from 5,000 to 7,000 different characters, a person meeting this minimal standard would not be able to fully function in Chinese society.

Because recognition of one character does not necessarily enhance recognition of other characters, the issue of degrees of reading comprehension arises when we study literacy in societies that use a nonalphabetic writing system. For a long time, scholars studying literacy in Europe, where the alphabet was used, tended to assume that anyone who learned the alphabet was automatically equipped to read. Of the many studies investigating rates of literacy in different societies during premodern times, few rest on substantive evidence concerning the quality of reading comprehension. From our modern perspective, the ability of an individual to sign his name on a contract or other document cannot be taken as proof of his ability to read a document; yet it is rare to find any historical information on the kinds of written materials that a person could read or on the extent of his comprehension. These gaps in our knowledge of historical literacy become more important as we consider the wide range of literacy skills that can coexist in any society, and the relativity of any definition.

It is undoubtedly the case that minimal requirements for literacy have risen with the industrialization and bureaucratization that have characterized many modern societies. Literacy tests for contemporary American adults distinguish three types of skills: prose literacy, document literacy, and *numeracy*—the ability to perform arithmetic operations. The newest of these is document literacy, the ability to read graphs, schedules, and tables, which became important as the emphasis on quantitative analysis increased in the 19th century. Recent evidence suggests that there is a significant level of functional illiteracy among Americans, when literacy is defined as the ability to synthesize the main points in a long newspaper article, read a bus schedule, or determine one's eligibility for a particular type of fringe benefit, yet it is entirely possible that the absolute levels of reading comprehension have remained constant over much of the 20th century. The raising of skill requirements, which continues to outgrow the educational achievement of American students, is thus a function of our rapidly changing technologically oriented society.

Although the ability to comprehend information in tabular or graph form is relatively modern, many premodern societies simultaneously supported different styles of writing, which contributed to the difficulties of acquiring full literacy. In East Asia, even after the invention of alternative scripts, Japanese and Koreans continued to regard Chinese characters as the prestigious form of literacy. Korean literati continued to use Chinese characters until the end of the 19th century. Japanese males in the elite warrior class during the Tokugawa era (1600–1868) learned to read and write in Chinese characters, as had their ancestors; females wrote in the syllabary. Similarly, Latin became the prestigious language for writing in Europe.

The fragmentation of power in Europe after the destruction of the Roman Empire encouraged the growth of distinctive dialects and languages, which impeded literacy growth. Latin served as a lingua franca uniting first the clergy then educated men across the many different spoken European languages. The distinction between a written and vernacular language, which persisted in the medieval and early modern periods, meant that, in order to be fully literate, individuals had to learn more than one language. Even though the Renaissance introduced materials written in the vernacular language, vernacular literacy in premodern and early modern Europe did not give individuals access to the higher culture, which continued to be written in Latin. Until the 18th century, Latin was the dominant language for philosophy, theology, history, and science; through it, Desiderius Erasmus, Francis Bacon, Rene Descartes, Baruch Spinoza, and Sir Isaac Newton communicated to a Europe-wide readership. The subject matter of vernacular printings was aimed at a much humbler readership. In 16th-century France, the vernacular Bible was beginning to be sold to rural villagers. Almanacs, little arithmetics, and "chapbooks" were the kinds of materials to be found circulating in European villages in the 16th, 17th, and 18th centuries, the content of which tended to be simple and repetitious. Substantial books, transmitting the elite culture, were rarely found in villagers' homes.

Most scholars would agree that the attainment of literacy was much easier in premodern Europe than in East Asia. Paradoxically, however, literacy was probably more widespread among elites in China, Japan, and Korea for much of the premodern period. Whereas western Europeans existed in a primarily oral culture before the 11th century, this was not the case in China, where a standardized writing system emerged with the creation of a unified empire (221 BC). English kings viewed literacy as a technical skill befitting clerks, but for Chinese emperors, literacy was the key to knowledge, which itself represented power. From a fairly early period, the Chinese developed a bureaucratic state that recruited officials through their possession of literacy skills. As early as the 7th century, educated Chinese could compete for government office by passing written examinations. From the 12th century on, the majority of government officials in China were recruited through examination. The examination system, which was based on the Confucian canons, ensured a wide geographical distribution of degree-winners through a system of regional quotas. The result

was the creation of an empirewide educated class, reared on a standardized curriculum. The Confucian orthodoxy was transmitted through a unified writing system that cut across the dialect and ethnic boundaries separating different Chinese communities from one another. The nonphonetic Chinese "logosyllabic" writing system thus helped produce a unified elite culture that would not have been possible had China adopted a phonetic alphabetic script. We need only compare the Chinese situation with the French one, where regional differences in vernacular languages persisted until the early 20th century.

The reasons for low levels of literacy in premodern Europe are also tied to its political framework and social structure. European monarchies were initially based on the feudal relations between a king and his warrior vassals, which were renewed each generation. Birth, not education, was the key to status and power. Medieval European society had relatively weak markets, which provided little incentive for literacy skills that would enable individuals to improve their marketing position. Not until the early modern era was there an increased incentive to acquire literacy, first in Italy (15th century), then in Sweden (17th century), and in England and France (18th century). Even as these countries achieved literacy rates that included 50 percent or more of the male population, their economies and political structures were being transformed. From the 12th century Italy became the first country in Europe to experience a commercial revolution. The Italian city-states capitalized on the Crusades to expand their trading empires to the eastern and southern shores of the Mediterranean; both Venice and Genoa, its leading competitor in the 14th century, were among the largest European cities of their time. Specialization in iron and copper production enabled Sweden to emerge as a leading producer of armaments in the 17th century. In England and France, centralized monarchies accompanied the rise of markets. During the 19th century, education was seen as a way to improve the quality of the English work force by inculcating habits of obedience and industry, not literacy per se. Yet literacy also rose as a result of an expansion in schooling. In some countries, the emergence of the modern nation-state, which advanced the standardization of the national language, was another enormous stimulus for the enhancement of literacy.

In parts of Africa, the Americas, and Asia, the imposition of European control in the post-Columbian period helped promote and shape the forms of literacy that prevailed. European colonizers brought with them administrative systems based on regulations written in their own languages, and stimulated major advances in bureaucratization which helped to promote literacy. Literacy transformed oral cultures in Africa, and often led to the amalgamation of formerly autonomous tribal units into states. By recording customary practice, colonizing regimes frequently "fixed" what had been fluid rules into a formal system of laws. Literacy in the language of the colonizers became a major determinant of status among the colonized populations, and this situation persisted even after the colonies obtained their independence. The languages of the imperialists were often retained as the preferred, sometimes the only, national language—examples include the use of Spanish and Portuguese in South and Central America, French in modern-day Vietnam, and English in India.

Studies of literacy suggest certain systematic variations across countries and time periods. Literacy tends to increase with a society's development of commerce and the emergence of a modern nation-state. Literacy rates tend to be higher among urban residents than peasants, among males rather than females. In premodern Europe, literacy rose earlier in Protestant than in Catholic societies, and in western rather than eastern Europe. The Scandinavians, Dutch, and British (especially the Scots) had the highest rates of literacy in early modern Europe. In 1868, as it embarked on a far-reaching modernization program, Japan already enjoyed relatively high literacy rates, with perhaps more than 40 percent of males and 10 percent of females obtaining some kind of formal schooling.

Whatever the debates concerning the extent of literacy in the premodern age, there is widespread agreement on the long-term historical trend, namely the linear progression of literacy over time. Literacy has been identified as an es-

sential skill for the citizens of modernizing societies; some scholars have posited that rising literacy precedes economic growth. With the social changes that underlie expansion of education come changes in demographic characteristics such as the age of women at marriage, fertility rates, and family structure. Literacy, which draws individuals into engagement with larger worlds beyond the boundaries of their local communities, can in the long run also influence the shape of a political system—some would say toward more democratic forms. In the 19th and 20th centuries, however, educational expansion has frequently been used to create a nationalist commitment to the goals of the modern state. The creation or reinforcement of a distinctive national written language, which sometimes accompanied the rise of nationalism, is to some degree counterbalanced by the increasing globalization of knowledge. Because of the growing prominence of English as the primary international language for science, technology, and commerce, many people today learn to read not just in their own language but also in English.

In the 1990s, there continues to be wide divergence in literacy levels around the world. As Table 1 indicates, illiteracy is still common in many underdeveloped countries in Africa, Asia, and the Caribbean, although it has been virtually eliminated in Europe.

Table 1

Illiteracy Rates in Selected Countries, 1990

Country	Percentage of Illiterates (age 15 and over)		
	Total	Male	Female
Afghanistan	70.6	55.9	86.1
Algeria	42.6	30.2	54.5
China	26.7	15.9	38.2
Egypt	51.6	37.1	66.2
Guatemala	44.9	36.9	52.9
Haiti	47.0	40.9	52.6
India	51.8	38.2	66.3
Iran	46.0	35.5	56.7
Morocco	50.5	38.7	62.0
Pakistan	65.2	52.7	78.9

Source: *Statistical Yearbook 1990*, comp. United Nations Educational, Scientific, and Cultural Organization (Paris, 1990), Table 1.3.

Evelyn S. Rawski

REFERENCES

Goody, Jack. *The Logic of Writing and the Organization of Society.* Cambridge: Cambridge University Press, 1986.

Ong, Walter J. *Orality and Literacy: The Technologizing of the Word.* London: Routledge, 1988.

Resnick, Daniel P., ed. *Literacy in Historical Perspective.* Washington, DC: Library of Congress, 1983.

Stock, Brian J. *The Implications of Literacy: Written Language and Models of Interpretation in the Eleventh and Twelfth Centuries.* Princeton, NJ: Princeton University Press, 1983.

Todd, Emmanuel. *The Causes of Progress: Culture, Authority and Change.* Translated by Richard Boulind. Oxford: Basil Blackwell, 1987.

Literature

Social historians of the 1960s and 1970s were suspicious of using literary evidence. One cultural historian, Christopher Lasch, accused them with some justice of finding it "a waste of time to read novels." The new social historians were eager to find more reliable evidence than literature provided. Some of them, in dealing with topics like the family, emphasized features such as size and structure, on which literary evidence shed little light, rather than internal relationships. Social historians' predominant concern with lower social groups made them suspicious of much literature that was obviously created by and for upper- and middle-class elements.

The further evolution of social history has brought literary evidence into much greater repute. Many social historians use literature as part of their inquiry into beliefs and private behaviors. Generally they continue to prefer to combine literary with other kinds of evidence, for they maintain some concern about literature's representativeness. Often they prefer very popular novels and short stories to "great works," on grounds that the former were more widely read and closer to the beliefs of relevant social groups. Some social historians, further, are borrowing techniques from deconstructionist or post-structuralist literary theory, in order to analyze fiction in terms of unintended meanings as well as explicit messages. Historians dealing with gender, in particular, share interests with scholars in literary and cultural studies in analyzing literature in terms of unconscious intent. By the same token, literary theorists pay increasing attention to the findings of social history in locating literary works in the particular social context of a historical period. This interdisciplinary connection may expand in the future.

Literary evidence, used with appropriate caution, has improved social historians' ability to deal with topics such as emotion, health, and family relationships. Problems of social class remain, as much available literature, even in modern periods, continues to privilege middle-class audiences. Even where representativeness can be established through readership data, literature unquestionably varies in its social role. Some fiction—and this was commonly true of Victorian middle-class stories—explicitly seeks to reinforce widely accepted values. Other fiction provides escape, offering alternatives to commonly held beliefs. Traditional Chinese culture was largely hostile to romantic love in actual family formation, but it generated many moving love poems; here, literary options played a complex social role, precisely because they did not mirror approved social experience. Chivalric love poems in the European late Middle Ages, in contrast, have been interpreted as launching a very gradual cultural conversion to a higher valuation of love in marriage.

The relationship between "real" beliefs and fiction continues to be complicated in later periods of social history. Working-class readers in Europe around 1900, even most loyal socialist voters, preferred escapist fiction to materials recommended by labor leaders and available in trade union libraries. Escapist fiction in the 20th century may subtly preach, but it also may encourage readers to relieve pressures created by "real life" through outright fantasy. New-style heroes like Superman provided escapist alternatives to constrictions in American men's real lives after 1938, but later changes including Superman's marriage reflected new social pressures toward family commitment.

Literature, in sum, provides a growing resource for social historians as they expand their topical range, while offering as well a number of challenging analytical problems. (*See also* Cultural History; Leisure)

Peter N. Stearns

REFERENCES

Radway, Janice. *Reading the Romance: Women, Patriarchy, and Popular Literature.* Chapel Hill: University of North Carolina Press, 1984.

Smith Rosenberg, Carroll. *Disorderly Conduct: Visions of Gender in Victorian America.* New York: Oxford University Press, 1986.

Stearns, Carol Z., and Peter N. Stearns. *Anger: The Struggle for Emotional Control in America's History.* Chicago: University of Chicago Press, 1986.

Vicinus, Martha. *The Industrial Muse: A Study of Nineteenth Century British Working Class Literature.* Totowa, NJ: Barnes and Noble, 1974.

Local History

Local history, long considered by scholars to be outside the mainstream of historical inquiry and of interest to amateur historians only, established credibility with the rise of social history. Historians studying marginalized groups and unexplored topics, the hallmarks of social history, turned to communities as their research laboratories. In scouring town records and documents to understand the processes of historical change, social historians changed local history: who does it, how it is done, and how it is perceived by the wider historical community. The traditional narrative of local events has been replaced by an analytical interpretation that places local history into a broader context of change. Social historians have illustrated that the genesis of change can be local. Moreover, they have demonstrated the role of human agency in historical change. Local history is a legitimate field of inquiry and no longer the domain of the antiquarian and genealogist alone, although some tensions still exist amid the purposes and methods of local history. The field's renaissance reveals an interesting conflict and tentative rapprochement between academic and amateur historians in the United States.

A schism between academic and amateur historians developed in the 1880s as American universities created departments of history. Here professors required students to document and analyze their findings and stressed the importance of national events. Conducting their research on national themes in national archives, historians found local repositories of little use and thus seldom interacted with local historians.

Moreover, academic historians scoffed at the work being done at the community level by amateurs and criticized local narratives that merely recounted the past. Professional historians dismissed local history as boosterism and a testimonial to the town's founding fathers. Contemporary local histories reflect this tendency, and provincialism has hampered the study of local history until recently.

Local historians published factual chronologies, vignettes of community life, and biographical sketches of prominent local figures, mostly men. This treatment left much history out of the written record. By the early 20th century, communities had experienced tremendous immigration, and developing tensions between natives and immigrants manifested themselves in political, social, and cultural movements. For native elites, the colonial revival celebrated America's early arrivals, and local histories sympathetically chronicled earlier times. These histories neglected populist activities—at work, home, and leisure—in favor of traditional military and political accounts. Excluded were conflict-ridden themes. Local history, much of it carried out under the auspices of the local historical society, gave greater significance to town fathers than to the contributions of ordinary people, many of whom were new arrivals. In this way, local history cultivated a mystique of exclusivity that persists.

The approach to local history taken by social historians, whose works began appearing in the 1970s, reversed this narrow version of events. New topics examined family and group activities and relationships among social classes. Historians exposed tensions at the community level and examined their broader implications in American history. These themes emerged as social historians analyzed town records, city directories, diaries, and other materials available locally. Social historians found the innovative use of local documents significant for understanding social change. A number of studies of colonial New England communities, appearing in the 1970s, demonstrated the vitality of this methodology. Although not directly tied to social history, the allure of quantitative analysis that developed at this time used manuscript censuses to examine the richness of community life, and "records linkage" became an important dimension of local social histories.

As social history gained acceptance and integrated with traditional academic history departments, awareness of the potential of the history of ordinary people grew. The 1970s were interesting times for the historical field. Social history's growing prominence coincided with a resurgence of interest in history as Americans celebrated the bicentennial of the American Revolution and historic preservation movements swept the country. The number of state and local historical institutions burgeoned during the decade.

As social historians ventured into local historical repositories to use historical records, they discovered other community artifacts that shed light on their interpretations of past events—photographs, architecture, locally manufactured products, and oral histories. A new generation of local historians, many educated in social history themes and methodology, greeted academic social historians. A partnership began that disproved the old rift.

A working relationship between local historians, many through local historical agencies, and academic historians has spawned innovative programs at the local level. The content of programs, exhibitions, and publications reflects the influence social history has had on the field in the past 25 years. Historical agencies and government-funded projects sought the participation of the academic community, and the number of scholars involved in community history projects grew in the 1980s.

Studies conducted by the American Association for State and Local History have found that the public increasingly calls upon the services of local and state historical agencies. New levels of demands have created some problems. Since many of these institutions have been underfunded and long neglected, they are unable to meet the expectations of their patrons. Once historians entered local repositories, they discovered the deteriorating condition of America's historical records. Conversely, curators and archivists found that not all historians are sensitive to the fragile condition of many early materials and the role of historical agencies to conserve artifacts for the future.

As historical institutions seek a wider public audience, to refute old claims of exclusivity, they find interesting responses to the new approaches of history. Some public audiences, schooled in more traditional history, miss the comfortable litany of names and events on which to hang historical change. Increasingly, however, general audiences are intrigued by the difference offered by social history and react enthusiastically. The marriage between local and social history offers ongoing opportunities both for research and for public presentations.

Marilyn Zoidis

REFERENCES

Gass, Marilyn, and Abigail Ewing. "New Directions for the Bangor Historical Society: The Remaking of a Nineteenth-Century Institution, 1864-1984," *Maine Historical Society Quarterly* (Spring 1987): 206–223.

Kammen, Carol. *On Doing Local History: Reflections on What Local Historians Do, Why, and What It Means.* Nashville: American Association for State and Local History, 1986.

Kammen, Michael, ed. *The Past Before Us: Contemporary Historical Writing in the United States.* Ithaca, NY: Cornell University Press, 1980.

Longue Durée

Inspiration for this entry comes from a 1958 article by the French historian Fernand Braudel. The purpose of the article was to persuade the rival social sciences to develop a common language and jointly constitute a "science of communication."

Arguing from the premise of a common human nature, fundamentally ahistorical and ascertainable only by the deconstruction of myth, kinship, and exchange systems, anthropologist Claude Lévi-Strauss agreed with Braudel that the key to an understanding of culture comprises the structures that endow it with the quality of wholeness. Wanting in Lévi-Strauss's structural anthropology, however, according to Braudel, was the idea of duration, without which vast sectors of culture remain incomprehensible.

Three different approaches to time prevail in cultural anthropology. There is a timeless Lévi-Straussian common-human-nature structural approach, a synchronic explanation in terms of a culture's constituent traits at a given moment, and a diachronic approach in terms of the organization of cultural traits at two different temporal intervals. None of the three approaches, maintained Braudel, addresses the question of the diverse rhythms of cultural change. Some aspects of culture are quick to change. Others change more slowly, so slowly that they present an appearance of stability, even immobility. Yet other elements, such as the unconscious Lévi-Straussian structures, may be changeless for tens or hundreds of thousands of years.

Culture has a basis in a common human nature. But individual cultures also exist, each occupying a particular space and with its own ways of relating to nature and nesting or lodging, and regulating the circulation of, people and things. Braudel defines a "culture area," indeed, as an abode (*logement*). It thus is a territory filled by previous and present human occupants with an organized mass of material and nonmaterial goods. The relative coherence in space of objects, institutions, and message systems confers upon the area a coherence in time.

By their concern for such coherences and/or interest in location theory, Conrad M. Arensberg and geohistorian Braudel concur in identifying the *pays* or count(r)y, the canton, and the province as three old units of cultural-territorial continuity throughout the world. The canton may be, in fact, a more recent innovation. But larger than any of the three units is the culture area. In 1500, according to anthropologist Gordon W. Hewes, there were in the world 76 culture areas. One also may follow sociologist Georges Gurvitch and historian of techniques André Leroi-Gourhan in identifying two basic forms of territorial organization: a linear *itinerant* space (pathways and routes) and a projective and ultimately *radial* space (a linkage of nests of human settlement by means of routes and solar markets).

But what is time? As an experientially knowable phenomenon, according to historian Gaston Roupnel and philosopher physicist Gaston Bachelard, it represents the passage of discontinuous instants. But space-time, a construct of human reason, exists, according to Roupnel, at three different levels—as a tumultuous time of a few instants and a confined space of a few points,

as a long space-time of social structures, and as a very long space-time of the biological and psychological realities of human destiny.

Opposed to their "fragmentations of duration," Braudel nonetheless similarly differentiated between the time of events, the time of social structures, and the time of "very long" Lévi-Straussian structures. He added to the above, however, a time of *conjonctures*.

The time of events is brief and episodic. The time of *conjonctures* is a time of cyclical fluctuations. Finally, the time of structures is a time of long duration. Immanuel Wallerstein (1991) adds that to each kind of time corresponds a particular kind of space. An episodic time reflects an "immediate geopolitical space," a cyclical time refers to an "ideological space," a structural time corresponds to a "large-scale space," and a very long structural time identifies an "eternal space." For Braudel, too, the idea of duration embraces the duration in space and time of a particular layout of cultural traits. Present of necessity in the concept of *presence* are the interdependent notions of place (where) and time (when).

Newtonian science depicts time as uniform or homogeneous, infinitely divisible, and continuous, allowing a distinction between time and space, each conceived as a separate container unaffected by the other. But modifying the Newtonian system, Albert Einstein identified time and space as principles relative to but not independent of each other. Social time, too, is conceivable only in relation to space, and space makes no sense except in relation to time. An absolute correspondence of the short, middle-duration, and long times may be impossible. But portions of the content of one category of time correspond to portions of the content of other temporal categories. Without events there would be no *conjonctures*, and without events and *conjonctures* there would be no structures, except perhaps structures of the Lévi-Straussian type.

The concept of *longue durée*, though sometimes diversely and informally interpreted, continues to influence the practice of social history as it urges attention to often very gradual processes of change and the need to attend to long sweeps of time to capture some central facets of a society's experience. (*See also Annales* School;

Anthropology; Civilization; Geography; Methodology)

Traian Stoianovich

REFERENCES

Braudel, Fernand. "History and the Social Sciences: The Long Term." Translation by Sian France of Braudel's 1958 article, in *Social Science Information* IX (Feb. 1970): 145–173; a second translation by Peter Burke, ed., *Economy and Society in Early Modern Europe: Essays from "Annales."* London: Routledge & Kegan Paul, 1972; New York: Harper & Row, 1972.

————. *The Mediterranean and the Mediterranean World in the Age of Philip II*, 2 vols. Translated by Siân Reynolds. London: William Collins Sons and Co.; New York: Harper & Row, 1972–1973.

Gurvitch, Georges. *The Social Frameworks of Knowledge.* Translated by Margaret A. Thompson and Kenneth A. Thompson, with an introductory essay by Kenneth A. Thompson. Oxford: Basil Blackwell, 1971.

Wallerstein, Immanuel. *Unthinking Social Science: The Limits of Nineteenth-Century Paradigms.* Cambridge, Eng.: Polity Press, 1991.

Love

Social historians are beginning to understand why love is a historically changing emotion. The modern experience with romantic love emerges as a distinct product of two transformations in modern Western culture.

First, in the late 18th century, during the onslaught of economic, political, and social changes, people began to attach greater importance to love along with the traditional economic and social reasons for getting married. To be sure, love had always been around; witness the courtly love prominent during the European Middle Ages. Furthermore, post-Reformation theology stressed new emphasis on love within the family. However, definable social change occurred much later. There is disagreement as to what groups started this. Some point to the young working class of 17th- and 18th-century England, who were freer to form love unions because they lacked property, while others see change beginning with the gentry and squirarchy. Still others place the credit in other cultures and regions. In any event, most researchers agree on a late 18th-century change, perhaps first in England, with Americans and Continental Europeans getting a later start. Here, more than writings on the family provide evidence for change. Law courts in Europe by the 1720s were beginning to dissolve marriage arrangements because of the parties' disavowed love, a reasoning unheard of a century earlier.

However, Americans led the further intensification of this change into the 19th century. Despite changing emotional norms and gender roles within the marriage, romantic love gained priority and glorification for both men and women in the American middle class. For this period, however, most evidence comes from the white middle class, with further research needed along class and racial lines. If in fact, as some have suggested, the changes wrought by industrialization affected classes differently, and economic changes precipitated a rise in affective concerns, then we should see some complexities based on class during the 19th century.

The second transformation occurred in the early decades of the 20th century. Where sexual pleasure was once considered distinct and less worthy a determinant of marital perfection, it now became intertwined with romantic love. Furthermore, distinct gender roles emerged, with women far more expressive of love, and men more involved with sex. These gender differences persist despite significant forces for social equality and emotional management in the later 20th century. One study has uniquely linked the "proper" female norms for romantic love and anger to an oscillating nonlinear progression related to waves of political liberation for women.

Most research on emotions and love, for the 19th and 20th centuries, has focused on women. This is apparently based on an overly simple assumption about men as more sexually oriented, less emotional, and largely concerned with the outside world. Research on men and men's culture is only just beginning, but it has challenged the imputed lack of love for men in the 19th century and suggested some new complexities for men in the 20th, while more clearly detailing some of the massive forces of change impinging on men's emotional norms.

The causes of this later transformation in love are yet unclear, and even the gender distinctiveness is a matter of dispute. The influence of mass media, changing work roles for women, new courtship patterns, massive shifts in gender relations, and new kinds of societywide emotional management all have been identified by social historians as probable factors.

The history of love has thus far focused mainly on Western societies. It has also emphasized relationships between husband and wife (or courtship partners). However, other work has applied to changes in love standards regarding older family members and particularly regarding children. Greater emphasis on love for children, though still debated among historians, may relate to new love standards and expectations for adults themselves. Many facets of the topic remain open to additional research, for various time periods, regions, and additional components of love relationships.

Love, as with emotions in general, has now become a topic in its own right, after being only a subtopic attached to focuses on divorce or the family. Social history continues to provide new insight to complement and challenge the traditional intellectual and literary histories of love, such as Irving Singer's recent three-volume *The Nature of Love* (1984–1988). As a result, we now know that the answer to the age-old question "What is love?" changes with time and place, and plays a significant role in other facets of social history. [*See also* Childhood; Courtship; Emotion (Emotionology); Family; Marriage/ Remarriage]

Mark T. Knapp

REFERENCES

Gillis, John R. *British Marriages, 1600 to the Present.* New York: Oxford University Press, 1985.

Journal of Social History. Special issue on the History of Love (Spring 1982).

Lystra, Karen. *Searching the Heart: Women, Men, and Romantic Love in Nineteenth Century America.* New York: Oxford University Press, 1989.

Siedman, Steven. *Romantic Longings: Love in America, 1830–1980.* New York: Routledge, 1991.

Stearns, Peter N., and Mark T. Knapp. "Men and Romantic Love: Pinpointing a 20th-Century Change," *Journal of Social History* (1993) 769–96.

Lower Middle Classes

The lower middle class or classes arose during the industrial revolution in western Europe and has grown fairly steadily, there and in other industrial and commercial societies, since that time. Social historians have devoted considerable attention to this class both because of its increasing importance and because it is extremely hard to define, posing an analytical challenge in terms of the criteria for social stratification. The lower middle class ranks, obviously, below the main groups of businessmen, managers, and professionals in wealth and status. Like the main middle class, however, it does not work with its hands and normally distinguishes itself from the working class. In income and sometimes in social origins, however, the lower middle class may be quite similar to manual workers. In this case, its principal definition involves cultural assumptions rather than measurable economic characteristics.

The first lower middle class, predating industrialization to some extent, consisted of small shopkeepers. This group grew with commerce, playing an important role in English cities even in the 18th century. Small shopkeepers were property owners and often aligned themselves with middle-class business attitudes. But they resented big business, which often competed, through institutions like department stores, with the shops. Shopkeepers also had close relationships with working-class patrons and could identify with workers' grievances. Important national differences arose among shopkeepers. American and British shopkeepers did not develop pronounced political partisanship, though they might be active on a local scale. German and French shopkeepers, in contrast, became highly politicized in the late 19th century, often backing conservative, even anti-Semitic groups that promised to attack big business and labor unions—forces that seemed to threaten the shopkeeper world. Many shopkeepers in Catalonia turned to the political left. Continued growth of big business in the later 20th century has limited the influence of small shopkeepers, though their political power continues to affect economic and political life in many countries.

A later lower middle class developed after about 1870, consisting of secretaries, telephone operators, department store clerks, and many other service personnel. Some teachers, nurses, and other near-professionals also fell into lower middle-class ranks; establishing the upper boundary of the group is difficult. This lower middle class became the fastest growing social class in advanced industrial societies. It tended to associate itself with many middle-class values—adopting small family size through birth control, spending more than workers did on respectable housing and so on. Encouraged by employers who sought to keep clerks and workers separate, through separate salary systems and benefit programs, for example, the majority of members of the lower middle class did not organize in trace unions, or organized separate from the working-class movement. On the other hand, lower middle-class people showed new leisure and consumer interests that marked them off somewhat from the mainstream middle class in the later 19th century—for instance, they were particularly quick to indulge in cigarette smoking. Again, the group continues to be difficult to define.

Recent work on the lower middle class, and particularly the modern, service-sector group, has included analysis of gender roles. Many lower middle-class jobs, even before 1900, were staffed by women. Other research has focused on how lower middle-class employees are regulated by management and are required to dress in certain ways and to manipulate their emotions to please customers. A special strand of lower middle-class alienation has also been identified, at least for the 20th century. Because lower middle-class people tend to share middle-class values, they anticipate social mobility for themselves and their children; and they are more likely to advance in school and in social position than members of the working class. However, many lower middle-class people do not advance as they had hoped, and may discover, toward middle age, that their dreams of success are doomed to frustration.

Because the lower middle class is hard to define and because it organizes less vigorously than workers or big business, less is known about its history than is true of its social neighbors above and below. Social historians continue to probe, with new work emerging fairly rapidly. (See also Alienation; Middle Class; Mobility; Stratification and Inequality)

Peter N. Stearns

REFERENCES

Benson, Susan Porter. *Counter Cultures: Saleswomen, Managers, and Customers in American Department Stores, 1890–1940.* Urbana: University of Illinois Press, 1986.

Kocka, Jurgen. *White Collar Workers in America, 1890–1940: A Social-Political History in International Perspective.* Translated by Maura Kealey. Beverly Hills, CA: Sage, 1980.

Lockwood, David. *The Blackcoated Worker: A Study in Class Consciousness,* 2nd ed. Oxford: Clarendon Press, 1989.

Nord, Philip G. Paris. *Shopkeepers and the Politics of Resentment.* Princeton, NJ: Princeton University Press, 1986.

Winstanley, Michael J. *The Shopkeeper's World, 1830–1914.* Manchester, NH: Manchester University Press, 1983.

Luddism

The term "luddism" refers to the practice of workers breaking or otherwise disabling machinery that they regard as threatening their security by undermining established job skills or work practices. As a general tactic of resistance, luddism is most characteristic of early phases of industrialization, and it has been carefully studied as part of the social history of protest in several countries. It often reflects a strong belief in values of skill and community at work—a moral economy different from the principles of industrialization.

More specifically, luddism refers to the collective actions of significant groups of British workers during the early 19th century. During the most intense years of action (1811–1816), luddism proper was confined to three industrial occupations—the Yorkshire wool croppers, the Lancashire handloom weavers, and the Nottinghamshire (and to a lesser extent Leicestershire and Derbyshire) framework knitters. Only the croppers directly resisted the introduction of new machinery—gig mills and shearing frames; the knitters and weavers faced various forms of exploitation, including low wages, high frame and loom rents, the introduction of lower craft standards and the hiring of semiskilled workers.

The term "luddism" derives from workers anonymously signing threatening letters to employers with the name "Ned Ludd" or "General Ludd." In April 1812, the most violent confrontation occurred in Yorkshire, when perhaps as many as 150 armed Luddites attacked the mill of William Cartwright, of Rawfords. The Luddites turned to violence, however, only after the failure of more peaceful forms of protest.

The Luddites were often bound together by tight discipline and secret oaths, and were protected by strong community loyalties. During this period trade union activity was illegal. Moreover, in 1812, the government made frame-breaking a capital offense. Luddite attacks were rarely random or purely spontaneous. Luddites usually chose their targets carefully. Resisting free-market conditions, the logic of machine-breaking constituted a defense of customary rights based on notions of a "moral economy." The extent to which luddism was linked to po-litical radicalism and to insurrectionary plotting is a matter of debate. As a movement luddism faded out after 1816, although sporadic incidents of machine-breaking continued. During the "Swing" riots of 1830, for example, agricultural laborers attacked threshing machines. (*See also* Moral Economy)

James Epstein

REFERENCES

Dinwiddy, John. "Luddism and Politics in the Northern Counties," *Social History* 4 (1979).

Hobsbawm, Eric. "The Machine Breakers," in *Labouring Men.* London: Weidenfeld and Nicolson, 1964.

Thomis, Malcolm. *The Luddites.* Newton Abbott, Eng.: David and Charles, 1970.

Thompson, E.P. *Making of the English Working Class.* New York: Viking, 1963.

M

Machismo

Machismo can be described as a set of beliefs surrounding honor and shame which came to serve as an ideal of manliness or a cult of virility particularly in Latin and Latin American societies. Tied up with male sexual prowess, courage, and competition among men, machismo includes the expectation that men be honorable, brave, able to handle events in the public world, and support and head a large family as well as a mistress and illegitimate children. Younger, unmarried men demonstrate their virility by displaying bravado, acting aggressive and arrogant, and attracting women. In addition, some authors associate machismo with dominance of and violence toward women.

While macho attitudes and behaviors can be found in several cultures, including the United States, southern Europe, the Middle East, and North Africa, machismo has been associated primarily with patterns of gender relations in Latin America. Some historians have argued that the roots of machismo lie in 16th- and 17th-century Spanish upper-class ideas and came to the New World with Spanish adventurers and soldiers who participated in the conquest. Although some scholars link machismo to lower strata of society, it can be found in every class. Machismo ideas, however, are not prevalent among indigenous groups in Latin America, which do not share Spanish ideas of acceptable gender relations.

Machismo cannot be discussed without considering its complement, marianismo. Marianismo, which derives its name from the cult of the Virgin Mary, is a set of beliefs that ideally guides women's behavior. Female duties include mother, moral leader of the family, and comforter to husband and children. Chastity, modesty, and shyness represent proper behavior for single women. Through these behaviors women derive a sense of superiority to men. Men, through their bravado as machos, frequently stray from Christian moral behavior. Women, then, are expected to be loving and forgiving to their men. Women's long suffering and prayer may be the only respite for their erring husbands, who, after all, cannot help themselves. Because these beliefs permeate society, both women and men receive reinforcement from family and neighbors for their behavior.

One can readily see the inherent contradictions between machismo and Catholicism in Latin America. Adultery, sexual licentiousness, and other manifestations of machismo go directly against Catholic ideas of proper behavior. Few works have traced machismo historically with any precision, although it is frequently mentioned when discussing gender relations in Latin America. While scholars have noted that machismo and consequent behaviors are commoner among mestizos (people of mixed Spanish and Indian heritage) than among indigenous groups, future work on machismo might investigate both the regional differences in macho ideology within Latin America, as well as how it has changed over time. (*See also* Gender Socialization)

Gina Hames

REFERENCES

Bingham, Marjorie Wall, and Susan Hill Gross. *Women in Latin America From Pre-Columbian Times to the 20th Century*. St. Louis Park, MN: Glenhurst Publications, 1985.

Brydon, Lynne, and Sylvia Chant. *Women in the Third World: Gender Issues in Rural and Urban Areas*. New Brunswick, NJ: Rutgers University Press, 1989.

Pescatello, Ann, ed. *Female and Male in Latin America*. Pittsburgh: University of Pittsburgh Press, 1973.

Stevens, Evelyn P. "Mexican Machismo: Politics and Value Orientations," *Western Political Quarterly* 18, 4 (December 1965): 848–57.

Magic

Social historians, particularly those interested in popular beliefs or mentalities, have paid renewed attention to magic and, ultimately, to its decline (though not its disappearance) in modern societies. They have tried to escape the idea that magic is a backward form of belief and practice, to understand its variety and functions in various societies. Magic is seen as a vital means that ordinary people, and often elites as well, used to counter disease—a part of traditional medical eclecticism. Its role in courtship and other family practices has been explored. Popular reliance on magic clearly survived a host of attacks from religious authorities—Christian leaders in Europe, Confucianists in China—because it meshed with popular values and practices. An appreciation of magic is fundamental to various topics in social history, but it is complicated by the deep-seated bias against the topic in Western intellectual life.

Historically, "magic" as a term has been used by literate elites to condemn ritual practices maintained through oral tradition; by practitioners of one system of rituals to question the spiritual efficacy of practices in another one; and as the adjective "magical," by intellectuals to characterize what they perceive to be unenlightened thought. As a social phenomenon magic can be defined as all performance of ritual aimed at the manipulation of the supernatural not sponsored by the dominant religious elite. Such a negative definition spotlights the cultural battle transcendent in social participation in rituals performed to coax some mundane result from the world of the unseen. It may not be completely accurate to describe magic as the religious practices of those who have lost a battle for cultural hegemony. Individual practitioners can and have claimed an ability to intercede in the spiritual world independent of preexisting ritual traditions. Intellectual elites have hidden from popular purview literate/numerate traditions of access to the invisible universe. Yet the characterization does help clarify both the meaning of the term "magic" within the Western intellectual tradition and the evolution over the centuries in the term's cultural substance.

Since the European Middle Ages intellectuals have sought to distinguish between "religion" and "magic," terms dichotomized respectively as the right and wrong ways to supplicate heavenly intervention. Augustine taught that all humans have within them a "religious seed," which leads to a misguided sense of satisfaction that rites performed to induce God's forgiveness actually have had some effect. Periodically, in the history of Christianity intellectuals influenced by Augustine have condemned all ritual performance as evil. Churches, however, have never gone beyond the condemnation as magical of all rites not traceable to a Christian source.

Nineteenth-century secular intellectuals replaced theology with science as the right-thinking path to understanding the unknown. But they maintained the Augustinian mistrust of the psychological satisfaction ritual performance provided. The dichotomy for them became one of magic versus science, which has stood as surrogate for opposing patterns of cognition described variously as primitive versus civilized, traditional versus modern, child versus adult in Freud's *Totem and Taboo*, and in a formulation that retains some contemporary currency, prelogical versus logical. Because the only way that magic ever worked was with the aid of the Devil, Christian intellectuals were convinced that all those who practiced magic should die. Because those who think in magical ways get in the way of progress, secular intellectuals have questioned the right of those who think this way to live.

T.M. Luhrmann's recent study of witchcraft in contemporary Britain, which reveals the appeal of New Age paganism to London's scientific elite, illustrates the futility of conceptualizing mutually exclusive modes of human thought and positing their preponderence among specific social populations. Contemporary intellectual awareness of the sterility of this type of dichotimizing, however, should not mask the role the procedure has played in rationalizing the suppression of subordinated cultures. Throughout the history of the West, "magic" has been the term employed by the reigning cultural elite to designate beliefs and practices they feel should be destroyed.

Sociologist Emile Durkheim once argued that a priest performed rites for a congregation, a magician for a clientele. In saying this he was observing the social outcome of the above cultural conflict. Delegitimized ritual traditions do not lose their audiences. These audiences lose their ability to participate in those rites publicly. Practitioners of the dominant system of rituals lay claim to the performance of all rites with some collective value. Their versions of the rites to insure a good harvest, to protect the community, to defeat an enemy army are the ones publicly performed, publicly reimbursed. Practitioners of subordinated systems are left to compete for the rewards for supplicating the supernatural for more private concerns. Once delegitimized, ritual traditions can only survive as cut-rate alternatives in the marketplace of supernatural services. The magician has only a clientele because the priest will not permit him a congregation.

Aspects of this process can be discerned in the histories of the heretical movements which gave rise to the medieval Inquisition. Catharism, a system of rituals whose appeal once rivaled that of Roman Christianity, survived suppression only in the form of clandestine rites practiced on the margins of Mediterranean society. Vigorous debate surrounds the question of when the countrysides of premodern Europe were Christianized. What is clear is that the pre-Christian diety Diana continued to be ritually invoked as a source of supernatural power by midwives and wise women until the witchcraze (1450–1650). And while the ritual observances of these women were pushed further and further out of the sight of the larger community, they never ceased to have some practitioners.

An almost paradigmatic example of how a claim for global spiritual authority could, through repression, be downsized into an advertisement for a market share is provided in Carlo Ginzburg's *Night Battles* (1983). Ginzburg details the story of the *benandanti*, an agrarian cult in early-modern Italy which demanded public respect in local communities for their nocturnal battles with demons for the harvest. Less than 100 years after the Inquisition frightened the *benandanti* away from their push for acknowledgment as a spiritual elite, we hear of individual *benandante* selling their services as diviners, healers, seers, and the like, activities scorned by their predecessors.

The effort on the part of anthropologists to distinguish among magic, witchcraft, divination, and so on, breaks down before the fact that rituals performed with these intents can be observed to have been performed by the same individuals. Historical research has also illustrated that the rules by which anthropologists seek to separate rites performed with a religious intent from rites performed with a magical intent are valuable mostly for what they reveal about the intellectual environment in which the anthropologists have operated.

Without always defining magic too formally, social historians have dealt with the subject in various ways, beyond tracing specific groups dealing with magic in medieval and early modern Europe. They have incorporated a more complex understanding of popular reliance on magic into studies of witchcraft—including the fact that some people, accused as witches, undoubtedly thought they had magical powers. They have studied historical roles and changes in magic in non-Western societies, such as China, where magic persisted as part of the culture of peasants and others in China's outlying provinces. They have also looked at positive, or "white," magic—the kind of magic most often utilized to propitiate the forces of nature through common rituals, rather than the rarer kind of magic used to attack. Well into the 18th century, studies of folklore reveal, ordinary people used magical rituals to make others fall in love with them, to promote conceptions, and of course to deal with illness. A host of common words and symbols expressed this casual but significant magical intent. Judith Devlin (1987) has shown how magical beliefs persisted among French peasants even around 1850, as a vital part of their mentality. Finally, beginning with the classic mentalities study by Keith Thomas (1971), social historians have discussed how changing official views, influenced by science, gradually made magical beliefs less popular or at least less easy to express openly, though the process of magic's decline and the impact of this decline have yet to be fully traced. (*See also* Christianity; Religion; Witchcraft)

Andrew E. Barnes

REFERENCES

Devlin, Judith. *The Superstitious Mind: French Peasants and the Supernatural in the Nineteenth Century.* New Haven: Yale University Press, 1987.

Ginzburg, Carlo. *Night Battles: Witchcraft and Agrarian Cults in the Sixteenth and Seventeenth Centuries.* Baltimore: Johns Hopkins University Press, 1983.

Ladurie, Emmanuel LeRoi. *Montaillou: The Promised Land of Error.* New York: Vintage Books, 1972.

Thomas, Keith. *Religion and the Decline of Magic.* New York: Scribner, 1971.

Walker, Barbara. *The Crone: Woman of Age, Wisdom and Power.* San Francisco: Harper, 1985.

Manners

Erasmus advised not to spit on or over the table, but underneath it. Since then, spitting has become ever more restricted, until it has now been banned altogether. Today, in the West, even the urge to spit has generally disappeared. This example shows that manners are a form of social control demanding the exercise of self-control, and that the word abbreviates ways of relating to others and oneself. Yet only recently have manners become a serious object of study, major obstacles being worries that the topic was too superficial and perhaps too strongly associated with certain behavioral problems of children and the nouveaux riches. Only after Norbert Elias (1978, 1982) had "opened the door," as Kasson (1990) puts it, with his pioneering two-volume work *The Civilizing Process,* did the topic gain ascendancy. Growing interest in linking social history with anthropology has also promoted the study of behavioral codes. Manners have become the object of an increasing number of studies, and they are increasingly taken to be an important part of any culture: within the relationships in which they grow up, people in various social groups are more or less attuned to the dominant manners of their society.

In all societies, a regime of manners mirrors and reinforces the distribution of power, status, or respect. The range of differences in respect, rank, and power, whether between social classes, sexes, or generations, can be deduced from such ratios as between formality and informality, strictness and elasticity, aloofness and intimacy, and commanding and negotiating manners. Moreover, via manners, all are confronted with demands on emotion management, with social constraints moving toward self-constraints. Transgressions are sanctioned in a variety of ways, ranging from blame gossip to excommunication, all involving a loss of face, respect, and self-respect. Thus, any particular regime of manners corresponds to a particular level of mutually expected self-controls, determining the range of accepted behavioral and emotional alternatives. Therefore, not only are manners the symbolic expression of institutionalized power and dependency relationships and the ensuing problems of living together, but also of the emotion management or self-regulation that is demanded from the individuals who are trying to cope with these problems.

Thus, changes in the spectrum of dominant manners refer to both social and psychological processes; they refer to changes in the regimes of power and emotions. It was from this perspective that Norbert Elias wrote his important book. Taking European mannerbooks from the 15th to the 19th century as pivotal to his analysis, Elias showed that in processes of state formation and growing interdependency, the pressures people excercised upon each other and themselves have on the whole developed in a specific direction: ever since the Middle Ages a wide range of elementary "animalistic" acts such as eating, drinking, and sleeping, as well as the more primary emotions and impulses, have become increasingly subjected to more—and more differentiated—regulations which have been standardized as laws and "good manners." Again and again, what was once seen as good manners, later became regarded as rude. Via manners, expanding social constraints toward self-constraints have pressed toward stronger and more automatic self-supervision, the subordination of short-term impulses to the commandment of a habitual longer-term perspective, and the cultivation of a more stable, even and differentiated self-regulation. As studied by social historians for western Europe and the United States, development can be viewed as a long-term process of formalization: more and more aspects of behavior and feeling were subjected to stricter regulations, partly formalized as laws and partly as manners.

This long-term trend reached its peak in the Victorian era, to be followed in the 20th century by a dominant process of informalization, when manners became increasingly relaxed, subtle and varied. The lessening of power inequalities and a growing expectation to proceed through mutual consent have been conducive to greater informality in manners. More and more manners have come to be ignored or attacked as rising groups came to be increasingly represented in the centers of power that function as a model for manners. These groups have demanded new behavioral alternatives for themselves, while at the same time limiting those of the old established groups. An example is a growing tolerance of cursing. Behavioral extremes, expressing large differences in power and respect, came to provoke moral indignation and were banned, while for the rest the codes of social conduct have become more lenient and more differentiated and varied. Rising mutually expected self-restraints allowed for an increase of socially accepted alternatives: as all kinds of formal rules and emotional controls were collectively taken into individual custody, they were subjected to a "controlled decontrolling." Emotions that according to these formal rules previously had been repressed and denied as dangerous, especially those concerning sex, violence, and death, were again discovered as part of a collective emotional makeup: there was thus an "emancipation of emotions." In increasingly dense networks of interdependency, more subtle, informal ways of obliging and being obliged have demanded greater flexibility and sensitivity to shades and nuances in manners of dealing with others and oneself. As manners turned from a set of general rules into guidelines differentiated according to the demands of the situation and relationship, they demand and allow for "doing it my way," that is, a process of individualization.

Reduced inequality of power chances will have always gone hand in hand with a relaxation of manners, but only in the 20th century have processes of social equalization and integration reached such a scope and degree that a long-term informalization process has got the upper hand. The fin de siècle, the Roaring Twenties, and the permissive societies of the 1960s and 1970s showed particularly strong spurts in this direction. For the United States, these spurts have been indicated by Hodges (1990) in an overview of changes in the literature on manners. On the whole, however, the study of the history of manners is still at an early stage. Changes not only in the 20th century but also in the 17th and 18th centuries "civilizing" transition and the extent to which middle-class manners trickled down are all open to additional scrutinizing in what has been recognized as a vital topic. The topic also can be profitably extended on a comparative basis to other social historians in Asia and elsewhere. [*See also* Civilization; Emotion

(Emotionology); *Longue Durée*; Mentalities; Ritual; Sense of Self/Individualism; Stratification and Inequality]

Cas Wouters

REFERENCES

Elias, Norbert. *The Civilizing Process*, Vols. I and II. New York: Pantheon Books, 1978 and 1982.

Hodges, Deborah Robertson. *Etiquette*. Jefferson, NC, and London: McFarland, 1989.

Kasson, John F. *Rudeness & Civility*. New York: Hill and Wang, 1990.

Wouters, Cas. "Developments in the Behavioral Codes Between the Sexes," *Theory, Culture & Society* 4 (1987): 405–427.

Manorialism

During the Middle Ages in western Europe, a distinctive economic form developed, a relationship between landlords and the peasants who worked the soil and raised the crops. At the time this type of relationship had no name, but it is now known as manorialism. It was found especially in medieval France and England. This form of agricultural organization was never universal and in fact probably involved a minority of all peasant laborers. But where it existed it was enormously influential. (Note: manorialism is sometimes, confusingly and erroneously, called feudalism.)

While manorialism has been most often defined in terms of medieval Europe, similar systems developed in many other times and places. Russia was characterized mainly by free farmers during Europe's Middle Ages, but then began to develop to the manorial system, with rigid serfdom, from the 15th century onward. A manorial system began to develop in the Middle East and North Africa by about the 12th century, as landlords seized local political and economic power. Systems similar to manorialism developed periodically in China, and long endured in Japan. Finally, the estates systems developed in Latin America after 1500 had many features in common with manorialism.

At its most basic, manorialism was characterized by agricultural land owned by a powerful lord, part of which was his own personal land, on which he had food grown for his own household and for market, and the rest of which was rented out to peasant tenants. In medieval Europe the lord's personal land was called the *demesne,* and the land he rented out was divided into *mansi*, units of land each theoretically capable of supporting one peasant family. The peasants paid their rents in a variety of different forms, which differed from individual to individual, but which were normally set amounts (not proportional to income or crop yield). These rents generally consisted of a few coins; some payment in produce, such as grain or chickens; and some payment in workdays, that is, one or two days a week on which the peasant would be obliged to work on the lord's demesne land rather than in his own fields. As well as having tenants work his land for him, the manorial lord might also have it worked by household slaves (until these vanished in the 10th century) or employ hired laborers (especially in the 12th century and later).

When manorialism first developed (probably during the 6th century, although the extreme shortage of documents from the period makes it difficult to pinpoint), it was a substitute for the slave-worked plantations that had characterized the Roman Empire. A combination of the high mortality of slaves when worked in gangs, the difficulty of obtaining new slaves with the breakdown of Roman trade routes, Christianity's emphasis on the virtue inherent in freeing slaves (though Christianity did not oppose slavery per se), and the struggles of the slaves themselves made agricultural slavery increasingly less viable, although slavery persisted in some places and in some forms, especially within the household, until the 10th century. Instead, early medieval peasants are usually considered serfs, distinguished from slaves because they could not be sold off their land and because they owed fixed dues rather than being subject to their lords' arbitrary demands.

Some of the serfs were descended from former slaves who had been granted their own plots of land to feed themselves and their families, so that the lords would not have the expense and difficulty of doing so. Other serfs were descended from freemen and women who had commended themselves to lords for protection and in order to have access to the agricultural land they needed to survive. Serfs, even though they were not slaves, were considered to be born into a dependent relationship with their lords from which it was difficult to escape, and they could not perform activities, such as appearing in court or entering the clergy, for which freedom was required. Servile dependence might be symbolized by the serf having to appear annually before his lord, on his knees, with a penny on his head. The lords of serfs often tried to regulate their marriages and inheritance.

By the 9th century, when a few great manorial surveys were made (especially of ecclesiastical estates), it is clear that even within servile status there was a great deal of variation, and a number of different terms were used to designate serfs. However, it is important to note that there were always free peasants as well, often living side by side with serfs in the countryside. Free peasants sometimes worked land that they themselves owned outright, and sometimes rented land from the same lords as the serfs, although renting per se did not make them into serfs. Up through the 10th century, the most important social and institutional distinctions were not made on the basis of wealth or of power, but rather on the basis of whether one was free or unfree.

During the 11th and 12th centuries, with the marked improvement of the agricultural economy, European manorialism underwent several important changes, starting with the rapid decline of serfdom. Peasants who resented their personal servitude might buy their way to freedom with a lump-sum payment of carefully hoarded coins; might run away and rent instead from a lord who allowed them their freedom; or might quietly attempt to pass as free. Landlords were often in competition with each other for peasant tenants as new fields were cleared and put under the plow. The newly freed peasants, however, frequently continued to rent from landlords in a manorial form of organization. That is, they lived on mansi on the lords' land and paid their rents in a combination of produce, money, and labor. It was at this point that the free/unfree dichotomy became less important, for virtually all peasants were free; rather, wealth and authority became the criteria by which society was divided.

Another change took place in manorialism in the late 12th and 13th centuries as rents increasingly were paid in coin (or in coin plus some produce). Landlords found it easier to use hired labor to work their demesne land than to enforce workdays on uncooperative workers who would have preferred spending their days working their own land; thus, they were willing to substitute monetary payments for these labor dues. In the 14th and 15th centuries manorialism declined rapidly, as nobles became more separated from the agricultural cycle and tended to live primarily from their rents.

The manorial system's chief advantages came from the association, or even partnership, that it created among peasants and between lords and peasants, even when the lords were most oppressive. Peasant workers who grew a small amount of extra food beyond what was needed to feed their families could sell that produce at market along with the larger amounts grown on their lord's demesne. While performing their labor dues, peasants could gain a first acquaintance with new and often expensive technology, such as iron plows, improved horse harnesses, and wind mills, all of which became widespread in the 12th century. Sometimes peasants also gained access to such equipment for their own use—for example, renting the lord's plow to work their own fields.

Comparative work on manorialism has particularly applied to Russia and eastern Europe, where harsh serfdom developed just as it was declining in western Europe. Comparative topics involve length-of-work obligations, extent of landlords' local political power, and the degree to which estate agriculture focused on sales to wider markets as opposed to local subsistence needs with some surplus for the lords. (*See also* Agricultural Systems; Corvée Labor; Feudalism; Haciendas/Encomiendas; Peasantry)

Constance B. Bouchard

REFERENCES

Bonnassie, Pierre. *From Slavery to Feudalism in South-Western Europe.* Translated by Jean Birrell. Cambridge: Cambridge University Press, 1991.

Duby, Georges. *The Early Growth of the European Economy: Warriors and Peasants from the Seventh to the Twelfth Century.* Translated by Howard B. Clarke. Ithaca, NY: Cornell University Press, 1974.

Duby, Georges. *Rural Economy and Country Life in the Medieval West.* Translated by Cynthia Postan.

Columbia: University of South Carolina Press, 1968.

Evergates, Theodore. *Feudal Society in the Bailliage of Troyes Under the Counts of Champagne, 1152–1284.* Baltimore: Johns Hopkins University Press, 1975.

Mariology

Narrowly defined as a subset of Roman Catholic theology, Mariology is the systematic reflection on the role of Mary, mother of Jesus, in the drama of salvation. Particularly important has been reflection on the special privileges which according to Roman Catholic doctrine have been granted to Mary, such as her Immaculate Conception, perpetual virginity, and bodily Assumption into heaven. Arising as a specialized field during the 17th century, Mariology has been especially the province of members of the monastic orders.

More broadly defined, Mariology is the study of devotion to and thinking about Mary throughout the history of Christianity. Early Christians saw in Mary's obedience to the will of God a reversal of Eve's disobedience (Irenaeus, d. 193), and at the Council of Ephesus (431), Mary was declared Theotokos, or Bearer of God, which was understood as ensuring the divine nature of the child to which she had given birth.

In the Middle Ages, with the rise of the cult of saints, Mary came to be venerated as Queen of the Saints, and by the 12th century, many had begun to trust in her ability to intercede with special effectiveness with her son and thus with God. The spread of Mariology at this point and later has highlighted the subject as part of social historians' efforts to grasp popular Christianity and its gender implications. The devotion to Mary that began to flourish at this time emphasized her universality and assumed that anyone anywhere could enlist her aid in any crisis. But it also emphasized the manifestation of her graces at particular places, and unique forms of devotions began to be associated with particular images and shrines. This flourishing of Marian devotion coincided with the cult of courtly love and its special focus on the lady of the manor. By the end of the Middle Ages, a number of special Marian prayers and devotions had arisen, the most important of which was the Rosary.

The most impressive monuments of the devotion to Mary that flourished in the later Middle Ages, however, were the great gothic cathedrals.

Several 16th-century Protestant reformers retained the doctrine of the virgin birth (that is, that Mary was a virgin at the time of Jesus' birth) and followed many earlier Christian thinkers in seeing Mary as a symbol of the church. But they and their followers tended to reject the idea that Mary or any other saint could intercede for anyone or that God had granted Mary any privileges besides that of being the mother of God's son. In the Eastern Christian churches, theologians tended to focus on Mary as a symbol of divine wisdom.

There are several studies of Marian devotion from the standpoint of the social sciences. Mart Bax and William Christian, Jr. (1989), have shown how local Marian devotions have been shaped by various interests and institutions within the Roman church and in society as a whole. Loreto Echeverría and Nicolas Perry have demonstrated how various repressive political regimes have profited from Marian devotion. Robert Orsi (1985) has demonstrated the importance of Marian imagery in helping immigrant communities adapt to their changing circumstances in the United States. Studies of Our Lady of Guadalupe, often considered a master symbol of Mexican culture, have shown the complexity of the Marian image and the usefulness of exploring Marian devotion in ethnic contexts. Recent feminist critiques have questioned whether Marian imagery can be consistent with the enhancement of the position of women in cult and society. (*See also* Christianity)

Sandra L. Zimdars-Swartz

REFERENCES

Bynum, Carol. *Jesus as Mother.* Berkeley: University of California Press, 1982.

Christian, W.A., Jr. *Person and God in a Spanish Valley.* 2nd ed. Princeton, NJ: Princeton University Press, 1989.

Orsi, R. *The Madonna of 115th Street.* New Haven: Yale University Press, 1985.

Perry, N., and L. Echeverría. *Under the Heel of Mary.* London: Routledge, 1988.

Warner, M. *Alone of All Her Sex.* New York: Knopf, 1976.

Zimdars-Swartz, S. *Encountering Mary*. Princeton, NJ: Princeton University Press, 1991.

Market Economy

Markets for the exchange of goods and services have existed in most societies in which there has been either a division of labor (e.g., between rural and urban producers) or trading for commodities unavailable locally. In a market economy, however, trade in goods, land, labor, and money is a widespread form of social activity governing the livelihoods of many people. Both as fact and as theoretical concept the notion is relatively modern; it followed from the expansion of European commerce from the 15th century onward and its long-term worldwide consequences. It is a basic characteristic of capitalist societies.

From the ancient world through the Middle Ages, markets were often specified places of exchange, licensed by governmental authority. Most traders were perceived as socially marginal; dealing was sinful, or potentially so. The commercial revolutions of the early modern period altered both the scale of market activity and ideas about it. In the 18th century the essayist Daniel Defoe attributed Britain's prosperity to its internal and foreign trade, and Adam Smith (*The Wealth of Nations* [1776]) argued that the division of labor in society and the ubiquitous exchange of goods among its members was the indispensable source of growing wealth. Orthodox economic theory (which Smith helped found) no longer perceived markets as marginal or threatening, but as the very heart of all economic activity.

Above all, markets appeared to be self-regulating mechanisms: supply and demand determined the prices of goods, while peoples' wish to earn profits motivated them to produce and sell. The ideal of the self-regulating market led 19th-century proponents of laissez faire (and many economists and politicians since) to press for minimal economic regulation by governments. It also powerfully influenced historical interpretations of the rise of market economies, which often accepted that a "natural" human propensity to pursue profit and self-interest was the force behind the increasing scope, complexity, and interdependence of modern market-based societies. Social history, however, has sought different explanations.

First, historians noted considerable resistance to the advent of unregulated markets. In 18th-century France and England, for example, popular food riots obstructed the movement of grain at times of scarcity and contested the power which "free" markets gave to dealers to determine the time, place, and price at which they would make grain, flour, or bread available for sale. In England, as E.P. Thompson showed, this resistance reflected a widespread ethical rejection of exchange dictated purely by market conditions, and revealed the existence of a "moral economy" driven by notions of fairness antithetical to the unrestrained pursuit of self-interest. Rioting in France forced the government to reverse, in 1770, several years' "liberalization" of grain markets and to restore a policy of regulation. Tensions in the early 19th-century United States also reflected concern about the advent of a market economy and the motivations and social relationships involved. Installing a market economy became a major point of sociohistorical change.

Second, social historians (following the example of anthropologists) have paid increasing attention to the mechanisms and practices of trade and its contexts. Coffeehouses, taverns, and retail stores, peddlers, street traders, and substantial merchants operated within wider social relationships, which could have much influence on the conduct and growth of trade. The work of Geoffrey Crossick and other scholars of 19th-century Europe has illuminated the complex connections between trading conditions and the political influence of groups such as small shopkeepers.

Attention to context also gives social history a say in issues once assumed to be the preserve of economic historians. Recent studies of rural society in the early United States, for instance, have divided into those strongly influenced by orthodox economic theory who see the growth of markets for goods, labor, and land as the cause of social and economic change, and those of social historians who see market growth itself as the result of deeper social patterns. Demography, family and household structures, land ownership, attitudes to neighbors and kin, and the "moral economy" of exchange, credit, and debt all helped determine when, why, and by whom participation in markets occurred. This sense of the creation of markets as a social and cultural process is also conveyed in such studies as William Reddy's *The Rise of Market Culture* (1984), about 18th- and 19th-century French manufacturing.

Above all, the social history of markets abandons the assumption of traditional economic theory, that participants in exchange bargain as equals. E.P. Thompson and others helped place class distinctions firmly on social historians' agendas; more recently, studies of race and gender have also shown that socially constructed patterns of power have influenced not just individuals' participation in economic activity but the whole character of markets themselves. Both in Europe and North America, for example, the 19th-century market for labor was shaped by changing attitudes about men's and women's social roles, and new presumptions that certain tasks were "unsuitable" for members of one or the other sex. Men and women, white and black, rich and poor participated in markets on unequal terms, terms not simply set by "economic" considerations.

In the rapidly growing field of the history of consumption, social historians have also been influential. Once more, they reject single or universal explanations of the wish to consume, and hence of the growth of modern consumer societies. Like anthropologists, they are seeking to locate the acquisition and use of consumer goods within a broader understanding of social relationships, exploring the ways in which the availability of consumer goods reinforced or, alternatively, helped alter patterns of social organization and interaction.

Future developments may take two complementary paths. The recent work referred to has treated the history of markets "from below," from the viewpoint of popular or culturally determined patterns of attitudes and economic behavior. This will continue; it is a relatively new area, and much remains to be explored. But social historians will also be concerned with the study of markets "from above"—examining the attitudes and policies of states and social elites. Together, the two approaches will increase our understanding of mar-

ket economies as cultural phenomena and arenas of power. [*See also* Capitalism; Commercialization; Consumerism; Economics (Economic and Social History); Merchants; Moral Economy]

Christopher Clark

REFERENCE

Braudel, Fernand. *Civilization and Capitalism, 15th–18th Century*, Vol. 3, *The Perspective of the World*. New York: Harper, 1984.

Marriage/Remarriage

Marriage is the socially formalized establishment of a publicly recognized relationship between spouses (marital partners)—a man (the husband) and a woman (the wife)—which includes sexual intercourse and is usually expected to produce children unless the woman is beyond childbearing age. Its consequent importance for social reproduction makes it an essential topic for study in all societies. It interacts with inheritance systems in ways that vary with the types of property to be inherited (fixed or movable, tangible or intangible) and with the degree to which adults depend on their network of alliances with others for assurance of livelihood, rather than on inherited property. In general, societies with high reliance on inherited property (often agricultural or pastoral) tend to display strong linealities and strict lineage control over the making and unmaking of marriages, while societies with high reliance on alliance networks (both foraging societies and urban commercial-industrial societies) tend to display bilaterality and at least some opportunity for self-selection of partners. The changeover to commercial-industrial life that began in western Europe in the early modern era and continues to spread around the world has therefore been accompanied almost everywhere by a loosening of earlier controls and sanctions, including redefinitions of the goals of marriage itself. This process has been studied in some detail for many societies, with special attention to northwestern Europe and its overseas offshoots in the settler societies of Australia, Canada, New Zealand, South Africa, and the United States because these changes first began to appear there.

A host of topics associated with marriage receives attention in social history, often in collaboration with other disciplines. The topics include: marriage ages; relationship with other kin; power, work, and emotional relations between spouses; and stability plus possibilities of divorce. These features change over time and vary from one society to another, shaping important agendas in sociohistorical research.

In almost all societies, marriage includes the co-residence of the spouses, usually with the husband's kin in patrilineal societies like those of traditional East Asia (patrilocality) or with the wife's kin in matrilineal societies like many Native American groups (matrilocality if with her sisters, avunculocality if with her oldest brother), possibly with the kin of either (ambilocality or utrolocality, as in largely bilateral Southeast Asia), or even with no older kin (neolocality, practiced mainly in bilateral societies). In most societies, both spouses' labors are primarily expected to benefit their own offspring, though matrilineal societies regard a man's sister's children rather than his wife's children as his primary obligation. Even in the few societies where spouses tend to live with their own blood kin rather than with each other (as among the matrilineal Ashanti of Ghana), a marriage is regarded as allying the kin of the spouses to each other for as long as the marriage lasts and/or any children born into that marriage are still living.

In most societies, most people marry. However, some women may be left unmarried in polyandrous societies. Unbalanced sex ratios are apt to mean celibacy for those of the more numerous sex, in monogamous societies. Societies whose members are concerned to limit the number of heirs are apt to display high celibacy and/or late marriage for at least one sex.

In some societies like those in the Middle East, marrying close kin is preferred because the resulting alliances reinforce kinship or lineage bonds. Marrying close kin is avoided in other societies because it is regarded as important either to establish wider circles of alliance, as in much of South Asia, or to weaken strong inmarrying lineages, as in medieval Europe. Marrying close kin, or even kin as distant as second and third cousins, can also help to reunite properties divided by the workings of an inheritance system.

Marriage payments have often been part of the social formalization of marriage. When made by the future husband or his kin to the future wife's kin (bride-price or bride wealth), a marriage payment usually enables one of her brothers or other male kin to marry, as in much of Africa. It may be paid in installments, the last of which may not be given until one or more children have been born. When made directly to the wife (dower), it may go into a conjugal fund set aside for her, her husband, and their children, as in Europe. Whoever receives it may also keep it as a fund for the wife's use if the marriage dissolves and she returns to her kin, leaving her children with her husband's kin, as in the Middle East. When made by the future wife's kin (dowry), it may go to the husband to be placed in a conjugal fund; or it may go to the husband's kin with the understanding that it guarantees support for the wife and any children she bears, as in much of South Asia. In societies like ancient Rome, which have recognized concubinage or consensual union as a socially acceptable status, it is generally distinguished from marriage by the absence of any marriage payments. Any children born into consensual unions normally lack an automatic right to inheritance from the father, which socially formalized marriage ordinarily conveys in all except matrilineal societies.

Since parents and other older kin in almost all earlier societies and many contemporary ones would co-reside with the newly married spouses and would expect to rely on grandchildren as well as children in their last years, they have usually taken a leading part in arranging at least the first marriage (and sometimes also later marriages) of their children. Given relatively brief life expectancies in earlier centuries (still real in regions where parental arrangement remains common, as in Africa and South Asia), they have usually tended to seek to marry daughters before age 20 at the very latest. They have often also sought to marry sons before age 22, unless late marriage for men would facilitate polygyny as in Africa or keep numbers of births somewhat limited in a limiting environment as in the Middle East.

Among major groupings of societies, only northwestern Europe and its overseas offshoots

443

saw large numbers of women marry at 23 or older prior to about the mid-19th century. This was part of the northwestern European family system. A family pattern which saw many adolescent girls as well as boys move out of their parents' homes to work in other households (and may have begun with the manor weaving halls and forestry crews of early medieval northwestern Europe) gave most nonelite young people an opportunity to find their own partners, even though elite families usually arranged their children's marriages for alliance-making purposes. The introduction of baptismal records by the bishop of Nantes in France in 1406 acknowledged the significance of each individual newborn not just to its kin but to the larger society of the living, through recording its entry into the even larger society of Christians both living and dead. This paved the way for formal recognition at the general Roman Catholic Council of Trent in 1563 that marriage concerned the partners even more than it concerned their parents. Self-selection (usually during the twenties) of partners who focus more on each other and their offspring than on their parents or siblings (and expect any property to be divided rather equally among all children of both sexes) became the norm even for most elites in northwestern Europe and its overseas offshoots by the early 19th century at latest.

As other societies in other parts of the world have become more diversified economically, with the spread of monetization, commercialization, and industrialization, their members have also tended to move toward both neolocality and self-selection of marital partners during the twenties. Self-selecting neolocal marital partnerships relying on a conjugal fund can provide reasonably good security for both the two spouses and their children in monogamous societies with low divorce rates. In polygynous societies, societies with large numbers of consensual unions, or societies with a significant divorce rate (whether the society practices monogamy, polygyny, or polyandry), wives and their children usually need guarantees other than a conjugal fund. Thus, the continuing prevalence of both polygyny and divorce in much of Africa contributes strongly to the continuing prevalence of close ties between siblings, as do the consensual unions of

much of Latin America, while the growing prevalence of divorce in Europe and its overseas offshoots tends to encourage greater reliance on blood kin (psychologically if not economically) and less reliance on a spouse. Conjugality (marriage) and consanguinity (kinship by birth) are always in tension with each other, even though every society relies on both. The real possibility of remarriage, even in societies which make little or no use of divorce, often increases that tension unless a society actively encourages seeking the next partner among the previous partner's closest kin. (*See also* Courtship; Demography; Divorce; European-Style Family; Family)

G. Robina Quale

REFERENCES

Carter, Hugh, and Paul C. Glick. *Marriage and Divorce: A Social and Economic Study*, rev. ed. Cambridge, MA: Harvard University Press, 1976.

Dupaquier, J., et al. *Marriage and Remarriage in Populations of the Past.* New York: Academic Press, 1981.

Fox, Robin. *Kinship and Marriage.* Harmondsworth, Eng.: Penguin, 1967.

Goody, Jack. *The Oriental, the Ancient and the Primitive: Systems of Marriage and the Family in the Pre-Industrial Societies of Eurasia.* Cambridge: Cambridge University Press, 1990.

Quale, G. Robina. *A History of Marriage Systems.* Westport, CT: Greenwood Press, 1988.

Marxist Historiography

Since the 1840s, Marxism's contribution to historical analysis has been threefold. Its practitioners have applied historical materialist criticism to non-Marxist scholarship, extending and refining its achievements. They have applied the same analytic method to existing Marxist theory—often with bitter zeal—to uproot error and push back the social frontiers it has explored. Most practically, they have tested Marxist theory and existing scholarly knowledge by study of concrete historical problems, which in recent decades has included path-breaking work in social history. Rather than rote application of the selective cookie-cutter of party dogma to the study of the past, as some have charged, the best Marxist history has synthesized these critical, theoretical, and practical aspects, working from real social relations toward better understanding of history's abstract meanings. Indeed, the course of Marxist historiography has been shaped by a relentless pursuit of historical method itself, at some moments abysmally incompetent, at others sublime. Nothing better proves Karl Marx's dictum, "There is no royal road to science."

Evaluation of the career of Marxist historiography requires recognition of the role of historical analysis as an aspect of class struggle, the sine qua non of Marxist theory and practice. Inevitably, Guyanese historian Walter Rodney told an academic conference shortly before his assassination in 1980 that every scholar acts as "an acolyte of the lords of production or an agent of social change." Though they might have doubted the voluntarism underlying Rodney's assertion, in Marxism's heroic age, every major theoretician and party leader recognized historical writing's role as a weapon of class struggle, deploying in to advance the goal of revolution. Yet as Marx's cautious *The Eighteenth Brumaire of Louis Bonaparte*, Friedrich Engels's *The Peasant War in Germany*, Leon Trotsky's *1905*, and especially V.I. Lenin's brilliant *The Development of Capitalism in Russia* attest, Marxists recognized that close, critical examination of existing social relations, not the pie-in-the-sky ravings of "utopian socialists" and Narodniks, would best advance their cause. Painstaking research, then, and scrupulous accuracy were critical to revolutionary victory.

With the triumph of the October Revolution (1917), however, and its paradoxical failure to spread beyond the Soviet Union, a defensive, self-affirming quality entered Marxist historical writing. Origins may be glimpsed in Trotsky's tendentious *History of the Russian Revolution*, not to mention Lenin and Trotsky's *apologia* on the Kronstadt insurrection; its consequences became plain after Stalin's advent, with the retouching of photographs, the suppression and falsification of documents, and the periodic wholesale revision of the historical record. As nothing before or since, Soviet historians justified American economic historian Charles Beard's argument that history is finally an act of faith.

Best scholarly intentions notwithstanding, between 1917 and 1956, Marxist historical writing remained yoked to the political needs of the Comintern or its Trotskyist opponents. On one hand, the Caribbean Trotskyist C.L.R. James recounted the bloody fate of a parasitic colonial ruling class in Santo Domingo, and of those who fought for, then betrayed the revolution. A half-century later, *Black Jacobins* remains a scholarly tour de force, but its presentist political agenda and romantic excesses are glaring. On the other hand, in the 1940s historian and Communist Party member Philip Foner told of the unholy alliance between *Business and Slavery* in antebellum America, while his colleague and comrade Herbert Aptheker recounted the long history of black slaves and white workers to achieve liberation. Again, the contribution of these studies is considerable and lasting; their political tendentiousness is inescapable. Here class struggle was incessant, and victory inevitable.

This was a motivation, if not a politics, which a host of conservative historians from Thucydides (d. c. 401 BC) onward might applaud. The problem was that Nikita Khrushchev's 1956 revelations made most Marxists outside the Soviet Union squeamish about offering up moral hymns to the revolutionary status quo. Some party member historians in western Europe and the United States had already suspected Stalin's crimes and had swallowed hard; the naive turned in their faces uncritically toward a brighter post-Stalin era. The wide-ranging research of Roy Zhores Medvedev, as well as Trotskyist biographer Isaac Deutscher, bears witness to the power of Marx's method against reactionary orthodoxy.

In the decade after 1956, ironically, Britain and the United States—politically paralyzed by Cold War hysteria—became twin centers of innovative Marxist historical scholarship. In England came forth the triumvirate of historians Christopher Hill, Eric Hobsbawm, and Edward P. Thompson, all variously disconcerted by the postwar world and Khrushchev's revelations. Linking Christian millennialism, political revolution, and social upheaval, Hill deepened the meanings and broadened the analytic scope of Tudor-Stuart history. Focusing upon the rebellious and downtrodden of early industrial Britain, among a wealth of other topics, Hobsbawm wove a tale of social contradiction, personal pride, and "labor aristocracy." Most startling of all was Thompson, a gentry-born Marxist whose love of culture and packrat archival instincts in 1963 produced the epochal work *Making of the English Working Class*, the first substantive contribution by a historian since Lenin to Marxist method and theory. Thompson's experiential redefinition of social class not only opened up large areas of life hitherto considered irrelevant to political analysis; his work also provided the theoretical underpinning absent in the work of Hill and others. It took several years for the Thompsonian revolution to wash outward from Britain's shores, but its impact proved profound.

In the United States, since 1965, historian Eugene D. Genovese's wide-ranging books and blistering critical essays have transformed the canon of historical scholarship almost single-handedly. Though he scrupulously noted the contributions of liberal predecessors, it was Genovese's brilliant exploration of the ideas of Italian Communist Antonio Gramsci that opened new vistas to the study of class formation and class struggle. Most important, perhaps, Genovese's discussion of hegemony ratified the British explorations of culture, religion, and ideology—though not the Thompsonian notion of class—stressing not just the potentially revolutionary character of the terrain, but the limits to revolution hegemonic struggle engendered. In a vast and still-growing body of work on the slave South, Genovese has analyzed the clashing "worlds" bondmen and masters made, situating those worlds within regional political economy and hemispheric relations of power. In tandem with Elizabeth Fox-Genovese, he has championed broader comparative analysis, seeking dynamics of slavery and sectionalism in the contradictory imperatives of merchant capital, and has even assaulted the conservative fortress of intellectual history to rescue "the mind of the master class." Without question, he remains the premier Marxist historian of our age.

By the mid-1970s, Anglo-American historians had moved from marginal to vanguard status, exerting a powerful pull on the direction of scholarship. Mainstream journals opened their pages to Marxian essays, and the post-Communist "New Left" created its own organs, including *Past and Present*, *Studies on the Left*, and *Radical History Review*. The recent "discovery" of a humanistic "Early Marx" made such developments more palatable, even trendy among liberals. With the knighthood of the Marxist classical historian Sir Moses Finley, and the creation of Genovese and Christopher Lasch's journalistic Tower of Babel, *Marxist Perspectives*, it seemed as if a generation of achievement was reaching full flower.

The practical impact of these accomplishments, however, verged on nil. After ten issues, *Marxist Perspectives* died a bitter, intellectually violent death in 1980. Its demise offered a powerful omen. Among other causes, the journal's popular front publishing strategy quickly tended toward a Marxism too watered-down to be recognizable. Similarly, Thompson's American popularizer, Herbert Gutman, abandoned the Briton's already wobbly notion of class, contributing subjectivist explorations of black and working-class culture and community instead. Where Thompson, Hobsbawm, and Genovese had struggled to solve the vexed question of the relation of base and superstructure in social analysis, the New Left increasingly turned its back on the problem, offering rather a culture-based populism which praised the triumph of will over power. The stirring tales of underdog resistance Gutman and his eclectic disciples told stole the Marxists' thunder. By 1990, an amorphous "radical" perspective, avowedly "influenced" by Marx, had marginalized Marxism once more. Those like Geoffrey de Ste. Croix, Bryan Palmer, or Tony Judt, who protested that there was too much water in the wine, were pilloried as throwbacks, cranks, or sectarians.

These scholarly developments, of course, reflected well the wildly optimistic cultural narcissism of the era. With the decline of Anglo-American communism after 1960, too, and the rise of increasingly abstruse and heretical "Western Marxism," even those who defended Marxist historical perspectives tended to verge on theoretical illiteracy. In France, where socialism and philosophy still flourish, different interpretive debates rage. Central to these is Jean-Paul Sartre's brilliant, neglected attempt to fuse Marxism and existentialism. In *Critique of Dialectical Reason*, he offered a method of overcoming the subject/object split which divides "radicals" and Marxists, testing his approach in a series of uneven, unwieldy biographical studies. To "structural

Marxist" followers of Louis Althusser, however, Sartre's nod to individual agency seemed mistaken. All sides admitted the restraining power of social structure, or the "practico-inert," as Sartre called it, but writing history based on it alone proved nearly impossible. Meanwhile, non-Marxist historians like Fernand Braudel were content to turn structural Marxism against its authors, jettisoning notions of class and exploitation, and demoting political conflict of all kinds. Other quarrels, some internecine, enveloped Marxist historians such as Thompson in Britain.

Currently, then, Marxist historical writing is in confusion and disarray, though the importance of individual Marxist sociohistorical studies persists. Despite important exceptions, Marxist writing has failed to penetrate many subdisciplines, such as biography and intellectual history. It has done little to utilize research tools such as quantitative methods or psychoanalysis. Interdisciplinary analysis has usually produced eclectic theoretical weakness. Confronted by scholars who trumpet the importance of race, gender, or other social variables, Marxists have usually mumbled a disastrously compromising response. The collapse of European communism, too, has only engendered more doubts on Marxism's validity as political strategy or historical method. Almost any social historian today concedes to being "influenced" by Marxism—but not too much! Solving these difficulties will require much time, and much criticism. Turning back to first principles of method might be the best way to start, beginning appropriately with Lenin's polemic "Better Fewer, But Better."

Lawrence T. McDonnell

REFERENCES

Abelove, Henry. *Visions of History*. Manchester: Manchester University Press, 1983.

Anderson, Perry. *Arguments Within English Marxism*. London: Verso Books, 1980.

Genovese, Eugene D. *In Red and Black: Marxian Explorations in Southern and Afro-American History*. New York: Pantheon Books, 1971.

Poster, Mark. *Existential Marxism in Postwar France: From Sartre to Althusser*. Princeton, NJ: Princeton University Press, 1975.

Tyrrell, Ian. *The Absent Marx: Class Analysis and Liberal History in Twentieth-Century America*. Westport, CT: Greenwood Press, 1986.

Masculinity

Masculinity is a concept whose familiarity has rendered it all the more elusive to scholarly analysis. While the term is almost always used in the singular form, the dictionary definition—"pertaining to men or males"—is universal. Most scholars and indeed most people using the term unthinkingly reify "masculinity" as a unitary and fixed phenomenon. Thus, such incongruous figures as Attila, Frederick the Great, and John Travolta have at one time or another been described as prototypically masculine. During the past two decades, however, a growing number of psychologists, sociologists, and social historians have questioned whether the Y chromosome dictates or even predisposes men to a single behavioral or psychological pattern. These scholars pointedly refer to "masculinities" and posit that the significant part of male gender behavior is and has been shaped by society and therefore might be studied as part of historical change. A significant example is the collection of essays edited by Harry Brod, a leader of the men's movement, entitled *The Making of Masculinities: The New Men's Studies* (1987).

This recent reassessment of "masculinity" was preceded and to some extent dependent on the feminist challenge to traditional conceptions of women. One of the most influential, though not the earliest such reconsideration, was Margaret Mead's *Sex and Temperament in Three Primitive Societies* (1935). Pointing to the aggressive behavior of Mundugumor women, Mead asserted that gender roles had not been predicated upon biological or psychological necessity, but had evolved as a product of social conventions. Mead's insight became dogma to the generation of feminist women who came of age during the sexual revolution of the 1960s. Women's historians contributed significantly to the feminist cause by revealing the important and widely varied roles of women in many different historical contexts. Women in the past had not, despite the fetters of patriarchy, behaved in a predictably "feminine" way.

That the same was undoubtedly true of men and of masculinity was perceived more slowly. Women's historians, initially intent on saving from oblivion the lives of women who had been overlooked in traditional chronicles, had little reason to turn their attention to men, who, since the time of Greek historian Thucydides (d. c. 401 BC), inhabited almost exclusively the pages of history books.

Moreover, no animating political ideology inspired hordes of scholars to write dissertations on the history of men. An important exception was the emergence of gay history in the wake of the gay-liberation movement of the 1960s and 1970s. In response to Freudian psychiatrists and other social scientists who had conceived of homosexuality as an errant path on the road to healthy masculinity, gay and lesbian historians attacked "hegemonic masculinity" itself as an oppressive force that stifled natural variations in human behavior. Much as feminist historians effectively challenged historical assumptions as to women's roles in the past, gay theorists and historians showed that men had always exhibited a wide range of gender-related behaviors and preferences. Jeffrey Weeks, in *Coming Out* (1977) and *Sex, Politics and Society* (1981), revealed that homosexuality itself did not acquire its modern meaning until the late 19th century.

The study of heterosexual men as gendered beings has lagged behind. Exceptions include psychologist Joseph Pleck's *The Myth of Masculinity* (1981), which offered a powerful indictment of psychological and sociological assumptions that all males are naturally drawn to a fixed "masculine identity." Among social historians, the seminal synthesis of men's history in Peter N. Stearns's *Be a Man! Males in Modern Society* (originally published in 1979; rev. ed. 1990), has gone virtually unchallenged.

The account begins in the Neolithic era, when men, whose larger bones and thicker muscles enabled them to run faster and hit harder, specialized as hunters, while women became charged with child rearing. Neolithic cultures consequently enshrined aggression as a positive trait associated with men, and nurturance, with women. Although crop cultivation superseded hunting as an economic activity during the agriculture revolution, the personality traits and skills associated with hunting were readily transformed into soldiering, for agricultural societies had to be protected from envious barbarians without and rebellious peasants within. Rulers fought to preserve their land, which they distributed to faithful retainers as property. Monarchs thus served as potent exemplars of martial masculinity, a role that became diffused to all property-holding men.

Even in these rigidly patriarchal societies, alternative conceptions of masculinity coexisted. It seems doubtful that peasants emulated the mastery and martial bearing of those whose lands they worked. Moreover, in nearly every society men have attained honor and prestige as shamen, priests, or scholars, positions whose religious and contemplative values exist in tension with the martial masculinity of the rulers. The ascendancy of Christianity, for example, greatly complicated the masculine norm in the West, for the stern patriarchs of the Old Testament were now superseded by a Christ who enjoined His followers to turn the other cheek and promised the meek that they would ultimately prevail.

The transformation of society through industrialization brought with it a special redefinition of gender roles. Middle-class sons whose fathers and grandfathers had cemented patriarchal authority through control of property now sought to make their own way in mercantile or professional activities in the new cities. Working-class sons whose fathers had taken pride in their craft accepted wage work in factories, where machines had devalued artisanal skills. Confronted with unsettling social changes, young men clung ever more tightly to old conceptions of masculinity and in so doing distorted them considerably. Wage earners who submitted to bosses and mutely tended machines demanded obedience at home and unloosed their tongues at the tavern. Middle-class men invested their increasingly sedentary labors with the competitiveness and emotional intensity of the primeval hunt. Recreations, too, such as sports, clubs, and fraternal lodges, often became exclusively male activities. For men whose sense of masculinity was imperiled, distance from women—whether emotional or physical—often proved reassuring.

During the 20th century, as corporations further circumscribed individual initiative, as feminism challenged notions of male superiority, and as women made gains in traditional male pursuits, some men sought refuge in traditional manhood, losing themselves in work or identifying with sports or movie heroes whose "masculinity" was in no way problematic. More recently still, others, American men especially, have been drawn to the "mythopoetical" movement, inspired by Robert Bly's best-seller *Iron John* (1990), a book that presumes that all men share a core masculinity whose roots extend to the dawn of man.

The persistence and vitality of traditional conceptions of "masculinity" constitute a significant challenge to social historians who have questioned the importance of biological or psychological bases of male behavior. This tension promises to invigorate this young field. Far more detailed and sophisticated research is necessary to show how and when society "constructed" specific norms and institutions, and how they adapted to new challenges. A host of specific issues also have yet to be resolved. Most work on 19th-century men, for example, assumes that fathers became increasingly unavailable for children, as work separated from home. But a complex, nuanced history of fatherhood has yet to emerge, which means that 20th-century history of the subject lacks an adequate baseline. Changes in male friendship after the 19th century constitute another topic inviting inquiry. The whole issue of comparative masculinity—how male standards in different cultures reacted to industrialization, for example—is virtually untouched, as most work has concentrated on the United States. As the realization that masculinity and male roles and relationships are socially constructed deepens, opportunities for historical analysis are rapidly expanding. (*See also* Cultural History; Women's History)

Mark C. Carnes

REFERENCES

Carnes, Mark C., and Clyde Griffen, eds. *Meanings for Manhood: Constructions of Masculinity in Victorian America.* Chicago: University of Chicago Press, 1990.

Filene, Peter G. *Him/Her/Self: Sex Roles in Modern America.* Baltimore: Johns Hopkins University Press, 1974.

Greenberg, David F. *The Construction of Homosexuality.* Chicago: University of Chicago Press, 1988.

Stearns, Peter N. *Be a Man! Males in Modern Society,* rev. ed. New York: Holmes and Meier, 1990.

Mass Culture

The concept of "mass culture" has only recently attracted the attention of social historians. Previously it was a subject of theory and investigation primarily among sociologists. Much as interest has grown among historians, so too it has expanded among literary critics. Thus, the study of mass culture has become a fertile ground of interdisciplinary study where scholars who identify with sociology, social theory, social history, communications, media, film, and literary and cultural criticism are all making contributions. For the purposes of this article, the following will serve as a general, if oversimplified, definition of mass culture: the cultural products of urban industrial society—ranging from mass newspapers to television—intended for and consumed by the masses, transmitted through modern mass media of communication, and shaped by this technology and mass marketing considerations.

In many ways the concept of "mass culture" is linked to another concept once popular in sociology, that of "mass society." The notion of mass society grew out of a tradition in social thought that dichotomized societies into categories like *gemeinschaft* and *gesellschaft*. These social theorists saw modern society undergoing a transition from intimate face-to-face communities to larger-scale, urban, industrial, and impersonal "mass" societies. In most cases they regretted the transformation, fearing the alienation and loss of individuality that might result. In this view, mass society produced a mass culture that was morally and intellectually barren. According to Theodor Adorno, Max Horkheimer, and other members of the famed Frankfurt School writing during the 1930s and 1940s, the rise of a mass culture of popular music, movies, advertising, radio, and eventually television deprived the masses of any creativity and originality. Coming out of fascist Europe, they also feared the antidemocratic and authoritarian possibilities of mass culture, where a ruling elite could manipulate the masses toward totalitarian ends. Even liberal democracies would suffer if people were indoctrinated by the mass media to pursue the interests of a political elite.

Another group of sociologists, gathered around Paul Lazarsfeld and Columbia University's Bureau of Applied Social Research during the 1940s and 1950s, posited a more optimistic view of mass culture as a counterbalance to the more pessimistic portrayal discussed above. Lazarsfeld and his associates argued that the effects of mass culture, particularly mass media, could be measured scientifically and, most importantly, that the process of transmission was more complex than the simple "stimulus-response" or "hypodermic-needle theory of media effects," which assumed that mass culture strongly affected all individuals in the same way. Rather, they proposed that audiences experienced mass culture through the mediation of opinion leaders and their own social and cultural needs. Although Lazarsfeld was not always approving of the impact of mass culture—he, for example, felt that mass media ironically might make citizens better informed but less likely to participate politically—his approach has spawned other efforts to probe the differential effects of mass culture on people, depending on their class, race, gender, and ethnicity. Many of these studies have appreciated the democratizing impact of mass culture in contrast to high culture, and have emphasized the ways that mass culture has complemented rather than replaced people's more indigenous cultural experiences.

The split between so-called pessimists and optimists has continued to inform recent studies of mass culture by historians and literary critics. The pessimists have persisted in seeing mass culture as an effort by capitalist and patriarchal elites to draw the masses into a hegemonic culture of standardized cultural symbols and political messages. The optimists have stressed instead how mass culture has integrated diverse individuals into a common culture with positive results and how individuals and social groups mediate the impact of mass culture, even at times turning it to their own ends.

The most extensive scholarship in the field of mass culture has come from literary critics and cultural historians, and the work of both has influenced social historians who are newer to the project. Cultural Studies, as it has been called in Great Britain, has been pioneered by members of the Birmingham Centre for Contemporary Cultural Studies under the intellectual leadership of Richard Hoggart and Stuart Hall and has focused on the impact of mass culture, particularly mass media, and on the theoretical relationship between material structure and ideological culture. Cultural historians, many of them American, have been important in bringing a historical perspective to the study of mass culture, often sharing with scholars in cultural studies a concern with texts and cultural products. Roland Marchand's *Advertising the American Dream*, Daniel Czitrom's *Media and the American Mind*, Lary May's *Screening Out the Past* (1983), and the essays in T. Jackson Lear's and Richard Fox's volume *The Culture of Consumption*, among others, have probed mass culture most intensively as a strategy of culture makers, and less intensively as an experience of culture consumers. Much of this literature assumes the successful cultural hegemony of cultural producers without actually investigating the audience's experiences or responses.

Social historians recently have brought their interest and sensitivity to the everyday lives of ordinary people to the study of mass culture and are helping to redress the imbalance in the cultural history literature. How social groups, differentiated by class, race, ethnicity, and gender, have experienced mass culture is the question social historians are uniquely prepared to probe. Several projects have focused on the relationship between strongly class-based leisure or outlook in the 19th century and seemingly more homogeneous cultural forms in the 20th century—such as television or mass sports. Relatedly, social historians have often used investigation of mass culture's impact not simply to understand the phenomenon itself, but also to gain further insight into fundamental questions in social history. For example, Kathy Peiss's (1986) study of the leisure activities of working women in New York from 1880 to 1920 argues that their involvement with mass culture, as represented by fashion, dance halls, nickelodeons, and Coney Island amusement park, led to the reorientation of American culture in the 20th century away from separate spheres toward heterosexual companionship. Similarly, Roy Rosenzweig (1983) and Lizabeth Cohen (1990) have suggested that working-class Americans' participation in mass culture and mass consumption facilitated rather than coopted (as the cultural hegemonists would have it) their political assertiveness as a class during the 1930s by helping them overcome divisions of race and ethnicity that long had undermined class-based collective action. Social historians dealing with western Europe have made similar efforts at understanding the reception of mass culture and its larger significance.

Investigations of mass culture are moving toward a new stage of more cross-fertilization between theorists, cultural historians, and social historians. Social historians consequently are becoming more conscious of the theoretical debates within cultural and literary studies and more appreciative of the importance of the text or cultural product than they had been. Future social histories of mass culture likely will be better informed by theory and more attentive to the content of people's cultural experiences, not just the social makeup and political responses of audiences. Hopefully, theorists and cultural historians likewise will prove more sensitive to the historical dimension of mass culture and the necessity of investigating—not just making assumptions about—the way ordinary people are affected by mass culture. (*See also* Class; Consumerism; Cultural History; Embourgoisement; Leisure; Mass Media; Popular Culture; Sociology)

Lizabeth Cohen

REFERENCES

Cohen, Lizabeth. *Making a New Deal: Industrial Workers in Chicago, 1919–1939*. New York: Cambridge University Press, 1990.

May, Lary. *Screening Out the Past: The Birth of Mass Culture and the Motion Picture Industry, with a New Preface*. Chicago: University of Chicago Press, 1983.

Peiss, Kathy. *Cheap Amusements: Working Women and Leisure in Turn-of-the-Century New York*. Philadelphia: Temple University Press, 1986.

Rearick, Charles. *Pleasures of the Belle Epoque: Entertainment and Festivity in Turn-of-the-Century France*. New Haven: Yale University Press, 1985.

Rosenzweig, Roy. *Eight Hours for What We Will: Workers and Leisure in an Industrial City, 1870–1920*. New York: Cambridge University Press, 1983.

Mass Media

While people used to go down to the train station to have their hands shaken or their babies kissed by a presidential candidate on a whistle-stop campaign, most now see and experience the presidency exclusively through the words and images of television, radio, and newspapers. While families used to create their own music at home with pianos, voices, or jugs, most now depend on radios, tapes, and CDs for musical entertainment supplied by professionals. Comedy and drama, once presented to and by live people in theaters, on vaudeville stages, and at the circus are now consumed for hours each day on television. The mass media—books, newspapers, magazines, recordings, movies, radio, TV, junk mail, computer networks—have for many people become the principal source of information about the world.

The mass media are the channels through which mass communication occurs. Unlike *interpersonal communication*, which takes place between two or three people, or *group communication*, which takes place between people in close physical proximity, *mass communication* describes the process whereby communicators deliver messages to a large number of physically separated people through a technologically based medium. Many trace the beginning of the mass media to the 15th century, when the German printer Johannes Gutenberg developed his movable type printing press, making books and other printed material (which no longer needed to be hand-copied) cheaper and more plentiful. The maturation of printing both served and catalyzed literacy among the growing middle class in western Europe. By the 18th century, printing had sired a new literary form, the novel, which was available to a wide audience, often in cheap, serialized forms. Newspapers began to flourish in this period as well, and in the first half of the 19th century "the penny press" provided timely information to anyone with a penny.

The operations of the early mass media depended upon an ability to reproduce cheaply messages and deliver them to the general public. This ability was greatly augmented by the discovery and harnessing of electricity and its attendant technologies. Today, mass-produced books (especially paperbacks), newspapers, and magazines bring the written word to every household. Radio, TV, and film bring drama and comedy to people who might seldom have gone to a theater, and information (including live broadcasts of events ranging from moon landings to warfare) to those who might never attend a lecture or even read a newspaper. Movies, records, tapes, and CDs make it possible for everyone to see and hear the same "performance." Computer networks make every home a research library.

Research into the mass media tends to cluster around two areas of concern. The first seeks to examine the elements and processes of mass communication itself. These studies concentrate on the principal features of the communication process: a *sender* (the communicator) acts as the source that delivers a message to a *receiver* (the listener, reader, viewer) over a *channel*, and the message might be altered or distorted by *noise* (misunderstood words, interruptions, etc.), and, in some cases, is responded to by the receiver in the form of *feedback* (messages delivered back to the sender). In the case of mass communication, each of these elements is part of a complex institutional system that employs a large cast of characters and technologies, all of which must be isolated and examined in order to understand fully the operations of the mass media.

Another area of concern for those who study the mass media, of particular salience in social history, is often referred to as "uses and effects." These studies concentrate on the audience for mass-mediated messages, a slippery subject since that audience sometimes numbers in the millions. They attempt to describe how people understand and are affected by media messages. Questions concerning the effects of advertising on shopping behavior, the effects of news coverage on voting behavior, and the media's overall impact on education and leisure are just a few of the many areas addressed here. Some of the most visible and controversial of the impact studies are those which examine the effects of the mass media (usually television) on children, and the relationship between media violence (usually in movies and on TV) and actual violent behavior.

The mass media have helped to blur traditional distinctions between "high culture" and "low culture." Books by Jane Austen and Danielle Steele are only steps away from each other in the chain bookstore at any mall; most record stores stock both chamber music and heavy metal. On the other hand, the mass media are also on a steady track toward specialization. General interest magazines with huge circulations that flourished earlier this century have in many cases either been repackaged (*The Atlantic*), scaled down (*Life*), or have ceased publication (*Look* and *Colliers*) in the wake of the onslaught of highly specialized periodicals aimed at specific target markets. Radio has followed the same pattern; most stations now are programmed with demographically specific musical categories like "urban contemporary," "country," or "light rock." Even TV, once the "national hearth" where culture was consumed by people across all economic, racial, educational, and gender lines, is now, thanks to multichannel cable packages, beginning to aim toward specific audiences. Mass media have also, by definition, reduced personal and community ties, often replacing spontaneous reactions with more silent, internalized responses (as when quiet, or when darkened movie houses replaced vaudeville).

It should be remembered that, while the mass media have democratized society in a way never before possible by making their messages accessible to nearly everyone, the nature of those messages is controlled by a select few, and most individuals lack much say in the process. Furthermore, advancing technology is often accompanied by higher price tags. The cost of CD players, cable subscriptions, and VCRs, for example, threatens to divide society into the information "haves," those who can afford access to the mass media outlets, and the "have nots," those who cannot.

Most study of mass media, particularly television, has been sociological rather than sociohistorical. Assessments of change over time are less common than assertions about what one new medium does with audiences. Nevertheless, several fine social histories exist, and the challenge for additional work is obvious. (*See also*: Leisure; Literacy; Mass Culture)

Robert J. Thompson

REFERENCES

Boorstin, Daniel J. *The Image: A Guide to Pseudo-*

Events in America. New York: Harper & Row, 1964.

Czitrom, Daniel J. *Media and the American Mind: From Morse to McLuhan*. Chapel Hill: University of North Carolina Press, 1982.

DeFleur, Melvin, and Everette E. Denis. *Understanding Mass Communication*, 4th ed. Boston: Houghton-Mifflin, 1991.

May, Lary. *Screening Out the Past: The Birth of Mass Culture and the Motion Picture Industry*. New York: Oxford University Press, 1980.

McLuhan, Marshall. *Understanding Media: The Extensions of Man*. New York: McGraw-Hill, 1964.

Postman, Neil. *Amusing Ourselves to Death*. New York: Viking, 1985.

Material Culture

As Thomas J. Schlereth (1982, 1990) and other scholars have noted, the concept of material culture is not culture but its product. Indeed, it is the use of the term "culture" in the expression that creates confusion in its definition. In the contemporary world, "culture" is studied from a multitude of disciplines so that dictionary definitions are not very helpful. For example, the *Oxford English Dictionary Supplement* defines culture as "the civilization of a people (esp. at a certain time of its development or history)." But the meaning of the word "civilization" is hardly more precise than "culture."

In 1952 the anthropologists A.L. Kroeber and Clyde Kluckhohn published *Culture: A Critical Review of Concepts and Definitions*, citing over 250 anthropologists, sociologists, psychologists, philosophers, and others in their quest for a more precise definition. While not claiming definitiveness the authors concluded with a formal definition as follows:

> Culture consists of patterns, explicit and implicit, of and for behavior acquired and transmitted by symbols, constituting the distinctive achievements of human groups, including their embodiments in artifacts; the essential core of culture consists of traditional (i.e., historically derived and selected) ideas and especially their attached values; culture systems may on the one hand, be considered as products of action, on the other as conditioning elements of further action.

Anthropologists, archaeologists, and ethnographers who investigate prehistoric eras without benefit of written documentation are, of course, dependent on artifacts. Artifacts, sometimes pottery shards as small as marbles, have been dug up and brought to the laboratory to be studied in relation to the broadest concept of culture. While archaeologists have long been associated with ancient civilizations and the aesthetics of the art produced by those cultures, in the last half of the 20th century there has been a major shift in scholarly emphasis to a greater concentration on social history, particularly on the everyday life of average people. And not only the everyday life of ancient Mediterranean peoples, but of peoples from all corners of the globe.

In the United States, it has been the historic archaeologists who have given the study of material culture a measure of academic sanction in fields other than anthropology and archaeology. James Deetz and Ivor Noel Hume, working in museums, have demonstrated to scholars in other disciplines the significance of objects in the study of social history. They have shown how artifacts that can be dated (ceramics of all sorts, for example) provide the groundwork for fundamental interpretations of historic houses and sites. In this case the archaeologists are often favored with written documentation to corroborate the evidence of the artifacts.

Traditionally, the realm of artifacts, "things," or objects has been the subject of study by museum curators and other collectors. Artifact identification in the United States has been greatly aided in recent years by the publication of a system for classifying manmade objects called *Nomenclature for Museum Cataloging*. As the cumulative effect of naming similar objects by the same name gains currency, and as museum collection data are entered into computer databases, it will become easier and easier to share information about and the identification of objects held in museums.

The worlds of the university and the museum have been separate in the United States since at least the last decade of the 19th century. It is the hope of many material culture scholars that the gap between these two institutions be closed. Thomas J. Schlereth (1982, 1990) of Notre Dame University has made great strides in closing this gap. Schlereth begins his definition of material culture with a definition of culture, in this case taken from the ethnohistorian James Axtell: "Culture is an idealized pattern of meanings, values, and norms differentially shared by the members of a society, which can be inferred by the non-instinctive behavior of the group and from the symbolic products of their actions including material artifacts, language, and social institutions." This definition clearly is not far from the old Kroeber/Kluckhohn definition of the 1950s.

In his recent book *Cultural History and Material Culture: Everyday Life, Landscapes and Museums* (1990), Schlereth has very elegantly posed three essential questions: What should students of material culture name what it is they do? Do the research strategies that have emerged recently constitute a field or a discipline? And what are the hypotheses that these students wish to answer?

Currently, three labels vie for acceptance: "material culture," "material history," and "material life." "Material culture" seems to have gained most acceptance among Americans; "material history," among Canadians; and "material life," among those historians and other scholars more inclined to accent the economic and social aspects of artifacts. Clearly, there is a dichotomy at the outset: is one studying the material or artifact per se, or is one using the material as one body of evidence in a larger set of other written and oral evidence?

The art historian Jules David Prown differentiates between a methodology, or a "mode of investigation," and a field of knowledge, or a "subject of investigation." Art history in Prown's view is both a mode and a subject while material culture is such an immense field to be unmanageable as a discipline standing alone. On the other hand, Dell Upton, an architectural historian, and John Michael Vlatch, a folklorist specializing in African American culture, urge that scholars follow Winterthur Museum historian E. McClung Fleming's techniques for studying artifacts—studying their properties of material, construction, design, function—reapplying these concepts to much larger artifacts such as buildings and landscape.

Fleming's approach analyzes these properties in four fundamental ways: He identifies the object with a complete description including its provenance, type of construction, likely date of construction, and materials from which it was made. Then, he evaluates it using contemporary standards of aesthetics and workmanship, usually by comparing it with similar examples. Thirdly, he puts it through a process of cultural analysis by which the artifact is evaluated in terms of its own culture. And finally, he interprets the artifact by making a determination of its significance in relation to both its intrinsic and our own culture.

Drawing on the concepts of these theorists, in Schlereth's own common sensible view, material culture can be defined as a mode of inquiry primarily (but not exclusively) focused on a type of evidence. Material culture thus becomes an investigation that uses artifacts (along with relevant documentary, statistical, and oral data) to explore cultural questions both in certain established disciplines (such as history or anthropology) and in certain research fields (such as the history of technology or the applied arts).

Schlereth divides practitioners of material culture into nine main categories: art historians, symbolists (from American studies in particular), cultural historians, environmental historians, functionalists, structuralists, behaviorists, definers of national character, and social historians. Indeed these categories are reflective of the emphasis on more and more specialization within the discipline of history and other social sciences. These specialists are interested in groupings of artifacts; they have differing views of history; and their objectives differ as do their research techniques and the formats in which their results are published.

Most of Schlereth's categories are self-explanatory, but some need further elaboration. For example, symbolists use artifacts as symbols for broader cultural meaning; Alan Trachtenberg's *Brooklyn Bridge: Fact and Symbol* is representative. Environmentalists tend to be cultural geographers who use the landscape itself as an artifact to look for sources of architectural ideas and building processes. J.B. Jackson (1909–1990) was one of its principal advocates, but Fred Kniffen and others have followed his lead.

Functionalists tend to be historians of technology of all levels from simple to very complex technological systems and their social consequences. Melvin Kranzberg, Merritt Roe Smith, Brooke Hindle are noteworthy advocates.

These various practitioners of material culture have used techniques that are primarily descriptive in nature but others—ethnologists, cultural geographers, social and economic historians—are moving into more analytical approaches borrowing concepts from Noam Chomsky, Claude Lévi-Strauss and other structuralist theoreticians. As Jules Prown puts it, that humans express their human need to structure their world through forms as well as through language is a basic premise of the structuralist approach to material culture. Henry Glassie is the foremost spokesman for this group; he sees the artifact as "an affecting presence, the perpetual mythic enactment of a culture's essential structure."

American studies scholars and other students of national character see objects as symbols of larger cultural ideas. Alan Gowans, for example, saw the "classical mind" of the 18th century embodied in architecture and furniture evidencing those principles of precision, self-containment, and measured control of environment that were at once vehicle for and expression of the urge for unity that transformed scattered colonies and provinces into the United States.

Finally, social historians such as Kenneth Ames have made compelling use of such mundane items of furniture as the umbrella stand and the parlor organ to illustrate a vast range of social values applicable to a particular time and place—in this case, Victorian America. To Ames, in relation to the parlor organ, "The nonverbal communicative aspect of material culture continues beyond its original context; tools developed for a society to attain its own goals become for the historian of a later period a means to identify and analyze those goals."

Social historians analyze both objects or "things" and pictorial and textual representations of things. There is a considerable body of historical work that has used mail order catalogues and probate inventories to address questions pertaining to a range of subject areas from the standard of living in a time and place to sleeping arrangements in a colonial home.

Most social scientists, if they use material culture at all, use it to illustrate ideas and concepts. But a growing number of them are seeing mate-rial—objects, works of art and design, housing types, landscapes—as evidence, as sources of ideas and concepts. No one yet has created a definitive methodology for studying and analyzing material culture, and indeed, because of the range of material, it may not be possible. But more and more scholars are taking seriously the notion that things can do much more than illustrate, that the analysis of objects is not only for the hobbyist collector and museum curator, but can go a long way in deepening our understanding of human experience.

Use of material culture evidence by social historians has been increasing, after an earlier period when, eager to avoid antiquarianism, many practitioners concentrated on other sources. Material culture most commonly forms part of an exploration of a particular group or time period; it is less often used as part of studying social change. The field, though still somewhat separate, interacts increasingly with other concerns in social history. (*See also* Archaeology; Cemeteries; Cultural History)

Elizabeth Hitz

REFERENCES

Deetz, James. *In Small Things Forgotten: The Archeology of American Life.* Garden City, NY: Anchor Books, 1977.

Fleming, E. McClung. "Artifact Study: A Proposed Model," *Winterthur Portfolio* 9 (June 1974): 153–161.

Gowans, Alan. *Images of American Living: Four Centuries of Architecture and Furniture as Cultural Expression.* New York: J.B. Lippincott, 1964.

St. Clair, Robert Blair, ed. *Material Life in America.* Boston: Northeastern University Press, 1988.

Schlereth, Thomas. *Cultural History and Material Culture: Everyday Life, Landscapes and Museums.* Ann Arbor: UMI Research Press, 1990; reprinted by University of Virginia Press, 1992.

———. *Material Culture Studies in America.* Nashville: American Association for State and Local History, 1982.

Matrilineal and Patrilineal Descent

Descent is the understood practice whereby successive lineal parent-child links are organized. The manner in which a single sex line is stressed is referred to as unilineal descent. When the kin group tracks its origins to a putative ancestor through males this usage is a patrilineage, conversely the tracing through females is a matrilineage. The corporate nature of these groups is evidenced by their allocative roles over persons and property and the concerns of inheritance and succession. Due to exogamy both sexes do not remain co-resident following marriage. Those lineages which include all of the collateral relatives from the apical ancestor are referred to as maximal lineages, while lineages which confer recognition to only three or four generations are called minimal lineages. When an ancestor is inferred rather than genealogically stipulated the resultant kin group may be referred to as a patriclan or matriclan. (The definitional boundaries of unidescent groupings is frequently a matter of confusion.)

In a patrilineage (read matrilineage for opposite gender kin placements), from the top down it appears that relatives are all those descended from an ancestor. One's mother is a relative but her kin who are connected through her are not the same kind of relatives as one's father's. A father's sister is a lineal relative while her children are not, as they belong to the kin group of her husband.

It is reckoned that patrilineal societies constitute 44 percent of the sample of descent-ordered ethno-units, while matrilineal societies represent 15 percent of the sample. The remainder are composed of descent types variously known as cognatic, ambilineal, bilineal, or double descent. One sample showed a strong correlation between horticultural and village communities and unilineal descent, a total of 380 out of 491. Descent forms constitute a major means of comparing family types in different societies, and thus play an important role in social history framework for family study. They have been less often examined in terms of change over time.

Unilineal descent groups are strongly associated with varieties of residence arrangements. Patrilocality is associated with patrilineage, and matrilocality and avunculocality, with matri-lineages. A patrilocal extended family may consist of a patriarch's wives, married sons with wives and children, and unmarried daughters. A man's extended patrilocal family with its dependents and descendants is based upon fraternal and fil-

ial bonds. The matrilocal extended family may mirror the patrilineal with the opposite mix of gender relations. With avunculocal residence the matrilineage males remain home through the wife's joining the residence of her husband's mother's brother.

Patrilocality is associated with pastoral nomadism, the use of the plow, or simple horticultural societies. Among pastoral nomads the fact that livestock is a form of property both mobile and dispersed puts a premium upon male solidarity and cooperation.

In and of itself matrilocality would not seem to confer any special advantages over patrilocality among horticulturalists. Harris (1990) suggests though from the examples of the Iroquois, Huron, and Mundurucu Indians that there are positive advantages with matrilocality in its correlation between internal peace through the scattering of males, female core cooperativeness, and male involvement in long distance trade and warfare.

Avunculocality seems to be associated with special prerogatives, possibly high ranking, which retain male political and economic controls within the matrilineage and succession and inheritance privileges to the sons of the matrilineage. Hence the incidence of avunculocality may represent a relatively developed and complex matrilineage. (*See also* Agricultural Systems; Family; Kinship; Land Tenure and Reform; Native Americans)

Frank McGlynn

REFERENCES

Barnes, John. *Three Styles in the Study of Kinship.* Berkeley: University of California Press, 1971.

Bohannon, Paul, and John Middleton, eds. *Kinship and Social Organization.* Garden City, NY: Natural History Press, 1968.

Goodenough, Ward. *Description and Comparison in Cultural Anthropology.* Chicago: University of Chicago Press, 1970.

Goody, Jack, ed. *The Character of Kinship.* Cambridge: Cambridge University Press, 1974.

Harris, Marvin. *Culture, People, Nature.* New York: 1990.

Schneider, David, and Kathleen Gough. *Matrilineal Kinship.* Berkeley: University of California Press, 1961.

Mechanization of Agriculture

Mechanization of agriculture refers to the process by which machine-age technology was developed and applied to the practice of agriculture. Labor-saving machines and mechanical devices, powered at first by horses and mules, later by inanimate sources of power, replaced hand tools and implements. Until mechanization, which began in England and the United States in the early 19th century, this aspect of agricultural technology had remained largely unchanged for centuries; many of the tools and implements used by late 18th-century farmers were essentially those used by farmers of classical antiquity.

The main thrust of the first wave of inventive activity was to substitute animal power for human. The result was the creation of a host of horse-drawn mechanical implements for use across a broad range of agricultural tasks and operations: improved plows, harrows, cultivators, and other ground-working equipment; mechanical reapers and threshers for harvesting and processing cereal grains; mowers, rakes, and hay loaders for harvesting forage grasses. These and many other labor-saving farm implements achieved widespread distribution by the middle third of the 19th century.

Development of machines reliable enough to inspire widespread adoption involved false starts and much experimentation. Often there was considerable time lag between the invention of a mechanical implement, and improvements and refinements that led to its widespread adoption. For this reason, mechanization did not have a major effect on American agriculture until the 1840s. Even after 1840 there was considerable unevenness in the pace with which new but proven machines were adopted. Farming with mechanical devices saved labor but was capital intensive. For example, seed drills, horse-drawn machines which sowed seeds at uniform depth and spacing, were in wide use by the 1850s. However, farmers continued to hand-broadcast seeds into the 20th century. Similarly, long after mechanical methods for harvesting grain had become standard, the grain cradle, the older, hand-powered implement for harvesting small grains, continued to be widely used.

In the late 19th century, inventive activity shifted to the development and utilization of inanimate sources of motive power for farm machines—first steam engines, then internal combustion engines. The result of these efforts was the tractor, a mobile source of inanimate power which, more than any other device, symbolizes the mechanization of agriculture. Noted for their power and versatility, tractors are capable of pulling heavy machines at speeds far greater than horses, while simultaneously generating the power necessary to operate the equipment. During the early stages of tractorization, horse-drawn equipment was retrofitted for use with tractors.

Tractors became ubiquitous on American farms during the first half of the 20th century. From just over 246,000 in 1920, the number of tractors on American farms expanded to over 2.3 million by 1945, and to 5.5 million by 1966. Motive power provided by tractors on American farms increased fivefold from the mid-1930s to the mid-1960s. Also, tractors permitted the elimination of draft animals, freeing farmers of the need to produce crops as feed for them. This greater productive capacity could be used to produce food for human consumption.

Mechanization transformed agriculture, expanding productive capacity while at the same time reducing labor requirements. The savings of labor and efficiencies of scale introduced by mechanization allowed fewer agricultural workers to produce crops at vastly higher levels than had been possible with the use of hand tools. Mechanization contributed immensely to the capacity of a small minority of the American population to produce agricultural commodities at levels sufficient to meet the needs of all.

Social historians of agriculture and rural life continue to examine the speed with which mechanization of agriculture proceeded and the determinants of that speed. Who were the adopters of new mechanical technologies and why did they adopt? Simply to save labor? How large were the productivity gains that resulted from mechanization? Further, what difference did these new labor-saving devices make in the lives of those who used them? Did they change traditional sex roles? How did mechanization contribute to changes in the nature of the family as an economic unit? What role did labor-saving agricultural technology play in the onset of a regime of lower fertility among agrarian populations? These are some of the main questions, issues, and themes pertaining to mechanization of agriculture that continue to be explored by social historians of the rural experience. (*See also* Animals; Food; Technology)

Kenneth E. Koons

REFERENCES

Danhof, Clarence. *Change in Agriculture: The Northern United States, 1820–1870.* Cambridge, MA: Harvard University Press, 1969.

Rogin, Leo. *The Introduction of Farm Machinery in Relation to the Productivity of Labor in the Agriculture of the United States During the Nineteenth Century.* Berkeley: University of California Press, 1931.

Schlebecker, John T. *Whereby We Thrive: A History of American Farming, 1607–1972.* Ames: Iowa State University Press, 1975.

Shover, John L. *First Majority–Last Minority: The Transforming of Rural Life in America.* DeKalb: Northern Illinois University Press, 1976.

Medical Eclecticism

The term "medical eclecticism" refers to a setting in which sick people, or those dealing with the sick, choose among a variety of medical options for care or cure. It is a practice that had been central to healing for several hundred years and has been revived in recent times, as an area of inquiry in the social history of health and medicine. A person in early 17th-century England, for example, could choose among doctors, local wisewomen, clergymen, traditional herbal remedies, magic, and astrology. Choice would depend on the financial resources of the sick person or family to some extent, but evidence shows that even fairly poor people chose expensive options while the rich might decide on cheaper practitioners. It was the exception, rather than the rule, for the sick to limit themselves to one practitioner, preferring instead a variety of options. This tendency was primarily due to the perception that disease had more than one cause, and illness was the result of a variety of both natural and supernatural forces.

Medical eclecticism depended on the lack of regulation governing medicine, as well as on distinctive beliefs about the strong links between mind and body, people and nature. In Europe, the use of magic was also fostered by popular religion, which taught that mental suffering was due to spiritual affliction; many clergymen had been respected practitioners of healing magic. An individual might thus select a clergyman to address the spiritual aspects of his/her disorder, an herbalist for medicine, and an astrologer to guide the forces of nature and indicate the proper timing of medication. For many centuries, the primary cause of disease, including mental disease, was considered to be disharmony between the body and the physical universe; thus, the eclectic practitioners shared the common goal of bringing the mind and body into harmony and, in theory, addressed themselves to all aspects of a person's life. The theory and practice of eclecticism were particularly widespread in the treatment of mental disorders during the 16th and 17th centuries due to the perceived powerful sympathy between mind and body and to reduce the imbalance among the body humors. Medical historians such as Michael MacDonald (1981) have shown via definitive case study analysis that physical remedies such as heat, purging, and bloodletting were frequently used for mental disorders.

Although medical eclecticism continues into the 20th century, social historians trace its decline, beginning in the 18th century, to western Europe and the United States. Causes of decline include professional rivalries, religious and political conflicts, and, to a lesser extent, scientific discoveries. The Church of England, for example, began to disdain the previously held notion that supernatural forces such as the Devil were responsible for illness. They championed instead the belief that secular causes were more influential determinants of sickness and health. The debate over causation of illness and misfortune led to political strife; eventually the secular view of illness prevailed, which reduced the sway of magical practitioners. Throughout the 18th century, physicians gained greater solidarity and education, dominating the preferences of the elite. This was the context in which more formal attacks on practitioners who were not doctors became possible.

In the United States, on the other hand, varieties of eclecticism were prevalent throughout the 19th century, due primarily to an anti-aristocratic sentiment, lack of licensing requirements, as well as a peculiar social environment promoting the concepts of individualism and "everyman as his own doctor." The climate led to a variety of medical sects throughout the 19th century in America. Many doctors practiced varieties of homeopathy, hydropathy, herbalism, and religious healing, to name a few, throughout the early and mid-19th century. Medical discoveries, new licensure, and educational action by the state and physicians forced some changes in popular belief and led to a focus on scientific medicine and a decline in choice of treatment options. By 1900, the regular physicians dominated medical practice and controlled the hospitals throughout the United States and Europe alike, as medical eclecticism declined further.

Nevertheless, even though Western medicine is dominated by the biomedical paradigm of disease causation and treatment, eclecticism persists among a variety of non-Western cultures in the 20th century. An excellent study of Taiwanese medicine highlights the pervasiveness of eclecticism, wherein the choice of treatment corresponds to the perceived etiology of disease, with remedies including herbs, tonics, diet, family intervention, rituals, and medications. The traditional folk healer is the shaman, believed to be one chosen by God to affect miraculous cures. Peasants have learned to include Western medicine as only one option among many in their search for healing. Social historians have explored the numerous and persistent alternatives to the Western biomedical model of disease and healing. Describing the process of change and explaining its causation, as well as exploring alternatives, sets the framework for much of the recent advance in the social history of health. (*See also* Magic; Medicine; Sectarians or Irregular Physicians)

Margaret Brindle

References

Thomas, Keith. *Religion and the Decline of Magic.* New York: Macmillan, 1971.

Kleinman, Arthur. *Patients and Healers in the Context of Culture.* Los Angeles: University of California Press, 1980.

MacDonald, Michael. *Mystical Bedlam: Madness, Anxiety and Healing in Seventeenth-Century England.* Cambridge: Cambridge University Press, 1981.

Medicine

The variety of medical practitioners and medical practices in the world today almost defy categorization; the varieties of each for which there is historical evidence is larger still. In Europe and North America, the medical field remained open to all until the later 19th century, as it still does in much of the rest of the world. All kinds of people practiced medicine: women as well as men, kin and neighbors as well as strangers, those who thought that they possessed special healing powers as well as those with a knowledge of local herbs, those who learned simply by trying to practice as well as those who learned from the experience of others, secular people as well as religious leaders, and those who were illiterate as well as those educated in universities. They might offer advice or treatment for money, favors, or kindness's sake; and they might do so incidentally, occasionally, often, or full time. Ordinary people—the patients themselves, and their neighbors and kin—have always been, and continue to be, the largest group of medical practitioners.

Medicine constitutes one of the fields most dramatically transformed by the rise of social history. Traditional history of medicine was a story of progress and great discoveries that assumed that modern medical changes were all to the good and that causation proceeded from the top down. Social history assumptions and findings generate a much more complex and lively picture that correspondingly integrates medical developments with a host of other features of society, from popular outlook to social class relations.

The variety of past medical practices and the relationships that existed among practitioners and between them and their clients have become the main objects of the attention of social historians of medicine in the last two decades. Most efforts to explore the social history of medicine have been devoted to the study of European and North American history, because that is where both the largest number of historians have been working and the most dramatic changes have occurred. Although there have been some exceptions, with important recent work on the social history of Asian, African, South American, and Australian medicine, this article will follow the current emphasis in the literature and focus on the development of European and North American medicine. The social history of medicine in these two regions reveals a general process sometimes termed "medicalization": a general shift from an open field to a government-regulated and -supported environment empowering experts trained in scientific medicine. Such a process has brought the loss of patient choice but benefits for health overall.

Given the variety of medical practitioners in the past, social historians of medicine have tended recently to stress how patient-dominated past practice was. With numerous and various practitioners available, a buyers' market existed for medical care. Patients with means and opportunity could choose among many kinds of practitioners and practices. While they suffered from a host of ailments, they had a wide range of medical resources to help them in their need. Popular assumptions about the body, which in contrast to 19th-century beliefs did not rigorously separate mental and physical disorders, contribute to making premodern medical history a major field of inquiry. Social historians successfully dispute traditional dismissal of this period through labels like "superstition" or "magic."

The transition to a practitioner-controlled medical field is generally held to have occurred sometime in the 19th century, although depending on the region under investigation and the definitions of the investigator, this might vary by decades, or even centuries. (The decline of magic, for example, began earlier.) Social historians of medicine have commonly portrayed the transition as a consequence of new forms of political organization. The transition began in the European Middle Ages. Beginning in the 12th century, some municipalities began to organize some kinds of medical practitioners into guilds, and to restrict certain practices to their members. Many towns and city-states also began to grant the university-trained physicians (who began to appear in the 13th century) special powers to supervise medical practice. With new forms

of medical organization and an emphasis on clinical experience in the 18th century, the apprentice-trained and university-educated practitioners began to have more in common, gradually coming to form a loose "medical profession," distinct from outsiders.

The rise of the modern nation-state and the human problems consequent on rapid urbanization, coupled with the powerful tools of medical chemistry and bacteriology of the later 19th century, brought about a closer alliance between the medical profession and government officials. Governments increasingly regulated medical practitioners, establishing a standard of scientific knowledge as the prerequisite for all practice. By the early 20th century, many nations had passed laws forbidding medical practice by those not qualified by standardized examination. As the right to practice medicine became limited to those educated in the universities, a series of long and bitter disputes were waged before women and minority groups gained entry into medical schools and so into the profession. As the profession unified, too, specialization within the profession became possible. Technological imperatives also began to take shape with the invention of a host of medical devices (including the x-ray, in the early 1890s), making medical specialism more common. By 1942, more than half of U.S. physicians (51 percent) were members of a specialty group within the medical profession, and now "general practice" is itself a specialty field, although general practitioners remain common in Europe.

Modern nation-states became involved in regulating medical practitioners for a variety of reasons, but many were coupled to the new problems consequent upon the dramatic rise in population and urbanization that began in the later 18th century. Crowded into small and dilapidated rooms, eating bad food, breathing filthy air, and having no access to clean water, the health of urbanites—especially the vast numbers of destitute and working poor—suffered terribly. Given government concerns about the connections between disease and poverty (the one causing the other, and vice versa), it was thought that keeping the poor rates down would be helped by lowering disease rates. The coming of Asiatic cholera in the mid-19th century brought a sense of urgency to policymakers who thought that ridding the cities of filth could lower the threat to all citizens that came from epidemic disease. Providing clean water and sewerage works became central to the public health campaigns of the later parts of the century. At the same time, fears of biological "degeneration" resulting from urban life, concerns about a citizenry fit to fight in the new wars that mobilized very large segments of the population, and extensions of the franchise to working people brought about government campaigns to improve the health of citizens more generally. Preventing the nonscientifically-trained from practicing became yet another branch of government health policy.

In addition to the effects of regulation on medical practice, the institution of the hospital has received much attention in recent years. Hospitals had come into being in the medieval period as particular kinds of hospices, charitable institutions to house and care for the sick poor. The Reformation brought an end to many hospitals in lands converted to Protestantism, while hospitals underwent renewal in Catholic lands. Some municipalities founded hospitals to care for the sick poor as part of their system of relief; by the later 17th century, military hospitals began to be built; and in the 18th century, "voluntary hospitals" were erected by groups of wealthy people. By the end of the 18th century, hospitals were so essential to local attempts to ameliorate the lot of the poor that in France the revolutionaries took over the hospitals from the church. By the later 19th century, most European hospitals were state-regulated if not state-run; in the United States, municipal and county hospitals continued to be mixed with proprietary hospitals. During the 19th century, too, hospitals became run more and more by the medical people who served in them, and decisions on admission and discharge were made increasingly for medical rather than charitable reasons.

Modern hospitals differ from earlier ones mainly in that they have become centers of medical treatment for all people, not just hospices for the sick poor. Again the transition began in the mid-19th century. With the development of anesthetic surgery (in the 1840s) and antiseptic surgery (in the 1860s)—which made surgery a possible form of medical treatment for a larger number of diseases—and with improvements in the qualifications of the nursing staff, hospitals became increasingly attractive as places to which one could go for medical attention and recovery. By the 1870s, many general hospitals were beginning to draw paying patients. After World War I in the United States and by the 1940s in Europe, paying patients predominated in general hospitals. Women even went to the hospitals for childbirth when mortality rates suggest that they may have been safer delivering their children at home. The profession has consequently become structured around the general practitioner/specialist (or hospital consultant) distinction, with the latter person gaining higher prestige and greater income.

As general practice and hospitals have become increasingly medicalized, so the question of how to make the new services available to the public has become a pressing concern. Local governments often provided relief to the sick poor, and guilds sometimes provided some help to their sick members. But by the 18th century, voluntary societies began to spring up into which a working person might pay some money regularly in return for medical "insurance" payments during sickness. By the 19th century, groups like the German "Krankenkasse" (sickness funds) were run by workers' unions, with employers as well as employees contributing. Many European governments became concerned about the amount of capital tied up in such funds, and began to regulate them in order to maintain their solvency. Gradually, for a variety of reasons, governments began to consider it good policy to bring all working people under such umbrellas. Between 1883 and 1911 (beginning with Germany and ending with Britain), most European governments passed acts requiring compulsory, government-regulated health insurance from the working-class segments of the population. Over the course of the 20th century, especially under pressure of war and depression, European governments began to prop up health insurance funds with tax money, and to extend coverage to virtually all citizens. In the early 20th century, too, the United States came close to introducing compulsory health insurance, but anti-German sentiment during World War I, the "Red Scare" after the Bolshevik Revolution, and growing concerns about professional autonomy turned the leaders of the medical profession against such government plans, and the plans failed. Only during the Great Society reforms of the 1960s did the U.S. Government begin to get involved in medical insurance, with the creation of Medicare and Medicaid.

Coupled with greater government involvement in regulating practitioners, in promoting hospitals, and in extending medical insurance has been a dramatic change in disease patterns. For millennia, most people have suffered from a wide variety of bodily discomforts, often from more than one at a time, and often accepting such discomforts as a part of the human condition. Such ordinary ills might be due to overwork, bad nutrition, worms and other parasites, accident and strain, and infection from others. Ordinary illnesses certainly affect what we would now call the "quality of life," but seldom caused death on their own. From the time that humans moved from the hunter-gatherer stage to living in settled communities, however, a large number of life-threatening diseases came to be transmitted from person to person, and sometimes became epidemic. On rare occasions, epidemic diseases might cause huge mortality crises. For example, epidemic plague in later 14th-century Europe may have killed 30 percent of the population in just a few years, while epidemic smallpox in Central America in the 16th century (brought over by the Europeans), together with slavery and other deleterious social conditions, helped to reduce the population to one-tenth of its original size in four or five generations. More commonly, endemic diseases—like generalized fevers and gastrointestinal illnesses or, in the 19th century, tuberculosis—cut down a large number of people every year. All these diseases preyed on infants and children, causing very high mortality rates early in life, and greatly lowering overall the average life expectancy. In short, until recently people tended to die from communicable diseases, which might linger but often killed quickly.

Within the last hundred years or so, however, disease patterns have changed, so that the major causes of death have become chronic, noncommunicable disease. The reasons for this shift lie mainly in new forms of food preservation and transportation, better housing, preventative vaccines, and especially the supply of clean water for drinking, washing, and carrying away wastes—in short, the increase in material wealth and the development of state-sponsored public health programs. The mortality rates from most communicable diseases had already fallen dramatically by 1920, before modern therapies were introduced (antibiotics, for example, came into production during and after World War II); modern medical treatments have helped to lower the incidence of communicable disease even further. While scientific medicine per se has not been the major cause of altered disease patterns, medical knowledge has also aided in the formulation of policies that have led to better conditions of life. On the other hand, growing anxiety about certain aspects of health and growing dependence on experts and government qualify any single history of progress. (*See also* Death; Health; Hospitals; Medical Eclecticism)

Harold J. Cook

REFERENCES

Bynum, W.F., and Porter, Roy, eds. *Encyclopedia of the History of Medicine.* London: Routledge, 1992.

Leavitt, Judith Walzer, and Ronald L. Numbers, eds. *Sickness and Health in America: Readings in the History of Medicine and Public Health*, 2nd ed. revised. Madison: University of Wisconsin Press, 1985.

McKeown, Thomas. *The Role of Medicine: Dream, Mirage or Nemesis?* Princeton, NJ: Princeton University Press, 1976.

Rosenberg, Charles E. *The Care of Strangers: The Rise of America's Hospital System.* New York: Basic Books, 1987.

Wear, Andrew, ed. *Medicine in Society: Historical Essays.* Cambridge: Cambridge University Press, 1992.

Meiji Era

The Japanese Meiji era began officially in 1868 with the abolition of the Shogunate and the restoration of the Meiji emperor. This period (1868–1912) encompasses major changes in the government, economy, and society of Japan. Prior to this period Japan had been a closed, isolated, self-sufficient society. The class structure had included the warrior/bureaucrat as the elite, the peasants, artisans, and merchants in descending order of respect. An underclass of slaves, priests, entertainers, and masterless samurai was not recognized officially as part of the social structure. Yet changes had occurred politically and economically as well as socially, which facilitated the transition to a modern nation under Meiji. Nonetheless, the Japanese were unable to prevent Western nations from establishing trade and diplomatic rights. This inability to protect the nation was a major factor in undermining the authority of the Shogunate.

The social history of the Meiji era deals with new relationships between state and society, with the impact of early industrialization, and with various kinds of social protest. The Meiji period has focused a great deal of sociohistorical work because of its key location between traditional and modern Japanese society.

During the transition to the Meiji era, one group from the elite class, a group of creative, intellectual leaders, dismantled the political and social structure which had been the basis of their status. The daimyo (feudal lords) and samurai (warrior/bureaucrats) lost the rights which had distinguished their class in society. Merchants were recognized, officially, as playing an important role in establishing the economic base and pursuing the modernization process of the nations. The peasants now owed their taxes to an impersonal central government rather than a local lord familiar with their conditions and problems. It was the peasants who furnished the revenue with which the government established modern communications, transportation, and heavy industry which were the basis of the economic transformation of Japan.

The economic changes included development of nascent business conglomerates. These were, in the main, family organized. As success in one area, such as textile manufacture, occurred profits were used to expand the business into money-lending (the basis of later banking enterprise), retailing, and brewing. Such developments, over time, led to the 20th-century conglomerates such as the Mitsui organization.

Politically, the new group in control was challenged by a popular rights movement. From this challenge, a constitution was developed which promised some freedoms, such as religion, education, and press; this constitution remained in effect until 1945. From the popular rights movements, as well, political parties were developed. While universal manhood suffrage was not achieved until 1925, a broadening of political participation occurred under Meiji. A draft for military forces was begun, with the British training the Japanese navy and the Germans developing the army. Western advisors helped in devising the school system, some university disciplines, and some industrial technology.

An antiforeign backlash occurred in the 1880s. Too many changes had occurred in a short period of time. In particular, too much Western borrowing had taken place; ironically, one motivation for the overthrow of the Shogun had been his inability to protect Japan from the West. Therefore, a reappraisal of the basic elements of Japanese society and culture began. The Japanese goal was modernization, not Westernization. As soon as a Western advisor had trained sufficient assistants, he was thanked and encouraged to return to the West. A period of consolidation followed; less experimentation was encouraged, and traditional values such as loyalty, obedience, and self-sacrifice were once more established within the education system. In this era the Japanese adapted some Western ideas, but did not become dependent upon the West.

Japan developed diplomatic and trade relations with other nations. A naval alliance was signed with Britain in 1902. To protect her interests, both political and economic, Japan waged war against China in 1895, and against Russia in 1905. With victories in these military encounters Japan achieved great power status.

It is in the Meiji era that Japan became a modern state. The Japanese achieved a remarkable transformation in roughly fifty years, with a minimum of social protest. By the death of the Meiji emperor in 1912, the goals of the Restoration had been achieved: Japan was a respected modern nation. (*See also* Japanese Industrialization; Japanese Popular Protest; State and Society)

Katherine Reist

REFERENCES

Hane, Mikiso. *Japan—A Historical Survey*. New York: Scribners, 1982.

Totman, Conrad. *The Collapse of the Tokugawa Bakufu, 1862–1868.* Honolulu: University of Hawaii Press, 1980.

Hane, Mikiso. *Peasants, Rebels, and Outcasts.* New York: Pantheon, 1982.

Menarche

Menarche, the onset of menstruation, varies historically and cross-culturally in both the age of onset and its social meaning. The age at which women first menstruate depends on nutrition, health, and genetics, and the different diets, living standards, gene pools, and treatment of women in the worlds' populations helps explain the wide variance in menarcheal age. Social historians can use average menarcheal age to evaluate the physical health and demographic potential of a group. The subject has important implications for the history of gender and sexuality, and it highlights the complex relationship between social history and human biology.

Traditional Islamic, Hindu, and Judeo-Christian legal works proscribed marriage before menarche, and reveal if not the actual average age of first menstruation, then at least when a culture considered a girl to have become a woman. European physicians from the 17th century onward queried groups of women to locate menarcheal age. Many 19th-century European and American hospitals examined female patients about their pubertal development. Twentieth-century anthropologists and researchers through longitudinal growth studies have gathered information on women's menstrual patterns across the world. In many places, however, menstruation has been considered a topic unfit for public discussion, leaving scant evidence for historical examination, although many patterns are now known.

Girls of higher socioeconomic groups usually menstruated earlier than their more poorly nourished counterparts. Regional differences exist as well, with menarche occurring earlier in the Mediterranean world than in northern Europe by as much as one year. Sources from classical India (500 BC–AD 500), recommending that a girl wed after her first menstrual period, place menarche from age eight to twelve. Girls in classical Greece and Rome and medieval Europe began menstruating around ages twelve to fourteen. The average menarcheal age in early modern Europe ranged from fourteen to eighteen depending on location and social class. The most controversial data are for late modern northern Europe, including an 1850 study in Denmark that has been interpreted to show an average first menstrual period occurring as high an age as seventeen. Other 19th-century studies confirm these late figures, such as the 1870 records of a London hospital placing the mean age at 14.96. Menarcheal age has dropped in industrialized nations, from 14.8 in 1890 to 12.8 in Japan and from 14.6 in 1920 to 13.3 in 1960 in Norway, a basic change in the framework for sexuality and reproduction, and for the experience of adolescence.

Although some cultures regarded menstruation positively, many others viewed menstrual blood negatively as having the power to do such things as destroy crops or curdle milk. These cultures therefore prohibited menstruating women from certain religious or sexual activities. Most nonindustrialized cultures practice initiation rituals for menarche ranging from festive welcomes to symbolic or physical mutilations. In the 19th century, many Westerners viewed menstruation as a debilitating state that made women unfit for education and professions. The American physician and feminist Mary Putnam Jacobi (1842–1906) was perhaps the most persuasive figure arguing scientifically against widespread misogynistic interpretations of female physiology. (*See also* Body; Demography; Marriage)

Lisa Cody

REFERENCES

Delaney, Janice, et al. *The Curse: A Cultural History of Menstruation.* New York: Dutton, 1976.

Tanner, J.M. *A History of the Study of Human Growth.* Cambridge: Cambridge University Press, 1981.

Mental Illness

In the premodern world, madness was attributed to the devil's influence, God's providence, or magic. In that fatalistic society the mad roamed unhampered, although the melancholic probably received kinder treatment than the furiously mad.

Social historians have emphasized the considerable tolerance for many forms of insanity, at least in the premodern West.

Even in supernatural explanations, commentators paid heed to natural causes. As Enlightenment thought in the 17th century diminished the role of demonological, theological, and magical forces, however, the idea that madness resulted from a failure to live within the rules of reason and natural law ascended. By mid-18th century, moral irregularities or excess passions became identified as causes of mental dysfunction and the responsibility for madness, or insanity, shifted from God to the individual.

The secularization of madness and the rise of scientific medicine coincided. Although lacking any notion of specific disease entities, 18th-century doctors adopted a somatic model of illness. They believed, first, that illness arose from a general imbalance within the body, often as a result of a diseased organ affecting some other part of the body and calling for bleeding or purging to restore bodily equilibrium. Second, the individual as well as the environment played a role in maintaining health. The application of theories about physical disease to mental dysfunctions required only the additional caveat that the mind as the agent of the immortal soul could not be diseased, only the brain. In this schema, either brain lesions (the physiological manifestation) or excess passions (individual or social factors) influenced the mind, which in turn affected the body, causing insanity.

Benjamin Rush, William Tuke, and Philippe Pinel helped disseminate this reconfiguration of Western ideas about insanity in the early 19th century. The American Rush prescribed bleeding, blistering, and other heroic measures to counteract the forces of bodily imbalance and their influence on mental functioning, but he was part of the rising world of humanitarian ways of thinking about insanity as well. Tuke, founder of the York Retreat in England, ignored the somatic side of madness. He favored addressing the psychological factors and established a widely imitated model of therapeutic care. But it was the Frenchman Pinel who was most influential in setting the stage for the changing definitions of insanity in the 19th century. While not rejecting the belief that madness arose from somatic causes, Pinel's observations that some patients exhibited no physical symptoms led him to the conclusion that psychological and environmental factors such as excessive passions or the strains of modern civilization were sources of insanity. Always less interested in identifying the causes of insanity than in establishing a system of thought and in treating its victims, Pinel advocated institutionalization, in asylums to remove the person from the social causes of the psychological malfunction. His detailed prescription of a regime of moral treatment (educational, occupational, religious, and recreational therapy) to strengthen the patient's ability to deal with his or her psychological shortcomings, and the social environment that caused them, carried the day.

This shift from theory to system left the 19th-century medical world intellectually tied to a somatic model while practicing a functional therapy. Doctors continued to look for physical causes and prescribed medical treatment for their patients, but with an unbridled optimism about the efficacy of intervention they promoted the asylum and moral treatment as the Western world's solution for insanity.

By the late 19th century, the asylum world was marked by pessimism because of the overcrowding of asylums with chronic patients, the rise of deterministic hereditarianism, and the separation of institutional psychiatrists from the more progressive medical world. Little new scientific knowledge about mental illness had emerged. Most doctors still believed that psychological and biological factors were somehow involved in mental illness, but none knew the nature of the connection.

At the dawn of the 20th century, doctors continued to struggle with defining mental illness. Somaticists' explorations of chemical imbalances, the endocrine system, and other possible physiological factors led to experimentations with insulin coma, metrazol convulsion, and electroshock therapies, as well as psychosurgery. Others explored the emerging psychodynamic theories, a school of thought which encouraged a less distinctive break between health and illness and fostered the practice of exploring life experiences. The development of psychotropic drugs in the 1940s emerged simultaneously with the widespread adoption of milieu therapy, once again blurring the lines between the somatic and psychological approaches.

The publication of the first edition of the American Psychiatric Association's *Diagnostic and Statistical Manual* in 1950 recognized the heterogeneity and bipolar character of the nature of mental illness. Today, mental disorder is defined either as a biologically rooted illness that results from a primary impairment of the brain function or as a psychologically based malfunction that manifests itself in a general inability (either neurotic or psychotic) to adjust to one's environment.

In the 1960s and 1970s controversy about the nature of mental illness marked both the historical and sociological assessments of psychiatry and mental illness. Progressive historians presented the history of mental illness as part of the story of reform, while some of the advocates of the new social history depicted the development of the medical model of insanity as serving the professionalization efforts of doctors and confinement in an asylum as serving the bourgeoisie's intent to control the behavior of the lower classes. The sociological arguments paralleled the historical. Mental illness, labeling theorists argued, is a social construct devised by doctors, with the approval of society, to control those whose behavior offends the ruling class. Opinions about mental illness, either as a medical phenomenon or a social construct, will continue to be complicated and controversial as long as they serve as indicators of a society's attitude about dependent peoples and affect the formulation of public policy.

Social historical work on mental illness continues to advance. Many social historians have refined social control models by exploring how different asylums actually function and why families entrusted members to them. They also deal with different kinds of patients—women and men received different kinds of treatment at some points, while minority groups like Irish immigrants and the elderly at certain times suffered disproportionate confinement to asylums. Social histories of mental health professionals relate to the general field, and some social historians are now tackling the origins and manifestations of certain forms of mental illness

itself, such as hysterical paralysis and anorexia nervosa. (*See also* Asylums; Professionalism; Social Control)

Constance M. McGovern

REFERENCES

Brumberg, Joan. *Fasting Girls: The Emergence of Anorexia Nervosa as a Modern Disease.* Cambridge: Harvard University Press, 1988.

Dain, Norman. *Concepts of Insanity.* New Brunswick, NJ: Rutgers University Press, 1964.

Grob, Gerald. *Mental Illness and American Society.* Princeton, NJ: Princeton University Press, 1983.

Jimenez, Mary Ann. *Changing Faces of Madness.* Hanover, NH: University Press of New England, 1987.

Rosenberg, Charles E. "The Therapeutic Revolution," in Morris J. Vogel and Charles E. Rosenberg, eds., *The Therapeutic Revolution.* Philadelphia: University of Pennsylvania Press, 1979.

Mentalities

In the 1990s the history of mentalities is still a relatively new field for social historians. It has developed only in the last quarter-century or so despite having close links to a much older history of culture. The history of mentalities, however, differs from a more traditional cultural history in both its subject matter and its methodology. Mentalities itself has no single definition accepted by all its practitioners. An early tendency was to consider it an intellectual history of nonintellectuals. The history of mentalities has also often been equated with the history of attitudes, especially with the outlooks of ordinary people on family, sex, death, crime, and bodies, concentrating on psychological states rather than material realities. But others endow the history of mentalities with a broader agenda that transcends a preoccupation with "attitudes about," and addresses instead the ways people thought about things, regarded the environment that surrounded them, and ordered that world in their own minds. Because of this continuing ambiguity, it is not too surprising that one can connect the history of mentalities to several related, if not identical, approaches to the doing of history: to a history of culture that centered on elites and identified great cultural periods such as the Renaissance; to social history; to popular culture; to the microhistory developed in the late 1970s and early 1980s by Italian historians (especially in the journal *Quaderni Storici*); to emotionology; and, since the 1980s, to intellectual history. This most recent tendency has helped produce a "new cultural history" which seems to overlap with a history of mentalities in various ways—in its emphasis on texts, rhetoric, and language, for example. This new cultural history is perhaps best known from work published in the journal *Representations*.

Because the history of mentalities is a field in flux as well as one which continues to generate much debate about proper boundaries and suitable objects, it is perhaps wisest to define its scope by reviewing the subjects historians have treated and by considering the several methodologies they have employed in their work.

The vast majority of scholarly energy in the history of mentalities has converged in the early modern world and on the European Continent. Historians have been relatively timid about breaking out of these chronological and geographical boundaries. Work in early modern history has centered on several topics, many of which fit rather easily under the rubric of popular culture. A hallmark of the early history of mentalities (that holds equally well for social history in general) was a deliberate turn away from elites and from elite-dominated areas, such as politics, and toward a consideration of the "people without a history" and everyday life. In examining popular belief systems, historians have postulated a "disenchantment of the world," arguing that in the 16th and 17th centuries people moved away from an extensive reliance on magic to a less eclectic, more structured, pluralistic, and religious understanding of the world. Others have contended that in the same period, in ways rather obscurely coupled to the Reformation, the opening of the Atlantic, and the scientific revolution, a split occurred between elite and popular cultures, isolating the "great" and "little" traditions from each other. Elite culture became more restrained and more formal as a means of separating itself from the unplanned and unruly elements of popular culture that continued to express themselves, for instance, in charivari and carnivals. Elites gradually distanced themselves, both spatially and psychologically, from the

masses by defining their own peculiar culture, while simultaneously trying to suppress the riotous, pagan, and superstitious elements of popular culture. This offensive included a war on magical practices (including magical healing) and against "pagan" popular customs such as maypole dancing and midsummer night bonfires. Elites attempted to substitute carefully constructed and orchestrated ceremonies in the place of popular festivities. The remodeling of elite culture also expressed itself in the reformation of manners. Courtly culture demanded the restraint of bodies. The rise of etiquette and a growing sense of shame attached to bodily functions, such as excretion, became the external marks of a civilized human being, accentuating the distance between the respectable behavior and personal self-control sought and prized by elites and the more traditional, festival-oriented spontaneity of the lower classes. Related threads in this development were an emerging sense of self and an identification of emotions as parts of an individual's personality.

Another crucial change that historians of mentalities have traced out was that of a major redefinition of family life. Several historians have found that from the 16th to the 18th century a more affectionate, or "companionate," type of marriage and family evolved. While it is hard to pinpoint why family relationships altered so drastically, some historians have singled out the importance of the rise of Protestantism with its emphasis on domestic relations, or newly developing commercial relationships that necessitated the creation of a "haven in a heartless world"—a family that offered significant emotional rewards as well as an emotional safe harbor from the hurly-burly of public life. The expression of emotions within families became more accepted, and some argue, sexual satisfaction within marriage increased as well. Thus, families became less exclusively economic, and more strongly affective in orientation and purpose.

Death and attitudes toward death are two other subjects that have attracted historians of mentalities. Significant historical shifts have been charted in the meaning of death, particularly as expressed in the staging of death rituals, of the celebration of funerals, and of attitudes toward cemeteries. The work of Philippe Ariès (*Hour of*

Our Death, 1981) has been especially influential in documenting the change from the "good" or "tamed" death of the Middle Ages to the "denied" or "forbidden" death characteristic of the 20th century. Others have shown how funerals and burial practices gradually came to shed their elaborate rites and rituals as the time of death receded into the future. Likewise, death became taboo in polite conversation. Some have suggested that as life became less precarious and as life spans lengthened, people began to reassess risks, to develop a heightened sense of security in this life (partly due in turn to the introduction of insurance, better medical and sanitary facilities, fire-fighting methods, and more abundant food supplies), and thus came to regard death as less imminent and universal, more remote in time, and devoid of all meaning. Death became merely "the end."

Another thread of historical analysis that fits both into the history of mentalities and the history of popular culture is microhistory (although paradoxically many of its practitioners, including the dean of microhistorical studies, Carlo Ginzburg, deny the association). Ginzburg's *The Cheese and the Worms* (1980) can be taken as the classic microhistorical text. Ginzburg used Inquisition documents to reconstruct the mental world of a 16th-century miller, Menocchio, who lived in a remote village in Italy, and who had fallen under suspicion of heresy. Ginzburg showed how Menocchio interpreted what he read by filtering it through his own experiences, creating a unique mental universe. Ginzburg then extrapolates (not *generalizes*) from Menocchio's case to discuss the cognitive constructions early modern peasants "thought with." The microhistorians trace individual persons and events in meticulous detail through the documents to build a collective biography which reflects the real choices and the real decisions made by real individuals in past times.

More recently historians have begun to explore rhetoric and texts, signs and symbols. They address how people expressed their ideas in their discourse, and they look at the symbols and signs people used to convey meanings. According to these historians, documents are not "transparent," that is, one cannot read them as accurate representations of what they purportedly depict.

Rather such texts were written with specific purposes in mind and were composed in a way to manipulate their audience. Scholars have devised "strategies of reading" to decode what texts really mean. Natalie Davis (1987), for example, in her study of pardon tales and their tellers, placed the fictional element of the tales at the very center of her analysis, arguing that how people composed stories was important to whether or not these stories would be regarded as credible or "good." Thus, many historians of mentalities labor at deciphering the hidden message of texts and documents, trying to read not only between the lines but "behind" them as well in order to comprehend how such narratives were composed and what their authors believed they were doing.

Other historians of mentalities have followed the anthropologist Clifford Geertz in doing "thick descriptions." They retell and analyze the action of rituals identified as "paradigmatic," that is, those which reveal the hidden forces that hold together society and endow it with meaning. Similarly, Geertz's idea that "master fictions" govern and glue together all polities, has stimulated a burst of activity on the "rites of power." Social historical scholarship has thus rediscovered politics. Historians have begun to analyze, for example, funeral rituals of monarchs, as well as coronation ceremonies and royal progresses, for clues as to how political authority is constituted, legitimized, and transmitted. The analysis of rhetoric has slowly yielded to a more encompassing attention to myths and symbols. Many historians of political culture have fixed their efforts on the French Revolution. Lynn Hunt (1984) has examined the "poetics" of political power, and Mona Ozouf has analyzed revolutionary festivals, while François Furet has insisted that "political discourse" is what the French Revolution and political culture were all about. The political cultures of fascism and communism have been less fully studied, although some have started to look at the importance, for instance, of war memorials and commemorative services in the 1920s and 1930s.

A related interest has crystallized around tradition. Most work here has argued that "'[t]raditions' which appear or claim to be old are often quite recent in origin and sometimes invented" (Hobsbawm and Ranger 1983:1). Traditions were invented to legitimize new groups coming to power, or to ease the trauma of change by providing a sense of continuity. In focusing on the invention of tradition some historians, encouraged by anthropologists, have been more adventuresome in escaping European and early modern restraints, turning their scrutiny on traditions in colonial areas or in non-European civilizations.

Another current preoccupation of historians of mentalities is the body and its representation. Michel Foucault, whose studies strongly influenced many facets of historical research and writing, produced several seminal works on the body and on sexuality. Basically, he argued that the body was an exhibition site where state power was acted out. He discussed the significance of executions, as well as other ways in which states "disciplined and punished" the socially marginal or undesirable, and showed how the body was subjected to the authority of physicians through a process of "medicalization." This line of investigation, of course, intersects with the study of political cultures: Hunt (1984), for example, looked at the body symbols—Hercules and Marianne—of the Revolution, while Dorinda Outram claimed that the body is "the most basic political resource" (1989:1). More recently, authors such as Thomas Laqueur have suggested that not only are gender roles (femininity and masculinity) constructed, but that "sex" itself has a history, and that Western society has moved from a "one-sex" model where the genitalia of males and females were seen essentially as inverted forms of the same organs, to a two-sex model that created the biological differences between the sexes.

These, then, are the topics and methods which have made up the history of mentalities over the last quarter-century. Despite a general enthusiasm for the field, critics have raised several serious objections to both the premises upon which mentalities are based and the methods used. First, as already suggested, the main body of work tends to be confined to early modern Europe, although this is beginning to change particularly under the impact of new fascinations with political culture, with texts, and with bodies. Attention to ceremonies, symbols, and rituals has also led some historians to employ the perspectives of anthropology, liberating them from a Eurocentric straitjacket.

Much early work in mentalities at least strongly implied that there was a massive alteration in how people perceived their world (from, for example, a magical to a more scientific stance) and that this metamorphosis occurred roughly within the chronological confines of the 16th and 17th centuries. Thus, change since then has been modest, perhaps even insignificant, or merely a series of minor variations on larger themes. Many modern historians have remained skeptical of the history of mentalities because it seems to offer little that illuminates 19th- and 20th-century history. Pioneering works indicated that changes in mentalities moved with glacial slowness and that significant shifts in mentalities were seldom. This orientation seemed at odds with what historians of the modern world felt they faced: a series of bewilderingly rapid innovations. Moreover, early mentalities studies tended to concentrate on elucidating the worldviews of peasants and socially marginal groups. Those concerned with elite culture, or with mass culture, or with a society having a strong written tradition, saw little of use. The emergence of a new emphasis on reading texts, and a new orientation toward political culture, may help win modern historians over to mentalities.

Deeper problems surface when we consider issues of causation. Early histories of mentalities tended to provide fascinating snapshots of small slices of history, of individual events, or of oddities such as a 16th-century miller who perhaps read the Qur'an, a lesbian nun, and a greyhound saint. But such studies appeared to ignore, or to reject as unimportant, one of the abiding interests of all historians (including social historians)—that is, the process and cause of change. Even those enthusiastic about the history of mentalities have admitted difficulties in tracing causal connections. All historians of mentalities implicitly or explicitly accept the reality of cultural phenomena and the centrality of cultural causation. But it has proved very troublesome in fact to chart transformations in mentalities without referring to *extra*cultural forces, such as major economic, social, and political pressures. One historian, Pierre Chanu, placed mentalities on a "third level" of history, above social and economic structures. Yet he felt that mentalities modified in response to upheavals in society and economics. Keith Thomas, in his influential book on *Religion and the Decline of Magic*, argued that "the abandonment of magic made possible the upsurge in technology, not the other way around" (p. 656-657) but then also accepted that technical advances or the amelioration of bad material conditions accelerated the retreat from a magical world. These problems of causation have persisted and have not, as yet, been well handled. Generally, historians have pulled back to some sort of economic determinism to explain cultural change.

Others have complained that it is very difficult to envision the range and the limits of a mentality. Part of this predicament lies in the continued unclarity about what a mentality is and what the objects of a history of mentalities legitimately should be. A sheer proliferation of faddish topics has attracted the voyeuristic interest of historians and readers, thereby doing much to discredit the approach. Many insist that such works fail to deal with the "big" issues in history, or, as Robert Darnton (1984) has pointed out, actually tend to dissolve the fabric of the past. Relatedly, others have maintained that a detailed study of individual topics—such as magic or sexuality—has rarely generated a generally believable or acceptable picture of something bigger—that is, a "whole" mentality. Historians who have charted major attitudinal adjustments toward death, toward child rearing, toward the disciplining (both external and internal) of the body, and toward the construction of gender and sex, have rarely been clear as to how such changes have played out in other areas of life. These critics also argue that studying the periphery (as the microhistorians do) does not automatically reveal the center, and that not all societies possess paradigmatic and defining rituals from which an observer can read off a society's deepest values. Also problematic has been the explanation of how mentalities can move from one group to another. Answers, such as those directed toward clarifying the disappearance of popular culture, tend to rely on some form of the "trickle-down theory," or to depend on the idea that elites sim-

ply suppressed popular activities, thus transforming popular lifestyles. This reading renders ordinary people unrealistically passive.

These, then, are the problems, but the promise remains great. Mentalities continues to offer a way to probe the collective psyche of historical groups, and to demonstrate the influence of intangibles that are as important to the functioning and the integrity of a society as are the politics of elites, the ideas of intellectuals, and the workings of the economy. (*See also* Anthropology; Body; Causation; Cultural History; Death; Discourse; Elites; Family; Festivals; Magic; Manners; Microhistory; Popular Culture; Ritual; Sense of Self/Individualism; Sexuality)

Mary Lindemann

REFERENCES

Darnton, Robert. *The Great Cat Massacre and Other Episodes in French Cultural History.* New York: Basic Books, 1984.

Davis, Natalie Z. *Fiction in the Archives: Pardon Tales and Their Tellers in Sixteenth-Century France.* Stanford, CA: Stanford University Press, 1987.

Hobsbawm, Eric, and Terence Ranger, eds. *The Invention of Tradition.* Cambridge: Cambridge University Press, 1983.

Hunt, Lynn. *Politics, Culture, and Class in the French Revolution.* Berkeley and Los Angeles: University of California Press, 1984.

Outram, Dorinda. *The Body and the French Revolution. Sex, Class and Political Culture.* New Haven and London: Yale University Press, 1989.

Thomas, Keith V. *Religion and the Decline of Magic: Studies in Popular Beliefs in Sixteenth- and Seventeenth-Century England.* New York: Weidenfeld & Nicolson, 1971.

Wilentz, Sean, ed. *Rites of Power: Symbolism, Ritual & Politics Since the Middle Ages.* Philadelphia: University of Pennsylvania Press, 1985.

Merchants

Al-Jahiz, a 9th-century Muslim writer, lauded merchants as the most noble of God's creatures, while St. Thomas Aquinas looked askance at those who engaged in trade. Some centuries later, the Muslim historian Ibn Khaldun expressed ambivalence about the role of merchants in society. This ambivalence was not shared by the English Thomas Mun who wrote a treatise extolling the virtues of merchants.

Twentieth-century social historians have debated the significance of such mental and cultural attitudes toward merchants on the development of commercial capitalism in Europe and elsewhere. The issues raised by these debates are pivotal for those who seek to explain why and how Western merchants and Western commercial practices had become dominant by the end of the 19th century. Historians who have focused on the global hegemony of European merchants have tended to view this hegemony as an inevitable process which was largely due to the dynamism of European merchants. Scholars who work on Asian and African societies have stressed the unevenness of this expansion over space and time. They have focused their attention on the ways that indigenous merchants have facilitated, resisted, and shaped European penetration. Particularly for the Middle East and Africa, they have also dealt with the great vigor of merchants in other societies in earlier periods. Historians who write global histories of trade and merchants have discussed merchants as cross-cultural migrants who carved out commercial and sometimes cultural zones centered around nodal points, usually cities and market or port towns. These nodal points and the fortunes of merchants associated with them changed periodically because of a variety of factors. The uniqueness of the European experience lies in the combination of factors—political, military, technological, and social—that facilitated the dominant, albeit contested, role of European merchants in the modern centuries.

The term "merchant" is problematic as it can designate those peddlers and large international merchants. Even in Europe, merchants include conservative elements as well as great risk-takers. Many merchants in 19th-century Europe, for example, opposed factory-based manufacturers as radical innovators. Perhaps the most unproblematic approach would be to define merchants as a social group engaged in the exchange of goods within the parameters of regional or international markets. More often than not, they are motivated by the economic rationale of making profit, and it is this rationale that propels them to cross cultural and geographic boundaries. Often, as well, merchants coexist uneasily with landed aristocracy, whose economic values

and methods may differ. Merchants are brokers that mediate between producers and consumers. They produce no goods but might at different historical junctures contribute to the process of production either through providing capital for producers, or through ownership of tools and materials of production. Generally, the existence of a well-defined merchant community presupposes a social division of labor that allows for the presence of markets and market towns.

Those writing on European social history have found that one of the key factors behind the hegemony of European merchants was the support afforded them by the European states. Beginning with the 15th century, Iberian and later northern European states developed mercantilist policies by using their military and technological resources to expand commercial frontiers. The Portuguese and Spanish states organized commercial companies and well-armed navies to maintain control of trade routes. During the 17th and 18th centuries, northern European states chartered joint stock companies in which their ruling elite, who were shareholders, organized protection for their merchants and often intervened militarily to maintain the monopoly of their merchants over certain trading regions. The centralizing states of early modern Europe actively sought the support of their merchants against their recalcitrant feudal nobility. For some historians, this stands in marked contrast to the attitudes of early modern states elsewhere. In China, Mughal India, and the Ottoman Empire, merchants were at best left to their own devices, and at worst actively discouraged through arbitrary taxation and confiscation from accumulating capital. This alliance between European merchants and early modern states explains in large measure their ascendance over Asian merchants.

Most historians concede the importance of this alliance to the expansion of European merchant capital. Many, however, do not find this unique to European societies in the early modern period but common in other societies in other historical periods. Among the many examples they cite are the Greek and Phoenician trade colonies around the Mediterranean as well as the various mercantile city-states and trading post empires around the rim of the Arabian Sea and the Indian Ocean in the medieval and early modern period.

While one could not argue conclusively that the political culture of Europe was uniquely favorable to merchants, there is little disagreement about the novelty in the way that European merchants organized themselves between the 15th and 17th centuries. Until then, long distance traders of common cultural origin formed diasporas in regions in which they operated. Some, like Muslim and Indian merchants in Africa and South Asia, combined proselytizing with trade and created cultural enclaves in the societies they encountered. Merchants around the Mediterranean and Indian Ocean formed short-term partnerships that pooled labor and capital. Cheques of exchange and the rudiments of a banking system existed in Muslim lands by the early medieval period. By the 14th century, both European and Asian merchants were involved in the organization of textile production providing rural and urban artisans with capital and materials. The organization of merchant firms remained until the 15th century, based on family, cultural, or ethnic group.

These methods of organization were modified and survived well into the 20th century. However, European merchants introduced a number of innovations in commercial practices in the 17th century. The joint stock company allowed merchants to pool large amounts of capital and spread risk. The development of a sophisticated banking system allowed for the easy flow of capital and for investment in the development of infrastructures at a global level. The mid-19th century ushered a period of Westernization of commercial practices fueled by the expansion of empire and advances in technology. The prime beneficiaries were European-based merchant and industrial companies.

This narrative of the hegemony of European merchants has been challenged by scholars working on Asian and African societies. They have shown that Asian merchants reacted and shaped their encounter with European merchants in ways that have made it necessary to modify this view. Some Asian merchants successfully resisted this hegemony through piracy or through organizing holy wars. Others were able to benefit through pressuring European merchants into accepting local partners and practices. Yet, others have had to succumb completely to the new threat. Thus, while these scholars do not deny the ascendence of the Western merchant over his Asian and African counterpart, they insist on underscoring the role of the latter in defining this encounter. (*See also* Commercialization; Latin American Merchants; Market Economy; Merchants; Middle Class)

Dina Rizk Khoury

References

Braudel, Fernand. *The Wheels of Commerce*. New York: Harper & Row, 1979.

Cipolla, Carlo, ed. *The Fontana Economic History of Europe*, 5 vols. Great Britain: Fontana, 1970.

Curtin, Philip. *Cross-Cultural Trade in World History*. New York: Cambridge University Press, 1984.

Steensgaard, Niels. *Carracks, Caravans and Companies*. Copenhagen: Institute of Asian Studies, 1973.

Subrahmanyan, Sanjay. *The Political Economy of Commerce. Southern India, 1500–1650*. Cambridge: Cambridge University Press, 1990.

Methodology

In the practice of social history, methodology, the ways and means to knowledge, is determined by the degree of abstraction and extent of analysis deemed necessary in dealing with a subject. Methodological approaches usually follow as a consequence of prior decisions about what the subject matter of social history really is, or should be, and the relationship of the speciality to history generally. Differences in views on these issues may be traced, in turn, to variations among and within national, philosophical, and disciplinary traditions. Additionally, availability of source materials for a particular subject can influence methodological choices. Finally, and to a lesser extent, considerations related to the mode of presentation and the intended readership can contribute to methodological decisions.

Social history is more abstract and analytical than the more traditional fields of history that concentrate on events and actions in a single historical context. Rather than exploring a particular episode—a carnival, ritual, strike, or crime—the social historian extracts data for a more general topic, such as social conflict or social order. To cite a distinction developed by the French *Annales* school, social history is part of the history of structures, not the history of events.

Similarly, the specific acts of individuals are not usually the focus of social history. For example, individual events such as births or crimes make very limited sense unless they are aggregated and related to the populations at risk to experience them. The investigator must raise people to the level of numbers in order to capture any patterning in behavior that is highly indeterminate for any individual. The histories of birth rates and crime rates are natural subfields within social history, which is sometimes said to be the history of groups, that is, collective behavior and the behavior of individuals defined by their affiliations with groups.

Quantitative methods have proved essential in describing the attributes and behavior of nonelite groups that did not generate large quantities of conventional documentation. Ironically, much of the quantitative work on what was called the new social history of the 1960s and 1970s derived from practical considerations about sources rather than from a methodological preference for quantification.

In addition to description, statistical methods provide a ready means for assessing the effect of a multiplicity of influences. But even seemingly straightforward studies of individuals involve a substantial degree of abstraction when the mode of inquiry is analytical. In statistical analyses, people are dissolved into components such as race, class, and gender, and the explanation aims at commenting on the relative influence of these elements. A white male worker, for example, is not just a summation of these separate variables.

Furthermore, individual attributes may attain importance through societal mechanisms in effect at the time. For example, a person's sex may influence his or her behavior, but the influence could be attributable to norms concerning gender roles or to the shared experience of those of a given gender. Beyond these extra-individual mechanisms, it matters whether individuals were consciously aware of the norms or experiences.

Just as individual episodes or actions are translated upward or downward, depending on the subject, they are also modified horizontally via a desire to make comparisons over time or space. That is, an investigation of urban history might focus on a number of cities, selected either to represent a larger universe of cities or to reflect important variations among kinds of cities. Whether sampling follows a random or archetypal strategy, comparison across units requires attention to comparability of measurement of the topics under scrutiny. Consequently, the historian cannot perfectly capture the reality of any one unit, since a common ordering framework obviates that possibility. In the same way, studies over time, especially very long periods, demand a higher level of abstraction than those that focus only on a single era.

Social history thus operates at several levels. Not surprisingly, there are discussions and disputes among practitioners in different disciplines concerning the level that should be the primary focus. Philosophically, the major division is between methodologically individualistic orientations and alternatives to such individualism. Individualism differs sharply from the other approaches in its focus on rational choice and its questioning of the reality or utility of extra-individual factors. Most of Anglo-American social science today fits within this tradition, most markedly the field of economics, a discipline that many recent sociologists and political scientists have found attractive.

One commentator has contrasted holistic and structuralistic alternatives to individualism. The former centers inquiry on the integrating unity generated by a whole society, set of circumstances, or collective mentality. Within this tradition are studies that draw on functionalist sociology, cultural anthropology, and varieties of European structuralism, as well as traditional historiography that insists on the irreducible distinctiveness of particular historical moments. In all of these variants, individuals are thus seen as part of a totality.

Structuralism is arguably a compromise between individualism and holism, although its focus tends to be on the trans-individual structuring of behavior rather than on individual action. In another formulation of this compromise, the structuralist approach asks how people lived the big changes, the implication being that they experience changes but do not, after all, actually make them. Still, conscious human beings can modify the structure, and stories are ideally told in terms of a dialectical relationship between action and structure.

Studies within both individualistic and nonindividualistic traditions require abstraction and analysis. Given its simpler assumptions and greater empirical orientation, individualism typically limits methodology to measurement issues. Methodological concerns are at the center of holistic and structuralistic approaches. Social historians correspondingly debate methodology more often than other historians. Discussions of the place of quantitative analysis, and more recently of other methodologies suitable for newer topics like ritual and mentalities (where methods drawn from cultural anthropology are used) follow from basic needs in the field. [*See also* *Annales* School; Economics (Economic and Social History); Quantification; Sense of Self/ Individualism]

Daniel Scott Smith

REFERENCES

Abrams, Philip. *Historical Sociology*. Near Shepton Mallet, Eng.: Open Books, 1982.

Burke, Peter. *The French Historical Revolution: The Annales School, 1929–89*. Stanford, CA: Stanford University Press, 1990.

Lloyd, Christopher. "The Methodologies of Social History: A Critical Survey and Defense of Structurism," *History and Theory* 30 (1991): 180–219.

Zunz, Olivier, ed. *Reliving the Past: The Worlds of Social History*. Chapel Hill: University of North Carolina Press, 1985.

Mexican Revolution

A social and political movement generally dated from 1910 to 1920, from the first outbreak of violence to the last violent overthrow of a Mexican president in this century, the Mexican Revolution was largely fought by peasant armies trying to recover lands and water rights lost during the rule of President Porfirio Díaz (1876–1911). A second motivating force, particularly in the northern portion of the country, was the drive to preserve communal autonomy in the face of rapidly encroaching central control. Workers also participated, especially those from the rapidly

developing mines of the north and from the cities. Leadership, however, came largely from discontented elites and from a middle class, both rural and urban, that was excluded from political power and blocked economically from significant upward mobility. Exceptions were the leaders of peasant armies—Francisco Villa of Durango and Chihuahua to the north and Emiliano Zapata of Morelos to the south.

The outbreak of the Revolution in 1910 was led by Francisco Madero of a northern landowning family. Spurred by foreign investment particularly from the United States, capitalistic development in both mining and agriculture had proceeded rapidly in the Porfirian period. Land alienation throughout the country and the migration of thousands attracted from the center and south to the economically developing northern region provided a huge reserve of landless wageworkers and eventually troops for the Revolution. Between 1910 and 1920, northern Mexico had experienced popular discontent—strikes in the mines, Indian uprisings, and agrarian protest, including armed attacks on landowners. Madero, in his campaign for the presidency in 1910, provided a national focus for discontent and made it possible for a countrywide movement to develop out of local and regional conditions. His candidacy was suppressed, in spite of his family's prominence, and after being jailed he fled to the United States, where he issued the Plan of San Luis Potosí.

The violence which followed, particularly between 1910 and 1917, encompassed much of the country, but the effective impetus continued to come from northern Mexico. After Madero's rapid triumph, leading to Díaz's resignation in 1911, the Revolution descended into six years of factional violence, and the presidency changed hands three times. Zapata's peasant forces soon resisted the northern upper-class leaders as tenaciously as they had fought against the Porfirian government. In 1914, at the Convention of Aguascalientes, they joined with Francisco Villa's northern forces, but were defeated by the Constitutionalists under Venustiano Carranza, also a northern landowner, and Alvaro Obregón, a small farmer from Sonora.

The Constitution of 1917 included key provisions preserving many of the social goals of the

Revolution, although certainly these were imperfectly carried out in practice. Article 27 returned all lands and waters to the nation and permitted it to grant private property rights. These rights, however, were subordinated to the needs of society, making possible a large land reform program which reached its height during the presidency of Lázaro Cárdenas in the 1930s. It also returned subsoil rights to the nation and separated them from surface ownership, leading to a long-lasting struggle with foreign investors and the nationalization of the oil industry by President Cárdenas in 1938. Workers were protected in Article 123, which provided for the right to organize and to strike, minimum wages and maximum hours, workers' compensation, and equal pay for equal work, regardless of nationality or gender. Article 3 made primary education free, obligatory, and secular, thus directly confronting the power of the Roman Catholic church, which had controlled most of the schools. The power of the church was confronted in other articles, which made marriage a civil ceremony, prohibited public worship outside of church buildings, and provided that all priests must be native-born.

Unlike many other revolutions, the Mexican Revolution did not have significant spillover effects into adjacent regions. Nevertheless, its importance in Mexican social history has generated considerable study, in terms both of causes and effects, some of which reveals dynamics shared by some other areas in Latin America in the 20th century. (*See also* Land Tenure and Reform; Landless Laborers; Peasant Rebellion; Revolutions; Rural Labor and Agricultural Protest)

Linda B. Hall

REFERENCES

Hart, John. *Revolutionary Mexico: The Coming and the Process of the Mexican Revolution*. Berkeley: University of California Press, 1987.

Joseph, Gilbert M. *Revolution from Without: Yucatán, Mexico, and the United States, 1880–1924*. Cambridge: Cambridge University Press, 1982.

Knight, Alan. *The Mexican Revolution*, 2 vols. Cambridge: Cambridge University Press, 1986.

Ruíz, Ramón Eduardo. *The Great Rebellion: Mexico, 1905–1924*. New York, Norton, 1980.

Womack, John, Jr. *Zapata and the Mexican Revolution*. New York: Knopf, 1969.

Microhistory

Microhistory evolved in Italy, France, and the United States during the late 1970s and 1980s in reaction to the prevailing trend in social history of studying large social groups through quantitative methods. In place of statistical data, microhistorians concentrate on a few revealing documents, such as the transcripts of trials or inquisitorial proceedings, which record the actual words of participants. Instead of examining aggregates of people—such as an entire social class or profession—they focus on individuals or small groups. Rather than analyzing structural continuities over long periods of time (the *longue durée*), they write narrations and concentrate on abrupt changes. Microhistorians favor comparative studies of individuals who experienced life as a series of events which required them to make choices about their own behavior and opinions. Most microhistorians also attempt to give a voice to persons whose low social status, illiteracy, or unconventional views make them otherwise lost to history.

A group of historians associated with the Italian journal *Quaderni Storici* first coined the term "microhistory" and explicated its theoretical underpinnings. According to them, microhistory has two distinguishing characteristics. The first involves the reduction of the scale of historical research in order to isolate and test abstract theories of social thought. To do this, a method of tracing the names of individuals through all available records from a particular locale was developed. By following names, microhistorians can reconstruct each individual's network of social relationships and determine the importance of various kinds of social interactions—that is, those determined by family, community, class, patronage ties, economic activity, culture, or ideology. The goal is to create a history in which the relationships, decisions, constraints, and freedoms faced by real people in actual situations would emerge.

The second characteristic consists of an attitude toward historical proof called the "evidential," or sometimes the "conjectural," paradigm. By employing a method similar to the detective's search for clues, the evidential paradigm supplements the normal scientific endeavor of discovering generally applicable laws derived from quantifiable investigations. Clues act as signs that indicate the presence of something that is otherwise hidden. For example, a detective finds fingerprints useful not because they reveal general principles of human nature but because each fingerprint differs from every other. The presence of a print at the scene of a crime allows a detective to identify possible suspects in the absence of an eyewitness. Likewise, the microhistorian uses isolated, seemingly insignificant clues to identify individual traits, behaviors, or beliefs in a particular historical situation. The microhistorian might argue that the testimony of a single talkative defendant is more revealing of the nature of witchcraft beliefs than the statistical analysis of a thousand witchcraft trials, in which alleged witches are classified according to the standard social categories of age, gender, class, and occupation. A verbal slip or misunderstanding might tell more about the real motives or beliefs of a person than repeated stereotypical statements. The evidential paradigm has also been applied to the study of famous persons, such as Galileo; here the microhistorians emphasize obscure, previously ignored documents, which do not fit into the general pattern generated by the bulk of the evidence.

Although the possibilities and potential topics for microhistorical treatment are virtually limitless, there have been several prevailing strains. One has concentrated on the relationships between various levels of culture: literate and nonliterate, written and oral, learned and popular. A second employs rigorous philological methods to reconstruct the meaning of a particular utterance or text in its original context and attempts to avoid anachronisms by assuming that the past is utterly alien to the present. A third employs the concept of the normal exception, which isolates for study persons whose behavior is exceptional according to the norms of their own society, such as rebels, heretics, and criminals. The normal exception permits historians to show how certain kinds of transgressions against authority may be abnormal to the dominant group but normal behavior for those on the periphery of society; it opens up history to include a wide range of human experience; and it reveals how the prosecution and persecution of abnormal persons serves as a commentary on the values of the dominant groups in society.

The most effective microhistories have been based on well-documented cases involving individuals whose experiences or thoughts appear to be revealing of more widespread social practices. For example, Carlo Ginzburg (1980) has investigated the case of a heretic miller in the 16th century to gain access to the cosmology of peasants, which was transmitted through oral means and therefore invisible to normal historical methods. To unveil the otherwise hidden emotional life of married couples, Natalie Zemon Davis (1983) has studied a celebrated dispute over the identity of a husband, and Gene Brucker (1986) has examined a bigamy suit. In making historians sensitive to the nuances of power and to the changes of voice in documents, microhistory offers great rewards; it allows scholars to uncover disjunctures between what those who created documents thought was necessary to record and what the scholar wants to know, and to indicate gaps between what the educated jurist, for example, meant when he asked questions and what the bewildered defendant understood in answering. A common criticism of the movement is that it has yet to demonstrate the significance of the various microhistories for broader historical trends and that it risks trivializing the past. Although microhistory is hardly a trivial endeavor, it remains to be seen whether the accumulation of individual studies will produce a coherent reinterpretation of any major historical period or group. [*See also Annales* School; Emotion (Emotionology); Local History; *Longue Durée*; Mentalities; Prosopography]

Edward Muir

REFERENCES

Brucker, Gene. *Giovanni and Lusanna: Love and Marriage in Renaissance Florence.* Berkeley: University of California Press, 1986.

Davis, Natalie Zemon. *The Return of Martin Guerre.* Cambridge, MA: Harvard University Press, 1983.

Ginzburg, Carlo. *The Cheese and the Worms: The Cosmos of a Sixteenth-Century Miller.* Baltimore: Johns Hopkins University Press, 1980.

————. *Clues, Myths, and the Historical Method.* Baltimore: Johns Hopkins University Press, 1989.

Muir, Edward, and Guido Ruggiero, eds. *Microhistory and the Lost Peoples of Europe.* Baltimore: Johns Hopkins University Press, 1991.

Middle Class

The middle class is a hotly contested category, variously used to describe manufacturing, commercial, and financial interests as opposed to both manual workers and the aristocracy. This broad definition, set mainly by economic power and function and somewhat equivalent to the term "bourgeoisie" as used by Marx, is often expanded by scholars to include market-oriented landowners. The German middle class, or *Mittelstand,* was seen from the outset also to encompass members of the learned professions such as the professorate or magistrature; these groups generally came to be accepted as part of the middle class in the late 19th century along with engineers and managers of large corporations. At the same time, a lower middle class, or petite bourgeoisie, of greengrocers, office workers, and lower-ranking functionaries developed, further expanding or complicating the definition.

A special definitional problem involves the upper middle class, or haute bourgeoisie. A very wealthy bourgeois segment developed in European (and other) cities before the industrial revolution, and could have political influence and links to the aristocracy far different from the bourgeoisie as a whole. With industrialization, particularly after 1850 in western Europe and the United States, a big business segment developed unusual economic and political power. Its origins were middle-class and other segments of the middle class (particularly some professionals) allied with it, but its activities and values could be quite distinctive, and certainly its wealth was. Determining the upper boundary line of the middle class, then, is a challenging task. The same holds true for the lower end, with regard to master artisans, for example, who owned property but worked with their hands and might lean more toward the working class than the middle class; but concepts such as *Mittelstand* and lower middle class facilitate analysis of these issues.

Finally by the 20th century in the United States the middle class had come to signify anyone falling between the abjectly poor and fabulously wealthy. The definition of America as a middle-class country effectively countered the Marxist concept of a working-class/bourgeois schism that had some political appeal both before and after the Russian Revolution of 1917.

The various specifics about who is included in the middle class relate to the basic definitional question: is the class to be defined by power and position (income, ownership, education, nonmanual labor) compared to groups above and below? Or is it to be defined more by shared cultures and values?

The emergence of a middle class is connected with the rise of commercial society. How much the traditional urban bourgeoisie in western Europe relates to the modern middle class is a key issue for medieval and early modern social history. The same question applies to traditional merchant groups in other societies. Traditional bourgeois had merchant and professional roles, but often corporate interests, economic values, and legal privileges different from a commercial middle class. The seeds of this class's emergence are seen in the commercial revolution of the early modern period and more specifically in the 18th century when commercial and market networks had become particularly dense in western Europe and the eastern coast of North America. Urbanization also influenced the rise of the middle class both by fostering commerce and by creating opportunities for nonaristocratic wealth outside the structures of landed society. The middle-class family often made its wealth in new cities where traditions of commercial restriction were less likely to hamper trade. Finally, farmers and commercially minded aristocrats made money from urbanization and from a financial and commercial point of view occupied some common ground with the urban middle class.

A middle class arose in non-Western countries as commerce and industry spread. The Japanese middle-class person was often a small businessman, but by the 20th century middle class had the same connotations as in America, pertaining especially to salaried workers. The middle class that arose under imperial domination accumulated capital under colonial rule; with independence after World War II these merchants and traders provided some of the impetus for further economic development and filled the shoes of departing European businessmen. Others in these newly independent nations dealt with the growing group of multinational firms. This middle class also financed much of the buying out of European owners. Communist countries, although theoretically classless, developed what the Yugoslav Milovan Djilas called the "new class," a cadre of functionaries who were well trained and privileged within Communist societies in the Soviet Union and China.

The middle class has also gained a reputation as a driving force in fighting for the creation of liberal political institutions rather early in its history. The English Revolution of the 17th century, the French revolutions of 1789 and 1830, and the revolutions of 1848 have been said to feature attempts at middle-class reform of absolutist and aristocratic institutions. Yet despite its growing wealth, the middle classes in Europe failed to attain complete political dominance in the 19th century because of weighted systems of voting and the continuing influence of the aristocracy. Karl Marx, who forcefully theorized the concept of class, saw the middle class in this heroic light as an agent of progress. He added, however, that by the mid-19th century the bourgeoisie had become parasitic on workers and oppressive of the modern political order as well. Rejecting liberal ideas of social harmony, Marx predicted that middle-class domination would soon be overturned by revolutionary struggle led by a class-conscious proletariat. Although superficially verified in the Russian Revolution, Marx's theories of class conflict in which the middle class was destroyed ultimately proved less viable than the United States consensus model of an inclusive and vast middle class of compatible interests. Moreover, by the late 19th century many liberal manufacturers allied themselves with agrarian interests to institute high protective tariffs that would insulate national markets in a time of economic turmoil due to uneven but increasing industrialization. Abandoning part of a liberal political and economic creed, middle-class interests lost some of their distinctiveness.

Social historians have devoted increasing attention to the importance of middle-class culture, as it emerged in the 18th and 19th centuries and gained increasing influence (though not full dominance) over other social groups. Middle-class ideas not only about politics, but about family structure, women's roles, children, and even the treatment of animals became standard fare in many Western societies, as popularized reading, schools, and other media served as transmitters. Internal structure within the middle class was often divided, with competing interests among lower middle class and bigger business, professionals and business, but promotion of common culture could proceed amid these tensions. The relationship between defining middle class in terms of power and function, and defining in terms of shared culture, forms a crucial instance of class analysis for modern social history.

The political role of the middle class in America, most notably in the 20th century, has yielded more jeremiads than analysis, and in general the social history of the 20th-century middle class is not well charted. Treatment of recent American middle-class history is further complicated by the fact that after 1945 about 85 percent of all Americans self-identify as middle class, which beclouds more precise definitions and measurements. Contrasting the vigorous middle class of the 19th century that actively engaged in reform in order to create the kind of political and social structures it envisioned, historians judge this group politically bankrupt in the 20th century as its members opt for enjoyment of cultural abundance rather than the stresses of political engagement. A few historians, however, point to a continuous radicalism and engagement that grew out of the middle class not only with such figures as Susan B. Anthony and Frederick Douglass but with those in the reform movements of the 1960s and 1970s. Rather than being moribund, the middle class continued to be a motor force in history through movements for such causes as civil rights, feminism, ecology, and peace. Party functionaries and intellectuals in communist societies also led several movements for political reform during this same period, which eventuated in the Czech springtime of 1968 and, many would say, ultimately to the fall of European communism late in the 1980s. Middle-class leaders also helped organize 20th-century independence movements in the colonized world and were ultimately able to gain a mass following for their cause.

Social and cultural historians have aimed for more wide-ranging analyses of the middle class than studies of political behavior alone afforded, and indeed the rise of a new social history after World War II opened new avenues from which to chart middle class life, including its activism. The middle class of the 18th century helped develop institutions such as coffeehouses, clubs, *salons*, learned societies, where they mingled with advanced members of the aristocracy, acquired social graces, and spread information. Seeking to distinguish itself from those both above and below (but especially from the aristocracy), the European middle class often emphasized its emotional commitment, sensibility, and hard work. Middle-class values also included social mobility and civic-mindedness or public "virtue." By the 20th century, as the middle class came to include more professionals, it regularized admission to its ranks through professional associations, which also came to shape middle-class identity.

Whereas the European aristocracy was seen as sexually reprobate and oriented toward lavish displays of sociability, the middle class nurtured a tightly knit and loving family life organized around an ideology of separate spheres. This ideology proposed a domestic role for women and a public, breadwinning role for men, with gender differences being marked by increasing differentiation in dress, wealth, and opportunity between men and women. Optimally, middle-class women raised the children, ran a household, managed servants, conducted social life, and faithfully performed their religious and charitable duties. But historians differ over whether men and women had different middle-class values because of their divergent ways of life, although most agree that the middle class saw women as mentally inferior and emotionally superior to men. Theorists like Thorstein Veblin judged that the bedecked and idle women of the middle class served merely to indicate the family's social status and wealth. Yet, life was not uniformly simple for this class, and it is important not to confuse upper middle class with the class as a whole. The increasing costs of maintaining a middle-class household and of educating children made the middle-class pioneer in the demographic transition of the late 19th and early 20th centuries wherein fertility rates dropped by some 50 percent in most parts of Europe and the United States. Widespread and effective contraception used by spouses (as opposed to that imposed by such social practices as a late age at marriage) was initially a middle-class phenomenon.

Historians see increasing social differentiation among the working and middle classes in the 19th century as heterogeneous neighborhoods gradually disappeared. Manual workers and members of the new service work force lived on close to subsistence wages during the 19th century, and their condition contrasted drastically with middle-class wealth that was generally untouched by progressive income taxes. The middle class sought out newly developed suburbs and the recently built streets that were part of 19th-century urban renewal. The middle classes also educated their children before compulsory education was effected late in the century, increasing differences that might have been slight a century or more earlier. Profiting from more abundant consumer goods and new institutions like mass marketing, the middle-class home became more ornate and its rituals more intricate by the turn of the 20th century.

Increasing social differentiation and the uneven prosperity in industrial society caused the middle class endless concern that often led to the development of social activism. Middle-class reformers created organizations to attack prostitution, destitution, illegitimacy, disease, sanitation, and myriad other social conditions, and they were instrumental in the democratization of primary education and the modernization of secondary school and university curricula. The many reform organizations were variously motivated, for instance, by fear of social disorder, by commitment to instill social values and work social improvement, by religious fervor to proselytize the lower classes, and by a belief that education was essential for social progress. Although many men practiced charity, women were associated with middle-class philanthropy. Gradually, however, government functionaries and politicians began programs to regularize the distribution of assistance, thereby welding citizens to the expanding nation-state. Historians of the United States still debate which sections of the middle class dominated the reform process across the 19th century.

Through reform the middle class was able to spread its various values, whether those of the household or those that guided industrialization. Entrepreneurs gave rural workers accustomed to agrarian routines a sense of industrial time and industrial discipline, often through harsh penalties such as withholding wages. Institutions such as the workhouse, the asylum, and prison were based supposedly on middle-class values of order, rationality, and rearranging of the spatial environment. Middle-class women in their charity work emphasized chastity, household cleanliness, and feminine obedience to social propriety and hierarchy. Authors like Charles Dickens harshly criticized these values in the 19th century, while in the 20th century the main character in Sinclair Lewis's novel *Babbit* represented the emptiness of middle-class values.

Historians of the United States have particularly observed the integration of ethnic and racial groups into the middle class and have debated what this meant for traditional ideas of social stratification and differentiation. Jews, they maintain, showed a high degree of social mobility into the middle class. African Americans developed a strong middle class under segregated conditions before the civil rights movement. This middle class founded such middle-class organizations as reading clubs, alumni associations of black colleges, and women's groups. In 1985 African Americans constituted almost 10 percent of American college students, and 45 percent of African Americans were homeowners. Moreover, both Jews and African Americans had commanding histories of fighting for liberal reforms, social justice, and equal opportunity for social mobility. Among people of color historians and sociologists have asked what class stratification has meant for group values and what the relationship is between so-called middle-class values and ideas of racial solidarity.

"Middle class" has become a term of increasing imprecision in postindustrial society, where manual labor is on the decline and where service and white-collar workers constitute the largest segment of the work force. Born as a defining term in the industrial age, the idea of a middle class was propagated to gain political and social distinction during the class's fledgling years and to propel liberal political change. By the late 20th century the term ranged from being a political rallying cry used to mobilize voters tired of social welfare programs for the "underclass," to a convenient, overarching explanatory motif of social change in modern times. Examples from the history of the middle class in nonliberal, non-Western, or underindustrialized countries are helping to restore interest and revive scholarship around this vexed concept. (*See also* Cultural Hegemony; Class; Liberalism; Lower Middle Classes)

Bonnie Smith

REFERENCES

Blumin, Stuart M. *The Emergence of the Middle Class: Social Experience in the American City, 1760–1900.* New York: Cambridge University Press, 1989.

Davidoff, Leonore, and Catherine Hall. *Family Fortunes. Men and Women of the English Middle Class, 1780–1850.* Chicago: University of Chicago Press, 1987.

Ghosh, Suniti Kumar. *The Big Indian Bourgeoisie. Its Genesis, Growth, and Character.* Calcutta: Subarnarekha, 1985.

Pilbeam, Pamela M. *The Middle Classes in Europe, 1789–1914. France, Germany, Italy and Russia.* Chicago: Lyceum, 1990.

Ryan, Mary. *Cradle of the Middle Class: The Family in Oneida County, New York, 1790–1865.* New York: Cambridge University Press, 1981.

Middle Eastern Family Life

Many scholars have relied on the normative version of family structure and obligations as described by Islamic law (the *shari'ah*) for the study of family life in the Middle East. Indeed, until the rise of social history, religious rules constituted the only basis for historical attention to the Islamic family. Even now, family history is less completely developed for the Middle East than for several other regions, though advances have been considerable.

Islamic law has served as a guide for Muslims in the region since the rise of Islam in the 7th century AD, and, as part of a dominant culture, has also helped shape the practices of the Christian and Jewish communities in the region. The salient features of Islamic law as it applies to family life set standards for family relationships. The *shari'ah* stresses the importance of the marital relationship: all adults are expected to marry (there are no celibate communities in Islam), and the husband and wife form the legal nucleus of a new family. Marriage is a contract entered into by a man and woman: its legal validity rests on the free consent of both parties and the payment of a bridal "gift" (*mahr*) by the groom to the bride, a gift which becomes her private property and over which she exercises total control. Once the marriage is established through contract, the husband and wife enjoy rather different rights and obligations; marriage is conceived of as a relationship of complementarity rather than equality. The husband is required to provide his wife with full material support and she reciprocates with obedience. The husband also can end the marriage at will. A man can repudiate his wife without citing grounds, and he need only pay any balance of the *mahr* and the costs of support for a three-month period, after which he is free of obligations to his former wife. Child custody rules reinforce a patrilocal and patrilineal family structure: in the event of a divorce or the death of the father, the mother enjoys only temporary rights of custody of young children, who will eventually go to the father or his family. Men are also permitted to marry up to four wives at a time, provided they treat them equally in terms of material support and attention, but women have no reciprocal rights. The *shari'ah* recognizes the importance of other family relationships: fathers are responsible for the material well-being of their children, and brothers have an obligation to impecunious sisters. The family described by Islamic law, however, is one in which the marital relationship looms the largest, however impermanent it may be.

Social historians, who have studied family life prior to the 20th century in a few urban areas, including Aleppo, Damascus, and Cairo, have begun to question whether the rights and obligations of the *shari'ah* describe family life as ac-

tually lived by the majority of the population of the region. The diversity of the region precludes any easy generalization: people of different social backgrounds lived in urban, rural, and pastoral nomadic milieus. Among some segments of the population, at least, family life was shaped by a set of considerations quite apart from the precepts of Islamic law. The ruling elites of the premodern era, for example, established large households that contained *harims* (harems), or "protected" areas in which multiple wives and slave concubines were lodged; the large size and grandeur of the household undergirded its political and economic weight. In such an establishment, the seclusion of women and the presence of a number of wives and concubines created homosocial worlds: the women (and the young children) of the *harim* formed their affective relationships among themselves and the marital relationship was of secondary importance. These women were not without influence and power within the wider family, however, insofar as they ran the household and could exercise influence in a number of ways, including through the arrangement of marriages.

Only a minority of families were wealthy enough, of course, to support a true *harim*. Most families, as far as we can know them through the records of the Islamic courts and the few scattered descriptions we have, lived in smaller groups and more modest houses. The seclusion of women and the practice of polygyny were luxuries beyond the reach of the majority of the population. Still, the emphasis Islamic law placed on the marital relationship was diluted by the prevalence of extended family, clan, and tribal ties. Family arrangement of marriage, often at an early age, and endogamous marriage, most often between paternal cousins, served to bind a clan together. Newly married couples commonly resided with the groom's parents, an arrangement which often persisted until the death of the husband's father. The political and economic life of the premodern period seemed to rest, to a great extent, on cooperation among the members of a family, most often an extended family in the urban environment that could expand in the pastoral nomadic areas to embrace a number of different clans organized as a tribe. Adherence to the dictates of Islamic law in family matters also varied, from observance of the law in many urban areas to reliance on extralegal custom in rural areas.

Anthropologists and historians, working in the 20th century, have helped us to understand the ways in which family life has been changing in the context of the sweeping transformations of the 19th and 20th centuries. The *harim* disappeared along with the old ruling elites and the system of household-based politics; the lifestyle of the upper classes came to resemble that of their European counterparts. The coherence and rationale of the extended family was undermined by the elimination of many former family-based economic activities (family farms, crafts that employed family labor). Despite these developments, however, the boundaries between family life and economic and political systems have remained permeable: family-based businesses and regimes with strong family identities (the Saudis, for example) remain, and much social life takes place within family circles.

The growing strength of Islamic movements in recent years as a source of cultural authenticity, and identity in the region has reverberated in family life as elsewhere. Conservative Islamic groups call for the "Islamicization" of family life in terms of stricter adherence to the *shari'ah* in matters of marriage and divorce as well as attention to gender complementarity, rather than equality. It remains to be seen, however, whether ideological pressure for a more "Islamic" family in which men are the breadwinners and women remain in the domestic sphere will triumph over countervailing economic pressures that increasingly draw women into the labor force. (*See also* Family; Islam; Marriage/Remarriage; Women's History)

Judith E. Tucker

REFERENCES

Esposito, John. *Women in Muslim Family Law.* Syracuse, NY: Syracuse University Press, 1982.

Fernea, Elizabeth. *Women and the Family in the Middle East.* Austin: University of Texas Press, 1985.

Marcus, Abraham. *The Middle East on the Eve of Modernity. Aleppo in the Eighteenth Century.* Cambridge: Cambridge University Press, 1989.

Rugh, Andrea B. *Family in Contemporary Egypt.* Syracuse, NY: Syracuse University Press, 1984.

Tucker, Judith E. *Women in Nineteenth Century Egypt.* Cambridge: Cambridge University Press, 1985.

Middle Eastern Industrialization

Earlier than in most non-Western areas, Middle Eastern manufacturers had to confront the expansion of the European economy. Already in the 17th century, they found their raw materials being drained away by European buyers who were paying higher prices. The severity of the competition increased after around 1750, when intensification of the workplace and mechanization allowed European producers to market cheaper, if often inferior, substitutes for locally made goods, especially textiles. Thus, imports of yarn into the Ottoman Empire rose about 18 times between 1820 and 1840 and tripled again by 1870. By the end of the century, imports were competing successfully in many industrial sectors.

Middle Eastern manufacturing suffered, but it hardly vanished. The "deindustrialization thesis" argues for its decline and disappearance; this view, however, is an incorrect oversimplification. It equates the disappearance of guilds and the absence of vast, mechanized factories with the lack of manufacturing activities. The craft guilds did disappear from most Middle Eastern lands by the late 19th century. And, it is true that most 19th-century industries remained small scale and were not located in big factories. But manufacturing, in the Ottoman Empire at least, survived and in some cases thrived, thanks in large part to an increasing population that provided an expanding internal market. Some industries that employed vast numbers of workers were scarcely affected by foreign competition—for example, those engaged in processing food, making home furnishings and constructing buildings. In other sectors, such as those producing footwear and textiles, manufacturers retained considerable proportions of their respective markets.

During the 19th and 20th centuries, Middle Eastern manufacturers generally have abandoned the international export market, in which they once had been important participants. There are several notable exceptions. Carpets and raw silk were exported abroad in significant quantities in the 19th century. Recently, in the 1980s, Turkey has sharply increased export production, making a variety of goods, mainly textiles, but also, for example, nails, for sale on a global basis. Overall, producers have focused on internal markets, seeking both to retain local customers and win them back (import substitution), using a combination of cheap labor and imported technologies that were relatively inexpensive. Hence, the guilds went under because they insisted on wages that made their goods uncompetitive in price.

Guilds were overwhelmingly male, but it is unclear if their disappearance meant a decline in male participation in the manufacturing work force. Child and female labor had been routine in earlier centuries, and it was commonplace in home, workshop, and factory production during the 19th century as well.

The partition of the Ottoman Empire after World War I badly hurt many producers as new political boundaries destroyed the integrity of a formerly unified economic region. Textile producers in Aleppo, for example, were cut off from their customers in Anatolia, a major market, when the separate states of Syria and Turkey emerged. In the French-occupied lands, Syria and Lebanon, policies of the Paris government deliberately dismantled local industries to promote the sale of French industrial goods.

During the 20th century, virtually all Middle Eastern countries have been experiencing extraordinary urbanization. This process enabled industrial entrepreneurs access to a comparatively larger and more concentrated labor supply than ever before. Manufacturing has grown steadily more important. In the late 1930s, manufacturing accounted for less than 10 percent of the total work force in the Middle East. By the 1970s, that share had doubled and even tripled in many states, including Turkey, Iran, and Egypt. The emergent factories have promoted the rise of a more self-conscious work force that has organized to articulate its grievances and express its collective point of view. At the same time, however, small-scale production remains important in many cities, including Cairo, Istanbul, and Tehran. The small workshop as well as the big factory is representative of Middle East manufacturing.

There has been little research by social historians into questions regarding Middle Eastern industrialization. Most inquiries, including those cited in the bibliography, are economic rather than social histories. There are some recent studies, by anthropologists, on the impact of women's wage work on the household and a few historical inquiries into the evolution of interethnic, interreligious relations in a changing industrial economy. Nearly all social history questions lie open to the researcher. (*See also* Guilds; Industrialization; Middle Eastern Urbanization and Cities; Ottoman Empire; Third World Urbanization; Working Class)

Donald Quataert

REFERENCES

Issawi, Charles. *An Economic History of the Middle East and North Africa.* New York: Columbia University Press, 1982.

Pamuk, Şevket. *The Ottoman Empire and European Capitalism, 1820–1913. Trade, Investment and Production.* Cambridge: Cambridge University Press, 1987.

Quataert, Donald. *Home, Workshop and Factory in the Ottoman Middle East, 1800–1914.* Cambridge: Cambridge University Press, forthcoming.

Shields, Sarah D. "Regional Trade and 19th-Century Mosul," *International Journal of Middle East Studies* (February 1991): 19–37.

Middle Eastern Medicine

Islamic medicine is largely based on the Greek medical knowledge of later antiquity and is more properly called Greco-Islamic or Galenic-Islamic medicine, reflecting the influence of Galen (AD 129/130–199/200) whose works dominated medical learning in the eastern Hellenic world. At the time of the Muslim conquests of the 7th century AD, the major centers of Greek medical learning in the eastern Mediterranean, then under Byzantine rule, were flourishing. The Muslim conquerors recognized the excellence of Greek learning, and the Umayyad and Abbasid caliphs subsequently sponsored the translation of a large portion of the available scholarly works into Syriac and Arabic. According to the Greco-Islamic medical theories, diseases were caused by imbalances of the four humors of the body: hot, cold, moist, and dry. The matters of the four humors, blood, phlegm, yellow bile, and black bile, influenced the temperament of individuals. When the balance was upset, the body would become ill. Thus, an excess of blood would produce a sanguine condition while an excess of phlegm would produce a phlegmatic condition, and so forth. The physician's role was to correct the balance, perhaps by prescribing foods or medicines with "hot" or "cold" properties or by removing excess blood. This system was essentially secular in character because it did not ascribe the causation of disease to supernatural influences. One of the most renowned of the many *hakims* (physicians) was Abu Bakr Muhammad ibn-Zakariyya al-Razi (Rhazes) (ca. 865–923). He is best known for his exceptionally precise (but not original) descriptions of diseases such as smallpox and measles.

Prophetic Medicine, a "science" that integrated medical knowledge derived from the *hadiths*, or sayings and traditions of Muhammad and his companions, local medical customs, magical beliefs, incantations, charms, and, of course, ideas and concepts drawn from Greco-Islamic medicine, must be considered an effort to incorporate Greek medical knowledge into an acceptable Islamic framework. The authors of Prophetic Medicine were generally not practicing physicians but *ulama* (specialists of Islamic theological and legal sciences), who worked out "religiously correct" compendia of medical lore. In recent years, many Prophetic Medical works have been printed and can be purchased in bookstores throughout the Islamic world.

Sufis (mystics) believed that illness should be treated through prayer or other religious observances and not by medical means at all. In addition, many people believed in astrological influences on disease causation. Astrological medicine was much practiced and most astrological manuals had sections giving medical advice. The obvious contradictions among natural causation, divine causation, and the planetary control of events were never entirely resolved. The average person sensibly subscribed to a variety of medical beliefs without great concern for such contradictions: in emergencies, all possibilities were to be tried. This eclectic approach resembles that described by social historians in ancient and medieval Europe.

Within the framework inherited from the Hellenic sciences, the Islamic scholars made a number of original discoveries—for example, in

the area of vision. The more important question for future research is, however, not whether the Islamic scholars made original discoveries or how the Greek sciences were translated into Arabic and then into Latin, but rather how to understand the process by which Islamic civilization appropriated, assimilated, and "naturalized" the Greek sciences.

When, in the 16th and 17th centuries, Muslim rulers became aware of the military and commercial expansion of the European powers, they did not hesitate to recruit European physicians to their courts. While European physicians of the era could treat most diseases no better than their Muslim counterparts, Muslim rulers, extrapolating from European advances in other fields of science and technology, assumed they could. The process of transmission of European medical knowledge accelerated in the early 19th century when Muhammad Ali, the modernizing ruler of Egypt, recruited Antoine-Barthelemy Clot to organize his medical services. Clot Bey founded a medical school in Cairo, where European medicine alone was taught. European physicians were subsequently called to Istanbul, Tunis, Tehran, and other Muslim capitals to organize modern medical schools and health services. By the early 20th century, the Greco-Islamic medical theories had been overturned by the experimental methods and systematic observations of modern Western medicine.

While most scholars of Middle Eastern medicine have concentrated on the study of the transmission of the Greek scientific tradition to Islamic civilization and of the medical texts of the great physicians, in recent years interest has shifted, and more work is now being done on the social history of medicine. The Society for the History of Social Medicine, associated with the Wellcome Institute for the History of Medicine, for example, publishes the *Journal of the Social History of Medicine*, which occasionally contains topics on the social history of Middle Eastern medicine. Topics of interest to social historians currently being researched include the history of popular medical practices; medical education; the functioning of hospitals; medical libraries; madrasas (schools) and mosques in which medicine was taught; the professionalization of medicine; the process of certification; the social status of physicians; physicians' participation in charitable institutions for the poor; the political, social, and economic contexts of medical pluralism; the relationship of professional medicine to Islam; and the role of women and minorities in the practice of medicine. Scholars have been increasingly conscious of the need to locate their topics of study carefully in time and place, that is, in their historical contexts, because of the recognition that medical practices have changed over time and vary widely according to region, social class, and, to a lesser extent, ethnicity. (*See also* Medicine; Sufism)

Nancy E. Gallagher

REFERENCES

Burgel, C. "Secular and Religious Features of Medieval Arabic Medicine," in Charles Leslie, ed. *Asian Medical Systems: A Comparative Study.* Berkeley: University of California Press, 1976.

Kuhnke, LaVerne. *Lives at Risk: Public Health in Nineteenth-Century Egypt.* Berkeley: University of California Press, 1990.

Omar, Saleh Beshara. *Ibn al-Haytham's Optics: A Study of the Origins of Experimental Science.* Minneapolis and Chicago: Bibliotheca Islamica, 1977.

Rahman, Fazlur. *Health and Medicine in the Islamic Tradition.* New York: The Crossroad Publishing Company, 1987.

Ullmann, Manfred. *Islamic Medicine.* Edinburgh: Edinburgh University Press, 1978.

Middle Eastern Popular Religion

Popular religion in the Middle East has not received nearly as much scholarly attention as the official traditions of the region's three major religions—Islam, Christianity, and Judaism. Perhaps the main reason for this relative neglect has been the nature of the sources. Whereas official religion rested on sacred texts whose meaning has been elaborated by a large body of scholarship, popular religion thrived for the most part outside the culture of the written word. Documentary evidence has therefore been less abundant and more indirect.

Popular religion further differed from official religious traditions in its comparative unorthodoxy. Although it more or less agreed with official religion on basic doctrine, it also had ideals, customs, and rituals of its own, which it frequently borrowed from unlettered or non-religious sources. It even contained elements which many religious authorities considered downright sacrilegious. As a result of this broad eclecticism, tension between popular and official religion has appeared as a recurring theme in Middle Eastern religious life.

Paralleling official religion, popular religion had its own organizations. Among Muslims, the best-known of these associations were the Sufi brotherhoods. Sufism represented the mystical strain of Islamic religious thought. Having originated in the early Islamic period, it established itself after AD 1000 as an accepted part of the Islamic religious scene. Throughout the Middle East, Sufi devotees grouped themselves into lodges, each of which was ultimately affiliated with a larger pan-Islamic order. Sufism exhorted all believers to live righteously, but never demanded their complete withdrawal from worldly activity. Sufi ritual was characterized by unrestrained fervor. Participants chanted, sang, danced to musical accompaniment, and entered trances. The most uninhibited worshipers whipped and stabbed themselves, and took intoxicants in spite of the Qur'anic prohibition against them.

Another prominent feature of Middle Eastern popular religion was the cult of saints. Whether living or dead, saints drew the reverence and admiration of the faithful. According to popular belief, they possessed extraordinary spiritual powers, including the ability to perform miracles and cure diseases. They might lead lives of extreme piety or engage in an austere spiritual regimen. Some saints, on the other hand, might be individuals who today would be classified as insane. These latter figures wandered through city streets, muttering predictions or making incomprehensible remarks, all of which people interpreted as a sign of holiness. Most saints were men, but a small number of women did manage to enter these exclusive ranks.

Saints were remembered long after their death. Across the Middle East, worshipers made pilgrimages to shrines which communities had erected in honor of local saints. A shrine might consist of a saint's tomb, or there might be a small building commemorating a saint's visit to the community. Believers journeyed to shrines usually to seek the saint's intercession with God on their behalf. Some pilgrims came simply to pray for favors from the saint.

Unlike ordinary humans, saints possessed a sort of spiritual energy (*baraka*) which they could pass on to their descendants, whether or not the latter were ever recognized as saints themselves. Believers sought this energy for its reputedly beneficial effects. They obtained it merely by touching the saint; or if the saint were not available, his clothes or personal possessions might serve the same purpose. The most popular method of acquiring *baraka* was to touch a saint's tomb.

Beyond the world of humans, popular religion conceived of a universe which was teeming with spirits, who roamed everywhere. Some spirits were good, and helped humans. But there were also malevolent spirits who caused endless mischief. To ward off these unseen enemies, people armed themselves with magical charms and talismans. As extra insurance, they routinely invoked the name of God to call down divine protection and neutralize potential dangers. God, of course, occupied the highest place in the popular cosmology. The faithful thought of God as an active deity who was constantly intervening in human affairs.

Aside from its meaning for the individual, popular religion found expression in events which involved the entire community. Festivals were held on such occasions as the birthday of the Prophet Muhammad and the end of the month of Ramadan. Saints' tombs, which were normally the scene of pilgrimages, sometimes hosted fairs. In moments of crisis, they might also receive public processions, which would plead for saintly assistance. Plays were yet another manner in which popular religious themes were presented for, and by, the community. Thus popular religion, despite its unofficial character, assumed a prominent role in the life of Middle Eastern societies, and may attract increasing attention as the social history of these societies gains ground. (*See also* Islam; Religion)

James Grehan

REFERENCES

Canaan, Tewfik. *Mohammedan Saints and Sanctuaries in Palestine.* London: Luzac, 1927.

Keddie, Nikki, ed. *Scholars, Saints, and Sufis.* Berkeley: University of California Press, 1972.

Reeves, Edward. *The Hidden Government: Ritual, Clientelism, and Legitimation in Northern Egypt.* Salt Lake City: University of Utah Press, 1990.

Trimingham, J. Spencer. *The Sufi Orders in Islam.* London: Oxford University Press, 1973.

Middle Eastern Urbanization and Cities

The Middle East boasts a strong urban tradition dating back to ancient times. Over the centuries its cities have tended to enjoy a privileged role in the life of the region. Although townspeople formed no more than 15 to 20 percent of the total population until the 20th century, it was in cities that the rulers and administrations usually made their seat, that learning and high culture flourished, and that long-distance trade and artisanal craftsmanship had their base. The cities extended their control over the peasantry in the countryside and syphoned off the agricultural surplus to support urban interests and luxuries.

Since the 19th century, with the process of modernization and the integration of the Middle East into the world economy, the level of urbanization and the size of cities in the region have grown dramatically. More than 50 percent of the population now resides in cities, and these are far larger than at any time in the past. While in 1800 most cities did not exceed 20,000 people, and only 4 or 5 boasted a population of 100,000 or more, today the region has several urban agglomerations surpassing one million, with Cairo ranking as a megacity of some 15 million people (having grown from about 250,000 in 1800). These transformations, which have reinforced the traditional predominance of the cities, reflect both the rapid natural increase of the population in general and the massive rural-urban migration. They have resulted, particularly in those primate cities that attract the bulk of migrants, in problems of crowding, acute housing shortages, squatter settlements, underemployment, and a breakdown of municipal services.

The physical form and the administration of the cities have also been transformed since the 19th century. The typical features of the premodern Middle Eastern city, with its tight-knit courtyard houses, winding alleyways, bazaars, walls, and gates, have given way to imported conceptions of urban design. Around the traditional settlements have grown European-type cities, with tall apartment buildings and wide streets organized on a grid pattern and capable of accommodating wheeled vehicles. Accompanying this process was the adoption of another European idea, that of municipal authority, which came to replace a diffuse setup in which central or provincial governments administered the cities indistinguishably from the areas around them, with informal urban networks and communal organizations handling many of the daily needs of the townspeople.

Given the urban origin and bias of most of the sources, cities have traditionally enjoyed particular attention in Middle Eastern historiography. Until recently the literature has tended to focus heavily on their physical aspects—their layout, markets, great houses, and monumental buildings—and on the world of their elites. In the 1970s and 1980s, however, historians have broadened the scope of inquiry considerably in search of a fuller understanding of the workings of urban communities and their place in the larger societies of which they were part. Guilds, neighborhoods, the family, charitable foundations, women, popular culture, migration, the economics of food, and other issues have become the focus of closer study, and new aspects of the region's cities and their past are gradually coming into view. (See also Cities; Middle Eastern Industrialization; Modernization; Third World Urbanization; Urbanization; Waqf-Charitable Foundations)

Abraham Marcus

References

Brown, L. Carl, ed. *From Madina to Metropolis.* Princeton, NJ: Darwin Press, 1973.

Costello, V.F. *Urbanization in the Middle East.* Cambridge: Cambridge University Press, 1977.

Goitein, S.D. *A Mediterranean Society,* 5 vols. Berkeley: University of California Press, 1967–1988.

Marcus, Abraham. *The Middle East on the Eve of Modernity: Aleppo in the Eighteenth Century.* New York: Columbia University Press, 1989.

Raymond, André. *The Great Arab Cities in the 16th–18th Centuries.* New York: New York University Press, 1984.

Middle Eastern Village Life

Most Middle Eastern people live in villages, and only recently have urban populations surpassed those of rural areas in some countries. Locations and types of villages in this largely arid region have been determined by sources and availability of water. Dry-farming villages have been distinguished from those practicing irrigated farming. Dry farming relies on seasonal rainfall and is characterized by extensive cultivation of grains. Irrigated farming relies on water from rivers and springs and concentrates on intensive cultivation of fruits and vegetables. Depending on local circumstances villagers may have practiced both types of agriculture. In addition to food crops, cash crops such as cotton and tobacco have also been important in Middle Eastern farming.

Until the 19th century villagers themselves decided what crops they would grow. Typically, the bulk of a village's production would be for local consumption, with surpluses to meet the fiscal demands of state agents and to sell in local and regional markets. A wide variety of village crafts were practiced (spinning, weaving, tool-making, etc.) but villages were rarely self-sufficient in an absolute sense and maintained petty trading relations with nearby towns, pastoral nomads, and other villages. Since food production was geared toward subsistence, premodern village practices usually guaranteed peasant cultivators access to sufficient land and water for household survival and reproduction. In extensively farmed grain-growing lands and in the Nile valley (where the annual flood inundated croplands) village land was periodically redistributed among peasant households. Hereditary ownership or use of specific plots of land was characteristic of areas requiring intensive labor and long-term investment—for instance, fruit or olive plantations whose trees had to mature for many years before bearing fruit.

Premodern Middle Eastern states claimed ultimate ownership over most agricultural land, particularly lands devoted to grain cultivation. In practice, peasants had hereditary rights to land use so long as they kept it cultivated and paid taxes on its produce. State authority over land was characteristically expressed through the institution of tax farming, whereby wealthy merchants and officials bid for the right to collect taxes of a specified region. By the 18th century tax farms had become practically hereditary, creating a layer of quasi-landlords between peasants and the state. But the existence of hereditary tax farms did not undermine cultivators' right of access to land.

Middle Eastern society prior to 1800 has some of the features associated with the Marxian concept of "the Asiatic mode of production," namely, subsistence-oriented villages linked to towns and wider markets via tribute-extracting state agents. But "the Asiatic mode of production" does not account for the role of pastoral nomads, who in some Middle Eastern regions levied taxes in lieu of weak or nonexistent urban-based states. In addition, rugged regions of the Middle East (such as the mountains of geographic Syria and Kurdistan) were dominated by communities of well-armed "tribal peasants." They enjoyed de facto autonomy of urban-based or pastoral nomadic power, and were taxed lightly if at all.

These generalizations are applicable to most of the Middle East from the 16th to the 18th centuries. But in the 19th and 20th centuries village life was radically altered by two interrelated processes: the integration of the Middle East into the capitalist world economy, and the replacement of older state structures with bureaucratic nation-states. These processes have drawn village producers into regional and international markets, have strengthened the role of the state in village life, and have consolidated the hold of towns over the countryside.

With the spread of regional and international markets, peasants came under pressure to produce cash crops. Depending on time or place peasants were drawn or coerced into cash cropping, but nearly everywhere they became increasingly dependent on the sale of their crops for subsistence. State agents intervened to ensure or to encourage the cultivation of such crops. Peasants' land-use rights were threatened as urban-based landlords (in Egypt, for instance) reorganized production on their estates to maximize profits. As tenant sharecroppers were hired and

fired at will by landlords, estate workers did not have subsistence guarantees. Monetization of the rural economy increased class stratification and contributed to landlessness. Peasants became indebted to urban landowners and money lenders. Out-migration from villages to towns became a major phenomenon as land-hungry peasants sought to supplement their incomes, sometimes settling permanently in urban areas. A new division of labor according to age and gender resulted, with farm work increasingly borne by women and children while men left the villages in search of wage work.

These transformations were accompanied by a struggle between social classes. Landlords and rich peasants were the beneficiaries of commercialization and consolidation of private property rights, and were usually allied with the state. But poor and middle peasants lost ground as a consequence. They sought individual solutions through labor migration, or they participated in collective resistance. The balance of power was against peasants, and major rural revolts were rare and usually crushed. Examples include the Babi rebellions of Iran in the 1840s, the Mount Lebanon revolt in 1858, and the Arab rebellion in Palestine in 1936–1939. More common were endemic forms of peasant resistance such as "rural brigandage" (Egypt, 1880s) and deliberate "laziness" and carelessness on the part of peasants whose labor was exploited by landlords or the state.

Since the 1950s nationalist regimes have implemented land reforms in the name of the peasantry. A close look at these reforms (Egypt, Syria, Iraq, Iran) indicates that the removal of large urban-based absentee landlords has mostly benefited wealthy peasants in the countryside. Under nationalist regimes, capitalist development in rural areas and the flow of people from countryside to town has accelerated. Most village families today depend to one degree or another on remittances and income from relatives who work in urban areas, or further afield in regional oil-producing states or in European countries.

Although today's villages may seem traditional to a casual observer, significant changes in relations of class, power, and gender distinguish them from their 19th-century predecessors. The continued importance of villagers is signaled by the fact that the integration of villagers and ex-villagers into national life and institutions is one of the major challenges facing Middle Eastern governments today.

The writing of social history has been late to develop in the field of Middle East studies, in part a legacy of the Orientalist tradition, which emphasized the study of elites through classical languages and literatures. Since the 1970s, however, social historians have made increasing use of Turkish and Arabic archives and have asked new questions of the traditional literary sources. Social history writing has had an urban bias reflecting the concerns and perspectives of written primary sources. Historians of rural life prior to the 20th century are forced to generalize based on a fairly small but growing number of local case studies. The database for the 20th century is more extensive due to increasing government bureaucratization and record keeping, and fieldwork undertaken by anthropologists during and after the colonial era. Historians of Middle Eastern village life usually work within paradigms established by the more developed fields of Asian and Latin American history (e.g., Brown 1990). (*See also* Community; Orientalism; Peasantry)

James A. Reilly

REFERENCES

Baer, Gabriel. *Fellah and Townsmen in the Middle East: Studies in Social History.* London: Frank Cass, 1982.

Brown, Nathan J. *Peasant Politics in Modern Egypt: The Struggle Against the State.* New Haven: Yale University Press, 1990.

Fernea, Elizabeth Warnock. *Guests of the Sheik: An Ethnography of an Iraqi Village.* Garden City, NY: Anchor Books, 1969.

Lawless, Richard, ed. *The Middle Eastern Village: Changing Economic and Social Relations.* London: Croom Helm, 1987.

Owen, Roger. *The Middle East in the World Economy, 1800–1914.* London: Methuen, 1981.

Midwifery

Before 1900, midwifery referred to the art of assisting in childbirth. Midwifery now means the practice of midwives, and this has been its focus of study by social historians who examine its place in the history of women, of medicine, and of childbirth.

Since ancient times, and until recently, birth had been a female-centered event. There are references to midwives in the Old Testament and in Hippocrates' writings. Female midwives provided comfort, delivered the baby, and cared for the family and household during confinement. Before 1700, male physicians or barber-surgeons attended parturient women only when the life of mother or baby had to be sacrificed in order to save the other. Male midwives began to attend normal deliveries of the English and French upper classes in the early 18th century and in America by 1800.

European and English midwives were placed under ecclesiastical control after the 13th century. In 1512, the bishop of London, wanting to ensure that infants were baptized before they died and desiring to alleviate concern that midwives would resort to magic, licensed midwives. Municipal regulation replaced ecclesiastical control by the 15th century in Germany and France. In England's American colonies, civil authorities regulated midwives in the early 18th century. Following English models, qualifications emphasized moral conduct rather than expertise. Midwives were to prohibit men in the birthing chamber, were required to attend all mothers in need, were to reveal the truth regarding infanticide and illegitimacy, and were forbidden to use witchcraft or perform abortions.

Self-selected or chosen by others, midwives learned their craft from predecessors or a formal training program. The Hotel Dieu in Paris opened the first school in 1631. By 1900, all European countries had private or public midwifery training programs. The first American hospital-affiliated school opened in 1911 at Bellevue in New York City, closing in 1936. Since then, several programs for nurse-midwives have developed in the United States, but they practice as part of an obstetrical team, not as independent practitioners.

During the 18th century, the British and French made significant advances in new obstetrics, promising greater safety in childbirth. Anatomical studies, development of techniques for turning malpositioned fetuses, and an increased understanding of the mechanisms of labor transformed obstetrics from an art into a science, interesting physicians in normal obstetrics. Male doctors, although widely accepted by the urban upper classes by 1800, were criticized as being instrumentalists who needlessly inflicted pain and death and offended female modesty. Emphasizing childbirth's dangers, doctors argued that their skill justified their presence. By 1860 male midwifery had won wide acceptance. A doctor's education, gender, and higher fees made him a status symbol to the patient. In addition, as religious certitudes declined, people's self-confidence in their own ability to manage health problems weakened, and they looked toward science with hope of a safer, more comfortable delivery.

Unique demographic patterns hampered American midwives and partially explain their demise beginning in the later 19th century. Midwives in Europe were fairly homogeneous, whereas in America there were ethnic, religious, racial, and linguistic differences. Geographic dispersion and poverty isolated American midwives and prevented them from building effective alliances to combat the encroachment of physicians. European midwives, however, were educated middle-class women who had the status of skilled reputable practitioners.

Early midwifery studies, like other medical histories, focused on medical progress, suggesting that as physicians entered the birth chamber and eliminated midwives, childbirth became safer. Achievements of famous physicians were highlighted, and midwives were characterized as being dirty, ignorant, and superstitious. Influenced by the feminist movement, midwifery was later studied within the context of the medical profession's search for autonomy and authority. American obstetricians have been viewed as self-serving, sexist, even misogynous doctors attempting to gain monopoly over the potentially lucrative field of obstetrics by laws and pressures to exclude midwives. Social historians, more recently, have looked for other factors to explain the demise of the American midwife. The promise of a safe delivery due to scientific obstetrics, the social changes due to urbanization, and the lower social status of the midwife combined to urge middle-class women to seek physicians as birth attendants. Recent focus has been on the role of patients and midwives and not just the power of the physician. Historians have begun to explore characteristics of the midwife and her relationship to her community, asking questions relating to ethnicity and race. A key question has been whether midwives or physicians had more favorable outcomes. Additional studies of midwives themselves are essential in order to understand the roles they played in their communities and within families. (*See also* Childbirth; Medicine; Women's History)

Carolyn Leonard Carson

REFERENCES

Donegan, Jane B. *Women and Men Midwives, Medicine, Morality, and Misogyny in Early America.* Westport, CT: Greenwood Press, 1978.

Litoff, Judy Barrett. *American Midwives, 1860 to the Present.* Westport, CT: Greenwood Press, 1978.

Shorter, Edward. *A History of Women's Bodies.* New York: Basic Books, 1982.

Migration

Human migrations are as old as our species. Since the movement of prehistoric *Homo sapiens* gradually settled the globe, agricultural and pastoral societies have depended on mobility to provide fresh fields and pasture land. In the ancient world, invasion, colonization, and slavery moved the largest masses of human beings. The most important large-scale international movements of the past five centuries began with the forced migrations of some 11 million enslaved Africans across the Atlantic Ocean to the Americas (1451–1870). European colonial settlements and plantation agriculture in Africa and Asia set off internal migration among the people of India, Indonesia, and Africa. The end of slavery in the British Empire, the United States, South America, and Dutch colonies set off even larger waves of migration as plantations sought alternative labor. In the 19th century, over 20 million Indians, Chinese, and Japanese moved as indentured coolie labor to work the fields of India, Southeast Asia, the Americas, and the Caribbean. Simultaneously, some 52 million Europeans immigrated between 1840 and 1930 to the Americas, Australia, and New Zealand. After the massive forced displacements of some 18.3 million people surrounding World War II, a fundamental shift occurred in the worldwide direction of migration. The movement of men and women from less developed countries to developed areas now far outweighs the movement of Europeans or North Americans abroad. The millions of people on the move today are attracted to the developed areas of Europe, the Americas, and the Pacific Rim. Their movement is only dampened by the simultaneous movement of capital into less developed areas where labor is inexpensive; this spread of industrial production worldwide augments the international flow of capital to employ a global labor force.

Detailed analyses show that itineraries of migration, defined simply as departure from village or town of birth, are embedded in virtually every historical society. Although few sources record precisely this elusive demographic phenomenon, migration pervaded historical societies in the West, enriching village populations, peopling cities, and repopulating regions devastated by war and disease. Because societies were not sessile in the past the incidence of migration flies in the face of modernization theory, which posits that geographical mobility is a byproduct of modernity and economic development.

Historical migrations may be categorized by distance and the degree of break with home society, and these categories help organize social history research on migration, its causes and its impact. *Local migration* maintains people within their market area; women who married a partner from the next village, families who took on a plot of land in a neighboring valley, and young people who worked as farmhands all moved in local migration systems. Although local migration did not change patterns of settlement or produce cultural diversity, it introduced young people to potential marriage partners, cemented regional cultures, and perpetuated the family in regions where exogamous marriage was the norm. In the history of Europe, the localized migration of young, single servants in husbandry served these functions. In southern and midland England for the period 1680–1730, 69 percent of rural men and 76 percent of rural women moved from their home parish, most of whom remained in their home county. Although local migration

was of premier importance in past centuries, it has waned over time relative to other kinds of mobility.

Circular migration routinely takes men and women away from home, but returns them at the end of a period of work. Circular migration moved thousands of people in harvest work who helped to supply cities with sustenance; it provided cities with seasonal labor and with young men and women to serve urban households. Because this type of movement rests on dramatic differences in pay between home area and destination, the earnings from circular migration maintain life in home areas, paying taxes, underwriting land purchase, and providing dowries. This kind of geographic mobility rises and falls with economic change, but remains important through the centuries. Circular migrants include early modern European harvest teams, 19th-century Chinese cane cutters in Cuba, African mine workers, and Bangkok pedicab drivers from northeast Thailand.

Chain migration puts men and women in contact with homeland people who have settled in at a new destination, and draws them to settle there. Visible chains of migration included Sicilian villagers in New York City, masons in 19th-century Paris from France's central highlands, and newcomers to the shantytowns of Rio de Janeiro. Chain migration is at the heart of the great voluntary population relocations in modern history, such as the European settlements of the Americas and the worldwide movement from countryside to city.

Career migration is mobility by the employer's logic, moving men and women to work locations on a bureaucratic map. Historically church, government, and armed forces produced the lion's share of career migrants; abbesses, bishops, national state administrators, Swiss mercenaries, college professors, and corporate managers are among career migrants. Career migration increased in importance with state bureaucratization in the 19th century and the proliferation of large-scale business organizations in the 20th.

Colonizing migrations take people far from home, and usually allow no return across the oceans and vast lands traveled by settlers. Since the movements of ancient and medieval times, most colonizing migrants have been farming peoples. The movements of 18th-century Germans into southeastern Europe, of 19th-century Russian farm families into Siberia, and of Scandinavian farmers into the upper Midwest in North America exemplify the colonizing migrations of modern history. Colonizing migrations, so important to the 19th century worldwide, are of decreasing importance.

Finally, *coerced migration* rarely allows return to the enslaved or terrorized peoples involved. The great migrations of enslaved Africans to the Americas since the 16th century constituted a massive expansion of the slave migrations in Africa, the Mediterranean basin, and Asia that have existed since ancient times. After slavery was banned in the 19th century, more voluminous movements of indentured contract workers ensued. The coerced migration of ethnic and religious minorities has a long history from the expulsion of the Moors and Jews from Spain in 1492 to the world tide of refugees at the close of the 20th century. Although the numbers of refugees and displaced persons reached a peak during and after World War II, that peak has been surpassed by the migrations on the Asian subcontinent with the division of Pakistan from India and the waves of refugees throughout the world that continue to reverberate with changes of political regime.

Changing migration itineraries are the human and social reflections of large-scale political and economic shifts. *Demographic changes* are fundamental to changes in migration because they redefine the home population. Historically, decreased infant mortality, decreased age at marriage, or increased proportions marrying have created crowded, restless generations more likely to earn their living away from home. The fast-growing populations of the Mediterranean basin seek their livelihoods in Europe and the Near East in the last years of the 20th century just as those of 19th-century Europe sought a future in the Americas.

Shifts in land-holding change the attachment of people to the land. The end of serfdom and slavery permitted landownership and free movement; the decline of landed peasantries worldwide has created a more proletarian population that is more mobile in its search for a wage. For example, only estate lords moved the enserfed people of central Europe until liberation in the 19th century; subsequently, localized movements were augmented by harvest team work, migration to western Europe, and immigration to North America.

Labor force demands create the need for working people in agriculture, rural industry, urban industry, and urban services, attracting them to these work sites. Historically, the demand for workers in agriculture has given way to expanded demands for labor in rural and urban industry and, most recently, in urban services. With the collapse of rural industries and growth of urban industries in historical Europe, for example, came massive rural-urban migrations.

Flows of capital underwrite shifting labor force demands in town and countryside. As specie from the Americas flowed into 16th-century Spain, French laborers came to earn their share of wealth; likewise, the capital-intensive auto industry of North America attracted southern blacks, recently arrived European ethnic groups, and native-born whites in the 20th century.

Finally, *shifts in migration patterns* operate within confines ultimately set by the state. Absolutist interests, mercantilist policies, laissez faire governments, and nationalist impulses all have shaped migration policies over the centuries. States have ousted religious and ethnic minorities, as with the French persecution of the Huguenots under Louis XIV; the United States and western Europe have attempted to restrict entry of nationals perceived as undesirable in this century. States have made wars and undergone regime changes that have displaced millions in the 20th century. Finally, governments negotiated bilateral treaties where labor demand was intense as in postwar Europe and the Middle East.

Although migration itineraries reflect social, economic, and political forces at work at any given time, the social organization of migration is intimately linked with migrants' networks of contact. Migration operates through social networks, and human relations are at the heart of geographic mobility; personally transmitted information determines where people go, how they find housing and work, and their initial social contacts. Migration streams manifest family, village, and regional solidarities; even labor recruiters drew upon networks among potential migrant workers. Migrants have not been economic atoms, but rather party to information about certain destinations, neighborhoods, and occupations. The current challenge for migration scholars is to link the history of migration systems to changes in the global economy, developing a double vision of microlevel and macrolevel change.

Historically, the decision to migrate is founded in family and related to life cycle. Those without relations, such as orphans, have been quickest to take to the road, forming a vagrant population inflated by hard times. In Western cultures, unmarried young people have been most mobile, and family groups with children have been least likely to move.

Gender is central to the migration process, distinguishing the likelihood of migration, work at destination, the social organization of migration, and reasons for moving. Women have been more likely than men to move in many Western societies because many women moved to work as servants, and women also moved to marry. Because tasks have been divided by gender, men and women have been affected by different economic crises and displacements. Moreover, they moved for different sorts of work opportunities—for example, men have historically performed construction and mining work while women have been the majority of domestic servants. The most significant migrant labor teams have been composed of men who built railroads, harvested grain, and cut sugar cane worldwide. Women, by contrast, have more often operated in smaller groups and by more intimate and protective arrangements in attempts to guard them from sexual exploitation and pregnancy; their movements more often have been under family auspices than those of men. Women's migrations have often been in response to men's need for wives and domestic labor. Moreover, women have been more likely to leave the countryside to avoid marrying a peasant or to follow a spouse than have men. Although women may have been more likely to leave home than men, some European records show that women moved fewer times than men during their lifetime, suggesting that single women have been less free to move about for work on their own.

Motives for migration are illuminated by the types of people who migrate, the broader forces inducing migration, and the social organization of mobility. Many early models assumed simple patterns of "push" or "pull," and in the main, migration patterns respond to a need for labor and to political and religious persecution. Yet, within this framework, the social structure of migration explains the impetus to move, plus the timing and destination of most migrants. Many migration historians find that migrant perceptions about opportunity are more significant in the decision to move than objective economic reality. This is one reason that it is not always the poorest groups who migrate. The information that each potential migrant possesses about destinations, employment, and social support explains the willingness to move and the attraction to certain locations. Moreover, much recent social history finds a wide mix of motives, expectations, and perceptions that shape the migrant experience and help explain what people decide to migrate as opposed to those who stay behind. As a basic phenomenon in social experience, migration attracts increasingly sophisticated historical inquiry. (*See also* Assimilation/Acculturation; Deindustrialization; European Migration; Immigration; Latin American Urbanization; Mobility; Modernization; Proletarianization; Protoindustrialization; Slavery; South Asian Migration; Urbanization; Women and Work)

Leslie Page Moch

REFERENCES

Curtin, Philip. *Death by Migration: Europe's Encounter with the Tropical World in the Nineteenth Century.* Cambridge: Cambridge University Press, 1989.

Goldscheider, Calvin, ed. *Rural Migration in Developing Nations.* Boulder, CO: Westview Press, 1984.

McNeill, William, and Ruth Adams, eds. *Human Migration: Patterns and Policies.* Bloomington: Indiana University Press, 1976.

Moch, Leslie Page. *Moving Europeans: Migration in Western Europe Since 1650.* Bloomington: Indiana University Press, 1992.

Yans-McLaughlin, Virginia, ed. *Immigration Reconsidered.* Oxford: Oxford University Press, 1990.

Military and Society

Most military history deals with strategy, tactics, logistics, weapons, leaders, and campaigns. The social history of the military focuses on the state-military symbiosis; on the recruiting, socializing, and motivating of military personnel; and on veterans and the consequences of military service.

The State-Military Symbiosis

Organization for warfare has for millennia been one of humankind's central activities. Our kinship-centered cooperative propensities, coupled with our effective use of verbal communication, offer better explanations of the military effectiveness of early human communities than those relying on theories of aggressiveness alone.

Simple, subsistence-level societies have not all waged war in the same manner. Cultural differences among such societies, such as the decision of some communities to house new couples in the wife's mother's community (matrilocality) as opposed to the husband's father's community (patrilocality), have been found to be strongly associated with a low level of local conflict (due to the constant breaking up of extremely localistic war bands) and a higher degree of effectiveness in longer range warfare (due to the creation of more cosmopolitan intercommunity trust and affiliation).

Military systems were also central to the emergence of ancient state-empires. These tended to emerge in fertile alluvial valleys as warlords came to dominate and fortify those central market towns with sufficient surplus to enable them to retain a professional military retinue, to centralize the acquisition and distribution of weapons, and to attack and hold other nearby towns and cities, while extending their power into the pastoral hinterland. Virtually all of the "budget" of the first known warlord, Sargon of Akkad, conqueror of Sumer, went to his army (as much as 70 percent of it would go for the military of the Roman Empire, Charlemagne, Edward III, and Louis XIV), but his willy-nilly military "pacification" produced secure trade routes, law courts, uniform weights and measures, and a common coinage. In the process, these warlords developed symbiotic relations with agrarian and mercantile elites. "Civilization" had arrived.

Some technological innovations transformed military ways; they socially transformed the social and political structure as well. Bronze weapons were expensive; hence Bronze Age armies were aristocracies; their states, oligarchies. The advent of cheaper iron weapons meant that men of more modest means would bear arms. In ancient Greece, this resulted in a more democratic polity. The stirrup enabled armored men to fight more effectively from horseback, but armor and large horses were expensive. Only an oligarchy could afford to field such a force in Europe, Asia, or Africa. By 1350, however, pikemen and crossbowmen had dealt the armored cavalry of feudalism devastating blows. The introduction of firearms into western Africa and Mauri New Zealand largely transformed the social and political structures of those peoples. In Europe, the Middle East, and Japan, firearms finished the mounted knights off as the rate of fire of the fuselier increased by tenfold between the early 16th and the late 17th centuries. By 1600 the ratio of infantry to cavalry in Europe had risen to almost eight to one. Military demands continued to inform the direction of much economic development in the clothing industry, the metals trades, nautical technology, land transportation, and high finance.

The early modern state emerged where monarchs were able to overcome the medieval constitutional traditions of sharing their power with a parliament of gentry and aristocracy. As commerce, new riches from the New World, and more efficient European farming techniques generated economic surpluses, these resources were taxed for military purposes. Intendants loyal to the French monarchy slowly helped to bleed power from the nobility to fuel royal ambitions throughout the 17th century. King Gustavus Adolphus successfully conscripted Swedes for the seven armies he flung against the Hapsburgs in the second quarter of that century, paying for the effort with the sale of war bonds and monopolies, the appropriation of farms, the rationing of food, and the debasement of Sweden's currency, all accomplished by a ruthless bureaucracy. In historian Charles Tilly's aphorism, "war made the State, and the State made war."

In the Netherlands, 16th-century Calvinist woolen manufacturers and merchants organized the first modern professional army. Their Spanish foe's army had been raised in the venture-capitalism fashion of most early modern forces; the Crown paid a fixed sum to professional military entrepreneurs to raise regiments, but the primary remuneration for these men in the course of the campaign was understood to be booty—under the maxim *bellum se ipsum alet* (war should feed itself). The Dutch force was conceived differently. Its mission was defensive and of an indefinite tenure, and its commanders sought to avoid the chaotic behavior characteristic of looting soldiers in order to maintain discipline; hence its men were paid regular salaries. Given that its employers included some of the world's first assembly-line manufacturers, it is not surprising that its infantry was trained to present the enemy with a continuous and lethal series of musket volleys by training manuals that offered a recruit dozens of by-the-number engravings of the steps that each rank of musketeers were to take simultaneously in their load-and-fire countermarch.

Conscription of Frenchmen in the 1790s for the Revolution's infantry advanced the role of the common soldier, joining political and technological change. The conscription act called on those with new rights to perform new obligations. Yet, the result of this massive and recurring mobilization was not to lead to greater democracy. The musket had not "made the democrat" (in J.F.C. Fuller's formulation), in Revolutionary France any more than it had in 16th century Japan, Russia, or Prussia. While it ended the battlefield supremacy of samurai and knight, they reemerged as the officer corps of the new standing armies.

While the intensity of warfare and the military participation rates of male citizens both increased throughout the 19th and the first three-quarters of the 20th century, the share of both GNP and the state's resources devoted to military expenditures began to decline. Social welfare and nonmilitary infrastructural development lobbies grew more and more effective, at the expense of the military-industrial complex. The ending of the Cold War in the late 1980s offered "peace dividend" prospects of an acceleration of this process.

The Recruitment Process

Military personnel have either been recruited as volunteers or conscripted by the state. At different times and places men and, more recently, women have had a variety of reasons for offering themselves for service, and, similarly, various states have displayed a number of different philosophical and technical approaches to the recruitment process, ranging from a total reliance on volunteerism to the most brutal sort of compulsion, with a host of intermediate formulae.

In the absence of conscription, individuals have chosen to serve for monetary reward or economic security, for adventure or glory, or for religious or political idealism. The mercenary forces of ancient Greece and Rome, of medieval and early modern magnates, and of the more modern armies of empire were largely motivated by economic considerations, but these could be intermingled with more culture-driven motives: Many Irish, Sikhs, and Gurkas in the service of the 19th- and early 20th-century British armed forces, for example, conceived of themselves as people with a warrior tradition, a self-image that was not lost on British recruiters. Similarly, the Crow, Pawnee, and Shoshoni braves who volunteered to serve as scouts for the U.S. Army of the 1870s felt both the push of tribal need and the pull of warrior tradition. Some members of the Untouchable caste (harijan) in India were recruited for British military service in India after the mutiny of elite Indian troops in the Bombay army in 1857. Untouchables certainly saw military service as a vehicle for social mobility, and the thought of being used against Brahmins may have been appealing to some as well. Black Americans first volunteered largely for ideological reasons during the Civil War, though for many recently freedmen there were also compelling economic motives. Thereafter, many found military service to be a clear avenue of economic and social mobility (though they faced disappointment at the hands of racist recruiters and commanders until the past generation).

Within socioethnic communities that do not especially see themselves as warlike or within subcultures and families not particularly impoverished, the individual act of volunteering in peacetime is not as easily explained. The first surge of wartime patriotic fervor in modern nation-states has led millions to enlist, but patriotic fervor could be inspired by other motives. Many colonial New England recruits during the French and Indian War were younger sons who had yet to inherit land of their own. Their response to offers of enlistment bounties, consequently, was informed by their desire to acquire a nest egg and personal independence from parental controls. Conversely, many Confederate volunteers who rode with guerrilla commander William Quantrill in western Missouri and Kansas during the Civil War were eldest sons of substantial slaveowners, defending their world against what they correctly perceived to be a serious threat of its survival. Most of those who served in the Continental Army were more interested in the size of the bounty being offered than with "The Cause."

In any event, patriotism alone does not explain why many select the military calling in peacetime, in a host of historical periods. The spirit of adventure and the martial spirit notwithstanding, economic security has clearly ranked as the primary motive behind peacetime enlistments in the history of voluntary military institutions.

When we approach the question of recruitment from the perspective of the recruiter, we find clear correlations between policy and sociopolitical structure. Thus, mercantilist reasoning led several early modern European states to seek foreign paid volunteers (mercenaries) in order to keep their own subjects employed productively on their farms and at their trades. Machiavelli argued for a militia drawn from both the propertied classes and the masses to defend liberty and the Florentine marches, but that reasoning did not impress 17th- or 18th-century rulers and their bureaucracies. In Great Britain, the secretary of the admiralty in 1740 spoke for them when he wrote that, given the natural division of labor in Britain's "advanced state . . . personal service neither is, nor ought to be, the duty of every citizen. Those . . . offensive and disagreeable public duties (among which we reckon personal service in the armies and navies of the state) must fall to the lot of that part of mankind which fills the lower ranks of

life." The solution was the creation of a professional military.

The modern nation-state rediscovered the power of local and regional loyalties in recruiting volunteers. Britain reorganized its regiments in 1873 by basing one of their two battalions permanently in locales with which they would thereafter clearly be identified. The virtue of this step for both recruitment and morale was quickly proved, and in the first two years of World War I Britain's massive volunteer army was raised largely through the private actions of committees and individuals drawing on "local pride," the "taproot of English nationality." The National Guard Association of the United States, created in the 1870s, was a lobby for volunteer units of the various states seeking resources from Congress. The regular army, recognizing the recruiting and political power of the Guard local roots, drew on this same source in the local basing of its Army Reserve units in the 20th century. Early 20th century Japanese military planners utilized the strong social bonds of village life to reinforce motivation in organizing army reserve units there.

Volunteerism was not always sufficient in raising military forces. Thus, Britain's citizenry were subjected to a conscription of sorts during the Seven Years' War and the Wars of the French Revolution and Empire. But the English Militia Act of 1757 and its later English and Irish counterparts, like the American Union Army drafts of 1863 and 1864, were essentially designed to spur enlistments by coaxing either service or payment to provide a substitution.

The conscription policies of other 19th-century nations offered fewer means to some eligible classes of avoiding service. The peasantry of Russia, Prussia, France, and certain Latin American dictatorships were subjected to long terms of service. Black Americans conscripted for segregated service during World Wars I and II faced both the fear and anger of southern whites and the distrust of white officers who regarded blacks as irresponsible and panicky. Social psychologists advising the American military in the 1940s recommended the integration of black and white units as a means of boosting morale and improving performance levels. They were supported by white officer combat veterans who had developed respect for their men and had become confident of their ability (a phenomenon reminiscent of the experience of many white officers and their black troops during the Civil War). The resulting integration of the services during the Korean War proved to be successful, and thereafter the American military, with its many bases throughout the South, prompted off-base desegregation.

Conscription lived again, in one form or another, in most of the NATO and Warsaw Pact nations during most of the Cold War era; its days may now be numbered.

Training and Socialization

The process of socializing military inductees into their service's norms and mores, while preparing them simultaneously to perform their new duties, has always had two dimensions—the goals and practices of the military, and the impact of the process on the inductees. Certain features of the former of these have been persistent and unmistakable. Discipline, collective action, the transmission of unit traditions, physical conditioning, and the acquisition of specific military skills have always been objectives of those responsible for the integrating of recruits into military forces.

Modern boot camps are presumed by some social psychologists who have described them to be sophisticated versions of this process of reorienting individuals into the regimen and mores of the warrior culture with its male bonding. But a recent study of Marine Corps basic training at Parris Island, South Carolina, in the 1940s and 1950s has established that marine officers had for generations felt it best to leave the process entirely in the hands of drill instructor sergeants (DIs) who trained the next generation of DIs without any formal manuals or officer-led instruction. As one officer put it: "Probably it's a good thing we don't know how it's done. If we knew, we might fiddlebitch and tinker with the process until we ruined it."

The military has always reinforced training with disciplinary codes and leadership methods to ensure that missions are accomplished. These codes and methods sometimes change, reflecting changes in the larger society's value system or new demands within the military itself. The

patterns of organizational authority within the modern military have especially changed since World War II. As the military became more technologically sophisticated, employing more military specialists, its need to reenlist such specialists grew, but these specialists were like free professionals, who were averse to arbitrary authority. Indeed, many former specialists indicated in the 1950s and 1960s that they had left their country's military because of its coercive ways, and soldier resistance movements, some blossoming into military unions, grew in the developed western states in the 1960s and 1970s. Hence, out of need, military elites slowly devised and provided less coercive forms of leadership than had prevailed before. This movement from coercion to persuasion accelerated in the United States when the draft was abolished in 1973 and the services had to rely entirely on volunteers.

Morale and Motivation

From the time that the first group of hunters drew on their supportive habits to collaborate in a successful war-band raid on their neighbors or the defense of their village, the small group camaraderie within military units has figured in the effectiveness of skirmishes, naval engagements, and pitched battles. And anything that disrupted that camaraderie was properly suspected of damaging military effectiveness.

John Lynn (*The Bayonets of the Republic: Motivation and Tactics in the Army of Revolutionary France, 1791–94*, 1984) has shown us how the French revolutionaries knew how to organize small groups of about 15 men into an *ordinaire* (messmates) under a corporal. When these men received their *marmites* of stew, they were often provided as well with revolutionary broadsides or songs that they would then read or sing by the evening campfire. French revolutionaries understood the importance of what modern sociologists call the primary group.

The results of this induced bonding were generally as intended. "A new comradeship and unity blossomed in our young lives," Emlyn Davies recalled of his early days in the 17th Royal Welsh Fusiliers in 1914. Canadian Major George Pearkes wrote home in 1917 that "it always seems to me that I'm not fighting for King and Country but just for [my] company, which seems to be everything to me these days."

German units may have been generally superior to comparable American units in World War II, or so Martin Van Crevald has argued, in part because American policies with regard to unit formation and casualty replacement practices resulted in a fighting force with lower small group cohesion and trust than German units, where cohesion was the conscious objective of commanders. But Omer Bartov's recent research offers an additional explanation for German morale—the strength and depth of Nazi ideology and socialization.

Many Americans entered Vietnam with a confidence in the rightness of their cause and the effectiveness of their weapons and leaders. This was often reduced after months of heavy combat in steaming-hot terrain to what one veteran called "a war waged for survival in which each soldier fought for his own life and the lives of the men beside him, not caring who we killed . . . or how many or in what manner." Their plight was made more perilous by the high command's practice of cycling too many career officers through too brief combat command tours of duty.

As the rate, range, and lethality of fire and the duration of exposure to it rose over the past five centuries, combatants have experienced more and more stress. After prolonged periods of combat, the din of battle and the sight of dying buddies produced "the shakes" and other symptoms of mental distress in many soldiers. In World War I their reaction was called "shell-shock"; in World War II, "battle fatigue." This phenomenon must have affected men before 1914, but the subject is not well researched.

The increasing lethality of combat might have been expected to lead to a greater unwillingness to respond to orders under fire. But while there is clear evidence of this among French forces in World War I, and some evidence of it in other armies of the 20th century, most troops have obeyed orders placing them in "the killing zone." Most mutinies continue to involve matters of pay or living and working conditions.

Consequences of Service

Military service has had both temporary and long-term effects on those who served. Some who appear to have been transformed by their experience, however, are better understood either to have possessed those propensities before entering the service or to have entered the service with traits or personalities that made them especially prone to experience the change. Combat veterans who suffered post-traumatic stress disorder (PTSD) long after their years of service certainly owed their distress to the trauma of combat, but not every veteran of heavy combat became a victim of PTSD. West German recruits who were given an "authoritarianism" questionnaire before entering basic training, again after completing 18 months of service, and still again two years after the completion of their service were found to have undergone a decline in their level of authoritarianism while in the *Bundeswehr*, but they then drifted back to their original, higher level after they had put that experience behind them. The process of self-selection into American airborne training and "Green Beret" service, due to values already possessed, proved to be more important than the training or duty assignments thereafter in explaining posttraining or postservice attitudes and values. In short, the impact of training and efforts to transform attitudes can be overstated. Militarization, if and when it occurs at all, has often been confused with the reinforcement of established values.

In some modern cases, at least, mobility opportunities in subsequent occupations improved as a result of military service (the case for minorities in the U.S. military in the 1940s and 1950s). One's perspective on the world could be altered as well. Certain American Revolutionary War soldiers seem to have experienced a change in political perspective: Officers who served outside their own states tended to adopt more cosmopolitan political positions after the Revolution, as did some enlisted men. Others who had not left their state but were similar in age, nativity, religion, social class, and county affiliation to those who had also exhibited an outlook altered by their army experiences; one group had seen more of the Confederation and its plight, and had seen the need of stronger bonds in the form of a new constitution. Service in the Prussian and German armies and navies appears to have made militarists of many veterans. In analyzing the interactions of the military and society, future scholars will continue to ask how military service affected those who served and how military institutions affected the societies they belonged to and vice versa. (*See also* Aristocracy; Feudalism; State and Society; Technology)

Peter Karsten

REFERENCES

Bushnell, John. *Mutiny amid Repression: Russian Soldiers in the Revolution of 1905–1906.* Bloomington: Indiana University Press, 1985.

Card, Josephina. *Lives After Vietnam: The Personal Impact of Military Service.* Lexington, MA: Lexington Books, 1983.

Lynn, John. *Bayonets of the Republic: Motivation and Tactics in the Army of Revolutionary France, 1791–94.* Urbana: University of Illinois Press, 1984.

Mann, Michael. *A History of Power to 1760.* New York: Cambridge University Press, 1986.

Redlich, Fritz. *The German Military Enterpriser and His Work Force,* 2 vols. Wiesbaden, 1964–65.

Smethurst, Richard. *A Social Basis for Prewar Japanese Militarism.* Berkeley: University of California Press, 1974.

Millenarianism

Millennialists (also called millenarians, millenarists, chiliasts) believe in an approaching cosmic upheaval that will destroy the present social order and establish a world of perfect peace, justice, and prosperity "for a thousand years" (millennium, Rev. 20:1–). The recurrence of popular millenarianism in various societies and periods makes it an obvious topic for sociocultural history. An apocalyptic (final revelatory) period of unprecedented suffering and disaster will usher in the new age. Millenarianism is perhaps the most dynamic and potentially disruptive of eschatological beliefs. If, for example, the eschatology means the total destruction of the earth and all physical existence, the task (until the atomic age) is God's, and believers tend toward a passive, even apolitical stance. But millenarianism anticipates a kingdom of heaven in this world, a belief with revolutionary implications since current regimes will be replaced by the reign of the saints and zealous servants of the Lord must play a key role. Thus, the salient element in millenarianism is not how long the new world would last, but that its establishment would take place on earth.

A major source of millenarianism grew out of diaspora Judaism's expectations of a return to the land of Israel. Later prophets linked Jewish redemption with that of the whole world, and the messiah, rather than leader of a national liberation, came to be seen as a cosmic savior with superhuman powers. Both Christianity and Islam grew out of messianic strains of Judaism and have strong millennial strains in their scriptural traditions. Similar beliefs in the imminent transformation of the world occur the world over (Africa, Melanesia, China), and mark some of the most antireligious movements of the modern world (Nazism, communism). The frequency, variety, and spread of millennial movements in the 19th and 20th centuries has made the phenomenon the object of not only religious but also historical, sociological, and anthropological studies.

The outstanding characteristics of these movements are their (1) linear attitude toward time and sense of its imminent consummation, which gives every moment and every deed vital importance in the unfolding cosmic drama; (2) dualistic vision of the universe, in which forces of evil (generally those now in power, even all nonmembers) are locked in mortal combat with those of good (the self-defined community); (3) emotional intensity, characterized by frenetic activity, visions, tremors, ecstatic dancing, and talking in tongues; (4) strong collective action and commitment—the millennial community plays a key role in bringing about the future society; (5) high profile role for women as visionaries and leaders; (6) proselytizing in order to save as many souls as possible; and (7) resilience in the face of their inevitably disappointed expectations. These general characteristics vary greatly, depending both on the group dynamics (personalities of the leaders) and the external conditions (political resistance, response of target populations). Among these variants, however, the most important historically galvanize popular protest against the current regime.

Millennial movements tend to follow the following pattern:

1. Preconditions: the collapse of cultural norms either from manmade or natural disasters, leaving people disoriented; these developments are then interpreted as the apocalyptic suffering.
2. Revelation: most often in the form a messianic leader with a vision of a new social order, the "revelation" galvanizes an initially small group of dynamic believers (often but not exclusively from a lower social class) who share in the charisma of the leader.
3. Community: in a spirit of total dedication and sacrifice a community forms around the bearers of the new revelation; this group may become extremely aggressive and expansive or reticent and secluded, but it always displays an intense sense of mission and cohesion marked by a radical break with past social behavior (rejection of family ties, antinomianism, promiscuous sexuality, or extreme asceticism), in varying degrees preparing for and celebrating by anticipation of the new world to come.
4. Disappointment: whether in the form of an expected date for divine intervention or the failure of a political coup by radical millenarians, or merely the waning of the period of expansion, all millennial movements have (so far) been forced to confront their disappointment when prophecy fails.
5. Adjustment or Disappearance: some, when not defeated and annihilated, disperse and lose all coherence; others, particularly smaller groups, adjust to new conditions in order to preserve the communal bonds already forged in the crucible of an imminent upheaval. These groups tend to reformulate both their expectations—stressing the need to continue while awaiting a recalculated future moment at which point—for example, in the case of a prematurely deceased messiah—he or she will return. In some cases, the group redoubles its efforts to proselytize at this moment of crisis, apparently seeking to deal with its "cognitive dissonance" by seeking reassurance in convincing others.

Because of their often popular makeup and highly unstable nature—the intensity of the emotions and actions stand in direct proportion to their sense of imminence—millennial movements leave few direct traces in the documentation. Authorities tend to be implacably hostile, suppressing both the existence and the memory of such groups, whereas those groups that do survive tend to write out of their past the mistaken prophecies that first brought them together and to create new, more socially acceptable and stable goals. This means, above all, that most of the long-range effects of millenarianism are unintended consequences, hence analyses of its impact must go beyond stated goals and primary characteristics. As a result, however, the historical study of the phenomenon remains largely conjectural, attempting to derive the characteristic patterns of such movements from fragmentary evidence. Only those current movements that sociologists and anthropologists can study provide hard data on the earliest stages of millennialism.

Historians of modern Europe have emphasized the movement from failed millennialism to revolutionary nationalism, and anthropologists have found that failed millennialism serves as both a means for dealing with the disruptions of modernization and as a gateway to more political forms of resistance and reform in the Third World. Historical studies of more distant periods pose more difficult problems: Christianity itself followed a classic millennial pattern (messiah [= christos], failed [crucified], reoriented [resurrection and Second Coming], wider efforts to proselytize [gentile mission], institutionalization [church] and eventual accommodation with the political structures once deemed irreparably evil [Christian Roman Empire]. But in this process of adjustment, the original (and dangerous) millennial impulse was systematically eliminated from ecclesiastical writings; there were even efforts to banish the most millenarian text—Revelation—from the canon. As a result many historians can write the history of Christianity with only a passing mention of millennialism.

But Christian millennialism, imbedded in the Bible, continued to generate movements that disturbed the ecclesiastical hierarchy with their disorderly enthusiasm and their powerful appeal. There is no Christian century for which we do not have evidence of millennial movements, and the indications from centuries with greater documentation suggest there may not be a generation that did not know such upheavals. Particularly in the last millennium (1000–2000), millennialism has shifted steadily away from a dependence on divine intervention toward an ever more central role for divinely inspired human activity; this culminated in the revolutionary movements of the modern world where God has been replaced entirely by human agency and historical processes. (*See also* Christianity; Nationalism; Religion)

Richard Landes

REFERENCES

Adas, Michael. *Prophets of Rebellion: Millenarian Protest Movements Against the European Colonial Order.* Cambridge: Cambridge University Press, 1979.

Emmerson, R., and B. McGinn, eds. *The Apocalypse in the Middle Ages.* Ithaca, NY: Cornell University Press, 1993.

Trompf, G.W., ed. *Cargo Cults and Millenarian Movements: Transoceanic Comparisons of New Religious Movements.* Berlin and New York: Mourton De Guyter, 1990.

Miners

Coal miners, because of the nature of their work and the communities in which they have traditionally resided, have a distinct history and culture as an occupational group. Immigrants from the British Isles initiated the mining of coal as an industry in the early American colonies. In the 1800s coal became a central commodity that literally fueled the industrial revolution, first in Britain and later in the United States; miners became an important but distinctive segment of the growing working class.

As the introduction of new mining methods changed the miner's job from a skilled or semi-skilled occupation to an unskilled one, wages and working conditions deteriorated. Increased immigration during the mid- to late 1800s provided the coal operators with cheap labor, as they were able to create ethnic divisions within the mining work force. Unskilled immigrants from southern and eastern Europe, as well as free and enslaved blacks, competed with the English, Welsh, and Irish miners who had preceded them into the mines. The company towns, where miners were often forced to live in company houses and spend their meager incomes at company stores, became true melting pots. Over time the collective misery of the isolated mining town, particularly in Appalachia and the western states, as well as the low wages and dangerous working conditions experienced by these ethnic and racial groups, helped miners overcome their differences. One of the ways in which these factors manifested themselves was in the militancy and solidarity with which miners generally approached their employers.

In the United States in particular, coal miners were one of the earliest groups of workers to form local and national associations for their mutual aid and protection. These groups, dating to the 1860s, evolved into some of the first significant American unions. This was a trend that would continue into the 20th century as the miners assumed a leadership role in the fledgling American union movement (through the United Mine Workers) and became known as the shock troops of American labor.

Because of their size and militancy, coal miners in many European countries and in Australia and southern Africa have received considerable attention from social historians, who deal not only with their protest efforts but with conditions of work and family life. Social historians also pay some attention to the decline of mining in many areas in the 20th century, as part of an analysis of deindustrialization and assessment of the changing bases of the labor movement in the industrial societies.

While the focus of most social and labor historians has been on coal miners, the social, economic, and cultural experience of the smaller number of miners employed in the hard-rock or ore mines of America has generally paralleled that of their counterparts in the coal industry. (*See also* Working Class)

Paul F. Clark

REFERENCES

Lewis, Ronald L. *Black Coal Miners in America: Race, Class, and Community Conflict, 1780–1980.* Lexington: University Press of Kentucky, 1987.

Long, Priscilla. *Where the Sun Never Shines: A History of America's Bloody Coal Industry.* New York: Paragon House, 1989.

Seltzer, Curtis. *Fire in the Hole: Miners and Managers in America's Coal Industry.* Lexington: University Press of Kentucky, 1985.

Mining/*Mita*

Colonial Spanish America was renowned as a source of gold, and even more of silver. Production of these metals was the work in part of forced laborers: enslaved blacks for gold, and drafted American natives for silver. In Mexico the draft was known as *repartimiento*, and in the Andes as *mita*. The systems were essentially the same. They were operated by the colonial government. They forced a percentage of the adult male native population of the mining zones to work each year, in return for a barely subsistence wage. And both had antecedents in forced labor systems of the Aztec and Inca states (*coatequitl* and *mit'a*, respectively), which eased their implementation by the Spaniards. Both, finally, have served as important targets in sociohistorical research in colonial Latin America.

The most notorious mining draft of colonial times was the mita of Potosí, the largest center of silver production in Spanish America until about 1680. This *mita* was organized in the 1570s by Don Francisco de Toledo, fifth viceroy of Peru. According to his final plan, of 1578, some 16 percent of men aged between 18 and 50 from the highland communities between Cuzco and Potosí were to go annually to Potosí to mine and refine silver ores. The actual total of the 1578 *mita* was 14,181.

These men were to spend a year in Potosí, though, at least in law, they had to work only four months of the twelve, with rest periods separating spells of labor. Because of the length of the absence from home, many men took their families with them. The Potosí *mita* caused, then, an annual migration of tens of thousands of native people. Many never returned home. A surprising number stayed in Potosí, the men often

becoming wage workers in mines and refineries, for far higher wages than those paid in the *mita*. Consequently, by about 1600, just over half the native silver workers in Potosí were unforced wage laborers. The balance between forced and unforced stayed roughly the same until the end of the colonial times. The *mita* men, however, always provided an essential subsidy of cheap labor for mine and refinery owners.

The Potosí *mita* disrupted central Andean native society not only by shifting many thousands from communities to Potosí, but also by causing many others to flee from the catchment area of the draft. Far more damage was done to native society by the flight and disruption caused by the *mita* than by the dangers of silver mining itself, in which mortality was lower than has often been imagined.

The same was true of the other large mining *mita* of the central Andes that allocated, also in the 1570s, to the mercury mines of Huancavelica. The initial number drafted here was over 2,000. Mining, and especially refining, mercury was more dangerous than producing silver, because mercury, especially as a vapor, is toxic. Many fled to avoid being sent to Huancavelica. But even there a body of unforced wage workers arose.

A few other small mining *mitas* always existed in the central Andes. But none compared in size or effect with those of Potosí and Huancavelica. (*See also* Latin American Ethnicity; Miners)

Peter Bakewell

REFERENCES

Cole, Jefrey A. *The Potosí Mita, 1573–1700. Compulsory Indian Labor in the Andes.* Stanford, CA: Stanford University Press, 1985.

Villamarín, Juan A., and Judith E. *Indian Labor in Mainland Colonial Spanish America.* Newark: University of Delaware, Latin American Studies Program, 1975.

Missionaries

Americans tend to identify missionaries with Christianity, although several other religions—notably Buddhism and Islam—have long and vigorous missionary traditions of their own. While this article will focus upon Christianity, it should be noted that missionaries of diverse faiths have profoundly influenced a great many cultures.

The missionary thrust of Christianity was central from the beginning, attributed in the New Testament to Jesus himself. His exhortation, "Go therefore and make disciples of all nations" (Matthew 28:19), has been called the Great Commission. In fact, much of the New Testament is missionary literature. The Acts of the Apostles recount some of the earliest efforts to spread the Gospel, and the canonical epistles were written to guide the newly established churches of the 1st and 2nd centuries.

Jesus disciples recognized two great responsibilities in their understanding of mission: the proclamation of the Gospel, with its attendant call to conversion, and the melioration of human suffering. This dual focus has characterized Christian missions for nearly two millennia, although the emphasis to be placed upon evangelism or social welfare has been a recurring debate among missionaries, especially since the late 19th century.

The most frequent criticism of missionaries is the charge of cultural imperialism, the claim that missionaries have sought to impose their notions of civilization upon converts, or worse, that missionaries have accompanied and abetted their conquering compatriots in search of political and economic hegemony. The spectacle of 16th-century *conquistadores* letting Native Americans be baptized before they were slaughtered, or 18th-century slave traders providing sermons to prisoners on their way to the blocks, or 19th-century Europeans and Americans carrying the "white man's burden" to beknighted people of other races—all of these episodes contribute to an image of missionaries as agents of imperialism.

The problem of "Christ and Culture," as theologian H. Richard Niebuhr put it, has challenged Christian missionaries since the 1st century. Christianity began as a movement within Judaism, and the earliest leaders of the church—Peter, James, Paul, and others—were Jews. As soon as Gentiles began to be converted the question arose regarding which of the dietary and other laws of Judaism should be incumbent upon Gentile Christians. The New Testament contains numerous references to the conflict, and to the extended discussions about which practices of the Hellenistic world were compatible with the new faith. The need for missionary sensitivity to other cultures, in short, began in the ancient Near East long before Christianity became the dominant religion of Europe.

Christianity came to Europe through the work of missionaries, some of whom, like St. Patrick of Ireland (born ca. 389) are still celebrated as national heroes. By the beginning of the 16th century, European interest in the New World was driven by a complex of motives—political, economic, and religious—but in a religious age motives were not easily separated. The year 1492 marked not only the voyage of Columbus, but a decisive Christian victory over Islam, which increased missionary fervor in European explorations. Sixteenth- and 17th-century expeditions were also driven by competitive interests arising from the Reformation, as Catholic Spain, France, and Portugal competed with Protestant England and Holland for religious as well as political and economic influence.

In America as elsewhere missionary activity occurred within a broader contest of cultures. Images of conquest and brutality suggest a powerful indictment of the missionary enterprise. But the historical record is more complex than these images alone convey. Missionaries have also been strong advocates for native peoples, sometimes arguing forcefully against the practices of their own countries, from Bartolome de Las Casas in the 16th century to workers in Central American base communities of the 20th century. Missionaries have been among the most sympathetic interpreters of foreign cultures, and they have developed innumerable schools, colleges, hospitals, agricultural projects, and reform movements, in addition to churches.

If missionaries have shared in cultural conflict and strife, they have also been among the world's great humanitarians, from Francis of Assisi to Mother Teresa. The historical record of missionaries is mixed, like that of most classes of human beings. What brings their record under so harsh a light, and generates such contempt or admiration, is their extraordinary claim to have been commissioned by God.

The study of missionaries has changed greatly under the impact of anthropology and social history. Earlier histories tended to take missionaries' claims at face value, and assumed that they dominated (benevolently or harshly) the peoples they served. Social history emphasizes the interactive quality of missionary activity; it looks at changes missionaries brought, in economic systems as well as religious beliefs (for modern missionaries often preached new work systems as well as religious and medical ideas), but also at ways in which local peoples used and adapted missionary activity. This interactive approach has proved important in providing new insights into missionary history in Latin America, the Pacific, and, increasingly, Africa. (*See also* Christianity; Missions; Religion)

James A. Gilchrist

REFERENCES

Axtell, James. *The Invasion Within: The Contest of Cultures in Colonial North America.* New York: Oxford University Press, 1985.

Marty, Martin E. *Pilgrims in Their Own Land: 500 Years of Religion in America.* New York: Penguin Books, 1984.

Neill, Stephen. *A History of Christian Missions,* 2nd ed. New York: Penguin Books, 1986.

Missions

Christian missions have been extremely important acculturating agents throughout the world. Here we refer to settlements among non-Christian peoples run by Christian missionaries who attempt to convert the members of the settlement. These types of missions existed throughout the Pacific Islands, Asia, Africa, and Latin America. Although the 16th and 17th centuries witnessed perhaps the largest number of conversions through missions (in colonial and Catholic Spanish and Portuguese America), missions reached their greatest extension in the 19th century, when Europeans both Protestant and Catholic penetrated to even the most inaccessible regions throughout the world and established missions.

Missions are especially important to social history because they are well-documented laboratories where two cultures, the European and the indigenous, met. Apologetic historians, often members of the missionary organizations themselves, have left copious works on the motives and struggles of the missionaries. Often these works have been taken at face value, showing the triumph of European civilization and Christianity. However, the documents record a different reality, with which one can reconstruct to a large extent the lifeways of societies about which we would otherwise know very little. Moreover, social historians and ethnohistorians have shown that the everyday reality of people who lived on the missions was often radically different than that described by the missionary historians. For example, demographic data from birth and death records show that settling the Indians of California to the missions in the 18th century exposed them to diseases and killed them off almost as quickly as they could be brought in. On the other hand, on the Chiriguano missions in 19th-century Bolivia, the records show that the missionaries (Franciscans in this case) had very little actual control over the daily running of the missions. Instead, for more than a generation the traditional chiefs wielded most effective power. We are beginning to realize that the missions did not serve merely as unidirectional acculturating agencies; rather, the missionized often took portions of the missionary message that appeared to appeal to them most and used them for their own ends. This occurred, for example, in South Africa, where the Methodist missionaries helped change local culture and in fact helped strengthen it against the onslaught of European capitalism.

The examination of missions by social historians is just beginning; a critical revision of the apologetic histories through the use of primary materials that still exist will yield many new discoveries. Moreover, scholars need to attempt to measure better the effect, if any, the missions had after they disappeared. Much work needs to be done especially on the missions of the 19th and 20th centuries, which up to this point have been the almost exclusive territory of anthropologists. A meshing of the two approaches, history and anthropology, would be particularly apt. (*See also* Christianity; Ethnography/Ethnohistory; Latin American Religion)

Erick D. Langer

REFERENCES

Comaroff, Jean. *Body of Power, Spirit of Resistance.* Chicago: University of Chicago Press, 1985.

Jolly, Margaret, and Martha Macintyre. *Family and Gender in the Pacific: Domestic Contradictions and the Colonial Impact.* New York: Cambridge Univeristy Press, 1989.

Langer, Erick D., and Robert H. Jackson, eds. *The New Latin American Mission History.* Lincoln: University of Nebraska Press, 1994.

Mobility

The history of social mobility is one of the central issues of social history. It was one of the first topics developed in the surge of the new social history in the United States, and also one of the early subjects open to quantitative investigation. Many historians have investigated the historical extent of, and the historical changes in, social mobility in its various dimensions—that is, elite mobility as well as social ascent from the lower classes; social mobility of ethnic, religious, and national minorities as well as sexual inequalities of social mobility; social mobility in preindustrial as well as industrial societies; and the various channels of social mobility such as education, business enterprises and bureaucracies, political parties, family networks, and marriage. A few general summaries of the history of social mobility exist for specific periods.

Definitions and Methods

What do historians mean by social mobility? First of all historians usually investigate only the social mobility of individuals. They usually do not explore under the heading of social mobility the grading-up or grading-down of entire social groups or entire social classes such as the decline of European aristocracy, the ascent of the middle class, the ascent of various professions, the decline of the urban artisanal elite. These changes in social hierarchies are to be taken into account in the study of social mobility. They are, however, usually not the main theme.

Moreover, the study of mobility also does not primarily focus upon geographical mobility of individuals as the term might suggest. To be sure, a good many studies by historians of social mobility do treat migration and geographical mobility as a factor in social mobility or, especially in local studies, the mobile as a group of historical individuals difficult to trace and, hence, creating severe methodological difficulties. The theme of transience has been particularly important in 18th- and 19th-century United States and European history. Wider studies of immigration have also tested causes (in terms of threatened downward mobility) and results (in terms of comparing mobility results for different immigrant groups) where geographic migration was involved.

Studies of social mobility per se mostly concentrate upon occupational mobility. If investigating career mobility, they trace the mobility of individuals between different occupational positions or their persistence in the same occupation. If they investigate mobility between generations, they compare the occupation of the father or the ancestors with the occupation of a historical individual. Occupation is usually seen as the central indicator of the situation of an individual in a historical society, though notably historians also deal with changes in the percentages attributed to occupations, which affects perceptions of mobility. Changes in income, in education, or in religious affiliations and social networks are not normally seen as secondary indicators of social mobility, if the occupation remained the same.

Starting from the occupation as the key indicator of social hierarchies, studies of social mobility by historians seek a highly differentiated impression from societies in the past societies. They try to explore hierarchies of occupations in taking into account differences of income, of properties, of educational training, of prestige, and of networks between occupations. They work to link various historical sources for this purpose and to trace individual persons through marriage license files, tax files, census materials, last wills, and records of churches and public administrations. During recent years, the competence of historians in linking various sources has grown.

The study of social mobility has also been criticized among historians for various reasons: Many historians argue that the sources which were normally used give us only an extremely crude idea of the historical reality. Data on only two or three points of time of a whole life and only on occupation or income in an often vague way are considered to be insufficient and unsatisfying. In addition, large parts of the population are excluded from the study of social mobility centering upon occupations. This is especially true for women, where historically mobility has mainly involved marriage. It is also true in a more fundamental way for societies in which large parts of the population did not yet have distinct and single professions; these mobility studies have less to say about peasant than about industrial settings. Moreover, critics object that the quantitative study of social mobility concentrated too much upon the objective side and neglected the entire subjective dimension of experiences, motivation, mentalities.

As a consequence, some new trends in the research on social mobility can be seen. The study of social mobility of women is starting, though even now only very few studies on gender differentials exist. It is already clear that the results are highly interesting, showing that the history of social mobility of women is clearly different from that of men. In addition, the study of social mobility has become highly sophisticated. Individual careers are explored in all details, especially in cases in which source materials are unusually rich. Some studies also try to include the subjective side and do trace the impact of mentalities (that is, perceptions of prestige or deterioration) and experiences on social mobility. Furthermore, the international and interregional comparative study of social mobility has become more frequent, using the rich results of about 30 years of historical research in this field.

Interdisciplinary Cooperation

Social mobility is one of the major fields of history in which research comes not only from historians but also from scholars of other disciplines. This is especially true for three crucial aspects of the history of social mobility: For the recruitment of the elites, above all for the political and administrative elites, political scientists have sponsored important investigations using the historical perspective. For educational opportunities in schools and in higher education, educationalists and sociologists have participated in the historical research. The most important contribution comes from the sociologists in the in-

vestigation of the overall trends of social mobility during the 20th century. A clear division of labor has emerged between sociologists and historians. Sociologists usually explore social mobility on the level of entire countries. They usually use cohort analysis, which is based on actual surveys and which follows up differences between the older and younger age cohorts, assuming that these differences represent the historical changes in social mobility. Historians usually explore social mobility on the local or regional level using the variety of sources already discussed. In selecting different types of cities and villages and in comparing local studies on an interregional and international level, historians also can investigate general tendencies of social mobility. Historians often use simpler quantitative methods of analysis which are less difficult to understand. The reader is obliged, however, to consult the sociological as well as the historical literature. Links between these two disciplines are disappointingly weak.

Main Debates

Two major debates have especially attracted the attention of the historians of social mobility: the debate on the rise of an open or a blocked society during industrialization and modernization and the debate on the advanced social mobility in the United States compared to the less mobile European society. The two debates are sometimes interrelated. American society sometimes is discussed as the more modern and, hence, more mobile society. But normally, this is a debate over peculiar American and European paths on a crucial aspect of modern society.

We begin with the first debate, the discussion on the increase of social mobility during the last 200 years. In this debate the rise of social mobility has various meanings. It sometimes means a more meritocratic recruitment, especially for the few most prestigious, most powerful, and best paid positions. It sometimes means more mobility between occupations, upward mobility as well as downward mobility, and job mobility as well as mobility between occupations in the same social class. Sometimes, the increase of social mobility includes the chances of both genders and of minorities. Sometimes it means a clear increase of the opportunities of the lower classes compared to the opportunities of the upper and middle classes and not just more social mobility for everybody. One has to make sure what meaning is used by individual authors.

The advocates of the rise of social mobility usually think of a general increase of mobile people, but often also of a rising number of upwardly mobile persons since industrialization. They argue that various major social changes should have led to more social mobility and to more social ascent: The general decline of the fertility rates during the late 19th and early 20th centuries made it possible for parents not only to invest more in the individual help and education of their children, but also to promote their own professional careers. The rapid expansion of secondary and higher education especially since the end of the 19th century enlarged enormously the chances for better training. The rapid increase of geographical mobility since the second half of the 19th century led to a widening of the labor market and to a greater variety of new chances. The fundamental changes of the active population from the predominance of agrarian work up to the 19th and early 20th centuries to the predominance of service work especially since the 1970s generated substantial social mobility between occupations. The distinct increase of the sheer number of occupations in all modern societies since the industrial revolution also must have led to more social mobility. The general change of mentalities, the weakening of the emotional identification with specific professions, social milieus, and also with specific local milieus, and the rising readiness for job mobility and for lifelong training further enlarged the number of socially mobile persons. The rise of the welfare state, the mitigation of individual life crisis and the guarantee of individual social security clearly improved the chances for further training and for the purposeful use of occupational chances. Deliberate government policies of enhancing educational and occupational opportunities for lower classes, for women, for ethnic and religious minorities, and for immigrants also should have had an impact on social mobility. In sum, a substantial list of factors in favor of an increase of social mobility during the last 200 years can be put forward from this side of the debate.

The advocates of stability or even decline in social mobility are a heterogeneous group. Arguments stem from very different ideas of social developments. It is sometimes argued that 19th- and early 20th-century industrialization not only led to a rising number and a fundamental change of occupations, but also to a class society in which the major social classes—the middle class, the lower middle class, the working class, the peasants, and in some societies also the aristocracy—tended to reinforce the demarcation lines to other social classes and, hence, to reduce rather than to enlarge the number of mobile persons. Other advocates of the skeptical view argue that the fundamental upheaval of modern societies during industrialization led to a unique rise of social mobility, of upward as well as downward mobility, and that modern societies thereafter became more closed since the generation of pioneers in business ended, as most occupational careers became more formalized and more dependent on formal education, as modern bureaucracies emerged and as mentalities adapted to the modern, highly regulated job markets. Other advocates argue for the stability of social mobility rates in a different and much more narrow sense: They argue that the long-term change of social mobility from the industrial revolution until the present was mostly structural, that is, it depended almost exclusively upon the redefinition of the active population rather than on the reduction of social, cultural, and political barriers. In this view social mobility remained stable if one abstracts from the changes simply induced by alternations in occupational structure (as peasants, for example, became workers—a real change, but not necessarily a case of upward mobility). Still other advocates of the long-term stability of social mobility posit a stable inequality of educational and occupational chances of lower classes, of women, of minorities in comparison with the educational and occupational chances of the middle and upper class, of the male population, or of the ethnic majority, respectively.

This long debate has led since the beginning of quantitative studies of social mobility after World War II to a large number of historical studies of social mobility and to a wide range of results. To sum up briefly, three main results ought to be mentioned. First, only in very rare cases could a clear decline of social mobility rates be found. Most studies show either stable or increasing rates of social mobility, depending upon the type of community and country and the generation and the period under investigation. There is no overwhelming overall evidence, neither for stability nor for decrease, of social mobility rates. Secondly, changes of overall social mobility rates do in fact depend to a large degree on changes in occupational and educational structure. So one can say that modern societies became more mobile to a large degree because education expanded so much and because occupational change became so frequent and normal. Finally, there is much evidence that the increase of educational and social mobility of lower classes and of women did not increase to the detriment of the educational and occupational chances of the middle and upper classes and of the men. Except for the eastern European countries in some specific periods, social mobility was usually not a zero numbers game.

The second debate on the more advanced social mobility in the United States is still older. It dates at least from the early 19th century, when the French social scientist Alexis de Tocqueville argued that the American society offered more chances of upward social mobility than did Europe. For a long time this debate was predominantly a moral one about the advantages and disadvantages of a mobile society. Only after World War II did it become a debate more over the fact of the American lead. Some social scientists attacked the idea of a more mobile American society. The American sociologist S.M. Lipset was the most prominent advocate against the American lead. He argued that industrialization and social modernization everywhere led to the same basic increase in social mobility. He believed that overall international figures on rates of social mobility and rates of social ascent after World War II did not prove any American lead in social mobility. This attack on an old myth was not only a debate among academics. It started in a period in which the American influence in the world reached its peak and in which the model of the American way of life in general was strongly discussed both in America and in Europe. Writers joined the skepticism about the American lead in social mobility. Simone de Beauvoir, the famous French intellectual, after travel in the United States also wrote that "there is almost no hope any more for the lower class to move up into this class" (i.e., into the upper class).

Other social scientists as well as writers defended the American lead. Ralf Dahrendorf, the well-known German sociologist, argued in the 1950s that "much direct evidence exists that this country [the United States] offers the opportunity of social ascent also to those who would have been stopped in Europe by the rigid social hierarchies." Three arguments were put forward in favor of the American lead. More detailed empirical studies by sociologists demonstrated that in some crucial aspects a clear American lead could be shown. This was especially true for the mobility into the professions. Higher education was more extensive and offered more chances than in Europe. Hence, the social ascent from the lower classes into the professions that are based on higher education was clearly more frequent than in Europe. In addition, comparative historical studies on late 19th- and early 20th-century American and European cities showed that in a special sense a modest American lead existed during that period: unskilled workers in fact moved up into white-collar positions in American cities somewhat more frequently than in European cities. Finally, historians demonstrated that the important difference between American and European societies could be found in the idea of social mobility rather than in the factual rates of mobility. Americans continuously believed that their country offered more opportunities than the rigid European societies.

The most recent studies tend to argue that a general lead of the American society no longer exists in comparison with Europe. To be sure, international comparisons show that strong and persistent differences in social mobility between cities and countries existed and still exist. Hence, it is difficult to accept the argument of a worldwide convergence of social mobility through industrialization and modernization. However, probably because of the fundamental social changes in Europe since World War II, there is no clear actual evidence for a general American lead in social mobility against the whole of Europe. Interestingly, while mobility research remains a vital facet of sociology and of European social history, it has for the moment declined among American social historians except for students of immigrant and racial minorities. (*See also* Assimilation/Acculturation; Immigration; Migration; Quantification; Sociology; Stratification and Inequality)

Hartmut Kaelble

REFERENCES

Erickson, R., and J.H. Goldthorpe. *The Constant Flux. A Study of Class Mobility in Industrial Societies.* Oxford: Clarendon Press, 1992.

Grusky, D.B., and R.M. Hauser. "Comparative Social Mobility Revisited: Models of Convergence and Divergence in 16 Countries," *American Sociological Review* 49 (1984).

Kaelble, Hartmut. *Social Mobility in the 19th and 20th Centuries. Europe and America in Comparative Perspective.* Lemington Spa, Dover, NH: Berg Publishers, 1985.

Lipset, S.M., and R. Bendix. *Social Mobility in Industrial Society.* Berkeley: University of California Press, 1959.

Thernstrom, S. *The Other Bostonians.* Cambridge, MA: Harvard University Press, 1973.

Modernization

The label "modernization" has been widely used: in the 1950s it was popularized as an approach to social history that helps to establish a general research agenda as well as methods and theories cutting across the social sciences. The label soon became a controversial point of reference. To many it signified breadth of coverage of countries and periods, the search for theories fruitful for area studies, and the introduction of social science concepts and rigor into historical studies. Proponents argued that industrial development, democratization, urbanization, the demographic transition, and other powerful forces of social change, which began to transform western Europe before the 20th century and have been spreading to far corners of the world, should be treated together as part of this general process. In contrast, numerous critics saw the label as an ideological challenge born of Cold War thinking. In their view, the very breadth of modernization limited its specificity and objectivity, while claims that the experiences of the West offered lessons elsewhere were aimed at casting doubt on the communist model or on autonomous Third World paths of development. They insisted that the world economic system, which made countries dependent, retards development; so lessons of earlier modernization are of little or no relevance. The literature applying and responding to modernization theory left a strong imprint on scholarship, explicitly to the 1970s and often implicitly, with fewer references to the label, in recent years.

At the core of the debate about the contribution of modernization studies and theory to social history were four far-reaching issues of the postwar era. First is the dispute about borrowing for development. In response to decolonization and the promise of large-scale foreign aid, experts weighed the prospects of less developed countries borrowing institutions from the West despite the absence of some historical preconditions for them. The critics insisted that modernization theory was Eurocentric and ahistorical, overlooking the social roots of the non-Western world in favor of blind copying, which they sometimes dismissed as neocolonialism. Others, however, seized the opportunity to examine varied topics such as bureaucratization in China, education and urban development before Japan's Meiji Restoration, and premodern commercialization around the globe to determine the extent of national differences and their relevance to subsequent economic growth. Research also focused on cases of borrowing both public and private institutions as a means of accelerating modernization.

The second issue is the struggle between capitalism and communism. Antagonists charged that modernization theory erroneously judges socialist societies by the standards of capitalist ones, failing to acknowledge a different and conflicting path of development. Advocates of developing the theory countered that problems of the city, the environment, and even the workplace largely reflect levels of economic development. From their perspective arose some of the most pointed critiques of communist policies, such as the lack of autonomy for experts or the restrictions on migration to cities. Such critiques often found the roots of policies in the underdeveloped social history of Russia or China and predicted that once more advanced stages of development were reached, imbalances in modernization would lead to a breakdown in much of the communist order. The collapse of the Soviet Union and other communist states offered conclusive support for this reasoning.

Third among the issues facing the social sciences is the tension between specialized research in one discipline or comparative, interdisciplinary, and wide-ranging approaches to social change. To some statistically oriented specialists only cross-national comparisons based on large data sets signify a contribution by modernization analysts. Critics disparaged claims to theoretical contributions in historical case studies due to omissions in much of the modernization literature, such as inattention to conflict, revolutions, or world dependency and a lack of clarity about definitions and measures. As studies under the modernization label declined, it seemed as if the critics had been convincing. Yet, scholars dissatisfied with the alternative of narrowly specialized research appreciated that modernization theory or something close to it would have to be pursued in order to show how changing levels of national development over a long time relate to many of the principal themes of social history such as changing types of economic organization and family structure.

Fourth, the debate over modernization raises the issue of the relationship between history and contemporary societies. At one extreme is the view that modernization is a universal social solvent, sweeping away the past and leading to accelerated convergence of lifestyles and ways of thinking as well as of organizations capable of competing in our increasingly integrated world. This approach is historical to the extent that it considers why countries varied in the timing and rate of their modernization, with most still incapable of achieving sustained modernization. At the other extreme is the argument that because the paths of economic development are so varied and the impact of that development on culture such as religion and attitudes toward authority is so weak, the world is best perceived strictly in terms of separate regions and national traditions.

Finally, and related to the fourth criticism, social historians dealing with modernization even in the West often object to its monolithic quali-

ties. Modernization theory can imply that all social groups and both genders move toward similar kinds of values, family structures, political behaviors, and the like, and that there is an integral relationship among political, family, economic, and other experience. Proponents of modernization as a description simply of patterns in western European or American social history have indeed argued that various social groups do move in some similar directions (for example, in reducing birth rates albeit at slightly different times) and that there are connections among economic changes, literacy developments, certain family values, and so on. In response, critics argue that while recent Western social history does expose people to some similar forces, like industrialization, the actual patterns of change are quite varied with consequences quite different from those modernization theory implies.

What is often overlooked in such controversies is that, unlike communism, modernization is not an ideology, but a label for a constantly changing effort to develop social science theory. It is not a school of thought with icons and believers, but a loosely associated set of developing ideas competing to determine which is most useful for research. As time has passed, more attention has been directed at international factors in development and at regional variations, especially the greater role of the state in latecomers to modernization and the lesser role of individualism in East Asian modernization. Such concerns drawn from recent developments continue to inform studies of social history and to ensure that what scholars of the past look for will often be linked to what seems to matter in our own times. Both quantitative and qualitative methodologies have improved, offering increased opportunity to compare many social variables systematically and with an eye to theory. While modernization is still widely criticized, it is also extensively used in the social history of various parts of the world. (*See also* Industrialization)

Gilbert Rozman

REFERENCES

Black, Cyril E., et al. *The Modernization of Japan and Russia.* New York: The Free Press, 1975.

Levy, Marion J., Jr. *Modernization and the Structure of Societies.* Princeton, NJ: Princeton University Press, 1966.

Rozman, Gilbert, ed. *The Modernization of China.* New York: The Free Press, 1980.

Monasteries/Nunneries

Monasteries and nunneries are social institutions that shelter communities of male and female monastics. Monastics are individuals who aspire to an awareness that makes explicit the sacred principles immanent in the profane world, such awareness permitting self-absorption with the holy. To cultivate this awareness, the monastic must free herself/himself from the distraction of social obligations. An essential consequence of the assumption of the monastic estate, then, is self-exclusion from normal social life. While monasticism has sometimes been studied from a doctrinal standpoint, as part of intellectual history, the social roles and social contrasts monasticism offers makes it an obvious target for a sociohistorical approach to religion.

"Renunciation of the world" should not be confused with social death. The monk's individual pursuit of the spiritual *center* of consciousness is part of the dialectic that determines the social *center* of the larger society. Patrick Henry and Donald Swearer (1989) observe that marginality places the monastic in a state of *liminality,* or being "betwixt and between," which invariably grants some form of spiritual authority in the surrounding community. While the *renouncer* may stand in social opposition to the *householder* (the *man-in-the-world*), as has been noted in Indian religions, the "anticulturalism" of the former has served to validate the "culture," the social correctness, of the latter.

Monastic traditions can be identified in Christianity and in the three southern Asian religions of Hinduism, Buddhism, and Jainism. Asceticism appears among the attributes of holiness in other world religions also, but only the above four emphasize the renunciation of sexuality as sanctifying.

Three ideal types of monastics can be identified. The *hermit* lives alone, removed from population centers, removed from daily contact with other monastics. The *cenobite* also lives isolated from urban life, but in the context of a community of other monastics. The *evangelist* takes shelter in and about the city, preaching his message in the context of a group of like-minded individuals. Most monastic traditions have favored the cenobitic type of monasticism, perceiving the other two types as demanding a level of self-discipline beyond the capacity of the ordinary monastic. Likewise, concerned to limit contact with secular society, most traditions have identified locations remote from human habitation as ideal for the establishment of communities. This has not resulted in monasteries remaining isolated, but in the creation of new transportation networks, as lay people have flocked to these remote sanctuaries seeking spiritual counsel.

More regularly monastics seek to distance themselves from the norms of the surrounding society through physical self-presentation and social behavior. Buddhist and Christian monastics shave their heads (tonsure). Jainist monastics have their hair pulled out by the roots. Almost all monastics adopt some special clothing or uniform. Before Muslim overlords suppressed the practice, the *Digambara* monks in the Jainist tradition wandered around sky-clad (naked). The austerities monastics perform, including fasting, living off leftovers from the plates of others, self-mortification, also should be mentioned here, since they contribute to the public perception of the monastic's special status.

As Mohan Wijayaratna insists in reference to the teaching of the Buddha on monastic celibacy, "Renouncing sexual relations was part of renouncing family life." The Western term "monk" in fact has its origins in the Greek word "monachos," which is a translation of the Hebrew word "lebado," which means "alone, solitary, without a wife." Sexual encounter, because it signals indulgence in sensual appetite, remains an act of pollution in every monastic tradition. But the motivation behind vows of celibacy has been a desire to suppress the countervailing pull of family life on the monastic's consciousness.

The social pressure on monastic communities to take in those with no place elsewhere in society makes comment on social recruitment difficult. Every society with a monastic tradition has in some way compromised that tradition through the expectation that monasticism provide shelter for groups of people whose marginality is not self-induced. Both the Christian and Buddhist traditions are littered with stories of wealthy and/or prominent men and women who give up the world. John Boswell's (1980) study of the abandonment of children in medieval Europe suggests that most of these people were younger sons and daughters and thus marginal to their parents' political and social needs. In Hindu society only a man in the *householder* stage of the life cycle is considered economically and socially productive. During the other three stages of his life he is expected to signal his marginality through the adoption of one of the three monastic ideals: as a youth he must spend some time learning the principles of religion in a cenobitic community; once his children are grown he is required to give up his householder status and become a hermit; in old age his religion demands that he leave his forest dwelling to become a wandering ascetic, earning food through the display of faith. In Buddhist Thailand also, the marginality of young men is controlled through the requirement that many of them spend some part of their youth in a monastery. Societies with a monastic tradition accept the idea of a religious vocation. But they also read a vocation into other forms of social marginality.

A comparative plenitude of social-historical research exist on female monasticism in Roman Christianity, very little on the topic for the South Asian religions. What can be said in general is that in all traditions female monastics are regarded as lower than and subject to male monastics. Even though the Buddha created the first female monastics, orders of Buddhist nuns have found it difficult to survive male monastic misogyny. In Hindu society charismatic women can attain the status of *guru*, or spiritual leader. Women can also choose to give up secular life and follow a spiritual leader. But since few religious retreats survive their founders, feminine religious orders such as exist in Roman Christianity and Buddhism have not developed. In Roman Christianity also, charismatic women can attain the status of holy women. Yet while they have established monasteries of female followers, rarely have they created monasteries of male followers. Despite separate status, however, convents can provide certain women a vital alterna-

tive to marriage; their abolition in Protestant parts of Europe in the 16th century formed part of a complex change in women's status that included greater dependence in marriage.

Monasteries have provided their societies with models of regulated, disciplined communities. Until the past few centuries they remained the only centers of literacy and written tradition. The lifestyles of monastics have served as paradigms by which laities measure their own progress toward spiritual enlightenment. But no consensus exists on the nature and import of the influence monasteries exert on secular society. Among the debates, scholars have argued over whether the celebration of "friendship" in medieval Christian monasteries did or did not represent a social acceptance of homosexuality. Students of Roman Christian monasticism have highlighted the structured role abbots play in keeping monasteries vital as institutions, and the essentiality of obedience as a monastic virtue. Scholars of Buddhism caution, however, against seeing the glorification of the abbot and of obedience in the Christian tradition as necessary traits of monasticism. They characterize the Buddhist *sangha*, or monastic community, as being less hierarchic, more democratic. Lastly, Lester Little (1983) provides an introduction to the enormous literature over the breakdown of the cenobitic and the reemergence of the evangelist type of monasticism in 12th- and 13th-century western Europe. (*See also* Buddhism; Charity; Christianity; Religion)

Andrew E. Barnes

REFERENCES

Boswell, John. *Christianity, Social Tolerence and Homosexuality: Gay People in Western Europe from the Beginning of the Christian Era to the Fourteenth Century.* Chicago: University of Chicago Press, 1980.

Elkins, Sharon K. *Holy Women of Twelfth-Century England.* Chapel Hill: University of North Carolina Press, 1988.

Henry, Patrick, and Donald Swearer. *For the Sake of the World: The Spirit of Buddhist and Christian Monasticism.* Collegeville, MN: Augsburg Fortress, 1989.

Little, Lester. *Religious Poverty and the Profit Economy in Medieval Europe.* Ithaca, NY: Cornell University Press, 1983.

McGuire, Brian Patrick. *Friendship and Community: The Monastic Experience, 350–1250.* Kalamazoo, MI: Cistercian Publishers, 1988.

Olivelle, J. Patrick. "Village vs. Wilderness. Ascetic Ideas and the Hindu World," in Austin Creel and Vasuda Narayanan, eds. *Monastic Life in the Christian and Hindu Traditions.* New York: Edwin Mellon Press, 1990.

Moral Economy

The idea that there was, or at least ought to be, an ethical dimension to the economic exchanges between ruling elites and their subjects was clearly present from ancient times in the writings of political philosophers from civilizations as diverse as those in Greece, India, and China. In the West, this notion was a matter of particular concern for 17th-century thinkers like Hobbes and Locke and for a number of the *philosophes* in the age of the Enlightenment. But the concept of the moral economy, as it has been understood and debated by social scientists in recent decades, derives largely from the writings of Karl Polanyi, particularly his early 1940s study of *The Great Transformation: The Political and Economic Origins of Our Time.* Drawing on his earlier fieldwork and writings on West African societies, Polanyi argued that the rise of capitalism in Europe and its concomitant valorization of the market nexus in societal exchanges led to a profound transformation in human perceptions and behavior. Profit maximization and personal advantage became the all-consuming drives of both the political elites and the rising mercantile classes which dominated the increasingly specialized societies of western Europe and later their overseas settlement colonies and tropical dependencies. The ethical grounding that had once undergirded human societies—and continued to do so to varying degrees in those areas of the globe where the market did not yet reign supreme—was undermined and discarded by the unbridled pursuit of competitive advantage in the market arena.

In the decades since Polanyi wrote, the concept of the moral economy has been elaborated, often in very different ways, by a number of authors. Though Polanyi's original arguments have been neglected, these reformulations of the moral economy have often been strongly challenged and in some cases dismissed by other social scientists. Perhaps the most influential of the more recent interpretations of the moral economy was set forth in *Past and Present* (1971) in a seminal essay by Edward Thompson entitled "The Moral Economy of the English Crowd in the 18th Century." Thompson himself and a number of scholars of the French Revolution, most notably George Rudé and R.B. Rose, had earlier stressed the importance of what were seen to be excessive price increases on staples, such as bread, as causes of social protest on the part of urban artisans and rural workers in the 18th century. But the "Moral Economy of the English Crowd" essay provided the fullest exposition of the consumer-oriented version of the moral economy approach to social unrest. Thompson argued that food riots, which had long been viewed as chaotic and marginal outbursts of protest on the part of the lower classes, represented premeditated, quite well organized, and clearly focused instances of political action. The grievances dramatized by these actions were generally seen as legitimate, and they were often tolerated by local officials, unless they became unduly violent or destructive. In Thompson's view, food riots and other actions aimed at preventing abuses by mercantile middlemen represented efforts by the urban and rural laboring classes to uphold the long-standing precepts of the moral economy. They were a means of defending paternalistic, consumer-oriented marketing patterns, which were regulated by custom and common law, against the practices and institutions that reflected the laissez faire doctrines of Adam Smith and other classical economists.

For some decades before Thompson's article appeared, Eric Wolf (1965) and a number of other scholars working on peasant societies mainly in colonized areas developed a rather different version of the moral economy concept. This approach has been the most fully elaborated in the writings of James C. Scott, who stresses relations of production rather than the consumer expectations that are central to Thompson. In *The Moral Economy of the Peasant* (1976), Scott argues that peasants approach the world with a "subsistence first" mentality, rather than with an eye to optimizing production or personal/family gain. In Scott's view the subsistence ethic shapes peasants' attitudes toward and responses to the demands of supra-village elite groups. The peasants judge the exactions of landlords, regional officials, or monarchs not according to how much rent or revenue these overlords take in absolute terms, but how much they leave relative to the peasants' output and subsistence needs. Thus, the peasants' definition of a "just" lord is one who recognizes their right to subsistence and regulates the timing and size of his rent or revenue demands to insure that the cultivator will retain enough food to support himself and his household. A moral economy is one in which elite demands fluctuate to take into account the impact of natural calamities and the depredations of marauding armies or bandit gangs on the level of agricultural production in any given year. Lords who insure that their peasant subjects retain enough for subsistence are viewed as legitimate and tolerable. Those whose demands are rigid and take no account of peasant subsistence needs are considered exploitative, unjust, and fair targets of peasant protest actions and rebellions.

A caricatured version of the moral economy approach to political economy as an argument for precapitalist utopia has proved an easy target for a number of social scientists, especially those espousing variants of rational choice theory. But more empirically based and less ideologically driven critiques of the various formulations of the moral economy have also appeared. These range from questions about the presumed homogeneity of peasant or urban laboring classes, the attachment of members of these groups to communal values and sanctions, and the extent to which elite rhetoric regarding obligations to the subject classes actually affected elite demands. Though the effectiveness of overarching moral economy prescriptions have been hard to validate, ethical components to elite-subject interaction, particularly within the nexus of patron-client systems, have been widely demonstrated. The questions raised by various proponents of the moral economy have also forced reevaluations of patterns of peasant resistance and protest that have laid increasing stress on the importance of everyday and avoidance modes of peasant and working-class defense and reprisal

in contrast to the almost obsessive focus on riot and rebellion in social science studies written in the 1960s and earlier. (*See also* Artisans; Capitalism; Food Riots; Market Economy; Peasantry; Protest)

Michael Adas

REFERENCES

Adas, Michael. "'Moral Economy' or 'Contest State'?: Elite Demands and the Origins of Peasant Protest in Southeast Asia," *Journal of Social History* 13, 4 (Summer 1980): 521–546.

Popkin, Samuel. *The Rational Peasant.* Berkeley: University of California Press, 1979.

Scott, James C. *The Moral Economy of the Peasant.* New Haven: Yale University Press, 1976.

Thompson, E.P. *Customs in Common.* London: Merlin, 1991.

Wolf, Eric. *Peasant Wars of the Twentieth Century.* New York: Harper, 1965.

Mortality Decline

One of the modern era's outstanding achievements has been the improvement in longevity and health over the last three centuries. The rapid rise in population growth since 1750 has been due in large part to mortality decline, first in western Europe and then, from the late 19th century, worldwide. Mortality improvements have been very much caused by reductions in the incidence of, and fatalities from, infectious and parasitic diseases and in diminished crisis mortality (i.e., years of severe excess mortality). History provides numerous accounts of destructive epidemics and plagues caused by such infections as bubonic and pneumonic plague, smallpox, typhus, typhoid fever, measles, diphtheria, scarlet fever, cholera, yellow fever, and influenza. A number of these diseases (such as measles and smallpox) became endemic, joining tuberculosis and a variety of other respiratory and gastrointestinal infections to keep "normal" mortality levels high.

Human beings are unusual among animal species in having most of their deaths caused by disease. This likely reflects a change in human ecological conditions from the Neolithic agricultural revolution of about 10,000 years ago, which brought people into close proximity with domesticated animals. It has been the control and modification of these disease processes which initiated the "epidemiologic transition"—from the age of pestilence and famine to the age of receding pandemics and finally to the age of degenerative and manmade diseases.

The timing of the mortality transition has varied. In western Europe, crisis mortality was stabilized in the 18th and early 19th centuries, partly because of government intervention and partly because of apparent ecobiological factors (e.g., the disappearance of the bubonic plague after 1720). After a plateau, there were further mortality reductions from the mid- to late 19th century, especially originating in declines in tuberculosis and gastrointestinal infections. Public health interventions (improved water supplies and sewage disposal, quarantine, compulsory vaccination) and better nutrition and standards of living had important roles. In this era the work of Louis Pasteur, Robert Koch, and others placed the germ theory of disease on a scientific footing. Specific microorganisms were now associated with specific diseases and conditions. Children and, with a delay, infants were particularly affected by control of many water- and airborne infections. Finally, after World War II, the advent of antibiotic therapy and improved medical and public health knowledge led the presently developed nations into a period when most deaths were from chronic degenerative diseases (e.g., cardiovascular disease, cancer) (Schofield, Reher, and Bideau 1991). Before the mortality transition, 50 percent or more of all deaths were caused by infectious and parasitic diseases. Now two-thirds to three-quarters of all deaths in low mortality, industrially developed nations are due to cancer and degenerative diseases. In addition, since World War II the mortality transition spread rapidly to the developing world with effective public health and enhanced medical technology.

A controversy surrounds the origins of the mortality transition in the developed world. Thomas McKeown (1976) has argued that population increase since about 1750 came solely from mortality reductions and that these reductions did not originate in medical intervention or even very much in public health activities. He concluded that improvements in nutrition, housing, and other aspects of standard of living were re-

sponsible. More recent research argues for a multiplicity of factors, including some effective public health interventions influenced to a degree by medical science. For example, the effectiveness of clean water and effective sewage disposal were being demonstrated in the 19th century in many urban areas before specific causative microorganisms were identified. The famous instance of Dr. John Snow removing the pump handle from a contaminated water supply during a cholera epidemic in 1854 London is a case in point. The 1892 cholera epidemic in Hamburg killed 1.4 percent of the population, while neighboring Prussian Altona and the sister port of Bremen, both with effective public health and sanitation, were virtually untouched. This was convincing evidence to contemporaries. McKeown's assertion that changes in fertility were not responsible for any significant part of the increase in population growth since 1750 is not always borne out. For example, the recent work by Anthony Wrigley and Roger Schofield on the population history of England (1541–1871) found changes in fertility were responsible for growth rate fluctuations. The rise in living standards was itself part of a general economic development which brought with it urbanization and industrialization. Urban growth had quite unfavorable mortality consequences. Cities, particularly large ones, were distinctly less healthy places to live up to the early 20th century. Excess urban mortality disappeared only when substantial public health infrastructure and programs were in place.

Table I provides some illustrative evidence. World population growth rates became moderate during the 18th and 19th centuries and then accelerated in the 20th century, sharply after 1950. The latter very rapid growth was caused by mortality decline (combined in some cases with increased fertility), concentrated in developing nations. The table also provides a time series of expectations of life at birth ($e(0)$) in six European nations and the United States. It shows substantial improvements between 1850 and 1950, when modern levels of survival were reached. The average increase in number of years of life expectation was 0.28 years per annum over the century before 1950 but only 0.16 years per annum thereafter. In contrast, a series of expec-

Table I

Mortality Decline Since 1750

Approx. Date	World Pop. Growth (% p.a.)	e(0) W. Europe and U.S.	Crude Death Rate Sweden	Infant Mortality Rate Sweden	e(0) Latin America
1750	——		27	204	
	0.42				
1800		37.4	26	200	
	0.51				
1850		41.5	20	149	
	0.54				
1900		54.3	16	98	27.2
	0.82				
1950		69.8	10	22	46.4
	1.87				
1965		72.3	10	14	55.8
	1.92				
1990		76.4	12	6	67.0

Western Europe includes Denmark, England and Wales, France, the Netherlands, Norway, and Sweden. For 1800, the results are only for Sweden. For 1850 and 1900, the results for the United States are for Massachusetts.

tations of life for Latin America exhibited improvements of 0.38 years per annum for the period 1900–1950 and 0.52 years per annum for the 40-year period 1950–1990. The table also provides series for crude death rates (deaths per 1,000 population per year) and infant mortality rates (deaths below age 1 per 1,000 live births per year) for Sweden, a nation with a long series of demographic data. Substantial improvements in overall and infant mortality were evident even from the beginning of the 19th century.

Overall, the achievement of low mortality and high life expectations has been a central aspect of modern economic growth and modernization. Although the pace has been uneven, the phenomenon has spread rapidly from the presently developed to the developing world. Indeed, mortality levels themselves are good indicators of development and the attainment of basic needs. Additional historical insight, both for Europe and elsewhere, will depend largely on painstaking and difficult work with local and parish records, genealogies, population registers, and other documents to reconstruct the past when regular censuses and other vital and demographic statistics were not collected or were of poor quality.

Social historians use findings on mortality decline extensively, and social historians who are demographers participate actively in debates over precise rates and causes. Research in social history focuses also on the results of mortality decline, in altering the age balance of populations, putting new kinds of pressures on families, shifting attitudes toward death and other basic beliefs. (*See also* Death; Demographic Transition; Demography)

Michael R. Haines

REFERENCES

McKeown, Thomas. *The Modern Rise of Population.* New York: Academic Press, 1976.

Omran, Abdel. "The Epidemiologic Transition," *Milbank Memorial Fund Quarterly* 49, 4 (Oct. 1971), Part I: 509–538.

Schofield, Roger, David Reher, and Alain Bideau, eds. *The Decline of Mortality in Europe.* Oxford: Clarendon Press, 1991.

United Nations. *The Determinants and Consequences of Population Trends.* Vol. I. New York: United Nations, 1973.

———. *Levels and Trends of Mortality Since 1950.* New York: United Nations, 1982.

Motherhood

Women have always borne and cared for children, but the institution of motherhood has changed over time in accordance with societal definitions and expectations regarding the maternal role. The social history of motherhood encompasses both the social construction of maternity and women's actual experiences as mothers.

Information on these aspects of motherhood has been gleaned from a variety of sources. For example, religious tracts and sermons, prescriptive literature addressed to women, medical treatises, and imaginative literature reveal the ideology of motherhood espoused by a given society at a particular period. Women's personal documents such as letters, diaries, journals, and autobiographies record the perceptions and reactions of individual mothers to maternity. All of these sources provide data about the expectations and experiences of motherhood among literate circles. Comparable information for other segments of society is far less accessible.

Social historians disagree in their interpretations of the history of maternity in Western society. Some argue that prior to the 17th century or even later, attentive, affectionate mothering was not emphasized, and relationships between mothers and children were formal and distant. Others discern more continuity in maternity and maintain that closeness and nurturing characterized earlier motherhood as well. Certainly some aspects of the experience of mothering have differed in accordance with the nature of women's social, economic, and religious circumstances. Changes in birthrates also affected the standards of motherhood.

The social history of American motherhood reveals clear evidence of change in the ideology of the institution. During the colonial period, feminine emotion was feared, and intense emotional attachments between mothers and children were discouraged. Large families and constant household duties deterred women from devoting extensive time and attention to individual children. This situation changed in the post-Revolutionary era with the emergence of the concept of republican motherhood, which stressed the civic and moral responsibility of mothers for raising virtuous future citizens. The ideology of American motherhood was further revised in the 19th century. Maternity and maternal love were idealized and redefined as eternal and sacred, and mothers were portrayed as instruments of their children's salvation. In the 20th century, the structure of motherhood has altered again, with a new and more comprehensive emphasis on the role of outside experts as sources of professional guidance and ostensibly superior knowledge about maternity. Changes in work roles have also altered patterns of maternal behavior. (*See also* Birth Control; Child Rearing; Family; Women's History)

Linda W. Rosenzweig

Badinter, Elisabeth. *The Myth Of Motherhood*. Translated by R. DeGaris. London: Souvenir Press (E & A), 1981.

Crawford, Patricia. "The Construction and Experience of Maternity in Seventeenth-Century England," in Valerie Fildes, ed., *Women as Mothers in Pre-Industrial England*. London and New York: Routledge, 1990, pp. 3–38.

Kerber, Linda. *Women of the Republic: Intellect and Ideology in Revolutionary America*. Chapel Hill: University of North Carolina Press, 1980.

Lewis, Jan. "Mother's Love: The Construction of an Emotion in Nineteenth-Century America," in Andrew E. Barnes and Peter N. Stearns, eds., *Social History and Issues in Human Consciousness: Some Interdisciplinary Connections*. New York: New York University Press, 1989, pp. 209–229.

Pollock, Linda A. *Forgotten Children: Parent-Child Relations from 1500 to 1900*. New York: Cambridge University Press, 1983.

Multiculturalism

The multicultural movement developed strongly in history and social studies teaching in the United States during the 1980s and 1990s. The basic premises were that the United States (and many other societies) could be understood only in terms of the histories and values of many ethnic, social, and other groupings, and that students from minority groups would gain better understanding and new confidence and self-esteem from a history focused on their own cultures of origin instead of a single mainstream history alone.

Multiculturalism related strongly to social history, urging attention to groups not in power and to causation and sources of information beyond the standard parade of political elites. Multiculturalism pressures promoted the inclusion of more social history materials in texts and curricula from primary school through college survey courses.

Multiculturalism derived more from political advocacy of various minority groups than from enthusiasm for social history per se. Some social historians, though favoring multiculturalism, worried that other facets of social history were not being introduced in history teaching and that basic features of social structure, and therefore a certain amount of coherence, were downplayed in favor of detailing one group after another. The linkage between social history and multiculturalism was promising but by no means complete.

Multiculturalism was attacked outright by educational conservatives in the United States, who argued that a single cultural criterion, deriving from the traditional elite, alone allowed history teaching to serve what they judged its primary function: to form cultural consensus and to insure attachment to vital national or civilizational values. Conservative attacks were often directed at social history research and teaching impact. They challenged social historians to formulate their teaching goals and strategies more clearly. (*See also* Teaching and Social History)

Peter N. Stearns

REFERENCES

Grant, Carl, and Mary Louis Gomez, eds. *Campus and Classroom: Making Schooling Multicultural.* New York: Guildford, 1993.

Stearns, Peter N. *Meaning over Memory: Recasting the Teaching of History and Culture.* Chapel Hill: University of North Carolina Press, 1993.

Music

Music is the most social of all the arts. As a performing art, it takes place in a ritual social context, not a solitary experience, as is true of reading, nor of people simply passing by one another, as in an art gallery. Musical contexts have maintained continuing relationships among people and established important institutional structures within the society. The opera gathered an elite public of both men and women that had no equal in 18th- or 19th-century society. Participation there involved both social and artistic concerns; the idea that people only went to the opera "to be seen" is a red herring, a cliché of late-Romantic ideology. Moreover, music was involved in an unusual variety of social contexts: the home and the school; the tavern and clubs; public institutions such as the church, municipalities, and national festivals; and the many cultural organizations that sponsored musical activities. Through looking at the network of social relationships that made up musical life, historians can gain important perspectives upon how groups interacted and defined public life.

By tradition, it has been conventional to discuss music within intellectual history as an aspect of philosophical or aesthetic movements such as neoclassicism, the Enlightenment, or Romanticism. But musical life had only limited or ambiguous relationships to intellectual life until well into the 18th century, since its learned tradition—the study of the physics and metaphysics of music—had little to do with musical practice, both performance and composition. The most important discourse in musical life was aural rather than written, and we know little of what was said. Thus, the entrance of musical topics into journalism and aesthetics toward the end of the 18th century was a change of great momentum for music. But even then, what was written was in large part a specialized form of musical journalism that kept its distance from literary and philosophical discourse.

Musicologists are very much alive to this problem; their present interests bear a much closer relationship to the methods of Roger Chartier, a leader in the French mentalities research, than to those of traditional intellectual historians. They start from social contexts in attempting to re-create musical practices—the hierarchy in a court or cathedral, the professional structure of the musical craft, and the norms of taste established in a particular community. They see a genre as a set of social expectations that composers then manipulated to their needs; they use the concept as an intermediary between the art and the society. Neal Zaslaw, for example, in his book *Mozart's Symphonies* (New York: Oxford University Press, 1989), looks into the traditions of the diverse cities where Mozart composed to explain how his approach to the genre evolved from being a light opener on a program to being a work of great intellectual substance.

One of the most important ways music can contribute to social history is in displaying the shape and the structure of elite groups. Concert societies and opera halls often left behind lists of subscribers, the proportions of whose social components can tell a lot about the uppermost classes of society, with a greater specificity and subtlety than is possible within macroscopic demographic treatment. During the 1780s, for example, the Paris Opéra included among its boxholders far more financiers—in both public and private posts—than the King's Theatre in London did. We can thereby see that because the English nobility had no parallel to the French tax farmers and royal secretaries, it possessed much stricter lines between its nobility and its bourgeoisie. Likewise, in the mid-19th century we can see the integration of nobility and bourgeoisie occurring in the musical events of the national capitals. The liberal professions played an important role in this process, as is suggested by Frédérique Patureau's (1991) book on the Paris Opéra between 1875 and 1914.

Elites played political roles just as much as social roles in musical activities. The opera was by definition a civic institution; in London in 1783 two-thirds of the male boxholders were or had been members of parliament. Jane Fulcher has likewise argued that the Grand Opera in Paris between 1830 and 1870 was essentially an ideological response to a political situation. William Weber's (1992) work on interest in old—"ancient"—music in 18th-century England has shown that such taste emerged essentially within a political context of opponents to the Whig regime.

Musical life is also a productive area in which to study the changing roles of men and women. Women have figured centrally in musical life, chiefly in informal roles knitting together musical communities and influencing taste. In late 18th-century London, for example, they were the "principal subscribers" who organized boxes. But as musical life became more formal in the course of the modern period men assumed much more central and important roles—that women could not assume—as directors of concert series, reviewers, indeed as connoisseurs. The canon of great composers that emerged beginning in late 18th-century England was dominated by men far more than ongoing tastes for contemporary music, based in salons, had been or continued to be.

Recent research on musicians has pointed in two different directions, with a breaking point around 1700. Before that time a significant number of court musicians played high roles as secretaries or diplomats; the early 18th-century German composer Agostino Steffani went beyond that to become bishop of Spiga in Asia Minor. Indeed, it was such men, and their lay colleagues, who led in the diffusion of music around Europe. After 1700 one is more impressed by the quite middle-class roles played by musicians as entrepreneurs, whose leadership was responsible for the dynamic growth of concerts and opera halls. The change in direction suggests how early they began developing markets for consumption—sheet music, instruments, lessons, and printed materials. As Cyril Ehrlich (1985) has shown in his history of the music profession in England, musicians generally followed a variety of trades, often in commerce.

Recent study of middle-class musical life is notable chiefly for demonstrating how widespread activity became in the provinces by the end of the 18th century. Research on England suggests a music society in almost every town of significance, with clubs rooted in both churches and assembly rooms, and one would suspect that similar work could profitably be done on France. The industrial working classes also developed a vigorous musical life in the 19th century. Dave Russell has shown how central brass bands became within the social life of workers in the North of England; one sees a vibrant, outward-looking culture in the competitions among these ensembles found from Brighton to Edinburgh. The German equivalent was choral societies, whose evolution was linked closely with industrial development. The social history of music has advanced rapidly through the efforts both of musicologists and social historians, though it has not yet become a mainstream sociohistorical concern. Developments in Europe have held center stage; there is little work on other societies. Research on working-class singing groups and other musical interests stands out amid a general lack of attention to the lower classes. Important efforts to deal with 20th-century popular music, including youth musical tastes, in a social history context has not yet produced a major study. The field, in sum, invites further work.

William Weber

REFERENCES

Ehrlich, Cyril. *The Music Profession in Britain Since the Eighteenth Century.* Oxford: Clarendon Press, 1985.

Fenlon, Ian, ed. *The Renaissance*, in Stanley Sadie, ed., *Music and Society.* Englewood Cliffs, NJ: Prentice-Hall, 1989.

Patureau, Frédérique. *Le Palais Garnier dans la société parisienne, 1875–1914.* Liége: Mardaga, 1991.

Weber, William. *The Rise of Musical Classics in Eighteenth-Century England.* Oxford: Clarendon Press, 1992.

Zaslaw, Neal, ed. *The Classical Era.* Englewood Cliffs, NJ: Prentice-Hall, 1989.

Music Hall

A robust, popular form of miscellaneous entertainment, music hall emerged in Britain in the 1840s and grew rapidly into a major leisure industry. Though its primacy was challenged from 1900 on, it remained an important branch of show business till the 1950s, and still survives as a particular comic style. Its history closely parallels that of American vaudeville and the French café-concert. Social historians have studied these forms, and their later decline, as central features of changing modern leisure.

Derived from amateur entertainments in the public house, music hall moved from the pub in the 1850s, occupying larger, more elaborate premises that better served an expanding urban population and the profit motive of its publican-entrepreneurs. Operations became highly commercialized with professional songwriters and performers, managers, agents, and a specialist press. Heavier capital investment brought the deluxe hall or variety theater of the 1880s, reproducing the house and stage design of legitimate theater and facilitating more spectacular productions, yet despite claims of increasing respectability, music hall remained embattled with reformers and licensing authorities over liquor, prostitution, and the morality of its entertainments. By 1914 the industry reached its heyday under large national combines, though overproduction, the cinema, and Americanized song and dance were threatening its predominance. Music hall survived World War I before being confronted with another powerful rival in radio. Yet, as with film, radio boosted the popularity of certain acts, and music hall laughed off many premature obituaries before the death blow of television and the new consumerism of the 1950s.

Among its great variety of acts, music hall's most distinctive idiom was the comic song, commonly an account of some episode in everyday life, enlivened by parody, double entendre, and the performer's active engagement with the audience. Audiences were predominantly working- and lower middle-class, with a high proportion of single young men and women. Improved amenities in the late century attracted middle-class families, when managerial controls had greatly reduced boisterous exchanges between audience and performer and the latter's alleged indecencies. Though the great stars still maintained an active intimacy with their audience, the transformation from pub to syndicated variety theater produced a generally more passive and homogenized public.

There is as yet no single, comprehensive scholarly study available, but the new interest in popular culture has advanced critical analysis of music hall as business and cultural form. The main interpretive issue, with mostly pessimistic conclusions, has been its function in sustaining or eroding an authentic working-class consciousness in an incipient mass culture. Attention to its representations of nation, race, and gender is growing, but important areas still underresearched include nonsong acts and the whole post-1914 period. As a prototype modern entertainment industry, music hall remains a major testing ground for the study of cultural production under capitalism. (*See also* Popular Culture; Vaudeville)

Peter Bailey

REFERENCES

Bailey, Peter, ed. *Music Hall: The Business of Pleasure.* Milton Keynes, Eng.: Open University Press, 1986.

Bratton, J.S., ed. *Music Hall: Performance Style.* Milton Keynes, Eng.: Open University Press, 1986.

Senelick, Laurence, et al. *British Music Hall, 1840–1923: Bibliography and Guide to Sources.* Hamden, CT: Archon, 1981.

N

Naming Practices

Names are important; names are identity. Names, however, denote an identity that is bestowed upon one by others, such as parents or associates (in the case of nicknames), for their reasons, not for those of the named. Thus, naming practices are a social invention and can be a social tool. Historians have just recently begun investigating how and why people transmit certain first names to their offspring.

In Christian society godparents performed the religious and social duty of naming their godchildren. In premodern England and France, godparents traditionally gave their own name to their godchildren. Thus, if parents wished to commemorate a certain name, they had to ensure that the godparent naming the child was so named. Unlike English and French godparents, Florentine godparents did not give their godchildren their own names. In fact, they did not have any freedom in the choice of the name given. Godparents simply transmitted the parents' wishes. In a recent survey of first names from Tuscan official records (including over 60,000

names of household heads drawn from the 1427 Catasto, a registry), David Herlihy (1988) noted a wide variety of sources for Tuscan names: classical, nonsensical, geographic, heroic, weather or time related, religious, and familial. Family and religious names predominated whenever a writer saw fit to explain the choice. According to Tommaso Guidetto, he named his son Manelo because it was an ancient family name and he wished to remake it.

This name remade has been the subject of investigation by Christiane Klapisch-Zuber (1985). Because so many ancestors and dead siblings were the source for so many names, Florentines thought that by giving a child a dead person's name that they could figuratively—if not literally—remake the individual. There was something even taboo about this process. Having a namesake who was still alive brought bad luck to both the child and the namesake. Florentines remade a name only once. To do it again, to rename a child with a name held by two dead relatives, also implied bad luck.

Saints' names have been popular choices for names in all Christian societies. Thirteen of the leading 15 first names in Tuscany in 1427 were those of saints. The church in the liturgy for baptism had always advised that children's names should be those of saints and not pagans. A more important reason to give a child a saint's name was to establish a guardian relationship for the child; considering the many threats to society in the late Middle Ages, children needed divine protection. Another reason to give children the name of a saint was to reflect the parents' own devotion. Parents hoped that the child would grow up in imitation of the saint they favored or admired.

Historians in the United States have traced shifts away from naming children after ancestors, toward greater secularism and individuality (by the late 18th and early 19th centuries), though they caution against oversimple interpretations of naming practices.

Naming practices can be as varied and interesting as there are cultures and people. Social historians have just barely scratched the surface as to why parents gave certain names to their children. (*See also* Ancestor Worship; Godparenting; Ritual)

Louis Haas

REFERENCES

Herlihy, David. "Tuscan Names, 1200–1530," *Renaissance Quarterly* 51 (1988): 561–82.

Klapisch-Zuber, Christiane. *Women, Family, and Ritual in Renaissance Italy.* Chicago: University of Chicago Press, 1985.

Scott-Smith, Daniel. "Child-Naming Practices, Kinship Ties, and Change in Family Attitudes in Hingham, Massachusetts, 1641 to 1880," *Journal of Social History* 18, 4 (1985): 541–566.

Narrative

One of the key questions raised by the gains of social history research involves the form of presentation this research should take. Most historical writing traditionally has been in a narrative mode. This involves, in turn, a fairly clear story line, with beginning and end. Classic historical narratives involved diplomatic negotiations, political campaigns or wars, with well-defined actors and a clear narrative view progressing from initial incidents to some sort of culmination in a treaty, an election victory, or a peace settlement. Causation, in the narrative mode, is usually handled as part of the story, rather than explicitly isolated in the analytical style of the social sciences. Not all history was narrative before the rise of social history—intellectual history had at best a much looser narrative form, since the sequence of ideas has a less obvious story format—but narrative presentations were both common and expected.

Some social history can also be presented in classic narratives. Riots or strikes have tidy story lines, and because protest formed an early entry to social history the issue of narrative was not immediately identified. Much social history writing, however, is not narrative. It involves laying out patterns, testing variables to explain change. Mobility studies or demographic history, based on quantitative patterns and formal causation analysis, do not lend themselves to narrative. Yet social historians have not generated a definite, defendable form of presentation to replace narrative.

For this reason, some social historians and also some critics have argued that the genre is inelegant and unclear, and have urged a return to narrative. In an essay originally published in 1979, the eminent social historian Lawrence Stone (1981) argued that, as social historians turned away from structural determinism, Marxist or other, and from a full commitment to quantification, they must inevitably reengage the narrative mode. He connected new narrative possibilities with growing interest in rituals, in mentalities, and in human emotions as part of social history. Some social historians have conscientiously experimented with unorthodox narratives to illustrate and dramatize social history findings. A massacre of cats by Paris artisans in the 1730s, for example, offers a vivid narrative line that can then be analyzed in terms of attitudes to animals and premodern protest forms.

Disputes about narrative have died down in recent years, as audiences become accustomed to diverse forms of historical presentation including formal analytical categories in addition to narrative. Interestingly, Lawrence Stone's subsequent work has continued to present unfolding patterns, more than narrative story lines. But concern about presentation in social history, especially as part of reaching wider publics and various teaching levels, persists. Museums like colonial Williamsburg, Virginia, for instance, use narrative illustrations in materials designed to communicate to visitors a sense of the patterns of ordinary people and daily life. More generally, discussions of effective presentation continue in a field still in process of definition.

Peter N. Stearns

REFERENCES

Darnton, Robert. *The Great Cat Massacre.* New York: Vintage Books, 1985.

Stone, Lawrence. *The Past and the Present.* Boston: Routledge & Kegan Paul, 1981.

National History

Most people think of history in national units—this is as true in France or China as in the United States. The rise of national histories in the 19th century was part of the movement to focus on political history and to use history to promote citizen loyalty; these motives persist. Social historians often write in a national history framework, sometimes merely assuming this framework, at other times questioning it. When a national state or a demonstrably national culture shapes social development, the national framework is clearly appropriate for social history.

But national history is not always suitable. Sometimes national boundaries are too small to encompass the real factors that mold social trends. Large geographical and economic regions may work better, as in Fernand Braudel's study of the Mediterranean. Some social historians and anthropologists are also identifying larger regions based on family types or on fundamental cultures—this last is a new thrust in the work of the Italian Carlo Ginzburg (1989), analyzing structures of popular mythologies from Siberia to Spain.

Still more social historians focus on subnational regions, arguing that particular economies and cultures shape experiences at this level far more than national factors do. Many *Annales* historians have worked on regional histories of France. American colonial social historians often picked on localities or regions, and the assumption that colonial social history must usually be divided at least in terms of New England, mid-Atlantic, and South is now commonplace, for levels of commerce, religious culture, and landholding patterns all varied widely. Regionalists often criticize even 19th- and 20th-century "American" social history as being defined mainly by the Northeast, assuming without testing that the patterns of this region formed a national norm. Work on the American West as a social history region is active, and the focus on the South, in terms not only of the slave and slaveholding patterns but also regional culture, is well established. Here, however, emphasis on a distinctive South has recently been countered by some careful work that argues that many southerners shared family ideals and other cultural values with the northern middle class. Even in this case, a regional versus national framework continues to spark a useful debate.

A final drawback of national history for social historians involves implicit emphasis on distinctiveness. American exceptionalists often contended that American values, social structures, or mobility patterns were unusual—that they responded to unique American conditions—without actually comparing with patterns elsewhere, and in some cases their claims were inaccurate. Modern German social history grapples with the notion of a German *Sonderweg*, or special path, in which German society, responding unusually to rapid industrialization, must be viewed as a preparation for the special experience of Nazism. Much recent social history demonstrates that important features of German social development need not be seen as terribly distinctive or viewed through the explanation-for-Nazism lens alone. A similar revision is beginning to move Spanish social history away from a preoccupation with the special experience of the Spanish Civil War, which had led to a sort of Spanish exceptionalism that could inhibit fuller comparisons.

Social history has not, in sum, dethroned the national framework, but it has helped provide alternatives and raise vital questions in what is, currently, an ongoing discussion about how to decide on appropriate geographical context for the major topics of social history. (*See also* American Exceptionalism; Fascism)

Peter N. Stearns

REFERENCES

Fox-Genovese, Elizabeth. *Within the Plantation Household: Black and White Women of the Old South.* Chapel Hill: University of North Carolina Press, 1988.

Ginzburg, Carlo. *Clues, Myths, and Historical Method.* Translated by John and Ann Tedeschi. Baltimore: Johns Hopkins University Press, 1989.

Goody, Jack. *Comparative Studies in Kinship.* Stanford, CA: Stanford University Press, 1969.

Stearns, Peter N., and Herrick Chapman. *European Society in Upheaval: Social History Since 1750.* New York: Macmillan, 1991.

Nationalism

Nationalism is not so much an ideology like other "isms" as it is an ethic, a pervasive modern assumption as to how the legitimate use of physical force in human affairs is constrained by people's identities and loyalties. The world is conceived to be a set of natural collectivities, normally resident in discrete territories and known as "nations." Between nations warfare is held to be always a possibility which might, under certain circumstances, be a legitimate course of action for one party or the other; within a single nation warfare is regarded as profoundly unnatural and, should it occur, as automatically calling into question the very claim to nationhood. The assumption is more often articulated in terms of the relationship between the nation and a more concrete entity, the state, which the German sociologist Max Weber defined in terms of a monopoly of the legitimate use of force within a given territory. The principle of nationality counsels statesmen to draw the boundaries of states, insofar as possible, along the boundaries of nations, and to ensure that the government of any state is composed of members of the nation to which it corresponds.

Of course nations are not natural. They are "imagined communities"—social constructions by groups seeking to legitimate their own acquisition or use of force or to delegitimate that of others. And the assumptions of nationalism are relatively modern. To understand how nationalism became the dominant modern ethic of coercion we should begin with the alternative social constructions which it replaced. As monarchies in early modern Europe made progress toward monopolizing force within their territories, they relied for legitimation primarily on claims of a divinely ordained right to rule backed by popular belief in semimagical powers of anointed kings. The fact that only a small proportion of the population were active participants in the polity no doubt made it easier for such means of legitimation to succeed. In the 18th and 19th centuries secularization undermined traditional dynastic claims to legitimacy in western Europe while polities expanded to include much more than narrow traditional elites. So the dysfunctionality of older legitimating myths is the context of the rise of nationalism.

Nationalists often stress the possession of a common and distinct language as evidence of nationhood. Actually, language is probably less useful in accounting for the success of particular groups in gaining recognition as nations than it is in explaining the general phenomenon of nationalism in the modern world. The universal literacy demanded in an industrial society, according to Gellner (1983), forces people out of the context-bound communication of the village into the world of impersonal communication appropriate to the abstract relationships of common nationality. Anderson (1983) points to the newspaper as enabling modern people to imagine themselves as communing with millions of persons they have never met, and the rise of "print languages" in the 16th and 17th centuries as alternatives to both the sacred languages (Latin, Arabic) by which elites associated themselves with more universal imagined communities and local dialects of ordinary folk.

Why have some groups whose territory did not correspond to the polity in which they lived, and not others, made an issue of their nationality? Part of the answer probably lies in the uneven spread of the benefits of industrialization. To take a simple case, the much greater strength of nationalism in Catholic Ireland than in lowland Scotland is no doubt due in part to the substantially greater lag of the former behind England in the 19th century. At the same time, upwardly mobile Scots probably enjoyed more access to opportunities in London than did their Irish Catholic counterparts. Although nationalist movements almost invariably celebrate peasant culture, they are usually led by urban intellectuals many of whom stand to benefit from the access to public employment which would result from their group's claim to nationhood being sustained.

The fact that the existing elite of the disadvantaged group making a nationalist claim is ordinarily the first group to benefit from the fulfillment of that claim does lend some color to the Marxist characterization of nationalism as a form of "false consciousness" into which the working classes are duped. Perhaps the tendency of dynastic and multinational states such as Russia and Britain to foster nationalisms of their own at the end of the 19th century is a better example. All these cases, however, illustrate the fundamental failure of Marxism to come to terms with nationalism rather than simply dismissing it.

Will nationalism continue to enjoy the unquestioned primacy which it held throughout the 20th century? The prospect of European integration, and the apparent alliance of Europeanists with subnational ethnic groups seems likely to compromise nationality as a model for political legitimacy in the very region where it originated. On the other hand, at the time of this writing, the political disintegration of the Soviet Union and Yugoslavia along ethnic lines suggests that nationalism is still very much alive.

Social scientists who are not historians sometimes confuse nationalism with ethnicity, begging the question why only a few hundred of the thousands of groups who might do so actually erect their ethnic distinctiveness into a claim for political self-determination. To avoid such confusion one must understand the phenomenon in time, and even conventional treatments by political and intellectual historians, which make clear the time-bound character of nationalism, are useful in that regard. Indeed, most formal histories of nationalism deal with diplomacy and doctrine primarily. Social historians, however, can make a distinct contribution to the study of nationalism by bringing to it both modern understandings of identity formation—what causes groups to become nationalist, and where nationalism fits a broader mentality. Social historians also adopt the discipline's usual skepticism of models of human nature as invariant in time and space. In doing so, they locate the topic at the interface of state and society, where empirical study of particular polities and ethnic groups in the past can clarify the applicability of the theoretical perspectives suggested above. (*See also* Cultural History; Ethnicity; National History)

David W. Miller

REFERENCES

Anderson, Benedict. *Imagined Communities: Reflections on the Origin and Spread of Nationalism.* London: Verso Editions, 1983.

Gellner, Ernest. *Nations and Nationalism.* Ithaca, NY: Cornell University Press, 1983.

Smith, Anthony D. *Theories of Nationalism.* London: Duckworth, 1971.

Weber, Eugen. *Peasants Into Frenchmen: The Modernization of Rural France from 1870–1914.* Stanford, CA: Stanford University Press, 1976.

Native Americans

The social history of Native Americans (or North American Indians) is still in its infancy. For over a century, anthropology was the primary academic field encouraging enquiry in Native American studies. In the past 30 to 40 years, ethnohistory, which is a melding of anthropological and historical method, has dominated. Ethnohistory is like social history in its intent to tell history from the bottom up, and like social historians, ethnohistorians must deal with the problem of how people at the bottom left behind few records of their own creation. The following overview of the field, which is based on literature in ethnohistory and social history, covers these subtopics: ethnic identity, historical demography, family, gender, class, and economic dependency.

Shifting cultural and political identities were probably commonplace in pre-Columbian North America. However, European contact accelerated this process as communities devastated by disease and warfare regrouped. At the time of European contact, there were several hundred cultural groups in North America, distinguishable by different languages, legends, social structures, and economies. Today, there are still several hundred tribes in the United States and Canada, distinguishable in most cases by their political status as federally recognized tribes. Intermarriage and post–World War II migration to urban areas have made Indian and tribal identities debatable issues. Moreover, in the 19th century other identities emerged as a common feature of reservation factionalism. To gain legitimacy for their views, many Indians began using terms like "fullblood," "mixed blood" ("metis" in Canada), "traditionalist," or "progressive." Social historians have just begun researching how Indians in the past identified the boundaries of their community and manipulated ethnic identity to fulfill larger goals.

Indian historical demography has mostly aimed to estimate the size of the population in 1492 and the extent of the subsequent population decline. Using a variety of methods, scholars have arrived at population estimates for the area above the Rio Grande ranging from under one million to 18 million. Not knowing more definitively the size of the population at the time of contact makes measuring the population decline difficult, but everyone agrees that it was catastrophic. Old World diseases, to which the Indians had no immunities, were the primary cause of the population decline. But also environmental disruption and increased warfare played a role. Unfortunately, few scholars have as yet drawn on the methods of social history to ask questions about Indian demography since 1492. There is much research still to be done on marriage, migration, fertility, household structure, and the life course.

Most research on native families has origins in anthropology and consequently focuses on kinship systems and the social obligations inherent in certain kin roles. Kinship and lineage systems varied greatly in native North America. Some tribes were matrilineal, others patrilineal, and others bilateral. Lineage determined clan, which determined property inheritance, available marriage partners, ceremonial roles, and mutual responsibility. Despite dramatic dissimilarities in native societies, it is safe to say that the family was in all cases the essential principle underlying the social, political, and economic structures of everyday life. Many scholars contend that after European contact Indians adopted the Euro-American model of a patriarchal, nuclear family. The suggested mechanisms for this transition include religious revitalization movements, government policies like the boarding school sys-

tem, and such "modernizing" influences as the introduction of wage work.

In native North America, gender was nearly as important as family in determining one's place in the community. Gender dictated each individual's economic role and prescribed appropriate behavior for men and women. Men usually went to war and hunted. Women planted corn, squash, and beans or gathered roots, berries, and nuts. Despite distinct boundaries between male and female, many Indian cultures allowed individuals to choose their gender identity. Given the name "berdache" by the French, some men essentially became women and did women's work. Similarly, women could opt to take on the male role. The historical literature on gender examines the changes resulting from European contact, usually arguing that women lost power and status through the introduction of capitalism or because Euro-American missionaries, schools, and policymakers successfully forced their own gender ideology on native people. Recent research on native women qualifies this interpretation and proposes that women continued to be influential community activists throughout the 20th century.

There has been little research thus far on social class in Native American history, probably because few native societies had such a concept. Age, gender, clan, and most importantly achievement—powerful visions, success in war, persuasive speaking abilities, and generosity—usually determined authority. Most native economies functioned according to the principle of economic reciprocity. Sharing was the dominant ethic, and people who accumulated wealth risked being ostracized or accused of witchcraft. European contact probably led to an inequality of wealth and imbalance of power within native communities. The horse, for example, arrived in the Americas with the Spanish and quickly became a symbol of wealth, achievement, and honor among Plains Indians. Indian participation in the European fur trade also may have elevated certain individuals to positions of power.

Scholars have devoted more effort to tracing the emergence of Indian economic dependency and point to the fur trade as crucial to this process. Although some tribes became powerful middlemen in the fur trade and benefited from their ability to control the trade throughout a large territory, the benefits were short-lived. As the fur trade exhausted beaver resources in one region and moved further west, tribes in the East could no longer trade in furs nor return to their old way of life. Euro-American settlement followed the fur trade, and land loss, the slaughtering of the buffalo, and disruptive government policies contributed to economic dependency.

Although researchers in Native American history were slow to incorporate the ideas and methods generated by social historians, much work has been done in the past few years, suggesting that Native American social history is a growing field. (*See also* Ethnicity; Latin American Ethnicity; Latin American Racism)

Nancy Shoemaker

REFERENCE

Sturtevant, William C., ed. *Handbook of North American Indians.* Washington, DC: Smithsonian Institution, 1978 to forthcoming.

Neighborhoods

"Neighborhood" is, on first glance, a self-evident term. It demarcates an urban residential area bounded in a way that sets it apart from other such districts. Concrete evidence of neighborhoods can be found by looking at any good city map, where names like "the Castro," "Chelsea," and "Montmartre" provide symbolic identities for discrete city quarters. But for social historians, a neighborhood is more than an intracity, bounded residential unit. That definition describes its geographical parameters in spatial terms, but social historians have become interested in exploring the ways in which neighborhoods function as loci for social relationships—especially those that develop between and among people of different genders and races, ethnic and religious groups, or economic and occupational categories.

Traditionally, social historians looked for the way these relationships played out elsewhere—in the family, at the workplace, or in the city at large. The neighborhood, however, offers a different kind of laboratory, where historians observe the social interactions that develop among people living in close proximity. By recognizing the special relationships formed in this way, so-cial historians have added another dimension to the analysis of people's daily lives: that where they live is as much a part of their identity as where they work.

For most social historians, the questions of where people live and how that affects their identity cannot be answered without attempting to understand the underlying relationships of power. Neighborhoods, as with any other social institution, tend to reflect and re-create the power hierarchies of the society at large. In this broader context, then, the neighborhood is an urban residential unit that embodies a set of relationships that are shaped by existing power structures. In any modern city, the juxtaposition of affluent, tree-lined streets and their poorer counterparts illustrates the reality of hierarchical space. While this point is visually obvious, social historians ask how these contrasts originated, what their impact has been, and how they change over time.

For example, the image of "rich" and "poor" neighborhoods that we recognize as paradigmatic in today's cities only materialized with the process of industrialization. In preindustrial cities, neighborhoods looked very different. Segregation generally occurred within neighborhoods rather than between them. The poorer families either lived on the top floor of houses or in housing units hidden in the inner courtyards behind more affluent residences. Thus, the poor were hidden in the interstices of apparently prosperous neighborhoods. This type of residential pattern fit the economic structure of the preindustrial city, where small-scale business and industry was carried on in the neighborhoods and sometimes in the homes where people lived. A hierarchy of space still existed, but its shape reflected an economic system in which the home and the workplace were still closely linked for all social classes.

This type of neighborhood began to change with the onset of industrialization and the consequent separation of home and workplace. In European cities, the construction of factories on the outskirts of the old city led workers and peasants to move to these areas to be near the new industrial jobs. As the men entered factories, their wives often stayed home, but no longer shared in the financial maintenance of the household. Although some women also entered factory work, the general pattern altered. As a result, the whole rhythm of neighborhood life changed, as men went off to work in the morning and their wives appropriated the streets during the daily pursuit of their domestic tasks.

By the early 20th century, then, residential patterns in the industrialized cities had changed dramatically. Workers and the factories in which they worked were isolated in neighborhoods outside the center, which were usually hastily thrown up and lacking in basic services. Often built near railroad stations, they were literally on the "wrong side of the tracks," an epithet that captures the sense of both segregation and hierarchy. On the other hand, affluent residents either continued to live in the commercial center of the city (the continental European model) or moved out of the city entirely (the American and British model) into new areas called suburbs. Literally "beyond the city," suburbs were explicitly envisioned to be a peaceful haven for affluent residents to escape the industrial world they had created.

Over the course of a century, then, the demands of industrial capitalist development reshaped existing residential patterns, with the help of city planners who encouraged the new segregation of classes. But that is only half the story. The evolution of segregated working-class neighborhoods often created new social ties between residents, who shared many of the same problems. In contrast to preindustrial neighborhoods, where poor residents were spread throughout the city, the concentration of workers in certain neighborhoods could lead to the development of strong social and sometimes political bonds. Residential ties tended to be stronger in these working-class neighborhoods, in contrast to more affluent areas, where residents had greater mobility and the resources to form ties and alliances that extended beyond the neighborhood. In fact, the importance of neighborhood networks to one's identity seemed to be in an inverse relationship to one's mobility. Thus, working-class women, for whom the neighborhood was virtually their only "public sphere," used it as a primary arena for expressing solidarity and collective discontent.

Ironically then, the residential pattern created by the development of industrial capitalism inadvertently encouraged the formation of a new kind of residential community. Put another way, working-class neighborhoods were often able to translate segregation and isolation from the rest of the city into internal solidarity and sometimes political opposition, although this solidarity was still limited by divisions between races, ethnic groups, and men and women. The result of this dynamic is that the neighborhood can be seen as an arena of struggle in which battles for social, economic, and political control take place.

While studies of working-class neighborhoods (or, in the United States, immigrant neighborhoods) have yielded important understanding, other aspects of the history of neighborhoods, and particularly neighbors' relations in terms of such values as the nuclear family and personal privacy, remain to be explored. This applies to middle-class and suburban neighborhoods and to the definitions and functions of neighborhoods in the mid- to late 20th century. (*See also* Cities; Community; Household Economy; Industrialization; Suburbanization; Working Class)

Pamela Radcliff

REFERENCES

Garrioch, David. *Neighborhood and Community in Paris, 1740–1790.* Cambridge: Cambridge University Press, 1986.

Slayton, Robert A. *Back of the Yards: The Making of a Local Democracy.* Chicago: University of Chicago Press, 1986.

Stovall, Tyler. *The Rise of the Paris Red Belt.* Berkeley: University of California Press, 1990.

Neolithic Revolution

The Neolithic Age (New Stone Age), which began in the 9th millennium BC, may be the most important period in human history since the emergence of our species. It was the epoch during which people domesticated plants and animals and established permanent villages. Domestication means the taming and manipulation of wild animals and plants. Doing so produces more food than having to hunt and gather wild varieties. It also means that people stayed in one place to raise their food and to store the surpluses that farming brought them. All civilizations, past and present, sprang from these innovations. So dramatic was the change in human life that the name "Neolithic revolution" has been applied to the era.

In reality the change was not sudden. As the last ice age ended and climate grew much warmer, human groups became increasingly sedentary. In several parts of the world they settled into specific territories and built more or less permanent houses. In many places such as Jericho near the Dead Sea, first occupied some 12,000 years ago, archaeologists have found settlements where wild food resources were so abundant that people lived by simply collecting them. Only when the populations in settlements grew too large to support by gathering did people begin to use the land and animals more intensively—by planting grain and raising animals. All evidence suggests that women were the first domesticators of plants, the first farmers. It was they who gathered plants and who bore and raised children. The many female figurines found near hearths and in food storage areas in these ancient houses is one piece of evidence among many. In the early Neolithic, and probably before, the idea of hearth and home, birth, and growing grain centered on women. Later mythologies all around the world tell of this idea.

The earliest Neolithic villages appeared in southwestern Asia, in the hilly country that lies between Iraq and Iran and in the Levant, during the 9th millennium BC. The basic foodstuffs here were large seeded grasses—wheat and barley—and animals such as sheep, goats, and cattle. From these areas farmers migrated to neighboring regions, spreading the idea of farming to peoples they encountered there. By 6500 BC, for instance, southeastern Europe had vast networks of villages stretching from Greece into the Ukraine on the east and the central Danubian river valley on the west. During the next millennium and a half pioneer farmers colonized the rest of the European Continent until they reached the British Isles around 5000 BC. Within the next 2,000 years, farming communities would develop into the civilizations of the major river valleys, Mesopotamia and the Nile. Meanwhile, the farmers of Europe created elaborate societies on their own, societies that built the large stone monuments of the Atlantic seaboard. Similarly, the idea of plant and animal domestication spread across Africa, into sub-Saharan regions by the 1st millennium BC. Here complex village cultures such as the Nok appeared.

In other parts of the world, similar processes brought forth settled villages and farming. These were independent of southwestern Asia. In Thailand and southern China, village life centering on growing rice and domesticated water buffalo developed by the 5th millennium BC, though earliest dates might be around 7000 BC. From there rice growing spread to India and the rest of southeastern Asia. The northern Chinese Neolithic dates to the 6th millennium BC, with villages established in the Huanghe (Yellow River) area. Millet was the main crop, with cattle, sheep, pigs, and dogs as domesticated animals. Over the next 2,500 years, sophisticated pottery-making traditions emerged, followed by a bronze technology. As villages grew larger, leaders appeared, accumulating wealth and power. By the late Neolithic Age some villages turned into towns and from these came the great historic civilizations of China. As in southwestern Asia, farming formed the base for all civilizations.

Across the world's oceans, in the Americas, domestication of plants and animals also took place. In Central and South America more than 100 plants were cultivated, many more than in other parts of the world, but fewer animals. In ancient Mexico, for example, only the dog, turkey, and some beetles were raised. In all the Americas, maize was the staple crop. It may have been propagated first in central Mexico or parts of western South America by the 6th millennium BC. Beans and squash have an even earlier history. As elsewhere, villages flourished, eventually giving rise to dense populations and high civilizations—Olmecs, Maya, and eventually Aztecs in Mexico, Chavin and finally Incas in Peru, among others. The story here is the same as elsewhere: all civilizations, all modern societies, derive from the human domestication of the natural world.

The development of settled villages and changes in work relationships between men and women were two obvious consequences of Neolithic revolution; so was a marked increase in human population. Elements of this sort form a framework for much of the social history of subsequent agricultural societies and civilizations. (*See also* Agricultural Systems)

Bruce Kraig

REFERENCES

Cole, Sonia. *The Neolithic Revolution.* New York: New American Library, 1970.

Wenke, R.J. *Patterns in Prehistory.* New York: Oxford University Press, 1990.

NEP Era

NEP, or New Economic Policy, has often been studied from the standpoint of government policy alone, as part of the aftermath of the Bolshevik Revolution in the Soviet Union. Social historians have explored additional facets of the policy's impact on major social groups, and also the more general atmosphere of experimentation that accompanied the policy in Soviet society and culture.

The period of Soviet history popularly known as NEP lasted from the adoption of the New Economic Policy in 1921 to the mass campaigns for collectivization and industrialization in 1929. The Bolshevik Party had successfully seized power in October 1917 and defended it in the bloody civil war that followed. But by 1921, the country's industrial base was devastated, its cities starved and depopulated. The policy of forcible grain requisitioning adopted during the civil war to feed the cities and the Red Army had resulted in reduced sowing, widespread hoarding, and outright rebellion among the peasants. Once the war ended, the Party sought to rebuild the shattered economy, repair relations with the peasantry, and increase the supply of food to the cities. In March 1921, the 10th Party Congress voted to abolish the system of grain requisitioning and replace it with an agricultural tax in kind. Peasants were given the right to trade their surplus grain, over and above the tax, on the free market. Over the next year and a half, the Party also voted to permit individuals and cooperatives to lease small enterprises from the state, to decentralize control of the economy, to introduce strict methods of cost accounting (profitability) into state-run enterprises, and to allow the limited use of hired labor and land rental in agriculture. In many industries, the former "bourgeois" managers returned to their old posts. The Party stabilized the financial system and restored the state budget. By 1922, the transition to commercial principles was complete.

NEP proved highly successful in restoring industry to its prewar level of production and in increasing agricultural output. The peasantry flourished, food was once again available through a thriving network of state stores and private retailers, and workers returned to the cities to rebuild ruined industries. Yet despite NEP's unquestionable economic success, it provoked intense debate throughout the 1920s. Party members argued fiercely about whether NEP signified a temporary, albeit necessary, retreat, or an advance toward socialism. Critics of NEP pointed to both a prospering class of businessmen and speculators (NEPmen) who flaunted their new wealth in the face of an impoverished working class and the growing strength of the richer peasants (*kulaks*) who hired labor, expanded their plots, and controlled the supply of grain to the cities. Both groups were seen as obstacles to the development of socialism. Other critics deplored cuts in state spending for social services, a reappearance of prostitution, and widespread unemployment, especially among women.

The NEP era was marked by great creative ferment in the arts, the law, education, and other areas of social life. Artists, workers, designers, architects, soldiers, writers, jurists, and Party members, animated by the prospect of building a new society, sought to remake life in every aspect. They created new revolutionary festivals and holidays to replace those of the Orthodox church. Red weddings and "Octobering" ceremonies replaced religious marriage and baptism. Parents rejected traditional Russian names in favor of Marks, Engelina, Parizhkommuna (Paris Commune), and Revmir (revolution and peace). The government approved a radical Family Code in 1926 that legislated equal rights for women, abolished illegitimacy, established divorce at the request of either party, and recognized cohabitation as the juridical equal of marriage. Many couples rejected marriage entirely. Numerous movements among writers and artists spawned new journals devoted to poetry, fiction, art, and criticism.

Political life, inside and outside the Party, was also marked by relative, although dwindling, freedom. Party members openly debated the future of NEP, the pace of industrialization, the organization of agriculture, foreign policy, and Party democracy. After Lenin's death in 1924, Stalin, Zinoviev, and Kamenev defeated Trotsky in a bitter struggle over control of the Party's leadership. Having destroyed the left wing of the Party, Stalin moved against its right wing. He launched a massive campaign to collectivize agriculture and industrialize the nation, bringing the economic and political freedom of NEP to an end by 1929.

Although NEP lasted less than a decade it continued to play an important role in subsequent economic and political debates. The model of NEP was used by Soviet economic reformers in the late 1950s and 1960s, and again by Gorbachev in the 1980s, to foster greater freedom, initiative, and efficiency. The NEP model has also influenced socialist planners throughout the world, shaping postwar debates and policy in Yugoslavia, Cuba, China, and Vietnam. (*See also* Russian Revolution; State and Society)

Wendy Goldman

REFERENCES

Carr, E.H. *The Bolshevik Revolution, 1917–1923*, Vol. 2. London: Macmillan, 1952.

Danilov, V.P. *Rural Russia Under the New Regime.* Bloomington: Indiana University Press, 1988.

Fitzpatrick, Sheila, Alexander Rabinowitch, and Richard Stites, eds. *Russia in the Era of NEP: Explorations in Soviet Society and Culture.* Bloomington: Indiana University Press, 1991.

Lewin, Moshe. *Political Undercurrents in Soviet Economic Debates: From Bukharin to the Modern Reformers.* Princeton, NJ: Princeton University Press, 1974.

Stites, Richard. *Revolutionary Dreams: Utopian Vision and Experimental Life in the Russian Revolution.* New York and Oxford: Oxford University Press, 1989.

Nobility

See Aristocracy

Nomadism

"Nomads" for this article are defined by their economic function of raising livestock by moving their herds to food instead of moving feed to the animals, although some societies maintained a high degree of mobility for hunting (Native Americans, Eskimos) or other purposes (Gyp-

sies). Of necessity, then, their production takes place outside of major urban areas. Nonetheless, they have been dependent upon settled populations for economic exchange for as long as their existence has been recorded. Although the camel-raising bedouin of the Middle East are those commonly known in the West, sheep-raising nomads of the Middle East and Asia, horse-raising nomads of central Asia, reindeer nomads of northern Europe, and cattle-raising nomads of Africa and the Eurasian steppes have also been historically important. Nomads raiding border areas often became the new ruling groups: the Arabs in the Middle East, the Mongols in China and the Middle East, and the Turks in the Ottoman Empire are prominent examples. Because nomadic traditions do not provide patterns for long-term rule over conquered areas, these nomads often encouraged urban development and incorporated the ruling traditions of the conquered people. The leaders of these conquering tribes then formed an elite class that received tribute from the population.

In general, nomads own land collectively, apportioning it for grazing according to ever-changing factors, which are ecological (rainfall, demography), political (power structures in the community), and external (rules of new state formations, changing areas of cultivation). Animals are usually privately owned by individuals or by households. Herds, not land, constitute wealth in these communities, and social organization arises from the ownership of animals and the need to move in order to feed them. Although the social structure varies considerably between groups, societies are frequently organized by tribes, whose membership is determined by birth, marriage, or other affiliation. In many cases women own household possessions and keep the income from butter-making, food-gathering, and craft production, but in societies where wealth is determined by livestock ownership, men are more powerful than women, who do not commonly possess herds. In some tribes, control over their sons' livestock increases women's power; in others the possession of certain skills and age affords them more authority in tribal decisions. There is wide divergence in the roles and status of women in nomadic societies, owing largely to the enormous variation in location, production, and traditions of these groups. Debate over women's roles still continues as outsiders try to understand the gender division of power and labor and the way nomadic women perceive their own experience.

Nomadic groups do not constitute separate societies encapsulated apart from the settled societies around them. One of the principal themes in the new social history of nomadism involves recognition of change in nomadic structures and in interactions with other groups. Although urban dwellers have often viewed nomads as a destructive force, recent scholarship has focused on the economic importance of nomads and their symbiotic relationship with the settled populations. Nomads in the past were important consumers of agricultural and manufactured goods produced in urban centers. They owned the primary means of transportation (camels), the most important articles of war (horses), and the readiest supply of meat, milk, and hides (cattle, sheep, goats). Indeed, nomads were so important to settled society that they often controlled market towns and oases in the Middle East (such as Mecca). Sheikhs, or tribal leaders, bought urban property, while urban merchants often invested in animals which they entrusted to nomads to raise. Poorer nomads also moved in and out of settled society, engaging in wage labor, trading in the markets, or stepping out to farm or hunt in order to acquire the capital to invest in herds.

In spite of this symbiotic economic relationship, conflict also has characterized the interaction between nomads and settled peoples. The opposition between these groups changed as the historical context evolved. When governments attempted to centralize control in the 19th-century Middle East, nomads rebelled against the imposition of new laws and the collection of taxes. At times when market agriculture brought high profits, cultivation spread and nomads raided the new farms which encroached on their grazing areas. If a government attempted to take over trading centers and trade routes, nomads revolted against the loss of their power base and economic prosperity. Notorious for their depredations, the nomads in the Syrion Desert engaged not only in random violence but more importantly employed warfare in competition over scarce resources or in protest over perceived wrongs. Some scholars have suggested that the Mongol nomads conquered settled areas in order to guarantee access to the urban markets upon which they depended for food and tools.

Like the broader culture, nomadic communities were affected by political changes such as colonization and new forms of government; by warfare, which threatened their population and their livestock; and by economic transitions, which altered the demand for their products and modified the methods of production. Nomads were seldom passive in these processes of change; they were not merely captured by modern global forces of colonialism and market economies. For example, although slave trade and colonialism disrupted nomadic life in East Africa, nomads used the resulting trade in ivory to recover after disease decimated their herds in the 19th century. Increasing animal production to meet the demands of the market combined with natural disaster to produce the famine in East Africa during the 1960s and 1970s. Changes within the societies followed as new class relations emerged in response to the cash-cropping in animal products. Barfield (1981) shows that the growth of cash-cropping in nomadic pastoral products led to a form of "agro-pastoral" combine with great concentration of wealth and the employment of lower-class nomads as wage laborers, while its absence promoted a more egalitarian political structure and stable nomadic population. (*See also* Agricultural Systems; Honor Codes; Market Economy; Military and Society; Pastoralism; Tribe)

Sarah Shields

REFERENCES

Barfield, Thomas J. *The Central Asian Arabs of Afghanistan: Pastoral Nomadism in Transition.* Austin: University of Texas Press, 1981.

Dyson-Hudson, Rada and Neville. "Pastoralism," in Bernard J. Siegel, ed., *Annual Review of Anthropology* 9 (1980): 15-61.

Khazamov, A.M. *Nomads and the Outside World.* Cambridge: Cambridge University Press, 1983.

Shields, Sarah D. "Sheep, Nomads, and Merchants in Nineteenth-Century Mosul: Creating Transformations in an Ottoman Society," *Journal of Social History* 25, 4 (1992).

Weissleder, Wolfgang, ed. *The Alternative: Modes and Models of Interaction in the African-Asian Desert and Steppes.* The Hague: Mouton Publishers, 1978.

Old Age

Continuities matter as much as changes in old-age history. Since the incidence of long-term disability and chronic disease increases with age, people have differentiated for centuries between a "green old age" (which is healthful and vital) and "senectitude," or "second childhood" (in which a person requires care). Gerontologists still distinguish between the "young-old" and the "old-old." Death marks life's finitude. Such biological realities have always colored perceptions of advancing years.

Adventurers, charlatans, and scholars have long sought to prolong life. But scientists have not yet discovered an elixir, nor can they separate cause and effect in senescence. Biological aging, experts believe, is played out at the genetic level, which partly explains why there has been no change in human life potential. Most people do not survive to the maximum life span, although 20th-century changes in life expectancy at birth, at age 40, and at age 60 have altered the meanings and experiences of old age.

There has never been a consensus in Western culture about which birthday, above 50 or under 80 (if any) signals old age. Senescence is not just biologically determined; it is also socially constructed. Centuries of motifs, folk wisdom, reinterpretations of classical texts, and "scientific" observation reflect the fears, hopes, struggles, successes, failures, and adaptations that people have felt and experienced. There have never been dramatic, sudden changes in attitudes or behavior. Modernization theory does not explain much: Turning points in the history of old age do not dovetail neatly with broader currents in economic, social, cultural, and political history.

Demographers estimate that two-thirds of the improvement in longevity since prehistoric times has occurred since 1900—hence, old age became a greater "problem" in this century. Yet the average life expectancy of U.S. men aged 40 in 1940 was only a year greater than in 1790. Forty-year-old women in 1940 on average could expect to live three years longer than ones in 1790.

A smaller proportion of blacks than whites live past age 65. The disparity has widened over time. By 1985, the elderly constituted 8 percent and 13 percent, respectively, of black and white populations. Similarly, immigration tended to make the United States "young" in the 1800s. Roughly a fifth of the older population was foreign-born in 1870. Immigration laws passed since the 1920s swelled the proportion of all foreign-born people who are old, from 9.7 percent in 1920 to 33.5 percent by 1960. The graying of the burgeoning U.S. Hispanic population will alter future patterns.

Historically, on average, women have lived longer than men. Despite this comparative advantage, they suffer a greater incidence of disease and disability. Divergent life expectancies create other differences. Older men have been more likely to be married than older women: in 1986, the figures were 77 percent and 40 percent. In the same year, half of all women over 65 were widows, a total five times greater than the number of widowers. The percentage of divorced older persons has risen.

Living arrangements have changed over time. A century ago more than 75 percent of all males over 65 were heads of household. With advancing age, many men and even more women reportedly live(d) with a child, in-law, or sibling. Few, however, went to an almshouse. Never has more than 5 percent of the population over 65 been in institutions. There has been a dramatic rise in the number of older people living alone. Roughly 40 percent of all women and 15 percent of all men over 65 lived alone in 1986. These figures represent a 68 percent increase since 1970, nearly 300 percent since 1900.

Demographics, however, have not been the sole force shaping images of old age. A deep stain of ageism has manifested itself in divergent ways over time. Unflattering images gained currency around the turn of the century. This focused expert attention on "curing" or at least ameliorating difficulties ascribed to late life. In recent decades, positive ideas about late-life potential were engineered. During the 1950s, a new set of euphemisms—"senior citizen," "golden agers"—came into vogue. Such Pollyannaish conceptions, however, typically ignored significant racial, class, and gender differences within the population.

Welfare laws fostered the sense that the elderly were vulnerable. Statutes based on Elizabethan poor laws held family members responsible for kin who were infirm or dependent. Local elites contributed funds to provide institutional support and financial relief for certain segments of the aged population—spinsters, widows, or hitherto self-sufficient citizens down on their luck. Religious groups operated more than 40 percent of all U.S. old-age social services in 1900.

Concern over old-age dependence was warranted. Employment during the last century became more difficult. Around the Civil War, roughly a quarter of all elderly men left estates worth less than $100. Most aged blacks died penniless. Nineteenth-century native-born elders tended to be better off than their foreign-born counterparts. Since Social Security, the extent of poverty has declined, although improvements in the aged's economic status vary by sex, race, and occupation. Older women remain more economically vulnerable than older men.

Since 1935, an impressive national aging network has emerged. The struggle for Social Security galvanized self-help social and educational groups to "salvage" old age. In the Great Depression, Francis E. Townsend and Upton Sinclair mobilized the old. The American Association of Retired Persons, which started modestly in 1958, now boasts more than 36 million members, making it the second largest social group in the United States after the Roman Catholic church.

Themes in the social history of old age have been developed since the 1970s not only for the United States but also in Europe and, in slightly more modest proportions, several other societies and periods. Attention to cultural standing, family and living arrangements, work and support command leading attention, in a modest but growing social history field. Some explicitly comparative efforts are beginning to emerge. (*See also* Life Course/Life Cycle; Retirement)

W. Andrew Achenbaum

REFERENCES

Achenbaum, W. Andrew. *Social Security.* New York: Cambridge University Press, 1986.

Cole, Thomas R. *Journey of Life*. New York: Cambridge University Press, 1992.

Fischer, David H. *Growing Old in America*. Oxford: Oxford University Press, 1977.

Gratton, Brian. *Urban Elders*. Philadelphia: Temple University Press, 1986.

Haber, Carole. *Beyond Sixty-Five*. New York: Cambridge University Press, 1983.

Stearns, Peter N. *Old Age in European Society*. New York: Holmes and Meier, 1976.

Oral History

"Oral history" refers to verbatim recordings of narratives. It falls within a broader category of evidence which social scientists call personal testimony, that is, statements which have as their subject matter the narrator's own experience. This category includes letters, diaries, court testimony, and memoirs. In most oral histories, an interviewer elicits the information from a subject either through prepared questions or through a less structured approach, recording the conversation on audio tape. Video-taped interviews and transcripts of court testimonies, however, constitute oral history as well. While the use of personal testimony has always been part of social science research, the widespread availability of new recording technologies in recent decades has led to an explosive growth in the collection and dissemination of oral evidence about individual and group experience. Social historians have formed part of this movement and have contributed to the growing numbers of oral history collections established in libraries and archives. While various kinds of historians dealing with recent history use interviews, social historians are particularly interested in oral history as a means of obtaining information about ordinary people and about aspects of life less frequently generating explicit written records, such as family behavior. Social historians concerned with anthropology, often dealing with less literate societies, use oral history to get at earlier time periods, as well as 20th-century experience. Oral history has been fundamental to the development of African social history, for example. The growth of oral history projects has prompted social historians to establish standards for the practice and use of oral history and to examine its relationship to other types of historical data.

An important distinction, however, must be made between personal testimony per se and elicited personal testimony. Though the line between these two types of evidence seems hazy, there is a difference between those narratives about the past voluntarily and single-handedly produced by individuals and those which historians have helped create. When a historian, attorney, or interviewer questions an individual about his or her past experiences the resulting evidence has been jointly created and must be evaluated in terms of its interlocutory dynamic. Oral history evidence should be evaluated in terms of the social and psychological relationship between the interviewer and the interviewee, the circumstances of the interview, and the cultural relevance of the questions being posed. Concerns about the accuracy of memory, and the desirability of supplementary with other evidence, are corollaries of oral history's limitations.

A seminal endeavor at oral history was that undertaken during the Depression by the Federal Writer's Project to record the memories of former slaves in the American South. Subsequently edited and published in 19 volumes by George Rawick (1972ff.), the 2,300 slave narratives collected by unemployed writers and journalists constitute an invaluable body of evidence about antebellum America; however, the Project's methodology was criticized by later historians and researchers. The FWP failed to establish standardized interviewing techniques, and the value of the results varied greatly. Like all initial documentations, this project suffered from a lack of methodological consciousness and rigor.

The process of conducting an oral history interview has a decisive impact on the type of evidence ultimately produced. The interview should ideally take place in a setting where few interruptions will occur and with equipment of a high enough quality to faithfully record the tone and inflections of both the interviewer's and interviewee's voices. Some debate exists among social historians as to the optimal structure of an oral history interview: whether tightly structured questions produce the best evidence or whether looser extemporaneous conversations are more desirable. Each has its advantages. The use of questionnaires has a greater likelihood of producing comparable data easily amenable to further quantitative analysis. Less structured interviews are usually employed when life histories are sought. In these autobiographical narrations, the subject has a more active role in constructing the direction of the tale, and greater meaning can often be extracted.

Another important methodological issue pertains to the reliability of oral history. When possible, secondary source verification of the information provided in any personal testimony evidence is essential. Still, some information cannot be verified. Reliability, however, represents less of a drawback than might be imagined and can be turned to the advantage of the historian. Human memory is both selective and fallible, but, as social scientists have observed, most selection and interpretation occur immediately after an event as part of an individual's coping process. The passage of time, though erosive to the recollection of details, may have little impact on the memory of major events in the life of an individual. If a historian is seeking to reconstruct the detailed daily habits of social groups in the past, personal testimony evidence from a diary would be more reliable than information recorded late in life. On the other hand, if information is sought about how individuals and groups reacted to a specific event or series of events, then an oral history interview conducted years after the fact would be a worthwhile resource because the lasting significance of the event will become apparent to the interviewer. Thus, an oral history interview will record not only the subject's subjective recording of selective events, but will also place the event into his or her life story. The event will be awarded, in a sense, explicative, reiterative meaning.

Since social history places greater emphasis on the experience of groups as opposed to individuals, the issue of the representativeness of oral history data is of central importance. One way to ensure that oral history data reflect the representative experience of the group in question is to use statistical sampling methods in the selection of subjects. Random, clustered, or stratified samples of oral history interviewees, for example, can assure that a representative unit of personal narratives can be assembled as evidence. On the other hand, such measures may not be necessary when the nature of human memory is considered. Studies using oral history evidence have shown that memories are not created in a vacuum but rather that individuals assign meaning to events through a shared discourse. Social scientists have found that when subjects are interviewed much of what they recount constitutes a retelling of narratives that have been passed along and shared within a given social or kinship group. Therefore, though an individual's experience may be unique, to some extent individuals are always a reflection of their group experience and, in a larger sense, the culture to which they belong. These phenomena must be taken into account by historians when analyzing oral history data.

To social historians, the value of the accumulation of oral history and of the methodology itself is that they can be used to document the experiences of groups who might otherwise leave little in the way of qualitative evidence about themselves and their community. Other types of personal testimony evidence, like diaries or autobiographies, tend to record the experiences of the educationally, financially, and socially privileged. Oral history projects, on the other hand, have focused on the experiences of the more ordinary members of society and therefore have proved to be a rich source for the study of popular culture and popular mentalities.

Montserrat Martí Miller

REFERENCES

Bertaux, Daniel. *Biography and Society: The Life History Approach in the Social Sciences.* Beverly Hills: Sage, 1981.

Crapanzano, Vincent, Yasmine Ergas, and Judith Modell. "Personal Testimony: Narratives of the Self in the Social Sciences and the Humanities," *Items* 40, 2 (June 1986).

Dunaway, David K., and Willa Baum, eds. *Oral History: An Interdisciplinary Anthology.* Nashville: American Association of State and Local History, 1984.

Fraser, Ronald. *Blood of Spain: An Oral History of the Spanish Civil War.* New York: Pantheon Books, 1979.

Frisch, Michael. *A Shared Authority: Essays on the Craft and Meaning of Oral Public History.* New York: State University of New York Press, 1990.

Grele, Ronald J. *Envelopes of Sound: The Art of Oral History.* Chicago: Precedent Publishers, 1975.

Organized Crime

The term "organized crime" has become a buzzword in the United States and elsewhere with as many definitions and meanings as there are people discussing it. Worldwide, in the eyes of many people, organized crime conjures up images of machine gun–toting gangsters such as Al Capone and drug-crazed Colombian cocaine traffickers. Social historians have dealt both with the nature of organized crime, and with often dramatic public perceptions.

Contrary to popular opinion, these Hollywood movie images depict a romanticized and incomplete picture of organized crime and the extent of the problem confronting law enforcement. Although sometimes violent, its preferred methods are usually less sanguinary. Although still involved in traditional activities such as prostitution, gambling, and drug trafficking, it is found as often in the boardrooms as in the backrooms. Its success can be seen in the recent estimate of the President's Commission on Organized Crime, which noted that organized criminal enterprises in the United States alone reaped an annual income of more than $100 billion. Its threat, as explained by the Pennsylvania Crime Commission in its 1990 report, *Organized Crime in Pennsylvania: A Decade of Change*, "lies not so much in the crime as in its organization."

Organized crime by definition tends to reflect the organization of culture of the larger "legitimate" society of which it is a part. Thus, organized crime takes different forms in different places. Although various definitions of organized crime are currently used by the U.S. Government, the definition most generally accepted by experts was stated by FBI director William Sessions in his 1988 testimony before the U.S. Congress. The key elements to focus upon when defining organized crime, he stated, are that the "group has some manner of organizational structure, engages in a continuing criminal conspiracy, and has as its primary purpose the generation of profit."

Many scholars cite the early street gangs of 19th-century New York, Boston, Philadelphia, and elsewhere as the origins of organized crime in America. These gangs, each with members of one particular ethnic background, mostly preyed upon their own kind and were involved in the hooliganism that typifies most youth gangs even to this day. Although generally a minor criminal nuisance, these gangs could on occasion become exceptionally violent and dangerous, as witnessed by the infamous Civil War draft riots that many contend were instigated by Irish street gangs.

With few exceptions, however, organized crime in 19th- and 20th-century America was quite parochial. During this period, a gang worked within its own neighborhood and rarely ventured into the territories of neighboring gangs, which were usually of a different ethnic background. Rarely would a gang operate citywide, and none operated nationally.

With the advent of Prohibition, all of this changed. On January 16, 1920, the 18th Amendment to the U.S. Constitution and the Prohibition Enforcement Act (Volstead Act) became effective, forbidding "the manufacture, sale or transportation of intoxicating liquors." Although organized crime had existed in the United States prior to this time, Prohibition along with new regulations on drugs created the economic fertilizer for the growth and flowering of national and international organized criminal enterprises that still exist today.

Prohibition required a change in the structure and activities of the organized criminal gangs that wished to profit by satisfying this artificially created shortage. If a gang was to acquire the alcohol that its neighborhood demanded, it had to learn to deal with other gangs, legitimate businesses, and state and federal officials with whom formerly it would never have dealt. From unsophisticated criminality, those gangs that learned to adapt to the new era of bootlegging became highly organized citywide, statewide, and sometimes even nationwide distribution networks. In short, the gangs that survived had to become as successful in managing their illicit bootlegging enterprises as their capitalist counterparts were in operating legitimate American business.

Although the repeal of Prohibition in 1933 marked the close of an era, it did not end organized crime. Instead, it merely forced the entities to diversify and use their new sophistication and capabilities in a variety of new schemes. Those that anticipated its repeal and/or succeeded in diversifying into new illegal or legal businesses became the new leaders in organized crime. The most enduring and successful organized crime group to do so has been the La Cosa Nostra (LCN), which presently includes 25 Italian American crime syndicates ("Families") and numbers thousands of members and tens of thousands of associates.

Although the U.S. Government was slow to acknowledge organized crime as a problem, the formation of the Federal Bureau of Investigation in the 1920s played heavily on (often exaggerated) public fears of organized crime and of immigrants. The 1970s and 1980s saw the enactment of a series of new laws specifically meant to address organized criminal activity, including the power to conduct electronic surveillance, limited immunity for prosecution, the Witness Protection Program, and the Racketeer Influenced and Corrupt Organizations Act, commonly referred to as RICO.

But organized crime has remained resilient. The traditional view of organized crime as synonymous with the La Cosa Nostra has been proved to be an oversimplification with the emergence over the last 20 years of new forms of organized crime throughout the country. They include a collage of ethnic and nonethnic groups that are organized for long-term criminal purposes and that sometimes link together in powerful criminal enterprises. They include motorcycle gangs, prison gangs, Colombian cartels, Jamaican Posses, Chinese Triad Societies, Vietnamese gangs, Russian emigré groups, and two major Los Angeles street gangs—the Crips and the Bloods—to name a few.

The emergence of these groups represents a new phase in the history of organized crime. Changing demographics and an expansive drug market have led many to organize in pursuit of lucrative profits to be made from drug trafficking, and have dramatically increased the growth and power of these organizations in a relatively short period of time. Many of these groups have armed themselves heavily with sophisticated weaponry and have achieved a level of violence that far surpasses that traditionally associated with the LCN.

From the Mafia of Italy to the Yakuza of Japan, organized crime has long been a challenge facing other countries as well, and it is becoming a potent new force in countries where its influence may have been limited before.

What the U.S. experience shows is that what we commonly refer to as organized crime may evolve from something quite simple—in the U.S. case, from urban street gangs. Shortages of a good or service—in this case, alcohol, from Prohibition—reformulated them into what we now know as modern organized crime. Many observers argue that even today, U.S. organized crime essentially makes most of its income by providing a limited number of goods or services that are otherwise unavailable to members of our society. In the U.S. case, these "shortages" or "deficits"—such as narcotics, prostitution, gambling, hard-core pornography, loan sharking, and money laundering—are generally illegal, and for the most part viewed by Americans as illegitimate.

As the countries of the former USSR and Eastern Europe face increasing economic shortages, many of these same principles are allowing organized criminal activities to flourish. Indeed, the enormous shortages of consumer goods and services of all kinds; the pervasiveness of second, or "underground," economies; the absence of effective law enforcement mechanisms; and a legacy of enormously corrupt systems have led many to conclude that Sessions's definition of organized crime may well apply to the very structures and fabrics of these entire societies. To the extent this is true, despite its growth and resilience in the United States and other more developed countries, "organized crime" may prove to be a far more destructive, dangerous, and intractable problem in these newly emerging countries than anything yet seen in the Western experience. As the U.S. pattern also underscores, even should shortages vanish tomorrow, one will be faced with the task of fighting organized criminal networks—however defined—well into the next century. (*See also* Crime)

Nancy Lubin

REFERENCES

Johnson, David. *Policing the Urban Underworld: The Impact of Crime on the Development of the American Police, 1800–1887.* Philadelphia: Temple University Press, 1979.

Nelli, Humbert S. *The Business of Crime*. New York: Oxford University Press, 1976, pp. 143–178.

Short, Martin. *Crime Inc.* London: Thames Methuen, 1984.

Orientalism

Until the 1978 publication of Edward Said's *Orientalism*, the word "Orientalism" denoted simply a scholarly or artistic preoccupation with the non-European civilizations of the Old World. Both before and after Said's work, Orientalism covered a variety of Western scholarly interests in Asia, including earlier and more recent forms of social history. Though little pursued in the United States until the 1930s, Oriental studies was a recognized discipline in many British and European universities. With thousands of manuscripts in non-European languages lying unread and unedited in European libraries, and hundreds of thousands more still mostly inaccessible in North Africa, the Middle East, India, and China, Europe's 19th-century Orientalists saw manuscript editing as a high calling and perfected methods for producing scholarly editions. For many Orientalists, interpretation was a secondary objective. The model for their work was the discipline of classical studies that had originated in the Renaissance. Academic Oriental studies were formally quite different from Orientalism in art, which usually combined the stylistic precision of academic realism with lurid, and often artificial, subject matter replete with camels, harem girls, ruined palaces, and exotic costumes. But both enterprises involved imagining non-European peoples and cultures at a time when the ruling elites of the Orientalists' countries were occupying themselves with solidifying imperialist rule abroad—for example, the British in India and Malaya, the French in Algeria and Indochina, and the Dutch in Indonesia. Though the scholarly Orientalists spent most of their time in manuscript collections, artists, novelists, and explorers trekked to distant places to record their impressions and feed a politically stimulated popular appetite for exotica.

Just as the Orientalist paintings and travel literature of the imperialist era found a receptive public, so did Edward Said's *Orientalism* (1978) a century or so later. Said maintained that Orientalism was not simply a congeries of scholarly and artistic enterprises, but a pervasive imperialist attitude to which scholars, artists, and novelists alike contributed by writing books that stereotyped the Oriental "other," whether Muslim, Chinese, or Indian, as exotic, weak, cruel, licentious, primitive, and passive. While pointing to a few Orientalists who actively facilitated colonial rule with their scholarship, like the Dutch specialist on Indonesian Islam Snouck Hurgronje, Said made the broader argument that all Orientalists were party to a socially constructed discourse of imperial domination. Though many Orientalists reacted to Said's theory by denying any complicity in imperialism, defending their impressive record in making little known texts available to Europeans and non-Europeans alike, and pointing out the highly selective character of his evidence, the more general response was to recognize his attack as an overdue corrective. That Said himself was a Palestinian (albeit a Christian educated in Anglo-American institutions) enhanced his voice as representing the intellectual victims of imperialism. At the same time, his high standing as a literary theorist (not as a scholar of Oriental studies) and his adaptation of the methodology of Michel Foucault helped his ideas gain widespread acceptance in intellectual circles.

Though many academic Orientalists, by the earlier meaning of the word, were angered by Said's recoining of the term and attack upon their motives and accomplishments, efforts to refute his allegations (for example, Maxime Rodinson's *La fascination de l'Islam* [1982]) fell largely on deaf ears. Whatever "Orientalism" had denoted before 1978, it definitely denoted something different after that date; whether Said created or uncovered this fresh understanding made little difference to those who welcomed it most warmly. For Arab and/or Muslim intellectuals, and, by extension, intellectuals from other imperialized lands, Said's construction of Orientalism provided a tool for understanding the powerful impact of European and American thought on giving authoritative, if distorted, shape to their histories and cultures. It also gave them a derisive epithet to use in their struggle to "decolonize" their histories. No longer would

European and American scholarship on the non-Western world be accepted as valid or estimable purely on the basis of Western academic criteria. In this respect, it is of considerable importance that Said's book was published on the eve of the Iranian revolution, which shattered Western theories of modernization and social revolution by demonstrating the vitality and political relevance of a non-Western religious tradition. Said's assertion that the intellectual edifice built by the Orientalists of the imperialist era, and perpetuated by American "regional studies" specialists of the Cold War era, was a fantasy of political, religious, and sexual wish-fulfillment seemed proved; and non-Western intellectuals thereby gained a healthy new sense of their ability to contest and reconstruct the intellectual configurations of their own histories and cultures received from Western hands.

In Western intellectual circles, the popularity of Said's *Orientalism* extended to people who knew little or nothing about Islam or the Arab world. Said had provided a vivid case study in the deconstruction of academic thought where it intersected with racism and imperialist politics. "Orientalism" consequently became a metaphor for all sorts of hegemonic intellectual constructions conceivable as instruments of capitalism and imperialism.

Richard W. Bulliet

REFERENCES

Rodinson, Maxime. *La fascination de l'Islam* (1982); English tr. with significantly revised introduction, *Europe and the Mystique of Islam.* Washington: Washington University Press, 1987.

Said, Edward. *Orientalism.* New York: Random House, 1978.

Ottoman Empire

The Ottoman Empire, which lasted from 1280 until its defeat in World War I, comprised at its height the areas presently known as Turkey, the Balkans, North Africa, and the Middle East. Although the Sultan and much of the population were Muslim, the Empire was ethnically, religiously, and linguistically diverse. Official Islam coexisted with a more commonly held faith which integrated mysticism and the traditional beliefs of the countryside with the state religion. Several features of Ottoman social structure and several major points of social change have promoted a growing amount of sociohistorical research on the Empire.

Until the 16th century, the peasantry produced for its own subsistence and for nearby urban centers, and its primary obligation was paying taxes to one of the military or bureaucratic officers of the Empire. Although the official who had the rights to these taxes (the timar holder) had few of the other privileges possessed by the feudal lords of Europe, illegal exactions were often carried out at the peasants' expense. The timar system began to change in the 15th century as the Ottomans introduced a slave army and slave bureaucracy. Peasants came under the control of an emerging class of taxfarmers and landlord/notables who employed their own militias, gained increasing autonomy, and collected taxes both for the state and for themselves.

Ottoman domains included sizable cities. Urban dwellers were merchants, craftsmen, officials, and laborers. Both men and women owned property, and often tended gardens or raised animals for their own consumption. Evkaf (charitable foundations) regularly created new public spaces in the cities, for commerce, for religious observance, and for serving the needs of the urban underclass. Ottoman cities were often divided into neighborhoods which reflected the diverse backgrounds and beliefs of the inhabitants. The boundaries between these districts were quite porous, as their inhabitants pursued day-to-day business dealings.

The Ottoman population confronted economic crises beginning in the 16th century when population increase, the discovery of New World silver, and the consequent speculation in precious metals led to extremely high prices. Many with fixed incomes revolted, creating political instability in the capital and sacking provincial villages. Flight from the countryside resulted in agricultural decline and ultimately contributed to consolidation of large plantations made up of abandoned holdings and employing landless wage laborers. The flexibility of the Ottoman Empire (apparent in such things as incorporating local customary law into its own legal system) allowed it to adapt to these crises and survive into the 20th century.

Europe's growing demand for agricultural products and the ready availability of European industrial goods beginning in the 18th century challenged the local methods of craft production in the cities and the countryside. Ottoman merchants and workers responded by focusing on products with strong local demand, by altering the way labor was carried out, by introducing new crops, and by terminating certain kinds of manufacturing. These changes limited the primary income for many wage earners and destroyed the auxiliary income of much of the rural population. Women became increasingly dependent upon male family members as the customary market outlets for their household production disappeared.

Nineteenth-century reforms in land tenure and the increasing involvement of Europeans in the Ottoman economy displaced many older patterns of living and producing. At the same time, by granting legal equality to all Ottoman subjects, the government overturned the millet system, which had defined the population according to religion and given considerable autonomy to religious groups to enforce their own laws. Together these changes elicited large-scale protest ranging from widespread smuggling, strikes, and machine-breaking to religious massacres, nationalist revolt, and tribal warfare. (*See also* Islam; Military and Society; Peasantry; Sufism; Waqf-Charitable Foundations)

Sarah Shields

REFERENCES

Inalcik, Halil. *The Ottoman Empire: Conquest, Organization and Empire.* Brookfield, VT: Variorum, 1978.

McGowan, Bruce. *Economic Life in Ottoman Europe: Taxation, Trade and the Struggle for Land, 1600–1800.* Cambridge: Cambridge University Press, 1981.

Quataert, Donald. *Social Disintegration and Popular Resistance in the Ottoman Empire, 1881–1908.* New York: New York University Press, 1983.

P

Parish Records

Parish records of baptisms, marriages, and burials began to emerge in increasing numbers in Europe during the Protestant and Roman Catholic Reformations of the 16th century. While Roman Catholic clergymen had kept lists of parish inhabitants and some registers of vital events well before this time in parts of Italy, religious revolutions of the 16th and 17th centuries gave new inspiration to systematic record keeping.

Parish records of vital events are used to reconstruct the demographic lives of the people of Europe and its colonies in the "prestatistical" era, that is, the era before regular censuses or government bureaus of vital events. Using the method of family reconstitution, historical demographers link together the different records of a couple from the time of their marriage, through the births of successive children, and ultimately to their deaths.

Parish records often yield information not only on vital events but on the people who experienced them, and the social setting. For example, marriage records often indicate occupations of the spouses, and the names and occupations of witnesses, thus giving greater insight into patterns of reproduction by social class and patterns of friendship. The quality of parish records in Europe, North America, and many colonial possessions of European nations varies widely. Although not all series are appropriate for detailed demographic uses, they are invaluable for the reconstruction of local microhistories. (*See also* Census; Christianity; Family Reconstitution; Local History; Microhistory)

Katherine A. Lynch

REFERENCES

Macfarlane, Alan. *The Family Life of Ralph Josselin.* Cambridge: Cambridge University Press, 1970.

———. *Reconstructing Historical Communities.* Cambridge: Cambridge University Press, 1977.

Willigan, J. Dennis, and Katherine A. Lynch. *Sources and Methods of Historical Demography.* New York: Academic Press, 1982.

Pastoralism

The domestication of animals—particularly horses and camels as well as cattle, sheep, and goats beginning in the 9th century BC—made possible one of the oldest and most widespread of human societal adaptations to the natural environment. Generally predominant in semiarid or desert regions, where rainfall is insufficient for sedentary agriculture, pastoralism has involved only minimal changes in the ecological contexts in which it has been practiced. Humans and the animal herds that provide their sustenance adapt to seasonal changes by migrating on a regular basis between steppe or savanna grasslands and hill and riverine areas. Movements are timed to insure that there will be sufficient water and plant cover for the pastoral group in question to pasture their herds in the areas they occupy at a given point in the annual migratory cycle. Pastoral groups tend to establish predictable migration routes and to return to the same grazing lands year after year. Thus, in both pasture areas and transit zones pastoral peoples develop a sense of territoriality, which has often led to violent clashes with groups that seek to obstruct their movement or encroach on their watering places or grazing lands.

Although pastoralism has proved a highly effective adaptive response to difficult environmental conditions, it can sustain only relatively small human groups on very extensive areas of land. This has meant that even though pastoralists have historically occupied large portions of the inhabited continents of the earth, they have in most time periods made up only a small fraction of the human population as a whole. Despite significant regional variations, most pastoral peoples have lived in kin-related bands—often called tribes—that range in numbers from 10 or 20 to 100 or more. In times of crisis or under exceptionally strong leaders, these bands have been combined in alliances numbering in the tens of thousands. But most nomads have lived most of their lives among their clanspeople, who were often linked to neighboring bands by common tribal ties.

Despite their small numbers relative to the much denser populations in areas where sedentary cultivation has developed, pastoral peoples have repeatedly played a major role in human history over much of the globe. Because stock raising did not require the long hours of labor that were needed for farming, males in pastoral cultures could devote much of their time to honing martial skills that made them formidable adversaries, both for neighboring nomadic groups and for the sedentary peoples whose civilizations spread on the fringes of the nomads' heartlands. Their skill as warriors was enhanced by the mobility inherent in their nomadic lifestyle. These attributes made it possible for pastoral peoples that were able to build alliances among far-flung nomadic groups to invade much more populous sedentary kingdoms and empires. Large-scale nomadic incursions into sedentary zones have at times radically altered the course of human history in core areas of civilized development like China, Egypt, and Greece. In some instances, such as repeatedly in Mesopotamia in ancient times, in the Indus region of northwest India in the 2nd millennium BC, and in the western Roman Empire in the 5th century AD, pastoral invaders have destroyed or contributed to the downfall of major sedentary civilizations. Often the nomadic conquerors have settled down in sedentary areas and worked with subjugated peoples to build new civilizations. At times, most notably in the vast Mongol imperium that spanned much of Eurasia in the 13th century, pastoral empires have linked diverse centers of sedentary civilization through trade and political overlordship.

Their martial exploits and sudden raids made pastoralists much feared by sedentary peoples. In addition, their very different lifestyles and much less complex material cultures contributed to the contemptuous attitudes often held by the nomads' "civilized" neighbors. But images of warlike barbarians often obscured the very considerable cultural achievements of pastoral groups as well as their ongoing and often mutually enriching exchanges with sedentary peoples. Pastoral peoples have depended heavily on their herds for their staple foods and for the materials used in their clothing, housing, transport, and art. Animal sacrifices or veneration have been central in most nomadic religions, and the size and quantity of nomads' herds have been the prime gauges of wealth and power. At the same time, all but the most isolated of pastoral peoples have maintained regular contacts with farming villages and urban centers. Most nomads traded with sedentary peoples for the grains, vegetables, clothing, tools, and weapons that they could not produce for themselves. In turn, pastoral peoples enriched the diet of sedentary peoples with meat and milk, guarded critical overland trade routes and the borderlands of sedentary empires, and were frequently key transmitters of ideas and technology from one center of sedentary civilization to another. Thus, the more dramatic invasions and conquests of pastoralists that have dominated recorded history should be seen as episodic extensions of much longer term symbiotic exchanges and cultural cross-fertilization. (*See also* Agricultural Systems; Animals; Civilization; Migration; Neolithic Revolution; Nomadism)

Michael Adas

REFERENCES

Grousset, René. *Empire of the Steppes: A History of Central Asia.* New Brunswick, NJ: Rutgers University Press, 1970.

Khazanov, A.M. *Nomads and the Outside World.* New York: Cambridge University Press, 1984.

Lattimore, Owen. *Studies in Frontier History.* Paris: Mouton, 1962.

Weissleder, Wolfgang, ed. *The Nomadic Alternative.* London: Mouton de Gruyter, 1978.

Paternalism

Paternalism can be defined as the system of relations between superiors and subordinates, whereby the subordinates are controlled more through informal and indirect methods such as moral pressure and the provision of benefits than through formal, direct methods such as contracts or wages. The term, which has been used frequently in labor history, comes from the Latin word for father (*pater*): just as a father in many societies had the right to control his wife, children, and servants, so employers or masters could assume the right to control those working under them.

In traditional society before the industrial revolution and the spread of individual rights, paternalism was rarely named or discussed, but simply taken for granted. Europeans and Americans in the 18th century used phrases such as "patriarchical principles" or the "natural rights of masters" to defend the privileges of the upper class. Scholars usually intend paternalism to include several components: hierarchy, authority, and reciprocity. Masters or employers believed that an inegalitarian hierarchy, stretching from those who worked up to those who ruled, constituted the natural order for society. Masters or employers also claimed the authority to control workers' lives, not just to supervise their labor on the job. As a Belgian industrialist in 1911 stated, "I claim to be master in my factory, as a priest is in his church and the teacher in the school." These aspects of paternalism were partially offset by reciprocity, the idea that superiors owed certain benefits to those below them. Guildmasters housed and trained apprentices, landlords frequently offered paternalistic benefits to serfs and peasants, and slaveowners claimed that they protected and provided for their slaves. Paternalism also used and reinforced age, gender, and racial or ethnic divisions, since superiors almost always have been older males of a privileged group, and those below, disproportionately younger, female, or of a different race or ethnic origin. Even labor historians who do not use the term "paternalism" often describe company housing or stores for workers or employer-provided welfare benefits. In exchange for these benefits, workers found they had to accept their employers' authority and give up the right to unionize or strike.

Benefits that control workers have been particularly common in new agricultural and industrial areas where labor is scarce or where it resists employers' discipline—for example, mining camps in the United States, France, and Zaire, plantations in South Africa and Malaya, and textile mills in England and South America. While paternalist labor relations often decline as more bureaucratic methods and labor unionism increase, company welfare benefits, company unions, and other methods of controlling employees may also emerge as more traditional ones disappear. Modern Japanese and U.S. corporations such as IBM can be seen as generous, but also at times as paternalist.

Paternalism, in short, is a common framework for relations between superiors and subordinates at work. Sometimes it involves nothing more than institutions designed to prevent worker mobility or protest, like company stores that run up heavy debts from the workers required to patronize them. On the other hand, paternalism of a more beneficial sort is often expected by workers. Both its heavy-handed presence but also its absence can inspire protest, as paternalism organizes diverse impulses on the employer side and evokes varied evaluations from the worker side depending on their perceptions of authority. Tracing changes in paternalism and in worker response forms an important part of the social history of work, in preindustrial and industrial societies alike. (*See also* Middle Classes; Working Class)

Carl Strikwerda

REFERENCES

Baron, Ava, ed. *Work Engendered: Toward a New History of American Labor.* Ithaca, NY, and London: Cornell University Press, 1991.

Genovese, Eugene. *Roll, Jordan, Roll: The World the Slaves Made.* New York: Random House, 1976.

Higginson, John. *A Working Class in the Making: Belgian Colonial Labor Policy, Private Enterprise, and the African Mineworker, 1907–1951.* Madison: University of Wisconsin Press, 1989.

Joyce, Patrick. *Work, Society and Politics: The Culture of the Factory in later Victorian England.* New Brunswick, NJ: Rutgers University Press, 1980.

Roberts, David. *Paternalism in Early Victorian England.* New Brunswick, NJ: Rutgers University Press, 1979.

Spencer, Elaine Glovka. *Management and Labor in Imperial Germany: Ruhr Industrialists as Employers, 1896–1914.* New Brunswick, NJ: Rutgers University Press, 1984.

Patriarchalism

Patriarchalism in its broadest sense refers to systems of social relations in which men formally or informally monopolize institutions of power and women have little access to sources of authority. Historians have found the fundamental and institutionalized gender inequality that patriarchalism denotes in many geographical regions and chronological periods from the first civilizations in Mesopotamia to the Western cultures of the late 20th century. Correspondingly, understanding the operation of patriarchy in family, economic, and political life; comparing various forms of patriarchy; and assessing changes in partriarchy including its applicability in modern society have set major analytical goals in social history.

Historians of all chronological periods have correlated patriarchalism with the organization of societies into family units based on households in which women were dependent on the men who were their fathers or husbands. Historians have been anxious to emphasize, however, that the universality of male dominance does not mean that patriarchalism has no history. This dependence of women on men has taken diverse forms—legal, political, economic, cultural, or some combination thereof. Social historians in particular have begun to recover historical variations in the construction of patriarchalism and women's experiences of it. Historians' efforts to recover the diversity of forms of patriarchalism as well as the myriad ways in which women have responded to the constraints upon them remain one of the most important challenges facing social history in the late 20th century. Yet the first steps toward the making of a history of patriarchalism have led to debate over whether "patriarchalism" is even a useful term or whether by emphasizing in broad terms the oppression of women it obscures more than it reveals.

The universality and origins of the patriarchal configuration of power have been much debated. In a classic formulation over a century ago, Friedrich Engels identified a causal relationship between the emergence of private property and "the world historic defeat of the female sex." Others have suggested that the exchange of women and the appropriation of their reproductive capacities preceded the concept of private property and were at the heart of the establishment of gender inequality. Anthropologists and historians have also searched for societies that were not characterized by patriarchalism in order to show that gender inequality is neither natural nor inevitable.

Whatever the causes, social historians have traced important differences in the form of patriarchalism in different times and places. Patriarchalism was most explicitly institutionalized in political, religious, and cultural as well as familial terms in the early modern West between the 16th and 18th centuries. Political theorists like Jean Bodin in late 16th-century France and Robert Filmer in mid-17th-century England articulated patriarchalism as the basis of absolutist monarchies. In making the analogy between the power of the father in the family and the king in the realm the fundamental justification for royal power, absolute monarchs also enhanced the authority of male household heads as husbands and fathers. During these same centuries, the religious changes associated with the Protestant and Catholic Reformations also tended to enhance the power of men over women by reinforcing the primacy of the household and valorizing wifely obedience. The emphasis on the absolute power of the father in the family was not unique to the early modern world, but it received unprecedented legislative and cultural endorsements during these centuries.

The consequences of this enhancement of patriarchalism for ordinary peoples' daily lives were very extensive. Some historians have seen the witchcraft craze in early modern Europe, for example, as one manifestation of the enhanced vulnerability of women in Western societies where patriarchalism was overtly mobilized to justify personal and political power hierarchies in terms of familial and national politics. Women were denied legal rights and were increasingly excluded from political participation and from many economic opportunities. The association between male head of household status and authority also meant, however, that men were at certain stages of their lives—as sons, apprentices, or servants—subject to the authority of the men who were heads of households, but their dependence was only a temporary prelude to their own gaining head of household status.

The liberal revolutions in France and America of the late 18th century have frequently been characterized as challenges to patriarchalism. In narrow political terms, liberal democracies did reject patriarchalism as a means of organizing political power with their emphasis on individualism and natural rights replacing the familial metaphors of earlier political systems. Clearly, however, in many senses gender inequality was merely reconfigured as women were denied the political and civil rights that were, in theory and

increasingly in practice in the 19th century, extended to all men.

Social historians are divided over the extent to which men's monopoly of power was perpetuated in the new liberal states. Citizenship, with the rights to political participation and legal equality that it implied, was profoundly gendered: only men could be citizens while women were urged to limit themselves to domestic roles and motherhood. In terms of access to employment opportunities, to education, and to many other sources of power and authority, women have been persistently disadvantaged throughout the 19th and 20th centuries. On the other hand, women haltingly gained many of the civil rights and benefited from the liberal emphasis on the individual rather than the family. Social historians, however, have shown how ideas like a family wage for men have continued to justify wage differentials between men and women as women remained culturally defined in terms of their relationships to men—as wives, mothers, and daughters—rather than as individuals.

In assessing the extent and impact of patriarchalism, social historians still face many challenges. Much more work still has to be done in identifying and explaining variations in the ways patriarchalism was constructed and maintained in different geographical and chronological areas, especially outside the West. Equally important, historians must examine changes in the nature of patriarchalism and explore women's experiences of and responses to particular systems of gender domination. The state of men and the construction of masculinity associated with patriarchy also draw increasing attention. (*See also* Masculinity; Women's History)

Julie Hardwick

REFERENCES

Engels, Friedrich. *The Origin of the Family, Private Property and the State.* New York: Viking Press, 1973.

Hunt, Lynn. *The Family Romance of the French Revolution.* Berkeley: University of California Press, 1992.

Lerner, Gerda. *The Creation of Patriarchy.* New York: Oxford University Press, 1986.

Pateman, Carol. *The Sexual Contract.* Stanford, CA: Stanford University Press, 1988.

Roper, Lyndal. *The Holy Household: Women and Morals in Reformation Augsburg.* Oxford: Clarendon Press, 1989.

Patronage

Patronage is an important social and political institution that has played a major role in the development of societies transhistorically and cross-culturally. It could be said that patronage is the most important vehicle of communication and political power in hierarchical societies, superseding in its power even the governmental structures of those societies. It has gained increasing attention as social historians have learned greater sensitivity in dealing with power relationships in premodern, and some modern, societies.

Patronage is both a social relationship between patron and client and an entire social system that generates power and complements other parallel systems. It can be defined as a reciprocal and asymmetrical relationship between unequals that continues over a period of time.

The partners in the relationship are usually of unequal social or economic rank. Each partner performs services for the other. The patron, or superior, uses his or her power, influence, wealth, and social position to assist, protect, and advance the inferior member by giving money or land, arranging interviews or audiences (for literary clients), and making introductions. The inferior is then put into the debt of the superior and is obligated to perform certain less tangible services. A lower-class client might perform the menial duties of a servant; a higher-class client who is a writer might compose panegyrics to honor the patron. Other client-duties include working to enhance the patron's prestige and power in various ways, such as campaigning for political office.

It is to the client's benefit to increase the patron's prestige because the prestige of the client is directly linked to the prestige of his or her patron, and a strong patron is better able to offer protection and favors.

The ways in which patronage is defined and conducted and the forms it takes depend upon the rules of the society and on the class and rank of the patron and client. Relationships of patronage can be formal and binding (e.g., freedmen and their manumitters in Rome; godparent and parent of a child in Sicily; peasant and dominant class in East Africa) or less well-defined (e.g., upper-class writers and their patrons in Rome; most contemporary Mediterranean patrons and clients).

In many societies, patronage relationships are called "friendship" (*amicitia* in ancient Rome, *amicizia* in contemporary Sicily). The "friends" in this relationship are rarely personal friends, but rather have political ties that can dissolve quickly if either party does not recognize and follow the rules implicit in this "friendship." The terms used to describe the parties to these "friendships" are designed to obscure the true relationships of the parties to each other. The word "friend" is applied indiscriminately to both patron and client to give the appearance of equality, but it really means two different things. Language thus does not denote actual social practice.

Patrons and clients can operate in a variety of settings. There can be dyadic pairs (a one-to-one relationship); vertical relationships, in which the patron of a client himself has a patron; multiple patrons for one client; interconnecting dyadic groups that depend on a broker to connect the groups; circles of patrons and clients, which were especially prominent in ancient Roman society in which upper-class literary clients would cluster together around one patron (e.g., Maecenas or Messalla), and find support from him and from each other. Patronage is rarely a simple reciprocal exchange, but a series of interconnecting alliances that is based on choice and competition and remains adaptable.

The metaphors applied to patronage highlight its qualities of dependence, bonding, and indebtedness. The client has been compared to a parasitic vine, a fish swimming toward a hook, and to a chameleonlike, changeable sea creature. Although patronage is beneficial to both parties, it is often contracted at a great cost to the client. It allows people of low status or means, however, access to money, networks of acquaintances, and power that they could not otherwise achieve in a highly stratified and immobile society.

It is difficult to analyze the role that patronage plays in societies, its relationship to the different institutions of a society (government, religion), and its relative importance. Some scholars view patronage as a universal phenomenon that is present in all times, places, and classes. Others argue that patronage is important only in certain types of societies, such as traditional or feudal societies, and that it has no place in the well-oiled machinery of the modern state. According to this view, patronage is important economically and politically in transitional societies in which kinship ties are no longer effective and the market forces and industrialization do not yet operate effectively. The intermediate position holds that patronage varies in importance and influence depending upon numerous factors.

Many peasants and early industrial workers protested the disappearance of what they viewed as natural patronage obligations by their superiors; this could be a key ingredient in an attack based in moral economy terms, on modern governance forms. Some groups, like immigrants in American cities, successfully re-formed patronage relationships (as with urban bosses), at least for a time.

Another scholarly debate involves those who analyze patronage as purely relational and sociologists who identify it as a system and a complex series of relationships that provide the vital link between the center of power and those on the periphery. This question is crucial for any analysis of economic, political, and social organization. The relationship between patronage and government is problematic: patronage can strengthen the smooth workings of government by allocating resources and maintaining social relations, but it can also weaken central government structures by undermining its laws.

A new approach to patronage is an analysis of the role that women play as patrons, even in societies in which they have a diminished role in politics and society. For example, in Hellenistic Greece and imperial Rome, women gained wealth and used it to become public patrons of towns and cities. The addition of women to analyses of patronage allows us to be more inclusive in our definition of patronage as an integral part of society that functions as a personal and flexible system of communication and distribution of resources in a way that is parallel to the official channels of government.

Patronage has been widely studied not only in Mediterranean but also in Asian societies, where some authorities argue that Western concepts can barely capture the network of patronage relationships that tied peasants and landlords and village headmen well into recent times. The decline of patronage—for example, attempts by European colonial governments to replace patronage relationships with "rational" government bureaucracies and tax procedures—constitutes a final subject of sociohistorical inquiry. (*See also* Clientage; Paternalism; Peasantry)

Barbara K. Gold

REFERENCES

Boissevain, Jeremy. "Patronage in Sicily," *Man* 1 (1966): 18–33.

Brown, Cedric C. *Politics, Patronage and Literary Traditions in England, 1558–1658*. Detroit: Wayne State University Press, 1992.

Campbell, J.K. *Honour, Family and Patronage: A Study of Institutions and Moral Values in a Greek Mountain Community*. Oxford: Clarendon Press, 1964.

Lytle, Guy F., and Stephen Orgel, eds. *Patronage in the Renaissance*. Princeton, NJ: Princeton University Press, 1981.

Pye, Lucian W. *Asian Power and Politics: The Cultural Dimensions of Authority*. Cambridge: Harvard University Press, 1983.

Pawnshops

A pawnshop lends money in return for an object of value or pledge that may be sold or auctioned by the pawnshop if the loan is not repaid. China, ancient Rome, and medieval Europe afford instances of the practice, but Renaissance Italy was the birthplace of the public institution known as the *monte di pietà* (Ital.), *monte de piedad* (Sp.), or *mont-de-piété* (Fr.). The term referred to the stockpile of charitable gifts serving as a bank for the poor. The *monte di pietà* established in Perugia in 1462 was the model for many others in central Italy. Franciscan preachers, particularly Bernardino of Feltre, reminded pious donors that the working capital given to *monti di pietà* could provide relief many times over, lessening the occasion for contact between poor Christians and Jewish moneylenders.

By 1500 the Franciscan position that *monti di pietà* should charge interest in order to defray costs was confirmed by papal decree, following a debate over church teachings on usury. Local municipal councils, usually of laity, managed the *monti di pietà* and ensured that loans were not used for immoral purposes such as gambling.

Pawnshops have taken various institutional forms. In Toledo, the *Arca de Misericordia y Monte de Piedad* was founded in the 1560s primarily to lend grain, but also money, to the poor. The *monte de piedad* founded in Mexico City in 1775 charged no interest, but users were urged to give alms for masses to be said for the soul of the founder. In Russia in the 18th century, owners of taverns or shops served as brokers for wet nurses, advancing them credit and taking in pawn the paybooks they received from the fosterage agencies of the foundling hospitals of Moscow and St. Petersburg.

In 19th-century London and in other major urban centers in Europe and America, dispensers of official charity found that pawnshops were used by the poor to convert clothes and other charitable gifts into cash to be used as the recipients saw fit. The interests of social historians have increased attention to the way poor people and workers used pawnshops as part of urban survival strategy and adjustments to economic and life-cycle fluctuations, particularly in early industrialization. (*See also* Charity; Poverty)

Thomas M. Adams

REFERENCES

Couturier, Edith B. "The Philanthropic Activities of Pedro Romero de Terreros: First Count of Regla," *The Americas* 32, 1 (July 1975): 13–30.

Pullan, Brian S. *Rich and Poor in Renaissance Venice: The Social Institutions of a Catholic State, to 1620.* Oxford: Basil Blackwell, 1971.

Ransel, David L. *Mothers of Misery: Child Abandonment in Russia.* Princeton, NJ: Princeton University Press, 1988.

Tebbutt, Melanie. *Making Ends Meet: Pawnbroking and Working-Class Credit.* New York: St. Martin's Press, 1993.

Peace Movement

Peace movements are defined chiefly as organized political reform groups which originated in the United States and Great Britain during the early 19th century. By century's end, peace activists had organized national groups throughout Europe as well as international organizations, which expanded the scope of their activism and reform agenda. Peace movements, shaped by the underlying social structures and political cultures of their societies, reflect a diversity of aims, methods, social composition, and ideology; however, peace activism has thrived most where liberal democratic practices and traditions of an activist citizenry prevailed. Largely composed of white women and men of the middle class whose political orientations ranged from liberal to left wing, these voluntary groups not only opposed war but sought positively to create peace. They provided systematic analyses of the causes of war and violence and sought to reform foreign policies, social institutions, or underlying cultural patterns.

Peace historians have defined peace advocates according to their forms of commitment to peace, which generally are encompassed by the terms pacifism, internationalism, and antiwar activism. The movements are most often studied as part of political and intellectual history, and their relationship with the leading emphases of social history is not always clear. From the sociohistorical perspective, the most significant categories of analysis are the distinctive social composition and reform qualities of peace organizations and movements. Having roots in 19th-century Quakerism and evangelical Protestantism, Anglo-American pacifism denotes the rejection of war and the commitment to nonviolent means to resolve conflicts. Quakers and some Protestants and Catholics comprise an inner core of pacifists who have provided continuity to peace movements. Pacifism of the 20th century is informed by Gandhian techniques of nonviolent resistance.

Internationalists have generally sought peace through disarmament and the development of international organizations and legal processes to create an international community which provides for the peaceful settlement of disputes between nations. Liberal democrats in the United States and Europe, who were concerned with stability and orderly progress, have included businessmen and government officials, and varieties of professionals such as legal experts, educators, and scientists. Organized in response to World War I and continuing to the present, radical peace workers combine pacifist and internationalist concerns, as well as a commitment to social justice. They go beyond internationalists' acceptance of the nation-state and envision a transnational community of peoples, rather than nations. On the political left, socialists and anarchists have participated in antiwar activism, contributing an economic and class analysis of war. Antiwar movements include various groups representing many shades of opinion which form in response to war or to a specific threat of war. Thus, peace movements are shaped by diverse approaches to peace which in turn draw upon various political religious ideologies.

As a field of historical inquiry, peace history dates to the work of noted social historian Merle Curti, who provided the first examination of peace groups in U.S. history. Subsequently, in the 1960s, historians fully established the field. Recent avenues for research include women's involvement in peace movements and their feminist/pacifist approaches to peace as well as comparative analyses of national peace movements.

Anne Marie Pois

REFERENCES

Alonso, Harriet. *Peace as a Women's Issue: The United States' Movement for Women's Rights and World Peace Since 1820*. Syracuse, NY: Syracuse University Press, 1992.

Cooper, Sandi. *Patriotic Pacifism: Waging War on War in Europe, 1815–1914*. New York: Oxford University Press, 1991.

DeBenedetti, Charles. *The Peace Reform in American History*. Bloomington: Indiana University Press, 1980.

Peasant Rebellion

Peasant rebellions are usually spontaneous uprisings of the simple tillers of the soil. They have been permanent features of all late-feudal and post-feudal societies, and they have been widely studied in social history.

Traditionally, peasants have constituted the most numerous social group in all societies, and they still do in states whose economy is based on agricultural production. Most peasants were and are settled food producers, although some of them also practice/practiced slash-and-burn agriculture. Originally only those with their own plots were referred to as peasants. Later this term was also extended to the landless members of the agricultural class. The term "peasant," however, was never used to refer to the agriculturists of such newly settled English-speaking lands as the United States, Canada, New Zealand, or Australia, who were and are independent farmers. Nor is this term applied to the rural proletariat of large modern estates—be these private enterprises, socialist state farms, or agricultural collectives. Their workers are more akin to modern wage laborers.

Peasants often rose against their social and economic superiors, but their "rebellions" have to be distinguished from modern "revolutions." Whereas the former are characterized by spontaneity, lack of formal planning, and the absence of dominant central ideologies (except where religious inspiration entered in), the latter display purpose, structure, and the directing vision of such more informed social groups as artisans, industrial workers, middle classes, and intellectuals. As such, peasant rebellions are closer to "slave insurrections" than to modern "revolutions."

Peasant rebellions had all sorts of local causes associated with manorial exploitation. Major uprisings, however, were outgrowths of rapid socioeconomic transformations or expectations of the same. This is best demonstrated by the case of pre-emancipation Russia, where, between 1825 and 1861, virtually every year saw an increasing number of local and regional rebellions. Historians have counted a total of 1,188, with one-third of them (474) taking place during the last six years of the pre-emancipation period.

In western and central Europe peasant rebellions occurred mostly from the 14th through the 16th centuries. In eastern and southeastern Europe they took place in the 17th through the early 20th centuries. This delay is even more evident in the case of Asia, Africa, and Latin

America, where such uprisings occurred largely during the past 100 years.

The first phase of peasant rebellions was occasioned by the transformation of the feudal-manorial system into money economy, which altered traditional economic relations and ended the system of mutual obligations. This breakdown of the manorial system, and not dire poverty by itself, produced widespread dissatisfaction and produced numerous uprisings.

The most serious French peasant insurrection was the *Jacquerie* of 1358—so named because of the nobles' custom of calling all peasants *Jacques*. It was actuated by the ravages of the Black Death and the Hundred Years' War, and by the growing influence of the "free air" of the towns. In this case the peasants were also enraged by their lords' inability to defend France while increasing their manorial dues. Led by a certain Guillaume Cale or Carle and Etienne Marcel, the peasants went on a warpath. They sacked castles and manor houses and massacred their inhabitants, but without any real chance of lasting success.

Almost simultaneously, England also witnessed growing social tensions. The imposition of a poll tax brought dissatisfaction to a climax and led to the massive peasant rebellion in 1381. Centered on southeastern England, the rebels were commanded by the ex-soldier Wat Tyler and the defrocked Wycliffite priest John Bell. They demanded economic and religious reforms, but their main goal was greater social justice. They terrorized the countryside, and even forced King Richard II to negotiate with them, but at the end they too were defeated.

The situation was similar in the German-speaking lands of the Holy Roman Empire, especially in the southern German states and in what later became Switzerland. In these lands the spirit of revolt was inspired by the growing disparity between the rich merchants and the impoverished peasants, and by the Swiss peasants' desire to end Habsburg dynastic control. The combination of social and political dissatisfaction led to a series of peasant rebellions and wars that lasted for over three centuries (1291–1648). They ended both feudalism and Habsburg rule, and resulted in the foundation of the Swiss Confederation.

In the southern German states the first significant peasant rebellion was headed by Hans Böheim in 1470, who denounced the feudal-clerical hierarchy and demanded greater social justice and religious reform. Böheim's defeat and execution by the bishop of Würzburg only added to the peasants' dissatisfaction, which by the early 1500s was also fueled by Martin Luther's anti-Rome and antiestablishment teachings. The result was the "German Peasants' War" of 1524–1525, which—led by Thomas Münzer—soon engulfed all of southern Germany. The peasants' excesses, however, turned even Luther against them. The defeat of this rebellion resulted in the worsening of peasant conditions and the restoration of serfdom. Some claim that this revolt had elements of a rudimentary proletarian revolution, but it was basically a peasant uprising, with the usual demands for social justice.

Conditions were also ripe for social eruption in 14th- and 15th-century Italy. The "Dolcino Uprising" of 1304, although largely religiously inspired, can be viewed as a major Italian peasant rebellion. Yet, because of the dominance of the cities, these disturbances usually took the form of urban revolts. The most renowned of these was the *ciompi* uprising (or carders' uprising) of Florence (1375–1382) under the leadership of Michael di Lando.

Social problems in east-central Europe were both similar and dissimilar to those of Germany. The dissimilarities stemmed partially from the lateness of the coming of serfdom to the region (ca. AD 1500), and partially from the growing antagonism between the expanding German settlers and the region's indigenous Slavic and non-Slavic people.

In the Czech kingdom of Bohemia, peasant dissatisfaction, fueled by Hussite religious egalitarian and growing anti-imperialism (later anti-Habsburgism), gave birth to a series of peasant rebellions, culminating in the so-called Hussite wars of the early 15th century. The most radical Hussites—the Taborites—preached social and religious egalitarianism, and demanded the abrogation of feudal exploitation. Although initially successful under Jan Žižka's and Prokop the Bald's leadership, ultimately they too were defeated. Moderate Hussitism survived into the

16th and early 17th centuries, but by that time serfdom had already been established in Bohemia, and it had become part of the Habsburg dynastic state.

The situation in the kingdom of Hungary (including Croatia, Slovakia, and Transylvania) was different only in the absence of Hussite religious radicalism. The first of a series of major uprisings took place in 1437 under the leadership of the Transylvanian-Hungarian nobleman, Antal Budai-Nagy, who died a heroic death in the course of the peasants' inevitable defeat. Next came the "Hungarian Peasants' War" of 1514, which started out as a crusade against the Turks, but which soon turned into a systematic massacre of the nobility. Although not as protracted as the German Peasants' War of a decade later, this so-called "Dózsa Rebellion" was similar in scope. Led by the nobleman György Dózsa, the peasants refused to move against the Turks, but turned against their own lords instead. They systematically burned, looted, and murdered, capturing several cities and fortresses, and even threatening the capital city of Buda. Their defeat was followed by their condemnation by the Diet of 1514 "to real and perpetual servitude." Following this defeat, Hungary experienced a few more spontaneous peasant uprisings—including the one led by the Croat Maté Gubec in 1573—but none of them threatened the existing social order.

In contrast to Bohemia and Hungary, the Polish-Lithuanian commonwealth escaped large-scale peasant uprisings. This may have been the result of the development of the so-called nobles' democracy, which placed most powers into the hands of the lower nobility, or *szlachta*. Even so, serfdom was introduced around AD 1500. Moreover, after the Union of Lublin between Poland and Lithuania (1569), it also moved into Lithuania, which in those days included Ukraine and Belorussia.

The situation in the Russian lands was different in that serfdom in the Western sense was consolidated only in the late 16th to mid-17th century. East Slavs were among the last to join the Christian world, wherefore their transformation from tribal to manorial society also came later. This process was slowed even more by Russia's vast spaces, which made it possible for peasants under increased exploitation to flee to the "Wild East" and to form themselves into so-called Cossack hosts. This process was speeded up by the Union of Lublin and by the introduction of the so-called prohibited years (1581) in Muscovite Russia. The former of these extended the Polish serfdom into Lithuania, Belorussia, and Ukraine, while the latter prevented the nominally free peasants from migrating even at the end of the agricultural year—St. George's Day—as has been their custom for centuries.

The climax to this process was the Law Code of 1649, which confirmed serfdom throughout the Russian lands. It was this process of enserfment that precipitated a number of major and hundreds of minor peasant uprisings during the 17th through the 19th centuries. The former of these included the Bolotnikov Uprising of 1606–1607, the Razin Rebellion of 1670–1671, the Bulavin Revolt of 1707–1708, and the Pugachev Rebellion of 1773–1774. These uprisings all display similar patterns in their origins, their leadership, and their ultimate demise. They were precipitated by extreme forms of exploitation, they were all led by peasant-turned-Cossack leaders, they all harvested the pent-up resentment of the peasant masses (mostly serfs), and they all ended in defeat.

The most significant of these uprisings was the Pugachev Rebellion of 1773–1774. Emelian Pugachev was a simple Don Cossack, who capitalized on grievances of the Russian serfs, Cossack groups, and various minorities to start his uprising that nearly overthrew Catherine the Great's pseudo-enlightened rule. In the course of this rebellion Pugachev proclaimed himself Emperor Peter III, established an "imperial court," announced the end to serfdom, taxation, and obligatory military service, and also declared his intention to exterminate all oppressive landlords and bureaucrats. At the end, Pugachev's rebellion also failed, mostly because of its own inefficiency, lack of coordination, and absence of real leadership—shortcomings that characterized all peasant uprisings. Its immediate impact was to scare Catherine sufficiently to give up the idea of peasant reform.

Ottoman Turkish manorialism differed from its European counterpart in that it did not recognize bonded serfdom, and because Ottoman feudal lords (*timaroits*) did not own their lands. Thus, during the 15th through the 17th centuries, Balkan peasants had more personal freedom than their brethren under Christian rule. Given these conditions, the Balkan lands did not experience major peasant uprisings. Most of those that occurred were local rebellions, connected with the activities of such Robin Hood–like figures as the Greek *klephts* and the Slavic *hayduks*. The lot of the peasants worsened in the 18th century, when the nonhereditary *timars* were turned illegally into the hereditary *chiftliks*, and the local lords increased their control over the peasants. With the coming of modern nationalism in the 19th century, however, most of the Balkan nationalist movements were peasant based, and thus they displayed elements of peasant rebellions. The most prominent of these were the Serbian Revolution of 1804–1813 and the Greek Revolution of 1821–1829.

During late medieval and early modern periods, peasant rebellions were part of an important, if generally unsuccessful revolutionary trend. Since the French Revolution, however, they came to be overshadowed by the urban revolutions of workers and intellectuals. This was paralleled by the peasants' gradual submergence in the new nations. Thus, peasant rebellions—except on the fringes of the Western world—became part of modern revolutionary movements. Yet, peasant movements and populist trends were still visible in the Russian revolutions of 1905 and 1917, as well as in the interwar political life of east-central and southeast European states. In the 20th century they also became dominant elements in various Asian, African, and Latin American revolutionary movements.

Anthropologists and social theorists have studied the role of the peasantry in modern revolutions. Theda Skocpol, for example, compared their role in the French, Russian, and Chinese revolutions, and stressed the centrality of this role. Eric Wolf, on the other hand, analyzed the peasants' role in such 20th-century revolutions as those of Mexico, Russia, China, Vietnam, Algeria, and Cuba. He concluded that while peasant rebellions per se are passé, the role of the peasants in revolutionary transformations in many parts of the world is still very much present. And this role will remain alive as long as the peasants constitute important segments of existing societies.

Forms of peasant rebellion clearly vary, from "social banditry," in which a few criminals gain peasant backing for attacks on the rich, to full-scale jacqueries. Land hunger and resentment at landlord obligations usually predominate, but taxation agents and other central state officials may be attacked as well. Loose ideologies, involving beliefs in peasant ownership and, often, some rough equality, are common, but formal political ideas usually are lacking. Often, peasants proclaim their loyalty to the king, claiming that the government should aid them in turn. Different types of peasants play different roles. The poorest, marginal in their communities, are not usually central figures. Rural artisans, however, can help provide leadership because of their wider contacts, and middling peasants, neither too rich to be satisfied or too poor to be incapacitated, usually provide key backing. Women often participate strongly, particularly in riots that protest lack of food or the movement of grain out of a famished region. Peasant risings usually begin locally, but they may fan out in fascinating patterns, spread by example and shared goals and grievances. Not a normal occurrence, peasant risings in their heyday played a major role in constraining elites and governments even when, as was most commonly the case, they failed to win their direct demands. (*See also Jacqueries; Manorialism; Peasantry; Revolutions*)

Steven Béla Várdy and Thomas Szendrey

REFERENCES

Blum, Jerome. *Lord and Peasant in Russia. From the Ninth to the Nineteenth Century.* Princeton, NJ: Princeton University Press, 1981.

Fourquin, Guy. *The Anatomy of Popular Rebellion in the Middle Ages.* New York: North Holland, 1978.

Hobsbawm, E.J. *Primitive Rebels. Studies in Archaic Forms of Social Movement in the 19th and 20th Centuries.* New York: Praeger, 1952; 2d ed., 1963.

Inalcik, Halil. *The Ottoman Empire. Conquest, Organization, and Economy.* London: Variorum Press, 1978.

Wolf, Eric R. *Peasant Wars of the Twentieth Century.* New York: Harper & Row, 1969.

Peasantry

The peasantry forms one of the most generally student topics in social history, ranging across many time periods and most of the world's inhabited regions (only a few areas, like North America, never had a significant peasantry). Perhaps the most widely (if not fully) accepted definitional characteristics of peasants has been offered by sociologist Teodor Shanin (1987), building upon the formative works of such figures as A.V. Chayanov, Robert Redfield, and Eric Wolf. He distinguishes peasants as small agricultural producers who labor mainly for their own consumption and produce a surplus sufficient to fulfill obligations to the state, landlords, and others in positions of economic and political power. Within this rural society, family farms form the fundamental unit of social organization, farming serves as the primary means of livelihood, and specific cultural patterns reflect, reinforce, and reproduce the peculiar features of the peasant community such as the preeminence of tradition, conformity, and social and legal norms. A final defining feature of peasants is their domination by powerful outsiders, as Shanin and others have argued, placing them in the role of exploited subordinates.

Not all scholars have accepted such definitional features without question or qualification, however, particularly that which views the peasantry's subordinate position as critical to understanding peasant status. Sidney Mintz, for example, while not rejecting the view that peasant society's political economy has been based, historically, "on expropriation of its surpluses by powerful outsiders," points out that it is insufficient to describe the peasantry merely "in terms of its asymmetrical relationships to external power" (1973:93). As he notes, economic and status differentiation in a community means that not all peasants are simply victims or prey; some (the wealthy or those who occupy positions of status and power) are also among the exploiters. One sector of the peasantry often profits by controlling another. Hence it is an oversimplification to view peasant societies as entirely homogeneous or egalitarian, for numerous and often competing sectors with divergent values, perceptions, and goals typically exist within the same community. Mintz also stresses the importance of understanding the interaction and association of these different peasant sectors with other rural groups (agricultural laborers, squatters, etc.) that share and help to shape rural life, since such relations serve to maintain the viability of the peasantry itself.

In addition to their attention to the internal structures and character of the peasantry, social historians and other scholars in peasant studies have been preoccupied with two broad, related questions, each stemming from earlier formulations on the nature of peasant society and encompassing a range of additional problems. The first question concerns the peasants' relationship to the larger world outside village communities and the role of external forces (exploitation, capitalist market relations, war, politics, state policies designed to promote capitalism, urban culture, and colonialism, for example) in bringing change or radical transformation to peasant societies. In their "search for modernity," historians have written extensively about the impact of capitalist penetration and expanding international markets on peasant family structure and social organization, land tenure laws, farming patterns, socioeconomic differentiation, and the division of labor. Such processes were already underway in Europe by the 17th century, but for peasantries throughout the world (in countries such as India, Burma, and Mexico, for instance), the 19th century in particular saw these economic forces dramatically alter existing survival strategies and social relations, compelling increasing numbers of peasants to produce directly for the market and often weakening their societies by undermining traditional forms of social control. Commercialization of agriculture and ties to world markets, while commonly limiting the peasantry's tactical advantages, have also brought about significant changes in class structure that produced new economic allies for peasants, especially in colonial states. Similar changes, adjustments, realignments, and transformations have continued up to the present time in large areas of Africa, Asia, and Latin America, where the vast majority of the world's peasants now live.

Peasants reacted to these new developments in a number of ways. Some did not survive the changes reshaping their world, but were forced off the land to find employment as migrants, rural laborers, or urban workers. This was in line with the classic Marxist argument that capitalism destroys the peasantry as an autonomous class. It has, however, proved far from a universal scenario, as seen, for example, in late 19th- and early 20th-century Venezuela, where capitalism actually created a peasant class. Indeed, one of the major contributions of social historians has been to show how peasants successfully adapted their traditional culture and cultural institutions to survive under new situations, thereby demonstrating that the persistence of older, local economic methods, forms of culture, and political action are as important as the broader economic, social, and political changes that were the focus of earlier scholarship. Depending on region and historical conditions, peasants adopt new strategies of avoidance, resistance, participation in local and national politics, and various forms of mobilization that have included ritualized protest, localized riots, direct confrontation with state agents, rebellion, and guerrilla warfare. But determining the precise conditions under which peasants are willing to risk confrontation and violence has proved difficult for scholars. As James Scott (1987) and others have pointed out in several recent studies, peasants are far more likely to offer constant yet subtle resistance than they are to rebel openly. Indeed, risk avoidance is yet another commonly accepted defining feature of the peasantry.

The second question that has occupied scholars centers precisely on this debate over peasant protest and violence, and stems in part from the fact that supposedly tradition-bound, conservative peasants have played such a prominent role not only in revolutions of the past, but also in most of the 20th century's massive social and revolutionary upheavals. One highly influential model popularized by James Scott posits a "moral economy" in which peasants share a moral universe intricately tied to the economy. Scott argues that peasants believe in a right to subsistence based on the fulfillment of minimal human needs within their economy, and peasant ideologies, commonly opposed to dominant world views, are created and sustained by such beliefs. Hence during times of change, when customary rights are violated and landlords cease to meet the peasantry's expectations of reciprocity, peasants will seek to reassert their traditional moral economy through a variety of methods including rebellion. Those who follow the moral economy model have shown that it can prove an effective ideology for supporting peasant revolution, particularly within relatively autonomous, isolated rural communities with strong precapitalist values.

Other scholars such as Samuel Popkin and Theda Skocpol have argued that moral economists provide a romanticized, ahistorical picture of the peasantry that is too narrowly focused on the peasant community and which take little account of internal divisions and class tensions that exist in these communities. A more complete and accurate analysis of peasant revolution, they continue, must take into account the role of political and military organizations in agrarian rebellions, the ways in which global (rather than purely localized) forces—in particular, the international expansion of capitalism and imperialism—may provoke revolutions, and the often critical factor of state organizations and their relationships to social classes. Peasants, in other words, are often only one part of the larger story of agrarian revolutions.

While peasant economic adjustments and protest dominate research on the peasantry, social historians have also expanded attention to peasant rituals and other manifestations of peasant belief systems, leading to debates over how peasants relate to wider cultural changes such as upper-class attacks on magic or the spread of nationalism. Peasant sexuality and family life have inspired important work as well, as have structures of village government as indications both of internal peasant hierarchies and of value systems. The problem of comparative history looms large in the agenda of peasant studies. Some conceptions of the peasantry assume basic similarities across many different times and periods, but other scholars point to the specificity of peasant family structures, ideas, and reactions. Finally, for modern history, the issue of the "end" of the peasantry has inspired attention; at what point in an industrial society like western Europe do the decline in peasant numbers and the changes in ideas and economic behaviors suggest that terming the farming population "peasant" becomes misleading? (*See also* African Peasantry; Asian Peasantry; *Jacqueries*; Land Tenure and Reform; Manorialism; Peasant Rebellion; Russian Peasantry)

Stephen P. Frank

REFERENCES

Ladurie, Emmanuel Le Roy. "Peasants," in *The Cambridge Modern History*, Vol. 13, appendix 7. Cambridge: Cambridge University Press, 1980.

Mintz, Sidney W. "A Note on the Definition of Peasantries," *The Journal of Peasant Studies* 1, 1 (October 1973): 91–106.

Scott, James C. *Weapons of the Weak: Everyday Forms of Peasant Resistance.* New Haven: Yale University Press, 1987.

Shanin, Teodor, ed. *Peasants & Peasant Societies*, 2nd ed. Oxford: Basil Blackwell, 1987.

Weller, Robert P., and Scott E. Guggenheim, eds. *Power and Protest in the Countryside: Studies of Rural Unrest in Asia, Europe, and Latin America.* Durham, NC: Duke University Press, 1983.

Peonage

Peonage refers to dependent labor on landed estates in Latin America. The word derives from "peon," a Spanish designation of the common foot soldier. Peonage emerged in Latin America in the second half of the 16th century as mestizos (people of mixed Indian and European heritage) and Indians who were escaping the labor and tribute exactions imposed upon their communities went to the Spanish-owned estates, called haciendas. The growth of hacienda peons marked the transition in colonial Spanish America from *encomienda* and state-supplied labor to the private acquisition of workers. Peonage remained a salient characteristic of rural labor relations until the land reforms of the second half of the 20th century.

Despite a common name, peonage differed widely from country to country and even, at times, from estate to estate. The Bolivian example from the early 20th century is typical. There were two types of peons on the haciendas. One were the *arrenderos,* or renters. They paid a token amount of money to rent parts of the hacienda lands and were obligated to serve as workers a certain number of days during the year (depending on the quality and quantity of land they were renting), for which they were paid small wages. In addition, children and wives served as shepherds and cooks, respectively, for the hacienda owner. The *arrenderos* also had to serve in other capacities, as in providing firewood and work in the hacienda house as stable boys and housekeepers. Many *arrenderos* in turn had their own peons, called *arrimantes*. These people sublet the *arrenderos'* lands and had to fulfill part of the *arrenderos'* obligations to the master as well as some labor obligations to the *arrendero.*

Other peonage systems, as in Chile or Mexico, had a category of permanent workers who paid no rent at all, whereas the hacienda maintained a much larger number of sharecroppers, whose tenure on the land was much less secure. Also, cow herders usually enjoyed more privileges because of their mobility than peons, who only engaged in agricultural tasks. While for a long time the peonage system was thought to be an essentially manorial system such as in medieval Europe, the relatively great mobility of Latin American peons and their ability to mitigate somewhat their exploitation has brought this view into question. The debate over debt peonage has brought this aspect into sharper focus. Debt peonage is a system whereby the owner kept the peon perpetually in debt and thus unable to leave the estate. However, peons did leave frequently without paying, and maintaining a debt peonage system was a relatively expensive method for the landowner because of the advances he had to give the peon to create the debt. Thus, debt peonage was used only in areas of acute labor shortage and where enforcement of legal norms was relatively effective, making escape difficult. These areas of debt peonage at the turn of the last century included places such as the Yucatán peninsula, southeastern Bolivia, and the rubber-harvesting regions of the Amazon jungle.

The demise of peonage systems occurred only in the 20th century in most of Latin America. The first country to rid itself officially of peonage was Mexico, in the aftermath of the Mexican Revolution. The social revolution in Bolivia in 1952 and the land reform measures abolished peonage throughout much of that country. Other Latin American countries followed suit, often combined with vigorous land reform measures. While peonage still subsists in certain areas of

Latin America, free wage labor has largely replaced it. (*See also Haciendas/Encomiendas;* Landless Laborers; Manorialism)

Erick D. Langer

REFERENCES

Bauer, Arnold J. "Rural Workers in Spanish America: Problems of Peonage and Oppression," *Hispanic American Historical Review* 59, 1 (Feb. 1979): 1–33.

Chevalier, François. *Land and Society in Colonial Mexico: The Great Hacienda.* Translated by Alvin Eustis. Berkeley: University of California Press, 1963.

Gonzalez, Michael. *Plantation Agriculture and Social Control in Northern Peru, 1875–1933.* Austin: University of Texas Press, 1985.

Katz, Friedrich. "Labor Conditions on Haciendas in Porfirian Mexico: Some Trends and Tendencies," *Hispanic American Historical Review* 54, 1 (Feb. 1974): 1–47.

Periodization/Sequences

Periods, eras, and epochs are working divisions of objective historical time used as frameworks of analysis. Any such framework involves the researcher in an act of "colligation"—that is, grouping together diverse events on the basis of some principle (e.g., common context, influence, process, or meaningful logic) that has temporal boundaries. In one approach, a period such as "the Renaissance" itself may constitute an object of inquiry. Alternatively, periods can be identified by major turning points (e.g., the French Revolution, the end of World War II) that the historical researcher argues shift the fundamental ways in which events proceed; a series of such major turning points can be used to identify sequences of historical periods (and, therefore, transitions between periods). Each period may itself be comprised of an internal sequence of events that unfolds from a point of departure to a point of resolution. (Such a sequence might be posited, for example, for the Cold War era from the late 1940s through the early 1990s.) History is thereby colligated as sequences of events that fit within larger-scale sequences of periods, and so on. In this approach, all events within a period do not necessarily share any single characteristic: history is marked by turning points, but a period between turning points does not necessarily have a coherent character. Indeed, periods only begin or end because of concrete events that are in principle open-ended and contingent: it is the events (and, perhaps, the willful play of historical actors) that establish periods, and not periods that determine events. By contrast, when a period such as the Renaissance is identified as a self-contained object of inquiry, colligation of events need not depend on sequences that nest within other sequences. Instead, events may be held to belong together on the basis of shared characteristics, regardless of whether they build on one another or lead in any particular direction. In this case, the character of a given period may be readily identifiable, while its beginning and ending are more nebulous, since they do not depend on any dramatic turning points. Periodization analysis may focus on causation, in which case beginning and end points are vital, or it may be more descriptive and interpretive in focusing on the issue of internal coherence.

This brief consideration of these two ideal typical alternatives shows that different approaches to periodization depend on different assumptions about the nature of historical time and the object of historical inquiry. The possibilities are diverse. A social history could be written to show how different people in different times and places have construed periods and sequences within the flux of historical time. In any such history, a major question would have to do with whether the periods and sequences are real characteristics of empirical history, simply awaiting discovery, or alternatively, whether they are the products of historical and methodological viewpoints that reside in the eyes of the beholders. Taking up the first possibility, philosophers of history and early sociologists once wanted to describe the "stages" of history as a totality. In a different approach, scientific historians in the tradition of Leopold von Ranke wanted to tell about history as it really was, but they still sought to establish grand narratives of the total movement of events. In either case, history written large would possess meaning independently of historical research, and the historian's choice of periodization would be an objective enterprise concerned with properly colligating events in ways that revealed the actual total historical process.

The rise of social history inevitably raised important questions about periodization, but many social historians long focused on other aspects of presentation. Some accepted standard periods derived from political history—witness the number of social histories that stop with 1914, for example, without asking whether World War I actually caused major changes in trends for the social history topic in question. Some simply worked on topics without much concern for periods, particularly when establishing a pattern, rather than dealing with change, formed the principal focus. With time, social historians' work on periodization has become more systematic and sophisticated, often challenging conventional divisions of time, but many routine approaches persist. Growing attention to issues of causation have improved periodization debates in social history, establishing characteristic differences between transition years, even decades in social history and the event-based calendars of conventional political accounts.

Recent approaches to social history lent greater complexity to the formulation of objective historical time. Fernand Braudel, famed historian of the *Annales* school, for example, has wanted to argue that various historical processes operate on different *scales* of objective historical time. In his formulation, (1) some periodizations might have to do with the short-term push of events such as political struggles; (2) others with much longer, "ecological," time spans of history of enduring social patterns in relation to things like climate and geography; and (3) finally, a middle scale of time capturing the changes in relatively stable social institutions and patterns that outlast any individual (for example, family structure patterns or modes of transportation). In this approach, social historians would not necessarily expect any neat alignment of, say, periods of political history and periods in the social history of sexuality. Periodizations might be of markedly different duration, and shifts between periods might occur at different points in objective time. Any given dimension of historical change might exhibit its own distinctive periodization.

With some affinities to the *Annales* approach, certain sociological theories of history, such as Marxism and some varieties of world-system theory, posit complex processes that operate under given general conditions. In such theories, the problem of periodization is a matter of identifying the central causal dynamics at work in history, and the points of their breakdown or shift to a new set of operative general conditions. As with the *Annales* approach, there are objective periods to be discovered. But *Annales* periods are defined by reference to empirical events, whereas Marxist periodization depends on using theory to identify "the engines" of history.

Such approaches to periodization are "realist" if they posit real periods *in* history. With the increasing influences of the humanities and empirical social sciences in the practices of historical inquiry, such realist assumptions have been challenged. Humanists have suggested that the approach chosen to conduct inquiry influences what appears as the object of historical investigation. The realist idea that history has an intrinsic meaning has been displaced by studies such as Hayden White's famous *Metahistory* (1973), which shows that historical writing is shaped by the internal structure of narrative as a kind of writing. In views such as White's, interpreting history is akin to reading a text. If, as many literary critics argue, there is no single meaning even to a given text such as a play or a novel, it seems even less likely that the flux of historical events has any intrinsic pattern to it. Any narrative structure that gives a meaningful account of history thus necessarily fits historical knowledge into a story that gives significance to history that does not depend upon historical knowledge alone. Under this argument, periodization and sequencing are interpretive acts of reading history. Inquiry need not be any the less illuminating, but the devices of periodization and sequencing have to be regarded as heuristics of inquiry which cannot be justified except by the understandings they yield. History may be about past events, but those events are placed into meaningful arrangements by the retrospective lenses of historians, and this is true whether historians (1) work to discover the (intrinsic) periodizations and sequences of interest to historical actors themselves or (2) seek to establish some objective (extrinsic) standard by which to identify periods and sequences.

Taken seriously, the humanists' claims mean that we must question whether "the Renaissance" actually took place, or whether it is simply one possible colligation of events that historians have found useful as a tool of analysis and a basis of argumentation. It is easy to take periodizations such as "the Renaissance" or "the postindustrial era" so seriously that they are treated as real things, rather than as the products of colligation. The dangers of such reification can be seen in the periodization that Marxist historians sometimes have used to mark off "feudalism" from "capitalism." Having posited two eras, Marxists could debate the question of the "transition" from one to the other. But detailed research draws into question whether there was ever a coherent phenomenon that might be called feudalism, much less an identifiable "period" of feudalism; nor is it evident that early modern capitalism originated out of any "transition from" feudalism. Even this brief discussion demonstrates the practical importance of the humanists' cautionary argument: seemingly obvious historical periodizations are themselves bound up with particular theories of history and historical processes.

The influences from social science are somewhat different. They have been of two major thrusts. First, both structuralist philosophers (such as Louis Althusser) and interpretive sociologists and anthropologists have argued that *social* time does not necessarily neatly align with objective, chronological time. They have pointed out that objective time itself is a social construction, like other socially constructed devices of measurement. If this is so, the practice of periodization using objective time may mask significant connections among processes and events that would be discontinuous if mapped on a scale of objective time. For example, events significant to the advancement of "the Enlightenment" may not all have happened within any neatly identifiable time period. Similarly, "the Cold War" has relevant originary events that precede any single identifiable "beginning" in the 1940s. For both structuralists and interpretivists, periodization by objective time thus may not be a particularly useful basis of colligation, because

"periods" are only intermittently connected by actions and processes that contribute to them, with the consequence that various "periods" (better, social processes or meaningfully connected action patterns) overlap and interpenetrate one another. For structural and interpretive approaches, objective periodization thus is only one tool of temporal historical analysis.

Second, quantitative social scientists interested in identifying causal regularities (and historians using similar methods) have drawn into question the idea that periodization would necessarily serve as the keystone to inquiry, and for related reasons. Grand social theories posit overarching processes at work in a single era (for example, market processes in industrial capitalism and the period industrial capitalism describes, or information in a postindustrial society). Such theories are increasingly undermined by empirical research that identifies not one, but a multiplicity of processes at work. Here, as with structural and interpretive approaches, periodization begins to have a more local or delimited character: researchers do not claim to identify the key epochs of history; instead, they hope to sort through the various phases that a region underwent under successive colonial regimes, or to find connections between a shift in the character of industrial production and changes in the status of women in a particular city. In such analyses, the problem of periodization is transferred from macrohistory to the analysis of connections among changes in discrete aspects of a relatively bounded sociohistorical phenomenon (a social movement, labor relations in a mining town, the history of an organization, and so forth).

In the final analysis, the humanistic warning against reification and the structural and interpretive social theoretical emphases on delimiting coherent spheres and conduits of social process find common cause with empirical social history, where debates about periodization and sequences can be informed by fine-grained analysis of one or another quantitative historical time series index (e.g., labor unrest over time, changes in economic conditions, state fiscal pressures, proportion of women in wage-labor positions). By use of sophisticated quantitative techniques, it is possible to examine time series data in order to identify the shifts and breaks and periods of constant trends or average tendencies. But quantitative analysis over objective time does not always neatly reduce to periods and sequences. Instead, there are a diversity of temporally located repetitive events, interactions between processes, conjunctures of events at the same time, shifts in tendencies, ruptures, and so on. Quantitative social history thus can temporally map a complex web of events and processes that go beyond basic questions of periodization and sequence to reveal a complex interaction of factors, no single one of which identifies a coherent period or sequence of periods. Even this sort of careful quantitative analysis leaves open the question of whether other analyses of the same events might yield important information that is masked by the operative time series indices. Qualitative evidence, as on cultural topics, promotes location of changes in trends as well, though the precision differs. Useful (indeed, inevitable) though periodizations may be, both the humanistic critique of historical practice and empirical social historical research suggest that we withhold any attribution of reality and instead recognize periodizations and sequences as conceptual tools that can be used to test various arguments about history. (*See also* Causation; Methodology)

John R. Hall

REFERENCES

Abbott, Andrew. "Event Sequence and Event Duration: Colligation and Measurement," *Historical Methods* 17 (1984): 192–204.

Carr, David. *Time, Narrative, and History.* Bloomington: Indiana University Press, 1986.

Dray, William H. *On History and Philosophers of History.* New York: E.J. Brill, 1989, esp. chap. 2.

Hall, John R. "The Time of History and the History of Times," *History and Theory* 19 (1980), 113–131.

Mandelbaum, Maurice. *The Anatomy of Historical Knowledge.* Baltimore: Johns Hopkins University Press, 1977.

Peronism

Peronism is closely identified with Latin American populism, which in turn has profound effects on a social historical understanding of the working class in the region from the 1930s to the present. Peronism, officially called Justicial-ism, was created by Juan Domingo Perón (1895–1974), who ruled Argentina from 1946 to 1955 and from 1973 to 1974. In addition to Perón's second wife Isabel's administration (1974–1976), a Peronist ruled Argentina from 1980 to 1984. In its original form, Peronism is known for a mixture of nationalism, the integration of the working class into national politics, and a multiclass alliance in the context of an authoritarian regime that provided for some reform but did nothing to fundamentally change society. Because of its popular appeal, Peronism differed from some earlier forms of Latin American authoritarianism; it must be studied from a social as well as a political vantage point.

Peronism arose in the post–World War II years, a special time in Argentine history when the country was awash in money from payments for agricultural exports that had been delayed until the end of the war. Colonel Juan Perón earlier, as secretary of labor during the military regime from 1943 to 1945, had garnered support from labor unions by intervening on their behalf in disputes with industrialists. Once in power, Perón backed his rhetoric by helping engineer a real rise in workers' wages. With his wife, Evita, a former actress and charismatic speaker, he created a network of social welfare agencies that increased his support among the lower classes. By the 1950s and especially after his wife's death in 1952, Perón's popularity began to slip. He was ousted by military coup in 1955. Even in exile, however, Perón kept the loyalty of a large proportion of an increasingly persecuted labor movement, making the country essentially ungovernable without the Peronists. He finally returned in 1973, when his party received an overwhelming majority of votes. His brief return to power before he died in office proved to be disastrous, precipitating the brutal military regimes which unleashed a "dirty war" against all opponents.

The Peronist legacy is thus manifold. It includes a concern for the working classes within an authoritarian system, in which there were some real gains in living standards for the lower classes as well as corruption and demagogy. It also established a system of government-worker relations in which the government was quite favorable to the workers, but only when it firmly controlled the labor movement. Peronism is also important because it integrated for the first time the workers into the body politic. Regimes that did not favor the workers found it impossible to extract the unions except through fierce (and ultimately temporary) repression. It also reconfirmed an important strain in Latin American political culture, in which charismatic leaders such as Juan Perón and Evita were essential to building a political system based on working-class support. Similar cases occurred in Mexico with Lázaro Cárdenas and in Brazil with Getúlio Vargas somewhat earlier, in the 1930s, but Peronism remains the best example of this type of regime. Most importantly, Perón found a way to make the working class into an important actor in Latin American politics, though the top-down means often provided the populists with greater benefits than the workers. Whether in fact Saúl Menem, elected president of Argentina in 1989 as a Peronist, can hold true to Perón's legacy is not clear.

The study of Peronism and other such movements can still yield many new insights into Latin American working-class history. Whether indeed Peronism was a multiclass alliance and what role the workers played in this alliance is being debated now. Moreover, the vast materials on Peronism can provide little-tapped but rich information on the political culture of the working class. Why laborers would opt for much rhetoric and a tepid reformism rather than the revolutionary actions presumed characteristic of an urban proletariat must be explored further as well. (*See also* Latin American Working Class; Strikes; Working Class)

Erick D. Langer

REFERENCES

Horowitz, Joel. *Argentine Unions, the State, and the Rise of Peron, 1930–1945.* Berkeley: University of California Press, 1990.

O'Donnell, Guillermo. *Modernization and Bureau-cratic-Authoritarianism: Studies in South American Politics.* Berkeley: University of California Press, 1979.

Page, Joseph. *Perón: A Biography.* New York: Random House, 1983.

Pilgrimage

Pilgrimage is ritualized procession to some site or shrine where the supernatural is perceived to intersect with the natural world. As an important popular religious expression, it has been increasingly studied by social historians and anthropologists. Pilgrimage may be in pursuit of divine intercession into a mundane situation—for example, supplication of mercy for sins committed or petition of a cure for a sick child. These types of motivations predominate within Christianity. Sites where holy people have spent time along their path to spiritual perfection can become places of veneration toward which pilgrims gravitate. Most pilgrimage sites in Buddhism have their origins as stopping points of the Buddha during his earthly peregrinations. Pilgrimage also may be a supreme act of faith, as in the Islamic requirement that every Muslim make the *hajj*, the pilgrimage to Mecca, if he or she has the means. Lastly, pilgrimage may be a search for the knowledge and wisdom to be gained through contact with a holy person or the place where a holy person has lived. This type of pilgrimage occurs regularly in Judaism. Whatever its goal, successful pilgrimage has as its social outcome a positive change in the cultural status of the pilgrim, though only in Islam is this transformation given formal acknowledgment (in the right of the returned pilgrim to add the term "*al-hajji*" to his name).

Pilgrimage has been described as a liminal state of existence. In pursuit of his or her goal, the pilgrim takes leave from normative society, and begins a journey through unknown time and space. Many pilgrimages give women greater religious equality than is normally the case. Bonds of fellowship, or *communitas*, are formed with others traveling toward the same goal. Victor and Edith Turner (1978) have contrasted the experiences of the pilgrim with those of the tourist and the mystic. Like the tourist, the pilgrim finds him- or herself free from communal obligations. For the pilgrim, however, social concern is replaced by spiritual concern, as the anxieties stimulated by the anticipated encounter with the divine supersede the pleasures attendant in adventuring. As the Turners observe, "if mysticism is an interior pilgrimage, pilgrimage is exteriorized mysticism." Like the mystic, the pilgrim embarks upon a mental voyage. But with the pilgrim, the mental journey is reinforced by a physical one.

According to all reports, modern improvements in transportation have helped facilitate pilgrimage as a devotional activity in all religions, though other kinds of travel now compete. Social historical research on this phenomenon, however, remains in a very early stage. (*See also* Buddhism; Christianity; Islam; Religion)

Andrew E. Barnes

REFERENCES

Morinis, E. Alan, ed. *Sacred Journeys: The Anthropology of Pilgrimage*. New York: Greenwood Press, 1992.

Orsi, Robert. "The Center Out There, In Here, and Everywhere Else: The Nature of Pilgrimage to the Shrine of Saint Jude, 1929–1965," *Journal of Social History* 25, 2 (1991): 213–232.

Turner, Edith et al. "Pilgrimage," in Mircea Eliade, ed., *Encyclopaedia of Religion*. New York: Macmillan, 1987.

Turner, Victor, and Edith Turner. *Image and Pilgrimage in Christian Culture*. New York: Columbia University Press, 1978.

Plague

The word "plague" has often been applied as a generic term describing any epidemic disease. The disease caused by the microorganism *Yersinia pestis,* and otherwise known as bubonic plague or the Black Death, however, remains historically most significant. Plague is primarily a disease of animals, mostly burrowing rodents, which when epizootic (that is, epidemic in animals) can be spread to human beings through a disease vector involving rats and fleas. The original focus, or home, of plague is the Eurasian steppe. From there plague has repeatedly swept outward to strike, at one time or another, almost every corner of the globe. Bubonic plague is a serious illness with about a 50 percent case mortality. Once introduced into the human bloodstream by the bite of a flea, the microorganism multiplies rapidly, spreading throughout the system and often causing typical lymph-node swellings, known as *buboes.* Infrequently, the infection settles in the lungs, where it can be transmitted

directly from person to person (without the intermediaries of rat and flea) by droplet infection (sneezing or coughing). If this happens, we speak of an epidemic of pneumonic plague, a disease with a 100 percent case mortality.

The history of plague has been written in numerous ways; medically and epidemiologically, of course, but also economically, socially, demographically, and as a history of mentalities. Work in English has concentrated on the European plague experience, converging on the cluster of outbreaks from 1347 to 1350, or focusing on plague in the Italies, or examining famous incidents, such as the Great Plague of London in 1665. Out of these events authors from several centuries have drawn their material for major literary works, including Boccaccio's *Decameron* (1353), Daniel Defoe's *A Journal of the Plague Year* (1723), and Albert Camus's *The Plague* (1948). Less information is available on the incidence and impact of plague in Asia or Africa. Plague continues to cause concern in central Asia today. Even in the late 20th century, plague is enzootic in several parts of the world, including the American Southwest and South Africa. Plague does not, however, constitute a major public health menace for areas of the world that enjoy adequate sanitary facilities and have high standards of personal and domestic hygiene. If treated promptly with antibiotics, plague can be cured. Social historians have addressed several themes in the history of plague. Despite much excellent work, the demographic consequences of plague remain disputed. Historians generally agree that plague during its initial incursion into Europe in the middle of the 14th century killed off between one-third and one-half of European inhabitants. Still, it must be remembered that some territories were more severely hit than others, while populations in several places escaped virtually unscathed. Plague persisted for a few centuries after 1347–1350, then disappeared from the European Continent forever after a last outburst in Marseilles in 1721. Yet plague was never actually endemic in Europe, rather Europe was continually reinfected with plague from the East. This repeated reintroduction of plague demonstrates how important and active were the trade networks and lines of communication that stretched between Europe and Asia in the early modern period.

The investigation of the economic consequences of plague has been to a large extent closely keyed to its demographic impact. The major and still unsolved question here is: Were people better off after the plague? The answers have varied. Some insist that plague helped alleviate an overpopulation problem (especially in 14th-century Italy), allowing survivors to acquire the use of more land or, because of severe labor shortages, to negotiate more effectively with their landlords for higher wages or more favorable terms of tenancy. Other scholars assert that landowners and governments used their political power to tighten existing regulations that limited freedom of movement, or introduce new strictures to tether a shrunken labor force to the land. Poor relief was increasingly linked to residence, thereby dampening workers' ability to move about in search of better jobs. In 14th-century England, for example, charity was extended only in a pauper's own parish.

Plague has also played a pivotal role in the history of public health. Many historians have argued that plague generated the first public health awareness. Under the pressure of plague, governments began in the 14th century to expand their range of actions and to intervene more vigorously in the private lives of their subjects. Thus, plague can be seen as an important component of the general process of state-building in early modern Europe. Plague called forth a series of public health measures, such as quarantines, the creation of boards of health, the erection of plague hospitals and *cordons sanitaires*.

The influence of plague on the human consciousness has also preoccupied many historians. Some have viewed plague in the 14th century as having a particularly debilitating effect on European civilization, signaling a major transformation in culture and fostering a more pessimistic outlook on life. More specifically, art historians have found echoes of plague in later medieval painting. The Dance of Death motif, for example, occurs with increasing frequency in the iconography of 14th- and 15th-century Europe. Plague has also raised questions about how readily, if at all, a scientific worldview came to replace a more religious one, and the extent to which civil conflicts during plague epidemics reflected a clash between faith and reason. More recently, historians have begun to explore how mentalities were affected and transformed by the experiences of plague, by studying, for instance, how plague became part of an age's "mental furniture" and found its way into popular discourse.

Thus, in these many ways plague has furnished and continues to furnish rich material for social history. While much work has been done on plague, there are still significant gaps. We know relatively little about plague outside of Europe. We need to learn more about how ordinary people grappled with the social and psychological consequences of plague. Finally, we still remain pretty much in the dark about the exact economic and demographic aftereffects of plague for all but a relatively few regions. (*See also* Asian Disease History; Charity; Health; Mentalities; Poor Relief)

Mary Lindemann

REFERENCES

Calvi, Giulia. *Histories of a Plague Year: The Social and the Imaginary in Baroque Florence.* Translated by Dario Biocca and Bryant T. Ragan, Jr. Berkeley and Los Angeles: University of California Press, 1989.

Cipolla, Carlo. *Faith, Reason and the Plague in Seventeenth-Century Tuscany.* London: The Harvester Press, 1979.

Dols, Michael. *The Black Death in the Middle East.* Princeton, NJ: Princeton University Press, 1977.

Herlihy, David. "Population, Plague, and Social Change in Rural Pistoia," *Economic History Review* 2, 18 (1965): 225–244.

McNeill, William H. *Plagues and Peoples.* New York: Anchor, 1976.

Slack, Paul. *The Impact of Plague in Tudor and Stuart England.* London: Routledge & Kegan Paul, 1985.

Plantation Economy

Initially, "plantation" referred to a plot of ground characterized by the movement of plants. Any colony had its plantations, every colonist was a planter. Only gradually did the term evolve its special meaning of an estate given to international market crops worked by gang labor with close supervision. From the beginning plantations described a variety of landholdings that have reflected the changing impetus of colonialism, evolutions of capitalism, and roles of agribusiness.

Long before plantations became synonymous with tropical plants and their costs in labor and land, plantations worked by slaves and based upon sugar had existed in the Mediterranean. The Portuguese were experimenting with slave-based sugar plantations in São Tomé on the West African coast by 1500. It was this initial experiment, introduced subsequently into northeastern Brazil and then into Barbados and the Lesser Antilles by the end of the 17th century, which created the Plantation Zone of the Americas.

The Plantation Zone running roughly from the Mason-Dixon line to the Rio Plata on the Atlantic coast and incorporating the Caribbean basin has been interpreted to show commonalities for the nations and regions which are encompassed. In one of the first definitions of this zone Charles Wagley defined it as "monocrop cultivation under the plantation system, rigid class lines, multiracial societies, weak community cohesion, small peasant properties involved in subsistence and cash crop production and matri-focal family forms." This definition should also emphasize that this is also the African American culture area of the New World. It was predominantly forced African labor and that of their descendants subjected to slavery and other harsh labor conditions which marked the plantation culture area. Wagley's definition is still of heuristic value, but recent works on plantation societies have emphasized the ranges of plantation regimes, the timing of their involvement in the world market, and the resultant effects upon the nexus of capital, labor, and land. It appears that the plantation as an abstraction is compatible with both conflict and cohesion in social life. The further attempt at formalizing plantation communities has led to new appreciations of the complex dichotomies and definitional interpenetration of peasant and proletariat in the plantation zone. And, again, household forms are not reproduced in a clear-cut way in plantation regions. Other variables have to account for the household varieties which are encountered.

This part peasant, part proletarian ambiguity of rural plantation societies has profound influence upon discussions of agricultural development, internal migration, ethnic diversity in the regional, and national politics of the region. The counterpart to these issues of analysis are found in the definitional concepts of the plantation economy itself. Is the plantation to be considered as a special type of capitalist enterprise? If so, what criterion should be applied? Some have argued that plantations have more in common, through relations of production and a seigneurial culture, with feudalism and manorialism than with capitalism. However Sidney Mintz, Immanuel Wallerstein, and others have forcibly argued that plantations and slavery are the essence of agribusiness and a capitalist mode of production.

In Philip Curtin's (1990) characteristics of Plantation Zones, six diagnostics are listed: (1) Most of the productive labor was forced. Most of the productive labor was introduced from elsewhere via slavery in the New World, East Africa, and Indian Ocean plus more subtle means of labor coercion. (2) "These populations were not self sustaining." (3) "Agricultural enterprises were organized in large scale capitalist plantations; typically these plantations had 50 to several hundred workers." (4) Though capitalist, these estates, particularly in the time periods and regions formed during mercantile capitalism, contained attributes which could be considered feudal. (5) "The Plantations were created to supply a distant market with a highly specialized product." A substantial investment in technicians, equipment, and overhead costs was required. The profits were due to overseas market demands. The plantation has been the transfer agent of metropolitan investment into the colonial periphery hence shaping profoundly the cultural and economic contours of the colony. (6) Political control was vested in metropolitan units whose social structure and interests were hardly synonymous with the peripheries.

Growing North Atlantic prosperity in the 19th century brought new demands and increasingly corporate-style plantations and their expansion into a global tropical production: coffee from Java and the Caribbean, Brazil, Colombia; tea from Assam and Sri Lanka; rubber from Indo-China and Malaysia; and sugar from Hawaii, Philippines, South Africa, Peru, and Australia. This expansion incorporated new populations of post-peasant labor, who were nominally free yet under harsh controls and often relocated regionally, continentally, or overseas, to the plantation sites.

The plantation's effects upon those zones in which it implanted and enforced have proven to be pervasive and long lasting. The plantation may have impoverished the states which were its hosts in large part by inhibiting the development of alternative forms of economic and social development. But today the plantation economic unit is a dwindling force in the world. Instead the plantation as metaphor is applied to new extractive industries such as tourism, branch plant manufacturers and mineral/exporting enclaves. (*See also* Agricultural Systems; Commercialization; Slavery)

Frank McGlynn

REFERENCES

Beckford, George. *Persistent Poverty: Underdevelopment in Plantation Economies of the Third World.* Oxford: Oxford University Press, 1972.

Curtin, Philip. *The Rise and Fall of the Plantation Complex.* Cambridge: Cambridge University Press, 1990.

Miles, Robert. *Capitalism and Unfree Labor: Anomaly or Necessity.* London: Routledge, Chapman & Hall, 1987.

Mintz, Sidney. *Sweetness and Power: The Place of Sugar in Modern History.* New York: Viking, 1985.

Stavenhagen, Rodolfo. *Social Classes in Agrarian Societies.* New York: Anchor Press, 1975.

Thomas, Clive. *The Poor and the Powerless: Economic Policy and Change in the Caribbean.* New York: Monthly Review Press, 1988.

Police

The police as a political and community-based institution has played an increasing role in the social history of Europe and other developing areas of the world. Preindustrial policemen did exist in some European and Asian countries, but the forces were small. A key focus of the social history of policing involves the shift from community responsibility for arrests (and considerable military involvement in keeping order) to the police, a trained governmental agency charged with law enforcement. Over the last two centuries, while professionalism and training have become the hallmarks of modern police forces in many cultures, the scope of their authority has varied significantly. In liberal democratic states, such as Britain, the police were charged with maintaining order while protecting individual rights. In contrast, other more authoritarian states such as Nazi Germany significantly expanded the police's role to emphasize political control and surveillance. Even in democracies such as the United States, the tension between the need for collective security and concerns about individual rights is far from resolved, and the police's role continues to be controversial.

In parliamentary governments such as Britain and the United States, police were created with legal and administrative constraints on their authority. Borrowing from the private policing experiments of Patrick Colquhoun and Henry Fielding in the 17th and 18th centuries, British prime minister Sir Robert Peel drafted the first police bill in 1828, and, the following year, a municipal force was created in London, setting a model which was copied in the United States, France, and Germany. Trained officers patrolled specific beats; their powers were legally circumscribed and their activities monitored by an administrative hierarchy.

In the United States, London's model of a municipal police was utilized in New York, Boston, and elsewhere. While similar in many ways, the United States was less successful in limiting police authority and creating professional officers. In Britain, for example, police administration was developed as part of the civil service, and officials were drawn from other areas of the government. In contrast, the American police were usually enmeshed in urban political machines, and political considerations heavily influenced appointments, policy, and operations. In matters of enforcement, the British police were more constrained in their use of force than their American counterparts. Also, in police training, British administrators emphasized professionalism and the uniform application of the law in an attempt to create officers aloof from their community and obedient to the administrative hierarchy. In contrast, American police, possessing a much broader mandate to interpret and enforce the law, were more influenced by local considerations or by racial or ethnic prejudices.

In the early 20th century, middle-class reformers in America became more critical of the police's political connections as well as their lack of efficiency when compared to their British counterparts. Through the appointment of commissions and strong chief administrators, Raymond Fosdick, Bruce Smith, and other reformers sought to maximize their control over departments and to make the police more responsive to centralized command. Senior officers were often passed over for appointments to high administrative office as legal professionals and college professors took their places. In their further attacks on political patronage, reformers advocated regular standards, examinations, and minimum educational requirements for promotion with court reviews of dismissals.

Ideologically, if not always in practice, the police in Britain and the United States tried to balance their duty to uphold the external order with the need to safeguard individual rights. In times of upheaval or in traditionally more authoritarian states, new police functions were created or enhanced, which emphasized collective security and state control. In czarist Russia, following a long tradition of state surveillance, the regular and political police were centralized under the Ministry of Internal Affairs following the assassination of Alexander II. A special department, the Osoby Otdel, dealt with political crimes, and drew many of its personnel from the regular police. Their investigative duties expanded to include the monitoring of not only dissidents in Russia but also émigrés and revolutionaries living abroad. With the fall of the monarchy in 1917, the new Soviet government adopted the same model for their secret police, the *Cheka,* and even expanded their punitive powers.

Even democratic states with model civil police forces could easily have these institutions converted into instruments of political surveillance and oppression. The police of Weimar Germany, for example, resembled the professional ideal advocated by American reformers. The *Kriminalpolizei* of Berlin were well-trained, highly educated officers that abhorred internal corruption as well as the use of violence against criminal suspects. In the unstable climate of the early 1930s, however, the Berlin police were easily attracted to the National Socialists who advocated civil order and control. In 1936, Heinrich Himmler became chief of all police forces in Germany, unifying regular police with Nazi units like the SS (Schutzstaffel) under one command, and regular police officials were dispersed throughout the organizational hierarchy. The powers of the police were greatly expanded to include criminal and political crimes with few limitations on police action and authority.

The social history of the police involves more than assessing the institution comparatively in light of different political structures. Social historians have dealt with police recruitment for the institution, which has often served as an important channel of social mobility. They have dealt with training, with methods (including the impact of patrol cars on police effectiveness), and with results in terms of crime patterns and arrests. Analyzing police choices in whom to arrest and what crimes to tolerate link police history with other aspects of urban social history. Finally, evolution of police functions has commanded significant attention. This can involve not only redefinitions of political policing but also the use of police for control of popular leisure activities, for dealing with vagrants and disorderly conduct, for providing informal welfare, and of course for dealing with the clearer categories of crime. In the United States, for example, the police moved away from some general discipline and community service functions at points in the 19th century, increasingly justifying their role in terms of crime fighting. Here is a final way to link, as police historian Eric Monkkonen put it, "cop history and social history." (*See also* Crime; State and Society)

Jared Day

REFERENCES

Hingley, Ronald. *The Russian Secret Police: Muscovite, Imperial Russian, and Soviet Political Security Operations.* New York: Simon & Schuster, 1971.

Miller, Wilbur. *Cops and Bobbies; Police Authority in New York and London, 1830–1870.* Chicago: University of Chicago, 1977.

Monkkonen, Eric. *Police in Urban America, 1860–1920.* New York: Cambridge, 1981.

Mosse, George L., ed. *Police Forces in History.* London: Sage, 1975.

Walker, Samuel. *A Critical History of Police Reform; The Emergence of Professionalism.* Lexington, MA: Lexington Books, 1977.

Poor Relief

Research on poor relief involves attention to the poor themselves, to class relations, and to larger social attitudes underlying policy. Social historians have associated changes in poor relief practices with rising commerce, declining community ties, and a growing central government. The documentary record of poor relief agencies provides a uniquely valuable source for a wide gamut of topics from food consumption patterns to social hierarchy and clientage.

The concept of "poor relief" can be taken very broadly to include all forms of aid, charity, and public assistance to the poor at all times, in all places. But here the focus will be on the modern, Western concept that emerged at the end of the Middle Ages and was to a large extent superseded by the modern welfare state (though contemporary welfare policies preserve many poor relief precedents). Poor relief has been a major topic for social historians of western Europe and America. Vast opportunities remain for further research and for comparative interpretations (including Russia and eastern Europe, for example, and lands subject to Islamic law).

The economic management of poor relief by lay authorities was a central theme of 16th-century charitable reform in western Europe, a movement that drew on rich medieval precedents. Writers from Ernst Troeltsch to W.K. Jordan attributed systematic reform to Protestantism, but in recent decades Natalie Davis, Brian Pullan, Bronislaw Geremek, and others have stressed the commonalities as well as the varieties of reform throughout Europe. In the interpretation of Marxist historians such as Catherina Lis and Hubert Soly, 16th-century conceptions of poor relief served the needs of an emerging mercantile economy and permitted urban elites to regulate the supply of labor. Changes in poor law arrangements, in their view, reflected the transition to capitalist forms of production.

England provided the most systematic poor relief of any country in Europe by the early 17th century. The "Elizabethan Poor Law" (1597 and 1601) required poor persons either to support themselves or to apply to their own parishes of settlement for aid. Overseers of the poor in each parish determined eligibility for relief and levied parish poor rates on property owners. Justices of the peace validated the rolls and compelled payments from those who failed to contribute.

Various local experiments, many of them modeled on the workhouse established in London's Bridewell hospital in the 1550s, inspired Parliament to make parish overseers responsible for organizing work for the able-bodied poor. But many parishes never erected bridewells, and local authorities saw fit to dole out relief to unemployed workers without necessarily "setting them on work." In the view of Paul Slack (1988), the English were able to establish a system so comprehensive because the country was relatively wealthy and could afford to raise the greater number out of the threat of destitution.

The extension of entitlement to "outdoor relief" in the Speenhamland reform of 1795 initiated a period of debate in England. The "new" poor law of 1834 instituted the principle of "less eligibility" and "the workhouse test," to make sure that recipients of relief would not be better off than those employed at a free-market wage. Scholars have recently qualified earlier generalizations about the harshness of the new system, while reaffirming the political impact of empirical social investigators such as Charles Booth, Seebohm Rowntree, and Sidney and Beatrice Webb, whose critique of the poor laws laid the foundation for the modern European welfare state.

Spain has been viewed as resistant to all change in the name of Catholic orthodoxy. But in a study of 16th-century Toledo, Linda Martz describes the efforts of reformers armed with the ideas of Juan Luis Vives and backed by the Spanish Crown. Resistance often won the day, but Spanish religious movements also generated new charitable initiatives. St. John of God (1495–1550) and his followers established hospitals for the lowliest as well as the most respectable of the poor. Domingo de Soto (1484–1560) argued against a new prohibition on the mobility of the poor in terms that were economic as well as religious: the poor should be allowed, he said, to migrate like ants searching out the richest part of the plant.

The relationship between attitudes and social realities has been a leading theme in much of the research on poor relief and policies toward the poor in France in the 17th and 18th centuries. Michel Foucault argued that the removal of marginal populations from public spaces into the *hôpital-général* of Paris in 1656 reflected a new value placed on rational order. But Jean-Pierre Gutton describes at least a century of previous efforts to confine the poor and set them to work and shows that the strategy of confinement always had its critics. Analyzing wills and testaments at Grenoble, Kathryn Norberg has shown how Counter-Reformation piety supported both individual almsgiving and bequests to institutions where the poor were confined. Finding a similar pattern at Montpellier, Colin Jones shows 18th-century donors supporting various forms of aid when they came to view the hospitals as inefficient. Olwen Hufton argues that, in spite of the interest of the elite in the reform of relief, the resources available from every quarter—including work projects and emergency relief from the royal government—were so limited as to throw the poor on their own to survive by "an economy of makeshifts."

The transition from the enlightened liberal paternalism of the 18th century to a far more limited and repressive policing of workers in a laissez faire industrial economy emerges clearly in Mary Lindemann's *Patriots and Paupers: Hamburg, 1712–1830*. A system that required an elite of volunteers to identify all the needy and to arrange relief, including the provision of work where appropriate, was overwhelmed by the demographic expansion and industrialization of the city and the region, and by the political upheavals of the Napoleonic period.

Recent studies of 19th-century poor relief have explored the gap between the official rationale provided for relief policies and the perspective of the poor who received relief. A study of Antwerp from 1770 to 1860 by Lis and Soly (1979) shows that the poor availed themselves of correctional institutions and insane asylums to provide sustenance to family members. This is a theme also explored in United States his-

tory: informal community support for the poor declined by 1800 as the poor increased in number. Lynn Hollen Lees has shown how mothers in 19th-century London exploited various private and public resources to supplement inadequate family income, circumventing the official rule that only the impotent poor receive help outside the established workhouse.

The evolution of poor relief in the United States has been shaped by notions of exceptionalism, but English law and English reform movements were influential at every stage. As in England, early 19th-century reformers condemned the practice of "outdoor relief" and extolled the merits of poorhouses. But by 1850, according to Michael Katz (1986), the poorhouse was viewed as a costly failure, and most states had greatly expanded their relief rolls in order to meet the crisis of Irish famine immigration and the dislocations of urban growth. In a further reaction against outdoor relief, the late 19th century saw the rise of the "scientific charity" movement. In *Public Relief and Private Charity* (1884), Josephine Shaw Lowell, a leader in the movement, urged the formation of charity organization societies everywhere to study the poor and coordinate the activities of those organizations that could best provide short-term relief without doing moral harm to the recipient.

The dramatic impact of the Great Depression of the 1930s on even the most self-reliant poor was documented by E. Wight Bakke in a 1933 study of the sequence of expedients that the unemployed of New Haven tried before resorting to relief. The federal government took over from insolvent local authorities, establishing various precedent-setting measures, supported through grants-in-aid to the states from the Federal Emergency Relief Administration (FERA). The idea of linking relief and work was embodied with partial success in the Works Progress Administration. Women's efforts to secure the welfare of children led to the provision of aid to dependent children under the terms of the legislation that established Social Security. At the same time, limitations on relief and recurrent attacks on "undeserving" welfare recipients suggest links to earlier policies and attitudes.

By 1948, when the United Nations adopted the Declaration of Human Rights, the principles of the New Deal in the United States and of the Popular Front in France influenced the provisions of article 22: "Everyone, as a member of society, has the right to social security and is entitled to realization, through national effort and international co-operation and in accordance with the organization and resources of each State, of the economic, social and cultural rights indispensable for his dignity and the free development of his personality."

According to the UN's *Human Development Report 1991*, over one billion people now live in absolute poverty. On a global level, the traditional concept of poor relief to maintain bare subsistence remains in the forefront even as idealistic statements of universal rights are linked uneasily with support for development plans and investment strategies. In richer countries, meanwhile, the notion of entitlement vested in poor citizens is contested. (*See also* Charity; Poverty; Social Control; Standard of Living)

Thomas M. Adams

REFERENCES

Katz, Michael B. *In the Shadow of the Poorhouse: A Social History of Welfare in America.* New York: Basic Books, 1986.

Lis, Catharina, and Hugo Soly. *Poverty and Capitalism in Pre-Industrial Europe.* Atlantic Highlands, NJ: Humanities Press, 1979.

Hufton, Olwen H. *The Poor of Eighteenth-Century France, 1750–1789.* Oxford: Oxford University Press, 1974.

Mandler, Peter, ed. *The Uses of Charity: The Poor on Relief in the Nineteenth-Century Metropolis.* Philadelphia: University of Pennsylvania Press, 1990.

Slack, Paul. *Poverty and Policy in Tudor and Stuart England.* New York: Longmans, 1988.

Popular Culture

Social historians have paid increasing attention to popular culture as a way of bringing the realm of culture into their investigations of the everyday life of ordinary people. Aware of the limitations of depicting people's historical experience primarily in terms derived from sociologists—emphasizing such matters as economic and social structure and demography—historians have turned to anthropology for suggestions as to how cultural activity may matter historically, and particularly how it may be a primary determinant, not simply a reflection of a social and economic reality. The kinds of topics that social historians have investigated as they have "gone cultural" vary widely, depending on scholars' particular interests as well as the era and locale they have chosen to study. So, for example, historians of early modern Europe have investigated popular religion and superstitions; historians of the 18th and 19th centuries, popular reading and public celebrations; and historians of the 20th century, leisure activities and mass culture.

Not all social historians interested in the realm of culture, however, are comfortable with the term "popular culture." Some worry about earlier antiquarian efforts that simply described circuses or fairs in the past without relating them to wider social meanings. More often, interested historians express concern about the false dichotomy implied between so-called elite and popular cultures. Even among those historians who embrace the notion of popular culture, it is not easy to find agreement on its definition. Some historians use "popular culture" and "mass culture" interchangeably, while others make significant distinctions. Sometimes those distinctions reflect a perspective that views "popular culture" as indigenous and emancipating in contrast to "mass culture," which is often assumed to be the imposition of a commercial, co-optive culture by a manipulative elite of capitalist and patriarchal culture makers. For other historians, "popular culture" represents the larger category of people's cultural experience spanning the centuries, whereas "mass culture" refers to the technologically and commercially sophisticated public culture of the last century, the balance of top-down or bottom-up influence varying with the interpretation. Finally, some historians prefer the term "popular culture" to avoid the derogatory implications of much of the "mass culture" criticism, which has viewed it as a corruption of a purer, high culture. These historians shun the use of "mass culture" entirely, distancing themselves from any effort to pass value judgments. When "mass culture" is subsumed under "popular culture" in this way, the historians involved usually hold the view that movies, radio, television, amusement parks, and other forms of modern mass culture are complex arenas much like carnivals or novel reading, where cultural consumers as well as cultural producers shape the experience.

Social historians who study popular culture have been influenced by the work of a number of theorists from other disciplines, particularly Clifford Geertz, Victor Turner, Antonio Gramsci, and Mikhail Bakhtin. Anthropologist Geertz has provided historians with a methodological model of "thick description," where close observation of cultural activity—a cockfight in Bali in his most famous example—reveals how people view themselves and their relationship to others. Fellow anthropologist Turner has contributed the theoretical concept of "liminality," where ritual events in a community are shown to be moments when the social hierarchy is temporarily inverted and the status quo thereby reinforced. Marxist social theorist Gramsci developed the notion of "cultural hegemony" to explain the complex way that elites retain power; subordinate groups are not coerced but in fact come to share the cultural orientation of dominant groups. Literary critic Bakhtin's concept of "dialogic" cultural process, where all texts embody part of the historical consciousness of their authors and audiences, has supported a cultural analysis where cultural artifacts or events convey past, present, and future struggles over power. Many popular culture studies are informed by one or more of these theoretical orientations.

Recent historical work in popular culture has challenged simplistic divisions between "popular" and "elite" culture and has used the theoretical perspectives discussed above, among others, to analyze popular culture for what it reveals about the interactions of ordinary people with more dominant groups, not just to isolate their culture as autonomous. The presence or absence of cultural autonomy, overlap, domination, emulation, or rejection has become a subject for investigation, not simple assumption. Two examples demonstrate this trend in the social historical literature.

Keith Luria (1991) has analyzed the cult of the Rosary, which grew enormously during the Counter-Reformation in France and has demonstrated that different social groups participated in this religious innovation and brought to it a multiplicity of meanings. For the church, the Rosary devotion and its confraternities taught disciplined religious behavior, particularly meditative prayer directed at one of the most charismatic figures of the faith, the Virgin. For village notable families who founded and supported the confraternities, the Rosary provided a way of allying themselves with reform groups within the church while also building their prestige vis-à-vis rival families and asserting greater cultural control over their communities. Village women, particularly of notable families, saw the confraternities as an opportunity to prove their piety while also utilizing their organizational and political skills. Poorer villagers gained a new means of expressing their religious enthusiasm and saw the Rosary confraternity processions as a vehicle for collective activity. Luria has avoided a simple elite versus popular culture analysis here. Rejecting interpretations that depict the cult of the Rosary as either imposed from above or rising autonomously from below, he argues for a shared cultural experience that different groups invested with their own meanings.

Another recent study by Lawrence Levine (1988) is also concerned with what popular culture reveals about relations between social groups. Levine has traced a transformation during the 19th century in how Americans viewed the plays of William Shakespeare. Shakespearean plays moved from being a part of mainstream cultural life—well integrated into public entertainment through their juxtaposition with other familiar performances of musicians, dancers, acrobats, and comics and enjoyed by heterogeneous audiences who actively participated by stamping, hissing, whistling, and the like—to being sanctified for "polite society" only. He shows how the ideological convictions and political agenda of an urban, cultural elite led by the turn of the century to the redrawing of cultural categories so that what once was a shared public culture became the property of the most privileged and educated in American society. In Levine's work, as in Luria's, popular culture is not isolated as a pure product of the common people, but rather is analyzed as a cultural territory where diverse social groups interact and often contest.

The field of popular culture is likely to develop further in this direction. Social historians' interest in the cultural lives of the populations they study will continue to attract them to investigating cultural practices and events. Their work will increasingly reflect the awareness, however, that the culture of ordinary people—whether defined by class, race, gender, or ethnicity—cannot be isolated from the culture of other social groups, including elites. "Popular culture," then, needs to be viewed as a place where interaction can be observed, not as an isolated expression of any one group's culture. One might wonder if this revisionism undercuts the validity of the notion of "popular culture" altogether, but that does not have to be the case. Historians should still be attentive to the crucial place of cultural activity in ordinary people's lives, and the concept of "popular culture" keeps them focused on it. That we are seeing more and more studies that bring a theoretically sophisticated and interactive interpretation of popular culture only validates the importance of the enterprise for larger historical understanding. Culture cannot be separated from issues of political power, economics, and social structure. (*See also* Anthropology; Cultural Hegemony; Festivals; Games; Leisure; Magic; Mass Culture; Mentalities; Street Life; Subcultures; Vaudeville)

Lizabeth Cohen

REFERENCES

Gans, Herbert. *Popular Culture and High Culture: An Analysis and Evaluation of Taste.* New York: Basic Books, 1974.

Geertz, Clifford. *The Interpretation of Cultures.* New York: Basic Books, 1973.

Levine, Lawrence W. *Highbrow/Lowbrow: The Emergence of Cultural Hierarchy in America.* Cambridge, MA: Harvard University Press, 1988.

Lipsitz, George. *Time Passages: Collective Memory and American Popular Culture.* Minneapolis: University of Minnesota Press, 1990.

Luria, Keith. *Territories of Grace: Cultural Change in the Seventeenth-Century Diocese of Grenoble.* Berkeley: University of California Press, 1991.

Pornography

Pornography remains a difficult topic for social historians because of its hidden nature, but it continues to be important as a facet of both popular culture and sexuality. The controversies that have surrounded pornography have led to the destruction of many primary sources and a readership which has refused to acknowledge their activities. Because of this, the essential concerns for social historians of who read pornography, what they read, and what they understood pornography to mean are still being explored.

The word "pornography" comes from the Greek *pornographos,* meaning "the writings about prostitutes." The Greeks did not define pornography as obscene. Instead, writing about prostitutes and other things sexual were accepted within the Greek culture. The current definition of pornography in Western culture, developed in the late 18th and early 19th centuries, centers upon the sexually profane. While representation of sexuality can be acceptable, in for instance medical texts, the portrayal of sexuality in ways that are taboo or for an inappropriate audience has created our understanding of pornography.

Social history offers a variety of ways to approach the topic of pornography. One approach charts the changes in cultural taboos that define pornography. The study of European pornography tends to take this focus. The proliferation of self-styled pornography in Europe was linked to innovations in printing and literature. The European discovery of the printing press in the 16th century encouraged the dissemination of sexually oriented materials, but even if these were considered obscene they were not labeled "pornography." "Aristotle's Masterpiece," a medical cum marriage guide, went through numerous reprintings until the 19th century. It was not generally labeled "obscene" even though it emphasized pleasure in marital sex. Published and outlawed at the same time, however, "Aretino's Postures," a series of sonnets and illustrations, went beyond the boundaries of acceptability. Both of these works seem to epitomize the Renaissance, however. "Aristotle's Masterpiece" brings the old master's name forth to justify new thoughts on sexuality. "Aretino's" explored the human body rather than religious themes, arguing against the hypocrisy in a society which allowed gambling, usury, and violence but not sexual recreation. Pirated copies of both works spread throughout Europe. "Aretino's" remained an underground publication, because of its explicitness in portraying human copulation. It did not depict elements associated with modern pornography, such as violence and multiple partnership, but the labeling of it as obscene shows us the divide between the licit and illicit in the early modern period.

The invention of the novel as a tool for middle-class self-definition seems to coincide with the development of the modern form of pornography. John Cleland's *Fanny Hill,* as the 18th-century story of a prostitute, falls within the confines of the old meanings of pornography—to write about harlots. As a work which takes the development of the compassionate marriage and the belief in self-improvement and sexualizes them, it fits the newer definition of pornography as the obscene within the culture. With the failure of the artisanal structure to protect the craft of printing, itinerant printers pirated *Fanny Hill* for quick funds, both in Europe and in America. Both by sexualizing what is normally not sexualized and by exploring culturally laden topics such as flagellation with its religious overtones, *Fanny Hill* works as a cultural source. Because of its popularity in spite of restrictions it also serves as a marker for proliferation of the new types of pornography. It allows the historian to see both the popularity of the profane and where the acceptable in the 18th century intersected with the taboo. *Fanny Hill* and similar works in various European countries open the subject, also vital for the 19th century, of how new forms of pornography related to sexual codes and standards and real sexual interests and beliefs.

Another way is to explore the history of social policy surrounding pornography—how society attempts to control the genre. Studies of pornography in 19th-century America, for instance, might focus on Comstockery, the 1870s legislation prohibiting the trade or circulation of the obscene. Obscenity was defined very broadly to include information concerning abortion, bawdy postcards, improper novels, and explicit works of art. Anthony Comstock, as a fringe member of the social purity movement, gained control of a government-sponsored post as a "special agent" to the Post Office, which he used to define and destroy over 160 tons of obscene materials. Legal battles involving George Bernard Shaw and Margaret Sanger, among others, helped raise awareness of the issues to the American public. Because of the definition of information concerning abortion and birth control as obscene, the history of women's rights intersects the history of the social policy of pornography. And because of his vigilance in destroying the obscene, the history of American pornography is hindered by a lack of source materials.

A third way that social history explores the issue of pornography is to project a current debate back onto the past to weigh its historic viability. This approach has been used successfully by those interested in Marxism and psychoanalysis. Discussions of the economy and the unconscious have allowed close examinations of recurrent themes in modern pornography.

The debate currently raging in American society concerns pornography's depiction of women. Coming from the feminist movement of the 1970s, this mode of analysis, posited by Andrea Dworkin, states that pornography and pornographers depict women as submissive, as desirous and deserving of violence, and as objects for masculine consumption. This depiction in fantasy carries over to the treatment of women in society, rendering violence against women acceptable. While social historians have toyed with this issue, they have not yet fully accessed its historical roots and significance. To do so, they would have to test the hypothesis that pornography contributes to the violence toward women over time, a difficult if not impossible task given the paucity of historical evidence concerning past use of pornography. Much work remains to be done in the social history of pornography. Exploring Dworkin's hypothesis is one approach. Exploring the cultural taboos exhibited in pornography and their meanings merits further analysis. Discovering who read pornography and how they understood it remains, however, the most significant task. (*See also* Body; Sexuality; Women's History)

Lisa Z. Sigel

REFERENCES

Kendrick, Walter. *The Secret Museum.* New York: Viking, 1987.

Marcus, Steven. *The Other Victorians*. New York: Norton, 1964.

Postindustrial Society

Like most other terms introduced by the prefix "post," "postindustrial society" is not an entirely satisfactory phrase. It denotes with some precision what it is not, but fails to specify what it is. Appropriately, even the most avid supporters of the concept of postindustrial society refuse to say quite when it began, just where it is flourishing, and precisely how the new society will develop. Thus, even Daniel Bell felt compelled to subtitle his otherwise self-confident exposition of the *Coming of Post-Industrial Society* (1973) a "venture in social forecasting" and to discuss the "coming" as a tendency rather than an accomplished fact.

Despite this vagueness, the term has come into wide use in recent years. For many scholars, journalists, and pundits it seems to capture the sense that much has changed in the advanced societies since World War II and that some different logic now governs their development. Clearly, previous ways of understanding society are no longer adequate, and a concept that defines itself by its difference from what preceded it appears highly attractive. On the other hand, it is the very power of earlier social theory—Marxism especially—that has kept theorists of postindustrial society from moving beyond a style of analysis that operates primarily by contrast. The importance of Marx is especially evident in Bell, who sees Marx both as the creator of the theory he rejects and as the prescient social theorist who anticipated Bell's own argument. In the first volume of *Capital*, Bell explains, Marx elaborated a vision of capitalist society characterized by recurring economic crises and increasing polarization between capitalists and workers, with intermediate classes disappearing or forced to throw in their lot with the two great, antagonistic classes. In the third volume of *Capital*, by contrast, Bell finds Marx commenting empirically upon the expansion of banking and credit and the growth in the number of engineers, supervisory personnel, and office workers. And, as if to confound all future critics, Marx proceeds to write in his notes for the fourth volume that "the size of the middle class increases and the proletariat will always form a comparatively small part of the populace. . . . This is indeed the true course of bourgeois society."

Virtually every major social theorist of the 19th and 20th centuries—including Saint-Simon, Comte, de Tocqueville, Weber, Sombart, Schumpeter, Veblen, Lederer, Aron, Touraine, and Dahrendorf—has contributed something to the slow elaboration of the concept of postindustrial society. For the notion to take hold, however, required quite specific circumstances. First, it was essential for scholars to develop a better understanding of the role of the service sector in economic development. This was not easily achieved, for the amazing productivity of the new technologies long mesmerized theorists, including economists, and so distracted them from a focus upon services. The breakthrough came in 1940, when the English economist Colin Clark published *The Conditions of Economic Progress*. Clark, like fellow economist John Maynard Keynes, sought a measure of total national income and to that end separated economic activity into three sectors: the primary sector, concerned with the production of food and the extraction of raw materials; the secondary sector, in which raw materials were manufactured into goods for sale; and the tertiary, or service, sector, which included everything from banking to advertising, from trucking to psychotherapy. Using this schema, it could be said that the industrial revolution had involved primarily the movement of people and capital from the primary to the secondary sector, from agriculture and the extraction of raw materials to manufacturing. As growth progressed still further, it would produce—and to some extent already had produced—a shift from both the primary and secondary sectors into the service sector. The most advanced economies were thus not necessarily those that produced the most coal, steel, or television sets, but those with the best developed financial and commercial institutions and those that could afford to specialize in the production of knowledge and culture and the delivery of services such as medicine and education.

Clark's argument went largely unnoticed during the first two postwar decades, when economic progress took the form of a broad extension of the techniques of mass production that enabled ordinary workers to reap some return in consumer goods from their increasingly productive labor. During this phase of growth social scientists continued to take note of such phenomena as the increase in supervision, the expansion of white-collar work, and the growing separation of ownership from control, but saw these as manifestations of assembly-line industrialism. The logic of industrialism was seen as virtually all-powerful—capable of eliminating social conflict, producing a convergence between capitalism and communism and bringing about "the end of ideology." Only later, when growth in the mass-production industries began to falter, did scholars begin seriously to ponder the meaning of the shift away from manufacturing in the advanced countries. Before that economic transformation became a cause for concern, however, more purely political events prompted a turn to speculation about "postindustrial" society. It was, in particular, the student protests of the 1960s, and 1968 especially, that caused social scientists to wonder what novel social structures had produced the oddly oppositional culture that seemed to flourish among the young. Several French writers—Touraine, Mallet, and Gorz—saw contemporary capitalism as creating, and hence depending on, a new class of highly educated technicians and the university as the setting in which this new class was nurtured. Student discontent was thus a preemptive rejection of the lifestyle and social function that membership in the new class would impose on them. It was an unusual distemper, however, for it was less economic than cultural in origin, more concerned with the quality of life and the scope it afforded for the expression and development of identity than with material circumstances. It was the product of a "postindustrial society" and reflected a "postindustrial" or, as it was otherwise called, "postmaterial" consciousness.

The need to explain the protests of the 1960s thus produced a flurry of writing on postindustrial society that culminated in the publication of Bell's book in 1973. Bell's book may be seen as something of a pivot, for it simultaneously climaxed the first major debate on postindustrialism while serving as the starting point for a second, and still ongoing, argument about the phenomenon. This more recent discussion has focused on two, rather discrete, issues. The first is the economic malaise from which the advanced nations in the West cannot seem to extricate themselves. Since the early 1970s, the leading Western economies have experienced relatively slow growth overall and a marked decline in those industries—like automobiles, steelmaking, and consumer electronics—that had fueled the postwar boom. The modest growth that has occurred, moreover, has been centered on services or on high-quality, specialized consumer goods. These economic difficulties have led a number of analysts to argue that the assembly line, the technological and organizational basis of the postwar boom, has played itself out and that further development must be based on something vastly different, on what some have labeled post-Fordism (referring to Henry Ford and his production system) and others have termed "flexible specialization." Whatever the label, the emerging economic organization will be weighted heavily toward financial, commercial, and personal services, characterized largely by the management of information, and its shrunken manufacturing sector will be devoted to the production by technically skilled workers of quality goods for specific and changing markets. The new economy will offer fewer jobs for manual workers, less security for those who do find work, and, in general, fewer rewards to those without technical skills and training. The second set of facts of which theorists of postindustrial society seek desperately to make sense is the apparent fragmentation of meaning and the increasing diversity of form that affect contemporary culture. These trends have often been termed "postmodern." Put very simply, "postmodernism" can be thought of as the reflection in the sphere of culture of an increasingly "postindustrial" economy and society.

There is as yet no genuine consensus on what postindustrial society means or what shape the new society will take; nor is there much agreement on "postmodernism." Still, the two terms dominate the current discourse on social, economic, and cultural change and show no sign of giving way to a more positive set of concepts based on any more coherent description of emerging social trends. These will surely change in the future, but for the moment one must come to terms with these unfortunately vague and unsatisfactory notions. They do at least convey the novelty of the present era and distinguish it from the recent past, and that is surely something. (*See also* Assembly Line; Lower Middle Classes; Working Class)

James E. Cronin

REFERENCES

Bell, Daniel. *The Coming of Post-Industrial Society: A Venture in Social Forecasting.* New York: Basic Books, 1973.

Harvey, David. *The Condition of Post-Modernity: An Enquiry into the Origins of Cultural Change.* Oxford: Basil Blackwell, 1989.

Inglehart, Ronald. *Silent Revolution: Changing Values and Political Styles Among Western Publics.* Princeton, NJ: Princeton University Press, 1977.

Kerr, Clark, et al. *Industrialism and Industrial Man.* Cambridge, MA: Harvard University Press, 1960.

Wright, Erik. *Classes.* London: Verso, 1985.

Potato

The potato plant was brought to Europe from its native South America toward the end of the 16th century. Its subsequent diffusion was inexplicably slow, even though the potato could be grown on lands and at altitudes at which other crops would not flourish, and even though a given amount of land devoted to this extremely nutritious crop can yield four times as many calories as the same amount of land devoted to grain. Even the threat of starvation was insufficient inducement for peasants to innovate. As late as the beginning of the 19th century, only 1.5 percent of cultivated land was devoted to the potato in France and Germany. In Ireland, however, it became such a major source of alimentation that by the 1840s one-third of the population depended on it for sustenance. Such dependence was risky: when the potato blight struck Europe in 1845–1846, the Irish were devastated. Millions either starved or emigrated, and the Irish population has still not recovered to its prefamine level.

Eventually the potato became a staple in the European diet, and a major source of nourishment for the common people. Without the po-

tato the course of the industrial revolution would surely have been impeded, inasmuch as the shift in occupational structure from agriculture to industry and the rapid growth of population were both predicated to a considerable degree on the rise in agricultural productivity. In other words, the potato made a significant contribution to the maintenance of the industrial labor force. Research on the potato, attitudes toward it, and results of its use provide social historians important insights into rural life and the humble dynamics of social change. (*See also* Demography; Food)

John Komlos

REFERENCES

O'Gráda, Cormac. *Ireland Before and After the Famine.* Manchester, Eng.: Manchester University Press, 1988.

Salaman, Redcliffe N. *History and Social Influence of the Potato.* Cambridge: Cambridge University Press, 1949.

Mokyr, Joel. *Why Ireland Starved: A Quantitative and Analytical History of the Irish Economy, 1800–1850.* Boston: Allen & Unwin, 1983.

Poverty

Poverty is a matter of degree, ranging from a lack of resources for survival to the relative sense of deprivation in comparison to more affluent neighbors. The causes of poverty are many, including natural conditions and occasional disasters, economic policies, legal and social discrimination, the inability to work, and the choices made by individuals. Poverty is, in short, a complex matter, and an enduring and controversial subject of social history.

Poverty becomes a public issue when it appears that something might be done about it. Efforts to alleviate poverty have two preconditions: the first is the belief that resources can be found to meliorate poverty; the second is that those who own or control such resources can be induced to employ them for the benefit of the poor. Similar ideas developed in Islam and other religions.

In the Western world, a sense of individual and public responsibility for the poor is at least as old as the Bible. While there are occasional references to poverty befalling the able-bodied who will not work, the dominant biblical perspective is that wealth is a matter of stewardship, and that justice and mercy require the sharing of resources to provide for the poor.

The biblical perspective informed the response to poverty in medieval Europe. While feudalism was hardly egalitarian, it nevertheless insisted—at least in theory—that the entire society comprised a web of reciprocal obligations, and that adequate provision for the poor was the responsibility of both its secular and religious members. Medieval law not only provided for charitable relief of poverty, but sought to regulate business practices such as usury and the setting of wages in order to ensure a measure of economic justice.

In modern times, English law has recognized the right of the poor to a subsistence income. The Henrician Poor Law of 1536 and the Elizabethan Poor Law of 1601 required each parish of the Church of England to raise a "poor rate," leaving the details of its administration to local vestries. Public rates were seldom generous, and settlement laws were enacted to resolve conflicts over responsibility for the transient poor, largely by restricting the movement of the poor themselves. Private charity helped to subsidize the public effort, especially in the wake of 18th-century evangelical revivals, with their emphasis on social reform as a corollary to spiritual renewal.

In general, public policy in western Europe, and by 1800 also in the United States, moved toward innovation in the treatment of the poor, despite persistence of charity and a sense of obligation. Communities began to seek ways to avoid supporting the poor, and upper classes increasingly insisted that poverty was the fault of the poor themselves. Assistance was designated for the "worthy poor"—those who simply could not work—with efforts to prevent aid to people who should be able to take care of themselves.

In Britain, the Speenhamland System, begun in 1795 and practiced in many parishes, indexed poor relief to the price of bread and provided supplements to wages to guarantee a minimum income. By the early 19th century, English practice reflected an uneasy combination of biblical responsibility and the new science of political economy. The prestige of the natural sciences made plausible certain claims about the "laws" of political economy with regard to wages, prices, and population, suggesting that government intervention on behalf of the poor would be ineffectual at best and probably counterproductive. This conflict "between sympathy and science," as historian Sydney Checkland calls it, and the displeasure of the upper and middle classes with the rising costs of poor relief, contributed to the tone and substance of the New Poor Law of 1834.

The New Poor Law reflected the ambivalence toward poverty which persists to the present day. The Act distinguished between the deserving poor, who were truly dependent, and undeserving, able-bodied paupers. Proponents of the Act argued that the old law was pauperizing the poor, removing incentives to work by sustaining the able-bodied at subsistence levels. To renew work incentives, the principle of "less eligibility" was established, whereby those on poor relief would receive less than the lowest wages paid to workers. Criteria for outdoor relief were tightened, and workhouses were encouraged so that the able-bodied could earn their benefits. The Poor Law of 1834, although widely criticized and occasionally amended, set the tone for English poor relief until the advent of the welfare state in the 20th century.

In the United States, support for the poor remained a local or state matter until the Great Depression of the 1930s. In the 19th century, the vast size of the country and the predominantly rural population meant that poverty was dispersed and much of it was invisible until it reached frightening concentrations in the expanding cities toward the end of the century. American individualism also resisted public action in diverse ways—in the Horatio Alger myths made plausible by a growing economy and real-life success stories; in the Protestant emphasis upon individual responsibility; in strong traditions of local control; in racial attitudes that took for granted the poverty of minorities; and in a Social Darwinism willing to see material success and failure as the evidence of personal virtue or vice.

The Great Depression, with its catastrophic unemployment rates, convinced many Americans that all poverty was not easily dismissed as the moral failure of individuals, and that only the federal government had the resources to address widespread poverty. Out of the New Deal came macroeconomic policies to stimulate employment and a variety of categorical assistance programs for dependent children, the aged, blind and disabled, the medically needy, and the temporarily unemployed. These Depression-era programs laid the foundations for American policy through the 1960s War on Poverty and down to the present day. Welfare measures in Europe expanded even more extensively, providing a variety of assistance to the poor.

Contemporary critics of antipoverty programs charge that they cost too much, undermine work incentives, break up families, and trap people in a culture of poverty—themes reminiscent of the English debates in the 1830s. Critics on the left argue that public welfare serves mostly to regulate the poor, alternately siphoning off dissent and ensuring the availability of low-wage labor, while governments, particularly in the United States, fail to establish full employment policies and provide adequate benefits for those who are unable to work.

Beyond the debate about programs and policies, social historians and sociologists have turned their attention to the poor themselves, seeking to describe their lives, their self-understanding, and their own initiatives. In this literature, which has precedents as old as the Victorian novel, poverty is brought down from the level of abstraction and becomes the context for depicting the lives, attitudes, and actions of people who are more than victims and the collective objects of public policy. Research on the distinctive family patterns, beliefs, and sheer survival strategies of the poor applies in principle to every society and time period. In practice, along with a bit of work on the rural poor on the margins of village life, most social history has focused on 19th- and 20th-century urban poor, in western Europe, the United States, and Latin America. Studies focusing on female poverty are also developing in this context. (*See also* Poor Relief; Welfare Capitalism)

James A. Gilchrist

REFERENCES

Himmelfarb, Gertrude. *The Idea of Poverty: England in the Early Industrial Age.* New York: Vintage Books, 1983.

Katz, Michael B. *In the Shadow of the Poorhouse: A Social History of Welfare in America.* New York: Basic Books, 1986.

Patterson, James T. *America's Struggle Against Poverty 1900–1985.* Cambridge: Harvard University Press, 1986.

Power

Social historians are vitally interested in questions of power and in how power relationships change. They explore not only political power but also power through wealth and ownership, through position in the family, and through various arrangements designed to deflect protest at work, on land and elsewhere. Many social historians also deal with power expressed in cultural hegemony, that is, with the way some groups create or enhance power by challenging alternate value systems and insisting on their right to define respectable behavior. Social historians dealing with changes in standards of crime or mental illness thus grapple with issues of power, as do those who analyze social structure. The growing range of social history thus extends the assessment of power from political rights to relations among age groups, among sexual preference groups, and between men and women. Power can serve as the central theme in a variety of social history's topical areas.

Much social history applied to the working class or slavery involves definitions of power relationships also in terms of the capacity to protest and the focus protest takes. Power struggles and protest failures here get to the heart of a society in a particular period.

A tension exists, however, between interests in power structures or patterns of hegemony and social historians' pervasive concern with agency. Some branches of social history see bitter contention over the balance between structure and agency, and specifically over whether power inequalities are given sufficient weight as against the ability of subordinate groups to serve as active agents in their own lives. Many historians of workers, ethnic immigrants, women, or even slaves stress their group's ability to shape many aspects of their community and their personal lives apart from the formal structures of power. Many radical critiques of social history contend that the field has moved too far from exploration of formal power structures, toward exaggerated interest in the results of active agency. The decline of Marxist analysis in social history further reduces emphasis on defining material structures of power.

The question of how to define structures of power expands into wider issues of causation. Many social historians must decide what really shapes the lives of various categories of ordinary people or the significance of powerlessness in the formal structures of a society. Precise balance between power hierarchy and human agenda will probably never win full agreement among social historians, for tension in the subject is endemic except for those few who see some groups or activities as entirely determined from above. The tension in emphasis provokes sometimes rancorous debate, but it also can be creative in reminding that absolute explanations, implying total subordination or complete ability to create a social framework apart from the dictates of power, are usually unproductive. (*See also* Elites; Marxist Historiography)

Peter N. Stearns

REFERENCES

Genovese, Eugene, and Elizabeth Fox-Genovese. "The Political Crisis of Social History," in Peter N. Stearns, ed., *Expanding the Past*. New York: New York University Press, 1989.

Judt, Tony. "A Clown in Regal Purple: Social History and the Historians." *History Workshop* 7 (Spring 1979): 66–94.

Prescriptive Literature

Prescriptive literature consists primarily of advice sermons, manuals, and periodical articles which offer information, instruction, and guidance on various aspects of human social behavior and experience. Topics covered in this literature include marriage and family relationships, child rearing, household management, fashion, career direction, manners, and morals. While prescriptive literature was published earlier, it proliferated in Western society during the 19th century in the context of urbanization, industrialization, and the expansion of the literate middle class, whose members comprised the major part of its readership.

Social historians use prescriptive literature as a source of information about past societal standards and values. They also use this material to illuminate the details of ordinary life in the past. Through the examination of changing trends in this literature, they raise questions regarding the direction of changes in social values.

However, advice manuals and prescriptive articles cannot be assumed to reflect reality directly. While these documents clearly reveal the values and concerns of their authors, they do not necessarily mirror either the behavior of their middle-class readers or the values of the wider culture. For example, prescriptive literature addressed to women has frequently been authored by men and often articulates conservative, male prescriptions for female behavior. A similar author-audience disjunction often characterizes advice and prescriptions directed toward working-class readers.

Thus, social historians must test generalizations suggested by prescriptive literature against other types of sources in order to determine the degree to which this literature illustrates actual human experiences at any period in the past. They must also examine a variety of examples of prescriptive literature on any specific topic in order to ascertain which of the ideas it contains are representative. (*See also* Cultural History)

Linda W. Rosenzweig

REFERENCES

Ehrenreich, Barbara, and Deirdre English. *For Her Own Good: 150 Years of the Experts' Advice to Women*. Garden City, NY: Anchor Books, 1978.

Hardyment, Christina. *Dream Babies: Three Centuries of Good Advice on Child Care*. New York: Harper & Row, 1983.

Mechling, Jay. "Advice to Historians on Advice to Mothers," *Journal of Social History* 9 (1975): 45–63.

Wishy, Bernard. *The Child and the Republic: The Dawn of Modern American Child Nurture*. Philadelphia: University of Pennsylvania Press, 1968.

Privacy

Concepts of privacy, and behaviors associated with privacy, have been incompletely but suggestively explored by social historians. Cultural anthropologists have long dealt with varieties in definitions of privacy, including personal physical space, among cultures.

In social history privacy has been explicitly researched as part of changes in social life in the United States and at least sections of western Europe in the decades around 1800. Previously, people displayed great unconcern for behaviors more modern Europeans and Americans would come to regard as private. Toilet habits, even in the upper classes, were fairly public. Courtship, up until a final pairing, was a group-centered activity. Shared bedrooms made other behaviors less private; even parental sex was incompletely concealed from children, which raises interesting questions about premodern psychological experience. Discipline, both of children and of social deviants, was also public, with shame a key ingredient.

In the later 18th century new concerns for privacy developed, though more among middle- and upper-class groups than among the lower classes. Love and courtship, including kissing, moved away from community life. Punishments were less open as public executions were banned, with private inner guilt encouraged more than public shame. Housing design changed to encourage privacy, between adults and children and then, by 1900, among individual children, particularly through individual bedrooms. Increased numbers of bathrooms per household, particularly in the United States, extended the trend further in the 20th century, as privacy for bodily functions continued as a major focus. Emotional privacy affected the definition of love particularly, but also other emotions where public control contrasted with private outpourings.

Causes for the intensification of privacy concerns have not been fully explored, though a relationship to the waning power of community and, later, the reformulation of family as a collection of individuals are clearly involved.

The history of privacy invites further exploration. It has not been applied to other periods or settings. Even the "modern" transformation needs refinement in terms of subcultures such as class or ethnic group. Implications of changes in privacy for other aspects of personality, or for the law, have yet to be explored. The relationship between privacy and loneliness (whose social history has yet to be seriously undertaken) is another theme touched by some novelists, but not yet by social historians. (*See also* Family; Houses and Housing; Love)

Peter N. Stearns

REFERENCES

Flaherty, David. *Privacy in Colonial New England.* Charlottesville: University of Virginia, 1982.

Gillis, John. *For Better, For Worse: British Marriages, 1600 to the Present.* New York: Oxford University Press, 1988.

Lystra, Karen. *Searching the Heart: Women, Men and Romantic Love in Nineteenth Century America, 1830–1900.* New York: Oxford University Press, 1989.

Professionalism

The terms "profession" and "professional" have expanded to cover a remarkable range of activities since the late 19th century. Once reserved for a handful of "learned professions"—divinity, medicine, and law—the term "professional" is now commonly applied to almost anyone who makes a living at an occupation, and nearly any occupation can be called a profession.

The "professionalization of everyone," as Harold Wilensky (1964) has called it, began in the 19th century in America. As early as the 1830s, French sociologist Alexis de Tocqueville pointed out that democratic societies, devoid of formal class structures, must rely upon other means to generate status and recognition for their members. Among the forms of recognition developed in America was the proliferation of titles. Given the prestige of the learned professions, it is hardly surprising that Jacksonian democracy should find more and more people calling themselves "doctor," to cite one example, and dispensing all manner of purported cures and remedies, often with little or no formal training.

After the Civil War, several factors combined to generate what Burton Bledstein (1978) has described as a "culture of professionalism" in America. Familiar developments occurred in western Europe. Technological innovation, industrialization, immigration, and the growth of large cities generated the need for people with increasingly sophisticated skills in law, medicine, social work, education, public health, management, and a host of other fields. The rising demand for professional training coincided with, and indeed helped to bring about, the emergence of the modern American university in the 1880s and 1890s, including professional schools to bridge the gap between traditional academic disciplines and the practical needs of the emerging professions.

Prestige and Status. By the beginning of the 20th century, American culture had become "professionalized," in the sense that professionalism was widely regarded as the standard for competence, and hence legitimacy and prestige, not only in the traditional professions but in almost any occupation. In this vein, as Bledstein notes, a plumber appeared before the American Public Health Association in 1891 to argue that "plumbing is no longer merely a trade. Its importance and value in relation to health, and its requirements regarding scientific knowledge, have elevated it to a profession. It is clothed with the responsibility of the learned professions and the dignity of the sciences."

In conferring status, "professional" identifies qualities that are denied not only to practitioners of trades, but also to "amateurs." An amateur does something occasionally, or for the enjoyment of it (Latin *amare*, to love), while the professional does the same thing for a living. The common presumption is that a professional is also more skilled than an amateur, and hence enjoys higher status in the field because of superior talent or more extensive practice or both.

The distinction between professionals and amateurs is most familiar in modern sports, where elaborate rules distinguish collegiate and other amateurs from professionals. The latter can earn millions of dollars a year playing basketball or baseball. Occasionally, the distinction becomes the source of controversy, as when an Olympic athlete—by definition an amateur—receives large sums of money to endorse a running shoe or appear on a cereal box. In this case one of the fundamental criteria of professional status is challenged, namely the prerogative to be paid for what one does, while the sanctity of amateur athletics is also challenged, precisely because amateurs are not to be paid for their talents.

The multiplication of titles in the Jacksonian period and the proliferation of "professions" in the populist age reflected an egalitarian impulse to enhance the status of various occupations and thereby diminish, relatively speaking, the status of the traditional professions. The claim to professionalism became, by the end of the 19th century, the paramount claim to status for an occupation.

This is not to say, however, that even the most venerable of the older professions were always well regarded by the public, or even by some of their own practitioners. Medicine in particular was held in low esteem through much of the 19th century. The American Medical Association was established in 1848, in part to correct the deplorable condition of medical education. Oliver Wendell Holmes, Sr., complained that "if the whole materia medica, *as now used*, could be sunk to the bottom of the sea, it would be all the better for mankind,—and all the worse for the fishes." Not until scientific advances gained momentum early in the 20th century and medical education was reformed along the lines described in the Flexner Report (1910) did the situation improve dramatically.

Specialization and Monopoly. By the early decades of the 20th century, as the professions developed more sophisticated methods and an increasingly complex body of knowledge, the public came to depend upon their expertise, and a reliance upon specialists of all sorts contributed to the growing prestige of the older professions along with the newer ones.

Sociologists have long been interested in the professions and their specialization. Not surprisingly, sociological models of the professions have been more exacting than the public's rather casual use of the term. While the models differ in detail, professions are said to be characterized by (1) a codified body of knowledge, especially requiring advanced learning; (2) a recognized body of practitioners who control access to admission and set standards for practice; and (3) an ideal of public service, often reflected in a formal code of ethics. Since the 1880s, professions have also been marked by organized associations of members, especially at the national level; professional schools, often located in universities; and journals that disseminate findings to members. Sociology itself developed the marks of a profession with the founding of a journal and a professional association in the 1890s.

Given the complexity of modern life, many individuals practice not only a profession, but a subspecialty within the profession. A physician is not just a doctor, but an internist, an obstetrician, or an otolaryngologist, and fellow physicians defer to specialists for medical judgments beyond their ken. The public, ill-equipped to evaluate the specialist's advice, must rely upon a practitioner's judgment, and must further rely upon the body of professionals to hold themselves accountable for the public welfare. It is this specialization that has given modern professions much of their influence, and their influence in turn has raised questions about the role of professions in society—questions about professional practice, authority, compensation, and ethics.

The public in effect grants a monopoly to various professions, in the form of responsibility for licensing and evaluation, because only professionals have the knowledge to determine how their field should be practiced. A kind of social contract is made between society and the professions: a profession is granted the right to practice, and reap the rewards of its practice, in exchange for demonstrating the ability to serve the public interest and police itself against wrongful conduct by individual or corporate practitioners.

Monopolies have advantages, however, and it is the privileged position of monopolies that contributes to the public's ambivalence about the professions. The most obvious advantage is the ability to control prices, either directly through price-fixing, or indirectly by limiting the supply of professional services. Physicians and attorneys argue that, given the large number of practitioners, there is plenty of room for competition. Critics reply that professional associations nevertheless limit the number of practitioners, and cite the fact that physicians and attorneys are among the highest paid members of society as evidence of monopoly power.

Ethics, Compensation, and Equity. Codes of ethics are supposed to demonstrate a profession's commitment to public service, in addition to setting the rules for relating to clients and fellow practitioners. But critics maintain that codes have often been so general as to have little impact on practice; and insofar as they have prohibited advertising and competition among practitioners, the codes have actually worked against the public interest by keeping prices high. Defenders reply that codes are general by their nature, and, especially in the 19th century, prohibitions against advertising and fee cutting (which have since been relaxed) served the public interest by limiting quackery and permitting competent doctors and lawyers to earn a living.

Not all professionals are highly compensated, of course. Teachers, nurses, social workers, and the clergy are among those whose compensation has been on a par with blue-collar workers, though some historians argue that the first three categories are not full professions in terms of control over training standards and entry. The first three of these professions comprise mostly women, and undoubtedly gender roles have played a part in keeping both wages and prestige relatively low. These conditions are in striking contrast to those in law and medicine, where prestige and compensation have been high, and where women have traditionally been small minorities and have only recently been admitted in significant numbers to professional schools and to practice.

Besides gender, another important influence on wages and salaries is the source of compensation. Teachers, social workers, and some nurses are typically paid out of public funds, or sometimes through the resources of voluntary organizations. Public spending is limited by the taxpayers' desire to minimize taxes, while private charitable agencies are constrained by the limits of voluntary giving. The contrast with physicians and lawyers is again striking. Physicians have, since the 1960s, been paid in increasing measure by third-party insurers, who have only recently begun to impose limits on compensation for physician services. A sizable number of attorneys, on the other hand, are employed by large corporations or relatively affluent individuals, or else they derive fees from third-party insurers through the awards or settlements made in the course of litigation.

The clergy presents a different case, the only one of the traditional "learned professions" that is not highly compensated. The Roman Catholic priesthood often entails voluntary limits on income, while Protestant clergy, for the most part, live modestly, and the rabbinate is somewhat better paid. From the days of Puritan New England, when ministers enjoyed high prestige and comparatively good compensation, the clergy have experienced a decline in relative prestige and an even greater decline in salaries relative to other professions. Among the reasons are the disestablishment of the churches, the proliferation of denominations, the increasing supply of clergy, and the dependence of salaries on voluntary contributions.

Expanding Scope and Interest. One of the newest vocations admitted to professional status is business. In the early 20th century, the ideal that professionals were motivated by public service was contrasted explicitly with the profit motive of business. People in business could not, by definition, be professionals. After World War I, however, as the growing complexity of industry required more sophisticated training of managers, and university-related business schools multiplied, it was increasingly argued that business should be considered a profession. Apologists maintained that business, too, served the public interest, and there was no inherent contradiction between the profit motive and social service. As various industries adopted codes of ethics, and business schools sought to demonstrate their own ideals of service to justify their place in the university, business managers came to be called professionals, and business itself was widely, if not universally, recognized as yet another profession.

The history of professions and the sociology of professions, both of which inform social history, are among the emerging fields of academic interest and research. This interest in the professions is due in large part to the pervasive role of professionalism in contemporary life. An understanding of professions and professionalism reveals a great deal about the perennial concerns of social science: the conditions of social status, the role of elites, the impact of gender and race, and the nature of the social contract itself. The social history of professions, which first operated in the shadow of sociological models, has increasingly explored variations on the standard "modernization" pattern, changes in the roster of professions, and the role of gender. Comparison of the evolution of similar professions in different modern societies also presents exciting analytical opportunities. (*See also* Judiciary; Medicine)

James A. Gilchrist and Daniel P. Resnick

REFERENCES

Bledstein, Burton J. *The Culture of Professionalism: The Middle Class and the Development of Higher Education in America.* New York: Norton, 1978.

Etzioni, Amitai. *The Semi-Professions and Their Organization: Teachers, Nurses, Social Workers.* New York: The Free Press, 1969.

Hatch, Nathan O., ed. *The Professions in American History.* Notre Dame: University of Notre Dame Press, 1988.

Larson, Magali S. *The Rise of Professionalism: A Sociological Analysis.* Berkeley: University of California Press, 1977.

Wilensky, H.L. "The Professionalization of Everyone?" *American Journal of Sociology* 70 (1964): 137–158.

Proletarianization

Proletarianization refers to increases in the number or proportion of wage laborers dependent for their survival on the sale of their labor power. The concept is derived from Chapters 25 through 32 of Karl Marx's *Capital,* which describes the creation of the English proletariat as a concomitant of the rise of capitalism. Although proletarianization evokes images of skilled artisans displaced by machines and forced to work for a pittance in insalubrious mills, in Marx's view it was also a consequence of enclosure of landed estates. Proletarianization generally implies the expropriation by a few of the means of production once controlled by many and an increase in the proportion of the labor force dependent for its subsistence on wage earning, whether in agriculture or in manufacturing. Proletarianization is a fundamental process in modern social history, first in Western society and then elsewhere. It creates a different structure for the lower classes than when modest property ownership was widespread (even when constrained by serfdom) and propertylessness was very rare as a lifelong characteristic. It also affects upper-class reactions, creating new anxieties and suspicions at least when the proletarianization process first becomes established.

When proletarianization occurs at the macro level, that is, when an entire country, a city, or an industry is affected, it often results in changes in the number of productive units and in the composition of the working population. Loss of control over the means of production and increases in the proportion of a population that lives by wage earning is considered to be proved empirically if the number of units of production—whether farms, firms, workshops, or factories—decreases while number of persons employed in the industry remains constant or increases, or if the number of units of production increases but the number of persons employed increases disproportionately. In other words, proletarianization is often illustrated by using aggregate data to show changes in the composition of populations under study, rather than by examining what actually happened to those who exercised control over the means of production or to those who were simply wage earners before proletarianization set in. Yet, the process by which a population or a labor force is transformed from one with some independence to one that is dependent is complex. Proletarianization can result from several economic and social changes that affect individuals in a variety of different ways.

A major contribution to conceptualizing the process of proletarianization was made by Charles Tilly. In his "Demographic Origins of the European Proletariat" (1984), he shows that proletarianization is most clearly understood as a product of three different types of changes. The proletariat can increase as a proportion of the total labor force due to (1) expropriation of the means of production by a few resulting in social mobility, (2) natural increase, and/or (3) migration. When owners of the means of production, whether peasant farmers or artisans, are forced to leave their land or give up their shops and to go to work for someone else, they experience downward social mobility. Through natural increase, an excess of births over deaths, among those already living as proletarians, the size of the proletariat increases. Through migration, the arrival of newcomers from outside the community who live by wage earning, the proletariat grows. Proletarianization in one locality may be the result of all three phenomena. Moreover, experiences in the life of a single individual may also reflect all three conditions.

Proletarianization is determined by changes in both the organization of production and the size of the potential labor supply. Tilly identifies four factors influencing the organization of production that lead to proletarianization. First is a demand for goods and services. Where demand increases, more workers are drawn into industry; where it declines, they are fired, laid off, or forced to look elsewhere for employment. Second is the increased cost of establishing new units. As factories and expensive machinery become prerequisites for going into business, some producers can no longer afford to modernize and stay in business; others cannot afford to start up. Third, concentration of capital contributes to proletarianization. Fewer firms controlling larger shares of the market force small producers out of business and into the ranks of the proletariat. Fourth, the coercive power of employers, whose positions are often supported by legal prerogatives and prohibitions, makes it difficult or impossible for wage earners to maintain or gain control over the work process and to become owners of the means of production in their turn.

Each of the four determinants of the rate of increase in wage labor—the demand for goods and services, the cost of establishing new units, the concentration of capital, and the coercive power of employers—contributes positively to the rate of proletarianization, but these are accelerated or mitigated by what happens to the potential labor force, those available to work. Thus, the rate of proletarianization is a function not only of changes in the organization of production, but also of changes in the number of persons and in the proportion of the total population in the labor force. Tilly identifies four factors that influence the potential supply of labor.

First, fluctuations in the demand for goods and services encourage or discourage entry into the labor force. Second, the rate of increase in the potential labor force is also affected by the opportunity cost of childbearing: to the extent that couples find it more advantageous to do other things with their time and money than to conceive and raise children, they are less likely to produce children. Fertility will therefore increase or decrease, enlarging or reducing the potential labor force, depending upon the "cost" of having children. Third, the existing level of proletarianization affects the rate of increase in the potential labor force. The hypothesized link between previous proletarianization and the rate of increase in the potential labor force is a lowering of the age at marriage with increased proletarianization, raising fertility and the availability of labor 15 or 20 years later. Fourth, fluctuations in natural increase; the excess of births over deaths, caused by changes in disease, nutrition, medicine, natural disasters, and wars; and civil disturbances also affect the rate of increase in the potential labor supply.

Many historical studies of proletarianization have been concerned with links between the spread of wage labor and the enormous growth in the European population after 1750. Proletarianization has been hypothesized as an element contributing to population growth by lowering the age at marriage. As more men and women became dependent upon wage earning to support themselves, they lost the incentive to wait to marry until after the deaths of their parents, when inheritance brought them the family farms or shops which they would run to support themselves and their children. The age at marriage dropped, and wives in the new generation had more children than their mothers. In particular, proletarianization in the form of cottage industry, especially spinning and weaving by villagers for urban merchants, has been seen as being responsible for European population growth in the 18th and 19th centuries. But historical studies have yielded mixed results. The spread of wage labor has not always been accompanied by lower ages at marriage or higher fertility.

Not only has the progress of proletarianization been seen as playing an important role in the demographic revolution, it is also regarded as being influential in the formation of working-class consciousness. As skilled artisans found their livelihoods threatened by machinery, an increased division of labor, restrictions on labor organizations, factory production, and loss of control over the process of production, a common feeling of desperation and injustice helped to unite them in a defense against the most devastating consequences of change (Thompson 1963). However, some labor historians have questioned the connection between proletarianization and the growth of working-class consciousness and labor militancy, pointing out that the connection is either much more complex than many analyses suggest or more often assumed than proved.

Interest in the link between proletarianization and labor militancy has not been confined to studies of the industrial working class. It has also been applied to analyses of changes in the organization of professions and white-collar work in the 20th century (Braverman 1975). In particular, the increased division of labor in the professions and the proliferation of jobs in the services sector have created a new working class of dependent wage earners and salaried employees. As the growth of white-collar work and of jobs in the services sector has outstripped the increase of jobs in manufacturing, the concept of proletarianization has been reexamined and redefined to emphasize control over resources, autonomy in decisionmaking, and bureaucratic processes. The implications of proletarianization for understanding economic change, labor, and society in the 20th century are only beginning to be explored.

While the effects of proletarianization in the 20th century may not yet be fully understood, the trend toward a labor force with ever larger proportions of dependent wage laborers nevertheless connects the economic and social history of the 20th to earlier centuries. Proletarianization was a fundamental consequence of the rise of capitalism and, in western Europe, began to take shape as early as the 16th century. The spread of commercial agriculture often made colonialism spread proletarianization in Asia, Europe, and later America by the 18th and 19th centuries. Whether the fundamental causes stemmed from changes in the organization of production or demographic conditions, today fewer people control the means of production and more support themselves and their children through salaried or wage work than in the past. The process of proletarianization is a repeated pattern, stitched with threads of often somber color into the tapestry of labor history in the modern era. (*See also* Commercialization; Marxist Historiography; Working Class)

Anne C. Meyering

REFERENCES

Braverman, Harry. *Labor and Monopoly Capital: The Degradation of Work in the Twentieth Century.* New York: Monthly Review Press, 1975.

Jones, Gareth Stedman. *Languages of Class: Studies in English Working Class History, 1832–1982.* Cambridge: Cambridge University Press, 1983.

Katznelson, Ira, and Aristide Zolberg, ed. *Working Class Formation: Nineteenth Century Patterns in Western Europe and the United States.* Princeton, NJ: Princeton University Press, 1986.

Mendels, Franklin. "Proto-industrialization: The First Phase of the Industrialization Process," *Journal of Economic History* 32, 1: 241–261.

Thompson, Edward P. *The Making of the English Working Class.* New York: Random House, Vintage Books, 1963.

Tilly, Charles. "Demographic Origins of the European Proletariat," in David Levine, ed., *Proletarianization and Family History.* Orlando: Academic Press, 1984. pp. 1–85.

Proletariat

See Working Class

Prosopography

"Prosopography," as the great dancer Martha Graham once remarked of the word "choreography," "is a wonderfully big word and can cover up a lot of things." It is also a word that confuses those who come upon it for the first time. The 1991 edition of the *Concise Oxford Dictionary* defines it as "a description of a person's appearance, personality, social and family connections, career, etc."—that is, a biographical essay, short or long, about a particular individual. Hundreds of great collections of such "prosopographical" essays—biographical dictionaries—have been produced for generations. But these great reference works are not prosopographical in the sense in which some social historians have come to use the word. The ambiguity of the term dates to 1971, when the Anglo-American historian Lawrence Stone published an influential essay called "Prosopography." In it Stone combined under the single umbrella term "prosopography" the older genre of compendia of biographies for reference, antiquarian, or commemorative purposes, with the newer practice of the systematic collection of biographical data for the purposes of social history, a technique more commonly known as "collective biography." Compilers of biographical dictionaries continue to call their work prosopography; historians of the ancient and medieval worlds tend to use the term "prosopography" to describe collective biography, while most historians of the modern world use the term "collective biography" as a label for the same thing and seldom use the word "prosopography."

Because social historians deal primarily with groups, rather than individual biography, techniques of collective biography have attracted considerable attention. Inadequate data and confusions over the effort involved have limited the use of formal prosopography, however, as opposed to less systematic group profiles. A full juncture between collective biography and social history remains to be effected.

As the historian Charles Tilly (1985) describes the logic of the process, collective biography involves "comparable observations on multiple units compounded into systematic collective accounts of unity and diversity." In concrete terms, this simply means examining the backgrounds of any distinct group of people in the past to discover what characteristics they had, or did not have, in common. The technique can also be used to compare two or more groups with one another. It is often used to test a specific historical hypothesis: for example, did the framers of the American Constitution share common economic interests, and did these interests influence their actions? By carefully examining the economic backgrounds of the framers, the historian Charles Beard (1914) decided in 1913 that a large proportion of them owned government securities whose value would be assured if a new Constitution was adopted, and thus had an economic interest in creating the Constitution. (Beard's thesis is now considered simplistic, but his collective economic biography inspired a generation of historical controversy and fruitful research.) In actual practice, the group characteristics to be researched might be of any kind that the researcher thinks significant—social, racial, economic, demographic, educational, religious, occupational, gender related, geographic, or others.

The nature of the group to be examined is limited only by the historian's broader interests and imagination. It might be something as commonplace as the members of a college class—or of successive college classes, in order to observe changes over time. The group might be small and elite, like the members of a business corporation, or it might be a large "mass" group, such as 18th-century Parisian rioters. The relevant data about the individuals who composed the group are normally gathered from a wide variety of sources, such as obituaries, church records, genealogies, birth and death records, wills, legal records, census data, and newspapers—the sources are limited only by the researcher's knowledge of the materials that might contain such information for the relevant historical period. Limitations of time make the procedure impractical for an in-depth investigation of all members of groups much larger than 200. Unless a research team is involved, collective biographies of groups larger than this should be based on investigation of individuals chosen from the group through a careful process of statistical sampling.

On its face collective biography seems like a very straightforward method. But it is full of traps. Ideally, a researcher should be able to draw a collective portrait of any group he or she chooses to investigate—the lords *and* the serfs of eastern Europe, the plantation mistresses *and* the slaves of the old American South. But as one researches deeper into the past, less and less of the historical record survives, even for individuals prominent in their times. It is very often extraordinarily difficult to establish firmly facts as elementary as the birth and death dates or the religious denominations of persons who lived only a century ago. The researcher will often be faced with large numbers of "unknowns" in a particular category of data, and should be wary of making generalizations without carefully considering the implications of gaps in the data. Collective biography demands an extremely careful evaluation of historical evidence. Even the most experienced historian can fall into error in following this method. For example, a gifted historian, with the help of two research assistants, once conducted a collective biography of the most studied group in American history, the signers of the Declaration of Independence and members of the Constitutional Convention. Two of the subjects (William Houston of Georgia and William Churchill Houston of New Jersey) bore the same name. (At most places in most times there are usually several people who have the same name.) In his collective biography the historian conflated the careers of the two men into one. Therefore, all his carefully tabulated background information on the most studied group in American history was slightly inaccurate. It was not a completely fatal error, but it illustrates the ease of error in a research technique that demands a high degree of accuracy, particularly where a statistical sample is used.

Any project involving collective biography requires careful preplanning. Since the method demands comparable observations it demands consistency in classification of the data. It is very often difficult to determine in advance the most useful categories of classification. For example, the occupations of individuals in a group seem a simple enough subject for classification. In practice, however, one often discovers that individuals followed multiple occupations—Thomas Jefferson, for instance, was both a lawyer and a planter. This case could be accounted for in a particular study by establishing a category for multiple occupations. A similar instance might involve someone who changed from one religious denomination to another. But it is best to make probes in the sources before establishing ironclad categories for classification, for it is very difficult to go back and alter them after the work is far advanced.

Use of computer database or statistical programs enables the modern researcher to manipulate quickly and easily amounts of data that were unmanageable by an individual researcher in the past. But few social historians are content to present only numerical data to their readers. A good "collective biography" of a particular group will also include "prosopographies" of individual members of the group whose typicality—or atypicality—adds an element of humanity and movement to the collective portrait that numbers alone can never convey. (*See also* Elites; Quantification)

James McLachlan

REFERENCES

Beard, Charles A. *An Economic Interpretation of the Constitution of the United States.* New York: Macmillan, 1914.

Brown, Richard D. "The Founding Fathers of 1776 and 1787: A Collective View," *William and Mary Quarterly* 3, 33 (1976): 465–480.

Stone, Lawrence. "Prosopography," *Daedalus* 100 (Winter, 1971): 46–79.

Tilly, Charles. "Retrieving European Lives," in Olivier Zunz, ed., *The Worlds of Social History.* Chapel Hill: University of North Carolina Press, 1985, pp. 11–52, esp. pp. 22–31.

Prostitution

Prostitution is notoriously difficult to define, a fact which has probably encouraged the multiplication of definitions. The German sociologist Iwan Bloch, writing in 1912, knew hundreds of these. One principle is paramount: definitions of prostitution tend to be functional in nature. The specific motive for constructing a definition inevitably affects its content, and this is especially true of moral, legal, and medical definitions of "prostitute."

The task of definition is of enormous importance, because it is essential to distinguish prostitution from other forms of nonmarital sex, including adultery and concubinage. All of these phenomena will assume different forms in different societies. A definition of prostitution that includes the three components of promiscuity, payment, and emotional indifference between the partners seems best suited to this distinction and flexible enough to allow for the great variety these forms of sexuality exhibit in different societies, both present and past.

That prostitution has a history has only recently been recognized, as part of the maturation of sociohistorical research. Until the late 1970s, most historians regarded it as a marginal topic, peripheral to the analysis of the achievements of upper-class men. Even among social historians it received little attention. Handbooks and reference works treated the phenomenon as isolated and essentially static: "the oldest profession." Now that a broader definition of history is winning acceptance, the study of prostitution promises to shed considerable light on the history of sexuality and the status of women. Beyond this, it illuminates the basic contours of political and social structure by contributing to an understanding of how various societies have been organized along class and gender lines. Research on prostitution has focused particularly on the 19th and early 20th centuries, in association with the impact of industrialization on women and men, but other periods gain growing attention as well.

The most important influence shaping this change has been feminist historiography. Feminist historians have shown how a gender-based distribution of power and economic resources has helped to create an environment favorable to venal sex. They have widened the field of enquiry by introducing new types of evidence, especially that provided by prostitutes themselves, as found in diaries, letters, and interviews, where this is available. These sources permit closer examination of the careers of individual prostitutes and of the factors that influence a woman's decision to become a prostitute, keep her in that profession for any length of time, and enable her to leave it or hinder her from doing so. For many prostitutes, the exchange of sex for money is a temporary and/or part-time pursuit, which is followed by reentry into lower-class society. While many women have been forced into prostitution, for others, prostitution represents a choice that makes a certain sense, given the available alternatives.

Feminist historians have also shown that prostitution cannot be understood as a phenomenon isolated from its social, economic, and political context. Prostitutes as a group are often not readily distinguishable from the rest of the urban poor in terms of social origins, place of residence, and living conditions. However, when a society adopts regulationist and repressive policies toward prostitution, its practitioners are often identified by various means, including official registration, forced residence, and the imposition of a particular item of clothing. All of these methods mark prostitutes as a separate group and inhibit their easy integration into their surroundings, a process also made more difficult by disease and addiction to drugs or alcohol.

Also of increasing influence is the work of Michel Foucault and his followers, who argue that sexuality is not, like the sexual act or anatomical gender, a biological fact and so cannot be accepted as a constant in human affairs. Instead, each society constructs sexuality after its own fashion, often defining as natural what is really a matter of convention. "Sexuality" itself is a concept of recent discovery, so that "homosexuality," for example, cannot be assumed to be universal. Foucault's argument is controversial, but at minimum it suggests that if sexuality is constructed differently in different historical settings, commercial sex will manifest itself in history with considerable variety.

These two approaches can be combined with other methods, including, for example, the categories of analysis developed by anthropologists studying traditional Mediterranean societies and the global approach to social history fostered by the French *Annales* school. Taken together, they open up for analysis society defined as a system of class and gender, a political economy of sex. A culture's definition of male and female roles cannot be understood in isolation. The status of prostitutes sheds light on the status of respectable women and vice versa. If women's role is largely relegated to the private sphere, this has certain consequences for the shape and scope of prostitution. When such an ideal is not attainable for all women, the denial of economic and educational opportunities attendant upon a narrow definition of appropriate female behavior tends to encourage women to resort to prostitution.

From another perspective, the practice of prostitution is closely connected with the status of women as marriage partners. If marriage functions as the ideal sexual and emotional relationship, prostitution may play a reduced role. However, even in cultures which strongly idealize wives' status, prostitution can flourish. If wives, however respected or cherished, are kept secluded in the home and are not, because of a difference in age or status, full partners with their husbands, a category of prostitute, identified as courtesans, *hetairai*, or geishas, may arise to fill male needs for sexual companionship.

Public policy provides an important illustration of the principle that various societies in history have experienced prostitution differently. The three policies most commonly adopted toward prostitution have been repression, regulation, and toleration. Regulation, which has typically meant official registration of prostitutes, medical examination, and the licensing of brothels, accepts prostitution as inevitable, because regulationists assume male sexual desire to be an uncontrollable natural force which is at best capable of being diverted away from respectable women toward prostitutes. Regulation therefore attempts to control prostitution, in order to maintain order, defend morality, and/or prevent the spread of disease. This policy was widespread in continental Europe of the 19th century, especially in France.

Repression often leads to the criminalization of prostitution and activities associated with it, such as public solicitation, procuring, and keeping a brothel. Repression was popular in Europe at the time of the Reformation, and has been the leading American response to prostitution, above all since the Progressive era. Tolerance broadly characterizes Greco-Roman antiquity and much of present-day Europe.

Rarely do any of these policies appear in their pure forms. A regulationist regime may display decidedly repressive elements, as we find with the 19th-century European systems. Suspected prostitutes were compelled to submit to medical examination and, if found to be infected, forced into a hospital that more closely resembled a prison. A repressive system may set aside certain zones (like the "red light" districts) for the practice of prostitution, a de facto form of regulation or even of toleration, depending on the degree of scrutiny exercised. This approach has been taken in various American cities over the last 150 years. A good example of how the policy of tolerance might display traits associated with the other two policies comes from ancient Rome. The Romans kept a register of prostitutes, entrusted junior magistrates with the oversight of brothels, and eventually imposed a tax on prostitutes, measures more consonant with a policy of regulation or even repression.

The reasons for such unevenness are numerous and complex. Policy advocates frequently have dissonant motives, which can translate into an ambiguous result, or even one that contradicts some of their aims. The 19th-century coalitions of feminists and moral reformers who attacked regulationism (in England, they helped abrogate the regulationist Contagious Diseases Acts) opened the way for a new approach that was typically both somewhat self-contradictory and more repressive. Changing perceptions, for example, of the moral or medical threat posed by prostitutes, may contribute to a mixed or rapidly shifting policy, as seen over the last two centuries with regard to sexually transmitted diseases such as syphilis and AIDS. The balance of political power may encourage a compromise, as in Italy in 1888, when opponents of the regulationist system then in place effected only a partial and temporary reform. Police could no longer inscribe prostitutes, but retained the power to register places of prostitution and keep them under surveillance: the pendulum swung back toward regulation only three years later. Government organs with dramatically different approaches may compete with each other in an uneasy seesaw, as in Wilhelmine Germany, where local authorities in such cities as Hamburg espoused a regulationist policy at odds with the preference of the imperial government for a repressive approach.

On a deeper level, ambivalence about prostitution and prostitutes explains much of the complexity and confusion that frequently characterize public policy. Prostitutes are often simultaneously pitied as helpless victims and reviled as corrupting predators, or the profession may be tolerated but its practitioners repressed. Attitudes toward prostitution can vary considerably within a culture: venal sex is often simultaneously argued to be a necessary evil deserving regulation, a victimless crime meriting tolerance, and an unacceptable moral vice and form of exploitation requiring repression.

This ambivalence rests in turn on ambivalence about human sexuality. The usual assumption, noted above, that male sexual desire is uncontrollable has been challenged on occasion by reformers, such as Stoics and Christians in Greco-Roman antiquity, Protestants and Catholics of the Reformation and Counter-Reformation, and moral purity crusaders of the late 19th century, who asserted a single standard of sexual continence for men and women. Attitudes toward female sexuality are typically even more complex. It is not unusual to find that women are thought dominated by sexual desire and yet, ideally, passionless, or considered morally superior to men yet sexually vulnerable and therefore in need of (male) surveillance and protection. When men regard a woman, no matter how virtuous, as easily corrupted, this attitude reveals both a vertiginous attraction toward and a deep fear of female sexuality. That prostitutes are regarded with extreme ambivalence occasions no surprise.

Ambivalence over prostitution and sexuality, taken together with differences of political constitution, social structure, and economic development, explains the extreme variety in the status and operation of prostitution in past societies. As a result, it is difficult to generalize about prostitution and policies directed at it. Untested assumptions have been commonplace. For a time, historians regarded the role of Christian teaching on this subject as uniform and its substance as monolithic. Christianity has therefore been assumed simply to encourage repression of prostitution. A more complex reality can be glimpsed in the experience of the French province of Languedoc in the Middle Ages. In the 13th century, aside from an isolated attempt at repression sponsored by Louis IX, prostitution was tolerated outside the town centers. The next two centuries saw the development of a system of municipal brothels, institutions that were regulated, often owned, and even operated by the towns. This system went into rapid decline in the 16th century, when the Reformation and Counter-Reformation fostered a repressive approach under the banner of moral and religious reform. Every one of these policies was accommodated, even justified, by reference to Christian moral teaching.

Two limitations of this article deserve special emphasis. Partly for reasons of space, it has not been possible to take adequate notice of male prostitution or prostitution in non-Western societies. Both phenomena are at this writing understudied. (*See also* Concubinage; Deviance; Family; Feminism; Greco-Roman Sexuality; Greek and Roman Family; Homosexuality; Marriage/Remarriage; Pornography; Sexuality; Women and Work; Women's History)

Thomas A.J. McGinn

REFERENCES

Corbin, Alain. *Women for Hire: Prostitution and Sexuality in France After 1850.* Translated by A. Sheridan. Cambridge: Harvard University Press, 1990.

Gibson, Mary. *Prostitution and the State in Italy, 1860–1915.* New Brunswick, NJ: Rutgers University Press, 1986.

Hobson, Barbara M. *Uneasy Virtue: The Politics of Prostitution and the American Reform Tradition.* Chicago: University of Chicago Press, 1990, rev. ed.

Otis, Leah L. *Prostitution in Medieval Society: The History of an Urban Institution in Languedoc.* Chicago: University of Chicago Press, 1985.

Rossiaud, Jacques. *Medieval Prostitution.* Translated by L.G. Cochrane. Oxford: Basil Blackwell, 1988.

Walkowitz, Judith R. *Prostitution and Victorian Society: Women, Class, and the State.* Cambridge: Cambridge University Press, 1980.

Protest

Protest in social history research is mainly popular protest—the contentious collective action that underdogs take to remedy grievances. Protest studies are central to social history research because they spotlight underdog political actions, motives, and beliefs as well as elemental power relations in past time. An academic growth industry since the 1960s, protest studies now make up a vast monographic literature whose problem is no dearth of facts but a glut. To get a handle on the facts, historians of protest combine generalizations together with a theory that orders them in an explanatory argument one can test with evidence. Generalizations about protest that available evidence permits describe collective actions, political intentions, capabilities to act in concert, and opportunities to get away with it.

But before historical generalizations, a few terminological definitions. Any action people take to achieve common goals is collective action. Any collective action they take against other people is contention. And any contentious collective action they take to remedy grievances is protest.

Protest is violent, moreover, when it wreaks physical harm on persons or property; it is popular when it involves underdogs as participants; and it is vigilante when it occurs without the sanction of public authority—either incumbent or insurgent.

Social history research by these definitions covers chiefly violent, popular, vigilante protest though most popular vigilante protest is nonviolent and most violent popular protest is authorized—by government or opposition. Social historians say more about tax revolt and food riot than about either petition and demonstration or guerrilla warfare and terrorism as well as more about overt protest that gains publicity than about covert protest (like backbiting, shirking, or sabotage) that escapes detection. Within those limits, however, social historians produce a wealth of empirical evidence on protest actions and the intentions, capabilities, and opportunities of the people who take them. The evidence refutes the volcanic or big bang view of popular protest as an eruption of mass rage and confirms a strategic view of it as "politics by other means."

Start with the contentious collective actions that define protest. Social history research finds them selective, methodical, and opportune in their target, technique, and timing. Their target is (as a rule) persons or authorities blamed for specific grievances; their technique is a standard procedure or stratagem—the work of militant minorities; and their timing coincides with the advent of allies or with government encouragement, toleration, weakness, or collapse.

To explain why popular protest is selective, methodical, and opportune in its target, technique, and timing, social historians note the intentions, capabilities, and opportunities of the participants as far as eyewitness and postmortem documentation allows. Here they find that their intention is to get or keep things they think they have a right to, not to turn the world upside down; that they have the capability to act in concert thanks to assets, organization, and knowhow; and that they have an opportunity to get away with it thanks to powerful allies or official laxity or both.

These generalizations—about protest actions and the intentions, capabilities, and opportunities that motivate and constrain them—may seem strange and even perverse to readers reared on the volcanic view (whose causal imagery of explosive aggression owing to unbearable frustration pervades journalism and social science), so consider the argument more closely.

Social history research finds that protest is selective in its target because the intention is to right specific wrongs blamed on private persons or public authorities, not to vent frustrations wholesale or to radically reconstitute state and society. Here the evidence is overwhelming. Peruse any competent study on protest, note what it says about who gets hassled and why, and you see that the target is always accused of injustice—of violating rights that the protesters claim. Other targets are not attacked. Violation of rights (to liberty, property, protection, sovereignty, subsistence, or remuneration) is what makes the wrongs that protest would repair by chastising wrongdoers. To explain protest, then, social historians rightly start with the grievances that motivate it.

Realizing grievances are violations of rights (breaches of social contract) suggests a convenient typology of protest actions but raises at once two thorny issues—ideology and violence—that no account of intentions can afford to ignore.

First the typology. Charles Tilly (1986) classifies protest actions by the rights being claimed. If the rights claimed are rights in conflict with corresponding rights of rivals, you have competitive protest; if the rights claimed are rights once established or enjoyed but then revoked or usurped, you have reactive protest; and if the rights claimed are rights announced yet not enjoyed, you have proactive protest.

Like any taxonomy, Tilly's scheme classifies, it does not explain—though it hastens a historical generalization he makes about Europe, namely, that types of protest characterize stages of state-making and economic organization: competitive protest is the preponderant type before 1600, reactive protest between 1600 and 1850, and proactive protest after 1850. Reactive protest (mainly tax revolt and food riot) takes on exponents of the national state and capitalist market, whereas proactive protest (mainly public demonstration and labor strike) takes those frameworks for granted and stakes new claims within them. Demonstrations and strikes on tap thus mean bureaucrats and businessmen are already on top. If types of protest follow trends in powerholding and production, competitive protest (such as blood feud and gang war) should revive as states come unstuck and economies collapse. Current history appears to confirm the prognosis.

Note that particular modes of protest can be different types of protest in different situations. Strike or demonstration can be proactive, reactive, or competitive (or even all three) depending on the intention—it can make various claims on different targets simultaneously. Guerrilla war or terrorism can do the same trick, but tax revolt or food riot can make only reactive claims (which mostly subside where national state and capitalist market eclipse local society) and today are largely extinct.

Considering ideology, social history research finds that the intention of popular vigilante protest is to get rights and get away with it, not to abolish the existing social order and institute a new one—and that when protest projects radical changes of state and society, the projectors are revolutionary intellectuals, not ordinary underdogs, whose idea of a good society is (as Barrington Moore [1978] says) the status quo with injustice left out. Underdogs and intellectuals have distinct aims, so protest often runs afoul of vanguard ideology.

Quick reference to fact is no substitute for comparative research but invites students to check for themselves. They should have no trouble seeing that tax rebels intend to stop new taxes from being levied; that food rioters intend to get breadstuff sold at a just price; or that labor strikers intend (as a rule) to get higher wages, shorter hours, or better working conditions conceded. But they might have trouble seeing that ordinary underdogs seldom voice socially radical demands unless revolutionary intellectuals contrive to put words in their mouth. Seeming counterexamples make the best evidence, so glance at some cases where revolutionary situations give underdogs the chance to claim what they want.

Rebels in the English Peasant Revolt of 1381 and the German Peasant War of 1525 demand abolition of villeinage—proposing to commute labor service into quitrent—but respect landlords' demesnes and even offer to work them for wages.

Social revolutionary clerics like John Ball and Thomas Müntzer attain only martyrdom—they affect historiography far more than events. Much later, peasant rebels in France of 1789 simply refuse to pay seignorial dues, wreck some châteaux, yet seldom hurt people, and kill no one, whereas in Russia of 1917 they stop paying rent on estate lands they farm, annex the rest to their village, pillage and burn dachas, but kill very few gentry. In town, the sans-culottes are government helpmates who go for cheap and plentiful bread; and the workers strike for higher wages, shorter hours, better working conditions, and job security. Where underdogs try to turn the world upside down (as in China's Taiping and Communist movements), they take orders from revolutionary intellectuals.

If the intention of protest is overwhelmingly reformist and not revolutionary, why is the history of protest so violent that all cases cited rack up a high body count? The question has no easy answer, but readers must note the obvious: when underdogs gang up to get their rights, redress means a change—of policy, polity, or society—that will injure vested interests, who may strike back. When protest gets violent, most of the casualties are protesters, not powerholders, whose subalterns do the most killing and wounding. Likewise, the revolutionary violence that kills millions owes mostly to new rulers bent on state power and social change, not to rebels out for redress. Stalin's collectivization of farming, for instance, cost more lives than all belligerents lost in World War I, while Mao's Great Leap Forward cost more, mainly through starvation. Rebels never cause such carnage, though when two sides tangle in a civil war, they can come close.

To explain popular violence, historians tease out its strategic and symbolic aims, noting that it both enforces demands and makes a statement. What they try to do, then, is decipher meanings coded in the grisly details—and find that popular violence (while gruesome and atrocious) is highly ritualized and typically imitates traditional punishments the authorities inflict. Students who have a taste for semiotics and a strong stomach can count on plenty of research material here.

But there is more to explaining protest than political intentions. Look now at capabilities to act in concert. Here social history research finds that protest is methodical in technique and mostly the work of militant minorities. Why? Because the modes of protest on tap come neatly packed in what Tilly calls repertoires, that is, feasible sets of rehearsed alternatives, and because it takes material assets, social organization, and strategic know-how to make repertoire items live options. Capabilities (the modes of protest people can use to claim rights) are collective action programs with standard operating procedures. The whole set of collective action programs people can perform in a pinch is their repertoire. When they gang up to get their rights, they do not run amok—they follow the script of a repertoire item.

Think about what this means. The modes of protest called *jacquerie* (peasant mutiny), tax revolt, food riot, public demonstration, labor strike, and such are collective action programs—coherent activities that require assets, organization, and know-how to conduct. Jacquerie means village militias gang up and confront seigniors, demand redress, swear violence if they do not get satisfaction, wreak damage until they get their way or get repressed, and return to obedience. Tax revolt follows a similar script but targets tax collectors (not seigniors, who may aid the rebels), wrecks their premises, and roughs them up—sometimes fatally. Food riot means people (mainly women) seize breadstuff and force sale at a price below market. Demonstration (show of political force) and strike (concerted work stoppage) are familiar routines today and have been for about two centuries.

As to the assets, organization, and know-how that make repertoire items live options, historians report something so obvious that only a theory can obscure it: protesters are not the wretched of the earth by and large, but solid citizens with the material, social, and strategic wherewithal needed to gang up and get satisfaction. Protesters have to pay their way as well as fight their way—which means they must have wealth and weapons. They have to hang together or they will all hang separately—which means they must have a command structure (albeit informal) to reward those who help out and punish those who hold out. And they have to know what they are doing—which means they must know how to go for what they want. Would-be protesters lacking these prerequisites have to acquire them; otherwise, they stay nonstarters, who are also a subject of social history research.

Skimming examples, again, is not comparative study, only a hint of it. But illustrations (even vignettes) always help. The backbone of the German Peasant War is the village elite of mayors, judges, innkeepers, blacksmiths, and rich farmers who sport pikes and muskets and conscript poor peasants into the movement. The sans-culottes comprise artisans, shopkeepers, entrepreneurs (the beer king of Paris is a militant), professionals, intellectuals, civil servants, and wage earners, though the 2,000 to 3,000 zealots who dominate Parisian neighborhood politics are mostly middle class. Russian peasant communities own two-thirds of the land outright, and when they grab the rest in 1917 and 1918 they make all households take part to ensure both success and equal liability in case of reprisal. Time and again, it is the strong not the weak who protest most—and most forcibly.

Social history research notes something else of extraordinary interest. Class position affects capabilities more than intentions. Fighting groups on both sides of the barricades (as Mark Traugott [1985] shows in detail) may have the same social composition.

Political intentions and capabilities to act in concert go far toward explaining protest but not far enough. Look now at opportunities to get away with it. The lesson social history teaches here is that protest depends on help from both friends and enemies—allies who give aid and comfort, opponents who waffle, give in, or cave in. Who would understand protest can never forget history's first commandment, namely that "chronology is king." Put together the parallel chronologies of protest and high politics and you see the pattern at once. Protest makes no progress where it has no powerful friends, only powerful enemies. It makes most progress where it has powerful friends or weak enemies or both. One cause of protest (as of war) is the hope of getting away with it, and what feeds hope is lack of power to resist it. The best test here is to see what happens when—thanks to a power shift in

government—protest suddenly loses strong allies and gains forceful enemies. Once again, the French revolutionary sans-culottes are a good example, being so heavily dependent on government patronage. As the dominant Jacobin party calls the sans-culottes in as helpmates in 1793, so it eases them out again in 1794; and when the Thermidorians supplant the Jacobins, they persecute the sans-culottes—showing them up as powerless and unpopular.

If our historical generalizations codify the findings of social history research on protest, the question remains: How do these findings cohere as an explanatory argument? The answer is situational logic. Explaining protest is deducing it from the protesters' situation—defined by their intentions, capabilities, and opportunities—on the assumption (the rationality principle) that people act in ways they expect to satisfy their intentions in view of their capabilities and opportunities. The findings on protest actions follow (in logic) from those on intentions, capabilities, and opportunities—taking for granted that people act as they do to get what they want under given constraints. Our aim here is not to decree how social historians should explain but to codify how they do explain—not to recommend a theoretical method but to recognize the one they use.

Readers who sense that this article mentions evidence only to illustrate a theory and sacrifices description to explanation are correct, though the slant is intentional. Evidence makes sense only in the light of a theory, which governs its selection and arrangement, and without which it is baffling. What saves the argument from vicious circularity is that our theory is testable—counterevidence could falsify it. Better that the theory be explicit and critically examined than implicit and uncritically assumed. We only can describe well what we already can explain.

Protest studies abound, though their market share of European social history research is down since the 1970s, owing to a shift of focus in human sciences from material conditions to cultural meanings as well as to success in making the major findings common knowledge among historians. If protest in Europe gets relatively less attention, however, protest in Asia, Africa, Latin America, and Oceania gets more, thanks in part to theoretical and comparative study of covert resistance to repressive regimes. The genre thrives. (*See also* French Revolution; Moral Economy; Peasant Rebellion; Strikes)

Rod Aya

REFERENCES

Cobb, Richard. *The Police and the People: French Popular Protest, 1789–1820.* Oxford: Oxford University Press, 1970.

Moore, Barrington, Jr. *Injustice: The Social Bases of Obedience and Revolt.* White Plains, NY: Sharpe, 1978.

Rudé, George. *The Crowd in the French Revolution.* Oxford: Oxford University Press, 1959.

Scott, James C. *Domination and the Arts of Resistance: Hidden Transcripts.* New Haven: Yale University Press, 1990.

Thompson, E.P. *Customs in Common.* London: Merlin, 1991.

Tilly, Charles. *The Contentious French.* Cambridge, MA: Harvard University Press, 1986.

Traugott, Mark. *Armies of the Poor: Determinants of Working-Class Participation in the Parisian Insurrection of June 1848.* Princeton, NJ: Princeton University Press, 1985.

Protoindustrialization

Since the early 1970s, lively debates centered on protoindustrialization have reinvigorated scholarly interest in the rural origins of European industrialization. The term "proto-industries" was coined by Franklin F. Mendels in 1972. While historians of Europe had long remarked upon the rapid expansion between the 16th and 18th centuries of export-oriented textile production in the countryside, Mendels renamed this phenomenon and suggested that it constituted a preparatory stage for factory-based industrialization. Building on the work of earlier scholars, Mendels argued that for merchants protoindustries served as a period of apprenticeship during which they acquire the business connections, managerial skills, and the capital necessary for later investments in centralized and mechanized production. On the labor side, the process weakened the ties of the work force to the land, aiding the formation of a rural proletariat.

Based on his own research on population trends and economic change in 18th-century Flanders, Mendels explained that protoindustries undermined traditional social controls on population growth. When land was the primary resource, members of each generation were expected to wait until their father retired or died before assuming control over the family farm, thus keeping the age of marriage high and families small. Growing home-based manufacturing challenged the dominance of agriculture. Wage work enabled children to marry younger. This decline in the age of marriage extended the years women bore children within marriage, leading to larger families and ultimately to population growth. Although, initially, agricultural households were drawn to manufacturing as a lucrative off-season activity to help sustain the viability of subsistence agriculture, demographic consequences of protoindustrialization forced the population to depend increasingly on wage work alone.

Mendels's hypothesis captured the imagination of social and economic historians because of the innovative ways that it integrated the study of economic development with a detailed analysis of family life. For many scholars, it provided an elegant model for understanding the articulations between international markets and household decisionmaking. Some social historians also extended the protoindustrialization ideas to discuss changes in consumer behavior and sexuality among rural manufacturing workers in 18th-century Europe. The popularity of Mendels's hypothesis led researchers to apply the model to rural industries around the globe, to radically different cultures and time periods. Others imported Mendels's hypothesis into their own research agendas, altering its original theoretical orientation. The most influential of the latter is the work of Peter Kriedte, Hans Medick, and Jurgen Schlumbohm (1981), who recognized the opportunity in these studies to revive an older Marxist debate on the transition from feudalism to capitalism.

Ironically, as the case studies proliferated, the hypothesis became a victim of its own success. Many researchers working on specific regions or specific industries have complained that the definitions and typologies do not suit their case. Moreover, for some regions, researchers have shown that protoindustrialization deterred successful industrialization. In themselves, such counterexamples do not undermine the hypothesis. Mendels's original statement accounts for these failures. Mendels was critical of the determinist logic of older explanations for industrialization. Observing that many regions now considered the backwaters of the European economy were actually casualties of the transition to the factory system, he argued that some protoindustrial regions "deindustrialized." Yet beyond serving as a category for "failed industrialization," what "de-industrialization" means is very unclear. Do these regions revert back to subsistence agriculture? Does rural manufacturing find ways to survive in an industrial economy? With a few exceptions, this aspect of the hypothesis has been ignored. So while the theory claims to represent the rise of the factory system as a dynamic and open-ended process, hinting at a fuller integration of the processes of underdevelopment, in practice, it replicates the deterministic logic that it initially criticized.

In the current debate, the future of the concept is in doubt. Some critics claim that the theory tries to explain too much, while others claim it explains nothing new at all. Defenders suggest the need for more restrictive conditions. Others hesitate. Limiting the scope of explanations may aid the theory by enabling it to hold true for a narrower range of conditions, but a diluted theory loses its original appeal. An acceptable compromise might retain the protoindustrialization hypothesis as a set of suggestive research questions while accepting its limitations as a general theory. Certainly, it is important to recognize the lasting contributions made by the past two decades of empirical research. For example, historians are more aware than ever before of the demographic dimensions of capitalist class formation, including the gendered politics of proletarianization. However, these empirical studies have raised a far more challenging problem for theorists. Conceived neither as case studies which demonstrate a general principle, nor as local studies in search of a grander synthesis, the new regional studies are reaching toward entirely different principles for explaining the patterns of capitalist development. No longer trying to discern an underlying unitary logic, they focus on how the contingencies of political and social struggles shape the possibilities for production. (*See also* Deindustrialization; Industrialization; Putting-Out System)

Tessie P. Liu

REFERENCES

Coleman, D.C. "Proto-industrialization: A Concept Too Many," *Economic History Review* 2, 36 (August 1983): 435–448.

Gullickson, Gay L. *The Spinners and Weavers of Auffay: Rural Industry and the Sexual Division of Labor in a French Village, 1750–1850*. Cambridge and New York: Cambridge University Press, 1986.

Kriedte, Peter, Hans Medick, and Jurgen Schlumbohm. *Industrialization Before Industrialization*. Translated by Beate Schempp. Cambridge and New York: Cambridge University Press, 1981.

Levine, David. *Family Formation in the Age of Nascent Capitalism*. New York: Academic Press, 1977.

Mendels, Franklin F. "Proto-industrialization: The First Phase in the Industrialization Process," *Journal of Economic History* 32 (1972): 241–261.

Sabel, Charles F. "Proto-industry and the Problem of Capitalism as a Concept," *International Labor and Working-Class History* 33 (Spring 1988): 30–37.

Psychohistory

Psychohistory emerged during the 1960s, primarily in the United States. Psychohistorians attempt to interpret psychological conditions in the past and to apply psychological, particularly Freudian, theory to past periods. While psychohistory has remained a minor current in American historiography, it continues to draw some attention, maintaining its own journal (*Psychohistory Review*).

Psychohistory has not overlapped consistently with social history, as the latter field has gained ground more rapidly. There are two reasons for the considerable separation. First, most psychohistorians have concentrated on individual biography, which may or may not relate to wider social changes, rather than larger group phenomena. One of the great works in psychohistory, psychologist Erik Erikson's study *Young Man Luther* (1962), deals with patterns of fatherhood and economic changes in the early 16th century as a backdrop to the family dynamic that in turn shaped Martin Luther's psyche. But the focus is on the individual, and this distinguishes most psychohistory from the dynamic that interests social historians. The second reason for a persistent gap involves the Freudian orientation of much psychohistory. Not only does this emphasize individual biography, Freudian theory also imposes a late 19th-century psychoanalytical model on the past in ways that many social historians find misleading. Interpretation of parent-child relations in terms of Freudianism may accurately describe conditions in the European upper middle class around 1900, but it may miss the mark for an earlier period.

Despite limited interaction, psychohistorians have contributed to social history in several ways. Key studies of childhood in the 1970s combined psychohistorical with sociohistorical concerns. David Hunt investigated patterns of child discipline in 17th-century France in terms of Erikson's psychological theories. His conclusions may have been somewhat anachronistic in insisting on the psychic harshness of early modern upbringing, but he mounted a challenging argument with interesting data about the way parents treated their children. Somewhat less successful were more sweeping efforts by Lloyd deMause (*A History of Childhood*, 1979) to show how most childrearing methods prior to the 20th century were psychologically injurious, because of rigid discipline, physical punishments, and lack of affection. In the judgment of most social historians, this approach misrepresents the complexity of pre-20th century parent-child relations and in the judgment of many current child psychologists it interprets the effects of physical discipline inaccurately as well.

Psychohistorians have also produced challenging interpretations of the impact of World War I and absent fathers on a generation of young Germans. Philip Greven, a leading American historian who has dealt both in psycho- and social history, has interpreted certain religious groups, initially formed in the colonial era, in terms of their persistent generation of characteristic personality types through religiously-inspired patterns of parenting.

Psychohistorians, in other words, continue periodically to address psychological characteristics of groups, often through attention to childhood, in ways that overlap with the interests of social history. Since the mid-1980s several psychohistorians have interpreted aspects of late 19th-century middle-class life, relating to sexuality, family, and emotion, by combining psychoanalytical theory with cultural and autobiographical data. The results have not always won full acclaim, either from social historians or from psychologists disenchanted with Freudianism, but they have affected our understanding of such phenomena as Victorian sexuality in practice.

Finally, as social historians return to new interests in personal standards, not only sexuality but also emotions and the physical senses, they suggest the possibility of group psychological portraits from a non-Freudian perspective. Here may be the basis for another stage in the off-again, on-again relationship with psychohistory. [*See also* Childhood; Emotion (Emotionology); Senses; Sexuality]

Peter N. Stearns

REFERENCES

Gay, Peter. *The Bourgeois Experience: From Victoria to Freud.* 3 vols. New York: Oxford University Press, 1984-1993.

Greven, Philip. *Spare the Child: The Religious Roots of Punishment and the Psychological Impact of Physical Abuse.* New York: Knopf, 1991.

Hunt, David. *Parents and Children in History: The Psychology of Family Life in Early Modern France.* New York: Basic Books, 1970.

Stearns, Carol Z., and Peter N. Stearns, eds. *Emotion and Social Change: Toward a New Psychohistory.* New York: Holmes and Meier, 1988.

Public History

Public history emerged as a distinct field in the second half of the 1970s. Clearly, historians have always had a public or, more precisely, a variety of public audiences. The term "public history" was first coined in 1975 by Professor Robert Kelley of the Public History Program at the University of California, Santa Barbara. The term, which has defied exact definition, is used to refer to applied as well as professional or even entrepreneurial history. One general definition consists of history that is done anywhere outside the classroom by anybody who's not employed in a university. Lacking sharply defined contours, the public history movement has nevertheless generated a national organization, the National

Council on Public History (NCPH), and a growing number of programs and courses devoted to the subject. The NCPH publishes *The Public Historian* quarterly journal, a quarterly newsletter, and other publications; sponsors an annual conference; and maintains a list of schools with public history programs and a syllabus exchange for public history courses.

Public history encompasses the following broad range of fields: preservation of archives and historical manuscripts; oral history; public records editing; historic preservation; documentary film production; museum exhibit development; state and local history; history of public institutions; presentation of history for public organization; public policy development; and corporate history.

The development of public history as a field has not lacked controversy. Public historians have rejected the refined definition of the professional historian as academic scholar. Practitioners of state and local history have taken issue with the notion promulgated by public historians that public history is a new endeavor.

What is clearly new about public history is its emphasis upon training graduate students for professional positions as archivists, preservationists, and the like. In this fashion, public history is moving in the direction of institutionalizing the practice of state and local history as fields within the academy. Thus, public history has in significant ways in its own terms offered a definition of professionalism as narrow as that of the academy. In some areas, especially applied history programs, public historians have turned what has long been a minor enterprise for historians—working for corporations or governments—into the major focus of historical efforts.

Within the ranks of public history, there have been significant differences as to the definition and direction of public history. Part of the public history rejection of narrow academic scholarship emanated from historians influenced by the social movements of the 1960s. A new generation of historians, practitioners of the new social history, addressed the history of social relationships, social structures, everyday life, private life, social movements, social conflicts, and social classes, both as distinct phenomena and in interrelationship with each other. Often populist in nature, these social historians have defined public history as an enterprise that aims to democratize history by seeking a broad public participation in the construction of its own history. Thus, public history includes this approach as well as other approaches that are more institutional and more concerned with the professionalization of the field.

Presentation of history for a wide audience often emphasizes social history themes. These themes have emerged strongly in museum programs designed to use artifacts to illustrate a wider social past. Many British social historians have engaged in extensive interaction with interested amateurs particularly around working-class topics, through the journal *History Workshop*. Public historians at sites such as Williamsburg and Sturbridge Village as well as the National Park Service have notably advanced the presentation of social history in the United States.

As a branch of public history, applied or policy historians trace trends and assess analogies relevant to defining current policy problems and developing solutions. Some of this policy history involves military or diplomatic subject matter, but otherwise a great deal of the new genre overlaps with social history in terms of assessing past policy impact on society and providing historical perspective on the nature of and reasons for current trends in such areas as family structure, adolescent sexuality, or retirement from work.

To illustrate public history in practice, the following three examples will be briefly outlined: the National Park Service, the American Association for State and Local History, and entrepreneurial history.

The National Park Service (NPS), a federal agency established in 1916, has administered historic sites since the 1930s, and now includes a wide array of historic and cultural sites, including presidential homes, Civil War battlefields, industrial locales, and much more. NPS historians conduct research about these resources, providing information and helping to clarify their significance, as well as assistance in shaping the interpretive presentation of walks, talks, and tours to the public. Historical research, often concentrating on social history topics and approaches, is critical in the development of museum exhibitry, audiovisual interpretations, books, and brochures. NPS historians also hold a variety of management and policy positions.

The American Association for State and Local History (AASLH) *Directory of Historical Societies and Agencies in the United States and Canada* identified 13,000 such organizations in 1986, up from 3,300 in 1970. A chief purpose of the organization is to help individuals and communities, especially through their historical organizations, identify, save, and use their significant historic resources. Most work in state and local history is done in historical societies, historic sites, museums, and public agencies. The majority of these organizations operate with relatively small annual budgets, although the range of organizations engaged in state and local history is very wide. They include small town and major metropolitan historical societies as well as quite a variety of state organizations and many other institutions. Efforts in training in social history have helped link these groups with analytical issues in the field.

Entrepreneurial history entails historical work in one form or another for clients outside the academy or the public sector; this work often deals with social history topics. Such historians form their own businesses or work for corporations, often managing their archives. There are a number of businesses operated by historians; many are listed in the *NCPH Directory of Historical Consultants* (1988). Ethical questions for entrepreneurial historians are inherent both in the uses to which projects they generate are put and in the findings which are expected by the client, the purchaser of services. For the historian in the private sector, the historical process encompasses more than an intellectual inquiry and presentation of findings and interpretations for the purpose of expanding knowledge on a given subject. (*See also* Local History; Oral History; Social History)

Martin Blatt

REFERENCES

Benson, Susan Porter, Stephen Brier, and Roy Rosenzweig, eds. *Presenting the Past: Essays on History and the Public.* Philadelphia: Temple University Press, 1986.

Grele, Ronald J. "Whose Public? Whose History? What Is the Goal of a Public Historian?" *The Public Historian* 3 (Winter 1981): 40–48.

Howe, Barbara J., and Emory L. Kemp, eds. *Public History: An Introduction.* Malabar, FL: Robert Krieger Publishing Company, 1986.

Leon, Warren, and Roy Rosenzweig, eds. *History Museums in the United States: A Critical Assessment.* Urbana: University of Illinois Press, 1989.

Samuel, Raphael. *People's History and Socialist Theory.* Boston: Routledge and Kegan Paul, 1981.

Public Schools

State schooling in many societies has been studied as a principal ingredient of the modern social history of education. Public schooling in the United States provides a more specific focus within this larger comparative context. Public schools in the United States are institutions which were locally organized and funded to educate children and some adults. Schools were created for a variety of reasons, such as promoting literacy, disseminating prioritized knowledge and beliefs, training a work force, and reinforcing political doctrines. The history of public schools reveals vital contributions from social history, and in turn helped develop American social history as a field of research.

Calvinists in colonial New England began early schools to promote biblical literacy and civil obedience. The enactment in Massachusetts of the famous "Old Deluder Satan Law" in 1647 required all communities over a specified size to establish and support schools. The success of the American Revolution brought an enhanced interest in public schools for the professed purpose of educating the newly democratic society. Although espousing varied goals, proponents such as Benjamin Rush, Thomas Jefferson, and Noah Webster concurred on the need for universal education for all male children.

The crusade for public schools was advanced by the common school movement of the 1830s and 1840s, led by reformer Horace Mann. Mann and other common school advocates, including both workingmen's groups and elites, promoted the further expansion of public schools. Similar to earlier proeducation movements, the motives and goals for the creation of common schools among competing interest groups varied greatly. The introduction of common schools did not greatly increase public school enrollments during the 19th century, but the idea of standardized public education became entrenched in society.

Since the early years of the Republic, public schools in most American cities were usually divided into two racially separate systems. The introduction of segregating Jim Crow laws throughout the South after the Civil War exacerbated this separation. Through both legislation or informal tradition, racial segregation continued as a prevailing norm in public schools until the 1960s or early 1970s.

Public schools became even more central in American life during the 20th century. A wave of child labor and mandatory school attendance laws and other reforms during the Progressive era of the early 1900s caused a significant increase in enrollments, in addition to other changes. Enrollments greatly expanded during the Great Depression of the 1930s, and public school attendance became the accepted occupation of childhood. Public schools continue today to be a common social and educational experience for most Americans, as well as a forum for political competition and conflict.

The historical study of public schools has experienced many changes and controversies. The consensus opinion among many historians of public education is that a historiographic divide developed around 1960. The field of educational history before 1960 was comprised of educational practitioners and professors in schools of education, who often glorified the purposes and successes of public schools. This "celebratory tradition" portrayed educators as the guardians of Christian morality and values, and public schools as the basis of American progress and prosperity. These historians usually concentrated their studies on the achievements of school leaders and reform movements and measured the success of public schools in terms of enrollments and financial allocations. Their approach to studying education highlighted the origins of public schools and stressed major leaders, events, and successes. Although voluminous scholarship on public school history was produced prior to 1960, it was usually descriptive and general,

rather than analytical. These earlier educational historians often failed to consider fundamental historical questions: why did public schools exist at all, which groups benefited from schools and which groups did not, and to what extent did public schools affect and change life in America?

In *The Social History of American Education* (1988), education historians William J. Reese and B. Edward McClellan cite the publication of Bernard Bailyn's *Education in the Forming of American Society: Needs and Opportunity for Study* (1960) as the beginning of more significant historical inquiry into public schools. Bailyn challenged many of the assumptions and generalizations common to earlier scholarship, and questioned the motivations and potential self-interests of professional educators writing the history of public schools. He criticized their writings as being too laudatory, and much too narrowly focused on institutional growth. He suggested that educational historians broaden their research to consider discussions of conflict and discontinuity, and to analyze public schools in the context of broader society. Bailyn called for incorporating the study of public education into the mainstream of historical scholarship. His research spawned a new generation of young scholars in the 1960s who were eager to explore other areas of educational history. Many of these Bailyn-inspired researchers during the next decade became involved in the social history movement.

Social history research in the area of American public schools was distinguished from earlier works by the introduction of new historical methodologies and philosophies. These included the use of quantitative analysis; the emphasis on the needs and desires of the working class, skepticism about the motives of school founders; and a deliberate avoidance of institutional and biographical studies. Prominent among this new social history research into public schools was Michael Katz's *The Irony of Early School Reform: Educational Innovation in Mid-Nineteenth Century Massachusetts* (1968). Katz's study of education in Beverly, Massachusetts, during the 1840s examines public attitudes and perceptions of public schools. Although his conclusions are often disputed, he successfully revised the field of educational history by dispelling the notion that public schools were enthusiastically accepted by all interest groups.

Despite controversies, the revisionist approach taken by Michael Katz and other historians succeeded in further stimulating research in educational history. Social historians during the 1970s and 1980s have inquired into many previously unexplored areas of public education. A 1974 study by David Tyack, *One Best System*, provided a comprehensive overview of the history of American urban education. More specific social history research has focused primarily on how economic class interaction affected public schools, such as Julia Wrigley's *Class Politics and Public Schools* (1982), Paul Peterson's *The Politics of School Reform, 1870–1940*, Ira Katznelson and Margaret Weir's *Schooling for All*, and David John Hogan's *Class and Reform*. William J. Reese in *The Power and Promise of School Reform*, David Tyack in *Public Schools in Hard Times*, and others focus on eras which are perceived watersheds for reform and change. Still other social historians have successfully linked the study of educational history with the historical studies of immigration, ethnicity, race, and gender. The introduction of social history methodology and the growing body of serious research on the history of public schools have successfully moved the history of education closer to the mainstream of historical scholarship. (*See also* Education; Literacy; Popular Culture)

David G. Hogan

REFERENCES

McClellan, B. Edward, and William J. Reese. *The Social History of American Education*. Urbana: University of Illinois Press, 1988.

Nasaw, David. *Schooled to Order: A Social History of Public Schooling in the United States*. New York: Oxford University Press, 1979.

Tyack, David. *One Best System: A History of American Urban Education*. Cambridge: Harvard University Press, 1974.

Wrigley, Julia. *Class Politics and Public Schools*. New Brunswick, NJ: Rutgers University Press, 1982.

Public Sphere

Scholars working on far-flung and disparate parts of the world have begun to analyze the emergence in the modern nation-state of "the public sphere"—that arena of collective opinion and activity that, together with the state and the individual, makes up contemporary civil society. The "public sphere" concept is closely related to a variety of social history concerns.

In Europe, creation of "the public sphere" has been identified with the emergence of the bourgeois nation-state, and thus analysts have timed its emergence to the rise of a capitalist order and the processes of industrialization. The most influential analysis has been provided by Jurgen Habermas. Habermas (1989) argued that the bourgeois public sphere that emerged in western Europe had at its heart a public opinion that was shaped by open access to information circulated through the print media and that functioned by exercising surveillance over the state. Recent research, however, suggests that earlier points of change or transition may be equally important, especially moments relating to the alterations in the relationship between monarch and state (e.g., the French Revolution, the accession of the Hanoverian dynasty in England, etc.).

Development of this revisionist approach for western Europe has focused on the nature of the dichotomy between "public" and "private" characteristic of the modern nation-state as it emerged in western Europe during the late 19th and early 20th centuries. Interested particularly in the "public" side of this dichotomy, sociologists and historians have followed the intellectual lead of the Frankfurt school and, especially, the work of Habermas, in tracing the development of a bourgeois "public sphere" that operated independently of the state. Meanwhile, feminist scholars interested in the "private" side of the dichotomy have explored the implications of familial and domestic hierarchies, as well as the distribution of power inherent in the distinction established between the public and private spheres. Both sets of scholars have sought to distill the essence of "the public" that was created in this period. A key concept for intellectuals and political figures at the time, the concept is under close critical scrutiny now, for "the public" was defined abstractly as an inclusive category. In the event and under promulgation by particular kinds of states, however, "the public" often has excluded broad categories of residents of a nation-state. Understanding the nature of this exclusion is fundamental to understanding the realities of power relationships in the contemporary world.

Furthermore, the nature and locale of activity influencing the development of the public sphere has begun to be described rather differently from its original caption. For instance, Habermas and other theorists looked to England for their model but abstracted their descriptions to include France and even Germany; scholars now agree that the distinct bourgeois class that emerged in England as consumers of print capitalism and, hence, participants in a public sphere was rather different from the professional classes who filled that niche in France. Similarly, there is no direct equivalent in England to the public sphere role played in France by the *salon* (organized, generally, by women). Moreover, the shift Habermas traces from an authority first derived by "the public" on cultural matters to the exercise of public opinion in political matters may have been less smooth, complete, and uncontested than Habermas supposed. Equally important for comparative analysis, imperial ideology differed in France and in England regarding the imperialized "Other" (and, therefore, the ostensible ability of the *indigene* in the colonies to participate fully in the political world of the metropole [the colonizing nation]).

In the world subject to imperialism, the process naturally proceeded differently, not least because industrialization has been a partial process, and because the power of the state was not rationalized by virtue of the relationship between state and individual citizen. Key moments under imperialism related, instead, to the state's refusal to recognize the legitimacy of arenas independent of the political structure designed by the imperial state. Nevertheless, the appeal of the rhetoric of democratic ideals, and the role of an independent "public" within those ideals, united the European metropoles and the colonies they controlled.

If a public/private dichotomy characterized the metropole, research developed independently for an area subject to imperialism—British India—has begun to delineate a related but significantly different pattern. There, the imperial state tried to distinguish a political realm which legitimized the state and its institutions (shaped by the assumptions at home about the separation of public and private) and defined all other activities as "apolitical." The activities deemed apolitical could be characterized, generally, as those relating to the local, familial, and/or domestic world, in which connections between people were expressed through kinship (including fictive kinship) and religious rhetoric, and in which the source of legitimate authority reposed outside the state. This world became known as the realm of community, in which "community" was given the gloss (much as the private world of western Europe) of "particular" and "special interest." Analysts are also beginning to argue that indigenous males in India and other colonies seized opportunities within their communities, to exercise much more direct and far-reaching control over domestic practices and the women who inhabited this world.

Distinctive from the state though this arena was, it was not "private" and apolitical. Instead, it became the repository of cultural memory and political consciousness as these evolved in resistance to the dominant mode of the imperial state. As such, this second arena becomes the focal point for political scientists, sociologists, anthropologists, and historians seeking to understand the reemergence in the late 20th century of regional ethnic and religious identities—bases of "community" that challenge the claims on citizens' loyalty put forth by the nation-state.

Finally, Habermas had argued a relatively smooth transition in western Europe from the independent exercise of public opinion regarding cultural matters (which became, over time, part of the private realm) to the exercise of public opinion in the public, political sphere. This suggested a profound difference with developments in the imperialized world, where cultural activity remained highly politicized and the site of much contestation. The nature of the cultural world in the metropole, however, may bear more similarity to the site of resistance in the colonies than had first appeared to Habermas and fellow analysts, and a number of analysts have begun focusing on this aspect of "public" activity.

The public sphere is likely to concern social historians for some time, as it historically has performed a critical function in the legitimation of power in the emerging nation-state, while also serving as the locus of resistance and contestation to the state. As a consequence, it should prove to be an important focal point for analysts interested in the relationships between state, community, and individual as these have emerged in the last few decades. By questioning the processes by which this intermediate sphere emerged, scholars are beginning to identify the important contributing factors and the underlying dynamics of the functioning of "a public" in ways that permit comparison and analysis across regional and cultural boundaries. (*See also* Community; Gender Socialization; Imperialism; State and Society)

Sandria B. Freitag

REFERENCES

"Aspects of 'the Public' in South Asia," *South Asia* 14, 1 (June 1991).

Habermas, Jurgen. *The Structural Transformation of the Public Sphere.* Translated by Thomas Burger. Cambridge, MA: MIT Press, 1989.

Landes, Joan. *Women and the Public Sphere.* Ithaca, NY: Cornell University Press, 1988.

LaVolpa, Anthony. "Conceiving a Public: Ideas and Society in Eighteenth-Century Europe," *Journal of Modern History* 64 (1992): 79–116.

Maza, Sarah. "Domestic Melodrama as Political Ideology: The Case of the Comte de Saois," *The American Historical Review* 94, 5 (December 1989): 1249–1264.

Punishment and Prisons

It is helpful to distinguish between formal and informal punishments. Formal punishments (with which this article will deal) are administered by institutions or organizations, usually after a hearing, and in accordance with a scale which matches transgressions and penalties. These are the punishments particularly explored in social history. Informal punishments are imposed by individuals or groups (parents, peers), and range from a word or facial expression which rebukes, to the infliction of physical pain. Punishment in the first of these two senses is one of the distinguishing features of civilization, necessitating a set of rules or laws, and a deliberative process, rather than random or immediate action. A few social historians have stretched connections between the two types of punishments

noting, for example, a decline in the use of shame in child rearing in the United States after 1800—about the same time that public punishments were transformed.

Philosophers, theologians, jurists, and social scientists have in the last two centuries identified several purposes in punishment. These are generally agreed to consist of four principal ends: retribution, deterrence, incapacitation and reformation, as well as some secondary objectives. The latter include restitution, penitence, denunciation, and the exercise of mercy. (Space does not permit further examination of these, and others. Works on the philosophy and theology of punishment should be consulted.)

In modern times, retribution has often been condemned as being retrogressive, and the resultant movement away from physical punishment, to incarceration, is a leading topic in social history. Critics have argued that to punish simply because a wrong has been done is to look only backward, and, that adding another ill to the one already committed is materially unproductive. There is, however, a positive and utilitarian side to retribution, which was recognized in some of the earliest societies, and which has again found advocates.

Retribution, as part of formal punishment, usually suggests proportion: the amount of punishment is matched to the gravity of the offense. In both the Judaeo-Christian traditions, and in Islam, retribution was a step forward because it restricted the harm that could be done to the wrongdoer. The *Lex Talionis*—"an eye for an eye"—means that one cannot take an arm and a leg as well. Redress, moreover, stopped with the retaliatory punishment of the offender, and did not extend to kin. The early Islamic insistence on individual and proportionate retribution replaced blood feuds and divisive clan and tribal wars with a unifying legal system. In the last 20 years, retribution—"just deserts"—has found support among some Western jurists as a means of restricting the state's right to punish to an equivalent of the actual harm done.

Deterrence is an unavoidable element in publicly administered or publicly known punishment. The memory of the pain experienced is supposed to deter an offender from repeating the misdeed, and the example of another being punished to dissuade those who might otherwise offend. The utilitarians (followers of Jeremy Bentham, an 18th- and early 19th-century English political economist) asserted that deterrence was a defensible justification for punishment, since it aimed to reduce future crime. To impose more punishment than was necessary for deterrence was, Bentham argued, a gratuitous act of tyranny. He was prepared to accept attempts at reformation through punishment, but conceived these in the form of a "calculus of felicity"—an effective balance between the pleasure of the crime and the pain of punishment, which would prevent the offender from relapsing.

Reformation through punishment was a religious objective for many centuries. The Christian church sought to reform errant monks, nuns, and other clergy through corporal chastisement and cellular confinement, combined with restrictions in diet, and exhortation. Both Christians and Muslims saw even the death penalty as reformatory, provided it could be made part of the process by which the condemned could be brought to penitence before death and therefore entry into the afterlife.

As a goal of secular punishment, reformation is relatively modern. In mid-16th century London a reformatory for minor offenders was established in the disused palace of Bridewell, and became the model for houses of correction throughout the country, and in the American colonies; Amsterdam's Rasp Huis had a similar influence on the Continent. Another wave of reformatory imprisonment, which led to penitentiaries, started at the end of the 18th century. Both sets of innovations occurred in the midst of economic and social change, and heightened concerns about offenders.

Although in reality the prisons and jails were usually sordid and hopeless, reformation was a major part of the penal rhetoric of most industrialized countries, from the latter part of the 19th century until very recent times. Various devices and formulas have been tried, including reformatories for juveniles, minimum-security (open) prisons for low security risks, industrial prisons, and psychotherapeutic communities. There have been experiments with different types of regime, such as military-type regimentation, extreme deprivation, occupational training, psychological counseling, and education. Noncustodial punishments such as probation, suspended and deferred sentences, reparation, and community service have all claimed reformatory properties.

Incapacitation, or destroying the offender's capacity to reoffend, may be found in the very earliest penal records. Prior to modern times, this type of prevention was corporal or capital. In a few countries the *Sharia* (Islamic law) even today seeks incapacitation through amputations. Amputation was never favored in common law (i.e., Anglo-American law), but occurred occasionally. A less severe form of partial incapacitation was, however, more widespread. Thieves, vagabonds, and other offenders were branded on their hands or faces, often with a letter or mark indicating the nature of their offenses. In times of limited government and record-keeping this may have been an effective means of prevention, since the branding, visible as it was, gave notice of the offender's character.

Capital punishment, the most severe form of incapacitation, has now generally been abandoned in Western nations. Among advanced countries, only the United States has this punishment, but it is widely used in Third World countries such as China and Iran. Long terms of imprisonment are the usual form of incapacitation where the death penalty has been abandoned, although many offenses which in the early 19th century were punishable by death are now treated as comparatively minor transgressions.

It is rare to find periods when one philosophy of punishment has totally predominated. The four main objectives have usually been combined in a pragmatic fashion. Retributive punishment often possessed deterrent properties as well, and it would have been hard to describe a public execution or flogging as wholly one or the other. Even reformation could be combined with other objectives, since imprisonment, for example, necessarily involves elements of incapacitation, retribution, and deterrence.

In their pure forms, however, there is a contradiction between penal objectives. Should an offender be released from prison when he has paid the penalty for his crime (retribution), or when he has been reformed? Should a sentence be determined by incapacitation, which might involve the prolonged confinement of a petty but habitual offender, or by retribution, which might indicate a lesser penalty? There are no easy answers, and these questions perplex the courts and lawmakers as much now as a century ago.

Many different punishments have been used over the centuries, some so ingenious and cruel that they prompt depressing reflections about mankind's sadistic obsessions. But three main types may be distinguished—corporal, custodial, and noncustodial. The first of these includes whipping, branding, and mutilation. These are easy and cheap to inflict, and have found particular favor (even today) in societies which have a limited apparatus of government, and in which public funds are scarce and certainly insufficient to maintain a prison system. A few countries have in modern times retained or revived corporal punishment for ideological reasons. This has happened in certain Islamic countries, for example.

The chief custodial punishment is imprisonment, although there were in common use until the 19th century detention devices such as the stocks, pillory, irons, and even cages. In China and other countries the penal yoke, a device locked around the neck, and resting on the shoulders, was used as a form of portable prison. Until very recent times, chain gangs and mobile prisons were used in parts of the United States, in order to employ prisoners at road and agricultural work, and, to some extent, to display their punishment and degradation.

The term "prison," strictly speaking, is generic, and encompasses all places of detention and, at least arguably, detention devices. The jail ("gaol"—same pronunciation—in British usage) is the oldest type of prison, references to which are found in ancient records. Until medieval times the jail was used in England almost entirely as a place of detention, rather than punishment. One was held in jail awaiting trial (or, for some unfortunates, the giving of evidence at a trial), or pending the execution of sentence. The wait for the latter was usually short, and it was by no means uncommon to be sentenced and hanged on the same day. Lesser offenders awaited the jailer's convenience to be flogged or branded.

From the 14th century onward jails were increasingly used for the detention of civil prisoners. Private creditors could get a court order committing a debtor to jail until he settled his obligations. The remedy appears absurd, since a prisoner was cut off from all possibility of earning a living and settling debts. There was another element which makes the process even more inexplicable to the modern mind—entry into jail meant an increase in debt, since jails were financed by user fees, and one could not depart until the jailer's tariff had been settled. Many hapless debtors starved to death, or were swept away by one of the periodic jail fevers. Detention was thought to be an effective means of forcing the disgorgement of concealed property, the sale of assets, or of inducing friends and relatives to settle the debtor's obligations. This use of the jail was curtailed in the latter part of the 19th century, but in certain forms has survived into modern times.

The notion of sending an offender to jail as a punishment was alien to medieval thought. Why resort to a practice which was so expensive, and possibly fatal, when minor offenses might swiftly and efficiently be dealt with by flogging, or the public disgrace of the stocks?

As for the greater offenders, there was little questioning of the doctrine that they should be executed. There was, in fact, some small recourse to the jail as a punishment in medieval times, and slow growth in this practice in succeeding centuries. There continues to be debate among historians about the causes of these changes.

In the United States the term "prison" refers to federal and state prisons, and "jail" to local (county and municipal) prisons. Federal and state government came late to the prison business preferring, until well into the 19th century, to pay counties to take their prisoners. The jail, as has been seen, was intended only as a place of detention or, later on, as a place of short-term punishment for minor offenders. As the notion of imprisoning felons gained support, the penitentiary was invented, and became the exclusive responsibility of the higher levels of government.

Punishment is now a major activity of government, involving enormous expenditures. By the early 1990s about 3 percent of the population of the United States was under some kind of penal supervision—prison, jail, parole, probation, or semicustody (halfway houses or home detention). The nation was imprisoning at a greater rate than any other developed country, and the numbers involved were larger than at any time in American history—1.2 million in custody and another 2.7 million on probation and parole. Even while the burden of building and operating such a vast penal estate significantly distorts public finance and administration, calls for yet more punishment continue to be made. Future historians will have a fascinating story to tell.

The rise of the prison has recently attracted most attention in the study of punishment, with scholars seeking information on the type of people imprisoned, the background to policy, and the experience of imprisonment. Earlier historical work which emphasized "progress" and humanitarian motives behind the rise of prisons has been revised, and more complex impulses behind the desire to isolate criminals have been examined. The social history of punishment and prisons since the move away from physical, and public, punishments—that is, during the past century—has been less fully developed, but is now beginning to receive more scholarly attention. (*See also* Asylums; Crime)

Sean D.M. McConville

REFERENCES

Foucault, Michel. *Discipline and Punish*. Harmondsworth, Eng.: Penguin, 1977.

Grupp, Stanley E., ed. *Theories of Punishment*. Bloomington: Indiana University Press, 1971.

McConville, Sean. *A History of English Prison Administration*. London and New York: Routledge (Vol. 1) 1981; (Vol. 2) 1993.

Morris, Norval, and David J. Rothman, eds. *The Oxford History of the Prison*. New York: Oxford University Press, 1993.

Rothman, David J. *The Discovery of the Asylum*. Boston and Toronto: Little, Brown, 1971.

Putting-Out System

The putting-out system was a decentralized form of industrial organization that prevailed before the introduction of technologies able to capture economies of scale that made larger production units (i.e., factories) more profitable. The system was most widely used in the labor-intensive processes of the textile sectors in symbiotic relationship with centralized operations, which completed the production process by bleaching, dying, fulling, or otherwise finishing the textiles for marketing.

The form of organization was predicated on the shortage of capital in the countryside, a scarcity which made it difficult for the would-be producers to purchase the raw materials on their own account. Instead, middlemen, sufficiently capitalized, provided the raw materials to the rural weavers and spinners, many of whom were still working in the agricultural sector at least on a part-time basis. The outputter, who was able to avoid the restrictions imposed by urban guilds, provided raw material and at times also such machinery as spinning wheels and weaving looms to the peasant-subcontractors. In addition, he provided the knowledge of the qualities demanded in distant markets and bore the risks associated with the undertaking. The workers retained their independence insofar as they monitored themselves while working in their cottages, and were free to employ family members, including children, for tasks such as combing wool or spinning. They were also able to avoid the high-mortality urban environment. If the peasant-artisans had sufficient money to buy the raw materials themselves, the system is known as the *Kaufsystem*, that is, the merchant did not enter the production process at the very beginning, but did so by purchasing the semifinished goods from the producers. The spread of the putting-out system producing goods for a distant market and concomitant demographic changes are often subsumed under the concept of protoindustrialization.

The putting-out system has been studied by social historians particularly in Europe, as part of understanding work rhythms and family work relationships before the industrial revolution. Expansion of the system was a vital precursor to the industrial revolution, in the 18th and early 19th centuries. The gradual demise of the putting-out system is also explored in terms of changes in the social history of work, a frequent decline in production jobs for women, and a shift in family-work relations. (*See also* Commercialization; Protoindustrialization)

John Komlos

REFERENCES

Kisch, Herbert. *Die Hausindustriellen Textilgewerbe am Niederrhein vor der Industriellen Revolution: Von der ursprünglichen zur kapitalistischen Akkumulation.* Göttingen: Vandenhoeck and Ruprecht, 1981.

Kriedte, Peter, Hans Medick, and Jürgen Schlumbohm. *Industrialization Before Industrialization. Rural Industry in the Genesis of Capitalism.* Cambridge: Cambridge University Press, 1981; first published in German in 1977.

Mendels, Franklin. *Industrialization and Population Pressure in Eighteenth-Century Flanders.* New York: Arno Press, 1981.

Quantification

No element amid the widespread changes in historical practice in the past few decades has occasioned so much rancorous debate as the use of quantification. Because quantification arose along with social history, these debates have had important bearing on sociohistorical methods and perceptions of the field.

At minimum, scholars who reacted against the application of quantification to historical investigation were troubled by the role of quantification in the sciences and especially in the social sciences, against which "the humanities" were to be set off; and by the seeming irrelevance of quantification to a discipline that focused on detailed accounts of unique instances, especially of events. For a period, the argument was further laced by charges that quantitative methods were crudely applied by historians who were newcomers to them and who did not understand the underlying logic of what they were doing, on the one hand, and by the countercharge that quantification's historical opponents were themselves not only ignorant of the tools but implacably hostile to quantitative reasoning in the human sciences even beyond history.

Historians writing of mass phenomena—wars, for instance, or elections—have of course always included numbers as important parts of their accounts. But these numbers were usually elements of description. The controversy over quantification began in earnest when, in the expansion of the historical profession in the United States and Europe in the 1950s and since, a self-conscious effort to import explanatory perspectives and methods from the social sciences became prominent. By the 1960s, historians were looking to econometric methods, no longer satisfied with the older institutional economics which itself employed mainly descriptive statistics. And they were looking to demography for techniques of analyzing the dynamics of human fertility, mortality, and migration from (often imperfect) lists of vital events and irregular population enumerations. And they were looking to sociology and social psychology for methods of discerning, counting, combining, and providing almost-causal explanation for the differential expression of attitudes and beliefs within populations. Finally, they were looking to political science for methods of analyzing the variation of electors' and legislators' votes.

What these interdisciplinary borrowings had in common, and how they differed from the older, descriptive uses of quantification that were acceptable to almost all historians, was that underlying the methods themselves were implicit or explicit models of human behavior within which the methods made sense. These analytic schemes had been developed in the social sciences as those disciplines refined their questions, and it was their analytic schemes to which the quantitative methods were directed. Were historians to be model builders, then, or were they, as humanists, to confine their activities to the investigation and interpretive description of unique instances? The numerical arrays and explicit methodological discussions that were the lightning rods for antiquantitativist discontent were only the visible signs of a deeper difference in intellectual style.

Historians by the 1980s had begun to treat this controversy in characteristic fashion, on the whole (but with some conspicuous exceptions), by softening its edges, and allowing a thousand flowers to bloom. Excitement about quantification among social historians has waned, though in key subfields (in and out of social history proper) the methodology remains vital, as examples below suggest. Discussion in historical methodology has generally allowed that historians rarely if ever are entirely innocent of implicit models even when they think they are simply following their evidence. And discussion within the fostering social science disciplines has tended to recognize that a strictly scientist characterization of their own progress (indeed, of the progress in the natural sciences, for that matter) is far too narrow: that they really do not proceed solely by evolving theory, deriving hypotheses, and rigorously testing these with empirical data. Quantitative methods, then, need not always offend traditional historical sensibility, and they do not. But, it is fair to say that most historians, including social historians, today do not carry out and are not trained to carry out quantitative analysis, and that many of the minority who do,

do so by preference to other methods. At the extreme, the journal *Historical Methods* focuses preferentially upon quantitative approaches (including mapping under this head). There is, however, no formal area in history defined by use of quantitative methods, as there is (for instance) in the case of oral history.

Acceptance (if often tacit and sometimes grudging) of quantification within the historical armamentarium has followed not only from methodological discussion and diplomatic negotiation within the profession, but also because many of the substantive areas that depend on quantification have gained legitimacy, especially but not exclusively as a result of the efflorescence of social history. As more historians have turned away from a near-exclusive focus on elites and on the history of ideas, they have focused on mass phenomena. The analysis of these typically demands the examination of repeated patterns; and to say this is very nearly to say that such investigation is inherently quantitative. Historical demography, for instance, seems now an inevitable component of macrohistorical investigation in many areas: the transition from the medieval period to the early modern, or the evolution of industrial and postindustrial societies, to name two broad transitions that are central to current sociohistorical study. And historical demography is simply unimaginable without rigorous and fairly sophisticated quantitative analysis.

Historians' ventures into quantification, although usually drawn from prior uses in the social sciences, are somewhat distinctive. They are distinctive in that they typically call upon evidence that is found rather than created, and in that interpretation—the imputation of meaning to pattern—rather than straightforward causal analysis is historians' most commonly avowed goal. Historians' use of quantification is rarely as mathematicized as at the leading edges of the social sciences. Historical data rarely enjoy the ideal properties for high-powered quantitative analysis: generalizability to a known population, uniformly inclusive recording, and unequivocal relationship of item to theoretical construct. To consider some particular quantitative methods that have especially attracted historians, then, conveys a sense of what is special about the way historians use quantity.

Of these, easily the oldest and perhaps the most commonplace within historical analysis is prosopography, or group biography. (Prosopography is, indeed, so old that many of its applications are only informally quantitative, from the perspective of mathematicized techniques, although an implicit model underlies the exercise itself.) Historical accounts have always dealt with collectivities—organized bodies and groups, movements, social categories, interests—but the focus has typically been squarely upon the common action. Prosopography presumes that the collectivity does not extinguish the particular concerns of those who compose it, and that something of these concerns can be inferred from the personal histories of these individuals. Accordingly, prosopographical accounts will summarize salient characteristics of a large number of members of a group and adduce from these shared characteristics the sense in which the behavior of the group fulfills the personal logic of the group's members. Finer-grained analysis distinguishes differential performance within the group of members of contrasting background. If the mathematics of prosopography are simple, the practical difficulties of gathering biographical data on large numbers of often obscure members of a given group, from a wide range of sources of varying reliability, are daunting—even when no formal questions are asked about the way that an appropriate sample of the appropriate universe of members has been defined.

Roll-call analysis, by contrast, is a far more mathematicized approach, seeking to discern latent and possibly counterintuitive connections among behaviors. The evidentiary base of roll-call analysis is considerably more straightforward and simpler to assemble than that employed in prosopography, since the key datum is utterly public and formally recorded (e.g., legislators' votes in legislative proceedings). In roll-call analysis, the key concern—the necessary interpretation based on the mathematicized modeling—is the basis for cohesion across the interpretively significant roll-call votes during a legislative session.

The mathematical operations of roll-call analysis essentially involve discerning, first, what characteristic patterns of voting by individual legislators on the various issues that came, one by one, before the legislature were, and, second, what the clusterings of legislators' voting patterns were. When the latter have been discerned empirically, they are often examined in the light of the political and social attributes of the legislators, and the economic and social characteristics of their constituencies. At its best, roll-call analysis can discover latent patterns of legislative behavior, giving grounds for inferring the ideological, partisan, economic, and social underpinnings of this behavior.

When historians use electoral voting data to infer the behavior of individual voters, employing a method called ecological regression, they are employing a model that explicitly relates individuals' behaviors over time to the aggregate pattern of group behavior (the group being electoral districts) seen over time. What electoral analysis employing ecological regression seeks to do is to examine voting totals on a number of substantively related elections within a relatively short period of time for a large number of electoral districts, together with uniform, reliable data on economic and social characteristics of those districts. The initial question that this form of analysis asks is not wholly unlike that in roll-call analysis: what are patterns of change on a district-by-district basis? What is sought is a sense of patterns of change over time, of "flows" into and out of voting or nonvoting, into and out of votes for one or another party, and so forth. Next, the correlates of these patterns are discerned, but at this point the model becomes more complex, because most analyses do not seek to explain what kind of districts changed in this way or that, but to infer what kind of voters changed in this way or that. The key to being able to do this (but with a necessary margin of uncertainty) is that both the vote proportions and the district characteristics are continuous variables.

If the logic of ecological regression is one that allows analysis to infer the behaviors of categories of individuals from behavior of areas, the logic of family reconstitution analysis is one that allows the accurate estimation of highly detailed demographic rates for whole areas by the painstaking (or, increasingly, automated) linkage of data on individual events. The events in question here are not votes but vital events (birth, marriage, and death), and the linking is by families, because focusing on the family allows one to carefully keep individuals "under observation" through their lives, or recognize that they have effectively disappeared from the data set. With family reconstitution, age-specific, marital-status-specific, and birth-order-specific fertility rates can be calculated, for those families that are securely within the vital records over the period in question. Even though (for small areas) the numbers of families for which reliable records can be assembled may be relatively few, the soundness of models of demographic behavior that are applicable to such finely detailed data commonly make it possible to generalize the findings to the society or culture from which they are drawn.

What do these four examples have in common? On the whole, they deal with large and carefully structured assemblies of data, although the range of sources and the form of assembly differ greatly. In each case, the data, assembled and treated quantitatively, are made to disclose patterns that are not visible in just one or a few instances. In each case, there is some sort of crossing of level of analysis: groups or aggregates are being understood with individual-level or event-level data, individuals are being understood with aggregate-level data. And in each case, although to differing degrees of overtness, models and assumptions about human behavior—often tying the behavior of individuals to that of aggregates—underpin the application of quantitative approaches. In no case is mere precision the purpose of quantification. In no case do the data, as they emerge from quantitative treatment, explain themselves—they always need interpretation. (*See also* Methodology; Prosopography; Sociology)

John Modell

REFERENCES

Clubb, Jerome M., Erik W. Austin, and Gordon W. Kirk. *The Process of Historical Inquiry: Everyday Lives of Working Americans.* New York: Columbia University Press, 1989.

Glass, D.V., and D.E.C. Eversley, eds. *Population in History.* Chicago: Aldine, 1965.

Hershberg, Theodore, ed. *Philadelphia. Work, Space, Family, and Group Experience in the Nineteenth Century.* New York: Oxford University Press, 1981.

Jarausch, Konrad H., and Kenneth A. Hardy. *Quantitative Methods for Historians.* Chapel Hill: University of North Carolina Press, 1991.

Willigan, J. Dennis, and Katherine A. Lynch. *Sources and Methods of Historical Demography.* New York: Academic Press, 1982.

R

Racial Segregation

Racial segregation, the attempt to control and subjugate one race by another through social separation, evolved slowly in the United States during the late 18th and early 19th centuries. Long treated in terms of formal policy, segregation offers an important social history vantage point in values and behaviors of whites and blacks.

In both the North and South, segregation was primarily an urban phenomenon. In rural areas, whites were able to use personal methods of race control, including direct surveillance, daily interaction, and paternalistic relationships. Cities were different. There blacks enjoyed more autonomy, anonymity, and relative freedom. For this reason, cities required a more impersonal system of race control.

Until the Civil War, racial segregation was more pronounced in the North than in the South. Very early on, northern cities developed legal and extralegal means to segregate their small black populations. In southern cities the separation of the races was less complete. Following the dictates of paternalism, the region's dominant social ideology, southern urban whites practiced more direct methods of race control than their northern counterparts. In an effort to monitor black behavior and to prevent the formation of a viable black community, civic leaders attempted to disperse black residents throughout their cities. In most cities, whites were only partly successful. Although blacks and whites often lived in close proximity to one another, whites were unable to watch blacks at all times. Through back alley grogshops and separate churches and places of employment, blacks secured a limited degree of freedom from white control. By mid-century, the emergence of autonomous black communities in several southern cities convinced most whites that urban life was incompatible with slavery. As a result, black urban populations declined in the decades before the Civil War.

After the war, southern racial segregation evolved more quickly. Several groups influenced its development. Southern whites, in an effort to reestablish their version of the antebellum status quo, applied a variety of legal and extralegal means, including violence, to exclude blacks from most public and private facilities. Northern whites, influenced by their region's policies of racial segregation and anxious to avoid conflict between southern blacks and whites, encouraged blacks to accept separate institutions as a gesture of compromise with native whites. Most newly freed slaves acquiesced. Defining freedom as the absence of white control, blacks apparently hoped that separate institutions would allow the black community greater autonomy.

Historians disagree on the social effects of segregation upon late 19th-century blacks. Recently, Howard Rabinowitz (1980) has observed that segregation was not uniformly negative in its results. Instead, most blacks viewed segregation as an improvement to the preexisting racial system, exclusion. In addition, many blacks effectively used segregation to better their own circumstances. Within the polarized racial environment, blacks gained a modicum of independence that enabled them to establish separate social, economic, cultural, and religious institutions.

Nevertheless, some social historians continue to emphasize the deleterious effects of segregation upon black society. According to Joel Williamson (1984), the mutual disengagement of the races contributed to the rise of white-sponsored racial violence. Moreover, blacks became increasingly alienated from the American mainstream, occasionally becoming psychologically disoriented from years of social denigration. According to Williamson, racism also took a collective toll on black society. Politically and economically vulnerable, individual slave communities failed to congeal after emancipation, leaving postbellum black society weak and lacking a moral center.

Social historians have yet to test Williamson's thesis with detailed analyses of southern communities. More research is obviously needed, especially studies that examine black communities from the close of Reconstruction to the Great Migration. To date, we know very little about how blacks survived this crucial period of their history.

Social historians also need to consider why turn-of-the-century white southerners abruptly fortified de facto segregation with a host of seemingly unnecessary legal restrictions. Decades ago, C. Vann Woodward (1955) attributed the origins of Jim Crow laws to the mutual erosion of northern liberalism and southern paternalism. Later, Howard Rabinowitz (1980) argued that a new generation of black activists, born in freedom and impatient to assert their rights, prompted whites to establish a more rigid form of race control. Though both arguments provide important insights, we still need to know more about the men who created and supported Jim Crow laws. Class may prove to be an important variable. The late 19th century was a period of growing restiveness among lower-class whites. Yet few historians have made the connection between their political activism and the emergence of Jim Crow.

Whatever its causes, segregation has shown remarkable staying power over the years. Despite recent civil rights legislation, segregation remains an enduring feature of contemporary race relations and racial subjugation. (*See also* African American Society; Civil Rights Movement; Jim Crow System; Racism; Reconstruction; Slavery; United States Urbanization)

Steve Tripp

REFERENCES

Woodward, C. Vann. *The Strange Career of Jim Crow.* New York: Oxford University Press, 1955.

Williamson, Joel. *The Crucible of Race: Black-White Relations in the American South Since Emancipation.* New York: Oxford University Press, 1984.

Rabinowitz, Howard. *Race Relations in the Urban South, 1865–1890.* Chicago: University of Illinois Press, 1980.

Racism

In recent centuries "racism" and "racist" have proved to be among the most frequently—and loosely—employed epithets for groups or individuals who show disdain for or express a sense of superiority toward other human groups. But the term is best seen as an extreme form of ethnocentrism that has developed in specific historical milieus. Properly understood, racism is rooted in the belief that there are innate, biologically based differences in abilities between human groups, which are delineated in varying ways depending on the racist proponent and time period in question. The biological, or in the 20th century genetic, grounding of racial differentiation, distinguishes racism from other forms of ethnocentrism and chauvinism that have been linked primarily to cultural attributes, as formal racist ideas affected popular beliefs in several settings. Alleged racial differences have been used to argue for the superiority and supremacy of certain groups and conversely to demonstrate the inferiority of as well as to justify the domination of others. Though much of the discourse on race and racial differences at the intellectual level has focused on demonstrating gradations in intelligence, less critical phenotypical distinctions, especially skin color, have been the dominant force shaping social interaction between groups distinguished by racial stereotyping.

Racism emerged as a major force shaping intersocietal and intergroup interaction in the post-15th-century era of European global expansion. Though attitudes toward intergroup differences that had a racist dimension can be identified in earlier periods, the European encounter with a bewildering diversity of human populations led to increasingly elaborate attempts to distinguish and rank them. In the early centuries of expansion, the extreme degradation of large numbers of Africans as a result of the slave trade gave credence to the notion that there were profound, innate, and permanent differences between what came to be designated as the various races of humankind. Trends current in science as it was practiced from the 18th century onward further reinforced the urge to demarcate, classify, and rank human groups along with the rest of creation. There was little agreement among racist writers on how to distinguish different racial groups, and consequently widely divergent opinions as to how many there were. But in the 19th century, both at the level of intellectual discourse and popular sentiment, there was widespread acceptance of the notion that the human species was made up of racial groups that could be readily distinguished on the basis of physical appearance.

Empirically verifying the distinctive physical features and varying aptitudes of different racial groups was a major enterprise for many, and often prominent, 19th-century scientists. But scientific racism only marginally affected the ideologies of race that were expounded by defenders of the slave trade or the systems of slavery that dominated the economies of the American South, the Caribbean, and Brazil. An even cruder variant of racism, based heavily on a very selective reading of the Bible and obvious economic imperatives, also developed among the relatively isolated Afrikaner ranchers and farmers that struggled with the indigenous peoples and British colonizers for control of South Africa. In the late 19th and early 20th centuries, race attributes were often conflated with national "characteristics," and the anti-Semitic strain of racist ideology became more virulent and prevalent, particularly in Europe. In Germany, the National Socialists blended the pseudo-scientific strains of racist thinking with a celebration of a misconstrued Aryan "racial" heritage and inflammatory stereotyping of the Jews. The massive scale of the horrific race persecution that resulted, and the bloody race wars that were fought on the Russian front and in the Pacific in the early 1940s, represented the culmination of centuries of racist polemic and discrimination and the beginnings of a global reappraisal and rejection of racism at both the level of intellectual discourse and social organization. While pseudo-scientific racism has declined, racism as an element in popular mentalities continues to be a significant factor in social patterns in many societies including the United States. Comparisons of the nature and extent of racism also form a revealing focus in social history for South Africa, the United States, Europe, and Latin America. (*See also* Ethnicity; Latin American Racism; Nationalism; Slavery)

Michael Adas

REFERENCES

Banton, Michael. *Race Relations.* New York: Basic Books, 1967.

Berghe, Pierre van den. *Race and Racism: A Comparative Perspective.* New York: Wiley, 1967.

Gould, Stephen. *The Mismeasure of Man.* New York: Norton, 1981.

King, James C. *The Biology of Race*. Berkeley: University of California Press, 1981.

Radical History

Radical history involves an effort to use history to further radical political causes, to attack conventions in history writing that from a radical standpoint seem inaccurately bound to the interests of elites, and often to seek to present history in ways that will interest a wider, and particularly a working-class, public. Radical historians have existed for a long time; for example, by the early 19th century a tradition developed in France of writing about the history of the French Revolution of 1789 in terms that would reflect and promote the current radical political fashion. But a self-conscious radical history movement emerged most clearly in the 1960s, associated with the political upheavals of that decade. In the United States (where radical history has been a distinct minority current), the journal *Radical Historian* was founded in 1969. A somewhat similar movement developed in Britain, with the formation of the journal *History Workshop* (1975), which featured writing by radical (often Marxist) historians; encouragement to writing by lay, working-class people reflecting on their own history; and efforts to present history, however authored, to a lay as well as an academic audience.

Radical history has close links with social history. Most radical historians deal with social history topics, particularly those associated with the lower classes and women. Many see in social history a systematic challenge to history written from the standpoint and in the interests of the status quo. Many social historians, correspondingly, approach their work as radical historians and make no particular distinction between the two genres.

Not all social historians have been radical historians, however; this was true even in the 1960s. And while many radical historians continue to embrace social history, even in the 1990s, some have bitterly criticized social history as it has developed. The criticisms include a belief that social history has become insufficiently ideological; a belief that social historians do not focus consistently enough on politics, and so distract from the radical cause; a contention that too much social history (some would add, particularly in the United States) has become enmeshed with social science methods that obfuscate its presentation and obscure any radical message; and an argument that too many social historians, even in dealing with the working class, have come to emphasize the adaptability and creativity of their subjects rather than stressing their oppression and focusing on their lack of power. As social history has become increasingly a mainstream research interest, the association between social and radical history has further dimmed—though it has by no means disappeared. Radical and social labels, then, formed for some similar (though not identical) reasons and at about the same period of time; they continue to coexist amid interesting tensions and periodic recriminations. Current movements—those, for example, in feminist history and some of the "new" cultural history, seek to revive on new grounds a link between social and radical causes, though interestingly they are sometimes criticized by more traditional radicals eager to focus on social class. (*See also* Marxist Historiography; Social History)

Peter N. Stearns

REFERENCES

Fox-Genovese, Elizabeth, and Eugene D. Genovese. "The Political Crisis of Social History: A Marxian Perspective," in Peter N. Stearns, ed., *Expanding the Past: A Reader in Social History*. New York: New York University Press, 1988, pp. 17–34.

Judt, Tony. "'A Clown in Regal Purple': Social History and the Historians." *History Workshop* (1979): 66–94.

Wiener, Jonathan. "Radical Historians and the Crisis in American History, 1959–1980," *Journal of American History* 76 (1989): 399–434.

Rancheros

The social structure of rural Mexico has been characterized historically by great complexity and regional diversity, and within it no social grouping is more difficult of strict definition than the rancheros. The Russian term *kulak* (a wealthy peasant) begins to convey something of the structural in-betweenness of the ranchero as against large landowners or simple peasants, and the traditional English category "yeoman farmer," with its implications of independence, comes closer still, but neither is finally a good approximation, while the American term "rancher" is further still from Mexican realities.

Rancheros have traditionally been identified as primarily mestizo (certainly non-Indian), independent middling farmers living mainly in the areas of central and northern Mexico, though ethnicity and geography are not in themselves the determining elements in their cultural identity. As agriculturalists, rancheros would on the whole produce both for their own subsistence and for a local market, certainly relying in the main on family labor and possibly on some hired help. They might own their lands outright or rent them from larger landholders, but would assert a degree of political and economic independence from landlord hegemony. Staunch Catholicism and conservative political attitudes have at times led large groups of such people into armed opposition to the government, as in the Cristero rebellion in western and central Mexico in the 1920s and 1930s, though they fought in all factions in the Mexican Revolution (1910–1920). Other traits strongly associated with ranchero life are cultural expressions such as mariachi music, and certain forms of masculine behavior (machismo), including consummate horsemanship, expertise with weapons, aggressivity, and a concern with personal and family honor. (*See also* Farmers; Mexican Revolution; Peasantry)

Eric Van Young

References

Jacobs, Ian. *Ranchero Revolt: The Mexican Revolt in Guerrero*. Austin: University of Texas Press, 1982.

Schryer, Frans J. *The Rancheros of Pisaflores: The History of a Peasant Bourgeoisie in Twentieth-Century Mexico*. Toronto: University of Toronto Press, 1980.

Reciprocity

Reciprocity refers to socially sanctioned expectations and obligations by individuals and social groups to exchange goods and/or services.

The first landmark study of reciprocity was that by the French sociologist and historian Marcel Mauss. In *The Gift* (1924), Mauss argued that the widespread pattern of giving, receiving, and repaying gifts in preindustrial societies was imbued with morally sanctioned rights, expectations, and obligations that transcended the flow of material goods. He interpreted reciprocity as a social and economic phenomenon that enhanced solidarity and mutual interdependence.

Reciprocity is an enduring feature of economic and social relationships in preindustrial and peasant societies. For example food sharing, highly valued in hunter and gatherer societies, serves to minimize the risk of hunger by individuals and domestic units, and underlies long-term social relationships and political alliances.

Reciprocity does not necessarily occur between social equals or imply harmonious and altruistic social relationships. Three patterns or modes of reciprocal exchanges have been recognized. Generalized reciprocity is characteristic of goods or services that circulate between close kinsmen (such as in a household). There is little or no obligation to immediately repay (reciprocate): the expectation is that what is given and received will eventually balance itself out. In balanced reciprocity carefully calculated exchanges are often accompanied by the obligation to reciprocate in the near future either with the same goods or services or with those of equal value. Negative reciprocity refers to unequal exchanges between parties socially distant from each other (e.g., strangers).

Scholars have recently paid increasing attention to how reciprocity structures relationships between peasant groups and political and economic elites, and this interest has brought reciprocity concepts more clearly into social history. Scott (1976) has argued for a peasant "moral economy" grounded on culturally defined obligations to provide services and rent to landlords and peasant expectations to receive assurances that their subsistence needs will be met. A violation of this social contract will generate strong resistance and, in some cases, open rebellion. Langer (1985) has also shown how reciprocal obligations permeated peasant and landowner relationships in southern Bolivia, and how landowner attempts to undermine these shared expectations were met by strong resistance. The "moral economy" and resistance literature, to which social historians, anthropologists, and others are contributing, is rapidly expanding. (*See also* Clientage; Moral Economy; Paternalism)

Harry Sanabria

REFERENCES

Langer, Erick. "Labor Strikes and Reciprocity on Chuquisaca Haciendas," *Hispanic American Historical Review* 65, 2 (1985): 255–277.

Mauss, Marcel. *The Gift*. Translated by I. Cunnison. New York: The Free Press, 1954 (orig. 1924).

Sahlins, Marshall. *Stone Age Economics*. New York: Aldine, 1972.

Scott, James C. *The Moral Economy of the Peasant: Rebellion and Subsistence in Southeast Asia*. New Haven: Yale University Press, 1976.

Slatta, Richard W. "Bandits and Rural Social History: A Comment on Joseph," *Latin American Research Review* 28, 1 (1991): 145–151.

Reconstruction

Reconstruction, the period in which the North attempted to transform the defeated South from a society based primarily upon black slave labor to a society based upon free labor, began before the end of the Civil War. In isolated federally occupied regions throughout the South, northern politicians, military officials, and businessmen joined with southern Unionists and ex-slaves to transform the South's society, politics, and economy. Bolstered by a series of federally imposed constitutional amendments and civil rights laws, these groups continued the purge on southern institutions for a decade after the war.

Although historians generally agree upon the federal objectives of Reconstruction, they disagree about its legacy. For over 20 years, the lines of the debate have been clearly drawn. Some argue that the war and Reconstruction destroyed planters' antebellum hegemony, creating a "New South" characterized by competitive market conditions, political unrest, and class and race conflict. Others argue that planters retained all aspects of their power—in large part because they were able to retain control over their former slaves. Given the nature of the issues, social historians have played an increasingly important role in the debate. In the last decade, as historians have become more adept at deciphering the worldviews of their subjects, many social historians have given a greater causative role to the freed people. Whatever power planters may have had, these historians—mostly notably Eric Foner (1989), John Scott Strickland, and Harold Woodman (1990)—have argued that newly freed blacks relentlessly pursued social and economic independence and equal citizenship. Although often frustrated in their quest, they gained considerable individual and community autonomy.

Unfortunately, we know far less about the goals and expectations of southern lower-class whites. Although they may have held the balance of power in the postwar South, historians have largely failed to subject them to the type of rigorous analysis that has come to typify most other facets of southern history. This may be changing. As social historians rediscover politics and as African Americans begin to emphasize the class dimensions of the postwar black experience, future analyses of Reconstruction will have to pay more attention to the strategic role lower-class whites played in the reshaping of the postwar South. Recent works that have begun this trend often endorse a common theme—that lower-class whites, like the freedmen, desired personal liberty and community autonomy. In their pursuit of these goals, they often frustrated the plans of both planters and the Republican coalition. As a result, race and class relations remained volatile throughout Reconstruction—and beyond. Although social historians have yet to develop any sort of synthesis for Reconstruction, the issues that they address—the role of the state, the interaction between race and class identities, the evolution of a new labor system, the impact of merchant and industrial capital upon traditional communities, the evolution of republican ideology—have made Reconstruction one of the more dynamic fields of historical inquiry in recent years. (*See also* African American Society; Racism)

Steve Tripp

REFERENCES

Burton, Orville V. *In My Father's House Are Many Mansions: Family and Community in Edgefield, South Carolina*. Chapel Hill: University of North Carolina Press, 1987.

Foner, Eric. *Reconstruction: America's Unfinished Revolution, 1863–1877*. New York: Harper Collins, 1989.

Wiener, Jonathan M. *Social Origins of the New South: Alabama, 1860–1885*. Baton Rouge: Louisiana University Press, 1978.

Woodman, Harold D. *King Cotton and His Retainers: Financing and Marketing the Cotton Crop of the South, 1800–1925*. Columbia: University of South Carolina Press, 1990.

Refeudalization

"Refeudalization" is a term used by historians of early modern Europe to describe the process by which the nobility in emerging centralized states strengthened and extended certain rights and jurisdictions that had feudal origins. These included the state's creation and sale of new fiefs, the granting of feudal titles of nobility associated with feudal property, and the protection of private jurisdictions. The term is of particular interest to social historians, because it implies that this largely legal and fiscal expedient of the state and the ruling families reflected deeper social and economic conditions.

For example, aristocratic families in the 16th, 17th, and 18th centuries adopted increasingly conservative economic strategies, characterized by a shift of investments from commerce and manufacture to agriculture and annuities. It is argued that these families often consolidated their economic control in the countryside by asserting their feudal rights and privileges, which caused greater subjection of the peasantry. In Italy, historians disagree about what this economic conservatism represents: either a failure of the medieval "commercial revolution" to develop into a modern industrial economy, or the domination of underlying feudal structures that were little affected by the few energetic commercial centers on the peninsula. Throughout Europe, social hierarchies became more rigid and unchanging, and it became harder to move into the upper ranks of the aristocracy, as private wealth was concentrated in ever fewer hands. This is sometimes attributed to a heightened emphasis on dynastic succession to feudal titles and property, and to the use of entail to prevent future generations from alienating family property, which was a nearly universal phenomenon among early modern European elites.

There is a lively historiographical debate, particularly among historians of early modern Italy, about the validity of the term. Did the proliferation of feudal titles and feudal jurisdictions indicate a return to earlier practices and systems (which were incompatible with strong, centralized government when first developed)? Or was the new emphasis on feudal forms merely an antique veneer given to more effective fiscal and administrative techniques of early modern governments? The feudal veneer, in evoking the heroic days of chivalry and empire, held strong cultural appeal for newly enriched elite families in search of an ideology that added legitimacy to their social and economic position. The term tends to mask important changes in social and economic strategies of early modern elites, whose behavior, although conservative, was by no means static or regressive. (*See also* Aristocracy; Feudalism)

Alison A. Smith

References

Jones, Philip. "Economia e società nell'Italia medievale: il mito della borghesia," in *Economia e società nell' Italia medievale*. Turin: Einaudi, 1980, pp. 3–189.

Sella, Domenico. *Crisis and Continuity: The Economy of Spanish Lombardy in the Seventeenth Century*. Cambridge, MA: Harvard University Press, 1979.

Reformation/Popular Religion

The social history of the Reformation became a flourishing field of research during the 1970s, when interest in the urban context of religious reform supplanted older questions about how social forces or class interests determined the Reformation. Many new studies of the urban Reformation explored how the religious interests of urban lay people predisposed them toward accepting new religious ideas, how social and political dissent within individual towns helped or hindered the reception and implementation of reform, and how the urban mentality left its imprint on the new churches that emerged from the religious upheaval. The burghers of 16th-century Europe, and Germany in particular, created a civic religion that brought the conduct of religious life firmly under secular control. Historians of the 1970s tended to regard the urban Reformation as a "people's reformation" and to emphasize the importance of social protest in creating impetus for reform. This view was modified by research of the 1980s which showed that such movements were invariably taken over by urban oligarchies or by territorial rulers who sought above all else to establish social order combined with magisterial control of the church. Imposition of control went hand in hand with the creation of a new bureaucratized clergy, so that classic Reformation doctrines of the priesthood of all believers and the rights of communities to elect their own pastors came to have little real meaning. Similarly, lay people were not trusted to interpret the Bible for themselves, lest they fall into the dangers of religious extremism (Anabaptism). In the course of time, the new Protestant pastorate met with continued lay hostility, its neoclericalism with a "Protestant anticlericalism."

A further aspect of the new social historical approach dealt with the peasantry's response to religious reform, and especially its understanding of how the word of God might be applied to adjudge matters of social justice. The major interpretative thesis that dominated discussion in the 1980s focused on the manner in which peasants and other disenfranchised groups in Germany and Switzerland appropriated Reformation ideas during the German Peasants' War, turning it into a near-revolution legitimated by the new religious ideology. The demands of the common man in town and country for greater communal participation in religious and political life constituted a "communal Reformation" (Blickle 1992), an expression of a more widespread movement of communalism in late-medieval and early modern history.

A third stream of interpretation ran counter to Blickle's thesis and involved studies exploring the popular reception of Reformation ideas. It encompassed a broad spectrum of topics: the impact of literacy and print on the spread of religious reform; studies of Reformation propaganda, both oral and visual; exploration of the short- and long-term impact of reform in the countryside (here the decisive and trend-setting thesis emanated from Gerald Strauss (1978)— that the slow and tenuous reception of the Reformation among the rural masses showed the Reformation to have been a failure); discussion of the extent and impact of Reformation educa-

tion; and especially the impact of the Reformation on women, the newest and most rewarding field of research.

Popular religion has been a more recent entrant into the social history of the Reformation. The impulse was given by anthropological studies which encouraged analyzing religion on its own terms rather than through the eye of confessional historiography. A fresh view of the nature and extent of the pre-Reformation religious system enabled an appreciation of how far this system was actually changed by the Reformation. The monastic system, saints, pilgrimages, and many religious practices may have been interrupted or repudiated, but study of popular rituals revealed that these were adapted in the service of religious reform rather than being completely uprooted. Ideas about sacrality and the sacred were modified; ritual life experienced changes in emphasis rather than a complete reversal to an antiritual and desacralized form of belief. The touchstone of these developments was the failure of the Reformation to change magical views of the world among the rural masses or to eradicate a tendency to rely on magic in times of adversity. Thus, more recent studies have focused on how far there was an accommodation between popular belief and an acculturating Protestantism to create syncretist forms of Protestant popular religion embedded in traditional forms of popular culture.

The difficulties of implementing religious reform directed the attention of historians of the 1990s to a new set of questions, embodied in the phenomenon of the "second Reformation." Syncretist and half-realized forms of reformation achieved by Lutheranism provoked a reaction by a second generation of Calvinizing Reformers, who sought to carry out more thoroughly what had been only imperfectly achieved by their predecessors. Attention was thus focused on the manner in which territorial rulers sought to impose new religious and social values on their subjects by a process of social disciplining and of confessionalization, associating allegiance to the emergent territorial state with inculcation of a confessional identity. Such studies have so far concentrated on expressions of intent by reforming rulers, rather than demonstrating their success. To this extent the problem posed by Gerald

Strauss about the success or failure of the Reformation remains firmly on the agenda for future social historical work. Most of the studies mentioned above have concentrated on Germany and Switzerland. However, the tendency to question the nature, extent, and speed of reform has also spread to other countries, with considerable rethinking about the social and intellectual impact of Calvinism in Europe, as well as a debate over the English Reformation. (*See also* Christianity; Evangelicalism; Religion)

Robert W. Scribner

REFERENCES

Blickle, Peter. *Communal Reformation: The Quest for Salvation in Sixteenth-Century Germany.* Translated by Thomas Dunlap. Atlantic Highlands, NJ: Humanities Press, 1992.

Cameron, Euan. *The European Reformation.* Oxford: Clarendon Press, 1991.

Hsia, R. Po-Chia. *Social Discipline in the Reformation. Central Europe, 1550–1750.* London and New York: Routledge, 1989.

O'Day, Rosemary. *The Debate on the English Reformation.* London: Methuen, 1986.

Prestwich, Menna, ed., *International Calvinism, 1541–1715.* Oxford: Clarendon Press, 1985.

Roper, Lyndal. *The Holy Household. Women and Morals in Reformation Augsburg.* Oxford: Clarendon Press, 1989.

Scribner, Robert W. *Popular Culture and Popular Movements in Reformation Germany.* London: Hambledon Press, 1987.

Strauss, Gerald. *Luther's House of Learning. Indoctrination of the Young in the German Reformation.* Baltimore: Johns Hopkins University Press, 1978.

Religion

Religion, meaning belief in superhuman or supernatural beings, long has been understood to concern peoples and nations as well as individuals and formal doctrines. Typically, religious "creation myths" are ripe with social themes. In Judaism, for example, the story of the earth's creation and of Adam and Eve is immediately followed by the long, unfolding epic of God's chosen nation—Israel—whose collective behavior is as important in seeking divine favor as the behavior of individuals. Similarly, the origin myth of the 16th-century Acoma Pueblo in New Mexico moves quickly from a story about Thought Woman, who nursed the world's first two sisters, to the acquisition of seeds for plants and animals, then to the birth of sons and daughters and to the creation of families and clans, all their interactions shaping society as well as relations with the gods.

Religions, large and small, also articulate social values through their rites and rituals. Indeed, the anthropologist Clifford Geertz (1960), describes religion as a "cultural system" whose symbols establish "powerful, pervasive, and long-lasting moods and motivations in men by formulating general conceptions of a general order of existence." This is as evident in conceptions of afterlife as in religious ceremonies. The ancient Egyptian nobility's careful preparation for life after death both fitted them for their future social life and justified the society they were leaving behind. Similarly, Christian pronouncements on heaven since the 18th century have stressed the theme of love, not merely between reunited couples but among all of heaven's residents, thereby also offering a guide to life for those still on earth.

Modern scholarship on the social history of religion dates from the studies of two late 19th-century sociologists, the German Max Weber and the Frenchman Émile Durkheim. In *The Protestant Ethic and the Spirit of Capitalism*, Weber stressed religion's capacity to shape society as capitalism originated in the 16th and 17th centuries, while in *Ancient Judaism* and the *Religion of India*, as well as other books, Weber emphasized the interaction of society with religious doctrine and authority. Weber's contemporary, Émile Durkheim, argued in *The Elementary Forms of the Religious Life* that religion contained the principal symbols of social values and stood at the center of social life at least down to the coming of modern times.

Recent scholarship continues to stress themes posed by Weber and Durkheim, while moving beyond them. Historians of early modern Europe still have not settled the debate about Weber's thesis. Economic historians observe that the capitalism of Catholic Spain, Portugal, and France differed little from that of Protestant England, Scotland, and the Netherlands, while historians of the family see substantial differences not only between Catholic and Protestant views on family life but among different kinds of Catholics and Protestants. Likewise, historians of Puritanism have long debated its impact—good or bad—on American society. Through the 1940s, they tagged Puritanism as the source of American anti-intellectualism and bigotry; more recently, they have stressed a greater variety of themes, ranging from the Puritans' commitment to community and pursuit of learning to their omnivorous missionizing and stubborn rhetoric of failure, doom, and rescue.

All of these specific debates on religion's social impact involve tracing what the doctrines and organizational forms of a major religion do to the ways groups of ordinary people think and behave. The Weber thesis thus argued that Protestantism helped create habits of savings and self-denial that furthered capitalism. More recent studies trace religion's impact in changing family behavior or sexual outlook. Religion becomes more than formal doctrines and theological leaders, but a living force whose impact on society must be examined in great detail.

Yet social history has also uncovered religion's remarkably persistent capacity to shape society even amid rampant modern industrialization and urbanization, quite counter to earlier convictions about the inevitability of "secularization" in modern times. Islamic fundamentalism, which first intertwined with Middle Eastern nationalism in the 19th century, toppled Western-style, nonreligious governments in Iran and Iraq in the 1970s and seriously threatened others in Egypt, the Sudan, and Algeria. In the United States, two contradictory movements stressed the primacy of moral issues in politics, a powerful Protestant and Catholic liberalism that underwrote civil rights and anti–Vietnam War crusades in the 1960s, and a conservative Protestant evangelicalism that helped bring Ronald Reagan to the White House in the 1980s.

Social history also has uncovered remarkable examples of religion's capacity to empower the powerless. Here, social history can show how people remake formal religions for their own purposes. Slaves in the Caribbean and Latin America frequently synthesized African religious customs with rites created in the New World to found new religious systems that dramatically remade their lives and societies in America. In the United States, where the destruction of traditional African religious systems was especially thoroughgoing, slaves and ex-slaves slowly converted to Christianity and championed biblical themes of equality and social justice, as well as exodus, that their European neighbors and owners had long bypassed. In India and Pakistan, Latin America, Africa, and post-Communist eastern Europe, ethnicity—a sense of national "people-hood"—has become closely entwined with religion to produce devastating ethnic and religious bigotry, reawaken waning religious and national traditions, and reinforce newly emerging intersections of religion and ethnicity.

Social history also highlights the composition and internal dynamics of religions. Wealth—and poverty—profoundly affect both the character of religion and its relationship to society. Though religion may empower the powerless, usually it has empowered the powerful. Both old and recent social histories emphasize the conjunction of religious authority and doctrine with wealth and traditional political authority in ancient and modern times. Although Christianity placed ethical constraints on rulers in both medieval Europe and 19th- and 20th-century Latin America, it also justified and upheld secular authority in both places. As a result, peasant revolts in both medieval Europe and modern Latin America have often involved as much bitter criticism of religion and especially of the church as of government.

Recent social history also stresses religious differences rooted in conceptions of gender and sex. Gender has been particularly important in shaping religious leadership, whether in so-called primitive societies studied by the first anthropologists or in major ancient and modern societies. Within Christianity, men monopolized formal authority down to the late 20th century, and even Christian denominations that permitted female ordination after 1960 have seen women occupy far fewer leadership positions than they do in secular politics. Gender and sexual orientation also define participatory roles. Transvestites filled special religious roles among 19th-century American Plains Indians such as shamans and diviners; male saints outnumbered female saints five to one in Roman Catholicism before 1700, probably because men enjoyed broader choices in religious careers than did women; yet women usually outnumbered men two to one in 19th-century U.S. Protestant congregations, where they also shaped the domestic religious milieu (with special implications for how and what children learned about religion), and dominated the societies that initiated America's distinctive antebellum and postbellum movements for social and moral reform.

Many developing trends in the intersection of social history and religion are summarized in recent studies of popular religion, meaning religion as practiced by the laity rather than by religious professionals. The essays of Natalie Zemon Davis in *Society and Culture in Early Modern France* (Stanford: Stanford University Press, 1975), describe the political and gender tension that frequently surrounded church rituals in Reformation-era France, often separating Catholics from Protestants, priests from politicians, men from women, and one kinship group from another. In contrast, David Hall's *Worlds of Wonder, Days of Judgment: Popular Belief in Early New England* (New York: Knopf, 1989) stresses the confluence of popular views about magic and "wonders" with Puritan doctrine, so that even the testimony of accused witches bespoke the terrifying preaching of Puritan ministers.

Popular religion is not merely a topic for premodern history. David Harrell's *All Things Are Possible: The Healing and Charismatic Revivals in Modern America* (Bloomington: Indiana University Press, 1975) reveals how thoroughly belief in direct supernatural power, including miracles, persisted both before and after World War II in the United States, though newspapers, television, and scholars seldom noticed it. Similarly, *Fundamentalisms Observed*, edited by Martin Marty and R. Scott Appleby (Chicago: University of Chicago Press, 1992), addresses the collective power of movements that claim to espouse "foundational" principals in Christianity, Islam, Buddhism, Hinduism, and Shintoism, and suggests that inattention to these movements—and exaggeration of secular "ideologies"—has produced substantial misreadings of world political dynamics in the late 20th century.

In all these works, the social histories that concern religion address central questions raised not only by Weber and Durkheim but by most religions themselves—the meaning of individual and collective life, not merely for the well known, but for each adherent in the milieu that life is lived. (*See also* Buddhism; Christianity; Evangelicalism; Islam; Popular Culture)

Jon Butler

REFERENCES

Bastide, Roger. *African Civilisations in the New World.* Translated by Peter Green. New York: Harper & Row, 1971.

Butler, Jon. *Awash in a Sea of Faith: Christianizing the American People.* Cambridge, MA: Harvard University Press, 1990.

Geertz, Clifford. *The Religion of Java.* New York: The Free Press, 1960.

Gutiérrez, Ramòn. *When Jesus Came, the Corn Mothers Went Away: Marriage, Sexuality, and Power in New Mexico, 1500–1846.* Stanford, CA: Stanford University Press, 1991.

McDannell, Colleen. *The Christian Home in Victorian America, 1840–1900.* Bloomington: Indiana University Press, 1986.

Weinstein, Donald, and Rudolph M. Bell. *Saints and Society: The Two Worlds of Western Christendom, 1000–1700.* Chicago: University of Chicago Press, 1982.

Renaissance Italy

One of the problems of the social history of the Italian Renaissance is that although social issues have increasingly become the focus of scholarship, the period was originally conceptualized by the 19th-century scholar Jacob Burckhardt in his *The Civilization of the Renaissance in Italy* as a period of intellectual history and to a great extent is still thought of as such. Thus, the Renaissance tends to be seen as a cultural revival that began in the 14th century typified by a renewed enthusiasm for and study of the classics, an emphasis on humanism (the study of ancient texts to empower and defend the importance of life in this world), and a series of artistic, literary, and intellectual breakthroughs that seemed to grow out of both. This rebirth (*renaissance*) wound to an end with the religious reform movements of the 16th century. Curiously, while much of the intellectual distinctness of the Renaissance has been undermined by a century of scholarship, the result has been rather than new definitions of the period that incorporate social history a tendency to ignore any overview in favor of studies focused on specific issues.

Some have seen this as a sign that the Renaissance as a distinctive period might well be ignored. But from the perspective of social history the period may well still have much to offer. Three themes have been particularly promising in recent research. First a major focus of scholarship since World War II has concentrated on the Italian Renaissance as an urban phenomenon. Certainly, cities were not new in the Renaissance, but the increasingly urban focus of life in the period created a particularly important break from the Middle Ages, where life had been predominantly rural. Second, in the Renaissance the social breakdown of society in that urban environment was decidedly different from that of the Middle Ages. It was more complex, and already in the 14th century it came to be so dominated by a different type of elite—merchants and bankers rather than nobles and clergy—that to a great extent this new elite not only conquered government and power but also conquered culture, values, and perceptions. Nobles and clergy, however, did not disappear. They merely lost their dominance for a time. And, in fact, the parabola of development across the Renaissance seems to have been one of a progressive ennoblement or aristocratization of merchants and bankers and an eventual amalgamation of the old nobility and the new elites.

Finally, life in the urban centers of the Renaissance, teeming with new social groups and new social pressures, problems, and possibilities was lived in the context of a number of different social and political institutions even if they often maintained traditional names. Thus, for example, although the debate about nature of the family remains intense it is clear that families functioned internally and in the context of the broader urban society of the time very differently than they had earlier. In turn, government became more complex and interfered more aggressively in life at every level from the economic to the sexual. Yet it was still a long way from being modern, with its emphasis on the honor of the state, its mythic origins, and its moral imperatives. Even culture was strongly influenced by the new ur-

ban and class realities of the period. The texts of the ancient world that had been read in the Middle Ages by ecclesiastics took on a rather different meaning when read by the urban secular elites of the Renaissance especially because much classical literature had been written for an educated secular elite living in an urban environment. Simply put, classical works spoke with a different voice to the Renaissance because, given similar social realities, intellectuals of the period could see and hear more in those texts. If a new urban environment, new elites, and new social structures helped to set the Renaissance apart, as those urban environments lost ground to the power realities of nation-states and as elites became ever more aristocratic in the 16th century, the Renaissance lost place in turn to a premodern world dominated by kings, powerful aristocrats, and a renewed emphasis on rural life. Significantly, however, many of the ideals of the Renaissance lived on to be taken up again in the more urban and bourgeois societies of 18th- and 19th-century Europe as the underpinnings of phenomena as diverse as liberalism, individualism, rationalism, and a class society dominated by the bourgeoisie. (*See also* Cities; Cultural History; Middle Class)

Guido Ruggiero

REFERENCES

Brucker, Gene A. *Renaissance Florence.* Berkeley: University of California Press, 1983.

Goldthwaite, Richard A. *The Building of Renaissance Florence. An Economic and Social History.* Baltimore: Johns Hopkins University Press, 1980.

Klapisch-Zuber, Christiane. *Women, Family, and Ritual in Renaissance Italy.* Translated by Lydia G. Cochrane. Chicago: University of Chicago Press, 1985.

Martines, Lauro. *Power and Imagination, City States in Renaissance Italy.* New York: Knopf, 1979.

Muir, Edward. *Civic Ritual in Renaissance Venice.* Princeton, NJ: Princeton University Press, 1981.

Reproduction and Class Formation

Reproduction refers to several processes that are important for the history of social classes. These include, first, the biological processes involved in human conception, birth, and development; second, the provision in everyday life for human needs such as food, shelter, and emotional support that have to be met in order to keep social life going; finally, the cultural processes such as religious training, schooling, and familial socialization whereby people learn about social relations.

The earliest studies of social class relations typically centered on the history of male workers in the workplace, understood as the locus of production. Only recently have the important connections between reproduction and class formation become the subject of historical study.

Social historians working on European working-class history first turned to demographic analysis to answer questions about how people became wage laborers and how the labor force was reproduced over time. Works like David Levine's *Family Formation in an Age of Nascent Capitalism* (1977), for example, traced the early disappearance of peasant classes in some areas of England and their replacement by a rural wage labor force long before the industrial revolution. Comparisons among Europe's various regions have shown that this process of proletarianization occurred at different times and paces. Often, the breakdown of peasant communities brought new patterns of family life and reproduction (such as earlier marriage and increasing illegitimacy), but the precise connections between the change to wage labor, on the one hand, and family and population change, on the other, are still disputed.

From a different theoretical perspective, historians of women and the family have brought increased attention to the interplay of productive and reproductive activities in everyday life. Books like Louise Tilly and Joan Scott's *Women, Work and Family* (1978) put new questions onto the historical agenda: how notions about and strategies for biological reproduction have changed over time; how families have pieced together their daily subsistence under changing historical circumstances and divided the work of both production and social reproduction among family members; how the rearing of children varied with and affected class identities.

Subsequent historical studies of European family life have demonstrated the close connections between family life and the world of social reproduction, on the one hand, and class identi-

ties and organizations, on the other. For example, Leonore Davidoff and Catherine Hall's book *Family Fortunes* (1987), on the English middle classes, illustrates the importance of the domestic life and the ideological support provided by evangelical religion for the evolution of middle-class identity in the late 18th and early 19th centuries. Michael Hanagan's analysis of mining communities suggests that, for French workers, the "private" decision to limit family size may have held greater consequence for their condition as a class than did the struggle to unionize.

Studies of social reproduction in other areas of the world have added new insights to our historical understanding of these regions and of connections between reproduction and class relations in colonial settings. In this tradition are works such as Margaret Strobel's *European Women and the Second British Empire* (1991), a study of colonizing women's activities, and Louise White's analysis of the connections between prostitution, urbanization, and class formation in colonial Nairobi in *The Comforts of Home: Prostitution in Colonial Nairobi* (1990). Historical research set in Africa, Latin America, and the United States is particularly important for its implications about the intersection of competing social identities in multiracial societies.

Sociologists and social historians have also explored questions about reproduction as a cultural process—in particular, the reproduction of cultural ideals and social relationships of inequality through such institutions as families (families including child rearing), schools, religious organizations, and leisure activities. Emphasis has differed: some social historians have argued that these institutions replicated existing class relations and allowed them to persist. This is the predominant view, for example, of Samuel Bowles and Herbert Gintis in their book *Schooling in Capitalist America* (1976) on the American educational system. Others have sought evidence of resistance or counter-hegemonic cultures in family or cultural institutions. For example, James Scott's study of peasant resistance, *Weapons of the Weak* (1985), or Herbert Gutman's analysis of the African American family, *The Black Family in Slavery and Freedom* (1976), emphasize the ways in which the realm of family and reproduction could undermine prevailing class relations.

Class formation, once regarded primarily as a consequence of changes in the occupational structure and formal political organization, now incorporates experiences grounded in family life, neighborhoods, and religious beliefs as well as in the workplace or party meeting. Future research on the connections between reproduction and class formation will no doubt continue to examine the many sites where class identity is built and where social identities like class are continually constructed and reconstructed over time and transmitted across generations. (*See also* Proletarianization; Public Schools; Working Class)

Mary Jo Maynes

REFERENCES

Bourdieu, Pierre. *Reproduction in Education, Society and Culture.* Beverly Hills: Sage, 1977.

Laslett, Barbara, and Johanna Brenner. "Gender and Social Reproduction: Historical Perspectives," *Annual Review of Sociology* 15 (1989): 381–404.

Tilly, Louise, John Gillis, and David Levine, eds. *The European Experience of Declining Fertility.* London: Blackwell, 1992.

Uno, Kathleen. "Women and Changes in the Household Division of Labor," in G. Bernstein, ed., *Recreating Japanese Women, 1600–1945.* Berkeley: University of California Press, 1991.

Republicanism

The term "republicanism" was first used in American historiography to identify the oppositionist political tradition that inspired resistance to British imperial reform measures leading up to the American Revolution. It has some relationship to studies of political culture in England and France in the same period, as these have evolved under the impact of social history. The "republican synthesis" (Shalhope 1972) built on contradictory approaches to intellectual history in post–World War II historical writing. Neo-Whig writers had challenged the materialist interpretations of the Progressive historians and insisted on the centrality of constitutional issues and principles to the imperial crisis. Consensus historians also described the Revolution in conservative terms, but they discounted the importance of ideological conflict: the fit between American social conditions and bourgeois liberal, Lockean ideas was so perfect that alternative ideologies were simply inconceivable. Republican revisionists combined the neo-Whig emphasis on the importance of political ideas with the consensus view that political values and behavior reflected the distinctive character of colonial American society. For revisionists, however, the point of studying political ideas was not simply to explicate the principled positions that led to the rupture of the British Empire, but rather to open a window on a profoundly different and unfamiliar world during a period of revolutionary change.

Republican revisionists radicalized the Revolution by projecting a wide array of anxieties and concerns into the constitutional and legal arguments of the imperial crisis. They emphasized the latent content of resistance rhetoric for anxious colonists who sought to explain and control social change. Key terms in this rhetoric—virtue, corruption, slavery—showed that colonists were fearful of modernizing tendencies in economic and social life as well as in British imperial administration. Seeking to rally fellow colonists to the patriot cause, resistance leaders invoked classical conceptions of virtuous citizenship and the public good. Freeholders who were anxious to preserve their economic independence and personal autonomy found these appeals compelling.

The crucial question raised by the republican synthesis was about the character of colonial society. Consensus historians had assumed that the broad distribution of property made the colonies "modern"—middle class, enterprising, individualistic, democratic, liberal—from their first settlement: the colonists had transformed John Locke's social contract theory into practice. But the republican revisionists proceeded from a far different conception of colonial America. The new social history had taught them that the colonies were part of a larger, transatlantic, Anglophone world, and that the premodern world was far different from our own. The republicanists' assault on Locke's influence over the Revolutionaries thus involved much more than conflicting intellectual genealogies. The effort to banish Locke from the American pantheon was a part of—or proxy for—a far-ranging reinterpretation of America's colonial past.

The revisionist project, bent on defining a particular republican political culture, was to demonstrate the historical "otherness," the premodernity, and the essentially "republican" character of colonial and Revolutionary America. The liberal America described by the consensus writers was displaced to a later period; colonial America was its inverse image, the republican antitype. The American Revolution was a radical, epochal movement because it somehow explained the transformation from one world to another.

Republicanism quickly assumed paradigm status in American historical writing. Its spectacular ascent was a tribute to the dynamism of colonial studies generally and specifically to a brilliant series of books that provided fresh readings of a massive array of neglected treatises, pamphlets, and newspaper essays. These works reinvigorated the history of Anglo-American political theory and helped illuminate the processes of Revolutionary mobilization and state-building. Yet the rise of republicanism is also a function of broader historiographical needs for fresh theory and satisfying narrative. The revisionists' challenge was, and remains, to reconcile their conception of fundamental historic change with all the apparent continuities in the social life, property relations, and even political practices of late colonial and early national America. Their solution was to appropriate theoretical constructs from symbolic anthropology and linguistics: the distinctiveness of the colonists' republican world was grounded in a coherent system of symbols, ideas, and assumptions that constituted their reality. This attractive and useful methodology buttressed the case for fundamental sociocultural change in Revolutionary America while stimulating revisionist interpretations for subsequent periods.

The limitations of the republican synthesis are now apparent. Ultimately, the ideological interpretation simply stipulates a radical transformation: where there is continuity in political thinking, the social referents must be fundamentally different; where social and institutional history is continuous, patterns of thought must have changed in a fundamental way. But if the recovery of neglected traditions of oppositionist thought helped explain the coming of the Revolution, closer study of the Revolution itself undercuts the revisionists' broad claims. Revolutionary American political thought cannot be reduced to a single discursive tradition, republican or liberal Lockean. Nor, in view of recent work on the expansion of markets and a market mentality in colonial America, is it possible to assume that the modernization of American society was the (unintended) consequence of Revolutionary political and constitutional change. Debate also continues about the nature, social constituency, and consistency of republicanism in the early 19th century, where it could serve threatened social groups, like (male) urban artisans, with a political rallying cry, but where it could also unite a broader social spectrum in new loyalties. (*See also* American Revolution; Liberalism)

Peter S. Onuf

REFERENCES

Bailyn, Bernard. *The Ideological Origins of the American Revolution.* Cambridge: Belknap Press, Harvard University Press, 1967.

Greene, Jack P. *Pursuits of Happiness: The Social Development of Early Modern British Colonies and the Formation of American Culture.* Chapel Hill: University of North Carolina Press, 1988.

Pocock, J.G.A. *The Machiavellian Moment: Florentine Political Thought and the Atlantic Republican Tradition.* Princeton, NJ: Princeton University Press, 1975.

Rodgers, Daniel T. "Republicanism: The Career of a Concept," *Journal of American History* 79 (1992): 11–38.

Shalhope, Robert E. "Toward a Republican Synthesis: The Emergence of an Understanding of Republicanism in American Historiography," *William and Mary Quarterly* 3, 29 (1972): 49–80.

Retirement

"Retirement" was defined in personal terms before it emerged as a major social institution during the 20th century. None of *Webster's Dictionary* 19th-century definitions applied exclusively to the aged, though the wealthy could enjoy "retiracy" in old age. The word remains ambiguous, even as "retirement annuity," "retirement income insurance," and "retirement plan"—terms that refer to institutional retirement arrangements—have entered the vocabulary.

Older people throughout most of history were expected to work while physically able. In late 17th-century Britain, reformers proposed pensions for workers over age 50. Miners, tailors, and metalworkers seemed particularly vulnerable. Wealthy landowners could sometimes retire at least partially, from ancient times onward. In 18th-century France, the urban old turned to begging. Continental farmers made contracts with middle-aged children to maintain control over their land. Almshouses in the United States in the early 19th century filled disproportionately with the elderly.

Some elderly did not retire but became "superannuated," defined by the English essayist Samuel Johnson in 1755 to mean "the state of being disqualified by years." Roughly a quarter of all males over age 65 were so disabled. Late 19th-century conceptions of "senility," moreover, diminished the aged's worth, and it was in this context that more systematic retirement developed in industrial areas.

Retirement programs arose in all industrializing societies. As in the United States, British companies' interest in retirement was stimulated by their desire for greater efficiency and productivity. There was, however, more concern than in Europe to promote old-age savings (through friendly and cooperative societies) and to involve the state in pension affairs. Class dynamics also were more evident. Germany's landmark old-age and invalidity scheme (1885) tried to garner working-class support for Bismarck's policies. Around 1900 state employees were the group most likely in France to opt for retirement.

In 1874, the Canadian Great Trunk system established the first corporate retirement plan in North America. A year later, the American Express Company permitted workers over age 60 who had served at least two decades to receive some compensation upon retirement. Subsequent initiatives were diverse. By 1910 only 60 plans were in place.

Workers toward the end of the 19th century became quite sensitive to the need to make plans for old age—though unemployment, disability, illness, and premature death loomed as greater threats. "Tontine insurance" (which divided funds among surviving policyholders after 20 years) represented two-thirds of all life insurance in 1900. Unions, fraternal groups, and friends offered (in)formal modes of retirement support.

The rate at which older men withdrew from the labor force represents the biggest controversy in the historiography of retirement. Conventional wisdom holds that there was some decline after 1875 in the proportion of men over age 65 who were gainfully employed. The revisionist interpretation shows a modest gain in older male employment patterns before 1935. Both camps agree that mandatory retirement plans initially had a minimal effect on older workers' employment behavior because they covered such a small proportion of the labor pool. Job transfers occurred informally. Managers and coworkers enabled aging workers to assume lighter loads and easier responsibilities as guards. That nearly 60 percent of all older men still worked in 1930 indicates retirement's privileged status.

The enactment of the Social Security Act in 1935 altered the meanings and experiences of retirement in the United States. The proportion of the elderly workers dropped dramatically. The 1935 Act protected only 60 percent of the labor force, but compulsory coverage subsequently was extended to farmers, military personnel, and the self-employed. By 1974, 93 percent of all people over age 65 were eligible for benefits. In the process, the system's 65-year-old-eligibility baseline became the benchmark for being "old" in America. Poor health still accounted for more than half of all retirements, particularly among those in low-paying jobs. Retirement by the 1970s was rewarding for many, but not all, older Americans.

Retirement's dimensions seem more complex when issues of race, ethnicity, and gender are taken into account. Slavery—and the racial discrimination continuing in its wake—made retirement in the black community a rare experience. Most older freed black men had to work longer than their white native-born (and foreign-born) peers. The growth of pensions for professionals and union members after 1948 made fringe benefits a more valid predictor of retirement security than ethnicity.

Gender differences in retirement, like racial ones, reflect variations in employment opportunities over the life course. Women found it difficult to save for superannuation. Social Security provided funds to expand mothers' pensions and children's welfare. Old-age assistance benefited elderly women. Given their sporadic career histories and sex discriminations in pay, wage-earning women typically accrued fewer retirement benefits than their male counterparts. Women remain poorer in old age than men because of differences in earnings histories and longer life expectancies. (*See also* Old Age)

W. Andrew Achenbaum

REFERENCES

Achenbaum, W. Andrew. *Old Age in the New Land.* Baltimore: Johns Hopkins University Press, 1978.

Graebner, William. *A History of Retirement.* New Haven: Yale University Press, 1980.

Hannah, Leslie. *Inventing Retirement.* Cambridge: Cambridge University Press, 1986.

Quadagno, Jill. *The Transformation of Old Age Security.* Chicago: University of Chicago Press, 1988.

Revolutions

Revolutions have been studied from many vantage points. Political factors are central. Ideologies usually play a substantial role. Explaining revolutions and exploring results in terms of social classes, lower-class beliefs, and other sociohistorical facets took shape several decades ago, particularly in dealing with the French Revolution of 1789 and then extending to other revolutionary settings. Debates over the relationship between social history and other kinds of history, including intellectual history, persist. Social history continues to be vitally involved in research on most aspects of revolution as a phenomenon. Social historians also try to understand why revolutions take different forms in different kinds of societies and why some societies (Germany, for example, compared to France and Japan compared to Russia) have been relatively immune to major revolution.

Three important elements of revolution need to be distinguished: a situation, a process, and an outcome. Revolution refers not simply to a drastic outcome to a social event, but also to the event itself. For every successful revolution resulting in dramatic social and political change, there are many failed revolutions that produce no such changes. Thus, it is necessary to distinguish a revolutionary situation from a revolutionary outcome. More than this, those revolutions that produced social transformations typically can be decomposed into a whole series of successive revolutionary situations; this whole bundle of events can be seen as part of a single revolutionary process. Although it is difficult to characterize revolutionary outcomes in any simple way, the great concentration of revolutionary situations and outcomes over the last four centuries can be linked to the twin processes of capitalism and state formation.

First, following Charles Tilly (1978), a "revolutionary situation" is a forcible transfer of power within a state in the course of which at least two distinct blocs of contenders make incompatible claims to control the state, and some significant portion of the population subject to the state's jurisdiction acquiesces in the claims of each bloc. In France, in 1789 the "Tennis Court Oath," in which elements of the Estates General proclaimed themselves a National Assembly possessing full sovereignty, marked the beginning of a revolutionary situation as soon as it was backed by the Parisian and provincial national guards.

With the outbreak of a revolutionary situation, a "revolutionary process" begins in which groups attempt to consolidate state power under their own auspices. Some revolutions, such as that of 1830 in France, exhibit only one revolutionary situation, and in this case, revolutionary situation and process coincide. But a revolutionary process may also be composed of several separate revolutionary situations. The coalition of groups that replace the previous government may be unable to either incorporate or to repress all the existing organized challenging groups, and when middle-class revolutionaries face workers or peasants whose goals are quite different. The failure of revolutionary coalitions to consolidate quickly and close the door to others is typical of revolutionary situations that yield dramatic revolutionary outcomes.

A characteristic feature of those major revolutions that dramatically change the relationship of social forces in the state is the presence of a series of revolutionary situations, one following the other in reasonably quick succession. Even after an initial revolutionary situation is terminated, state power remains fragmentary and partial and soon gives rise to further revolutionary situations. The French Revolution that began in May–June 1789 included such episodes of multiple sovereignty as the Federalist revolt in 1792, the Vendée in 1793, and the royalist uprising against the Directory in 1799.

Extended revolutionary processes present opportunities for new groups to mobilize power and to make their appearance on the political scene. Thus, in the French Revolution that opened in 1789, the sans-culottes (urban lower class) who had played relatively little role in French politics in the old Regime managed to organize and to exert influence in a Paris whose strategic importance had been magnified by the presence of the sitting legislature. A lengthy revolutionary process indicates the inability of those groups that initiated the revolutionary situation to bring it to a conclusion, and it presents opportunities for new groups to rise and to make their power felt. As Sidney Tarrow (1989) has suggested, previously unorganized groups have time to mobilize and proffer claims while political organizations have the opportunity to overbid other parties for the support of previously mobilized groups. In Russia in 1917, an extended revolutionary process facilitated the spread throughout most of the Russian Empire of a Bolshevik Party relatively little known before February 1917.

Although profoundly affected by social structure, the ability of organized groups to respond to pressing current needs can have important bearing on outcomes, particularly during periods of extensive and repeated multiple sovereignty. Although the old social order ultimately triumphed, the revolution of 1848–1851 in France exhibited several periods of multiple sovereignty: the February days began the revolution, the June days of 1848 witnessed the defeat of those Parisian workers enrolled in the National Workshops, and in December 1851, peasants, most of them in southern France, rose against Louis Napoleon's dictatorship. Yet, the conclusion of this revolution with the consolidation of power in Louis Napoleon's hands constituted only a relatively minor change in social and economic relations. While the revolution of 1848–1851 failed, the presence of a variety of clusters of multiple sovereignty suggests the real possibilities of serious social change contained within this revolutionary process. Many commentators have noted that France never subsequently came so near to socialist revolution as under the Second Republic, and the presence of clusters of multiple sovereignty reinforces such claims about its radical possibilities.

Radical or no, all revolutions end. The revolution's "outcome" occurs when power is stably consolidated into the hands of a single authority. Napoleon Bonaparte, Cromwell, and Lenin headed governments that consolidated power into the hands of a single authority. The ability of power holders to consolidate their hold over the state for a period of several years constitutes an "outcome" to a revolutionary process. The duration is somewhat arbitrary but the distinction is real. The reign of the Communist revolutionary, Béla Kun, in Hungary between March and August 1919 was too brief to be labeled the "outcome" of a revolutionary process. At the other end, it is possible to label the Bolshevik Party and Soviet institutions as bringing the end of the Russian Revolution, regardless of whether their power itself proves transitory in the wake of the unraveling of the Eastern bloc in the 1990s. Sooner or later all the outcomes of revolutions give way to new changes and different regimes.

Some outcomes of revolutionary processes result in revolutionary changes. Revolutionary outcomes occur when groups, previously excluded from power, become part of a new ruling coalition. Nonrevolutionary outcomes occur when those groups that held power before the revolution substantially reassert their hold after its consolidation. Revolution is often identified with a handful of "great revolutions": these were instances in which revolutionary situations multiplied and yielded revolutionary outcomes. But no revolution is total. Even in the most radical revolutions, some groups that had influence in the previous system—the ancien régime—retain their influence in the new order, and some prior patterns of social behavior persist. Large commercial landowners possessed great influence in ancien régime France, and their influence continued under the Napoleonic consolidation. In Russia, professional bureaucrats possessed considerable influence with the czar and retained their influence under the Bolsheviks, even though there was a substantial change in the personnel and composition of the bureaucracy. Whether an outcome is "revolutionary" or not, revolutions never end at exactly the same place where they begin. The very process of repressing protesters or strengthening military or police powers that ensures the defeat of revolution changes the pre-existing status quo.

Much attention has been devoted to those "great revolutions," characterized by sequences of multiple sovereignty, in which revolutionary situations yielded revolutionary outcomes. Although European lists differ, most include England between 1641 and 1649, France between 1789 and 1799, and Russia between 1917 and 1921. While much can still be learned from the study of these important events, such lists are often biased in favor of well-defined national states and against more decentralized state structures as well as emerging states. For instance, a focus that pays more attention to outcomes and influence and less to state forms might well include the Dutch revolution of 1567–1609 and the Greek revolution of 1821–1831 as among the major modern revolutions. A host of revolutions outside Europe in the 20th century provide obvious targets for social historians dealing with contemporary China, Mexico, Cuba, Iran, and elsewhere.

But regardless of the names on the list, a concentration only on those revolutionary situations with revolutionary outcomes and the consignment of all other revolutionary situations to the dust bin of history can mislead seriously. Ignoring failed outcomes makes it difficult to analyze the characteristics of success. It ignores the extent to which success or failure is not a structural characteristic of revolutionary situations but is contingent upon the events of the revolutionary process. Our definition of revolution points in a different direction; it defines a varied and extensive category of social events called "revolution-ary situations," which set in motion revolutionary processes, some of which have revolutionary outcomes.

Revolutionary situations are usually caused by a combination of factors that includes both external and internal forces. The most important external cause of revolutions has been the perpetual warfare carried on by and among modern Europeans. This system emerged definitively after the failure of the Hapsburg efforts to dominate Europe after 1648. Unlike the case in most other regions of the world, the failure of an imperial state to dominate the European system resulted in a system of warring states. State expansion and preservation forced rulers to increase their demands for money and conscripts upon already heavily burdened populations. Interstate warfare made it impossible for European rulers to devote their exclusive attention to subduing internal opposition. Unlike the great empires that dominated world systems, major European states found it necessary to grant some form of representation to those groups that could provide financial support for their state. Outside western Europe inroads of imperialism and international commerce, disrupting established states, provided external stimulus for revolution in Russia, China, Mexico, and elsewhere.

The most important internal cause of revolutions has been the spread of capitalism, which has threatened the established position of long-standing populations while creating powerful new moneyed groups that sought to limit the drain of warfare upon their financial coffers. Capitalism in its financial and industrial form promoted the rise of new social groups that needed state protection and support. In western Europe, foreign trade and usurious practices fostered hostility to commercial capitalists at the same time as they made capitalist structures increasingly indispensable. Many revolutions included groups protesting aspects of capitalism in the name of older values. In its industrial form, capitalism stimulated the growth of a new and extensive proletariat, some of whose elements, concentrated in the city and sharing many common experiences, were able to organize politically and exert significant pressure on rulers. The growth of industrial capitalism also threatened the position of many artisans and workers in domestic industry who sought to remedy their plight through political protest. Groups fighting against new work forms frequently contributed the worst violent revolutionary cadres.

Over the last four centuries, warfare and capitalism together have led repeatedly to revolutionary situations and, much more rarely, to revolutionary outcomes. The inability of ruling elites, faced with revolutionary situations, to effect a rapid reconciliation opened the way for greater mass participation in revolutions, and those popular groups most easy to mobilize benefited, at least initially, from the outbreak of extended sequences of multiple sovereignty. Where popular groups managed to institutionalize their power position, they created revolutionary outcomes that have exerted enduring influence over their own national history and often that of their neighbors.

One of the most difficult aspects of revolutions concerns the extent to which revolutions can be categorized as a whole. As a general rule, the shorter the revolutionary process and the smaller the number of revolutionary situations, the more likely the outcome of a revolution can be linked to its beginning and the whole treated as a coherent and unified effort. The revolution of 1830 in France, in which the period of multiple sovereignty lasted for about three days and which resulted in a rather minor redistribution of power within the upper classes, is perhaps more happily referred to as a "bourgeois" revolution than either the French Revolution of 1789–1799 or the English Revolution of 1641–1649. Whatever the initial hopes of those forces opposing the monarch in 1789 France and in 1641 England, they underwent great modification as a result of the momentum generated during the long revolutionary period itself. These revolutions must be understood not only in terms of the conflicts that generated revolutionary situations but also in terms of the new elements that emerged during prolonged revolutionary processes.

When revolutionary processes lengthen and state crises become almost endemic, existing organized groups seek to gain the advantage by incorporating strategically important groups that have not yet committed their loyalties or to stimulate partially mobilized groups by promising them further advantages. Many of the most precious legacies of revolutionary processes, such as democracy and religious toleration, may be better seen as a result of the bargaining occurring during the revolutionary process and not to the diverse goals proclaimed on the eve of revolutionary situations.

Revolutions formed one of the early research foci of social history; the role of different social classes in the French Revolution of 1789, for example, was studied even before the full rise of social history. The Russian Revolution has centered a disproportionate amount of social historical research on Russia in the 19th century. But the relationship between social history and revolution remains debated. Social historians have moved to a wider array of topics, though revolution still commands great interest. Disputes over the basic causes of revolution—whether best found in intellectual rather than social change, for example—continue to challenge any simple monopoly of social historians in the analysis of revolutionary experiences. (*See also* Chinese Communist Revolution; English Revolution and Civil War; French Revolution; Mexican Revolution; Revolutions of 1848; Russian Revolution)

Michael P. Hanagan

REFERENCES

Goldstone, Jack A. *Revolution and Rebellion in the Modern World.* Berkeley: University of California Press, 1991.

Kimmel, Michael S. *Revolution: A Sociological Interpretation.* Philadelphia: Temple University Press, 1990.

Skocpol, Theda. *States & Social Revolutions: A Comparative Analysis of France, Russia & China.* Cambridge: Cambridge University Press, 1979.

Tarrow, Sidney. *Democracy and Disorder: Protest and Politics in Italy, 1965–1975.* Oxford: Oxford University Press, 1989.

Tilly, Charles. *From Mobilization to Revolution.* Reading, MA: Addison-Wesley, 1978.

Revolutions of 1848

The Revolutions of 1848 spread across much of Europe, beginning in France and then hitting many German states plus Austria, Hungary, and many Italian states. The revolutions followed mounting agitation by liberals and nationalists, and a small but growing socialist current. They also roused popular protest against recent, severe food shortages and unemployment plus longer-standing grievances against growing commercialism in the economy. Each revolution had its own tone. The risings in Paris focused on a demand for democracy and abolition of the monarchy, along with artisanal pressure for jobs and protection against capitalist-induced changes in their work routines. Nationalism figured more strongly elsewhere. Tensions between middle-class rebels, concerned mainly with political gains, and lower-class demands for social change complicated all the revolutions.

All the major revolutions failed within a year. They taught most middle-class leaders to turn away from revolution and toward more gradual compromises that would work for liberal and national gains. Artisans learned that hopes for a restoration of the old craft economy were forlorn; new protest goals and methods were essential. Peasants in Germany and Austria, who won abolition of remaining manorialism, turned away from radicalism. Some factory workers gained new experience with radical protest during the revolution. The 1848 outbreaks were, however, the last phase of the major wave of revolution in west European history, marking a break between older forms of protest and new. In launching some new currents of protest—the first taste of Marxist socialism, the outbreaks by factory workers and some feminists, and demonstration of new political demands by some peasants—the protests conditioned later developments as well.

The revolutions of 1848 underwent substantial reinterpretation in the early phases of contemporary sociohistorical research, marking new understandings of social class relationships and the complex nature of early industrial protest. (*See also* Nationalism; Revolutions)

Peter N. Stearns

REFERENCES

Stearns, Peter N. *1848: The Revolutionary Tide in Europe.* New York: Norton, 1974.

Tilly, Charles, Louise Tilly, and Richard Tilly. *The Rebellious Century, 1830–1930.* Cambridge, MA: Harvard University Press, 1975.

Ritual

For anthropologists ritual has long been a key to meaning and value in unfamiliar societies. Social historians have increasingly become interested in the phenomenon of ritual for its own sake, or to decode distinctive cultural patterns in societies where it is especially salient, or to shed light on past political and social relationships. Ritual is widely understood to be formalized, repetitive, stylized, and symbolic behavior. Though specifically demarcated by place, time, and dress as well as in verbal and symbolic content, ritual events act persuasively upon everyday life through the expressive and symbolic use of the body, often through the multisensory experience of performance. This article uses ritual in this restricted sense, but one could note a number of fine historical explanations of quasi-ritualistic behavior such as the role of play in culture (Johan Huizinga 1950), the rise of table manners in Europe (Elias 1982), and the cult of cleanliness in Dutch culture (Schama 1981).

The study of political rituals pioneered by Marc Bloch in *Royal Touch* (1924) is again attracting the attention of historians. The politics of imperial mourning rites have been examined by Simon Price for imperial Rome in a volume edited by David Cannadine and himself (1987), and with thinner evidence by Gary Ebersole in *Ritual Poetry and the Politics of Death in Early Japan* (Princeton 1989). Both offer symbolic analyses that explain ritual in specific cultural contexts and relate it to the politics of succession. For the modern period, several writers deal with rituals invented by the state in a collection edited by Hobsbawm and Ranger (1983). Bernard Cohn traces British attempts to represent authority in South Asia. At first Mughal forms of rulership were adapted, including the ceremonial presentation of rewards and honors. After the suppression of the so-called Indian Mutiny in 1857–1858, when direct rule was instituted, new symbols and rituals were elaborated to underline the unstructured diversity of India and the indispensable hierarchical order supplied by the British *raj* under Queen Victoria. The Imperial Assemblage of 1877, an unprecedented ritual event that Cohn describes in the kind of detail historians rarely permit themselves, represented this order symbolically to its Indian and British participants. Another chapter, by David Cannadine, discovers that the so-called British penchant for public ceremonial, and skill at it, is actually quite recent, dating from the 1870s. It is a modern tendency, increasing as the power of the throne has diminished.

The problem of ritual efficacy dogs most of these studies. Did political rituals work as intended? How can efficacy be measured? Cohn sees the 20th-century ceremonies of the nascent Indian congress and Gandhi's antiritualism as unspoken tribute to the success of British ritualism, but such proof is very indirect. The difficulty is to know the relative importance of other forms of power. At least these studies indicate ritual's persuasiveness by showing links between political and other cultural symbols. Anthropologists working historically, like Maurice Bloch on Merina Madagascar and M.E. Combs-Schilling on Sherifian Morocco (*Sacred Performances* [New York, 1989]), have further shown that such links owe their strength to the implicit identification of relationships of the natural world with the arbitrary arrangements of human society. To be successful, ritual innovators must graft a political ideology buttressing the ruler onto native cosmic ideas. They must simultaneously harmonize local ritual practices with the central rites of state, if necessary by changing both.

Civic festivals, which like state rituals have a strong political component, have also proven to be a rewarding field of research. Carnivals in Italy reflect many centuries of changing political relationships between old and new leaders, among the various classes and age groups, and between townspeople and outsiders. Belying sociologist Max Weber's association of cities and rationality, carnivals decline not with urbanization and modernization but only when external state power makes them awkward reminders of local identity. Challenging sociologist Emile Durkheim's functionalist notions of ritual projecting ideal social solidarity in a state of equilibrium, the Venetian carnival offered a forum for diverse social groups to present competing identities, and flourished long after the city had lost its commercial dominance. The complexity of Edward Muir's (1981) picture of Venetian ritual, like Richard Trexler's *Public Life in Re-*

naissance Florence (New York, 1980), suggests that some state-centered studies lacking evaluation of the responses of all ritual participants may be one-sided.

Ritual, then, can be the expression of competitive social groups as well as what brings them together. It can also be a means of self-expression for the oppressed. As anthropologists have shown, Oceanians can respond to capitalist and Christian intrusion through cargo cults, Latin American peasants can rise to revolt under shamans, and Sudanese women can express a degree of household autonomy in male-dominated Muslim society through rituals of possession. Historian Natalie Davis has written in a similar vein about women's rites in 16th-century Europe, and the anthropologist Jean Comaroff has traced at book length South African Tshidi ritual cults before and after European dominance. Tame though such Christianized rituals of resistance look from the vantage point of South Africa in the 1990s, Comaroff's book suggests that research on rituals of resistance or adaptation offers promise for historians.

One of the problems of treating ritual historically is its apparent conservatism. Ritual need not always evolve along with social or political change: existing rituals may instead come to serve different purposes, or encode different messages. Maurice Bloch (1986) found in Madagascar an extraordinary continuity in ritual form. As the Merinas successively developed a centralized kingdom, came under Christian influence, were colonized, and became independent, the complex political ritual of circumcision, repeated in each family, served a series of different purposes yet retained the same sequence of acts. Such continuities amid change underline the danger of using ritual to read social conditions.

The conservative character of ritual has drawn historians' attention to the once-only ritual incident. A well-known example is the Carnival at Romans in 1580 described at length by E. Le Roy Ladurie. Normally carnival was a spring festival, a moment of license preceding the privation of Lent, a time given over to the wildness of youth, when a simpleton might be crowned for a day, and a rich man be obliged to ride on an ass. This carnival turned into a revolt against the rich. Another ritual transformed by politics was the St. Bartholomew's Day Massacre of 1572, a violent act that, Natalie Davis points out, was itself something of a rite. These works recall Victor Turner's extended case study of the schism among Ndembu, or Clifford Geertz's account of an Indonesian funeral that went wrong.

Undoubtedly the greatest quantity of material on past rituals has been produced when ritual was an object of contemporary controversy. Such written records are not uniquely Western—published commentaries on the Chinese Confucian classics of ritual are also voluminous—but as Peter Burke has pointed out, criticism of ritual is a major theme in post-Reformation Europe, both in Catholic and Protestant regions. Luther wanted simplicity and uniformity of rituals, and stressed the efficacy of belief in the Sacraments, not the prescribed ritual. Catholic clerics, in spite of their post-Tridentine support for invoking saints and burning incense and candles, were divided over the rightness of processions in time of plague, and the popular use of the mass to heal the sick. This concern with ritual indicates its importance to ordinary worshippers, who had developed rituals to satisfy a variety of social and psychological needs and who resisted change. The suppression of such unorthodox popular rituals was seen as vital to church reform.

The animus against ritual, extended to the secular realm, and in particular the sense of ritual as artificial and constraining, continue to be a strong current in writing in the West, and may have discouraged close examination of modern rituals. For in spite of Max Weber's catch phrase "the demystification of the world," rituals did not fade away after the Reformation. The very untraditional New England Quaker meeting and the Chinese Communist thought-reform confession are certainly rituals. The anti-Christian French revolutionaries developed elaborate postrevolutionary rituals, as analyzed by Mona Ozouf in *Festivals and the French Revolution* (Cambridge, MA, 1988), as did the Marxist-Leninist states of the 20th century. More recently the radical youth movements of the West in the 1960s and the democratic movements of the Communist East in 1989–1990 each invented their own rituals of protest. One might follow sociologists like Erving Goffman to argue that interpersonal contacts even today have a thoroughly theatrical and ritualistic character, but this is to stray beyond our restricted definition of ritual.

Social historians have discreetly kept out of theoretical debates about ritual's relationship to myth or to ordinary life, and about whether to read it as language or action. Wisely, they have not tried to squeeze ritual into such classifications as the irrational or the sacred and, when finding it meaningless or undecipherable—as do a few ethnographers and religionists—they have avoided the subject altogether. By engaging Weber and Durkheim in dialogue, they have escaped the oversimplifications of each. But historians have handicapped themselves by being only peripherally concerned with structures of meaning and their creation. Too often bound by conventional notions of power and culture, or generalizing reified modern Western categories of social analysis, they have not quite done justice to the power of ritual as post-Durkheimian ethnography did by the 1980s. Thus, no historian has presented a past ritual as an effective performative and symbolic integration of cosmic reality with the social setting, or as a powerful vehicle for transforming social status and relationships, or as the locus for the very construction of cultural identity—or as some or all of these in combination. (*See also* Anthropology; Ethnography/Ethnohistory; Feasts and Celebrations; Festivals)

Donald S. Sutton

REFERENCES

Bloch, Maurice. *From Blessing to Violence: History and Ideology in the Circumcision Ritual of the Merina of Madagascar.* Cambridge: Cambridge University Press, 1986.

Cannadine, David, and Simon Price, eds. *Rituals of Royalty: Power and Ceremonial in Traditional Societies.* New York: Cambridge University Press, 1987.

Comaroff, Jane. *Body of Power, Spirit of Resistance: The Culture and History of a South African People.* Chicago: University of Chicago Press, 1985.

Hobsbawm, Eric, and Terence Ranger. *The Invention of Tradition.* New York: Cambridge University Press, 1983.

Muir, Edward. *Civic Life in Renaissance Florence.* Princeton, NJ: Princeton University Press, 1981.

Rural Labor and Agricultural Protest

Rural labor is a special category in the study of agrarian protest. In many peasant societies rural laborers were so marginal that protest was difficult; both numbers and group structures were lacking. In special circumstances, however, propertyless laborers increased in numbers and gained greater self-consciousness. This phenomenon has been particularly studied in 18th- and 19th-century western Europe, where labor increased both on large estates, as in southern Europe and England, and as peasant proprietors expanded commercial operations, forcing smaller peasants into their employ.

In the 18th and 19th centuries, rural laborers participated in many agrarian protest movements. While the pattern of revolts varied, the events were often linked to new forms of popular alliances in communities in transition, resulting from linkages with dynamic market economies and the worldwide emergence of capitalism. From the 1770s to the 1870s in western Europe, such conditions favored loose but potentially potent alliances between peasant-owners, or "farmers," day laborers, artisans, and rural outworkers. The gradual disappearance of such revolts later in the 19th century marked a second transition, toward more modern forms of peasant protest based on mobilizing political support to influence economic policies in western European states.

Before 1789, rural laborers often joined the fray of tax protests, antifeudal revolts, and grain riots. Laborers were far from the most numerous or leading elements in such protest, however. Poor and dependent, they were often powerless and unorganized. The targets of protest often united entire communities in defense of communal interests, and the institutional role of parishes meant that even rural elites sought to defend collective rights by appealing to courts and to royal officials. The reforms of the French Revolutionary era brought a number of significant changes: abolition of feudalism, land reform, equal taxation, more political equality, and open markets. These reforms gave peasant-owners more rights as property owners, even as they served, indirectly, to deprive the poor of customary agricultural rights to pastures, commons, and forests. Free trade gradually changed the thinking of national elites, further discrediting popular ideologies of community rights and moral economy. However, rapid population growth, property subdivisions, and economic competition also created hardship for small producers. As marginal smallholders, laborers, and artisans became drawn into the orbit of national economies, they began to formulate a more open, popular set of community institutions and ideological outlooks. Agricultural revolts in the 19th century bore the imprint of such fluid political alliances in commercialized rural communities.

In England, enclosures and population growth had pauperized small peasants. In 1830 restive agricultural workers in the southeast launched a wave of labor riots led by a mythical but popular folk hero, Captain Swing. Laborers burned haystacks and smashed threshing machines of recalcitrant employers. Small farmers frequently supported their cause (if not their tactics): they suffered from rents owed the landlord, tithes owed the church, and inflated poor law taxes. They saw employment and higher wages for workers as preferable to higher poor law rates for unemployment relief. In many open parishes where laborers, farmers, and artisans lived in close communication, "swing" was a revolt of laborers and family producers. In later years, the decline of marginal farms, increased land concentration, and falling crop prices eroded such community alliances and left laborers isolated. Their protests against low wages in the 1870s followed the strategies of urban unions and the strike, but without enthusiastic support from others in their communities, the "revolts of the fields" were ineffective. As English workers left the land and as farming mechanized, rural protest largely disappeared.

In France, the Revolutionary land settlement and lack of enclosures meant that traditional rural protest in defense of communal rights persisted into the 19th century, as late as 1847–1848. But here, too, agrarian revolts were becoming tied to social alliances in regions oriented toward production for urban markets. The big revolt of 1851 started in central and southern districts where smallholders, day laborers, and artisans were engaged in production of cash crops, thanks to market links by roads, rails, rivers, and canals. Small-scale family producers and workers united on issues of crop prices and wages, as well as on demands for manhood suffrage to achieve political rights. Though savagely repressed, the revolt was a harbinger of modern rural political alliances. Thereafter, as in England, agrarian reform and the extension of male voting rights reduced discontent. But rebellions persisted in France because the population of small peasants and laborers remained in the countryside longer. In 1904–1906, poorly paid vineyard workers employed on the large wine estates of the Midi south formed a powerful labor federation that spawned vineyard strikes, and in the next year joined associations led by their winegrower allies that demanded (and after months of mass demonstrations, achieved) legislation to improve wine sales and market prices. In the winegrowers revolt of 1907 one sees precursors of later farmer protests targeting government legislation and agricultural policies.

In those regions where peasant-owners made a smooth transition to commercial production, rural disorders were rare (northern France, the Netherlands, Denmark). The extension of the vote gave peasants alternatives to protest as governments courted the farm vote with tariffs and pork-barrel legislation (Third Republic France, imperial Germany). In other districts not even the persistence of the rural poor produced revolt, since dependency or abject poverty often counseled submission. In England, the emigration of the miserable cottagers and industrial outworkers reduced the recruits for disorders. In contrast, in Prussia, large Junker (the landholding aristocracy) estates employed an army of farm laborers but kept them on a leash as bound cottagers entirely dependent on the landlords. At the other extreme, the big agrotowns of southern Spain and the Italian Mezzogiorno saw frequent violent strikes directed at the large estates by landless proletarians and harvest workers. Some of these protests had ideological as well as economic goals, often derived from anarchism. Their poverty, the lack of a phalanx of peasant and artisan allies, and the daunting political influence of their landowner-employers, however, meant that revolts, often messianic in their desperation, brought little lasting improvement.

Agrarian revolts were changeable, explosive, and passing; the 19th century would bring new influences in national politics, state policy, economic conditions, ethnic and religious identification, land reform, even in popular cultural values, which eventually dismantled the political alliances on which they were based, to be replaced by new forms of collective action. But their presence for over a century, in the form of potent alliances of smallholders, artisans, and agricultural laborers grounded in expanding networks of family production in commercial villages, suggests how persistent rural laborers were in defending their rights during the transition to agrarian capitalism. Finally, by the early 20th century rural labor in several areas joined proletarian currents such as unionism, socialism, and communism, providing a mass structural outlet for rural class conflict. (*See also* Aristocracy; Landless Laborers; Peasantry; Proletarianization)

Harvey Smith

REFERENCES

Frader, Laura Levine. *Peasants and Protest: Agricultural Workers, Politics, and Unions in the Aude, 1850–1914.* Berkeley: University of California Press, 1991.

Margadant, Ted W. *French Peasants in Revolt: The Insurrection of 1851.* Princeton, NJ: Princeton University Press, 1979.

Moeller, Robert G. *Peasants and Lords in Modern Germany: Recent Studies in Agricultural History.* Boston: Allen & Unwin, 1986.

Reed, Mick, and Roger Wells, eds. *Class, Conflict and Protest in the English Countryside, 1700–1880.* London: Frank Cass, 1990.

Snowden, Frank M. *Violence and Great Estates in the South of Italy: Apulia, 1900–1922.* Cambridge, Eng.: Cambridge University Press, 1986.

Russian Drinking

The alcoholic drinks of medieval Russia were fermented: *kvas* (a weak drink made from rye bread), beers (based on malted barley and often hopped), and meads (made from honey). Grape wines were drunk in the south or imported by the wealthy. *Kvas* was vital in the everyday diet, but drinks which could get you drunk were vital in social and religious rituals, both pagan and Christian. As foodstuff and as social lubricant, alcohol was therefore an item of necessity.

Distilled drinks appeared from the late 15th century, in the form of imported grape brandies, but Russians soon learned to distill from grain. Because of their superior potency, grain-based *vodkas* soon displaced fermented drinks in Russian ceremonial life, and the transfer of medieval traditions of binge-drinking to a distilled drink created a distinctively Russian style of drinking.

By the 17th century, vodka was that rarity in preindustrial society: an item of necessity that had to be purchased. Governments exploited this fact to turn vodka into a powerful revenue raiser. Ivan IV granted monopolies on the sale of vodka to government taverns, or *kabaks*, and his successors extended the monopoly to production and distribution. By the early 19th century alcohol revenues were the most important single source of tax revenues, generating almost one-third of ordinary revenue. Fiscal dependence on liquor sales made it difficult for governments to combat the growing problem of drunkenness. Binge-drinking was tolerable in the traditional community, where shortage of cash and the rigidity of the ceremonial calendar limited occasions for drunkenness; but in the towns, where cash was readily available and social norms less important than private inclinations, it posed serious problems of public health and public order. In 1652 and again in 1914, governments prohibited the sale and production of alcohol. Both attempts at reform failed as consumers resorted to surrogates or illegally distilled *samogon* (moonshine), while governments lost revenue.

Since Soviet governments reintroduced vodka sales in 1923, vodka has continued to generate huge revenues, the social problems associated with the binge-drinking of distilled liquor remain as severe as ever, and illegal distilling has become almost universal. Alcoholism was a major factor in the decline in public health evident by the 1970s; while increasing alcohol consumption sustained the illusion of continued economic growth. Gorbachev's attempt to reduce consumption in 1985 was as unsuccessful as previous attempts, and was abandoned within two years. (*See also* Drinking; Festivals; Popular Culture; Taxation and State Formation; Temperance)

David Christian

REFERENCES

Christian, David. *"Living Water": Vodka and Russian Society on the Eve of Emancipation.* Oxford: Oxford University Press, 1990.

Pokhlebkin, William. *A History of Vodka.* London: Verso, 1992.

Segal, Boris. *Russian Drinking: Use and Abuse of Alcohol in Pre-Revolutionary Russia.* New Brunswick, NJ: Rutgers Center of Alcohol Studies, 1987.

Treml, V.G. *Alcohol in the USSR: A Statistical Study.* Durham, NC: Duke University Press, 1982.

Russian Education

Education since the rise of Muscovy (the area around Moscow, first to free itself from Mongol control in the 15th century) was a struggle between native traditions of the Orthodox church and successive challenges from Europe. The heresy of Maxim the Greek in 1525, in which he was "forbidden to teach anyone," and the appearance of the obscurantist Domostroi in 1551 can be seen as early victories for the Muscovite church's curriculum of Slavonic primer, breviary, and psalter. After 1650 the arrival of Latin-educated Ukrainian humanists announced a century-long confrontation of two visions of education.

Although Peter the Great recognized the Latin education of the West, his eclectic borrowing did not directly attack the Orthodox ladder of literacy. Latin schooling became associated with the clergy, German and French military studies served the nobility, British mathematical learning guided the bureaucratic middling classes, and the vast peasantry held true to undisturbed Orthodox values. Catherine the Great's contribution was ambiguous. Her early reign encouraged classical and Enlightenment translations and experiments with boarding schools grounded in Lockean psychology. The 1780s, however, saw a religious revival, the purging of Ukrainian humanism, and the adoption from Austria of Russia's first national school system with a conservative social message. Her reign thus tacitly recognized a compromise: native clerical control over imported learning.

Alexander I created a ministry of education, increased the number of universities (only Moscow, 1755, previously counted as such), and provided national direction for schools maintained by the government and the church. Ironically, under the reactionary Nicholas I, modern Russian education was born. His emphasis on relatively small numbers of schools of classical studies and of technical and scientific education, and his nationalistic preference for a Russian professorate led to a uniquely Russian educational establishment based on Western learning and Orthodox values. His onerous controls over curriculum and student organizations also engendered the revolutionary intelligentsia. After his death the resources he marshaled could be expanded by a more reformist Alexander II to parts of the population he mistrusted.

By the end of the century the demands of the military, a vigorous education ministry, assertive municipalities, regional governments (*zemstva*), and the church began to eliminate the illiteracy that separated Russia from the West. Recent scholarship has clarified the contributions of prerevolutionary elementary educators (challenging excessive Soviet claims), suggesting that the new regime's task in the 1920s was but a mopping-up operation. Today the appearance of Russian academics like Mendeleev and Lobachevsky, literati like Tolstoy and Dostoevski, artists like Kandinsky and Chagall, or composers like Tchaikovsky or Musorgsky, seems less anomalous than they had previously, since schooling was widespread. One of the areas where social historians have enhanced understanding of Russian educational history lies in exploring the extent but also the impact of growing schooling and literacy among ordinary people in the later 19th century, with attention to the impact both on recruitment of an educated elite and on the outlook of workers and peasants.

Soviet educators destroyed much in their campaigns to secularize and proletarianize. They also created a uniform elementary education, spread technical learning in institutes and the workplace, and heavily subsidized all aspects of learning, bringing Soviet scholarship to world status. Unfortunately, Stalinism also sponsored pseudoscience in several fields (Lysenkoism in biology), promoted a debilitating social realism in the arts, imposed an ideological straitjacket on the social sciences, purged religion, and walked an uneasy tightrope in regard to the cultural, linguistic, and educational traditions of the numerous nationalities. Such policies isolated Soviet academia

from the dynamics of Western learning and again produced a disaffected intelligentsia. The national ideology of Marxism and common Soviet citizenship eroded, and tensions became increasingly visible in the breakup of the USSR in 1991. The 1990s would see the redrafting of educational values in each of the former Soviet republics. (*See also* Education; Literacy)

Max J. Okenfuss

REFERENCES

Alston, Patrick L. *Education and the State in Tsarist Russia.* Stanford, CA: Stanford University Press, 1969.

Eklof, Ben. *Russian Peasant Schools.* Berkeley: University of California Press, 1986.

Holmes, Larry E. *The Kremlin and the Schoolhouse.* Bloomington: Indiana University Press, 1991.

Okenfuss, Max J. "From School Class to Social Caste," *Jahrbuecher fuer Geschichte Osteuropas* 33 (1985): 321–344.

Russian Family, Demography

From earliest times, Russian population statistics have been closely tied to the country's stormy political history. Historians can only guess at the country's population before the 15th century. The Mongol invasion in 1237 and the plague of the Black Death in 1352 resulted in massive loss of life, but the exact impact of these events is unknown. From 1400 to 1600, the population rose steadily as the monarchy grew stronger and increasingly capable of defending its borders from nomadic invaders. By 1550, the tsars ruled a land of roughly 6.5 million people. In the late 1500s and early 1600s, Russia was rocked by a series of dynastic crises, peasant rebellions, and foreign invasions known as the Time of Troubles. The population around Moscow was decimated. Peasants died of famine, war, and disease, and thousands fled the war-torn regions.

Before the 16th century, peasants lived in isolated hamlets consisting of one to four households. Land was plentiful and family units were small. Peasant households were organized in a uniquely Russian institution called the commune (*mir, obshchina*), a form of self-government composed of male household heads which managed the common lands, engaged in joint economic projects, and collected taxes. Over time, as settlements grew and the peasants became increasingly bound to the land of the nobles, the commune played an important intermediary role between the peasants and their lords. By the end of the 16th century, both households and villages had considerably increased in size, and the commune took on the important role of distributing land in accordance with family size. This Russian custom of repartition acted both as a spur to high fertility and as a rough leveler of social inequality. Although most historians agree that the commune existed before the 16th century, its origins are subject to much debate. By the time of the emancipation of the serfs (1861), peasants lived in extended, multigenerational households. Peasant society was both patriarchal and patrilocal—women went to live in the household of their husbands, and children were vested with property rights through their fathers. For both the upper and lower classes in the 19th century, marriage was based on economics, not romantic love. Tasks within the family were divided by gender, and male and female spheres were quite separate. Among the nobility, parents tended to leave the care of children to nurses and governesses, although Western ideas about romantic and maternal love had a discernible impact on upper-class family life.

With the advent of industrialization in the 1880s, marital fertility began a long decline lasting until the present day. There were sharp drops in fertility during World Wars I and II as well as during the famine-stricken years of collectivization in the early 1930s. One-third of the male population was mobilized during WWI, and close to one million soldiers and two million civilians died. World War II also had a significant impact on the birthrate with losses of upwards of twenty million people, and the death of one in every three men. There were serious population losses in the 1930s due to Stalin's purges, the elimination of the *kulaks*, and the famine in the Ukraine. The 1937 census, which was subsequently banned from publication, showed a population of 164 million, although earlier demographic forecasts had predicted figures of 180.7 million; the difference gives some indication of population losses in those years. The new revolutionary government legalized abortion in 1920, but outlawed it again in 1936 due to concern about the plummeting birthrate.

In the 1920s, the government instituted a radical Family Code which sought to free women from the older repressive strictures of prerevolutionary Russian law. The Bolsheviks believed that, under socialism, the family would eventually "wither away." The first Family Codes legislated full equality for women, made divorce easy to get, and abolished illegitimacy. The Codes had a profound impact on the divorce rate, which soared in the late 1920s and early 1930s. Subsequent legislation in 1936 and 1949, however, reinstated a more traditional approach to divorce and to the family. Today, the divorce rate in Russia is roughly comparable to that of the United States.

Social historians have worked on various aspects of Russian demographic and family history. New work on changes in sexual patterns and some loosening of traditional patriarchal control focuses on the late 19th century, which also served as Russia's entry into demographic transition. Another focus involves interaction between family trends and social policy in the 1920s. More recent developments, like some of the earlier patterns, have been sketched, but not subjected to full sociohistorical synthesis. (*See also* Demographic Transition; Demography)

Wendy Goldman

REFERENCES

Blum, Jerome. *Lord and Peasant in Russia: From the Ninth to the Nineteenth Century.* Princeton, NJ: Princeton University Press, 1961.

Coale, Ansley, Barbara Anderson, and Erna Harm, eds. *Human Fertility in Russia Since the Nineteenth Century.* Princeton, NJ: Princeton University Press, 1979.

Levin, Eve. *Sex and Society in the World of the Orthodox Slavs, 900–1700.* Ithaca, NY: Cornell University Press, 1989.

Ransel, David, ed. *The Family in Imperial Russia: New Lines of Historical Research.* Urbana: University of Illinois Press, 1978.

Worobec, Christine. *Peasant Russia: Family and Community in the Post-Emancipation Period.* Princeton, NJ: Princeton University Press, 1991.

Russian Industrialization

In 1914, only four countries—Germany, France,

Britain, and the United States—possessed a larger industrial sector than Russia. Russia's appearance near the top of the industrial table was a relatively new phenomenon; it was only during the 1890s that Russia transformed itself into one of the leading industrial nations of the world. By any measurement, Russia's economic growth between 1890 and 1914 was impressive, yet paradoxically, despite this success, Russia remained a predominantly poor, agrarian society, with approximately two-thirds of the population still employed in the agricultural sector as late as 1914.

Russia did possess a manufacturing sector prior to the economic expansion of the 1890s. Indeed, since the time of Peter the Great, the Russian state played an important role in the promotion of industry, and historians have identified periods of sustained economic growth—in the textile industry, for example—during the 19th century. The Great Reforms of the 1860s (the liberation of the serfs, the introduction of a modern legal system) also helped lay the groundwork for Russia's economic expansion. Thus, when Count Witte became minister of finance in 1892, he could, to a certain degree, build on the work of his predecessors. What Witte added, however, was a sense of urgency; for Russia to remain a great power, he argued, it had to industrialize as fast as possible. Through a system of high tariffs, foreign loans, monetary stability, and high taxation, Witte presided over a period of unprecedented economic growth during the 1890s, ranging from 7 percent to 8 percent annually. Much of the investment was centered on the expansion of Russia's railways. Russia had already experienced a significant boom in railroad construction in the 1870s; now, during the 1890s, Russia enjoyed a second boom which saw its railway mileage increase from 17,000 in 1885 to 40,000 in 1905.

The 1890s also saw a major expansion in other industries as well, such as mining, metallurgy, textiles, and oil, and although there was a significant slowdown between 1900 and 1905, Russia enjoyed a second period of strong economic growth between 1906 and 1914. New centers of industry sprang up—in the Urals, Caucasus, and Urkraine—and the Russian economy became closely linked to the other economies of the world. Yet despite this impressive economic growth, Russia did not become a particularly wealthy country; thanks largely to its rapid population growth, Russia's per capita income remained extremely low in comparison to the other major industrial nations. As a result, Russia remained, one commentator concluded, the "poorest of civilized nations."

Perhaps the most controversial aspect of early Russian industrialization was the role of the state. Without question, whether through direct investment or indirect protection, the state played a pivotal role in Russia's economic expansion during the 1890s. The state encouraged foreign investment (a policy which resulted in Russia becoming the largest debtor nation in the world), promoted the construction of railways and introduced the gold standard in order to stabilize the ruble. Some historians contend that state intervention in the Russian economy was too great, that because the state assumed responsibility for supplying the demand for industrial goods, it drove away private investment. Recent research has shown, however, that the state's share in total net investment was not that impressive, and that the state's role in the economy—although still significant—has been exaggerated.

The relationship between the agricultural and industrial sector has also come under close scrutiny. The preservation of the village commune (the *mir*) has long been seen as a barrier to Russia's industrial development, primarily because it encouraged the collective, not individual, ownership of the land. Peasants also required special permission from the commune in order to work in a factory, thereby restricting Russia's labor market. However, new research suggests that, although the vast majority of peasants remained impoverished, agricultural productivity actually rose during the 1890s and that the negative impact of the commune on Russia's overall economic development has therefore been overstated.

Yet even if the peasantry was gradually becoming less poor on the eve of World War I, other problems associated with industrialization remained unresolved. For instance, Russia's corporate law was littered with contradictions and inconsistencies, thus making commercial transactions much more difficult to conduct. By encouraging heavy industry, the state antagonized its traditional base of support, the landed gentry, while simultaneously creating a new and volatile social class—the proletariat. The life of the Russian proletariat was especially harsh; workers lived in small, cramped quarters, were subject to arbitrary fines, and often worked long hours in unsafe factories. Russia's fast-paced industrialization, therefore, had led to significant economic expansion at the cost of greater social instability. Russian industrialization would continue, under greater state direction, after the 1917 Revolution. (*See also* Industrialization; Stalinism)

William E. Pomeranz

REFERENCES

Falkus, M.E. *The Industrialization of Russia: 1700–1914.* London: Macmillan, 1972.

Gatrell, Peter. *The Tsarist Economy: 1850–1917.* London: B.T. Batsford, 1986.

Rieber, Al. *Merchants and Entrepreneurs in Imperial Russia.* Chapel Hill: University of North Carolina Press, 1982.

Russian Nobility

The Russian nobility's status and influence derived from service to the state, not, as in the West, from the possession of land. The Russian nobility as a group rarely opposed the tsarist state, manifesting a political stance different from the premodern aristocratic traditions of western Europe. The Russian nobility's development as a privileged social estate proceeded hand in hand with the development of the autocratic state. Noble status was attainable by inheritance, by reaching a specified rank in military or civil service, or by receiving certain military or civil decorations. The nobility was formally endowed with individual and corporate rights, as opposed to obligations, only in 1785.

Among the many individual privileges enjoyed by nobles, the most valued was the right to own land to which peasants were legally attached. In their triennial provincial assemblies, nobles elected a broad range of local officials. The Great Reforms of the 1860s and 1870s abolished serfdom, introduced the principle of equality before the law, and created new local judicial and administrative posts; noble privilege was reduced to little more than the enjoyment of preferential treatment in entering and advancing in state service.

The Great Reforms led to a dramatic social transformation of the nobility, from a group that was overwhelmingly composed of full-time rural landowners who at some point in their lives had been in state service to a group that was predominantly urban and increasingly engaged in occupations that had traditionally been alien to the nobility. Between 1861 and 1914 nobles sold to members of other social estates 53 percent of the acreage they had retained after serf emancipation. The percentage of nobles belonging to landowning families fell from 80 in 1861 to 38 in 1905; the percentage of nobles belonging to families owning intermediate and large estates, from 46 to 16. This massive transfer of land was facilitated by the nobility's weak historical ties to their properties, by the vast cultural divide between the Westernized nobility and the traditional Russian rural population, the unprofitability of agriculture in Russia's historic core provinces, and by rapidly rising land prices. Despite the declining portion of the nobility involved in agriculture, in 1905 nobles still owned 52 percent of the properties and 68 percent of the acreage encompassed in intermediate and large estates. Nobles continued to dominate the higher and middle ranks of state service as well.

By 1897 only 14 to 22 percent of adult male nobles were full-time landowners and 36 to 38 percent were in state service; 40 to 50 percent were pursuing nontraditional careers in the free professions, education, the arts, commerce, and industry. With these new careers came an increasing demand for extended formal schooling. Between 1855 and 1904, noble enrollments increased by a factor of 2.2 in boys' academic high schools and 3.8 in universities. For the nobility, as for Russian society in general, achieved roles were replacing ascribed roles as determinants of social status, now that privilege had given way to legal equality as a basic principle of social organization. (*See also* Aristocracy; Emancipation of Serfs; Intelligentsia)

Seymour Becker

REFERENCES

Becker, Seymour. *Nobility and Privilege in Late Impe-*

rial Russia. DeKalb: Northern Illinois University Press, 1985.

Hamburg, Gary. *Politics of the Russian Nobility, 1881–1905*. New Brunswick, NJ: Rutgers University Press, 1984.

Jones, Robert. *The Emancipation of the Russian Nobility, 1762–1785*. Princeton, NJ: Princeton University Press, 1973.

Manning, Roberta. *The Crisis of the Old Order in Russia: Gentry and Government*. Princeton, NJ: Princeton University Press, 1982.

Raeff, Marc. *Origins of the Russian Intelligentsia: The Eighteenth-Century Nobility*. New York: Harcourt, Brace, 1966.

Russian Peasantry

The history of the Russian peasantry forms a vital part of Russian social history in general, because of the size of the class and its long, largely separate culture. Popular religion, the impact of the imposition of serfdom, basic agricultural methods, the importance of village organization and the communal culture that went with it—all have centered attention on the peasant class. While important work on Russian peasants deals with developments prior to the 19th century, including major episodes of peasant rebellion like the Pugachev rising of the 18th century, historians have particularly focused on conditions prior to the emancipation of the serfs (1861) and then on the complex patterns of continuity and change in peasant life from that point onward.

Under the terms of emancipation, ownership of collective peasant land was vested in the agricultural commune, controlled by male heads of households; peasants were held jointly responsible for tax and redemption payments, and still paid a "soul tax" from which other Russians had been exempted; mobility was limited by a system of internal passports designed to control peasant departures from the commune; most petty legal matters would be resolved in local, all-peasant class courts rather than in the reformed courts which tried cases involving other citizens; and peasants alone remained subject to corporal punishment, and could be fined, arrested, jailed, flogged, or even exiled to Siberia without trial by a judicial body. As a result of these provisions, the peasantry remained a distinct and legally inferior social estate within Russian society until the fall of the autocracy in 1917.

Some gradual improvements in their legal status did occur, however. For example, the government ended its policy of joint responsibility for tax payment in 1903, abolished corporal punishment in 1904, and, following the 1905 revolution, promulgated an agrarian reform (the Stolypin Reforms) allowing peasants to withdraw from the commune and consolidate their allotment holdings onto individual farmsteads. Hence peasants only began to gain equal rights before the law at the turn of the century, 40 years after their emancipation.

Throughout Russia as a whole, peasants received nearly 20 percent less land than they had farmed under serfdom—up to 40 percent less in some provinces. In addition, because serfowners determined which land would be given out, peasants often ended up with farms of poorer quality soil, sometimes cut off from access to forests or water. After emancipation, many rural communities were therefore forced to rent additional land in order to meet local needs and provide for a rapidly growing peasant population. It is little wonder, then, that a fundamental cause of rural unrest and agrarian revolution in 1905 and again in 1917 was the peasants' demand for more land. Recent research suggests a complex picture, however. Prior to the outbreak of World War I, agricultural productivity actually increased at a slightly higher rate than population growth in most of the Empire. There is also evidence that peasant purchasing power and consumption rose as a result of nonagricultural earnings. In some rural districts, so many men engaged in migrant labor that virtually all agricultural (and sometimes even administrative) tasks were left in the hands of peasant women. Still, despite signs of slight improvement in their economic conditions and a sizable group of prosperous farmers, most peasants remained poor, engaging in subsistence family farming, utilizing methods and tools tested by time, and largely unaffected by agricultural innovations.

The most important institutional structure in the lives of Russian peasants was the agricultural commune, nearly 70 percent of which were formed from a single village (others might include peasants from several settlements). Given de facto recognition by the emancipation legislation, this institution, through its assembly of male heads of households, held title to collective land that was periodically redistributed among commune families, and carried out a broad range of fiscal, administrative, police, and community functions including tax collection; military recruitment; maintaining public order; investigating crimes; upkeep of roads, bridges, churches, and a local grain store; fighting fires; mutual aid; poor relief; and welfare support for orphans and widows without kin. In its dual roles the commune directed and defended nearly all aspects of peasant life, but remained at the same time an administrative body utilized by the state for purposes of taxation and policing. Critics of the commune argued that it impeded economic development by perpetuating traditional farming methods and stifling individual incentive, while the commune's proponents (including the government) believed it to be a source for rural order and egalitarianism. With the Stolypin Reform of 1906, the state, hoping to create a conservative class of well-off, independent farmers, changed its position on the commune and sought to eliminate joint land tenure, encouraging peasants to claim title to their land and consolidate their holdings. The reform met with some success, but only a small fraction of peasants actually left their communes before 1917, and many returned to communal tenure following the revolution.

The peasant family provided the basic unit of social organization and economic production. Indeed, the emancipation legislation, as well as later laws, sought to strengthen the traditional peasant household. Family structure remained patriarchal throughout the tsarist period and beyond. Male heads of extended peasant families controlled the household economy (including the labor power of its members), decided most important internal family matters, and conducted relations between the household and commune or with officials from outside. The family patriarch could refuse to grant a passport to a son or daughter who sought to leave the village on outwork. Peasant men dominated not only their families, but rural society as well. Men held all administrative, police, and judicial posts in the countryside, limiting the women's sphere largely to domestic and certain farming chores, child rearing, and ceremonial life.

Although the Russian peasantry preserved many of their traditional social and economic practices well into the Soviet period, by the beginning of the 20th century peasant culture was being visibly altered by a number of forces stemming from within and outside of the village community. In this process, peasants themselves were often the primary agents of change. Nonagricultural earnings allowed many to improve their material well-being, for example. Brick houses began replacing the traditional wooden peasant home in the late 19th century, outfitted with chimneys, manufactured goods, and even urban-style furnishings. Young peasants—particularly those who had worked in cities—cast off traditional dress for the latest fashions and adapted elements of urban popular culture to their own. A rapid expansion of elementary schooling, the growth of rural literacy, and the spread of newspapers and popular literature provided greater access to the world outside the village. By the 1890s, increasing contacts with outsiders and urban life had brought a range of new ideas to the Russian village, as witnessed in the spread of cooperatives and other self-improvement movements.

External events also sparked rural revolution in 1905–1907, and again in 1917. The 1905 revolution witnessed the creation of the All-Russian Peasant Union, which sought to organize peasants and fight for radical land reform. Peasant politicization was another result, as significant numbers of peasants affiliated with political parties for the first time. War and urban revolution had a similar impact on the countryside ten years later. When the new government announced a postponement of any land reform until the war ended, agrarian unrest grew as peasants, in effect, gradually began to carry out their own reform, engaging in strikes, refusing to pay rents, seizing noble estates, burning manor houses and sometimes killing estate owners. When the Bolsheviks seized power in November 1917, they sanctioned the confiscation of landlords' estates and abolition of noble property rights. For the next ten years, then, the Russian peasantry seemingly received what they had long sought—a total redistribution of the land. Forced collectivization under Stalin, however, would put this dream to rest for over 60 years and destroy the peasantry as a class in Russia. (*See also* Collectivization; Peasant Rebellion; Russian Revolution)

Stephen P. Frank

REFERENCES

Eklof, Ben, and Stephen P. Frank, eds. *The World of the Russian Peasant: Post-Emancipation Culture and Society*. Boston: University Hyman, 1990.

Hoch, Steven L. *Serfdom and Social Control in Nineteenth Century Russia: Petrovskoe, Village in Tambov*. Chicago: University of Chicago Press, 1986.

Kingston-Mann, Esther, and Timothy Mixter, eds. *Peasant Economy, Culture, and Politics of European Russia, 1800–1921*. Princeton, NJ: Princeton University Press, 1990.

Worobec, Christine D. *Peasant Russia: Family and Community in the Post-Emancipation Period*. Princeton, NJ: Princeton University Press, 1991.

Russian Populism

The word "populism," when pertaining to Russia, is a precise translation of the word *narodnichestvo, narod* meaning people, which in the Russian context referred principally to the peasantry. Populism in other countries generally describes an agrarian movement or a movement involving mass participation of the lower classes. In Russia, populism refers to the revolutionary movement among the intelligentsia, which arose in the 1860s and achieved its high point in the 1870s. Socialist ideologists, such as Alexander Herzen and Nicholas Chernyshevskii, propounded the ideal of a system of peasant socialism, based on socialist instincts preserved in the Russian peasant commune. The leading revolutionary strategists of the 1860s and 1870s, Michael Bakunin and Peter Lavrov, called for a socialist revolution, based on the participation of the peasantry, which aimed at establishing a system of agrarian socialism organized as a confederation of communes. The populist revolutionaries of the 1870s propagandized and agitated in the countryside, but failed to foment a peasant revolution. At the end of the decade, devastated by arrests and hampered by police surveillance, they turned to terrorism. Their efforts culminated in the assassination of Emperor Alexander II, by members of the People's Will Party, on March 1, 1881. This event inaugurated a period of political reaction and police persecution that wiped out all but a few remnants of the revolutionary movement. In the 1880s, populists turned to more peaceful, cultural work, following what was called the doctrine of "small deeds."

Russian Populism experienced a resurgence during the revolutionary events from 1902 to 1906. In 1902, the neopopulists formed the Social Revolutionary Party. One leader, Victor Chernov, revised populist ideology to take into account the rapid industrialization of Russia and the appearance of an urban proletariat. The outbreak of peasant revolts in 1902 and 1903 and again in 1905 and 1906 restored hopes in a peasant revolution. The assassinations of hated tsarist officials by members of the Social Revolutionary Party played an important role in the disorganization of the power of the autocracy leading to the revolution of 1905. The Socialist Revolutionaries also agitated among factory workers.

The Socialist Revolutionaries enjoyed broad popular support in the agrarian population in the first decades of the 20th century. Socialist Revolutionaries, led by such figures as Victor Chernov, played an important role in the Provisional Government of 1917, and the party gained a majority of the votes in the elections to the Russian Constituent Assembly, which was dispersed by the Bolsheviks in January 1918. But the party was seriously weakened by struggles between left and right factions and poor organization. The left Socialist Revolutionaries participated in the Bolshevik government from the October Revolution until the Brest-Litovsk treaty of 1918, when they again took an oppositional stance. They were suppressed in 1922.

Russian populism figures in Russian social history concerning protest, the peasantry, and particularly the distinctive intelligentsia. The main lines of interpretation have been fairly firmly set, without major adjustment in light of specifically sociohistorical approaches. (*See also* Intelligentsia; Russian Revolution)

Richard S. Wortman

REFERENCES

Perrie, Maureen. *The Agrarian Policy of the Russian Socialist-Revolutionary Party from its Origins*

Through the Revolution of 1905–1907. Cambridge: Cambridge University Press, 1976.

Pomper, Philip. *The Russian Revolutionary Intelligentsia*. New York: Crowell, 1970.

Radkey, Oliver H. *The Agrarian Foes of Bolshevism: Promise and Default of the Russian Socialist Revolutionaries, February to October, 1917*. New York: Columbia University Press, 1958.

Venturi, Franco. *Roots of Revolution*. London: Grossett and Dunlop, 1970.

Walicki, Andrzej. *The Controversy over Capitalism*. Oxford: Oxford University Press, 1969.

Russian Revolution

Revolution entails a fundamental transformation of political, social, and economic institutions and of dominant myths and values. In this sense, the Russian Revolution was a series of transformations rather than an integrated process. In fact, one interpretation holds that this revolution should be understood principally in terms of the dislocations engendered by the initial stage of industrialization in Russia, which began in earnest in the 1890s and continued through the 1920s. But even if approached with a traditional emphasis on the events of 1917, the Russian Revolution was multifaceted. Politically, it encompassed two major conflagrations: the February Revolution, during which the government of Tsar Nicholas II was overthrown; and the October Revolution, when the Bolshevik (later renamed Communist) Party seized power in the name of the Petrograd Soviet. Socially, the Russian Revolution of 1917 emerged as a conflict between, on the one hand, the aspirations of the various political parties who represented the professional and landholding classes and, on the other, those of the overwhelming majority in the country, the peasants and workers.

Russians greeted the February Revolution with overwhelming approval. Nicholas II had consistently rebuffed proposals for even modest reform from representatives of the professional and landholding classes, and his policies toward peasants and workers mixed repression with indifference. Consequently, when disturbances in Petrograd at the end of February over food shortages escalated into a crisis of survival for the government, no significant group defended the autocracy. Instead, even before the tsar's formal abdication, oppositional forces began to create the institutions that would succeed tsarism. In short-term urban and rural politics, activists of all persuasions temporarily deferred their most pressing demands in favor of consolidating the revolution.

Beyond this unified opposition toward the old régime, however, lay serious differences. Mutual distrust between the upper classes and the masses led to a division of political authority known as Dual Power. In this arrangement, liberal representatives of the professional and landholding classes created the Provisional Government, an institution pledged to restoring civil order and military discipline; honoring Russia's commitment to World War I; and postponing major reform until after national elections to a proposed Constituent Assembly. These positions clashed with the aspirations of the moderate socialists who initially dominated the Petrograd Soviet, an elected council that spoke in the name of the masses. Yet the Soviet's fear of counter-revolution and lack of confidence in its own power caused it to temporize on the issue of reform. Thus, neither organ of Dual Power actively responded to the masses' desire for an immediate redistribution of political and economic benefits.

Mass organs, in which skilled workers exercised significant influence, more directly reflected the popular mood. During the first half of 1917, the gradualism of the moderate socialists largely prevailed in mass organs as it did in the Petrograd Soviet, but by mid-year workers and peasants pressed more stridently for social and economic reform. When industrialists resisted making concessions, general workers' meetings directly elected factory committees to represent their interests. Labor unions reorganized and became highly assertive, especially on issues of wages and living conditions. And in all localities, citizens elected representatives to political councils, called soviets. In the countryside, peasants by mid-1917 began to seize and redistribute land on their own initiative, and desertion became a serious problem in the largely peasant army.

It was to such discontent that the Bolsheviks addressed their principal message. Party leader Vladimir Lenin advocated accelerating the revolutionary process in his *April Theses*, which endorsed popular opposition to the war, outlined a restructuring of the economy, and called for a transfer of power to the soviets. In early July, the Bolsheviks supported a worker-organized Petrograd uprising known as the July Days, which, although unsuccessful, proved instrumental in raising the Bolsheviks' level of mass support. In the aftermath, the popular perception that only the Bolsheviks seriously pursued "peace, land, and bread" for the workers and peasants enabled them to displace their moderate rivals as the majority in the Petrograd Soviet as well as in mass organs. In August, a clumsy attempt by Prime Minister Alexander Kerensky to use military force to restore order permanently discredited the Provisional Government. Thus, on the night of October 25–26, 1917, the Bolshevik seizure of the Winter Palace faced negligible resistance. Their success in marshaling mass support thus enabled the Bolsheviks to seize political office, although an attempt at full revolutionary transformation still lay in the future. In 1918–1921, the Bolsheviks had to fight a debilitating civil war to retain political power, and only in 1921–1928 were they able to launch a full program of social and economic reforms, which lasted until the onset of Stalinism.

The Revolution has always been studied with awareness of major social factors involved. The rise of social history has increased attention to the goals of various social groups involved in the Revolution, including various segments of the working class and women. It has furthered debate about fundamental structural weaknesses in Russian society that led to revolution and about the relationship between the Revolution per se and subsequent, complex social changes and relationships into the 1930s and beyond. (*See also* NEP Era; Revolutions; Russian Working Class; War Communism)

William B. Husband

REFERENCES

Burdzhalov, E.N. *Russia's Second Revolution: The February 1917 Uprising in Petrograd.* Translated and edited by Donald J. Raleigh. Bloomington and Indianapolis: Indiana University Press, 1987.

Clements, Barbara, et al., eds. *Russia's Women: Accommodation, Resistance, Transformation.* Berkeley and Los Angeles: University of California Press, 1991.

Fitzpatrick, Sheila. *The Russian Revolution.* Oxford and New York: Oxford University Press, 1982.

Kaiser, Daniel, ed. *The Workers' Revolution in Russia, 1917: The View from Below.* Cambridge and New York: Cambridge University Press, 1987.

Lewin, Moshe. *The Making of the Soviet System: Essays in the Social History of Interwar Russia.* New York: Pantheon Books, 1985.

Russian Urbanization

As in other countries, urbanization in Russia has over the centuries signified more than just population growth and changes in physical structure. The city has been the locus of changes in political development, social organization, institutions, values, and behavior patterns. It has also been the product of practices by which urban inhabitants make the city in some measure their own place. The history of the Russian city and of the process of urbanization contains the chief antimonies of Russian culture: the West-Russia, official-unofficial, order-disorder, modernity-tradition, planned-spontaneous, autocracy-society, rapid growth-stagnation, monuments-transience.

Kievan Russia was known to the Vikings as a "land of cities." Towns arose for the exaction of tribute from the surrounding population and for the marketing of local wares. Larger towns such as Novgorod and Kiev were Eurasian trading depots situated on river highways. The medieval Russian town developed few autonomous institutions; city air did not make one free. By the 18th century, a network of urban centers provided revenue, grain, labor, and troops to serve the needs of a centralized empire.

Peter I introduced European rationalistic town planning in building St. Petersburg, and thereafter government-directed town planning reflected the glory of autocracy and empire, and the state's extensive powers created an "official" city of heavily administered institutions, residents, and activities. From the government perspective, the city became synonymous with public order, and a growing local bureaucracy superintended the comings and goings of a large number of temporary city dwellers. At the same time, an "unofficial" city of disorder, poverty, backwardness, transient residents, street life, and a popular oral and, later, print culture complemented the "official" city. Urban growth became less and less a product of state activity and more and more "spontaneous"; though urban populations were low, compared to total population, by the standards of China or western Europe in what remained a highly agrarian economy. To 19th-century writers such as Pushkin, Gogol, and Dostoevsky, St. Petersburg embodied the clash between modernity and tradition.

Fueled by commercial expansion, railroad building, and industrialization, the average annual rate of urban growth in tsarist Russia after 1867 was 2.3 percent, compared with 1.5 percent in the early 19th century and a world average of 1.5 percent for the last half of the 19th century. In 1914 approximately 12 percent of the Empire's population was urban. With populations exceeding one million by 1900, St. Petersburg and Moscow were among the world's ten most populous cities. At the end of the 19th century, large cities were characterized by great occupational diversity, large-scale immigration from the countryside, and a "dual economy" of small-scale production and distribution alongside large-scale capitalist commerce and industry.

Until the mid 19th century, municipal government operated to fulfill specific requirements of state administration. According to the first national municipal statute of 1870, the male electorate was divided into three curia according to tax assessments on trade, manufacturing, and real estate. Under the municipal statute of 1892, the franchise was severely restricted, and in most cities less than 1 percent of the population could participate in municipal elections.

However limited the electorate, a sphere of independent public activity arose, and by the end of the 19th century an intense cultural and political life emerged. From 1860 to 1900 the number of daily newspapers increased from 12 to 300. Russia's large cities boasted public schools, voluntary associations, libraries, museums, and theaters. As ethnic community ties strengthened, nationalism became a potent revolutionary force on the eve of the Russian Revolution in cities such as Baku, Odessa, Kiev, Tiflis, and Warsaw. At the same time an urban-based strike movement led by the better-paid, skilled urban workers played an important role in the revolutions of 1905 and 1917. As places of opportunity where inhabitants could free themselves from old bonds and habits of subservience, Russia's cities created the conditions of social and cultural ferment and political assertiveness which brought down the tsarist regime.

Urbanization during the Soviet era has had important continuities and discontinuities with tsarist traditions. State control of urban planning revived; spurts of rapid urban growth and the importance of large-scale migration from the countryside have continued. On the other hand, the state also assumed a major role in allocating housing, land, and industrial resources as well as in restricting population movement.

Urban stagnation and even deurbanization characterized the years of revolution and civil war (1917–1921). Urban real estate was municipalized in August 1918, and most dwellings came under the jurisdiction of the city soviet (council). Subsequent reallocation of housing space created the multifamily communal apartments, a pervasive feature of Soviet life in the big cities. In 1922 a sanitary minimum of nine square meters of living space was adopted; this remains the basic norm. In 1932 the internal passport system was adopted; city housing allocation and a residence permit were made dependent on employment.

City politics did not entirely disappear under Soviet rule. Urban plans of the 1920s revealed the conflict between urbanist and deurbanist schools. The deurbanists wanted a townless socialist society in order to abolish the contradiction between town and countryside. But with the implementation of the first five year plan in 1928, fundamental urban restructuring, let alone deurbanizing, was abandoned, and during the 1930s the average annual urban growth rate was a phenomenal 6.5 percent. All subsequent debate about the future form of the Soviet city was decreed redundant in 1931. Since the 1930s "politics" has largely transpired behind closed doors. For example, municipalities and industry, represented by powerful economic ministries, have competed over investment priorities, resource allocation, and location decisions. Although they have usually prevailed, the ministries have assumed responsibility for construction and maintenance of facilities that municipalities could not afford.

The predominance of public transport and public housing, the absence of private enterprise, and the limitation of retail functions have resulted in a less colorful urban landscape than that found in Western cities. The irony of the Soviet city is that in a society that used to trumpet the new, the city's treasures remain the monuments of old Russian culture. (*See also* Cities; Kievan Rus' Period)

Joseph Bradley

REFERENCES

Bater, James. *The Soviet City: Ideal and Reality.* Beverly Hills: Sage, 1980.

Bradley, Joseph. *Muzhik and Muscovite: Urbanization in Late Imperial Russia.* Berkeley and Los Angeles: University of California Press, 1985.

Brower, Daniel. *The Russian City Between Tradition and Modernity, 1850–1900.* Berkeley and Los Angeles: University of California Press, 1990.

Hamm, Michael F., ed. *The City in Late Imperial Russia.* Bloomington: Indiana University Press, 1986.

Hittle, J. Michael. *The Service City: State and Townsmen in Russia, 1600–1800.* Cambridge, MA: Harvard University Press, 1979.

Morton, Henry W., and Robert C. Stuart. *The Contemporary Soviet City.* Armonk, NY: M.E. Sharpe, 1984.

Russian Women

Russian social historians have long concentrated on the peasantry and working class, and on patterns of social protest. Women's history has developed rapidly since 1970, however, adding significantly to Russian social history and making Russia, in turn, an important comparative case for women's history more generally.

The legendary matriarchy of the Amazons, rumored to have flourished in the 7th century BC, was based in the area that eventually came to be known as southern Russia. Later evidence suggests that the women of the early Slavic tribes served alongside men as warriors and hunters. Yet by the 9th century, with the development of Kiev, Russia's first great city-state, the ancient traces of matriarchy and sexual equality had been supplanted by a patriarchal society organized around tribal/clan lines. In Kievan Rus', women's property rights were limited to their dowries,

daughters were not permitted to inherit if there were sons, and a firm sexual division of labor prevailed at every social level. Christianity, adopted in the 10th century, reinforced women's subordination to men in both the family and the larger society. The church struggled for centuries to eradicate and replace popular pagan beliefs and practices. By the 17th century, the church had successfully wrested control of marriage and family life, although the pre-Christian traditions that gave women a more important role were never entirely destroyed.

With the Mongol conquest of Russia in the 13th century, Kiev was destroyed, its population taking refuge in the north and northeast. Although historians have debated the effect of Mongol rule on women, all agree that life became extremely difficult for both sexes. The Mongols plundered and leveled the cities of the realm, destroyed trade, and exacted heavy tribute. The upper-class custom of secluding women in separate quarters (the *terem*) and forbidding them to appear in public or mix socially with men first appeared during the period of Mongol domination.

As the influence of the church increased so did the strictures on female behavior and sexuality. The Domostroi, a 16th-century church treatise on the household, decreed that a woman must be strictly subordinated to her husband and obedient to his wishes. A husband had the right to punish his wife physically for any infractions. Women were instructed to avoid social contact and restrict their conversation to domestic matters. The *Ulozhenie,* or legal collection, of 1649 reinforced and codified both serfdom and the subordination of women. It provided no penalty for a husband who murdered his wife, but decreed a horrible death for the woman who killed her husband. By the 17th century the position of women had reached a nadir. The *terem,* enshrined as a basis for family honor, had become a virtual prison for upper-class women who left its confines only to attend church.

Peter the Great's reign (1682–1725) marked a turning point in the status of upper-class women. After a lengthy tour of Europe, Peter instituted a series of cultural reforms aimed at forcing Russia's upper classes to adopt Western customs. He abolished the *terem,* brought women out of seclusion, and encouraged the sexes to mix socially in public. Peter's turn toward the West marked the beginning of Russia's long, fruitful, and frequently ambivalent engagement with Western ideas and models. Catherine the Great (1762–1796), strongly influenced by Enlightenment thinkers like Locke, Voltaire, and Rousseau, promoted vigorous educational reform. Challenging the rigid culture of Orthodoxy with a new secular outlook, Catherine established the first schools for young women and expanded female educational opportunities. Yet neither Western cultural reforms, the presence of a female tsar, or the diffusion of Enlightenment ideas had much bearing on the lives of the peasants. By the mid-17th century, Russia's peasants had been effectively bound to the land of the nobility in a long, bloody process of enserfment marked by immiseration, flight, and rebellion. Although all Russian women, at every level of society, lacked social, economic, and political power, the gulf between upper- and lower-class women was nonetheless enormous. By the 19th century, the vast differences among such women were even reflected in the languages they spoke: the upper classes spoke French, the lower classes, Russian. The fashions and ideas that circulated at the upper levels of society had little effect on the largely illiterate mass of peasant women or the persistent forms of patriarchy that defined village life.

The peasantry constituted the vast majority of the Russian population. As late as the 1920s, fully 84 percent of the population was peasants, living and laboring within an agricultural system that was centuries old. Certain features of peasant social life maintained a striking continuity from the 18th century through the emancipation of the serfs in 1861, the revolution of 1917, and into the 1920s. The most essential of these was the family/household (*dvor*), the basic unit of social and economic life. The *dvor* was a kin-based, patrilocal unit composed of one or more family groups that often spanned several generations. Women who married went to live in their husbands' households; men remained in the *dvor* of their fathers. A *dvor* might thus include a group of brothers and their wives and children as well as parents and grandparents. Its ability to survive and prosper depended on its size and its number of male workers. Richer households tended to be large, with many able-bodied sons. Widows with small children featured prominently in poor households.

The household held the land, livestock, implements, buildings, and other property in common; property was not divided into definable shares. Unlike the European peasantry, where a single individual inherited property, Russian peasants did not struggle over the household's property when its head (*domokhoziain*) died, for the entire family "inherited," or more precisely, retained the land and property in its collective possession. If a household grew to a certain size, it might split into two, a process known as *razdel*. Like inheritance, the process of partition revealed the difference between male and female property rights. According to peasant customary law, all male members of the *dvor* were entitled to an equal share of the property in the event of a split, but the women had no rights at all. Women did not receive their own share, and were not considered full household members because they could not, in the view of the peasants, "perpetuate a family." According to the peasants, "Every daughter is someone else's booty."

A woman, however, was not entirely dispossessed. She was entitled to her dowry, and if her father died, her brothers were required to provide one. She frequently had the right to keep a separate income from garden produce, poultry, dairy products, needlework, and spinning. The cow was often part of a woman's dowry and thus exempt from a property inventory in the event of *razdel*. In some areas, women controlled small plots of land and provided their daughters with dowries.

Widows usually had greater rights than other women and were sometimes permitted a share in the *dvor's* property. In some regions, a widow could become a *domokhoziain* and control the property of the household, but in others, she had no rights at all. Sometimes a widow received a fixed portion of the property, ranging from one-seventh to a full share. Yet even with a full share, a widow alone or with small children would find it almost impossible to survive on her own.

The household itself was managed according to strong patriarchal principles. The *domokhoziain* exercised control over all the members of the family, and although he did not own the property of the *dvor*, he had the final say in its management. A woman only became the head of household if she was widowed in a single-family *dvor* with no adult males, if her husband worked outside the village for long periods of time, or if he was chronically ill or disabled. Yet even if a woman attained this position, she was still limited in her rights and powers. According to peasant custom, she could not sell or buy cattle, tools, or machines, or lease or rent land without her husband's consent.

A woman's limited rights made her position in the *dvor* less secure than a man's. A married woman's tie to the *dvor*, for example, frequently depended on the presence of her husband or her male children. If her husband died, leaving her childless, his family could disown her. Even a widow with children could be thrown out of the *dvor* by his family. Yet a woman could not easily choose to leave her husband's *dvor*. Divorce was almost impossible in prerevolutionry Russia, and even if a woman was successful in separating, she often had nowhere to go. In the countryside, she could not live apart from the household, and her natal family had no material interest in taking her back. Thus, despite women's crucial contributions to the productive and reproductive life of the peasant household, they held little power. Subject to the strict control of their fathers, husbands, and father-in-laws, they had limited property rights, little say in the household, and no say in the political decision-making bodies in the village. Wife-beating was endemic, and fathers were notorious for sexually abusing their daughters-in-law. Subordinated to the patriarchal household, women's place in peasant society was perhaps best summed up by the popular saying, "A chicken is not a bird, and a *baba* is not a human being."

Not surprisingly, the initial impetus for women's emancipation did not originate within the peasantry but within the educated upper classes. In the 1830s and 1840s, a small group of Russian writers, influenced by Western authors, were successful in promulgating new romantic ideas about marital love and "freedom of the heart" among noble women. In the late 1850s and early 1860s, the "woman question" emerged as a subject of lively discussion. Educated circles

engaged such issues as equal educational rights for women and the companionate ideal of marriage. After the state established secondary schools for wealthy girls in 1858 and 1860, reformers and state officials continued to debate how far women should be allowed to advance.

New demands for women's rights paralleled discussion of the emancipation of the serfs and were likewise linked to the economic crisis of the regime. The nobility, indebted and economically troubled, found it increasingly difficult to support its daughters and unmarried female relations. Such difficulties prompted new concern for women's inability to maintain an independent existence outside of marriage. Thus, the first advocates for women's emancipation came from the upper classes and largely concerned themselves with issues relating to upper-class women. They sought to expand women's educational and economic opportunities. After 1868, they helped to establish limited access to higher education for women. Their victories, although noteworthy, affected only a tiny minority of Russia's women.

The increasingly ossified, autocratic state system, the enormous gap between rich and poor, the obstacles to all forms of democratic protest, and the impossibility of reform turned many educated young people toward nihilism, populism, and other forms of radicalism. Although radical groups tended to subordinate the "woman question" to larger social concerns, they all professed and attempted to practice principles of female equality. In 1863, N. Chernyshevskii published his famous *What Is to Be Done*, a novel that extolled sexual freedom, equality, and personal emancipation. It quickly became a bible for future generations of radical youth.

In the 1870s, the radical movement entered a new phase as young people fanned out into the countryside to "go to the people" (*v narod*). Although women's issues were largely subsumed by efforts to incite, educate, and ultimately liberate the peasantry, the populists, or *narodniki*, continued to adhere to radical ideas of women's emancipation. The government moved quickly to crush the movement, and after a series of mass arrests and trials many radicals turned underground to terrorism. Women played leading roles in these radical movements, motivating and inspiring those around them. The preponderance of radical female leaders was, in the words of one historian, "a unique phenomenon in European history."

In the 1880s and 1890s, rapid industrialization led increasing numbers of peasant women to the cities to work in the factories. Women were 25 percent of the labor force in 1880, and fully 40 percent in 1914. By 1912, the huge textile factories were almost half women. Conditions for working women were terrible, marked by low pay, sexual harassment, poor housing, and no provisions for either pregnancy or nursing. Infant mortality was the highest in Europe: fully two-thirds of the babies of Russian workers died before they reached the age of one.

After 1900, advocates of women's emancipation split even more sharply along class lines: feminists agitated for a limited women's suffrage, temperance, charity, and philanthropy; socialists organized around questions of labor. In 1908, the first All-Russian Women's Congress was held, an event noteworthy largely for the friction between bourgeois feminists and radicals, who found little common ground. A suffrage movement comparable in militancy to that of America or England never developed in Russia, and after 1907, the movement began to fall apart. Ironically, the only parties to support women's suffrage unequivocally were Marxists. The moderate and liberal parties, the political and class counterparts of the suffragettes, were loathe to support the issue. The bourgeois women's political dilemma was perfectly captured in the public confrontation between Paul Miliukov, the leader of the liberal Cadet Party who refused to support women's suffrage, and his wife, Anna Miliukova, the leader of the suffrage campaign.

Within the Russian Social Democratic Workers Party (later to split into Bolsheviks and Mensheviks), Alexandra Kollontai began actively to organize women workers, although the party remained ambivalent about the idea of separate women's organizations. In 1903, the party platform included a plank calling for full equality of rights for men and women. In 1913, after a period of repression and decline for the labor movement, the party launched a special effort to organize working women, publishing *Rabotnitsa*, a paper devoted to the interests of working-class women.

Russia's working-class women were active throughout World War I in a series of increasingly disruptive strikes, food riots, and labor disturbances. By 1917, they constituted 43 percent of the industrial work force. With almost 15 million men mobilized for war, women entered sectors of the work force—munitions, metal, chemicals, and mining—that were previously bastions of male labor. The February 1917 revolution that deposed the tsar was sparked by the working women of Petrograd who rioted for bread on International Women's Day.

After the October 1917 revolution, the Bolsheviks immediately initiated ambitious legal reforms to establish equal rights for women and eliminate the power of the church. In a far-reaching Family Code aimed at encouraging the "withering-away" of the family, they established civil marriage, the right to divorce at the request of either spouse, and an end to joint marital property. Abortion was legalized in 1920 and made available, free of charge, through clinics and hospitals. The party created a special organization, the Zhenotdel, to work on issues of concern to working-class and peasant women, and it established maternity clinics, literacy programs, counseling centers, and legal outreach programs to educate women about their new rights. In the countryside, the Land Code of 1922 overturned centuries of patriarchy and customary law by decreeing equal rights for women in the household and in the governing institutions of the village.

Bolshevik theorists believed that under socialism the state would have no reason to interfere in relations between the sexes. Womens' work within the home—child care, housework, food preparation—would be transferred to the realm of waged labor through daycare centers, public laundries, and dining facilities. Free to develop their potential, unhampered by domestic duties, women would enter the public world of waged labor on an equal footing with men. Women and men would come together and separate freely on a new basis of mutual respect and affection. The family, gradually deprived of its various social functions, would slowly "wither-away."

The 1920s witnessed an ongoing struggle between the poverty of the new state and its attempts to realize its revolutionary ideals. The New Economic Policy (NEP) launched in 1921 proved painful for women as the state cut back on social services in an attempt to rebuild the shattered industrial base. Thousands of women lost their jobs to demobilized veterans. In a shift to cost accounting, managers fired women in the hope of avoiding the generous maternity benefits established by Soviet law. Millions of homeless children, spawned by the long years of war and the famine of 1921, proved a terrible drain on state resources, diverting money from day care centers and preschool programs. Much of the new legislation aimed at freeing women from the shackles of the family had unintended social consequences. New provisions for easy divorce caused the divorce rate to soar, and many women were abandoned by their husbands. Left to fend for themselves and their children, they faced a harsh labor market and an impoverished system with few social supports.

Stalin's rise to power at the end of the 1920s marked the end of the revolutionary socialist experiment with women's liberation. Stalin eliminated the Zhenotdel in 1930. Subsequent legislation in 1936 not only made abortion illegal and divorce more difficult to obtain, but enacted a series of pronatalist measures designed to bolster the birthrate. The party officially declared the idea that the family would "wither-away" to be an anathema, replacing it with a new reliance on a strong socialist family. Women, who entered the work force in record numbers during the state-sponsored industrialization drive of the 1930s, assumed a double burden of both work and motherhood. Although the state provided day-care centers, the majority of its resources were targeted toward the development of heavy industry. The project of transferring women's domestic work to the realm of waged labor was largely abandoned.

By 1939, women constituted 39 percent of the labor force, rising to 56 percent at the end of World War II. The collective farms were run and managed almost solely with the labor of women during the war. One man in every three died in the war, leaving a significant number of women without husbands. Total losses of more than 20 million people depressed the birthrate and damaged social life in general. Women's rates of labor participation remained high after the war, although both vertical and horizontal sex segregation of the labor force persisted. Despite high rates of participation, women continued to be responsible for arduous domestic duties, which were multiplied by the state's persistent underfunding of light industry, food services, and consumer goods. Abortion was legalized again in 1955, but because contraceptives were unreliable and scarce, it functioned as the main form of birth control.

By the 1980s, Russia had one of the highest rates of female labor participation in the world: over 90 percent of women of working age either held jobs or attended school. Yet women earned, on average, only two-thirds of men's wages, and were still concentrated in occupations where pay was 25 to 30 percent lower than the national average. Women clustered at the bottom of every occupation and every industry. Fully 44 percent of women did unskilled manual work, and in agriculture, women did 98 percent of the manual work. In general, the greater share of women in a particular industry, the lower the pay. Thus, despite legislation that explicitly decreed equality between the sexes and enacted an enviable package of protective labor laws that granted paid maternity leave, breaks for nursing mothers, paid leave to care for sick children, and other health and safety features, Russian women were still far from equal with men in their working lives.

The breakup of the Soviet Union in the early 1990s and the move toward privatization have had negative effects for women. Cutbacks in industry have led to large-scale unemployment for the first time since the 1920s, with a disproportionate impact on women. The increased scarcity of consumer goods have made women's daily round of provisioning even more exhausting. The new explosion of pornography has done little to "liberate" sexuality for women. Firms now discriminate against older, less attractive women, frequently demanding that job applicants interview in scanty clothing. Inflation and the headlong devaluation of the ruble have given immense social importance to hard currency, thus giving new impetus to prostitution among Western businessmen. Cutbacks in health care, social services, child care, and the service sectors have all worked to the particular disadvantage of women. (*See also* Russian Revolution; Women's History; Women and Work)

Wendy Goldman

REFERENCES

Atkinson, Dorothy, Alexander Dallin, and Gail Lapidus, eds. *Women in Russia*. Sussex: Harvester Press, 1978.

Clements, Barbara, Barbara Engel, and Christine Worobec, eds. *Russia's Women. Accommodation, Resistance, Transformation*. Berkeley: University of California Press, 1991.

Engel, Barbara. *Mothers and Daughters. Women of the Intelligentsia in Nineteenth Century Russia*. Cambridge: Cambridge University Press, 1983.

Glickman, Rose. *Russian Factory Women. Workplace and Society, 1880–1914*. Berkeley: University of California Press, 1984.

Stites, Richard. *The Women's Liberation Movement in Russia. Feminism, Nihilism, and Bolshevism, 1860–1930*. Princeton, NJ: Princeton University Press, 1978.

Russian Working Class

Research on the working class has provided a major focus in the social history of Russia. Initially focused on working-class involvement in revolutionary movements before and during 1917, scholarship has broadened to examine a wider range of issues and to consider working-class experiences and roles under the Communist regime. Comparative work has developed as well, finding parallels as well as differences in the history of Russia's working class when placed against experiences elsewhere in Europe.

As state-encouraged industrialization in Russia gathered force in the late 19th century, the "cancer of proletarianism" that officials and social elites had openly feared but had hoped to avoid began to appear. Growing strikes and worker receptivity to socialist intellectuals culminated in a massive nationwide outbreak of social and political unrest in 1905. Although the government tried to channel workers' anger and aspirations into legal channels by authorizing strikes and trade unions and establishing a representative Duma (parliament), the half-hearted

realization of these reforms tended to aggravate workers' discontent.

Many conditions contributed to the alienation of Russian workers from the autocracy and the social order. Some historians have pointed to an elemental rebelliousness characteristic of workers with roots still in the peasantry. Certainly, migration to the city created feelings of disorientation and bitterness among many workers. More generally, the harsh authoritarian regime of the Russian factory, the poverty of workers' material lives, and the limited social protections and civil and political rights caused many workers to feel excluded and humiliated.

Revolutionary commitment, however, was not simply a natural response to civic exclusion, subordination, poverty, and social deracination. Drunkenness, violence, hooliganism, itinerancy, and escape into the diverting popular literature of detectives and bandits were far more widespread and sustained among workers than involvement in socialist or labor movements. Nonetheless, many workers, especially during times of upheaval as in 1905 and 1917, showed a readiness to challenge collectively the established order and expressed a consciousness of alternatives. Skill, literacy, and prolonged urban residency facilitated the mobilization of many Russian workers, as in other countries; feelings of mastery and self-respect, which often came with the acquisition of skill, clashed with everyday indignities and with political and social powerlessness. Although often motivated by different experiences and values, peasant migrants, women, and youths also played an important part in the revolutionary upheavals in Russia, though they were less organized and disciplined. The influence of intellectuals, and not just socialists, must also be underscored: they not only helped workers to organize but exposed workers to important ideas about democratic rights, moral value, and human dignity, as well as class and socialism.

The relationship between workers and the new Bolshevik state was troubled. Efforts to limit the autonomy of factory committees and trade unions and to increase labor discipline, political restrictions on the press and on other civil liberties, and the humiliating conditions of the peace settlement with Germany contributed to provoking workers' protests, to which the regime responded with concessions but also repression. Workers were especially discontented with material conditions after October, as industrial collapse continued, unemployment rose, real wages fell, and food and other commodities remained scarce. Compounding these problems, the composition of the working class changed in the first years of Bolshevik power, as the most politically supportive workers left the factories to join the army and to take state and party posts, and many workers simply returned to their villages.

Throughout the 1920s, workers remained an ambivalent ally of the new regime, though material conditions improved considerably. Workers who were enthusiastic about socialism were often discontented with the compromises of the New Economic Policy (NEP)—the return of social inequality symbolized by rich NEPmen and exclusive cafés, and the widespread moral disorder indicated by widespread criminality, hooliganism, and prostitution. Skilled workers, particularly, resented the new regime's efforts to raise productivity by means of higher output norms, increased demands for labor discipline, reintroduction of piece rates, and shock work campaigns (which many older skilled workers viewed as "rate busting"). Additionally, observers often noted high rates of labor turnover, low levels of work discipline, and widespread hostility to foremen and engineers ("specialists").

During the 1930s, the working class was partly remade as rapid industrialization and forced collectivization brought huge numbers of peasants into industry. But workers remained a fragmented class, diverse in social backgrounds, experience, skill, age, and gender. Different workers responded differently to the Stalinist revolution, and workers were to be found among its enthusiasts, beneficiaries, and victims. The renewed spirit of class war and the enthusiasm of economic construction appealed to many workers, especially the young. Large numbers of workers benefited from rapid promotion into positions of management, into the Communist Party, and into technical schools and universities. But many older skilled workers fought vigorously, though largely in vain, to defend their traditional work cultures and shopfloor autonomy, and many rural migrants resented a system that had driven them off the land and subjected them to the discipline and authoritarianism of the factory.

Paralleling these changes and conflicts was the poor ideological and cultural integration of workers into the official political culture of the new society. Heavy drinking, preferences for escapist entertainment over political meetings, persistence of religious practices, and growing consumerism appear to have characterized the mental world of most workers during the 1920s and 1930s alike, though the study of workers' culture remains fragmentary.

The Bolshevik Revolution influenced both the development of the working class in Russia and its historiography, which focused attention on explaining the exceptional radicalism of Russian workers and on examining mainly the political relationships between workers and the "workers' state." Recently, historians have started to examine workers' social and political lives not just at the workplace or in the political arena but at home and in their neighborhoods. They have also begun to question simplistic interpretations of workers' consciousness by looking more closely at cultural life, out of which emerged values and norms that helped workers to give meaning to their experiences, and at the ideas and vocabularies, such as class, democracy, and socialism, that workers encountered and often embraced. (*See also* Bolshevism; Russian Revolution; Working Class)

Mark D. Steinberg

REFERENCES

Bonnell, Victoria. *Roots of Rebellion*. Berkeley: University of California, 1983.

Chase, William. *Workers, Society and the Soviet State*. Urbana: University of Illinois, 1987.

Kaiser, Daniel, ed. *The Workers' Revolution in Russia, 1917*. Cambridge: Cambridge University Press, 1987.

Kuromiya, Hiroaki. *Stalin's Industrial Revolution*. Cambridge: Cambridge University Press, 1988.

S

Saloons

The saloon is a retail establishment where alcohol is sold and consumed on the premises. Most narrowly defined, saloons refer to American beer halls which flourished after the Civil War and were victims of Prohibition in the 1920s. There were, and are, similar institutions in Europe, such as the English pub or the German beer garden. More broadly conceptualized, saloons reflected the changing sphere of work and leisure during industrialization and thus play a significant role in the social history of industrial cities and modern leisure. More generally still, saloons provide an example of a popular institution bounded in time, whose rise and fall can reveal a good bit about social patterns in a particular period.

The line between work and leisure was relatively diffuse in the preindustrial period, and drinking on the job was overseen—not prohibited—by the boss. For instance, rum was a part of sailors' daily rations well into the 19th century. Prior to the 1820s in the United States, it was considered impossible to build a house without liquor on the job site. Mixing labor and drink-

ing died with the craft system of production, beginning about the 1830s, a victim of employer temperance efforts. However, as employers gained more control over the workplace, they exercised less control over workers' leisure hours.

Saloons spread to meet the needs of workers in crowded urban environments. More than a place to drink, they provided, in many ways, the living rooms of the working classes. Saloons offered a respectable forum to socialize, find jobs, read the paper (often in immigrants' native tongue), and enjoy the nickel lunch. Successive waves of European immigrants established their own drinking places, and saloons provided a natural constituency for the urban political machines—which in turn generated jobs and opportunity for immigrants.

The saloon not only reflected the increasing division between work and leisure, but also the divergence between middle-class and working-class cultures. As the 19th century progressed, many in the middle class became openly concerned that drinking was a habit best abandoned, even in leisure hours. Attempts throughout the 19th century to regulate saloons and drinking revealed the cultural fault lines of American society. The would-be reformees largely resisted local attempts to regulate drinking, but ultimately lost the national struggle over Prohibition in 1920. Prohibition ended in failure in 1933, and public drinking reemerged more respectable than ever.

After Prohibition, however, the saloon was displaced by the tavern. The causes for this change have yet to be pinned down in social historical research. The saloon was a product of the streetcar city, with its vibrant and insular working-class neighborhoods and culture. In contrast, the tavern is less of an all-male institution than the saloon, and may reflect the growing access of women to public life. Lastly, public drinking has been on the decline since 1945, a victim of a higher standard of living that allowed people their own living rooms in which to drink. (*See also* Drinking; Working Class)

John Hinshaw

REFERENCES

Duis, Perry. *The Saloon: Public Drinking in Chicago and Boston, 1880–1920.* Urbana: University of Illinois Press, 1983.

Rosenzweig, Roy. *Eight Hours for What We Will: Workers and Leisure in an Industrial City, 1870–1920.* Cambridge: Cambridge University Press, 1983.

Samurai

Samurai, or *bushi,* are the military elite who first appeared in the Japanese countryside in the 10th century and dominated Japanese government from the 12th to the 19th centuries. Although the nature, size, organization, and economic base of the samurai class changed over the centuries of its existence, certain characteristics remained constant: its martial nature, its dominant political position (after 1192), and its organization along lord-vassal and kinship and fictive kinship lines.

The earliest evidence of the samurai class comes from the mid-10th century. Although the tradition of a fighting elite goes back to the protohistorical tomb building period in the 5th

to the 7th centuries, the samurai class rose in the Heian period of civilian rule (794–1185) because of the central government's inability to maintain law and order in the countryside. Thus, local officials created militia to maintain regional security. These local officials, that is, the regional leaders of the samurai, were often descendants of emperors, who sent their surplus family members to the provinces.

The scion of one such family, Minamoto no Yoritomo, founded the first of Japan's three shogunates in 1192. His government used military power, lord-vassal relations, and values like honor, loyalty, and the importance of the collective good to control subordinate samurai chieftains all over Japan. They in turn used their own and the shogun's military power and his overall authority to administer locally. During this period, Japan had two overlapping governments: one civilian, centered on the emperor, and one military, based on Yoritomo's network of authority. Over the following 150 years, power gradually shifted from the civilian to samurai elite.

Kamakura authority was overthrown in the mid-1300s and replaced by the Ashikaga shogunate. It was during this period that Japanese feudalism most resembled its European counterpart. Peasants were bound to the land and made payments in kind to their samurai overlords. The samurai, without civilian competition, controlled fiefs that were organized along vassal-lord lines into larger regional coalitions. In the last 100 years of the Muromachi period, central shogunal authority broke down, regional samurai power increased, and endemic warfare broke out. A new type of samurai leader called *daimyō,* the closest Japanese equivalent to the European feudal lord, arose to control the coalitions and to lead increasingly larger samurai armies; this in turn led to the recruitment of new soldier/samurai from outside the existing samurai class.

By the late-1500s, the most successful of these *daimyō*/generals commanded large armies equipped with Western-style rifles. As armies increased in size and weaponry became more deadly, *daimyō* commanders began to cut off the upper samurai from their small fiefs, that is, from their own semi-independent estates worked by their own peasants, and to force the samurai to move into castletowns as salaried employees. Warrior officials, who rotated periodically from the castletown to administer the villages, replaced samurai fiefholders as local tax collectors and overlords.

The Tokugawa authorities who established the last shogunate in Edo (now Tokyo) in 1603, established an era of peace that lasted well into the 19th century. The Tokugawa decided to use Confucian values to turn samurai into literate soldier-administrators. Thus, samurai learned to read and write using Confucian texts. It was during the Tokugawa period that *bushidō*, "the way of the warrior," was transformed to emphasize values such as benevolence, hard work, frugality, service, and moral leadership as well as martial skills and virtues. Samurai during the Tokugawa period were for the most part the hereditary, salaried administrators of the shogun's or the *daimyō's* domains.

The new Meiji government that replaced the Tokugawa in 1868 was led by ex-samurai from powerful domains in western Japan; nevertheless, one of the government's first steps was to abolish the class from which its leaders came. During the period 1868–1878, samurai lost their hereditary positions as officials and soldiers, their stipends, and their right to wear swords, the symbols of their position. Although samurai, because of their educational attainments, held a disproportionately large number of government and business positions after 1868, the problem of unemployed samurai led to several rebellions and bedeviled the Meiji government for the first decade of its existence. Japan's prewar military leaders used samurai values to train recruits. Today, samurai serve largely as the Japanese equivalent of cowboys in popular culture. (*See also* Aristocracy; Chinese Gentry; Confucianism; Feudalism; Japanese Popular Protest; Meiji Era)

Richard J. Smethurst

REFERENCES

Duus, Peter. *Feudalism in Japan*. New York: Knopf, 1969.

Hall, John Whitney. *Government and Local Power in Japan*. Princeton, NJ: Princeton University Press, 1966.

Scapegoating

The term "scapegoat" comes from the biblical passage commanding the Israelites to place symbolically their collective sins on the head of a goat which is then sent out to "bear the iniquities of the people upon him to a solitary land" (Lev. 16:6–22). It has come to mean anyone who must bear responsibility symbolically or concretely for the sins of others. Psychologically, the tendency to find scapegoats is a result of the common defense mechanism of denial through projection. Some societies have ritualized the process of scapegoating, of expelling a person or creature who then carries evil and misfortune from out of their midst. In many instances, this expulsion entailed human sacrifice (e.g., the Greek *pharmakos*). Human victims were chosen for a variety of reasons—often the particularly ugly, old, ill, poor—but even kings and gods could become victims. Crucial to these human sacrifices is the unanimity of the action—for example, victims stoned by the whole community—which characterizes "sacred violence." Some analysts contend that this unanimity moves the community from uncontrolled reciprocal violence to directed and ritually limited violence. In some senses the first steps toward social cohesion may be built upon such rituals. As an acknowledgment of the vital role that the victim plays in the life of the community, scapegoats often receive specially favored treatment before their expulsion/execution and have a sacred aura.

In more modern societies, where human sacrifice and the kinds of rituals noted in tribal and peasant cultures have been abandoned, scapegoating remains a powerful if less conscious and more sporadic activity. Families may designate one "insane" member to bear responsibility for collective dysfunctional interactions; small communities may select marginal members who threaten their sense of orderliness and proper behavior and heap both verbal and physical abuse on them; scapegoating of this sort is a vital part of the social history of deviances. Larger social units may target an entire group for victimization, and particularly when gathered in crowds, burst into collective violence against them. Studies of racism and anti-Semitism have emphasized that, in societies marked by strong class conflict, one finds a tendency to "identify with the aggressor" (i.e., the unattackable ruling elite) by making someone else the victim (women, Jews, gypsies, deviants, darker-skinned minorities). The scapegoating of a marginal or minority community thus serves as a kind of escape valve for the violent resentments of a population itself oppressed either by disasters (plague, famine, cultural collapse, etc.) or by a dominant ruling class.

Anti-Semitism has been widely studied in social history. Starting in the 11th century, European society became a "persecuting" society in which Jews, witches, heretics, lepers, and sexual deviants became collective victims of a culture in the process of a painful, ongoing social transformation. Often the onset of such attacks came at the prompting of newer elites, who solidified their authority and often eliminated rivals by directing social resentments against them. With the advent of more modern secularized elites, the focus shifted somewhat to other races and minority groups, but retained the obsession with Jews. On the sociopolitical plane as well, the Jews made a particularly useful scapegoat, since they not only provided an easy target which could not fight back, but in trampling them, the ruling elites debased or eliminated communities that were both religiously and politically less authoritarian and violent than their own. The basic theme of the most vehement anti-Semitic tract, the Protocols of the Elders of Zion (1903), is that the Jews were undermining the natural rulers of mankind—the Christian aristocracy—by seducing the populace with false promises of constitutional government and human rights.

The most significant element of modern, unconscious scapegoating is an underlying conspiracy of unspoken guilt—the victim is a concrete image of the repressed consciousness of the sacrificers. The resulting paranoiac tendencies of the latter are then projected onto the former who can then be portrayed as malevolent conspirators bent on domination of the scapegoating community. Few social and psychological phenomena are so clearly marked by bad faith: the elites manipulate popular anxieties to distract the people from the real source of their misfortune. The favorable response such efforts meet among those who are solicited as the aggressors, despite the long-term negative effects on them (perpetuation of their condition), reflects the power of "sacred" violence to stir hearts and cloud minds. Modern historians have also studied particular groups and periods when scapegoating proved particularly important. Anti-Semitism among small shopkeepers in Europe after 1890 focused on Jews' anxieties about commercial competition and trade union activity. The spread of the Ku Klux Klan in the 1920s in many American states, which used blacks, Jews, and Catholics as scapegoats, resulted from a sense among many white Protestants that familiar 19th-century values were being destroyed. Scapegoating often highlights groups or time periods in economic or cultural crisis. (*See also* Jews; Lower Middle Classes; Racism)

Richard Landes

REFERENCES

Girard, René. *The Scapegoat.* Baltimore: Johns Hopkins University Press, 1986.

Hamerton-Kelly, R.G., ed. *Violent Origins: Walter Burkert, René Girard & Jonathan Z. Smith on Ritual Killing and Cultural Formation.* Stanford, CA: Stanford University Press, 1987.

Maccoby, Hyam. *The Sacred Executioner: Human Sacrifice and the Legacy of Guilt.* New York: Thames & Hudson, 1982.

Perera, S.B. *The Scapegoat Complex: Toward a Mythology of Shadow and Guilt.* Toronto: Inner City Books, 1986.

Pulzer, Peter. *The Rise of Political Anti-Semitism in Germany and Austria.* New York: Wiley, 1964.

Science

The history of science is not tightly connected to social history, though it probably should be. Most history of science is written as intellectual history, with ideas causing ideas, greater thinkers stimulating other thinkers. Some social and science historians have worked to widen this view of causation, seeking to identify social groups interested in science and wider shifts in popular culture that helped cause, as well as resulted from, scientific change. One focus, in the history of Western science over the past four centuries, has involved the social composition and role of the great academic associations that were heavily involved both in scientific innovation and in dissemination of scientific ideas; the Royal Society of London is a case in point, from the 17th century onward. It remains true, however, that most historians of science have yet to connect very seriously with the work of social historians.

Results of scientific change are another matter, and many social historians have dealt with these. The relation between new scientific thinking and changes in medicine form an important part of the social history of medicine, not only in the modern West but in earlier Arab and Chinese history. New scientific ideas may promote wider changes in popular belief systems, as in the decline of the legitimacy of belief in magic in Britain by the later 17th century. Science and the history of mentalities here are closely related.

Another contact between science and society, increasingly explored by social historians, involves seeing science as a social construct that can reinforce power inequalities or that results from power inequalities. Here too, it is recognized that the links between science and social history are somewhat indirect since the people of greatest interest to social historians have generally been forced to work at the periphery of scientific practice or excluded from it altogether. The individuals who took part in the scientific revolution of the 16th and 17th centuries were predominantly white, male, and well-to-do. The same holds for the scientific philosophers of ancient Greece or the Arab Muslim world. Indeed, only upper-class intellectuals had the time or the money to pursue what was initially for the most part a hobby for the more intellectual of the upper crust. Even today, the ranks of the scientific profession are predominantly white and male. But it is precisely these characteristics which lie behind one of the key roles science has played in social history, serving as a means of rationalizing and expressing cultural prejudices against women, minorities, and the economically disadvantaged.

Like all generalizations, however, this one requires qualification. Up until the 19th century, women enjoyed a modicum of participation in European science through informal devices such as the salons of 17th- and 18th-century Paris. As science professionalized, however, and thus became an increasingly public rather than private activity, women lost much of what little access and status they had achieved. Unable to attend universities or join scientific academies (the Italian academies being a notable exception), women were effectively barred from much of science. The situation in America was somewhat better than in Europe owing to the development of women's colleges. Still, American women faced both hierarchical segregation in low paying, low recognition jobs and territorial segregation in particular scientific fields perceived as suitably feminine, such as botany and psychology.

In an ironic twist, not only did women find themselves effectively excluded from significant participation in science (with respect to both numbers and job types); science was employed to demonstrate that the very nature of women rendered them antithetical to the scientific enterprise. Perceptions of intellectual and temperamental sex differences grew during the 18th century and were given the imprimatur of science through the work of anatomists intent on ranking races and sexes along a single axis of social worth. In so doing, they found a satisfactory scientific justification for the prevailing social order in which white males dominated. Changes in "scientific" representations of human anatomy newly stressed male-female differences. Those sex differences, moreover, developed into a set of dualities such that women were rendered inherently unsuited for science, being repositories of "unscientific" values. Ultimately, these distinctions were enshrined in a theory of sexual complementarity, in which the domestic, nurturing, emotional woman attended to affairs of the home and family while the public, competitive, rational man involved himself with the affairs of business, politics, and intellectual inquiry.

The work of Charles Darwin served as the foundation for some of the most destructive instances of science as a means of social control. In Darwinist thought, Victorian era intellectuals found legitimating grounds for discrimination on the basis of both class and race. Evolutionary theory and quantification were seized upon to fulfill the need for a scientific means of substantiating the intuitively obvious superiority of upper-class white males. Thus, from the second half of the 19th century onward, much time and energy was devoted to the fine art of using scientific measurements to rank both races and genders according to mental ability and social worth. These efforts ranged from craniometry (the measurement of head size) to modern IQ tests. Again, not surprisingly, whites ranked ahead of other races, while men ranked ahead of women. Other racist translations of Darwinism fed the xenophobic fear of immigrants in the United States which the eugenics movement both reflected and reinforced, helping to win passage of the 1924 U.S. Immigration Restriction Act. This legislation tightly restricted immigration from southern and eastern Europe on grounds that "races" in these areas were probably inferior.

Science, then, has both reflected society's biases and served as a key instrument in their development. Further insights will no doubt emerge as a result of increased synthesis of social, intellectual, and cultural history. Only through such multifaceted investigation will we continue to expand our understanding of the importance of science for members of society who at a more superficial level might seem to have only a marginal stake in it. It may well be precisely this marginal direct involvement which has allowed various pernicious causes to enlist science in their aid.

Exploration of particular social distortions resulting from science do not, of course, exhaust the science-society relationship. Renewed attention to science as a factor in shaping broader attitudes and to social change as an ingredient in fostering scientific innovation is overdue. Science and society, and so social history, are not separate, but we have not found entirely satisfactory methods of combining their historical analysis. (*See also* Feminist Theory; Magic; Professionalism; Racism; Reproduction and Class Formation; Social Control)

Stuart Shapiro

REFERENCES

Gould, Stephen Jay. *The Mismeasure of Man*. New York: Norton, 1981.

Kevles, Daniel J. *In the Name of Eugenics: Genetics and the Uses of Human Heredity*. New York: Knopf, 1985.

Merchant, Carolyn. *The Death of Nature: Women, Ecology, and the Scientific Revolution*. San Francisco: Harper Collins, 1989.

Rossiter, Margaret W. *Women Scientists in America: Struggles and Strategies to 1940*. Baltimore: Johns Hopkins University Press, 1982.

Schiebinger, Londa. *The Mind Has No Sex? Women in the Origins of Modern Science*. Cambridge: Harvard University Press, 1989.

Scientific Management

Scientific management originated with the application of "scientific" principles to the art of industrial management in the late 19th century. As they perfected the new machinery and equipment for the American industrial revolution, many mechanical and industrial engineers, especially Frederick W. Taylor, quickly discovered a "labor problem." Their perfection of the "mechanical" element of production led to their examination of the "human" element which could not or would not keep pace with nor match the efficiency of their modern industrial machines. In the 1880s and 1890s, they began to explore financial, psychological, and social incentives to increase managerial control of the workplace and to spur workers on to ever increasing output.

By 1900, Frederick Taylor became the principal innovator and "father" of his new system of scientific management. Born in 1856 to a prominent Quaker family, Taylor's adult years spanned the maturation of the American industrial economy. Although destined for Harvard, Taylor developed eye problems at Exeter and entered the mechanical world of the industrial workshop. He apprenticed as machinist and patternmaker at the Enterprise Hydraulic Works in 1874. Although Taylor later received a mechanical engineering degree from the Stevens Institute of Technology, his apprenticeship was a traditional path to an engineering or management career. When he completed his shop education in 1878, he joined the Midvale Steel Company and began an innovative 12-year period of shop-floor experimentation which eventually resulted in his system of scientific management. From 1890 through 1901, with uneven success, he managed his own firm, served as a management consultant, and worked at Bethlehem Steel Company.

Through the last decade of the 19th century, Taylor presented several major papers to the American Society of Mechanical Engineers and initiated his important synthesis of managerial innovations and reforms. Taylor's papers touched on a wide range of topics—piece rates, belting, and cutting metals. According to Daniel Nelson (1980), his 1901 synthesis of management ideas fell into five broad categories of managerial innovation and reform. These included (1) systematic management procedures, (2) production cost control, (3) functional foremanship, (4) time study, and (5) wage incentives. In 1903, he published "Shop Management," an extensive guide to modern management practice. Later, in 1911, a more popular work, *The Principles of Scientific Management*, capped his national and international reputation as the "father" of scientific management.

Taylorism went to the root of the labor-management relationship, best captured in the labor slogan "a fair day's labor for a fair day's pay," where workers and managers differed on the nature of the wage-effort bargain. In three broad principles, Harry Braverman (1974) succinctly captured the essence of scientific management. First, scientific managers gathered together, organized and classified, the worker's traditional knowledge about work. Second, once gathered, organized, and classified, all "brain work" was relocated in a centralized planning department. This was "the separation of conception from execution." Third, using the task idea, the scientific manager determined the workers' specific tasks and communicated these to the workers.

Although contemporary management and industrial relations experts claim that they have superseded the primitive forms of Taylorism, scientific management became an important component for the managerial control of the workplace in the 20th century. To be sure, the social science and human relations approaches to management have attempted to soften the rough edges of scientific management. Nonetheless, until the American industrial crisis of the 1980s, Taylor's premises have constituted the basis of an industrial regime characterized by rigid blue-collar/white-collar divide, monotonous and degraded work, and tight management control over the industrial workplace. Study of scientific management focuses a great deal of the social history of work in late 19th- and early 20th-century America and, through imitation, elsewhere in the industrial world including the Soviet Union.

Social historians use the official principles of Taylorism and the organizers of assembly lines as springboard for inquiry into the reactions of workers and the impact on labor protest. (*See also* Assembly Line)

Stephen Meyer

REFERENCES

Braverman, Harry. *Labor and Monopoly Capital: The Degradation of Work in the 20th Century.* New York: Monthly Review Press, 1974.

Nelson, Daniel. *Frederick W. Taylor and the Rise of Scientific Management.* Madison: University of Wisconsin Press, 1980.

Taylor, Frederick W. *The Birth of Scientific Management.* New York: McGraw-Hill, 1966.

Sectarians or Irregular Physicians

American medicine and education were in a primitive state relative to European practice in the early 1800s. Disease etiology was largely unknown, and physicians, often equating symptoms with disease, attempted dramatic and frequently harmful treatments such as powerful emetics and bloodletting, or bleeding patients. In addition to heroic treatments, the status of physicians was further compromised by social factors. The Jacksonian era, for example, fueled a disdain for privileged groups such as physicians in favor of an individualism that rejected formal education and fostered the notion of every man being his own doctor. The social climate hardly supported "elitist" education, and the state of American medical education, primitive though it was, declined still further during the early 1800s. Medical licensure was revoked by several states in 1820 and rescinded by the majority of states by 1840. Thus, virtually anyone could be a self-proclaimed physician. The lack of standards governing medical education coupled with a general anti-intellectualism, rugged individualism, and the rural nature of America fostered the rise of medical sectarianism, or "irregular physicians." The sectarians comprised roughly 10 percent of all physicians between 1830 and 1860, and by 1870, operated approximately 15 out of the 75 existing medical schools.

These irregular physicians played a significant role in American medical history during this period reflecting important popular beliefs about health and medicine that remain to be fully explored. While sectarian groups existed in Europe, they did not influence the "regular" practice of medicine as profoundly as their American counterparts, largely because of the better status of European medical education. In America, the sectarians brought new appreciation for preventive medicine and forced the regular physicians toward improved standards in education. In addition, a major impetus behind the organization of the American Medical Association was to protect the interests of the "regular" physicians from the influences of the sectarians. And the sectarians were an element in malpractice escalation of the mid-19th century, as sectarian physicians testified unabashedly against the regular practitioners in court.

The first popular group of sectarians, arising in the early 1800s, were the Thomsonians. They believed that all disease was caused by cold, and could therefore be treated with one remedy. They advocated the use of natural means and botanicals to restore heat to the body and promoted the notion that, in a democracy, the individual should cure himself. The Thomsonians advocated the role of physician as educator and contributed to their own demise. Their strength began to wane by 1840. The Eclectics, who denied the importance of scientific training but were conventional in many respects, followed. This group incorporated many of the methods of the Thomsonians and campaigned against the excessive methods of regular physicians.

By 1840, the homeopaths had gained national prominence. Unlike the Thomsonians, the homeopaths were founded by German immigrants and did not advocate the notion of every man being his own physician. In place of "heroic" treatments, however, the homeopaths taught the importance of small doses of medication and promoted the law of similiars—fighting the disease by producing symptoms similar to the body's natural defense. The homeopaths were particularly popular among women who comprised nearly two-thirds of their patients and sought their domestic remedies. Founded in America

in 1825, the homeopaths numbered nearly 2,500 strong by the start of the Civil War.

The third most popular group of sectarians were the hydropaths. Immensely popular in America from 1840 to 1870, the hydropaths promoted both preventive medicine and a wide variety of water therapy in favor of medical treatments. The *"Water Cure" Journal* was a means of spreading hydropathy and, like many of the sects, placed special emphasis on the role of women as providers of health care in the home. John Harvey Kellogg became the most prolific writer on hydrotherapy, adding nutritional advice to the sect's literature and promoting the preventive and curative aspects of the therapy well into the 20th century.

The sectarians were generally more popular among women than men. Industrialization wrought confusion concerning women's roles. The emphasis on domestic treatment and the notion that it was up to the individual to keep himself well was consistent with the new ideas about womens' role in the home and led to particular interest among women in health reform. Though not a formal sect, the health reform movement countered the practices of regular physicians and, through reform journals and lectures, advocated prevention through physiology, proper nutrition, and hygiene. The women's health reform movement founded the American Physiological Society, through which many women articulated both their feminism and the central role of women in society.

The influence of industrialization was also evident in the popular osteopathic and, later, chiropractic sects. The osteopaths advocated the notion of the body as a machine illness caused by mechanical misalignment. The chiropractics were an outgrowth of the osteopaths, and both groups advocated educational requirements sufficiently to obtain licensure in every state by the turn of the century. Finally, the Christian Scientists grew in popularity by the end of the 19th century. Advocating mind over matter, the Christian Scientists urged their converts to heal themselves, metaphysically.

By the turn of the 20th century, the state of medical education and practice had improved considerably, muting the attacks on professional physicians. Asepsis and technological changes such as anesthesia and x-ray advanced the status of the regular physicians, as well. The regular physicians became better organized, and the American Medical Association sought new licensure and educational standards. In the main, they sought to close the "irregular" physicians' schools and deter the irregular's ability to practice. Social changes such as urbanization and the resultant growth of hospitals fostered reliance on formal care rather than on self-help. In the process, several groups of sectarians such as the osteopaths were absorbed into the ranks of the regular physicians. Others, such as the homeopaths, adapted their educational requirements and practices toward the requirements of the mainstream. And the budding patent medicine industry absorbed much of the remaining demand for self-help.

The sectarians, then, once a viable source of competition for regular physicians, diminished in number as they were replaced with an ever more powerful medical elite. As hospitals became the locus of health care in the 20th century, the sectarians were denied access. Those sects who survived did so largely due to assimilation into the mainstream of standard practice. The balance between official pressure and changing popular belief in the demise of the sectarians continues to challenge the American social history of medicine. (*See also* Medical Eclecticism; Medicine; Professionalism)

Margaret Brindle

REFERENCES

Risse, Guenter, Ronald Numbers, and Judith W. Leavitt. *Medicine Without Doctors.* New York: Science History Publications, 1977.

Starr, Paul. *The Social Transformation of American Medicine.* New York: Basic Books, 1982.

Verbrugge, Martha H. *Able-bodied Womanhood.* New York: Oxford University Press, 1988.

Sense of Self/Individualism

As descriptions of social and personal standards, individualism and sense of self have been explored by social historians, but far from systematically. Historian Alain Corbin, for example, has noted that French people became individualistic only in the later 19th century, but he does

not fully define the change. Historians dealing with naming practices have seen the increasing trend, in western Europe and the United States around 1800, to choose nonancestral names for children as a sign of increasing attention to children as individuals. Child discipline, switching toward inner guilt and away from social shame, and a bit later the effort to provide each child with a separate room may also be markers toward individualism in Western society, particularly in the middle classes, but again no systematic synthesis has emerged.

The idea of individualism as a historical topic far antedates social history. By the 19th century commentators on American or Western civilization often noted and sometimes criticized a pronounced individualistic strand. This was a theme of conservative Russian intellectuals by the 1870s, eager to preserve more communitarian and authoritarian values in their country by criticizing western Europe. Comparisons of Western individualism with more group-oriented Japanese maintain this theme in the later 20th century. Intellectual historians have long tried to trace the rise of greater individualism in Western society. Jakob Burckhardt, the great 19th-century Swiss historian, found it in the artists and politicians of the Italian Renaissance. Others trace it to the Protestant Reformation. Concern for individual rights and criteria of individual well-being form parts of 18th-century Enlightenment political philosophy and 19th-century liberalism. Individualism is also linked to a capitalist value system, as in Max Weber's interpretation of Protestant Christianity.

How these themes translate into social history remains complex. What groups internalized new kinds of individualism and when and why? New disdain for the poor, on grounds that they should aid themselves, entered into social class relationships in western Europe by the 17th century, and in the United States by the 19th. New aspirations for social mobility for oneself or one's children may suggest new individualism by the 19th century. The family was increasingly defined as an arrangement among individuals, not as a separate entity, though this notion probably affected men earlier than women. Individualistic motives almost certainly developed more slowly in the working classes than in the middle class.

The more recent social history of individualism also raises questions. With Western influence, greater individualism may have spread to other societies in the 20th century. African novelists as well as social scientists have explored the tension between new individualistic interests and traditional obligation to the extended family. In Western society some sociologists see new forms of individualism, creating progressive loosening of 19th-century rules on polite behavior and language as people seek individual outlets through cursing or distinctive dress. Assertions of individual expression create tensions with family solidarity. On the other hand social historians have noted efforts to adjust individualism to the needs for 20th-century "team play" in corporate management structures, and to new efforts to limit individual emotional intensity in favor of social conformity. Here, too, the individualism theme raises important questions that await a full-scale treatment.

In contrast to scattered research on individualism, sense of self is a concept social and cultural historians have introduced to describe one part of the extensive changes in Western mentality that took shape in the 17th and 18th centuries. Without, as yet, fully specifying the social groups affected, mentalities historians see a new ability to identify oneself as separate from family and community, and also to see the individual personality as a controllable creation expressing the self. According to the new sense of self, emotions no longer buffet individuals because of humors or evil spirits beyond their control. People can identify their personal reactions and control them to create a pleasing and effective character. American and English diaries form one source from the 1600s and 1700s used to display the new sense of self expression and control; the diary itself was a new form of writing suggesting self-consciousness.

Ultimately, social historians may further define the use of new sense of self and explore the concept to pin down phases of the emergence of novel kinds of individualism. The concomitance in time of the new sense of self and efforts to name children more individualistically constitutes the kind of link that might be spelled out in relating early modern mentalities changes to individualistic developments in the past two centuries. [*See also* Cultural History; Emotion (Emotionology); Mentalities; Naming Practices]

Peter N. Stearns

REFERENCES

Lasch, Christopher. *The Culture of Narcissism.* New York: Warner Books, 1983.

Sabean, David W. *Power in the Blood: Popular Culture and Village Discourse in Early Modern Germany.* Cambridge: Cambridge University Press, 1988.

Stearns, Carol Z., and Peter N. Stearns, eds. *Emotion and Social Change, Toward a New Psychohistory.* New York: Holmes & Meier, 1988.

Senses

As early as 1938 Lucien Febvre, one of the *Annales* pioneers, was calling for a history of the senses and perception, to include such fields as the study of emotional systems and the configurations of certain fundamental sentiments—fear, pity, cruelty, love—in an effort to reconstitute people's "mental tools" in the past. As a framework for this history, Febvre emphasized the growing rationalization of conduct since the dawn of the 16th century as well as a decline in the uses of touch and smell. According to Febvre, Renaissance men and women smelled, inhaled, and licked more than their descendents, who submitted more to the primacy of sight and hearing. At the same time, Norbert Elias (1939) detected a civilizing process at work in the history of the West since the Middle Ages. According to Elias, the progressive diversification of social relations elicited an internalization of increasingly rigorous norms, particularly evident in the heart of court society. In the course of centuries, this process translated primarily into a decrease in the tolerance thresholds of the senses and an increasing delicacy.

Historians of the aesthetic are logically impassioned by the study of the senses, but from a completely different perspective from that adopted by Lucien Febvre or Norbert Elias. To appreciate this difference it suffices only to examine the many works devoted to the mechanics of sight structuring 18th-century English gardens or the systematic studies led by Michael

Baxandall—and this is but one example—on the manner of observing the works of the *Quatrocento*. Such works sketch the beginnings of a history of art founded on the interaction that develops between the perspective of the artist and that of the viewer—in brief, between creation and reception.

At the same time, certain anthropologists have emphasized the importance of the hierarchy of the senses and the balance established between them, which allow a richer examination of culture. As early as 1844, Karl Marx wrote that "the culture of the five senses is the work of all history" and that capitalist society is at root a mutation of sensibility. In the *Genealogy of Morals* (1887), Friedrich Nietzsche developed at length the theme of instinctual repression in civilization, and Sigmund Freud, in turn, emphasized this mutilation in his *Civilization and Its Discontents*. Recently, and this is again but one example, a team of researchers, under the impetus of David Howes (1990), have sought to deepen this anthropology of the senses; they ask of historians the possibility of constructing a social history of the senses.

Such a task should be subdivided. It would be appropriate, in the first place, to study simultaneously systems of belief or scientific conviction that arrange the representations of the sense organs and the dominant discourse on the hierarchy of senses during each historical era. It would be especially important to understand the deep roots of the exclusion of touch, smell, and taste, having long been qualified as the animal senses, doorways to sin. It would also be necessary to perceive the aims that guided the magnification of sight and hearing, exalted, from Plato to Kant, because of their aesthetic power and the importance of their social uses.

Aiming to construct a history of the senses at least in Western history (the development of Asian standards concerning smell and cleanliness remains an important comparative challenge), researchers must delimit how such a hierarchy induced a whole system of norms. Since the codification of classical hygiene, the uses of the senses (*percepta*) have been objects of apprenticeship. In Catholic lands, the penitentials—confession manuals—created a discipline for the senses, especially of sight, well

known today among specialists. Codes of civility—revisiting Norbert Elias here—imposed thresholds of tolerance. At the end of the 19th century, the codification of sexual perversions, analyzed recently by Michel Foucault in *The History of Sexuality, Volume I*, developed proscriptions of certain sensual practices, since then relegated to the field of pathology.

These apprenticeships and injunctions determine the sensory *habitus* of individuals; they condition the forms of attention and the canons of modesty. Thus, for the historian, the goal is to construct, for each historical era, a sensory archeology surpassing a simple inventory of the visual, sonorous, and olfactive environment. We know, at present, very little about the uses of smell, the forms of touch, or the welcome reserved for daily sounds. The ephemeral nature of the sources—the distance that separates the spoken of the experienced and the silence of the inexperienced—hampers the researcher. One route open to this unknown domain may be the discourse on loss and the social study of handicaps; in brief, the history of the blind, deaf-mutes, and anosmatics (people with no sense of smell).

The links woven between the social imagination and the use of the senses constitute another field open to historians. The social uses of the senses were, in effect, very often decreed by those holding power. An evident relation exists between the social hierarchy and the pattern of sensuality. The dominant classes of the 19th century knew very well, thus, to distinguish themselves by the delicacy of their sensory standards while decreeing the sensory inferiority of the people associated, by this fact, to animalism, death, and sin.

Thus, the changes in sensory standards most thoroughly investigated thus far relates to relationships among social classes in a setting of rapid transition, as well as to the larger redefinition of delicacy suggested in earlier general theory. Standards of smell changed considerably, beginning with the upper and middle classes, from the late 18th century onward in Western society. Smells that had been widely accepted now became disgusting, prompting new attention to perfume, to bathing, to toilet training, and to public health regulations. Reliance on sense of smell may have declined accordingly. More tentative research suggests changes in standards applied to touching and perhaps to hearing during the same decades, again toward greater refinement but also as a means of labeling lower classes (and, in some instances, racial and ethnic minorities) as inferior.

A sensory message can thus constitute, in itself, a claim to power. Jacques Attali (1977) has noted that the organization of sounds—the appropriation and the control of noises—represents so many attributes of power, so many ways of creating or consolidating a community. The audible band of signs translates the structures of a society; aiming at the monopolization of oral messages, the power to deafen by the organ, the bell, factory machines, or the amplifier proves determining. Furthermore, a relation forms between the limits of a territory and the means of making oneself heard there. It is important in that perspective to pay attention to the sonorous form of knowing.

Here, in a few lines, are the contours of a history of hierarchies, norms, and sensorial uses, or, if one prefers, systems of appreciation, thresholds of tolerance, and degrees of delicacy: a history rendered more difficult by the ephemeral nature of the sources but spurred on by the pleasures of the adventure that constitute, for the historian, the invention of sources. [*See also* Animals; Anthropology; Art; Cleanliness; Emotion (Emotionology)]

Alain Corbin

REFERENCES

Attali, Jacques. *Bruits*. Paris: Presses Universitaires de France, 1977.

Baxandall, Michael. *Painting and Experience in 15th Century Italy*. Oxford: Oxford University Press, 1972.

Corbin, Alain. *The Foul and the Fragrant: Odor and the French Social Imagination*. Cambridge, MA: Harvard University Press, 1986.

Green, Nicholas. *The Spectacle of Nature: Landscape and Bourgeois Culture in Nineteenth-Century France*. Manchester, Eng.: Manchester University Press, 1990.

Howes, David. "Les Cinq sens." Special issue of *Anthropologie et Sociétés* (1990).

Lowe, Donald M. *History of Bourgeois Perception*. Chicago: Chicago University Press, 1982.

Servants

Live-in domestic service was characteristic of the 18th- and 19th-century middle- and upper-class way of life. Domestic service was also the largest category of women's employment in Europe, the United States, and Latin America until the early 20th century. Predominantly a male occupation in the largest and wealthiest European households in the 18th century, the servant class not only grew but became overwhelmingly female by the mid-19th century. The French Revolution of 1789 did much to alter the legal and social relationship of servants and masters in Europe, but rather than ending this kind of personal servitude, the Revolution ushered in a period of rising wealth for the middle classes and expanding employment of live-in female servants. Domestic service represented a traditional occupation for young rural women. In the rural parts of the United States, the hiring of female "help" to assist in the household on a seasonal basis was common in the 19th century. Forty-eight percent of Michigan farmers and 36 percent of Wisconsin farmers reported in 1895 that they hired female help in the summer. But in the United States, as in Europe and Latin America, domestic service was increasingly an important channel of migration to the cities. By the end of the 19th century, domestic service was more clearly delineated as a permanent status in urban America, and black women played an increasingly important role as servants to the white upper and middle classes. (By 1920, black women constituted 39 percent of all servants in American cities of more than 100,000 population.)

Domestic servants in the 19th century were primarily young and female, most often from rural or small-town backgrounds. They earned very low salaries, but were supplied with room and board. They were often housed two to a bed in the attic rooms of Parisian apartment buildings or forced to sleep in the kitchen. The work was not attractive in itself, but it was easy to secure a position as a servant, and service provided young women with an opportunity to move into a large city. When Lucy Maynard Salmon of Vassar College surveyed domestic servants in the United States in 1890, she concluded that servants found compensation in the fact that by "living in" they could save most of their salary.

Domestic service was often spoken of as an occupation suitable to women's place in society. If work was merely a stage in a woman's life cycle between childhood and motherhood, then domestic service was as appropriate an occupation as any of those available to women. The household provided a sheltered environment for women—so it was thought—and young women received a kind of apprenticeship in the skills of marriage and motherhood. Only a minority of live-in servants in the 19th century were career domestics, but many women worked in that capacity until they married or moved on to some other occupation. The women who became servants had few options because of their lack of education, and housework could be a dead end if one did not escape to marriage because it did not provide any formal occupational training. "Housework soon unfits one for any other kind of work," commented one servant. "I did not realize what I was doing until too late." European servants, however, were more literate than the rural population from which they were recruited, suggesting that a period in service had exposed them to useful skills such as reading and writing.

The all-encompassing nature of the work and the servant's live-in situation tended to create an oppressive environment. In 1906, a French association of servants attempted to have the domestic's workday limited to 15 hours at a time when the average for other workers was close to 10. A French servant complained in the early 20th century that she worked for two teachers who "have two days off a week, a twelve-day holiday at Easter, four months or more of summer vacation; but I am given only a half-day every five weeks, and if I ask to go out at any other time, they begin to talk about firing me."

The occupation isolated servants, who most often worked alone or with only one other servant, in a middle- or upper-class household. Service exposed a young woman to exploitation by employers and at times to the sexual domination of her master. A high percentage of prostitutes and women admitted to public hospitals for the delivery of an illegitimate child were servants. Powerless to control her living and working situation, a servant's only alternative was to change jobs frequently, which the majority of servants did.

As servants changed positions, the question of how to hire and keep a servant became as important to the well-brought-up middle-class girl as the choice of a husband. "I must not do our household work, or carry my own baby out; or I should lose caste," wrote the wife of an English doctor. "We must keep a servant." A manual for housewives warned that "without a single exception, servants are the greatest plague connected with housekeeping."

The rising expense and the difficulties of keeping live-in servants undoubtedly reinforced a desire for a more private family life and led middle-class employers to hire fewer live-in servants over time. But although live-in domestic service has declined as a characteristic of middle-class life in industrialized countries since the late 19th century, its history remains a significant chapter in the experience of working-class women. Servanthood remains a vital topic in the contemporary social history of Latin America and parts of Asia.

The changing nature of domestic service, its role in the lives of women and in family structures, and the causes and impact of the gradual decline in service have also attracted social history research. Comparative analysis has also developed, in an area whose unexpected significance continues to draw scholarly attention. (*See also* Domesticity; Women and Work)

Theresa McBride

REFERENCES

Dudden, Faye. *Serving Women: Household Service in 19th-Century America.* Middletown, CT: Wesleyan University Press, 1983.

Katzman, David M. *Seven Days a Week: Women and Domestic Service in Industrializing America.* New York: Oxford University Press, 1978.

McBride, Theresa. *The Domestic Revolution: The Modernization of Household Service in England and France, 1820–1920.* New York: Holmes & Meier, 1976.

Sexuality

Does sex have a history? If it does, does it have a social history? These are questions that are still asked and remain the focus of much debate. Yet after a pattern of accelerating research since the 1970s it seems evident that both sex and sexuality have to some extent escaped what has been labeled the "essentialist" objections to their historical study. The essentialist position argued that sex is a biologically determined enduring reality and that sexuality is a relatively fixed and limited complex of private activities of little or no significance; thus, neither sex nor sexuality had much in the way of a history, and what little there might have been hardly warranted the interest of historians.

The rejection of the essentialist perspective has been in large part due to the work of feminist and gay scholars. Central was their adoption of "gender" as a special technical term to describe the cultural constructs that different societies built around perceived sexual differences. Implicit in the use of the term was the understanding that a great deal of what people perceived as making up male, female, or other intermediate categories of gender was a social and cultural construct rather than a biological given. Moreover these constructs, because they had changed over time, needed to be studied in their historical dimension. From that starting point it was relatively easy to argue that sex and sexuality were also largely social, cultural, and perceptual constructs built upon more or less limited and limiting biological and psychological bases. That meant that both had a history. And as the social world has seemed to play an important aspect in the shaping of perceptions and culture on these matters it meant that a social history of sexuality could be and should be written.

At the least it is being written. Like all things relating to sex, however, that social history is not without controversy. In fact, one of the hottest areas of controversy at present turns around a position taken by the more radical opponents of the essentialist vision. They argue that sex and sexuality have no history at all before the modern period simply because both are modern inventions and therefore did not exist in earlier times. Thus, precisely because sex and sexuality are not enduring biological givens they have little history being a product of the recent past. Many of these radical modernists, as they might be termed, are following the work of the innovative

and controversial French philosopher Michel Foucault. In his uncompleted multivolumed work, *The History of Sexuality,* he argued rather paradoxically that sex had only a modern history in his introductory volume, and then in the two volumes completed before his death he discussed sex largely in the context of the ancient world.

Yet paradoxical and contrafactual as it may seem, the position of Foucault and his followers has some merit. Foucault was concerned that the modern definition of sexuality with its emphasis on sex as a form of fixed essence within an individual that defined and drove that individual was rooted in deterministic presuppositions tied to the 19th-century transformation of medicine, biology, and psychology from subjects of study to disciplines. According to those new disciplines one acted in certain ways because one *was* either male or female; either "homosexual," "heterosexual," or "bisexual." Literally, there was little room for decision in these areas—one largely was what one was, and to a great extent the new disciplines of the 19th century allowed no other options. That vision and the complex "discourse" (as Foucault termed it) on sexuality that developed around it, he argued, severely distorted any understanding of the history of the social and cultural constructs of pleasure and power that had developed around the body in earlier periods. Thus, to a great extent his rejection of a history of sexuality before the modern world (even as he was writing such a history) was aimed at finally destroying the essentialist position which he associated with the limiting structures of 19th-century thought.

Foucault was certainly correct to assert that if we persist in defining sex and sexuality by the terms of a 19th-century discourse we will have not a history of sex or sexuality but the vision of that century rewritten on the past. Yet this fundamental realization should not be pressed too far. Just as we write histories of ancient governments or medieval families realizing that neither those governments nor those families should be confused with modern ones, so too we can write histories of the social constructs of sex and sexuality realizing that 19th-century definitions need not apply—much as one might well assert they no longer apply today. The problem is to construct a definition of sex and sexuality that can serve as a unifying theme (like gender) without constructing a trap that will overly distort our understanding of the historical diversity of the past. Foucault, himself, made an attempt to do this by focusing his projected history of sexuality on what he labeled the "pleasures of the body," and others have followed his lead with impressive results. It may be, however, that this definition is at once too broad and too narrow. Too broad in that it seems it would include pleasures that in many societies might be seen as completely unrelated to sex such as eating, sleeping, playing sports, and so on. Certainly all these things might be associated with sexuality, but the point is that they often have been seen as unrelated and separate. One might well imagine how different our society would be if high school athletes were forbidden the pleasures of the body involved with sports because they were too young for sex or entrepreneurs were forbidden the pleasures of the body associated with a business lunch because such contacts were seen as too intimate! On the other hand, "pleasures of the body" might be seen as too narrow, for in most societies the emotions associated with sex and sexuality have been passionate but not necessarily pleasant nor necessarily concerned with the body alone.

It may be simply that at this stage research has not yet revealed clearly enough the parameters of what we will want to cover with the terms "sex" and "sexuality" to develop a good definition. Still, when such a definition is developed it will probably work out from something like a specific group of passions associated with the body and its erotic contact with other bodies (or avoidance thereof) in a specific society and culture. Two elements are key here. This complex of passions associated with the body, of course, cannot be seen as necessarily isolated within the body. Such passions will have ramifications or be perceived as having ramifications well beyond and thus will invariably involve larger constructs of behavioral norms, values, and ideals as well as more or less formal restrictions. In turn erotic contact with other bodies involves a social setting, and a great deal of the way in which such contact occurs will thus be a social construct. Obviously, in the end both the broader context of the passions involved and the social contact involved will intertwine to make sexual-

ity a very complex and significant construct in most societies. It may be, however, that we will also find that even such a definition in certain places at certain times will be too alien to apply, and thus occasionally we might well wish to sacrifice it for others more true to the times.

Beyond the problems of defining sex and sexuality in a way that will allow a meaningful history to be written about them, a second much discussed issue turns on the quality of the historical records available for the study of such subjects. The problem is not so much a lack of documentation as that the extensive and varied records that exist seem to be so biased. Often they seem to be concerned primarily with concealing, transforming, or idealizing material dealing with sexuality. This has led some to claim that a history of sex is impossible—that is, because the documentation is so biased, interpreting it in any meaningful way is impossible. Perhaps, however, this problem is more a product of the still early stage of research on the subject and not as daunting as it seems at first. We must remember that even apparently straightforward references to politics or war are virtually never as transparent as they might seem. In fact a good rule of thumb might be that anything that is worth recording so that it becomes a part of the historical record is worth distorting to make the historical record come out right. Whether speaking of sex or politics, the records of the past are usually attempting to tell what *should* be told and remembered. The hopeful thing about both sex and politics is that enough was written about each from a wide enough range of perspectives that some fairly precise histories can be written. The real problem for the history of sexuality is that, unlike the history of politics, where the broad parameters have long been set and the scholarly debate thus can concentrate on rethinking and refining, for the history of sexuality we have only recently begun to look carefully at the records.

Thus, the history of sexuality still looks quite radically different depending upon the type of sources used. And rather than a sign of weakness, it can be argued that this is largely a reflection of a field that is rapidly developing. Perhaps the most important types of sources used to date have been prescriptive literature (i.e., literature that describes or prescribes how people were ideally to behave), medical literature (i.e., literature that describes how the body was supposed to function), law (i.e., rules that theoretically governed how bodies interacted within a community), literature (i.e., the fictional representations of how people and bodies interacted), and finally regulatory and criminal documents (i.e., records that preserve accounts of how societies attempted to discipline sex). One result of using these types of documents seems to have been a focus on the disciplining and controlling of sexuality in the past. Sex seems almost to have been more a social danger than a pleasure. Certainly one should not underestimate the fact that it has been so continuously seen as a danger (even if the nature of its dangerousness has changed over time), but we also need to know more about the other side of the equation if we are to understand its impact in specific societies—how people viewed it and experienced it as a pleasure and what complex of passions were seen as being necessary to make that pleasure work.

The discipline and control of sex, however, has opened up a very fruitful rethinking of the nature of discipline and control in society—from the level of the internal discipline of values and conscience to the social controls of family, neighborhood, and community often expressed in terms of honor, to the controls of religion, morality, and shared values, and on out to the more traditionally recognized controls of laws and governments. Tellingly, from the perspective of sex and sexuality most of these disciplining forms look slightly different, and thus the perspective of the history of sex and sexuality is helping to add new dimensions to more traditional fields of historical study. Of course, adding new dimensions is not always appreciated, and that has added another level to the controversy about the value and validity of the study of sex and sexuality in historical terms of any kind whether it be political or social. But such debates it may be hoped will only increase the sophistication of such studies, and as new sources are considered and more subtle questions asked, significant new vistas on social history and history in general should be developed as a result of investigating the social history of sexuality.

Important histories of sexuality have been developed for western Europe, the Mediterranean world, the United States, and Russia. Traditional impressions that relied too heavily on the officially stated views of a dominant social class—most obviously, middle-class Victorianism in the 19th century—have been greatly modified, as social and gender divisions have been explored. The relationship of sexuality to other expressions and activities, the definitions of gender associated with sexuality, and the importance of sexuality in personal expression have all received considerable attention. Debates about changes in sexuality have focused not only on the 20th century but also on the early Christian period, on the Renaissance, and on the 18th century, where many scholars have discerned a major revolution in sexual behavior and expectations. Sexual deviance and violence are also receiving growing attention. (*See also* Homosexuality; Masculinity; Victorianism; Women's History)

Guido Ruggiero

REFERENCES

Brown, Peter. *The Body and Society. Men, Women, and Sexual Renunciation in Early Christianity.* New York: Columbia University Press, 1988.

D'Emilio, John, and Estelle Freedman. *Intimate Matters: A History of Sexuality in America.* New York: Harper & Row, 1989.

Laqueur, Thomas. *Making Sex. Body and Gender from the Greeks to Freud.* Cambridge, MA: Harvard University Press, 1990.

Muir, Edward, and Guido Ruggiero. *Sex and Gender in Historical Perspective. Selections from Quaderni Storici.* Baltimore: Johns Hopkins University Press, 1990.

Peiss, Kathy, and Christine Simmons, with Robert A. Padgug. *Passion and Power. Sexuality in History.* Philadelphia: Temple University Press, 1989.

Shamanism

Shamanism is a vast subject on which little satisfactory historical work has been done. This is because it involves oral and gestural behavior that the composers of written records rarely treat in detail or with sympathy. Moreover, the term is used inconsistently. Most loosely, "shamanistic" has been applied to any so-called primitive religion—for example, pre-Hellenic. Most restrictively, the term according to Mircea Eliade (1991), refers to a complex of beliefs and practices centered in Siberia since prehistoric times, including ecstatic trance, magical flight, communication with spiritual beings, and the use of such animal spirit familiars as bears. It is more satisfactory to follow anthropologists, who see shamanism as a form of spirit-mediumship: a culturally accepted state of voluntary dissociation in which the practitioner, usually understood to be possessed by a benevolent spirit, tries to manipulate unseen spirits and forces in order to heal patients and solve other community and individual problems. In this broader sense it has been witnessed in recent times in every continent (though not every country) outside Europe.

Evidence from both ends of Eurasia gives some support to an idea of Eliade's that poetry originated in (Siberian) shamanism. According to Glosecki (1989), Anglo-Saxon and Old Norse literature exhibits numerous shamanic "reflexes" from earlier Germanic tribal culture: such works as *Beowulf* are filled with evidence of shamanic initiation, ecstasy, and therapy, along with vestiges of animism and references to spirit helpers. Similarly, the earliest Chinese long poem, the *Songs of Ch'u*, shows shamanic influence in its poet-hero's voyage to distant cosmic realms and in passages evidently copied from shamanic utterances.

Perhaps because of the efforts of Christian missionaries, Europe, at least by the time of *Beowulf*, was markedly freer of shamans than East Asia—though Carlo Ginzburg (1991) has argued that a shaman tradition underlies magical beliefs in late medieval Europe. In East Asian religion, the shamanist substrate has continued to be close to the surface, and shamans have long worked out a *modus vivendi* with Taoism and Buddhism, and in Japan, with Shinto. Shaman practitioners have resisted Confucian attacks on their presumed immorality, greed, and deceptiveness for millennia, and today they are no less Confucianized than the rest of East Asia, and seem to have outlasted formal Confucianism. There are occasional reports of shaman practices in the People's Republic of China.

The richest historical evidence is not about shamanism but what scholars thought of it. Most Chinese accounts reveal nothing so clearly as their authors' Confucian dislike of the obviously backward peoples that practice shamanism, a dislike heartily shared by their Nationalist and Communist successors. The modern Russian case is similar. In the late 19th century Russian scholars viewed Siberian shamans as fakes and swindlers; and then after the turn of the century, more as hysterics and psychopaths. Under Stalin, Soviet scholars often combined both points of view. Only in recent decades has a new generation of scholars, some of them Siberian, examined the shamans in the light of social and psychological theory. They have, however, inherited the notion that shamans are virtually extinct remnants of society undergoing transformation by modern science and progress—a view that has now been confidently maintained for over a century.

Yet there is good evidence that shamans or spirit mediums, far from being throwbacks to a prehistoric past before priestly and scriptural power, do play a leading role in social and cultural change. Examples from Korea and Indonesia are suggestive. As Confucianism gradually spread through Korean society, there was a shift in gender roles, with shamanism becoming the province of women. Korean women had previously enjoyed a relatively superior position in East Asia, in terms of natal residence after marriage, rights of inheritance, and participation in ancestor worship. Confucianization limited but did not end their relative autonomy. Instead there was a bifurcation of ritual activities. As men increasingly monopolized dignified ancestral worship, women managed household rituals with the help of ecstatic shamans, who were and are generally female. Shamanism, writes Laurel Kendall, thus helped Korean women to retain their household status. Recent Wana history as described by Jane Atkinson (1989) offers another case of shaman adaptability. In the 19th century, the Wana ethnic group in what is now Indonesia was organized under regional chiefdoms, but this political system has given way to small, relatively egalitarian communities led by shamans. Open in the past to Islamic influence, the Wana have in the present century adopted the idea of a supreme being from Islamic or Christian sources, perhaps under the influence of the state. As in Korea, shamans have adapted so as better to serve the weak.

It is possible that social historians, freed of past prejudices and geographic limits, will find other cases in which shamans have a history and social meaning, and are neither inexplicably surviving prehistoric relics nor an inert substrate underlying dynamic formal religions. (*See also* Health; Magic; Popular Culture; Religion)

Donald S. Sutton

REFERENCES

Atkinson, Jane Monnig. *The Art and Politics of Wana Shamanship.* Berkeley: University of California Press, 1989.

Balzer, Marjorie Mandelstam, ed. *Shamanism: Soviet Studies of Traditional Religion in Central Asia.* Armonk, NY: Sharpe, 1990.

Eliade, Mircea. *Shamanism: Archaic Techniques of Ecstasy.* Princeton, NJ: Princeton University Press, 1964.

Ginzburg, Carlo. *Ecstasies: Deciphering the Witches' Sabbath.* New York: Pantheon, 1991 [1989].

Glosecki, Stephen O. *Shamanism and Old English Poetry.* New York: Garland, 1989.

Siblings

Siblings have not been extensively treated in sociohistorical research. We know far less about emotional and functional contacts among brothers and sisters in the past, particularly during childhood, than is desirable. Despite the salience of the theme (particularly in tensions between brothers) from the Old Testament's Cain and Abel onward and the attention paid in contemporary psychological research, the sociohistorical record remains sparse. The lack of sibling history confirms that the vast expansion of social history coverage does not preclude significant new targets.

Social historians may have neglected siblings from a belief that other family relationships, such as parent-child or spouse-spouse, take precedence, or they may have assumed that sibling interactions do not change substantially over time. Surely, however, changes in inheritance patterns produced shifts in sibling relationships before and during adulthood. So might changes in marriage customs that reduced the need to marry off the oldest daughter before younger sisters could seek a turn. Here is an essentially new topic awaiting sociohistorical exploration in various time periods and cultures.

One historical case has been partially probed. Part of the idealized family culture of the 19th-century American middle class stressed the importance of cooperative and affectionate relations among brothers and sisters. Biographical evidence suggests the kinds of tensions that could contradict the goals of harmony; sibling competitiveness among Henry, William, and Alice James provides a notorious example of psychological conflict. Nevertheless the assumption of sibling harmony, including shared recreations around the piano or on the lawn, had some real power. Sibling relations changed, however, around 1900. Smaller family size reduced sibling interaction in favor of direct relations between children and parents. Older siblings no longer took much care of younger ones, a major change for sisters especially. More individualistic strategies, such as housing siblings in separate rooms, limited interchange as well. In this context both child-rearing experts and middle-class parents began to worry intensely about sibling rivalry and the real dangers it posed both to children's physical safety and to adults' mental health. The tenor of family life was significantly altered by the expectation of tensions among siblings and the nuisance and expense of counterstrategies. Whether these same changes affected relationships among siblings as adults has yet to be determined. The significance of the change is, however, sufficiently well established to warrant additional historical study of the subject more generally. (*See also* Childhood; Family)

Peter N. Stearns

REFERENCES

Dunn, Judy, and Carl Kendrick. *Siblings: Love, Envy and Understanding.* Cambridge: Harvard University Press, 1982.

Stearns, Peter N. *Jealousy: The Evolution of an Emotion in American History.* New York: New York University Press, 1989.

Strouse, Jean. *Alice James. A Biography.* New York: Houghton Mifflin, 1984.

Singlehood

Singlehood refers to the states of not-yet-married, never married, divorced, or widowed. The majority of the world's population marries, but for those who do not, the reasons are complex and involve social and cultural factors as well as matters particular to individual or family circumstance.

The costs of supporting a family and the structure of the domestic economy shape marital choices. In societies where the household is the principal unit of economic production as well as consumption, the rate and age of marriage are tied to the vitality of the economy as a whole. Where not, the structure of economic opportunity shapes that of marriage. Single men and women must be attached to households or live independently. How society arranges this and what resources are available for household formation influence patterns of singlehood. Social opportunities available to spinsters and bachelors affect their numbers, as does the stigma (or lack thereof) attached to the unmarried state. Society's needs with regard to population have some influence.

The marriage market acts to encourage marriage or singlehood. The sex ratio of men to women in marriageable age groups may be high or low. The means of mate selection and cultural definitions of eligibility mediate between the absolute number of men and women in the population pool and the number of mated couples emerging from it. Historical and cross-cultural evidence suggests that when the authority for selecting marital partners rests with the family of origin, early and universal marriage results. A system of individual determination operates less efficiently because men and women must be old enough to make a mature choice, learn appropriate courtship rituals and skills, and undergo a trial-and-error process of mate selection. In addition to such cultural ideals as beauty, potential fertility, or character, eligibility includes nativity, ethnicity, class or caste, and religion, as some groups are endogamous, marrying only among themselves.

Changes in methods of mate selection and definitions of eligibility affected western Europe and the United States around the 18th century

or before. There developed a pattern of marriage characterized by high age at marriage (mid-twenties for men and early twenties for women) and a high rate of singlehood (in the range of 10–15 percent). This rate began to decline by the early 20th century, as people married more and earlier. By mid-century, the numbers remaining unmarried through life were significantly reduced (to below 5 percent in some areas). As of the early 1990s, the American pattern seems to be both high marriage rates and increasing singlehood of all kinds.

Social historians have studied rates of singlehood in different societies and changes in these rates over time. They have begun to study the economic conditions and cultural standing of single people, with due attention to gender, though much work remains to be done. (*See also* Marriage/Remarriage)

Lee Chambers-Schiller

REFERENCES

Chambers-Schiller, Lee. *Liberty, A Better Husband. Single Women in America, The Generations 1780–1840.* New Haven: Yale University Press, 1984.

Faderman, Lillian. *Odd Girls and Twilight Lovers: A History of Lesbian Life in 20th Century America.* New York: Columbia University Press, 1991.

Kitch, Sally L. *Chaste Liberation. Celibacy and Female Cultural Status.* Urbana: University of Illinois Press, 1989.

Uhlenberg, Peter R. "A Study of Cohort Life Cycles: Cohorts of Native Born Massachusetts Women, 1830–1920," *Population Studies* 23 (1969): 407–420.

Vicinus, Martha J. *Independent Women: Work and Community for Single Women, 1850–1920.* Chicago: University of Chicago Press, 1985.

Slavery

The history of slaves, particularly in the American South, formed one of the central early interests of social historians in the United States, as they explored slave conditions and outlook, relations between masters and slaves, and slave protest both individual and collective. The social history of slavery has progressively broadened to include important comparative dimensions, attention to the social dimensions of the end of slavery, and additional features of the slave experience itself. Overall, the history of slavery, even as it expands, constitutes one of the best developed areas in social history, contributing methods and insights to many other branches of history and to other disciplines as well.

From the perspective of world history slavery proves striking neither by its peculiarity in the sense of being uncommon nor by its victimization of a single cultural or phenotypical group. It has existed from time immemorial and, at one time or another, on every continent. It can be found in hunting and nomadic societies as well as in sedentary ones. In some cases slavery underpinned civilizations and was associated with human progress; in others, it survived at or near the margin of society, one form of labor coercion among many. All great civilizations of antiquity in Europe, Asia, pre-European Africa, and pre-Columbian America embraced slavery. Christianity, Judaism, Islam, and other of the world's principal religions have sanctioned it. It remained legal in the Western Hemisphere until 1888 and in several Persian Gulf states for more than a decade after World War II. It continues today despite the prohibition of national and international bodies in regional backwaters and as part of the underground world market.

As a social status, slavery bears marked similarity to other forms of human dependence. It implies the violent domination of one human being by another. Slaves have lost control of their productive and reproductive capacities. The ideal slave becomes a mere extension of the master's will. The Western tradition, heavily influenced by Roman law, has emphasized the property element in slavery. But ownership of human beings by itself proves insufficient to distinguish slavery from other types of human relations such as serfdom, helotage, and even marriage in which extreme proprietorial claims on persons are made. Unlike other statuses, slavery embodies the contradiction of a dead being, someone who has been forcibly disembedded from society and therefore exists deracinated, stripped of any claim to society's protections, in a highly personalized and individuated relation to an all powerful other. Because slaves lack the social belonging of kinship ties or citizenship do they characteristically fall victim to dehumanization and ritualized degradation. Justification for the large-scale enslave-

ment of outsiders has always rested on difference, whether of religion, ethnicity, color, or race. Pejorative stereotypes like the Sambo can be found in virtually every slave society. Slaves bear the stigma of outsiders, even when procured from within society by means of punishment, self-enslavement, kidnapping, abandonment, or birth. Most slaves, however, have been procured in war; the act of enslavement substitutes for death.

A distinction should be drawn between slave societies and societies that merely have slaves. The former imply the crucial role of the master-slave relation in the organization and maintenance of the larger society. A slave society need not require that slaves do most or all of the work nor that they comprise a majority of the total population or nearly so. Marxist scholarship has tended to view slavery as one of many species of dependent labor in which the means of labor control is nonmarket or extra-economic. Accordingly, a slave society is defined by a specific set of productive relations in which a ruling class maintains itself largely by the extraction of a surplus product from slave labor. By this definition classical Greece, classical Rome, and most of the slaveholding plantation economies of the Americas qualify as slave societies, although in the cases of classical Greece and probably classical Rome, the antebellum southern United States, and colonial Cuba slaves failed to reach a majority of the total population. Most slaves in human history, however, have done more to consume an economic surplus than to produce it. Emphasis on the economic aspect of slavery in imperial Rome and in the Americas has obscured the broad range of key roles played by slaves in other societies at other times. Precisely because slaves are considered to exist suspended, outside of society, have they often provided masters with a human instrument of greater flexibility and value than other dependents for whom society offers protection and competing claims. And even a small minority of slaves in a society can determine its politics or value system by how they confer power, status, and honor on elites. Throughout history slaves have labored in fields, mines, galleys, and brothels but have also represented their masters in positions of influence and authority. For example, palace slave eunuchs contributed to the fall of the Han Dynasty in China.

Kings of the Mali empire in West Africa used royal slaves to serve as local governors. Slave armies spearheaded the advance of Islam. The Ottomans enslaved Christian boys to raise the formidable Janissary infantry. Enslaved Christians formed a large part of the Mameluke warrior elite in Egypt, which overthrew the Ayyubid dynasty in the mid-13th century. Powerful absentee landlords in Muscovite Russia often turned over their vast estates to slave administrators. Even American slave societies produced elite slaves, including agricultural foremen who directed operations on the most sophisticated plantations.

Although slavery receded in rural Europe after the fall of the Roman Empire, it continued strong during the Middle Ages in many urban areas and in the lands of the Mediterranean basin. On Mediterranean islands slaves of various colors and cultures worked together on large agricultural estates that served as the prototype for slave plantations in the Americas. By the time of Columbus, the majority of the world's slaves still lived outside of Africa. The word "slave" itself (Latin, *sclavus*) derives from the identification in Europe as early as the 9th century AD of the condition with the mass enslavement of the central and eastern European Slavic peoples. Islamic expansion during the Middle Ages reduced increasing numbers of Slavs, other Europeans, and east and west Africans to enslavement. In fact, Muslims originated the long-distance trade in west African slaves. From the 7th century to the 12th century, millions of African slaves crossed Saharan routes to satisfy Muslim demand. Females outnumbered males; household employment seems to have prevailed. The transatlantic slave trade, probably the largest forced migration in world history, rose within the context of western European colonization of the Americas, the attendant elaboration of a global market, and capitalist development. Slavery emerged as the central labor form in Brazil and the circum-Caribbean region, where it became primarily associated with large-scale commercialized agriculture and with Africans or persons of African descent. The susceptibility of the indigenous peoples of the Americas to waves of European and African epidemic diseases precipitated a crisis of labor supply that was ultimately resolved by the trans-

atlantic slave trade. The extreme force permitted masters to impose gang labor contributed to the widespread and profitable use of African slaves on plantations. Europe's seemingly insatiable appetite for sugar, more than for any other crop, fueled the growth of the plantation system; sugar, more than any other crop, fueled the demand for African slaves.

During the entire history of the transatlantic trade, from the time of Columbus to the mid-19th century, about 10 million, mostly male, African slaves from various cultural and linguistic groups entered the Americas. The Portuguese, who had cut into Islamic sources of west African slaves as a result of their maritime explorations of the 15th century, delivered more slaves to the Americas than any other nationality. The Portuguese colony of Brazil received more slaves than any other country, about 40 percent of the total. Not until about the mid-19th century did the number of European migrants to the Americas surpass the number of imported Africans. The extent of African slave influence on the evolution of American cultures remains an underexplored subject. Clearly, the strength and character of these influences had much to do with a country's participation in the Atlantic slave trade. A minor participant like the United States and the colonies that became the United States, which received less than 7 percent of the total, had weaker links with Africa than did Brazil. Still, in varying intensities, every American slave society showed continuities with an African past in its art, crafts, language, cooking, housing, music, and religious practices. Large numbers of slaves acquired from a specific African region over a period of time could impart a strong ethnic flavor to specific slave societies. Massive slave imports from the Bight of Benin in the 19th century explains the pronounced Yoruban influence in Cuba. The strength of Akan culture in Jamaica derived from a sizable 18th-century trade with the Gold Coast.

Slave treatment defies easy generalization. It varied widely over time according to a complex of cultural, economic, political, environmental, and biological factors. By definition slaves lived exposed and vulnerable to their masters. But such an intimate relation could also breed mutual trust and affection. In any individual case slave treatment could swing wildly between benign paternalism and capricious brutalization. Sexual exploitation of female slaves occurred in every slave society. Laws designed to protect slaves from gross abuse rarely resembled practice. In some slave societies, masters could kill their slaves with impunity. Masters in societies where domestic or household slavery prevailed often had greater power over their slaves than did masters in the plantation societies of the Americas. In the case of precolonial Africa, famines, endemic diseases, warfare, castrations, and ritual sacrifices took a heavy toll in slave lives. Frontier areas and urban environments tended to provide slaves with greater freedom of movement. Most slave societies had slaves who hired themselves out and lived almost free by remitting regular payments to their masters. Every slave society qualified the power of masters over their slaves. Community or peer pressure seems to have restrained masters more effectively than laws. Manumission offered slaves a life after social death. Every slave society practiced it, some far more than others. Masters recognized how powerful an incentive the prospect of freedom could be. They used manumission to reward meritorious service, to relieve themselves of economic burdens, to liberate lovers and offspring, and to fulfill political or religious obligations. After manumission freed people usually remained in a clientage relationship with their former masters. Classical Greece and Rome developed liberal policies of manumission. The Roman *peculium*, which had variants in most slave societies, promoted slave self-purchase by allowing slaves conditional use of property for their own benefit. Islamic law explicitly encouraged manumission and, like Roman law, presumed freedom to be man's natural state. Spanish law may have drawn on Roman and Islamic antecedents in authorizing the institution of *coartación*. It allowed a slave to have his value fixed by a third party so that he could purchase his freedom in installments. Once a slave was *coartado*, his master's dominion was supposedly limited in direct proportion to the amounts paid. To judge by the experience of Spanish American slavery, urban, domestic slaves might avail themselves of this legal opportunity, but illiterate and isolated plantation slaves could rarely do so. Frequency of manumission

fails to correlate directly with such other measures of treatment as the material conditions of life (e.g., housing, clothing, diet) or the presence of a stable slave family. The antebellum southern United States had one of the lowest manumission rates in the history of slavery, yet its slave population reproduced itself naturally at an unprecedented rate. Slaveholders responded to the legal end of the external slave trade in 1808 by improving slave material well-being. The slave population became overwhelmingly Creole or native-born with relatively balanced sex ratios. Two-parent nuclear slave families appear to have been the norm, slave separations notwithstanding. By contrast Latin American slave societies had higher manumission rates and acquired a reputation for mildness. Yet with the intensification of labor under the plantation system, their slave populations suffered high rates of natural decrease. Continued operation of the Atlantic slave trade meant higher proportions of African-born slaves and a disproportionate number of male slaves. Recent quantitative studies have demonstrated a strong link between slave mortality and sugar production. The traumas of forced migration, plantation regimentation, imbalanced sex ratios, disease and poor diet, and deliberate sexual abstinence all combined to restrict slave reproduction and, by extension, the slave family.

Slave behavior, individually and collectively, wherever slavery existed, ranged a spectrum from docility to rebelliousness. Nowhere did slaves fully internalize their degraded status or meekly submit to their master's will. In reality, conflict and mutual dependence characterized the master-slave relation. What masters bestowed as privilege, slaves claimed as customary right. What masters called stealing, slaves called taking. In struggles over everything from naming practices to the *peculium* slaves countered dehumanization and attempted to redeem themselves from social death. They married, established lineages, and built communities, albeit precariously. Even slave eunuchs created fictive kin. Day-to-day resistance could take the form of sabotage, arson, theft, shirking, poisoning, destruction of stock and tools, feigned sickness, assassination, suicide, and self-mutilation. Flight was commonplace. Short-term absenteeism reached epidemic proportions in many slave societies, despite savage punishment. Some runaway slaves found freedom in urban ghettos; others, in the most forbidding stretches of wilderness. Communities of runaway slaves or maroons developed in ancient and modern slave societies. They grew so powerful in central Jamaica in the late 18th century and eastern Cuba in the early 19th century that colonial authorities were forced to contract peace treaties with them. In the United States maroon bands operated out of swamps and other hostile locations from Virginia to Florida to Louisiana. Palmares, the largest maroon community in the history of the Americas, formed in northeastern Brazil in the 17th century. Before its destruction in 1695, it had many thousands of members and challenged Portuguese hegemony in the region. For most of their history, however, maroons possessed neither the overall unity nor the inclination to end slavery per se, however much they struggled against their own enslavement. Individual slaves, for example, might escape their bondage to enter a maroon community that sanctioned forms of dependency including slavery. In the Americas maroon communities largely aspired to restore a traditional and hierarchical African or modified-African society in a new setting. Maroons did not always have good relations with plantation slaves and could act in concert with whites as agents of repression.

The imposing forces arrayed against slaves failed to prevent collective slave violence, although massive slave rebellion that comprised a thousand or more slaves proves rare throughout history. Ancient Greece appears to have had no such rebellions. Republican Rome faced three: the first Sicilian slave war (137?–132 BC), the second Sicilian slave war (104–100 BC), and the famous Spartacus revolt (73–71 BC). The great revolt of the Zanj (slaves of East African origin) in AD 869 involved thousands of slaves engaged in agricultural reclamation of the salt flats of Basra in southern Iraq and took the Abassid caliphate more than a decade to suppress. The only successful slave revolution in world history erupted in 1791 in the French plantation colony of Saint Domingue and led to the creation of Haiti, the second independent nation in the Americas. Conditions that favored collective slave resistance include master absenteeism, sharp reversals in working conditions, high concentrations of slaves, real or perceived weakening in the forces of control, divisions within the ruling class or between elite social groups, favorable terrain for establishing lines of communication and conducting subversive activity, and sufficient space within society for the creation of a viable slave leadership. Few instances of collective slave violence lacked privileged slaves in leadership roles. Hence, accommodation does not necessarily preclude collective resistance but rather can be a prerequisite to it. A slave driver headed the largest slave revolt in U.S. history, which numbered at least several hundreds of slaves and broke out in the sugar region of territorial Louisiana in 1811. Slave artisans figured prominently in Gabriel's conspiracy of 1800 in Richmond, Virginia. Three of the largest slave revolts in the history of the British Caribbean, in Barbados (1816), in Demerara (1823), and in Jamaica (1831), all had elite slave leaders. Numerous slave revolts in the Americas consisted of African slaves of a common ethnicity or religion. Akan slaves rose repeatedly in 18th-century Jamaica. The Stono rebellion of 1739 in South Carolina, the largest slave revolt in colonial North America, appears to have been comprised of Catholic Congos. In 1835 Hausa and Yoruban Muslim slaves came together in one of the most serious revolts in Brazilian history. To encourage division, slaveholders purposely acquired ethnic mixes of slaves. Ethnic tensions surfaced in the Islamic world between European and African slaves. In ancient Rome rivalry between slaves of Germanic origin and Spartacus, a Thracian, appears to have weakened his rebellion. The composition of many of the larger slave uprisings warns against the imposition of ideological uniformity on the insurgents.

In the Americas, some rebellions and conspiracies developed sophisticated chains of command as arrangements were made and deals were struck between slaves rural and urban, mulatto and black, African and Creole, privileged and unprivileged. The specific reasons for collective slave resistance could differ markedly from one rebel group to another, or from the leadership to the soldiery. Analysis of variance within movements helps to account for so many tragic failures. In every slave society rebel slaves formed ties with other oppressed groups. In the Americas disaffected whites occasionally contributed to collective slave resistance. In most of the larger movements free people of color figure conspicuously.

Not until the second half of the 18th century in Britain did an organized movement to abolish the institution of slavery arise. It would lead to the abolition of the slave trade to Britain's colonies in 1807, to a program of gradual emancipation in 1833, and eventually to a global antislavery crusade. Slavery was abolished everywhere in the Americas in about a hundred years, ending finally by legislation in Brazil in 1888. Recent scholarship on this complex process has tended to eschew any explanation that would focus narrowly on either humanitarian ideals or economics and to argue instead for a complex of cultural, economic, and political factors. Economics in a strict accounting sense had little to do with the transition from slave to free labor anywhere in the Americas. In every case, it appears, plantation slavery continued to be profitable at the moment of abolition. In Britain a fortuitous conjunction of the egalitarian elements of evangelical Protestantism and the economics of the Manchester School generated a powerful ideological thrust against slavery by identifying it with sin, evil, moral turpitude, and economic backwardness. There it became a popular social movement that both shaped and drew strength from the forces that were redefining the relationship between capital and labor during the industrial revolution. But the antislavery movement also unfolded on a broad, ever-shifting terrain of political and ideological contention that involved the beliefs and initiatives of many social groups, free and slave, on both sides of the Atlantic. In this respect the slave revolution in Saint Domingue can be seen as a turning point in the history of slavery in that it marked an integration of American slave revolts into the revolutionary politics and ideology of Europe. Much particularist resistance to enslavement mobilized Saint Domingue's oppressed masses, but the revolutionary process also manifested an ecumenical crusade against the system of slavery itself and thereby bore witness to the revolutionary politics and ideology of the wider world.

Saint Domingue's rebel leaders certainly asserted the rights of their people by looking well beyond the referent of their own insular community. The triumph of the slaves and their creation of a black nation in what had been the world's most valuable slave colony raised a standard by which subsequent collective slave resistance, wherever it occurred in the Americas, would be reckoned. Slaves everywhere now had evidence that they could win a confrontation with their supposedly invulnerable masters; masters everywhere now had evidence that collective slave resistance, no matter how small in its beginnings, could turn their world upside down. The birth of a radical new ideology in Europe that radiated outward to groups across the Atlantic decisively conditioned the discrete struggles that brought about emancipation. But the initiatives of the slaves themselves also form a vital part of the story. Whatever the explanation, the ending of a status that had been ubiquitous in history and continued to be profitable ranks as one of the most remarkable and dramatic shifts in moral sensibility in the making of the modern world. (*See also* Emancipation; Protest)

Robert L. Paquette

REFERENCES

Davis, David Brion. *The Problem of Slavery in Western Culture.* Ithaca, NY: Cornell University Press, 1966.

Davis, David Brion. *Slavery and Human Progress.* New York: Oxford University Press, 1984.

Genovese, Eugene. *Roll, Jordan, Roll: The World the Slaves Made.* New York: Pantheon Books, 1974.

Patterson, Orlando. *Slavery and Social Death: A Comparative Study.* Cambridge: Harvard University Press, 1982.

Phillips, William, Jr. *Slavery from Roman Times to the Early Transatlantic Trade.* Minneapolis: University of Minnesota Press, 1985.

Social Class

See Class

Social Control

The question of how well past societies treated those whom they deemed dangerous or unfit has become a legitimate historical one only since the emergence of social history in the last 25 years. The histories of persons considered deviant—including those convicted of crimes, the insane, the poor, orphans, and wayward children—have been the subject of interest since revisionist historians began discarding the older Whig interpretations of institutions and professions designed to confine, control, or educate potentially troublesome groups. The previous Whig, or "progressive," view, that the dominant medical, philanthropic, and legal institutions were guided by benevolent reform impulses, was almost wholly discarded for the view that the rise of public and private institutions to confine deviant and oppressed populations was the result of prevailing cultural attitudes of aversion and fear. Some of these historians further argued that a pragmatic need to control persons who were seen as interfering with the rational and orderly workings of economic and political systems was the basis for their confinement in institutional settings. Efforts to reform the insane, the poor, and the prisoners, along with efforts to educate the children of immigrant families, were viewed as tantamount to efforts to control them by these revisionist historians. The term "social control" implies a stern, if not malevolent, attitude toward persons considered dangerous or unfit by society; the belief in the reality of this punitive attitude has informed the histories associated with the social control hypothesis.

The first and still foremost exponent of the social control hypothesis was Michel Foucault, whose influence has spread far beyond his readership over the last 25 years. In *Madness and Civilization* (1988) Foucault argued that confinement of the insane in western Europe beginning in the 17th century grew out of a need to control nonproductive members of the growing market economy. The insane came to symbolize this nonproductivity, inheriting the stigmatized role of the lepers in European society. Foucault discarded earlier more positive versions of the rise of science and reform, and in so doing he created a new paradigm out of which social historians would fashion related versions of the history of asylums, psychiatry, almshouses, prisons, and other institutional solutions to human problems. In the United States the earliest, and perhaps most influential, exponent of the social

control thesis was David Rothman, whose *Discovery of the Asylum* (1971) offered a penetrating analysis of the asylum-building movement in the Jacksonian period. According to Rothman, the American asylum, which by the end of the 19th century housed the poor, orphans, and the insane, represents society's attempt to impose order and stability on deviant populations in order to compensate for the wildly changing Jacksonian social order.

Rothman's work gave historical vividness to Foucault's argument that asylums were created to serve the needs of those outside their walls. Together their works sparked new interest in the history of institutional responses to the insane and the poor. In this context, the asylum became an object of great interest for social historians. Asylum histories include Anne Digby's *Madness, Morality and Medicine, A Study of the York Retreat, 1796–1914*, which examined the York Retreat in England in the 19th century. In *A Generous Confidence: Thomas Story Kirkbride and the Art of Asylum Building, 1840–1883*, Nancy Tomes offered a study of the Pennsylvania Hospital for the insane in the 19th century. In *Homes for the Mad: Life Inside Two 19th Century Asylums*, Ellen Dwyer looked at two public asylums in New York State in the 19th century. All these works shared a common interest in presenting a complex picture of asylums as places where reform intentions served the wider needs for institutional control of troublesome populations.

The period before the asylum has been the subject of far less historical argument than the asylum-building period, both because primary research about persons who were deviant, but not confined, is more difficult to undertake than is research about confined populations, and also because evidence of social control is not immediately presented by persons free to go at large in their communities. One of the few historians to look at madness in the period before the asylum was Michael MacDonald, whose *Mystical Bedlam* is a descriptive account of one man's practice with the insane in an English village in the 17th century. MacDonald showed how a combination of magic, astrology, and folk medicine provided an effective worldview out of which madness was understood and treated. He argued that the replacement of this early cosmological view with a secular, medical one ultimately led to confinement of the insane in madhouses in England at the end of the 18th century. MacDonald's research did support an important theme offered by the social control revisionists: the systematization and rationalization of the treatment of the insane was not necessarily beneficial for the insane themselves. In American history, Mary Ann Jimenez, in *Changing Faces of Madness: Early American Attitudes and Treatment of the Insane* (1987), examined the treatment of the insane in England in the 18th and early 19th centuries. She found a similar tolerance for nonviolent insane behavior that MacDonald found in England in the 17th century, along with a complex mixture of supernatural, magical, and homeopathic remedies for insanity that colonists fashioned to diffuse the threat of madness.

Michael Katz has looked at two cultural institutions through a social control lens: public education and public welfare. In *The Irony of Early School Reform: Educational Innovation in mid 19th Century Massachusetts* (1968), Katz looked at the rise of public education in Massachusetts in the middle of the 19th century and argued that public commitment to schooling grew out of the need to discipline and assimilate children of immigrant families in order to prepare them for their role in an increasingly complex and demanding labor force. Katz similarly argued in *In the Shadow of the Poorhouse: A Social History of Welfare in America* that public welfare grew out of a need to make poverty a moral lesson as well as to provide structures of control—from the 19th century almshouse to 20th-century cash relief programs—that would effectively regulate the labor market and preserve social order.

Another subject of interest to social historians interested in themes of social control has been the history of prisons. Foucault again established a new direction for this history in *Discipline and Punishment* (1977), when he argued that the modern prison system offers a far more thorough and systematic punishment than the public spectacles of torture and execution it replaced at the beginning of the 19th century. In spite of the more benevolent look on the modern face of punishment, the abuse of power cen-

tral to the operation of the penitentiary system in the 20th century condemns the prisoner to recidivism, Foucault argued. The criminal justice system also has been the focus of historians looking at gender bias in legal system and judicial proceedings. Lyle Koehler in *A Search for Power: The Weaker Sex in Colonial Massachusetts* argued that the system of justice in colonial America served as a mean of controlling women; whereas N.E.H. Hull in *Female Felons: Women and Serious Crime in Colonial America* argued that it did not constitute a system particularly oppressive to women, but rather a system of social control effective for both sexes. David Rothman continued his saga of institutions in America with *Conscience and Convenience: The Asylum and Its Alternatives in Progressive America,* in which he offered a fresh analysis of Progressive institutional reforms, including penitentiaries, the juvenile justice system, and mental hospitals. Rothman argued that the zeal of Progressive reformers obscured the oppressive nature of the institutions they created, which functioned systematically as effective instruments of social control.

Finally, the history of substance use and abuse has been told from the perspective of social control. David Musto in *The American Disease: Origins of Narcotic Control* (1987) argued that efforts to regulate drug use in the Progressive era were a direct result of racist and nativist sentiments which linked drug use with ethnic and racial minorities and sought to control these groups through drug legislation. Similarly, W.J. Rorabaugh argued in *The Alcoholic Republic* that legal efforts to regulate alcohol consumption grew out of an effort to control immigrant populations by controlling their drinking habits.

The social control hypothesis is based on an assumption that the movement to confine or regulate the behavior of persons considered deviant by the larger society does not have the well-being of such persons as a dominant motive. Historians writing on these issues borrow from sociological theory to demonstrate how broader concerns for order and repression of deviant groups covertly inform and eventually overwhelm reform efforts to provide organized, institutional solutions for social problems. While the history of mental institutions may have been thoroughly mined, the history of other institutions, such as prisons, both adult and juvenile, has been largely unexplored. The history of legal restrictions of personal behavior, including sexuality, is another area ripe for the emergence of the social control hypothesis.

Social control theory has also been applied to the history of leisure, with work on efforts to reform and restrict popular leisure in the 19th century a primary focus.

Social control theory deals not only with the direct objects of reform—the criminals, the insane, and so on—in arguing that institutions reputedly designed to help them are often constructed to restrict them in new and subtle ways. The same theory argues that social control is also directed at the "normal" majority, in trying to define criteria for deviance that will keep the majority in line and methods of emendation that will, by the stigmas attached, help motivate discipline.

Social control theory is widely accepted as an approach in social history, but it has also encountered criticism and is seldom presented quite as starkly as during its initial formulations in the 1970s. Critics of social control argue that some extreme versions of social control inaccurately neglect real, objective problems, implying that all insanity, for example, is simply a social construct designed to discipline. They note that many lower-class people actively collaborated with some of the social control reforms, seeking asylums for certain family members, for instance; social control is thus not simply an imposition from the top down. They deal with varieties of policy and results among social control institutions; not all asylums in the 19th century were alike. Finally, they note that social control is hardly a modern invention, even though its forms have changed with the decline of community and religious supervision and the growth of the state. Social control theory survives in driving home the more nuanced view of reform efforts and institutions and in pointing out some characteristic changes in social control methods during the past two to three centuries. (*See also* Asylums; Education; Punishment and Prisons)

Mary Ann Jimenez

REFERENCES

Foucault, Michel. *Discipline and Punish: The Birth of the Prison.* Translated by Alan Sheridan. New York: Pantheon Books, 1977.

Jimenez, Mary Ann. *Changing Faces of Madness: Early American Attitudes and Treatment of the Insane.* Hanover, NH: University of New England Press, 1987.

Katz, Michael B. *The Irony of Early School Reform: Educational Innovation in mid 19th Century Massachusetts.* Cambridge: Harvard University Press, 1968.

Musto, David. *The American Disease: Origins of Narcotic Control.* New York: Oxford University Press, 1987.

Rothman, David. *The Discovery of the Asylum: Social Order and Disorder in the New Republic.* Boston: Little, Brown, 1971.

Social History

Social history has become a leading branch of historical research and teaching, in the United States and internationally, over the past 30 years. Part of social history's surge has involved wider-ranging definitions of the field—for social history itself has a pedigree that stretches well beyond its recent success. This is one reason that references to social history in the 1970s and 1980s often included the label "new"—to distinguish it from older, more prosaic versions that were sometimes derided as "pots and pans" history. Definitions of the new social history are not always as precise as might be desired, for the field is more a collection of topics and analytical styles than the result of single methodologies. Nevertheless, most social historians share some sense of their common scholarly mission and of how their work differs from other kinds of history. This same sense has attracted various criticisms from more traditional practitioners, to which social historians have responded in recent years, in the process amplifying their own statements of purpose.

A good bit of the history written before the middle of the 19th century included what would now be considered social history components. The ancient Greek historian Herodotus included many comments on popular customs and rituals, along with accounts of wars and politics; the same was true of the great Islamic historian Ibn

Kahldun, writing in the 14th century. These historians, and later European historians like Voltaire and Edward Gibbon, made no hard and fast distinctions between political events and other social developments. This broad tradition continued in some major 19th-century work, such as the study of the Renaissance by the Swiss historian Jakob Burckhardt; this work, though not heavily focused on the lower classes, included considerations of popular protest and certainly a range of behaviors, including personal manners and popular beliefs, besides politics. By current social history standards Burckhardt's classic treatment of the Renaissance is biased toward the elites and unduly taken with the historical role of individuals, but it unquestionably includes much relevant material and many fascinating insights about connections among various social institutions and attitudes.

The dominant emphasis of European and United States history writing in the 19th century turned, however, to a fascination with politics as the focal point of the past, and to descriptions of political developments—election campaigns, changes in monarchs, and diplomatic alliances—as the principal means of presenting this same past. The actions of individuals and elites, within a fairly restricted field of behavior, dominated the discipline, and the informal but not inconsiderable social history features of earlier historical writing withered. History's teaching agenda, relatedly, became strongly nationalist, and much of the past was squeezed into heroic lessons about each nation's origins, progress, and triumphs.

In this framework, in turn, a minor strand of social history emerged anew, by about 1900 in the United States. Various books were published dealing with the history of the American family and with childhood in the past, which reflected some dissatisfaction with the narrow vision of American history dominant in academic research and in school and college courses. Between 1927 and 1930, this interest in social history topics gained solid academic backing with the publication of the 12-volume *History of American Life* series, edited by Arthur M. Schlesinger and Dixon Ryan Fox. Books in this series included much familiar political narrative, but they also paid consistent attention to women and to city life, and devoted some space to African Americans, families, and other topics beyond the conventional historical fare. No explicit definition of social history was ventured, however, and this interest trailed off somewhat amid the political excitements of the next three decades.

Much of the work in this intermediate period of social history, from 1900 to the 1960s, fell into essentially an antiquarian mode. Titles such as the *Curious Punishments of Bygone Days* correctly evinced an interest in exploring certain topics simply to show the weirdness of ancestral ways; other books evoked more admiring nostalgia. In neither case was there any overriding analytical purpose. Even Schlesinger's *American Life* series, in its social history chapters, typically listed behavior patterns, neither relating them to the larger treatment of politics nor finding any compelling integrative themes. One chapter in a book on the 1865–1878 period thus listed home interiors and domestic art, dress styles, dietary innovations including the introduction of oatmeal, the surge of outdoor sports, and Barnum's 1871 circus—all summarized, in a brief concluding epitaph, as illustrating American fondness for "showy results." Social history in this reading became a catalogue of data on the "way they lived." An English scholar, G.M. Trevelyan, captured some of the same spirit by describing social history as "history with the politics left out"—a collection of topics, in other words, that might be interesting but whose purpose was not entirely clear during decades when the real moving spirit of the past was assumed to be political action. Small wonder that social history of this sort maintained a distinctly subordinate place in the discipline as a whole. As late as 1968 an article on social history in the *International Encyclopedia of the Social Sciences* could note the lack of vigor surrounding social history in the United States, in contrast to major strides in Europe and particularly in France.

By 1970, however, it was possible to identify the distinctive features of traditional social history, including its penchant for vignettes and scattered data, and to contrast those to the newer genre now taking shape in the United States. In 1942 Carl and Jessica Bridenbaugh offered a series of impressions of conditions in Philadelphia in the past; their menu included a few statistics, considerable description of building aesthetics, and praise for the energy of the merchant elite. Several decades later Sam Bass Warner, a new social history urbanist, probed the same city: his purpose was to convey what it meant for people to live there; his data included elaborate statistics; and his analytical structure included recurrent efforts to fit Philadelphia into a larger urban typology. The new social history, clearly, claimed a sense of purpose and structure that the older "pots and pans" version had lacked, even while dealing with some of the same topics.

Prepared by some 1950s work on immigrant history and to some new questions about lower-class participation in American political culture, the social history surge in the United States emerged clearly in the 1960s. Harvard University established a PhD field in social and economic history by 1961. Several new colonial historians, including John Demos, Kenneth Lockridge and Philip J. Greven, Jr., produced vital studies of colonial family and community relationships, sometimes linked to political developments in the same period but always treated as significant primarily in their own right. Research by Herbert Gutman on the American working class, by Eugene D. Genovese on southern slavery, and by Stephan Thernstrom on social mobility patterns defined the range of the field still further. *The Journal of Social History* and *Historical Methods Newsletter* both began in 1967, serving as clear heralds of the new field. Finally, American researchers such as Charles Tilly, sometimes borrowing heavily from sociology, began to contribute to social history analysis outside the United States, dealing with lower-class protest, peasant conditions, and soon, with popular rituals as well.

Three basic forces prompted this surge of social history in the United States. The first was a belated acquaintance with European historiography, and particularly with the strides in French sociohistorical work since the 1920s under the banners of the *Annales* school. French social historians had long been probing peasant conditions, popular material culture, and a variety of other topics, with particular attention to the medieval and early modern periods. Their work also spilled over into studies of other areas, such

as Italy and Latin America. Americans working not only on France but also in area studies programs dealing with Asia, Latin America, or Africa increasingly encountered and assimilated elements of the French approach. Work by Eric Hobsbawm and E.P. Thompson on the British working class, appearing in the 1960s, also provided direct inspiration. European work of this sort not only provided examples of sources, methods, and topics, but also offered ample evidence that sociohistorical work was intrinsically important. Thompson, for example, wrote of his desire to rescue the history of lower-class groups from "the enormous condescension of posterity," and many practitioners elsewhere heartily agreed.

The second source for the rise of social history, already operating in Europe and affecting a crucial generation of American historians during the 1960s and 1970s, followed from political ferment. The rise of the civil rights movement, followed by the revival of feminism and the emergence of gay rights crusades, inevitably inspired interest in the historical patterns of these same groups. History could lend dignity to the political cause, by showing that groups besides the white male elite had contributed to the past and by showing past examples of suffering and effective struggle alike. This political impulse, though sometimes diffuse, led many American social histories to define their specialty as "history from the bottom up," devoted to providing a full and usually friendly record for the activities of a host of lower-class and minority groups in the past. Some of the principal contributions of social history, by the same token, continue to involve attention to African Americans, immigrants, women, sexual preference groups, the elderly—a host of crosscutting population segments somewhat removed from society's governing elites.

"Bottom-up" social history entailed not only a redefinition of major historical topics, it also called for reassessments of historical causation—toward consideration of the role of various population segments, and not just formal leadership; and it forced imaginative quests for new kinds of historical sources that would reveal the lives and thinking of these same segments. One of the central and enduring impulses of the new social history involves the insistence on the active agency for the groups under examination; the past is no longer a pattern of leadership (benign or exploitative) shaping a passive population mass. On virtually any topic, from formal politics to the working of insane asylums or slave plantations, interaction becomes the key, as the presumably powerless play a definite historical role.

The third source for the rise of social history resulted from growing interdisciplinary connection between many younger historians, sociologists, and other social scientists. This connection enhanced historians' concerns for expanding the topics open to historical inquiry, so that their subject material would compare more systematically with that of sociology; it brought concern for innovative methodologies, particularly in the quantitative area; and it generated attention to some common theoretical problems and models in dealing with social patterns and with social change.

The interdisciplinary impulse toward expanding historical topics added facets of social behavior to the "bottom-up" interest in a wide range of social groups. Here was a key source of the rapid development of family research—quickly a staple in American social history—and the flowering of social mobility studies. Additional topical interests came later, continuing the sociology-history interchange. Social histories of old age, for example, related to work in gerontology, while the history of emotions reflected the concomitant revival of emotions sociology.

Methodologically, interdisciplinarity initially involved quantification applied to family structure research, mobility studies, crime, and of course demography. For a time the new social history was equated with quantitative history pure and simple. After the mid-1970s, however, quantification declined somewhat, and new links with anthropology guided interests in ethnographic sources and other kinds of qualitative materials where historians and anthropologists shared some common methodological concerns.

Finally, the social science impulse propelled social historians to a strong interest in analysis and at least middle-level theory. "New" urban historians looked for city typologies in the past, and family historians defined primary structural categories. Social historians used social science

theory, testing it on historical data, and added theoretical statements of their own about patterns of development over time. Save in some very early efforts, dealing, for example, with long-ignored minority groups, pure description would not suffice. Social history was, at its best, fiercely analytical, probing causation, turning points, and interactions.

The central definition of the new social history emerged from these various impulses. Social historians emphasized processes of change—like the introduction of a new birth rate level—over event-based description. They applied analytical skills to virtually every significant feature of human behavior in the past that was not simply a biological constant. They attended to the history and the historical role of a variety of social groups. The result was a constant tendency toward topical expansion, as new groups—like youth or homosexuals—were added to more established categories and new behaviors—like leisure—added to the initial list of not-strictly-political topics. The further result was a growing recognition that social historians' view of the past—in terms of the forces that shaped it and the styles necessary to present it—differed from those previously dominant in the wider discipline of history. Individuals, events, and precise dates counted for less, and ideas no longer operated independent of social interaction; in contrast, diverse groups and evolving processes counted for far more, in this new vision.

Social historians were by no means united. They disagreed over specific interpretations. They settled on no single methodology, particularly after the flirtation with numbers subsided. They argued over causation, with some urging the centrality of political and economic factors, others urging attention to culture or mentalities. They disputed political preferences: bottom-up historians often maintained lively sympathy for their subjects, but other social historians might explore elites with great sympathy and certainly saw no reason for their findings to advance a current radical cause.

Social historians did agree on the importance of expanding history's topical range and on reassessing the conventions of earlier work, not only concerning causation of change but also basic periodization. They agreed, then, that social history involved not only a redefinition of topics and of the justifications for assigning significance to topics, toward the inclusion of ordinary people and ordinary facets of life, with the expansion of source materials that this entailed, but also that the new field compelled a reformulation historical presentation itself. Even political history, in this vision, required reassessment, toward greater attention to inputs from below and more ability to define key processes or stages in political alignments or state functions, making political history more compatible with, indeed an essential part of, the social history enterprise. This aspect of social history increasingly reshaped older historical fields. Labor history, for example, converted from a concentration on institutional development and formal ideologies to a study of the working classes, inside and outside formal organizational experience.

The social history vision, finally, was applied to study of every historical period and geographical area, by scholars around the world. Area studies programs in the United States, dealing with Africa, Asia, and Latin America, built in a strong social history component as part of the attention to peasantries and the strong interdisciplinary framework. Sources here included particular emphasis on oral history and material artifacts, and a distinctive set of analytical problems including modernization and dependency theory formulations. Nevertheless not only topics but also theoretical issues were shared, around such concepts as the "moral economy," initially developed in dealing with the emerging British working class but then applied to peasant history in various areas. In a few cases, though on the whole too few, specific comparative work developed, with the history of slavery heading the list.

Both the distinctiveness and the success of social history—plus, at times, a certain brashness in touting the new genre over more conventional versions of the craft—raised a number of objections. Many conventionally trained historians simply did not understand what the new breed was driving at: if they did not contribute to new interpretations of World War I or the Civil War, what function did they serve? New methods, new sources, and new conversations with other disciplines might easily seem suspect.

Redefinitions of causation—as, for example, the "great man" interpretation of history in terms of single leadership roles virtually disappeared—and reassessments of periodization (as the Renaissance tended to decline slightly when European history was staked out from a sociohistorical vantage point) clearly challenged long-standing habits. Social historians' multiplication of topics and local case studies and their failure to agree on causation gave an impression of incoherence in the field that increasingly bothered social historians themselves, leading by the 1980s to new calls for synthesis.

By the 1980s, indeed, social history faced renewed critique even as it had solidified as a field. By this point, about 35 percent of all practicing historians in the United States claimed to be social historians, and social history figured centrally in any definition of the discipline in the United States. Teaching and textbooks, though slower to change, also picked up strong social history components, while again at the research level the number of specialist journals continued to expand. Topical innovation continued—studies of masculinity added to women's history, a thriving subfield built around changes in the culture and symbolism of death, medical history and, more tentatively, legal history were reinterpreted from a social history vantage point, and emotions history entered the lists. Finally, even problems of synthesis were increasingly addressed. Charles Tilly called attention to the possibility of singling out "big changes" that set new social frameworks in motion, like the development of capitalism and a stronger state in early modern Europe; more detailed social history could work within the patterns these changes stimulated. Other social historians picked up the challenge of gender theory as the basis for at least partial synthesis. The plea to "put the state back in" by adding politics to a social history framework produced important results. The field, in sum, remained lively, innovative, and expanding.

Attack on social history by this point centered primarily on its implications for teaching. A new group of educational conservatives, closely associated with the Republican-dominated presidencies of the 1980s, urged that history should teach inspiring example and should focus on the achievements of American democracy. Diversities, group behaviors, and causations, and the whole idea of using history to stake out new knowledge rather than treading across already-hallowed ground, seemed anathema to this approach. History should deal with the great moments in western European and American history, and nothing more; its presentation style should emphasize inspiring narratives, not analytical modes. This challenge emphasized a continuing gap between social history research and normal classroom teaching of history. It did not deflect social history's scholarly momentum, and in many ways it reflected the field's success, but there was no question that it produced some bitter contention and some issues as yet unresolved.

On balance, however, the emergence of a well-defined social history approach constituted one of the leading developments not only in the historical discipline but in the social sciences more generally over the past generation. Social history had added greatly to the knowledge of human behavior and the nature of social change, and had produced numerous plausible explanatory models and generalizations beyond the new data themselves. Well into the 1990s the excitement of the field continued. Early in its surge, the great British social historian Eric Hobsbawm had claimed, quite accurately, that "it is a good time to be a social historian." Most practitioners 30 years later maintained the claim. (*See also Annales* School; Causation; Methodology; Periodization/ Sequences; Quantification; Teaching of Social History)

Peter N. Stearns

REFERENCES

Gardner, James B., and G.R. Adams, eds. *Ordinary People and Everyday Life: Perspectives on the New Social History.* Nashville: Society for State and Local History, 1983.

Himmelfarb, Gertrude. *The New History and the Old.* Cambridge: Harvard University Press, 1987.

Stearns, Peter N., ed. *Expanding the Past: A Reader in Social History.* New York: New York University Press, 1988.

Stearns, Peter N., and Herrick Chapman. *European Society in Upheaval: Social History Since 1750*, 3rd ed. New York: Macmillan, 1992.

Zunz, Olivier, ed. *Reliving the Past: The Worlds of Social History.* Chapel Hill: University of North Carolina Press, 1985.

Social Mobility

See Mobility

Socialism

The term "socialism" refers to a movement or theory of social organization advocating the common ownership and/or control of the means of production and distribution. Socialism first arose in reaction to the economic and social changes associated with industrialization and the rise of capitalism, and its theorists have generally emphasized the importance of cooperation, planning, and public ownership as opposed to the competition and profit seeking of individual entrepreneurs under capitalism. Socialist movements developed first in Europe but by the 20th century spread to various parts of Asia, Africa, and Australia.

Socialism is a challenging topic for social historians. The importance of socialism in modern political history is unquestionable. Until the rise of social history, socialism was usually studied in terms of doctrine, political maneuverings, and/ or relationships with trade unionism. Significant comparative work developed, dealing with differences in strength and organization between, say, German and French socialist movements. A useful comparative discussion also took shape around the issue of why socialism in the United States, uniquely among industrializing countries, never developed very significantly.

Romantic (utopian) *socialism* emerged in France in the 1830s with the writings of Henri de Saint-Simon, Charles Fourier, Pierre Leroux, and their followers. Reacting against the individualism of the Enlightenment and of liberal political economy, the romantic socialists sought to articulate the vision of a society bound by ties of love and affective solidarity. Socialism at this point had an economic component: its exponents were fiercely critical of competitive capitalism and laissez-faire economics, and they looked to collective control of the economy. But more important was the belief that it is in community, and not in isolation, that humans can best realize their potential and achieve full human emancipation. Many of these early socialists encouraged communitarian experimentation, particularly in the United States. A few had working-class followers, particularly among artisans. But socialism before 1848 was essentially a bourgeois movement critical of capitalism and seeking working class support.

Marxist socialism. In the writings of Karl Marx and Friedrich Engels socialism was presented as the ideology of the working class, or proletariat. The struggle of labor against capital would create a revolutionary class consciousness, they argued, and would lead eventually to proletarian revolution and the establishment of a classless society. Marx and Engels presented this theory as "scientific," arguing that unlike their "utopian" predecessors, they had described the historical process by which the good society would emerge.

The earliest writings of Marx and Engels offered suggestive reflections on human nature, freedom, and alienation. But after 1848, as prospects for revolution waned, Marx devoted himself to his great economic treatise, *Capital* (Vol. I, 1867), the aim of which was to demonstrate the necessity of the breakdown of capitalism as an economic system.

By 1900 Marxism had become Europe's predominant socialist theory. It flourished especially among the parliamentary socialist parties—and nowhere more than in Germany, where by 1912, the Social Democratic Party received over 30 percent of the votes. But success posed problems. A growing split within the socialist movement between revolutionary theory and reformist practice came to a head in 1914 with the outbreak of World War I. Socialists had long proclaimed international working-class solidarity. But when war came, the socialist parties of Germany, Austria, and France all voted to support their governments. Nationalism proved stronger than class, and international solidarity turned out to be a myth. In this context two new forms of socialism appeared to challenge orthodox Marxism: evolutionary democratic socialism and Leninist socialism.

Evolutionary democratic socialism emerged in Germany in the 1890s with the "revisionist controversy" and in England somewhat earlier with the creation of the Fabian Society. Both revisionism and Fabianism were responses to a rising standard of living and to the electoral success of left-wing parties (not only in national elections but in forming many city governments). The Fabians shunned high theory and put their hopes in gradualism and practical reforms ("gas and water socialism"). Eduard Bernstein, the principal theorist of revisionist Marxism, called on German socialists to abandon their revolutionary rhetoric and to recognize theoretically what they had already accepted in practice—that Germany could attain socialist goals without revolutionary violence.

After World War I revisionist socialism triumphed among German Social Democrats. Although it went into eclipse with the rise of Hitler, it was reborn after 1945. The Labour Party in England derives directly from Fabianism, and most continental European socialist parties have followed the revisionists in abandoning the ideal of full state ownership and settling for state action to ensure greater equality and social justice. Strong socialist movements in Scandinavia built welfare programs through a reformist approach. Within western Europe, then, and also in Australia democratic socialism has meant parliamentary struggle for better social conditions through social welfare legislation and public control of a mixed economy.

Leninist socialism (or communism) appeared around 1900 in opposition both to orthodox Marxism and to revisionist parliamentarianism. At its center was a voluntaristic theory of revolution which owed something to the conspiratorial activity of earlier Russian radicals. In *What Is to Be Done?* (1902) Lenin argued that, left to themselves, industrial workers would never progress beyond reformist "trade union consciousness." A vanguard of professional revolutionaries was needed to organize the mass of workers and peasants and to push them into revolution. Breaking with their more orthodox Marxist rivals, the Mensheviks, Lenin and his Bolsheviks eventually seized power in Russia (October 1917). Following World War II communism was imposed on eastern Europe, and the Leninist example of a communist seizure of power in an agricultural country and the pursuit of industrialization and socialism "from above" inspired imitation in China. For a time the Soviet Union became the model for rapid industrialization in much of the Third World. But the human costs were enormous; and the lack of genuine democracy made a mockery of "socialist" planning. Attempts to reform the system from within failed, and the fall of Gorbachev in 1991 marked the end of Leninist socialism in most parts of the world.

In the 1990s socialism is at a crossroad. The policies and pronouncements of Europe's democratic socialist leaders are scarcely distinguishable from those of their opponents, as reformist socialists embrace feminist and ecological concerns. At the same time Leninist socialism is bankrupt, its ideology too often used to mask political oppression and economic exploitation. Some now argue that as a workers' movement socialism is "dead," that we need to reconceptualize socialism to take account of the claims of women, of consumers, of oppressed minorities and nationalities, and of the environment. Those who still take seriously the promise of socialism must wrestle with these issues.

Conventional histories of socialism tended to assume that socialism and working class were synonymous, at least until 1917 in western Europe. Social historians of the working class, however, have raised new questions about the different meanings socialism could have for different kinds of workers and about the important groups of workers never attracted to socialism at all. They also urge the necessity of focusing on aspects of working-class life quite apart from socialist politics, including not only family activities and leisure but also competing loyalties like nationalism. The "new labor history" is not content to assume that socialist leadership accurately defines all we need to know about the working classes. It also notes that leaders sometimes pushed on workers bourgeois values, like temperance or birth control, that might change worker habits but that also might provoke annoyance. Social history, in sum, complicates the interpretation of socialism and places it in broader contexts. It adds depth to questions about what kinds of workers sought revolutionary change, what groups mainly looked to socialism to provide pragmatic reforms like laws facilitating unions or limiting hours of work. Growing interest in women has added additional facets to the history of socialism, in noting that while many socialist leaders advocated women's rights, some of the same leaders assumed that in a socialist society women would concentrate on domestic tasks and leave production jobs to men.

The effort to separate socialism from real working-class history should not be pressed too far. Socialism was and remains a vital expression for many workers. It taught them new protest goals and organizational skills, and for a minority provided mobility into positions of political leadership when other mobility channels were blocked. At its height, between the late 19th century and the rise of mass affluence in the later 20th century, European socialism also provided a network of social institutions—including libraries, dance halls, and even advice to the lovelorn. These features too must be embraced in a sociohistorical approach to one of the leading political currents of modern times. (*See also* Marxist Historiography; Unions; Working Class)

Jonathan Beecher

REFERENCES

Geary, Dick, ed. *Labour and Socialist Movements in Europe Before 1914*. New York: St. Martin's Press, 1989.

Howe, Irving, ed. *Essential Works of Socialism*. New York: Bantam, 1971.

Laslett, John, and S.M. Lipset, eds. *Failure of a Dream: Essays in the History of American Socialism*. Berkeley: University of California Press, 1984.

Lichtheim, George. *A Short History of Socialism*. New York: Praeger, 1970.

Lidtke, Vernon. *The Alternative Culture: Socialist Labor in Imperial Germany*. New York: Oxford University Press, 1985.

Sociobiology

Sociobiology emerged in the 1970s as a field devoted to studying human behaviors in society that were rooted in invariant biology. Sociobiologists attribute key gender characteristics, for example, to basic biology, arguing that men are by nature (due to their capacity for recurrent production of sperm) sexually profligate while women are naturally (due to their finite number of eggs) sexually conservative. Arguments of this sort relied on evolutionary functionalism: the natural sexual duality of men and women best served the species by combining the male's widespread search for potential mates with the female's desire to form families and thus nurture the children who were born.

Sociobiologists frequently wrote on topics, such as gender and sexuality, that were also central to social history. Their approach clashed with the assumptions of social historians, who were particularly interested in tracing the social and cultural origins of human characteristics—the specific construction of major gender traits, for instance—and their capacity to vary and change. Social historians did not neglect basic biological features, but they pointed to evidence of change even in such basics as age of puberty or of menopause, depending on historical circumstance. The gap between sociobiology and social history in explaining human and social behavior was so wide that effective dialogue was impossible. Sociobiologists, in the view of social historians, resolutely ignored historical findings in their generalizations about fundamental traits. While the most fervent sociobiology declined somewhat by the 1990s, other disciplines that studied human behavior, including some branches of psychiatry and psychology, similarly neglected findings about variety and change in the search for genetically or chemically caused universals in the species. (*See also* Body; Menarche; Sexuality)

Peter N. Stearns

REFERENCES

Fausto-Sterling, Anne. *Myths of Gender: Biological Theories About Women and Men.* New York: Basic Books, 1985.

Goldberg, Steven. *The Inevitability of Patriarchy.* New York: Morrow, 1973.

Sociology

Sociology examines the influence that societal institutions, values, and norms have on the ways people think, feel, and behave, and, conversely, the effects that people's ideas, sentiments, and actions have on these social constructs.

Defined as the process of mutual conditioning of social institutions and human actions, the subject matter of sociology is inherently historical, regardless of whether a study focuses primarily on large-, or macro-, scale social structures, or on local-, or micro-, level social relations and personal lives. It might therefore seem self-evi-

dent that there cannot be anything but *historical* sociology, one that considers the interactive effects of social structures and social action on the patterns and transformations of social life, and is attentive to its temporal and spatial dimensions. But in fact, since the inception of modern sociology, this orientation has at most coexisted with the prevailing, distinctly ahistorical, approaches.

One important reason for this situation derives from sociology's intellectual lineage, and specifically from the ambiguities concerning the fundamental character of society and the status of knowledge acquired about it, received as a legacy from the main founders of modern sociology. The ways these 19th-century European social philosophers approached the social world and tried to make sense of it refracted divisive political debates about the social costs and benefits of the emerging urban-industrial society, and intellectual controversies regarding the status of the social sciences as *nomothetic* (natural sciencelike, i.e., analytical and generalizing) or *idiographic* (interpretive and particularizing, i.e., time and place specific).

Four major themes/orientations (discussed below), associated with particular founders to a significant extent inform the sociological agenda to this day. The double-mindedness of the classical thinkers regarding the nature of social phenomena and methods of sociological study has been preserved within each of these broad traditions. Within these traditions a variety of disciplinary subfields have emerged since World War II (over 30 such sections focusing on different aspects of social life—e.g., family, law, organizations, deviance, social stratification, religion, state and politics, community, etc.—were registered with the American Sociological Association in 1991), and have provided legitimacy to both historically oriented subfields (a minority, although steadily expanding in the last decade and a half) and to basically ahistorical (mainstream) sociologies.

1. *Primacy of the Economic Base and Class (Group) Conflict.* This sociological theme/tradition is associated with Karl Marx (1818–1883). His theory, called "historical materialism," is predicated on two central assumptions: the mode in which economic production is organized and the antagonistic relations between (two) major so-

cial classes derived from it (the so-called *base*) can account for all other facets (political, ideological, cultural—the so-called *superstructure*) of society; and societal transformations follow a historical sequence whereby each subsequent socioeconomic formation proceeds from the contradiction between base and superstructure that ripened in the preceding epoch.

Marx's writings contain two different interpretative strands of this model. One, basically ahistorical (also called "scientific"), tends toward reductionist, economic-determinist explanations of concrete social orders, and toward evolutionary-linear and teleological view of long-term social change (it has continued first and foremost in Soviet Marxism-Leninism, but also among some Western sociologists). The coexistent historical perspective in Marx's work views the economic base as restrictive rather than prescriptive, societal structures as much more complex, and social actors as more autonomous than posited in the two-class model. This orientation (also called *open*, or *humanistic*, Marxism), has attracted a greater number of Western sociologists, especially from the rebellious generation of the 1960s, who reexamine, expand, or modify Marxian central themes and assertions, regarding both macrostructures (states, classes) and social actors in their local environments (e.g., workers, members of racial and ethnic groups, men, and women).

2. *Rationalization of Society: Its Triumphs and Discontents.* This theme/orientation has been associated with German sociologist Max Weber (1864–1920). Although, unlike Marx, Weber never produced a unified social theory, his studies on such diverse themes as sociology of law, religion, state, power, authority, status and social stratification, bureaucracy, and the origins of modern capitalism share the general underlying theme of the expanding rationalization of Western society. Rationalization is a process made up of several developments such as secularization, professionalization, and overall regularization of the everyday life, all of which provided the prerequisites for a stable administrative system, systematized legal order, and efficient organizations, but also for the spread of institutions of control and surveillance.

Equally influential have been Weber's writings on the methodology of the social sciences. While he considered nomothetic sociology as possible and desirable, Weber did not agree that it could adopt the methods of the natural sciences. Since, in Weber's view, humans are unique in using the symbolic (cultural) system to orient their actions, understanding of social processes is not possible without accounting for the *subjective meanings* social actors attach to their worlds; in consequence, the social sciences require a particular method of investigation (the so-called *ideal-type analysis*).

Of all classic schools, Weber's sociology was the most consistently historical in method and practice. Nevertheless, there inheres in his writings a detectable ambivalence, or tension even, between the two orientations, likely a reflection in his attempts to integrate elements of opposed intellectual traditions. In the matter of methodology, Weber wished for objective, scientifically rigorous, and valid sociology, but at the same time his emphasis on the inescapable subjectivity of human perceptions (including those of the social scientist) undermined this possibility. He insisted on the underdetermined, contingent nature of causality, yet at the same time referred to bureaucratization as the irrevocable fate of the industrial world. Those ahistorical leanings in Weber's writings have been brought to the fore, in particular, in the works of Talcott Parsons (1902–1979), whose influence on sociological theory in the United States reigned practically unchallenged during the two postwar decades. The historical-interpretive orientation of the Weberian tradition has been continued during that same period by a few outstanding scholars, but it was only since the 1970s that a renewed interest in historical sociology, the same that revived Marxist orientation, has not surprisingly turned younger scholars directly (i.e., without the Parsonian mediation) to Weber's methodological writings and his studies on the above-mentioned subjects.

3. *Social Differentiation and "Organic" Solidarity.* This theme/tradition derives from work of Emile Durkheim (1858–1916). If Weber's orientation was programmatically the most historical among the founders of modern sociology, then Durkheim is affiliated most closely with the sci-

entist paradigm. This approach, called *positivistic,* posits, in Durkheim's famous phrase, the treatment of "social facts as if they were things," wholly external to the individuals, and fully accountable for in rigorous scientific investigation. Consequently, sociology is postulated as a science capable of formulating generally applicable theories (understood as sets of interrelated causal statements) about society. Arguably the most influential of Durkheim's prolific writings has been his evolutionary model of the progressive functional differentiation of the social structure (a result of the increasing division of labor) that causes the nature of social cohesion to transform. Namely, the *mechanical solidarity* typical for simple or little differentiated societies, based on similarity of individuals and embracing moral consensus, is replaced by *organic solidarity* characteristic of complex, heterogeneous societies, based on differences between individuals or groups interlinked through systematic relations of exchange, and on (postulated) *moral individualism,* that is, individual autonomy self-restrained by the precept of cooperation.

From the viewpoint assumed here, both Durkheim's methodology and his theory of social evolution are distinctly ahistorical (although, in tune with the prevalent contemporary understanding, he himself considered the latter as the evolutionary, therefore "historical," model). Durkheim's legacy has inspired two parallel developments in sociology, both bearing the same ahistorical mark. One has been a tendency toward abstract grand theorizing (Parsons's structural-functionalism, elaborated from a combination of the Durkheimian and Weberian orientations, is the most outstanding case; there have also been smaller-scope theories constructed within the same framework—of deviance, law, religion, family, community, etc.). The other development, equally inattentive to social dynamics embedded in time and place, has been narrow empiricism based on scientific methods such as representative sampling and complex statistical analyses of large sets of aggregate data. (It was this kind of sociology, for that matter, that enchanted social historians in the 1970s—rebels against what they perceived as ills of their own discipline—which was a platform for the forma-

tion in 1977 of the Social Science History Association.)

But Durkheim's writings also contain an ambiguity, specifically in his theory of social evolution, which harbors a potential for historical sociology as defined earlier. It could be argued that Durkheim's postulate of "moral individualism," as the necessary cohesive element for the adequate functioning of differentiated and heterogenous society, implodes the presumed externality of social facts, and centers attention on the actors as autonomous, or choosing individuals, and their interactions with social environment. This is where historical sociological analysis enters in. As things stand, however, historicization by sociologists of the Durkheimian/Parsonian orientation still lies in waiting; not counting the appliers of the general model to a historical case without feedback, thus far there have been but a few practitioners of historical sociology in this tradition.

4. *Industrial Urbanism and a Loss of Community.* This theme/tradition in sociology originates in the works of the 19th-century European social philosophers Ferdinand Tönnies (1855–1936) and George Simmel (1858–1918). What Durkheim perceived as a basically positive evolution from homogeneous, mechanically linked to heterogenous, organically cohesive society, for these thinkers represented a loss. In Tönnies's classical counterposition, this societal change was depicted as the replacement of *Gemeinschaft* (in German, literally "community") by *Gesellschaft* (perhaps best translated as "association"). The former, typical for preindustrial society, refers to social relationships that are contained within a limited locality, stable, intimate, and based on a thorough knowledge of each individual's life situation. The latter, characteristic of urban-industrial society, is the opposite: it denotes the spatially diffuse, contractual, impersonal, and instrumental or task-oriented relationships that supplant close-knit communal bonds. This conceptual framework was later adopted and elaborated by the so-called Chicago School of urban sociology, and particularly by Robert Park (1864–1944), Louis Wirth (1897–1952), and Ernest Burgess (1886–1966), who applied it to the study of "human ecology" and (L. Wirth) to a general theory of "urbanism as a way of life."

Like the previous ones, this sociological tradition, too, contains at its source both ahistorical and historical strands. The Chicago School, for example (and, for that matter, early American sociology in general), was strongly informed by the general theory of social evolution (equated, as in the case of Durkheim, with a "historical" approach). At the same time, however, the Chicago sociologists produced a plethora of richly textured studies of urban neighborhoods and immigrant communities, attentive to processes of "structuration." Wirth's classical theory of "urbanism as a way of life" has since been reexamined on the basis of the accumulated research, and has been modified in different ways. The tradition of historically minded urban ethnography has found followers in several sociological subdisciplines, such as community sociology, immigration and ethnic studies, racial groups and relations, family sociology, and the sociology of deviance and social control.

The ambivalences about history in sociology have determined a fluctuating relationship with social history (or sociological history) since its serious inception three decades ago. Initially, social historians borrowed heavily from sociological concepts and methods, and interaction was expected to expand as historians became, for example, better versed in quantification. Studies in mobility and protest overlapped the disciplines. By the late 1970s the connection had cooled, and social historians began turning more to anthropology. Recently a revival has occurred, with growing sociological interest in historical approaches and with social historians, dealing with such subjects as life cycle and emotion, interacting extensively with sociological researchers. (*See also* Methodology; Quantification)

Ewa Morawska

REFERENCES

Abrams, Philip. *Historical Sociology*. Ithaca, NY: Cornell University Press, 1982.

Bourdieu, Pierre, and James Coleman, eds. *Social Theory for a Changing Society*. New York: Russell Sage Foundation, 1991.

Lee, David, and Howard Newby. *The Problem of Sociology. An Introduction to the Discipline*. London: Unwin Hyman, 1989.

Nisbet, Robert. *The Sociological Tradition*. New York: Basic Books, 1966.

Skocpol, Theda, ed. *Vision and Method in Historical Sociology*. New York: Cambridge University Press, 1984.

Smith, Dennis. *The Rise of Historical Sociology*. Philadelphia: Temple University Press, 1991.

South Asian Cities

Cities emerged in South Asia with the birth of civilization. As the remains of Mohenjodaro and Harappa indicate, they evolved in the Indus civilization in the third millennium BC. A second phase of urbanization occurred in the early historical period (ca. 500 BC) and persisted into the early 7th century AD. Thereafter, another lull set in before cities rose to prominence again, this time with the advent of Muslim empires. From AD 1200 onward, and particularly during the height of the Mughal Empire from the 16th through the early 18th centuries, cities flourished, the scale and richness of Agra and Delhi far surpassing their European counterparts.

Indus cities can be traced back to an indigenous preurban phase. Rather than seek their beginnings in the urban revolution experienced earlier in West Asia, current research is therefore aimed at uncovering the so-called core trends of urban genesis—social stratification, the emergence of an archaic state, craft and occupational specialization, and settlement patterns indicative of the development of urbanization. Compared to archeological, anthropological, and historical work conducted on other early civilizations, much less has been done to date regarding the central-place roles performed by Indus cities, as nodes in marketing and trade systems, and as political, administrative, and religious centers. Until the Indus script is deciphered, the archeological record remains the only source of information, better at shedding light on some aspects of these first cities than others.

The cities of the early historical period—Patna and Banaras in the north and Madurai in the south—are also beginning to be noticed. Initial research, based on spadework and oral and written sources, has already produced wide-ranging generalizations about urban economy, society, administration, and life. Surprisingly, the urban boom of the Muslim periods of rule has not generated attention commensurate with its importance; cities and towns not only formed an integral part of Islamic lifestyles but also prospered in many quarters of the rising all-India empire. Although sparse, the literature includes significant studies of urbanization in the Mughal period and of such urban centers as the capital city of Shahajahanabad (old Delhi) and the trading port city of Surat in western India. Another city that has finally received its due is Vijayanagara, the capital of the Hindu kingdom of the same name that dominated much of the southern peninsula from the mid-14th through the 17th centuries.

The colonial urban past (later 18th–mid-20th centuries) is also just beginning to be mapped. By digging into the abundant source materials of this era, researchers have explored a range of urban settings—for example, the great metropolitan centers of Bombay, Calcutta, Madras, and Delhi as well as the smaller cities of Ahmedabad, Banaras, Dacca, Hyderabad, Lucknow, and Karachi. As urban biographies, most of these studies offer portraits of the city itself or of its morphogenesis. A different approach utilizes the city as backdrop, as the locus for testing fundamental propositions regarding the effects of colonialism on indigenous society. As yet rare are conceputalizations of the city as process, as a unique container shaping and organizing experience, an approach that has advocates in American and European urban history. And only lately have there been considerations of cities as constituent units of larger networks, that is, central places linked to their immediate localities and to other nodes in the region and in the subcontinent. Another promising line of inquiry that has produced provocative results is the analysis of colonial cities and port cities as distinctive types, as phenomena related to the peculiarities of colonialism in the subcontinent.

The investigation of the urban past of South Asia, as this brief historiographical survey reveals, is still in its incipient stages. The limited coverage partly reflects the understandable preoccupation of South Asian studies with rural history because of the overwhelmingly agrarian and rural nature of the subcontinent. In part, it shows the newness of this genre of historical writing—the new urban history, after all, dates back to the rise of new social history of the 1960s.

But there is also much about urban history that is not novel because its theoretical and conceptual foundations were partly built by an earlier generation of social scientists (geographers and sociologists mostly but also demographers and anthropologists). Consider the influence exerted by German sociologist Max Weber's pronouncements on Asian cities, or by Robert Redfield and Milton Singer's anthropological formulation of cities as "orthogenetic" or "heterogenetic," or by Bert Hoselitz's notion of the "parasitic" versus "generative" cities, or Sjoberg's more specifically historical idea of the "preindustrial city." Consider also the extent to which urban studies have been (and still are) shaped by the ethnocentric assumption common to all these formulations regarding the universalizing tendencies of the Western pattern of urbanization or by the construction in these notions of a rural/urban dichotomy or of a rural/urban continuum. Yet another inherited bias is the conception of cities as integrative institutions, that is, magnets for migrants from rural areas; incubators of modernization, Westernization, and industrialization; and administrative, political, commercial, and religious centers with far-reaching influence over their hinterlands.

South Asian cities continue to attract scholarly attention, especially that of social scientists concerned with present-day urban conditions and "overurbanization." Indeed, although the level of urbanization in the subcontinent remains comparatively low—except for Pakistan, less than 25 percent throughout the region and below 10 and 7 percent in Bangladesh and Nepal, respectively, in 1981—the absolute size of the urban population is staggering. Four Indian cities, Bombay, Calcutta, Madras, and Delhi, are currently projected to be among the 25 megalopolises in the world with populations exceeding 10 million in the year 2000, indicating that, for South Asian cities of the present and of the past, much remains to be said and done. (*See also* Cities; Third World Urbanization; Urbanization)

Anand A. Yang

REFERENCES

Ballhatchet, Kenneth, and John Harrison, eds. *The City in South Asia: Pre-Modern and Modern.* London: Curzon Press, 1980.

Basu, Dilip K., ed. *The Rise and Growth of the Colonial Port Cities in Asia.* Lanham, MD: University Press of America, 1985.

King, Anthony D. *Colonial Urban Development: Culture, Social Power and Environment.* London: Routledge & Kegan Paul, 1976.

South Asian Collective Action

The truism regarding violence and unrest in Asia is that Chinese history has been dramatically shaped by such collective action, while South Asia (the subcontinent now divided into the nation-states of India, Pakistan, Bangladesh, and Sri Lanka) has not. China's pronounced turbulence had even accorded to peasant rebellion a fundamental role in Chinese political philosophy, signifying the withdrawal of "the mandate of heaven" from a ruler. It has been argued, by contrast, that the South Asian social system—notably the institution of caste—precluded this kind of turmoil. Certainly, large-scale rebellions and revolts proved the exception in South Asia, and changes in political rulers resulted from traditional battles between kingly pretenders. But social historians have found a number of forms of collective action that constitute overt and covert resistance or contestation, and make it clear that the hierarchical form of social organization presumed to be caste did not preclude significant examples of collective action in the subcontinent.

Historians studied the most obvious expressions of South Asian collective action first, especially those 19th-century events marking the consolidation of British rule; these included the Mutiny/Revolt of 1857 (which began as a mutiny in the Oudh Army and spread to become an armed revolt waged throughout much of north Indian agrarian society), and the Deccan Riots of 1875 (in which peasants attacked moneylenders). Various occasions of resistance waged by cultivating "tribes" were studied as well, especially the Santal uprisings (attacks on moneylenders and claims laid to villages in mid-century) and the Chipko ("Hug the Trees") movement (in which women, especially, resisted the state's environmental encroachment as it imposed commercialized forestry on the Uttarakhand area). Other events examined in the early writings by South Asian social historians included movements that blurred the boundaries between peasant and religious movements, especially the early 19th-century Faraidi movement (staged by Muslim peasants in Bengal who resisted landlords, generally Hindus) and the Mappillahs of western India (who, in a series of rebellions over the late 19th and early 20th centuries evoked the heroic Islamic imagery of a *jihad*—holy war—to shape several peasant rebellions against Hindu landlords and even the 1920s Non-Cooperation Movement against the British). This historiography has drawn conclusions and analytical comparisons consistent with the study of unrest in other parts of the world—examining, especially, the exploitation of the peasantry by urban-based moneylenders and absentee landlords—and has been characterized by much the same split between Marxist and non-Marxist scholarship and interpretations.

More recently, innovative methodologies and assumptions brought to the study of collective action have revealed more nuanced conclusions and theoretical implications. The first innovation has been pioneered by a collective of leftist scholars based primarily in India and self-named the Subaltern Studies School. (The term "subaltern," arising from the word used for a British enlisted man and expanded on theoretically by Italian socialist theorist Antonio Gramsci and others, has come to stand, in South Asian social history, for those persons who were relatively powerless in any given relationship.) Working on resistance, rebellion, and other forms of collective action, this group has pioneered the application of discourse analysis, a technique of studying texts for their implied meanings drawn from literary criticism, to illuminate such issues as peasant constructions of M.K. Gandhi, definitions of community as held by small-town residents in north India, British and rebel views of each other during resistance movements, and the like. Informed especially by the theories of Gramsci and French philosopher Michel Foucault, discourse analysis of collective action sees it as having been shaped especially by the state's imposition of a hegemonic discursive frame. Impelled by contemporary concerns, the focus of this group has now begun to shift to the postcolonial state, and to the roots of contemporary political hegemony in nationalist discourse.

Another innovative approach has involved contextualizing expressions of violent collective action by identifying the cultural matrix in which they are embedded. This scholarship has involved the study of folksongs (as evidence of popular opinion on political and social change) as well as festivals and other civic ceremonials (involving peaceful collective action in the form of processions and the like). Thus, the explication of violent resistance has been linked, by these scholars, to the broader social history of popular culture, and used to illuminate the larger developments identified in political narratives (such as identity formation, delineation of community boundaries, cultural nationalism, and the like). Perhaps for this reason, the social historians embarked on this project have paid more attention to towns and to ideological movements relating to such issues as religion and caste (rather than peasant-focused causes). In general, this body of research has credited cultural expressions of counterdiscourse with successfully resisting the imposition of a hegemonic frame, whether attempted by the imperial state or the nationalist movement.

A third innovation has been based on the premise that collective action need not be overt and violent to constitute resistance and contestation. Inspired by the theoretical arguments posed by historian Michael Adas and economic theorist James Scott, this approach has looked for forms of "everyday resistance" in the very organization of agrarian life, and the efforts by peasants and agricultural workers to resist the oppressions of local power holders. This approach has been used, as well, to examine the way merchants, courtesans and other women structure their lives to resist dominant values that run counter to their own. While not yet systematically worked out to formulate a consistent theoretical position, this approach, too, has proved fruitful in delineating the role played collectively by actors in the social history of the South Asian subcontinent. (*See also* Chinese Social Protest; Japanese Popular Protest; Moral Economy; Popular Culture; Protest)

Sandria B. Freitag

REFERENCES

Freitag, Sandria B. *Collective Action and Community: The Emergence of Communalism in North India.* Berkeley and Los Angeles: University of California Press, 1990.

Guha , Ranajit, ed. *Subaltern Studies,* Vols. 1–8. New Delhi: Oxford University Press, 1982–present.

Haynes, Douglas, and Gyan Prakash. *Contesting Power: Resistance and Everyday Social Relations in South Asia.* Berkeley and Los Angeles: University of California Press, 1992.

Siddiqi, Majid. "History and Society in a Popular Rebellion: Mewat, 1920–1933," *Comparative Studies in Society and History* 28 (1986): 442–467.

South Asian Colonialism

The European quest for commercial access to the fabled wealth of India that led to Columbus's discovery of America in 1492 also gave rise to the voyage of Vasco da Gama around the southern tip of Africa and on to the Indian port of Calicut in 1498. Within a generation of that landfall, Portuguese naval power had become dominant in the Indian Ocean basin, and Portuguese forts were established at a host of strategic positions therein. In 1510, the port of Goa on the west coast of India was established by Afonso de Albuquerque as the capital of all the Portuguese settlements in the east, and that city and a small surrounding territory remained in Portuguese hands until 1961. But, despite their commercial ascendancy in India throughout the 16th century, the Portuguese never tried to acquire direct control over large territories; and only in Ceylon (now Sri Lanka) did their domains extend much more than a day's march from one of their coastal strongholds.

With the formation of the English and Dutch East India companies, in 1600 and 1602, respectively, new powers entered into competition for Indian trade, mainly in textiles, spices, and a variety of luxury goods. The French soon followed and, later and more ephemerally, so did other European powers. Neither Portuguese manpower nor their naval strength sufficed to stave off their north European rivals, and most of their possessions passed into the hands of those adversaries. Initially, the other Europeans, like the Portuguese, sought trade in preference to territory. But they had to deal with a host of Indian rulers, especially after the decline of the Mughal Empire early in the 18th century; and to gain favor among those rulers they often found it expedient to offer them military assistance in internal Indian conflicts. For a time, French diplomacy was particularly adept, especially in peninsular India, and French artillery officers were much in demand by Indian rulers. To frustrate French designs and protect their own growing trade, the British forged a number of counteralliances and were soon embroiled in a series of wars in India involving both the French and various Indian states. During one such struggle British forces, led by Robert Clive, gained several decisive victories, most notably over a combined French-Mughal force at the Battle of Plassey in 1757. The outcome of that victory was the Mughal grant to the British of the right to collect land revenue from their rich province of Bengal. Thenceforth, the effects of Western colonialism on Indian social history became especially pronounced. Plassey marked the beginning of an inexorable, albeit unplanned, process of British territorial expansion in India. Less than a century after Plassey, the British were masters throughout the subcontinent.

Supremacy in India proper, however, did not put an end to the British expansion; for they felt it necessary either to gain direct control over a girdle of highland territory on the flanks of their possessions on the Indo-Gangetic Plain or to establish protectorates over docile buffer states such as Nepal, Sikkim, and Bhutan. In Afghanistan, their intervention in favor of a claimant to the throne embroiled them in a civil war (1839–1843) that ended in one of the worst defeats in British military history. But a second Afghan War (1878–1881) achieved what the first failed to do and established Afghanistan as a British protectorate, at least until the third and final Anglo-Afghan War in 1919, after which the British again recognized Afghan sovereignty. The same concession was granted to Nepal in 1923. To the east a succession of wars (1824–1826, 1852, and 1885) led to the piecemeal acquisition of the entire Burmese Empire, which became a province of India, and so remained until 1937, when, in recognition of its cultural distinctiveness, it was made a separate crown colony.

The effect of British conquest on India was economically, culturally, and spiritually devastating. As the industrial revolution made England, for a time, the workshop for the world, cheap British manufactures flooded Indian markets, and millions of weavers, who, only decades earlier, could barely keep up with the European demand for their superior textiles, were no longer able to sell their wares. Similar fates befell other artisans. Agriculturists also suffered as the British put in place a class of big landholders (zamīndārs) who had to turn over specified amounts of land revenue to the government but could extract from the peasantry far more in rent than they were obliged to pay out. The introduction of cash crops often led to indebtedness of cultivators after bad harvests, moneylending at high interest rates, frequent forfeiture of land used as collateral for debts, and widespread impoverishment of the peasantry.

At first, the East India Company sought to discourage the activities of British missionaries (though evangelists from other countries were not similarly hindered); but this policy gradually changed and, beginning in the 1830s, proselytization spread rapidly in India, especially among depressed castes and tribal people. The mantle of moral superiority assumed by many missionaries, together with the new ideas in respect to science and other branches of learning that were promoted as the British extended their influence into the domain of education, undermined the faith of the Indian intelligentsia in the values of their own culture and demoralized the erstwhile ruling elite.

But not all effects of British rule were negative, and this provides an additional focus for work in social and cultural history. In Bengal, contact with Western thinking acted as a catalyst for what came to be known as the Hindu Renaissance, spearheaded by Ram Mohan Roy, who, in 1828, founded the Brahmo Samaj, the first of many religious revival and reform movements that subsequently sprang up over many parts of India. New literary and artistic forms emerged as Indians absorbed various aspects of Western culture. From the 1840s onward there was a rapid expansion of the economic infrastructure, as improved roads and a vast network of railroads, telegraphs, and irrigation canals laced the Indian countryside.

Changes in the political domain, however, came more slowly. The first major political convulsion, the so-called Indian Mutiny of 1857 (actually 1857–1859), took the British completely by surprise. This uprising by Indian troops spread like wildfire across northern India and was soon joined by numerous royal families who had accepted British rule and saw in the revolt a chance to regain their lost power. The struggle, waged with great brutality on both sides, was ultimately won by the British. Two immediate political results were the deposition and exile of the last Mughal "emperor," and the replacement of East India Company rule by that of the British Crown, a precursor to the declaration of Queen Victoria as Empress of India in 1877.

As the range of British economic interests and other activities in India expanded, their need for educated Indian assistants grew commensurately. Notwithstanding the legacy of distrust left by the Mutiny, relations of mutual dependence of ruler and ruled intensified. To make the case for a more enlightened government, an Englishman, Allen Octavian Hume, helped establish the Indian National Congress (INC) in 1885. In time, the INC evolved into a political party and grew increasingly more strident in calling for greater rights for Indians in all spheres of life, especially for an enhanced role in government and, in 1929, for complete independence. While the INC sought from the outset to represent all Indians, many Muslims foresaw that, with the gradual advance of democratic institutions, their position as a minority community would leave them at the mercy of India's large Hindu majority. This consideration was instrumental in the forming in 1906 of the Muslim League. The following decades witnessed a series of major constitutional reforms in India, each of which expanded the roles of Indians in government at both the provincial and the all-India level. But, while the British yielded power on the one hand, they divided the opposition on the other by acquiescing, first to the Muslim demand, and then to the demands of other religious communities and interest groups, for separate electorates for reserved seats in the central and provincial legislatures.

Of all the reforms, the 1935 Government of India Act was the most far-reaching. Seen as a steppingstone to full independence, this Act greatly expanded the franchise (extending the vote, in particular, to women), and increased the powers of the various legislative bodies (while retaining veto rights for the viceroy and provincial governors), and ushered in a period of vigorous political confrontation between the INC and the Muslim League, the former led by Mahatma Gandhi and Jawaharlal Nehru and the latter by Mohammed Ali Jinnah. This culminated in the demand by the latter in 1941 for the establishment of a separate state of Pakistan as the territorial home for the Indian Muslim "nation."

Indian participation in World Wars I and II also had a major impact on internal and external politics. Contributions to the Allied cause in those conflicts were such that India was made, even though not yet independent, a charter member of both the League of Nations and the United Nations, which greatly enhanced its international stature. When, in 1939, Britain failed to consult the INC and declared war on behalf of India, the Congress responded by boycotting the war effort. This did not, however, prevent millions of Indians from participating individually in the struggle. Nor did it call a halt to negotiations between Britain and the major Indian parties in respect to independence. The British Labour Party, which came into power in 1945, promised speedy independence for India. Attempts by the last British viceroy, Lord Louis Mountbatten, to find a formula whereby the divergent interests of the INC and the Muslim League could be reconciled and the territorial integrity of India maintained proved futile. Recognizing that compromise was impossible, the Congress leaders eventually bowed to the demands for partition; and, on the night of August 14–15, 1945, two new dominions, India and Pakistan, were born. Momentous though that event was, it was marred by unprecedented communal violence as millions of Muslims fled India for Pakistan and comparable numbers of Hindus and Sikhs sought refuge within the truncated state of India. Independence for Burma and Sri Lanka was much more peacefully achieved in January and February of 1948. (*See also* Colonialism; Imperialism; South Asian Regionalism)

Joseph E. Schwartzberg

REFERENCES

Kumar, Dharma, ed. *The Cambridge Economic History of India, Vol. II, c. 1757–c. 1970.* Cambridge: Cambridge University Press, 1983.

Metcalf, Thomas R. *Modern India, An Interpretative Anthology.* New Delhi: Sterling Publishers, 1990.

Sarkar, Sumit. *Modern India, 1885–1947.* Calcutta: Macmillan India Ltd., 1983.

Schwartzberg, Joseph E., ed. *A Historical Atlas of South Asia* (updated 2nd impression). New York: Oxford University Press, 1992.

Spear, Percival. *The Oxford History of Modern India, 1740–1947.* Oxford: Clarendon Press, 1965.

South Asian Demography and Family

In comparison to the situation in other parts of the developing world, the demographic history of South Asia since the mid 19th century is remarkably well documented. The region's various kinship systems are also relatively well understood.

From time immemorial India has been among the most densely settled portions of our planet. One estimate holds that the population had already reached 100 million during the apogee of the Mauryan empire in the 3rd century BC. While this obviously cannot be substantiated, the figure is not unthinkable for a high civilization based largely on the intensive cultivation of rice. Over the following two millennia the population underwent long periods of slow growth, marked by high birth rates, slightly in excess, on average, of high death rates, interspersed by periods of dramatic population loss occasioned by times of marked political instability and, locally, by such Malthusian checks as famine, pestilence, war, and natural catastrophe. The first comprehensive census, taken in 1881, showed a population (probably undercounted) of 254 million, with another 2.8 million in Ceylon. (Other parts of South Asia were not to take censuses until considerably later.) Population growth continued to be slow until 1921, with large areas of actual famine-induced decline in most decades. The 1921 figure was 319 million for India and 4.5 million for Ceylon. Thereafter, population began to grow at a steadily increasing rate as public health measures, the spread of modern medicine, and famine relief strategies caused death rates to plummet, while birth rates fell only marginally from their traditionally high levels of almost 50 per 1,000 per year. When India and Pakistan gained their independence in 1947, their combined population was around 415 million, with birth rates of about 43, death rates of 30, and rates of natural increase of about 1.3 percent per year.

Since independence, all the countries of South Asia have instituted family planning programs; but some have pursued them with much greater vigor than others. Popular acceptance, however, has not always been commensurate with government efforts. In particular, resort by India to various coercive tactics to promote male and female sterilization programs during a period of emergency rule (1975–1978) led to a widespread political unrest and a retrenchment of the population control program. Nevertheless, Indian birth rates have been steadily, if not rapidly, declining and stood at 31 in 1991, as against a death rate of only 10. Considerably greater strides, however, have been taken by Sri Lanka (formerly Ceylon), which has one of the most advanced government-sponsored welfare programs in the developing world. There, birth rates and death rates have fallen to 21 and 6, respectively. At the opposite end of the spectrum, so far as South Asia is concerned, is Afghanistan, with estimated rates of 48 and 22. Pakistan (43 and 13), Nepal (42 and 17), and Bangladesh (37 and 13) all still have dangerously high rates of natural increase. That of Pakistan, 3 percent per year, is such that it would take a mere 23 years for the country's population to double. South Asia as a whole had a population of 1.14 billion in 1991, 21 percent of the world's total, and an overall growth rate of 2.2 percent (with a doubling time of 31 years).

Accompanying the foregoing changes have been significant reductions in the rates of infant mortality, ranging from 19 per 1,000 per year for Sri Lanka to 182 for Afghanistan, with a regional average of 95 (as compared with 9 in the United States); and in total fertility rates (the average number of children a woman may be expected to have, assuming she lives through her childbearing years), ranging from 2.5 for Sri Lanka to 7.1 for Afghanistan, with a regional average of 4.4 (versus 2.1 in the United States). There has also been a dramatic rise in life expectancy at birth from only about 35 years at the time of independence to a regional average of 57 years today, with a range from a low of 41 years in Afghanistan to a high of 70 in Sri Lanka. Finally, there has been a slow but steady increase in urbanization. For South Asia as a whole the proportion of the population living in urban areas has increased from about 16 percent in 1947 to 23 percent in 1991, still well below the average of 37 percent for the developing world and 43 percent for the world as a whole.

The age composition of South Asia's population is marked by a high proportion of young persons (38 percent below age 15 versus 22 percent in the United States) and a low proportion of the elderly (4 percent above age 65 versus 12 percent in the United States). The sex composition displays a strong male bias, attributable to selective neglect of females and generally difficult conditions of life for women. For every 1,000 males in 1991 there were only 929 females (versus 1,058 in the United States). Male life expectancy is several years greater than that of females, in marked contrast to most countries of the world.

Almost all South Asians marry. Divorces are very rare; but the commonly wide age discrepancy between males and females at marriage makes for high rates of widowhood. Polgynous marriages are legal, but rare, among Muslims. Among non-Muslims in India such marriages are no longer sanctioned, though those that have already been consummated remain legal. South Asian families tend to be large, and households often include more than one married couple, for example, a father and his sons and their respective spouses. This type of "joint family," eating at a common hearth and sharing the earnings of all, is looked on as the ideal. Its rupture is traumatic. While kinship systems vary greatly from one region, religion, and social group to another, bonds of kinship tend everywhere to be quite strong. Kinship by blood and marriage is supplemented by various forms of "fictive kinship," for example, that of viewing all members of one's village as brothers and sisters, even, for some purposes, across caste lines. Within the household, each adult member has well-defined social and economic roles, with concomitant expectations of respect and deference for those of higher status. Rules as to whom one may marry are often complex and vary by religion, caste, and region. North Indian Hindu males, for example, must marry females from outside their natal village and a circle of surrounding villages. Marriages among first cousins within one's own village are favored in southern India and are permitted in Islamic society. Almost everywhere most marriages are arranged, often by professional matchmakers, though so-called love marriages are slowly becoming socially acceptable in large urban areas. Problems of growing concern are insistence, especially among urbanized north Indians, on exorbitantly high dowries and pro-male bias in the rearing and care of children. (*See also* Birth Control; Demography; Family; Marriage/Remarriage)

Joseph E. Schwartzberg

REFERENCES

Cassen, R.H. *India: Population, Economy, Society.* New York: Holmes & Meier, 1978.

Dyson, Tim, ed. *India's Historical Demography: Studies in Famine, Disease, and Society.* London: Curzon Press, 1989.

Kapadia, K.M. *Marriage and Family in India,* 2nd ed. London: Oxford University Press, 1958.

Mitra, Asok. *India's Population: Aspects of Quality and Control,* 2 vols. New Delhi: Abhinav Publications, 1978.

Schwartzberg, Joseph E., ed. *A Historical Atlas of South Asia* (updated 2nd impression). New York: Oxford University Press, 1992.

South Asian Festivals

The social history of festivals and fairs in the South Asian subcontinent is rooted in the amateur ethnography conducted by British administrators, who hoped to control Indian society both physically and intellectually through knowledge. Local administrators produced a variety of descriptive materials: some were intended for scholarly study by other ethnographers at home in England and in the subcontinent (documenting particular practices of a people or place); some contributed to the body of general administrative knowledge (e.g., the lists of fairs and festivals appended to the gazetteer created for each district, a massive project produced in the late 19th century); and some were designed to facilitate local control (e.g., the "District Notebooks" compiled in the early 20th century, which described in detail how religious observances and other festivals were staged in order to prevent expansion and innovation). These analyses never constituted simple descriptions; the depictions always supported a particular (if changing) set of assumptions about Indian society and how it is organized. (Indeed, a relatively new kind of social history often called the "sociology of knowledge" has been developed to study this genre of information. Represented best, perhaps, by the recent work of Bernard Cohn (1987) and Christopher Pinney (1990), this analysis has probed the processes by which evidence was gathered and organized to support an interpretation of Indian society that fit the colonial ideology of rule.) Festivals played an important part in this construction of knowledge, as they supported a picture of vast mobs gathered together to express blind and unreasoning religious devotion.

Academic successors to these studies were pioneered by anthropologists and consequently focused through the 1970s on rural festivals, which tended to be more domestically oriented and smaller in scale. The classic account in this genre is McKim Marriot's (1967) amusing analysis of Holi, the ubiquitous festival celebrated throughout India as a "ritual of reversal," in which those lowest in the social hierarchy (emboldened by drinking bhang, a marijuana-based beverage) fling colored water and powders, even cow dung, at those in power. Marriot argued, however, that this ostensible reversal of normal power relationships actually reinforced the status quo by emphasizing that this was the *only* occasion on which resistance could be expressed.

Ground-breaking work by historians might be dated to 1977, when Breckenridge, Appadurai and Stein underscored the role played by South Indian temple festivals in regulating power relationships and redistributing resources; this work attracted the attention of social historians to the role of festivals in urban life and in the conduct of the state. Changes over time in the composition and conduct of processions have proved to be particularly crucial pieces of historical evidence for social historians, because these public ceremonials provide the most regular and sustained expressions of the values and viewpoints held by the polity. Festivals reflected changes in value systems; they were used as a yardstick to determine legitimacy and appropriateness; and they became the focal points of contestation. They created, as well, the symbolic vocabulary used on other occasions, in protest activities.

A significant body of work has begun to emerge on the array of processions staged in South Asian urban spaces, especially those connected to the Fall Dassehra festival, during which events are enacted from the story of Ram (avatar of the god Vishnu). Although most work has been focused on these Ramlilas, the same areas in north India witnessed a similar development and expansion of Muharram, a processional observance mourning particular events important to Shi'as (a minority community of Muslims) but used in many urban places to serve more generally as a collective expression of Indian Islam. The process described here for Ram's story, therefore, may stand in for a larger set of developments important for the social history of British India. Lasting from 10 to 41 days, these Ramlilas—dramatized tellings of Ram's coronation, exile, battles with demons to save his devoted wife Sita, and eventual triumphant return to his role as king—provide numerous occasions to enact the central values and favorite stories of the South Asian polity.

Two examples will suggest the social history implications of Ram-related festivals. Nita Kumar (1988), in the context of a social history of the artisans of Banaras, traced significant changes in a staging of the Nakatayya festival, in which the cutting off of the nose of a forward demoness was elaborated by a lower-class neighborhood into a popular festival of reversal. By the early 20th century, enactment of this event became the occasion for wild costumes, "lewd" tableaux, unrestrained behavior in the streets, and the shouting of verses ridiculing local power holders. Coterminous with the nationalist movement, an elite effort to sanitize and contain this festival sedated its expressions by the 1940s and 1950s.

In much the same period, Sandria Freitag (1990) has examined anxious British administrative documentation tracing an increased politicization of Ramlila (and other) processions: traditional figures being paraded and represented in tableaus were joined by images of nationalist leaders, heroic figures from the 1857 Mutiny/Revolt, and even representations of concepts such as Bande Mataram ("Mother India"). The changing content of this entertaining but critically important form of communication, then, enables analysts to gauge what mattered both to those who sponsored and to those who participated as audience for these processions. As a consequence, festivals document important ideological and organizational changes that form society and its historical narrative. (*See also* Community; Festivals; South Asian Popular Culture)

Sandria B. Freitag

REFERENCES

Cohn, Bernard. *An Anthropologist Among the Historians, and Other Essays.* New Delhi: Oxford University Press, 1987.

Freitag, Sandria B. *Culture and Power in Banaras: Community, Performance and Environment, 1800–1980.* Berkeley and Los Angeles: University of California Press, 1990.

Kumar, Nita. *The Artisans of Banaras: Popular Culture and Identity, 1880–1986.* Princeton, NJ: Princeton University Press, 1988.

Marriott, McKim. "The Feast of Love," in Milton Singer, ed., *Krishna: Myth, Rites and Attitudes.* Chicago: University of Chicago Press, 1967.

Pinney, Christopher. "Colonial Anthropology in the 'Laboratory of Man,'" in C.A. Bayly, ed., *The Raj: India and the British, 1600–1947.* London: National Portrait Galley Publications, 1990.

Stein, Burton, ed. *South Indian Temples: An Analytical Reconsideration.* New Delhi: Vikas, 1978; originally published as a special issue of *Indian Economic and Social History Review,* 1977.

South Asian Gender

Historically, gender distinctions have been sanctioned by all major South Asian religions and reinforced by social institutions. Waves of conquerors—Aryans, central Asian Muslims, Europeans—have carried into India new cultural and social institutions as well as new gender ideologies.

The *varna*, or early caste system, of ancient India divided men into four broad classes: priests, kings and military leaders, merchants, and laborers. Women were born, married, and had children within these *varnas* and performed the work roles associated with household and family. Men from the first three *varnas* were termed "twice-born," signifying their initiation into full-scale participation in religious life. The idealized conceptualization of the twice-born man's life cycle included four stages: student, householder, retiree, and ascetic. Neither women nor *shudras* (laborers) participated in these four stages. Women's life stages were determined by marriage. From childhood they learned about household work; the sacrament of marriage marked entry into the roles of wife and mother. If the husband died before the wife she was regarded as inauspicious for the remainder of her life.

Shudras were also limited in their life stages, but one cannot equate the lives of *shudras* with those of higher caste women. The daughters, wives, and widows of the twice-born enjoyed the high status and wealth of their husbands. They were required to live according to codes designed to uphold family honor and perform household religious ceremonies to ensure the family's good fortune. There is ample evidence that the system produced strong and capable women whose life histories seemed to belie the roles allotted to them by religious treatises. Many of these women experienced a dramatic loss of status when their husbands died. They were then barred from many religious ceremonies and rituals including marriage. By contrast, *shudra* men and women were laborers from birth and were not accorded the same religious status and duties as the twice-born men and their mates.

In practice, individuals identified with *jati*, rather than the broad category of *varna*. One was born into and married with the same *jati*. In the south cross-cousin marriage was preferred whereas in the north marriage partners were sought among strangers. The negative effects of customs such as dowry and the preference for sons were exacerbated when marriage took the female away from her kin.

In the 19th century, *jatis* became political associations and often enforced ritual behavior as well as gender ideology. As caste associations sought upward mobility for their members they frequently emulated gender rules formulated for the higher castes. According to a process termed Sanskritization, child marriage, female seclusion, and prohibitions on widow remarriage became even more widely practiced.

Islam, a religion that entered India through trade and conquest (ca. AD 800–1100), introduced a new gender ideology. Muslim women had the right to worship Allah and read the Qur'an, as well as the right to inherit and own property. Preference was for marriage with close family relations and theoretically the agreement of the daughter was sought before the contract was sealed. Sex segregation and female seclusion were part of Muslim social life, and the militaristic ethos of the new Muslim kingdoms reinforced these practices. Seclusion of women was already practiced in the warrior states of northern India and among many families of high status; once these customs were sanctioned by the rulers they became even more entrenched. This has led some historians to blame those customs which have excluded females from full participation in public life (e.g., child marriage, polygyny, and neglect of education) on Muslim invasions.

The British rulers introduced another gender ideology in the 19th century and reinforced it through taxation, opportunities for career advancement, and grants to educational institutions. They too maintained sex segregation and sexual difference but characterized their system as higher on an evolutionary scale than that which they found in India. Unlike previous invaders, the British brought women with them—wives, daughters, missionaries, teachers, and medical women. Employment with the British Raj (the imperial government) was largely limited to men but acceptance of a new gender ideology was necessary for these men to gain promotion. British women, both wives of officials and missionaries, helped establish new institutions (e.g., the Dufferin Fund to train medical women) that employed women. Women were now strongly encouraged to enter the public sphere—to seek education, perform social service, work in a "ladylike profession" (teaching or medicine), and engage in petition politics. While the British

claimed they had introduced significant reforms to improve the status of women (e.g., abolishing *sati* [widow burning] and allowing widow marriage), they also reinforced old customs with the weight of a new formal legal system (e.g., conjugal rights were now enforced by the courts).

The struggle for freedom involved both men and women. Led by Mahatma Gandhi, the Indian National Congress was pledged to using a nonviolent strategy. Gandhi acknowledged the influence of his religious mother and the English suffragettes on his tactics. He challenged Indians to turn the "weakness of women" into strength and insisted women be included in all phases of the fight for freedom. It was the Gandhian movement of the 1920s and 1930s that brought women into public political life.

Since 1947 women have played significant roles in all the countries of South Asia. The political achievements of women such as Prime Ministers Indira Gandhi of India (1966–1977, 1980–1985), Sirimavo Bandaranaike of Sri Lanka (1960–1965, 1970–1972), Benazir Bhutto of Pakistan (1989–1990), Khaleda Zia of Bangladesh (1991), make this region of the world unique. At the same time, many studies and reports emphasize the absence of "gender justice" and the low survival rate of women in relation to men (94:100). The answers to this seeming paradox are best sought in historical developments, social institutions, and economic policies.

In these lands of compulsory heterosexuality only male transvestites (*hijras*) have found a niche. India, Pakistan, and Sri Lanka all punish male homosexuality with imprisonment under the Unnatural Offenses Law; there are no laws prohibiting lesbianism. Since conventional gender ideology involves a denial of the existence of same sex relationships, there is little evidence regarding practice.

In South Asia today there are no significant movements designed to break down sex segregation and bridge gender differences. However, this need not be seen in negative terms. Sex segregation may ultimately serve the interests of those seeking a greater degree of gender equality. (*See also* Caste System; Hinduism; Islam; Women's History)

Geraldine Forbes

REFERENCES

Mandelbaum, David G. *Women's Seclusion and Men's Honor.* Tucson: University of Arizona Press, 1988.

Miller, Barbara D. *The Endangered Sex.* Ithaca, NY: Cornell University Press, 1981.

South Asian Migration

Migration, beginning with the coming of Indo-Europeans in the 2nd millennium BC, has a long history in South Asia and a long tradition of adding to its ethnic, linguistic, and cultural diversity. People from very early on have also moved abroad, scattering across Asia and Africa. And over a thousand years ago, Tamil invaders and immigrants from southern India began pushing into Sri Lanka. In the colonial diaspora of the 19th century a few million people shifted to other parts of the British Empire. The so-called Indian Tamils of Sri Lanka (to be distinguished from the earlier migrants known as the Tamils of Sri Lanka) were part of this exodus. Massive event-specific movements—involving refugees crossing national boundaries because of changing political alignments (e.g., independence and partition of India and Pakistan and later the creation of Bangladesh) or people moving because of famines or floods (e.g., Bangladesh)—constitute yet another chapter in the history of migration.

The colonial period also witnessed considerable internal migration, particularly of people moving from the countryside to major urban and industrial centers, such as Bombay, Calcutta, Madras, and the emerging urban-industrial complexes of the late 19th and early 20th centuries. Largely seasonal or circular in nature much of this movement comprised labor migration. Other migration streams flowed toward plantations, newly developed lands, and mining areas. The largest movement was of women involved in marriage migration, typically moving to join their husbands because of local traditions of village exogamy or caste endogamy.

Comparatively, the volume of migration in South Asia has been considered to be small. Recent census data for India indicate that over 90 percent reside in the state in which they were born, and well over 80 percent within the boundaries of the district of birth. In other words, well over 10 percent of the population, in sheer numbers over 50 million people, were enumerated outside their district of birth, a percentage that has been steadily rising in the 20th century. And if those who live in a village or town other than the place of their birth are designated migrants, almost a third of the population can be counted as migrants.

Most migrants have historically moved within rural areas; a small percentage have been involved in rural-to-urban migration and an even smaller number in urban-to-urban migration. Women constitute an enormous proportion of all migrants.

Although the current preoccupation with diaspora studies has led to a surge of interest in international migration, internal migration, particularly its patterns at the national and regional levels, continues to generate the most attention. Much of this literature relies on statistical analyses of macrolevel data; case studies at the microlevels are rare. And, as for other parts of the world, the emphasis is primarily on rural-to-urban migration; questions regarding urbanization and linkages between city, town, and village generally take analytical priority over other kinds of concerns.

Such spatial and analytical biases reflect the data utilized in most studies: census materials that are amenable to quantification and informative regarding the patterns and flow of migration. Much of the data relate to place of birth information that designates a person enumerated at a place other than that of his or her birth as a migrant. (Until 1961 Indian censuses did not report on intradistrict movement.) These indirect place of birth data have little to say regarding different kinds of mobility (e.g., marriage migration, or political, economic, social, or casual movement). Neither is there much regarding the socioeconomic identity of migrants, nor much about the number of moves made by people. Generated every ten years, census data, furthermore, make comprehensive temporal analyses of migration difficult.

A dominant mode of analysis well into the 1970s (and still enjoying some currency) has been to relate internal migration to processes of modernization or economic development. Such an approach keys on rural-urban movement as the most critical migration because its emphasis is on delineating the relationship between migration and urbanization and industrialization. The spotlight therefore is on the receiving communities (city, town, factory, etc.) or on the migrants themselves. Another tendency is to link movement to uneven development, to attribute migration to a mix of push and pull factors (e.g., scarce resources and abundant labor in the places of origin and rich capital and scarce labor in the places of destination). Migrants in this approach are conceived of as driven by economic motivations to make "rational" choices.

Largely ignored in the literature are other types of migration—rural-to-rural, urban-to-urban and urban-to-rural—and other kinds of questions—particularly those of interest to social historians. Note the virtual absence of historical and ethnographical studies examining the sociocultural factors involved in mobility. And although the relationship between migration and ethnicity has been explored, most of the research has been fitted into the modernization framework. Migration, according to this view, ignites the volatile mix created by India's multiethnic society, uneven regional development, and territorial units (states) organized by historical, cultural, and linguistic regions. Movement, because it entails crossing ethnic lines, sets off this mix resulting in conflict pitting "outsiders" against local "sons of the soil"—for instance, Bengalis in Assam, Kerala migrants in Madras, Tamil migrants in Bombay, or Hindu migrant laborers in Punjab. Similar dynamics are perceived at work in violent confrontations in Pakistan, Bangladesh, and Sri Lanka, where clashes between the Tamil minority and the Sinhala majority have plunged the nation into crisis.

One encouraging development is the growing interest in sending communities. Initial findings drawn from village studies have produced some surprises: migration appears not to have benefited sending villages economically and socially, but to have intensified poverty and exacerbated local imbalances of gender and age. Much more needs to be done generally on the effects of migration on family structure and gender roles, and much, much more, on the little studied subject of marriage migration. And for all the topics and themes mentioned here, social historical

works are few and far between. The detailed attention social historians have paid to population movements in Europe, Africa, and the Americas is not yet available for South Asia, particularly before very recent decades. (*See also* Migration)

Anand A. Yang

References

Connell, John, Biplab Dasgupta, Roy Laishley, and Michael Lipton. *Migration from Rural Areas: The Evidence from Village Studies.* Delhi: Oxford University Press, 1976.

Gosal, G.S., and G. Krishan. "Patterns of Internal Migration in India," in Leszek A. Kosinski and R. Mansell Prothero, eds., *People on the Move: Studies on Internal Migration.* London: Methuen, 1975, pp. 193–206.

Weiner, Myron. *Sons of the Soil: Migration and Ethnic Conflict in India.* Princeton, NJ: Princeton University Press, 1978.

South Asian Popular Culture

Although the term "popular culture" has been much debated in the scholarly literature, South Asianists have identified a range of activities that point to distinctive characteristics. One example might be the music subgenre *biraha*, which began as a style of folk music, played solely in villages by the *Ahir* (cowherding) caste, especially at weddings. While keeping much of its distinctive form and instrumentation, over the last four or five decades the style of *biraha* has evolved into a form of music broadly popular in cities, recognized and promulgated by All-India Radio and the cassette industry. Particular performers enjoy "star" status over much of (urbanized) India. Live performances are still the norm, however, and, generally speaking, performance venues remain those accessible to lower-caste /class audiences—for example, bazaars, street corners, temple courtyards (when performers serve as an opening act for temple renewal ceremonies), open fields, and the like. Lyrics refer to issues of the day, are marked by raucous humor, and include personalized references to members of the audience, who come forward with contributions for the musicians during each performance. Perpetuation of the genre and, indeed, of each performance group is ensured by the social organization of performance through *akharas,* a form of organization that can be traced back several centuries for performance troupes as well as physical fitness or wrestling bands, but which was expanded around the turn of the 20th century as a way of structuring voluntary activities. Members of a performing *akhara* are connected by fictive kin ties to each other, and dyadically to the leader through ties of devotion and discipline. The standard performance format is, literally, one of artistic battle. Two performing groups, representing different *akharas,* "face off" on two separate platforms, with the audience seated in between. First one group performs, then the other, and the audience ultimately decides the "winner" of the contest.

Competitiveness, public accessibility through enactments in open spaces, commentary on contemporary events that expresses and shapes shared values, the amalgamation of sociability and organizational forms to ensure perpetuation are all characteristics that help define popular culture. They also provide valuable historical evidence, which partly explains why social historians have focused on popular culture. Studies of urban popular culture, particularly, have delineated the aspects of everyday life, including forms of entertainment (especially music, street theater, wrestling, etc.) and other leisure-time activities, as well as the "invention" of Sunday as a day off. Conceptions of space, as these relate to popular culture activities, have begun to be explored as well, ranging from urban-dwellers' "mental templates" to their varied uses and claims to open, public space (contrasted with conceptions of domestic space). The interaction of mass consumer culture (especially that represented by the music and stars of Hindi film) has also begun to be documented. Consistent with the scholarship on popular culture for other world regions, the place of fairs and festivals in popular culture has claimed scholarly attention, as have devotional activity and the capacity of popular culture heroes and concepts to be harnessed to ideological movements for lower-class/caste uplift and resistance.

A number of conclusions have begun to emerge from these studies. First, the activities pursued have formed the focal point for significant forms of voluntary association (or sociabil-

ity) capable of perpetuating cultural forms and messages from generation to generation. At the same time, because popular culture also provided fundamental avenues along which competition and contestation could be routed, these forms could be tapped for other purposes, including the construction and invocation of community identity. Second, the patronage required to support performers, religious specialists, and other practitioners or facilitators of popular culture has devolved in significant ways down to the lower classes themselves. In South Asia, the 18th and early 19th centuries saw a devolution of patronage from the courts to the corporate communities (composed especially of merchants and dispersed courtiers) located in the newly emerging urban centers. In the late 19th and early 20th centuries these middle-class patrons tried first to co-opt many expressions (e.g., a festival for the elephant god Ganpati in Bombay was turned into a Hindu nationalist observance). By the 1930s this elite then began trying, simultaneously, to sanitize or contain expressions of popular culture, and to withdraw from physical participation in these activities. The result, since the 1960s and 1970s, has been popular culture activities more exclusively supported and shaped by lower-class audiences themselves. Third, the increasing global ties among those with Indian ancestry has fostered both a transnational flow of video- and audiotape cassettes and a broadened frame of reference and audience that is reshaping popular culture into "public culture" (spawning, in part, a new journal by that name to document this postmodern, postcolonial phenomenon). (*See also* Caste System; Community; Festivals; Leisure; Popular Culture)

Sandria B. Freitag

REFERENCES

Chakrabarty, Dipesh. "Open Space/Public Place: Garbage, Modernity and India," in "Aspects of 'the Public' in Colonial South Asia," special issue of *South Asia* 14, 1 (June 1991): 15–32.

Kumar, Nita. *The Artisans of Banaras: Popular Culture and Identity, 1880–1986.* Princeton, NJ: Princeton University Press, 1988.

Marcus, Scott L. "The Rise of a Folk Music Genre: Biraha," in S. Freitag, ed., *Culture and Power in Banaras.* Berkeley and Los Angeles: University of California Press, 1990, pp. 93–116.

Masselos, Jim. "Spare Time and Recreation: Changing Behaviour Patterns in Bombay at the Turn of the Nineteenth Century," *South Asia* 7, 1 (June 1984).

O'Hanlon, Rosalind. *Caste, Conflict and Ideology: Mahatma Jotirao Phule and Low Caste Protest in Nineteenth Century Western India.* Cambridge: Cambridge University Press, 1985.

South Asian Regionalism

In India and neighboring countries of contemporary South Asia (excepting such minor states as Bhutan and the Maldives) regionalism is an important political reality, often posing a serious threat to national unity. The roots of that regionalism run very deep. In contrast to patterns in China, in which a single powerful state has been the norm and political fragmentation the exception, the history of India is one in which, notwithstanding the overarching cultural unity provided by Hinduism, pan-Indian empires were exceptional and relatively short-lived, while varying and sometimes extreme degrees of political disunity were the norm.

Evidence of a keen awareness of regional diversity abounds in ancient Indian texts, extending as far back as the Vedic hymns composed over a period of centuries beginning in the mid-2nd millennium BC. There one finds abundant reference to the opposition of a group of invading Aryans and darker-skinned peoples, the presumed ancestors of India's present-day speakers of Dravidian languages and of numerous tribal peoples. As the Aryans consolidated their hold over north-central India, especially the middle Gangetic plain, they referred to their new homeland as Madhyamoā Di's, the central country, and invested it with a particularly sacred status, which it retains to this day. Awareness of regional distinctiveness is also apparent in numerous passages from the *Mahābhārata* and the *Rāmāyana*, the two great epic poems of ancient India. As a final illustration, each of another group of texts called the *Purānas* (literally, "ancient writings") contains a long encyclopedic section noting the names of scores of regions of India, grouped within the general framework of seven or eight macroregions, that still have cultural relevance for Indians.

Over the millennia, numerous invaders—Greeks, Scythians, Arabs, Turks, Mongols, Afghans, and others—penetrated the Indian subcontinent, especially through the Khyber Pass and other routes through the mountains on India's northwestern frontier. Many of these peoples carved out territories in which they established their supremacy. Although, with the passage of centuries, most such groups became Indianized, they remained sufficiently distinctive to put their cultural stamp on a region. For example, Rohilkhand, in the Indian state of Uttar Pradesh, signifies the country once ruled by the Rohilla Afghans. Similarly, the Indian state of Assam derives its name from the Ahoms, a group related to the Thais, who conquered the Brahmaputra River valley in the 13th century.

Of all the outside conquerors prior to the coming of the British, none was more successful than the Mughals, who ruled over much of India from 1526 to the mid-18th century. The provinces (*sūbahs*) that they established were sufficiently long-lasting and politically integrated to create yet another basis for regional sentiment, especially when, as in the cases of Kashmir, Gujarat, Bengal, Orissa, or Sind, those provinces were based on the recognition of a preexisting, essentially linguistic regional identity. While some Mughal provinces were essentially maintained as political units under British rule, most British provinces were arbitrarily bounded, based on the historical circumstances attending their annexation. As a result, they were culturally quite heterogeneous. When the Indian National Congress was agitating for independence, an important point in its political platform was the call for provinces organized on a linguistic basis. A concession to this demand was made in the creation of the essentially linguistic provinces of Orissa and Sind in 1935. Following independence, the demand for linguistic states escalated. Andhra (later Andhra Pradesh) was established as a Telugu-speaking state in 1954 and, following the Report of the States Reorganization Commission, the map of India was completely redrawn on linguistic lines in 1956. Even so, not all demands for new states were then met. Bombay State was partitioned into Maharashtra and Gujarat only in 1960; Punjab was partitioned in 1966; and other changes occurred in northeast India in subsequent years. An unfortunate concomitant of the establishment of Indian states along linguistic lines is what have been termed "nativistic movements," that is, movements to discriminate against "foreigners" (those whose mother tongue differs from the dominant language of the state), by limiting their access to certain types of political office, employment, or welfare benefits. More extreme expressions of nativist sentiment call for expulsion of unwelcome migrants, and numerous bloody riots have occurred in pursuit of that objective, especially with respect to Bengalis in Assam. Similar movements exist also in Pakistan.

The creation of linguistic states and provinces did not always suffice to meet the regionalist demands of specific linguistic groups. During the 1950s and 1960s, for example, agitators in the south Indian state of Tamil Nadu (literally, "country of the Tamils"), which has a particularly rich cultural legacy, were in the vanguard of a movement for the separation of "Dravidistan" from India. A somewhat similar situation existed in respect to the linguistic region of Bengal, which was partitioned between India and Pakistan in 1947 on the basis of religion. The successful struggle for secession from Pakistan in 1971 waged by Bangladesh (literally, "country of the Bengalis"), resulted largely from a profound sense of linguistically rooted cultural regionalism. While the neighboring Indian state of West Bengal now shows no sign of wishing to secede from India, many Hindu Bengalis did believe, as Indian independence approached, that union with their primarily Muslim fellow Bengalis in what was to become East Pakistan would have been preferable to union with fellow Hindus within the proposed dominion (later republic) of India.

The force of religious regionalism, which made the partition of India inevitable, has abated somewhat since 1947. Nevertheless, it remains extremely potent in several parts of South Asia. The most important largely religiously based regional movements, all accompanied by considerable and prolonged violence, are the struggles of the Sikhs for an independent state of Khalistan, including the whole of the Indian state of Punjab; of the Muslim Kashmiris, for either an independent state or union with Pakistan;

and of the Hindu Tamils in Sri Lanka, for an independent state of Tamil Eelam, a struggle abetted to some degree by fellow Tamils in India. In each of these cases religious identity is reinforced by linguistic distinctiveness, compounding the difficulty of finding a satisfactory resolution of the struggle.

Tribal and clan affiliation also underlies regionalism in various countries of South Asia, especially in the mountain belt along the subcontinent's frontiers with the rest of Eurasia. Afghanistan, in particular, is a country in which loyalty to one's tribe, and even to one's clan, commonly takes precedence over loyalty to the state. This fact is a major reason why establishing a unified front against the Marxist regime established with Soviet backing in 1979 proved so difficult. Other areas in which culturally distinct tribal groups have been engaged in protracted struggles for either independence or greater autonomy include Nagaland and other states in the far northeastern part of India, and the adjacent Chittagong Hills region of Bangladesh. In the Chota Nagpur region, including portions of the Indian states of Bihar, Orissa, and Madhya Pradesh, a movement to create a multitribal Jharkhand state has waxed and waned for decades.

A final basis for regionalism is the sense of economic neglect in certain relatively backward areas that, prior to Indian independence, were indirectly ruled or treated as "princely states," rather than directly ruled as provinces of "British India." Failure by the new state governments to redress the inherited economic imbalances was a common source of resentment and led to several unsuccessful attempts by certain areas to separate themselves from the states of which they were a part. (*See also* South Asian Colonialism)

Joseph E. Schwartzberg

REFERENCES

Crane, Robert I., ed. *Regions and Regionalism in South Asian Studies: An Exploratory Study.* Durham, NC: Duke University Press, 1967.

Fox, Richard G., ed. *Realm and Region in Traditional India.* Durham, NC: Duke University Press, 1977.

Schwartzberg, Joseph E., ed. *A Historical Atlas of South Asia* (updated 2nd impression). New York: Oxford University Press, 1992.

Spate, O.H.K., and A.T.A. Learmonth. *India and Pakistan*, 3rd ed. London: Methuen, 1967.

Spanish Civil War

The Spanish Civil War began in July 1936 as a military uprising led by General Francisco Franco against the newly elected Popular Front government. Since the abdication of Alfonso XIII in 1931, Spain's new democratic republican regime (known as the Second Republic) had undertaken policies directed at ameliorating endemic social, economic, and political problems. The Republic implemented a program of land reform, restructured the army, mandated the separation of church and state, and granted a measure of autonomy to the industrialized region of Catalonia. These policies alienated the right without moving quickly enough to satisfy the leftist political and labor parties burgeoning in Catalonia and in conflict-ridden Andalusia.

The insurgents were supported by most of the army, the church, monarchists, the *Falange* (Spanish fascist party), the landed classes, and aid from Italy and Germany. Parts of southern Spain and Galicia fell quickly to the Nationalists, while the Republic struggled to maintain control. Popular militias formed around political parties and labor organizations, and along with volunteers from abroad, remnants of the army, and scant amounts of aid from the Soviet Union and Mexico, were able to defend the Republic for nearly three years, in what amounted to full-scale social conflict.

But the social, political, and military situation was a complex one with layered conflict in some areas. In Catalonia, war unleashed a social revolution that included the collectivization of factories and agricultural production. The government moved to legalize the revolution but was unable to prevent an internal civil war between anarchosyndicalists and communists from exploding on the streets of Barcelona in May 1937.

Between 1936 and 1939, Spain became a testing ground for German, Italian, and some Soviet weaponry. Battles and political repression took the lives of some 440,000 persons; 160,000 additional persons emigrated in fear of the new regime's reprisals. Postwar cultural repression was especially harsh against the Catalans, who were perceived by Franco to be leftist and separatist.

The Spanish Civil War was essentially a class and ideological conflict. The significance of the war went well beyond the country's borders, adding to international tensions that led to World War II. The legacy of the war on the Spanish mentality has been profound, as evidenced in art, literature, music, and the political and cultural movements which became active as censorship and repression eased in the 1960s.

The extensive historical work done on the Spanish Civil War was at first primarily by English and American writers and then since the 1960s by Spaniards themselves. Many studies focused on the political aspects of the conflict, but important research early related the Spanish Civil War to deeper social tensions involving popular mentalities, landholding patterns, and other distinctive characteristics of 19th- and early 20th-century Spain. The sociohistorical research of recent years has been limited almost exclusively to the study of labor movements. At the same time, many social historians seek to expand beyond the Civil War to deal with other features of modern Spanish social history not so wrapped up in this traumatic event. (*See also* Fascism)

Montserrat Martí Miller

REFERENCES

Carr, Raymond. *The Spanish Tragedy.* London: Weidenfeld & Nicolson, 1977.

Linz, Juan, and Alfred Stepan, eds. *The Breakdown of Democratic Regimes: Europe.* Baltimore: Johns Hopkins University Press, 1978.

Orwell, George. *Homage to Catalonia.* London: Secker & Warburg, 1986.

Preston, Paul, ed. *Revolution and War in Spain. 1931–1939.* London: Methuen, 1984.

Thomas, Hugh H. *The Spanish Civil War.* New York: Harper & Row, 1977.

Spanish Conquest

The Spanish overseas conquests of the 15th and 16th centuries were organized and led by private individuals, with the monarchy playing only an occasional role in the process. The peoples of the Caribbean islands were so quickly decimated by disease, essentially disappearing by 1550, that no true conquest was ever really undertaken there. Nonetheless, Spanish settlers established basic patterns of organization and behavior in the Caribbean that they would transfer intact to the mainland. While heroics or dastardly Spanish conquerors have long figured prominently in textbook histories, social historians focus on group characteristics and interaction with native peoples.

The city functioned as the essential political unit. An expedition into a new area characteristically founded a city to bestow legitimacy on itself, endowing the enterprise with a recognized political status from which to challenge any rival claims. Colonists invariably sought out gold and silver mines in order to have a commodity to trade with Europe and also established commercial farms and ranches to feed their rapidly growing cities. Old World epidemic diseases decimated the natives, who had never been exposed to them. The survivors became personal retainers of individual Spaniards or had to provide periodic labor service for the settlers.

New expeditions were organized in the most recently established colonies. The conquests of Cuba, Puerto Rico, and Jamaica were launched from Santo Domingo; that of Mexico proceeded from Cuba. Subsequent ones radiated out from Mexico and Peru. The ventures were led by experienced colonists of standing who aspired to become governors of new provinces. The leaders regularly recruited kinsmen and other trusted associates, often from their home provinces in Spain, to function as their lieutenants. Leaders commonly went greatly into debt, even selling off their holdings, to finance their undertakings. Colonial merchants invested by advancing them additional necessities on credit.

The great majority of participants were recent arrivals in the Americas. Prospering colonists did not join these ventures. The rank and file overwhelmingly belonged to the middle sectors of Spanish society, with only titled nobles and peasants being dramatically absent. Members of the gentry; professionals such as notaries, physicians, and clerics; merchants; clerks; diverse artisans; mariners; a scattering of blacks and mulattoes—both slave and free—and a few foreigners were included among them.

The salient division of forces was between cavalry and footmen, with the cavalry typically constituting only a small fraction of the membership. The men were not under military discipline nor organized into ranks. They received no training upon joining the expedition and gained no salary. They signed on for a share of any rewards. A well-equipped man usually received one share; one with a horse merited a double share. Established colonists could invest in expeditions without themselves joining by equipping a member—which would probably entitle them to a half-share—or by contributing a horse (worth a full share). The leader and his associates claimed a number of shares each. All parties were very sensitive to the final distribution of booty, and rancor commonly resulted. A failed expedition could leave everyone in debt and result in revolts by the dissatisfied men.

The Spaniards enjoyed an overwhelming technological advantage against most native societies. Their metal weaponry and armor were not duplicated by the indigenous peoples, who instead used wooden clubs and arrows and javelins tipped with obsidian or other sharp rocks. Against most peoples, the Spaniards sought close combat, where they could use their swords and horsemen with lances to best advantage. Except against mobile hunting-and-gathering societies, which characteristically did not fight in formation in open territory, they did not make great use of gunfire.

The Spanish method of warfare, which stressed killing and desolation of towns and croplands, was especially effective against the sedentary empires of the Aztecs and Incas. The agricultural peoples of these vast and densely populated regions had for centuries fought in open areas in tight, very hierarchically organized formations, and they seemingly put more emphasis on capturing rather than killing their opponents. Their armies made little use of tactics, and entire units fell out of action when their commanders were killed or seized.

Many distinct ethnic groups made separate deals with the Spaniards, once they saw that the intruders might be a military match for the local people that had long subjugated them. Thus, the Spaniards did not have to fight all of the societies, but rather just the imperial centers.

Most subject peoples withdrew into neutrality or even offered the Spanish active support.

The epidemic diseases—particularly smallpox, measles, and typhus—that the Europeans and Africans brought with them ran rampant during and sometimes even before the conquests, killing vast numbers of people, disrupting lines of authority, and confusing and discouraging the afflicted, for their opponents were not similarly affected.

The Spanish experienced much less success against chiefdoms and hunting-and-gathering societies because they lacked empires whose leaders the Spaniards could capture and rule through. These peoples also fought in ways that were less susceptible to the Spanish mode of warfare. They were more mobile and adaptable, fought to kill, and commonly used bows and arrows, avoiding close combat.

The majority of conquerors remained in the colonies, where most of them enjoyed prestige and political power they could not attain in Spain. They well appreciated that enduring wealth derived from effective use of the land, resources, and people of the regions they had taken over. Most set up estates and businesses, recruiting family members and skilled individuals to join them. (*See also* Colonialism; Mining/*Mita*)

John E. Kicza

REFERENCES

Altman, Ida. *Emigrants and Society: Extremadura and Spanish America in the Sixteenth Century.* Berkeley: University of California Press, 1989.

Clendinnen, Inga. *Ambivalent Conquest: Maya and Spaniard in Yucatan, 1517–1570.* Cambridge, Eng.: Cambridge University Press, 1987.

Hassig, Ross. *Aztec Warfare: Imperial Expansion and Political Control.* Norman: University of Oklahoma Press, 1988.

Lockhart, James. *The Men of Cajamarca: A Social and Biographical Study of the First Conquerors of Peru.* Austin: University of Texas Press, 1972.

Powell, Philip Wayne. *Soldiers, Indians, and Silver: The Northward Advance of New Spain, 1550–1600.* Berkeley: University of California Press, 1952.

Sparta

Spartan social arrangements were designed to foster a citizen military elite, the Spartiates, dedicated to the maintenance of a large subject population. Attention to Spartan social organization has long formed part of the standard historical approach to this important Greek city-state. At an early age, boys were removed from their parents and subjected to a program of training characterized by austerity, discipline, and group solidarity; later, they married and eventually left the all-male barracks to establish their own households. Girls, residing with their parents until marriage, received a public education, though in later life a woman's primary role was as wife and mother of warriors. Marriage customs permitted the exchange of women, probably, along with certain apparently eugenic practices, in order to maximize the quality of male offspring. By the 4th century BC, as a result of the decline of citizen numbers, Spartiate women came into much land, but the extent to which this development was translated into actual influence is not clear.

Of the subject peoples, the *perioikoi*, "those who dwell around," occupied up to 100 independent towns enjoying local self-government. They provided soldiers for the Spartan army, reportedly in numbers equal to the Spartiates, and were subject to taxation. Settled on inferior lands, they also evidently owned their own slaves—not, however, helots, but chattels. Besides farming, the *perioikoi* may have engaged in industry, a likely function being the manufacture of armor. Militarily, the situation of the *perioikoi* in the districts surrounding the interior allowed them to serve as a buffer insulating Sparta from the outside world.

Probably a remnant of previously conquered populations, the helot slaves, or "captives," unlike the *perioikoi*, were established on the lands of the Spartiates themselves. Although apportioned to individual citizens, the helots were formally owned by the state in the sense that it alone could manumit. Their work extended to agriculture, pasturage, domestic service, and baggage-carrying on Spartan military expeditions. Not as servile as chattels, helots could own personal property and maintained a semblance of family life. Formally, helots were responsible to their masters to turn over a fixed amount of produce, with which the Spartiates, thus freed from all nonmilitary duties, paid their dues to the state. Far outnumbering the Spartiates, the helots posed a constant threat to security; the government's response was to declare "war" annually upon them and to terrorize them with random killings. Even so, revolts did occur, and Sparta's internal and external policies were seriously inhibited as a result. (*See also* Athenian Democracy; Greco-Roman Stratification; Slavery)

Nicholas F. Jones

REFERENCES

Cartledge, Paul. *Sparta and Lakonia. A Regional History, 1300–362 B.C.* London, Boston, and Henley: Routledge & Kegan Paul, 1979.

Forrest, W.G. *A History of Sparta 950–192 B.C.* London: Hutchinson & Co., 1968.

Spinsterhood

See Singlehood

Sport

Today's mass obsessions with sports Superbowls and World Cups have prompted historians to investigate the spectacles and contests of societies past. Most research expands the notion of "sport" to include not only physical competitions themselves but also related phenomena such as theories of exercise and training, notions of body culture, and changing rhythms of work and leisure. Scholars have typically tied change or continuity in sport's "interior" (e.g., game forms, equipment, ideologies) to some wider context (e.g., political economy, race or gender relations). They have examined sport in Africa, Asia, South America, and the Middle East, but the bulk of work has focused on the Western tradition, especially the Anglo-American experience, which heavily influenced today's most popular sports.

Although ancient, medieval, and Renaissance societies had rich (and sometimes sophisticated) sporting cultures, the last three centuries contain the most noteworthy historical development: the transformation of traditional agrarian pastimes into the commercial spectacles of urban-industrial societies. Rules, records, roles (such as spectator, player, administrator), facilities, and equipment have become much more formal, precise, and rational. For instance, the annual Shrovetide football match at Derby, England, had no real boundaries, no formal rules, and no limits on team size (500 to 1,000 might play per side). By contrast, today's brands of football (American, British, Canadian, Australian) each have established rules, standardized equipment and facilities, carefully plotted tactics, well-defined positions and roles, and myriad statistics and records to quantify and compare performances across time and space.

As some sports became more formal, they also went national and international. For instance, in 1850 Americans played many local versions of baseball. By 1880, the "New York" version had swept the country to become the national pastime. A similar process occurred with Canadian hockey in the last quarter of the century, with the "Montreal" game driving local versions of shinny or hurley to the frozen backwaters. This process of national or international standardization—where *some* games became *the* games—typically included the rise of bureaucratic leagues or governing bodies that sought order and control of rules and records. Many of today's strongest organizations arose during the "long" 19th century, when the bulk of metamorphosis occurred: in England, the Marylebone Cricket Club (1787), Football Association (1863); in American baseball, the National League (1876).

The context for this transformation was a capitalist system that slowly changed the economic, social, and cultural landscapes of Europe and North America. Rationalized production of agricultural and material goods disrupted traditional patterns of work and leisure; so did accompanying Puritan, evangelical, and bourgeois work ethics. Urban growth, fueled by massive immigration, raised widespread concerns about health and morality, some of which focused on sports like cockfighting and cudgelling. At the same time, innovations in communications and transportation, state funding of urban play space and education, and real increases (for some) in leisure time and discretionary income opened up markets for new or reformed sport products.

If capitalism provided a base for a new sport structure, then the main agents of change were entrepreneurs and professional experts who packaged and sold events, equipment, instruction, facilities, and attitudes. James Figg, who in 1720s

London began teaching pugilism (including forms of boxing, stick and swordplay) as a "Science of Defence," was the forebear of giants like Albert Spalding, who built a world-class sporting goods firm in the late 1800s, or Constance Applebee, who brought British field hockey to American college women in 1901.

Entrepreneurs and experts had great influence over the course of sport, but they were not alone. While participation and influence have always been uneven, today's games are the products of negotiations among players, spectators, commentators, coaches, and administrators, as well as among classes, races, genders, and nationalities.

For instance, workers (and their gentry allies) long resisted suppression of traditional pastimes, especially the violent animal sports; cockfighting and dogfighting continue today in many underground venues. Similarly, 19th-century working-class males like New York's John Morrissey made bare-knuckle prizefighting (then illegal) a ritual of resistance to bourgeois morality, turning "scientific" training to illicit ends, and launching their own careers in gambling, politics, or entertainment. Along similar lines, if cricket or football served British colonial agents as a medium for teaching a peculiar form of imperial "teamwork," victories by native clubs in Calcutta or the West Indies could foster impressive levels of resistance and local pride. Amateurism contained similar contradictions. In the last third of the 19th century, elites like Caspar Whitney invented amateurism as a safe haven of competition for the respectable classes. Nonetheless, some of the most aggressive "amateurists" were working-class refugees like James E. Sullivan, the bulldog of the American Amateur Athletic Union.

Gender and race relations have likewise influenced the direction of sport. Although women and blacks have experienced limited and often segregated access to sport, their struggles, victories, and defeats represent negotiations with dominant groups. Physical educators like Senda Berenson constructed women's basketball (1892) in reaction to commercial, violent, and spectacular male models. At the same time, however, many men promoted and embraced brutality in football, boxing, or hockey as an antidote to cul-tural softening and effeminacy. Likewise, the careers of Jack Johnson, Jackie Robinson, and Muhammad Ali say much about the shifting nature of discrimination and opportunity in American life.

Although historians have focused on transformations in sport during the last two centuries, one can also discern long residuals from the past—continuities in forms and meanings that have crossed time and context. These include notions of sport as craft and community; gambling practices; the framing of games within festival, carnival, and spectacle; the erotic appeals in athletic performance.

Sport history emerged slowly as a branch of social history, partly because many historians considered it a frivolous research interest and partly because traditional, antiquarian approaches still thrive in the form of purely descriptive accounts of individual sports heroes, teams, or statistics. Sports' importance in modern society has propelled a major expansion of serious, analytical scholarship, several important journals, and some intriguing debates about the meaning of sports to key groups in modern society (including spectators, whose history is just beginning to gain attention) and about changes in sports' role even within the modern era. (*See also* Leisure; Popular Culture)

Stephen Hardy

REFERENCES

Baker, William. *Sports in the Western World.* Urbana: University of Illinois Press, 1988.

Guttmann, Allen. *Sport Spectators.* New York: Columbia University Press, 1986.

Holt, Richard. *Sport and the British.* Oxford: Clarendon Press, 1989.

Rader, Benjamin. *American Sports.* Englewood Cliffs, NJ: Prentice-Hall, 1990.

Stalinism

The term "Stalinism" conveys a totalitarian system in which the bureaucracy is efficient and highly centralized, and in which the police act with unbridled license to enforce the dictator's unchallenged personal rule. Recent research, much of it using a social history rather than purely political focus, has cast serious doubt on this commonplace definition not only because it is inaccurate but also because it ignores the social policies which were essential components of Stalinism and the rapidly changing social realities which shaped Soviet society and politics during Stalin's rule (1928–1953).

Stalin's political victory in 1928–1929 resulted from his skillful manipulation of the Communist Party's bureaucracy and three policies which promised the realization of socialism in the USSR: cultural revolution; collectivization; and rapid, planned industrialization.

Cultural revolution had destructive and constructive components. The former entailed eliminating the political and economic power of alleged "bourgeois" groups in society. In industry, this was accomplished by political show trials of engineering and managerial personnel charged with economic sabotage in the service of capitalist restoration, and by mobilizing workers to expose "saboteurs" in their enterprises. In the professions, similar tactics were employed. By removing experienced, educated personnel, the "class-war" policy had many negative effects. In 1931, the party leadership abandoned it.

The constructive aspect was intimately linked to its destructive component. Stalin announced in 1928 that replacing "bourgeois specialists" necessitated the creation of a socialist intelligentsia. The government embarked on a mass educational campaign to provide working people with the educational and technical skills necessary to become economic administrators, engineers, technical personnel, or skilled workers. This policy of "proletarian advancement" was part of a broader educational reform designed to eliminate illiteracy and raise society's educational level. The number of educational institutions at all levels increased dramatically as did the proportion of children of proletarian origin who attended school. The policy initiated a period of rapid, upward social mobility for working people.

Collectivization sought to break the power of the peasant commune, destroy the three-field system and the practice of strip farming, and create a scientific basis for Soviet agriculture. To enact the policy, the state employed coercion more than incentives. Peasants often violently resisted the policy and its enforcers. Class war also extended to the villages, where the state sought to break the power of *kulaks* (rich peasants) and all who opposed collectivization. The effects on the rural economy were severe. They contributed significantly to the famine of 1932–1933. Millions of peasants fled the villages to escape collectivization and repression. To halt the exodus, the state withheld internal passports from the peasantry thereby limiting their right to leave the village and making peasants second-class citizens. Although 90 percent of peasant households were collectivized by 1936, the productivity of collective farms was less than that of peasants' small private gardens. Peasant discontent with party-appointed collective farm chairmen ran deep. The policy's negative consequences affected all of society. Food rationing lasted from 1928 to 1935, and food shortages generated popular discontent.

The cornerstone of Stalin's policies was rapid, planned industrialization. Despite significant problems, the accomplishments of the first Five-Year Plan (1928–1932) were unparalleled in history and created the economic basis for Soviet industrial development.

The unemployment crisis of the 1920s gave way to a labor shortage despite the influx of millions of former peasants, women, and youths into the work force. The size of the working class mushroomed. The demand for labor was so great that labor turnover often exceeded the size of the work force. High levels of geographical mobility characterized the period. Industrialization provided the stimulant to rapid urbanization. Existing cities' populations increased sharply, and new cities were constructed. Between 1926 and 1939, the proportion of the population living in urban areas jumped from 13 percent to 25 percent. A severe housing shortage gripped urban areas, where residents lived in overcrowded apartments, dormitories, and makeshift dwellings. Rationing, poor housing, and scarce consumer goods resulted in a low living standard in cities until 1935.

From 1932, the leadership sought to curtail the Stalin revolution's often disruptive consequences. The need for competent industrial personnel hastened the end of class war and the restoration of "bourgeois specialists." The power and prestige of industrial managers and technical staffs were enhanced. Educational opportunities continued to expand, but the need for competent personnel resulted in tighter traditional admission criteria based on performance. From 1932, social and economic stratification widened as the economic and political power of the elite rose sharply. Their economic success stood in marked contrast to the low, albeit improving, living standard of the population's vast majority.

The period's seeming calm masked deepening social discontent. Local officials' arbitrary interpretations of policy engendered many citizens' antipathy and many national leaders' suspicions. Unsatisfactory levels of industrial productivity and efficiency slowed economic growth. In 1935, the leadership launched the Stakhanovite campaign, the goal of which was to increase industrial productivity and efficiency. This was to be accomplished by rewarding workers who exceeded production norms while simultaneously urging workers to pressure management to achieve these goals. Conflict between workers and management increased as workers blamed management for their enterprises' problems. So too did intra-working-class tensions as many workers resented their co-workers' increased productivity, which raised production quotas for all workers.

The mid-1930s witnessed the enactment of conservative legislation regarding divorce and abortion, which had been available on demand. The new laws made divorce difficult to obtain and severely restricted the right to abortion. The changes were partly a reaction to the nation's steadily declining birth rate, itself a consequence of the fact that the vast majority of women worked. Women bore a double burden since they were responsible for virtually all aspects of domestic life.

Between 1928 and 1936, two variants of Stalinism existed. The first lasted until 1932, and was characterized by revolutionary policies designed to deepen class war, accelerate centralized economic planning, and provide opportunities for social mobility. The second gave primacy to social stability, economic productivity, and the rationalization of political administration.

Mid-1936 marked the onset of mass political repression. Traditionally, scholars have interpreted the repression of 1936–1939 as being a plan devised by Stalin to secure absolute power. This argument has been based more on assumptions than evidence. Recent research indicates that the repression's goal was to remove those political and economic personnel who obstructed efforts to centralize and make more efficient the bureaucracy. To accomplish these goals, rival groups within the political leadership relied either on the police or on mobilizing popular discontent with officials to "unmask" alleged "enemies of Soviet power."

Both interpretations agree that the effect on society was dramatic. The arrest, imprisonment, or execution of many officials and citizens entailed both personal tragedies for the victims and their families and opportunities for social mobility for those who replaced them. The campaign to "unmask enemies" often revealed the depth of popular frustration with officials, frustrations rooted in the officials' misuse of power for personal gain and their ignoring citizens' legal rights and human needs. Social tensions fueled the repression, which had contradictory social effects. On the one hand, many citizens feared that they would become victims, a fear which affected all aspects of their public and private lives. On the other hand, labor discipline and productivity fell sharply as many workers refused to heed their bosses' directives since the latter were viewed as "enemies." A significant proportion of industrial officials were repressed during the period. From 1939, the enactment of strict labor policies sought to reverse the decline of time and labor discipline and productivity, and enhance managerial power. Because many "enemies" were allegedly spies, xenophobia reached a fever pitch.

How many people were repressed and how many died during this period cannot yet be ascertained. Nor is it possible to determine which social or occupational groups were most affected. What the available evidence does suggest is that the repression fell most heavily on the political elite at all levels of society. To isolate the victims, the labor camp network (*Gulag*) expanded markedly. Although repression, violations of legal norms, and arbitrary rule antedated 1936, during the mass repression of 1936–1939, these characteristics became the defining features of Stalinism.

From 1939, a conservative variant of Stalinism emerged. The need for a stable bureaucracy and the prospect of war extinguished the remnants of revolutionary Stalinism. The fanning of class tensions gave way to calls for social unity. Soviet nationalism replaced the revolutionary internationalism of earlier years. Leaders demanded respect for hierarchy and discipline. Religion, once condemned as counterrevolutionary, was tolerated.

World War II profoundly affected Soviet society. More than 20 million citizens (one-eighth of the population) died; 1,710 towns and 70,000 villages were destroyed; and 25 million people became homeless. Millions of children lost one or both parents. The male-female ratio was severely distorted. Almost 32,000 industrial enterprises and 100,000 collective and state farms were destroyed as was much of the transportation system. The economic destruction during the war equaled 20 times the USSR's 1940 GNP.

From 1945 to Stalin's death in 1953, the imperatives of economic reconstruction and national security became the defining features of conservative Stalinism. Because productive enterprises were the first to be restored, the standard of living remained low. Rationing, housing shortages, and scarce consumer goods defined the citizenry's material lives. As the Cold War deepened, so too did xenophobia.

Stalinism was not a static political ideology but rather one in which competing political visions vied for primacy. Which vision was in the ascendancy was often determined by the social, economic, and political realities of the moment. (*See also* Collectivization; Russian Industrialization)

William Chase

REFERENCES

Getty, J. Arch. *Origins of the Great Purges.* Cambridge: Cambridge University Press, 1985.

Hindus, Maurice. *Red Bread.* Bloomington: Indiana University Press, 1988.

Kuromiya, Hiroaki. *Stalin's Industrial Revolution.* Cambridge: Cambridge University Press, 1988.

Rittersporn, Gabor. *Stalinist Simplifications and Soviet Complications.* Chur, Switzerland: Harwood Academic Publishers, 1991.

Siegelbaum, Lewis. *Stakhanovism and the Politics of Productivity in the USSR, 1935–1941.* Cambridge: Cambridge University Press, 1988.

Werth, Alexander. *Russia at War, 1941–1945.* New York: Carroll and Graf, 1964.

Standard of Living

The standard of living is a concept used to denote well-being. It enables one to measure change over time, and to assess cross-sectional differences between different societies or between different regions or classes of the same society, at a point in time. It has three components: material, biological, and psychological. The first of these is the common interpretation of the concept, and is defined in terms of the command over goods and services, measured by real per capita income. The other two components are defined in terms of how well the human organism thrives in its socioeconomic and epidemiological environment. Frequency and duration of sickness, life expectancy, and physical stature have all been used as indicators of biological well-being.

Measurement of the standard of living is made extremely difficult by the paucity or poor quality of the relevant historical evidence. Even the calculation of real per capita income, necessary to trace change over time, requires accurate and geographically representative price and wage indexes, which are scarce before the 20th century. There are many other problems associated with the construction of such series: daily wages cannot be accurately converted into annual income, nor personal income into family income; moreover, wage data are typically limited to a few occupations. We also do not know enough about the length of the workday, the incidence of unemployment, and the prices of some nontradeable goods, such as rents. These difficulties are compounded by the "index number problem," that is, the fact that the results can be influenced by which base year is chosen for the series. Analogous problems arise when one compares different societies at the same point in time. The exchange rate may not reflect true purchasing power parity, and the societies might be at different levels of commercialization.

Differences in how different segments of a population fared over time also complicate historians' efforts to quantify well-being. Women and children, and such groups as aristocrats, slaves, and subsistence farmers, generally did not participate directly in market activity and therefore were isolated from short-run market forces reflected in prices and wages; hence real-wage indexes are not relevant measures of their well-being. Because of these uncertainties, conventional indicators of well-being are seldom definitive.

Consequently, the so-called standard of living debate continues to rage among historians, generating considerable research in 19th-century social and economic history. The disagreement is between the "pessimists," who argue that the well-being of a fairly large segment of society was decreasing during the industrial revolution in Britain, and the "optimists" who argue the opposite with equal certitude. All agree, however, that in the long run the standard of living improved enormously. The discussion is complicated by the fact that during the initial phases of industrialization, as economist Simon Kuznets has shown, the distribution of income becomes more skewed.

To gain additional insight into these issues, and as the classic standard of living issues have declined as a social history focus, some economic historians have turned to the physical sciences to assess changes in the biological well-being of the human organism. This research program is still in its beginnings. An examination of anthropometric evidence indicates that as part of its adaptability to its socioeconomic environment, human physical stature has undergone cyclical change during the course of the last quarter of a millennium. In Europe a downturn in physical stature occurred in response to demographic pressures in the second half of the 18th century and again in the second quarter of the 19th century. On American soil a major downturn has also been identified beginning among the birth cohorts of the 1830s; this decline was probably caused not only by rapid population growth and urbanization, but also by the inability of the agricultural sector to keep pace with the expansion of the industrial labor force. Thus, it is becoming evident that the various compo-

nents of the standard of living need not always move procyclically.

Social historians have paid increased attention to mentalities and to expectations involved with changing consumer behavior in assessing what the various components of standard of living mean, in addition to efforts to measure changes and variations in absolute levels. Why some groups use extra income on housing while other groups devote extra income to entertainment or affording more children constitute the types of questions investigated under this heading. (*See also* Anthropometric History; Food; Health; Houses and Housing; Material Culture)

John Komlos

REFERENCES

Boot, H.M. "Salaries and Career Earnings in the Bank of Scotland, 1730–1880," *Economic History Review* 44 (1991): 629–653.

Komlos, John. "The Height and Weight of West Point Cadets: Dietary Change in Antebellum America," *Journal of Economic History* 47 (1987): 897–927.

———. "The Secular Trend in the Nutritional Status of the Population of the United Kingdom, 1730–1860." *Economic History Review*, forthcoming.

Mokyr, Joel. "Is There Still Life in the Pessimist Case?: Consumption During the Industrial Revolution, 1790–1850," *Journal of Economic History* 48 (1988): 69–92.

Riley, James C. *Sickness, Recovery and Death*. Iowa City: University of Iowa Press, 1989.

Sen, Amartya. *The Standard of Living*. Cambridge: Cambridge University Press, 1987.

Steckel, Richard. "Stature and Living Standards in the United States," National Bureau of Economic Research, Working Paper No. 24, April 1991.

State and Society

Since the 1960s many social historians have tried to link political and social history by investigating the changing relationship between state and society. This effort gained momentum partly in reaction to criticism that in their eagerness to explore new terrain social historians had lost sight of politics. Some historians also drew inspiration from Marxist debates about the state in capitalist societies. Above all, historians felt the influence of sociologists and political scientists who were rebelling against society-centered explanations for political behavior—that is, seeing politics and governmental institutions as direct reflections of societal structures, conflicts, and change—that had long dominated their disciplines. By 1985, when Peter Evans, Dietrich Rueschemeyer, and Theda Skocpol published a collection of essays entitled *Bringing the State Back In,* state-centered explanations had won new respectability in the social sciences. Historical developments during the 1970s and 1980s further reinforced this trend. As the welfare state came under attack and Keynesian economic policy lost its luster, and as postcolonial states outside the West assumed an extraordinary variety of forms, it became harder to believe states were mere products of evolutionary, societal change. States appeared to be more diverse, more subject to dynamic processes of their own, and more important in explaining societal change itself than social scientists had appreciated. In this context the state had become a legitimate subject, and the interplay between state and society, a major theme, in social historical research.

In taking up these issues, scholars hardly started from scratch. For over a century historians had written about politics and state-building with considerable interest in the influences of social and economic change. Much of this older literature found new readers as historians and social scientists used it as source material for making new arguments about state-society relations. More important, scholars drew on ideas from major social theorists of the 19th century. From Karl Marx they borrowed notions of how states became arenas of class conflict and instruments of class rule. From German sociologist Max Weber they learned to see the state as a cultural, organizational, and legal entity—as authority, bureaucracy, and rules—that evolved not just in response to societal pressures but also in accord with an internal developmental logic. And from French sociologist Alexis de Tocqueville's studies of France and the United States historians were inspired to explore how state structures and political culture could affect all kinds of seemingly nonpolitical aspects of life, such as the relationship between men and women, parents and children, or teachers and students.

Although the field of state-society studies continues to evolve in fresh ways, several approaches have taken firm shape since the 1970s. One approach has explored the relationship between state-building and large-scale structural changes in society. Historian-sociologist Charles Tilly has studied state-building in Europe with an eye toward its links to the growth of capitalism and changes in the structure of social protest. Over the course of several centuries social rebellion inspired rulers to strengthen and expand the state, which in turn led later rebels to invent new forms of social protest. Sociologist Theda Skocpol (1979) has taken a more explicitly Weberian approach to state-building in her comparison of the French, Russian, and Chinese revolutions. She has argued that these revolutions occurred not simply because of social conflicts in the countryside, which were common elsewhere, but because state authority in these societies collapsed under the pressure of international crises. The revolutions then became occasions for refashioning the state and greatly expanding its capacities, which in turn enabled new elites to enforce new social relations in the countryside. Skocpol's emphasis on state autonomy, international context, and the reciprocal interplay between social structures and state capacities has had a major impact on the field. Several Latin Americanists have also broken ground in the study of state formation, a process they see crucial to the periodization of the social history of this region.

One of the most remarkable effects of the new literature on state-building has been in the unlikely territory of American history. Traditionally, Americans have stressed how much their institutions of government have differed from the centralized, more statelike regimes of continental Europe. Yet a number of American historians and social scientists have used themes that Skocpol developed in her study of revolutions to look anew at governmental change during the Civil War, the Progressive era, the New Deal, and after World War II. In an influential study of federal policy during the Progressive era, Stephen Skowronek (1982) argued that between 1900 and 1920 an American state of courts and parties (where power was located in the patronage networks of the two major parties and key issues decided in courts) gave way to a new administrative state of regulatory commissions, executive authority, and greater presidential power. Controversy abounds over these matters, and historians disagree with one another particularly over how autonomous state officials have been from powerful business interests. No consensus reigns as to whether in the course of the 20th century the American state continued to differ from its European counterparts as much as it had before. But American historians and social scientists now debate questions about state-society relations with as much conceptual rigor as they do in Europe, and this in itself marks an important shift in American intellectual life.

Another approach to state-society relations has stressed the cultural dimensions of state power. In a seminal essay on royal ceremonies in England, Java, and Morocco, the anthropologist Clifford Geertz showed how important the symbolics of power—as conveyed through rituals, gestures, and images—proved to be in enhancing the charismatic authority of state officials. Historians have explored this insight in many societies and periods, though especially in the monarchies of medieval and early modern Europe. More is known about what rulers created than how people responded to symbolic representations of political authority. Still, historians have discovered a great deal about rituals, myths, festivals, iconography, and language itself as tools to make the otherwise amorphous notion of state authority vivid in people's minds. Historians of the French Revolution in particular have shown how cultural issues, far from being marginal, lay at the center of creating a new political culture. And historians of 19th- and 20th-century societies have looked at how leaders invented traditions to give their regimes legitimacy. Symbolism of every sort—from the cut of a candidate's clothes to the linguistic subtleties of legislative debate—remain as essential to the chemistry of state-society relations today as they did a millennium ago.

Although a great deal of the work on state and society has focused on state formation, many historians, like Tocqueville before them, have looked at the state as part of the explanation for particular types of social change. This approach—seeing the state as cause, rather than consequence—has had an important impact on the historical study of the working class. In trying to explain why working-class radicalism took the forms that it did at different times in a single country, or in different countries in roughly comparable times, historians have paid increasing attention to the effects of state structures, political culture, and government action. Historians of the United States, for example, have seen the decentralized structure of American government and the early introduction of universal suffrage for white men as crucial for the growth of urban political machines that tied workers to middle-class parties. By contrast, in Germany and France, where industrialization preceded democratization, the delay in suffrage rights fed the growth of separate, radical, working-class parties. In making these kinds of arguments, historians have by no means lost sight of how the social and economic dimensions of working-class life were important to the way workers' movements evolved. But they have acquired a new appreciation for state-centered factors—for the state as cause.

The rediscovery of the state has had a similar impact on the study of race and ethnicity, though this literature is less developed than that on the working class. Katherine O'Sullivan See has argued for the importance of state structure, international relations, and party politics in explaining why ethnic conflict took the shape that it did in Northern Ireland and Quebec. Recent comparative studies of race relations have stressed political and state-centered factors as well. John Cell, for example, has argued that segregation in the United States and South Africa had political rather than economic origins, as conservatives used state authority and segregationist policies to hold onto their own declining political power. Studies of regional and linguistic nationalism in Europe have also viewed the state—its centralization, the capacity of government leaders to integrate political and economic elites, their role in cultural policy—as critical in shaping ethnic movements.

One of the most active fields of research during the 1980s has developed around questions of gender, family, and the state. Historians have looked at how gender relations, especially patriarchal ones, influenced state formation—how the state was "engendered" from medieval times on. Studies of the French Revolution examined the new ways that men, despite their egalitarian convictions, used the state to reinforce patriarchy. Recent work on women's suffrage movements have paid close attention to political and organizational factors, and not just broad social trends, to explain the differing fates of these struggles internationally. The bulk of the work in this general field, however, has focused on the welfare state—its origins, its impact on family life (particularly in taking over some traditional family functions), and its role in reflecting and transforming gender relations. This is another instance of seeing the state, at least the modern state, as a cause of social change. Here again, comparative studies have made an impact. Historians have argued, for example, that in the late-19th century middle-class women played a prominent role in the development of social welfare activities in Britain and the United States, where state officials had not yet built a strong administrative apparatus for social policy, as opposed to France and Germany, where they had. Scholars have also turned to political factors, along with economic and demographic ones, to explain why British welfare policy in the 20th century discriminated against women more than was the case in France. Specialists on U.S. welfare policy have looked at how gender ideology and the federal structure of the American state combined to give policies toward child care and pregnancy, for example, an especially conservative character.

For all the progress historians and social scientists have made in the field of state-society relations, much work remains to be done. Studies of both the creation and effects of public policy can often reveal a lot about the interplay of state officials, governmental structures, and societal groups over time and across cultures. Many areas of public policy, however, await the kind of comparative historical treatment that historians of social welfare policy have recently accorded their field. Immigration, housing, transportation, health, policing, and even education, on which much has been written, all beg for more comparative historical analysis. Military historians are just beginning to reconsider issues in their field in such a manner. Much more could be done to situate foreign-policy making in its larger social historical context. Historians of popular culture have a great deal to contribute as well, since governments have come to play important roles in subsidizing, even shaping, mass communications, television, radio, film, the arts, and sports. Although economists and political scientists have recently made headway in analyzing the social and organizational dynamics of contemporary economic policy, historians can do more to address these themes in the past. In addition to studies of discrete policy areas, work is also needed that compares state-society relations across policy areas. Finally, as people in most countries, and especially in Europe and the former Soviet Union, struggle with new ways to distribute authority between local region, nation-state, and supranational bodies, social historians need to ask new questions about how people have come to define their local, ethnic, national, and international identities.

With its variety of facets and approaches the field of state society relations offers a rich agenda in social history. Many social historians see the linkage between state and society as a channel for creating larger synthesis within social history—the basis for long-term periodization, for example, as with Charles Tilly's work—as well as a means of relating social history to the interests of other kinds of historians. Basic differences in perspective, however, remain. Historians of some periods or regions have welcomed this approach more readily than have others. A great deal of the research on state-society relationships has in fact concentrated on the modern period. In reasserting the political dimension of social history, some historians define politics very broadly to include any kind of power relationship, although such a definition may make it difficult to conceptualize state-society relationships clearly. Some social historians, finally, while welcoming the effort to put the state back in, worry that the political aspects of peoples lives might become the only ones that matter in historical research—an outlook against which some social historians rebelled a generation ago. Some important topics in social history do indeed have relatively little to do with the state. By the same token the emphasis on state-society relations in recent research has provoked a rethinking of issues in social history once deemed unpolitical, and it has inspired a more sociohistorical approach to topics in political history. These recent trends in historical inquiry will no doubt continue, along with the debate this exciting new approach to social history has stimulated. (*See also* Revolutions; Russian Revolution; United States Politics and Society; Welfare State)

Herrick Chapman

REFERENCES

Bright, Charles, and Susan Harding, eds. *Statemaking and Social Movements: Essays in History and Theory.* Ann Arbor: University of Michigan Press, 1984.

Gordon, Linda, ed. *Women, the State and Welfare.* Madison: University of Wisconsin Press, 1990.

Skocpol, Theda. *States and Social Revolutions: A Comparative Analysis of France, Russia, and China.* New York: Cambridge University Press, 1979.

Skowronek, Stephen. *Building a New American State: The Expansion of National Administrative Capacities, 1877–1920.* New York: Cambridge University Press, 1982.

Wilentz, Sean, ed. *Rites of Power: Symbolism, Ritual and Politics Since the Middle Ages.* Philadelphia: University of Pennsylvania Press, 1985.

State and Society (Asia)

The analysis of state and society in South Asia is intimately tied to the history of Orientalist discourse. The annexation of India to the British colonial empire, beginning in the second half of the 18th century, produced a particularly marked tendency on the part of European analysts to see in India a deep gulf between society and the state. Most British observers saw Indian history as marked by a very high degree of political fragmentation and instability, punctuated only by the occasional ephemeral establishment of centralizing empires. The establishment of British rule in India, first under the aegis of the East India Company, and later (from 1858) under the British Crown, represented for many Englishmen the gift of political order to India. Beneath this political order, the concept of Indian "society" as a self-regulating construct distinct from the state, with its own bounded internal logic, exercised a profound influence on the British.

The foundations of this indigenous social order were in the eyes of most Englishmen rooted in three concepts: village, religion, and caste. Charles Metcalfe, an East India Company servant, characterized Indian villages in 1810 as "little republics." The British often portrayed Indian villages as largely self-regulating units bound together by customary relationships and obligations. But they also tended to see these villages as part of a larger indigenous pattern of social order in India shaped by religion and caste. Though the wellsprings of caste society were found in the legal and religious principles embodied in the ancient Sanskrit texts (many of which were translated by European Orientalists), 19th-century British administrators tended to see these principles as embodied also in living caste hierarchies, defined by the social precedence of Brahmans. Later 19th-century scholars, such as Max Muller, elaborated a vision of Hinduism as an ancient, ordered system of religious ideas with its own internal logic, while British administrators described and ranked Indian castes in census reports and official ethnographies as part of an ordered social system. The concept of a self-regulating Indian society, rooted in custom, caste, and religion, in fact empowered and legitimized for the British the concept of a rational, overarching colonial state, providing a framework of political unity.

Such ideas survived the British departure from India in distinctive Western academic traditions of writing about state and society in South Asia. Perhaps the most influential recent work in sustaining the image of South Asian society as a self-regulating, largely apolitical entity shaped by religion and caste is Louis Dumont's *Homo Hierarchicus.* Published in 1970, Dumont's book argued that Indian society historically contained its own internal hierarchical logic shaped by concepts of purity and pollution, and that caste, as the hierarchical social expression of these concepts, provided the essential unity of Indian society. Politics were viewed by Dumont as products of separate principles, always in tension with the fundamental principles of social ordering that defined the essence of Indian civilization.

This underlying view of a structure of social ordering intrinsically in tension with instruments of state political power has found expression in a large number of works on premodern Indian society. Some, such as the Dutch Sanskritist J.C.

Heesterman (1985), have seen this internal tension as central to Indian tradition. Perhaps most influential in recent years has been Burton Stein's (1980) application of the concept of the segmentary state to premodern India, a vision of the state as a ritual integrator of segments, drawing on unifying hierarchical religious ideas, rather than political structures, to unify state and society. Unity between state and society in such a vision was achieved not primarily by integrative political and economic structures, but by the replication of rituals of ranking and power linking kings and temples, Brahmans, and local power holders at various levels of political structures. The preeminence of society as a self-regulating structure of relationships, shaped by religion and caste, has remained in such work as defining the distinctive forms of South Asian civilization.

Considerable recent work, however, has called into question much of this inherited wisdom. Perhaps most thoroughgoing has been the critique of the Orientalist roots of the separation of Indian state and society. As Ronald Inden (1990) has argued, the search to find the social and cultural "essence" of Indian civilization in village, caste, and religion grew out of the European denial of agency to Indians as makers of their political order. More substantively, Nicholas Dirks (1987) has attacked Dumont's essentialist vision of caste, arguing that caste itself can only be understood in relation to changing historical patterns of kingship and state authority. The concept of a society regulated by its inner cultural and religious logic has thus increasingly been called into question.

Recent scholars have also sought to chart the impact of the colonial vision itself on modern Indian history. However self-serving for colonial interests, the conceptual colonial separation of the state from Indian society produced its own distinctly colonial political structure in India, and encouraged the emergence of new forms and conceptions of popular religious and social organization. Historians have traced the emergence of communalism, the political competition between religious communities so prominent in 20th-century India, as itself an outgrowth (at least in part) of the conceptual separation of state and society articulated by the colonial power. As Sandria Freitag (1989) has argued, local arenas of religious ritual and public performance independent of the patronage of the state produced new conceptions of political community under colonial rule. Independent India's concept of a secular state, a political construct standing theoretically above a society of religious communities, itself grew in part from colonial conceptions of state-society relations. Though shaped profoundly by the history in India of colonial rule, the analysis of state and society thus remains important for modern Indian social history. (*See also* Caste System; Colonialism; Hinduism; Orientalism; South Asian Colonialism)

David Gilmartin

References

Dirks, Nicholas. *The Hollow Crown: Ethnohistory of an Indian Kingdom.* Cambridge: Cambridge University Press, 1987.

Freitag, Sandria. *Collective Action and Community: Public Arenas and the Emergence of Communalism in North India.* Berkeley: University of California Press, 1989.

Heesterman, J.C. *The Inner Conflict of Tradition: Essays in Indian Ritual, Kingship and Society.* Chicago: University of Chicago Press, 1985.

Inden, Ronald. *Imagining India.* Oxford: Basil Blackwell, 1990.

Stein, Burton. *Peasant State and Society in Medieval South India.* Delhi: Oxford University Press, 1980.

Stratification and Inequality

Inequality consists of the uneven distribution of attributes among a set of social units: individuals, categories, groups, regions, or something else. Social historians interest themselves especially in the uneven distribution of costs and benefits—*goods*, broadly defined. Relevant goods include not only wealth and income but such various costs and benefits as control of land, exposure to illness, respect from other people, liability to military service, risk of homicide, possession of tools, and availability of sexual partners. Like social scientists in general, social historians have paid little attention to the uneven distribution of other attributes such as genetic traits and musical tastes except as they correlate with the uneven distribution of goods in this broad sense. Goods vary in the extent to which they are *autonomous* (observable without reference to outside units, as in accumulations of food) or *relative* (observable only in relation to other units, as in prestige). On the whole, inequalities with respect to autonomous goods reach greater extremes than with respect to relative goods.

Estimating the inequality of any two social units presents three major problems: identifying and bounding the units to compare, weighing the importance of different goods, and deciding whether the weighted differences are "large" or "small." Generally speaking, all three judgments require a theory of the larger social structures in which the two units are embedded. The difficulty compounds with the summary measurement of inequality and its changes among many units, for example (as in many analyses of long-term change), among all households in a national population or (as in many world-system analyses) among all the world's states. There social historians usually adopt two linked strategies: (1) choosing a single criterion good (e.g., current income) they regard as correlating with a number of other inequalities, (2) comparing the actual distribution of that good with a standard of absolutely equal distribution; such widely used devices as the Gini index and the Duncan dissimilarity index illustrate the combined strategy.

Although historians sometimes apply the term loosely to all sorts of inequality, *stratification* designates the rare form of inequality that clusters social units by layers, or *strata*, which are homogeneous with respect to a wide range of goods (both autonomous and relative), and which occupy a single well-defined rank order. A true system of stratification resembles a skyscraper, with its summit and base, its distinct levels, its elevators and stairways for movement from level to level, and its array of multiple graded niches.

Large organizations, such as armies, sometimes stratify internally: they establish bands of homogeneous rank that reach across the whole organization, segregation among ranks, and rituals of succession from rank to rank. As a consequence, localities depending on large, stratified organizations (e.g., company towns, military bases) likewise sometimes fall into ranked strata. But no general population larger than a local community ever maintains a coherent system of stratification; even the so-called caste system of India accommodated great variation in rank orders from village to village. In general, rank orders remain inconsistent, apparent strata contain considerable heterogeneity, and mobility blurs dividing lines. Stratification is therefore a matter of degree.

Inequality is likewise a matter of degree, but for the opposite reason—because it is ubiquitous. Whatever the criterion of equivalence, no two social units ever possess precisely equivalent arrays of goods for more than an instant. Possession of different sorts of goods, furthermore, couples loosely enough that the same social unit moves in several directions simultaneously; inequality is always in flux. Any unified, fixed model of inequality—and, *a fortiori*, of stratification—we impose on social life caricatures a dynamic reality. As with other useful caricatures, then, the secret is to sketch a model that brings out salient features of its object, but never to confuse model with reality.

Three main families of models purporting to describe and explain inequality vie for attention in social history: (1) societal, (2) individualistic, and (3) structural. *Societal* models of inequality assume the existence of an overarching ideology, culture, or value system that orders activities by their worth, and parcels out rewards accordingly. Such models include John Millar's 18th-century vision of progress toward a democratic society rewarding merit and effort, Max Weber's definition of various "societies" by their dominant belief systems, and Talcott Parsons's evolutionary model of functional differentiation.

Thus, in 20th-century America, runs one sort of societal argument, entertainers make more money than social workers because Americans collectively value mass entertainment more than professional help to poor people. Some societal models stress functions, suggesting for instance that doctors generally have greater wealth than janitors because doctors perform a more indispensable function rather than because they have managed, with state aid, to monopolize an expensive service and its clientele. Because they lapse easily into tautology, rest on the hazy entities called "societies," and yield few verifiable propositions, societal models of inequality have for some time been losing their appeal among social historians.

Individualistic models assume that the essential units of inequality are persons, and that inequality takes the form of placement in hierarchies. They range from Pitirim Sorokin's original popularization of a vertical-horizontal stratification space to contemporary human capital models à la economist Gary Becker which say that investment in job-relevant training pays off in location within hierarchies of income and occupational attractiveness. Many analysts in this tradition adopt a distinction between vertical and horizontal mobility; *vertical* moves change a person's rank, however measured, while *horizontal* moves change a person's group membership or geographic location. A major specialty within sociology and social history, the study of *status attainment*, builds on that geometric analogy; assuming that income, education, and occupation form closely correlated unilinear hierarchies, status-attainment investigators examine the relationship between some point of origin (often father's occupation) and some destination (often son's highest-ranking or most remunerative occupation), treating the essential problem as explaining the relationship between destination and origin through the effects of inheritance, education, experience, gender, nationality, and race.

Although the idea that every concrete change of social position has both rank-altering and locus-altering components is useful, the implication that each component reduces to a single dimension has caused a series of intellectual disasters, including the effort to analyze social mobility as if beneath all the disorder of observed inequality lay a true linear order of status, rank, prestige, wealth, or power. In fact, inequality forms complex lattices of division and interconnection, more like the structure of a molecule than that of a skyscraper.

Starting with precisely that observation, *structural* models of inequality à la Karl Marx or Harrison White begin with characteristic relations among individuals or other social units and derive from their compounding the complex configurations of inequality. In Marx, for example, we see the contrast between the schematic (and incomplete) portrayal of class structure in his *Capital* and the proliferation of classes in his writings on the French revolutions of 1848 to 1851. In both cases, Marx presented class structure as emerging from the relations of production, notably between landlords and peasants or capitalists and workers, but his political writings allow for fractionation, complexity, and coalition depending on organization and experience.

Contemporary structural analysts, many of them non-Marxist or anti-Marxist, typically treat inequality as an outcome of conflict, competition, and bargaining within well-defined limits set by existing relations among actors. Harrison White's vacancy-chain analysis, for example, examines the way the opening of a vacancy within a connected structure (say the creation of a new job) cascades through the structure as occupants of other positions struggle to take advantage of the new opportunities offered by those who vacate their present positions to move into newly opened places. Although they still lack a synthesis comparable to those available for societal and individualistic models, structural models of inequality offer the greatest promise for analyses in social history.

Positions often cluster so that large numbers of people have similar goods, and stand in similar relations to other clustered sets of people. *Social classes*, for example, bring together people who occupy similar positions with respect to the organization of production: peasants, industrial wage workers, petty entrepreneurs, landlords, and so on. The classification male/female, on the other hand, builds a large set of social distinctions on anatomical, physiological, and reproductive differences. We can usefully place the principal kinds of cluster along a continuum between *self-reproducing* and *subdividing extremes*, considering the extent to which the cluster acquires new members through biological reproduction within the cluster or forms as a subdivision of biologically reproducing populations. The most prominent instances are the following:

relatively self-reproducing: religion, class, imputed origin (race, ethnicity, nationality, slavery/freedom);

intermediate: party affiliation, patron-client network, state service;

relatively subdividing: gender, age, sexual orientation.

Although socially constructed categories and imputations of character unquestionably influence the division of populations by race, ethnicity, or nationality, once they exist marriage and birth commonly reinforce their boundaries; divisions by age, on the other hand, pervade every self-reproducing population. Strict segregation of whole rounds of life by race, ethnicity, and nationality is common, and strict segregation by age is quite rare. The distinctions are obviously relative: The pair slavery/freedom, for example, becomes more subdividing to the extent that enslavement selects for gender (as in the Mamluk capture of boys for incorporation into their military order), while connected sets of women and their children (black Caribbean families being a prominent example) sometimes maintain themselves in substantial independence of adult males. Although every known large population has incorporated strong forms of gender inequality, furthermore, subdividing bases of inequality vary greatly in the extent to which they are explicit and precise. In Western industrial countries, for example, only with the recent political mobilizations of homosexuals have divisions by sexual orientation become explicit, public, and legally sanctioned.

The distinction matters because relatively self-reproducing bases of inequality usually incorporate strong mechanisms of inheritance, which greatly increase the likelihood that inequalities will persist over generations. Theorists of gender, age, and sexual orientation have sometimes argued that ideology and socialization combine to make them more profound bases of inequality than religion, class, or imputed origin, but so far the evidence indicates that, over a wide range of goods in large populations, inequalities usually run deeper with respect to self-reproducing divisions than with respect to subdividing divisions; institutions of inheritance play a large part in that difference.

All durable structures of inequality originate in the collective exercise of power—including the power to label others as different—by connected clusters of social units. Commonly a single cluster adopts a device that subordinates one or more other clusters, then the interaction among the clusters produces contested but durable social categories, power relations, and inequalities in entitlement to goods; in the case of relatively self-reproducing structures, however, both small-

scale mobility across the crucial divisions and differential natural increase among them likewise affect the pattern of inequality. Often the more powerful clusters adopt an ideology of worthiness (for example, distinctions among the wealthy, the middle classes, the deserving poor, and the undeserving poor, with appropriate ideas concerning differences in their moral and religious performances) that presumably justifies and explains their own advantages.

Such a sequence describes the imposition of theocratic power on ostensibly pagan peoples, the relegation of old people to poverty or reduced power, and the formation of proletariats under capitalism. In an Essex village, for example, Keith Wrightson and David Levine show how local property holders not only elaborated an ideology of religious respectability and disrespectability, but also subjected their own previously dissolute behavior to its requirements, as they instituted more controls over a growing and increasingly stigmatized group of landless laborers. In all forms of inequality, even where the goods involved are autonomous (e.g., wealth or income), relations among unequals rather than solo performances by members of one category or another underlie the system. Asymmetrically, victors and victims shape each other.

Analyzing English capitalist experience, for example, E.P. Thompson has forcefully argued that class is a continuous interactive process (in this case relating landlords and merchant capitalists to landless laborers) rather than a static structure given by the organization of production. The grand debates among social historians, indeed, concern the articulation and relative weight of belief and consciousness, on the one hand, and day-to-day relations of production, on the other, in that process of interaction among classes. At a materialist extreme we see complete determination of class by capitalist-worker relations at the point of production, mitigated (or obscured) only by false consciousness, while at an idealist extreme we see nothing but class discourse that causes itself. All realities lie somewhere in between.

Less fundamental than the structure-culture tension in determining social stratification, the question of complexity also affects social historians in this area: how many groups must be defined within the basic stratification system? Some historians of early modern England argue that there were only two social classes: the aristocracy and everybody else. Others, however, would note important power and cultural divisions within the "everybody else" category, creating hierarchies among both urban and rural social groups. Social historians must recurrently decide on what the basic power and cultural configurations of ideology are, for a given society and period, as well as what their own heuristic needs require in terms of presenting inequality alignments—all toward deciding how many groupings along the spectrum to present. Some societies and periods, further, require greater complexity than others—for example, when one basis for inequality yields to another, old and new hierarchies coexist for a time period.

Powerful social units often cement their control of goods, especially autonomous goods, by the establishment of property rights, or enforceable prior claims to the disposition of specific goods. Property rights rest on the readiness of third parties in cases of dispute to intervene on behalf of one claimant; secure property rights most often depend on some sort of governmental authority, which is why widespread seizures of previously protected property occur chiefly in times of rapid contraction or expansion of state power.

Extensive property rights both sustain and magnify inequality, since they allow those who have acquired extensive authorized control over individual goods to enjoy that control while depending on a collective good—state intervention—to protect it to a degree that their own resources would not permit. When property rights extend to inheritance, they further reinforce self-reproducing forms of inequality.

The most powerful property rights are those that govern the production and reproduction of goods, as when landlords in an agrarian system exercise rights not only to most of the land but also to a portion of peasant household labor. To the extent that a small cluster of persons monopolizes such rights, inequality will be extensive. Even at the small scale of the household, the basic principle seems to hold: to the degree that women exercise autonomous ownership of property or generate larger shares of household income through activity unsupervised by other household members, they command greater power in a wide range of household decision-making.

Under capitalism, merchants monopolized control over the production and distribution of a wide range of services and manufactured goods. The short-run consequence was generally a sharp increase of inequality between capitalists and workers, which became general inequality to the extent that the entire population divided between the two classes. During the 1940s and 1950s, students of national income such as economist Simon Kuznets inferred, indeed, that aggregate disparities of income commonly increased in early capital-concentrated industrialization, then diminished as the benefits of industrialization spread within any particular population. Subsequent historical work (e.g., by Hartmut Kaelble and Jeffrey Williamson) has generally confirmed increasing inequality during early industrialization, but has left uncertain the extent of leveling thereafter. The closely related "standard of living controversy" has likewise produced some agreement among social historians that a wide range of workers experienced declines in real income during major periods of capital concentration without resolving under what conditions, how extensively, and how soon higher productivity (agricultural or industrial) resulted in real-income gains. On the overall course of inequality during industrialization, social historians still have their work cut out for them.

Because it deals with what actually happened over long stretches of capitalist expansion, social history has much to contribute to general analyses of inequality. It also has much to learn from current debates. Social historians deal generally with the intersections between large-scale processes such as proletarianization or state formation, on one side, and small-scale social life, on the other. Social historians formed their craft as a skeptical complement to political history and economic history—skeptical about the straightforward determination of political action by economic organization, skeptical about the direct determination of social relations by political and economic position. Yet within the economic sphere social historians have remained surprisingly susceptible to simple technological determinism, to the assumption that owners of productive means choose the most efficient available technologies, that technologies determine the organization of production, that the organization of production causes the fundamental inequalities of wealth and income, that workers' options therefore reduce to placing themselves somewhere on a continuum from enthusiastic commitment through grudging acquiescence and open resistance to revolution. Such a view denies workers significant influence over the organization of production except through revolution or sabotage.

This strangely prevalent perspective fosters the illusion of capitalist omnipotence in the face of widespread evidence that in early industrial capitalism employers acted primarily as merchants, exploiting their workers mercilessly, but doing so primarily by driving down prices for goods rather than prescribing or supervising the conditions of their production. It took a long time, for example, before owners of glassworks knew more about the production of glass than their skilled workers did, a long time before employers stamped out the subcontracting arrangements whereby foremen in metal production recruited and paid their own workers, a long time before miners started receiving an hourly wage with the supervision it implies rather than collective payment per ton brought to the surface, a very long time before labor unions became heavily involved in negotiating pensions, vacations, health benefits, and wages rather than the very conditions of employment and work. Even today the social organization of long-distance migration (e.g., from Korea, Mexico, or Turkey) profoundly affects the workers actually available to different groups of employers, hence the sharp segregation of jobs by gender, race, and national origin in all Western countries.

The analysis of culture—of shared understandings and their objectifications—occupies an important place in social history's agenda concerning inequality. Culture shapes the rituals by which people affirm or challenge specific inequalities, the interpretations they make of each other's intentions, the inferences they draw concerning the likelihood of future actions and consequences of action. Shared understandings strongly affect the relative valuation of different sorts of goods, hence the extent to which participants in a set of social relations interpret inequalities as large or inequitable. They likewise influence the ways in which people publicize their own positions and code other people's positions. Because so much sociohistorical analysis has suffered under the burden of stratification models, from the assumption of strict, unitary hierarchies, or in the grip of technological determinism, the cultural study of inequality promises to be a major field for new discoveries. Any good social history in this regard will contribute as well to our shared understanding of contemporary social life, not to mention its origins. (*See also* Class; Cultural History; Mobility)

Charles Tilly

REFERENCES

Granovetter, Mark, and Charles Tilly. "Inequality and Labor Processes," in Neil J. Smelser, ed., *Handbook of Sociology.* Newbury Park, CA: Sage, 1988, pp. 175–222.

Kaelble, Hartmut. *Industrialisierung und soziale Ungleichheit.* Gottingen: Vandenhoeck & Ruprecht, 1983.

Williamson, Jeffrey. *Did British Capitalism Breed Inequality?* Boston: Allen & Unwin, 1985.

Wright, Erik Olin. *Classes.* London: Verso, 1985.

Street Life

This is among the most basic levels of study for social historians, but it is by no means a simple area of investigation. Local, or community, culture has proven to be quite different from, and often contradictory to, generic national values. In some working-class and ethnic communities petty crime has been shown to be an accepted and even positive part of daily life, especially if these crimes are victimless or perpetrated against the outside. Petty criminals are often seen as local heroes, and prostitution, gambling, bootlegging, and shoplifting can be deemed acceptable and economically necessary. Evidence suggests that this is consistent across various areas of study from Victorian history in Britain to the study of racial segregation in America. At the street level, more formal aspects of culture have been appropriated and modified to reflect community life. Sport in black American communities in the 20th century is a good example, where blacks formed community baseball leagues which mirrored the white professional leagues and produced local heroes such as Josh Gibson and Satchel Page. While on one hand more formal aspects of culture have been appropriated at the community level, it is also the case that dominant culture has taken aspects of street life and sanitized them for more general consumption. This is evident in the history of blues and other forms of popular music and England's punk movement of the 1970s.

The study of street life has revealed that pubs, pool halls, music halls, pawnshops, corner stores, and various voluntary organizations have played a more important role in the definition of community standards than their expressed functions might suggest. They act as gathering places where community values are established and perpetuated. At the street level, simple definitions may obscure deeper, more important "hidden" functions of groups and businesses.

While street life may appear to be an impenetrable area of research, its study, in many fields, produces important alternative views which make generalizations about societies very difficult. For example, the desires of the "mob" in the French Revolution have been shown to be quite different from those of the middle-class leadership. Victorian middle-class values coexisted with both pornography and prostitution. In America in the 1920s and 1930s Prohibition was law, but speakeasies enjoyed tremendous popularity and support. These contradictions make the study of street life very rewarding. However, most studies of this basic level of social interaction have been confined to working-class or ethnic groups, and there is a pressing need to study other classes and dominant groups in relationship to less formal areas of their lives, as it may reveal the foundations upon which more traditional aspects of history are based. (*See also* Drinking; Prostitution; Vaudeville)

James W. Martens

REFERENCES

Mayhew, Henry. *London Labour and the London Poor*, Vols. I–IV. New York: Dover, 1968.

Pearson, Geoffrey. *Hooligan: A History of Respectable Fears*. London: Macmillan, 1983.

Ruck, Rob. *Sandlot Seasons: Sport in Black Pittsburgh*. Chicago: University of Illinois Press, 1987.

Rudé, George. *The Crowd in History, 1730–1948*. New York: Wiley, 1964.

Walkowitz, Judith. *Prostitution and Victorian Society: Women, Class and the State*. Cambridge: Cambridge University Press, 1989.

Strikes

The strike—the collective withdrawal of labor to support a demand by workers—was known in biblical times. It emerged as a significant form of social behavior, however, only with industrialization and the concomitant separation of employee from manager. Some strikes, such as the United States Steel Strike of 1919 and the British General Strike of 1926, are major national events. Describing them was a central feature of traditional labor history. The rise of the new labor history, with its stress on work experience, has been associated with a reduction in interest in strikes as part of labor movement history. A general overview is, however, best provided by a third approach which examines the long-term development in the character of the strike. Social historians though not always concerned with the story of individual strikes have been vitally interested in larger patterns and changes, and what the causes of pattern and change reveal about worker conditions and expectations.

Most accounts rely heavily on the statistics which the government agencies of most capitalist nations began to collect toward the end of the 19th century. To look further back and at other countries, historians have increasingly analyzed newspaper and police records to build up data on incidents of collective action. Strictly speaking, strikes are actions initiated by workers, with lockouts being the employer's equivalent. In practice, the distinction is hard to draw: it takes two sides to make a quarrel. The organized lockout has become rare in many countries, but it remains a significant tactic in some, such as Sweden and Germany, where employers have a high degree of solidarity; the rationale is to prevent unions from whip-sawing each company in turn.

The amount of strike activity can be described in terms of secular trends and waves. Under the former, there have been three main patterns. In the first, the number, size, and duration of strikes have remained more or less constant over a long period; the prime example here is the United States. Second, there are cases where strikes have grown shorter but also larger, as in France and Italy. Third, in Germany and the Nordic countries, the number of strikes has sunk to very low levels; a few large stoppages still occur, but labor peace is the norm. The explanation turns on the nature of labor's insertion into the economy. In the United States, collective bargaining between unions and employers covers not only wages but a variety of other benefits, and the strike remains a lengthy battle. In France and Italy unions do not have strike funds, and all-out stoppages are rare. The strike is used instead as a short demonstration of purpose. In the third pattern, unions have an established place in the industrial order, and are often described as one of the "social partners." There is a tacit exchange of rising real wages and low unemployment for industrial quiescence, and the strike remains a weapon of last resort.

Second, strike activity moves in waves. There were major peaks in the late 19th century, after World War I, and during the 1960s, with substantial falls during the 1920s and 1980s. The similarity of timing of these waves in many countries led to the search for a common cause, which was found in the concept of long cycles of economic growth. Capitalism has progressed through cycles lasting about 50 years, and workers' protests have been associated with the peaks of these cycles. The explanation remains controversial. Strike patterns reflect short-term influence as well as long-run ones, and there are some apparent anomalies. But the long wave seems to be an important condition promoting strikes, even though its effects may be overlaid or counteracted by other forces.

The idea of waves is also important in a global context. Levels of strikes fell in the industrialized world during the period after 1945. But there were increases in all forms of collective labor protest in industrializing nations such as Korea. The overall level of conflict has not fallen as capitalism has developed.

The character of strikes has changed, however. Before the late 19th century, strikes were largely artisanal in nature—the actions of small groups of skilled workers, often concerned with the conditions of labor as well as wages. With the growth of mass production, new groups of semi- and unskilled workers were drawn into collective action against employers. The ostensible reason for strikes was increasingly the level of wages. Stoppages became larger as workers used their industrial muscle. A third phase has also been suggested in which the typical figure is the worker in an advanced facility like a chemicals factory. Strikes become smaller and more sophisticated, as workers use their strategic position in the production process. This development seemed to affect France and Italy in particular from the 1960s, but evidence that it was a distinct phase was not convincing.

Changes in character were also associated with changes in industrial distribution. The use of the strike in the 19th century was confined to manual workers, generally those in coal, construction, and heavy industry. During the 20th century new groups of workers learned to use the strike, notably those in white-collar sectors and the public sector. These groups struck less often than the former leading sectors—and the decline of these sectors is one reason for the overall decline in strike levels—but they nonetheless used tactics that would in the past have been unthinkable.

Finally, in Western countries but to a lesser extent in the Third World, the strike gradually became the property of the trade union. This was not always so, and many early strikes involved unorganized workers who may subsequently have joined a union. This development was part of a wider process in which industrial tactics became more routine and predictable.

These changes in the nature and extent of strikes reflect fundamental structural forces such as the progress of industrialization, more immediate economic circumstances, and a variety of strategic decisions by workers, unions, and employers. Strikes are only one index of collective behavior, but they have been a particularly significant one. (*See also* Protest; Unions; United States Labor Movement; Working Class)

Paul Edwards

REFERENCES

Cronin, James E. *Industrial Conflict in Modern Britain.* London: Croom Helm, 1979.

Edwards, P.K. *Strikes in the United States, 1881–1974.* Oxford: Blackwell, 1981.

Geary, D. *European Labor Protest, 1848–1939.* New York: St. Martin's, 1981.

Shorter, E., and C. Tilly. *Strikes in France, 1830–1968.* Cambridge: Cambridge University Press, 1974.

Silver, B. "World-Scale Patterns of Labor-Capital Conflict," in I. Brandell, ed., *Workers in Third World Industrialization.* London: Macmillan, 1991.

Subcultures

The concept of subcultures is essential to social history, with its attention to social classes or other groups out of power. Most social historians dealing with peasants or workers, with ethnic groups, or even with age groups such as youth identify cultural features different from the dominant culture. In the 19th century, thus, workers in Britain became aware of dominant middle-class values but deliberately preserved elements of a separate culture, or subculture even though they had little chance to gain wider legitimacy for their values. A youth subculture developed in many parts of Europe and North America by the later 19th century, even within the middle class. A homosexual subculture has developed in the 20th-century United States.

The idea of subculture has some contact with Antonio Gramsci's notion of a dominant or civic "hegemonic" culture issued by a ruling class like planters in the pre–Civil War South, or the industrial middle class. Subcultures reflect the beliefs of various groups not fully captured by the dominant culture, capable also of influencing it, but not powerful enough to replace it.

Some subcultures seem more defiant of mainstream values than is actually the case. Middle-class utopian movements after 1850, in the United States, blasted middle-class beliefs in marriage and property but unwittingly upheld other beliefs about gender roles or sexual or emotional propriety (women, thus, were kept domestic and inferior). Other subcultures are traditionally very separate, like gypsy culture in western Europe.

The importance of subcultures to social history steadily grows as greater attention is given to group beliefs and to cultural causation. No theoretical definitions of subcultures are available in social history. Attention to contemporary fad groups, like punk rockers or motorcycle gangs, sometimes involves use of the term "subculture," here applied to rather small categories and often with little attention to relationships to the wider culture save the obvious claim of defiance. Journalists and anthropologists interested in describing varieties of popular culture do not use terms like "subculture" exactly as social historians do. It is clearly desirable to work toward sharp definitions and former overall characterization of subcultures and their contacts with dominant cultures in different periods of social history. At present subculture is an essential category but a potentially vague catchall in the juncture between social and cultural history. (*See also* Cultural Hegemony; Utopian Communities)

Peter N. Stearns

REFERENCES

Hunt, Lynn. *The New Cultural History.* Berkeley: University of California Press, 1989.

Spurlock, John. *Free Love: Marriage and Middle-Class Radicalism in America, 1825–1866.* New York: New York University Press, 1989.

Suburbanization

Suburbanization refers to the development of residential communities on the urban fringe and the decentralization of certain commercial and retail activities. The suburbanization pattern is a product of industrialization and a vital aspect of modern social history. In the United States, suburbanization is closely tied to changing social values and technological innovation, particularly in the area of transportation.

Prior to the 19th century, suburbs in Europe as well as the United States resembled slums, housing the city's poorest citizens and most obnoxious industries. Because people generally walked to work, a residence in the city center was preferred. As technological advancements improved access to the city, however, the periphery became increasingly attractive as a residential choice.

By the 1830s, the development of omnibuses, commuter railroads, and ferries allowed people to live in the suburbs and work in the city. The high cost of these conveyances, however, restricted their use. With the introduction of the street railway in the 1850s and its mechanization and electrification in the 1880s and 1890s, suburban residence came within reach of the city's growing middle class.

As technological advances made suburbanization possible, the increasing complexity and heterogeneity of urban life made suburban life attractive. The developing value system of the middle classes figured as well, in growing suspicion of the poor, anxiety about crime, and greater concern about health and sanitation. As large numbers of immigrants entered America's industrializing cities to work, the middle class responded by creating homogeneous communities in the suburbs. In addition, because it brought them closer to nature, people believed suburban living was virtuous and moral. By 1900, a suburban residence had become the preferred choice of America's middle classes. The resulting communities, however, tended to exclude people on the basis of race and religion as well as economic standing. In Europe, somewhat similar impulses resulted from the in-migration of rural workers, although low suburban housing costs created some working-class suburbs as well.

The physical pattern of suburbanization changed dramatically with the introduction of the automobile in the 1920s, although many of the social characteristics remained the same. In these early automobile suburbs, lots were larger, prices higher, and admittance restricted to upper middle-class whites. Following World War II, widespread automobile ownership and permissive federal monetary policies enabled large numbers of middle-class, lower middle-class, and some working-class Americans to move to suburbs. These communities remained predominantly white due to the prevailing prejudices of residents and the policies of local and federal government.

Commercial activity suburbanized from the late 19th century onward. The introduction of the truck in the 1920s and the interstate highway system in the 1950s promoted the suburbanization of business. By 1980, many American and European cities were surrounded by suburban office parks and shopping malls that mixed work, shopping, and residence in development nodes scattered throughout the urban periphery. By 1990, the development of these "outer cities" had become a common urban characteristic, and many American cities had more office space located outside their central business districts than inside.

Suburbanization on the U.S. or European model is not a worldwide phenomenon. Even in some European cities people live near the city center in substantial numbers. In Latin America, Africa, and the developing world, urban services extending beyond the city center are quite rare. In these societies, the poor live in the suburbs, while the middle class live and work downtown. (*See also* Cities; Racial Segregation; United States Urbanization; Urbanization)

Steven J. Hoffman

REFERENCES

Fishman, Robert. *Bourgeois Utopias*. New York: Basic Books, 1987.

Jackson, Kenneth. *Crabgrass Frontier*. New York: Oxford University Press, 1985.

Sufism

The word "Sufism" is synonymous with Islamic mysticism. The Arabic word for wool (*suf*) describes the fabric of the clothes worn by individual mystics who are called *Sufis*. Islamic mysticism first developed within the 8th and 9th centuries in Iraq, Egypt, and Iran. Muslim men and women dedicated their lives to Sufism as a spiritual quest for understanding and direct personal communion with the supreme and sole Islamic deity Allah. Sufism shaped individual and communal identity as well as social organization in the Islamic world.

The first source for the Sufi's mystical experience was the Qur'an, the core of Islamic belief for all Muslims which is regarded as the literal word of Allah revealed in Arabic to the Prophet Muhammad (d. 632). A Sufi might choose to live in isolation or in the world. Sufis most often married and were urged to avoid the celibate example of Christian monks. Some lived on alms, but most worked or were simultaneously members of the class of male religious scholars known in Islamic society as the *ulama*. The medieval reconciliation of Sufism with orthodox Sunni Islam achieved its final and most important synthesis in the work of the medieval theologian and mystic al-Ghazali (d. 1111).

The earliest Sufis demonstrated marked ascetic tendencies. They rejected what they perceived as the corrupt material world and wore their woolen cloaks as a sign of their spiritual commitment. One of the most famous of the early Sufis, a woman named Rabi'a al-Adawiyya (d. 801), became a model of piety for later mystics. Rabi'a refused to marry because she believed a husband would distract her thoughts from God. Rabi'a's choice to remain celibate made her an exception to the Sufi rule. Her life exemplifies the Sufi theory that outer bodily forms are irrelevant when the soul approaches the divine. Rabi'a's later male biographers found her spiritual legacy so unusual for a woman that they opted to define her as a man. Such a posthumous categorization suggests that Rabi'a's exceptional lifestyle and piety defied medieval Islamic notions of gender.

The spread of Sufism in the medieval and premodern period influenced the social history of the entire Islamic world from North Africa to India. As the doctrines of the Islamic mystical experience increased in complexity, Sufi orders, or brotherhoods, developed. Each brotherhood (*tariqa*) traced its origins to one master (*shaykh*) and his followers whose teaching and example were kept alive in a human chain of instruction perpetuated over generations. Hundreds of Sufi orders proliferated throughout the medieval Islamic world. Sufism became a major force in the spread of the Islam in North Africa, central Asia, and India. Sufi masters played a key role in directing their followers to convert non-Muslims. The success of Sufism on the Islamic frontiers may have had much to do with the charismatic powers of Sufi masters. Some were thought to have the ability to work miracles and were revered as saints. Their tombs became places of veneration and pilgrimage throughout the Islamic world.

Sufi brotherhoods held frequent communal gatherings in their lodges and developed special religious rituals geared to the remembrance of Allah in chants, music, poetry, and rhythmic movement. These observances offered a point of access to the mystical experience for the larger Islamic community. Muslim women had a less pronounced role in Sufi brotherhoods founded by men. They might participate as associates or lead their own exclusively female gatherings.

Sufism bound the Muslim community into new and complex networks of social interaction. Islamic mysticism became part of the grass-roots organization of premodern life which insured Islamic cultural continuity in periods of political decline, decay, and invasion. Identification of the individual with a Sufi brotherhood often indicated social status, profession, or geographical location in the Islamic world. Thus, Sufi brotherhoods embodied both a spiritual and social force in Islamic history.

The study of Sufism by social historians has begun to document the complexity of medieval and premodern socioeconomic structure in Middle Eastern history. These relatively new analyses in Western scholarship on Islamic mysticism suggest that Sufism had more than spiritual and philosophical implications in Islamic society. Examination of Sufi membership and practice reveals much about a phenomenon that touched the daily lives of the Muslim male and female nonelite. The study of Sufism by social historians also provides a critical key to forms of popular religious expression in the Islamic world to the present day. New directions for research on the social history of Sufism feature interdisciplinary methodologies drawn from anthropology, psychology, and gender studies.

In the 19th and 20th centuries the power of Sufi orders diminished throughout the Islamic world due to the combined pressures of secularism and nationalism. In Turkey, Sufi brotherhoods were outlawed in 1925 as a way of demonstrating the new republic's break with its Islamic and Ottoman past. Throughout the Islamic world Sufism continues to attract many Muslims as a form of popular Islamic religion. (*See also* Islam; Popular Religion)

Denise A. Spellberg

REFERENCES

Lings, Martin. *A Sufi Saint of the Twentieth Century.* Berkeley: University of California Press, 1973.

Schimmel, Annemarie. *Mystical Dimensions of Islam.* Chapel Hill: University of North Carolina Press, 1975.

Smith, Margaret. *Rabi'a the Mystic and Her Fellow Saints in Islam.* Cambridge: Cambridge University Press, 1928.

Trimingham, J. Spencer. *The Sufi Orders in Islam.* New York: Oxford University Press, 1971.

Suicide

Suicide is the act of taking one's own life, or self-murder. For sociologists and psychiatrists, suicide has long been a cardinal issue. Only recently, however, have social historians begun to reveal how this private, enigmatic act can serve to illuminate such important themes as the history of age, gender, and death, the impact of industrial and urban change, and the sweep of cultural change over the past four centuries or more. In general, social historians have addressed themselves to the work of the early sociologists of suicide.

Emile Durkheim's *Suicide* (1897), the classic text on the sociology of self-slaughter, reinforced the 19th-century interpretation of suicide. This attributed the contemporary rise in suicide rates to the passing of the old social order and its replacement by an urban-industrial society, in which the familial or religious bonds that held society together were unraveling. Durkheim declared, in a word, that modern society was a killer. The interpretive tradition embodied in Durkheim's *Suicide* had a deep and abiding impact on later sociological research. The Chicago School of urban sociologists underscored the thesis that suicide is an expression of the social disorganization of the modern city. Ruth Cavan's *Suicide* (1928) found that suicide rates were highest in the central lodging-house areas, where the family, school, and church were weak. The urban thesis also influenced the occasional historian. Louis Chevalier, in *Laboring Classes and Dangerous Classes* (1973), embraced the "uprooting hypothesis"—that large numbers of the 19th-century poor, torn from their rural roots, migrated to Paris, victims of "urban pathology" in the shape of crime, madness, and suicide.

More typically, however, social historians have thrown into question the assumed causal link between urban-industrial society and self-slaughter. Nineteenth-century Philadelphia, according to Roger Lane (1979), grew less not more violent. If suicide rates rose, as they did from the 1870s, this reflected not urban disorganization, but an industrial discipline (learned in schools, factories, and offices) which effectively curbed external aggression (homicide) and redirected it inward (suicide). Lane thus offers a modified urban thesis, replacing the connection between suicide and disintegration with that between suicide and integration.

The most impressive history, to date, of suicide in Victorian and Edwardian England, by Olive Anderson (1987), poses a more fundamental challenge to the view that high suicide rates are an index of "the suffering and rootlessness bred by urban industrialism." Those most prone to doing away with themselves were not the victims of the new industrial economy. The highest suicide rates were found in rural villages and nonindustrial county towns and resorts, not in industrial cities. Assessment of individual suicides, moreover, convinced Anderson that they lived in a social network of relations, landlords, and lodgers. She would doubtless endorse Richard Cobb's (1979) statement that the impression given by the *garni* (lodging-house) dwellers of Paris, from among whose ranks many suicides came, "is not at all that of people recently uprooted, insecure, unassimilated in the vast anonymity of an alien and forbidding capital."

More recently still, in a study of suicide in England between 1500 and 1800, MacDonald and Murphy (1991) discarded the Durkheimian obsession with the suicide rate, and sought, rather, to decode "the meanings implicit in social actions and in texts." The historical records were examined for what different groups thought about suicide, how they responded to self-destruction, how suicides tried in their notes to influence the interpretation of their own death. Thus, in the historical investigation of suicide, attention has shifted from social causes outside the influence of the actors involved, to the meaningful choices and responses made by suicides and their entourage.

Historians have paid much less attention to psychoanalytical explanations of suicide; to theories of repression, early childhood loss, and incomplete mourning. Only Howard Kushner (1989), in a study of American suicide, has confronted these mental conflicts, as part of a pioneering advocacy of a theory of suicide which integrates sociological, psychological, and organic approaches; a synthesis of culture, mind, and body.

For the future, social historians might try to develop a theory of suicide that unites a material account of social structure with the individual motives for suicide, one that incorporates the determined and chosen dimensions of suicidal behavior. My own preferred framework for this approach is that of the individual life cycle or life course. An investigation of how dying by suicide was related to the impact of the various transitions of the life course may well provide important clues to the enigma of suicide, as social historians amplify what is proving to be an exciting new field of historical inquiry. (*See also* Death; Life Course/Life Cycle; Urbanization)

Victor Bailey

REFERENCES

Anderson, Olive. *Suicide in Victorian and Edwardian England.* Oxford: Clarendon Press, 1987.

Cobb, Richard C. *Death in Paris.* Oxford: Oxford University Press, 1978.

Kushner, Howard I. *Self-Destruction in the Promised Land: A Psychocultural Biology of American Suicide.* New Brunswick, NJ: Rutgers University Press, 1989. (Reprinted as *American Suicide.* Rutgers, 1991).

Lane, Roger. *Violent Death in the City: Suicide, Accident, and Murder in Nineteenth-Century Philadelphia.* Cambridge, MA: Harvard University Press, 1979.

MacDonald, Michael, and Terence R. Murphy. *Sleepless Souls: Suicide in Early Modern England.* New York: Oxford University Press, 1991.

Swedish Population Data

Sweden is known for the high quality of its population records. Like other parts of Europe, Sweden's series of parish records of baptisms, marriages, and burials became more numerous in the 17th century along with the growing power of the state Lutheran church. The Swedish clergy was required to keep a catechetical examination register (*husförhörslangd*) to record each parish-

ioner's ability to read and recite passages from the Lutheran catechism. Gradually, however, these registers came to hold vast amounts of information on individuals whom they listed by households, as in a modern census. Data eventually included names, literacy levels, infirmities, or moral failings, as well as vaccination information. Clergy members updated the register whenever changes in a household occurred as the result of birth, marriage, death, or migration.

Sweden was also one of the earliest European societies to carry out periodic censuses. Beginning in 1749, Swedish clergy were required to compile annual data on vital events as well as a census of their parishes. These data were then collected at the county and finally the national level. While clergy were responsible for annual records of births, marriage, deaths, and migration, census data were eventually collected only triennially. The existence of extraordinarily detailed census and vital event data as early as the 18th century, including information on causes of death, makes it possible to study Sweden's population and medical history in great detail. Major projects utilizing these data are ongoing. (*See also* Census; Literacy)

Katherine A. Lynch

REFERENCES

Hofsten, Erland, and Hans Lundström. *Swedish Population History.* Stockholm: Central Bureau of Statistics, 1976.

Johansson, Egil. "Literacy Campaigns in Sweden," in R.J. Arnove and H. Graff, eds., *National Literacy Campaigns: Historical and Comparative Perspectives.* New York: Plenum, 1987.

Kälvemark, Ann-Sofie. "The Country That Kept Track of Its Population," in Jan Sundin and Erik Söderland, eds., *Time, Space and Man.* Stockholm: Almqvist and Wiksell, 1979.

Syndicalism

Syndicalism, also called anarchosyndicalism or revolutionary syndicalism, was the doctrine of direct action against employers and the general strike for the overthrow of capitalism that prevailed in the French trade union movement before 1914. A similar doctrine was espoused by unions in Italy, Spain, and Latin America as well as by the Industrial Workers of the World in the United States and the New Zealand Federation of Labour. By extension the term also describes militant rank-and-file movements against employers such as the shop stewards movement that erupted in Britain during World War I.

Syndicalism originated in France, where it was adopted by the CGT (Confédération générale du travail), the national trade union federation, in the 1906 Charter of Amiens. The CGT sought both immediate gains and the elimination of employers through the general strike that would place unions in control of industry. The general strike was also endorsed as a revitalizing social myth by the philosopher Georges Sorel. The failure of attempts at general strike thwarted by government repression produced a crisis of leadership, resulting in a more realistic approach to organization in the CGT after 1909.

Contrary to its mythology, syndicalism owed much to political socialism—to the republican socialism of 1848 and the Paris Commune and to the formation of the Marxian *Parti ouvrier,* or workers' party, in 1880. In order to maintain unity in the face of splits and political opportunism among socialists, the trade unions asserted their independence on the basis of their belief in emancipation by the general strike. Many new leaders were anarchosyndicalists, who advocated electoral abstention and military desertion. They were not representative of most members, who supported the Socialists and were ready to defend the Republic in 1914.

The first social historian to study syndicalism was Peter Stearns (1971), who questioned its impact on strikes and workers. He found that French strikes in the period were not more demanding, violent, or indeed more general than those in Britain or Germany. He noted the decline of strikes after 1910, which he attributed to a combination of employer strikebreaking and to concessions granted in collective bargaining, and concluded that syndicalism was not representative of workers, who were becoming increasingly moderate as they adapted to industrialization.

It did not follow, however, from the failure of the general strike that syndicalists had no influence on strikes or that workers were becoming more moderate. The greatest growth in the CGT occurred after 1906 when new categories—coal miners, railway engineers, postal clerks, and teachers—were radicalized. The crisis of syndicalism after 1909 was due not to real-wage gains or the success of collective bargaining, which was minimal and declining, but largely to the defeat of the general strike by strong radical governments.

Quantitative studies by Charles Tilly and Edward Shorter and by Gerald Friedman suggested ways in which syndicalism influenced strikes. Tilly stressed the role that sympathetic governments played in the outbreak and mediation of strikes. Comparing American and French strikes in this period, Friedman found that a class-oriented syndicalism produced strikes that were larger in size and rates of participation, including the unskilled and more factories, than those organized by more exclusive craft unionists in the United States.

The complete history of French syndicalism remains to be written. Little work has been done on individual unions or industrial federations or on industrial relations in individual firms or sectors. The impact of syndicalism on working-class culture and daily life is obscure. Nor has the connection of postwar syndicalism with the rise of communism been fully explored. (*See also* Anarchism; Socialism; Strikes; Unions; Working Class)

Bernard H. Moss

REFERENCES

Amdur, Kathryn. *Syndicalist Legacy: Trade Unions and Politics in Two French Cities in the Era of World War I.* Chicago: University of Illinois Press, 1986.

Moss, Bernard. *The Origins of the French Labor Movement: The Socialism of Skilled Workers (1830–1914).* Berkeley: University of California Press, 1976.

Shorter, Edward, and Charles Tilly. *Strikes in France, 1830–1968.* Cambridge: Cambridge University Press, 1974.

Stearns, Peter N. *Revolutionary Syndicalism and French Labor: A Cause Without Rebels.* New Brunswick, NJ: Rutgers University Press, 1971.

T

Taoism

Taoism (Daoism) was retrospectively named by historians to include a rather broad range of Chinese thought. The scholars who were regarded Taoists probably never had and never would have organized themselves into a so-named school, for as highly individualistic thinkers, they were categorically against any form of institutionalization.

While names of some Taoists are mentioned in records, together with a few fragments of their statements, only two sets of major works of Taoism survive, namely those attributed to Chuang Chou and Lao-tzu.

Chuang Chou was active in the 4th century BC. The works attributed to him are a number of essays, most of which were written in the form of metaphors and allegories, where it preached that knowledge is relative and even agnostic. Judgment of values is at best subjective, determined by the observance of one's own situation and criterion. Anything or any effort arbitrarily developed is against nature and therefore artificial. Society may be necessary, but only as long as one lives as a free individual.

Lao-tzu probably was a senior contemporary of Confucius. The concise work attributed to Lao-tzu, called Tao-teh-ching, is most plausibly a composition of the late 4th century or in the 3rd century BC. Being concise and ambiguous, this work remains the most difficult among the Chinese classics for readers to fathom. Tao-teh-ching contains dialectical arguments of relativism. Yet, any human action or any effort for particular purposes or even any phenomenon observed represents actually only one of two sides, while the counterpart of such phenomena and the counteraction of such action is really dialectically related to its proper side. Also, no action and nonbeing are more fundamental than action and being. In regard to social life, society is meaningless, as the real life is individualistic. Law, order, and knowledge are useless and even harmful for real life—at best, one can tolerate small communities, isolated from each other. Therefore, Tao-teh-ching actually is more radical than the works of Chuang Chou. The paradoxes raised in the Tao-teh-ching are often ambivalently interpreted as the foundations of military strategy of dialectical struggles, such as guerrilla warfare.

Both Taoist works are usually regarded a counterweight to Confucian humanistic positivism and its social concerns. Ironically, in Chinese intellectual history, the interaction between Confucian and Taoist positions often resulted in mutual influences that were complementary. The philosophy of Chuang-Lao Taoism eventually was absorbed by a religious movement initiated in the late 2nd century AD, and eventually organized into an institutional religion, also named Taoism. Its theology, however, was developed from several origins, among which the Taoists' philosophy was only one, while ancient shamanistic folk faiths probably could be regarded the most crucial fountainhead of Taoist religion.

According to traditional Chinese intellectuals, Taoism is a supplementary and complementary system of the Confucian orthodoxy. Confucian positivism prevails while one is actively taking part in state and social affairs. Taoism prevails while one lives in retirement or has no chance to participate in societal leadership. The dialectical argument of Taoism also provides China with a useful viewpoint to appreciate dynamic changes in society. Priests of the Taoist religious sects, however, do not have the prominent roles or status of the Confucian scholars, though at times they influenced popular religious belief considerably. Popular Taoism and its overlays of shamanism are often studied as part of Chinese mentalities history. (*See also* Magic; Popular Culture; Religion)

Cho-yun Hsu

REFERENCES

Lau, D.C., trans. *Laotzu: Tao te ching.* Beijing: Chinese University Press, 1982.

Schwartz, Benjamin I. *World of Thought in Ancient China.* Cambridge, MA: Harvard University Press, 1985.

Watson, Burton, trans. *Chuang-tzu.* New York: Columbia University Press, 1968.

Taxation and State Formation

Social history has generally moved away from understanding states as simply the outcome and instrument of class dynamics. States are more often seen as autonomous actors, interacting with social classes. This has inspired interest in the relationship between state and society; and taxation has emerged as the critical nexus between the two. War has been the principal reason for taxation, hence taxation, state development, and military matters are closely related, with particular attention focusing on the period AD 1000–1800; modern taxation history has yet to be fully addressed in a sociohistorical context.

Early autocratic forms of taxation and state formation may be identified in countries such as Russia, Castile, the Ottoman Empire, Tokugawa Japan, and China. In these areas we find, owing to powerful military forces, a strong state developing quite early, able to collect taxes through force. Political power concentrated in the hands of suppressors of warlordism, ruthless tax collectors beholden to foreign rulers, or commanders of expanding, centralized militaries. Such states were quite powerful in relation to the major social classes (even the upper classes); taxes were collected forcibly; and opposition, should it appear, was firmly crushed. Imperial and monarchal bureaucracies developed to govern, defend, and expand the territory. Key social classes were often closely integrated with the state, either as administrators, as managers of state-owned enterprises, or as merchants and manufacturers loyal to the state (which was the main purchaser of military equipment and luxury goods). States following this pattern were powerful, coercive, and durable. They could rule arbitrarily; meaningful representative government and the rule of law were absent; kingship was often divine, or at least caesaropapist. Power was often somewhat limited by administering taxation through private contractors (tax farmers, *multezim, publicani*), who paid the state fixed amounts, and could legally retain whatever else they extracted. State revenue was lowered by peculation; and state power was reduced by these semi-independent contractors (as opposed to beholden functionaries) within the apparatus. Though tax farmers enjoyed some measure of independence, as long as they and the state maintained mutual interests, the power of the state remained formidable.

These areas might be usefully contrasted to

medieval western Europe. Although military chieftains and empires were in evidence—witness the Carolingian and Holy Roman empires—revenue was based exclusively on the royal demesnes and administration depended on the all too unreliable basis of personal loyalty. Central authority was never clearly established; ambitious vassals assumed increased power at the expense of nominal sovereigns. A balance of power emerged between the crown and local centers of power—a balance between chaos and autocracy. Taxation and state formation followed a distinct pattern stemming from a partially mistrustful, partially cooperative, relationship between crown and social classes. Unable to collect taxes forcibly, monarchs had to *negotiate* with social classes in order to obtain revenue for the state and warmaking. Negotiations became routinized, formalized, and, by the late Middle Ages, institutionalized. Parliaments (*Landtage*, estates, diets) emerged throughout western Europe as forums for taxation. Representative assemblies exchanged revenue for increased control of lawmaking and war.

These states were *constitutional* in nature: government comprised a royal chancery, a parliament of the higher social classes, and royal officials in the localities, who were appointed in consultation with local elites. The contrast to the early autocracies is marked: Russian, Chinese, and Ottoman monarchs ruled without formal need to consult their social classes; the grasping Western monarch faced a parsimonious parliament, fierce opposition, and perhaps even a march to the scaffold. In order to regulate taxation and other dealings between state and society in the West, elaborate legal thinking developed, which served as a basis for personal liberties, the rule of law, and enduring commitment to this early form of representative government. This pattern of taxation and state formation may be called constitutional, as opposed to autocratic or imperial.

Taxation systems had important consequences for the economy and for nation-building. The imposition of taxes in the Middle Ages forced many elites to adopt rational methods of calculation and accounting to their estates and property, which, in turn, aided in the shift to modern economic methods. Through the nexus of national parliaments, disparate localities became increasingly cognizant of involvement in a larger whole. In such areas, disintegration into regional separatism was prevented. An instructive case is that of Spain, which did not develop a national parliament. Instead it relied on revenue from its heartland (Castile) and from foreign holdings, including those in the Low Countries and the New World. The result was a strong autocratic state centered in Castile, which was poorly integrated with the political, social, and cultural realities of other regions of Spain (especially Catalonia). Regionalism came to a head when, in the mid-17th century, Castile sought to extend taxation over the entire Iberian peninsula. This led to long wars, the collapse of Spanish power in European affairs, and an enduring legacy of separatism.

New taxation problems emerged in Europe as costs of warfare increased sharply in the early modern period. Parliaments were unable or reluctant to provide adequate revenue to field large numbers of soldiers with modern equipment. Increased taxation fed peasant discontent, though this was sometimes offset by the decline of manorial dues. In countries that had to use large amounts of domestic resources for war (e.g., France and Brandenburg-Prussia), monarchs dismantled parliaments and other aspects of constitutionalism and replaced them with powerful structures to extract revenue and build strong armies. These states became increasingly bureaucratic, military-centered, and autocratic. Forcible extraction replaced constitutional negotiation; royal tax officials became provincial governors, intendants, and commissars; and the state managed and developed the economy in order to increase revenue.

Although monarchs in military-centered autocracies gained considerable power over taxation, problems nonetheless surfaced. This was the case in France, where fiscal problems led to efforts at tax reform, which in turn led to elite opposition (including the tax farmers), state paralysis, and, when combined with peasant rebellions, the momentous Revolution of 1789. But not every country faced these problems. England, with less warfare, did not have the taxation levels of France or Brandenburg-Prussia. Constitutional methods of taxation endured and merged with public debt (as they had in the Netherlands) as central means of war finance. Constitutional structures survived as the main method of taxation, and, as modernization of state and economy proceeded, they formed a sound basis for modern democratic government.

It is perhaps hackneyed but nonetheless accurate to say that scholarship on these dynamics, in almost every country and epoch, is in an early stage. Social history, and the linkage between social factors and the state, will be enriched by future research for quite some time. (*See also* Aristocracy; Comparative History; French Revolution; State and Society)

Brian M. Downing

REFERENCES

Gilbert, Felix, ed. *The Historical Essays of Otto Hintze.* New York: Oxford University Press, 1975.

Strayer, Joseph R. *On the Medieval Origins of the Modern State.* Princeton, NJ: Princeton University Press, 1970.

Tilly, Charles, ed. *The Formation of the National States in Western Europe.* Princeton, NJ: Princeton University Press, 1975.

Teaching of Social History

Two major areas of concern define the issues surrounding the teaching of social history at the college and university level, and at the precollege level as well. The first and more theoretical area, which centers on the establishment of a rationale for the integration of sociohistorical material into history curricula, emerges from current and related debates over the nature of the historical canon and over conflicting definitions of historical literacy. These discussions have created a problematic climate for history instruction generally and for social history specifically. The second area, which focuses on more practical pedagogical matters, arises from certain characteristics of the field itself: social history differs from more traditional history in important ways, and those differences translate into several specific concerns with regard to curriculum design and classroom instruction.

A number of recent critical analyses of the undergraduate history curriculum have suggested that fundamental knowledge concerning the Western heritage and the American past has been, or is in the process of being, systematically eliminated in favor of the inclusion of less important information drawn from an untraditional, multicultural context. These discussions suggest that major works of significant, original Western thought have been supplanted in basic, required history courses by inferior, derivative texts chosen on the basis of current standards of political correctness. Thus, for example, recently designed courses such as Stanford University's Cultures, Ideas, and Values, which incorporates several minority and non-Western sources as part of the assigned readings on the European past, have been compared unfavorably with Columbia University's more established and traditional Western history course which is organized around Great Books and with the University of Chicago's extensive requirements in the history of Western civilization.

While educators who support contemporary efforts to expand the historical canon cite the relevance and value of a broader approach in the context of an increasingly interdependent world, their opponents perceive the incorporation of untraditional perspectives as a threat to American cultural identity. These critics reiterate the importance of exposing students to a common core of agreed-upon knowledge about Western and national events, achievements, and ideas as a means of insuring a future commitment to democracy and to civic participation.

Closely linked to this concern is the widely held perception that historical literacy, defined as the mastery of traditional information organized chronologically, usually according to political developments, has declined dramatically since the early decades of the 20th century. Here precollege as well as undergraduate education has been targeted. Bolstered by the findings of the 1986 National Assessment of History and Literature, which highlighted the inability of a national sample of 17-year-old high school students to answer a set of factual questions about various aspects of American history, this perception has generated efforts to define specific lists of facts, concepts, and generalizations that, if properly taught, would insure an appropriate level of historical literacy. Advocates of such an approach would assign the responsibility for conveying this material to instructors who teach introductory-level college courses as well as to those who teach at the elementary and secondary levels.

The discussions regarding the expansion of the canon and the decline in historical literacy have created a conservative climate which has hampered efforts to introduce new historical material, including the research of social historians, into required courses at either the undergraduate level or earlier. Thus, for example, while both high school and college survey texts may include some coverage of topics in women's history, black history, and immigrant history, material of this type typically continues to be presented as peripheral to the "real" history that constitutes the major narrative. Indeed some literacy advocates view the rise of social history, which represents a new kind of historical inquiry in terms of both content and approach, as at least partially responsible for the serious problems they perceive in contemporary history education. Such critics assert that efforts to teach sociohistorical material detract from the urgent task of covering more fundamental and important facts about a common Western and national past, and thus contribute to both deteriorating standards and unacceptable knowledge gaps.

In this conservative context, history is usually defined as a narrative collection of facts dealing primarily with national heroes and inspirational triumphs. Historical literacy is equated with the memorization of those facts, and the rationale for history education is derived from its perceived political contribution to the maintenance of cultural cohesion. Although such arguments do not reflect accurately either the viewpoints of most historians or the nature of contemporary historical research, collectively these criteria pose a formidable challenge to the effort to construct a rationale for integrating the findings of social historians into history curricula.

By defining the discipline in this limited fashion and equating historical literacy with the mastery of a circumscribed set of traditional "basics" drawn primarily from Western political history, the proponents of these views effectively foreclose any opportunity for the study of sociohistorical material in the context of required secondary school or introductory undergraduate courses, which represent the only formal historical study most students will ever experience. As advocates of traditional literacy, they restrict exposure to social history to those comparatively few students who might elect advanced courses at the college or university level. Inasmuch as the range of topics and the methodology that distinguish social history currently define the cutting edge of the discipline, the exclusion of the field in favor of more traditional content portrays history incompletely if not inaccurately.

However, the restrictive definitions of the nature of the discipline and of basic historical knowledge offered by literacy advocates do not reflect the views of most historians, past or present. Historical scholars have defined their craft more broadly, as an analytical process for the examination and interpretation of change over time in diverse social, institutional, and ideological contexts. When history is construed in accordance with this definition, as a way of thinking about the past, of raising questions and pursuing answers through the study of pertinent data, toward the goal of understanding social change, it is not difficult to argue that both precollege and undergraduate history curricula can and should devote attention to new research findings and techniques as well as to more traditional content.

The findings of social historians exemplify such material. As a new field, social history has extended the parameters of traditional historical inquiry to encompass rigorous scholarly research on aspects of the past that were not previously regarded as having a history. This work has produced important new knowledge about the activities of ordinary people and the private side of human experience. Social historians have broadened the range of sources for historical research, and they have emphasized the importance of focused analysis of societal change rather than the presentation of chronological narratives. Sociohistorical research has also integrated insights drawn from other social science disciplines and from literary and cultural studies. Thus the field has permanently altered the contours of our understanding of both historical reality and historical methodology.

These characteristics, which delineate the uniqueness of social history, also underscore its incompatibility with an approach that seeks to restrict the historical canon to traditional Western and national material, and to construe historical knowledge in terms of a narrow conception of literacy. But in the context of a more comprehensive approach to the discipline, one which corresponds with the views of its modern practitioners, social history represents an important body of instructional material to which all history students can appropriately be introduced. Certainly the goals of history instruction are not identical to those of the field's professional practitioners, and basic history classes do not exist as training grounds for future history professors or even for undergraduate history majors. Nevertheless, unless required history courses inform students that the past is more than a saga of great leaders and momentous events and that the traditional documentary sources have been augmented by a wide variety of new data, they do not present a history that accurately reflects the current state of the discipline.

In addition to closing the gap between historical scholarship and the study of history, the teaching of social history has the potential to enhance student interest in and understanding of the past. Because the field encompasses topics that are intrinsically interesting and relevant to students' own lives—for example, family relationships, work and leisure values, health and medical practices, and the experience and expression of human emotions—it can involve them more fully in historical study. It can also increase their recognition and comprehension of the process of social change over time and of the connections between past and present societies, through a focus on phenomena with which they have concrete, personal experience. In this sense, then, as well as in terms of its illumination of new aspects of the past, social history instruction can potentially contribute to the development of a more comprehensive kind of historical literacy than that envisioned by current advocates of a narrow, fact-based literacy.

Beyond the issues involved in the articulation of a rationale for the incorporation of social history into history curricula, several salient practical issues arise in conjunction with both precollege and undergraduate instruction. One such concern emerges from the fact that histori-cal change in the areas studied by social historians has generally been a very gradual process. For example, child-rearing patterns, attitudes toward aging, and the ideology of popular consumer culture have evolved over a period of years or decades rather than as a result of a particular event or an action by a political leader. Consequently, chronology in social history differs from traditional historical periodization which is based primarily on political, economic, or intellectual developments. Social historians organize their findings instead according to time periods defined by major trends, such as the evolution from preindustrial work patterns to those which accompanied early industrialization. Teaching social history, then, involves the introduction and explanation of an unfamiliar chronological structure based on trends, processes, and decades as opposed to individual events and specific dates.

Secondly, many of the "facts" of social history are actually generalizations derived through the examination of diverse primary sources, each representing a specific illustration of the phenomenon under study. Such sources often reflect the impact of a wide range of influences—geographical differences, or differences in gender or social class, for example. Thus, even at the basic factual level, sociohistorical material represents the synthesis of a large amount of specific information, expressed in terms of broad trends and processes. The basics of social history, then, embody a different sort of material from those of more traditional history, a disparity which can create problems for students when they first encounter the field. Without the familiar indicators of names, dates, and specific events as guides to their study, many students feel insecure about the nature of the information they are expected to know and frustrated by the comparative absence of individual actors and memorable occasions.

The characteristic level of generalization in sociohistorical material poses a particular challenge for young people whose abstract thinking skills have not developed fully—a category which can include college students as well as those at the secondary level. However, many of the data on which the generalizations are based pertain to familiar phenomena with which students have actual personal experience. As a result, although in some ways the study of social history may demand more of students than is required by other types of history, it may be more comprehensible for them as well. Because the subject matter stresses familiar themes, the content of social history offers a potentially more supportive context for the development of real understanding of both the nature of social change and the nature of historical scholarship.

Like good historical scholarship, valid history education requires attention to the importance of accuracy and objectivity if the study of the past is to be meaningful. These issues have special implications in the context of social history instruction. Because the overwhelming majority of people who participated in the ordinary daily activities of life in the past left no record of their feelings about experiences like work satisfaction and the meaning of leisure or the role of sex and the impact of crime on their lives, many unanswered questions remain, even in areas such as family history where social historians have conducted extensive research. It is especially difficult for scholars to make accurate assessments about the nature of these kinds of experiences in premodern society. Thus, students need to understand clearly that, while basic trends can be discerned, social history, like all history, represents an interpretive approach rather than a finished body of conclusive information about the past.

Because so much of the subject matter in social history has direct personal relevance for students, the issue of objectivity merits particular attention. For example, students may respond to discussions of preindustrial patterns of community or family interactions with either nostalgia for an apparently simpler and more satisfying lifestyle, or revulsion toward what seems to have been a harsh and difficult experience of human existence. Obviously the task of evaluating earlier societies is more complex than this sort of either-or dichotomy suggests. The tendency to judge the activities of people in the past from a subjective, contemporary point of view is not peculiar to the study of social history, but it may be more pronounced in this context because so many social history themes and topics resonate in students' own lives. Therefore, the task of converting spontaneous evaluative responses into

rational judgments based on accurate perceptions of the societal conditions and beliefs that generated specific practices and behaviors must be consciously addressed as an integral component of instruction.

Finally, social history instruction involves attention to issues of linkage and integration with other approaches to the past, as well as to matters that reflect the field's distinguishing characteristics. Despite clear differences in topic and approach, the findings of social history relate to more traditional subject matter in important ways. To some extent, these links have been developed at the research level. Scholars have considered various interactions between state and society in the past—for example, the effects of political change on the lives of peasants and the impact of worker protests on political and economic developments. They have also examined the connections between broader developments like urbanization, industrialization, and demographic trends, and people's private emotional experiences, such as anger and jealousy.

However, a complete elaboration of the links between social history and traditional political, economic, and intellectual history remains to be accomplished as the field continues to develop in new directions and social historians explore ways to synthesize and combine their findings. Hence, the establishment of these connections represents an unfinished task for scholars, and it poses a challenge to be addressed at the teaching level as well.

Social history instruction has addressed these pedagogical considerations in various ways. Some survey courses utilize periodization based on major sociohistorical developments such as the transition from preindustrial to industrial society in the Western world or in a particular national context, and focus exclusively on the attendant changes in key areas such as family life, work and leisure patterns, education, health, and crime. Others integrate and relate coverage of traditional areas and that of selected trends in social history, and blend new and conventional chronology. This approach requires rigorous selectivity with regard to both sociohistorical material and more traditional subjects, as well as a readiness to eliminate some standard topics to permit the inclusion of new themes. Topical approaches often involve a concentration on one or more major social history themes which define the course structure, but also include the examination of connections between these areas and other subjects.

Social history has already had noticeable impact on the teaching of history, at both college and high school levels. Social history materials, particularly associated with women and minorities, have entered standard textbooks. Standards in history teaching are currently disputed, however. Further, social historians themselves have been much less active in defining teaching strategies than in research. The full relationship of social history to the redefinition of history teaching has yet to be achieved, and many opportunities for imaginative connections await further attention. (*See also* Education; Public Schools; Social History)

Linda W. Rosenzweig

REFERENCES

Hirsch, E.D. *Cultural Literacy.* Boston: Houghton Mifflin, 1987.

Ravitch, Diane, and Chester E. Finn, Jr. *What Do Our 17-Year Olds Know? A Report on the First National Assessment of History and Literature.* New York: Harper & Row, 1987.

Rosenzweig, Linda W. "Teaching Social History," *Social Education* 46, 5 (May 1982).

Schlesinger, Arthur M., Jr. *The Disuniting of America: Reflections on a Multicultural Society.* New York: Norton, 1992.

Stearns, Peter N. *Meaning over Memory: Recasting the Teaching of Culture and History.* Chapel Hill: University of North Carolina Press, 1993.

Technology

The relevance of technology for social history begins long before the industrial revolution. Basic technical innovations created the context for agricultural rather than hunting and gathering societies. Inventive cultures like China (where innovations from wheelbarrow to paper were introduced) created distinctive political structures and population concentration. Improvements in agricultural technology had a profound effect on medieval social relations in northern Europe. The heavy plough, the horse harness and nailed horseshoe, and the three field system of crop rotation resulted in surplus production but required cooperative land management on the part of peasant farmers, a combination which provided the economic foundation of manorialism. Surplus crops combined with faster animal transport to produce greater urbanization, since peasants could increase output from their fields and had the means to purchase manufactured goods. Eventually, mechanization of agriculture would promote heavy urban migration, providing the labor required by new factories.

Johann Gutenberg's development of a printing press with movable type in the middle of the 15th century is a major item in the social history of culture and the spread of literacy. The increased availability of books and pamphlets enabled Martin Luther and his supporters to propagate their arguments far more effectively than would otherwise have been possible, thus helping to launch the Protestant Reformation. Pamphleteering in particular became a popular means of widening knowledge and discussion of important issues in Europe and later in America.

Developments in military and navigation technology, accumulating in western Europe by the 15th century in part by borrowing from the Middle East and China, set the stage for major commercial expansion and, through this, substantial social change. With technology-based dominance of the seas, Europe gained new access to world markets, which in turn promoted manufacturing and the growth of wage labor. Some societies, acquainted with European technology, decided against fully imitating it, a case in which cultural and political values affected technology in turn.

As European and especially British industrialization began to accelerate in the second half of the 18th century, so too did industrial protest, some of it directed against technological change, like the English Luddism of the early 19th century. Luddism, however, was far from a homogeneous movement, and while some protesters lived up to the image of workers literally attacking deskilling automation, others were mainly demonstrating their displeasure over other issues.

The harsh, numbing conditions of factory life along with the environmental degradation that often accompanied it exacted a heavy spiritual as well as physical toll on workers. As always, though, conditions varied and the slower industrialization and urbanization of the European Continent engendered somewhat less human despair than the pace of technological change in Britain. The industrial revolution in the United States in the 19th century produced varied factory conditions as well. While some of this variation was attributable to the type of work involved, some of it was a matter of managerial discretion, with a fair degree of consensus developing as to the desirability of productivity enhancing improvements such as electric lighting.

A fair degree of consensus also developed regarding the scientific and technological backwardness of non-Western peoples. Europeans and later Americans took it as their duty to "civilize" these "unfortunates" primarily by using their advanced knowledge and tools to ensure the full economic exploitation of the natural riches of, for instance, Africa. After World War II, modernization theorists contended that these victims of Western imperialism needed to replicate Western patterns of industrial development. Repeated failures produced a countermovement which argues for "appropriate" technology compatible with indigenous conditions and cultures.

Technology combined with organizational rationalization to generate further social change in the 20th century, even in the established industrial centers. Exemplary in this regard was the sophisticated, finely tuned assembly line of the Ford Motor Company. Just as important for the working class, though, was the impact of the cars themselves. With the advent of the mass-produced automobile early in the 20th century, where one lived no longer automatically reflected where one worked or socialized. The automobile brought mobility and dispersion, creating the conditions for suburbanization. At the same time, new communication technologies—especially films and later television—served to bind industrialized societies together in a different way. Whereas geographical communities had previously woven the social fabric, now the standardized tastes of mass consumption as suggested and reflected by mass media served as social adhesive.

The automobile is just one instance of the importance of technological change revolving around the home. Industrialization, mass production, and the modern household technologies of the consumer culture relieved men and children of the housework for which they had once been responsible while altering the shape and efficiency rather than the amount of work done by women. This trend reflected the value placed on family privacy and autonomy and the assumed existence of a full-time housewife to care for the household.

The decreasing self-sufficiency and increasing self-determination of the American family generated increased interest in contraception—another area of technological innovation beginning with the vulcanization of rubber in the 1840s. It was the middle class, though, that demonstrated this concern most strongly because of the high marginal impact of children—now an economic liability—on their standard of living. Decades later, the birth control pill would stoke the fires of sexual liberalization in the 1960s and 1970s.

The next step in technology-based societal transformation has been labeled postindustrialism or the information society, to name but two. While the extent of this socioeconomic reshaping is still an open question, issues of disenfranchisement and worker control are already being raised. Future investigations of late 20th-century social history will need to highlight new questions related to information technology, but within the enduring contexts of autonomy, empowerment, and human relationships.

As the above examples suggest, technology is usually related to social history as a basic cause of change. A major set of inventions stimulates new social patterns, though responses may vary depending on the group involved (Luddites, for example, as opposed to profit-seeking entrepreneurs in the early industrial revolution). Basic periods in social history are shaped in large part by the introduction of new technologies. Technological change affects not only work but also, as 20th-century history reveals, very personal and familial behaviors. Differences among societies (as well as their mutual attitudes) reflect technology differences as well. Social historians debate how much technology matters, as compared with other causes such as politics or culture, in shaping societies, but there is no doubt of considerable impact. The understanding that technological change speeds up with industrialization reflects a similar agreement on the role of technology in shaping modern social history.

The history of technology itself, however, does not have as clearcut a relationship with social history. Much technology history is written in terms of the individual genius of inventors or of purely scientific factors shaping innovation. Explanations of why technologies develop and spread, or fail to spread, are only beginning to connect with social history, in a field that often concentrates simply on describing past technologies or listing the order of inventions. Understanding how social changes help promote or retard technology is a vital facet of social history (or of the history of technology socially construed), and it is only beginning to take shape. (*See also* Industrialization; Luddism; Modernization)

Stuart Shapiro

REFERENCES

Adas, Michael. *Machines as the Measure of Men: Science, Technology, and Ideologies of Western Dominance.* Ithaca, NY: Cornell University Press, 1989.

Cowan, Ruth Schwartz. *More Work for Mother: The Ironies of Household Technology from the Open Hearth to the Microwave.* New York: Basic Books, 1983.

Mumford, Lewis. *Technics and Civilization.* New York: Harcourt Brace Javonovich, 1963.

White, Lynn, Jr. *Medieval Technology and Social Change.* New York: Oxford University Press, 1962.

Zuboff, Shoshanna. *In the Age of the Smart Machine: The Future of Work and Power.* New York: Basic Books, 1988.

Temperance

Although temperance now connotes organized efforts to reduce or eliminate a society's consumption of alcoholic beverages, it originally meant general moderation in one's appetites and activities. Before the early 19th century, many temperance advocates believed that the moderate use of alcohol was both beneficial and necessary to the preservation of health, and it was this belief that shaped their efforts to reform alcohol use. Consequently, early temperance advocates counseled against excessive drinking or urged the avoidance of spirituous liquors like whiskey and

gin in favor of the moderate use of less potent beverages like wine and beer. Through arguments drawing on religion, science, economic self-interest, and patriotism, temperance supporters hoped to convince potential drinkers of the dangers of immoderate alcohol use. This approach, called moral suasion, aimed at persuading rather than forcing people to change their behavior.

Temperance societies appeared on a large scale in Great Britain and the United States in the first half of the 19th century, and somewhat later in other countries, when demographic and economic change disrupted customary patterns of social organization and alcohol consumption. To convince prospective members of the pitfalls of drinking, societies held meetings, sponsored lectures, and published tracts and pamphlets which detailed the destructive effects of alcohol on individual, family, and society. To help members avoid drinking, temperance societies organized lectures, picnics, outings, holiday celebrations, and other social events as alternatives to tavern life and alcohol-centered recreation. As drunkenness and its social consequences appeared to increase in the first half of the 19th century, temperance advocates changed their position on moderate drinking, arguing that total abstinence from all alcoholic beverages—beer and wine included—was the only adequate safeguard against drunkenness and dissipation. They now insisted that consuming any quantity of alcohol would inevitably lead to uncontrolled or excessive drinking and its attendant dire consequences. By the 1830s and 1840s, many societies in Great Britain and the United States instituted the "pledge" as an indication of and commitment to total abstinence. The pledge was a signed document which served as both a symbolic affiliation with the temperance cause and a personal promise of sobriety. Temperance reformers began moving away from moral suasion and toward more coercive measures to insure that their warnings would be heeded. If consuming even small amounts of alcohol endangered individuals and society, then preventing widespread drunkenness could not be left to argument, example, and persuasion. Reformers attempted to give their beliefs the force of law by working to enact legislation which would limit or prohibit the manufacture, sale, and use of alcohol. Organizations such as the

Women's Christian Temperance Union and the Anti-Saloon League emerged in the late 19th century to coordinate efforts to ban alcohol. In the United States, tenacious support for prohibition measures led in 1919 to the passage of the 18th Amendment to the Constitution. This amendment prohibited the manufacture, sale, or transportation of alcoholic beverages, and ushered in the Prohibition era, which lasted until 1933, when the 21st Amendment repealed the ban on alcohol.

Social history has explored many aspects of temperance: the characteristics of society membership, the relationship between social class and alcohol reform, and the connection between temperance and industrialization. Historians have attempted to identify the ethnic, religious, and gender characteristics of temperance societies to determine why particular groups supported or opposed alcohol reform. Many social historians point to the class basis of reform, arguing that a person's socioeconomic status was a good predictor of his or her position on temperance. Another approach is to examine temperance in the context of industrialization. Since temperance societies often thrived in areas being transformed by industrialization, some historians contend that employers demanded sobriety of workers as a way to increase productivity, output, and thus, profits. Other scholars argue that working-class support for temperance was not mere capitulation to employers, but labor's attempt to produce a sober, disciplined resistance to exploitation by industrial capitalism. To illuminate the social history of temperance, future work should incorporate these perspectives with further research on the religious and gender basis of alcohol reform and comparative studies of temperance activities in areas other than Great Britain and the United States. (*See also* Drinking; Saloons; Social Control; United States Reform Movements)

Scott C. Martin

REFERENCES

Barrows, Susanna, and Robin Room, eds. *Drinking: Behavior and Belief in Modern History*. Berkeley: University of California Press, 1991.

Blocker, Jack S. *American Temperance Movements: Cycles of Reform*. Boston: Twayne Publishers, 1991.

Harrison, Brian. *Drink and the Victorians*. Pittsburgh: University of Pittsburgh Press, 1971.

Tyrell, Ian. *Sobering Up: From Temperance to Prohibition in Antebellum America, 1800–1860*. Westport, CT: Greenwood Press, 1979.

Tenancy

Tenancy can be studied in many societies practicing commercialization, including England in the 18th-century enclosure period as well as the United States. When commercialization is less advanced or abundant labor encourages more restrictive arrangements, as in parts of the American South, Latin America, and southern Europe, sharecropping has been the prevalent form of tenancy. The history of the tenant farmer belongs to the inarticulate. Since traditional sources are biased in favor of elite groups, most information on tenantry from 1850 to 1920 comes from the U.S. manuscript census returns. The meaning of "farm tenant" varies from state to state, and even from county to county. Generally, however, tenants farmed land owned by someone else. Cash tenants paid their rent in cash; sharecroppers either paid their rent with part of their crops or worked for the landowner and received part of the crops as wages. This seemingly inconsequential difference in the method of payment has incredible social repercussions because tenantry is more than an economic institution; it is social, political, and cultural. The procurement of the necessities of survival defines the relationships of people to the land and to each other.

American tenantry, widely studied by social and agricultural historians, provides important examples of change and variety, and indicates the range of topics involved. Tenant farming in America had roots deep in the colonial period. Settlers moving to Virginia in the 1600s were permitted to occupy farms as tenants until they could afford to pay for the land. By the 20th century tenant farming was well established throughout the United States. Large numbers of white farmers in the Midwest were tenants. As the mechanization of agriculture increased land productivity and costs, acquiring a farm became more difficult, and farmers remained tenants for longer periods of time. Even greater proportions of southerners farmed land that was not their own. In the United States as a whole, the total percentage of tenants operating all farms in 1900 was 35.3—in the North Atlantic states, 20.8; North Central states, 27.9; Western states, 16.6; South Atlantic states, 44.2; South Central states, 48.6. By 1910, half the tenant farmers in the country lived in the cotton South, and more than half the farms in eight southern states were farmed by tenants. Many of these landless farmers were black.

Although tenantry did not spring up suddenly after the Civil War, tenant farming did expand to replace slavery as the predominant farm labor system in the South. By 1890 three-fourths of all laborers in the cotton fields were tenants. The percentage of tenants operating farms in the South increased from 36.2 in 1880 to 55.5 in 1930. By that year nearly half of all white and more than two-thirds of all black farm operators were tenants. Almost one out of every four southerners lived in a tenant family.

During and after Reconstruction, control of land was the central issue, but closely related was control of labor. With emancipation southern white planters lost their slave laborers, field workers, and skilled artisans. Immediately after the Civil War planters tried to hire and work black laborers in gangs as under slavery. Wage labor would give them more control over farm workers than renting their land to independent farmers would provide. Black workers, preferring landownership themselves, rebelled against this gang system.

Freedmen forced white landowners into concessions because of the scarcity of money and the refusal of former slaves to be worked as gang labor. The result was tenantry. Large sections of land were parceled out and rented in smallholdings among white and black farmers, fragmenting the antebellum plantation system. Contracts were signed between employer and employee. The usual arrangement involved an exchange of part of the crop at the end of the season. Sometimes it was the sharecropper who provided the landowner with part of the harvest. More often the landowner gave the sharecropper a portion of the crop as a wage. The key issue decided by contracts was control of labor. Who scheduled the worker's daily chores and

activities, the tenant or the landowner? A renting tenant had more control over his time and activities than someone working for a wage. Sharecroppers had little control over what crops were planted or how they were sold.

In the post–Civil War South tenantry represented large-scale competition in the economic sphere between African Americans and whites, and racial tensions flared. For African Americans coming out of slavery, those who made it into the tenantry system took a step up. Within tenantry differing gradations and statuses depended upon such factors as ownership of farming tools, equipment, or work animals, and whether the rent was paid in cash or a share of the crop. Even at the lower end of these gradations, tenant farmers were economically and socially better off than day laborers (the majority of former slaves). As farm tenants, black families gained some control of the land and their own lives and could pursue the Jeffersonian ideal of the independent yeoman. Yet, going further to actual ownership remained limited. Despite the Homestead Act (1862) and some congressional action, land was not effectively made available to former slaves. Just as former slaves were becoming tenants, many white yeoman farmers were losing their lands and being forced into tenantry as well. The status of white tenants declined as the number of black tenants swelled. The tenant system after the Civil War involved stark levels of poverty. In some cases it amounted to enforced servitude because the tenants were permanently in debt to the landowners.

A myth persists that sharecropping and tenantry harmed families, especially African American families. To the contrary, southern tenancy helped strengthen the family. Farming was a family affair. Tenantry reinforced the patriarchal culture of the South; men dealt with men on business matters, including landlord/tenant interactions between white and black men. Landowners rented to men, preferably men with families where everyone could work. Moreover, cultural mores dictated gender divisions in agricultural labor; since plowing was considered a man's job, landlords rarely rented out land to a woman (unless she had older sons). Thus, tenantry reinforced strong families, black and white, with a male as the head.

For black families, tenantry as a system affected the ability to organize politically. Whereas during slavery blacks lived together in slave quarters where they could be policed easily, tenantry scattered black families into the countryside, where tenant houses stood amid cotton or tobacco fields. Blacks then lived away from the supervision of whites, but dispersion made political organization much more difficult.

New Deal legislation in the 1930s marked the beginning of the end of the tenant system. The federal government began paying landowners money to plant fewer crops. This program encouraged landowners to evict southern tenant farmers from the land. Good cotton prices and yields between 1935 and 1939 allowed a landowner to improve his returns per acre by 91 percent if he replaced tenants with wage laborers. The growth in farm mechanization also made wage labor more efficient. During World War II tenants found employment in the armed forces or in northern industries. Full mechanization gradually replaced tobacco and cotton farm tenants, and the South's tenant system was broken. Broken but not eliminated, tenantry throughout the world continues today. In the United States vestiges of the tenant farm system remain in the South and Midwest. Some midwestern tenant farmers who own their own equipment are even wealthy. As commercial enterprises and agribusiness monopolize available land, however, many tenants in the United States cannot find land to work. Tenantry continues to be an important and changing aspect of social history of modern agriculture, in the United States and elsewhere. (*See also* Agricultural Systems; Farmers; Landless Laborers)

Orville Vernon Burton

REFERENCES

Bode, Frederick A., and Donald E. Ginter. *Farm Tenancy and the Census in Antebellum Georgia*. Athens: University of Georgia Press, 1987.

Burton, Orville Vernon. *In My Father's House Are Many Mansions: Family and Community in Edgefield, South Carolina*. Chapel Hill: University of North Carolina Press, 1985.

Daniel, Pete. *Breaking the Land: The Transformation of Cotton, Tobacco, and Rice Cultures Since 1880*. Urbana: University of Illinois Press, 1985.

Kim, Sun Bok. *Landlord and Tenant in Colonial New York: Manorial Society, 1664–1775*. Chapel Hill: University of North Carolina Press, 1978.

Ransom, Roger L., and Richard Sutch. *One Kind of Freedom: The Economic Consequences of Emancipation*. Cambridge: Cambrige University Press, 1977.

Third World Urbanization

The increasing numbers of Third World city dwellers (i.e., absolute *size* of the urban population) and the growing proportion of total population residing in cities in the Third World (i.e., *level* of urbanization) have been dramatic in the 20th century. Bairoch (1988) estimates the Third World urban population at the beginning of this century at under 100 million, increasing to well over one billion by 1985. Existing cities have gotten much larger (e.g., Mexico City will have grown from a little more than 3 million in 1950 to a projected 26 million by the end of the century), and new cities have emerged (e.g., Brasilia). This tenfold increase in the numbers of urban residents has been accompanied by an equally remarkable shift in the distribution of the Third World population from rural areas to cities: the overall *level of urbanization* in Africa, Asia, and Latin America has increased from about 9 percent urban to almost 30 percent urban since the beginning of the 20th century. While these summary statistics mask significant differences across regions (e.g., the urban percentage in Latin America is about 67 percent) and within regions (e.g., the urban percentage in Paraguay is less than 30 percent), they are useful in characterizing patterns in the world's less developed countries as a whole. Some of the factors leading to increased urbanization in these areas of the world are identical to those underlying urbanization anywhere during the modern era (e.g., increasing urban-based industrialization), but many conditions are substantially different; the differences are vital to the comparative social history of modern urbanization. The most important differences are the direct and indirect effects of the rapid population growth characteristic of most Third World countries, especially since the 1950s.

High rates of natural increase, coupled with declining mortality rates, created what became known as the Third World population explosion. While rates of natural increase were generally lower in urban than in rural areas, they were still high enough to produce significant increases in the numbers of urban dwellers. Equally important in the growth of Third World cities has been tremendous rural-to-urban migration. Poor, rural Third World residents are pushed from their small villages by extreme poverty, shortages of land, scarcity of fuel, and a lack of educational, health care, and other social services. At the same time they are pulled to cities by the prospect of finding wage labor in the limited urban manufacturing sector or in the growing "informal" and "underground" economies. Cities are also made attractive to the rural poor by national policies that generally favor them, over rural areas, for social expenditures in public education, health care, and other social needs. While migration obviously swells the absolute size of the urban population, it is this shift from rural residence to urban residence that accounts, primarily, for the dramatic increases in the *levels* of urbanization across countries in the Third World.

Although Westerners often think of urbanization in Asia and Africa as being a relatively recent phenomenon (in comparison with the early industrialized countries of Europe and North America), this is not accurate. Earlier civilizations on these continents produced exceptionally large cities for their time. For example, between 1800 and 1700 BC Babylon probably had a population in excess of 200,000. Of course these earlier civilizations were not in the Third World. The term, "Third World," like "less developed countries" and "periphery," are concepts that have meaning only in relation to a "First World," "more developed countries," and "core." Thus, Third World urbanization must be understood in terms of the expansion of the capitalist system from western and central Europe, beginning in the 16th century, and its gradual incorporation of the Third World. The dynamic political, economic, and cultural relationships across core and periphery have profoundly shaped the character of Third World urbanization. Some reasonably large cities in the Third World faded into relative obscurity as they became more integrated into, and subordinated to, the modern world economy (e.g., Esfahan, in Persia, was

among the world's five largest cities in 1700); some were transformed into or emerged as colonial or neocolonial export and administrative centers (e.g., Calcutta); and some appeared suddenly in response to world market demands or geopolitical requirements (e.g., Potosi, Bolivia). Although cities have always been an important aspect of Third World countries' relationship with the world economy, overall levels of urbanization have remained much lower than in more developed countries. Indeed, as recently as the 1970s low level of urbanization was regarded by social scientists as a prime indicator of a country's underdevelopment.

Today it is the quality of Third World urbanization, not its level, that causes concern. In the late 20th century, the immense size, high population density, and often squalid living conditions found in many cities in the Third World are regarded as signs of "underdevelopment" in the same way as small gross national product, high population growth rates, and low levels of literacy. Problems of urbanization include "urban primacy," "overurbanization," housing shortages, and unemployment. Urban primacy refers to the existence in a country of one extremely large city in the absence of other large and medium-size cities. Bangkok, Thailand, with a population 15 times that of the next largest Thai town exemplifies the primate city. Though theoretically regarded as an obstacle to economic growth, research has so far not shown that countries with primate cities are any less likely to experience developmental success than countries with normal distributions of cities of different sizes.

What is more problematic about primate cities is the immense numbers of people living in them, their poverty, and the fact that many continue to grow rapidly. In such cities there are often problems with inadequate water supplies, ineffective sewerage treatment, air pollution, and inadequate housing. In fact, in many Third World cities there are found large numbers of people living in makeshift dwellings in areas not intended for residential habitation. Such "squatter settlements" are a common feature of cities in Latin America, some parts of Asia, and in Africa. Unable to find employment in better paying industrial jobs or in the civil service, many residents of such communities survive by working long hours in labor-intensive service sector jobs in the "informal sector." Such work is not subject to regular hours, minimum wage, or even minimal benefits. Urban planners and policymakers often regard squatter settlements and informal sector workers as evidence that Third World countries are "overurbanized"—that is, that they have more people living in cities than ought to be there, based on the level of industrialization. Research in many different Third World cities, however, disputes the view that these people's activities are marginal. Ethnographies and social histories of the residents of squatter settlements and other such communities indicate that the work they perform is often essential, not only for their own survival, but that also of their fellow urbanites who are fortunate enough to have jobs in the formal sector. Their work is also connected to the profitability of transnational corporations. The cheap services produced by informal sector workers in Third World cities, many of whom are women, allow formal sector workers to survive on lower wages than would otherwise be possible. (*See also* African Urbanization; Chinese Urbanization; Cities; Community; Dependency Theory; Latin American Urbanization; Urbanization; World Economy/Dependency Theory)

Michael Timberlake

REFERENCES

Bairoch, Paul. *Cities and Economic Development: From the Dawn of History to the Present*. Translated by Christopher Braider. Chicago: University of Chicago Press, 1988.

Drakakis-Smith, David. *Urbanization in the Developing World*. London: Croom Helm, 1986.

Gilbert, Alan, and Josef Gugler. *Cities, Poverty, and Development: Urbanization in the Third World*. New York: Oxford University Press, 1982.

Sethuraman, S.V., ed. *The Urban Informal Sector in Developing Countries*. Geneva: International Labor Organization, 1981.

Timberlake, Michael, ed. *Urbanization in the World-Economy*. Orlando, FL: Academic Press, 1985.

Time

Society may be said to be organized around attitudes toward time. Technology and social organization have transformed temporal rhythms and how time was allocated. These two factors came together in the advent of the industrialist and the modern clock, and it is here that the social history of time has focused particularly.

The cadence of preindustrial societies was often set by the agricultural cycle and was marked by feasts and fasts organized by the clergy. The dominant attitude toward time was the notion of recurrence—the eternal repetition of nature—and the desire to merge past and present. The ancient measures of time, the calendar and poor clocks, allowed for irregular work habits, and labor was frequently interrupted by play. Long, but often irregular, workdays were interrupted by seasonal slowdowns and long waits for improved weather, the erratic arrival of goods, or simply the erratic demand for labor.

The advent of market capitalism began a long process of intensifying and regularizing the pace of work and with it the suppression of numerous feast days, initially in western Europe. The modern clock, with its capacity to measure minutes and (later) seconds accurately, allowed a new acceleration to the tempo of life in the 18th century. The driving compulsion was no longer to deny time; rather the object is to "gain" and "save" it. Segmented time—unlike the broad durations of the past—became a means of quantifying the economic value of labor. Along with the division of labor and the mechanization of work, clock time made possible the treatment of labor power as a commodity—as so many units of time. The value of a product or service was now measured by the time necessary to produce it. The clock has made modern people anxious of empty time and has intensified the tempo of life at both play and work. Clock time became a tool of industrialists to regulate the flow of production by eliminating the gaps in the traditional workday and assuring a continuity and uniformity of output. The clock, in part, allowed the employer to impose the work ethic upon the masses. From the 18th-century British industrialist Josiah Wedgewood, with his fixed factory hours, to the early 20th-century American engineer Frederick Taylor, with his stopwatch, management capitalized on the power of the clock to regularize and intensify the pace of work.

As a result, laborers increasingly experienced

hours from which traditional pleasures were purged, which diminished the pride of skill. More and more, a day's work meant merely the selling of time rather than a way of life. Nineteenth-century employers placed a monetary value on the hour and sought to increase its economic output. Laborers responded in kind: they demanded overtime pay and a cap on the length of the workday. Thus, they hoped to gain economically from their increased productivity, to make a job last longer, and often to share work among a larger group of wage earners. Workers became aware that time was a scarcity to be protected and increased in value. They too realized that time was money.

But workers and employers not only adjusted to the new economic realities of work time. They attempted to recapture leisure hours and the more relaxed pace lost during industrialization and to "repackage" it. A common strategy of the wealthy was to defer leisure to a later period in life—as in early retirement (when financial independence was assured)—or to concentrate free time and a leisurely pace of life in lengthy holidays. In contrast, the strategy of workers was to liberate hours from daily toil and to free a day or two from labor each week (e.g., Saint Monday). With insufficient resources to "save" time (in reality, income), the worker sought to "spend" free time in frequent, regular, and necessarily short doses. By the end of the 19th century, these different time strategies had largely merged around the familiar ideas of the eight-hour workday, the weekend (of at least a day), paid vacations, and retirement. The goal increasingly became that of uniform durations of work, compressed into as few hours as necessary to maintain production and income. Leisure time was radically segmented from work.

This change in the uses of time was in part an accommodation to the exigencies of industrial capitalism, especially the separation of work and home which made necessary segmented time. These new attitudes toward time also reflected a growing attitude toward work as a mere economic means to practically the only remaining arena of personal freedom—leisure. Separate leisure time compensated for work that sometimes had lost its autonomy and pride of skill. But the desire for a regular short workweek was also a

quest for the right of predictable work and permanent settlement against the roller coaster ride of wageless leisure and debt-driven toil that often characterized older patterns of seasonal and migratory work. Moreover, reduced work time represented a concrete demand for liberty. This meant freedom not only from the fatigue and boredom of industrial work but also from the increasingly authoritarian environment of the modern factory or office. In an increasingly democratic age, many understood leisure as a right of citizenship. The wage earner's embrace of segmented time reflected also a positive quest for family life in shared blocks of domestic leisure time. In effect, the objective was to reclaim family time lost when work and home were separated in industrialization.

The repackaging of time did not follow naturally from increased labor productivity. It was discontinuous, occurring in brief and often sharp changes, usually only after years of political and intellectual ferment. Employer resistance to short hours was almost always stiffer than it was to higher pay. Free time threatened to slow the turnover of capital and inventory and to choke off profits. Competition dissuaded individual employers from unilaterally reducing hours. Elites also feared that reduced work time would undermine work discipline and cultural standards (especially if males had more leisure time). Indeed, ruling classes were far more willing to concede time free from work to the woman (because of her family and domestic "duties") and to the child (to assure a minimal education and physical development).

Thus, reductions in work time were won often only in rounds of national (and even international) political or industrial bargaining. For example, in the 1840s industrial countries in Europe placed limits on the working hours of factory workers (e.g., instituting a 10-hour day in English cotton mills and a 12-hour day in French industry). By the 1880s the increasing integration of the world economy produced a movement for an international workday, which culminated in the nearly universal eight-hour workday after World War I.

Since the 1920s, despite great gains in productivity, there has not been a corresponding reduction in work time. In addition to traditional economic and political constraints, the growth of mass consumerism placed a brake on additional free time. The eight-hour workday became a norm essential for both adequate time to consume and sufficient hours to earn the money required for an open-ended pursuit of goods. Spending became a compensation for meaningless work and thus bound the wage earner to steady and long hours of work. In the United States one apparent result has been the lengthening of the work year by a month since the late 1960s, as families work more to accommodate consumer needs in a period of stagnation. In Europe, however, since the 1960s efforts to free time from labor have been more successful, especially in extending holidays and early retirement. During the same period, the ideal of regular blocks of work and free time has been undermined by the growing demand for flexible work schedules from both wage earners and employers. This adjustment reflected changing needs across the life course and an increasingly more competitive world economy. Thus, despite the common desire for time free from the hurried pace of industrial life and for free periods tailored to individual needs, economic pressure has continued to intensify the use of time. (*See also* Consumerism; Industrialization; Leisure; Working Class)

Gary Cross

REFERENCES

Bienefeld, M.A. *Working Hours in British Industry: An Economic History.* Cambridge: Cambridge University Press, 1972.

Cross, Gary, ed. *Worktime and Industrialization: An International History.* Philadelphia: Temple University Press, 1988.

Le Goff, Jacques. *Time, Work, and Culture in the Middle Ages.* Chicago: University of Chicago Press, 1980.

Landes, David. *Revolution in Time: Clocks and the Making of the Modern World.* Cambridge, MA: Harvard University Press, 1983.

Schor, Juliet. *The Overworked American.* New York: Basic Books, 1991.

Tribe

The term "tribe" is one of the most egregious in social science. It has been used in such a variety of manners, some of which are often contradictory, that some anthropologists and social historians have abandoned its usage as either meaningless or perverse. Yet anthropologists still return to this term in at least two senses, which although different are linked. One usage is to employ the tribe as a stage in global political history occupying the second tier in the steps from "bands" to "tribes" to "states." The second usage situates tribal social organization as a stage in cultural evolution. The linkage between these usages suggests the problems for anthropology and history.

If we consider the vast congeries of social forms which are accepted as "tribal" in a generic sense of the evolutionary or stage constructs, what are their commonalities? Their respective subsistence forms may be as diverse as swidden cultivators, pastoral nomads, equestrian hunters of the Great Plains and the Pampas, or the intensive cultivators such as the Pueblos of the southwestern United States. All of these instances are products of the Neolithic revolution: the domestication of plants and animals which gave rise to corporate groups, which allocated areas to garden and livestock to members defined by kinship and residence. Theirs was a simple household economy, of multiplex relations based upon kinship. The kinship nexus embedded through production the consumption of resources, rank, and religious expression. The division of labor was simple and allocated through age, gender, and kin roles. The tribal adaptation not derivative of the Neolithic's long-term return of social surplus in a small-scale social order was represented by intensive hunters and fisherfolk such as the northwest coast Indians who harvested fish.

The anomaly in this reading of the tribal world is the effective nonexistence of the tribe as a bounded sociopolitical unit with recognized allegiances from its designated belongers. Within the pure, pristine tribe what mattered was to whom you were related and where you resided. Outside the corporate kin unit and its marital alliances there was a lack of social cohesion. "If we do not marry you, we fight you" need not be taken literally to suggest the ambiguous, shadowy, and potentially hostile universe beyond the womb of kith and kin.

What then of those instances of tribe which are associated with ethnic, linguistic, or cultural designations? It is here where the transformative element of the tribe becomes inherent in its usage. There are cases where the kinship order gives way to a stratification which admits initially that if all are kinsmen some are more purely, truly, and legitimately kin than others. At this point the issue of tribe becomes a processual case in a dynamic of social evolution. There are also the conditions which replicate this case from external impetus where expanding states either incorporate tribes, thereby making of the term an administrative category, or where kinship societies which are buffeted and impacted by neighboring states begin to agglomerate and centralize under the external threat and its internal exasperations.

The use of "tribe" to describe contemporary ethnic, regional, or folk groupings should be resisted in favor of terms which more adequately represent the racial, class, and other social divisions of the modern world. (*See also* Hunting and Gathering; Nomadism; Pastoralism)

Frank McGlynn

References

Fried, Morton. *The Notion of Tribe.* Menlo Park, CA: Cummings Publishing Company, 1975.

Friedman, Jonathan, and Michael Rowlands, eds. *The Evolution of Social Systems: Proceedings of a Meeting of the Research Seminar in Archaeology and Related Subjects Held at the Institute of Archaeology, London University.* London: Duckworth, 1977.

Godelier, Maurice. *Perspectives in Marxist Anthropology.* Cambridge: Cambridge University Press, 1973.

Sahlins, Marshall. *Tribesmen.* Englewood Cliffs, NJ: Prentice-Hall, 1968.

Upham, Steadman. *The Evolution of Political Systems: Sociopolitics in Small Scale Sedentary Societies.* Cambridge: Cambridge University Press, 1990.

Tribute

Tribute is the payment that conquered peoples must give to their conquerors or payments made by those who perceive themselves to be militarily inferior to those they consider superior in exchange for not submitting politically. The tribute payments can be made in money, labor, or other goods and services. In this article, we shall only be concerned with the first definition, for this type of relationship is especially suited to analysis from social historians.

Tribute has been an almost universal custom throughout history, since the conquerors saw tribute payments and the siphoning off of resources from another society for their own as a reason for conquest, as well as an important symbolic gesture which reaffirmed the superior relationship with the conquered. Great civilizations such as the Chinese, Romans, and Aztecs engaged in this practice. In certain places, tribute became one of the main sources of revenue.

This was the case, for example, in Spanish America, where in the core areas of the Empire (Mesoamerica and the Andes) tribute was the single largest source of income for the Spanish colonial state. The Indians paid tribute to the state beginning in the 16th century after the *encomienda* (a type of privatized tribute to the conquistadores) had been abolished in the late 16th century. Even after independence in Peru, Ecuador, and Bolivia Indian tribute constituted the largest source of income for much of the 19th century. Although in Peru tribute was abolished in 1845 on the national level, it continued to be charged by local officials. In Bolivia, tribute was abolished only in 1874, but even today, anthropologists have found, many ethnic groups pay tribute in lieu of land taxes.

Tribute in fact does not establish, as one might think, a one-sided relationship. The state often begins to rely heavily, as in the case of the Andes, on tribute payments, giving the tribute payers certain leverage. In the case of the Andes, the state, in return for receiving tribute payments, guaranteed the land and other Indian village resources from outsiders. State officials realized that without these resources the Indians would not be able to pay. In this sense, a pact between the Indians and the state evolved, which was only broken with the advent of liberalism in the second half of the 19th century. Liberal governments, exalting individualism, broke up the Indian communities and changed the tax structure once income from other sources, such as guano and silver, made tribute income expendable. (*See also* Clientage; Taxation and State Formation)

Erick D. Langer

REFERENCES

Gibson, Charles. *The Aztecs Under Spanish Rule.* Stanford, CA: Stanford University Press, 1964.

Platt, Tristan. "Liberalism and Ethnocide in the Southern Andes," *History Workshop Journal* 17 (Spring 1984): 3–18.

Tupac Amaru, Jose Gabriel Condorcanqui (1738–1781)

Tupac Katari, Julian Apasa (1750–1781)

During the colonial period of Latin American history and especially during the last half of the 18th century as the Crown intensified capitalist relations with native peoples, undermining their access to land, resources, and the sociopolitical mechanisms required to preserve their ways of life, resistance and rebellion against colonial oppression became commonplace. Tupac Amaru and Tupac Katari led the largest and most significant rebellion against Spanish authoritarianism to occur prior to Latin American independence in 1821. Focused in the sprawling viceroyalty of Peru, Spain's oldest and wealthiest American colony, the "Great Rebellion" as it was called broke out in the provinces of Cuzco, sacred center of the former Inca Empire, and in La Paz, the Aymara Indian stronghold of Upper Peru (Bolivia) some 1400 kilometers eastward. The rebellion's scope, intensity, social composition, and objectives provide social historians with an extraordinary window onto the dynamics of the later colony and its peoples.

The Tupac Amaru rebellion, initiated on November 4, 1780, with the capture of a local Spanish magistrate of Tinta, Tupac Amaru's natal province south of Cuzco, was the culmination of years of frustration on the part of the protagonist to secure from the Crown legal validation of his direct descent from the royal Inca line as well as part of a larger effort of Inca cultural recovery and revival of the idea of a unified Incario, or area of the former Inca Empire which had been destroyed by the Spanish conquest of the 16th century.

By imprisoning, placing on trial, and executing the judge Antonio de Arriaga, Tupac Amaru hoped to demonstrate to the native peoples of southern Peru that his leadership could counter Spanish economic abuses which drove peasants off their land and reduced them to abject poverty. As the rebellion moved south and east out of Tinta and later developed into a loosely connected regional movement extending into Upper Peru and even the Río de la Plata region east of the Andes Mountains, it was informed by different social groups with varying objectives which have resulted in a substantial historiography as to the true meaning and significance of the Great Rebellion.

The rebellion in Upper Peru was dominated by Julian Apasa (Tupac Katari), an Aymara commoner socially far removed from his noble Quechua counterpart, Tupac Amaru. A charismatic man, Tupac Katari's hatred of material exploitation of native peoples was combined with a moral outrage against whites, whom he felt to be Spanish at heart. This lack of distinction between Creoles and Spaniards set him apart from Tupac Amaru, who assiduously courted *mestizos* (mixed bloods) and other near whites by invoking himself as the representative of the Crown. Both men closely identified themselves with the myth of *Inkarrí*, the ancient Andean creator god whom the people believed would return to restore justice and social harmony that native culture had lost with the conquest.

The Tupac Amaru and Tupac Katari rebellions, both recorded with utmost seriousness by the Crown, which resulted in trials of both families, produced massive amounts of historical materials (located in the Peruvian and Spanish archives) with which to consider the paradigms and methods traditionally used to explain peasant unrest and agrarian movements generally. Initially viewed as failed movements for Latin American independence and then as pure vestiges of Inca nationalism, since the 1970s scholars have sifted through demographic, quantitative, and even symbolic data to devise and sometimes substantially revise the historiography of Andean peoples, using these tumults as a window on more normal times. These sociohistorical inquiries make it clear that, despite the powerfully cohesive features of the Inkarrí myth, the inherently divisive structure of the late colonial Andean world practically guaranteed dissension between the two leaders as well as the extension of regional rivalries. Within the revolts themselves, centuries of distrust came to bear on the chieftains, as Inca nobles viewed Tupac Amaru as an imposter and a competitor while mestizos and Creoles (American-born whites) cautiously supported him because of his opposition to taxation. Yet over time, as whites defected, they were supplanted by a nativist, Incaic element which was more radical and violent and sought to remove all vestiges of white rule. Only the personal charisma of the two chieftains, both of whom were regarded by many of their followers as native messiahs, kept their fragile coalitions together as effective fighting forces. The Tupac Amaru army was estimated at 60,000 men by the Spaniards.

Significantly, during the months of November and December, 1780, Tupac Amaru ceased insisting that he was acting against "bad government" on behalf of the king and instead began to stress his own authority as the returned Inca. The sociohistorical approach to such a shift uses census data and trial records to demonstrate that the rebel leader was not simply reacting defensively to destructive external forces such as increased taxes but rather was drawing on strategies derived from long-standing patterns of Inca resistance to state authority as well as adapting to evolving social patterns among his followers. The defection of whites from his banner and the rabid fanaticism displayed toward him by the peasant masses led Tupac Amaru to abandon his attack on the capital city of Cuzco in January 1781, and to reorient the rebellion toward La Paz. There, in a ceremony of reincarnation Tupac Katari had taken power according to the dictates of the Inkarrí myth. His appearance posed both a threat and an opportunity for Tupac Amaru. Although Katari accepted the overlordship of the powerful Quechua chiefs, the more radical Kataris sponsored a race war directed at all whites which threatened to polarize further the fragile social coalition the Tupacamarus had constructed.

In March 1781 the Katari forces, rebuffed in their quest to capture La Paz, were forced into retreat. Disputes with the Tupacamaru commanders (who may have betrayed them) and Spanish military strength led to Katari's capture

and subsequent execution for sedition in November 1781. Earlier, Spanish authorities had capitalized on hostilities within Tupacamaru ranks to locate and capture Tupac Amaru who was tried and convicted before being dismembered alive in full view of his partisans in May 1781. The Crown ordered the Tupacamaru family eradicated from human memory as a warning to others, thus closing a bloody chapter in Andean social relations.

The sociohistorical approach to upheavals such as the Tupac Amaru and Katari rebellions focuses less on the revolts themselves than on the cultural history, peasant relations, and ethnic divisions that divided native peoples. Rather than seeking meaning in the failed efforts of native rebels against the formidable resources of the Spanish state, social historians examine these ruptures within the longer context of continuous oppression. Unlike Spaniards, peasant leaders invoked the traditions of their forefathers to stiffen resistance against royal extortion.

Tupac Amaru in Quechua means "shining serpent." To his followers, Tupac Amaru came to symbolize, as native chroniclers had long foretold, "a world turned upside down," where serpents (Incas) emerged from their netherworld after three centuries of colonialism to "devour" their Spanish oppressors. The Tupac Amaru and Katari rebellions are but the most notorious and extensive examples of resistance against Spanish colonialism in the Andean area. As Western investigators clarify the nature and meaning of belief systems the fuller significance of these rebellions to the larger epoch of colonialism will emerge. Eventually, the Andean experience will inform both paradigms and methodologies concerning peasants and their overlords. (*See also* Peasant Rebellion)

Leon G. Campbell

REFERENCES

Campbell, Leon G. "Recent Research on Andean Peasant Revolts, 1750–1820," *Latin American Research Review* 14 (1979): 3–49.

Stern, Steve J., ed. *Resistance, Rebellion and Consciousness in the Andean Peasant World: 18th to 20th Centuries.* Madison: University of Wisconsin Press, 1987.

U

Ulama

Ulama compromise the religiously educated elite of Muslim society. Though often compared with the clergy of Christian society, Muslim *ulama* enjoy neither sacramental nor official legitimation, nor are they found in all Muslim societies, since day-to-day practice of the religion does not require their presence. Nevertheless, they are integral to the normative order of Islam as conveyed in most religious texts, and their history is fundamental in the social and political patterns of Islam.

Lexically, *ulama* is the plural of the word *alim*, which is an active participle of a verb meaning "to know," hence the literal sense of *ulama* as "people of knowledge." What these people know are the *ulum al-din*, or "sciences of the faith," into which category fall religious jurisprudence, Qur'an interpretation, the traditions of the Prophet Muhammad, Qur'an reading, and so on. Yet there was no clear standard for assessing the extent or accuracy of this knowledge before the 11th (5th Islamic) century when institutions of higher Muslim learning called *madrasa* began

to proliferate on the basis of earlier models in eastern Iran. From the 13th century onward, most *ulama* received their training, and certification of their learning, from a madrasa, although personal master-student relationships remained central to madrasa education.

The emergence of the *ulama* as a core social elite took place during the 3rd and 4th Islamic centuries in a context of rapid religious conversion and associated urban growth. As Arab Muslims became increasingly detribalized in the urban centers that originated, in the conquest era, as garrison sites, and non-Arab converts to Islam flocked to these same locations in order to experience and benefit from the presence of a large Muslim community, as well as to escape ostracism by their former coreligionaries, demand for guidance in the practice of the Islamic religion burgeoned. Yet the religiously defined Arab government, the caliphate, had neither policies nor institutions for answering this demand. There was no Islamic church. Consequently, ascetics, pietists, and mystics of many different sorts became subjects of veneration in different localities. However, though these individuals afforded the faithful examples of pious living, actual knowledge about Islam was increasingly understood to reside in the hundreds of thousands of sayings and actions attributed to the Prophet Muhammad and his closest associates. Each report of such a saying or action was called a *hadith* and came to be accompanied by an introductory litany enumerating the sequence of oral transmission from the days of the Prophet to the time of recital. Though this was not the only type of knowledge the *ulama* commanded, it grew into being the core of their knowledge; and the training of an *alim* centered on years of listening to, and memorizing or recording, thousands of hadith.

The social importance of ascetics and mystics continued, with the two categories largely falling together during the 11th century in the form of organized Sufism. But the growth of influence of the *ulama* overshadowed this religious current. Though social background initially made little difference in determining who might become learned, teaching usually being freely available to all comers, during the 10th century the *ulama* increasingly took on a castelike complexion with extensive intermarriage and hereditary succession to positions of religious eminence. Particularly in the east (Iran and Iraq, and somewhat later Egypt and Syria), major families of *ulama* achieved social and religious dominance on a local, usually urban, basis. Many such families also gained wealth through intermarriage with landowners and merchants eager to gain religious cachet. Other wealthy families, including rulers, courted piety by permanently endowing religious institutions that supported *ulama* pretensions. The popularity and rapid spread of madrasas after the 11th century affords examples of such patronage and testifies to the desire of the *ulama* for institutionalization of the educational process that defined admission to their ranks.

Institutionalization also made it easier for governments to co-opt *ulama* into quasi-bureaucratic roles, most notably through service as religious judges, or *qadis,* the breadth of whose activities, during the Ottoman period, included many nonreligious civil matters. From Morocco

to India a pattern emerged after 1500 of semiofficial *ulama* enjoying close relations with government; other *ulama*, including some of the most eminent, whose importance remained local and largely free of government entanglement; and leaders of Sufi brotherhoods, who often, but not always, had the credentials of *ulama*. Though the original independence of the *ulama* from government influence was somewhat compromised in this period, they retained their theoretical supremacy as interpreters of the Islamic law, the *shari'a*, to which every Muslim government paid at least lip service. In some areas, such as West Africa, *ulama* independence remained even stronger and provided a basis for political action.

The course of modernization in the 19th and 20th centuries saw the deliberate destruction of the institutional infrastructure of the *ulama*, particularly the madrasas, and a concerted effort by authoritarian governments, encouraged by Europe, to tame the *ulama* (called *mullas* in Iran and *hojas* in Turkey) and curtail their social influence. The Iranian Revolution demonstrated the failure of this program in a country where madrasas remained strong and independent, but in many other countries leadership of the growing Islamic political tendency has fallen to graduates of secular universities without formal religious training as most *ulama* remain quiescent following government desires. (*See also* Islam)

Richard W. Bulliet

REFERENCES

Bulliet, Richard W. *The Patricians of Nishapur.* Cambridge, MA: Harvard University Press, 1972.

Eickelman, Dale. *Knowledge and Power in Morocco: The Education of a Twentieth-Century Notable.* Princeton, NJ: Princeton University Press, 1985.

Green, Arnold. *The Tunisian Ulama, 1873–1915.* Leiden: E.J. Brill, 1978.

Mottahedeh, Roy. *The Mantle of the Prophet.* New York: Pantheon, 1986.

Underclass

Beginning in the 1970s, journalists and social scientists began to use the term "underclass" to identify a new phenomenon they observed emerging especially among very poor, inner-city African Americans in the United States. Sociologist William Wilson (1987) described ghetto neighborhoods from the 1970s on as "populated . . . by the most disadvantaged segments of the black urban community . . . who are outside the mainstream of the American occupational system." Members of this new "underclass" saw their economic opportunities cut off by plant closings, relocations, or automation while more successful working- and middle-class blacks, benefiting from civil rights gains, improved their economic position and left inner-city areas.

According to Wilson, the underclass increasingly occupied inner-city neighborhoods whose abandonment by the more successful removed important sources of role models and social control from these areas. In earlier years the "integration of different segments of the urban black population" prevented isolation of the very poor, "provided stability to inner-city neighborhoods and reinforced . . . mainstream patterns of norms and behavior." Without these influences, members of the underclass "engaged in street crime and other forms of aberrant behavior," while underclass "families . . . experienced long-term spells of poverty and/or welfare dependency."

Although social scientists and journalists vary in their definitions of "underclass," the term emerged in the 1970s as a replacement for the "culture of poverty" theory which scholars applied to the very poor in the 1950s and 1960s. Use of the poverty culture concept declined markedly in the 1970s after critics, including social historians, questioned its veracity and value. While several social scientists used "underclass" as early as the 1960s, it replaced the culture of poverty in the next decade as the key label for the poorest.

As a concept "underclass" drew much from culture of poverty theory; it also revised and added to it. Both concepts assumed the emergence of a near-permanent, dependent class. In either case, these concepts accounted for only part of those in poverty; those with the fewest resources become dependent on the state and pass on their dependency and other undesirable traits to future generations. Both terms reflect the neutral language of the social sciences; they also fit well into the long tradition of invidiously identifying some of the poor as different, dysfunctional, and

undeserving of help. While the "underclass" was a focus particularly in the United States some economists, discussing the secondary labor market to which many immigrants in western Europe were confined, also applied it to the contemporary social history of other areas.

While culture of poverty scholars linked its emergence to the early stages of capitalism, "underclass" theory traces its rise to the post-1960s period. Wilson and others also speculate more fully on the causes of poverty by tying it to major structural economic changes, such as decline of manufacturing.

Despite its theoretical rooting in the late 20th century, some historians have applied the concept of underclass to earlier periods when massive economic dislocations also took place. Kenneth Kusmer (1987) found the economic turbulence of the 1870 to 1930 period produced an "underclass" made up of a diverse group of unemployed. Their numbers "grew dramatically in size and assumed a distinctive form"—"the tramp." Most of these homeless tramps were young, white, native-born Americans who "had little in common with that of the peasants who had emigrated from southern and eastern Europe." While some tramps escaped a permanent life of poverty, life on the road quickly eroded their physical and mental strength and could lead to "a life of begging or the hand-to-mouth existence of the odd-jobber."

Other social historians have questioned when the underclass appeared as well as the causes of this phenomenon. An analysis of a large Philadelphia public housing project dated the emergence to the period from 1945 to 1960 (Bauman, Hummon, and Muller 1991). While most earlier residents lived in two-parent, working families, after 1952 the project "increasingly harbored [female-headed] families where breadwinners, who were often underemployed or jobless, barely survived on abysmally low paychecks or public assistance." Structural changes in the economy helped account for these conditions; public housing policies also played a major role by isolating troubled families and by prohibiting such traditional survival strategies such as taking in boarders or extended kin. The public housing project then accumulated a growing population with "underclass" characteristics: "low aspirations, poor education, family instability, illegitimacy, unemployment, crime," and addiction.

Other social historians challenged elements of underclass theory. In a study of Birmingham's black poor from 1929 to 1970, Robin Kelley (1991) found class divisions in the African American community long isolated the poor from the working and middle classes. Moreover, rather than the image of an apathetic, demoralized, and pathological underclass portrayed by underclass theory, Kelley found Birmingham's black poor "developed strategies of survival and resistance that grew out of their specific social and historical locations, and those strategies changed as conditions changed."

Social historian Michael Katz (1989) questions the very use of the term "underclass." Although he finds Wilson's work valuable as a hypothesis that requires much more testing, others simply use the term "as a crude synonym for inner-city blacks over whom they cast the old mantle of the undeserving poor." To Katz and others, such a term "deflects attention from comprehensive social policies and encourages targeted approaches that historically have isolated their beneficiaries and reinforced the stigma attached to poverty and relief."

Most social science studies of the underclass rely heavily on statistical evidence and a top-down approach. While Wilson and other scholars add significantly to our understanding of the causes of new poverty, ethnographic approaches such as Kelley's provide more insight into the organizational life and politics of the poor. The issues of periodization in underclass history and possible links with earlier groups of urban poor continue to challenge social historians.

James Borchert

REFERENCES

Bauman, John, Norman Hummon, and Edward Muller. "Public Housing, Isolation, and the Urban Underclass," *Journal of Urban History* 17 (May 1991): 264–292.

Katz, Michael. *The Undeserving Poor*. New York: Pantheon Books, 1989.

Kelley, Robin. "Resistance, Survival, and the Black Poor in Birmingham, Alabama," Institute for Research on Poverty—Discussion Papers No. 950-91. Madison: University of Wisconsin, 1991.

Kusmer, Kenneth. "The Underclass in Historical Perspective," in Rick Beard, ed., *On Being Homeless*. New York: Museum of the City of New York, 1987, pp. 21–31.

Wilson, William. *The Truly Disadvantaged*. Chicago: University of Chicago Press, 1987.

Unions

Although they often assume a variety of larger social and political roles, trade unions are formal organizations that represent the interests of workers to their employers. Trade unions represent workers by negotiation, through collective bargaining, and by confrontation, through strikes. Trade unions should be seen as legal institutions regulated by governments, as economic organizations that claim jurisdiction to represent different sections of the labor force, and as political organizations that often have formalized relations with national political parties and, sometimes, with organized industrialists.

Trade unions generally emerged in the 18th and 19th centuries in Europe and the United States. In the late 19th century, the growth of trade unions was so rapid and so general that Kenneth Boulding (1953) has seen them as part of an "organizational revolution" that transformed modern life. Legal recognition was usually the driving force behind the rapid fire spread of trade union organizations as well as of other organizations. With legal recognition went legal restriction. French trade unionists were among the most constrained. The U.S. law of 1884 that legalized trade unions recognized the corporate character of union locals but not of federations, thus weakening the ability of national organizations to build solid organizations. Later, this law was interpreted by the courts to forbid unions to engage in political actions. Some have detected the roots of revolutionary syndicalism in this founding legislation. Among the least constrained were British unionists. Although modified importantly in 1927 and after, the Trade Disputes Act of 1905, precluding legal actions against trade unions, placed them in an exceptionally strong and practically unique legal position.

The first trade unions were organized by "craft," according to the specific skill that the worker possessed. In some countries, federations of local unions, trades councils, union centrals, *Bourses du travail* (labor exchanges), and *Camere del Lavoro* (labor chambers) were the first form of large-scale union organization, but these usually gave way to national organizations. In countries like Denmark, England, and the United States, where unions were established early, national craft unions proved durable; industrial unions were established with considerable difficulty; and craft unions still remain in important sectors of the economy. In countries where unions were legalized later, after, or during the period of heavy industrialization, such as France, Germany, and Italy, national trade union federations successfully promoted the transformation of craft unions into "industrial" unions, organized by industry, and few pure craft organizations remain.

In countries where large industrial unions were dominant, formal affiliation to political parties was common, usually to socialist parties, but occasionally to confessional and even to liberal parties. Socialist parties often led the way in founding trade unions. But whether parties founded national unions or, as in the case of the UK, unions founded political parties, within a few decades, the two organizations came to recognize the value of a considerable sphere of mutual autonomy. Indeed, in the years following World War II, many feared that large trade unions meeting together with large industrialists to set economic policy constituted a threat to parliamentary democracy. Among Western industrialized nations, only in the United States was there no large socialist or labor party associated with trade unions.

The history of trade unions developed well before the rise of social history, and involved attention to institutional development and ideology. Social historians deal with unions as part of a wider study of protest or the working class. They add range, as in dealing with the frequent tension between male-dominated unions and women workers. Trade union history remains an important entry to working-class history, not only in the industrial nations but also in the burgeoning social history of areas like modern Africa. At the same time, tension persists in studying trade unions, with some work remaining resolutely in the category of political/intellectual history and other work struggling for wider connections to sociohistorical scholarship to what is sometimes called the "new" labor history. (*See also* Class; Strikes; Socialism; Syndicalism; Working Class)

Michael P. Hanagan

REFERENCES

Boulding, Kenneth E. *The Organizational Revolution: A Study in the Ethics of Economic Organizations.* New York: Harper Brothers, 1953.

Marks, Gary. *Unions in Politics: Britain, Germany, and the United States in the Nineteenth and Early Twentieth Centuries.* Princeton, NJ: Princeton University Press, 1989.

Middlemas, Keith. *Politics in Industrial Society.* London: Andre Deutsch, 1979.

Tomlins, Christopher L. *The State and the Unions: Labor Relations, Law, and the Organized Labor Movement in America, 1880–1960.* Cambridge: Cambridge University Press, 1985.

United States Demography

In 1790, the first United States census counted 3.9 million people. By 1990, there were 248 million Americans, living in 50 states. Such growth is very rapid, and had started as early as 1700, for at that time the colonial population was only about 250,000. Fifty years after the first census, the total number of Americans was 17 million. By 1890, the total stood at 63 million, and by 1940 had reached 132 million. Until 1860, population growth was extremely rapid, from a combination of high birth rates and immigration. From 1790 to 1840, the increase was more than fourfold, while growth between 1840 and 1890 was just under that. Since 1890, the population has not quite doubled in each half-century. The slower growth since 1890 is the result of lower birth rates and reduced immigration. All these patterns form a vital changing framework for American social history.

Perhaps the most distinct influence on the American population has been immigration. The United States has often been referred to as a nation of immigrants. By the time the first census was taken, immigration had long been a part of American history. Sizable numbers of English and Africans had crossed the Atlantic, the latter involuntarily, along with smaller numbers of Germans, Irish, Dutch, and others. In what was later to become the southern part of the United States, a small Spanish presence was evident. From 1770 until 1820, revolutions in America and France reduced travel to the United States. Then, between 1820 and 1920, over 30 million people moved to the United States, mostly from Europe, though some came from China and Japan. First came the Irish and Germans in the middle of the 19th century. The Chinese began to arrive in California shortly after the gold rush in 1849, but prejudice ended their immigration via the Chinese Exclusion Act in 1882. From 1890 to 1915, many immigrants arrived from southern and eastern Europe, with yearly totals exceeding a million six times between 1905 and 1914. During this period, Japanese became the principal immigrants from Asia. After 1917, quotas, economic depression, and wars effectively cut the flow of migrants to the United States, until 1965, when a new immigration policy was implemented. Immigration has been important not only because it brought millions of people of different backgrounds to the United States, but also because those who moved often were good for the economy. The vast majority were adults, and most were young males, in the 19th century, when labor was needed. Recently, immigrants have been skilled workers, and have come from countries outside Europe.

Migration within the United States has also been important. By 1912, little more than a century after the country was founded, the population, which had once mostly lived within 150 miles of the Atlantic, had expanded across the continent. The westward expansion of the United States population came at the expense of Indians, who had long occupied the land, and other nations, such as Spain, France, and Mexico, who claimed land that Anglo-Americans wanted. Migration to the cities paralleled westward expansion. In 1800, only about 5 percent of Americans lived in cities, and the largest, Philadelphia, held only 62,000. In 1880, New York became the first city to count one million residents. Another three cities had reached that mark by 1920, when half the population lived in cities, large and small. By 1990, over seven of every ten Americans are urban residents, though many live in suburban communities that surround urban cores that have not changed much since 1920. Until 1900, most African Americans lived in the rural South. Then, changes in southern agriculture and the lure of northern jobs triggered a move to cities in the North, and during World War II, to the West. The vast majority of African Americans outside the South today are urbanites, while those in the South have moved increasingly to cities.

From 1800 to the present, Americans have experienced, along with many other people, changes known as the demographic transition. This refers to reductions in fertility and mortality that are unprecedented in history. Starting about the time of the Revolution, some Americans began to limit the size of their families. By the end of the 20th century, virtually all Americans practice some sort of family limitation. The result is a decrease in the average number of children born to a family from about eight to about two. Mortality did not improve much until 1880, but since then life expectancy at birth has risen from about 40 to over 70 years. Much of this is the result of major reductions in infant mortality. In 1900, over 190 of every 1,000 babies born died before their first birthday; the corresponding figure today is under 10. Children today have a better chance of living to age 60 than they would have had of living to age one in 1900. (*See also* Baby Boom; Census; Cities; Death; Demographic Transition; Divorce; Fertility; Immigration; Marriage/Remarriage; Mortality Decline; Urbanization)

Robert V. Wells

REFERENCES

Nugent, Walter. *Structures of American Social History.* Bloomington: Indiana University Press, 1981.

Taylor, Philip. *The Distant Magnet: European Emigration to the United States.* New York: Harper & Row, 1971.

Vinovskis, Maris A., ed. *Studies in American Historical Demography.* New York: Academic Press, 1979.

Wells, Robert V. *Revolutions in Americans' Lives: A Demographic Perspective on the History of Americans, Their Families, and Their Society.* Westport, CT: Greenwood Press, 1982.

———. *Uncle Sam's Family: Issues in and Perspectives on American Demographic History.* Albany: State University of New York Press, 1985.

United States Ethnic Diversity

Throughout much of the American past historians were loath to explore ethnic diversity systematically lest they reveal abiding ethnic cleavages or complicate identification of an Anglo-American cultural mainstream. Instead they wrote of "immigrant gifts" that contributed to securing the work of the Founding Fathers, or of the speedy, if jarring, assimilation of immigrants that served to enhance, but did not change, society. Only in the decades after 1945, as a result of shifting cultural authority and changing political preoccupations, was there a social atmosphere hospitable to the investigation of how ethnic diversity in its American context came to be a principal source of the processes differentiating our society, culture, and politics from those of other nations.

Historical attention to ethnic groups has become a major preoccupation of American social historians, fascinating them as social class has attracted European analysts. Ethnicity, as it complicates or supersedes class structure, correspondingly figures strongly in any statements of a distinctive American social tradition.

Ordinary Americans have long understood the salience of diversity in daily life, past and present. Deeply enshrined in folk memory is the vision of America as a land of immigrants. To be sure, voluntary immigration is only one of the ways the American population has been formed. Slave trading, penal transportation, and conquest and incorporation were also important. Furthermore, the conception of the American as foreigner should not be taken too far back into the prenational period. By the time the United States was established in 1789, a colonial melting pot already had gone a significant way toward homogenizing the largely English, Scot, and Irish settlers around a common history, based on settling the frontier, a national liberation struggle, and the political process of creating a new state, on which gradually to build an identity.

More than any other process, however, voluntary immigration does account for the spectacular diversity of the American population. According to official sources, 4.7 million entered the United States as immigrants between 1820 and 1975, and perhaps another 10 million have come since 1975. (The fact that a significant proportion of contemporary immigration is illegal limits precision on the recent figure.) Immigration achieved epic proportions at three distinct points, each geared to socioeconomic crisis and political strife in the lands of emigration and to the availability of inexpensive farmland and to regional and sectoral labor shortages in the United States. Between 1841 and 1860 millions of Irish, Germans, and British came to these shores. Later in the century, even larger numbers of southern and eastern Europeans arrived, particularly Italians, Poles, and Russian and Polish Jews. Immigration restrictions helped interrupt this flow but were relaxed after World War II, and by 1975 immigration, now from Asia, the Caribbean, and the Americas, was again reaching mass proportions. These new Third World immigrants have vastly augmented the small populations from the same regions which had slowly gathered alongside the Euro-American groups. Each immigrant wave set in motion various ethnic prejudices within the established population. Each prompted a complex mixture of ethnic identity (sometimes newly created, among groups whose traditional loyalties were localistic) and adaptation to "American" ways.

The impressive volume of immigration is not unique, at least in comparative terms. Other lands, Argentina, for example, have absorbed a greater percentage of foreigners relative to their total populations. But none has absorbed so many different peoples. (The *Harvard Encyclopedia of American Ethnic Groups* has entries for 132 ethnic groups.) This diversity has profoundly influenced politics, culture, and social structure. The American narrative may well be conceived as the story of the development of the capacity, amidst the tensions associated with democratization and modernization, to create an organized citizenry out of these migrated, conquered, incorporated, and stolen peoples from every corner of the globe.

The American pattern of socially absorbing individuals as members of large, complex ethnocultural groups, has been facilitated by historical contingencies and conscious policy. It has mattered greatly that in contrast to other pluralistic societies, such as Canada and the Soviet Union, American ethnocultural groups have rarely been associated with separate internal regions and historic homelands. American pluralism did not evolve out of the fusion of adjacent territories inhabited by culturally distinct peoples, but out of forced or voluntary displacement. Territorially based ethnic separatism has thus far not been an American problem. Moreover, such displacements, when combined with the absence of a territorial base and with a vast expanse of useable land that gave rise to many centers of economic development and much internal migration, have discouraged the long-term survival of culturally distinct groups. The realistic assumptions of the Constitution also have played a role. The Constitution allowed for group competition and conflict by establishing a framework of routine political processes and governmental institutions with finely detailed, balanced powers. The Bill of Rights protected individuals and, by extension, the groups to which they belonged, against all manner of religious, political, intellectual, and social impositions.

Still, the conflicts associated with American pluralism have often revealed the major fault lines of the social order. Democracy and capitalism spread economic and political rewards broadly, though never equally, and removed some of the bitterness from societal competition. But competition at every social level within what has been a relatively harsh capitalist order, unmediated by the constraints of deference and *noblesse oblige* that lingered in Europe from the premodern social system, frequently produced ethnocultural animosities. Electoral politics has mostly been organized along a variety of shifting ethnocultural lines, generating resentments that were bound up with and exacerbated existing prejudices. The process of nation-building also created abiding tensions. In most western European nation-states the forces that created a sense of common peoplehood antedated the emergence of centralized state structures. In contrast, the United States became a state before its citizens felt it necessary consciously to forge themselves into a united people. The work of nation-building was long retarded by the weakness of the central government among a heterogeneous citizenry distrustful of concentrated power. It has been accelerated in times of war and acute social strain when passions and fears often guided the process. Indeed American nationalism has always possessed a Janus-faced quality: here, beckoning immigrants to come and lend their labor to the development of the fairest, most democratic of countries; there, warning ethnic groups that they must give up the culture they came with and conform to standards and ways of life they found when they arrived. (*See also* African American Society; Asian Americans; Assimilation/Acculturation; Ethnicity; Immigration; Nationalism; United States Demography)

David A. Gerber

REFERENCES

Bodnar, John. *The Transplanted: A History of Immigrants in Urban America.* Bloomington: Indiana University Press, 1985.

Reimers, David M. *Still the Golden Door: The Third World Comes to America.* New York: Columbia University Press, 1985.

Thernstrom, Stephen, ed. *The Harvard Encyclopedia of American Ethnic Groups.* Cambridge, MA: Harvard University Press, 1980.

United States Labor Movement

The organized labor movement in the United States is one of the oldest such movements in the world. The precursors of American unions—among them guilds and benevolent societies—were brought to this continent by British immigrants. By the 1790s, artisans and craftsmen in the colonies had transformed these organizations into the first American labor unions. Each of these organizations was based on the principle that collective action gave workers significantly more influence over their work lives than individual dealings with an employer. Conspicuous among these early organizations were unions of shoemakers, printers, bakers, and carpenters in the emerging cities of Philadelphia, New York, and Boston.

Employers were initially successful in having these early unions outlawed by the courts as illegal conspiracies in restraint of commerce. Despite numerous efforts to establish permanent organizations beyond the local level throughout the first half of the 19th century, it was not until the 1850s that American workers were able to form anything resembling regional or national unions. Individual groups of workers like the typographical workers and the molders formed fledgling national unions during this period. These early unions, along with other groups of workers, in turn, formed the first significant labor organizations transcending a single occupation in the 1860s. Two of the first such groups were the National Labor Union and the Knights of Labor.

As the industrial revolution progressed throughout the 1800s, the body of workers in the United States gradually diverged into two general categories—the skilled or craft workers who practiced a trade and the unskilled or semi-skilled workers who were most often employed in factories and mills. The earliest and most effective unions were made up exclusively of craft workers. These unions generally showed little interest in the ranks of the nonskilled workers which were quickly growing as a result of immigration, mostly from southern and eastern Europe. Those labor groups that tried to organize these nonskilled workers, such as the Knights of Labor and later the Industrial Workers of the World, failed after some short-lived success.

Because of their ability to organize and endure over the long run, the ideology of the early craft unions basically established the philosophy that guides the American labor movement today. Rather than opposing the free enterprise system and attempting to reform or even overturn it, as the Knights of Labor and the Industrial Workers of the World advocated, the craft unions generally accepted the system of private enterprise. Their goals centered around promoting their members' interests within the existing economic and political system, through a basically adversarial relationship with employers. This pragmatic approach came to be labeled "business unionism." In 1886, many of these craft organizations banded together to form the American Federation of Labor (AFL).

While these unions experienced relatively steady, if somewhat modest, success in improving employment conditions for their members, millions of unskilled, industrial workers suffered at the hands of their employers due to the lack of union protection. It would not be until the mid-1930s, when a dissident group of leaders from several AFL unions split from the federation and formed a rival coalition, the Congress of Industrial Organizations (CIO), that indus-

trial workers would come under the union banner on a large scale. With the beginning of World War II membership in new CIO unions in industries such as automobile and steel had grown to approximately 3.8 million, compared to the AFL's membership of 4.2 million.

After a rivalry of almost twenty years, the two federations merged in 1955 to found the AFL-CIO, the labor federation representing the vast majority of national unions in the United States today.

While the structure and composition of the labor movement has changed significantly since the 1930s, the basic philosophy guiding the American labor movement has remained largely intact. Contemporary American unions, unlike their counterparts in many other parts of the world, remain wedded to the free enterprise system. Within this system their basic function is to improve the wages, benefits, and working conditions of their members. Until the recessions of the 1980s and the 1990s, American workers experienced some of the highest living and working standards of any workers in the world. The last decades of the century, however, have seen the labor movement on the defensive as they have fought falling memberships and weakened bargaining power.

American unions have, over time, reshaped the business unionism approach to better protect and serve their members. Two particular trends are especially significant in this regard. First, since the beginning of the 20th century American labor organizations have steadily become more involved in the political arena, an activity the earliest craft unions eschewed. In order to protect their workers' basic rights to union protection and to gain greater government involvement in areas vital to their members such as economic policy, welfare benefits, and safety and health on the job, unions developed legislative agendas and political action programs. Increasingly, throughout the 20th century, unions have become active in the legislative and electoral processes. Some unions have extended this activity into areas of more general social concerns such as civil rights, education, and the environment. This type of activity has been labeled "social unionism," as opposed to the strictly "business unionism" approach of the past.

A much more recent development, beginning in the 1970s and gaining momentum through the 1980s and the early 1990s, has involved efforts by both labor organizations and employers to move away from the adversarial relationship that has characterized union-management relations for nearly two centuries. While not all employers or unions are convinced that fostering cooperation between the parties is in their best interests, a variety of programs designed to do this, including labor-management committees, have appeared on the labor relations scene.

Much historical work on the American labor movement has focused on institutional development and trade union programs. Social historians have added to the study of the labor movement by giving fuller attention to types of workers who joined and did not join, to relations between leadership and rank and file, and, on a comparative basis, to the reasons for the particularly bitter, adversarial tone of labor-management relations in the United States especially in the 20th century. Labor movement history continues, however, to display tension between institutional emphasis and relationship to wider social currents. (*See also* Protest; Unions; Working Class)

Paul F. Clark

REFERENCES

Filippelli, Ronald L. *Labor in the USA: A History*. New York: Knopf, 1984.

Gutman, Herbert G. *Work, Culture, and Society in Industrializing America*. New York: Knopf, 1976.

Montgomery, David. *The Fall of the House of Labor*. New York: Cambridge University Press, 1987.

Strauss, George, Daniel G. Gallagher, and Jack Fiorito, eds. *The State of the Unions*. Madison, WI: Industrial Relations Research Association, 1991.

United States Political Culture

United States political culture, a concept defined in the post–World War II period, refers to a method of studying the public life of the nation (or smaller units such as regions, communities, groups, or political parties) by evaluating the attitudes, beliefs, behaviors, and ceremonies that inform and give meaning to their political processes. In the same relation to politics as culture is to society, U.S. political culture moves beyond the objective world of voting, turnouts, issues, and electoral winners and losers to incorporate the more subjective arenas of the sentiments held by Americans about the fundamentals of the public power that governs them. This approach forms a key link between social and political history.

Research on political culture assumes that such attitudes are not random but instead display patterns, just as it assumes that individuals as well as elites assimilate into their political being and personality their society's public habits. The study of American political culture is linked to the recent development of social history in four specific ways. These are, first, the intention of evaluating individual perceptions of the political system; second, the efforts of students of political culture to move beyond the opinions of elites and elected leaders; third, the use of other disciplines such as sociology, anthropology, and psychology to demonstrate culture; and, lastly, the application of the concept of political socialization as a means of understanding the transmission of culture.

The application of this method and its results have been extremely varied, and a monograph with the subtitle "political culture" does not assure any systematic use of its methods. Even before the naming of political culture there had been methodologically informal studies which focused on U.S. political culture. Among the first of these was Frenchman Alexis de Tocqueville's generalizations about the nation's equality published in 1832 in *Democracy in America*. Like later students, de Tocqueville investigated the political mentality of a new nation that seemed in both its governmental practice and national mentality to display stunning differences from his aristocratic homeland of France in its commitment to "equality of condition as the fundamental fact from which all others seem to be derived." In the same vein nearly a century later Margaret Mead in her 1943 study *And Keep Your Powder Dry* discovered a national character based on a core of traits and a homogeneous political culture that included competitiveness, shrewdness, flexibility, and hard work.

Today's students of American political culture are usually less holistic, though they search for the same collective expression of values. Some depend on public opinion surveys to discover contemporary attitudes toward the government, not insofar as a specific policy or administration is concerned, but rather in terms of the emotional, affective relationships toward the state. Thus, a sample of Americans was asked "if you think you as a citizen have an obligation to pass on anything to the next generation, what is it?" In 1940 the typical answer to this attitudinal survey was good citizenship and participation. By 1990 the number of "don't knows" had increased and the usual answer to the open-ended question centered on economic stability.

From polling has come the identification of a "civic culture" in the United States, a political culture which is (perhaps was) notable for a high sense of political efficacy and importance among citizens, high levels of participation, and a general satisfaction among the citizenry with their system. Originally, such generalizations were based on comparisons with other nations, and some students of U.S. political culture believe that the civic culture defined by Gabriel Almond and Sidney Verba (1963) in the 1950s has disappeared.

Since the 1960s historians have used political culture as a means of understanding national politics not as the event-laden story of presidential administrations, of elections affected by extraneous events, and of partisan platforms offered as much to run as to stand on. Instead employing computerized studies of voters to discover what Samuel Hays has called "the social analysis of politics," their conclusions posited new views of 19th-century voters as influenced not by economic issues but by their membership in ethnic and religious groups.

More in keeping with the design of political culture as an investigation of how the U.S. political system is imbedded in a particular orientation to public life is the work of recent historians such as Ronald Formisano, Harry Watson, and Daniel Howe. In 1974 Formisano discovered in the postrevolutionary generation of the early 1800s a "deferential-participant" mentality that explained the manner and meaning of public life. Three years earlier Harry Watson had turned to local history at the county rather than the state level to probe the values and expectations held by citizens about what government

should be and what civic duties meant to a generation of North Carolinians in Cumberland County during the Jacksonian period.

Meanwhile, Daniel Howe in his study *The Political Culture of the American Whigs* focused on a political party as an institution available for investigating the "moods, metaphors, values and style of Whig politics" which in his conclusion revealed the elaboration of a culture of modernization and self-control quite different from that of Democrats. Like many studies of U.S. political culture which deal with geographic or partisan segments, the representativeness and connection to a broad mentality of U.S. political culture remained unexplored.

Given the interdisciplinary nature of political culture some researchers have employed anthropology to probe political culture and in studies such as Jean Baker's *Affairs of Party* (1983) election day behavior and the ceremonies of politics such as torchlight parades serve as rituals and symbolic occasions into which Americans have placed information about their public norms. Properly evaluated, even the persistently military idiom of American campaigns, election routs, and paper bullets reveals generalized attitudes about, in this case, the partisan competition of U.S. political culture.

There is no single interpretation of U.S. political culture at the present time. Still the pursuit of the meaning of public life continues in particularized studies, which are available for cross-national comparison. (*See also* Popular Culture; Republicanism; State and Society; United States Politics and Society)

Jean Baker

REFERENCES

Almond, Gabriel, and Sidney Verba. *The Civic Culture*. Princeton, NJ: Princeton University Press, 1963.

Baker, Jean. *Affairs of Party*. Ithaca, NY: Cornell University Press, 1983.

Formisano, Ron. *The Transformation of Political Culture: Massachusetts Parties, 1790s–1840s*. New York: Oxford University Press, 1983.

Pye, Lucien, and Sidney Verba. *Political Culture and Political Development*. Princeton, NJ: Princeton University Press, 1965.

United States Politics and Society

Traditionally, historians divided America's past into periods marked by significant political events, such as presidential elections and administrations. Social historians have employed a different approach. By examining the demography, socioeconomic status, and culture of groups who did not participate in national politics, social historians have explored long-term trends and changes in American life. Having discarded the "presidential synthesis," we can now see the development of American politics and society as the product of ideological changes, economic pressures, and the interaction of different groups of people.

Deemphasizing crown policy and colonial charters, social historians have established that migration patterns, family structure, religion, and economic needs—both English and colonial—largely shaped the colonial societies established by the English, Scottish, Irish, and Dutch peoples who wrested land from Native American tribes. Groups of migrants from different regions in Europe, with various religious backgrounds, brought distinctive cultures to different North American colonies. Local conditions encouraged the further diversity of regional societies and political cultures. High death rates in Virginia and Maryland, for example, undermined hierarchy and prevented the rise of a political elite until the end of the 17th century, while the remarkable longevity of the founders of Massachusetts helped to preserve a system of tightly knit corporate governance.

Turning from exclusive examinations of political events in order to study religion and ideology, historians of the revolutionary period argue that, in the mid-17th century, the popular religious experience of the evangelical Great Awakening encouraged the colonists, unsettled by a volatile economy, to unite in resistance to English control. Historians like Bernard Bailyn and J.G.A. Pocock have explored the key transatlantic concept of "republicanism," which convinced colonists that English political corruption must be rejected in favor of a republic of sovereign people to preserve traditional liberties. Their republican ideas spurred colonists to fight the American Revolution, after which they attempted to institutionalize their political ideology in the Constitution. Gradually, different economic and social factions organized into political parties, and created the first American party system.

While Andrew Jackson's presidency has often dominated studies of the early 19th century, social historians have concentrated on exploring the effects of economic growth to understand the sweeping social and political changes that characterized the period. Small factories began to replace individual artisans in the Northeast; the invention of the cotton gin sparked the growth of southern cotton culture; and canals, turnpikes, and railroads fueled western expansion. This "market revolution," Nancy Cott and Mary Ryan have argued, removed women from the production of goods, prompting the rise of a "cult of domesticity" restricting women to the home. In the Northeast, economic growth created tension between increasingly divided workers and manufacturers and drew European immigrants, which exacerbated ethnic tensions. In the South, the booming cotton market guaranteed the expansion of slavery, while rising slave prices cemented the dominance of wealthy planters. Sean Wilentz has suggested that Jackson won the presidency in 1828 with the support of workers, small producers, farmers, and southern yeomen, who, feeling threatened by the economic transformation, formed the powerful new Democratic Party and ushered in the second American party system.

Historians examining ideology, ethnicity, and economics have explored the causes of the Civil War. They have argued that, on the national level, the rapidly expanding northern system of free labor clashed with the southern slave system in the West, and that, on the local level, native-born Americans struggled to retain political power as immigrants poured into the booming North. The Whig Party disappeared and the Democratic Party tore apart as each found itself able to address adequately neither the tension between immigrants and native-born Americans nor the conviction of both northerners and southerners that the opposite section threatened their respective ways of life. As Iver Bernstein noted in his study of the 1863 New York City Draft Riots, the war also revealed economic and class tensions in the North, raising questions about the nature of the postwar world.

Rethinking interpretations of Reconstruction that concentrated on northern political power, historians like Eric Foner and Thomas C. Holt have recently explored the influence of African Americans and yeoman southerners on southern society and politics in the late 19th century. Other historians have rejected the old rudimentary idea of simple class struggles in the "Gilded Age," examining instead the complex economic and social consequences of modernization for the nation. They have studied the growing political involvement of African Americans, farmers, laborers, immigrants, and women in this period through voting, labor unions, populism, and reform movements.

Historians of the 20th century have tried to move away from the historical dominance of the world wars, and have suggested instead that new organizational and cultural patterns have defined the century. Recent studies of the Ku Klux Klan and of the movements led by Huey Long and Father Charles Coughlin, for example, indicate that these organizations revealed popular attempts to reject modern industry and bureaucracy and the moral decay they seemed to foster.

The concentration of social historians on historically neglected groups of people has significantly broadened our understanding of American society. While opening up new aspects of the past, however, the rejection of traditional political history has often made historians disregard the vital influence of society on politics. While some have offered glimpses of the effects of ethnicity and local prejudices on 19th-century voting patterns, and have explained certain political events in terms of social upheaval, the constant interaction of social patterns and local, state, and national politics remains largely unexamined. Kinship patterns affected American politics long after the colonial period, for example, and, as Drew Faust has suggested in a study linking the collapse of the Confederacy to the disaffection of southern women, disqualification from voting does not necessarily mean that women and other disenfranchised groups did not significantly affect political events. Social history can be used to illuminate not only the lives of previously unstudied groups but also their effect on the nation's political direction.

Examination of complex relationships between voting patterns and social groups and trends, plus emphasis on key political events rather than one presidency after another, do help relate social and political history in the United States, despite important tasks of integration still to achieve. The relationship between American society and politics changes over time, becoming periodically more interactive in times of crisis and also constantly adjusting to shifts in political structure and culture. Further, the relationship has become steadily more intense during the 20th century with the growing importance of the American government and its assumption of an increasing role in social issues. In contrast to the previous century, changes in political culture and organization during the 20th century have reduced voter participation, emphasized federal over state and local politics, and increased the importance of media presentations. (*See also* Reconstruction; Republicanism; United States Political Culture)

Heather Cox Richardson

REFERENCE

Foner, Eric, ed. *The New American History*. Philadelphia: Temple University Press, 1990.

United States Professionalization

There is a vast sociological and historical literature on the development and theory of professionalism. Much of the writing consists of case studies of separate professional groups. Until very recently, a central theme in the literature has been an attempt to define the distinguishing characteristics of a profession. Among the suggested criteria, three seem to rule. First, a profession claims to rest on a distinct body of relatively abstract and organized knowledge. Second, a profession emphasizes its moral commitment to service to the public good, rather than to an interest in personal financial gain. A third element involves the relative autonomy of professionals to determine entry requirements, set fees, determine standards, and establish working conditions. Professions have thus moved to create licensure and certification, define their ethical norms, and establish special forms of education, journals, and associations.

Modern studies of professionalism, however, stress the failure of these definitions to describe the complexity of professional development. For example, specialized training and an abstract knowledge base are not confined to professionals; no one is more specialized than a computer repairman. Nor can one equate professionals with an advanced degree, for professional poets or musicians do not require college training. Similarly, most professionals have little independence or autonomy in determining their working conditions or setting the terms of their employment. Many scientists, engineers, teachers, and countless other professionals are as subject today to the rule of corporate management or administrative bureaucracy as is the average assembly line worker. And although experts in medicine, law, and dentistry frequently exhibit pecuniary greed, they are counted among the professions, while business executives are not. Clearly, the process of professionalism that has historically granted more privilege and higher status to some forms of work than to others is determined by class, race, and gender, as well as by level of knowledge or commitment to the public good. The most recent studies of professionalism advise that scholars give up the effort abstractly to define the term "professional," in recognition of the socially constructed process by which certain occupations have been awarded professional status.

The concept of "professional," as we know it, began in the 19th century. It depended largely on class relationships, and was first associated with well-bred English gentlemen with a classical education who worked as clerics, physicians, or lawyers. In the United States, however, professional aspiration and development was greatly influenced by the forces of egalitarian ideology, a relatively open society, and market capitalism. The tension between democracy and professionalism that marks our history led in the Jacksonian period to a withering attack upon professional exclusivism. Between about 1830 and 1880, many states repealed their licensing laws and refused to set educational requirements or restrict entry into the established professions. Lawyers, doctors, and ministers faced new competition, while rapidly expanding educational institutions opened opportunities to those who could not have claimed professional status on the basis of wealth or family standing. Yet the period between 1880 and 1920 witnessed the reestablishment of American professionalism, encouraged by the growth of technology, massive industrialization, centralization of business enterprises, and middle-class fear of labor discontent. During the Progressive period, many reformers envisioned the growth of bureaucracy and the rise of "nonpartisan" experts schooled in scientific "objectivity" as the best hope for renewing American democracy.

Further strengthened by the effects of World War II, professionalism was increasingly portrayed as a positive and inevitable consequence of life in a complex world. Scientific research became closely tied to corporate profit or to government financing and direction. Newly emerging professions, most prominently in psychology and counseling, staked out claims to professional recognition. By the end of the 1950s, American professions offered a wide road to upper mobility, job satisfaction, service to the social good, and a secure income. They also had built great barriers to legitimate their vested interests and to justify social inequality.

Influenced by the new political climate of the 1960s, the history of professions was shaped by awareness of the way that professions enlarged their power and income through monopolistic practices, while limiting access on the basis of class, race, and gender, and engaging in bitter struggles between competing branches within the professional area. The history of the relatively low-paid and low-status work done by nurses, teachers, social workers, and librarians within the feminized "semi-professions" is a good case in point, as is the history of racial minorities within all the professional groups. These criticisms rest on a new political and social consciousness. Yet the model that links professional development solely to capitalist, racist, and patriarchal imperatives is not in itself sufficient to account for all the richly diverse elements within the history of professionalism in the United States. While the newest scholarship studies the systemic nature of professionalism, it also notes the limits of professional power and the willingness of the public to accord special status and privilege to trained experts.

The social history of American professions demands analysis of a tangled mass of contingent forces and interdependent relations. In addition, our theoretical model of modern professional development is still limited by the lack of comparative studies of the nature of the process in socialist or communist countries. The history of professionalism is determined by larger social, economic, political, and cultural forces. It is largely a history of social stratification and of the work of elites. But professionalism is also the main way of structuring expertise in technical and industrial societies, and thus crucial to our understanding of the division of labor in general.

Research on professionalism in the United States uncovers much that is common to professions in other societies in recent centuries. Relatively little explicit comparative work has been done. However, the United States sometimes has evinced a particular distrust of professional claims (as in the Jacksonian era) but also perhaps a particular willingness to be guided by professional expertise (the result perhaps of a relatively weak government until recent decades). Thus, American doctors, by the late 19th century, achieved a professional status far above that of their European counterparts. Dealing with specific professional histories and with larger context and impact invites more focused comparative work, to place American patterns in clearer perspective. (*See also* Medicine; Professionalism; Sectarians or Irregular Physicians)

Dee Garrison

REFERENCES

Abbott, Andrew. *The System of Professions: An Essay on the Expert Division of Labor.* Chicago: University of Chicago Press, 1988.

Bledstein, Burton J. *The Culture of Professionalism: The Middle Class and the Development of Higher Education in America.* New York: Norton, 1976.

Brumberg, Joan Jacobs, and Nancy Tomes. "Women in the Professions: A Research Agenda for American Historians," *Reviews in American History* 30 (June 1982): 275–296.

Hatch, Nathan O., ed. *The Professions in American History.* Notre Dame, IN: University of Notre Dame Press, 1988.

Larson, Magali Sarfatti. *The Rise of Professionalism: A Sociological Analysis.* Berkeley: University of California Press, 1977.

United States Reading/Literacy

Scholars interested in literacy in the United States continue to debate the most basic issues of their subject, from how it is defined to how it is measured. In part, these debates grow from different interpretations of the consequences and effects of literacy: is the movement from an oral to a print culture progressive or destructive? Is literacy a tool used by people for empowerment or by authorities to establish social control? These debates are complemented by equally diverse views on what sources best measure literacy. For example, Kenneth Lockridge's (1974) pioneering study of literacy in colonial New England used the numbers of signatures or marks on wills to estimate literacy levels. Lockridge found that signing rates for men increased from 60 to 90 percent between 1660 and 1790. Women's signing rates were much lower: 31 percent before 1670 and 46 percent by the 1790s. Expanding upon Lockridge's study, scholars have found higher signing rates by using other legal documents such as deeds.

Yet even the practitioners of quantitative studies recognize their limitations. Legal documents are biased toward property holders, and thus underrepresent poor and working-class whites and free African Americans. Scholars also question whether signatures measure reading and writing ability. Examining the social forces affecting literacy acquisition, E. Jennifer Monaghan argues that a woman's mark on a will may reflect her inability to read and obscure her ability to write. Colonial law required boys and girls to learn to read, but until the 1690s only boys were taught to write. Monaghan notes that even limited reading ability would have had a great impact on a colonial woman's life, enabling her to claim time for herself instead of in service to others and to engage in her religious devotions.

Monaghan's study demonstrates the way in which exploring who was literate leads to questions about the uses of literacy—what did people read and how did they use their reading? Perhaps the most controversial issues for scholars of reading history surround the years from the early Republic to the Civil War. This was the era of the "democratization of literature" and the "reading revolution" as improved education led to higher literacy and technological innovations increased the availability of print materials.

Scholars debate the effects of these changes as heatedly as they do those of literacy. For example, Ronald J. Zboray challenges the notion of a democratized literature by noting that, though more literature was produced and sold at reduced prices, few people could afford its cost: a hardcover novel that cost a dollar represented one-sixth of a skilled male worker's weekly salary and over one-half of a woman's. However, paperback novels ranged in price from six to fifty cents, making them more accessible to people who chose to spend their limited resources on reading materials. Cathy N. Davidson (1989) argues that the early American novel became an important source of self-education for the disenfranchised groups of the Republic—women, the poor, and the working class—whose experiences were often the subject of these texts.

Scholars also question whether changes in the production of literature affected the nature of reading itself: did reading change from the often public "intensive" reading of a few cherished books to the "extensive" private consumption of numerous texts? Examining hundreds of copies of early American novels, Davidson found evidence that readers did not simply consume and dispose of their "cheap" texts. Signatures marking possession and inscriptions describing how a book was purchased or received as a gift show that these texts were an important part of their readers' libraries and lives. Barbara Sicherman has also found intensive reading patterns among readers from the late Victorian period. The letters and diaries of the Hamilton family record their public reading practices—reading aloud to each other and as members of a reading group. The Hamilton family's responses to their reading raise questions about the effect of gender on the reading process. Male readers admired traditional romantic heroines as models of true womanhood while female readers were drawn to adventurous plots with independent and socially conscious women characters. Many of the Hamilton women pursued professional careers and credited their reading with providing them with role models.

While most studies of literacy in the United States focus on the colonial period and the 19th century, several recent works also deal with recent decades and assess the "crisis of literacy" in contemporary America. Many of these studies emphasize how literacy definitions continue to change, as social demands evolve, leaving impressions of deterioration when in fact the real force includes altered demands. The relationship between current assessments and a firm sense of historical precedent seems increasingly important. (*See also* Literacy; Public Schools)

Amy M. Thomas

REFERENCES

Davidson, Cathy N., ed. *Reading in America.* Baltimore: Johns Hopkins University Press, 1989.

Graff, Harvey. *The Legacies of Literacy.* Bloomington: Indiana University Press, 1987.

Kaestle, Carl F., and Helen Damon-Moore, et al. *Literacy in the United States.* New Haven: Yale University Press, 1991.

Lockridge, Kenneth. *Literacy in Colonial New England.* New York: Norton, 1974.

United States Reform Movements

Historical work on American reform ranges from studies of colonial almshouses to the development of public welfare policies during the 20th century. Most attention has focused on reform efforts of the 19th and 20th centuries, but work in the colonial period demonstrates the persistence of efforts to distinguish between the "deserving" poor and the "undeserving" poor.

In a recent work, Robert H. Walker (1985) defines reform as "directed social change," especially attempts to increase democracy and equality. He suggests three "modes" of reform. The "largest element within American reform" involves mainstream political and economic efforts aimed at "eliminating special privilege and undue poverty." The second mode, which includes abolitionism, the civil rights movement, and feminism, focuses on groups "separated from the mainstream and denied a measure of participation in social, political, and economic life." The third includes the wide variety of efforts to create or describe "an alternative order."

Work on 19th-century reform is particularly rich. Historians, investigating the character and composition of reform organizations, have described the middle-class evangelical background of reformers and the private, voluntary nature of reform organizations. While individual voluntary associations focused on problems like prostitution, religious ignorance, or alcohol, the broad goal of the organizations making up the "benevolent empire" was to Christianize American life. At a time when most organizations were small-scale in nature, voluntary reform offered an impressive example of a national, organized effort to reshape American society. Some historians see this benevolent empire functioning much like an established church in other cultures.

The prominence of women in voluntary reform has prompted studies of female benevolence. Historians agree that 19th-century norms associating morality with women justified their reform work in the public sphere. Though the class background of these women can generally be described as middle class, detailed analyses of specific reform organizations suggests that more affluent, better connected women, often members of mainline evangelical churches, tended to support more conservative reform organizations, while less well connected and economically secure women, some Hicksite Quakers, became members of more radical associations. Social and economic differences also helped shape female strategies. Although all women were denied the vote, elite female reformers had access to legislators and secured legislation and funds to support their work. Reformers lacking social connections relied on techniques like petitioning to influence politicians.

As the efforts of reform-minded women suggest, reform and politics were intimately connected. The emergence of popular politics ensured that moral and religious questions took on political dimensions. Generally, historians see connections between the Whig Party and the benevolent empire not only in terms of membership and issues but in terms of attitudes.

A heated debate has focused on the relationship between class and motivation. Because the rise of voluntary reform coincided with the development of modern capitalism, many historians have hypothesized that reform was the means by which bourgeois reformers imposed social control on the lower classes. Neo-Marxism and the work of French philosopher Michel Foucault, for example, inspired a portrait of abolitionists as unwitting collaborators in the creation of bourgeois capitalist dominance. Critics of such a characterization highlight the moral principles of reformers and have explored reformism from psychological and psychoanalytic perspectives. They suggest that the reform commitment resulted from the desire for a new personal identity rather than the desire to control others.

Though the debate continues, with social control theory used to analyze reformers, there are efforts to view reform in a less polarized fashion. One historian has suggested substituting "discipline" for the term "social control." Although he acknowledges the reality of social control, especially in reform efforts connected with politics, he points out that evangelicals sought self-discipline as well as discipline over others. Reformers hoped to liberate individuals to act as morally responsible beings, to facilitate self-discipline rather than rely on a system of external control. The nature of the relationship between evangelical reform, capitalism, and personal identity is still unresolved, however.

Historians of 20th-century reform agree that American welfare policies developed more slowly and were more modestly funded than they were in other Western industrialized nations. Most work has focused on the development and implementation of public policies, the motivations of reformers, and the professionalization of reform. This top-down analysis has recently been supplemented by efforts to understand reform programs from the perspective of those served and to uncover the social and cultural resources of different groups who are the objects of varied reform efforts. Much research remains to be done on this broad subject.

Historians' concentration on the Progressive period, the New Deal, and the 1960s implicitly suggests a cyclical view of reform. This perspective prompts analysis of the various forces promoting and discouraging opposing reform. The persistence of cultural ambivalence to poor people may explain the general character of much of American reformism, but many questions about reform, especially during the 20th century, await further research. (*See also* Charity; Social Control; State and Society)

Julie Roy Jeffrey

REFERENCES

Hewitt, Nancy A. *Women's Activism and Social Change: Rochester, New York, 1822–1872.* Ithaca, NY: Cornell University Press, 1982.

Katz, Michael. *In the Shadow of the Poorhouse: A Social History of Welfare in America.* New York: Basic Books, 1986.

Patterson, James T. *America's Struggle Against Poverty, 1900–1985.* Cambridge, MA: Harvard University Press, 1986.

Trattner, Walter I., ed. *Social Welfare or Social Control.* Knoxville: University of Tennessee Press, 1983.

Walker, Robert H. *Reform in America: The Continuing Frontier.* Lexington: University Press of Kentucky, 1985.

United States Urbanization

Urbanization, understood most simply as the multiplication, growth, and increasing demographic preponderance of towns, cities, and metropolitan areas, has been one of the most fundamental and transforming long-term trends in American history. The evolution of a demographically rural nation into a demographically urban one during the past 200 years could hardly have been more dramatic. At the time of the first national census in 1790, there were only 24 American communities exceeding the census-defined urban population threshold of 2,500 inhabitants, only 5 exceeding 10,000, and only one, Philadelphia, as large as 40,000. Among them, these two dozen small cities and towns accounted for only 5 percent of the American population. Two centuries later, there are nearly 2,400 cities in the United States exceeding 10,000 inhabitants, and 284 census-defined Metropolitan Areas in whose central cities, secondary urban centers, and suburbs reside fully 77.5 percent of the nation's population. Slightly more than half of all Americans live in the 39 Metropolitan Areas that exceed one million, and more than 18 million live in the Consolidated Metropolitan Statistical Area centered on New York, a city whose population in 1790 was but 33,000.

Urbanization in this demographic sense has been continuous since the first census (the 1810s being the only decade in American history in which the urban or metropolitan proportion of the population did not increase to some degree), but its pace and pattern have varied in response to episodes or stages of economic development, swings in the business cycle, foreign and domestic rural crises, changes in foreign immigration laws, and the shrinking pool of potential domestic rural-urban migrants. A modest trend toward cities and towns may be discerned even before the first census, but the first era in which urban growth decisively outpaced rural growth was the generation immediately preceding the Civil War, a period of rapid industrial expansion and high levels of foreign immigration, the latter consisting mainly of flight from famine and economic crisis in Ireland and Germany to city-based jobs in the United States. It took the half-century following the first census for the urban proportion of the population to double from 5 percent to 10 percent, but in the 20 years between 1840 and 1860 it doubled again to 20 percent, and the number of cities and towns increased to nearly 400. This was also the period in which the United States acquired large cities that rivaled the capitals of Europe. Philadelphia exceeded half a million inhabitants by 1860, and New York City and Brooklyn, though still politically independent from one another, had grown together into a de facto metropolis of more than a million people.

The Civil War and the depression of the mid-1870s probably slowed the pace of urbanization somewhat, but by 1900 the urban proportion had doubled again to 40 percent, and by 1920, after a generation of vastly increased foreign immigration, extensive migrations of black and white Americans from rural areas to cities, and the industry-stimulating effects of World War I, a majority of Americans were living in the nation's 2,700 cities and towns. The Great Depression of the 1930s brought urbanization to a near halt, but World War II and the postwar economic boom quickened its pace once again. If the overall rates of urbanization have moderated in the postwar era, it is a reflection only of the weight of the extant urban mass, the effect of the massive demographic transfer of earlier generations. In this era, indeed, the most notable migrations have been from city centers into suburbs, a process responsible for the sprawling metropolises and metropolitan corridors only partly captured by new census definitions. This process is best understood not as deurbanization but as metropolitan deconcentration, the creation and growth of new human environments as different from the farms and villages of the preurban era as were the first concentrated cities.

Building upon basic patterns of urbanization, social historians have illuminated in a variety of ways the distinctive character of urban experience, and the distinctive contributions of cities to American development. They have amplified attention to diverse urban groupings. Indeed, something of a debate has arisen, particularly in the United States, as to whether urban history is a branch of social history or something more. Shared interests, in any event, have steadily expanded. (*See also* Cities; United States Demography; Urbanization)

Stuart M. Blumin

REFERENCES

Berry, Brian J.L., ed. *Urbanization and Counterurbanization.* Beverly Hills: Sage, 1976.

McKelvey, Blake. *American Urbanization: A Comparative History.* Glenview, IL: Scott, Foresman, 1973.

Weber, Adna Ferrin. *The Growth of Cities in the Nineteenth Century: A Study in Statistics.* New York: Macmillan, 1899.

United States Women's History

U.S. women's history boasts a long intellectual tradition reaching back to the post-Revolutionary years when women authors, educators, and activists first bolstered their attempts to improve women's lives with narratives of women's pasts. These writers established links between scholarship about women and women's political concerns so strong that women's history today cannot be understood outside this context. Within it, women's history and social history also share a special relationship. At turn of the 20th century, women were among the pioneers in the "new" social sciences. Concerned with a range of social problems, including those affecting women, women scholars saw in the social sciences a way to support social change. Yet, these women found their work marginalized in feminized "applied" branches and excluded from masculine "academic" research. Likewise, women's pasts—including those of women scholars—generally remained outside the field of historical inquiry. As late as the 1960s, few U.S. historians recognized women's history as a legitimate academic field, and fewer still had thought about the process or theory of writing women's history. That situation soon changed. The women's movement ignited the field: women historians, gaining hard-won access to professional opportunities, responded to the feminist call to recover women's pasts. So too did the concurrent growth of social history, which built on many of the same questions and methodologies developed by earlier pioneers. In fact, many women's historians embraced social history for the same reasons an earlier generation had been attracted to the social sciences.

Social history illuminated women's lives in a way that traditional political history did not. Within frameworks of political history, women's history became contribution history—recovering notable women whose accomplishments could be evaluated by the same standards as those applied to men. Because most of the experiences that constituted women's lives were considered unimportant, the majority of women remained outside history. Social history's emphasis on "ordinary" people held the potential to make more women visible, while its concentration on a broadly defined "social arena" provided a means to bring their lives into history. New work on demography, family life, slavery, and industrialization opened up ways to explore women's pasts. Yet, here too, women generally remained peripheral, even when they appeared in the analysis.

Women's historians moved women to the center and examined the ways that historical processes affected them. The first wave of the "new" women's history, for instance, built on work in the "new" social history centering on industrialization, but concentrated, specifically, on the effects of industrialization on women. Some argued that women's status depended on their role as producers in preindustrial households. As production moved outside of the home and women became simply consumers, women's status also deteriorated. Others claimed that capitalist development mitigated patriarchal oppression, creating a feminine space—a separate sphere—that resulted in greater power within and, ultimately, outside the household. The result was a rich body of literature that expanded our understanding of how women's work and the social value attached to it changed over time. We learned, for instance, that the importance attached to motherhood and women's duties in the home increased in the early 19th-century United States; that, at the same time, responsibility for and knowledge about women's health and reproduction was appropriated by male professionals; that women always engaged in work sex-typed by their contemporaries as "male"; and that the kinds of work seen as "male" and "female" changed over time. Other historians carried these themes into the 20th century, revealing the tenacity of gender-based discrimination even as women gained access to more and new kinds of employment as well as continued efforts to regulate women's power over their bodies.

One troubling tendency, particularly in the earlier works, was to cast women as passive victims, not actors who themselves shaped historical events. In response, some social historians expanded on the idea of a woman's separate sphere, focusing on women's own words and their efforts to direct their lives within externally imposed limits. The characterization of women as isolated within their homes, for instance, was taken apart. Studies showed that women's earnings—from petty commodity production to occasional wage work—were central to households, rural and urban, from the colonial period to the late 20th century. Women, moreover, formed relationships with each other that not only sustained them emotionally and materially but, ultimately, created a female network that supported political action. Indeed, the fact that United States women had been politically active and influential long before they obtained the vote challenged political history's traditional emphasis on political parties and suffrage and expanded no-

tions of "the political." What emerged were strong women who worked long hours, who fought hard for women's political rights, and who sought to ameliorate the poverty and despair of others around them.

Yet, as certain critics contended, these women were almost too good to be true. They seemed to live in a world completely divorced from the oppressive social practices that previous scholarship had stressed. Even the reformers and activists who confronted social injustice seemed insulated from its pernicious effects. Some women's historians discounted these criticisms, arguing that separate spheres and the resulting sense of sisterhood—both the camaraderie and the sense of shared political purpose—did, in fact, define women's lives. Others maintained that this was a celebratory approach that obscured as much as it revealed about women's lives.

One critique of separate spheres and sisterhood emanated from historians interested in race and class. The approach, they argued, universalized from experiences of a particular group, middle-class white women, as if they applied to all women. It thus ignored the ways that race, class, and ethnicity shaped all women's lives. Building on the insights of earlier studies of women and industrialization, new work on poor women and women of color painted a very different picture of women's lives, a picture that highlighted diversity and conflict among women. For these women, who had always juggled work inside and outside the home, the notion of a "separate sphere" made little sense. Their standards of proper female behavior differed considerably from those of middle- and upper-class white women. For instance, African American women, regardless of their class, continued to combine work and public service with the roles of wives and mothers, while working-class women who participated in the emerging consumer culture of the 19th and 20th centuries claimed both public space and an open sexuality. And their politics, grounded in concerns shaped by race, class, and ethnicity, were often in conflict with those of middle- and upper-class white women, whom they saw not as sisters but as slaveowners, employers, white supremacists, and reformers with the power to enforce unwanted restrictions on their lives. Even middle- and upper-class white women differed on notions of womanhood; some in the 19th century advocated a feminine version of the active man, while others in the 20th century adopted both the consumer culture and the same "manners and morals" of many of their working-class sisters. This commentary, guided by political concerns inside and outside the academy, drew on a range of scholarship from various fields including new work in Third World women's history and comparative women's history. It also owed much to the growing quantity and sophistication of social history, the insights of which cast women's history in a different light. As social history revealed more about how traditional historical paradigms made "ordinary" people invisible, it also became increasingly clear how women's history paradigms rendered many "ordinary" women invisible. Their visibility enriched and, ultimately, transformed women's history, for the recognition that all women did not share a common gender experience problematized two of the field's central categories—"women" and "gender."

While some were developing the argument that race, class, and other axes of power were crucial to understanding women's history, others were developing the idea that gender was implicated in the history of all power relationships. Much of women's history since the late 1960s is built around the assumption that male and female roles are socially constructed, not biologically determined—a concept now commonly known as gender. By historicizing practices previously considered "natural," this approach initially provided the critical wedge to question dichotomies—"nature" versus "culture," "work" versus "family" and "private" versus "public"—that had marginalized women and devalued their lives. At first, the focus was on challenging the hierarchies and the male/female associations implicit in these dichotomies. Studies emphasized, for instance, that women's reproductive work was just as important as men's productive labor or that the association of productive labor with men was inaccurate because women had always participated in work of this kind. But, as some maintained, revealing these dichotomies as "false" did not necessarily negate their power: the presence of women in the "male" public sphere was not enough to alter the power arrangements that continued to structure "public" and "private" as gendered spaces, thus marginalizing women. This critique cited two related problems. First, the "male" side remained the unexamined standard against which the "female" side was explained. Second, gender was confined to the analytical work of interpreting women's position, when ideas about gender were actually embedded in all social relations and the exercise of power generally. In this view, gender was as much about the history of male privilege and the maintenance of a range of social hierarchies—for instance, colonialism, slavery, and relations of race and class.

Some women's historians have criticized "gender history," arguing that it denies women historical agency and obscures the nature of patriarchal oppression by casting men as victims. Given the struggles of the recent past, these concerns underscore the need to maintain the links between women's history and feminist politics. In this context, expanded analytical applications of gender are powerfully compelling. By drawing connections among a range of power relationships and by revealing the ways that social relations are politically constructed, they can promote a truly inclusive feminist politics and move women's history from the margins to the center. As a result, women's history now stands poised to recast not just social history, but history in its broadest sense. (*See also* African American Women; Feminism; Women's History)

Laura F. Edwards

REFERENCES

DuBois, Ellen, and Vicki Ruiz, eds. *Unequal Sisters: A Multicultural Reader in Women's History.* New York: Routledge, 1990.

Hull, Gloria T., Patricia Bell Scott, and Barbara Smith, eds. *All the Women Are White, All the Blacks Are Men, But Some of Us Are Brave.* Old Westbury, NY: The Feminist Press, 1982.

Scott, Joan Wallach. *Gender and the Politics of History.* New York: Columbia University Press, 1988.

Urban History

See Cities

Urbanization

Historians have generally approached the study of urbanization from two perspectives. One defines urbanization as simply the combination of processes causing the creation and growth of cities, including rates of migration from the countryside. The other emphasizes the impact of cities on society as a whole, viewing urbanization as the extension of urban structures and values to the majority of a given population. Whereas the first approach has been applied to the development of cities throughout human history, the second has usually focused on the modern era, from the 18th century to the present, often stressing the relationship of urbanization to other broad social processes such as capitalism and industrialization. Both approaches have in common a core definition of urbanization as a process of population concentration.

Social historians have utilized both perspectives in analyzing the history of urbanization. In doing so, they have tended to center their studies on a few fundamental aspects of city development. Many historians have looked at the city as an economic mechanism, considering the ways in which concentrations of wealth have led to urban development. The technology of urbanization, including subjects like housing, transportation systems, and utilities, has also been widely studied. The view of the city as primarily a population concentration of a certain size has given demographic history a key role in the study of city growth. Other historians have been intrigued by the development of specifically urban cultures, or the impact on the city of both local and national politics. Finally, most historians agree on the importance of studying the growth of cities in relation to the surrounding countryside, other urban centers, or in their national and international contexts.

Urbanization in the Ancient and Medieval Worlds

The first cities in human history arose in the Middle East and Central America several thousand years before the birth of Christ. Historians have mostly abandoned earlier theories basing the origins of cities in the preliminary rise of settled agricultural communities. Jane Jacobs has even argued that urban settlements preceded and in fact gave rise to agriculture. Excavations of one of the earliest known cities, Jericho, have revealed the existence of sophisticated urban structures and rudimentary grain cultivation at roughly the same time. Increasingly, historians have emphasized demographic pressure on resources in bringing about new levels of population concentration and thus the origin of urban civilization. By the beginnings of the 1st millennium BC important urban centers had developed in Egypt, Mesopotamia, Central America, northern China, and the Indus River valley of India.

These early cities combined a number of functions. They were centers of production and exchange, whose inhabitants worked in agricultural, commerce, and handicrafts. They were military strongholds, equipped with contingents of soldiers and defensive walls. They were centers of both political and religious authority, whose kings and priests ruled over the adjacent countryside. In general, these cities performed the typically urban function of bringing diverse peoples and functions together in a new synthesis.

The growth of the urban centers of ancient Greece and Rome represented an important new stage in the history of urbanization, though agricultural economies could afford no more than 20 percent of the population in cities. From 1000 to 500 BC Greek society underwent an urban revolution, as communities like Athens, Sparta, Corinth, and Thebes developed into significant urban settlements. Unlike many earlier cities, these did not emerge in major river valleys but instead on rocky coastlines, and early in their history emphasized maritime trade and conquest as keys to their power. The Greek cities made important advances in urban planning and design, but their most important innovation was the city-state, involving urban autonomy and limited representative government, plus urban control over agricultural hinterland.

Rome succeeded the Greek cities as the leading urban settlement in the ancient Mediterranean. Rome's rise to prominence was far from inevitable: initially, it had neither a fortress nor a port, was not a religious center, and did not occupy any important trade routes. In the 6th century BC the Etruscans gave Rome its first urban forms, and the city began a series of alliances and conquests that brought it mastery first of Italy and then ultimately of the Mediterranean world. Its military supremacy brought ever increasing wealth and population, so that by the reign of Augustus imperial Rome had close to one million inhabitants. The Empire's maintenance of military garrisons, commerce, and good transportation networks facilitated the creation and growth of many other urban centers throughout the Mediterranean. Although these cities gradually lost much of their autonomy as the Empire grew more autocratic, they remained important centers of government, commerce, industry, and culture.

The decline and collapse of the Roman Empire ushered in a long period of deurbanization in Europe and the Mediterranean. As the Empire weakened it lost the ability to protect city dwellers from barbarian invaders, a process which culminated in the sacking of Rome itself by Alaric in AD 410. Higher taxes and prices, along with declining trade and industry, also served to reduce the urban population. By the 6th century AD the cities of the Roman world were shrinking noticeably.

For the next several hundred years urban life stagnated in the former Empire. While historians have mostly rejected the earlier view that the Germanic invaders completely destroyed Roman urban civilization in Europe during the Dark Ages, many cities declined in size or were abandoned as the economy shifted to a rural one based on feudal agriculture. Urban life fared better in other parts of the Empire. Cities in the Byzantine east did not suffer the same drastic dislocations experienced in the west, retaining important continuity with the Roman experience. Constantinople long remained a vision of the glory of imperial Rome. However, Byzantine society did undergo a shift away from cities and toward great landed estates after the 6th century. The Arab conquests of the 7th and 8th centuries fostered city life more insistently. Islam had a strong urban theme, and cities like Baghdad, Alexandria, and Cordoba became vibrant commercial and intellectual centers. China also continued to develop substantial cities and a distinct urban culture.

Not until the 11th century did significant urban growth resume in Europe. Population growth in this period both overcrowded the countryside and created more demand for the manufactured goods produced by townspeople, thus providing more urban jobs; here were important sources of urbanization. In addition, the growth of international trade and the increasing attempts of kings to reduce the power of feudal lords interacted to produce an important new phase of urbanization. From the 11th to the 14th centuries many towns contained up to 10,000 inhabitants, while several large cities counted populations of over 50,000. Cities developed most rapidly in northern Italy and the low countries, where Venice, Milan, Florence, Bruges, and Ghent became the largest cities on the Continent. Although this phase of urbanization came to an end in the 14th century with the depopulation and economic crisis caused by the Black Death, its advances were by no means entirely erased. In fact, some historians have argued that these crises, although decreasing the overall size of the urban population, increased rates of urbanization by concentrating more people in cities.

Urbanization in Early Modern Europe

During the period from 1500 to 1800 European cities not only grew markedly in size but came to exercise an unprecedented influence over society in general. As a result, some historians have considered this era the true beginning of historical urbanization. Paul Hohenberg and Lynn Lees (1985) have characterized these years as a distinct and fundamentally new period in urban civilization. Clearly a notable increase of the urban population took place. The number of European cities with more than 10,000 people increased from 154 in 1500 to 364 by 1800. Large national capitals in northern Europe like London, Paris, and Amsterdam grew especially rapidly, while in regions like northern Italy urbanization seems to have declined. By 1800 several cities had over 200,000 residents, and London was rapidly approaching the size of imperial Rome at the height of its power.

A few key factors combined to produce this new phase of urbanization. The rise of a merchant capitalist economy fueled by national and international commerce but centered in a few major cities provided new levels of urban capital and resources. The growing power and centralization of large nation-states tended to concentrate this wealth, as well as large new populations, in the capital cities. As in earlier periods, rural demographic expansion both provided new urban recruits and new markets for urban manufactures.

In some ways this period of urban growth resembled that of medieval Europe, if on a larger scale. Few cities achieved prominence in the early modern era that had not already been substantial towns for centuries. One very important new innovation, however, was the development of protoindustrialization, or rural cottage industry, in the 18th century. Most historians now agree in locating the beginnings of modern industry in the countryside, as merchant capitalists sponsored rural industries like textiles to escape the restrictions and high costs of urban guild labor. Protoindustrialization redefined the economic relationship between urban and rural areas in the 18th century. Following upon the stagnation of the 17th century it proved a disaster for some cities. However, as Jan DeVries (1984) argues, other cities, especially in northern Europe, benefited by coordinating relations between urban and rural economies, placing themselves at the center of networks that ultimately embraced the whole of Europe. While other cities declined, these centers seized the lead in a new pattern of urbanization, one that was to lay the foundations for the industrial revolution. Furthermore, urban cultural influences expanded, also affecting many rural areas in terms of cultural as well as economic forms; urban styles, songs, and entertainers gained growing audiences. Here was an instance of urbanization in its broader sense.

Although Europe took the lead in urbanization during this period, one can find significant examples of city development in other parts of the world. In general, non-European urbanization was closely related to the rise of strong central states. Japan was one of the most urbanized societies outside Europe in the early modern era. Under the Tokugawa shogunate Edo (Tokyo) reached a population of one million by the early 19th century, with Osaka and Kyoto claiming

roughly half that number. As in Europe, stable national rule and extensive commerce combined to produce a climate favorable to the growth of cities. In China, India, and Latin America, on the other hand, cities grew primarily as seats of government.

Thus, at the beginning of the 19th century northern Europe stood poised to take a world lead in urbanization. This process, in combination with industrialization and the triumph of the nation-state, brought Europe to the zenith of its world dominance by the outbreak of World War I.

The City in the Era of the Industrial Revolution

The industrial revolution dramatically increased the numbers of Europeans living in cities. From 1800 to 1890 the percentages of people living in cities larger than 20,000 doubled in Belgium and France, tripled in European Russia, and quadrupled in Germany. The undisputed leader in this process was Britain, the first nation to industrialize. Industrial cities like Manchester and Liverpool grew by roughly 500 percent and 700 percent, respectively, during the 19th century, and London expanded from one million to five million inhabitants. By the end of the century a majority of the British people lived in cities.

During the 19th century industrial production became more mechanized and moved from rural cottages into urban factories. Technological innovations, such as railroads, made centralized manufacture in cities more efficient. At the same time, the concentration of workers in factories facilitated greater control over them by their employers. These factors combined to produce a new phenomenon, the factory city, or "Coketown," as Lewis Mumford (1961) has termed it. Urban centers like Manchester and Lille emphasized industrial production for national and international markets above all other aspects of city life. Although these cities symbolized the industrial revolution, others also felt the impact of this new system of production. National capitals like London, Paris, and Berlin became centers of industry.

Most of the new urbanites were migrants from the countryside, prompted to leave their home by the decline of employment in agriculture and rural industry, as well as by the lure of city jobs. Social historians once debated the balance between push and pull explaining the new influx of people—largely young—into the cities. The revolution in the rural economy undoubtedly forced many people out, reluctantly, but there was freedom and excitement in the cities as well which might attract young adults. Certainly, the resultant rise of a large urban industrial working class constituted one of the great changes in 19th-century European society. Rapid urbanization and their own poverty caused numerous problems for these new arrivals, especially in the early 19th century: severely overcrowded housing, inadequate sanitation systems, intense pollution, and cultural disorientation. The poor quality of working-class urban life shocked contemporary observers and led to high rates of disease and death.

The growth of 19th-century cities also produced an important urban middle class. This was an extremely diverse group, including not only the great captains of finance and industry, but also educated professionals, government officials, and shopkeepers. Its needs for housing and office space gave 19th-century cities much of their physical appearance. Although some historians have overstated the prominence of this class in national politics, by the end of the century it did enjoy strong and growing influence in western Europe. This was especially true in Britain, where the desires and views of the urban middle classes became a symbol of Victorian culture.

The industrial revolution of the late 18th and 19th centuries witnessed the birth of a new society in Europe, and the city was its cradle. The city loomed large in the 19th-century imagination, symbolizing both the grandeur and the inadequacies of the human achievement. Even the majority of Europeans who remained in the countryside felt its presence, as it increasingly defined the nature of modern civilization.

The Urban Explosion of the 20th Century

During the 20th century the majority of the peoples of Europe and North America have become city dwellers. By 1960 the percentage of national population living in cities of more than 20,000 residents had reached 48 percent in France, 52 percent in West Germany, 60 per-

cent in the Netherlands, and 69 percent in the United Kingdom. Even more spectacular has been the growth of cities in Africa, Asia, and Latin America. By the end of this century most of the world's largest cities will be located in the Third World. If one defines urbanization as the dissemination of urban structures in society as a whole, then in the 20th century it has become a global process.

This expansion has brought important shifts in the structure of urban growth. Increasingly this process has become dominated by suburbanization. The existence of settlements adjacent to city limits is a phenomenon dating back to the ancient world. In the 19th century, however, the growing social and functional specialization of urban space, plus more rapid means of urban transportation, facilitated a growth of suburban communities. In many parts of Europe and North America the suburbs grew faster and contained more inhabitants than the cities upon which they depended. The mass use of the automobile for urban transportation after World War II further strengthened this trend, leading to the rise of cities like Los Angeles, which seemingly had abolished the central city altogether in favor of an endless array of suburbs.

In this context the phrase "urban explosion" has a double meaning. In addition to characterizing rapid growth, it also suggests that in the transition from compact urban core to megalopolis anything recognizable as a city has disappeared. Some historians have suggested that, in achieving unprecedented levels of city development, the process of urbanization itself has come to an end and that the far-flung nature of contemporary urban areas fundamentally contradicts the very concept of population concentration. However, even the decentralized cities of the late 20th century have retained population densities far greater than those of the surrounding countryside, not to mention both the benefits and problems that for so long have characterized urban life. Urbanization has been a major force in the history of humankind, and it is therefore difficult to believe that in this particular instance the 20th century has brought about the end of the process. (*See also* Cities; Third World Urbanization)

Tyler Stovall

REFERENCES

DeVries, Jan. *European Urbanization, 1500–1800.* Cambridge, MA: Harvard University Press, 1984.

Dyos, H.J. *The Study of Urban History.* New York: St. Martin's Press, 1966.

Hohenburg, Paul, and Lynn Lees. *The Making of Urban Europe, 1000–1950.* Cambridge, MA: Harvard University Press, 1985.

Konvitz, Josef. *The Urban Millennium.* Carbondale: Southern Illinois University Press, 1985.

Mumford, Lewis. *The City in History.* New York: Harcourt, Brace & World, 1961.

Utopian Communities

Utopian communities (also called intentional communities, communes) try to establish ideal arrangements for living and working. Historians have studied the social forces that create the desire for communitarian living, the inner life of communities (relations among members, success at meeting members' needs), and the influence of outside society on the community. With the rise of social history, attention to formal utopian ideas has been transformed by these wider concerns. Utopianism must be understood in its relationship to more formal protest, not only in its frequent attempt to recall older social relationships but also in its articulation of variants of new standards developing in society at large— for example, concerning family or sexuality.

Ideas for improving human society have flourished since the Renaissance. Thomas More's novel *Utopia* (1516) gave its name to this entire genre of thought. Utopian ideas and communities have proliferated during periods of social upheaval as alternatives to isolation and social fragmentation. They usually attempt cooperative living and working to achieve equitable relations and material security. Often this has meant abolition of private property. Utopians have also attempted various changes in family structure, ranging from celibacy to group marriage to free love.

Both religious and secular utopians (in Europe and the United States alike) viewed America's vast resources, cheap land, and lack of strong institutions as perfect conditions for uto-pian experiments. One of the first and most successful of religious communitarian movements, the Shakers, arrived in 1774. Religious utopian societies usually demand profound commitment like the sacrifice of property or family life, or strict adherence to religious doctrine, and they often last relatively long periods of time. These strengths appeared in Mormonism, which began in 1830 and included communitarian elements.

Many nonreligious utopias were established during the early years of American industrialization (1800–1860). Like Robert Owen's New Harmony, in Indiana (1825–1827), secular, democratic utopias have typically demanded less of their adherents and survived shorter periods. There were approximately 300 utopian societies in the United States during the 19th century, practicing ideas as diverse as spiritualism, individualism, and socialism.

Two major developments occurred during the 20th century. European Jews settling in Palestine during the 1920s began to establish communal settlements known as *kibbutzim.* The kibbutz movement drew inspiration from Zionist, Marxist, and utopian ideas. Residents of kibbutzim in the late 1970s accounted for about 3.5 percent of Israeli Jews. In the United States the 1960s and 1970s witnessed the formation of thousands of communes committed to social change, spiritual fulfillment, or concern for the environment. Although usually small and transitory, the communities established during this time included a number of successes like Twin Oaks (established 1966) and The Farm (established 1970). At present there are more than 1,000 intentional communities worldwide.

Utopianism, through the lens of social history, involves not only attention to minority currents in various modern societies but also assessment of often complex relationships to mainstream values. (*See also* Subcultures)

John C. Spurlock

REFERENCES

Gorni, Yosef, et al., eds. *Communal Living: An International Perspective.* New Brunswick, NJ: Transaction Books, 1987.

V

Vaudeville

The word "vaudeville" may have originated as the French "voix de ville," or "street songs" of the Vire Valley (Vaux de Vire), France. In America, vaudeville was first called "variety" and signaled a collection of unrelated acts, a continuous talent show of performances, that could be drawn from the circus or the elocution class or the tavern. It served many of the same functions as the popular music hall in Britain in the same time period. Vaudevillians played in barns and tents, in "free and easies" and honky-tonks, and in schoolhouses and grand theaters. During the 19th century, frontier communities were more than willing to attend any kind of entertainment, and audiences were untroubled by the sometimes bizarre juxtapositions of performances on a single evening's bill.

Minstrel shows and burlesques (or satires) began as separate entertainments in America. The minstrel show had a three-part form. The first part included a blackface company seated onstage in a semicircle with an interlocutor, or leader, and two end men, Tambo and Bones, at the right and left wings of the half-circle. There were riddles and jokes in dialect and dances. The second part of the show, called the "olio," was a succession of variety acts. The conclusion was a "walk around" of song that included the entire ensemble. This three-part structure was later transformed into musical theater's three-act format.

Minstrel performers appeared in vaudeville, and vaudeville absorbed many of the songs and comedy of the minstrel tradition. In fact, vaudeville took in virtually every form of entertainment from circus to Wild West show.

In the 1840s, Tony Pastor, called "the father of vaudeville," made a determined effort to elevate vaudeville from its rough and raucous performances for mostly male audiences into family fare. Pastor initiated "ladies' matinees" and gave away turkeys and pigs as free dinner door prizes. Some vaudeville stars gave women in box seats souvenir handkerchiefs.

By the time the Keith-Albee "circuit" of theaters and bookings was in place, managers across the country were expected to fill out ratings charts and report whether an entertainer had used "blue," or unamusing material. An entertainer might be reprimanded, or fired, for using such material, but since audiences rewarded comedy with applause, a performer could simply substitute another joke.

Vaudeville entertainers represented a variety of tastes and talents. Lillian Russell, George M. Cohan, and Jenny Lind offered popular songs and operatic solos. African American performers like "Black Patti" (Sissieretta Jones) rivaled European divas, while others read Shakespearean soliloquies or played ragtime music. From 1880 to 1910 ethnic comedy flourished on vaudeville bills, and audiences laughed at "greenhorns" of all nations. Cross-dressing was considered daring and delightful. The Russell Brothers played Irish maids in petticoats, and the music hall star Vesta Tilley performed in tuxedo and top hat as "Berty from Brighton." Tilley took out patents on her "boater" (brimmed straw hat) and vest, and women who chose to be daring dressed like a "guy." Long before Marlene Dietrich or Greta Garbo or Josephine Baker wore men's evening clothes in the early 1900s, vaudeville stars of the 1880s and 1890s "invented" the style.

Vaudeville was the first home of performers like W.C. Fields, Sophie Tucker, Will Rogers, Fanny Brice, Al Jolson, and the duo (George) Burns and (Gracie) Allen, all of whom later went on to enjoy successful careers in radio and/or movies.

From 1913 to 1932, the Palace Theater in New York City was the most well known vaudeville house, and to perform there was the high point of any vaudevillian's career. In 1932 the Palace was converted into a movie house, but even then, vaudeville acts often appeared between films. Early television shows like Ed Sullivan's "Your Show of Shows" (1949–1954) were really contemporary versions of vaudeville, proof that American audiences still liked the fast pace of quick change and the stunning variety of disconnected acts.

Changes in the workplace and in the composition of the work force led to new forms of leisure entertainment. Social historians have studied American vaudeville and English Music Hall, and also popular entertainments in western Europe, as evidence of social class, ethnic diversity, and racial stereotypes. The extent to which entertainments distracted from class-based protest and the extent to which popular theater was manipulated by commercial interests have drawn considerable attention from scholars in recent years. The decline of popular theater in favor of motion pictures, which operated in more anonymous settings, and the interest of middle- and upper-class people in "slumming" at popular theater, constitute other important topics in the social history of leisure and leisure's functions at the turn of the century. (*See also* Music Hall; Popular Culture)

Lillian Schlissel

REFERENCES

Bailey, Peter, ed. *Music Hall: The Business of Pleasure.* Stratford, Eng.: The Open University Press, 1986.

Peiss, Kathy. *Cheap Amusements: Working Women and Leisure in Turn-of-the-Century New York.* Philadelphia: Temple University Press, 1986.

Sobel, Bernard. *A Pictorial History of Vaudeville.* New York: Citadel, 1961.

Spitzer, Marian. *The Palace.* New York: Atheneum, 1969.

Toll, Robert C. *On with the Show: The First Century of Show Business in America.* New York: Oxford University Press, 1976.

Victorianism

"Victorianism" is a term used to describe middle-class culture in 19th-century Britain. It is also often applied to the United States and, sometimes, to western Europe. Victorian culture emphasized middle-class beliefs in science, a rather optimistic version of religion (stressing a benign God and downplaying hell and damnation). Victorians also stressed important differences between men and women, arguing that women were naturally suited to domestic roles and moral guidance, and men, for work in the world. Strong emphasis on the home served as a Victorian anchor. As a cultural framework, Victorianism inevitably affects the central concerns of many social historians dealing, for example, with attitudes toward and self-perceptions of women. At the same time, Victorian cultural emphases need to be carefully tested, to ascertain how they were received by their middle-class audience and how they selectively affected lower-class attitudes as well. Nor should the label "Victorianism" be used to conflate American and British, as is commonly done; different regional versions of Victorian outlook may have shaped different beliefs and behaviors in the Western world.

The most explicit debate about Victorianism has centered on sexual standards. Some Victorian popularizers, writing for a wide middle-class audience, frowned on sexuality, particularly for women, leading to assumptions that Victorian culture was strikingly prudish. But other popularizers, while warning against sexual excess, recognized the validity of sexuality within marriage; and middle-class couples seem to have developed some latitude in their interpretation of sexual norms. Victorianism, in sum, is not always easy to capture, particularly when treated as part of social rather than purely intellectual history.

Several historians also work on the "end" of Victorian values, and the reasons for and results of the change. In the United States, the 1920s have been widely identified as a time of significant values change, with the dislocations and cultural protests such change entails. (*See also* Cultural History; Sexuality)

Peter N. Stearns

REFERENCES

Coben, Stanley. *Rebellion Against Victorianism: Impetus for Cultural Change in the 1920s.* New York: Oxford University Press, 1991.

Seidman, Steven. *Romantic Longings: Love in America, 1830–1980.* New York: Routledge, 1991.

Stearns, Peter N. *American Cool: Constructing a Twentieth-Century Emotional Style.* New York: New York University Press, 1994.

Voluntary Associations

Unlike the group into which one is born, such as a family or a tribe, voluntary associations require a conscious act of affiliation. Examples include the secret societies of traditional China, the trade guilds of medieval Europe, the labor and reform organizations of the 19th-century United States, and the tribal unions of modern West African cities. If voluntary associations have appeared in many places and historical contexts, however, they have been chiefly associated with industrial societies and pluralistic democracies. Why this is so has precipitated long-standing debates among sociologists and political scientists.

During the last third of the 19th century, social theorists such as T.S. Cooley, Ferdinand Tönnies, and Emile Durkheim categorized human societies along an ascending evolutionary continuum: primitive societies, at the lower end, were characteristically held together by personal bonds; and modern societies, by contractual and formal ties among people with common interests. Voluntary associations were thus by definition associated with societies at more advanced stages of economic, technological, and social evolution.

Some sociologists explained that industrialization and urbanization inevitably eroded traditional bonds of kinship and family; city life threw many people together and increased the frequency and variety of social interactions, thereby giving rise to a diverse associational life. Other scholars pointed to the tangible benefits of collective enterprise among workers and farmers who had been victimized by industrial corporations. Still other sociologists, emphasizing the anomic character of modern life, argued that individuals who had become lost in the "lonely crowd" of the city flocked to clubs and associations out of psychological desperation.

This debate over the sociological, economic, and psychological functions of voluntary associations was often overshadowed by a debate as to their political significance. The guilds of the late Middle Ages, which emerged in cities where royal prerogatives were less entrenched, often mounted successful challenges to monarchs and noblemen. That voluntary associations served as counterweights to tyranny has most frequently been cited in the context of the United States. French sociologist Alexis de Tocqueville, commenting on the "immense assemblage" of political and philosophical clubs, farmers' organizations, and labor societies in Jacksonian America, maintained that such organizations prevented the federal government from encroaching on individual liberties. Almost a century later German sociologist Max Weber identified the profusion of organizations as a central "characteristic" of American political life. Its democracy, he wrote, entailed not of a "sand heap of individuals, but rather a buzzing complex of strictly exclusive, yet voluntary associations." Writing in 1918, he proposed that Germany, having been misled by Prussian authoritarianism, would do well to adopt the American "club pattern" as a basis for its own "re-education." On the eve of the Japanese attack on Pearl Harbor, Arthur Schlesinger, Sr., similarly described America as a "Nation of Joiners," whose many voluntary associations would serve as an antidote to Nazism and fascism. With the onset of the Cold War, American theorists further enshrined America's democracy as a system where a "plurality" of interests, most of them organized through voluntary associations, came together to hammer out a political consensus.

But during the 1960s scholars disillusioned with the Vietnam War came to doubt that American pluralism functioned effectively, and for a time, interest in voluntary associations waned, especially among practitioners of the new social history. However, a fundamental injunction of the "new" social history—that society be examined from the bottom up—resulted in a scramble to find information about everyday people whose lives were missing from the history books—and from the public archives. Social historians soon discovered the rich (and ne-glected) repositories of documents that had accumulated in church and union basements, in lodge reading rooms, in immigrant and reform society libraries. These documents revealed, for example, that the clubs of the immigrant bosses, however corrupt, fulfilled important needs; that seemingly inconsequential church societies provided the emotional bonds that enabled women to take on the reformation of society; that the bizarre rituals of fraternal orders shaped new conceptions of masculinity. Although the scholars who have advanced these and other insights have eschewed the grand theorizing of their intellectual forebears, their work has changed the terms and shape of those debates. (*See also* United States Reform Movement; Women's History)

Mark C. Carnes

REFERENCES

Carnes, Mark C. *Secret Ritual and Manhood in Victorian America.* New Haven: Yale University Press. 1989.

Ryan, Mary. *Cradle of the Middle Class: The Family in Oneida County, New York, 1790–1865.* Cambridge: Cambridge University Press. 1981.

Weber, Max. *From Max Weber: Essays in Sociology,* ed. H.H. Gerth and C. Wright Mills. New York: Oxford University Press. 1946.

W

Waqf Charitable Foundations

From the early period of Islamic rule in the Middle East until the 20th century the main source of financial support for religious and communal institutions came from charitable donations. The Muslim institution of the *waqf*, or "pious endowment," provided a regulated means for individuals to dedicate private property for the maintenance of public causes such as houses of worship, shrines, schools, water facilities, and poor relief. An individual could endow in perpetuity real estate that he owned or even cash for the support of an institution of his choosing, and could designate in his deed of endowment how he wanted the income derived from his donation to be used. The endowed property was added to the other assets of the institution, all of which were managed as a charitable foundation. The administrator of the foundation and his assistants rented out the properties, collected the rents and interest payments, disbursed the wages of the institution's staff, and in general looked after its upkeep and economic needs.

Over the centuries a vast network of public institutions supported by such endowments came into being in the region, primarily in the cities. The absence of substantial or any government funding for this network placed the burden of maintaining it on communities and their philanthropic impulses. Men of wealth, including rulers and government officials, established new mosques, colleges, and water fountains, and made the initial donations of real estate, often on an impressive scale, to support them. Smaller donors helped replenish the assets of these institutions by adding to them a house, shop, or monetary contribution. Governments traditionally provided some limited oversight of the foundations' activities, but in general the system remained a diffuse one composed of thousands of separate foundations, each with its own assets and staff, operating independently of each other with little official control. Beginning in the 19th century, however, governments in the region steadily seized control of the charitable foundations and their assets. Today special government ministries manage waqf properties in many countries. With this growth of governmental jurisdiction came also a sharp decline in new endowments, as the state increasingly assumed the provision of services, including those previously funded through the waqf.

The study of the waqf has focused for many years on the institutional arrangements and legal codes governing the workings of the foundations, and on individual documents of endowment, especially the more grandiose ones. More recently social historians have been directing attention to the broader social and economic role of the waqf in Middle Eastern society and to the dynamics of the institution. They have been inquiring who the donors and the beneficiaries of the enormous body of endowments were, how the foundations functioned in practice as economic enterprises, and what effects the process of endowment had on urban development and the economy in general. The most promising documentation on these issues is found in the archives of the Ottoman Empire, especially in the registers of the Muslim law courts, where many of the waqf transactions and accounts were recorded. Although the research into these and other sources is still in its beginnings, case studies of charitable foundations in different localities and periods point to certain general patterns.

Most endowments were composed of modest donations of a property or two, and the donors included a good proportion of women. The Christians and Jews also resorted to waqf endowments for the support of their communal institutions, although to a lesser extent than the Muslims. Some donors, especially the founders of new institutions, used their endowments in part as family trusts to provide income for relatives. In their aggregate the charitable endowments constituted a significant transfer of wealth from the better-off to the larger community, with members of the religious establishment (the *ulama*) being the main direct beneficiaries of the revenues. The foundations managing these endowments were involved in a whole array of business transactions, and while many of them proved enterprising and enduring, financial difficulties appear to have been fairly common, as illustrated,

for instance, by the state of the foundations in 18th-century Aleppo. Large acts of endowment often contributed to urban development by initiating the building of new commercial complexes to serve as sources of financial support. But the endless process of endowment also removed a vast body of urban and rural property from the sales market, creating legal and economic complications whose legacy still confronts present-day governments in the region. (*See also* Charity; Islam; Middle Eastern Urbanization and Cities; *Ulama*)

Abraham Marcus

REFERENCES

Baer, Gabriel, and G. Gilbar, eds. *The Social and Economic Aspects of the Muslim Waqf,* forthcoming.

Barnes, John. *An Introduction to Religious Foundations in the Ottoman Empire.* Leiden: Brill, 1986.

Gil, Moshe. *Documents of the Jewish Pious Foundations from the Cairo Geniza.* Leiden: Brill, 1976.

Marcus, Abraham. *The Middle East on the Eve of Modernity: Aleppo in the Eighteenth Century.* New York: Columbia University Press, 1989.

War and Population

Mortality. The demographic impact of wars is an important facet of social history in many historical periods and settings. The first way in which war and population are related is through combat casualties. Until the 19th century, the *direct* demographic consequences of military losses have been limited. When armies were composed of mercenaries, they were manned frequently by alien recruits. Since the 1790s in Europe, mass conscription has brought combat losses home to the populations engaged in hostilities.

The scale of those losses, though, has been traditionally smaller than the swath cut through populations by major epidemics. For example, perhaps 600,000 soldiers were killed in the Thirty Years' War (1618–1648); in the same period, deaths due to epidemic diseases were much more numerous. It is true that warfare spread epidemics, but in considering *direct* losses, we must recognize that until the 20th century, loss of life in war was dwarfed by the toll of natural disasters. In this century, medical treatment has reduced battlefield deaths, but the technology of violence has vastly increased the killing power of arms, culminating in nuclear weaponry.

The age and sexual composition of direct war losses have important demographic repercussions. In World War I, perhaps 9 million men died on active military service, of the 70 million who served. The vast majority were under the age of 30, as was the case in World War II. The result, especially in countries like Russia, which suffered perhaps 20 million deaths in World War II, was to pinch the age structure inward for males in their early to middle adult years. These distortions were, until recently, also sex specific. The preponderance of females in certain age cohorts, again in Russia since 1945, for example, is a direct outcome of selective decimation by sex in war.

Direct war losses were registered long after hostilities ended in most modern conflicts. Damaged and diseased men, whose disabilities dated from military service, were more likely to succumb to their condition, or to have reduced resistance to other infections or diseases.

Indirect losses attributable to war occurred when civilian life was so disrupted that death rates rose above peacetime levels. Atrocities, like the Armenian and Jewish genocide of the two world wars, are extreme cases. Less shocking, but still evident, were rising death rates during the Thirty Years' War in Europe, or in localized conflicts, such as the Russo-Swedish War of 1788–1790, the Crimean War of 1854–1856, or the Franco-Prussian War of 1870–1871.

Twentieth-century developments are more complex. In some cases, notably Germany in World War I, and all of eastern Europe in World War II, civilian mortality rates skyrocketed. But in western Europe, death rates were not noticeably higher than in the prewar periods, with some notable exceptions, such as the Dutch hunger winter of 1944–1945, a truly manmade famine. Almost always, the elderly suffered, having little to contribute directly to the war effort. Babies, representing the nation's future, were more important to society, and thus attracted resources to defend their health in wartime.

Migration. The second area in which the impact of war is particularly striking is in population movement. Here the effects are either to

cause a ripple effect outward away from the epicenter of conflict, or to bottle up normal peacetime migratory flows when warfare seals borders or disrupts merchant shipping.

War as a creator of refugee flows is a feature of military conflict from time immemorial. Either in terms of expulsions or as the seizure of captives as slaves or barter, warfare has moved populations in irregular ways. In more recent times, the effect of war has been more mixed—either to constrict migratory flows, as occurred during and after World War I, or to create permanent exchanges of population, as in the Palestinian exodus from Israel in 1947–1948, or the westward movement of ethnic Germans after World War II.

It is important to recognize that migration can also lead to war. The inflow of Jewish refugees before and after World War II to Palestine has been a source of armed conflict. Ethnic tensions, which can explode, as in the collapse of Yugoslavia, in armed conflict, reflect population movements which occurred long before the clash of arms it indirectly provoked.

Nuptiality. War destroys marriages and creates the conditions for new ones. Since a substantial number of migrants have usually been young unmarried males, one demographic effect of war-induced population movement is the disruption of nuptiality. Wars which move populations out of their homes can disturb in powerful ways marriage patterns—witness African demographic patterns in the Ethiopian civil wars. Wars which trap populations in their homes paradoxically can keep potential marriage partners within the reservoir of spouses-to-be and thereby buoy up nuptiality rates.

The volatility of war periods, especially in recent years, has had the effect of increasing marriage rates at moments of uncertainty and anxiety. Some young people marry under these unusual circumstances who would not have done so ordinarily. The result at times is an increase in the divorce rate, when couples reunite after the conflict is concluded, and realize the mistakes they may have made.

Fertility. The most powerful effects of war on the birth rate has usually been indirectly through its impact on marriage rates. However, there are two ways in which war has deflected fertility trends. The first is through severe malnutrition, leading to amenorrhea. The second effect is the clustering of compensatory "baby booms" after war, which may do more than simply make up the deficit in births caused by the separation of spouses. After World War II, such a baby boom led to the single most sustained increase in fertility in the West in 100 years. Some scholars see here the effect of war in deepening the cultural supports for maternity and family life in general, as a kind of "inner migration" at times of social turbulence. (*See also* Demography; Military and Society)

J.M. Winter

REFERENCES

Notestein, F., ed. *The Future Population of Europe and the Soviet Union.* Geneva: League of Nations, 1944.

Wall, R.M., and J.M. Winter, eds. *The Upheaval of War. Family, Work and Welfare in Europe, 1914–1918.* Cambridge: Cambridge University Press, 1988.

Urlanis, B. *Wars and Population.* Moscow: Progress Publishers, 1971.

Winter, J.M. *The Great War and the British People.* London: Macmillan, 1985.

War Communism

War Communism designates the economic policies of the Soviet government from June 1918 to March 1921. The policies were a series of ideologically guided improvisations to replace market relationships with nonmarket allocation of resources and distribution of products and to mobilize human and productive resources in response to economic deterioration and war. Antecedents may be found in the state regulation of wartime economies, particularly in Germany, during World War I, and in several measures of the first eight months of Bolshevik rule, before the outbreak of civil war.

The policies of War Communism consisted of six basic components: (1) confiscation or nationalization of private assets, real estate, the banking system, and industry; (2) abolition of private trade and monopolization of consumer goods by the Food Commissariat; (3) elimination of the value of money by uncontrolled inflation and by a substitution of transactions in kind for monetary transactions; (4) seizure of farm surplus by armed food detachments and Committees of the Poor; (5) centralization of economic decisionmaking and allocation of supplies, primarily through the Supreme Economic Council, created December 15, 1917, and state agencies, called *glavki*, which ran industry by command; and (6) mobilization of labor through periodic "drafts" for civilian work.

Although requisitioning did increase the centrally controlled supply of grain from 0.85 million tons to 6.6 million tons during the period 1917–1918 to 1920–1921, by all accounts War Communism was an economic disaster. An economy already devastated by war and revolution experienced declines in living standards, real wages, labor productivity, livestock, and sown acreage. Overall industrial output dropped to 20 percent of prewar levels. When sailors in the port of Kronstadt mutinied, Lenin announced a New Economic Policy (NEP), which replaced the requisitions with a tax in kind and sanctioned the return of the market in the spring of 1921.

Like NEP and the First Five-Year Plan, War Communism has become a critical episode in the debate over the role of ideology in Soviet policies. Lenin himself indicated, albeit later, that war and devastation forced adoption of makeshift policies. Foreign blockade, the needs of defense, and the loss of important sources of raw materials, fuel, grain, and manufactured goods disrupted normal channels of production, supply, and distribution; at stake was survival. Yet, policy statements of Lenin and other leaders, as well as economists, indicated that War Communism was not just a temporary expedient but desirable ideologically. The government printing press was extolled as "the machine gun which attacked the bourgeois regime in its rear—its monetary system." Even allowing for hyperbole which made a virtue of necessity, the Bolsheviks believed at the time that they were building true socialism, eradicating the remnants of bourgeois life and launching the "Red Guard assault on capital."

War Communism has also become an important period in the debate over the role of society in Soviet policies and as such is of particular interest to social historians. War Communism was not wholly government fiat but was also shaped by initiative "from below." Factory-organized food teams had gone to the countryside to exchange manufactured articles for food even before the first government grain requisitions, and at first Bolshevik food policy had considerable support among urban workers. The Decree on workers' control (November 27, 1917) and nationalization represented government response to pressure from below. The former legitimated growing syndicalism by giving stronger powers of supervision to already existing factory committees. For owners and managers who did not cooperate, confiscations by local soviets and factory committees were the next step, and until June 1918, the majority of such "wildcat nationalizations" were not decreed, and not even desired, from above. For workers, nationalization contained an irony: the more industry was nationalized, the *less* it was put under workers' control. From this perspective, War Communism was an attempt by the central authorities to control, standardize, systematize, and stiffen a bewildering variety of ad hoc and undisciplined direct actions.

The grain requisitions prompted fierce resistance among the peasants, as a major revolt in Tambov testifies. The city population devised a variety of survival strategies. Although many basic provisions and public services were offered free (bread, rent, utilities, transport), ration cards were issued in the cities according to a "class principle." "Bagmen" risked armed train guards to bring food surpluses to sell or barter in the city outside state procurement and distribution channels. One escape from starvation in the hungry cities was a return to villages, and the urban population declined by 33 percent. Such survival strategies contained an irony: state policies to eradicate the private trader made virtually everybody a private trader.

A poster of the time blared: "We will drive humanity to happiness with an iron hand!" For more than a generation, to its admirers the legacy of War Communism, indistinguishable from that of the civil war, was the "heroic period of the Russian Revolution"—leatherjacketed commanders, shouting orders. To its critics, including, recently, writers in Russia, War Communism contains the "sources" of the command

economy, "barracks communism," and the statization of all public life. (*See also* Bolshevism; Market Economy; NEP Era; Russian Revolution)

Joseph Bradley

REFERENCES

Chamberlin, William Henry. *The Russian Revolution. Vol. 2: 1918–1921: From the Civil War to the Consolidation of Power.* New York: Grosset and Dunlap, 1976.

Chase, William J. *Workers, Society and the Soviet State: Labor and Life in Moscow, 1918–1929.* Urbana and Chicago: University of Illinois Press, 1987.

Koenker, Diane P., William G. Rosenberg, and Ronald Grigor Suny, eds. *Party, State, and Society in the Russian Civil War: Explorations in Social History.* Bloomington: Indiana University Press, 1989.

Lih, Lars T. *Bread and Authority in Russia, 1914–1921.* Berkeley and Los Angeles: University of California Press, 1990.

Malle, Silvana. *The Economic Organization of War Communism, 1918–1921.* New York: Cambridge University Press, 1985.

Welfare Capitalism

Welfare capitalism may be distinguished from laissez faire capitalism on the one hand and socialism on the other. Laissez faire is the reliance upon market mechanisms in the private sector to determine the prices, quantities, and distribution of nearly all goods and services, except in such areas as military procurement where the state is considered the sole legitimate contractor. Socialism, by contrast, may be defined as a system in which the state rather than the market determines the prices, quantities, and distribution of most goods and services.

Welfare capitalism as a socioeconomic system relies largely upon the market, but differs from laissez faire in that it supplements market mechanisms to promote a more adequate distribution of such welfare requirements as food, housing, education, and health care. Welfare measures in a capitalist economy are not always administered by the state. Indeed, the history of welfare capitalism includes the efforts of charitable organizations, businesses, and the state, all functioning within the context of a capitalist economy.

Private, voluntaristic welfare activities predate capitalism. Religious bodies have provided food and shelter, and sometimes education, from ancient times, and continued this tradition in the midst of economic dislocations arising from modern capitalism. In some European countries where there has been an established church, and in parts of colonial America, religious welfare activities were quasi-public—the state assigned certain functions to the churches and either subsidized them directly or gave churches the authority to raise their own resources, as in the English Poor Laws of the 16th to the 18th centuries.

Voluntary associations of workers have been another form of welfare activity under capitalism. English Friendly Societies—a type of credit union—provided mutual support for workers in the late 18th and early 19th centuries, and included nearly a million members by 1815, at a time when modern trade unions were still prohibited by law. Societies of this type developed in all industrializing nations and served members and their families, as did the later trade unions, but their resources were limited by the members' low wages, and they did not address the needs of the poor who were not members.

By the 1880s, as industries grew larger and required sizable, disciplined work forces, a few businesses began to experiment with welfare capitalism of their own design. Among the most famous of these experiments was the model town created by George Pullman in Hyde Park, near Chicago. Beginning in 1880, the railroad car magnate bought 4,000 acres on which he built a town named for himself. Compared with the squalor of many urban working-class communities, Pullman was a showcase with its decent houses, parks, athletic fields, public sanitation, a library, and a theater. At its peak in 1893, the town had 12,000 residents. But workers increasingly resented the company's control over their lives, from the prohibition of alcohol to the approval of political candidates to the company-owned church. When a nationwide depression occurred and Pullman laid off workers and cut wages and hours for the rest, while holding rents constant, the workers struck. The Pullman Strike of 1894 was a dramatic episode in American labor history, involving federal troops and marshals against the new American Railway Union, and it underscored the tensions between welfare and social control in business-sponsored versions of welfare capitalism. Similar tensions developed in paternalistic welfare networks in European big business.

As the 19th century drew to a close, it was becoming apparent to many in labor and government, and even in business, that voluntaristic and business-sponsored initiatives would not be sufficient to meet the welfare needs of advanced capitalist societies. Social unrest among the laboring poor and the unemployed grew increasingly ominous, and the fear of socialist revolutions drove even the conservatives in business and government to consider alternatives to the laissez faire state. During the 1880s, Germany under Bismarck began the first state-sponsored social welfare programs for workers in a modern capitalist society, including provisions for sickness, accident, and old age insurance. Bismarck and other conservatives were explicit about their motivation for supporting limited state welfare initiatives: the socialist alternative was intolerable.

"Socialism" is itself a somewhat elastic concept which has figured prominently in the development of welfare capitalism. As various welfare measures began to be instituted piecemeal in the late 19th and early 20th centuries, Marxists denounced them for the very reason that capitalists supported them—namely, that they were intended to prevent the advance of socialism. Critics on the right, meanwhile, who were committed to laissez faire, decried the same measures on the grounds that they were socialistic by definition, using government coercion as a means of redistributing wealth. Standing between the Marxists and the laissez faire capitalists have been those proponents of the welfare state who argue that it is simply an arm of welfare capitalism, and therefore an alternative to socialism, along with some reformist socialists who welcome the welfare state as embodying, however incompletely, elements of their vision of democratic socialism.

In the midst of innumerable debates over political economy, the modern welfare state has emerged. The term was used in 1941 by William Temple, then Archbishop of York, to describe a state which "is a servant and instrument of God for the preservation of justice and for the promotion of human welfare." During World War II, British leaders sought to develop a consensus regarding the state's responsibilities in social welfare, defining these in contrast to both communism and fascism, and after the war, Great Britain became a more comprehensive welfare state than it had ever been before.

Most advanced capitalist nations now represent some version of the welfare state, ranging from the comprehensive "middle way" of Sweden to the comparatively modest provisions of the United States. The rise of Margaret Thatcher and Ronald Reagan in the 1980s points to the continuing controversy over welfare and the state a century after Bismarck. Yet, as the 20th century draws to a close, welfare capitalism has become the norm; the question is what form it will take.

Social historians have studied welfare capitalism from two angles. First, they have participated in debates over the origins of welfare systems and why some societies developed different welfare emphasis and timing than did others. Different working-class organization and outlook served as one of the kinds of variables involved. Second, social historians increasingly look at ways welfare systems have affected, and been used by, lower-class groups; here, the welfare state serves as a major instance of state/society evaluation, in which what the state does must also be interpreted in light of the interests and actions of various social groups. (*See also* Poverty; Welfare State)

James A. Gilchrist

REFERENCES

Checkland, Sydney. *British Public Policy, 1776–1939: An Economic, Social and Political Perspective.* New York: Cambridge University Press, 1983.

Heclo, Hugh. *Policy & Politics in Sweden.* Philadelphia: Temple University Press, 1987.

Schottland, Charles I. *The Welfare State: Selected Essays.* New York: Harper & Row, 1967.

Trattner, Walter. *From Poor Law to Welfare State: A History of Social Welfare in America*, 4th ed. New York: The Free Press, 1989.

Weinstein, James. *The Corporate Ideal in the Liberal State.* Boston: Beacon Press, 1969.

Welfare State

The modern welfare state is the result of government efforts to alleviate the full effects of market forces on social life: it is based on state-provided, noncommodified social services. Differences in the needs of classes and interest groups as well as disparities in their ability to exert political influence have created substantial variations in the character of welfare states. Differences among welfare states exist with respect to the democratization of administrative structure, the degree of public funding of social insurance programs, the extent of coverage, and the mechanisms used to identify and relieve poverty. From the social history standpoint, the rise of welfare states marks a substantial change in state-society relations, including the enhanced role of the state in causing social patterns. While welfare states have been studied mainly as part of Western social history, many features of this state have developed in other societies.

Before the rise of the centralized welfare state in the 19th century, most social services were undertaken at the local level by political authorities, mutual aid societies, private charities, and church institutions. The growth of an extensive market society gradually doomed local or regional approaches to social welfare, at a time when the growth of more centralized states and expanding administrative bureaucracies rendered possible more centralized approaches. Yet, the previous history of local welfare profoundly shaped the formation of national welfare policy. British welfare debates were strongly influenced by the peculiar institutions of the Elizabethan Poor Law, the celebrated "43rd of Elizabeth" of 1601, that had created separate, municipally administered, local organizations for the care and supervision of the poor. On the Continent, older traditions of corporative responsibility for welfare also influenced social policy. Bismarck's social insurance legislation was based on the assumption that if workers were required to contribute they should have some share in deciding how their money was spent. The provision of the 1884 law which allowed workers to elect representatives to the insurance administration made sense against a background of still vital corporative traditions. As a result, Germany in the years before

1914 was to have among the most democratically administered welfare systems in the industrial world.

The commercialization of agriculture, the rise of protoindustry, and the growth of casual labor in industry created unparalleled social problems. Both rural and urban elites required day laborers, yet falling wage rates, rising prices, or unemployment could all lead laborers to the brink of disaster, while elites frequently quarreled over the responsibility for their upkeep. The outcome of these conflicts were embodied in both local and national welfare institutions. Different assumptions concerning the goals and purpose of welfare systems were adopted early in the formation of national insurance systems and these assumptions have had persistent influence. The British National Insurance Act of 1911 established the principle that insurance should be self-financing and that benefits should be based on contributions, and these principles remained enshrined as goals long after the fiscal framework supporting them had eroded. At the very beginnings of the welfare state in early 20th-century Denmark and Sweden, quarreling rural and urban elites agreed upon the principles of universal coverage, substantial subsidies from public revenues, and the payment of equal benefits to all. Thus, the most egalitarian elements of the modern Scandinavian welfare state stem not from socialist demands but from elite compromises made at the very beginning of the centralized welfare state. The social bases of many welfare states often involve strong guidance from upper classes, as well as responses to demands from below; the precise balance is an important social history focus, into quite recent times.

While a wide variety of approaches to the funding and organization of the welfare state were tried over the course of the 19th century, the concept of social insurance gradually came to the fore. Basically, the insurance idea was based on a policy of "forced savings," usually combined with government subsidies. It entailed collecting money from a large number of productive workers and/or their employers and putting aside this money, usually along with government supplements, to provide for accidents, sickness, and old age. Napoleon III had been one of the early advocates of government promoted and subsidized insurance, but Bismarck was the first to make it compulsory and to extend it widely. In 1884, Bismarck introduced compulsory social insurance against sickness, and in 1889 the program was extended to include old age pensions. In the United Kingdom, the National Health Insurance Act of 1911 provided national health insurance and pioneered in the introduction of unemployment insurance. The insurance principle was widely imitated: most of western and northern Europe adopted some form of compulsory social insurance in the years before World War I. Among advanced industrial nations, the United States was very slow, adopting compulsory social insurance only in 1935. (Social historians have begun exploring reasons for comparative differences of this sort, as well as the differing social experiences that resulted.)

The insurance principle was based on the needs of workers and employers in urban, proletarianized industry, and most modern welfare states retain important elements of the founding purposes. In many European countries, social insurance was initially restricted to leading heavy industries. Social insurance developed in the more stable heavy industries because, unlike many other industries, engineering, metal working, and coal mining possessed a core of permanent workers who had acquired industry-specific skills and abilities and were liable to remain in the industry long enough to reap the benefits of their contributions. Social insurance supported employers' efforts to secure a stable work force while often winning sympathy from organized trade unionists, usually craft trade unions, because their own mutual aid societies proved inadequate faced with rising life expectancies.

The adaptation of social insurance to heavy industry had serious long-term implications for the development of welfare states. The social insurance principle worked best in industries that offered continuous, lifetime employment and where workers were able to take advantage of these opportunities. It was least effective in temporary or seasonal industries or for women or other minorities who were often assigned temporary jobs. Because social insurance was based on employment, it doubly neglected women who were mothers and housekeepers and did not receive wages. It further paid little attention to children and dependents who did not work. Gradually, those insurance programs which had ignored wives and children added provisions for them, but these always received less than permanently employed workers, the principal focus of such programs. Too often, when male wage earners died or when families dissolved, women and children were left to "need"-based social programs, which usually entailed humiliation and inferior care.

In some states, particularly in France where birth rates declined early, but becoming more general as European fertility declined after 1900, a different, more family-oriented approach was also applied. In France, family allowances, calculated on the base workers' wage, were paid to mothers' based on family size. Further, attention was devoted to reducing infant mortality by providing paid maternity leaves, free infant medical care, and subsidized child care centers of working mothers. While such services undoubtedly benefited most married women with children, they often tended to ratify a gendered division of labor in which men were expected to work on a permanent basis and women on a temporary basis.

Social historians have contributed to discussion of the origins of the welfare state. They have also attempted to assess its impact on major social classes, on protest, and on the family. A generally favorable attitude toward the welfare state shifted among social historians during the 1970s, with growing concern about the state's limitations and also its coercive power over lower-class behavior including families. New challenges to welfare states amid growing costs during the 1970s and 1980s add another state-society topic for current social history in the Western world. Very recent work, however, concerned about growing social problems in capitalistic societies, has returned to a more favorable view of the welfare state. (*See also* Charity; Poor Relief; Social Control; State and Society; Welfare Capitalism)

Michael P. Hanagan

REFERENCES

Ashford, Douglas L. *The Emergence of the Welfare States*. Oxford: Basil Blackwell, 1986.

Baldwin, Peter. *The Politics of Social Solidarity: Class Bases of the European Welfare State, 1875–1975*. Cambridge: Cambridge University Press, 1990.

Esping-Andersen, Gøsta. *The Three Worlds of Welfare Capitalism*. Princeton, NJ: Princeton University Press, 1990

Flora, Peter, and Arnold J. Heidenheimer, eds. *The Development of the Welfare States in Europe and America*. New Brunswick, NJ: Transaction Books, 1987.

Gordon, Linda. "The New Feminist Scholarship on the Welfare State," in Linda Gordon, ed., *Women, the State and Welfare*. Madison: University of Wisconsin Press, 1990.

Korpi, Walter. *The Democratic Class Struggle*. London: Routledge & Kegan Paul, 1983.

Swaan, Abram de. *In Care of the State: Health Care, Education and Welfare in Europe and the USA in the Modern Era*. Cambridge: Cambridge University Press, 1988.

Weir, Margaret, Ann Shola Orloff, and Theda Skocpol, eds. *The Politics of Social Policy in the United States*. Princeton, NJ: Princeton University Press, 1988.

Westernization

The West as a geographical, political, and cultural concept was developed in 19th-century Russia. It denoted the country's western neighbors—foremost Germany, France, England—whose superiority impressed Russian intellectuals eager to "westernize" their backward country. Redefined in the 20th century, "the West" came to mean the leading democratic countries of western Europe led, after World War II, by the United States, representing both the democratic tradition and their superior military and political power. Since 1945 the Western way of life has become the model which, in the judgments of many observers, all non-Western peoples must follow in order to be respected in the modern world. The term "Westernization" thus describes the expansion of Western civilization around the globe.

Westernization affects all aspects of life, providing political ideals of freedom and democracy while setting the expectations of material welfare worldwide. Western science and technology have become universal property; so have Western business methods, institutions of higher learning, modes of transportation, urban architecture, styles of dressing and personal appearance, or popular entertainment, with English as the common medium of communication. The metropolitan centers around the world look remarkably alike, radiating, with the help of satellites, their Western standards into distant villages through radio and television. The contemporary worldwide economic and political interdependence is the product of Western civilization.

Expansionism is a common human aspiration, found in all parts of the world. But only the Westerners acquired the means to carry that ambition to its ultimate limits. Nowhere else did geography and history produce such exuberant cultural creativity.

Until the 17th century Europe could be considered backward as compared with imperial China, Mughal India, or the Islamic states. Adapted, after the 15th century, to the rising nation-states, Western skills of social cooperation allowed an unprecedented mobilization of both human and natural resources for prevailing in the ceaseless competition in all aspects of life, but foremost in political power. Imperialist overseas expansion was part of that competition.

In the 16th and 17th centuries the peoples of the Western Hemisphere and of Southeast Asia fell victim to the superior power of Spanish, Portuguese, Dutch, French, and English explorers. In the 18th century the British took over India; in the 19th century the Chinese empire was humiliated. By the end of that century, with Africa divided into European colonies, Western imperialism reached its peak. In the fierce power contests of the 20th century, the West under American leadership consolidated its superiority by creating the present worldwide interdependence. However brilliant in their own settings, no other people in the world, no other civilization, had developed sufficient resources to match Western power and to stop its triumphant ascent.

The sources of Western power, however, did not lie in brute force, but in the human values and elaborate civic organization sustaining economic growth, industrial development, and governmental authority, the bases of modern military strength. With the help of the Judeo-Christian religion the keen competition within Western civilization accustomed its peoples to the discipline of hard work and close coopera-

tion with fellow citizens as well as machines. Responsible civic awareness also promoted democratic government. Many historians (mostly but not exclusively Western) argue that no other peoples, no other civilization, had evolved such disciplined social integration and such solid respect for human rights. Implicitly Westernization propagated these premises of Western superiority around the world.

The effect of Westernization on non-Western peoples has been mixed. On the one hand, they were deprived of shaping their future by their traditional resources; they lost their freedom of cultural or even political self-determination. Some, like the Amerindians, faced near extinction; others became colonial subjects. Those who retained their independence, like the Russians or the Chinese, were forced to Westernize themselves against their will. Only the Japanese possessed in their own traditions the capacity to absorb Western achievements without losing their cultural continuity. On the other hand, the West has shared many of its boons with the rest of the world, providing support for more human life on earth than existed ever before (at growing risks to the environment) and imparting its skills through many development projects to those willing to learn them. It enlarged creative opportunities for all humanity, while also adding to its problems.

From the start Westernization provoked hostility. Anti-Westerners highlighted the discrepancy between ideals and reality in Western practice, while glorifying their indigenous traditions; they cried out against exploitation or even resorted to armed counterattack. But anti-Western self-assertion paradoxically needed Western weapons and organizing skills in order to become effective—with no success. Anticapitalist communist totalitarianism constituted an effort to catch up to Western achievements; its failure inspired further Westernization under Soviet leader Gorbachev. Decolonization also strengthened the Western impact. By the end of the 20th century the Western ascendancy stands unchallenged.

Underneath the Western impact, however, traditional ways continue; most non-Western societies are trapped in depressing cultural disorientation which saps their efforts to escape from their helplessness. The Westernized world also suffers from the profound inequality between the "developed" (mostly Western or fully Westernized) and "developing" countries (all non-Western and located in the "Third World"). Westernization continues to work for the benefit of the West.

As a phenomenon, Westernization, both before and during the contemporary era, poses two particular challenges to the social historian. First, social historians of non-Western areas must assess the adaptive power of ordinary people and social institutions, to determine how much Westernization occurs and under what degree of compulsion. Second, social historians generally, if they use the Westernization concept (and many are uncomfortable with it, lest it oversimplify complex processes), must decide whether it refers primarily to elite culture, institutions, and economic behaviors or whether it also captures patterns in the wider society. Some "Westernizations" involve elites far more than masses and need careful assessment from the social history standpoint. (*See also* Economic Development; Imperialism; Modernization)

Theodore H. Von Laue

REFERENCES

Jones, E.L. *The European Miracle.* New York: Cambridge University Press, 1981.

Von Laue, Theodore H. *The World Revolution of Westernization.* New York: Oxford University Press, 1987.

Westward Movement/United States Expansion

Although some historians have examined the 18th- and 19th-century movement to western frontiers, most scholarly attention has focused on expansion to the trans-Mississippi West during the 19th century. Traditionally, historians have either emphasized the formal aspects of territorial expansionism, war, and diplomatic maneuvers or the informal migration of white men west.

When social historians began to reexamine American history, they transformed the understanding of the westward movement. In the 1970s increasing attention was paid to gender as a component of western expansion. Studies of middle-class white women during and after the overland migration detailed female participation in and contribution to migration and settlement. Heated debates arose over the persistence and relevance of middle-class gender roles in the West. Were women conservative forces in their communities as conventional gender roles might suggest or did living in the West free them from eastern norms? These sorts of debates were updated versions of a long-standing argument over whether the West was an exceptional region or merely an extension of the East.

The heat of these inconclusive debates cooled as historians turned to consider the importance of class, ethnicity, and race during the period of expansion. Studies, whether of working-class women (like the white and Chinese prostitutes found in many mining communities), Native American tribes, Mexican Americans, or European immigrants on the Great Plains, raised new questions. Some historians focused on western social mobility, particularly in urban areas which had not received much attention, and in mining towns, now seen as far more important to regional development than the agricultural frontier. These analyses tested and usually found wanting the notion of the frontier as a place of special opportunities. Other work dealt with the character of non-Anglo cultures and/or the nature of cultural contact between groups, especially between white settlers and Native Americans or Mexican Americans.

While historians emphasized the ability of non-Anglo groups to resist wholesale cultural domination, they generally detailed the negative impact of American expansion. Mexican Americans, for example, were denied rights of citizenship assured by the treaty of Guadeloupe Hidalgo and, in many places, were dispossessed of their land. By the 20th century many had become poorly paid wage laborers. Similarly, promises made to Native American tribes were routinely broken, and the Indians were ultimately confined to reservations where they were expected to adopt white culture.

A more complex understanding of the interaction of different groups suggests the limitations of a view primarily emphasizing the east to west movement of white Americans. Historians have studied Asian migration, the movements of Indian tribes and Mexican Americans within the West, and the northward flow of Mexicans across what one historical geographer has called "one of the world's great cultural borderlands." The view of the West as a region where peoples and cultures mixed has increasingly replaced the one-sided notion of westward expansion or a western frontier.

Another area of exploration during the post-1960 period has dealt with the importance of the West as myth. The popularity of Freudian ideas originally prompted studies in the 1920s and 1930s; new work ranges from analyses of literature and film to art.

By the 1980s and early 1990s, the contours of western history had changed so dramatically that the media and scholars both were talking about the "new western history." Key themes of "new western history" include the idea of the West as a region, and "a place undergoing conquest and never fully escaping its consequences." This perspective places the conquest of the West in the context of European expansion. Some historians have developed the themes of violence, oppression, labor activism, and class conflict while others have analyzed western expansionism as part of larger stories like the spread of world capitalism. Several accounts stress environmental consequences of white settlement in the West.

While the work on expansion lacks the unity once provided by Frederick Jackson Turner's frontier thesis, new questions focusing on the social, ethnic, and racial character of the westward movement have revitalized the field. Some historians point to the neglect of political, cultural, and religious questions, however, and future research may turn to explore topics in these areas. (*See also* Frontier Societies; Frontier Thesis)

Julie Roy Jeffrey

REFERENCES

Limerick, Patricia Nelson. *The Legacy of Conquest: The Unbroken Past of the American West.* New York: Norton, 1987.

White, Richard. *Roots of Dependency: Subsistence, Environment, and Social Change Among the Choctaws, Pawnees, and Navajos.* Lincoln: University of Nebraska Press, 1983.

Wet-Nursing

Wet-nursing is the practice of a woman caring for and breastfeeding a child not her own. This practice was widespread in the past, and in fact is still utilized in the present, especially in eastern Europe and the Middle East. It is still utilized, however, in isolated cases in the modern industrial world.

In the past the wet nurse sometimes remained in the child's household, but usually parents sent their children to the wet nurse's home. This could be miles away from the family home. Children remained with the wet nurse until weaned, at about two years of age, though sometimes they stayed longer after weaning. Parents could find wet nurses on their own, though usually they went to a broker of the sort who also furnished household servants. Sometimes the intermediary between the parents and the wet nurse was the wet nurse's husband. Although wet-nursing was common to all classes, usually only the aristocracy, middle classes, and urban artisans utilized wet-nursing because of the expense involved.

Most wet nurses came from the lower classes, especially the peasantry. Because urban dwellers required so many wet nurses, the practice represents a significant economic interchange between city and countryside. Margherita Datini, who procured wet nurses for her husband's business in Renaissance Florence, was constantly searching the Tuscan countryside to find suitable wet nurses.

Wet-nursing and wet nurses appear frequently throughout the records of ancient and premodern Europe. Juliet's wet nurse, in Shakespeare's play, is the most familiar example from literature, though Plutarch records that Cicero had one as did Moses. Expenses for wet-nursing appear frequently and in great detail in Renaissance account books. Premodern correspondence, even official correspondence, mentions the practice. Governments tried to regulate the business in their laws. Tax lists record wet-nursing as an occupational category. The bureaucratic records of foundlings' homes richly record the employment of wet nurses. Chronicles even note their presence.

As a consequence, researchers frequently stumble across mentions of wet-nursing in ancient and premodern European records but without really understanding its significance or scope. Historians who have examined wet-nursing in their research on the family and childhood typically see it in a negative light, calling it a brutal inhuman practice because it trafficked in babies and exploited the poor peasant women who breastfed the children of the urban elite. There is evidence that wet-nursed babies had higher than average mortality rates. Moreover, since most nurslings were away from home for almost two years, wet-nursing possibly represents a form of parental neglect in the ancient and premodern world. Attacks on wet-nursing by reformers and government officials from the 18th century onward helped put the practice in a bad light, and wet-nursing did begin to decline in Europe after 1800.

Modern condemnations of wet-nursing are, however, somewhat anachronistic, failing to see the full reality of the structures of life in the ancient and premodern eras. In eras without adequate artificial means of feeding infants, working mothers needed wet-nursing to combine their work and child rearing. Fathers whose wives had died in childbirth needed wet-nursing to feed their infant children. Society needed wet-nursing to feed foundlings. The wet nurse was essential for the maintenance of the ancient and premodern family and society.

Recent work on wet-nursing in ancient Rome, Renaissance Italy, and Enlightenment France indicates that wet-nursing was neither an aberration of the rich nor an example of how premodern parents did not care for their children. It was normal societal practice at all socioeconomic levels, though particularly in cities, and represented a form of premodern child care. Wet nurses then were the primary child care providers for many ancient and premodern European infants and toddlers.

While a child might be with a wet nurse for years, evidence from premodern European diaries indicates that parents would frequently visit their children at the wet nurse. And within the constraints of wet-nursing, parents and children did develop significant and lasting emotional bonds.

During the Enlightenment, Paris had four public institutions that served as clearinghouses for the hiring of wet nurses. In 1751 some 12,000 women applied to just one of these institutions to serve as wet nurses. In 1780 some 25,000 babies were born in Paris and the surrounding regions, and 20,000 of them were sent to wet nurses. Out of some 90,000 inhabitants of 18th-century Hamburg, 5,000 women listed their occupation as "wet nurse." In late 19th-century Russia some 30,000 women a year applied to the various public agencies hiring wet nurses. Clearly, if these isolated figures are any indication, wet-nursing represented a significant aspect of women's work and child care in the ancient and premodern world. (*See also* Child Rearing; Motherhood)

Louis Haas

REFERENCES

Fildes, Valerie A. *Wet Nursing: A History from Antiquity to the Present.* Oxford: Basil Blackwell, 1988.

Ransel, David L. *Mothers of Misery: Child Abandonment in Russia.* Princeton, NJ: Princeton University Press, 1988.

Sussman, George D. *Selling Mother's Milk: The Wet-Nursing Business in France, 1715–1914.* Urbana: University of Illinois Press, 1982.

Widows

Widowhood defines women in terms of their relationship to the social institutions of marriage and the family: a widow is a woman whose husband has died and who has not remarried. Widows in Western society, which is patriarchal, patrilineal, and usually patrilocal, tended to be quite vulnerable, because their access to economic and social supports was reduced, if not cut off. This has also been true in Latin American history. The legal status of widows varied greatly according to time, place, and the class and occupation of their husbands, and some had much greater success than others in creating replacement support systems. Social historians have worked both on some of the common problems of widows, and also on reasons for change and variations.

In much of traditional European society, the dowry that a woman brought to her marriage was supposed to be used to support her after the death of her husband (her husband's patrimony would be inherited by his male heirs), although she did not always have control over it. The widow of a feudal lord, for example, could find herself and her dowry the pawns in a political conflict and be prevented from exercising any control over her property that she may have had in theory. On the other hand, the widow of an urban merchant or craftsman might have complete control over her own dowry as well as her husband's commercial interests, and be legally independent and autonomous. Widows were also regularly named as the guardians of their minor sons. Because of their control over property, widows wrote most of the surviving female wills, producing some of the most valuable extant sources for the history of women's kinship ties, piety, and social sensibilities.

Younger widows would often remarry (to recover the support and status of the married state), but children from their first marriage were rarely permitted to accompany them to their new home. Older women with children would usually choose not to remarry and to live instead with one or more of their adult children. A widow's allegiances tended to become more complex and idiosyncratic toward the end of her life if the number of her direct descendants, and hence marital ties to other families increased. For some, therefore, widowhood was empowering, because it was the only time in women's lives when they had access to the control of property (if not outright ownership of it) and could use that control to create social supports of their choosing. For the poor, however, and for women with few surviving relatives, widowhood was a tragically precarious stage of life. For these women, pensions and other forms of social welfare developed in the 20th century provided an indispensable safety net. Studies of widows in modern history have focused on patterns of residence—whether they lived independently, with adult children (increasingly, daughters), or in institutions, including almshouses. (*See also* Marriage/Remarriage; Old Age; Women's History)

Alison A. Smith

REFERENCES

Anderson, Bonnie S., and Judith P. Zinsser. *A History of Their Own: Women in Europe from Prehistory to the Present*, 2 vols. New York: Harper, 1988.

Metcalf, Alida. "Women and Means: Women and Family Property in Colonial Brazil," *Journal of Social History* 24, 1 (1990).

Witchcraft

Belief in witches and witchcraft has formed an important part of the mentalities of people in many societies. Witchcraft phenomena were long neglected by historians because they involved ordinary people and could be dismissed as "mere" superstitition, but recent historians have paid much greater attention to witchcraft because of what it reveals about popular culture. Research has dealt with a number of different periods and places, often in conjunction with anthropological inquiries. The most thoroughly examined aspect of witchcraft remains, however, the witch hunts that spread over many parts of Europe and North America during the 16th and 17th centuries. Social historians have explored witch beliefs during that period, the motives behind persecutions, and the cessation of witchcraft trials as part of a major cultural and social transition in the Western world around 1700.

During the 16th and 17th centuries, more than 100,000 men and women were tried for witchcraft in Europe and New England. Many of them were convicted and then burned or hanged. People had used witch beliefs to explain misfortune throughout the medieval period, but fear of witchcraft and the frequency of witch prosecutions rose dramatically during the early modern period. This was due in part to the religious tensions caused by Reformation and Counter-Reformation, as people became convinced that the adherents of rival confessions were servants of Satan and thus witches. Political and ecclesiastical authorities exploited such tensions to attack their enemies. But accusations of witchcraft were founded just as securely in social conflict: they expressed not only fears about the supernatural world, manipulated by church officials and rulers, but also social tensions between ordinary men and women.

Recent scholars have shown that personal conflicts within individual towns and villages underlay many witch accusations. Accuser and accused were usually neighbors with a recent history of disagreement: the accused had typically requested a loan or gift, perhaps of food or a household implement; the accuser had refused, but then felt guilty for having done so; in an attempt to shift guilt onto the aggrieved neighbor, the villager who had refused the original request now blamed the spurned neighbor for any subsequent misfortune, such as crop failure or the death of livestock, claiming that the wronged person had resorted to witchcraft as a form of revenge.

Neighborly conflicts became particularly acute, historians argue, during the 16th and 17th centuries, as a result of social and economic transformation. The emergence of a market economy and increasing social mobility made for a less communitarian ethos, just as economic transformation swelled the ranks of poverty-stricken people who needed support from their neighbors. In time, new institutions such as the work house were developed to cater for such people. But during an interim period, witchcraft accusations served a double function: on the one hand, in defense of traditional values, they suggested that unneighborly behavior had unpleasant (sometimes fatal) repercussions; on the other, they legitimized new and less communitarian values by sanctioning the prosecution of those who made unwelcome demands on their neighbors. It was during that period of adaptation that witchcraft cases proliferated. While witch accusations performed a positive function in enabling men and women to channel fear and guilt, witch trials were also profoundly negative in their effects on the local communities in which they originated. The accusations, recriminations, and paranoia which accompanied a trial ripped apart the social fabric; lingering hostilities could fracture towns and villages long after the trial had run its course. Moreover, in cases where an initial accusation developed into a witch panic, many locals could end up being accused, convicted, and executed. Communities were often decimated by witch hysteria.

Witch accusations were directed, for the most part, against women. Christian mythology had traditionally associated women with evil in general and witchcraft in particular, but witch accusations became notably more gender-directed during the 16th and 17th centuries. The disproportionate vulnerability of women to witch accusations in the early modern period may have been linked to demographic change. During the 16th century, Europeans began to marry much later than before; a growing number of men and women never married at all. In a culture which saw the patriarchal family structure as a primary guarantor of social stability, this trend represented a fundamental threat to order. Particularly disturbing was the presence of unmarried women, especially those whose fathers had already died: these spinsters challenged the expectation that men would protect and control women, first as daughters and then as wives. Fears aroused by the emergence of this threat to patriarchal control may help to explain the predominance of women among accused witches. Recent research suggests that women who violated social norms by inheriting property and thus wielding a form of power usually reserved for men were especially vulnerable to witch accusations. Older women, freed from the recurring cycle of pregnancy and lactation, were disproportionately represented among the accused, as were widows, who, depending on their economic circumstances, constituted either a challenge to expectations of female dependency or an irritating drain on community resources. Midwives, whose skills were both respected and feared, and whose medical prowess tended to be confused with occult knowledge, were also vulnerable to witch accusations. (*See also* Charity; Christianity; Community; Inheritance Systems; Magic; Market Economy; Midwifery; Singlehood; Widows; Women's History)

Richard Godbeer

REFERENCES

Karlsen, Carol. *The Devil in the Shape of a Woman: Witchcraft in Colonial New England.* New York: Norton, 1987.

Klaits, Joseph. *Servants of Satan: The Age of the Witch Hunts.* Bloomington: Indiana University Press, 1985.

Levack, Brian. *The Witch-Hunt in Early Modern Europe.* New York: Longman, 1987.

Macfarlane, Alan. *Witchcraft in Tudor and Stuart England*. London: Harper & Row, 1970.

Midelfort, H.C. Erik. *Witch Hunting in Southwestern Germany, 1562–1684*. Stanford, CA: Stanford University Press, 1972.

Women and Work

One of the most important areas of investigation to emerge with the development of women's history in the last 30 years has been women's work. Building on the studies of a few earlier scholars whose own interests were sparked by the feminist movement of the early 20th century, historians began to investigate what sorts of tasks women had done in the past and how major economic changes such as the development of commercial capitalism, the industrial revolution, or the creation of colonial trading networks had affected women's work. By doing so, they hoped to understand how contemporary structures of work—in which women in the Western world receive about 60 cents for every dollar men earn and women in developing countries generally work much longer hours than men but receive little or no independent pay—had developed.

These investigations quickly led to a realization that the definition of "work" is itself gender-biased; in most societies of the past, men's tasks have been more likely to be defined as "work," and women's, as "helping out," "assisting," or "housework." When women's activities were thought of as work, they were still not as highly valued as men's, even if they took the same amount of skill, effort, and time. This realization has led historians of women's work in two directions.

First, they have searched for the roots of these gender divisions and the reasons why women's labor has been undervalued. Focusing primarily on western Europe, some scholars have suggested that commercial capitalism played a key role by making people equate work and wage labor; because women's tasks such as child care and housekeeping were generally unpaid, they were increasingly not thought of as work. When much wage labor was transferred to factories with the industrial revolution, and particularly where, as in western Europe and the United States, only a minority of factory workers were women, tasks within the household were regarded even less as work, including those which were paid; women who labored in factories were described as "workers," but those who took in laundry or boarders were not. This bias against work within the household—work which was generally done by women—became enshrined in statistics in the late 19th century; as economists began to measure things like "gross national product" or to ask about people's occupations, they only measured or counted work which was paid and which was one's full-time occupation. A woman who raised five children, sold eggs from her chickens and vegetables from her garden, fed and laundered the clothes of three farmhands, and worked in the fields whenever she had time, would appear in census or tax records as "housewife" or "not working." This was not simply a matter of labeling, but could have a very negative effect on the woman's economic well-being as her work did not make her eligible for a government pension or a private retirement fund.

Studies of more recent trends in developing countries have also indicated that the introduction of wage labor and capitalized agriculture and industry have decreased the value attached to the work women do. Projects to improve agricultural production have been directed by and to men and so have concentrated on cash crops rather than on the subsistence crops which women produce; that these development projects have not reduced the threat of famine is unsurprising.

Because wage labor appears to have had a negative effect on the value of women's work, many scholars have explored societies where most labor was unpaid and went to support the family economy in an attempt to discover a time or place where women's work was valued equally with that of men. Pre-agriculturalist hunter-gatherers, medieval Europe, colonial and frontier America, and some Pacific islands have all been held up as "golden ages" for women's work, though as yet no culture has been found which regarded women's work the same as men's. As these investigations have revealed, the reasons for this lie beyond the realm of economics, and cannot be discovered by looking at work alone. Laws which restricted or handicapped women;

marital traditions which prevented wives from acting independently; misogynist ideas about women's mental, moral, and physical weaknesses; the physical hardships of pregnancy and breastfeeding; and ideologies which defined female labor as the property of men all worked (and in most parts of the world, continue to work) to disadvantage women as workers. The most recent studies of women and work have thus generally given up a search for a "golden age" and instead have begun to link women's work opportunities and patterns not only to economic developments but also to other types of social, political, and ideological change. They have investigated ties between women's work and, for example, the growth of large-scale slavery in 1st-century BC Rome, daughters' and sons' appearances in court in 14th-century England, Protestant ideas about the family in 16th-century Germany, changing standards of cleanliness in households and clothing in 20th-century America, or funds established for pilgrimages and marriages in postcolonial Ivory Coast.

The second direction historians of women's work have taken is to broaden their own definition of "work" to gain a more complete picture of all the types of activities women were engaged in which supported themselves and their families. Though traditional economic analysis often makes a sharp distinction between "productive" and "reproductive" labor (and generally pays much more attention to the former), this distinction in some ways misrepresents pre- or nonindustrialized economies where the household and workplace were or are not separate. It also misrepresents women's work rhythms, because women often carried out "productive" labor such as the making of cloth or craft items and "reproductive" labor such as cooking or child care simultaneously. Therefore, studies of the broad range of women's work now include analyses of housework; breastfeeding practices; care of children, the sick, and the elderly; and investment activities as well as more traditional types of rural and urban labor.

These studies have found certain patterns in female labor across cultures and time periods. Whether viewed positively or negatively, as biological or cultural, a woman's primary concern has traditionally been the welfare of her children and family, so that her work has been adapted so far as possible to the needs of her family. This means that she changed jobs, moved into and out of the labor force, worked part-time, or learned new skills as her family situation changed, and so did not develop as strong a sense of work identity as a man who more likely stayed in one occupation his entire life. What work men did and do is generally determined by their class, training, skills, race, energy level, ingenuity, and the types of employment available, but women's work was and is determined by all these factors and personal ones such as marital status and number and ages of children. Therefore, there are often great differences in the impact of changes such as industrialization on young single women as opposed to older married women.

Women's work has also been shaped more by ideas of morality and propriety than men's, with women excluded from certain tasks because they were not regarded as "proper" for women, though often these exclusions were justified in terms of strength or training. (Women's long exclusion from professional medical practice or the military are two examples of this.) Women have generally been paid much less than men for the same tasks, and occupations in which the majority of workers were or are female have lower wages and status than those in which the majority of workers are male. In fact, women's entry in large numbers in any occupation actually lowers wages and status, a change which has been traced in the early 20th century for secretaries and telephone operators.

Whatever culture or century they are studying, then, social historians have discovered that women's work is absolutely essential to the operation of the economy. It is generally low status, badly paid, frequently shifting, and perceived as marginal, but these factors make it no less essential. Further research will no doubt reveal more information about why this is so and, particularly in studies of more recent history, suggest ways to make the structure of work more equitable. Another fruitful line of research growing out of the investigation of women and work is a broader analysis of the relationship between gender and work, that is, examining not only how women's work experience was shaped by the fact that they were women, but also men's, by the fact that they were men. At the same time, women's work roles in the past have changed women's work, but in different ways depending on region. These complexities, under the larger umbrella of inferior work statutes, requires careful analysis. Explaining change and variation and assessing their impact on women and men alike form key methods of getting beyond generalizations and diatribes in this important social history topic. (*See also* Child Labor; Child Rearing; Chinese Gender Relations; Domesticity; Feminism; Gender Socialization; Household Economy; Housework; Industrialization; Marriage/Remarriage; Proletarianization; Prostitution; Protoindustrialization; Reproduction and Class Formation; Women's History; Working Class)

Merry E. Wiesner-Hanks

REFERENCES

Afshar, Haleh, ed. *Women, Work, and Ideology in the Third World.* London: Tavistock, 1985.

Hanawalt, Barbara, ed. *Women and Work in Preindustrial Europe.* Bloomington: Indiana University Press, 1986.

Jones, Jacqueline. *Labor of Love, Labor of Sorrow: Black Women, Work and the Family from Slavery to the Present.* New York: Basic Books, 1985.

Kessler-Harris, Alice. *Out to Work: A History of Wage-Earning Women in the United States.* Oxford: Oxford University Press, 1982.

Tilly, Louise A., and Joan W. Scott. *Women, Work and Family.* New York: Methuen, 1987.

Woman's History

The writing of women's history—a history that takes women as its subject matter—has developed over many centuries while constantly changing its form, transforming its methodology, and increasing in popularity, especially in the 20th century. Inspired by feminist or protofeminist concerns that women be regarded as equal to men, women's history first focused on women's achievements, but by the 19th century it also addressed issues of women's condition under the law, in economics and politics, and in the functioning of society. Amateurs and a few professional historians carried women's history across a mine field of rebuke as history professionalized from the mid-19th century on. By the late 20th century, the field was still disputed, but increasing numbers of people in the profession writing this kind of history allowed for criticism to be met more forcefully and for the genre as a whole to become more sophisticated and innovative.

Christine de Pisan's *Book of the City of Ladies* (ca. 1405) was a prototype of historical writing on women until the era of professionalization. De Pisan introduced her subject matter by citing the slanders against women that prompted her to write on their behalf. The body of this work proceeded to narrate the lives of exemplary, heroic, and accomplished women in the past. Over the next few centuries such works contributed to the humanistic project of constructing the outlines of a secular self, only a female one. By the French Revolutionary period massive compendia of notable women's lives were appearing in western Europe, including May Hays, *Female Biography* (6 vols., 1803); Fortunée Briquet, *Dictionnaire historique des françaises* (1804); and Mary Bentham, *Biographical Dictionary of Celebrated Women of Every Age and Country* (1804).

The French Revolutionary era raised questions of liberal rights and the status of history, firmly defining rights as masculine but leaving the question of history open in the new regime. Would much history continue to tout dynastic grandeurs? Should it be erased as a history of monarchist crimes? Did it contain the lost voice of the people and the story of fledgling nationalism? French writer Germaine de Staël was among those who entered the fray with histories of literature, of Germany, and of the French Revolution. But her most pertinent writing for the development of women's history was the novel *Corinne* (1807), which contested the generally masculine voice of history and the masculine subject matter that focused on dynastic politics and military engagements. A political liberal, she implicitly touted nonetheless the old regime days when salonières directed intellectual debate and shaped knowledge, and this allied her in women's historiography with writers like Félicité de Genlis who reveled in social histories of court life, women's learning, and salons. Both these writers were indebted to the tradition of citing notable women, and indeed de Staël wrote biographical articles on women like Sappho, but their writing also charted a new path directed to carving out big chunks of society and culture and looking for the activities of women there. Women in households or salons were not just notable but interesting and often anonymous figures from the past. As these works proliferated in the 19th century in the work of such authors as Mary Lamb, Alice Morse Earle, and hundreds of others, women's daily activities acquired historicity.

The creation of a historical profession, however, served to contest the expansion of historical subject matter. Challenging the grip on the past of romantic writers in the first half of the 19th century, German historian Leopold von Ranke emphasized the use of official documents, especially those in state archives, as the basis of history. German historical training came to focus on the discovery, evaluation, and compilation of this kind of document, and taught in small seminars, this historical methodology soon discredited amateur historical writing and university lectures to large and disparate crowds that conspicuously featured many interested women. But the most important impact on the experimentation then taking place in amateur historical writing was to undermine the widening scope of history to include such topics as women and the nonpublic world. English historian J.R. Seeley's characterization, "History is past politics," became a sacred dictum.

The scientific spirit that professional historians espoused meant that history was in principle untainted by such issues as class, race, and gender. Thus, in England and the United States substantial numbers of women received advanced training in history, but many of them departed sufficiently from the restrictions on acceptable subject matter to help professionalize the writing of women's history. Mary Bateson at Newnham College, Cambridge, for instance, used her considerable expertise to write about the double monastery (1899), where men and women held comparable power. Trained at the University of Michigan and Bryn Mawr, Lucy Maynard Salmon of Vassar College published her study of domestic service in the 1890s and throughout the early 20th century wrote on cookbooks, laundry lists, and other aspects of domestic life. Salmon was committed to the seminar method, but she contested the narrow definition of a historical document as something one found in an official archive. Her "History in a Backyard" opened with the scenario of a scholar being unable to go to a European archive one summer and proceeded to discuss the ways in which domestic artifacts could be evaluated as historical material. Salmon encouraged her students to support local archives and historical societies, further broadening the definition of historical material and democratizing access to records.

Salmon, like many other historians writing the history of women at the turn of the 20th century, was a suffragist, and the fact that millions of women obtained the vote in the first half of the century seemed only to intensify the writing of women's history and the formation of document collections that would make this possible. French feminist Marguerite Durand, Dutch physician Aletta Jacobs, French stenographer Marie-Louise Bouglé, and American activist Mary Beard were among those who founded important collections of books and documents and sought to build archives and libraries to serve women's history. On the eve of World War II many of these projects were very advanced if not already completed.

Historians argue that World Wars I and II along with the Cold War between the Soviet Union and the United States militarized the human spirit and effectively quashed feminist consciousness that had propelled the earlier writing of women's history. Indeed some of the most prominent studies of women written immediately after World War II such as Mary Beard's *Woman as Force in History* (1946) were undertaken by historians who were already accomplished in the field. After 1945 it was more usual for women trained in universities to avoid topics on women (if they ever considered studying them in the first place), and the percentage of women scholars actually declined in the 1940s and 1950s. Rectifying this situation became one focus of women's activism in the new feminist movement of the 1960s and 1970s.

This movement again drew attention to the inequities women experienced in all aspects of life simply because of their sex. In an age when sociological and Marxist theory shaped ideas, feminists maintained that women constituted a class with a common past. The neglect of this past in the academy became one more sign of their unequal condition. As early as the late 1960s traditionally trained women professors in North America began offering courses in women's history. Jill Conway and Natalie Davis at the University of Toronto offered a comparative course that yielded a mimeographed bibliography widely circulated in the 1970s. In the United States Gerda Lerner at Sarah Lawrence College also introduced women's history into the curriculum and was instrumental in starting a master's program in women's studies. Much information about these innovations, including course syllabi and sample bibliographies, spread along informal networks.

Women's history benefited from the democratization of education that had occurred in the universities since the 1950s, because as women reestablished their presence in the student body, they formed a constituency for these new courses. It was also increasingly linked with the rise of social history, benefiting from its wider framework and enriching it in turn. Although the women professoriate generally had middle-class backgrounds, many were from working-class families. In many countries the so-called elite universities shunned women's history, while newer ones like the polytechnics in Britain provided the kind of intensely intellectual atmosphere that welcomed new programs and ideas. Collectives of mixed amateur and professional historians also wrote and taught women's history, and night classes of adults also proved a receptive audience. By the 1990s there were thousands of courses in the United States and even some named-chairs in women's history, while in western Europe there were few if any chairs in the field but many active scholars. Graduate training in women's history was also a thriving enterprise by the 1980s.

Women's history became institutionalized regionally, nationally, and internationally, as well as being housed in individual universities. In 1973 the Berkshire Conference sponsored its first women's history conference at Douglass College, Rutgers University, which ultimately led to the publication of *Clio's Consciousness Raised* (1974), edited by Mary Hartman and Lois Banner. Founded in 1930 for women historians who felt themselves discriminated against in national

organizations like the American Historical Association, the Berkshire Conference's programs had become one of the largest international scholarly meetings by the 1990s. Although women's history was weaker institutionally in western Europe than in North America, scholars organized conferences dealing with women's experience in the work force, in the French Revolution, in the field of education, and in assorted national histories. Collaborative international publications included Michele Perrot, ed., *Storia della donna*; Karen Offen, et al., eds., *Writing Women's History* (1991); and the journals *Gender and History* and *The Journal of Women's History*. Extraordinary library and archival facilities in Amsterdam, London, Paris, and other capital cities were devoted to the history of women and often received government financing. Women activists in eastern Europe and in many non-Western countries found historical and other scholarship on women a luxury not yet available to them given the other areas that urgently needed their help.

Women's history also furthered democratization in the academy by drawing attention to layers of society generally excluded from the definition of history as "past politics." Indebted to innovations in quantitative and social history during these decades, women's history searched out what its practitioners considered the most invisible subjects, notably working women, prostitutes, and the poor. Monographs such as Joan Scott and Louise Tilly's *Women, Work, and Family* or surveys such as Sheila Rowbotham's *Hidden from History* or *Becoming Visible*, edited by Renate Bridenthal and Claudia Koonz, uncovered the lives of many unknowns to provide important insights into women's daily experiences and into the shape of society as a whole. Women's history in the 1970s sought knowledge of women's reproductive, work, and family lives, thus broadening historical questions to include areas beyond politics. Its findings influenced history as a whole in such works as Philippe Ariès's multivolumed *History of Private Life*, which specifically included the kind of attention to women's history that innovative social historians like Ariés had hitherto neglected.

Critics soon challenged the dominance of social history in the field and forcefully suggested that women's history take new directions. Some apparent challenges, however, seemed in fact to urge continued expansion of the social history–women's history link. First, books like *But Some of Us Are Brave* (1982), edited by Gloria Hull, Patricia Bell Scott, and Barbara Smith, maintained that black women were invisible in the writing of both black and women's history. Other women of color added their voices, insisting that race was an important historical category and one that was not covered in the innovations of the 1970s. At the 1988 Wingspread Conference on the training of graduate students in American women's history Rosalyn Terborg-Penn gave a speech consisting of one sentence: "I have only one thing to say: Race." Second, other historians maintained that issues of sexual orientation and sexuality were critical not only to understanding everyday life but the exercise of political power. Although fewer studies of lesbians than of women of color appeared, books like Estelle Freedman and John D'Emilio, *Intimate Matters* (1988), and Martha Vicinus, et al., eds., *Hidden from History* (1990) provided solid scholarly interpretations. A third change was proposed most forcefully in Joan Scott's article "Gender: A Useful Category of Historical Analysis," which first appeared in the *American Historical Review* (1986, Vol. 91, pp. 1053–1075). Influenced by poststructuralist theory, Scott suggested that scholarship in women's history had in general produced only ghettoization. This ghettoization occurred primarily because "women" was not something real but part of a binary coupling of the terms "women" and "men." Because these categories were defined in terms of one another and because they lacked an essential reality, investigation into women's "experience" was in large part a self-defeating and misguided enterprise. Instead, history should explore the operation of the category "gender" to understand the ways in which such terms as "men" and "women" produced social, economic, and political inequalities and yielded power.

By the 1990s women's history was one of the largest fields in publishing in the United States and Britain, but it was one in which a rough, early consensus about scholarship had given way to increasingly difficult challenges and multiple calls for new directions. As of this writing historians debate whether they should focus on women's history, gender history, or feminist history—each of them a way of writing women's history fraught with historical concerns. Scholars working on non-Western countries are particularly anxious about the universal status given to the history of women in the West and are debating the terms on which this dominance can be turned around. Finally, as universities in the United States face the restructuring of academic decisionmaking because of financial turmoil, the future of women's history, which is less institutionally secure than other fields, may be jeopardized. (*See also* African American Women; Chinese Gender Relations; Latin American Women; Russian Women; Widows; Women and Work)

Bonnie Smith

REFERENCES

Davis, Natalie Z. "Gender and Genre: Women as Historical Writers, 1400–1820," in Patricia Labalme, ed., *Beyond Their Sex: Learned Women of the European Past.* New York: New York University Press, 1980.

———. "History's Two Bodies," *The American Historical Review* 93 (February 1988): 1–30.

Offen, Karen, Ruth Roach Pierson, and Jane Rendall, eds. *Writing Women's History: International Perspectives.* Bloomington: Indiana University Press, 1991.

Smith, Bonnie G. "The Contribution of Women to Modern Historiography in Great Britain, France, and the United States, 1750–1940," *American Historical Review* 89 (June 1984): 709–732.

Zinsser, Judith. *A Glass Half Empty: The Impact of Feminism on History.* Boston: Twayne, 1992.

Work Ethic

In the Western world, the idea of work being motivated by moral considerations rather than by a simple need to fill one's belly has long been presumed to date from the Protestant Reformation or at least from the Calvinist phase of that upheaval. Until quite recently, in fact, the terms "work ethic" and "Protestant ethic" have often been used interchangeably to describe those who seem to "live to work" rather than "work to live." This "Protestant/work" ethic was thought to govern both the propensity to accumulate capital of the bourgeois entrepreneur and the inspired assiduity of the artisan or manual worker. Since World War II, however, the tendency to ascribe worker motivation to a Puritan ethic of work or indeed to any single, monolithic ethic at all, has come under attack. Some scholars today question whether some work ethic ever affected the behavior of most workers. Others, while admitting the relevance of ethical motivation in the workplace, argue that just as "work" can no longer be defined simply as "paid labor," so different ethics inspire different kinds of work.

The idea of a "Protestant ethic" of work was first given explicit formulation by the early 20th-century German sociologist Max Weber. In his well-known study *The Protestant Ethic and the Spirit of Capitalism* (1921), Weber ascribed the famous homilies (e.g., "Time is money") of the American sage Benjamin Franklin to the indoctrination Franklin had received from his stern Calvinist father. The elder Franklin apparently liked to quote Proverbs, xxii: 29 from the Bible to his son: "Seest thou a man diligent in his business? He shall stand before kings." Weber argued that "the real Alpha and Omega of Franklin's ethic" was the belief that "virtue and proficiency" in work constituted "a calling" of a religious nature. He concluded that it was this belief which generally motivated the "earning of money within the modern economic order."

The English economic historian R.H. Tawney, while observing that Weber had overstated his case for a "Protestant ethic" of work, nonetheless went on to make an equally sweeping argument for the impact of a Puritan "work ethic." Tawney wrote in his *Religion and the Rise of Capitalism* (1926), "The labor which [the Puritan divine] idealizes is not simply a requirement imposed by nature, or a punishment for the sin of Adam. . . . It is not merely an economic means, to be laid aside when physical needs have been satisfied. It is a spiritual end, for in it alone can the soul find health, and it must be continued as an ethical duty long after it has ceased to be a material necessity."

American scholars have understandably taken an interest in Tawney's Puritan "work ethic," while recognizing that the original religious inspiration has been, if not entirely absent, at least submerged since the 18th century. Daniel Rodgers, in his *Work Ethic in Industrial America,*

1850–1920 (1978), for example, argues that, in 19th-century American countinghouses and factories alike, "the central premise of the work ethic was that work was the core of moral life. Work made men useful in a world of economic scarcity. It staved off the doubts and temptations that preyed on idleness, it opened the way to deserved wealth and status, it allowed one to put the impress of mind and skill on the material world."

Modern skepticism. Social historians who study workers and the work they do are increasingly skeptical of theories of worker motivation which stress moral imperatives. Patrick Joyce (1987), one of the most prolific modern scholars of work, says that of the many "hardy old perennials of very dubious historical validity" which bedevil his field, "none . . . is hoarier than the Protestant work ethic." H.E. Moorhouse, another contemporary historian of work, denies that there is any "intrinsic meaning," religious or secular, "to any piece of labor."

If the "Protestant work ethic" is irrelevant, so is the notion that "the dominant values of capitalist society . . . present some 'work ethic' which is . . . paramount in the messages emanating from the major institutions of society." Moorhouse also takes issue with the recent slimmed-down version of the work ethic, which equates it with a craft or professional ethic and seeks to explain the "blue-collar blues" as a consequence of deskilling.

Universal theories of worker motivation seem to many social historians to be particularly inappropriate in an era when the very concept of work is undergoing substantial revamping. In a time when even some forms of consumption are being described as "work," says Moorhouse, it can only be assumed that workers will be bombarded by society with "different messages about work." Class, gender, and ethnic cultures will have an impact, as will "precise occupational ideologies formed in varying workplaces . . . from union rule books to workgroup norms." Nor should it be assumed that job satisfaction resides only in the artisan workshop or that worker alienation is to be found only on assembly lines. Ethics of work are often job- or profession-specific. Some jobs motivate workers because they demand strength or courage (furnace-tending in steel mills), others because they are in companies on the cutting edge of new technology (the aerospace industry).

It should be noted, however, that if contemporary social historians of work are determined on banishing the old notions of universal ethics of work, whether religious or secular, they are equally quick to recognize that they still have a way to go in providing satisfactory substitutes. "The critical study of 'the work ethic,' . . . especially in its contextualized and particular manifestations such as the Victorian 'gospel of work,' must be acknowledged as a serious gap in the literature," acknowledges Patrick Joyce. Changes over time, including alterations and continuities in middle-class work values in the 20th century, also pose a challenge for sensitive sociocultural histories. Finally, comparative possibilities have increasingly emerged with interest in differences between Japanese or Korean work cultures and those of Western societies and the relevant historical roots. (*See also* Capitalism; Middle Class)

Bruce Vandervort

REFERENCES

Joyce, Patrick. *Work, Society and Politics. The Culture of the Factory in Late Victorian England.* Brighton: Harvester, 1980.

———, ed. *The Historical Meanings of Work.* Cambridge: Cambridge University Press, 1987.

Kaplan, Steven L., and Cynthia J. Koepp, eds. *Work in France: Representations, Meaning, Organization and Practice.* Ithaca, NY: Cornell University Press, 1986.

Reddy, William. *The Rise of Market Culture. The Textile Trade and French Society, 1750–1900.* Cambridge: Cambridge University Press, 1984.

Rodgers, Daniel T. *The Work Ethic in Industrial America, 1850–1920.* Chicago: University of Chicago Press, 1978.

Working Class

The word "worker" first appears in English in John Wyclif's translation of the Bible from the Latin (1382). The term "working class," on the other hand, emerged for the first time in English only in 1813, appropriately enough in a book entitled *A New View of Society*, by the utopian socialist Robert Owen. Wyclif's "worker" was, not surprisingly, an agricultural laborer (*operaio agrario*), while Owen's "working class" comprised "workers"—men, women, and children—whose work and workplaces increasingly were being shaped by the industrial revolution of the 18th century. Owen reckoned that in 1813 the "poor and working classes" of the British Isles numbered some 12 million persons. This figure probably would have accounted for the whole of the nonagricultural labor force of Britain and Ireland, including the artisans and home workers of the "old" working class who still represented the great majority of the manual workers, as well as the factory workers of the new industrial labor force.

This new industrial labor force, or "proletariat," wrote Karl Marx in his *Communist Manifesto* (1848), had been "called into existence" by the bourgeoisie by way of the industrial and French revolutions it had made. Three years after the *Communist Manifesto* was published, factory labor in England, homeland of the industrial revolution, accounted for perhaps half of the country's 5 million manual workers. Although Marx would not live to realize it, this was as large as the factory proletariat would ever bulk in the composition of modern society. In ascribing to it the role of "gravedigger of the bourgeoisie," Marx had assumed that industrial capitalism's demand for labor would so swell the ranks of the proletariat that it would come to represent the overwhelming majority of humankind. In 1900, less than two decades after Marx's death, however, artisans still accounted for a significant percentage of the working population in some countries. Even more important, in the more advanced industrial nations, the growth of white-collar employment had already begun to outstrip that of the factory work force. Since the beginning of the 20th century, the percentage of industrial workers in the labor forces of most industrialized nations has continued to decline, precipitately in the last decade with the onset of deindustrialization in many countries.

New Trends in Historiography

Until fairly recently, however, the main preoccupation of social historians of the working class has been the industrial proletariat, especially the trade unions and socialist parties which grouped its organized "vanguard." Although it never became the social behemoth Marx had predicted, the industrial working class nevertheless has been in the thick of Western politics during most of the modern era, both as historical actor and object. Its painful birth as a class created guilty consciences among the bourgeoisie, thus assuring the social question a place near the top of most national political agendas well into the 20th century. And, concentrated as it was in highly productive, highly profitable, and often strategic industries, the industrial working class possessed a capacity for political and economic mischief that guaranteed it attention from the authorities out of all proportion to its actual size. Finally, it may be of relevance that one side in the recent Cold War made its entrance onto the historical stage as the party of the proletariat of the Russian lands and, latterly, claimed to represent the "workers of the world." Given all this, it is not unreasonable that the industrial working class, rather than the artisans or commercial employees or office workers, should have for so long exercised such a pull on social historians.

Nonetheless, the social historians who responded to this pull often ended up misrepresenting the working classes of the various industrialized—and Third World—nations as monoliths whose aspirations and interests (whether they knew it or not) were incarnate in the industrial proletarians in their ranks and in the unions or parties who acted in their name. One of the most notable features of the New Social History of the working class, which began to surface in the 1970s, has been its refusal to treat the working class as a bloc. As one recent labor historian has put it: "Generalizations about *the* working class have been . . . undermined by the analysis of individual trades and crafts, and of conflicts within them: conflicts as often between skilled and unskilled, male and female, as between workers and their employers." The same writer notes that studies of the working class at national level are now being "supplemented by local and regional studies, a point of considerable significance, given the fragmented history of labour, even in individual nations."

Gender divisions and conflicts have perhaps received more attention from the "new" social historians of the working class than any other aspect of "the fragmented history of labour." The extensive research carried out in recent years in this subfield has led one prominent labor historian to conclude that "perhaps the greatest dividing line within the European working class on the eve of the First World War was that of sex."

Other contemporary scholars have highlighted the importance of skill differentials to segmentation of the working class, stressing at the same time the status anxiety of artisans and other skilled workers faced, as they increasingly were in the 19th century, with speedups, increased oversight, and deskilling, or proletarianization. The latter factors are also thought to have played a major role in fostering discontent and protest among artisans and other skilled workers, who often led the way in Europe and North America (and in Third World countries as well) in forming unions, founding cooperatives, fomenting strikes, or rallying support for socialist parties. The term "aristocracy of labor" was coined to denote skilled, relatively well-paid workers in factories and the crafts whose lifestyles and bargaining power could isolate them from other workers. Finally, propertyless rural workers bear a complex relationship to the urban working class, which they often supply through migration.

Analysis of working-class behavior has also been deepened by a recent focus on the daily lives of workers, their attitudes toward religion and culture, and their practices and traditions on the shop floor and in the community, and at work and play.

Coverage of this broad array of subtopics has been aided and enhanced by a remarkable cross-fertilization of disciplines. Modern social historians frequently employ data or techniques borrowed from such fields as sociology, psychology, demography, cultural anthropology, linguistics, and literary criticism.

Not surprisingly, these trends in the New Social History have not been well received by all historians of the working class. Perhaps the most frequent objection is that voiced in strident tones in 1979 by the prominent historian of the French left, Tony Judt. The "new" social history, he said, was a "new positivism" which ignored politics or reduced them "to events of marginal significance." Its focus on providing "a serial description of 'long-term social change'" was, Judt concluded, "an insulting denial to people in the past of their political and ideological identity."

A number of problems, some quite familiar to the "old" school, others more congenial to the "new," continue to exercise social historians of the working class. Treatment here is selective but, hopefully, representative of major concerns.

Problems of Working-Class Social History

Periodization. "New" social historians see less of a clear distinction between preindustrial and industrial labor than their predecessors did. The current tendency is to downplay the idea of a brusque takeoff into industrial revolution around 1750–1780, in favor of the notion of a glide from protoindustrialization (e.g., the putting-out industry, concentrated textile production in such areas as medieval Flanders or Renaissance Florence) into broader-gauge factory production. A number of contemporary social historians have drawn attention to the accumulation of skills and experience with team production which took place over the centuries of widespread home production under the putting-out system and have concluded that at least some key elements in the industrialization process were already in place well before the mid-18th century. This suggests that it may be time to posit a new, earlier date for the "making" of E.P. Thompson's (1966) English working class, and, by extension, the working classes of continental Europe as well.

Once past the industrialization threshold, however, the periodization of working-class history seems to have become more rather than less tricky. Modern social historians no longer find economic cycles or levels of industrial development (e.g., the transition from textile-led growth to new leading sectors such as chemicals, steel, electricity) satisfactory benchmarks for determining stages in working-class history. Political and cultural factors probably deserve more attention than they have received. For example, it has been argued that, despite Germany's more advanced industrial economy, French workers around 1900 were actually more "mature" than their German counterparts because in France political and ideological modernization had preceded economic and technological change.

This problem poses particular difficulties for efforts at comparative working-class social his-tory. If levels of economic development or of industrialization are no longer sound bases for comparison, what is? One suggestion is that perhaps behavioral changes such as the raising or lowering of the average age of marriage or of the average number of children born to working-class families are surer guides to the periodization of working-class history.

Where is the worker's homeland? Debate has raged since Marx's time over the extent to which the working class can be defined in terms of national citizenship. This is one controversy that has altered little with the coming of the New Social History. The orthodox Marxist view held that the worker's only homeland was his class. Historian Peter Stearns, albeit from a different standpoint, has argued in a similar vein. "[T]he national framework causes [historians] more trouble than it is worth," he has written, adding that "a docker can be more accurately understood as a docker than as a Frenchman or a German." Scholars who have studied working-class reactions to national and international crises, such as the coming of war in 1914, however, render a different verdict. Jolyon Howorth, for example, in his study of the inability of French and German workers to make common cause against the growing threat of war in 1900–1914, concludes that "nationalism occupied the hearts and guts" of workers at that crucial juncture in working-class history.

Workers' Protest. The various forms of workers' protest against exploitation, working conditions, or denial of basic rights have been a staple of historical research since the 19th century. The study of workers' protest was, of course, at the heart of the the "old social history" of the working class, with its emphasis on unions and socialist parties, but it remains a topic of considerable interest to new social historians as well.

The "old" social historians tended to explain the incidence of worker protest as a product of either immiseration or class consciousness. The unrest caused by grinding poverty might produce explosions of rage, riots, or even strikes, but for these more "primitive" forms of protest to be transformed into sustained working-class movements, consciousness of class and class interests was required. This generally meant the intervention of some external agency, for example, a vanguard party such as the Russian Bolsheviks, possessor of the theory and praxis required in order to guide the workers from mere protest to thoroughgoing revolution.

"New" social historians tend to downplay both immiseration and consciousness as sources of worker protest. The notion of a direct relationship between protest and impoverishment has been the easiest target. For some time, historians have been aware that some of the more significant outbursts of worker protest have coincided with rising wages, including real wages. For example, the prodigious growth in union and Socialist Party strength in Germany from the late 1890s down to the eve of World War I occurred at a time when the German economy generally was on the upswing.

Other new social and labor historians have taken aim at the view that worker protest, in order to be meaningful, must stem from a highly developed class consciousness. English labor historian Dick Geary (1989) has contested this view in a characteristically bold (some might say reckless) statement. "It could . . . be argued," he writes, "that the basic motivation of both Russian and English workers [in 1917] was identical and nothing more than a desire to fill their bellies; but the rectification of these immediate material grievances entailed different strategies because of the surrounding circumstances which differed so greatly. . . . It was the framework, not different 'levels of consciousness,' which made the difference."

Some national working-class concerns. Of the large number of important questions that have bedeviled social historians in attempting to profile national working-class movements, some of the more interesting have arisen in studies of the pre-1917 Russian working class. This is also a field which demonstrates with exceptional clarity the differences between the "old" and "new" approaches to the social history of the working class.

Russia. One student of the history of the Russian working class has remarked that the difference between historians of the Russian labor movement and those of its Western counterpart is that "the former sets out to explain why workers turned out to be revolutionary and the latter why they did not." Perhaps surprisingly, despite the seemingly endless stream of books on the 1917 Revolution and the history of the USSR, historians may be no closer to understanding why Russian workers turned out to be revolutionary than they were at the time the events took place.

A major problem, of course, has been the lack of access to archives and to the oral witness of participants in the events. In addition, too many historians of the period have been unduly influenced by the terms of reference and standpoint of the (heretofore) official Marxist-Leninist historiography. Because of this, attention has for some time been focused so extensively upon the vanguard party (the Bolsheviks) which supposedly provided workers with the leadership and inspiration required to enable them to transcend their natural economism and take to the revolutionary path, that we have only a very sketchy understanding of the structure and composition, to say nothing of the agenda, of the working class itself.

We know something of the worker elite, the supposedly most conscious and disciplined elements, which followed the lead of the Bolshevik Party. Marxist historiography in general and Soviet historiography in particular have tended to give short shrift to those very considerable parts of the Russian working class from the beginning of industrialization in the 1870s down to 1917 who were new to urban life and factory labor, or were female, or who maintained close links to the peasant milieu. These workers, it was felt, were inherently more conservative than their fellow toilers who had been resident in urban centers for some time and had become a genuine industrial proletariat. The besetting sin was to have kept close ties to the soil.

The more conventional Western Marxist historians and Soviet historians in general have tended to repeat Marx's view of the reactionary nature of the peasantry. Some recent historians of the Russian working class see this as a major weakness in the traditional historiography. They find it odd that Russian Marxists who exalted the peasant *mir* as a means whereby Russia, unlike other European nations, could skip the capitalist stage on the road to socialism, should then reverse field and condemn peasant influence upon the Russian working class as reactionary. These revisionist historians argue that the peasantry was a strong revolutionary force throughout the modern period in Russia and contributed considerably to the militancy of the Russian working class by transmitting its collectivist values and strong sense of social justice to those of its sons and daughters obliged to seek work in the city.

Greater access to Russian archives in the post-Glasnost era will no doubt enable historians to develop a much fuller portrait of the Russian working class, one that will take into account its important residual links to the countryside, its strong sense of community in the urban setting, and its evolving agenda as a class as opposed to a party clientele and paramilitary force.

While the most intense focus on the social history of the working class focuses on the industrialization period, considerable attention has been given to the fate of working-class behaviors and beliefs in the later 20th century, around arguments about whether a distinct social class persists or gives ground, as well as numerical strength, to other social allegiances. The rise of new unskilled and immigrant working-class groups feeds into 20th-century history as well. Finally, attention to the emergence of working classes in Japan and other Asian, Latin American, and African countries extends the range of social history and, gradually, brings new opportunities for comparison. (*See also* Embourgeoisement; Industrialization; Marxist Historiography; Proletarianization; Russian Revolution; Unions)

Bruce Vandervort

REFERENCES

Berlanstein, Lenard. *The Working People of Paris, 1870–1914.* Baltimore: Johns Hopkins University Press, 1984.

Evans, R.J., ed. *The German Working Class.* London: Croom Helm, 1982.

Geary, Dick, ed. *Labour and Socialist Movements in Europe Before 1914.* Oxford: Berg, 1989.

Magraw, Roger. *History of the French Working Class, 2* vols. London: Blackwell, 1992.

Mitchell, Harvey, and Peter N. Stearns. *Workers and Protest.* Itasca, IL: Peacock, 1971.

Thompson, E.P. *The Making of the English Working Class.* New York: Pantheon, 1966.

Tilly, Louise A., and Joan W. Scott. *Women, Work and the Family.* New York: Holt, Rinehart and Winston, 1978.

World Economy/Dependency Theory

World economy theory and dependency theory, though arrived at independently, are conceptually linked because they both try to explain differential economic development throughout the world primarily through the mechanism of trade. Both theories use Marxist concepts and utilize them to understand exploitation on an international level.

Dependency theory emerged from the work of economist Raul Prebisch, who, in his work for the United Nation's Economic Commission on Latin America in the 1950s, showed that the raw material-exporting countries of Latin America maintained a trade deficit with the industrialized North Atlantic economies. Prebisch concluded that this deficit was built into the structure of trade, for processed goods inevitably cost more than raw materials. Marxist theorists in the 1960s used this insight to provide a rebuttal of modernization theory then in vogue among social scientists. They argued that commerce between industrialized countries and Latin America meant not, as modernization theory asserted, the gradual economic development of Latin American economies, but instead their further subjection to the North Atlantic economies. As a result of their colonial experience which introduced capitalism, the Latin American economies (also called satellites) were tied in a dependent and exploitative relationship with the European metropoli. This web of exploitation between metropolis and satellite is also reproduced on the local level within Latin America itself. The capital city, as the administrative center and often the export/import trade entrepôt, acts in many ways as a metropolis to the surrounding countryside, thus reproducing patterns of exploitation within the region as well. This meant that local elites might become relatively wealthy within the Latin American context, but that the overall system drained resources and capital from the region. Thus, this international division of labor—with Latin America producing the raw materials in return for manufactured goods from the North Atlantic—kept Latin America underdeveloped, explaining the apparent contradiction between its vast resources and its persistent poverty.

A somewhat more sophisticated analysis pioneered by scholars such as the Brazilian sociologist Henrique Cardoso shows that development can in fact occur within a dependent country. "Associated-dependent" development, including some industrialization, took place in many Latin American countries during the Great Depression of the 1930s, when trade with the metropolis was weak. However, to sustain this development, the Latin American bourgeoisies eventually had to ally themselves with multinational capital, thus recreating in slightly different form the ties of dependency. Despite the increasing sophistication of this approach, much of the dependency model has been rejected in the past decade. Some key insights into the nature of colonial or semicolonial economic development have been integrated into an understanding of Latin America and other parts of the Third World, especially Africa, where this model has also been applied.

World economy theory was generated by sociologist Immanuel Wallerstein during the 1970s, and since has been enhanced by numerous scholars from a variety of disciplines including social history. Dependency and world economy theories are very similar, since the primary factor in unequal relationships around the world in both is trade. There are many important differences as well. World economy theory is somewhat more complex in its categorization and takes into account state power and labor conditions as important variables in different categories of regions within the world economy.

World economy theory argues that the rise of an aggressive, capitalist economy in western Europe from about 1500 onward, itself the result of political consolidation and other changes, created a durable set of relationships with economies of other societies. Western Europe became the dominant, or core, economy, exporting finished goods, controlling the bulk of profits from growing world trade. Opposite this core economy were peripheral, or dependent, economies, which exported cheap raw materials (like silver or foodstuffs) to the core, buying higher-priced luxury and manufactured goods in turn. Colonial Latin America is a prime example of this kind of economy. Not all societies were initially sucked into the unequal terms of world trade (Wallerstein calls these external), but over time, not only Latin America but also the southern colonies of British North America, Africa, India, parts of eastern Europe, and other areas became increasingly peripheral. Peripheral status is often part of colonialism, but it can often survive a decolonization process. Many independent states preside over dependent economies.

Peripheral societies are characterized not only by dependent economies, but also by weak governments (lacking big revenues and also faced with substantial foreign intervention), small merchant classes, and a coercive labor system such as slavery or extreme forms of serfdom (including the hacienda regime in Latin America and the tightening of serfdom in eastern Europe). Coerced labor is essential to keep production costs down, in turn a prerequisite of international trade.

World economic theory assumes that economic relations are primary in historical explanation, at least in the modern centuries. Labor systems, politics, and other relationships (including, some theorists argue, deteriorating economic roles for women in peripheral societies) follow from position in the world economy. A variety of topics in social history has been explored from a world economy perspective, including labor relations in Latin America, challenges to traditional African peasant societies, and exploitation of women. Many explanations of industrial "lag" in certain parts of the world continue to reflect the assumptions about the special burdens of economic peripheralization.

The relationships in the world economy tend to persist; it is very hard to escape the periphery, though Wallerstein does allow for gradual change. Many world economic theorists see core-periphery relationships continuing to the present day, engulfing large parts of societies such as Africa in the long-term economic stagnation and inability to industrialize.

Social historians have also criticized both dependency and world economy theories. They have argued that categories such as peripheral or satellites generalize too broadly, omitting the complexity of labor and other relationships in so-called dependent economies. Many Latin American historians, for example, point to significant internal economic development, plus large pockets of peasant autonomy, even at the height of Latin America's "dependency" in the late colonial period. Against the general categories and the economic determinism of both theories, these social historians argue for the need to examine actual social and economic patterns on a case-by-case basis, in which international trade position is merely one factor among many. World economy in particular remains widely discussed, but its ascendancy is declining in sociohistorical works in areas such as the African peasantry or Latin American economy and society.

Many scholars, however, continue to assert the utility of the framework in organizing basic social comparisons in modern world history, and certainly, since the decline of modernization theory, no other general formula has rivaled the global sweep of world economy or dependency theories in the social history field. Correspondingly, social historians dealing with many topics, such as recent peasant history, regularly grapple with the dependency framework whether they accept it or not. (*See also* Commercialization; Imperialism)

Erick D. Langer and Peter N. Stearns

REFERENCES

Wallerstein, Immanuel. *The Modern World System*, 3 vols. New York: Academic Press, 1974–1986.

Cardoso, Henrique, and Enzo Faletto. *Dependency and Development in Latin America*. Translated by Marjory Mattingly Urquidi. Berkeley: University of California Press, 1979.

Stern, Steven J. "Feudalism, Capitalism, and the World-System in the Perspective of Latin America and the Caribbean," *American Historical Review* 93, 4 (Oct. 1988): 829–872.

Frank, Andre Gunder. *Capitalism and Underdevelopment in Latin America*, rev. ed. New York: Monthly Review Press, 1969.

World History

World history as a genre has surged at several points during the 20th century, and since the mid-1980s has been gaining ground again as an orientation for historical synthesis and for teaching at both secondary and university levels. World history, as the name implies, covers historical developments on a global basis, rather than focusing on single regions, nations, or civilizations.

It seeks to develop a framework for understanding the major developments in all areas of the world from the emergence of agricultural societies (or even before) to the present. World historians like Arnold Toynbee used a rise and fall of civilizations approach, seeking common patterns in the emergence of new, vigorous societies, their maturation, and their ultimate decline. More recent world historians have been less sanguine about uncovering general laws; rather, they have emphasized contacts among civilizations, using world history to trace the diffusion of technologies, ideas, artistic styles, even diseases. The leading interpretive issue in world history today involves balancing the importance of separate civilizations or regional cultures, which have their own historical dynamic, with growing interest in large-scale, multicivilizational contacts and parallels. World history periodization is increasingly determined by changes in the nature and intensity of contacts among a number of otherwise different societies, as in the spread of world religions after the 3rd century AD or the growth of commercial links among Asia, Africa, and Europe after about AD 1000.

Much world history has been written in terms of the achievements of great thinkers, artists, kings, and generals. This features the conventional political and intellectual monuments and characteristics of major civilizations. The approach assumes that the way to assess a civilization is through particularly dazzling regimes—like the rule of Manu Mansu in the African kingdom of Mali, or Suleiman the Magnificent in the Ottoman Empire—and particularly creative philosophers. Many leading issues in presenting world history, furthermore, like how to wean world history from excessive emphasis on the West and on Western-centered standards, have little to do, necessarily, with social history. But the rise of social history has challenged world history since the 1980s. Characterizing major civilizations and culture groups now must include topics like labor systems, family forms, and conditions of women, as well as the ideas of Confucius or Buddha. Comparisons among civilizations—a vital analytical approach in world history—now routinely involves social history topics. The contacts among civilizations almost invariably include the beliefs and behaviors of ordinary people, including the impact of international diseases, religious ideas, or commercially inspired changes in labor structures. Because world history, however defined, is a challenging, complex subject, fitting social history in remains a task to be completed. It is still tempting to organize the subject around upper-class culture and government forms. Some attempts have tended to rely on a relatively conventional emphasis for premodern world history, spiced perhaps with vignettes about women's place in Islam or pre-Columbian America, while turning to more systematic social history when the account reaches the most recent centuries, with changes among ordinary people due to new technology, imperialism, and other modern forces. This approach conduces to notions of a changeless, unvarying mass—particularly, a standardized, immobile peasantry—in the long centuries dominated by agriculturally based societies, with all the action concentrated among elites. Ordinary people emerge as a measurement of historical change, perhaps even a cause of historical change, only as agricultural societies began to draw to a close. Here too, however, growing understanding of the importance of social history, and the range of sociohistorical topics and comparisons, in agricultural as well as industrial centuries, increasingly generates more insistent attention to social history throughout world history coverage.

Recent attempts at world history synthesis, including the growing attention to basic international forces of disease, technological diffusion, and religious belief, attempt to force a more comprehensive approach on the basis of sociohistorical considerations. A great deal of research remains necessary, to develop comparable social histories for all major periods and areas. It is not yet possible, for example, to provide as much depth in the coverage of women's history for some major civilizations as for others. Figuring out how to present changes in international contacts, as the result of new exchanges of goods or new cultural confrontations, in social history terms also remains challenging. Opportunities for effective conceptualization are considerable as well, as two of the most important emphases in contemporary history teaching

attempt to combine more fruitfully. (*See also* National History; Teaching of Social History)

Peter N. Stearns

REFERENCES

McNeill, William. *The Rise of the West: A History of the Human Community.* Chicago: University of Chicago Press, 1963.

Stearns, Peter N., Michael Adas, and Stuart Schwartz. *World Civilizations: The Global Experience.* New York: HarperCollins, 1992.

World Wars

The two world wars broke new ground in the sad history of human conflict. War became global, involving peoples of every continent. And war became total: the major belligerent countries mobilized whole populations and vast economic resources for the purposes of military destruction. The line between front and homefront disappeared, especially during World War II when tactics of rapid movement, massive aerial bombardment, and Nazi genocide made many civilians more vulnerable than soldiers. In both wars people died in numbers hitherto scarcely imagined—about 8.5 million in World War I, and at least 50 million in World War II. These wars also produced social change, which is why they are examined by social historians and tested for their role in shaping distinct periods in recent social experience. Some effects came immediately, such as the wave of revolutions that swept through eastern and central Europe at the end of World War I. Other effects, on gender relations or economic behavior, for example, were subtler and harder to see. Most historians agree, however, that many fundamental values most people in the West took for granted in the 19th century—patriotic loyalty, a belief in progress, a respect for leaders, a confidence in human rationality—never had the same appeal after Verdun, Hiroshima, and Auschwitz.

Although books on the world wars could now fill libraries, only recently have historians made great headway in writing detailed, scholarly social histories of these events. This delay stems in part from restricted access to archives, and in part from a tradition in social history to look at social change over long spans of time rather than during events such as wars, natural disasters, and revolutions. Since the 1960s, however, historians have made strides in analyzing popular experience during and after the world wars. Just what role these events played in shaping change in the 20th century has become a central issue in social history.

The first area of extensive research emerged from debates about the causes of World War I. Historians had long argued about the diplomatic and military origins of the war. But in the 1960s several historians in Germany reopened the controversy by suggesting that the German government played the leading role in causing the war in 1914 and that it did so for social and economic reasons. The rise of the socialist movement and the intensification of class conflict after 1890, these historians argued, inspired conservative leaders to stress nationalistic ambitions as a way to unify the country and strengthen their own political position at home. By the 1970s historians explored similar links between social conflict and foreign policy in Russia, France, Britain, and elsewhere. Scholars also took a new look at the social and economic context for Hitler's aggression, as well as British and French appeasement, in the 1930s. No consensus emerged on these matters, as historians continued to debate the relevance of social pressures, as opposed to more purely diplomatic and political ones, in inspiring government action on the eve of both wars. But this wave of scholarly debate paved the way for new work on the social history of the wars themselves.

That work has tended to focus either on soldiers or on people at the homefront. Most of the work on the former has looked at the men in the trenches of the western front of World War I, where astonishing casualty rates in a four-year stalemate produced a psychology of bitterness and alienation in soldiers that cut across class, ethnic, and national lines. Historians have made inventive use of letters, diaries, trench newspapers, literary testimonies, and psychological reports to explore the mental world of the combat soldier and postwar veteran. Much of this scholarship makes important connections between trench experience and participation in paramilitary and pacifist movements in the interwar years. Much more work remains to be done on the

social history of military experience in World War II, although historians in the United States have begun to exploit government studies of soldiers that were done at the time. New work has appeared on the psychology and sociology of the resistance in Nazi-occupied Europe, work that explores who resisted and why. In all this literature on combat during the wars, one issue looms especially large: whether soldiers' nationality, religion, ethnicity, age, class, and gender played a major role in determining the way they understood their experience, or whether the form of combat itself evoked more universal reactions.

Studies of the homefront have explored a wide variety of issues. A good deal has been done in business-state relations, especially during World War I. Never before had governments assumed so much authority over the production and distribution of goods and services. Overall the two wars greatly expanded the role of government in economic life, from taxation and public welfare to centralized planning and nationalized industry. Methods of control, however, varied by country and by war. In France it took World War II to inspire business and government elites to make the break with 19th-century laissez faire orthodoxy, whereas in Britain and Germany World War I had a decisive effect. In the United States it took the Cold War to consolidate the military-industrial complex that had taken shape in World War II. Much more work remains to be done on the social and cultural dimensions of these changes, especially during World War II. Until recently, for example, historians in Germany and Japan have tended to stress 1945 as a new beginning for their countries, "year zero" as the Germans called it. American authorities, eager for new friends in a Cold War world, encouraged this view. But new studies have pointed to important continuities in personnel, ideas, and institutions that help explain the postwar economic success of these defeated nations.

A similar body of work has emerged on working-class experience and labor relations during the wars. Although conscription and wartime shortages subjected working-class families to hardship and tragedy, both wars created new opportunities for labor movements, since governments needed people to work as never before. Trade unions emerged from World War I with newfound influence, only to lose it in the 1920s. During World War II, labor's fortunes varied enormously: workers regained power in democratic societies but suffered severe repression in Germany, Italy, Japan, and the Soviet Union. In nearly every country World War II set the stage for dramatic changes in labor relations thereafter. Although historians have explored these changes in most countries, more work remains to be done on the subtler effects of the war on class relations more generally and on working-class identity. Some historians have seen wartime experience as important in accounting for the quite distinctive quality of class identity in the United States, France, and Japan, for example, in the postwar era. However, just how important the war years really were, as opposed to longer-term patterns, remains unclear.

Gender relations have also emerged as a major focus of recent studies of the homefront. Wartime mobilization both reinforced and challenged conventional notions of gender. Men went to war, women stayed home. But some women also engaged in combat, especially in the anti-Nazi resistance and in the Soviet army. More important still, women in every major belligerent country in both wars entered the labor force in huge numbers, often with hopes of keeping their jobs when peace returned. Demobilization, however, and the widespread assumption that men had a right to reclaim their jobs, forced women either back into the home or into less desirable niches of the labor force. War also disrupted patterns of courtship and married life. Few families in France and Germany escaped the loss of a son or father or uncle in World War I. The same could be said of Germany and the Soviet Union in the second war. Conscription alone could play havoc with family life. Divorce rates soared for a time in Europe after 1945. Still, the long-term effects on gender relations remain unclear. Conventional norms remained in force after both wars, though many women resented it. Some historians argue that the bitterness women felt about the restoration of old patterns after 1945 fed a feminist rebellion in the next generation. Much remains to be learned about war as a gendered experience for women and men, and especially for children, whose lives during the wars have scarcely been explored.

Race and ethnicity also shaped the choices people faced during the wars and the meaning they ascribed to their experience. In both wars Britain and France conscripted soldiers from the populations of their colonial empires. During World War I Poles served in the armies of Germany, Austria-Hungary, and Russia, and hence on opposing sides. The Soviet army of World War II was a vast multiethnic collectivity, as was the American army in its own way. Many of the repercussions of multiethnic conscription are well known. Historians of American race relations have pointed to the war years as important in raising the political aspirations of African Americans, a significant part of the context for the later civil rights movement. Colonial peoples in Asia and Africa acquired ideas, experience, and resentments that fed anticolonial movements after both wars. World War II certainly accelerated the disintegration of the British and French empires; defeat in the first war put an end to Germany's extra-European empire. Beyond these general outlines, however, the social and cultural effects of wartime experience on ethnic groups both within and outside Europe remain a relatively unexplored field of research. Much more needs to be done, too, on the impact of the war on ethnic identity in the Pacific theater of the war.

One exception to this weakness in the literature is work on European Jews in the 1930s and 1940s. The Holocaust has inspired a good deal of scholarly research. An enormous body of official German government documents, combined with the records of other governments and many personal testimonies, have given historians a wealth of material to work with. Debate has emerged over several issues that fall within the domain of social history: the nature of Jewish resistance, the role of bystanders and accomplices in the genocide, and the breadth of popular support for or resistance to anti-Semitism in wartime Europe. There remains a need for more work on these questions, especially with a comparative perspective. And much remains to be learned about how people came to understand the Holocaust, and what they made of their understandings, after the war.

Collective memory, in fact, is just emerging as a major field of inquiry in the social history of the wars. Historians are exploring how commemoration—from battlefield tourism to ceremonies, parades, monuments, and museums—shaped popular conceptions of these wars after 1918 and 1945. Governments, activists, and intellectuals created myths about the recent past, sometimes even consciously, in their efforts to forge the postwar future. Historians, too, played a part. Postwar memory-making had its own contemporary political logic, but it also reflected the influence of wartime propaganda activities. Commemoration, postwar memory and amnesia, and the dynamics of propaganda and even advertising are likely to emerge as an important focus of research. These subjects could well bring the wars into the center of debates about popular culture in the 20th century.

Finally, more work needs to be done on the wars as turning points in the history of nationality, identity, and the state. War inspired governments to rally diverse populations around new conceptions of national identity. At the same time many governments, including that of the United States with its internment of Japanese Americans, singled out nationality groups for imprisonment and persecution. Internationalism, too, gained new legitimacy as a focus of identity, especially in Europe at the end of World War II. Just how various social groups and nationalities responded to these contradictory influences remains to be investigated, especially in a comparative framework. (*See also* Military and Society; State and Society; Welfare State; Women and Work)

Herrick Chapman

REFERENCES

Blum, John Morton. *V Was for Victory: Politics and American Culture During World War II.* New York: Harcourt Brace Jovanovich, 1976.

Higgonet, Margaret Randolph, et al. *Behind the Lines: Gender and the Two World Wars.* New Haven: Yale University Press, 1987.

Leed, Eric J. *No Man's Land: Combat and Identity in World War I.* New York: Cambridge University Press, 1979.

Marwick, Arthur. *Total War and Social Change.* New York: St. Martin's Press, 1988.

Rousso, Henry. *The Vichy Syndrome: History and Memory in France Since 1944.* Translated by Arthur Goldhammer. Cambridge, MA: Harvard University Press, 1991.

Y

Youth/Adolescence

Youth, that stage of life between childhood and adulthood, has been an ever changing concept that has biological, social, cultural, psychological, and historical dimensions. In preindustrial societies youth passed directly from childhood to adulthood, usually celebrated by a coming-of-age ritual, without experiencing the period of extended schooling and age segregation associated with industrial society. Societal perceptions of youth also changed dramatically in Europe and the United States as the preindustrial family was transformed by rapid urbanization and the decline of agriculture and preindustrial forms of work. Youth experienced an increasing age segregation and extended dependency during this demographic transformation of industrializing countries. As youth labor decreased and extended schooling became common in industrially advanced societies, the obligations and duties of adulthood were postponed. Therefore, it is necessary to look at the historical development of age categorization. This has correspondingly been an important facet of social history, though

it was more lively in the 1970s, in the wake of youth rebellion, than in recent years.

Youth history before 1800 has formed an important part in studying village festivals, where in Europe youth groups had special roles and required special outlets for expression. Youth service in apprenticeship and the widespread practice of sending youth out to other households are other important premodern topics.

In the preindustrial period several of the conditions tied to modern concepts of youth were not present, and labels used to describe youth were quite general. Although the concept "adolescent" existed long before the 19th century, it lacked the age specificity it acquired in the late 19th century with all the legal, cultural, and social characteristics such a designation implied. The primary designations for age categories were work related with little of the social, psychological meaning of today. As Joseph Kett (1977) has argued, status rather than age was more important in determining the stage of life. Youth from the lower social orders were part of the household economy. They learned what they needed to know in the family and were sent away from families at age 14 or earlier to take up adult tasks as apprentices, agrarian laborers, and household help. Only socially privileged male youth began to experience an extended youth in the mid-19th century, since they were not sent out to work and often continued schooling into their teen years.

Linguistic designations for preindustrial youth were class and gender specific. In Germany, for example, adults used separate designations for upper-class boys (*Jungling*) and girls (*Jungfrau*). Jungling implied a romantic image of youthful innocence, idealism, and vulnerability. Until they became an adult concern at the turn of the century, lower-class youth had no general linguistic designation. They moved in bourgeois consciousness directly from childhood to adulthood, from the designations for boys (*Knaben, Burschen*) to work designations such as apprentice (*Lehrlinge*) or casual laborer (*Hilfsarbeiter*). Only in the late 19th century did the new more all encompassing term "adolescent" (*Jugendliche*) come to designate all youth after age 14.

During the last half of the 19th century, most industrially advanced countries began to separate youth from adult society. As the agricultural population declined and labor shortages faded in industrializing states, authorities passed child labor laws to protect jobs for adults and to satisfy reformers who argued that youth should not work in factories. Youth were further separated from adult society when the inception of mass compulsory education dictated schooling into the teen years for all youth in the late 19th century. But education beyond the elementary grades (extended primary, vocational, or secondary) remained a middle- and upper-class and male experience until the early 20th century in most countries.

Beginning in the 1890s, social reformers, educators, and government authorities, concerned about the larger number of working-class youth and their often semi-autonomous condition, began to extend the adolescent experience to all youth. Only later in the 1890s did the term "adolescence" become a widely used designation for youth in official and public discussion in France, Germany, Britain, and the United States. Ado-

lescence became a more clearly defined preparatory stage before adulthood. Some scholars, such as John Gillis (1974) and Joseph Kett (1977), have argued that authorities invented adolescence in order to give credence to attempts to subordinate and isolate youth. Others, such as Harvey Graff (1985), maintain that the term originated from actual observation of youth behavior and was therefore an empirical discovery. No matter which position one adopts, a common concern existed among authorities that lower-class youths' greater autonomy and independence that accompanied industrialization and urbanization represented a threat to society and governments needed to provide an ordered environment in order to overcome youths' unruly or troubled nature. G. Stanley Hall's 1904 psychological study of adolescence promoted societal concerns for adolescents in Europe as well as the United States. Hall's view that juvenile delinquency was a result of troubled development, a storm and stress period typical of this stage of life, led many reformers to demand that adolescents be provided with age-specific institutions and special care. By the turn of the 20th century, earlier in industrially advanced Britain, this image of the vulnerable, victimized adolescent coexisted alongside the perception of the dangerous teen.

The adult perception of adolescents as that of the threatening "teenager" in the United States and its equivalent, the "Halbstarke" (half-strong) in Germany, prompted social reformers, governments, and religious organizations to set up numerous youth organizations that further separated adolescents from adults and extended the adolescent phase to almost all youth in developed societies. This institutionalization of youth resulted in an enormous expansion of youth organizations in the early 20th century. A pioneering Boy Scouts was established in England in 1908 by General Baden-Powell and then spread to the European Continent and the United States. In some countries, the United States, for example, the secondary school was to prepare the adolescent for adulthood. Where the secondary schools were restricted to a few privileged youth, as in Europe, vocational schools were to mold youth for adult responsibilities.

A final decisive division of the adult and youth worlds came with the legal separation of the two through special youth legislation, legal terminology, a distinct youth court system, and separate youth reformatories. Until the early 20th century, courts throughout the world had treated juvenile offenders as adults. Britain experimented with nonpunitive institutionalization in the last quarter of the century and instituted reformatory prisons, known as Borstals, in 1900 to deal with older juvenile offenders. Pioneer juvenile courts were first set up in Chicago, Illinois, in 1908. Europeans soon followed with juvenile court officials and eventually with juvenile courts. The objective was to separate youthful offenders from the hardened criminal in the hope that more lenient, rehabilitative treatment might reform youth.

In modern society adolescence does not necessarily end with the teen years because of extended schooling. Youth often remain dependent on their parents and isolated in educational institutions into their twenties. But life-course patterns have changed in the late 20th century, with youth often combining school and work rather than work following school as they did in the early 20th century. With youth gaining some limited financial autonomy through early work, their dependence on their parents has been reduced. Consumer societies have responded to and promoted youths' autonomy by aiming much advertising at the adolescent rather than the adult. The youthful image has become the ideal among many adults. The impact of youth peer culture, though not fully analyzed as yet in social history, becomes a vital topic.

Linguistic and life-course analysis are now the dominant trends in the study of youth. The life-course approach emphasizes alterations in the sequencing of school, work, courtship, marriage, and parenthood. The timing of these events shape other events. For example, John Modell (1989) has argued that the overlapping of school and work in the United States has brought about a greater independence among adolescents. Youth are, according to this argument, asserting more control over their life course. Those approaching youth from a linguistic perspective argue that the terms used to describe youth are either a means for society to control youth or they reflect a recognition of a changed youth experience. In either case, the study of youth

images will reveal the position of youth within a society. (*See also* Childhood; Education; Life Course/Life Cycle; Youth Movements)

J. Robert Wegs

REFERENCES

Gillis, John. *Youth and History: Tradition and Change in European Age Relations, 1770–Present.* New York: Academic Press, 1974.

Graff, Harvey. "Early Adolescence in Antebellum America: The Remaking of Growing Up," *The Journal of Early Adolescence* 5:4 (1985), pp. 411–427.

Kett, Joseph. *Rites of Passage: Adolescence in America 1790 to the Present.* New York: Basic Books, 1977.

Modell, John. *Into One's Own: From Youth to Adulthood in the United States, 1920–1975.* Berkeley: University of California Press, 1989.

Wegs, Robert J. *Growing Up Working Class: Continuity and Change Among Viennese Youth, 1890–1938.* University Park: Penn State Press, 1989.

Youth Movements

Although Sigmund Freud never employed the term "youth movement," he hypothesized in *Totem and Taboo* that the origins of human society were to be found in the collective actions of young people. This earliest and most momentous of "youth movements" supposedly occurred in a primeval clan dominated by a single adult male. The young men of the clan, frustrated that this primal patriarch restricted their sexual access to females, formed a conspiracy and killed him. Then, abashed by their deed and fearing that rivalry for the females would lead to further violence, they established laws (taboos) prohibiting sexual intercourse among clan members. These laws provided the legal and cooperative foundation upon which all society rests, or so Freud claimed.

Freud's speculation has been challenged by anthropologists and psychologists alike, but it nevertheless illustrates several issues that have long concerned social scientists. The first is whether youth or, more precisely, adolescence, represents an inherently turbulent stage of life. The second is whether youth movements endanger society or help preserve it.

That young people are especially unruly is a commonplace of even ancient texts; but the idea was first codified by the American psychologist G. Stanley Hall in *Adolescence* (1904). Anthropologist Margaret Mead refuted Hall by pointing to the tranquil passage of Samoan girls into adulthood; adolescence, Mead maintained, was a peculiar product of modern industrial life.

During the past few decades, social historians have challenged the views of both Mead and Hall. Mead's assumption that turbulent adolescence was peculiarly a condition of modern societies was confuted by examples of volatile youth movements in premodern Europe and America; and Hall's notion that adolescence was always stressful failed to explain why disruptive youth movements were far more common in modern societies than in premodern ones. Social historians have generally concluded, first, that youth (especially adolescence) may be an innately unstable stage of life—perhaps because issues of identity are unresolved, or because young people have yet to receive either the full imprint of socialization or the benefits of adult status; and second, that this universal tendency emerges as a historical force only in certain contexts.

Revolutionary youth movements were generally uncommon in agricultural societies, where patriarchal authority was reinforced by its control of land. Dynastic China provides an example. Emperors and their familial surrogates, fathers, supervised a remarkably stable system of land tenure; from this position of authority they successfully inculcated Confucian precepts of deference to elders and submission to the conventions of ancient sages.

Traditional and peasant societies in Europe and America were similarly resistant to organized youth rebellions. Fathers' possession of land exerted a powerful restraint on sons, who could not begin families without a "marriage portion," a grant of land sufficient to sustain a family. Sons who no doubt chafed at their delayed entry to adulthood commonly expressed their frustrations by joining informal youth groups such as the Lords of Misrule in England, the Abbeys of Misrule in France, and Bruderschaften in Germany. Although these groups staged carnivals and festivals that mocked traditional institutions and forms of authority, they also imposed rigid norms of behavior and courtship that in many ways corresponded to the roles young people would perform as adults.

Population growth and the enclosure of farm lands during the 16th century drove more and more young people from the land of their fathers. Youth groups that had once vented frustration over the strictures of state and family now took on overtones of political rebellion. Historian Emmanuel Le Roy Ladurie has described the youth groups of 16th-century southern France as "cells for insurrection." By the late 18th and early 19th centuries large numbers of restless young people had crowded into industrial cities, forming an unstable element that could readily be enlisted in revolutionary causes. Young people's zeal was further stimulated by Romantic philosophies that counterposed the innocence of youth to the corruption of adults who upheld social convention.

The Western world during the 19th century was jolted by a series of young people's rebellions. Historian John Plamenatz has described the republican revolution of 1830 in France as being composed of "mostly young men tired of their elders" (*The Revolutionary Movement in France, 1815–1871* [1952]). The Young Italy movement, founded the following year by Giuseppe Mazzini, excluded all persons over age 40. Several years later Ralph Waldo Emerson called upon American youth to "obey your hearts" and "lead the leaders" in creating a revitalized Young America. Organized groups of young people played prominent roles in the revolutions of 1848, in American abolitionism, and in anarchist attacks on the Russian czars. It is little wonder that by the close of the century G. Stanley Hall would conclude that the young were naturally inclined to mayhem.

At about this time, too, conservatives recognized the necessity of directing youthful energies into patriotism and character reform. Most of the leaders of the English Boy Scout movement, founded by General Baden-Powell, were high-ranking military officers, and the Boy Scouts relentlessly advocated middle-class values and religious sensibilities. In the United States, the YMCA and the American Boy Scouts instilled morality and hard work. In Germany the *Wandervogel*, composed of young boys who seemingly defied bourgeois convention by leaving their heads and knees uncovered, similarly transformed youthful rebelliousness into acceptable forms. Revolutionary states of the 20th century also sought to solidify their power by enlisting young people: the Soviet Union by creating Konsommol, a Communist youth organization; and Nazi Germany, the Hitler Youth.

During the 1940s and 1950s sociologist Talcott Parsons updated Hall by claiming that adolescent movements eased the transition to adulthood in modernizing societies ("Age and Sex in the Social Structure of the United States" [1949]). Youth culture and youth movements were thus "functional," for they served as sources of new ideas even as they directed youthful energies into safe channels.

These views prevailed until the 1960s, when outbursts of student activism throughout the world called into question Parsons's belief that youth movements were socially beneficial. Students in the United States protested, sometimes violently, against the Vietnam War; some joined avowedly revolutionary organizations such as the Students for a Democratic Society; others, shaving a decade off Mazzini's cautionary message, warned against trusting "anyone over thirty" and spawned a highly visible "counterculture." Student radicalism flared up in European universities at about the same time. The revolutionary potential of young people was highlighted in Communist China from 1966 to 1969 when the Red Guard, consisting of millions of college and high school students, went on a bloody rampage against all vestiges of Confucian culture.

Scholarly interest in organized youth movements has declined since the 1970s. Whether youth movements should be perceived chiefly as a threat to society or as a means of its growth and renewal remains unresolved, though the topic remains a vital facet of social history. (*See also* Generations; Protest; Youth/Adolescence)

Mark C. Carnes

REFERENCE

Gillis, John R. *Youth and History: Tradition and Change in European Age Relations, 1770–Present.* New York: Academic Press, 1981.

Index

Items in this index involve specific names (e.g. people, events, institutions) referred to in the text as well as more general concepts (e.g., domesticity, modern society, new religions) covered in the *Encyclopedia*.